T0189299

Lecture Notes in Computer Science   10251

Commenced Publication in 1973
Founding and Former Series Editors:
Gerhard Goos, Juris Hartmanis, and Jan van Leeuwen

More information about this series at http://www.springer.com/series/7407

Liran Ma · Abdallah Khreishah
Yan Zhang · Mingyuan Yan (Eds.)

Wireless Algorithms, Systems, and Applications

12th International Conference, WASA 2017
Guilin, China, June 19–21, 2017
Proceedings

 Springer

Editors
Liran Ma
Texas Christian University
Fort Worth, TX
USA

Abdallah Khreishah
New Jersey Institute of Technology
Newark, NJ
USA

Yan Zhang
University of Oslo
Oslo
Norway

Mingyuan Yan
University of North Georgia
Dahlonega, GA
USA

ISSN 0302-9743   ISSN 1611-3349 (electronic)
Lecture Notes in Computer Science
ISBN 978-3-319-60032-1   ISBN 978-3-319-60033-8 (eBook)
DOI 10.1007/978-3-319-60033-8

Library of Congress Control Number: 2017942990

LNCS Sublibrary: SL1 – Theoretical Computer Science and General Issues

Printed on acid-free paper

This Springer imprint is published by Springer Nature
The registered company is Springer International Publishing AG
The registered company address is: Gewerbestrasse 11, 6330 Cham, Switzerland

Preface

The 12th International Conference on Wireless Algorithms, Systems, and Applications (WASA 2017) was held during June 19–21, 2017, in Guilin, Guangxi, China. The conference is motivated by the recent advances in cutting-edge electronic and computer technologies that have paved the way for the proliferation of ubiquitous infrastructure and infrastructureless wireless networks. WASA is designed to be a forum for theoreticians, system and application designers, protocol developers, and practitioners to discuss and express their views on the current trends, challenges, and state-of-the-art solutions related to various issues in wireless networks.

The technical program of the conference included 70 regular papers together with nine short papers, selected by the Program Committee from 238 full submissions received in response to the call for papers. All the papers were peer reviewed by the Program Committee members or external reviewers. The papers cover the various topics, including cognitive radio networks, wireless sensor networks, cyber-physical systems, distributed and localized algorithm design and analysis, information and coding theory for wireless networks, localization, mobile cloud computing, topology control and coverage, security and privacy, underwater and underground networks, vehicular networks, Internet of Things, information processing and data management, programmable service interfaces, energy-efficient algorithms, system and protocol design, operating system and middle-ware support, and experimental test beds, models, and case studies.

We would like to thank the Program Committee members and external reviewers for volunteering their time to review and discuss conference papers. We would like to extend special thanks to the steering and general chairs of the conference for their leadership, and to the finance, publication, publicity, and local chairs for their hard work in making WASA 2017 a successful event. Last but not least, we would like to thank all the authors for presenting their works at the conference.

April 2017

Liran Ma
Abdallah Khreishah
Yan Zhang
Mingyuan Yan

Organization

Steering Committee

Xiuzhen Cheng	The George Washington University, USA, Co-chair
Zhipeng Cai	Georgia State University, USA, Co-chair
Jiannong Cao	Hong Kong Polytechnic University, Hong Kong, SAR China
Ness Shroff	The Ohio State University, USA
PengJun Wan	Illinois Institute of Technology, USA
Xinbing Wang	Shanghai Jiao Tong University, China
Wei Zhao	University of Macau, SAR China
Ty Znati	University of Pittsburgh, USA

General Chair

Feng Zhao	Guilin University of Electronic Technology, China

Program Co-chairs

Liran Ma	Texas Christian University, USA
Abdallah Khreishah	New Jersey Institute of Technology, USA
Yan Zhang	University of Oslo, Norway

Publication Co-chairs

Mingyuan Yan	University of North Georgia, USA
Donnell Payne	Texas Christian University, USA
Junggab Son	Kennesaw State University, USA

Publicity Co-chairs

Chunyu Ai	University of South Carolina Upstate, USA
Wenjia Li	New York Institute of Technology, USA
James Comer	Texas Christian University, USA

Finance Chair

Xiaoling Tao	Guilin University of Electronic Technology, China

Local Chair

Xiaohuan Li	Guilin University of Electronic Technology, China

Webmasters

Sarah Allen	Texas Christian University, USA
Jaron Householder	Texas Christian University, USA

Program Committee

Syed Hassan Ahmed	Kynugpook National University, South Korea
Abdulrahman Alhothaily	George Washington Universit, USA
Ashwin Ashok	Georgia State University, USA
Yu Cai	Michigan Technological University, USA
Bin Cao	Harbin Institute of Techonolgy, China
Ionut Cardei	Florida Atlantic University, USA
Mihaela Cardei	Florida Atlantic University, USA
Yacine Challal	Université de Technologie de Compiègne, France
Songqing Chen	George Mason University, USA
Siyao Cheng	Harbin Institute of Technology, China
Wei Cheng	Virginia Commonwealth University, USA
Yu Cheng	Illinois Institute of Technology, USA
Hongwei Du	Harbin Institute of Technology Shenzhen Graduate School, China
Qinghe Du	Xi'an Jiaotong University, China
Xiaojiang Du	Temple University, USA
Xinwen Fu	University of Massachusetts Lowell, USA
Zhangjie Fu	Nanjing University of Information Science and Technology, China
Chunming Gao	University of Washington, USA
Xiaofeng Gao	Shanghai Jiao Tong University, China
Yong Guan	Iowa State University, USA
Xiali Hei	Delaware State University, USA
Yan Huo	Beijing Jiaotong University, China
Soo-Yeon Ji	Bowie State University, USA
Donghyun Kim	Kennesaw State University, USA
Hwangnam Kim	Korea University, South Korea
Yanggon Kim	Towson University, USA
Sanghwan Lee	Kookmin University, South Korea
Fan Li	Beijing Institute of Technology, China
Feng Li	Indiana University, USA
Hongjuan Li	George Washington University, USA
Pan Li	Case Western Reserve University, USA
Qun Li	College of William and Mary, USA
Wei Li	Georgia State University, USA
Wenjia Li	New York Institute of Technology, USA
Yingshu Li	Georgia State University, USA
Zhenhua Li	Tsinghua University, USA

Jie Lian	University of Virginia, USA
Zhen Ling	Southeast University, USA
Benyuan Liu	University of Massachusetts Lowell, USA
Peixiang Liu	Nova Southeastern University, USA
Yang Liu	Beijing Institute of Technology, China
Xiang Lu	Chinese Academy of Science, China
Zhihan Lu	University College London, UK
Jian Mao	Beihang University, China
Manki Min	South Dakota State University, USA
Aziz Mohaisen	SUNY Buffalo, USA
Nam Nguyen	Towson University, USA
Linwei Niu	West Virginia State University, USA
Jian Ren	Michigan State University, USA
Na Ruan	Shanghai Jiaotong University, China
Sushmita Ruj	Indian Statistical Institute, India
Kewei Sha	University of Houston - Clear Lake, USA
Zhiguo Shi	Zhejiang University, China
Houbing Song	West Virginia University, USA
Junggab Son	Kennesaw State University, USA
Zhou Su	Waseda University, Japan
Xiaohua Tian	Shanghai Jiao Tong University, China
Chaokun Wang	Tsinghua University, China
Guodong Wang	South Dakota School of Mines and Technology, USA
Honggang Wang	University of Massachusetts, USA
Huihui Wang	Jacksonville University, USA
Li Wang	Beijing University of Posts and Telecommunications, China
Licheng Wang	Beijing University of Posts and Telecommunications, China
Shengling Wang	Beijing Normal University, China
Wei Wang	San Diego State University, USA
Yu Wang	University of North Carolina at Charlotte, USA
Yuexuan Wang	University of Hong Kong, SAR China
Lifei Wei	Shanghai Ocean University, China
Wei Wei	Xi'an University of Technology, China
Alexander Wijesinha	Towson University, USA
Yang Xiao	University of Alabama, USA
Kaiqi Xiong	Rochester Institute of Technology, USA
Guobin Xu	Frostburg State University, USA
Kuai Xu	Arizona State University, USA
Wen Xu	Texas Woman's University, USA
Minhui Xue	NYU Shanghai, China
Qingshui Xue	Shanghai Jiao Tong University, China
Qiben Yan	University of Nebraska Lincoln, USA
Ming Yang	Southeast University, China
Qing Yang	Montana State University, USA
Jianguo Yao	Shanghai Jiao Tong University, China
Dongxiao Yu	Huazhong University of Science and Technology, China
Jiguo Yu	Qufu Normal University, China

Wei Yu	Towson University, USA
Sherali Zeadally	University of Kentucky, USA
Bowu Zhang	Marist College, USA
Lichen Zhang	Shaanxi Normal University, China
Haojin Zhu	Shanghai Jiao Tong University, USA

Additional Reviewers

Ai, Yutong	Li, Ruinian
Aranzazu-Suescun, Catalina	Li, Ting
Bachir, Abdelmalik	Li, Wanyi
Boussaha, Ryma	Liang, Yi
Boyanapalli, Uday Bhaskar	Mei, Bo
Cao, Lijuan	Miao, Dongjing
Chu, Xu	Qiu, Linhai
Cobb, Crystal	Steinberg, Andrew
Duan, Zhuojun	Song, Tianyi
Gao, Qinghe	Tahir, Shahzaib
Ghose, Sarbani	Wei, Wei
Gu, Zhaoquan	Wen, Hui
Guo, Jin	Wu, Jiajia
Han, Meng	Wang, Jinbao
He, Zaobo	Wu, Mingli
Hu, Chunqiang	Wang, Yingjie
Huang, Yan	Xiao, Yinhao
Kim, Yanggon	Yao, Wenyan
Kim, Yeojin	Yang, Shuhui
Ko, Euiseong	Zhang, Cheng
Li, Hanshang	Zhang, Kai
Li, Hong	Zhao, Wei
Li, Hongjuan	Zheng, Xu
Li, Ji	

Contents

Simultaneous Wireless Information and Power Transfer for Multi-hop Energy-Constrained Wireless Network

Shiming He[1,2], Kun Xie[3(✉)], Weiwei Chen[3], Dafang Zhang[3],
and Jigang Wen[4]

[1] School of Computer and Communication Engineering, Hunan Provincial
Key Laboratory of Intelligent Processing of Big Data on Transportation,
Hunan Provincial Engineering Research Center of Electric Transportation
and Smart Distribution Network, Changsha University of Science and Technology,
Changsha 410114, China
smhe_cs@csust.edu.cn
[2] Hunan Provincial Key Laboratory of Network Investigational Technology,
Hunan Police Academy, Changsha 410138, China
[3] College of Computer Science and Electronics Engineering,
Hunan University, Changsha 410082, China
cskxie@gmail.com
[4] The Institute of Computing Technology, Chinese Academy of Science,
Beijing 100080, China

Abstract. As a new wireless communication technology, simultaneous wireless information and power transfer (SWIPT) can perform the information decoding at the same time energy harvesting. It can prolong the life time of the energy-constrained wireless node. Current works of SWIPT mainly focus on one-hop and two-hop wireless networks. When SWIPT is applied in multi-hop energy-constrained wireless network (MECWN), each hop node needs to allocate the optimal information and power, and the different allocation of information and power affects the network topology and thus the route selection, which is challenge. This paper concurrently considers SWIPT and routing selection in MECWN to improve the performance. For forming a link in a path, we design a novel allocation model to allocate information and energy each hop. For choosing a next hop node and path, we propose a novel energy cost metric to choose the transmission mode and evaluate the energy consuming of SWIPT link. Based on the metric, we propose an energy-aware SWIPT routing algorithm which allocates the information and energy of link during path finding process. Our performance studies demonstrate that our proposed algorithms can efficiently support SWIPT in MECWN to significantly decrease the energy consuming.

Keywords: Simultaneous wireless information and power transfer · Resource allocation · Routing algorithm · Network energy

© Springer International Publishing AG 2017
L. Ma et al. (Eds.): WASA 2017, LNCS 10251, pp. 1–12, 2017.
DOI: 10.1007/978-3-319-60033-8_1

1 Introduction

As a new wireless communication technology, simultaneous wireless information and power transfer (SWIPT) [1] can perform the information decoding at the same time energy harvesting. SWIPT is benefit from a promising radio frequency (RF)-based energy harvesting technology where the ambient RF radiation is captured by the receiver antennas and converted into a direct current (DC) voltage through appropriate circuits (rectennas) [2]. SWIPT refers to using the same wireless electromagnetic wave for information decoding and energy harvesting at the receiver. SWIPT is introduced as an attractive solution to prolong network lifetime [3–5].

Clearly, SWIPT will have a profound impact on the design of energy-constrained wireless network (equipped with batteries), which is attributed to its following advantages: (1) it can provide reliable energy without being affected by the dynamics of environments; (2) it eliminates wires or plugs between the charger and receiver; (3) it does not interfere with the normal operations of sensors such as sensing, packets delivering and receiving.

Current works of SWIPT generally focus on information and energy allocation problem, how many percent of received power is used to information decode or energy harvest, assuming the network nodes are in one-hop [3–6] and two-hop [7–10] wireless network. It is unclear what performance gain can be achieved if nodes are in multi-hop energy-constrained wireless network (MECWN). In order to verify the performance of SWIPT in multi-hop energy-constrained wireless network, this paper considers the problem of SWIPT in MECWN.

However, when SWIPT is applied in MECWN, each hop node needs to allocate the optimal information and energy, and the different allocation of information and power affects the network topology and the route selection, which is challenge. Some of the challenges are as follows.

First, the end-to-end path includes multi-hops in multi-hop energy-constrained wireless network, and each hop needs to allocate the information and energy. To minimize the end-to-end transmission power, the information and energy allocation of each hop needs to be considered in the path totally.

Second, the information and energy allocation affects the neighbor node set and network topology, which further decides the routing selection. The neighbor node set is changed as the change of information and energy allocation.

Third, SWIPT makes the routing more complicated than only information transmissions (IT). There are two transmission mode between nodes, SWIPT and IT. Which transmission mode of link may produce better performance? It desires careful design to choose the transmission mode along with the finding of the routing path and information and energy allocation in multi-hop energy-constrained wireless networks.

In summary, routing, information and energy allocation and transmission mode chosen are inter-dependent. To enable SWIPT in multi-hop energy-constrained wireless networks and fulfill the full potential of both techniques, these problems need to be systematically solved together.

This paper concurrently considers SWIPT and routing selection in multi-hop energy-constrained wireless network to improve the performance. For forming a link, we design a novel information and energy allocation model for routing. For choosing a next hop node and path, based on the allocation model, we proposes a novel routing metric and routing algorithm. Our contribution in this work can be summarized as follows:

- We introduce a novel information and energy allocation model for forwarding which forms a better link in a path. Based on the allocation model, we propose an information and energy allocation algorithm (IEA) to solve information and energy allocation problem.
- We propose a novel energy cost (Ecost) metric to choose the transmission mode and evaluate the energy consuming of SWIPT link. Based on the metric, we introduce an energy-aware SWIPT routing algorithm (ESWIPTR) which allocates the information and energy of link by IEA algorithm during finding path.
- We have carried out extensive simulations to evaluate the performance of our proposed solution. The simulation results demonstrate the effectiveness of our solution and the significant energy cost gains by incorporating SWIPT in multi-hop networks.

The rest of this paper is organized as follows. We introduce our network models and a motivation example in Sect. 2. We present our detailed algorithms on information and energy allocation and routing in Sects. 3 and 4. Simulation results and analysis are given in Sect. 5. We conclude the work in Sect. 6.

2 System Model

In this section, we first introduce our network models, then present a motivation example.

2.1 Network Models

We consider a multi-hop energy-constrained wireless network, as shown in Fig. 1. There are N nodes in the network. Each node is supported by battery. The residual energy of node i is denoted as Er_i. If the residual energy Er_i of node i is lower than Er_{min}, the node i will refuse to forward information for other nodes in order to prolong its own life time, which is an inactive node. For example, the residual energy of node 4 is lower than Er_{min}. The node 4 is an inactive node and the link l_{43} l_{45}, l_{47}, and l_{4D} are inactive. The node is an active node, while its residual energy is higher than Er_{min}.

All nodes are equipped with single antennas and have equivalent characteristics and computation capabilities. The data flow may traverse multiple hops in the network. A flow $F(S \rightarrow D)$ goes through a pair of source node and destination node, denoted as S and D.

There are two transmission modes between any two nodes in the network considered, information transmission (IT) and SWIPT transmission, as shown in Figs. 2 and 3.

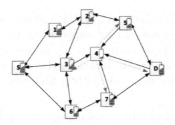

Fig. 1. Network model

Information Transmission (IT). IT is widely employed in current wireless networks, where a send node transmits its signal to a receiver node, and the RF signal is all fed into the signal processing circuit to information decode, which can be a decode and forward (DF) relay node.

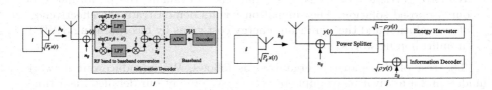

Fig. 2. Information transmission.   **Fig. 3.** SWIPT

At the sender side, the complex baseband signal is expressed as $x(t)$. It is assumed that $x(t)$ is a narrow-band signal with bandwidth of B Hz, and $E[|x(t)|^2] = 1$, where $E[\cdot]$ and $|\cdot|$ denote the statistical expectation and the absolute value, respectively. The transmitted signal propagates through a wireless channel h_{ij} with channel gain $|h_{ij}|^2$. h_{ij} captures the effects of path-loss, shadowing, and fading within the channel between i and j. Figure 2 shows the standard operations at an information receiver with coherent demodulation (assuming that the channel phase shift is perfectly known at the receiver). n_{ij} is the antenna noise and $n_{ij} \sim CN(0, \sigma_{ij}^2)$, where $CN(\mu, \sigma^2)$ denotes the circularly symmetric complex Gaussian (CSCG) distribution with mean μ and variance $\sigma\mu^2$, and $\sim$ stands for "distributed as".

The received RF band signal $y(t)$ is first converted to a complex baseband signal and then sampled and digitalized by an analog-to-digital converter (ADC) for further decoding. The noise introduced by the RF band to baseband signal conversion is denoted by z_{ij} with $z_{ij} \sim CN(0, \eta_{ij}^2)$. For simplicity, we assume an ideal ADC with zero noise. The discrete-time ADC output is then given by

$$\bar{y}[k] = \sqrt{P_{ij}} h_{ij} x[k] + n_{ij}[k] + z_{ij}[k] \tag{1}$$

where $k = 1, 2, \ldots,$ denotes the symbol index. The signal-to-noise ratio (SNR) is given by

$$\gamma_{ij}^{IT} = |h_{ij}|^2 P_{ij} / (\sigma_{ij}^2 + \eta_{ij}^2) \tag{2}$$

SWIPT Transmission. SWIPT still involves two nodes. The sender i transmits the signal $x(t)$ to the receiver with power P_{ij}. The received RF signal at the receiver j is

$$y(t) = \sqrt{P_{ij}} h_{ij} x(t) + n_{ij}(t) \tag{3}$$

We consider the power splitting (PS) mode [4], as shown in Fig. (3). The receiver j splits the received RF signal into two streams with the splitting ratio $\rho_{ij} \in [0, 1]$ by the power splitter. After that, $\sqrt{1 - \rho} y(t)$ is used for the EH circuit.

$$y^{EH}(t) = \sqrt{1 - \rho} y(t) \tag{4}$$

According to [5], the harvested power at the receiver is

$$E_{ij}^{eh} = \varepsilon(1 - \rho_{ij})(|h_{ij}|^2 P_{ij} + \sigma_{ij}^2) \tag{5}$$

where $\varepsilon \in [0, 1]$ denotes the energy converting coefficient of EH circuit.

In the meantime, the other RF signal $\sqrt{\rho} y(t)$ is fed into the signal processing circuit. Then the baseband signal at the receiver node can be expressed as

$$y^{ID}(t) = \sqrt{\rho} y(t) + z_{ij}(t) \tag{6}$$

Then, the signal-to-noise ratio (SNR) at the receiver can be derived as

$$\gamma_{ij}^{SWIPT} = \rho_{ij} |h_{ij}|^2 P_{ij} / (\sigma_{ij}^2 + \eta_{ij}^2) \tag{7}$$

Benefiting from the SWIPT, the node 4 can be charged from the previous node, and the link l_{43}, l_{45}, l_{47}, and l_{4D} become active again. In MECWN, a SWIPT routing path could be a combination of SWIPT links and IT links. For example, in Fig. 4(b), the flow is $F(S \rightarrow D) = S \xrightarrow{IT} 3 \xrightarrow{SWIPT:0.3} 4 \xrightarrow{IT} D$, where the second hop link l_{34}^{SWIPT} adopts SWIPT transmission mode, while the first hop link l_{S3}^{IT} and the third hop link l_{S3}^{IT} adopt the IT mode.

2.2 Motivation Example

To help understand the significance of our problem, we give a motivation example to show that only information transmission cannot achieve the good performance in multi-hop energy-constrained wireless networks.

Figure 4 is an multi-hop energy-constrained wireless network with 9 nodes. The small bar in each node denotes the residual energy. For simplicity, we assume that the SNR and harvested energy of each link can be calculated by Eq. (2) or Eqs. (5) and (7) depending on the transmission mode. The parameters are similar as the simulation setting in Sect. 5.

Initially, the flow $F(S \rightarrow D)$ has four available IT routing paths $Path_1 = S \xrightarrow{IT} 1 \xrightarrow{IT} 2 \xrightarrow{IT} 5 \xrightarrow{IT} D$, $Path_2 = S \xrightarrow{IT} 3 \xrightarrow{IT} 2 \xrightarrow{IT} 5 \xrightarrow{IT} D$, $Path_3 = S \xrightarrow{IT} 3 \xrightarrow{IT} 6 \xrightarrow{IT} 7 \xrightarrow{IT} D$, and $Path_4 = S \xrightarrow{IT} 6 \xrightarrow{IT} 7 \xrightarrow{IT} D$ as shown in Fig. 4(a). According to Eq. (2), to make sure that the forwarder node successful decodes data, the energy cost of links in these four paths can be calculated

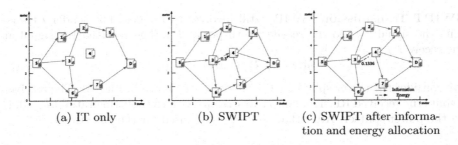

(a) IT only   (b) SWIPT   (c) SWIPT after informa-
                                    tion and energy allocation

Fig. 4. Motivation example.

directly: $P_{s1} = 23.61\,\mathrm{uW}$, $P_{s3} = 4.02\,\mathrm{uW}$, $P_{s6} = 33.23\,\mathrm{uW}$, $P_{12} = 2.02\,\mathrm{uW}$, $P_{25} = 4.02\,\mathrm{uW}$, $P_{32} = 21.36\,\mathrm{uW}$, $P_{36} = 21.02\,\mathrm{uW}$, $P_{5D} = 23.62\,\mathrm{uW}$, $P_{67} = 13.93\,\mathrm{uW}$, and $P_{7D} = 31.62\,\mathrm{uW}$. The energy cost of each path are $P_{Path_1} = P_{s1} + P_{12} + P_{25} + P_{5D} = 53.27\,\mathrm{uW}$, $P_{Path_2} = P_{s3} + P_{32} + P_{25} + P_{5D} = 53.02\,\mathrm{uW}$, $P_{Path_3} = P_{s3} + P_{36} + P_{67} + P_{7D} = 70.59\,\mathrm{uW}$, and $P_{Path_4} = P_{s6} + P_{67} + P_{7D} = 78.78\,\mathrm{uW}$, respectively. We select the minimum energy cost path $Path_2$ as the final path, and the energy cost is $53.02\,\mathrm{uW}$.

In Fig. 4(b), the node can harvest energy from other nodes to increase its residual energy. Benefiting from the SWIPT, the node 4 can be charged from the previous node 3, and the link l_{43} l_{45}, l_{47}, and l_{4D} become active again. The available SWIPT routing paths include more three paths $Path_5 = S \xrightarrow{IT} 3 \xrightarrow{SWIPT:0.3} 4 \xrightarrow{IT} D$, $Path_6 = S \xrightarrow{IT} 3 \xrightarrow{SWIPT:0.3} 4 \xrightarrow{IT} 5 \xrightarrow{IT} D$, and $Path_7 = S \xrightarrow{IT} 3 \xrightarrow{SWIPT:0.3} 4 \xrightarrow{IT} 7 \xrightarrow{IT} D$. The splitting ratio ρ of link l_{34}^{SWIPT} is 0.3. The energy cost of links in these three path are $P_{34} = 41.15\,\mathrm{uW}$, $P_{4D} = 4.02\,\mathrm{uW}$, $P_{45} = 12.82\,\mathrm{uW}$, and $P_{47} = 21.58$, respectively. The energy cost of these three path are $P_{Path_5} = P_{s3} + P_{34} + P_{4D} = 49.19\,\mathrm{uW}$, $P_{Path_6} = P_{s3} + P_{34} + P_{45} + P_{5D} = 69.17\,\mathrm{uW}$, $P_{Path_7} = P_{s3} + P_{34} + P_{47} + P_{7D} = 85.69\,\mathrm{uW}$, respectively. Therefore the minimum energy cost path is $Path_5$ with $49.19\,\mathrm{uW}$. The energy cost decreases about 8.3% compared with that in Fig. 4(a).

With the above-selected routes, we apply allocation to improve the network performance. In Fig. 4(c), we change the split ratio ρ of link l_{34}^{SWIPT} to 0.1336. The energy cost of link l_{34}^{SWIPT} reduces to $28.69\,\mathrm{uW}$, and the forwarder node 4 can successfully decode information. The energy cost of $Path_5$ reduce to $36.72\,\mathrm{uW}$. The energy cost decreases about 25.3% compared with that in Fig. 4(b).

The above example demonstrates that considering only information transmission, routing and information and energy allocation is not enough for achieving the maximum performance in multi-hop energy-constrained wireless networks. Information and energy allocation interacts with routing selection, and these elements should be simultaneously considered.

To solve the problem, we propose a solution framework which is formed with two important components: information and energy allocation model, and SWIPT routing.

3 Information and Energy Allocation

As shown in the motivation example of Sect. 2.2, the information and energy allocation can reduce energy cost and thus increase the transmission performance. The main function of information and energy allocation is to decide how many the transmission power and split ratio are, that is, how many percent of power for information decoding and how many percent of power for energy harvesting in the total transmission power. For practical implementation of the information and energy allocation in a multi-hop energy-constrained wireless network, we need to follow two basic constrains: (1) The information after splitting can be successfully decoded. (2) The receiver node can further forward packet to destination.

Algorithm 1. Information and Energy Allocation Algorithm (IEA)

Input: $i, j, R_{min}, P_{max}, Pc_j, |h_{ij}|^2, \sigma_{ij}^2, \eta_{ij}^2$
Output: ρ_{ij}, P_{ij}
1: Initialization. Set $\rho_{ij}^0, P_{ij}^0, a^1, b^1 \in \mathbb{R}, \mu > 0, 0 \leq \phi \ll 1, \upsilon \in (0,1), \eta > 1, k \leftarrow 1$.
2: Solve the problem (8). Based on the $\rho_{ij}^{k-1}, P_{ij}^{k-1}$, solve the no-constrained problem

$$\min_{\rho_{ij}, P_{ij}} L(\rho_{ij}, P_{ij}, a, b, \mu) = P_{ij} + \frac{1}{2\mu}(\min\{0, \mu(E_{ij}^{eh} - Pc_j) - a\}^2 - a^2)$$
$$+ \frac{1}{2\mu}(\min\{0, \mu(\gamma_{ij} - R_{min}) - b\}^2 - b^2) \qquad (8)$$

to get the ρ_{ij}^k, P_{ij}^k.
3: Check the stop criterion, if $\beta^k \leq \phi$, stop the loop and return ρ_{ij}^k, P_{ij}^k; otherwise, goto step 4.

$$\beta^k = (\min\{(Pc_j - \varepsilon(1 - \rho_{ij}^k)(|h_{ij}|^2 P_{ij}^k + \sigma_{ij}^2)), \frac{a^k}{\mu}\}^2$$
$$+ \min\{(R_{min} - \rho_{ij}^k|h_{ij}|^2 P_{ij}^k/(\sigma_{ij}^2 + \eta_{ij}^2)), \frac{b^k}{\mu}\}^2)^{1/2} \qquad (9)$$

4: Update μ, if $\beta^k \geq \upsilon\beta^k$, $\mu := \eta\mu$.
5: Update the lagrange multiplier a, b, according to

$$a^{k+1} = \max\{0, a^k + \mu(Pc_j - \varepsilon(1 - \rho_{ij}^k)(|h_{ij}|^2 P_{ij}^k + \sigma_{ij}^2))\}$$
$$b^{k+1} = \max\{0, b^k + \mu(R_{min} - \rho_{ij}^k|h_{ij}|^2 P_{ij}^k/(\sigma_{ij}^2 + \eta_{ij}^2))\} \qquad (10)$$

6: $k \leftarrow k + 1$, goto step 2.

In the allocation problem, the first constrain is that the information after splitting can be successfully decoded, that is, the SNR of received information should be larger than a SNR threshold R_{min}.

$$\gamma_{ij}^{SWIPT} \geq R_{min} \qquad (11)$$

The second constrain is that the receiver node can further forward packet to destination, which means that the harvest energy E_{ij}^{eh} of receiver node should larger than the receiver node's forwarding power Pc_j for forwarding to next hop node. The forwarding behavior doesn't reduce its residual energy.

$$E_{ij}^{eh} \geq Pc_j \tag{12}$$

The transmission power is no larger than the maximum transmission power P_{max}. The splitting ratio ρ is in the range of 0 to 1. Then, the allocation objective is to minimize the transmission power. Therefore, the information and energy allocation problem can be described as follow:

$$\begin{aligned} &\min_{\rho_{ij}, P_{ij}} P_{ij} \\ &s.t.\,(11),(12) \\ &0 \leq P_{ij} \leq P_{max} \\ &0 \leq \rho_{ij} \leq 1 \end{aligned} \tag{13}$$

We exploit the lagrange multiplier algorithm to solve the problem (13). By introducing lagrange multiplier a, b, we have the lagrange function.

$$\begin{aligned} L(\rho_{ij}, P_{ij}, a, b, \mu) = &P_{ij} + \tfrac{1}{2\mu}(\min\{0, \mu(E_{ij}^{eh} - Pc_j) - a\}^2 - a^2) \\ &+ \tfrac{1}{2\mu}(\min\{0, \mu(\gamma_{ij} - R_{min}) - b\}^2 - b^2) \end{aligned} \tag{14}$$

Inspired by the PHR algorithm proposed by Rockfellar, the information and energy allocation algorithm (IEA) of the problem can be described, as shown in Algorithm 1.

4   Energy-Aware SWIPT Routing

To quantify the energy cost of a link in multi-hop energy-constrained wireless networks, in this section, we first introduce a new routing metric, called energy cost (Ecost). Based on the metric, we propose an energy-aware routing algorithm to better exploit the benefit of SWIPT for a higher transmission performance.

In multi-hop energy-constrained wireless networks, there are two transmission modes (IT and SWIPT). If the node i transmits to the node j with IT, the energy cost $Ecost(i, j)^{IT}$ of the link l_{ij}^{IT} is equal to the transmission power. The SNR of node j should be larger than the SNR threshold R_{min}. Therefore, the energy cost $Ecost(i, j)^{IT}$ can be calucated as Eq. (15).

$$Ecost(i, j)^{IT} = P_{ij} = (\sigma_{ij}^2 + \eta_{ij}^2)R_{min}/|h_{ij}|^2 \tag{15}$$

If node i transmits data to node j with SWIPT, a part of power from node i is transformed to energy in node j, which is not consumed in the transmission. We should subtract this part. Therefore, the energy cost $Ecost(i, j)^{SWIPT}$ of the link l_{ij}^{SWIPT} is equal to the transmission power deducted by the harvested energy of node j.

$$Ecost(i, j)^{SWIPT} = P_{ij} - E_{ij}^{eh} \tag{16}$$

Based on Eqs. (15) and (16), the routing metric of link is defined as the minimum energy cost among all transmission models. The routing metric of a path is the sum of all links' metric in the path.

$$Ecost(i,j) = \min\{Ecost(i,j)^{SWIPT}, Ecost(i,j)^{IT}\} \tag{17}$$

Based on the metric, the node i can decide to take IT or SWIPT and determine the splitting ratio. The combined problem of routing, information and energy allocation, and transmission mode chosen can be described as problem (18).

$$
\begin{aligned}
&\min_{\mathbf{r},\rho,\mathbf{P}} \sum r_{ij}(P_{ij} - E_{ij}^{eh}) \\
&s.t.\ (11),(12), \forall i,j \\
&\sum_j r_{ij} - \sum_j r_{ji} = \begin{cases} 1, i = S. \\ -1, i = D. \ \forall i \\ 0, other. \end{cases} \\
&0 \le P_{ij} \le P_{max}, \rho_{ij} \in [0,1], r_{ij} \in \{0,1\}, \forall i,j
\end{aligned} \tag{18}
$$

In this paper, we modified dijkstra routing to implement our energy-aware SWIPT routing algorithm (ESWIPTR) to establish the minimum energy cost path, as shown in Algorithm 2. The derived Ecost metric is applied to construct the SWIPT path. Given a graph $G(V, E)$, the algorithm calculates the minimum energy cost paths from all nodes to a destination d. In the algorithm, we refer to $Ecost(i, d)$ simply by $Ecost_i$ for convenience. The estimate $Ecost_i$ is an upper-bound on the metric of the minimum energy cost path from i to d. In addition, we also keep its corresponding forwarder F_i, which stores the next forwarder used for i to reach d. We use Pc_i to store the forwarding power. The key idea of the algorithm is that each node $i \in V$ keeps the $Ecost_i$ as the node metric. At each round of the while loop, the node with the minimum metric from Q is settled. Let this node be j. For each incoming edge $(i, j) \in E$, we check if the metric $Ecost_i$ is larger than the metric $Ecost_j$ of the node just settled. If that is the case, we calculate the node temporary metric $Ecost'_i$ by temporarily setting j as the forwarder of node i according to Algorithm 1. If $Ecost_i$ is larger than the temporary metric $Ecost'_i$, then node j is set as the forwarder F_i, metric $Ecost_i$ is updated accordingly, and the forwarding energy Pc_i is set to P_{ij}. After node i is settled, the forwarder F_i and forwarding energy Pc_i are obtained.

5   Simulation Results and Analysis

In our simulation, we assume that the full energy of node Er_{full} equals to one energy unit. All nodes' residual energy Er satisfy stochastic distribution from 0 to Er_{full}. The energy threshold for forwarding Er_{min} is set to 0.4. The maximum transmission power P_{max} set to 100 mw. R_{min} is set to 20 dB. Specifically, the propagation gain from node i to node j is modeled by $|h_{ij}|^2 = 1/(1 + ||i - j||^\alpha)$, where $||i - j||$ is the distance (in meters) between i and j and α is the path-loss exponent. The path-loss exponent is set to 2.7 which corresponds to the urban

---

Algorithm 2. The pseudo code of ESWIPTR (G, d))

Input: $G(V, E), d, R_{min}, P_{max}$
Output: Path from i to d, with each hop (i, j) and ρ_{ij}, P_{ij}
1: **for** each node i in V **do**
2:     $\text{Ecost}_i \leftarrow \infty$
3:     $Pc_i \leftarrow \infty$
4:     $F_i \leftarrow \text{NIL}$
5: **end for**
6: $\text{Ecost}_d \leftarrow 0$
7: $Pc_d \leftarrow 0$
8: $S \leftarrow \emptyset$
9: $Q \leftarrow V$
10: **while** $Q \neq \emptyset$ **do**
11:     $j \leftarrow \text{EXTRACT-MIN}(Q)$
12:     $S \leftarrow S \bigcup \{j\}$
13:     **for** each incoming edge $(i, j) \in E$ **do**
14:         use algorithm 1 with $i, j, R_{min}, P_{max}, Pc_j, |h_{ij}|^2, \sigma_{ij}^2, \eta_{ij}^2$ to get ρ_{ij}, P_{ij}
15:         $\text{Ecost}'_i \leftarrow P_{ij} - E_{ij}^{eh} + \text{Ecost}_j$
16:         **if** $\text{Ecost}_i > \text{Ecost}'_i$ **then**
17:             $\text{Ecost}_i > \text{Ecost}'_i$
18:             $F_i \leftarrow j$
19:             $Pc_i \leftarrow P_{ij}$
20:         **end if**
21:     **end for**
22: **end while**

---

cellular communication environment. We assume that all nodes have the same noise set of parameters, i.e., $\sigma_{ij}^2 = \sigma^2, \eta_{ij}^2 = \eta^2$. Moreover, we set $\sigma^2 = -50\,\text{dBm}$, $\eta^2 = -70\,\text{dBm}$ in all simulations. The energy converting coefficient of EH circuit ε is set to 0.65. A direct link between two nodes may be not available (e.g., coverage extension scenario, physical barriers). The barriers rate br is the percent of unavailable direct link due to barriers, where $br = 30\%$.

There is no existing work studying SWIPT with routing in multi-hop energy-constrained wireless networks. We implement SWIPT schemes in an multi-hop network which is our proposed Algorithm 2, denoted as SWIPT. We also implement an additional schemes based on IT without considering SWIPT. The IT scheme is denoted as IT, where we use the Eq. (15) as the routing metric and apply Algorithm 2 to find the path with the minimum energy cost for flow.

Source and destination node are set at the diagonal corner of the square area, that is, source node is at (0,0) and destination node is at (50,50).

Energy cost is used to evaluate the performance. Energy cost is the routing metric from source to destination. We also calculate the routing metrics from all other nodes to the destination. Aggregative energy cost is the sum of routing metrics of all nodes. Various factors affect the performance. We perform simulation to analyze the effect of node density.

First, we investigate the convergence property and analyze the performance of the proposed algorithm. Note that in order to reach equilibrium in the Algorithm 2, the variables have to converge first in the Algorithm 1. For clarity, we show the convergence of the power variable on the Algorithm 1, in which the input variables are $P_{max} = 1000\,\text{mW}$, $Pc_j = 10\,\text{mW}$, $|h_{ij}|^2 = 0.0635$. And the inner variables of Algorithm 1 are $\mu = 0.5, \phi = 0.01, \upsilon = 0.5, \eta = 1.2$. Figure 5 shows the convergence of the Algorithm 1. We can see that the variables fluctuate in the first 40 iterations and reach equilibrium after 40 iterations.

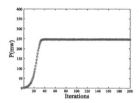

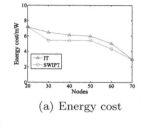

(a) Energy cost

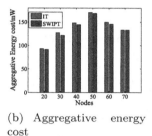

(b) Aggregative energy cost

Fig. 5. Convergence property of Algorithm 1.

Fig. 6. Energy results with different node density.

To investigate how the node density impacts the network performance, we vary the number of nodes from 20 to 70 in the network. When the number of nodes increases, the resource of forwarder nodes becomes richer. Therefore, the energy cost under two routing schemes decrease, as shown in Fig. 6(a).

When the number of nodes increases to 30, the energy cost of SWIPT starts to be lower than that of IT. Because of the increase of inactive forwarder nodes, forwarding packet through the lower energy nodes by SWIPT can be better than through active forwarder nodes by IT. The gains between SWIPT and IT are between 10% and 19%. When the number of nodes is 70, the gain can be ignore because of the dense active forwarder nodes. The node can find better forwarder nodes without SWIPT. The aggregative energy cost experiences two period. First, due to the increase of number of nodes, the aggregative energy cost increases because it is the sum of all nodes' energy cost. Second, due to the increase of active forwarder nodes, a node's energy cost decreases significantly. Although the number of all nodes increase, the aggregative energy cost decreases. From the aspect of all nodes, 10% to 23% nodes can decrease its energy cost by SWIPT. Therefore, the SWIPT is more suitable for medium node density.

6   Conclusion

To fulfill the full potential of SWIPT in MECWN, we propose a solution in which energy-aware routing at the network layer, transmission mode choosing at the MAC layer, and information and energy allocation at the physical layer can work coherently together to minimize the network energy consuming. Our solution firstly effectively exploits SWIPT technique to improve the performance of MECWN networks with transmission mode choosing and information and energy allocation. The simulation results demonstrate that SWIPT can achieve a large energy gain.

Acknowledgments. This work was supported by National Natural Science Foundation of China (Nos. 61572184, 61502054, 61303045, 71331001, 71420107027), the Science and Technology Projects of Hunan Province (No. 2016JC2075), the Open Research Fund of Hunan Provincial Key Laboratory of Intelligent Processing of Big Data on Transportation, the Research Foundation of Education Bureau of Hunan Province, China (Nos. 16C0047, 16B085), the Chinese Postdoctoral Science Foundation (No. 2013M541045), and the Scientific Research Fund of Hunan Provincial Transportation Department (No. 201446).

References

1. Varshney, L.R.: Transporting information and energy simultaneously. In: IEEE International Symposium on Information Theory (ISIT), pp. 1612–1616 (2008)
2. Valenta, C., Durgin, G.: Harvesting wireless power: survey of energy-harvester conversion efficiency in far-field, wireless power transfer systems. IEEE Microwave Mag. **15**(4), 108–120 (2014)
3. Zhang, R., Ho, C.K.: MIMO broadcasting for simultaneous wireless information and power transfer. IEEE Trans. Wirel. Commun. **12**(5), 1989–2001 (2013)
4. Liu, L., Zhang, R., Chua, K.C.: Wireless information and power transfer: a dynamic power splitting approach. IEEE Trans. Commun. **61**(9), 3990–4001 (2013)
5. Zhou, X., Zhang, R., Ho, C.K.: Wireless information and power transfer: architecture design and rate-energy tradeoff. IEEE Trans. Commun. **61**(11), 4754–4767 (2013)
6. Xiang, Z., Tao, M.: Robust beamforming for wireless information and power transmission. IEEE Wirel. Commun. Lett. **1**(4), 372–376 (2012)
7. Liu, Y., Wang, X.: Information and energy cooperation in OFDM relaying. In: IEEE ICC 2015 - Wireless Communications Symposium, pp. 1–6 (2015)
8. Liu, Y., Wang, X.: Information and energy cooperation in OFDM relaying: protocols and optimization. IEEE Trans. Veh. Technol. **65**(7), 5088–5098 (2016)
9. Huang, G., Zhang, Q., Qin, J.: Joint time switching and power allocation for multicarrier decode-and-forward relay networks with SWIPT. IEEE Sig. Process. Lett. **22**(12), 2284–2289 (2015)
10. Diamantoulakis, P.D., Ntouni, G.D., Pappi, K.N., Karagiannidis, G.K., Sharif, B.S.: Throughput maximization in multicarrier wireless powered relaying networks. IEEE Wirel. Commun. Lett. **4**(4), 385–389 (2015)

Leveraging Scheduling to Minimize the Tardiness of Video Packets Transmission in Maritime Wideband Communication

Tingting Yang[1,2,3($\boxtimes$)], Zhengqi Cui[1,2,3], Rui Wang[1,2,3], Zhou Su[1,2,3($\boxtimes$)], and Ying Wang[1,2,3]

[1] Navigation College, Dalian Maritime University, Dalian, China
[2] School of Mechatronic Engineering and Automation,
Shanghai University, Shanghai, China
[3] Information Science Technology College,
Dalian Maritime University, Dalian, China
yangtingting820523@163.com, zhousuasagi@gmail.com, wy_dlmu@163.com

Abstract. In this paper, we investigated the scheduling issue of the vessel's uploading data to the infostations through the maritime communication network, to optimize the dispatching process by Dynamic Programming. We mapped it as a single-machine minimized total weighted tardiness scheduling problem, subjecting to intermittent network connections in communication, packet generation and due time limitations. The route of the ship, the duration of generation, as well as the due date of the data packet is a priori known. Especially, the time-capacity mapping method is used to convert the problem of intermittent resource scheduling in the sea to continuous scheduling problem. We proposed a Dynasearch algorithm based on time-capacity mapping, and further the proposed algorithm is verified by MATLAB.

Keywords: SDN · Dynasearch scheduling · Maritime communication networks

1 Introduction

In recent years, facing the increasingly scope of the maritime transport systems and complex maritime situation, the maritime communication gradually reflects an important role. Maritime wideband communication system is distinct from the current maritime communication systems, which consists of ground and satellite systems. The newest satellite systems can achieve wideband transmission, whose data rates up to 432 kbps. However, due to the high cost of satellites communication (e.g., voice service costs USD$ 13.75 per minute for Iridium [1]). Taking the legacy VHF communication for an example has the maximum data rate approximately 9.6 kbps [2]. Therefore considering the problem of reducing costs, the establishment of maritime wideband communication system is a fundamental section that we must pay attention. In order to make the system be controlled more finely, Software Define Network (SDN) can be a good solution.

© Springer International Publishing AG 2017
L. Ma et al. (Eds.): WASA 2017, LNCS 10251, pp. 13–22, 2017.
DOI: 10.1007/978-3-319-60033-8_2

Software Defined Networking is a new way of modifying the network. Nearly a decade, the SDN has increasingly became a hot research direction carrying out the separation and control of the network [3]. SDN separates the control and data transmission in network devices and logically centralizes the governing of the network. This paradigm makes the development of new services and applications versatile. Moreover, SDN also has brought certain new concepts in networks such as Network Operating Systems (NOS) which represent a promising approach for realizing the full potential of computer communication networks, High Level Network Operating Languages and Network Functions Virtualization (NFV) [4]. SDN has revolutionized the way which the network built. Based on SDN system, maritime wideband communication systems targets the incorporation of wireless communications and informatics technologies into the navigation transportation system, making the navigation pattern to be safer and more efficient [5]. If a maritime wideband communications system is established, communications will be more convenient in case of maritime distress and safety system, urgency and general communication, and communication performance will be more easily promoted based on SDN field studies [6].

According to the connectivity of maritime wideband communication system is intermittent, a huge number of vessels can not always take part in the communication. So in the limited communication periods scheduling, the schelding is necessary. In this paper, we only concerned the single machine occasion which is about the problem of single-machine total weighted tardiness scheduling [7] to sort the data.

The extensive applications of scheduling in various trades and traffic communication have aroused people's interest [8]. Those are harnessed in the field of operations research, applied mathematics, computer science, production management science, artificial intelligence and engineering science. Study on the problem of single machine scheduling is a guide to research complex problem and provides an approximation algorithm for dealing with complex scheduling problems [9]. For example, many job shop problems can be solved using the decomposition method, and its sub-problems become a single problem.

The plight mentioned above is seldom discussed, easily overlooked, in the scheduling scenario of transport tasks for maritime wideband communications. This is an open issue, and of significance in the maritime efficient scheduling for video transmissions in maritime wireless communication networks area [10]. We have done some basic research in this area, It is more efficient and stable in the area of shipboard and ship interactive information, and provides the theoretical basis for multi-ship cooperative communication in the field of maritime wideband communication system. Considering to find a ductile transmission sequence, which satisfies both the external conditions of delay and the internal conditions of the information classification according to the classification of weights. Since all the constraints are NP-hard problems, we adopt a dynasearch algorithm based on neighborhood searching. In the context of time-depending, dynasearch is a recently proposed neighborhood search technique [11] that allows a series of moves to be performed at each iteration of a local search algorithm, generating in that way an exponential size neighborhood. Congram et al. applied dynasearch to the classical single machine total weighted tardiness problem. In the field of maritime scheduling, due to the multiple, complicated data and which the weight level is a lot in the maritime communication, the similarity of the dynamic search and the characteristic of narrowing the domain scope are particularly suitable for application. We used a lot of ideas on shore-based network scheduling aspects, communications, etc. from below references [13–18].

The remainder of this paper is organized as follows. System model is given in Sect. 2 and problem formulation is presented in Sect. 3. Actual dynamic programming algorithms are proposed in Sect. 4. In Sect. 5, simulation results are given employed to demonstrate the performance of our approaches. We conclude this paper with future work in Sect. 6.

2   System Model

The vessel's route is from the origin port to the destination port, during which the ship will generate a monitor video randomly and discontinuously, the task in order to transmit the monitor video is considered as a job. Videos could be uploaded to content server of administrative agencies by infostations deployed along route line. In the process of transmission, the packet type is based on the weight, the start time and the end time of the transmission, and the time required for the transmission. The infostations distributed along the navigation path, each infostation has coverage. The vessel in the infostations' coverage transmit monitoring video, in the outside of infostations' coverage sort the data. In order to optimize the result, we use dynamic programming to solve the scheduling problem, such as swapping the sequence of the jobs instead of the traditional search method. The vessels running route within the communication system is shown as followed (Fig. 1):

2.1   Time-Capacity Mapping

In our previous work, Dr. Yang put forward this idea in the information scheduling of maritime wideband network. The time is regarded as discrete and intermittent. In contrast, the capacity is continuous. This paper is based on the scheduling problem of this model, due to the intermittent network connectivity, a vessel may confront several infostations en route. We map the time indices into virtually cumulative capacity values, as shown in Fig. 2.

The time-capacity mapping function $f(t)$: $[T_I, T_o] \rightarrow [0, 1, \cdots \sum_{h=1}^{H} \sum_{k=1}^{K} A_{h,k}]$ is shown as:

$$
f(t) = \begin{cases} \sum_{m=1}^{(t-T_{h_t}^i)/T_F} A_{h_t,m} + \sum_{l=1}^{h_t-1} \sum_{m=1}^{K_l} A_{l,m} \\ \qquad if \ h_t \geq 1 \ and \ T_{h_t}^i \leq t \leq T_{h_t}^o \\ \sum_{l=1}^{h_t} \sum_{m=1}^{K_l} A_{l,m} \qquad otherwise \end{cases} \tag{1}
$$

where $A_{h,k}$ means the capacity of the kth frame within the hth infostation, while $T_I(T_O)$ represents the departure (arrival) time. $h_t = \arg \max_h \{T_h^i \leq t\}$.

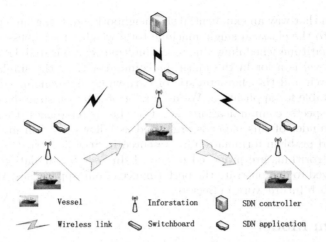

Vessel	Inforstation	SDN controller
Wireless link	Switchboard	SDN application

Fig. 1. An illustration of the network topology

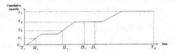

Fig. 2. Time-capacity mapping

After time-capacity mapping process, the issue could convert from time based scheduling to capacity based scheduling over a continuous horizon [12], such that the job-machine scheduling theory can be applied to solve the resource allocation problem at a low computational complexity, to be discussed in the following section. Since the parameters t are used in the subsection Time-capacity mappings, in order to distinguish them, we use t' for the relationship of $t \overrightarrow{f(t)} t'$.

2.2   Ds-swap Neighborhood

The dynasearch neighborhood we use is based on the swap neighborhood which gives the best results compared to other ones for the $1|| \sum_{j=1}^{n} w_j T_j$ problem, and probably for the generalized problem that we consider. We shall represent a solution by a permutation $\sigma = (\sigma(1), ..., \sigma(n))$ of the set $\{1, 2, ..., n\}$, meaning that job $\sigma(j)$ is the jth job to be scheduled. Given a permutation $\sigma = (\sigma(1), ..., \sigma(i), ..., \sigma(j), ..., \sigma(n))$ the swap neighbor consists of all $\frac{n(n-1)}{2}$ permutations $\sigma' = (\sigma(1), ..., \sigma(j), ..., \sigma(i), ..., \sigma(n))$, with $1 \leq i < j \leq n$, that can be obtained from r by swapping two jobs. The ds-swap neighborhood, introduced in [11], it is not difficult to see that this neighborhood has size $2^{n-1} - 1$.

3   Problem Formulation

Our goal is to let the infostations on the shore receive data more efficiently, that is, minimize the product of weights and delays by rescheduling the data task. A network centralized controller is employed, with the ability to schedule resource allocation problem.

In this section, we give the formal expression of the vessel weight tardiness minimization problem (VWTMP) for scheduling problems. The problem can be stated as follows. There are a set of n jobs seem as the transmission of monitor video, each job j has a due date d_j and a positive weight w_j. The processing time $f_j(t')$ of each job j depends on its starting time of execution t' and is given by a function f_j. We shall denote $f_j(t')$ by $p_j^{t'}$. So, if a job j immediately starts after a job i, its duration is $p_j^{c_i}$, where c_i represents the completion time of job i. We denote by c_j the completion time and by $T_j = \max\{C_j - d_j, 0\}$ the tardiness of job j. The objective is to find a schedule which minimizes the total weighted tardiness.

$$\exists N sequence \{\sigma_1(1), ..., \sigma_1(n)\}, ..., \{\sigma_n(1), ..., \sigma_n(n)\},$$
$$result[x] = \sum_{j=1}^{n} W_{\sigma_x(j)} T_{\sigma_x(j)} \tag{2}$$
$$\sigma_* = \arg\min result[x], 1 \le x \le 2^{n-1} - 1$$

This problem is strongly NP-hard since it is a generalization of the single-machine total weighted tardiness problem. Indeed we use dynasearch programming. The method of neighborhood search is used to obtain the solution of an approximate optimal solution, which greatly reduces the computational cost.

4   Proposed Algorithms

In order to achieve effective resource allocation with low computational complexity, We propose a dynamic programming algorithm based on sequence scheduling, which combines the parameters of time-dependend processing and the idea of ds-swap (here we consider only a single swap).

4.1   Ds-swap-Neighborhood with Dynasearch Programming

To search this exponential neighborhood in an efficient way, i.e. to find the best neighboring permutation of job among the $2^{n-1} - 1$ candidate permutations (i.e. we use steepest descent local search), We use a backward enumeration scheme in which jobs are appended to the beginning of the current partial sequence and are possibly swapped with jobs already scheduled in the partial sequence. We denote $(x)^+ = \max\{x, 0\}$ for any integer x. Let $\sigma = (\sigma(1), ..., \sigma(i), ..., \sigma(j), ..., \sigma(n))$, be a permutation. We denote (σ_i, t') the best possible way to schedule jobs $\sigma(i), \sigma(i+1), ..., \sigma(n)$ by applying a series of independent swaps on the subpermutation $(\sigma(i), \sigma(i+1), ..., \sigma(n))$, assuming that the first job scheduled in that sub-permutation (which is not necessarily $\sigma(i)$) is scheduled at time t'. We take only into account the total weighted tardiness of jobs $\sigma(i), \sigma(i+1), ..., \sigma(n)$ and forget jobs $\sigma(1), \sigma(2), ..., \sigma(i-1)$ when dealing with (σ_i, t'). We note $F(\sigma_i, t')$ the corresponding total weighted tardiness of jobs $\sigma(i), \sigma(i+1), ..., \sigma(n)$ in the state (σ_i, t'). We shall put $(\sigma_{n+1}, t') = \phi$ and $F(\sigma_{n+1}, t') = 0$ for any time t' to simplify the description of the algorithm below. Now the state (σ_i, t') must be obtained either by appending the job $\sigma(i)$ in front of the state $(\sigma_{i+1}, t' + p_{\sigma(i)}^{t'})$ or by appending the sequence $(\sigma(j), \sigma(i+1), ..., \sigma(j-1), \sigma(i))$, obtained by swapping jobs $\sigma(i)$ and $\sigma(j)$, in front of the state (σ_{j+1}, t'') for some job $i+1 < j \leq n$ and time t'' (to be determined later). We have for the first case

$$F(\sigma_i, t') = w_{\sigma(i)} \left(t' + p_{\sigma(i)}^{t'} - d_{\sigma(i)} \right)^+ + F\left(\sigma_{i+1}, t' + p_{\sigma(i)}^{t'} \right) \tag{3}$$

For the second case, let t'_k be the starting time of the kth scheduled job for $i \leq k \leq j$ after having swapped $\sigma(i)$ and $\sigma(j)$. By definition of $F(\sigma_i, t'), t'_i = t'$. Then since jobs $\sigma(i)$ and $\sigma(j)$ have been swapped, $t'_{i+1} = t'_i + p_{\sigma(j)}^{t'_i}$. Finally, $t'_k = t'_{k-1} + p_{\sigma(k-1)}^{t'_{k-1}}$ for $i+1 < k \leq j$. Thus we have

$$
\begin{aligned}
F(\sigma_i, t') = &\ w_{\sigma(j)} \left(t'_i + p_{\sigma(j)}^{t'_i} - d_{\sigma(j)} \right)^+ \\
&+ \sum_{i<k<j} w_{\sigma(k)} \left(t'_k + p_{\sigma(k)}^{t'_k} - d_{\sigma(k)} \right)^+ \\
&+ w_{\sigma(i)} \left(t'_j + p_{\sigma(i)}^{t'_j} - d_{\sigma(i)} \right)^+ \\
&+ F\left(\sigma_{j+1}, t'_j + p_{\sigma(i)}^{t'_j} \right)
\end{aligned} \tag{4}
$$

If $j = i + 1$, the sum is empty.

We want to calculate $F(\sigma_1, 0)$. Notice that a forward enumeration scheme is not possible in ourcase, since we do not know what is the completion time of the last job in an optimal solution. In our implementation of the dynamic programming algorithm, an array stores the values of F already computed in order to reduce the number of recursive calls. The optimal set of independent swaps can be retrieved by examining an array which stores, for each job j and each time t' for which a value $F(\sigma_j, t')$ was computed, the position of $\sigma(j)$ in the state (σ_j, t'). The algorithm is given as followed.

We obtain the time complexity of the result is $\theta(n^4)$, so as to obtain the optimal solution in the case where the complexity is as small as possible, and give the most feasible job permutation.

5   Performance Evaluation

In this part, We consider the comparison between dynamic search algorithm and some common algorithms. In simulation comparison, we choose some significant parameters such as processing time, task waiting time and the number of tasks.

In the three simulation diagram, the vertical axis is expressed as the sum of the delay times the weight.

Algorithm 1. *Ds-swap Dynasearch*

---

phrase 1 : Time-capacity Mapping

$$f(t) = \begin{cases} \sum_{m=1}^{(t-T_{h_t}^i)/T_F} A_{h_t,m} + \sum_{l=1}^{h_t-1} \sum_{m=1}^{K_l} A_{l,m} \\ \quad \text{if } h_t \geq 1 \text{ and } T_{h_t}^i \leq t \leq T_{h_t}^o \\ \sum_{l=1}^{h_t} \sum_{m=1}^{K_l} A_{l,m} \quad \text{otherwise} \end{cases}$$

$\overline{t \; f(t)} \; t'$

phrase 2 : Ds-swap Neighbourhood

Initially:alreadycomputed$[i][t']$ =false,swaps$[k][t'] = k$ $\forall i \in \{1, ..., n\}, t' \in \{0, ..., (n-1)p\max\}$
$\forall k \in \{1, ..., n\}, t' \in \{0, ..., (n-1)p\max\}$

function $ds - swap - neighborhood(\sigma)$
function $dyna(i, t')$
if $i = n$ then
return $w_{\sigma(n)} * (t' + p_{\sigma(n)}^{t'} - d_{\sigma(n)})^+$
else if computed$[i][t']$ then
return dynacomputed$[i][t']$
end if
result$[i] := w_{\sigma(i)} * (t' + p_{\sigma(i)}^{t'} - d_{\sigma(i)})^+ + dyna(i+1, t + p_{\sigma(i)}^{t'})$
for $j = i + 1$ to n do

result$[j]=:$
$$\begin{aligned} &w_{\sigma(j)} * (t' + p_{\sigma(j)}^{t'} - d_{\sigma(j)})^+ \\ &+ \sum_{i<k<j} w_{\sigma(k)} * (t'_k + p_{\sigma(k)}^{t'_k} - d_{\sigma(k)})^+ \\ &+ w_{\sigma(i)} * (t'_j + p_{\sigma(i)}^{t'_j} - d_{\sigma(i)})^+ \\ &+ dyna(j+1, t'_j + p_{\sigma(i)}^{t'_j}) \\ &/ * t'_{i+1} = t' + p_{\sigma(j)}^{t'_j} \end{aligned}$$ and $t'_k = t'_{k-1} + p_{\sigma(k-1)}^{t'_{k-1}}$ for

$i + 1 < k \leq j * /$
end for

phrase 3 : Generate The Sequence

$j* :=$arg min$i \leq j \leq n$ result$[j]$
swaps$[i][t'] := j*$
alreadycomputed$[i][t']$ =true
dynacomputed$[i][t']$ =result$j*$
return dynacomputed$[i][t']$
end function
$dyna(1, 0)$
$time := 0$
for $k = 1$ to $n - 1$do
if swaps$[k][time]! = k$ then
$swap\ job\ \sigma(k)\ with\ job\ \sigma(swaps[k][time])$
k:=swaps$[k][time]$
end if
$time := C_k$
end for
return σ
end function

In Fig. 3 the processing axis can be seen as independent variables indicates the number of tasks, it varies from 30 to 50, with the increase of the number of tasks. The total delay weight multiplied by the three algorithms are increasing, but the increase of the dynamic search algorithm is the slowest. That is to say when the task increases when the algorithm is still very stable.

In Fig. 4, AHT is equal to average processing time. The average processing time requires for horizontal variables task processing, it varies from 10 to 14 second. Increasing the average processing time will make the task delay increase,

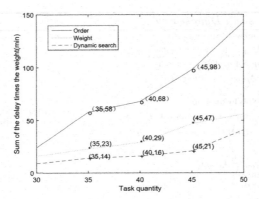

Fig. 3. Delay times weight versus task quantity

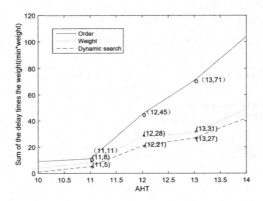

Fig. 4. Delay times weight versus task AHT

and the dynamic search algorithm index still increased most slowly. The weight sorting algorithm and dynamic search algorithm will be relatively close to the average processing time.

In Fig. 5 indicates the influence of the average waiting time on the results. The task average waiting time varies from 320 to 440 second. Task average waiting time is longer, the delay will be shorter, so the value of the variable will be reduced. The increase in the average waiting time will reduce the number of tasks that exceed the deadline. The cumulative effect of delay does not occur, thus reducing the weight of the impact of the results. By comparing with other algorithms, the dynamic search algorithm is still the best method, which shows that the algorithm is very stable.

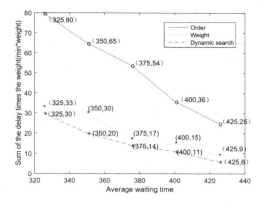

Fig. 5. Delay times weight versus average waiting time

6   Conclusion

In this paper, we done a deep exploration of the scheduling problem of uploading data to infostations in marine environment. In order to minimize the total weighted tardiness, time-capacity mapping based dynamic search algorithm is proposed. In simulation part, we compared our schemes with the other two traditional transmission methods. The simulation results showed that the dynamic search algorithm has a more effective consequence in transferring time, which has an extremely prefect time complexity that nearly $\theta(n^4)$. All in all this potential field also has a flamboyant future, we have a strong wish to devote in the collaboration of multi-ship and valid scheduling tasks of multi-transfer mode. In addition, priority options for maritime emergency missions such as search and rescue and certain information of diabolic accidents will also be pondered.

Acknowledgement. This work was supported in part by Research Project for FY2017 of International Association of Maritime Universities, China Postdoctoral Science Foundation under Grant 2015T80238, Natural Science Foundation of China under Grant 61401057, Natural Science Foundation of Liaoning Province under Grant 201602083, Science and technology research program of Liaoning under Grant L2014213, Dalian science and technology project under Grant 2015A11GX018, Research Funds for the Central Universities 3132016007 and 01760325. Dalian high-level innovative talent project under Grant 2016RQ035, Open Research Project of the State Key Laboratory of Industrial Control Technology of Zhejiang University, China under Grant ICT170310.

References

1. Delta Wave communication LLC: INMARSAT BGAN SERVICE RATES, single and dual SIM data allowance plans. www.deltawavecomm.com/
2. Bekkadal, F., Yang, K.: Novel maritime communications technologies. In: IEEE MMS Symposium (2010)

3. Zhang, C.-K., Cui, Y., Tang, H., Wu, J.: Software define network (SDN) research progress. J. Softw. **26**(1), 62–81 (2015)
4. Thomas, R.H., Schantz, R.E., Forsdick, H.C.: Network operating systems. In: Proceedings on Local Area Networks: An Advanced Course (1978)
5. Yang, T., Shen, X.S.: Maritime Wideband Communication Networks: Video Transmission Scheduling. SpringerBriefs in Computer Science. Springer, Cham (2014)
6. Yang, T., Liang, H., Cheng, N., Shen, X.: Towards video packets store-carry-and-forward scheduling in maritime wideband communication. In: IEEE GLOBECOM (2013)
7. Maheswaran, R., Ponnambalam, S.G.: An investigation on single machine total weighted tardiness scheduling problems. Int. J. Adv. Manuf. Technol. **22**(3–4), 243–248 (2003)
8. Feng, D., Tang, L.: With maximum weighted satisfaction dynasearch algorithm. In: Management Sciences (2006)
9. Eiselt, H.A., Sandblom, C.L.: Single machine scheduling. In: Eiselt, H.A., Sandblom, C.L. (eds.) Decision Analysis, Location Models, and Scheduling Problems, pp. 353–365. Springer, Heidelberg (2004)
10. Yang, T., Liang, H., Cheng, N., Deng, R.: Efficient scheduling for video transmissions in maritime wireless communication networks. IEEE Trans. Veh. Technol. **64**(9), 4215–4229 (2015)
11. Congram, R.K., Potts, C.N., Van de Velde, S.L.: An iterated dynasearch algorithm for the single-machine total weighted tardiness scheduling problem. INFORMS J. Comput. **14**(1), 52–67 (2002)
12. Liang, H., Zhuang, W.: Efficient on-demand data service delivery to high-speed trains in cellular/infostation integrated networks. IEEE J. Sel. Areas Commun. **30**(4), 780–791 (2012)
13. Zheng, X., Cai, Z., Li, J., Gao, H.: A study on application-aware scheduling in wireless networks. IEEE Trans. Mob. Comput. **pp**(99), 1 (2016)
14. Zheng, X., Cai, Z., Li, J., Gao, H.: Scheduling flows with multiple service frequency constraints. IEEE Internet Things J. **pp**(99), 1 (2016)
15. Zheng, X., Cai, Z., Li, J., Gao, H.: An application-aware scheduling policy for real-time traffic. In: IEEE International Conference on Distributed Computing Systems, pp. 421–430 (2015)
16. Du, Q., Zhang, X.: Statistical QoS provisionings for wireless unicast/multicast of multi-layer video streams. IEEE J. Sel. Areas Commun. **28**(3), 420–433 (2010)
17. Duan, Z., Li, W., Cai, Z.: Interference-controlled D2D routing aided by knowledge extraction at cellular infrastructure towards ubiquitous CPS. Pers. Ubiquit. Comput. **19**(7), 1033–1043 (2015)
18. Duan, Z., Li, W., Cai, Z.: Distributed auctions for task assignment and scheduling in mobile crowdsensing systems. In: The 37th IEEE International Conference on Distributed Computing Systems (ICDCS 2017), no. 5, pp. 1–5 (2017)

Optimal Power Scheduling for SIC-Based Uplink Wireless Networks with Guaranteed Real-Time Performance

Chaonong Xu[1($\boxtimes$)], Kaichi Ma[1], Yida Xu[1], and Yongjun Xu[2]

[1] China University of Petroleum, Beijing 102249, China
xuchaonong@cup.edu.cn
[2] Institute of Computing Technology, Chinese Academy of Sciences,
Beijing 100190, China
xyj@ict.ac.cn

Abstract. The k-SIC technology can support at most k parallel transmissions, thus it has the prominent capability of providing fast media access, which is vital for real-time industrial wireless networks. However, it suffers from high power consumption because high interference has to be overcome. In this paper, given the real-time performance requirement of an uplink network supporting k-SIC, we study how to minimize aggregate power consumption of users by power scheduling. We prove that the problem is solvable in polynomial time. A universal algorithm with complexity of $O(n^3)$ is proposed for k-SIC, where n is the number of transmitters. For the special case of $k = 2$, another algorithm with complexity of $O(L^4)$ is presented, where L is the frame length. Simulation results reveal that both the aggregate power consumption and the maximal transmit power will be exponentially declined with further relaxation of the real-time performance.

Keywords: SIC · Uplink network · Schedule · Power control · Low power · Real time

1 Introduction

Wireless networks have been applied widely in industry. Currently, most of the practical monitoring systems are based on the single-hop uplink networks, where UEs (User Equipment) are laid to sense environment and then the sensory data is transmitted to and aggregated in a base station.

Real-time performance is an important performance metric for uplink network. For example, in some industrial wireless monitoring systems, especially for systems involving sensory data fusion or emergency alarm, UEs must access wireless channel in time. In other words, rapid channel access is required. MPR (Multi-Packet Reception) can support multiple parallel transmissions from different UEs, it is thus helpful for rapid channel access. SIC (Successive Interference Cancellation) technology supports MPR by exploring the structure of the interference signal. Its principle is as follows: Once a signal is decoded successfully, it will be subtracted from the received signal, the decoding of subsequent signal is thus immune from the signals that have

© Springer International Publishing AG 2017
L. Ma et al. (Eds.): WASA 2017, LNCS 10251, pp. 23–36, 2017.
DOI: 10.1007/978-3-319-60033-8_3

been decoded before. The process goes on until no signal can be decoded any further. Because of its implementation simplicity, SIC technology has attracted interests of researchers from both cellular networks [1] and WLANs (Wireless Local Area Networks) [5]. For example, it is a key component in NOMA (Non-Orthogonal Multiple Access), which may be adopted by future 5G standards.

Although SIC is effective in boosting real-time performance, since high interference has to be overcome, SIC suffers from tremendous power consumptions, which poses a huge challenge for energy-constrained UEs [3, 4]. Therefore, minimizing power consumption under given real-time performance is of great significance [6, 10].

In this paper, we consider a single-channel uplink network that consists of a base station (receiver) and multiple UEs (transmitter)[1], and the base station installs a k-SIC receiver. Given the requirement of the real-time performance, we try to find an algorithm that minimizes the aggregate power consumption of all UEs.

We solve the problem by combining transmitters scheduling and power allocating together. On one hand, since UEs in the same group transmit concurrently, the transmitters scheduling aims to determine how to group the UEs. On the other hand, the component of power allocating sets the transmit powers for UEs, so that all UEs in the same group can be decoded successfully. In other words, minimized aggregate power consumption could be achieved by joint optimization of transmitters scheduling and power allocating, or alternatively, power scheduling [7, 8].

We show that the above problem can be solved by sequentially solving two sub-problems, i.e., power allocating of k-SIC and transmitters scheduling in multiple slots. Our technique contributions are as follows: (1) We formulate the problem of minimizing aggregate power consumption for SIC-based real-time uplink wireless network by combining transmitters scheduling and power allocating. (2) We propose a universal algorithm with complexity of $O(n^3)$ for k-SIC, where n is the number of transmitters. For 2-SIC, another algorithm with time complexity of $O(L^4)$ is also presented, where L is the frame length required by the real-time performance.

2   System Model

We consider a single-hop, single-channel uplink network consisting of n single-antenna UEs $u_1, u_2, \ldots, u_n$, and a single-antenna base station. The base station is equipped with a k-SIC receiver. A k-SIC receiver can decode at most k signals at one time, provided that SINR of every signal after interference cancellation is beyond the decoding threshold of the receiver.

In the considered network, time is divided into frames, and each frame includes multiple time slots. In the beginning of a frame, transmitters with data to transmit will notify the base station in the Information Collection (IC) sub-frame. The base station computes the optimal power scheduling scheme and then broadcasts them in the BC (Broadcast) sub-frame. In the following data subframe, all transmitters will transmit their

---

[1] UEs and transmitters are used interchangeably in this paper.

data based on the optimal scheduling scheme. Note that IC and BC could be executed on control subchannel, while DATA is executed on data subchannel.

The channel gain gauges the loss of signal power as it travels through the channel. We assume that channel gain of each node keeps constant during a frame time. Only in the section of performance evaluations, the following channel gain model for wireless signal is used,

$$CG = -20log(f) - 26log(d) + 19.2,$$

where f is the frequency in Megahertz, and d is the Euclidean distance between transmitter and receiver in meters. Using the channel gain model, the channel gain of each transmitter can be known based on its Euclidean distance with the receiver.

We add no constraint of maximal power because it makes the optimal solution intractable. However, since our aim is to minimize aggregate power consumption, the optimal transmit powers of UEs could not be very high. In other words, the constraint of maximal power is useless in this paper.

We use frame length to gauge the real-time performance of the uplink network, where the real-time performance is better if the frame length is smaller. In general, a frame consists of multiple time slots with fixed time duration. Take LTE-FDD (Long Term Evolution, Frequency Division Duplex) for example, the duration of one frame is 10 ms, and that of a time slot in LTE-FDD is 0.5 ms. In this paper, the duration of a time slot is not specified, since the duration could be set according to application requirements.

3   Minimal Power Scheduling Algorithm for 2-SIC

Definition 1. Real-time Minimal Power Scheduling for 2-SIC (RMPS-2SIC) Problem. Given a 2-SIC receiver and n transmitters $u_1, u_2, \ldots, u_n$ with channel gains $G_1, G_2, \ldots, G_n$ respectively. Without loss of generality, assume $G_1 \geq G_2 \geq \ldots \geq G_n$. At most two transmitters can transmit in parallel. Noise power is n_0 for all transmitters. Configure the transmit powers $p_1, p_2, \ldots, p_n$ such that the aggregate power consumption of the n transmitters is minimized under the following constraints: (1) Every transmitter is scheduled only once in a frame; (2) The number of time slots in a frame is not larger than the designated value L; (3) SINR for any transmitter is above the given decoding threshold γ.

The problem is thus formulated as

$$\min_{\{s; p_1, \ldots, p_n\}} \sum_{i=1}^{n} p_i$$

$$\text{s.t. } FL(s) \leq L; \quad 0 \leq Nb(s[j]) \leq 2 \ j \in [1..L]; \quad \frac{G_i p_i}{I_i + n_0} \geq \gamma \ p_i \geq 0 \ i \in [1..n];$$

where s represents the transmitters scheduling scheme, $s[j]$ represents the set of all transmitters which are scheduled in the j'th slot, and I_i is the power of interference when decoding signal of u_i. Apparently, the interference is only decided by s if $\{p_1, p_2, \ldots, p_n\}$ are already known. $FL(s)$ is the number of time slots in the scheduling scheme s. L is for gauging the real-time performance, which should be at least $\lceil n/2 \rceil$ for a 2-SIC receiver, and $Nb(s[j])$ is the cardinality of $s[j]$.

RMPS-2SIC is formulated as a joint optimization problem of power allocating and transmitter scheduling. We prove that its optimal solution can be found by sequentially solving two sub-problems, i.e., power allocating for 2-SIC and transmitters scheduling in multiple slots for 2-SIC.

3.1   Minimal Power Allocating for 2-SIC

Definition 2. Minimal Power allocating for 2 Parallel Transmitters (MPC2PT): Given an uplink network which consists of a 2-SIC receiver and two transmitters u_1, u_2 with channel gains as G_1, G_2, and n_0 is the noise power. Without loss of generality, assume $G_1 \geq G_2$. Configure transmit powers p_1, p_2 for u_1, u_2, so that the sum of their power consumptions is minimized, in the premise that u_1, u_2 transmit in parallel and both of them are decoded successfully.

If $G_1p_1 \geq G_2p_2$, signal from u_1 must be decoded first because $\gamma > 1$ is necessary for successful decoding. Thus, the problem is formulated as

$$\min_{p1,p2} \ p_1 + p_2$$

$$s.t. \ \frac{G_1p_1}{G_2p_2 + n_0} \geq \gamma; \ \frac{G_2p_2}{n_0} \geq \gamma; \ G_1p_1 \geq G_2p_2; \ p_1, p_2 \geq 0; \tag{1}$$

On the other side, if $G_1p_1 \leq G_2p_2$, signal from u_2 must be decoded first, and thus the problem can be formulated as

$$\min_{p1,p2} \ p_1 + p_2$$

$$s.t. \ \frac{G_2p_2}{G_1p_1 + n_0} \geq \gamma; \ \frac{G_1p_1}{n_0} \geq \gamma; \ G_2p_2 \geq G_1p_1; \ p_1, p_2 \geq 0; \tag{2}$$

Lemma 1. The minimum of Formula (1) is not larger than that of Formula (2).

Proof. Assume the optimal solution to Formula (2) is $(\bar{p}_1, \bar{p}_2)$. Order that $\tilde{p}_1 = \frac{G_2\bar{p}_2}{G_1}$ and $\tilde{p}_2 = \frac{G_1\bar{p}_1}{G_2}$, so $\frac{G_1\tilde{p}_1}{G_2\bar{p}_2 + n_0} = \frac{G_2\bar{p}_2}{G_1\bar{p}_1 + n_0} \geq \gamma$, $\frac{G_2\tilde{p}_2}{n_0} = \frac{G_1\bar{p}_1}{n_0} \geq \gamma$ Besides, since $G_1\tilde{p}_1 = G_2\bar{p}_2 \geq G_1\bar{p}_1 = G_2\tilde{p}_2$, $(\tilde{p}_1, \tilde{p}_2)$ is therefore a feasible solution of Formula (1).

It can be easily verified that $\tilde{p}_1 + \tilde{p}_2 - \bar{p}_1 - \bar{p}_2 = \left(\frac{G_1 - G_2}{G_1 G_2}\right)(G_1 \bar{p}_1 - G_2 \bar{p}_2) \leq 0$, therefore, the object value of Formula (1) at $(\tilde{p}_1, \tilde{p}_2)$ is no more than the minimum of Formula (2), i.e., the minimum of Formula (1) is not larger than that of Formula (2). $\square$

Theorem 1. The optimal power configuration for MPC2PT is $p_1^* = \frac{\gamma n_0 (\gamma + 1)}{G_1}$ and $p_2^* = \frac{\gamma n_0}{G_2}$.

Proof. We use Lagrange relaxation method to find an analytic solution to Formula (1). Order that $L(p_1, p_2, \lambda_1, \lambda_2, \lambda_3) = p_1 + p_2 + \lambda_1(\gamma G_2 p_2 - G_1 p_1 + \gamma n_0) + \lambda_2(-G_2 p_2 + \gamma n_0) + \lambda_3(G_2 p_2 - G_1 p_1)$. Based on the KKT condition, we get:

$$\frac{\partial L(p_1, p_2, \lambda_1, \lambda_2, \lambda_3)}{\partial p_1} = 1 - \lambda_1 G_1 - \lambda_3 G_1 = 0;$$

$$\frac{\partial L(p_1, p_2, \lambda_1, \lambda_2, \lambda_3)}{\partial p_2} = 1 + \lambda_1 \gamma G_2 - \lambda_2 G_2 + \lambda_3 G_2 = 0;$$

$$\lambda_1 \left(\frac{G_1 p_1}{G_2 p_2 + n_0} - \gamma\right) = 0; \quad \lambda_2 \left(\frac{G_2 p_2}{n_0} - \gamma\right) = 0; \quad \lambda_3 (G_2 p_2 - G_1 p_1) = 0;$$

In general, $\gamma > 1$ is necessary for decoding, thus $G_1 p_1 > G_2 p_2 + n_0 > G_2 p_2$. Therefore, $\lambda_3^* = 0$, and thus

$$\begin{cases} 1 - \lambda_1 G_1 = 0 \\ 1 + \lambda_1 \gamma G_2 - \lambda_2 G_2 = 0 \end{cases}.$$

So, $\lambda_1^* = \frac{1}{G_1}$ and $\lambda_2^* = \frac{G_1 + \gamma G_2}{G_1 G_2}$. Based on the complementary slackness condition, we get $\frac{G_1 p_1^*}{G_2 p_2^* + n_0} = \gamma$, and $\frac{G_2 p_2^*}{n_0} = \gamma$, i.e., $p_1^* = \frac{\gamma n_0 (\gamma + 1)}{G_1}$ and $p_2^* = \frac{\gamma n_0}{G_2}$. $\square$

One natural intuition is that the farther a transmitter is from the receiver, the more power consumption it has to pay, which is consistent with Theorem 1.

3.2 Minimal Power Scheduling for 2-SIC

Based on the optimal solution to MPC2PT, we present algorithm 1 for solving RMPS-2SIC based on the MWM (Maximum Weight Matching) of a graph.

We construct a weighted graph which includes n real graph nodes and $2L - n$ virtual graph nodes. Note that the n real nodes correspond to the n UEs.

```
Algorithm 1. Optimal algorithm of RMPS-2SIC {
1. Construct graph GH including n real and 2L-n virtual
   graph nodes;
2. For any two real graph nodes i and j {
3. If G_i > G_j, the weight of their connecting edge is set
```
as $-\left(\frac{\gamma n_0(\gamma+1)}{G_i}+\frac{\gamma n_0}{G_j}\right);$ else set it as $-\left(\frac{\gamma n_0(\gamma+1)}{G_j}+\frac{\gamma n_0}{G_i}\right);$ }
```
4. For any real graph node i and a virtual node {
```
   the weight of their connecting edge is $-\frac{\gamma n_0}{G_i};$ }
```
5. Find a MWM(GH) generated by Edmond's blossom algo-
   rithm;}
   //setting transmit power based on MWM(GH)
6. for any edge in MWM(GH) which connects i and j {
7. if(both i and j are real graph nodes){
8.     if G_i > G_j,
```
$(p_i, p_j) = (\frac{\gamma n_0(\gamma+1)}{G_j}, \frac{\gamma n_0}{G_i});$ else $(p_i, p_j) = (\frac{\gamma n_0(\gamma+1)}{G_i}, \frac{\gamma n_0}{G_j})$ }};
```
   else the transmit power of the UE corresponding to the
```
   real graph node is $\frac{\gamma n_0}{G}$, where G is its channel gain;}

The output of Algorithm 1 can be mapped to power scheduling scheme as follows: For two real graph nodes i and j, u_i and u_j will transmit in parallel if they are matched in MWM(GH). If a real graph node i is matched with a virtual node, u_i will monopoly a time slot.

Theorem 2. Algorithm 1 solves RMPS-2SIC.

Proof. First, the output of Algorithm 1 is a feasible solution to RMPS-2SIC, i.e., it satisfies all constraints of RMPS-2SIC as follows:

(1) Since there are at most $2L$ graph nodes, MWM(GH) has at most L edges. Based on the mapping scheme, the frame length is thus at most L.
(2) Signal from every UE can be decoded correctly based on the power allocation mapped from MWM, which is in line 8.
(3) Every graph node will appear only once in a matching, and thus every UE will be given only one transmit chance.

Second, the power scheduling scheme mapped from the output of Algorithm 1 gets the minimal aggregate power consumption. Its proof is based on the following facts:

(1) Based on the structure of GH, transmitters scheduling strategies and maximal matchings of GH can be mapped one-to-one. Therefore, we only need to focus on all maximal matchings of GH.
(2) For any edge in GH, its weight is the inverse of the minimal aggregate transmit power of the two graph nodes it connects. Therefore, for the transmitter scheduling scheme mapped from a maximal matching, the inverse of the weight sum of the maximal matching is the least power consumption of the scheme.

(3) The Edmond's blossom algorithm finds a MWM(GH).

Put all above facts together, Algorithm 1 outputs an optimal solution to RMPS-2SIC.   □

The time complexity of Algorithm 1 is equal to that of the Edmond's algorithm, which is O (L^4).

4 Minimal Power Scheduling for κ-SIC

In this section, we try to find a minimal power scheduling algorithm for k-SIC based uplink networks. Similar to RMPS-2SIC, Real-time Minimal Power Scheduling for k-SIC (RMPS-kSIC) Problem can thus be formulated as

$$
\min_{\{s;p_1,...,p_n\}} \sum\nolimits_{i=1}^{n} p_i
$$
$$
s.t.\, FL(s) \leq L; \quad 0 \leq Nb(s[j]) \leq k \; j \in [1..L]; \quad \frac{G_i p_i}{I_i + n_0} \geq \gamma p_i \geq 0 \forall i \in [1..n]; \tag{3}
$$

Obviously, $L \geq n/k$ is required.

In the following sections, similar with that in RMPS-2SIC, we also show that RMPS-kSIC can be solved by sequentially solving two sub-problems, i.e., minimal power allocating for k-SIC and transmitters scheduling in multiple slots for k-SIC.

4.1 Minimal Power Allocation for k-SIC

Definition 3. Minimal Power allocating for r Parallel Transmitters (MPArPT): Given an uplink network which consists of a k-SIC receiver and r transmitters $u_1, u_2, \ldots, u_r$ with channel gains as $G_1, G_2, \ldots, G_r$. Without loss of generality, assume $G_1 \geq G_2 \geq \ldots \geq G_r, r \leq k$, and n_0 is the noise. In the premise that $u_1, u_2, \ldots, u_r$ transmit simultaneously and are decoded successfully, configure transmit powers $p_1, p_2, \ldots, p_r$ for $u_1, u_2, \ldots, u_r$ so that the aggregate power consumption is minimized.

The problem is thus formulated as

$$
\min_{\{p_1,...,p_r\}} \sum_{i=1}^{r} p_i
$$
$$
s.t.\, \frac{G_i p_i}{I_i + n_0} \geq \gamma; \; p_i \geq 0; \quad \forall i \in [1..r];
$$

Similar with that in Sect. 3.1, we have to determine the expression for all I_i before solving MPArPT. Obviously, I_i is dependent on the decoding order. Using the similar proof as that in Lemma 1, we can easily prove that the optimal decoding order is the descending order of channel gains. In other words, if the optimal solution of MPArPT problem exists, it can only be achieved by decoding the transmitters' signals on the descending order of their channel gains.

Lemma 2. The optimal decoding order for MPA*r*PT is the descending order of channel gains.

Proof. We notate the decoding order as $\langle 1, 2, \ldots, r \rangle$ if u_i is decoded before u_{i+1} for $\forall\, i \in [1, r-1]$.

Assume that the optimal decoding order is $\langle s_1, s_2, \ldots, s_r \rangle$ but $\langle 1, 2, \ldots, r \rangle$, and the optimal transmit power of the decoding order is $(\bar{p}_{s_1}, \bar{p}_{s_2}, \ldots, \bar{p}_{s_r})$ for MPA*r*PT. Assume that s_i is the first distinct element between $\langle s_1, s_2, \ldots, s_r \rangle$ and $\langle 1, 2, \ldots, r \rangle$, i.e., $s_l = l$ for all $l \in [1..r-1]$ and $s_i \neq i$. Therefore, there must exist an integer $j \in (i, \ldots, n]$ which satisfies $s_j = i$. Order that $\tilde{p}_{s_i} = \frac{G_{s_j} \bar{p}_{s_j}}{G_{s_i}}$ and $\tilde{p}_{s_j} = \frac{G_{s_i} \bar{p}_{s_i}}{G_{s_j}}$. If we exchange s_i and s_j in $\langle s_1, s_2, \ldots, s_r \rangle$, we get a new decoding order $\langle 1, 2, \ldots, i-1,$ $s_j, s_{i+1}, \ldots, s_{j-1}, s_i, s_{j+1}, \ldots, s_k \rangle$.

If $\langle \bar{p}_{s_1}, \bar{p}_{s_2}, \ldots, \bar{p}_{s_{i-1}}, \tilde{p}_{s_j}, \bar{p}_{s_{i+1}}, \ldots, \bar{p}_{s_{j-1}}, \tilde{p}_{s_i}, \bar{p}_{s_{j+2}}, \ldots, \bar{p}_{s_k} \rangle$ is adopted as the transmit power vector for new decoding order, all constraints of MPA*r*PT are still satisfied. Besides, since $\tilde{p}_{s_i} + \tilde{p}_{s_j} \leq \bar{p}_{s_i} + \bar{p}_{s_j}$, the minimal aggregate power consumption under the decoding order $\langle 1, 2, \ldots, i-1, i, s_{i+1}, \ldots, s_{j-1}, s_i, s_{j+1}, \ldots, s_k \rangle$ must be no larger than that under $\langle s_1, s_2, \ldots, s_k \rangle$, which contradicts the assumption.   □

We repeat above processes until all r signals are decoded successfully. Obviously, the decoding order index for u_i is i, or in other word, the decoding order is $\langle 1, 2, \ldots, r \rangle$. Therefore, MPA*r*PT can be now reformulated as follows based on Lemma 2,

$$\min_{\{p_1, \ldots, p_r\}} \sum_{i=1}^{r} p_i$$

$$\text{s.t.} \quad \frac{G_1 p_1}{\sum_{i=2}^{r} G_i p_i + n_0} \geq \gamma; \quad \frac{G_l p_l}{\sum_{i=l+1}^{r} G_i p_i + n_0} \geq \gamma \ \ l \in [2..r-1]; \quad \frac{G_r p_r}{n_0} \geq \gamma; \quad (4)$$

Definition 4. Power Threshold Vector for *r*-SIC (PTV-*r*) is a vector $\hat{X} = (\hat{X}_1, \hat{X}_2, .., \hat{X}_r)^T$ which satisfies equality group

$$\frac{\hat{X}_l}{\sum_{i=l+1}^{r} \hat{X}_i + n_0} = \gamma \ \ l \in [1..r-1]; \quad \frac{\hat{X}_r}{n_0} = \gamma;$$

where $\hat{X}_i > 0$ for $\forall i \in [1, .., r]$, and $\gamma > 1$.

Obviously, $\hat{X}_1 \geq \hat{X}_2 \geq .. \geq \hat{X}_r$. PTV-*r* is in fact the minimal received powers required for r signals if the r signals are to be successfully decoded by a k-SIC receiver. The assertion is proved by Theorem 3.

Theorem 3. For the following inequality group

$$\frac{x_l}{\sum_{i=l+1}^{k} x_i + n_0} \geq \gamma \; l \in [2..k-1]; \; \frac{x_r}{n_0} \geq \gamma; \tag{5}$$

any of its solution $(\tilde{X}_1, \tilde{X}_2, .., \tilde{X}_r)^T$ satisfies $\tilde{X}_i \geq \hat{X}_i$ for $\forall i \in [1,..,r]$.

Proof. It can be proved by mathematical induction as follows.

(1) $\tilde{X}_r \geq \hat{X}_r$ because $\tilde{X}_r \geq \gamma n_0 = \hat{X}_r$.

(2) Assume $\tilde{X}_i \geq \hat{X}_i$ for $\forall i \in [l+1, r]$, therefore, $\tilde{X}_l \geq \gamma \left(\sum_{i=l+1}^{r} \tilde{X}_i + n_0 \right) \geq \gamma$
$\left(\sum_{i=l+1}^{r} \hat{X}_i + n_0 \right) = \hat{x}_l$.

In conclusion, Theorem 3 is thus proved. □

Theorem 4. The optimal solution to MPArPT is $(\frac{\hat{X}_1}{G_1}, \frac{\hat{X}_2}{G_2}, .., \frac{\hat{X}_r}{G_r})$.

Proof. Since $\hat{X}_1 \geq \hat{X}_2 \geq \ldots \geq \hat{X}_r$ and $G_1 \geq G_2 \geq \ldots \geq G_r$, based on Lemma A.1 in Appendix, we can know that $\sum_{i=1}^{r} \frac{\hat{X}_i}{G_i} \leq \sum_{i=1}^{r} \frac{\hat{X}_i}{G_i'}$, where $(G_1', G_2', \ldots, G_r')$ is any permutation of $\{G_1, G_2, \ldots, G_r\}$. On the other hand, for any solution $(\tilde{X}_1, \tilde{X}_2, .., \tilde{X}_r)$ to Formula (5), since $\sum_{i=1}^{r} \hat{X}_i \leq \sum_{i=1}^{r} \tilde{X}_i$, we can know that $\sum_{i=1}^{r} \frac{\hat{X}_i}{G_i} \leq \sum_{i=1}^{r} \frac{\tilde{X}_i}{G_i}$. Thus, $\sum_{i=1}^{r} \frac{\hat{X}_i}{G_i} \leq \sum_{i=1}^{r} \frac{\tilde{X}_i}{G_i'}$. Since $\left(\frac{\hat{X}_1}{G_1}, \frac{\hat{X}_2}{G_2}, .., \frac{\hat{X}_r}{G_r} \right)$ is a feasible solution to MPArPT, and $(\frac{\tilde{X}_1}{G_1'}, \frac{\tilde{X}_2}{G_2'}, \ldots, \frac{\tilde{X}_r}{G_r'})$ can represent any feasible solution to MPCrPT. Therefore, $(\frac{\hat{X}_1}{G_1}, \frac{\hat{X}_2}{G_2}, .., \frac{\hat{X}_r}{G_r})$ is an optimal solution to MPCrPT. □

$(\frac{\hat{X}_1}{G_1}, \frac{\hat{X}_2}{G_2}, .., \frac{\hat{X}_r}{G_r})$ is not only Pareto optimal but also globally optimal for MPArPT. Besides, for user u_i with channel gain G_i, if its signal is to be decoded by a k-SIC receiver and its decoding order index is r where $r \leq k$, its transmit power should be at least $\frac{\hat{X}_r}{G_i}$, which is the key to Algorithm 2 in the following sections.

4.2 Power Scheduling in Multiple Slots for k-SIC

Lemma 3 reveals a vital attribute of the optimal power scheduling scheme for RMPS-kSIC.

Lemma 3. If $n \leq kL$, we have:

(1) The number of transmitters in any slot is either $\lfloor n/L \rfloor$ or $\lceil n/L \rceil$ for the optimal power scheduling scheme for RMPS-kSIC.

(2) The optimal power scheduling scheme includes $L\lceil n/L\rceil - n$ slots, each of which has $\lfloor n/L\rfloor$ parallel transmitters, and $L - L\lceil n/L\rceil + n$ slots, each of which has $\lceil n/L\rceil$ parallel transmitters.

Proof. Assume there is a slot S_1 which has less than $\lfloor n/L\rfloor$ parallel transmitters in the optimal power scheduling scheme, therefore there must exist another slot S_2 which has no less than $\lceil n/L\rceil$ transmitters. If the transmitter whose decoding index is 1 in S_2 is moved to S_1, we get a new power scheduling scheme. Besides, based on Theorem 4, the aggregate power consumption of the new power scheduling scheme is less than that of the optimal scheme, which contradicts the optimality.

Similarly, there could not have a slot which has more than $\lceil n/L\rceil$ transmitters. Therefore, Lemma 3.(1) is proved.

To prove Lemma 3.(2), assume there are q slots each of which has $\lfloor n/L\rfloor$ parallel transmitters. Since $q\lfloor n/L\rfloor + (L - q)\lceil n/L\rceil = n$, therefore, $q = L\lceil n/L\rceil - n$.   □

Theorem 5. For an uplink network of n transmitters and two integers k_1 and k_2, if $L \geq n/min\,(k_1, k_2)$, the optimal power scheduling schemes of RMPS-k_1SIC and RMPS-k_2SIC must be same.

Proof. Based on Lemma 3, the optimal power scheduling scheme of RMPS-k_1SIC must be a feasible solution to RMPS-k_2SIC, and vice versa. So the two optimal power scheduling strategies must be same.   □

Theorem 5 shows that if $n \leq kL$, the optimal power scheduling scheme relies only on L but k.

Based on the definition of PTV-k and Theorem 5, we propose an optimal algorithm for the RMPS-kSIC problem, which converts RMPS-kSIC into the problem of finding a MWM of a balanced complete bipartite graph.

```
Algorithm 2  Optimal algorithm for RMPS-kSIC {
1. GH = ∅;   Compute PTV-⌈n/k⌉ as X̂₁,X̂₂,..,X̂⌈n/k⌉.
2. Add n graph nodes with label uᵢ where i ∈ [1,n] into part
   I of GH;
3. If (n%L!=0) {
4.     For (i=1;i<n%L+2; i++)    Add a graph nodes with la-
   bel Tᵢ₁ into part I of GH; }
5.     Add L⌊n/L⌋ graph nodes with label Tₕⱼ where h ∈ [1,L]
   and j ∈ [2,⌈ⁿ⁄ₗ⌉] into part II of GH;
6. For any graph node uᵢ and Tₕⱼ in part I and II {
7.     Add an edge (uᵢ,Tₕⱼ) with weight −X̂ⱼ/Gᵢ; }
8. Find a MWM(GH) using Kuhn-Munkres algorithm;
9. For any (uᵢ,Tₕⱼ) in MWM(GH), uᵢ will be scheduled in the
   h'th slot with power p̂ⱼ/Gᵢ; }
```

In the above algorithm, the edge (u_i, T_{hj}) represents that u_i will be scheduled in the h'th slot, and its decoding order index is j. MWM(GH) corresponds to a feasible power scheduling scheme. Now Theorem 6 tells us that the scheme mapped from MWM(GH) is the optimal.

Theorem 6. Algorithm 2 outputs an optimal solution to RMPS-kSIC problem.

Proof. Our proof is based on the following facts.

(1) Based on the construction of GH, and the mapping scheme that the edge (u_i, T_{hj}) in GH means that u_i is scheduled in the h'th slot, any feasible user scheduling schemes in the optimal decoding order can be mapped to a maximal matching of GH, and vice versa. In other words, they have a one-to-one mapping relationship.
(2) For the edge (u_i, T_{hj}) in GH, $\hat{x}_j / G_i$ is the minimal transmit power allocated to u_i if its decoding order index is j.

By taking the above two facts together, for any maximal matching of GH, its inverse weight sum is equal to the minimal aggregate power of all UEs for the corresponding power scheduling scheme. So the MWM(GH) can be mapped to the optimal solution to RMPS-kSIC. ☐

5 Performance Evaluations

Some simulation parameters are as follows in default: The noise power spectral density is -169 dBm/Hz, and the noise bandwidth is 200 kHz, thus N_0 is -116 dBm. The frequency of signal is 2.4 GHz, and the decoding threshold γ is 2. The regular transceiver that does not support SIC is represented by $k = 1$.

An uplink wireless network which consists of 30 transmitters and one base station is constructed, where the base station is situated at the center of a square with edge length being 120 meters, and all transmitters are placed uniformly in the square.

Based on Lemma 3, the aggregate power consumption will be larger if the frame length is smaller. Therefore, we evaluate the performance by setting the frame length

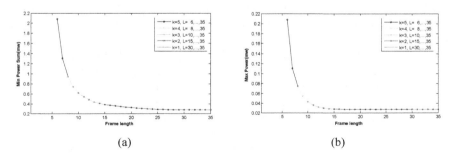

(a)   (b)

Fig. 1. (a) Aggregate power consumption with real-time performance (b) Maximal transmit power with real-time performance

from $\lceil 30/k \rceil$ to 35, i.e., the real-time performance requirement varies from the tightest to the easiest. Besides, k is set as 1, 2, 3, 4, 5 in all experiments for clear evaluations.

Just as illustrated by Fig. 1(a), for same frame length, the aggregate power consumption has no relation to k. The fact is consistent with Theorem 5.

The aggregate power consumption decreases exponentially with the increasing of frame length. From Fig. 1(a), we can find that the aggregate power consumption is 1.3 mW when $k = 5$ and $L = 7$, while it is 2.1 mW when $k = 5$ and $L = 6$. In other words, the power saving is prominent for cases where n approximates kL. However, it will diminish exponentially if the frame length grows.

With different values of k and L, the maximal transmit powers among the 30 transmitters are illustrated in Fig. 1(b). Obviously, the smaller is k, the less is the maximal transmit power. Besides, if the real-time performance requirements are same, the maximal transmit powers are also same, and have no relation to k if $n \leq kL$. It also decreases exponentially if the real-time performance is even slightly relaxed. Take for example $k = 5$ and $L = 6$, the maximal transmit power is 0.21 mW. If $k = 5$ and $L = 7$, it is only 0.11 mW. The maximal transmit power will decrease exponentially if the frame length continues to grow. All of these facts are consistent with Theorem 5.

The results of the above experiments reveal that, comparing to the number of parallel transmitters supported by the SIC receiver, the requirement of real-time performance has tremendous impacts on both the aggregate power consumption and the maximal transmit power. Besides, both the aggregate power consumption and the maximal transmit power are exponentially decreased with the relaxation of the real-time performance requirement.

For typical cases of k, the maximal transmit power is acceptable. For example, if the value of k is 3 and 4, the maximal transmit power is only 0.04 mW and 0.07 mW respectively, which are completely acceptable in nowadays even for low-power RF (Radio Frequency) chips. In other words, with the optimal power scheduling scheme, SIC technology is even suitable for low-power applications.

6   Conclusions and Future Works

Although SIC has a broad prospect for its inherent quality of supporting real-time application, the high power consumption has also been denounced. The focus of this paper is the tradeoff between the power consumption and the real-time performance for SIC-based uplink wireless networks. Specifically, given the requirement of real-time performance, we want to achieve the least power consumption. We formulate the problem based on the power scheduling technology. Our conclusions are as follows. (1) The problem is solvable in polynomial time, and an optimal power scheduling scheme is given in this paper. (2) The factor of real-time performance has a major affection on the power consumption than other factors, such as the number of parallel transmitters supported. (3) With the optimal power scheduling schemes, SIC technology is even suitable for low-power applications.

In future works, we will consider the case when the transmit powers are discrete. In that case, the problem may be NP-hard [9], and heuristic algorithm may be developed for solving the problem.

Acknowledgments. This paper has been supported by National Scientific Foundation of China (61173132), Science Foundation of China University of Petroleum, Beijing (ZX20150089).

Appendix

Lemma A.1 Assume $a_1 \geq a_2 \geq \ldots \geq a_n$, $b_1 \leq b_2 \leq \cdots \leq b_n$, then the optimal solution to the problem

$$\min_{X_{ij}} \sum_{i,j=1..n} X_{ij} a_i b_j$$

$$\text{s.t. } \sum_{i=1..n} X_{ij} = 1 \ \forall j \in [1..n]; \quad \sum_{j=1..n} X_{ij} = 1 \ i \in [1..n]; X_{ij} \in \{0,1\};$$

is $X_{ij} = \begin{cases} 1 & \text{for all } i = j \\ 0 & \text{for all } i \neq j \end{cases}$.

Proof. We prove it using mathematical induction.

It is easy to prove the case $n = 2$ since $a_1 b_1 + a_2 b_2 \geq a_1 b_2 + a_2 b_1$.

Assume that the lemma is true when $n = k - 1$.

For $n = k$, order that $\beta_i = b_i - b_1$ for $\forall i \in [2..k]$. We now only need to prove that $a_1 b_1 + a_2(b_1 + \beta_2) + \ldots + a_k(b_1 + \beta_k) \leq b_1 a_{i1} + (b_1 + \beta_2)a_{i2} + \ldots + (b_1 + \beta_k)a_{ik}$, where $(a_{i1}, a_{i2}, \ldots, a_{ik})$ is any permutation of $\{a_1, a_2, \ldots, a_k\}$.

Case 1. $a_{i1} = a_1$. The lemma can be proved by the induction assumption of $n = k - 1$.
Case 2. $a_{i1} \neq a_1$. Since $(a_{i1}, a_{i2}, \ldots, a_{ik})$ is any permutation of $\{a_1, a_2, \ldots, a_k\}$, therefore, $a_{i1} + a_{i2} + \ldots + a_{ik} = a_1 + a_2 + \ldots + a_k$, and there exist a $j \in \{2, \ldots, k\}$, $a_{ij} = a_1$. Thus, $b_1 a_{i1} + (b_1 + \beta_2)a_{i2} + \ldots + (b_1 + \beta_k)a_{ik} = b_1(a_1 + a_2 + \ldots + a_k) + \beta_2 a_{i2} + \beta_3 a_{i3} + \ldots + \beta_k a_{ik} = b_1(a_1 + a_2 + \ldots + a_k) + \beta_2 a_{i2} + \beta_3 a_{i3} + \ldots + \beta_{j-1} a_{i(j-1)} + \beta_j a_1 + \beta_{j+1} a_{i(j+1)} + \ldots + \beta_k a_{ik} \geq b_1(a_1 + a_2 + \ldots + a_k) + \beta_2 a_{i2} + \beta_3 a_{i3} + \ldots + \beta_{j-1} a_{i(j-1)} + \beta_j a_{i1} + \beta_{j+1} a_{i(j+1)} + \ldots + \beta_k a_{ik}$.

Thus, the case can be proved if $\beta_2 a_2 + \beta_3 a_3 + \ldots + \beta_k a_k \leq \beta_2 a_{i2} + \beta_3 a_{i3} + \ldots + \beta_{j-1} a_{i(j-1)} + \beta_j a_{i1} + \beta_{j+1} a_{i(j+1)} + \ldots + \beta_k a_{ik}$.

The above inequality can be proved by the induction assumption for $\{a_1, a_2, \ldots, a_k\}$ and $\{\beta_1, \beta_2, \ldots, \beta_k\}$.

In conclusion, the lemma is proved. $\qquad \square$

References

1. Zhang, X.C., Haenggi, M.: The performance of successive interference cancellation in random wireless networks. IEEE Trans. Inf. Theory **60**(10), 6368–6388 (2014)

2. Yang, Z., Ding, Z., Fan, P., Al-Dhahir, N.: General power allocation scheme to guarantee quality of service in downlink and uplink NOMA systems. IEEE Trans. Wirel. Commun. 15 (11), 7244–7257 (2016)
3. Sen, S., Santhapuri, N., Chouhury, R.R., Nelakuditi, S.: Successive interference cancellation: a back-of-the-envelope perspective. In: Proceedings of Hotnets 2010, CA, USA, 20–21 October 2010
4. Weber, S.P., Andrews, J.G., Ying, Y.X., de Veciana, G.: Transmission capacity of wireless ad hoc networks with successive interference cancellation. IEEE Trans. Inf. Theory 52(8), 2799–2814 (2007)
5. Halperin, D., Anderson, T., Wetherall, D.: Taking the sting out of carrier sense: interference cancellation for wireless LANs. In: Proceedings of ACM MobiCom 2008, San Francisco, USA, 14–19 September 2008
6. Xu, C., Li, P., Sammy, C.: Decentralized power allocating for random access with successive interference cancellation. IEEE J. Sel. Area Commun. 31(11), 2387–2396 (2013)
7. Karipidis, E., Yuan, D., He, Q., Larsson, E.G.: Max-min power allocating in wireless networks with successive interference cancellation. IEEE Trans. Wirel. Commun. 14(11), 6269–6282 (2015)
8. Yuan, D., Vangelis, A., Lei, C., Eleftherios, K., Larsson, G.E.: On optimal link activation with interference cancellation in wireless networking. IEEE Trans. Veh. Technol. 62(2), 939–945 (2013)
9. Goussevskaia, O., Wattenhofer, R.: Scheduling with interference decoding: complexity and algorithms. Ad Hoc Netw. 11(6), 1732–1745 (2013)
10. Harpreet, D., Howard, H., Viswanathan, R., Valenzuela, H.: Power-efficient system design for cellular-based machine-to-machine communications. IEEE Trans. Wirel. Commun. 12(11), 5740–5753 (2013)

A Novel Collision Analysis
for Multiple-Subcarrier Frequency-Domain
Contention

Yu Zeng and Qinglin Zhao[(✉)]

Faculty of Information Technology,
Macau University of Science and Technology, Macau, China
cardwhen@yahoo.com, qlzhao@hotmail.com

Abstract. Frequency-domain contention is a promising technique that can significantly improve channel utilization. Recently, a novel multi-subcarrier frequency-domain contention protocol called WiFi-BA has been proposed to solve the collision issue between data transmissions in single-subcarrier frequency-domain contention protocols. In this paper, however, we reveal that WiFi-BA has serious design defects, which will cause a new type of collision between data transmission and contention signal. We then analyze the root cause leading to such a collision and provide solutions to fix it.

Keywords: 802.11 · Frequency-domain contention · Multiple-subcarrier

1 Introduction

IEEE 802.11 networks [1] perform channel contention in time domain. It is well known that the time-domain contention leads to poor channel utilization, because the channel is forced to remain idle during the contention process. Ref. [2] pointed out that more than 30% reduction in throughput is due to the idle time. Ref. [3] shows that the channel utilization becomes lower and lower when the PHY data rate increases.

Recently, a frequency-domain contention protocol, which is called time to frequency (T2F) [4], has been proposed to solve the low channel utilization issue in conventional time-domain contention. T2F employs the orthogonal frequency-division multiplexing (OFDM) subcarriers for channel contention. It is a single-subcarrier frequency-domain contention protocol. In T2F, each subcarrier is allocated with a unique number. Each node chooses one subcarrier from all available subcarriers, and then signals on its chosen subcarrier and at the same time listens to all available subcarriers. By sorting all active subcarrier numbers, each node can independently find the winner whose chosen subcarrier number is the minimum. For example, in Fig. 1(a), node A chooses subcarrier 6 from all available k subcarriers, while node B chooses subcarrier 4; nodes A and B know subcarriers 4 and 6 are chosen, and then node A infers its failure and node B infers its victory. T2F can significantly reduce the contention time to 10.4 s from 150 s on average in 802.11, and therefore have received considerable attention [5–12].

© Springer International Publishing AG 2017
L. Ma et al. (Eds.): WASA 2017, LNCS 10251, pp. 37–46, 2017.
DOI: 10.1007/978-3-319-60033-8_4

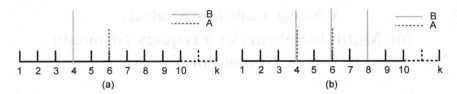

Fig. 1. (a) Single-subcarrier frequency-domain contention and (b) multiple-subcarrier frequency-domain contention

The single-subcarrier frequency-domain contention easily leads to a type-1 collision (we call in this paper): multiple winners, who choose the same minimum subcarrier, transmit data simultaneously. For example, in the case of Fig. 1(a), if nodes A and B choose subcarrier 4, both nodes will infer that they are winners, and therefore transmit data simultaneously, leading to a collision. Note that although there are 64 subcarriers in 802.11 a/g, the number of available subcarriers is very limited due to power leakage (e.g., only 8 subcarriers are adopted for contention resolution in [7]). Therefore, given the limited number of available subcarriers, when the number of nodes is large, the probability of generating multiple winners will increase remarkably, leading to serious type-1 collisions.

To overcome the type-1 collision, the multiple-subcarrier frequency-domain contention protocol has been proposed. WiFi-BA (bitwise arbitration) [7] is such a typical representation. Different from T2F, in WiFi-BA, each node can choose multiple subcarriers. The great amount of combinations that choose multiple subcarriers from a set, can remarkably reduce the type-1 collision. In WiFi-BA, while signaling on multiple subcarriers, each node also detects all active subcarriers. WiFi-BA has the following *matching rule* (we call in this paper; see Sect. 3 in [7]): if a node finds that the observed active subcarriers match its chosen subcarriers, the node infers that it is a winner and will transmit a data in the next slot immediately (in this paper, we call an OFDM symbol time a time slot); otherwise, it will continue contending for channel by signaling on its chosen subcarriers.

Unfortunately, although overcoming the type-1 collision, the matching rule in WiFi-BA easily leads to a type-2 collision (we call in this paper): the winner starts transmitting data, while other nodes signal on subcarriers to contend for channel, leading to a collision between data transmission and channel contention. The main reason is: different nodes will make inconsistent arbitrations, according to the same active subcarrier spectrum (each node can observe) and different multiple subcarriers (different nodes choose). Figure 1(b) shows an example of the type-2 collision. In this example, node A chooses subcarriers 4 and 6, while node B chooses subcarriers 4, 6, and 8. Then the superposed subcarrier spectrum, which is subcarriers 4, 6, 8, matches node B's choice but mismatches node A's choice. As a result, in the next slot, node B will transmit a data, while node A will signal to contend for channel, leading to a collision. The type-2 collision motivates us to study WiFi-BA.

The rest of the paper is organized as follows. Section 2 outlines the WiFi-BA protocol. Section 3 classifies the relationship among multiple subcarriers to reveal the reason leading to the type-2 collision. Section 4 provides solutions to overcome the WiFi-BA design defect. Finally Sect. 5 concludes this paper.

2   Overview of WiFi-BA

In WiFi-BA [7], each node has two antennas: one for regular data transmission and another for listening to the channel. WiFi-BA adopts the OFDM technique, where the whole channel is divided into L subcarriers (e.g. $L = 64$ in 802.11 a/g). Let k denote the number of available subcarrier. In general, k takes a small value due to power leakage (e.g., k = 8 in [7]). WiFi-BA is a multiple-subcarrier frequency-domain protocol, i.e., each node will choose multiple subcarriers from k available subcarriers for channel contention.

With the help of Fig. 2, we here outline WiFi-BA. Before transmission, each node performs a clear channel assessment (CCA) for a time duration. If the channel is sensed idle, the node starts contending for channel: it first enters a stage of frequency-domain collision probe, and then enters a stage of time-domain arbitration phase. At the end of the channel contention, the winner initiates a data transmission. Below, focusing on the channel contention process, we explain the adopted three schemes sequentially: binary mapping, frequency-domain collision probe, and time-domain bitwise arbitration. After that, we present the design defect of WiFi-BA.

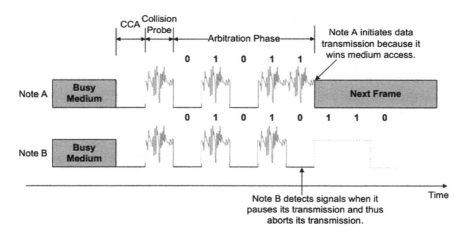

Fig. 2. An overview of WiFi-BA [7].

2.1   Binary Mapping

In this stage, each node will generate a binary code indicating its chosen subcarrier number and then use it in the stage of collision probe.

In this scheme, each node randomly picks a number from $[1, 2^k - 1]$ for contention, where k denotes the number of available subcarriers (k = 8 by default). The value of this random number represents node's contention priority, and the larger the value is, the more likely a node accesses channel. We use a k-bit binary code to represent the random number. The binary code is mapped to subcarriers with bit '1' indicating that the corresponding subcarrier is selected by the node, and bit '0' indicating that the corresponding subcarrier is not selected by the node. As shown in the left part of Fig. 3, the binary code of node A is 01011010, representing that it has selected subcarriers 1, 3, 4, 6. The binary code of node B is 01010110, representing that it has selected subcarriers 1, 3, 5, 6.

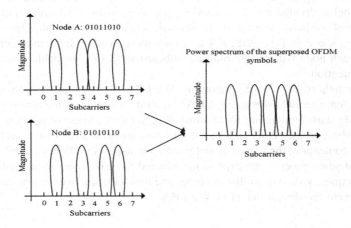

Fig. 3. Collision detection in the frequency domain.

2.2 Frequency-Domain Collision Probe

In this stage, each node detects whether there exist other nodes for channel contention. We call this operation the collision detection. Each node uses the superposition of binary codes to detect collision.

When entering this stage, according to its binary code, each node generates an OFDM symbol through inverse fast Fourier transform (IFFT), and then transmits it, thereby activating these selected subcarriers. At the same time, each node listens to the channel and performs FFT on the received signals, which is a superposition of all transmitted OFDM symbols. The FFT result will show all subcarriers activated by contenders, which is called the power spectrum of the superposed OFDM symbols. For example, the right part of Fig. 3 shows that subcarriers 1, 3, 4, 5, 6 have been activated. Transmitting all activated and deactivated subcarrier numbers into a binary code, we obtain 01011110. In this paper, we call such a binary code the superposed binary code.

Next, each node compares the superposed binary code with its chosen binary code to detect collision. WiFi-BA has the following *matching rule*:

- If two codes match well, the node infers that it is a winner, and will transmit a data in the next slot.
- Otherwise, it infers that there exist other contending nodes (i.e., a collision is detected), and will enter the stage of bitwise arbitration for continuing channel contention.

In the example of Fig. 3, the superposed binary code (i.e., 01011110) matches neither node A's code (i.e., 01011010) nor node B's code (i.e., 01010110). Therefore both nodes collide each other in this stage, and will enter the stage of bitwise arbitration.

Remarks: WiFi-BA does not detect the collision where two or more nodes choose the completely same binary code, because the probability of two nodes choosing the same binary code (i.e., the probability of the type-1 collision) is very low. For example, if a node chooses one binary code from $[1, 2^k-1]$, another node chooses the same binary code with probability $\frac{1}{(2^k-1)^2}$ only.

2.3   Time-Domain Bitwise Arbitration

When detecting a collision in the collision probe stage, a node enters the arbitration phase. Starting from the most significant bit of its selected binary code, the node performs the following operations.

− If the bit is '1', the node transmits its OFDM symbol and applies the matching rule as in the collision probe stage. According to the result of the matching rule, the node either transmits a data or continues checking its next bit in the next slot.
− If the bit is '0', the node does not transmit its OFDM symbol in the current slot. At the same time, it detects signals. When detecting a signal, it exits the arbitration phase and then aborts this-round contention; otherwise, it continues to check the next bit.

As the bitwise arbitration processes proceeds, most contending nodes gradually abort their transmissions. Finally, the node (whose binary code matches the superposed binary code) wins the channel and then initiates a data transmission.

Figure 2 gives an example of the arbitration phase. In this example, node A's code is 01011010 and node B's code is 01010110. In the collision probe stage, both nodes detect the presence of each other and then enter the arbitration phase. Because the first four bits of the two codes are the same, both nodes continue to check the 5-th bit. At this moment, node A finds that the superposed code matches its own, while node B detects a signal. As a result, node A starts to transmit a data while node B exits the arbitration phase in the next slot.

2.4   Design Defect of WiFi-BA

WiFi-BA can remarkably reduce the type-1 collision, namely, two or more nodes transmit datum simultaneously. However, it introduces considerable the type-2 collisions, namely, one node is transmitting data, while other nodes are transmitting contention signals. In Sect. 3.2, we will show that the type-2 collision might occur frequently.

The type-2 collision can occur at the beginning (shown in Sect. 4.1) or in the middle (shown in Sect. 4.2) of the arbitration phase.

3 Four Multiple-Subcarrier Relationships

In this section, we first define four multiple-subcarrier relationships and then reveal that the complicated multiple-subcarrier relationships will lead to frequent occurrences of type-2 collisions.

3.1 Four Relationships

In this section, according to the relationship between binary codes that nodes pick, we define the relationship between nodes. In a binary code, bit '1' denotes that the corresponding subcarrier is selected, while bit '0' denotes that the corresponding subcarrier has not been selected.

Taking 8-bit binary codes as an example, we define four relationships between two nodes.

- Identical type. If two nodes pick the same subcarriers, we define the relationship between them as an identical type. For example, 10101010 and 10101010.
- Containing type. If node A selects all the subcarriers that node B selects, but it also selects some subcarriers that node B do not selects, we define the relationship between them as a containing type. We say that node A is *a containing node* and node B is *a contained node*. For example, node A picks 10101010, while node B picks 10101000.
- Cross type. If node A's subcarriers only contain parts of node B's subcarriers and node B's subcarriers only contain parts of node A's subcarriers, we define the relationship between them as a cross type. For example, node A picks 10101010, while node B picks 10100101.
- Totally-different type. If each of nodes A and B picks subcarriers that the other does not pick, we define the relationship between them as a totally different type. For example, 10101010 and 01010101.

3.2 The Severity of the Type-2 Collisions

In this section, taking the containing type as an example, we reveal that the severity of the type-2 collisions in WiFi-BA.

Assume that k is the number of total available subcarriers. Let P_i, $1 \leq i \leq k$, denote the probability that a containing node selects i subcarriers from k available subcarriers. For k binary bits, we have $\binom{k}{i}$ codes where i bits are 1 and k-i bits are 0, among 2^k different codes in total. P_i is calculated by

$$P_i = \binom{k}{i} \frac{1}{2^k}.$$

Let Q_i, $1 \leq i \leq k$, denote the total number of possible containing types, under the condition that a containing node has selected i subcarriers from k available subcarriers. For k binary bits, we have $\binom{k}{i}$ binary codes where i bits are 1 and k-i bits are 0. Given i binary bits, we have $2^i - 2$ different codes (except 0 and $2^i - 1$) that have a containing relationship with $2^i - 1$; for example, when i = 2, codes 01 and 10 have a containing relationship with 11. Q_i is calculated by

$$Q_i = \binom{k}{i} (2^i - 2).$$

Table 1 shows P_i and Q_i in the containing type when k = 8. From this table, we can see that P_i may take a very high probability and Q_i may take a very large value. For example, $P_4 = 0.2734$ and $Q_6 = 1736$. In Sects. 4.1 and 4.2, we point out that the containing type is an important reason causing the type-2 collision. The high value of P_i and Q_i implies that the type-2 collision will occur frequently in WiFi-BA.

Table 1. P_i and Q_i in the containing type.

i (k = 8)	1	2	3	4	5	6	7	8
P_i	0.0313	0.1094	0.2188	0.2734	0.2188	0.1094	0.0313	0.0039
Q_i	0	56	336	980	1680	1736	1008	254

4 Solutions to Overcome the Type-2 Collision

In this section, we only need to consider the type-2 collision due to the containing and cross types and give solutions. The reason is as follows. In the four multiple-subcarrier types in Sect. 3.1, if all nodes are identical types, we cannot differentiate them; if all nodes are totally-different types, it will not incur any collision.

4.1 Type-2 Collision Due to the Containing Type

We consider an example of the type-2 collision due to the containing type. In this example, node A picks a code: 11110000, and node B pick a code: 11000000. The two nodes form a containing relationship and the superposed code is 11110000.

We note that if all nodes form a containing relationship, in the collision-probe stage, the containing node will infer its victory and all contained nodes will infer that there exist other contending nodes. Then, the type-2 collision occurs at the beginning of the arbitration phase, where the containing node starts transmitting data and the contained nodes transmit contention signals for bitwise arbitration.

There are two methods to solve the problem.

– Method 1. In this method, we need additional information that notifies all contained nodes of listening to the channel at the beginning of the arbitration phase. As illustrated in Fig. 4, at the first OFDM symbol time of the arbitration phase, while the containing node transmits data, we force all nodes (entering the arbitration phase) to listen to the channel. to listen to the channel. We dictate that once these contained nodes sense channel busy in the first OFDM symbol time, they should abort their arbitration phases immediately, thereby avoiding the type-2 collision. In this manner, we can avoid the type-2 collision immediately.

- Method 2. In this method, we did not introduce additional information, but force the containing node to execute its arbitration phase until its final 1-bit. At that time, all nodes finish the arbitration phase and therefore we can avoid the type-2 collision. However, this method will consume a long contention time. For example, in the above two-node example, node A, whose code is 1111000, is the containing node and should keep executing its arbitration phase until its 4-th bit.

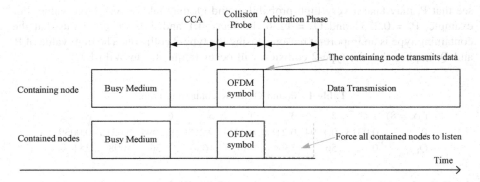

Fig. 4. Solution to solve the type-2 collision occurring at the beginning of the arbitration phase.

4.2 Type-2 Collision Due to the Cross Type

We consider an example of the type-2 collision due to the cross type. In this example, nodes A, B, C, respectively, pick codes 11111100, 10100010 and 11110000, where nodes A and C form a containing relationship, node pairs, A and B, as well as B and C, form a cross relationship. The superposed code is 11111110.

In this example, the type-2 collision occurs during the arbitration phase. With the help of Fig. 5, let us outline the contention process. In the collision-probe stage (see Fig. 5(a)), the superposed code mismatches any of the three nodes. Then they enter the arbitration phase.

- In the first OFDM symbol time (see Fig. 5(a)), the mismatching occurs again as in the collision-probe stage.
- In the second OFDM symbol time (see Fig. 5(b)), node B senses the channel busy without transmitting a signal because node B's 2nd bit is 0, and hence will abort its arbitration phase; node B's code matches the superposed code and hence infers its victory; and node C's code mismatches the superposed and infer that there still exists other contending node.
- In the third OFDM symbol, node A starts transmitting data and node C continues transmitting contention signal, incurring a type-2 collision.

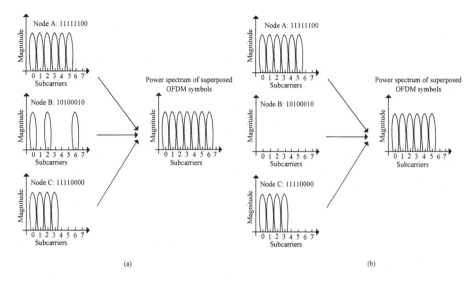

Fig. 5. (a) No winners appear in the collision-probe stage and in the first OFDM symbol time of the arbitration phase, and (b) node A wins in the second OFDM symbol time of the arbitration phase but will incur the type-2 collision in the third OFDM symbol time.

In this case, we can apply Method 2 in Sect. 4.1 to solve the type-2 collision, instead of Method 1 in Sect. 4.1, because we cannot generally predict the precise symbol time when the type-2 collision occurs.

5   Conclusion

Frequency-domain contention has received considerable attentions. WiFi-BA is a novel multi-subcarrier frequency-domain contention protocol. In this paper, we are the first to point out the design defect of WiFi-BA. We then classify the multi-subcarrier relationships to show the severity of the design defect and provide solutions to overcome it.

Acknowledgment. This work is supported by Macao FDCT-MOST grant 001/2015/AMJ, and Macao FDCT grants 104/2014/A3 and 005/2016/A1.

References

1. IEEE Std. 802.11-2007, Part 11: Wireless LAN Medium Access Control (MAC) and Physical Layer (PHY) Specifications, June 2007
2. Jardosh, A.P., Ramachandran, K.N., Almeroth, K.C., Belding-Royer, E.M.: Understanding congestion in IEEE 802.11 b wireless networks. In: Proceedings of the 5th ACM SIGCOMM Conference on Internet Measurement, p. 25. USENIX Association (2005)

3. Tan, K., Fang, J., Zhang, Y., Chen, S., Shi, L., Zhang, J., Zhang, Y.: Fine-grained channel access in wireless LAN. In: ACM SIGCOMM Computer Communication Review, vol. 40, no. 4, pp. 147–158. ACM (2010)
4. Sen, S., Choudhury, R.R., Nelakuditi, S.: Listen (on the frequency domain) before you talk. In: Proceedings of the 9th ACM SIGCOMM Workshop on Hot Topics in Networks, p. 16. ACM (2010)
5. Sen, S., Roy Choudhury, R., Nelakuditi, S.: No time to countdown: migrating backoff to the frequency domain. In: Proceedings of the 17th Annual International Conference on Mobile Computing and Networking, pp. 241–252. ACM (2011)
6. Zhang, H., Zhao, Q., Dang, P., Dai, H., Ma, Z.: A weighted T2F scheme for WLANs. In: Kim, Kuinam J., Wattanapongsakorn, N. (eds.) Mobile and Wireless Technology 2015. LNEE, vol. 310, pp. 75–82. Springer, Heidelberg (2015). doi:10.1007/978-3-662-47669-7_8
7. Huang, P., Yang, X., Xiao, L.: WiFi-BA: choosing arbitration over backoff in high speed multicarrier wireless networks. In: 2013 Proceedings IEEE INFOCOM, pp. 1375–1383 (2013)
8. Feng, X., Zhang, J., Zhang, Q., Li, B.: Use your frequency wisely: explore frequency domain for channel contention and ACK. In 2012 Proceedings IEEE INFOCOM, pp. 549–557 (2012)
9. Wang, L., Wu, K., Xiao, J., Hamdi, M.: Harnessing frequency domain for cooperative sensing and multi-channel contention in CRAHNs. IEEE Trans. Wirel. Commun. 13(1), 440–449 (2014)
10. Misra, S., Khatua, M.: Semi-distributed backoff: collision-aware migration from random to deterministic backoff. IEEE Trans. Mob. Comput. 14(5), 1071–1084 (2015)
11. Shen, W.L., Lin, K.C.J., Cheng, W.J., Qiu, L., Chen, M.S.: Concurrent packet recovery for distributed uplink multinode MIMO networks. IEEE Trans. Mob. Comput. 15(12), 3014–3027 (2016)
12. Huang, P., Yang, X., Xiao, L.: Dynamic channel bonding: enabling flexible spectrum aggregation. IEEE Trans. Mob. Comput. 15(12), 3042–3056 (2016)

Wi-Dog: Monitoring School Violence with Commodity WiFi Devices

Qizhen Zhou[1], Chenshu Wu[2], Jianchun Xing[1(✉)], Juelong Li[3], Zheng Yang[2], and Qiliang Yang[1]

[1] PLA University of Science and Technology, Nanjing, China
zhouqizhen2016@163.com, xjc@893.com.cn, yang@greenorbs.com
[2] Tsinghua University, Beijing, China
wu@greenorbs.com, yql@893.com.cn
[3] Technical Management Office of Naval Defense Engineering, Beijing, China
lijuelong@126.com

Abstract. Monitoring school violence is critical for the prevention of juvenile delinquency and promotion of social harmony. Pioneering approaches employ always-on-body sensors or cameras with limited surveillance area, which cannot provide ubiquitous violence monitoring. In this paper, we present Wi-Dog, a non-invasive physical violence monitoring scheme based on commodity WiFi infrastructures. The key intuition is that violence-induced WiFi signals convey informative characteristics of intensity, irregularity and continuity. To identify school violence from violence-alike actions (*e.g.*, jump, lie down and run), we develop a precise noise reduction method by selecting sensitive antenna pair and subcarriers. Moreover, a wavelet-entropy-based segmentation method is proposed to detect movement transitions in the distance, and the complete local-global analysis is further adopted to improve overall performance. We implemented Wi-Dog using commercial WiFi devices and evaluated it in real indoor environments. Experimental results demonstrate the effectiveness of Wi-Dog with average detection accuracy of 0.9.

Keywords: Channel state information · Physical violence · Wireless sensing · Abnormal activities

1 Introduction

School violence, as the leading cause of juvenile delinquency, has become an increasingly serious social issue and attracted extensive academic research. According to the reports of the National Center for Educational Statistics, 28% of total 4326 examined adolescents were reported bullying victimization, whose physical and mental health were severely affected [5]. To curb the prevalence of school violence, governments have introduced relevant policies to deal with. A key enabler for effective school violence prevention is to automatically detect the instantaneous physical violence with existing available infrastructure. Wearable sensor based scheme provides a possible solution [19]. However, the always-on-body requirements of dedicated sensors (*e.g.*, data glove [8], RFID [4] and

© Springer International Publishing AG 2017
L. Ma et al. (Eds.): WASA 2017, LNCS 10251, pp. 47–59, 2017.
DOI: 10.1007/978-3-319-60033-8_5

smartphone [10]) make users difficult to comply with. Camera based detection is another type of monitoring scheme [2,3,20]. Pre-mounted cameras continuously collect and analyze the video frames of interested areas, yet they bring underlying privacy issues and only operate in a clear line-of-sight (LOS) view.

In this paper, we show for the first time that WiFi signals can be exploited to monitor physical violence. WiFi signal is pervasive nowadays with widely deployed WiFi infrastructures on campus, which delivers the idea of ubiquitous device-free surveillance into a practical solution. The key intuition is that abrupt physical violence along with rapid movements of body parts could generate distinct features in received signals. To acquire abundant information about abnormal dynamics induced by physical violence, we take advantage of fine-grained Channel State Information (CSI) on commercial WiFi devices. Comparing with pioneer works which mainly focus on the recognition of repetitive actions [12,15,21] or single-person abnormal behaviors [13], physical violence has three significant features [10]: (1) intensity (*i.e.*, the attacker intends to harm the victim), (2) irregularity (*i.e.*, physical violence can be random which performs uncertain actions) and (3) continuity (*i.e.*, the violence is focused on particular children and occurs continuously). Velocity is a natural choice to build up relationships with activities [9,16]. However, existing approaches cannot be directly used in violence detection due to the lack of analysis of violent process.

We present Wi-Dog, a non-invasive physical violence monitoring scheme on commercial WiFi infrastructure, to protect adolescents from rampant school violence, just like a loyal dog does. We seek to advance the state-of-the-art on WiFi based sensing by deriving precise motion-induced Doppler shifts from imperfect WiFi devices and further identifying the physical violence based on local-global analysis. In a nutshell, our contributions are summarized as follows:

- We investigate the characteristics of violence-induced WiFi signals through complete local-global analysis. To our best knowledge, we are the first to propose a non-invasive physical violence monitoring scheme on a single link with commercial WiFi devices. We envision this capability as a significant complement for future violence threat warning applications.
- To present obvious characteristics of physical violence, a novel CSI data processing method is proposed by selecting antenna pairs and sensitive subcarriers. Moreover, we develop a wavelet-entropy-based indicator to monitor slight transitions of movements in the distance. The core technologies in Wi-Dog can be applied to various gesture recognition schemes.
- We conduct extensive experiments and validate Wi-Dog in classroom and corridor environments by imitating real physical violence with different volunteers. Experimental results show that Wi-Dog can monitor the imitated physical violence with a high True Detection Rate of 0.94 (0.85), along with a low False Alarm Rate of 0.08 (0.11) in corridor (classroom) environment.

In the rest of the paper, we introduce the background in Sect. 2, then we elaborate the detailed methodologies in Sect. 3, evaluate the performance in Sect. 4. We present related works in Sect. 5 and conclude in Sect. 6.

2 Background

2.1 Channel State Information

With slight firmware modification, commodity WiFi NICs could report a group of 30 selected subcarrier channel measurements to upper layers in the format of CSI [6]. As the transmitted signal in reality arrives at the receiver through N different paths, $H(f,t)$, the superimposed response of each individual path, can be written as:

$$H(f,t) = \sum_{n=1}^{N} \alpha_k(t)e^{-j2\pi f \tau_k(t)} \tag{1}$$

Where f is the carrier frequency, $\alpha_k(t)$ and $\tau_k(t)$ denotes the attenuation factor and time of flight for the k-th path at time t, respectively.

2.2 PLCR Model

In prior works [9,16], Doppler frequency shifts have been utilized to realize human tracking and action recognition, which actually reflect the rate of variation of each signal propagation path length. For the k-th path, an instantaneous displacement $d_k(t)$ caused by moving objects in a short time interval t can be expressed as $d_k(t) = c\tau_k(t)$, where c is the speed of light. We further relate $\tau_k(t)$ to the Doppler frequency shift f_{D_k}: $\tau_k(t) = d_k(t)/c = \frac{1}{f}\int_{-\infty}^{t} f_{D_k}(x)\mathrm{d}x$, where $f_{D_k} = -\frac{1}{\lambda}\frac{d}{dx}d_k(x)$, λ is the wavelength of WiFi signal. The complex value $H(f,t)$ can be expressed in another form:

$$H(f,t) = H_s(f) + \sum_{k \in P_d} \alpha_k(t)e^{j2\pi \int_{-\infty}^{t} f_{D_k}(x)dx} \tag{2}$$

where P_d denotes the set of dynamic path ($f_D \neq 0$), $H_s(f)$ represents the sum of static components ($f_D = 0$). To eliminate phase noises, the unwrapped instantaneous CSI power is derived as:

$$|H(f,t)|^2 = \sum_{k \in P_d} 2|H_s(f)\alpha_k(t)| \cos(2\pi \int_{-\infty}^{t} f_{D_k}(x)dx + \phi_{sk})$$

$$+ \sum_{k,l \in P_d} 2|\alpha_k(t)\alpha_l(t)| \cos(2\pi \int_{-\infty}^{t} (f_{D_k}(x) - f_{D_l}(x))dx + \phi_{kl}) \tag{3}$$

$$+ \sum_{k \in P_d} |\alpha_k(t)|^2 + |H_s(f)|^2$$

Through Hilbert Transform, we can extract Doppler frequency shifts for further time-frequency analysis.

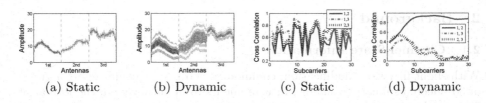

(a) Static   (b) Dynamic   (c) Static   (d) Dynamic

Fig. 1. The amplitudes and cross correlation in two environments.

3 Methodologies

In this section, to derive precise motion-induced Doppler shifts, we first propose a novel CSI processing method by selecting sensitive antennas and subcarriers. For precise action segmentation, we then present our advanced segmentation method based on wavelet entropy, to discern slight transitions in the distance. After that, to explore the properties of physical violence, we present local-global analysis for the feature extraction and classification.

3.1 CSI Processing

Bandpass Filtering: Raw CSIs contain high amplitude impulses and burst noises with high frequency and significant static interferences with low frequency. To obtain sanitary CSI data with a target frequency shift, a three-order Butterworth filter is a natural choice to remove irrelevant signal components in $|H(f,t)|^2$. Considering real physical assaults are extremely intensive, the lower cutoff frequency is set to 1 Hz, while the upper cutoff frequency is set to 80 Hz to keep more high-frequency action information.

Antenna and Subcarrier Selection:

Observation 1: The CSIs with higher variances in static are likely to possess less dynamic environment responses, which is shown in Fig. 1a and b. It indicates that background noises contribute a lot to variations of amplitudes, rather than useful dynamic information.

Observation 2: In Fig. 1c and d, the antennas with lower cross correlation of 30 subcarriers in static are likely to possess higher correlation in dynamic environment. The reason is that the same subcarriers of different antennas are affected by the background noises with various degrees, leading to similar variations in waveforms, which we term "relevant noise".

Selection Strategy: We present our strategy for selection of antenna pairs and subcarriers as follows: For antenna selection, we first calculate the standard deviation σ and mean cross correlation C for each antenna in static. Then, the Antenna Selection Indicator (ASI) is defined as $C\sigma$. The antenna pair with the lowest ASI is selected as the sensitive antennas. For subcarrier selection, to find a trade-off between sensitivity and robustness, we choose 20 subcarriers with the

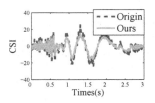 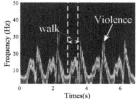 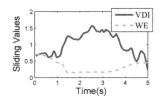

Fig. 2. The PCA result with selection strategy.

Fig. 3. CSI spectrogram of fighting.

Fig. 4. The sliding values of VDI and WE.

lowest cross correlation values in static and with the highest cross correlation values in dynamic environment, respectively. The final selected subcarriers are chosen from the intersection of 40 subcarriers. The criterion of our subcarrier selection scheme is not to select those subcarriers with the lowest variance in static, because we are unaware beforehand whether the variation is induced by location-dependent movements. To reduce dimensions of CSI data, we apply Principle Component Analysis (PCA) to extract common variations of selected subcarriers and choose the first principal component for further processing, which contains major information about human actions and contributes to increase the proportion of reflecting power in spectrogram. Figure 2 shows the PCA result of all 90 subcarriers, which still contain non-negligible "relevant noise". Clearly, our processing method provides a smooth waveform with informative changes and weakly noises.

Short-Term Fourier Transform (STFT): To effectively analyze the CSI waveforms in the time-frequency domain, STFT is adopted to generate the spectrogram which shows the energy of each frequency component with time. We use the normalized FFT magnitudes and a sliding window approach for suitable time-frequency resolution of 1.93 Hz and 0.5 ms. A Gaussian window with a size of 3 is further applied to smooth spectrogram. Figure 3 shows fine-grained spectrogram with two volunteers imitating real physical collisions. One volunteer who plays the role of an attacker is asked to aggressively push the victim walking towards to him, and the victim is asked to respond as realistic as possible. The process iterates five times. We are inspired to monitor physical violence based on following observations: First, physical collisions are always *intensive* which lead to distinct variations of power in corresponding frequency bands. Second, real violence assaults could burst out anytime but keep *continuity* for a long time. Third, the distribution of energy of reflect signal is *irregular* due to random movements of body parts.

3.2 Action Segmentation

To identify the violence-induced fluctuations, the key issue is to discern the transition points in CSI time series. Most existing works utilize the sliding average value and variance of CSI amplitude to detect human motion, which is labor intensive and might be indispensable due to changing locations. Correlations between different subcarriers [9] have shown to be effective in reflecting the presence of human walking. However, we argue that it is insufficient to differentiate temporal fluctuation caused by micro-motions nearby from macro-movements in the distance. Therefore, we resort to wavelet entropy (WE), a new method of complexity measurement for signals [17,18], which is capable of monitoring micro-energy response and quantifying the order-disorder states of the reflected signals. WE possesses unique advantages as follows: On the one hand, comparing with the periodic motions of human objects, the signals reflected from drastic actions of body parts are highly non-stationary and correspond to more randomness in time and frequency domain. WE could precisely reflect the intensity level of energy variations of target frequency bands. On the other hand, WE is a feasible and location-independent indicator, which is suitable for our dynamic experimental scenes.

We define wavelet entropy as: $WE = -\sum_{j<0} p_j ln(p_j)$, where p_j represents the normalized ratio of wavelet energy E_j at the j-th scale, $\sum_{j=-1}^{-N} p_j = 1$. In practice, we select db6 wavelet due to its better orthogonality. We adopt a sliding window method to calculate WE with the sliding window width of 100, half of which is used as the step size. As is shown in Fig. 4, lower WE denotes the simpler components of frequency and the more orderly changes of movements, vice versa. To further improve the robustness of detection system, we propose a light-weight Violence Detection Indicator (VDI) consisting of wavelet entropy WE and cross correlation C as: $VDI = [\max(WE)\text{-}WE]e^C$, with a 5-point median filter. The higher VDI means the higher intensity level of activities and the more frequently signal changes. We select transition points which are the local minimum values closed to the predefined threshold.

3.3 Action Recognition

The action recognition step aims to efficiently characterize the features of violence attacks and precisely detect the presence of violent events. Hence, we identify suspected violent events from two perspectives, *i.e.*, the *local view* and the *global view*. The purpose of local analysis is to identify violent actions from mild human activities, while global analysis is to evaluate the complexity of signals in a given time interval.

Local Analysis: Note that dominant power strengths of frequency bins caused by human torso reflect the major trends of human movements. We adopt the percentile method, a state-of-the-art PLCR extraction method, to estimate the torso movement speed. The cumulated percentage $P(f,t)$ of energy $F(f,t)$ at a given frequency f and time t is calculated as:

$$P(f,t) = \frac{\sum_0^f F(f,t)}{\sum_0^{f_{max}} F(f,t)} \tag{4}$$

where selected frequency values f should not be singular at time t and satisfy $P(f,t) \geq 0.75$.

Therefore, several features of intensity can be extracted from both the total spectrogram and dominant speeds, including:

(1) **The area of the surrounded curve (ASR)** denotes the area of the speed curve surrounded with axis. The rationale is violence-alike actions produce relatively enormous velocity along with high peaks of amplitudes in a short time duration. The efficiency of ASR depends on previous segmentation step.

(2) **The power changing rate (PCR)** is proposed to reflect the increase of kinetic energy based on the observation that abnormal drastic motions typically have high Doppler energy content within a specific frequency band. We give out the mathematical formula of PCR as follows:

$$PCR = \frac{|\sum_{t \subseteq [t_0-1,t_0]} \sum_{f \subseteq [f_l,f_u]} F(f,t) \cdot f - \sum_{t \subseteq [t_0,t_0+1]} \sum_{f \subseteq [f_l,f_u]} F(f,t) \cdot f|}{min(\sum_{t \subseteq [t_0-1,t_0]} \sum_{f \subseteq [f_l,f_u]} F(f,t) \cdot f, \sum_{t \subseteq [t_0,t_0+1]} \sum_{f \subseteq [f_l,f_u]} F(f,t) \cdot f)} \quad (5)$$

where $F(f,t)$ represents the FFT power coefficients of a specific frequency f at time t, f_u and f_l is the upper bound and lower bound of the interested frequency band, t_0 refers to the time when transition point is detected.

(3) **Peak amplitude bandwidth (PAB)** chooses the $1/2$ and $1/4$ peak amplitude bandwidth to reflect the divergence between peak values and valley values of FFT magnitudes. The reason is that energy of intensive assaults disperses in a wide band around the frequency of peak amplitude.

(4) **High-frequency duty ratio (HDR)** is often used to measure the ratio of high level of the time. Considering violent actions are always along with rapid high-frequency changes, we count the number of times when FFT coefficients $F(f,t)$ meanwhile exceed preset frequency f and a predefined threshold.

The SVM classifier using the features extracted above is then applied to identify violence-alike actions, which is originally designed for binary classification. We use LibSVM toolbox [1] with Gaussian Radial Basis Function (RBF) kernel in the training process, and set the cost parameter C and gamma g in kernel function to be 4 and 0.0884 through 10-fold cross-validation.

Global Analysis: Global analysis starts to be considered only when violence-alike action is detected. We adopt two features to represent the characteristics of continuity and irregularity of complex physical violence:

(1) **Detection Confidence** is calculated to reflect the continuity of human activities. As is shown in Fig. 3, violent events always last for a relatively long time due to the escalation of the conflict, while other normal movements (*e.g.*, lying down and sitting down), even with abrupt acceleration, seem unlikely to occur several times within a short time duration. To quantify the continuity of actions, let J be a sequence of segmented slices, the predicted

violence probabilities of following segments are calculated. We give out a detection confidence C_T as:

$$C_T = sgn(T) - \prod_{j \subseteq J} (1 - P_j) \tag{6}$$

where P_j denotes the probability of violent action in the j-th segments. The formula indicates that with the increase of the number of violence-alike segments within time duration T, the higher possibility of violence events will be, which could efficiently reduce the rate of false alarm.

(2) **Lempel-Ziv complexity** is a feasible indicator to reflect the irregular degree between the vicinity segments. Physical violence may result in irregular patterns due to various extents of attacks, while rapid macro-movements, *e.g.*, running and frog leaping, have repetitive profiles. In such case, Lempel-Ziv complexity [7] is a natural choice which measures the dissimilarity by counting the number of different patterns. To avoid excessive coarseness, we adopt multi-scale Lempel-Ziv complexity.

Finally, a simple decision tree is adopt to discern physical violence, which sets the criteria of continuity and irregularity.

4 Evaluation

In this section, we interpret the experimental setups and the analysis of system performance and parameters.

4.1 Experimental Strategy

Experimental Setup: Specifically, we use a Thinkpad X200 laptop with a single antenna as the sender and a Lenovo T460 laptop with three antennas as the receiver. Both laptops are equipped with Intel 5300 NICs and set up to in monitor mode on Channel 165 at 5.825 GHz. The package rate is set to 1000 pkts/s. We evaluate Wi-Dog with 5 volunteers (4 males and 1 female) in a multipath-affected classroom surrounded with tables and chairs, and a narrow corridor with the width of 1.5 m. We place the sender and the receiver at the height of 0.8 m corresponding to the height of human torso and separate them by a distance of 1.5 m for an appropriate detection range.

Data Collection: We collect abundant CSI data of (1) 5 mild interactions (*e.g.*, shake hands, make bows, talk with body language, hug and high-five), (2) 5 normal human actions (*e.g.*, fall, lie down, walk, run and play exergames) performed by one volunteer with the other one standing by and (3) long-time physical violence assaults imitated by two volunteers of each group with necessary protective equipments. Each volunteer iterates the specific behaviors ten times for 50 sets in 3 days. The ground truth is acquired according to the video recordings and volunteers' feedback.

Metric: We evaluate the performance of Wi-Dog based on two metrics:

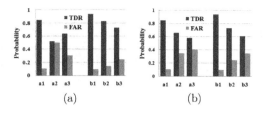

Fig. 5. System performance with (a) selection and (b) local-global analysis.

- **True Detection Rate (TDR)** is the probability that the physical violence is accurately detected. Higher TDR contributes to an effective emergency alert system.
- **False Alarm Rate (FAR)** is the proportion that the system wrongly alarms when there is no violent assault happening, which can be defined as the ratio of wrongly detected violence and accurately detected violence. Lower FAR helps to diminish the waste of public resources.

4.2 Overall Performance

In Fig. 5a, we depict the overall performance of Wi-Dog by comparing three selection methods in two scenarios. $a1, a2, a3$ denotes the average TDR and FAR of (1) our processing approach, (2) a fixed subcarrier of two antennas and (3) all 90 subcarriers from 3 antennas in classroom, respectively, while $b1, b2$ and $b3$ shows the same approach applied in the corridor. Clearly, if we take all antennas and subcarriers into account, the average TDR is only around 68% with FAR of 28%. With advanced selection strategy, Wi-Dog achieves a considerable TDR of 85% with a FAR of 11% in classroom with serious multipath, and a higher TDR of 94% with a lower FAR of 10% in the corridor. It indicates that sensitive antennas and subcarriers help to improve the accuracy and robustness of Wi-Dog. Even though system may achieve acceptable TDR and FAR on a fixed subcarrier of two antennas, just as $b2$ shows. The accuracy and robustness cannot be ensured due to frequency-selective fading and severe multipath effect, just as $a2$ shows.

Figure 5b shows the performance of Wi-Dog with local-global analysis. We illustrate the importance of local-global analysis (*e.g.*, $a1, b1$) by comparing the results with only global analysis (*e.g.*, $a2, b2$) and only local analysis (*e.g.*, $a3, b3$). We find that only considering local features would detect intensive events, but lead to high FAR of 40%. Moreover, TDR and FAR provided by isolated global analysis could still maintain at an acceptable level, which implies the necessity of complexity analysis for violence detection. Taking both aspects into consideration, the TDR rise to an obviously high value with the decline of FAR.

4.3 Parameter Study

Impact of Sliding Window Size: As precise segmentation is essential for the overall performance, an appropriate sliding window size of VDI is needed

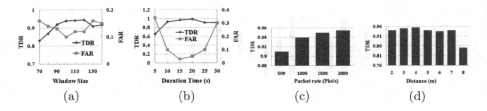

Fig. 6. The impact of various parameters.

to sensitively monitor state transitions. Overlarge window size would decrease sensitivity of detection, while results induced by tiny window size would be affected by burst interferences. Figure 6a depicts the trends of TDR and FAR varying with window sizes, which verifies our previous guess.

Impact of Duration Time: We further evaluate the performance with changing duration time T. Intuitively, longer duration time could contain more underlying violence actions, which would improve the performance significantly. As is shown in Fig. 6b, we observe the ideal phenomenon of rising TDR as well as decreasing FAR with longer T. This is because intensive actions like fall and run would be wrongly detected. However, when duration time T exceeds 20 s, FAR has an obvious rising trend while TDR has a slight decline. We explain that even physical collisions would generate some similar patterns and present some kind of regularity. Furthermore, longer time duration would generate relatively higher possibility of violence with continuous middle-intensity movements during exergames.

Impact of Packet Rates: As we choose a clean channel 165 and set up both laptops in monitor mode to avoid uncontrolled packet losses, we further conduct experiments with different packet rates to see if more CSI measurements would improve the performance. Figure 6c indicates that a higher packet rate results in better accuracy with 500, 1000, 1500 and 2000 Pkt/s. To avoid underlying data overflow and maintain accuracy, we choose 1000 Pkt/s.

Impact of Performing Distance: We test the effects of distance in the mid-perpendicular of a single link, with the distance from 2 m to 8 m. Figure 6d shows the TDR for two volunteers performing actions at different distances. We observe that Wi-Dog could precisely detect violence events in corridor with the average accuracy of 94% at a distance of 7 m.

5   Related Work

Wi-Dog is related to the previous research in three categories: wearable sensor based, camera based and wireless sensing based.

Wearable Sensor Based: Wearable sensor based systems are both widely used and commercially available owing to the rapid development of sensor technology.

For example, [4] recognized free-weight activities by attached RFID tags and further assess the exercise quality from a local-global perspective. [19] developed a fall detection system by monitoring the variation of 3-dimension acceleration data, with a specific wearable device placed on human's waist. [8] utilized a multi-sensor integrated glove to identify abnormal behaviors of paralysis patients. [10] explored the possibility of using a smartphone to detect abrupt physical attacks. However, all these methods require per-user worn sensors, while Wi-Dog aims to achieve contact-free violence detection.

Camera Based: Camera based violence detection system using fixed cameras to capture pictures or video frames to identify human violence. [2] firstly presented an approach to analyzing violence relying on the information of motion trajectory and acceleration. [3] further studied on aggressive fighting using extreme acceleration pattern as discriminant feature. [20] designed a novel image descriptor for violence with spatial features and temporal features. Even so camera based schemes address the problem of wearing extra devices, the issues of privacy and limited monitoring scope still matter.

Wireless Sensing Based: Wireless sensing based schemes attract extensive attentions in recent years. We adopt CSI-based schemes because fine-grained CSI is available in ubiquitous WiFi devices. In recent studies, CSI was utilized to track the location [14] and synchronous gestures [21], recognize walking postures [15] and even slight movements like breathe [12] and finger movements [11], which depends on the observation that the repetitions of certain activities would generate periodic features, while violent behaviors can be random and irregular. RT-Fall [13] used the sensitive phase difference to detect fall with distinct power decline pattern in transition points. However, we discard the phase information of CSI power due to the impact of carrier frequency offsets. As CARM [16] and WiDar [9] both extracted PLCRs from time-frequency analysis, Wi-Dog makes one step further in accurate feature extraction of velocity, including a selection strategy of antennas and subcarriers as well as a segmentation method. Furthermore, Wi-Dog improves the robustness through complete local-global analysis.

6   Conclusion

Wi-Dog is a non-invasive physical violence monitoring scheme on a single link with commercial WiFi devices, which analyze the local-global characteristics of CSI waveforms. We propose a novel CSI processing method to choose reliable antenna pairs and sensitive subcarriers. Moreover, a feasible Violence Detection Indicator (VDI) is developed to monitor slight transitions of behaviors in the distance. We prototype Wi-Dog on commodity WiFi devices and evaluate the overall performance in both LOS and NLOS scenarios. Experimental results demonstrate the accuracy and robustness of Wi-Dog. We consider Wi-Dog as an early step towards general emergency detection for wireless sensing, including, but not limited to terrorist threat warning, fall detection for the elderly and exercise quality assessment. We envision this capability as a significant complement for future violence threat warning applications.

References

1. Chang, C.C., Lin, C.J.: LIBSVM: a library for support vector machines. ACM Trans. Intell. Syst. Technol. (TIST) **2**(3), 27 (2011)
2. Datta, A., Shah, M., Lobo, N.D.V.: Person-on-person violence detection in video data. In: Proceedings of 16th International Conference on Pattern Recognition, vol. 1, pp. 433–438. IEEE (2002)
3. Deniz, O., Serrano, I., Bueno, G., Kim, T.K.: Fast violence detection in video. In: 2014 International Conference on Computer Vision Theory and Applications (VISAPP), vol. 2, pp. 478–485. IEEE (2014)
4. Ding, H., Shangguan, L., Yang, Z., Han, J., Zhou, Z., Yang, P., Xi, W., Zhao, J.: Femo: a platform for free-weight exercise monitoring with rfids. In: Proceedings of the 13th ACM Conference on Embedded Networked Sensor Systems, pp. 141–154. ACM (2015)
5. Evans, C.B., Fraser, M.W., Cotter, K.L.: The effectiveness of school-based bullying prevention programs: a systematic review. Aggress. Violent Behav. **19**(5), 532–544 (2014)
6. Halperin, D., Hu, W., Sheth, A., Wetherall, D.: Tool release: gathering 802.11 n traces with channel state information. ACM SIGCOMM Comput. Commun. Rev. **41**(1), 53–53 (2011)
7. Mateo, A., Roberto, H., Daniel, A., Daniel, A.: Interpretation of the lempel-ziv complexity measure in the context of biomedical signal analysis. IEEE Trans. Bio-med. Eng. **53**(11), 2282–2288 (2006)
8. Nelson, A., Schmandt, J., Shyamkumar, P., Wilkins, W., Lachut, D., Banerjee, N., Rollins, S., Parkerson, J., Varadan, V.: Wearable multi-sensor gesture recognition for paralysis patients. In: 2013 IEEE SENSORS, pp. 1–4. IEEE (2013)
9. Qian, K., Wu, C., Yang, Z., Yang, C., Liu, Y.: Decimeter level passive tracking with wifi. In: Proceedings of the 3rd Workshop on Hot Topics in Wireless, pp. 44–48. ACM (2016)
10. Sun, Z., Tang, S., Huang, H., Huang, L., Zhu, Z., Guo, H., Sun, Y.: iProtect: detecting physical assault using smartphone. In: Xu, K., Zhu, H. (eds.) WASA 2015. LNCS, vol. 9204, pp. 477–486. Springer, Cham (2015). doi:10.1007/978-3-319-21837-3_47
11. Tan, S., Yang, J.: WiFinger: leveraging commodity WiFi for fine-grained finger gesture recognition. In: Proceedings of the 17th ACM International Symposium on Mobile Ad Hoc Networking and Computing, pp. 201–210. ACM (2016)
12. Wang, H., Zhang, D., Ma, J., Wang, Y., Wang, Y., Wu, D., Gu, T., Xie, B.: Human respiration detection with commodity wifi devices: do user location and body orientation matter? In: Proceedings of the 2016 ACM International Joint Conference on Pervasive and Ubiquitous Computing, pp. 25–36. ACM (2016)
13. Wang, H., Zhang, D., Wang, Y., Ma, J., Wang, Y., Li, S.: RT-Fall: a real-time and contactless fall detection system with commodity wifi devices. IEEE Trans. Mob. Comput. **16**(2), 511–526 (2016)

14. Wang, J., Jiang, H., Xiong, J., Jamieson, K., Chen, X., Fang, D., Xie, B.: LIFS: low human effort, device-free localization with fine-grained subcarrier information. In: Proceedings of the 22nd Annual International Conference on Mobile Computing and Networking, pp. 243–256. ACM (2016)
15. Wang, W., Liu, A.X., Shahzad, M.: Gait recognition using wifi signals. In: Proceedings of the 2016 ACM International Joint Conference on Pervasive and Ubiquitous Computing, pp. 363–373. ACM (2016)
16. Wang, W., Liu, A.X., Shahzad, M., Ling, K., Lu, S.: Understanding and modeling of wifi signal based human activity recognition. In: Proceedings of the 21st Annual International Conference on Mobile Computing and Networking, pp. 65–76. ACM (2015)
17. Wang, Y., Li, W., Zhou, J., Li, X., Pu, Y.: Identification of the normal and abnormal heart sounds using wavelet-time entropy features based on OMS-WPD. Future Gen. Comput. Syst. **37**, 488–495 (2014)
18. Wang, Y., Yu, X., Zhang, Y., Lv, H., Jiao, T., Lu, G., Li, Z., Li, S., Jing, X., Wang, J.: Detecting and monitoring the micro-motions of trapped people hidden by obstacles based on wavelet entropy with low centre-frequency UWB radar. Int. J. Remote Sens. **36**(5), 1349–1366 (2015)
19. Wu, F., Zhao, H., Zhao, Y., Zhong, H.: Development of a wearable-sensor-based fall detection system. Int. J. Telemed. Appl. **2015**, 2 (2015)
20. Zhang, T., Jia, W., Yang, B., Yang, J., He, X., Zheng, Z.: Mowld: a robust motion image descriptor for violence detection. Multimedia Tools Appl. **76**(1), 1419–1438 (2017)
21. Zhou, Z., Yang, Z., Qian, K., Wu, C., Shangguan, L., Xu, H., et al.: Tracking synchronous gestures with wifi. In: The 25th International Conference on Computer Communication and Networks, Waikoloa, Hawaii, USA (2016)

Energy-Efficient Contact Detection Model in Mobile Opportunistic Networks

Yueyue Dou[1], Feng Zeng[1(✉)], and Wenjia Li[2]

[1] School of Software, Central South University,
Changsha, China
{douyueyue,fengzeng}@csu.edu.cn
[2] Department of Computer Science, New York Institute of Technology,
New York, USA
wli20@nyit.edu

Abstract. Contact discovery is important to energy conservation in mobile opportunistic networks. In this paper, we propose an energy-efficient contact detection model with contact process following the Poisson distribution. Based on the proposed model, we find out the relation between the total number of effective contact detections and the interval of contact probing, and obtain the trade-offs between energy consumption and contact probing efficiency in different situations. Experiment is done, and the result shows the reasonability and correctness of the proposed contact detection model. Based on this work, the mobile devices can have the contact probing interval set according to the environment for energy conservation.

1 Introduction

Mobile devices with short range wireless network interfaces become increasingly popular and enable new peer-to-peer applications [3]. One of such applications is the mobile opportunistic network (OppNet) [2,4,16,17] in which the radio links between mobile devices are inconstantly changed with time elapsing and contacts (i.e., communication opportunities) are intermittent [6,8]. The typical scenario in this kind of networks is that two users carrying portable devices with wireless network interfaces (e.g., Bluetooth, Wi-Fi, etc. [9]) walking past each other and exchanging data during the period of time they are in communication range.

To enable the above scenario, mobile devices first need to discover each other. And the absence of any infrastructure implies that a continuous, or at least periodic, process for detecting the environment i.e., the neighbor discovery process, has to be run on mobile devices [3]. However, infrequent probing may miss many of their contacts. On the other hand, continuous or frequent probing for contacts may consume considerable amounts of energy [7], which highlights the need for energy-saving in OppNets [1], since mobile devices are commonly powered by batteries. Some related studies [12] have shown that the energy consumption of the Bluetooth discovery protocol is the limiting factor for wide deployment

L. Ma et al. (Eds.): WASA 2017, LNCS 10251, pp. 60–70, 2017.
DOI: 10.1007/978-3-319-60033-8_6

of such ad-hoc networks. Hence, designing an energy-saving contact detection mechanism is critical to the OppNets.

In this paper, we investigate the double detection process between two devices in OppNets and propose an energy-efficient contact detection model based on the Poisson distribution model. Then, we analyze the relationship of the total number of effective contact detections and the detection interval and then achieve the trade-offs between energy consumption and detection effectiveness in different situations. Based on these analysis, users can configure the detection interval according to their state, the surrounding environment, such as the number of other users around so as to obtain more effective detections with less energy consumption, and thus conserve energy and make energy consumption more effective.

The rest of the paper is structured as follows. In Sect. 2, we summarize the related work in this area. Then we give a detailed description on our proposed energy-efficient contact detection model in Sect. 3. Following that, we evaluate the correctness of our proposed energy-efficient contact detection model by conducting extensive experiments in Sect. 4. Finally, Sect. 5 concludes the paper.

2   Related Work

Nowadays, the research in OppNets is mainly focused on two aspects: neighbor discovery and the opportunistic transfer of data. While the latter operation has received more attention. Many energy-saving mechanisms are proposed to reduce energy consumption in data transfer process, since the mobile devices are commonly driven by batteries. Yao *et al.* in [18] proposes an efficient routing algorithm by making the isolated nodes enter the low power consumption dormancy state, then they will be timely awaken when there are other nodes entering into their communication range, which achieves the goal of saving energy. In [13], the authors propose an energy efficient social-based routing protocol to reduce the load of nodes while maintaining the delivery ratio within an acceptable range by limiting the chances of forwarding in traditional social-based routing.

However, the neighbor discovery process is also an energy-consuming process. In OppNets, information is opportunistically exchanged between mobile devices when encounter each other. In order to enable such information exchange, mobile devices must have knowledge of other devices in their vicinity [10]. So devices must probe the environment to discover the neighbors. However, if the device keeps frequent contact probing, it will consume large amounts of energy. Wang *et al.* [14] make measurements on a Nokia mobile phone and conclude that the neighbor discovery process is as energy-intensive as making a phone call. Hence, it is quite significant for mobile devices in OppNets to design an energy-efficient contact detection mechanism because of limited power supply.

Some studies have tried to reduce energy consumption in the contact probing process. Qin *et al.* [11] investigate the impact of contact-probing schedule on link duration and the transmission capacity of DTNs, and propose a model for calculating the optimal contact-probing rate with limited energy and then adjust the

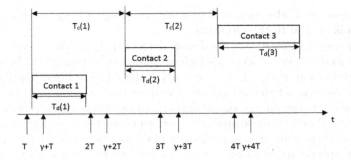

Fig. 1. The double detection process between two devices with the constant interval T

probing rate. Via simulation experiments, the correctness of this model is validated. Two adaptive algorithms for dynamically adjusting the Bluetooth parameters based on past perceived activity in the ad-hoc network were introduced in [3]. The simulations experiments show that the proposed adaptive algorithms reduce energy consumption by 50% and have up to 8% better performance over a static power-conserving scheme. In order to investigate the trade-off between energy efficiency and the contact opportunities in OppNets, Zhou *et al.* [19] propose a model to investigate the contact process and quantify the detecting probability, using the Random WayPoint model. The correctness of the model is verified by conducting simulation experiments. And the result show that the trade-off points are different when the speed varies. Finally, the trade-off between the total number of effective contacts and the energy efficiency is obtained. Wang *et al.* [15] point out that among all contact probing strategies with the same average contact probing interval, the strategy which probes at constant intervals achieves the minimum missing probability. In this paper, we use a constant detection interval in the contact detection process.

In addition, Gao *et al.* [5] validate that the contact process between each node pair follows a homogeneous Poisson process by real trace data. In this paper, we model the contact process of nodes based on the Poisson distribution model and study the relationship between the energy efficiency and the total number of effective detections.

Through the analysis of the relevant work and research above, we propose an energy-efficient contact detection model based on the Poisson distribution model in which users can set the detection interval T according to their state, the surrounding environment, such as the number of other users around so as to obtain more effective detections with less energy consumption, and thus conserve energy and make energy consumption more effective.

3   Energy-Efficient Contact Detection Model

In OppNets, contacts between nodes are intermittent, the links between nodes are constantly changing. The nodes can exchange data with each other when they are in communication range of each other. Due to these characteristics of OppNets, nodes have to probe the environment to find the contact for data exchange. In this section, we proposed a model to investigate the contact process.

3.1 System Model and Assumptions

In OppNets, every device probes the environment with a certain contact probing algorithm. Assume the scenario that a device A probes its environment, other devices which hear the probe respond device A with some information. Then, A can choose the device to exchange data based on these information. And devices are in contact with each other when they are within a predetermined communication range. The interval during which nodes are in contact is called the contact duration, which is expressed as T_d, and the interval of two continuous contacts is called the inter-contact time, which can be expressed as T_c, as shown in Fig. 1. And if neither device probes the environment during a contact duration between device A and B, then this contact is called a missed contact.

Furthermore, we assume that a contact between device A and B, which plan to exchange data, is detected, then this detection is valid and the effective detection probability is expressed as P_{ed}; On the contrary, if this contact can not be detected, then this detection is invalid and the invalid detection probability is expressed as P_{miss}.

In addition, assume that both devices are using the same fixed contact detection interval of T and each probe consumes equal energy so that the energy consumption rate of the device can be converted to the average probing frequency. For a given device, assume that the contact durations $T_d(t)$ are $i.i.d$ stationary random variables with CDF (Cumulative Distribution Function) of $F_{T_d}(t)$.

3.2 Invalid Detection Probability

In this section, we try to calculate the invalid detection probability. As we mentioned earlier, a contact between device A and B is missed only if neither device probes the environment during the contact. Consider the case when two devices A and B are independently probing the environment using the same fixed T. Then, the probability that neither A nor B discovers the other during a contact is $P_{miss}(T)$. Suppose one device probes at $T, 2T, \cdots, nT.$, and the other probes at $y, y + T, \cdots, y + (n-1)T$. Without loss of generality, we can assume that $y < T/2$ .Then, the probability that during a contact, neither device discovers the other is given in Eq. (1) [15]:

$$P_{miss}(T, y) = \frac{1}{T} \left[\int_0^y F_{T_d}(x)dx + \int_0^{T-y} F_{T_d}(x)dx \right] \tag{1}$$

Since the two users probe independently, y is uniformly distributed in $[0, T/2]$, and the average missing probability is:

$$
\begin{aligned}
P_{miss}&(T)\\
&= \frac{2}{T} \int_0^{\frac{T}{2}} \frac{1}{T} \left[\int_0^y F_{T_d}(x)dx + \int_0^{T-y} F_{T_d}(x)dx \right] dy \\
&= \frac{2}{T^2} \left[\int_0^{\frac{T}{2}} \int_0^y F_{T_d}(x)dxdy + \int_0^{\frac{T}{2}} \int_0^{T-y} F_{T_d}(x)dxdy \right] \\
&= \frac{2}{T^2} \left[\int_0^{\frac{T}{2}} \int_0^y F_{T_d}(x)dxdy + \int_{\frac{T}{2}}^{T} \int_0^y F_{T_d}(x)dxdy \right] \\
&= \frac{2}{T^2} \int_0^T \int_0^y F_{T_d}(x)dxdy
\end{aligned}
\tag{2}
$$

In OppNets, the number of contacts with other devices in a certain period of time is random due to the randomness of the human movement. Then the number of contacts is consistent with the Poisson distribution. For a certain device, the average contact duration in a certain period x is $E\{T_d(x)\}$. In order to simplify the calculation, we assume $\lambda = 1/E\{T_d(x)\}$, and the number of contacts with other devices in this period can be expressed as $x/E\{T_d(x)\}$, that is λx. Hence, $F_{T_d}(x)$ of each device can be expressed as $F_{T_d}(x) = 1 - e^{-\lambda x}$. Using Eq. (2), we have:

$$
\begin{aligned}
P_{miss}(T) &= \frac{2}{T^2} \int_0^T \int_0^y F_{T_d}(x)dxdy \\
&= \frac{2}{T^2} \int_0^T \int_0^y (1 - e^{-\lambda x})dxdy \\
&= \frac{2}{T^2} \int_0^T (y + \frac{1}{\lambda}e^{-\lambda x} + \frac{1}{\lambda})dy \\
&= \frac{(\lambda T - 1)^2 - 2e^{-\lambda T} + 1}{\lambda^2 T^2}
\end{aligned}
\tag{3}
$$

From Eq. (3), we can find out that the probability of invalid detection have relationship with the average contact duration and the detection interval T. Moreover, the invalid detection probability tends to 0 when the detection interval T approaches 0; and the invalid detection probability gradually approaches 1 when T increases to infinity. Hence, it is reasonable.

3.3   Trade-Offs in Energy Consumption and Detection Efficiency

In the previous subsection, we get the invalid detection probability $P_{miss}(T)$. Based on this, we can figure out the relationship between the total number of effective detections and T so that we can configure the T value with the goal to conserve energy. Here, we define the total number of effective detections as the total number of effective contacts detected by a device which plan to transmit

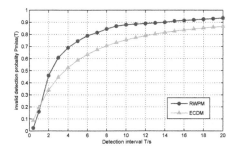

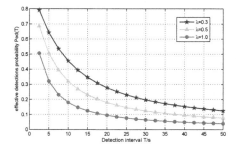

Fig. 2. Comparison ECDM and RWPM

Fig. 3. Relation between detection interval and effective detection probability

data over a period of time T_P, and we express it as S_e. Hence, we can calculate S_e with Eq. (4):

$$S_e = P_{ed}(T) \times T_P \times (n - 1) \tag{4}$$

Where $P_{ed}(T)$ represents the effective detection probability, n represents the total number of mobile devices in OppNets. Due to $P_{ed}(T) = 1 - P_{miss}(T)$, we can calculate $P_{ed}(T) = \dfrac{2e^{-\lambda T} + 2\lambda T - 2}{\lambda^2 T^2}$ based on Eq. (3). And S_e can be solved with Eq. (5):

$$S_e = \frac{(2e^{-\lambda T} + 2\lambda T - 2) \times T_P \times (n - 1)}{\lambda^2 T^2} \tag{5}$$

As we assumed earlier, both devices use the same fixed T and each probe consumes equal energy so that the smaller the value of T, the higher the detection frequency and the more energy consumption; similarly, the larger the value of T, the lower the detection frequency and the less energy consumption. Hence, we define the energy consumption of each contact probing as $E = 1/T$. Based on this definition, we can figure out the relation between S_e and E and the S_e can be recast as:

$$S_e = 2E^2 \times \frac{(e^{-\lambda/E} + \lambda/E - 1) \times T_P \times (n - 1)}{\lambda^2} \tag{6}$$

From Eq. (6), we can find out that S_e have relation with the number of mobile devices n, the average contact duration $1/\lambda$ and energy consumption E. It can be found out that when E approaches 0, S_e approaches 0 from Eq. (7).

$$
\begin{aligned}
&\lim_{E \to 0} S_e \\
&= \lim_{E \to 0} \frac{2E^2 \times (e^{-\lambda/E} + \lambda/E - 1) \times T_P \times (n - 1)}{\lambda^2} \\
&= \lim_{E \to 0} \frac{2E \times (Ee^{-\lambda/E} + \lambda - E) \times T_P \times (n - 1)}{\lambda^2} \\
&= 0
\end{aligned} \tag{7}
$$

And when E approaches infinity, $P_{ed}(T)$ approaches 1, as shown in Eq. (8).

$$\lim_{E\to\infty} P_{ed}(t) = \lim_{E\to\infty} \frac{2e^{-\lambda/E} + 2\lambda/E - 2}{\lambda^2/E^2}$$

$$= \lim_{E\to\infty} 2 \times \frac{\lambda/E^2 e^{-\lambda/E} - \lambda/E^2}{-2\lambda^2/E^3} \tag{8}$$

$$= \lim_{E\to\infty} \frac{1 - e^{-\lambda/E}}{\lambda/E} = \lim_{E\to\infty} \frac{\lambda \times e^{-\lambda/E}}{\lambda} = 1$$

Then, we can obtain $S_e = T_P \times (n-1)$.

Finally, in order to find the trade-offs in energy consumption and detection efficiency under different average contact duration, we define the effective detection efficiency of energy as H, which can be calculated as follows:

$$H(E) = \frac{S_e(E + \Delta E) - S_e(E)}{\Delta E} \tag{9}$$

It is known that when energy consumption is at the equilibrium point, the increase in the number of effective detections caused by the increase of the energy is not conspicuous. On the other word, it is not worth to pay a relatively large amount of energy to achieve a smaller effective number of detections.

Defining the effective detection efficiency expectation is μ, we hope $H(E) \geq \mu$. Hence, the trade-off is $H(E) = \mu$. And according to the continuity of Eq. (6), we have:

$$H(E) = \frac{S_e(E + \Delta E) - S_e(E)}{\Delta E}$$

$$= \frac{S_e(E) - S_e(E - \Delta E)}{\Delta E} = S_e{'}(E) \tag{10}$$

$$S_e{'}(E) = \frac{2(\lambda e^{-\frac{\lambda}{E}} + 2E e^{-\frac{\lambda}{E}} - 2E + \lambda) \times T_P \times (n-1)}{\lambda^2} \tag{11}$$

Then $H(E) = S_e{'}(E) = \mu$, we can formulate the relation between E and μ. Further, we can obtain the trade-offs of the corresponding detection effectiveness and energy consumption according to the user's μ so as to configure the T to conserve energy.

4   Performance Evaluation

To evaluate the correctness of the proposed contact detection model, extensive experiments have been done in Matlab. In the experiment, we compare the proposed energy-efficient contact detection model based on the Poisson distribution model (ECDM) with the invalid detection probability based on the random waypoint model (RWPM) [19] as the detection interval varies in the Matlab platform. The value of n should be configured, in the experiments, $n = 100$. In addition,

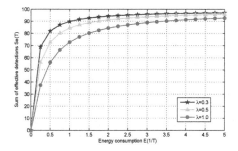

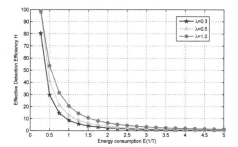

Fig. 4. Relation between energy consumption and the total number of effective detections

Fig. 5. Relation between effective detection efficiency and energy consumption

another parameter T_P, appears in Eq. (4), is set to be 1 s for simplicity reasons. Since S_e increases with the increase of T_P, but T_P has no effect on the trend of S_e. Then the effective detection probability under different circumstances can be compared by setting the different values of λ. In the end, the trade-offs in energy consumption and detection effectiveness can be obtained with the value of μ, then users can configure the detection interval based on the trade-offs.

4.1 Model Validation

The validation of the proposed model is conducted in this section and the result show that the trends of $P_{miss}(T)$ calculated based on our proposed model and $P_{miss}(T)$ verified in [13] are consistent with T varies from Fig. 2. Hence, the proposed model is reasonable and correct.

As shown in Fig. 2, the invalid detection probability increases as T increases and the $P_{miss}(T)$ approaches 0 when T increases to infinity, it is reasonable. In this subsection, we set $\lambda = 0.7$, that means $E\{T_d(x)\} \approx 1.43$ s. When $T < 1.43$ s, $P_{miss}(T)$ approaches 0; And $P_{miss}(T)$ increases as T increases. It can be found that $P_{miss}(T)$ from ECDM is bigger than the RWPM when $T < 1.32$ s and the $P_{miss}(T)$ from RWPM is bigger than the ECDM when $T > 1.32$ s. This is reasonable because users move with purposes in the ECDM, while in RWPM, users move randomly. Hence, the contacts in ECDM are more than that in RWPM. When T is small, that is to say that the detection is frequent, the missed contacts in ECDM is relatively more than in RWPM, and $P_{miss}(T)$ is relatively big as well. However, when T is comparatively big, (on other words, probing infrequently), S_e in ECDM are more than in RWPM, and $P_{miss}(T)$ is smaller meanwhile. But the $P_{miss}(T)$ in both models approach 1 as T increases.

4.2 Trade-Offs in Energy Consumption and Detection Efficiency

On the basis of previous work, this section investigates the trade-offs of energy consumption and detection effectiveness. First, the effective detection probability is obtained based on Eq. (3), then we can get the relation between T and P_{ed}

with different T settings. Regardless of the average contact duration, it can be found that the trend of P_{ed} is the same, as shown in Fig. 3. However, in the case of the same T, the longer the average contact duration, the greater the P_{ed}. The main reason is that the longer the average contact duration, the easier the contact is detected. Furthermore, as T increases to infinity, P_{ed} approaches 0.

Figure 4 shows the relationship, which is obtained according to Eq. (5), between E and S_e with different settings of λ. From Fig. 4, we can find out that S_e increases as E increases with different setting of λ. And the smaller the value of λ(the longer the average contact duration), the more S_e in the same value of E. In addition, it can also be seen from the figure that, at the beginning, S_e increases rapidly as E increases, but the increase of S_e is gradually reduced and the latter is almost no increase when the E continues to increase.

Finally, the relationship between the effective detection efficiency H and the energy consumption E is obtained according to the Eq. (8), and the trade-off can further be found out according to the user's setting of μ at different values of the average contact duration, as shown in Fig. 5.

Figure 5 shows that the $H(E)$ decreases as the E increases, and the smaller the value of λ (the longer the average contact duration), the lower the $H(E)$. From Fig. 5, the trade-offs in energy consumption and detection effectiveness can be found according to users setting of μ. For example, when μ is set to be 50, λ is 0.3, 0.5, 1.0, respectively, then we can figure out the equilibrium point are 0.365, 0.439, 0.529, and the corresponding T are 2.736 s, 2.277 s, 1.889 s. To summarize, users can set the detection interval T according to the effective detection efficiency expectation, their state and the surrounding environment (e.g., the number of other users around, etc.) so as to obtain more effective detections with less energy consumption, and thus conserve energy and make energy consumption more effective.

5   Conclusion

In this paper, we propose an energy-efficient contact detection model with contact process following the Poisson distribution for the OppNets. Then, we validate the reasonability and correctness of the proposed contact detection model by conducting extensive experiments. Based on the proposed model, we find out the relation between the total number of effective contact detections and the interval of contact probing, and obtain the trade-offs between energy consumption and contact probing efficiency in different situations. Finally, the mobile devices can set the detection interval according to the environment to save energy, which is quite beneficial for restricted energy resource in OppNets where nodes are often powered by batteries.

References

1. Anastasi, G., Conti, M., Di Francesco, M., Passarella, A.: Energy conservation in wireless sensor networks: a survey. Ad Hoc Netw. **7**(3), 537–568 (2009)

2. Dai, Y., Yang, P., Chen, G., Wu, J.: CFP: integration of fountain codes and optimal probabilistic forwarding in DTNS. In: 2010 IEEE Global Telecommunications Conference (GLOBECOM 2010), pp. 1–5. IEEE (2010)
3. Drula, C., Amza, C., Rousseau, F., Duda, A.: Adaptive energy conserving algorithms for neighbor discovery in opportunistic bluetooth networks. IEEE J. Sel. Areas Commun. **25**(1) (2007)
4. Fan, J., Chen, J., Du, Y., Gao, W., Wu, J., Sun, Y.: Geocommunity-based broadcasting for data dissemination in mobile social networks. IEEE Trans. Parallel Distrib. Syst. **24**(4), 734–743 (2013)
5. Gao, W., Li, Q., Zhao, B., Cao, G.: Social-aware multicast in disruption-tolerant networks. IEEE/ACM Trans. Netw. (TON) **20**(5), 1553–1566 (2012)
6. Hossmann, T., Spyropoulos, T., Legendre, F.: A complex network analysis of human mobility. In: 2011 IEEE Conference on Computer Communications Workshops (INFOCOM WKSHPS), pp. 876–881. IEEE (2011)
7. Kohvakka, M., Hannikainen, M., Hamalainen, T.D.: Energy optimized beacon transmission rate in a wireless sensor network. In: IEEE 16th International Symposium on Personal, Indoor and Mobile Radio Communications, PIMRC 2005, vol. 2, pp. 1269–1273. IEEE (2005)
8. Li, Y., Bartos, R.: A survey of protocols for intermittently connected delay-tolerant wireless sensor networks. J. Netw. Comput. Appl. **41**, 411–423 (2014)
9. Motani, M., Srinivasan, V., Nuggehalli, P.S.: Peoplenet: engineering a wireless virtual social network. In: Proceedings of the 11th Annual International Conference on Mobile Computing and Networking, pp. 243–257. ACM (2005)
10. Nakayama, H., Ansari, N., Jamalipour, A., Kato, N.: Fault-resilient sensing in wireless sensor networks. Comput. Commun. **30**(11), 2375–2384 (2007)
11. Qin, S., Feng, G., Zhang, Y.: How the contact-probing mechanism affects the transmission capacity of delay-tolerant networks. IEEE Trans. Veh. Technol. **60**(4), 1825–1834 (2011)
12. Su, J., Chin, A., Popivanova, A., Goel, A., De Lara, E.: User mobility for opportunistic ad-hoc networking. In: Sixth IEEE Workshop on Mobile Computing Systems and Applications, WMCSA 2004, pp. 41–50. IEEE (2004)
13. Tian, C., Li, F., Jiang, L., Wang, Z., Wang, Y.: Energy efficient social-based routing for delay tolerant networks. In: Cai, Z., Wang, C., Cheng, S., Wang, H., Gao, H. (eds.) WASA 2014. LNCS, vol. 8491, pp. 290–301. Springer, Cham (2014). doi:10.1007/978-3-319-07782-6_27
14. Wang, W., Motani, M., Srinivasan, V.: Opportunistic energy-efficient contact probing in delay-tolerant applications. IEEE/ACM Trans. Netw. **17**(5), 1592–1605 (2009)
15. Wang, W., Srinivasan, V., Motani, M.: Adaptive contact probing mechanisms for delay tolerant applications. In: Proceedings of the 13th Annual ACM International Conference on Mobile Computing and Networking, pp. 230–241. ACM (2007)
16. Wu, J., Xiao, M., Huang, L.: Homing spread: community home-based multi-copy routing in mobile social networks. In: 2013 Proceedings IEEE INFOCOM, pp. 2319–2327. IEEE (2013)
17. Xiao, M., Wu, J., Liu, C., Huang, L.: Tour: time-sensitive opportunistic utility-based routing in delay tolerant networks. In: 2013 Proceedings IEEE INFOCOM, pp. 2085–2091. IEEE (2013)
18. Yao, Y.K., Liu, W.H., Zheng, W.X., Ren, Z.: An energy-saving routing algorithm for opportunistic networks based on asynchronous sleep approach. In: Applied Mechanics and Materials, vol. 441, pp. 1001–1004. Trans Tech Publications (2014)

19. Zhou, H., Zheng, H., Wu, J., Chen, J.: Energy-efficient contact probing in oppor-
    tunistic mobile networks. In: 2013 22nd International Conference on Computer
    Communications and Networks (ICCCN), pp. 1–7. IEEE (2013)

Modeling of Random Dense CSMA Networks

Yuhong Sun[1(✉)], Tianyi Song[2], Honglu Jiang[1], and Jianchao Zheng[1]

[1] School of Information Science and Engineering, Qufu Normal University,
Rizhao, 276826 Shandong, China
sun_yuh@163.com, jianghonglu88@163.com, jianchao_zheng1991@163.com
[2] Department of Computer Science, The George Washington University,
Washington, DC 20052, USA
tianyi@gwmail.gwu.edu

Abstract. In Carrier Sense Multiple Access (CSMA) media access control (MAC), two nodes that are within the range of one another can not simultaneously transmit packets. Modeling the concurrently transmitting nodes is the key to analyzing the performance of a CSMA network. In this paper, we study the density of concurrently transmitting nodes and propose a Modification of Modified Hard Core Point (MMHCP) model to accurately estimate the density of concurrently transmitting nodes. Our MMHCP best the popular Matérn CSMA model and the Modified Hard Core Point (MHCP) model by avoiding the underestimation and overestimation issues, respectively. We conduct extensive numerical analysis and simulations to evaluate the accuracy of estimation of our MMHCP. Furthermore, we study the impact of the density of initial Poisson Point Process (PPP) on the mean of aggregate interference. The simulation results demonstrate that our model is more accurate than MHCP and Matérn CSMA.

Keywords: CSMA · Stochastic geometry · Poisson point process · Density · Interference

1 Introduction

Carrier Sense Multiple Access (CSMA) is a class of Media Access Control (MAC) protocols that is designated to improve the probability of successful transmission while avoiding collisions between nodes when they attempt to transmit packets over the shared medium. Under CSMA/CA, a transmitter continuously senses the channel state prior to transmitting. If the channel state is idle, the transmitter starts transmitting packets. Otherwise, it waits for a while before it starts sensing the status. By this way, the network can achieve a higher probability of successful transmissions. For a wireless network with densely deployed access points (APs), over dimensioning network planning has been suggested due to the low cost of a wireless networking technologies. However, over dimensioning planning can cast a negative impact on the overall network capacity. Moreover, the behavior of the CSMA networks becomes more complicated as the number

© Springer International Publishing AG 2017
L. Ma et al. (Eds.): WASA 2017, LNCS 10251, pp. 71–82, 2017.
DOI: 10.1007/978-3-319-60033-8_7

of access points increases. Therefore, it is crucial to design a model to predict the impact of the cumulative interference produced by the access points that operate over the same channel [1]. Note that under the rules of medium access, packet transmissions on one node are prohibited by other nodes. Thus, we focus on the model of concurrently transmitting nodes in a time slot on the same channel.

In this paper, we investigate the transmitting density in a dense CSMA network. The transmitting density, which indicates the density of active nodes, is one of the most useful parameters when it comes to measuring the network performances such as the network throughput [1], the aggregate interference [2], and the probabilities of successful transmissions [3], etc. We further study the mean aggregate interference from our numerical analysis and simulations. Our multi-fold contributions can be summarized as follows.

- We analyze the traditional models and demonstrate the underestimation and overestimation of the density for dense CSMA networks.
- We propose a model to accurately express the retaining probability in dense CSMA networks.
- Given that nodes being retained by the same probability, we get the density expression for the simultaneously transmitting nodes in dense CSMA networks.
- We analyze the mean of aggregate interference in CSMA networks based on the proposed model.

2   Related Work

In a CSMA network, a node y is in the contention domain of node x if the power received by x from y is above certain detection threshold. The nodes that are in the same contention domain are called neighboring nodes. Note that the contention domain is determined by the network configurations. Under CSMA MAC, wireless nodes may transmit packets at the same time if no on-going transmission is sensed from their common neighbors, which is termed as the hidden terminal problem [4]. To avoid such a problem, a timer is set for each node. When a node senses that the medium is idle, its timer reduces by one time unit. The node is not allowed to transmit its packet until its timer expires. The principle is that a node has the privilege to transmit only if it has the least remaining time on its timer among all the nodes in its contention domain.

To model such a CSMA network, the use of stochastic geometry is introduced to analyze the network performance from a statistical perspective. In particularly, Poisson Point Process (PPP) is widely used in modeling cellular networks [5,6] and ad hoc networks [7,8] for its tractability in analyzing the interference, probabilities of coverage, and other performance metrics. However, PPP is accurate for very sparse networks as the distributions of the atoms of a PPP are independent, which usually is not the case in wireless networks. For example, in heterogeneous cellular networks, the locations of base stations are modeled by Poisson Cluster Process (PCP) [9] or Ginibre Point Process (GPP) [10] in order to reflect the dependence in the locations of the base stations. Similarly, for the exclusion of CSMA nodes, the hard core point process has been applied to model the simultaneously transmitting nodes [1,3,11].

A hard-core point process is a point process such that the distance between any two points is greater than a special value h. Matérn proposed two ways by thinning a PPP dependently to obtain such a point process. Both approaches can generate a homogenous point process, while type II has a higher packing density. Furthermore, Matérn type II can be approximated to an inhomogeneous PPP to model the mean aggregate interference [12]. Therefore, most methods adopt the Matérn type II to model the CSMA networks.

Matérn type II point process is implemented as follows. Let $\Phi = \{x_i\}_{i \in (1,n)}$ be a homogeneous PPP with density λ. Each point x_i is marked by a random variable u_i that is uniformly distributed on $[0,1]$. The marks are independent and identically distributed, or i.i.d, and independent of the positions of x_i. If the ball that centers at x_i with radius h does not consist of any points with mark less than u_i, the point x_i is retained in the hard point process. The points that are not retained will be deleted from the PPP.

A natural modification of Matérn II model, named Matérn CSMA was proposed in [3]. Let $\hat{\Phi} = \{x_i, m_i\}$ be an initial marked PPP with density λ on R^2, where $\Phi = \{x_i\}$ denotes the locations of potential transmitters, and $\{m_i\}$ are i.i.d. marks uniformly distributed on $[0,1]$. A random variable e_i is used to denote whether the nodes in Φ can access the medium. Note that $e_i = 1(\forall x_j \in Neighbor(x_i), m_i < m_j)$, where $Neighbor(x_i)$ denotes the set of nodes close to x_i in the sensing range. The point process $\Phi_m := \{X_i \in \Phi : e_i = 1\}$ is referred to as the Matérn CSMA point process [1]. It defines the set of transmitters retained by CSMA as a non-independent thinning of the PPP. This model captures the key requirement that a retained node never has another retained node in its contention domain. When the transmitting power on each node is different, the model is more accurate than the traditional Matérn II model. For the sake of argument, we will refer to both standard Matérn II model and the Matérn CSMA model [3] as Matérn model in the rest of our paper.

As shown in Fig. 1, both Matérn models lead to an underestimation of the density. In Fig. 1, node x_1 is not retained as it detects its neighbor x_2; moreover, node x_2 is not retained either as it detects its neighbor x_3, i.e., $m_1 > m_2 > m_3$, where m_i is the mark of x_i. As a result, neither x_1 nor x_2 can be retained in the thinning scheme. However, if x_3 is not the neighbor of x_1, and if x_3 does not detect any on-going transmissions of its neighbors, a more reasonable MAC will allow x_1 and x_3 to transmit simultaneously in order to obtain a better throughput. Such a retaining scheme shows that Matérn CSMA model is conservative.

ElSawy et al. in [13] investigated the problem of underestimation of the Matérn CSMA model, and proposed another Modified Hard Core Point (MHCP) process. In MHCP, a node x_i has the privilege to transmit in a time slot for the following two reasons. First, node x_i has the lowest mark in its contention domain, which is the same condition as that of the Matérn model. Second, node x_i has the second lowest mark in its contention domain, and node x_j the lowest

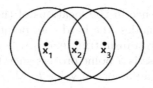

Fig. 1. Density underestimation in Matérn CSMA

while x_j is not the node with the lowest mark in contention domain of itself. Such a scheme can avoid the omittance of nodes, as shown in Fig. 1. However, in a network with dense nodes, MHCP may lead to the problem of overestimation as shown in Fig. 2. In fact, when we consider the nodes with second lowest mark, the nodes with the lowest mark may be retained for the same reason, resulting in two nodes being retained at the same time in one domain. As shown in Fig. 2, assume that $m_1 > m_2 > m_3 > m_4 > m_5$, the node x_1, x_2 and x_3 are retained for the same reason, which causes collisions.

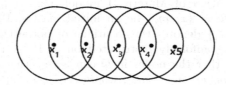

Fig. 2. Density overestimation in MHCP

Simple Sequential Inhabitation (SSI) is an alternative to model the dense CSMA networks. In [2], Busson and Chelius used SSI to model the spatial distribution of potential interference sources. However, analyzing the model turned out to be very challenging as SSI only give the point density when the underlying PPP density tends to be infinity. What is more, analytical expression can not be derived.

Given the overestimate and underestimate issues in modeling the transmitting nodes in CSMA networks, we consider a more accurate scheme. The basic idea is very intuitive and simple. That is, in the initial PPP, a node x_i is retained under the following conditions: (1) x_i has the lowest mark in its contention domain; (2) x_i has the second lowest mark in its contention domain, meanwhile, node x_j has the second lowest mark and x_j is not retained. We name our proposed model a modification of MHCP (MMHCP).

3   Network Model and Symbols

3.1   Network Model

We use a marked PPP $\tilde{\Phi} = \{(x_i, m_i, F_i)\}$ to indicate the potential transmitters, where $\{x_i\}$ is a homogeneous PPP over the plane with density λ_p denoting the locations of the transmitters and $\{m_i\}$ being their marks that are uniformly distributed over $[0, 1]$. The virtual power emitted from x_i towards x_j is denoted by $\{F_i = (F_i^j : j)\}_i$. The contention domain of a node, also called the neighborhood of a node, is defined as $N(x_i) = \{(x_j, m_j, F_j) \in \tilde{\Phi} : (F_i^j)/l(|x_i - x_j|) \geq p_0, j \neq i\}$, where $p_0 > 0$ is the sensing threshold of the network and $l(.)$ is the path loss function. For simplicity, we denote the neighborhood of node x_i as C_i.

We assume that the receivers are randomly distributed over the plane. Each transmitter's receivers are uniformly distributed within its Voronoi cell. A receiver associates with its transmitter only if the transmitter is the one with the strongest average received power. The transmitting power and fading are combined into a virtual power F in this paper: $F = p \cdot G$, where p is the transmitting power, and G is the fading factor that is subject to an exponential distribution with μ, $\mu \geq 0$. The path loss function is $l(r) = r^\beta, \beta > 2$, where r is the distance between a transmitter and the receiver, and β is the path loss exponent. The sensing threshold for each node is p_0 such that $F/l(r) \geq p_0$. Since the transmitting power is the same for each node, we can get a distance r_e as the distance threshold of sensing for a node. We call r_e as exclusion radius.

3.2   Notations

For the sake of argument, we list our mathematical notations here. Node x_i is abbreviated as i, and i, j, and k are used to denote different nodes.

We use C_i to denote the nodes set in the contention domain of node i. For the same transmitting power of each node, the nodes in C_i are just the points in a disc centered at x_i with the exclusion radius. To determine whether a node is privileged to transmit, several probability symbols are needed:

Probability of a node i being retained is denoted by $P_{retain}[i] = P[i \text{ is retained}]$.

Probability of a node i having the lowest mark in C_i is denoted by $P_{min}[i]$.

Probability of a node i having the second lowest mark in C_i is denoted by $P_2[i]$.

Probability of a node i with the second lowest mark in C_i being retained is denoted by $P_{2\_retain}[i]$.

Probability of a node j having the lowest mark in C_i and not being retained, conditioned on that node i has the second lowest mark, is denoted by $\hat{P}^i[j]$.

Suppose there are n nodes around node x_i in the initial PPP, $P_{min}[i]$ and $P_2[i]$ are equivalent in denoting x_i with a certain mark in $\{m_i\}, i \in (1, n)$. Due to the uniform distribution of the marks among the n points coexisting with x_i in C_i, the probability that x_i has a certain mark is $1/(n + 1)$. At the same time, since we adopt homogeneous PPP, the average number of points in C_i is $\lambda_p S_{C_i}$, where S_{C_i} is the area of C_i. With the same transmitting power, S_{C_i} can be the area of a disc with radius r_e. Hence, the probability can be derived as follows.

$$P_{\min}[i] = P_2[i] = = \sum_{n=0}^{\infty} \frac{1}{n+1} P[|C_i \setminus \{x_i\}| = n]$$

$$\stackrel{(a)}{=} \sum_{n=0}^{\infty} \frac{1}{n+1} \frac{e^{-\lambda_p \pi r^2} \cdot (\lambda_p \pi r^2)^n}{n!} \tag{1}$$

$$= \frac{e^{-\lambda_p \pi r^2}}{\lambda_p \pi r^2} \sum_{n=0}^{\infty} \frac{(\lambda_p \pi r^2)^{n+1}}{(n+1)!} = \frac{1 - e^{-\lambda_p \pi r^2}}{\lambda_p \pi r^2}$$

where $|.|$ denotes the size of a set, and (a) holds because the points follows Poisson distribution. If we let $N = \lambda_p \pi r^2$, the above probability can be written as $\frac{1-e^{-N}}{N}$.

Suppose x_i has the second lowest mark in C_i, and x_j has the lowest mark, while there is at least a node x_k in C_j with a lower mark than m_j. It is equivalent to say that there is at least a node with lower mark than m_j in C_j-C_i (shadow of Fig. 3). The probability is $Pro[\exists k \in (C_j - C_i), m_k < m_j] = \sum_{t=1}^{\infty} \frac{t}{n+t+1} \frac{M^t e^{-M}}{t!}$, where $M = \lambda_p \int_0^r (2\pi z - 4z \cos^{-1}(\frac{z}{2r}) + \frac{z}{r^2}\sqrt{4r^2 - z^2})dz$, denotes the average number of the C_j-C_i. The derivations can be found in [13]. We use $P_{C_j - C_i}(k)$ to indicate the similar scenario in the following of the paper. Therefore, the probability of a second lowest mark node being retained is

$$P_{2\_retain}[i] = P_2 \times P_{C_j - C_i}(k)$$

$$= \sum_{n=0}^{\infty} \frac{1}{n+1} \frac{e^{-N} N^n}{n!} \sum_{t=1}^{\infty} \frac{t}{n+t+1} \frac{e^{-M} M^t}{t!} \tag{2}$$

$$= \frac{M(1 - e^{-(N+M)})}{N(N+M)} + e^{-N}\left(\frac{(M-N)(e^{-M} - 1)}{NM} - 1\right)$$

where $N = \lambda_p \pi r^2$ denotes the average number of nodes in C_i, and M is the average number of nodes in C_j-C_i, and it can be manipulated in a closed form. We further plug it into (2) to get the probability of a node with the second lowest mark being retained in MHCP. The whole retaining probability for any node is $P_{mhcp} = P_{min} + P_{2\_retain}$, which is consistent with that in [13].

4   Retaining Probability of Nodes in MMHCP

Combining the analysis of Matérn CSMA and MHCP model in [13], we propose the MMHCP model, where the simultaneously transmitting nodes (retained nodes) in CSMA include those nodes with the lowest marks, and the nodes satisfying that it has the second lowest mark in the domain of itself, while the node with the lowest mark has not been retained. It can be formally expressed as: $\Phi_t = \{x_i : \forall x_j \in N(x_i), x_i \neq x_j, m_i < m_j\} \cup \{x_i : \exists x_j \in N(x_i), m_i > m_j, \forall x_k \in N(x_i) \setminus \{x_i, x_j\}, m_k > m_i, and \ x_j \ is \ not \ retained\}$. The probability of a node been granted to transmit is $P_{retain}[i] = P_{min}[i] + P_2[i] \cdot \hat{P}^i[j]$.

For $\hat{P}^i[j]$, it can be interpreted that conditioned node i having the second lowest mark in C_i, node j has the lowest mark in C_i and is not retained. In other words, node i has the second lowest mark in C_i, and node j is not retained only since there is at least a node k in $C_j - C_i$ (shadow) and k is retained (node k may have the lowest mark, or k has the second lowest mark while the node with the lowest mark is not retained in C_k). ElSawy $et\ al.$ in [13] considered the reason for j not been retained is that nodes existing in shadow, while in fact even nodes exist in shadow, j may be retained. Namely, when j is the second lowest and the lowest k is not retained, j is retained, which makes i not be retained.

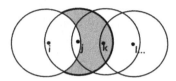

Fig. 3. Node i is retained, if m_j is the only mark lower than m_i in C_i and j is not retained. Other nodes are omitted in the figure.

We further modify the probability in [13] as follows. Suppose there are n nodes and node i in C_i, and t nodes in the shadow, where n and t follow two Poisson distributions with parameter N and M, respectively. Firstly, we analyze the probability of j not been retained, given that j has the second lowest mark in C_i. Following the analysis above, we know j is not retained for the following reason: m_j is not the lowest in C_j, except that although m_j is not the lowest in C_j, m_j is the second lowest and the lowest node k is not retained. Because in such a case, j should be retained too. According to [13], we know that the probability of j not having the lowest mark in C_j equals to $P_{2\_retain}[i]$ in (2). We consider the probability of m_j being the second lowest in C_j under the condition that m_j being the lowest in C_i. It equals the probability of j having the second lowest mark in $(n + t + 1)$ nodes :

$P(j\ has\ the\ second\ lowest\ mark\ in\ C_j | j\ has\ the\ lowest\ mark\ in\ C_i) \triangleq P_2'[j] = 1/(n+t+1)$. The probability of i being retained is $P_{retain}[i] = P_{min}[i] + P_2[i] \times \hat{P}^i[j] = P_{min}[i] + P_2[i] \times (P_{(C_i - C_j)}[m_j\ is\ not\ lowest] - P_2'[j] \times (1 - P_{retain}[k])) = P_{min}[i] + P_{2\_retain}[i] - P_2[i] \times P_2'[j] \times (1 - P_{retain}[k]))$. $P_{retain}[k]$ is the probability of node k been retained and can be obtained the same way as above. In a dense nodes distributed network, the rule is iterated until the current node is definitely to be retained or not. However, for the randomness of the nodes distribution in a network, we cannot know the exact number of the nodes in such an iteration chain beforehand. Thus the ultimate result is hard to obtain.

To simplify such a problem, we assume the probability of each node being retained is the same in a network, and we only need to get an average probability of retaining a node. Hence, $P_{retain}[i] = P_{retain}[j] = P_{retain}[k] = ...$, and the problem is simplified as $P_{retain}[i] = P_{min}[i] + P_{2\_retain}[i] - P_2(i) \times P_2'(j) \times (1 - P_{retain}[i])$.

We get

$$P_{retain}[i] = \frac{P_{\min}[i] + P_{2\_retain}[i] - P_2[i] \times P_2'[j]}{1 - P_2[i] \times P_2'[j]}$$

Here, $P_{2\_retain}[i]$ is given in Eq. (2), we denote $P' = P_2[i] \times P_2'[j]$. Since n and t are distributed as Poisson with parameter N and M, we get

$$P' = P_2[i] \times P_2'[j] = \sum_{n=1}^{\infty} \frac{N^n e^{-N}}{n!} \frac{1}{n+1} \sum_{t=1}^{\infty} \frac{M^t e^{-M}}{t!} \frac{1}{n+t+1}$$

According to the deduction of $P_{2\_retain}[i]$ from [13], we can obtain

$$
\begin{aligned}
P' &= \frac{Me^{-(N+M)}}{N} \left(\sum_{n=1}^{\infty} \frac{N^{n+1}}{(n+1)!} \sum_{t=1}^{\infty} \frac{M^{t-1}}{t!} \frac{1}{n+t+1} \right) \\
&= \frac{1}{M}(P_{2\_retain}[i] - \frac{Me^{-(N+M)}}{N} \cdot \frac{e^N - 1}{N})
\end{aligned}
\tag{3}
$$

Finally, we get

$$P_{retain}[i] = \frac{P_{\min}[i] + P_{2\_retain}[i] - P'}{1 - P'} \tag{4}$$

where $P_{\min}$ and P_{2_retain} are given by (1) and (2), and P' can be obtained by

$$P' = \frac{1 - e^{-(N+M)}}{N(M+N)} + \frac{e^{-N}}{M}(\frac{(M-N)(e^{-M}-1)}{NM} - 1) - \frac{e^{-(N+M)}(e^N - 1)}{N^2}.$$

Proposition 1. *If the probability of a node i being retained in MMHCP is denoted by $P_{mmhcp} = P_{retain}[i]$ as (4), the probability of a node being retained in MHCP of [13] is P_{mhcp}, and the probability of a node being retained in Matérn CSMA is P_{matern}, then we get $P_{matern} \leq P_{mmhcp} \leq P_{mhcp} \leq 1$.*

Proof. The last '$\leq$': The retaining probability is obviously less than 1 in a network, and '$=$' holds only when the network is sparse enough. Then, let us prove $P_{matern} \leq P_{mmhcp}$, namely $\frac{P_{min}[i] + P_{2\_retain}[i] - P'}{1-P'} \geq P_{min}[i]$. We need that $P_{min}[i] + P_{2\_retain}[i] - P' \geq P_{min}[i] - P_{min}[i]P'$ holds. Since P' reflects the probability of j having the second lowest mark in shadow while $P_{2\_retain}[i]$ reflects the probability of node j having not the lowest mark, $P_{2\_retain}[i] \geq P'$, so it is proved.

Then, we prove $P_{mmhcp} \leq P_{mhcp}$, namely $\frac{P_{min}[i] + P_{2\_retain}[i] - P'}{1-P'} \leq P_{min}[i] + P_{2\_retain}[i]$. Since $P_{min}[i] + P_{2\_retain}[i]$ is the probability of been retained in MHCP, and is less than 1. Let $a = P_{min}[i] + P_{2\_retain}[i]$, $b = P'$, we know $\frac{a-b}{1-b} < a$. The proof is completed.

We can conclude that the probability of a node being retained in MMHCP is lower than that in MHCP, and higher than that in Matérn CSMA. The underlying reasons are as follows. Matérn CSMA is conservative and does not retain any nodes other than the nodes with the lowest mark in the contention domain. The MHCP model retains a node with second lowest mark only because the neighbor with the lowest mark of such a node has a neighbor with a lower mark. While in MMHCP model, when we consider a node with the second lowest mark retained or not, we check whether any neighbour of the lowest mark neighbour is retained. Hence, the MMHCP model can alleviate the overestimation in MHCP. Knowing the probability of being retained, the density of simultaneously transmitting nodes in CSMA can be represented as $\lambda_{mmhcp} = \lambda_p \cdot P_{retain}[i]$. Such a density is affected both by the initially density λ_p and the exclusion r_e (determined by the threshold of the sensing power), illustrated in Figs. 4 and 5.

5   Mean of Aggregate Interference

The probability of successful transmission is a significant metric in performance analysis of a wireless network. For a receiver on the plane, the transmission is affected mainly by the aggregate interference that is the accumulated signals sent by concurrent transmitters at the same time. If the transmitters are distributed as a PPP, the aggregate interference can be expressed as a closed form. Furthermore, based on the theorem of Slivnyak [14], a stationary point process seen from an arbitrary location is same whether there is a point at that location or not. Therefore, we need only consider the conditional distribution of points 'seen' from a *typical receiver*, which is referred to as a receiver at a typical location [14]. For instance, we set the location at the origin, and the distance between a transmission could be easier.

For Matérn type II, authors in [12] proposed that the mean interference of the point process can be approximated by a PPP with the same density. On the other hand, from the Compbell theorem [15], the mean of the aggregate interference is same for any stationary point process with same density. It is only related to the density of nodes, fading, and path loss, independent of the position of each node. So we can take the mean aggregate interference of a PPP with the same density to approximate the Matérn CSMA, MHCP, and MMHCP to analyze the mean of the aggregate interference.

We compute the mean of aggregate interference suffered from a typical node (positioned on the origin). In CSMA, the transmitter is not interfered within its contention domain, which is a disc centered at this node with the exclusion radius. So the nearest interferer is far from the typical receiver at least $dis = r_e - R$, where R is distance between the receiver and its intended transmitter, and r_e is the exclusion radius. Here we only consider that r_e is much greater than R. Following the association law, the intended transmitter is the closest one. Considering the transmitting power p, a general fading G, from [14], the mean of aggregate interference of a typical receiver can be expressed as $E[I] = E[p]\lambda \int_{R_2} l(y)dy \int_0^\infty (1 - G(s))ds 2\pi\lambda \int_{dis}^\infty \frac{r}{l(r)}dr$. Therefore, with the exponential distribution of $G(s) = 1 - e^{-\mu s}$, $\mu \geq 0$, we can get $E[I] = \frac{2\pi\lambda}{\mu} \int_{r-R}^{\infty} \frac{r}{l(r)} dr$. Given the density λ of the PPP and $l(r) = r^\beta$, the mean of the aggregate interference can be expressed as $E[I] = \frac{2\pi\lambda}{\mu} \int_{r-R}^{\infty} \frac{r}{r^\beta} dr = \frac{2\pi\lambda}{\mu} \cdot \frac{1}{2-\beta} \cdot (r-R)^{2-\beta}$. And the approximation of the mean of the aggregate interference is taken by replacing λ with λ_{matern}, λ_{mhcp}, and λ_{mmhcp} respectively.

6   Simulation

The density analysis and interference approximation can be numerical evaluated and simulated using MATLAB.

At first, we realize a CSMA network inherited from a PPP with different densities in a rectangle with 10×10. Then we thin the PPP by CSMA MAC. A node is retained if the minimum distance between it and all of the previously retained points is greater than r_e.

To analyze the slope of the CSMA density with the density of initial PPP, we repeat 100 times by setting the initial PPP density from 0.1 to 2.8. The trend is shown in Fig. 4. By numerical analysis, we can see that the Matérn CSMA model underestimates the density, while MHCP model overestimates the density. The MMHCP curve is closer to the simulation than the other two. At the same time, it is shown that when the density of initial PPP is small (0.1 – 0.3), the differences among the models are trival. When the density of PPP is large (more than 0.5), the curves differ much, which implies that with the CSMA network being denser, a more accurate model to estimate the intensity is necessary.

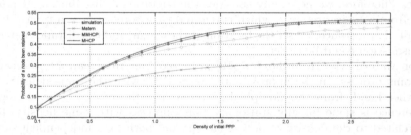

Fig. 4. Density of CSMA follows the density of initial PPP

For the trend of the estimated density following the exclusion r_e, we take a fixed density of initial PPP as 0.5 and set exclusion radius from 1 to 16, and repeat the simulation for 100 times. The curves are shown in Fig. 5, where we can see the trend of density of CSMA following the exclusion radius.

For the mean of aggregate interference, we set $\mu = 1$, $\beta = 4$ and compute the mean of the aggregate interference. The receiver is set at the center point of the rectangle, and the nearest transmitter is the intended sender, other transmitting nodes are treated as interferers. The mean of aggregate interference is taken as the average of 100 times experiments, illustrated in Fig. 6. It can be seen that the MMHCP has a better approximation to the simulation.

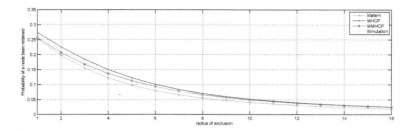

Fig. 5. Density influenced by the exclusion radius

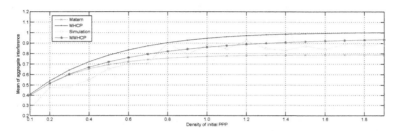

Fig. 6. Mean of aggregate interference

7   Conclusion

In this paper, we study the model of dense CSMA networks with randomly distributed nodes. Because the Matérn CSMA point process underestimates the density of the simultaneously transmitting nodes and the MHCP in [13] overestimates the density, we propose to further modify MHCP to alleviate the overestimation of the density. We give a more accurate density estimation for the simultaneously transmitting nodes in dense CSMA networks. Given the initial density of the PPP and exclusion radius, we express the density estimation in a closed form by regarding the retaining probability for each node being same. The simulation results demonstrate that the density from MMHCP model is closer to the actual distribution of nodes in CSMA than Matérn model and MHCP. The impact of the density of nodes on the mean of aggregate interference is also studied in our numerical analysis and simulation, from which we can see that MMHCP is more accurate in modeling the network behavior than MHCP and Matérn CSMA.

Acknowledgments. This work is supported by NSF of China under Grant 61373027 and 61672321 and Shandong Province Higher Educational Science and Technology Program (J15LN06).

References

1. Alfan, G., Garetto, M., Leonardi, E.: New directions into the stochastic geometry analysis of dense CSMA networks. IEEE Trans. Mob. Comput. **13**(2), 324–336 (2014)
2. Busson, A., Chelius, G.: Point processes for interference modeling in CSMA/CA ad-hoc networks. In: Sixth ACM Symposium Performance Evaluation of Wireless Ad Hoc, Sensor, and Ubiquitous Networks, pp. 33–40 (2009)
3. Nguyen, H.Q., Baccelli, F., Kofman, D.: A stochastic geometry analysis of dense IEEE 802.11 networks. In: 26th IEEE International Conference on Computer Communications, pp. 1199–1207 (2007)
4. Boorstyn, R., Kershenbaum, A., Maglaris, B., Sahin, V.: Throughput analysis in multihop CSMA packet radio networks. IEEE Trans. Comm. **35**(3), 267–274 (1987)
5. Andrews, J.G., Baccelli, F., Ganti, R.K.: A tractable approach to coverage and rate in cellular networks. IEEE Trans. Commun. **59**(11), 3122–3134 (2011)
6. Dhillon, H., Ganti, R., Baccelli, F., Andrews, J.: Modeling and analysis of k-tier downlink heterogeneous cellular networks. IEEE J. Sel. Areas Commun. **30**(3), 550–560 (2012)
7. Weber, S., Andrews, J.G., Jindal, N.: An overview of the transmission capacity of wireless networks. IEEE Trans. commun. **58**(12), 3593–3604 (2010)
8. Venkataraman, J., Haenggi, M., Collins, O.: Shot noise models for the dual problems of cooperative coverage and outage in random networks. In: 44th Annual Allerton Conference on Communication Control, and Computing, Monticello, IL, USA, pp. 2642–2650 (2006)
9. Suryaprakash, V., Møller, J., Fettweis, G.: On the modeling and analysis of heterogeneous radio access networks using a poisson cluster process. IEEE Trans. Wirel. Commun. **14**(2), 1035–1047 (2015)
10. Deng, N., Zhou, W., Haenggi, M.: The ginibre point process as a model for wireless networks with repulsion. IEEE Trans. Wireless Commun. **14**(1), 107–121 (2014)
11. Baccelli, F., Blaszczyszyn, M.B., Muhlethaler, P.: An aloha protocol for multihop mobile wireless networks. IEEE Trans. Inf. Theory **52**(2), 421–436 (2006)
12. Haenggi, M.: Mean interference in hard-core wireless networks. IEEE Commun. Lett. **15**, 792–794 (2011)
13. ElSawy, H., Hossain, E., Camorlinga, S.: Characterizing random CSMA wireless networks: a stochastic geometry approach. In: IEEE ICC, pp. 5000–5004 (2012)
14. Baccelli, F., Blaszczyszyn, B.: Stochastic Geometry and Wireless Networks. NOW publishers, Breda (2009)
15. Haenggi, M.: Stochastic Geometry for Wireless Networks. Cambridge University Press, Cambridge (2012)

Throughput Maximization in Multi-User Cooperative Cognitive Radio Networks

Lei Lu[1], Wei Li[2], Shengling Wang[1], Rongfang Bie[1(✉)], and Bowu Zhang[3]

[1] Beijing Normal University, Beijing, China
lulei@mail.bnu.edu.cn, {wangshengling,rfbie}@bnu.edu.cn
[2] Georgia State University, Atlanta, USA
wli28@gsu.edu
[3] Marist College, Poughkeepsie, USA
bowu.zhang@marist.edu

Abstract. In Cooperative Cognitive Radio Networks (CCRNs), primary users and secondary users are mutual beneficial through setting up cooperative transmission. But, in most of the existing work, only the SUs working as the relays can have the opportunities to access primary users' channel, which may incur a waste of resource or a throughput reduction if the relays have light data traffic. In this paper, to tackle this issue while fully exploiting cooperative transmission, we propose a novel scheme GMLDF-Cooperation to achieve multi-path cooperation transmission of primary transmitters and provide all secondary users with a chance to send their own data. Our theoretical analysis and simulation results can validate the effectiveness of the proposed algorithm.

Keywords: Cognitive radio network · Cooperative transmission · Relay selection

1 Introduction

As one of the promising approaches, cognitive radio technique has been proposed to enhance spectrum utilization and satisfy the ever increasing demand of wireless service. Moreover, in order to improve the coverage area and the throughput of Cognitive Radio Networks (CRNs) [1–7], cooperative communication technique is brought to form Cooperative Cognitive Radio Networks (CCRNs), in which secondary users (SUs) help relay primary users (PUs)' data and then are awarded channel access opportunities for their own transmission. Such a cooperation can benefit both the PUs and the SUs, achieving a "win-win" situation.

In past years, a number of relay selection schemes have been proposed for CCRNs [8–16]. In [12,13,15,17], a best SU is chosen as the relay for a primary

This work has been supported by the National Natural Science Foundation of China (Nos. 61472044, 61472403, 61571049), and the Fundamental Research Funds for the Central Universities (No. 2014KJJCB32).

© Springer International Publishing AG 2017
L. Ma et al. (Eds.): WASA 2017, LNCS 10251, pp. 83–95, 2017.
DOI: 10.1007/978-3-319-60033-8_8

transmitter (PT)-primary receiver (PR) pair according to different performance criteria and cooperation constraints. However, utilizing only one relay may not effectively improve the transmission performance for the PT-PR pair. Thus, to further exploit cooperative transmission between the PT and the SUs, "multi-relay" selection schemes are proposed [8,10,11,14,16]. In [8,10,14,16], a set of SUs are selected to perform "multi-path" cooperative transmission for the PT-PR pair. With such "multi-path" cooperative transmission, the PT's data can be forwarded within a shorter time period. Besides, in [11], a network formation game-based multi-hop relay selection algorithm is proposed to set up a multi-hop path from the PT to the PR.

Notice that in the cooperation model of the all above work, only the relays (i.e., the selected SUs) can obtain the opportunity to transmit their own data, which may incur the following issues: (i) a waste of channel resource may happen when the relays have little data to transmit or the channel condition from the relays to the SAP are worse than that of other SUs; and (ii) the throughput of a secondary network may be reduced if the relays have only a bit of data to send. Therefore, to avoid resource waste and throughput reduction, a different cooperation model is designed [9] to allow all SUs to access the PT's channel for their own transmission. But, in [9], only one relay is employed for the PT-PR pair. Motivated by the key idea of [9], in this paper, we intend to design a "multi-relay" selection scheme to establish "multi-path" cooperative transmission for a PT-PR pair while taking into account energy consumption.

In this paper, we first establish a cooperative transmission model, in which a set of SUs could be selected to relay primary transmitter's data and all SUs are allowed to access the primary transmitter's channel. Based on this model, we formulate the problem of jointly selecting a relay set for the PT-PR pair and allocating transmission time for the SUs as an optimization problem, in which our objective is to maximize the average expected throughput of the secondary network. Then, we propose a novel scheme **GMLDF-Cooperation** to solve the optimization problem by applying Lyapunov optimization theory, in which our results can be found by minimizing the corresponding Lyapunov drift-plus-penalty function. In addition, we validate the performance of our proposed scheme via both theoretical analysis and intensive simulations. The multi-fold contribution of this paper is briefly summarized as follows.

- We formulate the joint problem of relay selection and channel allocation as an optimization problem with considering throughput improvement and energy consumption.
- We utilize Lyapunov optimization theory to design a novel scheme **GMLDF-Cooperation** to solve the optimization problem.
- We conduct both theoretical analysis and numerical experiments to evaluate the performance of our proposed scheme.

The rest of the paper is organized as follows. The system model and problem formulation are presented in Sects. 2 and 3, respectively. In Sect. 4, a greedy algorithm is proposed for relay selection and channel allocation. After reporting the simulation results in Sect. 5, we conclude this paper in Sect. 6.

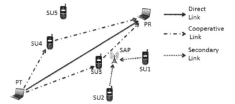

Fig. 1. An example of CCRN.

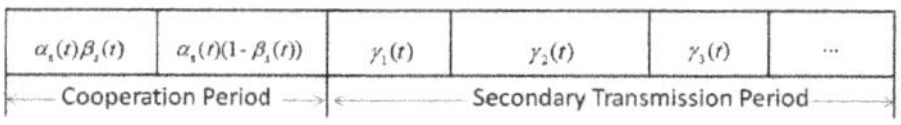

Fig. 2. Time division of a time slot.

2   System Model

Consider a CCRN consisting of one primary transmitter-receiver pair and a secondary network in which there are a set of secondary users denoted by N_S and a SAP as shown in Fig. 1. The primary transmitter (PT) communicates with the intended receiver (PR) over a licensed channel, while each SU has data to send to the SAP. Suppose that time of the network is discretized into time slots. In each time slot, the SAP conducts centralized control for relay selection and channel allocation among SUs through the information collecting from the PT and SUs over a common control channel. To improve the data transmission rate while saving energy consumption for the PT, the SAP intends to select a subset of SUs to cooperate as relays for the PT; in return, the SUs are offered the opportunity to access the licensed channel to send their data during the idle time period. Notice that there exists an upper bound denoted as $\mu(\mu \geq 2)$ of the number of relays in the cooperation because the encoding complexity would become too high if the number of relays is too large [18]. We assume that all SUs in the secondary network can sense the same spectrum environment and that the relays cooperate to transmit in DF mode [19].

For each SU i denoted to be $SU(i)$, let $Q_i^T(t), Q_i^N(t) \in \{0, 1, 2, \cdots\}$ represent its queues on the transport layer and the network layer in time slot $t(t = 0, 1, 2, \cdots)$, respectively [9]. For each SU i, new packets arrive at the transport layer according to an i.i.d Poisson process with an arrival rate λ_i. Formally, let $A_i(t)$ be the number of packets arriving at SU i's transport layer in time slot t, for which there exists a finite constant A_i^{max} such that $A_i(t) \leq A_i^{max}$ for all t [20]. We use $R_i^N(t)$ to denote the number of new packets admitted from the transport layer into the network layer. Note that $R_i^N(t)$ is usually bounded by a positive constant $R_i^{N,max}$ to avoid infinite data packets into the network layer [20]. We also assume that channel fading is independent and i.i.d across time slots, and is also independent across different users. Suppose that the PT, the PR, and the SUs are relatively stationary in the CCRN, thus the channel gain can remain at a constant value during a time period. Since the length of a time slot is not too short [21], the time division during a time slot is meaningful for all users. Without loss of generality, the length of a time slot and the channel bandwidth are normalized to 1, respectively. When the PT directly transmits to PR, the data transmission rate is expressed as

$$R_{tr}(t) = \log_2(1 + \frac{P_t|h_{tr}|^2}{N_0}), \tag{1}$$

where P_t is the PT's transmission power, N_0 is the white noise power, and h_{tr} is the channel gain between the PT and the PR [22].

In order to improve the data transmission rate, the PT could employ one or multiple secondary users forming a relay set $S(S \subseteq N_S$ and $|S| \leq \mu)$ to forward its data via awarding the channel access opportunity to all SUs in N_S. Specifically speaking, if the cooperative transmission in DF mode can improve the transmission rate from the PT to the PR, the PT exploits the cooperative transmission; otherwise, the PT uses the direct transmission. Once a cooperative transmission is adopted, a time slot t will be split into a cooperation period $\alpha_s(t)$ $(0 < \alpha_s(t) < 1)$ and a secondary transmission period $1 - \alpha_s(t)$ as shown in Fig. 2. The cooperation period is used to transmit the PT's data and the secondary transmission period is allocated to SUs to transmit their own data. Furthermore, the cooperation period is divided into two sub-periods: (i) the PT transmits the data to the relays of S in the first sub-period $\alpha_s(t)\beta_s(t)(0 < \beta_s(t) < 1)$; and (ii) the relays decode the received data and then forward it to the PR in DF mode in the second sub-period $\alpha_s(t)(1 - \beta_s(t))$. The transmission rate between the PT and the relays in S during time slot t is determined by the worst link, which is expressed as

$$R_{ts}(t) = \alpha_s(t)\beta_s(t) \log_2(1 + \frac{\min_{i \in S} P_t|h_{ti}|^2}{N_0}), \tag{2}$$

where h_{ti} is the channel gain between the PT and SU i. The transmissoin rate from each relay in S to the PR during time slot t is computed by

$$R_{sr}(t) = \alpha_s(t)(1 - \beta_s(t)) \log_2(1 + \frac{\sum_{i \in S} P_i|h_{ir}|^2}{N_0}), \tag{3}$$

in which P_i is the transmission power of SU i, h_{ir} is the channel gain between SU i and the PR.

The secondary transmission period is further divided into one or several sub-periods, where we use $\gamma_i(t)(0 \leq \gamma_i(t) < 1)$ to represent the sub-period allocated to SU i. Note that if $\gamma_i(t) = 0$, SU i cannot get any transmission time. The transmission rate between SU i and the SAP during slot t is

$$R_i(t) = \gamma_i(t) \log_2(1 + \frac{P_i|h_{i0}|^2}{N_0}), \tag{4}$$

where h_{i0} is the channel gain between SU i and the SAP.

3   Problem Formulation

With cooperative communication, all the data received by the relay set S from the PT in period $\alpha_s(t)\beta_s(t)$ must be delivered from S to PR in period $\alpha_s(t)(1 - \beta_s(t))$, in which the transmission rate of such a two-hop cooperative transmission in DF mode is determined by the worse link. Thus, we can compute the transmission rate of the two links as

$$R_{ts}(t) = R_{sr}(t). \tag{5}$$

The transmission rate over the relay set S is expressed as

$$R_{tr}^s(t) = \min\{R_{ts}(t), R_{sr}(t)\} = R_{ts}(t). \tag{6}$$

The PT determines to use cooperative transmission if and only if its transmission rate is increased via the cooperative transmission, therefore we have the following cooperation constraint for the PT.

$$R_{tr}^s(t) \geq R_{tr}(t). \tag{7}$$

The summation of sub-periods in the secondary transmission period satisfies

$$\sum_{i \in N_S} \gamma_i(t) \leq 1 - \alpha_s(t), \tag{8}$$

which means that the total time allocated to SUs cannot exceed $1 - \alpha_s(t)$.

For a given queue $Q_i(t)$, we define *mean rate stable* in Definition 1.

Definition 1. *Queue $Q_i(t)$ is mean rate stable if $Q_i(t)$ satisfies the equation* $\lim_{t \to \infty} \frac{\mathbb{E}[Q_i(t)]}{t} = 0$.

Given a scheduling strategy, the queues $Q_i^T(t)$ and $Q_i^N(t)$ evolve as follows.

$$Q_i^T(t+1) = \max\{Q_i^T(t) - R_i^N(t), 0\} + A_i(t), \tag{9}$$

$$Q_i^N(t+1) = \max\{Q_i^N(t) - R_i(t), 0\} + R_i^N(t). \tag{10}$$

Furthermore, let $R_i^{N,ave} = \lim_{T \to \infty} \frac{1}{T} \sum_{t=0}^{T-1} \mathbb{E}[R_i^N(t)]$ and $R_i^{ave} = \lim_{T \to \infty} \frac{1}{T} \sum_{t=0}^{T-1} \mathbb{E}[R_i(t)]$, thus we have the following theorem.

Theorem 1. *$Q_i^N(t)$ is mean rate stable for each SU i if and only if the long-term average expectation input rate (i.e. admitted rate) is no more than long-term average expectation output rate (i.e. transmission rate). That is,*

$$R_i^{N,ave} \leq R_i^{ave}. \tag{11}$$

Proof. **Necessity:** According to the queue evolution Eq. (10), we have $Q_i^N(t+1) \geq Q_i^N(t) - R_i(t) + R_i^N(t)$, i.e., $Q_i^N(t+1) - Q_i^N(t) \geq R_i^N(t) - R_i(t)$. Therefore, during the T time slots, we have $Q_i^N(T) - Q_i^N(0) \geq \sum_{t=0}^{T-1} [R_i^N(t) - R_i(t)]$. Then, by dividing by T and taking expectations, we have

$$\frac{\mathbb{E}[Q_i^N(T)] - \mathbb{E}[Q_i^N(0)]}{T} \geq \frac{1}{T} \sum_{t=0}^{T-1} (\mathbb{E}[R_i^N(t)] - \mathbb{E}[R_i(t)]).$$

If $Q_i^N(t)$ is mean rate stable, it holds that $\lim_{T \to \infty} \frac{1}{T} \sum_{t=0}^{T-1} (\mathbb{E}[R_i^N(t)] - \mathbb{E}[R_i(t)]) \leq 0$, which indicates that $R_i^{N,ave} \leq R_i^{ave}$.

Sufficiency: For $\forall \epsilon > 0$, $Q_i^\epsilon(t)$ is defined as a queue with $Q_i^\epsilon(0) = Q_i^N(0)$, and $Q_i^\epsilon(t)$ evolves as the following: $Q_i^\epsilon(t+1) = \max\{Q_i^\epsilon(t) - R_i(t), 0\} + R_i^N(t) + [R_i^{ave} - R_i^{N,ave}] + \epsilon$, which shows that if $Q_i^\epsilon(t) \geq Q_i^N(t)$, then $Q_i^\epsilon(t+1) \geq Q_i^N(t+1)$, i.e.,

$Q_i^\epsilon(t) \geq Q_i^N(t)$ for all $t \in \{0, 1, 2, \cdots\}$. According to Rate Stability Theorem [23], we have

$$
\begin{aligned}
0 &\leq \lim_{t\to\infty} \frac{\mathbb{E}[Q_i^N(t)]}{t} \\
&\leq \lim_{t\to\infty} \frac{\mathbb{E}[Q_i^\epsilon(t)]}{t} \\
&= \lim_{T\to\infty} \frac{1}{T} \sum_{t=0}^{T-1} \left\{ \mathbb{E}[R_i^N(t)] + R_i^{ave} - R_i^{N,ave} + \epsilon - \mathbb{E}[R_i(t)] \right\} \\
&= \epsilon.
\end{aligned}
$$

When $\epsilon \to 0$, we can obtain $\lim_{t\to\infty} \frac{\mathbb{E}[Q_i^N(t)]}{t} = 0$.

Thus, in order to ensure rate stability of $Q_i^N(t)$, $R_i^{N,ave} \leq R_i^{ave}$ must be satisfied. In addition, $R_i^N(t)$ satisfies

$$R_i^N(t) \leq \min\{R_i^{N,max}, Q_i^T(t)\}. \tag{12}$$

Moreover, to avoid the energy consumption from exceeding the total available energy, the constraints for energy consumption are taken into account. Formally, we use E_i^{ave} to denote the average available energy of SU i during a time slot, which is pre-determined and is proportional to its total available energy amount. In time slot t, SU i's energy consumption consists of two parts: (i) the cooperation energy consumption $E_i^c = \Phi_i^s(t)\alpha_s(t)(1 - \beta_s(t))P_i$; and (ii) the secondary transmission energy consumption $E_i^s = \gamma_i(t)P_i$, where $\Phi_i^s(t) \in \{0, 1\}, \Phi_i^s(t) = 1$ if $i \in S$, and $\Phi_i^s(t) = 0$ if $i \notin S$.

For any SU i, there exists an energy constraint to request that the long-term average expected energy consumption of SU i is no more than E_i^{ave}, which is expressed as

$$\lim_{T\to\infty} \frac{1}{T} \sum_{t=0}^{T-1} \mathbb{E}[E_i^c + E_i^s] \leq E_i^{ave}. \tag{13}$$

In order to satisfy constraint (13), we make use of a virtual queue $Q_i^E(t)$ for SU i, which updates as follows,

$$Q_i^E(t+1) = \max\{Q_i^E(t) - E_i^{ave} + (E_i^c(t) + E_i^s(t)), 0\}. \tag{14}$$

The virtual queue is mean rate stable using the analysis similar to that in Theorem 1. In addition, SU i's energy consumption in time slot t should be bounded by a positive constant E_i^{max}; that is,

$$E_i^c(t) + E_i^s(t) \leq E_i^{max}. \tag{15}$$

Accordingly, we can formulate the joint problem of the relay selection and secondary transmission scheduling in the CCRN in (16), in which our objective is to maximize the long-term average expectation throughput of the whole secondary network.

$$\max: \lim_{T \to \infty} \frac{1}{T} \sum_{t=0}^{T-1} \sum_{i \in N_S} \mathbb{E}[R_i^N(t)] \tag{16}$$

subject to: (5)(7)(8)(11)(12)(13)(15),

where $\Phi_i^s(t), \alpha_s(t), \beta_s(t), \gamma_i(t)$ are variables calculated by the SAP.

4   A Greedy Algorithm

To solve the optimization problem (16), we develop a scheme termed **GMLDF Cooperation** (Greedily Minimizing Lyapunov Drift-plus-Penalty Function based Cooperation) in this section, which maximizes the objective function of (16) while ensuring the stability of the secondary network via greedily minimizing the corresponding Lyapunov drift-plus-penalty function. The main idea of our proposed scheme is motivated by reference [23]. Generally speaking, we first define Lyapunov function (17) as a scalar measure of secondary network congestion in the CCRN and compute the difference in the Lyapunov function from one slot to the next one (namely, Lyapunov drift). Then, the objective function of (16) is mapped to a function penalty term. Next, by incorporating the penalty term into the Lyapunov function, drift-plus-penalty expression is obtained and minimized in every time slot in a greedy manner. Finally, via implementing our proposed scheme over a period of time, we can get the final results for problem (16). Note that the proposed scheme can be performed as an online algorithm because it only requires the knowledge of the current network state. Let $\mathbf{Q}(t) = (\langle Q_1^N(t), Q_1^E(t)\rangle, \cdots, \langle Q_{N_S}^N(t), Q_{N_S}^E(t)\rangle)$ denote the queue state of the system at the beginning of time slot t. To measure the congestion in the system, we define the Lyapunov function as

$$L(\mathbf{Q}(t)) \triangleq \frac{1}{2} \sum_{i \in N_S} [(Q_i^N(t))^2 + (Q_i^E(t))^2]. \tag{17}$$

Then, we get the Lyapunov drift as the conditional expected change in $L(\mathbf{Q}(t))$ over time slot t, i.e., $\Delta(t) = \mathbb{E}[L(\mathbf{Q}(t+1)) - L(\mathbf{Q}(t))|\mathbf{Q}(t)]$. The congestion in the backlogs becomes lower when minimizing the Lyapunov drift greedily. To maximize the throughput of the secondary network, we map Eq. (16) to a penalty term $-V \sum_{i \in N_S} \mathbb{E}[R_i^N(t)|\mathbf{Q}(t)]$ and add it to the Lyapunov drift, where $V > 0$ is a control parameter to balance the tradeoff between the network throughput and networking delay as analyzed in Theorem 2. The Lyapunov drift-plus-penalty function is the left-hand-side of inequation (18) and needs to be minimized.

$$\Delta(t) - V \sum_{i \in N_S} \mathbb{E}[R_i^N(t)|\mathbf{Q}(t)] \leq B - V \sum_{i \in N_S} \mathbb{E}[R_i^N(t)|\mathbf{Q}(t)]$$

$$+ \sum_{i \in N_S} \mathbb{E}[Q_i^N(t)(R_i^N(t) - R_i(t))|\mathbf{Q}(t)]$$

$$+ \sum_{i \in N_S} \mathbb{E}[Q_i^E(t)(E_i^s(t) + E_i^c(t) - E_i^{ave})|\mathbf{Q}(t)], \tag{18}$$

where B is a positive constant that satisfies the following condition for all t:

$$B \geq \frac{1}{2} \sum_{i \in N_S} \mathbb{E}[(R_i^N(t))^2 + (R_i(t))^2 + (E_i^s(t) + E_i^c(t) - E_i^{ave})^2 - 2R_i^N(t)\widetilde{R_i(t)}|\mathbf{Q}(t)], \quad (19)$$

in which $\widetilde{R_i(t)} = \min\{R_i(t), Q_i^N(t)\}$. According to the fact that $R_i(t)$ is bounded within one time slot and the assumption that $R_i(t) \leq R_i^{max}$ for all $i \in N_S$ and $t \in \{0, 1, 2, \cdots\}$, we can choose the value of B via Eq. (20) to satisfy (19).

$$B = \frac{1}{2} \sum_{i \in N_S} \left\{ (R_i^{N,max})^2 + (R_i^{max})^2 + (E_i^{max} - E_i^{ave})^2 \right\}. \quad (20)$$

In order to obtain the final results, we need to minimize the right-hand-side of the inequation (18). Note that the scheduling strategy in time slot t only affects the other three terms except B in the right-hand-side of inequation (18), thus minimizing the Lyapunov drift-plus-penalty function can be accomplished by greedily minimizing

$$-V \sum_{i \in N_S} \mathbb{E}[R_i^N(t)|\mathbf{Q}(t)]$$

$$+ \sum_{i \in N_S} \mathbb{E}[Q_i^N(t)(R_i^N(t) - R_i(t))|\mathbf{Q}(t)]$$

$$+ \sum_{i \in N_S} \mathbb{E}[Q_i^E(t)(E_i^s(t) + E_i^c(t) - E_i^{ave})|\mathbf{Q}(t)]. \quad (21)$$

The minimization of Eq. (21) can be further decomposed into instant admission control and network control problems including relay selection and secondary transmission scheduling in each time slot. The major steps are detailed in the following.

(1) Admission Control at SUs. Each SU i chooses $R_i^N(t)$ in time slot t as follows:

$$R_i^N(t) = \begin{cases} 0, & \text{if } Q_i^N(t) > V, \\ \min\{R_i^{N,max}, Q_i^T(t)\}, & \text{otherwise.} \end{cases} \quad (22)$$

(2) Centralized Control at SAP. The SAP first collects the current network information from PUs and SUs, and then solves the optimization formulation (23) to get the optimal relay selection and secondary transmission scheduling strategy in the current time slot.

$$\min \sum_{i \in N_S} \gamma_i(t) \left\{ Q_i^E(t)P_i - Q_i^N(t) \log_2(1 + \frac{P_i|h_{i0}|^2}{N_0}) \right\}$$

$$+ \sum_{i \in N_S} Q_i^E(t)\Phi_i^s(t)\alpha_s(t)(1 - \beta_s(t))P_i. \quad (23)$$

subject to:

$$\Phi_i^s(t)\alpha_s(t)(1 - \beta_s(t)) + \gamma_i(t) \leq \frac{E_i^{max}}{P_i}, \quad (24)$$

$$\sum_{i \in N_S} \gamma_i(t) + \alpha_s(t) \le 1, \tag{25}$$

$$I_{tr} \le \alpha_s(t)\beta_s(t)I_{ts}, \tag{26}$$

$$\alpha_s(t)\beta_s(t)I_{ts} = \alpha_s(t)(1 - \beta_s(t))I_{sr}, \tag{27}$$

$$0 \le \gamma_i(t), \alpha_s(t) < 1, \Phi_i^s(t) \in \{0,1\}, \forall i \in N_S, \forall t,$$

where $I_{sr} = \log_2(1 + \frac{\sum_{i \in S} P_i |h_{ir}|^2}{N_0})$, $I_{ts} = \log_2(1 + \frac{\min_{i \in S} P_t |h_{ti}|^2}{N_0})$, and $I_{tr} = \log_2(1 + \frac{P_t |h_{tr}|^2}{N_0})$. According to inequation (26) and Eq. (27), we have

$$\frac{1}{I_{ts}} + \frac{1}{I_{sr}} \le \frac{1}{I_{tr}}. \tag{28}$$

From Eq. (23), one can see that for a given SU in S, the optimization formulation (23) is a linear programming problem and can be solved easily. Therefore, the value of the function (23) is just decided by S and can be denoted as $f(S)$. In other words, we can first select a relay set and then solve the problem (23). More specifically, the PT picks the candidate SU set K_0 in which SU i's channel gain meets $|h_{ti}| \ge |h_{tr}|$ according to the inequation (26). Based on K_0, the SAP selects one SU that can ensure that the PT's transmission rate satisfies inequation (28) and minimize $f(S)$, and moves the selected SU from K_0 to S. The SAP repeatedly selects the remaining SUs in K_0 and moves them to S one by one to form the relay set until $f(S)$ can't be less or the number of SUs in S is more than the upper bound μ. Finally, the relay set S is the final result. The pseudo-code is presented in Algorithm 1.

Algorithm 1. Greedy Relay Selection Scheme

1: $K_0 = \emptyset; S = \emptyset; Min = \infty; flag = 1;$
2: **for** each $SU(i) \in N_S$ **do**
3:     **if** $SU(i)$ satisfies $|h_{ti}| \ge |h_{tr}|$ **then**
4:         $K_0 = K_0 \cup SU(i)$
5:     **end if**
6: **end for**
7: **while** $K_0 \ne \emptyset$ and $|S| \le \mu$ and $flag == 1$ **do**
8:     flag=0;
9:     **for** each $SU(i) \in K_0$ **do**
10:         **if** $SU(i) \cup S$ satisfies inequation(28) and $f(SU(i) \cup S) < Min$ **then**
11:             $flag = 1;$
12:             $Min = f(SU(i) \cup S);$
13:             $MinSU = i;$
14:         **end if**
15:     **end for**
16:     **if** $flag == 1$ **then**
17:         $S = S \cup SU(minSU);$
18:         $K_0 = K_0 \setminus SU(minSU);$
19:     **end if**
20: **end while**
21: **return** S;

After receiving the relay set S in time slot t using Algorithm 1, the SAP can determine the values of $\Phi_i^s(t)$, $\alpha_s(t)$, $\beta_s(t)$, and $\gamma_i(t)$ through solving the optimization problem (23).

(3) Queues Update: In time slot $t+1$, the queues can be updated according to Eqs. (10) and (14), respectively.

Theorem 2. *(Performance Theorem) Suppose the Lyapunov optimization technique based scheme GMLDF-Cooperation is implemented over all time slots $t \in \{0,1,2,\cdots\}$ with initial condition $\mathbf{Q}(t) = (0,0,0,\cdots,0)$ and with a control parameter $V > 0$, we have: (1) each SU i's queue backlog $Q_i^N(t)\{i=1,2,3,\cdots\}$ is upper bounded for all t:*

$$Q_i^N(t) \leq Q_i^{max} \triangleq R_i^{max} + V. \tag{29}$$

and

$$\lim_{T\to\infty} \frac{1}{T} \sum_{t=0}^{T-1} \sum_{i\in N_S} \mathbb{E}[Q_i^N(t)] \leq \frac{B + V * R^{max}}{\epsilon}, \tag{30}$$

where $R^{max} \geq \sum_{i\in N_S} \mathbb{E}[R_i^N(t)]$ for all t. ϵ is a positive number that satisfies $\mathbb{E}[(R_i^N(t) - R_i(t))] \leq -\epsilon$ and $\mathbb{E}[(E_i^s(t) + E_i^c(t) - E_i^{ave})] \leq -\epsilon$ under some scheduling policy over a given time slot. indicating that average queue size is indeed $O(V)$; (2) the virtual energy queue $Q_i^E(t)\{i=1,2,3,\cdots\}$ is mean rate stable, i.e.,

$$\lim_{t\to\infty} \frac{\mathbb{E}[Q_i^E(t)]}{t} = 0. \tag{31}$$

indicating that constraint (13) is satisfied; and (3) the long-term average expectation secondary users throughput satisfies the following bound for all $t \in \{0,1,2,\cdots\}$:

$$\lim_{T\to\infty} \frac{1}{T} \sum_{t=0}^{T-1} \sum_{i\in N_S} \mathbb{E}[R_i^N(t)] \geq R^* - \frac{B}{V}, \tag{32}$$

where R^* is the optimal value of the secondary users' throughput.

According to Theorem 1 of [20], Eq. (29) can be proved; and from Theorem 4.2 of [23], Eqs. (30), (31), and (32) can be proved. Due to the space limitation, we omit the proof process in this paper.

5   Simulation

In this section, we conduct an intensive simulation to evaluate the performance of our proposed scheme GMLDF-Cooperation. We set a network area of 1000m×1000m, where the SAP is deployed at the central point of the network area, the PT and the PR are placed at the midpoint of two opposite boundaries of the network area, and the SUs are distributed uniformly and randomly within the network area. The channel gain is computed according to the path loss model proposed in [2], i.e., $|h(d)_{i,j}|^2 = 1/d^\eta$, where d is the distance between nodes i and j, and $\eta = 3$ is the path loss coefficient. The transmission and noise power levels are $P_t = P_i = 0.1w$, and $N_0 = 6.70 \times 10^{-10}w$. The length of time period is $T = 3000$ time slots. For each SU i, the packet arrival rate at the transport

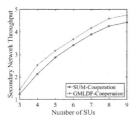
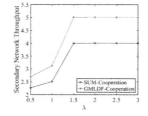
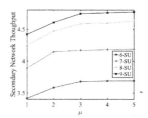

Fig. 3. Throughput vs. number of SUs.

Fig. 4. Throughput vs. Poisson rate.

Fig. 5. Throughput vs. μ.

layer follows a Poisson process with a mean rate λ_i. Moreover, $R_i^{N,max} = 2$, $E_i^{ave} = 0.04$, and $E_i^{max} = 0.08$. Under this network scenario, we compare the throughout of the secondary network of our scheme GMLDF-Cooperation and SUM-Cooperation that is a single-relay selection scheme using Lyapunov optimization [4], in which a higher throughout of the secondary network indicates a better spectrum utilization in a CCRN.

The parameter settings of Fig. 3 are $\lambda_i = 1$, $\mu = 3$, and $V = 100$. As shown in Fig. 3, the throughput of both two algorithms gradually grows up when the number of SUs becomes larger. The reason is that with more SUs in the CCRN, the PT is able to select a better relay to help improve its transmission rate. On the other hand, the throughput of GMLDF-Cooperation is higher than that of SUM-Cooperation, because with more selected relays in GMLDF-Cooperation, the cooperation period becomes shorter and the SUs can send their own data in a longer secondary transmission period.

In Fig. 4, we set $\mu = 3$, $V = 2$, the number of SUs is 9, and $\lambda_i = \lambda$ for every SU i. From Fig. 4, it can be seen that the throughput of the secondary network in both two schemes increases with λ and becomes nearly stable when λ is greater than a certain value. This is because: (i) when the Poisson mean rate λ increases, more packets are admitted into the secondary network, leading to a higher throughput; but (ii) when λ becomes large enough, the length of the queue on the transport layer Q_i^T increases quickly and the admission rate is mainly constrained by $R_i^{N,max}$, resulting in a saturated secondary network. Besides, our proposed scheme outperforms SUM-Cooperation schemes as the PT's transmission can be completed in a shorter cooperation period with more relays and the secondary transmission period is longer for SUs.

Furthermore, we exam the impact of the upper bound of the number of relays on the throughput, and present the results in Fig. 5, in which $\lambda_i = 1$ and $V = 100$. The results of Fig. 5 can be explained from the following two aspects. On one hand, when the value of μ increases, more relays can be selected to forward data for the PT and the length of cooperation period is reduced, leading to a longer secondary transmission period for SUs to improve their throughput. On the other hand, with a fixed value of μ, if there are more SUs in the CCRN, a more proper relay set can be formed to enhance the PT's transmission rate, obtaining a longer secondary transmission period for the secondary network.

6   Conclusion

In this paper, we deeply investigate the joint problem of relay selection and channel allocation in CCRNs to improve the throughput of the secondary network. Generally speaking, there are the following novelties: (i) a multi-path cooperative transmission is established for a primary transmitter-primary receiver pair to improve transmission rate; (ii) all secondary users can be awarded the channel access opportunity to avoid wasting channel resource and reducing throughput; (iii) a scheme GMLDF-Cooperation is proposed using Lyapunov optimization theory. In our future research, we will extend this work to consider the performance improvement of current GMLDF-Cooperation scheme and the cooperative transmission in a multi-hop CCRN.

References

1. Li, W., Cheng, X., Jing, T., Cui, Y., Xing, K., Wang, W.: Spectrum assignment and sharing for delay minimization in multi-hop multi-flow crns. IEEE J. Sel. Areas Commun. **31**(11), 2483–2493 (2013)
2. Cai, Z., Ji, S., He, J., Bourgeois, A.: Optimal distributed data collection for asynchronous cognitive radio networks. In: IEEE ICDCS (2012)
3. Duan, Y., Liu, G., Cai, Z.: Opportunistic channel-hopping based effective rendezvous establishment in cognitive radio networks. In: Wang, X., Zheng, R., Jing, T., Xing, K. (eds.) WASA 2012. LNCS, vol. 7405, pp. 324–336. Springer, Heidelberg (2012). doi:10.1007/978-3-642-31869-6_28
4. Cai, Z., Ji, S., He, J., Wei, L., Bourgeois, A.: Distributed and asynchronous data collection in cognitive radio networks with fairness consideration. IEEE Trans. Parallel Distrib. Syst. **25**(8), 2020–2029 (2014)
5. Cai, Z., Duan, Y., Bourgeois, A.: Delay efficient opportunistic routing in asynchronous multi-channel cognitive radio networks. J. Comb. Optim. **29**(4), 815–835 (2015)
6. Yan, M., Ai, C., Han, M., Cai, Z., Li, Y.: Data aggregation scheduling in probabilistic wireless networks with cognitive radio capability. In: IEEE GLOBECOM (2016)
7. Zhang, L., Cai, Z., Li, P., Wang, X.: Exploiting spectrum availability and quality in routing for multi-hop cognitive radio networks. In: Yang, Q., Yu, W., Challal, Y. (eds.) WASA 2016. LNCS, vol. 9798, pp. 283–294. Springer, Cham (2016). doi:10.1007/978-3-319-42836-9_26
8. Zhang, J., Zhang, Q.: Stackelberg game for utility-based cooperative cognitiveradio networks. In: MobiHoc (2009)
9. Long, Y., Li, H., Yue, H., Pan, M., Fang, Y.: Spectrum utilization maximization in energy limited cooperative cognitive radio networks. In: ICC (2014)
10. Wang, L., Tang, Y., Luo, W., Sun, W.: Resource allocation in OFDM-based cooperative cognitive radio networks with two-way amplify-and-forward relay. In: WiCOM (2015)
11. Li, W., Cheng, X., Jing, T., Xing, X.: Cooperative multi-hop relaying via network formation games in cognitive radio networks. In: INFOCOM (2013)
12. Jing, T., Zhu, S., Li, H., Xing, X., Cheng, X., Huo, Y., Bie, R., Znati, T.: Cooperative relay selection in cognitive radio networks. IEEE Trans. Veh. Technol. **64**(5), 1872–1881 (2015)

13. Yan, Y., Huang, J., Wang, J.: Dynamic bargaining for relay-based cooperative spectrum sharing. IEEE J. Sel. Areas Commun. **31**(8), 1480–1493 (2013)
14. Chen, J., Lv, L., Liu, Y., Kuo, Y., Ren, C.: Energy efficient relay selection and power allocation for cooperative cognitive radio networks. IET Commun. **9**(13), 1661–1668 (2015)
15. Zheng, G., Ho, Z., Jorwieck, E.A., Ottesten, B.: Information and energy cooperation in cognitive radio networks. IEEE Trans. Signal Process. **62**(9), 2290–2303 (2014)
16. Simeone, O., Stanojev, I., Savazzi, S., Bar-Ness, Y., Spagnolini, U., Pickholtz, R.: Spectrum leasing to cooperating secondary ad hoc networks. IEEE J. Sel. Areas Commun. **26**(1), 203–213 (2008)
17. Karaca, M., Khalil, K., Ekici, E., Ercetin, O.: Optimal scheduling and power allocation in cooperate-to-join cognitive radio networks. IEEE/ACM Trans. Netw. **21**(6), 1708–1721 (2013)
18. Wang, L., Tang, Y., Yuan, B., Zhu, D.: A stackelberg game for DSTC-based cognitive radio networks with multiple cooperative relays. In: INCoS (2016)
19. Yang, D., Fang, X., Xue, G.: Hera: An optimal relay assignment scheme for cooperative networks. IEEE J. Sel. Areas Commun. **30**(2), 245–253 (2012)
20. Urgaonkar, R., Neely, M.J.: Opportunistic cooperation in cognitive femtocell networks. IEEE J. Sel. Areas Commun. **30**(3), 607–616 (2012)
21. Vutukuru, M., Balakrishnan, H., Jamieson, K.: Cross-layer wireless bit rate adaptation. In: SIGCOMM (2009)
22. Laneman, J.N., Tse, D.N.C., Wornell, G.W.: Cooperative diversity in wireless networks: Efficient protocols and outage behavior. IEEE Trans. Inf. Theory **50**(12), 3062–3080 (2004)
23. Neely, M.J.: Stochastic network optimization with application to communication and queueing systems. Synth. Lect. Commun. Netw. **3**(1), 1–211 (2010)

Load-Balancing Software-Defined Networking Through Hybrid Routing

Gongming Zhao, Liusheng Huang$^{(\boxtimes)}$, Ziqiang Li, and Hongli Xu

School of Computer Science and Technology,
University of Science and Technology of China, Hefei, Anhui 230027, China
{zgm1993,lzqrush}@mail.ustc.edu.cn, {lshuang,xuhongli}@ustc.edu.cn

Abstract. In recent years, software defined network (SDN) has become a promising technology to improve the network utilization. However, due to the limited flow table size and long deployment delay, it may result in low network performance in datacenter networks, which makes the user experience much worse. In this paper, we first propose a novel Tag-based Rule Placement Scheme (TRPS) for wildcard routing. Then, we study the Hybrid Routing problem by Joint Optimization of Per-Flow Routing and Tag-based Routing (HR-JPT). Besides, an approximation algorithm (RRJD) is proposed to solve the HR-JPT problem. The simulation results on Mininet platform show that our proposed algorithms are efficient for software-defined networking.

Keywords: SDN · Load balancing · Per-flow routing · Tag-based routing · Hybrid routing · Flow table constraint

1 Introduction

SDN is a new networking paradigm that decouples the control plane and data forwarding plane of network devices. More specifically, the controller constitutes the control plane of an SDN, and determines the forwarding path of each flow in a network with the centralized control manner. SDN switches constitute the data plane of an SDN, and response for data forwarding of each flow. Because the controller has global visibility and full control capacity over the whole network, SDN users can composite application programs run on top of the controller to monitor and manage the entire network (*e.g.*, traffic engineering, heavy hitter identification and proper routing) in an efficient and centralized manner. Thus, SDN has been used in different fields, such as campus networks and datacenter networks.

However, with the growth of Internet services, many large-scale data intensive applications (*e.g.*, video conferences, cloud services and financial data analysis) have become popular. Large-scale networks are experiencing more and more bursty flows. For example, in a practical datacenter network with 1500 server operational clusters, the average arrival rate will reach 10^5 flows per second for the core switches [6]. That means, if we perform per-flow routing (*i.e.*, one rule

© Springer International Publishing AG 2017
L. Ma et al. (Eds.): WASA 2017, LNCS 10251, pp. 96–108, 2017.
DOI: 10.1007/978-3-319-60033-8_9

for one flow) in that situation, it may require tens of thousands flow rules on each switch. However, due to the high price and energy-consuming of Ternary Content Addressable Memory (TCAM), an SDN switch usually contains a few thousand of flow rules [3]. Besides, recent testing results show that it usually takes 3.3 ms delay to insert a single flow rule into the flow table on a commodity switch [5]. On the other hand, deployment delay is critical for many applications, *e.g.*, the authors of [12] showed that 100 ms delay causes a 1% drop in revenue at Amazon and 400 ms delay causes a 5–9% decrease in traffic at Google. Thus, considering the flow table and deployment delay constraints, *per-flow routing is impractical to large-scale networks.*

To solve the flow table and deployment delay constraints problem, the classical design principle is destination host-based aggregate routing (*i.e.*, wildcard routing). However, now many datacenter networks contain millions of virtual or physical hosts, this scheme also requires tens of thousands TCAM rules to deploy host-based wildcard routing in large-scale networks [7]. Thus, the deployment delay and table size constraints in large-scale networks cannot be solved by destination host-based aggregate routing, especially for core switches, which may encounter a vast number of flows. Besides, the network performance (*e.g.*, load balancing) cannot be guaranteed by aggregate routing.

Thus this paper first studies wildcard routing and proposes the tag-based wildcard routing (TRPS). Then, we focus on the hybrid routing by joint optimization of per-flow routing and tag-based routing (HR-JPT). To the best of our knowledge, our work is the first to deploy hybrid routing by joint optimization of per-flow routing and tag-based routing under flow table size and deployment delay constraints for load balancing.

2 Tag-Based Rule Placement Scheme (TRPS)

A typical datacenter network architecture usually consists of three-level trees of switches. Typically, a three-tiered design can support tens of thousands of terminals. Under this circumstance, the bottleneck of the datacenter networks usually is the core switches, which encounter a massive number of flows [2]. Besides, due to the development of Open vSwitch and Overlay technologies, the resource shortages of edge switches have been eased [11]. Thus, our proposed scheme mainly concentrates on solving the deployment delay and flow table constraints of the core switches (or internal switches).

An openflow-based flow rule mainly contains match fields, priority, counters and actions. Match fields match against packet headers and consist of the *in_port*, *vlan_id*, *eth_dst*, *eth_src*, *ip_dst*, *ip_src* etc. Note that, with the update of the openflow protocol, the number of supported match fields are increasing and have some reserved match fields. Thus, we can define a *SwID* field (choose one reserved match field) as a new match field to perform the tag-based rule placement scheme (TRPS). The work [2] showed that the operation of adding or deleting a tag is easy for the controller, so the tag-based method is practical.

We illustrate TRPS by an example, as shown in Fig. 1. The controller first assigns four unique *SwID*: v_1, v_2, v_3, v_4 to corresponding switches. Next, The

Flow Table (v_1)

Dst	SwID	Action
*	SwID = v_2	Output=2
*	SwID = v_3	Output=3
*	SwID = v_4	Output=2
Dst = 3.0.0.1		Output=3
Dst = 2.0.0.1		SwID=v_4

Flow Table (v_4)

Dst	SwID	Action
*	SwID = v_1	Output=4
*	SwID = v_2	Output=4
*	SwID = v_3	Output=3
Dst = 3.0.0.1		Output=2
Dst = 2.0.0.1		Del SwID Output=1

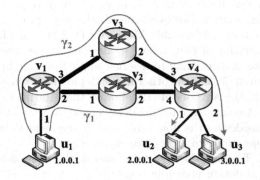

Fig. 1. Illustration of tag-based rule placement scheme. The left two plots denote the flow table of switch v_1 and v_4, respectively. The $SwID$ rules are pre-deployed when the topology is created. The Dst rules are reactively deployed based on the controller commands. When v_1 receives packets whose destination is u_2 with IP address 2.0.0.1, this switch will set $SwID = v_4$ for this flow and forward this flow based on switch level. When v_1 receives packets whose destination is u_3 with IP address 3.0.0.1, this switch will forward this flow based on per-flow level.

controller installs the tag-based switch level routing rules into switches. We only list *dst* match field and $SwID$ match field in Fig. 1 for simplicity. Due to the limited space, we only analyze switch v_1 to illustrate switch level rules. V_1 installs three switch level rules for other three switches, respectively. For example, the rule "$SwID = v_4, output = 2$" denotes that the flows labeled $SwID = v_4$ will be forwarded to port 2. Note that, all the flows labeled this $SwID$ have the same egress switch v_4. After all the proactive rules are installed, there will have three proactive rules on each switch. There arrive two flows: one is from 1.0.0.1 to 2.0.0.1 (denoted by γ_1) and the other is from 1.0.0.1 to 3.0.0.1 (denoted by γ_2). We assume that the controller decides to let γ_1 forwarded by tag-based routing and let γ_2 forwarded by per-flow routing. Thus, the controller only needs to interact with the ingress switch v_1 and egress switch v_4 to install tag-based routing rules. For the ingress switch v_1, we install a rule that matches flows with destination 2.0.0.1, the action of this rule is to attach $SwID = v_4$ so that they can be forwarded by tag-based routing rules. For the egress switch v_4, we install a rule that forwarded flows to the port 1, which matches flows with destination 2.0.0.1, so that these flows can reach the destination terminal. For γ_2, the controller needs interact with v_1, v_3, v_4 to install three rules for γ_2, which is same as the traditional per-flow routing rules.

By building rules on switch level, TRPS has the following advantages compared with other schemes:

(1) Reduce the number of required flow rules. The number of switches is always much smaller than the number of hosts in a network. For example, there have n switches and m hosts ($m \gg n$), if we build rules on host level, for the core switch, there need $m \times (m - 1)$ rules at most. Even we build destination host-based rules, the core switch also needs m rules. But using TRPS, there need $n - 1$ rules at most for the core switches.

(2) **Decrease the deployment delay.** TRPS combines the proactive routing and reactive routing. Since the switch level routing has been deployed in advance, the controller only needs to install 2 rules on the ingress and egress switches for each request. Let ψ denote the average length of all the paths, obviously, ψ increases along with the growing network and is usually greater than 5. The traditional scheme needs install ψ rules on average for each request. That means, our proposed wildcard routing scheme is efficient to reduce the deployment delay.

(3) **Relieve the load of the controller.** For the same reason, the controller only needs to send flow-mod commands to the ingress and egress switches with TRPS. That means this proposed scheme can relieve the load of the controller.

Comparing with other wildcard routing scheme, TRPS can achieve smaller deployment delay and similar network performance while using fewer flow rules.

3   Definition of Hybrid Routing (HR-JPT)

Although TRPS can save TCAM resources, reduce the deployment delay and relieve the load of the controller compared with other wildcard routing schemes, **if we deploy tag-based routing rules for all the flows, the network performance may become worse comparing with per-flow routing scheme.** Thus, in this section, we study the problem of *hybrid routing by joint optimization of per-flow routing and tag-based routing (HR-JPT)* to make use of the limited flow rules.

3.1   Network Model

An SDN typically consists of three device sets: a terminal set, $U = \{u_1, ..., u_m\}$, with $m = |U|$; an SDN switch set, $V = \{v_1, ..., v_n\}$, with $n = |V|$; and a cluster of controllers. The controllers response for route selection of all the flows and not participate in the packet forwarding in a network. These switches and terminals comprise the data plane of an SDN. Thus, in the view of the data plane, the network topology can be modeled by a directed graph $G = (U \cup V, E)$, where E is the link set in the network. For ease of expression, let $c(e)$ and $T(v)$ denote the capacity of link $e \in E$ and the number of available rules of switch $v \in V$ in graph G, respectively.

3.2   Hybrid Routing by Joint Optimization of Per-Flow Routing and Tag-Based Routing (HR-JPT)

There arrives a set of bursty flows, denoted by $\Gamma = \{\gamma_1, ..., \gamma_{|\Gamma|}\}$, in the network. By collecting the flow statistics information from switches, the controller can estimate the size (or intensity) of each flow $\gamma \in \Gamma$ as $f(\gamma)$. We also assume that each flow is unsplittable for simplicity. We use $\mathcal{P}_\gamma$ represents several feasible paths from source to destination for each flow $\gamma \in \Gamma$. Flow γ can be forwarded by a tag-based path and the tag-based path $h(\gamma) \in \mathcal{P}_\gamma$. One tag-based path can be shared by many flows and should be classed as default path (wildcard path). Note that, the $h(\gamma)$ is pre-deployed on switch level (may be the shortest path from ingress switch to egress switch) as illustrated in Sect. 2. Let $\mathcal{P}'_\gamma = \mathcal{P}_\gamma - h(\gamma)$ denote the feasible per-flow paths set of flow γ. Besides, let p_{ie} denote the set of ingress and egress switches of path $p \in \mathcal{P}_\gamma$.

We formulate the HR-JPT problem into a non-linear program as follows. Let variable $y_\gamma^p \in \{0,1\}$ denote whether the flow γ selects the feasible path $p \in \mathcal{P}_\gamma$ or not. z_v^u denotes whether a tag-based flow rule need to be installed for the terminal u on switch v or not. H is the union of all the $h(\gamma)$. Due to the deployment delay is linearly associated with the number of rules that will be installed on each switch, we can use converting factor $\omega(v)$ to combine the two constraints as one constraint for simplicity. For example, the number of available rules $T(v)$ on switch v is $2\,\mathrm{K}$ and we want to be able to forward these flows within $3.3\,\mathrm{s}$ (denoted by T_0). It takes $3.3\,\mathrm{ms}$ (denoted by t_0) to insert a rule [5]. Considering the flow table constraint, we can only install $2\,\mathrm{K}$ rules at most. Considering the deployment delay constraint, we can only install $3.3\,\mathrm{s} \div 3.3\,\mathrm{ms} = 1\,\mathrm{K}$ rules at most. So, let $\omega(v) = 0.5$ to satisfy both constraints. In other words, we set:

$$\omega(v) = \min\{\frac{T_0}{t_0 \cdot T(v)}, 1\}, \quad \forall v \in V \tag{1}$$

HR-JPT solves the following problem:

$$\min \quad \lambda$$

$$S.t. \begin{cases} \sum_{p \in \mathcal{P}_\gamma} y_\gamma^p = 1, & \forall \gamma \in \Gamma \\ y_\gamma^p \le z_v^{d(p)}, & \forall v \in p_{ie}, p \in H \\ \sum_{\gamma \in \Gamma} \sum_{v \in p : p \in \mathcal{P}'_\gamma} y_\gamma^p + \sum_{u \in U} z_v^u \le \omega(v) \cdot T(v), & \forall v \in V \\ \sum_{\gamma \in \Gamma} \sum_{e \in p : p \in \mathcal{P}_\gamma} y_\gamma^p f(\gamma) \le \lambda \cdot c(e), & \forall e \in E \\ y_\gamma^p \in \{0,1\}, & \forall p, \gamma \\ z_v^u \in \{0,1\}, & \forall u \in U, v \in V \end{cases} \tag{2}$$

The first set of equations means that each flow will be assigned a feasible path from the source to the destination. The second set of inequalities denotes that, the tag-based rules will be deployed if at least one flow chooses this tag-based path as its route. As illustrated in Sect. 2, we only need to install rules on the ingress and the egress switches. The third set of inequalities denotes the flow table constraint and deployment delay constraint. The fourth set of inequalities expresses that the traffic load on each link e does not exceed the $\lambda \cdot c(e)$, where λ is the load balancing factor. Our objective is to minimize the load balancing factor, λ.

Theorem 1. *The HR-JPT problem defined in Eq. (2) is an NP-hard problem.*

Proof. We consider a special example of the HR-JPT problem, in which there is no flow table constraint and deployment delay constraint. Then, we are able to deploy routes of all the flows in an SDN so as to achieve the load balancing under link capacity constraint. In other words, this becomes an unsplittable multi-commodity flow with minimum congestion problem [4], which is NP-Hard. Since the multi-commodity flow problem is a special case of our problem, the HR-JPT problem is NP-Hard too.

4   Algorithm Description for the HR-JPT Problem

4.1   Approximation Algorithm to Solve HR-JPT

Due to NP-hardness, this section presents an approximation algorithm to deal with the HR-JPT problem. We design the Rounding-based Route Joint Deployment (RRJD) algorithm to solve the HR-JPT problem which is NP-hard. To solve this problem in polynomial time, we relax this assumption to suppose that each flow can be split and forwarded through multiple paths. By relaxing this assumption, y_γ^p and z_v^u are fractional. So we can solve it in polynomial time with a linear program solver (*e.g.*, CPLEX). Assume that the optimal solution is denoted by $\widetilde{y}$, and the optimal result is denoted by $\widetilde{\lambda}$. As the linear program is a relaxation of the HR-JPT problem, $\widetilde{\lambda}$ is a lower-bound result for this problem. More specifically, for each flow $\gamma \in \Gamma$, we select a feasible path $p \in P_\gamma$ with the probability of $\widehat{y}_\gamma^p$ for flow γ. If $\exists p \in P_\gamma, \widehat{y}_\gamma^p = 1$, this means that flow γ selects $p \in P_\gamma$ as its finally route path. For the tag-based routing, $\widehat{x}_v^u = \max\{\widehat{y}_\gamma^p, \forall d(p) = u, v \in p_{ie}, p \in H, \gamma \in \Gamma\}$. By this way, we have determined the final route paths for all the flows. The RRJD algorithm is formally described in Algorithm 1.

Algorithm 1. RRJD: Rounding-based Route Joint Deployment

1: **Step 1: Solving the Relaxed HR-JPT Problem**
2: Construct a linear program LP_1 based on Eq. (2)
3: Obtain the optional solution $\widetilde{y}$
4: **Step 2: Route Selection for Load Balancing**
5: Derive an integer solution $\widehat{y}_\gamma^p$ by randomized rounding
6: **for** each switch $v \in V$, each terminal $u \in U$ **do**
7:     $\widehat{x}_v^u = \max\{\widehat{y}_\gamma^p, \forall d(p) = u, v \in p_{ie}, p \in H, \gamma \in \Gamma\}$
8: **for** each flow $\gamma \in \Gamma$ **do**
9:     **for** each route path $p \in P_\gamma$ **do**
10:         **if** $\widehat{y}_\gamma^p = 1$ **then**
11:             Appoint path p for flow γ

4.2 Approximate Performance Analysis

We give two famous lemmas for probability analysis.

Theorem 2 (Chernoff Bound). *Given n independent variables: $x_1, x_2, ..., x_n$, where $\forall x_i \in [0,1]$. Let $\mu = \mathbb{E}[\sum_{i=1}^{n} x_i]$. Then, $\mathbf{Pr}\left[\sum_{i=1}^{n} x_i \geq (1+\epsilon)\mu\right] \leq e^{\frac{-\epsilon^2 \mu}{2+\epsilon}}$, where ϵ is an arbitrarily positive value.*

Theorem 3 (Union Bound). *Given a countable set of n events: $A_1, A_2, ..., A_n$, each event A_i happens with possibility $\mathbf{Pr}(A_i)$. Then, $\mathbf{Pr}(A_1 \cup A_2 \cup ... \cup A_n) \leq \sum_{i=1}^{n} \mathbf{Pr}(A_i)$.*

We define a variable α as follows:

$$\alpha = \min\{\min\{\frac{\widetilde{\lambda} c_{\min}}{f(\gamma)}, \gamma \in \Gamma\}, \min\{T(v), v \in V\}\} \quad (3)$$

Link Capacity Constraint. The load of link e from each flow γ is defined as a variable $x_{e,\gamma}$. we have:

$$\mathbb{E}\left[\sum_{\gamma \in \Gamma} x_{e,\gamma}\right] = \sum_{\gamma \in \Gamma} \mathbb{E}[x_{e,\gamma}] = \sum_{\gamma \in \Gamma} \sum_{e \in p: p \in \mathcal{P}_\gamma} \widetilde{y}_\gamma^p f(\gamma) \leq \widetilde{\lambda} c(e) \quad (4)$$

Combining Eq. (4) and the definition of α in Eq. (3), we have

$$\begin{cases} \frac{x_{e,\gamma} \cdot \alpha}{\widetilde{\lambda} c(e)} \in [0,1] \\ \mathbb{E}\left[\sum_{\gamma \in \Gamma} \frac{x_{e,\gamma} \cdot \alpha}{\widetilde{\lambda} \cdot c(e)}\right] \leq \alpha. \end{cases} \quad (5)$$

By applying Theorem 2, we assume that ρ is an arbitrary positive value. It follows

$$\mathbf{Pr}\left[\sum_{\gamma \in \Gamma} \frac{x_{e,\gamma} \cdot \alpha}{\widetilde{\lambda} \cdot c(e)} \geq (1+\rho)\alpha\right] \leq e^{\frac{-\rho^2 \alpha}{2+\rho}} \quad (6)$$

Now, we assume that

$$\mathbf{Pr}\left[\sum_{\gamma \in \Gamma} \frac{x_{e,\gamma}}{\widetilde{\lambda} \cdot c(e)} \geq (1+\rho)\right] \leq e^{\frac{-\rho^2 \alpha}{2+\rho}} \leq \frac{\mathcal{F}}{n^2} \quad (7)$$

where $\mathcal{F}$ is the function of network-related variables (such as the number of switches n, etc.) and $\mathcal{F} \to 0$ when the network size grows.

The solution of Eq. (7) is expressed as:

$$\rho \geq \frac{\log \frac{n^2}{\mathcal{F}} + \sqrt{\log^2 \frac{n^2}{\mathcal{F}} + 8\alpha \log \frac{n^2}{\mathcal{F}}}}{2\alpha}, \quad n \geq 2 \quad (8)$$

Lemma 1. *The proposed RRJD algorithm achieves the approximation factor of* $\frac{4\log n}{\alpha} + 3$ *for link capacity constraint.*

Proof. Set $\mathcal{F} = \frac{1}{n^2}$. Equation (7) is transformed into:

$$\mathbf{Pr}\left[\sum_{\gamma \in \Gamma} \frac{x_{e,\gamma}}{\widetilde{\lambda} \cdot c(e)} \geq (1+\rho)\right] \leq \frac{1}{n^4}, \quad \text{where} \quad \rho \geq \frac{4\log n}{\alpha} + 2 \qquad (9)$$

By applying Lemma 3, we have,

$$\mathbf{Pr}\left[\bigvee_{e \in E} \sum_{\gamma \in \Gamma} \frac{x_{e,\gamma}}{\widetilde{\lambda} \cdot c(e)} \geq (1+\rho)\right] \leq n^2 \cdot \frac{1}{n^4} = \frac{1}{n^2}, \quad \rho \geq \frac{4\log n}{\alpha} + 2 \qquad (10)$$

The approximation factor of our algorithm is $\rho + 1 = \frac{4\log n}{\alpha} + 3$.

Flow Table Constraint. Note that, the approximate performance analysis of the **deployment delay constraint** is same as the analysis of the flow table constraint, we omit it due to limited space. Similar to Link Capacity Constraint, we define random variable δ, $t_{v,\gamma}$ and $\mathcal{F}$. we have:

$$\delta \geq \frac{\log \frac{n}{\mathcal{F}} + \sqrt{\log^2 \frac{n}{\mathcal{F}} + 8\alpha \log \frac{n}{\mathcal{F}}}}{2\alpha}, \quad n \geq 2 \qquad (11)$$

We give the approximation performance as follows.

Lemma 2. *After the rounding process, the total number of flow rules on any switch v will not exceed the constraint $T(v)$ by a factor of* $\frac{3\log n}{\alpha} + 3$.

Proof. Set $\mathcal{F} = \frac{1}{n^2}$. $\mathcal{F} \to 0$ when $n \to \infty$. With respect to Eq. (11), we set

$$\delta = \frac{\log \frac{n}{\mathcal{F}} + \log \frac{n}{\mathcal{F}} + 4 \cdot \alpha}{2 \cdot \alpha} = \frac{6\log n + 4 \cdot \alpha}{2 \cdot \alpha} = \frac{3\log n}{\alpha} + 2 \qquad (12)$$

Then Eq. (12) guarantees with $1 + \delta = \frac{3\log n}{\alpha} + 3$, which concludes the proof.

Approximation Ratio. With these analyses, we know the approximation factor for link capacity constraint and flow table constraint (deployment delay constraint) is $\frac{4\log n}{\alpha} + 3$ and $\frac{3\log n}{\alpha} + 3$, respectively. More specifically, by using the proposed RRJD approximate algorithm, we can scale flows by a factor of $\frac{4\log n}{\alpha} + 3$ to satisfy the link capacity constraint and by a factor of $\frac{3\log n}{\alpha} + 3$ to satisfy the flow table constraint (deployment delay constraint). For example, let $\alpha = 100$, n = 100, then the approximation factor for link capacity constraint and flow table constraint (deployment delay constraint) is 3.08 and 3.06, respectively.

5   Simulation Results

5.1   Performance Metrics and Setting

The proposed scheme and algorithm focus on datacenter networks, so we choose the fat-tree topology [7] in the simulation, which has been widely used in many datacenter networks. The fat-tree topology has 16 core switches, 32 aggregation switches, 32 edge switches and 128 servers. We also assume that each server performs 15 VMs (Virtual Machines) for simulating the realistic scenario. Thus, the total number of terminals is 1920 and we set all links are 1 Gbps for simplicity. Each simulation will be executed 100 times and average the numerical results. We use the power law for the flow-size distribution, where 20% of all flows account for 80% of traffic volume.

Since this paper studies both the wildcard routing and the hybrid routing, we let TRPS denote all the flows are forwarded by tag-based routing. The RRJD denotes the hybrid routing by joint per-flow routing and tag-based routing. We compare these two proposed methods with four other methods: (1) The first one is the per-flow routing (**PFR**). We adopt the multicommodity flow (MCF) method using randomized rounding for unsplittable flows in an SDN. Note that, the method may drop some flows to satisfy the flow table constraint and deployment delay constraint. (2) The second one is **OSPF** protocol, which is the host-based routing [10]. This benchmark is mainly compared with TRPS (both are wildcard routing scheme). (3) The third one is DomainFlow [9] (denoted by **DFW**). DFW divided the network into two parts, one part using OSPF (wildcard rules) and another part using per-flow routing rules. This benchmark is mainly compared with RRJD (both are hybrid routing scheme). (4) The last one is the optimal result for the linear program LP_1 based on Eq. (2), denoted by **OPT**. Since LP_1 is the relaxed version of the HR-JPT problem, OPT is a lower-bound for HR-JPT.

We mainly adopt 5 different metrics for performance measurement. The first two metrics are the maximum/average number of required flow rules on all the switches. After executing these algorithms, we can obtain the number of used flow rules on each switch, and compute the maximum/average number of used flow rules on all the switches. To measure the network performance, the next two metrics are link load ratio (LLR) and network throughput (NT). LLR can be obtained by measuring the traffic load $l(e)$ of each link e. Then, LLR is defined as: $LLR = \max\{l(e)/c(e), e \in E\}$. The smaller LLR means better load balancing. NT can be obtained by measuring the total traffic amount through the network. The last metric is the communication overhead to/from the controller, which can reflect the overhead of the controller.

5.2   Simulation Evaluation

We run 6 sets of experiments to test the 5 different metrics of these algorithms. The flow table constraint is 5 k [3]. The first two sets of experiments observe the maximum/average number of required flow rules by increasing the number of flows. The results are showed in Figs. 2 and 3. Due to the flow table constraint, the maximum number of flow rules is 5 K. Both figures show that the wildcard routing (*i.e.*, OSPF and TRPS) require fewer rules than other methods. Besides, our proposed TRPS wildcard routing can reduce the maximum/average number of required rules by about 20%/65%. Note that, due to TRPS can significantly reduce the number of rules for the core switches and have less impact on the edge switches, the performance of the average number of required rules is much better. These two figures indicate that TRPS needs fewer rules than OSPF.

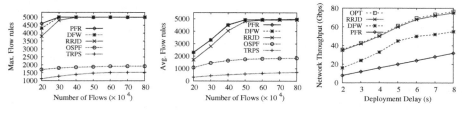

Fig. 2. Max. num. of flow rules vs. num. of flows

Fig. 3. Avg. num. of flow rules vs. num. of flows

Fig. 4. Network throughput vs. deployment delay

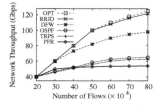
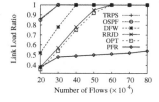
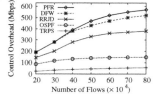

Fig. 5. Network throughput vs. num. of flows

Fig. 6. Link load ratio vs. num. of flows

Fig. 7. Communication overhead vs. num. of flows

The third set of experiments observes the network throughput by changing the deployment delay constraint. The default number of flows is 40 W. The result in Fig. 4 indicates that RRJD can improve network throughput by about 43% compared with DFW. The performance of PFR is worse due to the low speed of per-flow routing.

As illustrated in Fig. 5, the fourth set of experiments measures the change of the network throughput by increasing the number of flows. Our proposed RRJD can improve the network throughput by about 30%/90% compared with DFW/PFR while using a similar number of rules. Besides, the network throughput of OSPF and TRPS are similar while our proposed TRPS can reduce the required number of rules by about 65% on average (illustrated by Fig. 3). The worse performance of PFR indicates that per-flow routing is impractical for large-scale networks.

The result of the fifth set is presented in Fig. 6. PFR has exceptionally low link load ratio because of the flow table constraint and many flows are dropped. Our proposed RRJD can reduce link load ratio by about 23% compared with DFW while using a similar number of rules. Besides, all the above three figures show that the performance of OPT and RRJD is very similar, that means, the proposed algorithm can elegantly solve the HR-JPT problem and get a feasible solution that closing to the lower-bound OPT.

The last set of simulations evaluates the communication overhead between the controller and switches. The wildcard routing (OSPF and TRPS) can greatly reduce the control overhead, because many flows can be forwarded by wildcard rules without being reported to the controller. Our proposed TRPS can reduce overhead by about 75% compared with OSPF, this is because of switch-based rules and proactive rules. Our proposed RRJD can reduce overhead by about 30% compared with DFW, this is also due to the use of proactive rules and switch-base rules (Fig. 7).

From these simulations, we can make some conclusions. (1) Our proposed TRPS (the version of only tag-based wildcard routing) is better than OSPF (terminal-based wildcard routing). For example, TRPS can reduce the number of required rules by about 65% on average and reduce the overhead by about 75% compared with OSPF. (2) Our proposed RRJD increases network throughput by about 43% (or 30%) compared with DFW by changing the number of rules (or changing the deployment delay). Moreover, RRJD can reduce the communication overhead by about 30% and reduce link load ratio by about 23% compared with DFW. (3) The performance of our proposed RRJD is similar with the lower-bound OPT, which means the approximation algorithm is efficient to solve the NP-Hard problem.

6 Related Works

Since routing is a critical issue to achieve better network performance in an SDN, there are many related works to handle the routing problem. The obvious way is to deploy one individual rule for each flow to provide the fine-grained route selection. Al-Fares et al. [1] designed a dynamic flow scheduling for datacenter networks that sets up a new TCAM rule for every new flow in the network. However, as the networks are experiencing more and more flows while the commodity switches only contain a few thousand TCAM rules [3], per-flow routing is impractical to large-scale networks.

Some works devoted to aggregate traffic (i.e., wildcard routing). iSTAMP [8] use part of the TCAM rules for aggregation traffic. But it may encounter the aggregation feasibility problem in a network for these works. Some works considered the wildcard routing. Work [10] adopted the destination terminal-based aggregate routing. However, now many datacenter networks contain millions of virtual or physical end terminals, this scheme also requires tens of thousands TCAM rules to deploy terminal-based wildcard routing in large-scale networks [7]. Moreover, these works suffered from worse network performance due to that many flows will be forwarded by the same path, which might cause link congestion.

To achieve the balance between network performance and flow table constraint, some works studied the combining of per-flow routing and wildcard routing. Devoflow [3] combined pre-deployed wildcard rules and dynamically-established exact rules, DomainFlow [9] divided the network into two parts, one part using wildcard rules and another part using exactly matching rules. However, these works did not mention the details of how to deploy default paths and mainly adopted the OSPF protocol as the wildcard routing. The performance of OSPF protocol cannot be guaranteed.

7 Conclusion

In this paper, we proposed a novel tag-based rule placement scheme (TRPS) for wildcard routing and studied the hybrid routing problem that joint optimization of per-flow routing and tag-based routing (HR-JPT). The testing results have shown high efficiency of TRPS (compared with other wildcard routing schemes, *e.g.*, OSPF) and HR-JPT (compared with other hybrid routing schemes, *e.g.*, DFW). In the future, we will consider the update scheme and online algorithm.

Acknowledgments. This paper is supported by the NSFC under No. 61472385 and U1301256, and NSF of Jiangsu in China under No. BK20161257.

References

1. Al-Fares, M., Radhakrishnan, S., Raghavan, B., Huang, N., Vahdat, A.: Hedera: dynamic flow scheduling for data center networks. In: NSDI, vol. 10, p. 19 (2010)
2. Banerjee, S., Kannan, K.: Tag-in-tag: efficient flow table management in SDN switches. In: International Conference on Network and Service Management, pp. 109–117 (2014)
3. Curtis, A.R., Mogul, J.C., Tourrilhes, J., Yalagandula, P., Sharma, P., Banerjee, S.: Devoflow: scaling flow management for high-performance networks. In: ACM SIG-COMM Computer Communication Review, vol. 41, pp. 254–265. ACM (2011)
4. Even, S., Itai, A., Shamir, A.: On the complexity of time table and multi-commodity flow problems. In: 1975 16th Annual Symposium on Foundations of Computer Science, pp. 184–193. IEEE (1975)
5. Huang, H., Guo, S., Li, P., Ye, B., Stojmenovic, I.: Joint optimization of rule placement and traffic engineering for QoS provisioning in software defined network. IEEE Trans. Comput. **64**(12), 3488–3499 (2015)
6. Kandula, S., Sengupta, S., Greenberg, A., Patel, P., Chaiken, R.: The nature of data center traffic: measurements and analysis. In: ACM SIGCOMM Conference on Internet Measurement 2009, Chicago, Illinois, USA, November, pp. 202–208 (2009)
7. Lu, X., Xu, Y.: Sfabric: a scalable SDN based large layer 2 data center network fabric. In: 2015 IEEE 23rd International Symposium on Quality of Service (IWQoS), pp. 57–58. IEEE (2015)
8. Malboubi, M., Wang, L., Chuah, C.N., Sharma, P.: Intelligent sdn based traffic (de) aggregation and measurement paradigm (istamp). In: IEEE 2014 Proceedings of the INFOCOM, pp. 934–942. IEEE (2014)

9. Nakagawa, Y., Hyoudou, K., Lee, C., Kobayashi, S., Shiraki, O., Shimizu, T.: Domainflow: practical flow management method using multiple flow tables in commodity switches. In: Proceedings of the Ninth ACM Conference on Emerging Networking Experiments and Technologies, pp. 399–404. ACM (2013)
10. Network, M.Y.O.: OSPF Network Design Solutions (2003)
11. Wang, A., Guo, Y., Hao, F., Lakshman, T., Chen, S.: Scotch: elastically scaling up SDN control-plane using vswitch based overlay. In: Proceedings of the 10th ACM International on Conference on Emerging Networking Experiments and Technologies, pp. 403–414. ACM (2014)
12. Wei, C., Buffone, R., Stata, R.: System and method for website performance optimization and internet traffic processing. US Patent 8,112,471, 7 Feb 2012

A New Greedy Algorithm for Constructing the Minimum Size Connected Dominating Sets in Wireless Networks

Chuanwen Luo[1], Yongcai Wang[1], Jiguo Yu[2], Wenping Chen[1(✉)], and Deying Li[1]

[1] School of Information, Renmin University of China,
Beijing 100872, People's Republic of China
chuanwen_luo@163.com, {ycw,chenwenping,deyingli}@ruc.edu.cn

[2] School of Information Science and Engineering, Qufu Normal University,
Rizhao 276826, Shandong, People's Republic of China
jiguoyu@sina.com

Abstract. Finding the Minimum-size Connected Dominating Set (MCDS), i.e., the communication backbone with the minimum number of nodes is a key problem in wireless networks, which is crucial for designing efficient routing algorithms and for network energy efficiency etc. This paper proposes a new greedy algorithm to approach the MCDS problem. The key idea is to separate nodes in CDS into *core* nodes and *supporting* nodes. The core nodes dominate the supporting nodes in CDS, while the supporting nodes dominate other nodes that are not in CDS. The proposed algorithm is verified by simulation, the simulation results show that the CDS constructed by our algorithm has smaller size than the state of the art algorithms in [10].

Keywords: Wireless network · Minimum-size · Connected dominating set · Unit disk graph

1 Introduction

Wireless (adhoc, sensor) networks play critical role in many areas, such as environmental monitoring, disaster forecast, etc. [1]. The wireless communication adopts a broadcasting nature, which can cause the problem of *message flooding*. The key way to avoid flooding is to find a communication backbone. The connected dominating set (CDS) [2,3] is one of the good choices to construct virtual backbone of the network, which can be used for data aggregation and processing data [4,5]. As the number of nodes in the CDS grows, the negative effect of retransmissions increases. Hence, virtual backbone network with smaller number of nodes are highly desired, which leads to the minimum connected dominating set (MCDS) problem. The literature [6] proves the MCDS problem is

This work was supported in part by the National Natural Science Foundation of China Grant Nos. 11671400, 61672524; the Fundamental Research Funds for the Central University, and the Research Funds of Renmin University of China, 2015030273.

L. Ma et al. (Eds.): WASA 2017, LNCS 10251, pp. 109–114, 2017.
DOI: 10.1007/978-3-319-60033-8_10

NP-hard. The literatures [7–10] design the approximation algorithms for solving MCDS problem. The proposed algorithms in [7–9] follows a general two-phased approaches. In the first phase, a dominating set is constructed, and the nodes in the dominating set are called *cores*. In the second phase, additional nodes are selected, called *connectors*. Together with the cores, they form a CDS. In [10], Al-Nabhan et al. extended the above two-phased algorithms and proposed three four-phased centralised algorithms to construct CDSs in wireless network with approximation factor of 5. Recently, CDS has more effective applications, such as energy-harvest sensor networks [11,12], battery-free networks [13].

In this paper, we propose a novel scheme for constructing minimize-size CDS. The proposed algorithm is verified by simulations, which shows that it is more effective in reducing the CDS size than the state of the art algorithms in [10]. The rest of the paper is organized as follows. Section 2 presents our greedy algorithms for constructing a CDS. Section 3 gives the results of simulations, which shows out the performance of the algorithms. Section 4 concludes this paper.

2   Greedy MCDS Construction

In this paper, a wireless network is modeled by an unit disk graph $G(V, E)$, where V is the set of all nodes in the network; E represents the set of links in the network. If the Euclidean distance of any two nodes u and v is smaller than 1, then there is an undirected edge e_{uv} between two nodes. Each node $v \in V$ has a unique ID. $N(v)$ is a set of all neighbors of v. Let $N^i(v)$ be the ith hop neighbors set of v, in which each node is only i hops away from node v. A dominating set (DS) for an undirected graph $G(V, E)$ is a node subset S of V such that each node $v \in V$ is either in the set S or has a neighbor in the set S. A CDS is a DS that induced a connected subgraph in G. If a CDS has the minimum size among all CDSs, then we called it as minimum CDS (MCDS).

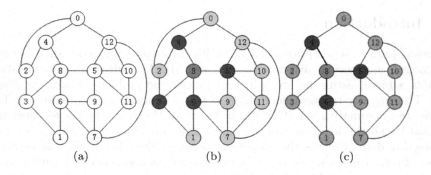

Fig. 1. The process of CDS construction by our algorithm. (Color figure online)

In this section, we propose a greedy MCDS construction algorithm. We first give an example to show the key idea. We illustrate the CDS construction process by Fig. 1, which is the same network example G in [7]. Initially all nodes are marked as white and each node has an unique ID, as shown in Fig. 1(a). In the first phase of our algorithm, we can know that node 8 has the largest value of $\frac{|N^2(v)|}{|N(v)|}$ among all nodes in the graph. Hence, node 8 is marked black and all neighbors in $N(8)$ are colored red and all neighbors in $N^2(8)$ are colored yellow. As shown in Fig. 1(b), nodes 3, 4, 5 and 6 are colored red and nodes 0, 1, 2, 7, 9, 10, 11 and 12 are colored yellow. None of nodes become connector in the second phase of the algorithm since only one black node 8 is added into independent set. In the third phase, for all red nodes, node 5 has the maximum number of yellow neighbors, then node 5 is marked green and its yellow neighbors 9, 10, 11 and 12 are colored red. After that, node 6 and 4 have the same number of yellow neighbors and the ID of node 6 is larger than node 4, therefore, node 6 is marked green and its yellow neighbors 1 and 7 are colored red. Then node 4 is marked green and nodes 0 and 2 are colored red. Finally, we obtain a CDS that contains nodes 4, 5, 6 and 8, and the CDS in this example is exactly the MCDS, as shown in Fig. 1(c).

2.1 Independent Set S_1 Construction

In this section, we construct the set S_1 such that the hop-distance between any two nearest nodes of S_1 is exactly three hops, which is an extension of [10].

The details of S_1 construction process as shown in Algorithm 1. After the algorithm terminates, the nodes in V are either black, red, or yellow. We can obtain that an independent set S_1 that is composed of black nodes and that any red nodes is definitely dominated by a black node and that any yellow node has two hops distance from a black node. The nodes in the set S_1 are called *core* nodes.

Algorithm 1. S_1 Construction

Input: $G(V, E)$
Output: S_1
1. Sets of S_1, $N^1(v)$, $N^2(v) \leftarrow \emptyset$;
2. $Color_v = white$;
3. Choose an initiator $v \in V$ with the maximum $\frac{|N^2(v)|}{|N(v)|}$ among all nodes;
4. $Color_v = black$; $S_1 = S_1 \cup \{v\}$;
5. The nodes in $N(v)$ are marked red; the nodes in $N^2(v)$ are marked yellow; the nodes in $N^3(v)$ are marked blue;
6. For each blue node w, delete red nodes from the set $N^2(w)$ and delete yellow nodes from the set $N(w)$;
7. Select blue node w with the largest value $\frac{|N^2(w)|}{|N(w)|}$ among all blue nodes and set $v = w$;
8. Repeat line 4-7 until all nodes in V are black or red or yellow;
9. return S_1;

2.2 Connecting S_1 Nodes

In this section, we propose a new algorithm for connecting all black nodes in the set S_1, in order to form the backbone of the CDS.

Before we describe the algorithm for this section, we introduce some terms and notations. For any subset $U \subseteq S_1$, let $q(U)$ be the number of connected components in $G(U)$. The set U is initially equal to empty set, and the initial value of $q(U)$ is $|S_1|$. The subset $M \subset E$ contains all edges that each edge consists of a red endpoint and a yellow endpoint.

The detail illustration as shown in Algorithm 2. After the algorithm terminates, any two black nodes are connected by a path that consists of black nodes and blue nodes.

Algorithm 2. Connecting S_1 nodes

Input: S_1
Output: C (The set of connectors)
1. Sets of U, $C \leftarrow \emptyset$, $M \leftarrow$ the subset of E, contains all edges that each edge consists of a red endpoint and a yellow endpoint;
2. $q(U) = |S_1|$;
3. Select an arbitrary $v \in S_1$ as the initiator to start the algorithm;
4. $U = U \cup \{v\}$; $q(U) = q(U) - 1$;
5. **while** $q(U) > 1$ **do**
6.   Select arbitrary node v from the set U;
7.   **if** there exists a node $u \in N^3(v) \cap (S_1 \backslash U)$ **then**
8.   Select an edge $e_{xy} \in M$ such that $x \in N(u)$ and $y \in N(v)$;
9. $M = M \backslash e_{xy}$, $Color_x = blue$, $Color_y = blue$, $C = C \cup \{x, y\}$;
10.   For each node $w \in N(x)$ or $w \in N(y)$, set $Color_w = red$;
11.   **end**
12. $U = U \cup \{u\}$, $q(U) = q(U) - 1$;
13. **end**
14. **return** C;

2.3 Dominating Set S_2 and CDS Construction

After executing above two algorithms, we have got a backbone of CDS and some yellow nodes have changed into red. However, there are still some yellow nodes not being dominated since they have two hops distance from some black node or some blue node. In this section, we propose a novel greedy algorithm for acquiring a supporting set S_2 in which the nodes are used to dominate remaining yellow nodes. And the nodes in the set S_2 are called *supporting* and are marked green. After that, we can obtain a CDS that is union of S_1 (black nodes), connectors (blue nodes) and S_2 (green nodes).

The detail illustration as shown in Algorithm 3. After the algorithm terminates, we obtain a CDS that is composed by black nodes, blue nodes and green nodes.

Algorithm 3. CDS Construction

Input: S_1, C
Output: S_2, CDS
1. Sets of $S_2 \leftarrow \emptyset$, $CDS \leftarrow S_1 \cup C$, $RED \leftarrow$ contains all red nodes in V;
2. Select a red node $v \in RED$ with the maximum number of yellow neighbors and set $Color_v = green$, $S_2 = S_2 \cup \{v\}$;
3. For each node $u \in N(v)$ and $Color_u = yellow$, set $Color_u = red$;
4. For each node $w \in RED$, updates the yellow neighbor set;
5. Repeat line 2-4 until no yellow nodes are left in the graph;
6. $CDS = CDS \cup S_2$;
7. return S_2, CDS;

---

3   Simulation

In this section, we show the simulation results, with each representing an average of 100 runs. First, we investigate the performance of our algorithm. After that, we compare the performance of our algorithm with the performance of three algorithms in [10]. We used MATLAB R2013a for each simulation.

In the experimental setup. We model the wireless network as a set of nodes deployed randomly in a fixed square area A. In the detection area, each of the N nodes has equal probability of being placed. The number of nodes N and transmission range R have been considered as tunable parameters. The induced graph of underlying network is a UDG and the nodes in the network have the same maximum transmission range. Figure 2(a) shows that the CDS size decreases as

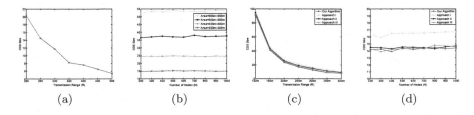

| (a) | (b) | (c) | (d) |

Fig. 2. (a) The average performance of our algorithm when R varies between 200 m to 500 m. (b) The average performance our algorithm for $R = 80$ m, when N varies between 200 and 1000 nodes. Comparing the performance of our algorithm with the performance of algorithms Approach I, Approach II and Approach III in [10]. (c) R changes between 100 m to 400 m, and N is fixed at 1000 nodes in $1000*1000$ m^2 square area. (d) The average performance of four algorithms, when (d) $R = 80$ m and N varies between 200 and 1000 nodes in the $300*300$ m^2 detection area.

the transmission range R increases. Figure 2(b) shows that the CDS size grows as the field area grows. As shown in Fig. 2(c) and (d), the simulation results show that the CDS constructed by our algorithm has smaller size than the three algorithms in [10].

4   Conclusion

This paper studies greedy algorithm to construct a minimum CDS in wireless networks. The key idea is to separate nodes in CDS into *core* nodes and *supporting* nodes. The core nodes dominate the supporting nodes in CDS, while the supporting nodes dominate other nodes that are not in CDS. To minimize the number of both the cores and the supporters, we proposes a three-phase greedy centralized algorithm. Simulation results show that the algorithm generates CDS with smaller size than the state-of-the-art algorithms.

References

1. Blum, J., Ding, M., Cheng, X.: Applications of connected dominating sets in wireless networks. Handb. Comb. Optim. **42**, 329–369 (2004)
2. Ephremides, A., Wieselthier, J.E., Baker, D.J.: A design concept for reliable mobile radio networks with frequency hopping signaling. Proc. IEEE **75**(1), 56–73 (1987)
3. Misra, R., Mandal, C.: Ant-aggregation: ant colony algorithm for optimal data aggregation in wireless sensor networks. In: 2006 IFIP International Conference on Wireless and Optical Communications Networks, p. 5. IEEE (2006)
4. He, Z., Cai, Z., Cheng, S., Wang, X.: Approximate aggregation for tracking quantiles and range countings in wireless sensor networks. Theoret. Comput. Sci. **607**, 381–390 (2015)
5. Cheng, S., Cai, Z., Li, J., Fang, X.: Drawing dominant dataset from big sensory data in wireless sensor networks. In: IEEE INFOCOM, pp. 531–539 (2015)
6. Clark, B.N., Colbourn, C.J., Johnson, D.S.: Unit disk graphs. Ann. Discret. Math. **48**, 165–177 (1991)
7. Wan, P.J., Alzoubi, K.M., Frieder, O.: Distributed construction of connected dominating set in wireless ad hoc networks. In: IEEE INFOCOM, vol. 3, pp. 1597–1604 (2002)
8. Wan, P.J., Wang, L., Yao, F.: Two-phased approximation algorithms for minimum CDS in wireless ad hoc networks. In: 2008 The 28th International Conference on Distributed Computing Systems, ICDCS 2008, pp. 337–344. IEEE (2008)
9. Misra, R., Mandal, C.: Minimum connected dominating set using a collaborative cover heuristic for ad hoc sensor networks. Parallel Distrib. Syst. **21**(3), 292–302 (2010)
10. Al-Nabhan, N., Zhang, B., Cheng, X., Al-Rodhaan, M., Al-Dhelaan, A.: Three connected dominating set algorithms for wireless sensor networks. Int. J. Sens. Netw. **21**(1), 53–66 (2016)
11. Shi, T., Cheng, S., Cai, Z., Li, J.: Adaptive connected dominating set discovering algorithm in energy-harvest sensor networks. In: IEEE INFOCOM, pp. 1–9 (2016)
12. Shi, T., Cheng, S., Cai, Z., Li, Y., Li, J.: Exploring connected dominating sets in energy harvest networks. IEEE/ACM Trans. Netw. (2017). doi:10.1109/TNET. 2017.2657688
13. Shi, T., Cheng, S., Li, J., Cai, Z.: Constructing connected dominating sets in battery-free networks. In: The 36th Annual IEEE International Conference on Computer Communications INFOCOM (2017)

Study on the Impulse Radio mmWave for 5G-Based Vehicle Position

Xuerong Cui and Juan Li[✉]

China University of Petroleum (East China), Qingdao, China
lijuanlijuan@sina.com

Abstract. The device to device (D2D) ability of the fifth generation of wireless mobile communications (5G) provides a new approach to determine the real-time location of vehicles especially in the environment without global navigation satellite system signal. Millimeter-wave transmission has drawn great attentions and it is regarded as a key technique in 5G cellular networks. In this paper, two impulse radio pulses of millimeter-wave are introduced, and the ranging precisions are simulated and analyzed.

Keywords: Vehicle ranging · 5G · Millimeter-wave · Waveform

1 Introduction

In recent years, with the rapid development of wireless communication technology, the applications of wireless sensor networks are more and more widely [1]. The important premise of these applications is to obtain the precise position of the targets. Therefore, the precise positioning of targets becomes the key problem to be solved urgently.

Currently, Global Navigation Satellite System (GNSS), such as Global Positioning System (GPS) and BeiDou Satellite positioning system (BDS), are widely used in vehicles [2] but they are fairly accurate only in flat open areas. That is because GNSS can only work in Line Of Sight (LOS) environment, and it fails to operate in Non-Line of Sight (NLOS) tunnels or in downtown areas where blockage of satellite signals is frequent. GNSS must be integrated with other positioning techniques such as local wireless position, INS (Inertial Navigation System), digital map, and so on. In [3] a CAPS (Chinese Area Positioning System) based on UWB (Ultra Wide-Band) pseudolite signals was proposed.

Before the future fifth generation of wireless mobile communications systems (5G), the networks of 3G or 4G cannot be used for CCA or EWM application, because there is no real-time communication ability, that is to say, each message will be delivered through the cellular base station, which will introduce insufferable time delay against the rapid velocity of CCA system needed. On the other hand, the location precise of cellular is about several hundred meters and it is not enough for vehicular safety system. Fortunately, in order to support a variety of innovative services, the emerging 5G cellular networks will provide the ability of Device to Device (D2D) real-time communication, at the same time, millimeter-wave (mmWave) transmission is regarded as a key technique, which can provide the location precise of centimeter or millimeter level.

L. Ma et al. (Eds.): WASA 2017, LNCS 10251, pp. 115–123, 2017.
DOI: 10.1007/978-3-319-60033-8_11

In order to meet the explosive increase demand of Gbps data transmission rates and the severe spectrum shortage in conventional cellular bands, the mmWave communication technique has become one of the possible candidates for 5G. Recent studies have demonstrated the feasibility of mmWave in 5G cellular networks. In [4], the motivation for new mmWave cellular systems, methodology, and hardware for measurements are presented and a variety of measurement results show that 28 GHz and 38 GHz frequencies can be used when employing steerable directional antennas at base stations and mobile devices. Conducted over a 28 GHz, Samsung Electronics [5] has achieved an uninterrupted and stable connection at 1.2 Gbps in a mobile environment from a vehicle traveling at over 100 km/h. The paper of [6] used real-world measurements at 28 GHz and 73 GHz in a dense urban deployment of New York and derived detailed spatial statistical models of the urban channels. It is found that, even in highly NLOS environments, strong signals can be detected 100–200 m from potential cell sites.

About the waveform of 5G, in [7], the key findings of the European research project 5GNOW are provided, including unified frame structure, multicarrier waveform design including a filtering functionality, sparse signal processing mechanisms, a robustness framework, and transmissions with very short latency which can support the highly varying set of requirements originating from the 5G [8]. Compared the time-frequency efficiency of very small bursts frames among the three candidate multicarrier waveforms of 5G: filtered Cyclic Prefix - Orthogonal Frequency Division Multiplexing (CP-OFDM) - the choice for 4G, (Filter Bank Multi Carrier) FBMC - heavily discussed in recent years, and Universal Filtered Multi-Carrier (UFMC) - a new contender making its appearance recently. There two literatures both talked about short latency or tight response time requirements which may be used for vehicle to vehicle communications [9, 10].

However, in the above literatures, the Impulse Radio (IR) waveform is not discussed. The potential of IR-pulse to solve positioning problems is apparent because of its multipath resolution capability. The IEEE 802.15.4a [11] is the first international standard that specifies a wireless physical layer to enable precision ranging, which specifies two optional signaling formats, that is, IR-UWB and chirp spread spectrum (CSS) UWB. The IR-UWB system is used for ranging, and the CSS-UWB is used for data communication. At the same time, there is little study on ranging or positioning performance of different mmWave waveforms in 5G cellular. Therefore, in order to provide some reference to the future waveform design, this article focuses on several different waveforms of mmWave used for positioning.

The remainder of this paper is organized as follows. In Sect. 2, the two different kinds of IR mmWave are introduced. Section 3 introduces the position estimation method. Some performance results are presented in Sect. 4, and finally Sect. 5 concludes the paper.

2   Waveform of IR mmWave

The mmWave bands that have attracted particular interest are the Local Multipoint Distribution Services (LMDS) bands at 28 GHz, 38 GHz and the V-band at 60 GHz, where 1 GHz, 2 GHz and 7 GHz of bandwidth is available respectively [12]. Both [5] and [6] used the 28 GHz Bands. One advantage of lower frequencies is that the signals have better penetration ability, so 28G is analyzed in the ranging period of this paper.

There are two kinds of waveforms discussed in the article, one is Gauss pulse, and the other is Inverse Fast Fourier Transform (IFFT) pulse.

In the simulation, Pulse Position Modulation (PPM) is used to modulate the signals, which can be expressed as

$$s(t) = \sum_{-\infty}^{+\infty} p(t - jT_f - c_j T_c - a_j \varepsilon) \tag{1}$$

where j and T_f are the frame index and frame duration, respectively, and the PPM time shift is ε, with the data a_j either 0 or 1. If $a_j = 1$, the signal will be shifted in time ε, otherwise there will be no time shift.

2.1 Gaussian Pulse

Gaussian function and its derivatives pulses are easy to be produced, which can generate different waveforms of mmWave. Gaussian pulse and its derivatives can be expressed as (2)

$$
\begin{aligned}
g_0(t) &= Ae^{-\frac{2\pi t^2}{\alpha^2}}, \\
g_1(t) &= A(-\frac{4\pi t}{\alpha^2})e^{-\frac{2\pi t^2}{\alpha^2}}, \\
g_2(t) &= A\frac{4\pi}{\alpha^4}e^{-\frac{2\pi t^2}{\alpha^2}}[-\alpha^2 + 4\pi t^2], \\
g_3(t) &= A\frac{(4\pi)^2}{\alpha^6}te^{-\frac{2\pi t^2}{\alpha^2}}[3\alpha^2 - 4\pi t^2], \\
&\vdots
\end{aligned}
\tag{2}
$$

where $g_0(t)$ is the Gaussian pulse; $g_k(t)$ is the kth derivatives of $g_0(t)$, and $k \geq 1$; A is the coefficient to normalized the pulse energy; α is the shaping factor, which will affect the bandwidth and center frequency of pulse f_{peak}. The relationship between α, k and f_{peak} can be derived from the Fourier Transform, as shown in (3). Thus, changing α or k, may produce different pulses with different Power Spectral Densities (PSD).

$$f_{peak} = \sqrt{k}\frac{1}{\alpha\sqrt{\pi}} \tag{3}$$

Figures 1 and 2 are simulated with pulse duration time $T_p = 0.5$ ns, and $\alpha = 0.11e$ -9 for 28 GHz, 0.081e-9 for 38 GHz; and 0.051e-9 for 60G GHz. Thus, a smaller value of α results in a shorter pulse duration, higher center frequency and larger bandwidth.

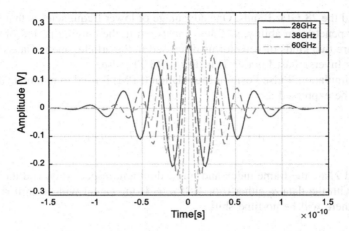

Fig. 1. Waveform of Gaussian 15th derivatives function.

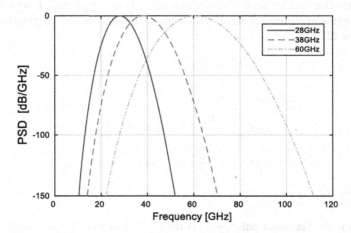

Fig. 2. PSD of Gaussian 15th derivatives pulse.

2.2 IFFT Pulse

Normally speaking, the ideal pulse can be obtained by the Inverse Fast Fourier Transform (IFFT) transform from the desired spectrum mask. Assuming the maximum power is 10 W, the ideal PSD should written as (4)

$$P(f) \approx \begin{cases} \sqrt{\frac{10T_p}{f_H - f_L}} & f_L \leq f \leq f_H \\ 0 & \text{otherwise.} \end{cases} \tag{4}$$

where f_L and f_H are the desired lowest and highest frequencies respectively. The IFFT of expression (3) is the ideal pulse as shown in (5),

$$p(t) = \frac{\sqrt{10T_p}}{2\pi\sqrt{f_H - f_L}} \left(f_H \text{sinc}(2f_H t) - f_L \text{sinc}(2f_L t)\right), \quad t \in \left[-T_p/2, T_p/2\right]. \quad (5)$$

where $\text{sinc}(x) = \sin(\pi x)/\pi x$. Obviously, a bigger value of T_p produces a better PSD matching the desired spectrum mask.

Figure 3 is simulated for 28 GHz pulse with $f_L = 27.5$ GHz, $f_H = 31.5$ GHz, and T_p is set to 0.5 ns and 5 ns respectively. T_p determines the number of side lobes in a pulse duration, when $T_p = 0.5$ ns, there are no side lobes, as the T_p increases, more side lobes will appear. Figure 4 is simulated for 28 GHz pulse and 60 GHz pulse with $f_L = 57$ GHz, $f_H = 64$ GHz. When $T_p = 5$ ns, there are more side lobes, and the PSD fits the desired spectrum mask better.

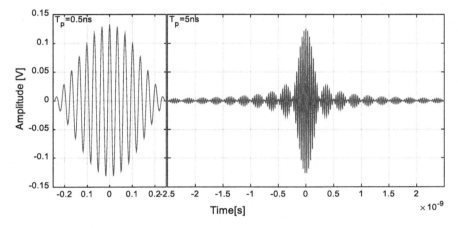

Fig. 3. Waveform of IFFT.

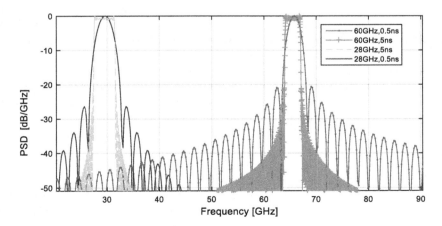

Fig. 4. PSD of IFFT.

3   Position Estimation Methods

3.1   Positioning Technologies

Positioning technologies can be classified into range based and non-range based. For example, Time of Arrival (TOA) and Time Difference of Arrival (TDOA) are range based methods, while Received Signal Strength (RSS) finger print and Angle of Arrival (AOA) are non-range based. Range based positioning is the most suitable for the mmWave wave as it can take full advantage of the high time resolution available with very short pulses. On the other hand, the finger-print positioning methods need the prior information to build the finger-print database, which is different to be used in vehicle positioning.

Accurate TOA or range estimation is the key to precise positioning, and there are two main approaches for wireless ranging, the first is correlation receiver, and the second is energy detection. Correlation receiver is more accurate than energy detection, so the former is analyzed.

3.2   Correlation Receiver Ranging

At the receiver, the received signal can be written as

$$r(t) = s(t) * H(t) + n(t) \tag{6}$$

where $s(t)$ is the transmitted signal, and $H(t)$ is the impulse response which can be expressed as follows,

$$H(t) = X \sum_{n=1}^{N_c} \sum_{n=1}^{K(n)} \alpha_{nk} \delta(t - T_n - \tau_{nk}) \tag{7}$$

where X is a log-normal random variable representing the amplitude gain of the channel, N_c is the number of observed clusters, $K(n)$ is the number of multi-path contributions received within the nth cluster, α_{nk} is the coefficient of the kth multi-path contribution of the nth cluster, T_n is the time of arrival of the nth cluster and T_{nk} is the delay of the kth multi-path contribution within the nth cluster.

The goal of range estimation is to get the unbiased estimate of the time $\hat{\tau}$ for TOA by observing the received signal $r(t)$. A correlator receiver is used to correlate the received signal $r(t)$ with a reference template $s(t-\tau)$ and calculates the propagation delay $\hat{\tau}$ corresponding to the position of the correlation peak as following:

$$\hat{\tau} = argmax_\tau \int r(t)s(t - \tau)dt \tag{8}$$

At the same time, the straight line range between the transmitter and receiver can be calculated according to this time delay $\hat{\tau}$, that is, $\hat{d} = \hat{\tau} * C$ where c is the speed of light.

4 Performance Results and Discussion

In this section, the Mean Absolute Errors (MAE) as shown in (9) and the successfully located percentage (SLP) as shown in (10) are examined for different waveforms and different SNRs in the AWGN channel. MAE is defined as

$$MAE = \frac{1}{N} \sum_{n=1}^{N} \left| D_n - \widehat{D}_n \right| \qquad (9)$$

where D_n is the nth actual distance, $\widehat{D}_n$ is the nth distance estimated, and N is the number of range estimates. SLP is defined as

$$P(x) = \frac{1}{N} CountIF(\left| \hat{D}_n - D_n \right| \leq x) \qquad (10)$$

where *CountIF* is a function to count the number of simulation that the estimated error is not larger than a given value x. For example, $P(0.002)$ is the percentage which the error of ranging estimations are less than 2 mm.

In order to compare the 2 waveforms in the method of correlation receiver, 2000 realizations for each of SNR = 0, 1... 20 dB were generated. Figure 5 presents the MAE of the range estimation, which shows that the waveform of Gaussian Pulse is better than the ITTF pulse in most cases. When SNR > 16 dB, the MSE of Gaussian Pulse and ITTF pulse are almost the same, which is nearly to 0.1 mm.

Figure 6 presents the SLP of the range estimation, which also shows that the waveform of Gaussian Pulse is better than the ITTF pulse for any SNRs. For example, When SNR = 0 dB, the SLP of Gaussian Pulse is 60%, but it is 6 dB for ITTF pulse to

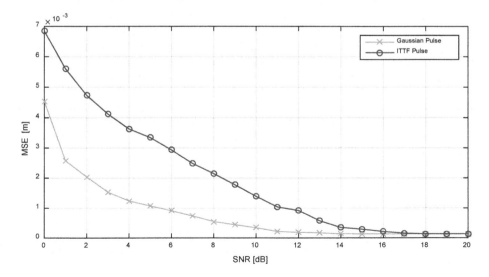

Fig. 5. Simulation result of MSE based on correlation receiver.

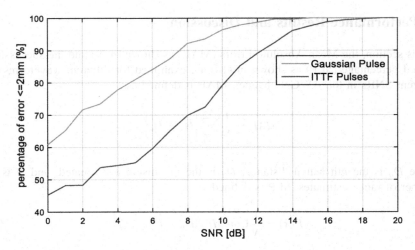

Fig. 6. Simulation result of SLP based on correlation receiver.

reach 60%. As the SNRs increasing, the SLPs for the two pulse will increase. When SNR >= 13 dB, SLP of Gaussian Pulse will reach nearly 100%, and for ITTF pulse when SNR >= 18 dB, SLP reaches nearly 100%.

5 Conclusions

In order to meet the demands of 5G used in the vehicular environment, two different IR-Pulses are introduced. Both the time and frequency domain characteristics of each waveform are analyzed. A ranging method based-on correlation receiver is used to test ranging the precisions of different waveforms. It shows that the Gaussian Pulse is better than the ITTF pulse. With the ranging result here, the location of vehicle can be get via the methods of positioning, for example CHAN, Taylor series, Fang, Least Square and so on. The study results of different waveforms can be used in D2D communication of emerging 5G cellular networks, which will provides a new approach to determine the real-time location of vehicles, especially in the environment without GNSS signal.

Acknowledgment. This work was supported by the National Natural Science Foundation of China under Grant No. 61671482, the Fundamental Research Funds for the Central Universities Nos. 16CX02046A, 17CX02042A, and 14CX02212A and the Nature Science Foundation of Shandong Province No. ZR2014FL014.

References

1. Huang, Y., Chen, M., Cai, Z., Guan, X., Ohtsuki, T., Zhang, Y.: Graph theory based capacity analysis for vehicular ad hoc networks. In: 58th IEEE Global Communications Conference, GLOBECOM 2015, 6–10 December 2015. Institute of Electrical and Electronics Engineers Inc. (2015)

2. Wang, X., Guo, L., Ai, C., Li, J., Cai, Z.: An urban area-oriented traffic information query strategy in VANETs. In: Ren, K., Liu, X., Liang, W., Xu, M., Jia, X., Xing, K. (eds.) WASA 2013. LNCS, vol. 7992, pp. 313–324. Springer, Heidelberg (2013). doi:10.1007/978-3-642-39701-1_26

3. Xiao, Z., Bai, J., Ma, G.Y., Fan, J.T., Yi, K.C.: Research on positioning enhancement scheme of CAPS via UWB pseudolite. Sci. China-Phys. Mech. Astron. **55**, 733–737 (2012)

4. Rappaport, T.S., Shu, S., Mayzus, R., Hang, Z., Azar, Y., Wang, K., Wong, G.N., Schulz, J.K., Samimi, M., Gutierrez, F.: Millimeter wave mobile communications for 5G cellular: it will work! IEEE Access **1**, 335–349 (2013)

5. Gozalvez, J.: Samsung electronics sets 5G speed record at 7.5 Gb/s [Mobile Radio]. IEEE Veh. Technol. Mag. **10**, 12–16 (2015)

6. Akdeniz, M.R., Yuanpeng, L., Samimi, M.K., Shu, S., Rangan, S., Rappaport, T.S., Erkip, E.: Millimeter wave channel modeling and cellular capacity evaluation. IEEE J. Sel. Areas Commun. **32**, 1164–1179 (2014)

7. Wunder, G., Jung, P., Kasparick, M., Wild, T., Schaich, F., Yejian, C., Brink, S., Gaspar, I., Michailow, N., Festag, A., Mendes, L., Cassiau, N., Ktenas, D., Dryjanski, M., Pietrzyk, S., Eged, B., Vago, P., Wiedmann, F.: 5GNOW: non-orthogonal, asynchronous waveforms for future mobile applications. IEEE Commun. Mag. **52**, 97–105 (2014)

8. Schaich, F., Wild, T., Yejian, C.: Waveform contenders for 5G - suitability for short packet and low latency transmissions. In: 2014 IEEE 79th Vehicular Technology Conference (VTC Spring), pp. 1–5 (2014)

9. Guan, X., Huang, Y., Cai, Z., Ohtsuki, T.: Intersection-based forwarding protocol for vehicular ad hoc networks. Telecommun. Syst. **62**, 67–76 (2016)

10. Huang, Y., Guan, X., Cai, Z., Ohtsuki, T.: Multicast capacity analysis for social-proximity urban bus-assisted VANETs. In: 2013 IEEE International Conference on Communications, ICC 2013, 9–13 June 2013, pp. 6138–6142. Institute of Electrical and Electronics Engineers Inc. (2013)

11. http://standards.ieee.org/getieee802/download/802.15.4a-2007.pdf

12. Ott, D., Talwar, S.: Exploring next generation wireless (5G): transforming the user experience. IDF13, ACAS002 (2013)

Detect SIP Flooding Attacks in VoLTE by Utilizing and Compressing Counting Bloom Filter

Mingli Wu[1], Na Ruan[1(✉)], Shiheng Ma[1], Haojin Zhu[1], Weijia Jia[1], Qingshui Xue[2], and Songyang Wu[3]

[1] Department of Computer Science and Engineering,
Shanghai Jiao Tong University, Shanghai 200240, China
{mingliwu,ma-shh}@sjtu.edu.cn, {naruan,zhu-hj,jia-wj}@cs.sjtu.edu.cn
[2] School of Computer Science and Information Engineering,
Shanghai Institute of Technology, Shanghai 200240, China
xue-qsh@sit.edu.cn
[3] The Third Research Institute of Ministry of Public Security,
Shanghai 200240, China
wusongyang@stars.org.cn

Abstract. As a new generation voice service, Voice over LTE (VoLTE) has attracted worldwide attentions in both the academia and industry. Different from the traditional voice call based on circuit-switched (CS), VoLTE evolves into the packet-switched (PS) field, which is quite open to the public. Though designed rigorously, similar to VoIP service, VoLTE also suffers from SIP (Session Initiation Protocol) flooding attacks. In this paper, two schemes inspired by Counting Bloom Filter (CBF) are proposed to thwart these attacks. In scheme I, we leverage CBF to accomplish flooding attack detection. In scheme II, we design a versatile CBF-like structure, PFilter, to achieve the same goal. Compared with previous relevant works, our detection schemes gain advantages in many aspects including low-rate flooding attack and stealthy flooding attack. Moreover, not only can our schemes detect the attacks with high accuracy, but also find out the attacker to ensure normal operation of VoLTE. Extensive experiments are performed to well evaluate the performance of the proposed two schemes.

Keywords: SIP flooding attack · CBF · Count · Filter

1 Introduction

As a voice call paradigm, VoLTE has attracted worldwide attentions of the public. Different from the traditional CS call, VoLTE evolves into PS field, determining to provide more reliable and rich user experience. The transition brings many benefits, such as multimedia support including high quality voice and video call, less set-up time, and less end-to-end delay. Also, compared with VoIP, which

© Springer International Publishing AG 2017
L. Ma et al. (Eds.): WASA 2017, LNCS 10251, pp. 124–135, 2017.
DOI: 10.1007/978-3-319-60033-8_12

has dominated in PS voice telecommunication services, VoLTE gains its obvious advantages in higher voice quality, less drop-out rate, and faster set-up time for dedicated LTE resource reservation. However, the prevalence of VoLTE also involves it into various attacks, especially flooding attacks exploiting the spoofed SIP messages attempting to undermine the IMS (IP Multimedia System) or UEs (User Equipments), which is a tricky problem remaining to be solved.

Kim et al. [1] successfully exploit the SIP signal bearer in VoLTE to achieve free data transmission in forms of Mobile-to-Mobile and Mobile-to-Internet. Same loopholes are also revealed in [2]. Since the dedicated VoLTE SIP signal bearer is free and bandwidth reserved [2], even normal users would be tempted to send data through it, resulting in flooding attacks to IMS.

In case of SIP flooding attack detection, many works have been proposed. Tang et al. [3,4] propose a SIP flooding attacks detection and prevention scheme by integrating a three-dimensional sketch design with the Hellinger Distance (HD) technique. One obvious drawback of their scheme is that it needs a training period lasting even for $10\,\mathrm{s} \times 10 = 100\,\mathrm{s}$. However, in the case of attacks may occur at any time, it is impractical to ensure the training set is not contaminated by vicious SIP messages. Another drawback is that it is incapable to detect stealthy flooding attack. Stealthy flooding attack is a kind of attack that is difficult to be distinguished because the attacker patiently increases the flooding rate in slow pace. Sengar et al. [5,6] also propose the statistical detection mechanism called vFDS based on sudden surge caused by incomplete the handshaking processes in SIP. In their scheme, training phase is also needed to provide a baseline.

In order to thwart the above serious flooding attacks, in this paper, we propose two novel flooding attack detection schemes enlightened by CBF, a data structure widely used in many fields. In scheme I, we demonstrate there are plenty of remaining spaces in it to be exploited to detect the SIP flooding anomalies. To utilize CBF to accomplish our detection goal, we illustrate the lower bound of CBF and evaluate the overflow risk caused by repeated insertions of elements. However, due to the limited size of unit counter in CBF, there are still concerns whether the repeated insertion will lead to new overflow issue of CBF, which has been discussed in Fan's work [7]. On basis of his work [7], proof of concept is conducted to validate the low overflow risk due to repeated insertions.

To extend the detection capability concerned about multi-attributes flooding attack, we propose scheme II. Inspired by CBF, we create our own data structure named PFilter to detect the attacks. PFilter is like horizontally compressed CBF and gains strong capability in filtering SIP messages. PFilter is able to filter out large portion of normal SIP messages and prevent suspicious ones by virtue of a dynamic threshold. To get an appropriate threshold, we take exponentially weighted moving average (EWMA) to estimate the normal average transmission level during sampling period.

To sum up, the contributions we make in this paper are as follows:

(1) We demonstrate the remaining capacity of Counting Bloom Filter can be utilized to thwart SIP flooding attack.

(2) We design PFilter, a versatile structure, which gains great capability to filter out a large portion of normal SIP stream and prevent vicious messages.
(3) Extensive experiments are implemented to evaluate the performance of our two schemes, and results demonstrate their effectiveness.

The remainder of this paper is organized as follows. Section 2 introduces the preliminaries of our detection schemes. Section 3 describes the attack model and our two SIP flooding detection schemes. In Sect. 4, we perform our experiments and evaluate the performances of our schemes. Section 5 reviews the prior related works. Finally, in Sect. 6, we conclude this paper.

2   Preliminaries

In this section, Counting Bloom Filter will be introduced from its structure, parameter configuration to overflow issue.

A Bloom Filter is a space-efficient probabilistic data structure to test whether an element is a member of a particular set. The feather of Bloom Filter is that false positive (e.g., an element not in the set but wrongly being taken as a set member) matches are possible while false negative (e.g., an element in a set but not being taken as a set member) ones are not. The false positive probability of Bloom Filter is

$$f = (1 - e^{-nk/m})^k \tag{1}$$

where n is the number of elements in the set, m is the length of the bit array, and k is the number of hash functions.

Given m and n, the optimal value of k that minimizes f is

$$k = \frac{m}{n} \ln 2 \tag{2}$$

The idea of Bloom Filter is that it uses k independent hash functions h_1, h_2, $\cdots$, h_k to hash each item x_i in the set to position $h_1(x_i)$, $h_2(x_i)$, $\cdots$, $h_k(x_i)$ in a bit array of m bits that are initiated as 0. The hashed bits are set to 1 and the range of this array is $\{0, 1, 2, \cdots, m - 1\}$. When examining whether an element belongs to this set, one can just check the k corresponding bits. Only all the k corresponding bits are 1 will the element be taken as a legal element, otherwise not. It does not support element deletion, Fan et al. [7] suggest Counting Bloom Filter to remedy this defect by adding a counter to record the number of each bit in the bit array. When deleting an element, the numbers of the corresponding bits of the element in the k counters will decrease by 1. The corresponding numbers will increase by 1 for add.

Practically, the arithmetic overflow due to the limited size of each counter in CBF is also an important factor supposed to be considered. In CBF, the 4-bits counter can only support 15 insertions at most during a period. Once a particular position has been hashed to more than 15 times, then the counter will overflow, resulting in adverse implications to the later operation on CBF. The probability that any count is greater or equal to i is

$$Pr(max(c) \geq i) \leq m \cdot (\frac{eln2}{i})^i \tag{3}$$

In their work, the authors demonstrate that the probability of overflow is minuscule when allowing 4-bits per counter. In this paper, we will take the unit length as 4-bits following the most common practice.

3   Attacks and Defense Mechanisms

In this section, we will describe the attack model and the two defending schemes. In scheme I, we take CBF to authenticate the incoming SIP messages and exploit its remaining capacity to thwart the flooding attacks. To remedy its poor scalability in detecting multi-attributes flooding attack, we design PFilter, a compressed CBF-like data structure we utilize in scheme II.

3.1   Attack Model

In VoLTE, the attacker is able to craft the source information of SIP messages to avoid being captured. They launch flooding attack on IMS by transmitting excessive INVITE messages at the victims' identities. In addition to INVITE, other SIP attributes, such as ACK, BYE, REGISTER, can also be exploited to mount flooding attacks. If the attacker simultaneously floods multiple SIP attributes messages, then it will result in multi-attributes flooding attack.

3.2   SIP Message Authentication

Since attackers are capable of crafting SIP messages by modifying the source information, an intuitive and effective method is to authenticate every SIP message. To achieve this authentication goal, very SIP message should carry a secret key released by the VoLTE carrier and is supposed to be updated periodically. The key agreement could be accomplished through IMS-AKA suggested in GSMA official document. The key can be the signature of each UE in VoLTE. All the secret signatures should be stored in CBF to achieve the authentication goal and the IMS server will check all signatures the coming SIP messages carry by referring CBF. Therefore, the attacker cannot be an imposter who sending SIP messages at other victims' identity.

3.3   Defense Scheme I: Simply Count by CBF

In VoLTE SIP flooding attacks, abnormal users and vicious attackers always attempt to send excessive SIP messages to achieve most benefits. In addition to the authentication function, CBF gains an advantageous ability to count the number of repeated insertions for an element during a certain period. We demonstrate this property of CBF and take advantage of its remaining capacity to detect the flooding messages.

A. Remaining Capacity

Though each counter in CBF can only be counted for at most 15 times and have already been counted for its primary counting usage, it still remains sufficient remaining spaces for us to count the incoming SIP messages.

For an arbitrary counter in CBF, the probability that it holds count i is

$$P(i) = \binom{n \cdot k}{i} \cdot (\frac{1}{m})^i \cdot (1 - \frac{1}{m})^{n \cdot k - i} \tag{4}$$

According to Eqs. (2) and (4), the expected number of counters that hold count i is

$$\begin{aligned} c_i &= m \cdot P(i) \\ &= m \cdot \binom{n \cdot k}{i} \cdot (\frac{1}{m})^i \cdot (1 - \frac{1}{m})^{n \cdot k - i} \tag{5} \\ &= m \cdot \binom{m \ln 2}{i} \cdot (\frac{1}{m})^i \cdot (1 - \frac{1}{m})^{m \ln 2 - i} \tag{6} \end{aligned}$$

Thus, the ratio that the counters holding i account for all the none-zero counter is

$$h(i) = \frac{c_i}{m - c_0}$$

Then the remaining capacity ratio for that counters containing i is

$$r(i) = h(15 - i) = \frac{c_{15-i}}{m - c_0}$$

Given a large $m = 33,547,705$(how this number is chosen will be explained in the evaluation part), then we can see $r(14) \approx 0.693$, $r(13) \approx 0.240$, $r(12) \approx 0.056$, $r(11) \approx 0.010$, $r(10) \approx 0.001$. Therefore, $r(i \geq 10)$ almost equals 1. It means that in CBF, counters whose remaining capacity are no less than 10 are almost 100%. However, there are still two factors supposed to take into account. One is the lower bound concern and the other is the overflow issue.

B. Lower Bound of CBF

For each element in a particular set that has been stored in CBF, the lower bound is defined as the minimum number its k hashed counters contain.

Theorem 1. *Assuming that $k \geq 12$, then among the k counters that a legal element hashed to Counting Bloom Filter, there is high probability that at least one counter contains 1, where m is the length of the counters in Counting Bloom Filter, m_0 and m_1 is the number of counters containing 0 and 1 respectively, k is the number of hash functions.*

Proof. In Counting Bloom Filter, for a legal element, the probability that at least one counter in its k hashed counters contains 1 is

$$\begin{aligned} p &= 1 - \binom{k}{0} \cdot (\frac{m_1}{m - m_0})^0 \cdot (1 - \frac{m_1}{m - m_0})^k \\ &= 1 - (1 - \frac{m_1}{m - m_0})^k \tag{7} \end{aligned}$$

As long as $(1 - \dfrac{m_1}{m - m_0})^k$ is small enough, then we can deduce that $p \approx 1$. Since c_i is an expected value of m_i, we can use c_0 and c_1 to estimate the m_0 and m_1. Given $m = 33,547,705$, then we know $c_0 = 1.69 \times 10^7$ and $c_1 = 1.16 \times 10^7$. Substitute m_0 and m_1 with c_0 and c_1 respectively in (7), then we can get

$$p = 1 - 0.303929^k \tag{8}$$

Since k is an integer, if we expect $p < 0.999999$, then we can easily get $k \geq 12$. It implies that if $k \geq 12$, the probability that at least one of the k counters contain 1 will approach 1.

According to Theorem 1, the probability that every legal element in the set corresponds to at least one counter contains 1 is high. This is a great property can be utilized to count how many SIP messages a UE/subscriber has sent during a sampling period, for this particular counter only belongs to this element, otherwise the original count before the repeated insertion into this counter will exceed 1.

C. Overflow Risk

Though CBF gains a good lower bound, there are still concerns whether the repeated insertions of elements will cause the overflow issue because of the limited 4-bit size per counter. Based on formula (3), we can further deduce that

$$Pr(max(c) \geq 15) \leq 1.0579 \times 10^{-14} \times m$$
$$Pr(max(c) \geq 14) \leq 6.3957 \times 10^{-13} \times m$$
$$Pr(max(c) \geq 13) \leq 1.2454 \times 10^{-11} \times m$$
$$Pr(max(c) \geq 12) \leq 1.2452 \times 10^{-10} \times m$$
$$Pr(max(c) \geq 11) \leq 3.7239 \times 10^{-9} \times m$$

Still, given $m = 33,547,705$, then $Pr(max(c) \geq 11) \leq 0.125$. Since the remaining capacity of CBF $r(i \geq 10) \approx 1$, then even when $Rmax = 4$, the probability that CBF will overflow is low.

Though the overflow risk is low, we take our ejection strategy to eliminate the negative effects of malicious messages. When the lower bound for a message exceeds $Rmax$, it implies this message is an abnormal one and we will delete all its previous insertions to eject it, then put it into a blacklist to prevent its further intrusion.

3.4   Defense Scheme II: Count by Lightweight PFilter

Scheme I is capable of detecting any abnormal user who has sent excessive SIP messages. However, due to the memory consumption, it cannot be easily scaled to detect multi-attributes flooding attack and still hold the overflow risk even it is low. Therefore, in this part, we propose another effective scheme based on PFilter, a data structure inspired by CBF. It is noteworthy that the length of PFilter is far less than that of CBF, so it is lightweight.

A. PFilter

PFilter is like a horizontally compressed CBF that also exploits k_p hash functions h_1, h_2, $\cdots$ h_{k_p} to profile each element x_i into position $h_1(x_i)$, $h_2(x_i)$, $\cdots$ $h_{k_p(x_i)}$ of an array with range $\{0, 1, 2, \cdots, m_p - 1\}$. When a SIP message comes, the system will extract the signature of it and profile it into PFilter. In CBF, counters still holding 0 accounter for a large part of CBF. However, PFilter does not rely on the 0 counters but a threshold to accomplish the judgement. Therefore, it is much more space efficient. The tricky question arises how to choose a good and reliable threshold, which is critical to our detection effects.

B. Filter Threshold

Since the SIP flooding attacker always intends to send excessive messages, these malicious messages will outnumber normal users and deviate from the normal level. By virtue of PFilter, we can compact all messages into it and find out the outlier. The tricky question arises how to choose a good and reliable threshold, which is critical to our detection effects. Fortunately, we find that EWMA is pretty appropriate to create the dynamic threshold adapted with the stochastic SIP stream.

Denote α_i as the measured average number of messages each VoLTE user sends during sample round i, R_i as the estimated one and β_i as the average skewed distance between the α_i and R_i. Then

$$R_i = (1 - \lambda_1) \cdot R_{i-1} + \lambda_1 \cdot \alpha_i \tag{9}$$

Because the traffic is frequently fluctuate over time, we are also supposed to estimate the skewed distance

$$\beta_i = (1 - \lambda_2) \cdot \beta_{i-1} + \lambda_2 \cdot |\alpha_i - R_i| \tag{10}$$

In (9), the average measured transmission times is

$$\alpha_i = \frac{N_i}{U_i}$$

where N_i is the message number, U_i is the caller number in round $i (i \geq 1)$. And $0 < \lambda_1 \leq 1$, $0 < \lambda_2 \leq 1$ are the weight factors. In (9) and (10), λ_1 and λ_2 are constant factors that determine the memory depth of EWMA. The closer they are to 1, the more weight EWMA lays in the current measurement. A value of $\lambda_1 = 1$(or $\lambda_2 = 1$) implies EWMA only cares about the current measurement.

Given the estimated average threshold R_i and the estimated average skewed distance β_i, we can further calculate the average number of messages each counter in PFilter holds during sampling period i is

$$Thre_i = \frac{k_p \cdot U_i}{m_p} \cdot min\{R_{i-1} + \lambda_3 \cdot \beta_{i-1}, Rmax_i\} \tag{11}$$

$\lambda_3 \geq 1$ is a magnification factor of skewed distance and $Rmax_i$ is the maximum number of messages a legal UE can transfer. Note that since $Thre_i$ is the threshold, $Thre_i < 1$ is not allowed, otherwise it will be automatically revised to 1 in case of threshold disfunction caused by low SIP stream.

To prevent threshold pollution, we take a self-adapted strategy that $Thre$ will only be updated according to formula (9) (10) on condition that there is no attack being detected during the current sampling period, otherwise it will keep its own value.

C. Messages Filter

PFilter takes its responsibility to filter out flooding messages from the normal ones. In analogy with CBF, we take the similar strategy that as long as one of k_p counters contains a count less than the threshold $Thre$, then this message will be taken as a normal message. The reason why we can take this strategy is flooding SIP messages will conspicuously stand out in normal messages crowds. The observation is that the more drastic the flooding attack goes, the more prominent the attack messages become compared with normal messages. Even for low rate flooding attack, they will still outnumber the normal ones, thus crossing the line of PFilter.

4   Experiments and Evaluation

4.1   Experiment Set up

To evaluate our proposed mechanisms, we design our testbed comprised of three computers. In this design, one computer plays the role of normal users by sending normal SIP messages, another one as IMS server in VoLTE handling the incoming SIP messages. The third computer functions as attacker sending flooding SIP messages. We perform our defense mechanisms on the computer playing as IMS server.

4.2   Evaluation

In our scheme, we empirically choose $\lambda_1 = \lambda_2 = 0.8$. For $Thre$, we set $\lambda_3 = 2$ to slightly enlarge the skew distance and we set the maximum transmission times as $Rmax = 4$. For hash functions, we take $MurmurHash3$ functions with independent seeds. $MurmurHash3$ function is non-cryptographic hash function used for hash-based lookups. It has been widely deployed in many famous applications, such as Hadoop, libstdc++, Nginx. One more benefit of $MurmurHash3$ is that it cares nothing about the length of input.

We randomly mount INVITE flooding attacks with varying flooding rate from 10 cps(call per second) to 100 cps. For each flooding rate, we perform 500 attacks to obtain a good evaluation of PFilter. It is noteworthy that the normal call generation rate randomly varies from 700 cps to 3200 cps, which is much more frequent than most relevant works. We take the extreme values to thoroughly evaluate the performance of PFilter.

A. Scheme I: Simply Count by CBF

In scheme I, we randomly generate $n = 1,000,000$ UEs in VoLTE and each UE maintains its unique secret signature. We also set the tolerated false positive rate as $f = 10^{-7}$. Then according to formula (1) and (2), we can get the length of CBF is $m = 3,354,7705$ (it is the reason we take this number in Sect. 3.1) and the number of hash functions is $k = 23$. According to formula (8), it is obvious that $k = 23 > 12$ and the lower bound for CBF that the probability at least one of the k counters for a legal message contains 1 indeed approaches $p = 1$. We also compare real measured $\dfrac{m_i}{m}$ with $\dfrac{c_i}{m}$ to examine the validity of our estimation to substitute m_i with c_i in (8). It turns out the two sets of data share great similarity, and the results are shown in Table 1. The similarity also confirms the selected hash functions perform in good state.

Table 1. A comparison between $c_i/m(\%)$ and $m_i/m(\%)$

i	1	2	3	4	5	6	7	8	9	10
c_i/m	34.540	11.840	2.706	0.464	0.064	0.007	$<10^{-3}$	$<10^{-4}$	$<10^{-5}$	$<10^{-6}$
m_i/m	34.546	11.835	2.705	0.465	0.063	0.007	$<10^{-3}$	$<10^{-4}$	$<10^{-5}$	0

As long as the lower bound of one message exceeds $Rmax$, then this message will be taken as illegal one. In our more than five thousands flooding attacks at varying rate from 10 cps to 100 cps, the detection rates are always 100%, the false detection rates stay 0, and no overflow issue resulting from the repeated insertion is detected. It is not a surprise because the functional CBF relies on an absolute counting strategy and we also exploit the timely ejection approach to eradicate the adverse effects incurred by the flooding messages. Therefore, for one attribute flooding attack in SIP, CBF is sufficient to detect and find out the attacker. However, the cost for detecting multi-attributes flooding attack is high. For example, to detect INVITE and BYE flooding attack, an extra CBF for BYE messages should be created and the cost is $m * 4 = 134,190,820bits$.

B. Scheme II: Count by Lightweight PFilter

In this scheme, we set $m_p = 500$ and $k_p = 3$. For each counter, we set the length as 8-bits. PFilter is able to filter out a large portion of normal SIP messages and we can easily find out the attacker from the small portion. We achieve high detection rate in different flooding rates, as is shown in Table 2. As we can see in this table, even when the flooding rate is as low as 10 cps, our scheme can efficiently detect this anomaly with detection rate (DR) at 76.4%. Figure 1 shows how PFilter functions to detect INVITE flooding attack at 15 cps. In Fig. 1(a), we get $Thre = 22.4$ by the estimation of equation (11). As long as one of the three entries contains a count less than 22.4, the message will be filtered out as a normal one. The dynamic feather of $Thre$ is depicted in Fig. 1(b) for 20 flooding attacks, with all the $k_p = 3$ counts of the attack message exceeding $Thre$. Because of this feather, $Thre$ can be self-adapted with the high random and fluctuant SIP traffic.

We also compare our detection results with Tang's work [3] even when we get the measurements in extreme condition describing in the above section.

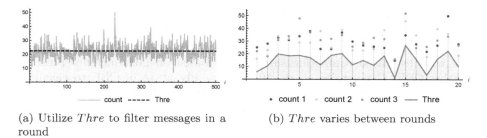

(a) Utilize *Thre* to filter messages in a round

(b) *Thre* varies between rounds

Fig. 1. An example of how *Thre* works for PFilter

The results can be found in Table 2. Our scheme could still detect flooding rate at 15 cps with DR at 97.1% even when normal VoLTE call randomly fluctuates between 700 cps and 3200 cps, compared with 88% in Tang's between 30 cps and 80 cps. The reason why we do not choose more drastic flooding rate as [3] is that since our scheme can detect flooding rate at 100 cps, it is certain we can detect more drastic flooding attack.

Table 2. Detection results: Tang's [3] *vs* Our's

Flooding rate	DR (Tang's)	DR (Our's)
10	–	76.4%
15	88%	97.1%
35	100%	100%
50	100%	100%
75	100%	100%
100	100%	100%
500	100%	–

Compared with scheme I, the low-rate flooding attack detection rate in scheme II is lower. However, when it comes to the multi-attributes flooding attack detection, we can simply apply other PFilters to detect other SIP attributes anomalies at small costs because it is much more memory saving compared with CBF. For example, in addition to INVITE flooding attack detection that costs $m_p \times 8 = 4000bits$, if the attacker also launch BYE flooding attack, the memory cost will be another $4000bits$. It is obvious that $4000 \times 2bits < 134,190,820bits$, so it is much cheaper than scheme I.

5   Related Work

Generally, network-based intrusion detection systems can be divided into two categories: signature-based NIDSs and anomaly-based NIDSs [8].

Signature-based NIDSs rely on a context-aware "blacklist" containing various signatures that describe known attacks. Many signature-based NIDSs adopt Bloom Filter to solve the storage and computation issues. Roh et al. [9] propose whitelist-based countermeasure scheme based on none-member ratio by utilizing CBF. Geneiatakis et al. [10,11] take advantage of CBF to calculate session distance of SIP to detect anomalies with the assumption that flooding attack is associated with incomplete sessions.

Tang and Cheng [12] address the stealthy attack by combining sketch with wavelet techniques. Akbar et al. [13] leverage Hellinger distance to low rate and multi-attributes DDoS attack. In Golait and Hubballi's work [14], the authors also detect the anomaly by generating the normal profile of SIP messages as a probability distribution.

Ryu et al. [15] derive the upper bound of the possible number of SIP messages, and detect the SIP flooding attacks by checking whether this upper bound has been challenged. Mehić et al. [16] also calculate the maximum number and type of SIP messages that can be transferred during established VoIP call without raising an alarm from IDS (Intrusion detection system).

6   Conclusion

In this paper, we propose two effective schemes to detect and prevent SIP flooding attack. In scheme I, we demonstrate CBF can be exploited to keep track of how many SIP messages a VoLTE user transmit during a certain period, thus detecting the attacker. In scheme II, we design PFilter, a more lightweight data structure, to accomplish the detection goal. Not only can our schemes detect the flooding anomalies, but also find out the attackers to alleviate their adverse effects. Another advantage is that no training period is needed, so both schemes have no fear of baseline pollution. Also, the two schemes function well in low-rate flooding attack detection and keep immune to stealthy flooding attack.

Acknowledgments. This work is supported by Chinese National Research Fund (NSFC) Key Project No. 61532013; National China 973 Project No. 2015CB352401; Shanghai Scientific Innovation Act of STCSM No.15JC1402400; 985 Project of Shanghai Jiao Tong University with No. WF220103001; SIT Collaborative innovation platform under Grant No. 3921NH166033; NSFC No. 61170227 and No. 61672350.

References

1. Kim, H., Kim, D.,. Kwon, M., Han, H., Jang, Y., Han, D., Kim, T., Kim, Y.: Breaking and fixing VoLTE: exploiting hidden data channels and mis-implementations. In: Proceedings of the 22nd ACM SIGSAC Conference on Computer and Communications Security, pp. 328–339. ACM (2015)
2. Li, C.-Y., Tu, G.-H., Peng, C., Yuan, Z., Li, Y., Lu, S., Wang, X.: Insecurity of voice solution volte in LTE mobile networks. In: Proceedings of the 22nd ACM SIGSAC Conference on Computer and Communications Security, pp. 316–327. ACM (2015)

3. Tang, J., Cheng, Y., Hao, Y.: Detection and prevention of SIP flooding attacks in voice over IP networks. In: 2012 Proceedings IEEE INFOCOM, pp. 1161–1169. IEEE (2012)
4. Tang, J., Cheng, Y., Hao, Y., Song, W.: SIP flooding attack detection with a multidimensional sketch design. IEEE Trans. Depend. Secur. Comput. **11**(6), 582–595 (2014)
5. Sengar, H., Wang, H., Wijesekera, D., Jajodia, S.: Fast detection of denial-of-service attacks on ip telephony. In: 2006 14th IEEE International Workshop on Quality of Service, pp. 199–208. IEEE (2006)
6. Sengar, H., Wang, H., Wijesekera, D., Jajodia, S.: Detecting VoIP floods using the hellinger distance. IEEE Trans. Parallel Distrib. Syst. **19**(6), 794–805 (2008)
7. Fan, L., Cao, P., Almeida, J., Broder, A.Z.: Summary cache: a scalable wide-area web cache sharing protocol. IEEE/ACM Trans. Netw. (TON) **8**(3), 281–293 (2000)
8. Meng, W., Li, W., Kwok, L.-F.: EFM: enhancing the performance of signature-based network intrusion detection systems using enhanced filter mechanism. Comput. Secur. **43**, 189–204 (2014)
9. Roh, B., Kim, J.W., Ryu, K.-Y., Ryu, J.-T.: A whitelist-based countermeasure scheme using a bloom filter against SIP flooding attacks. Comput. Secur. **37**, 46–61 (2013)
10. Geneiatakis, D., Vrakas, N., Lambrinoudakis, C.: Performance evaluation of a flooding detection mechanism for VoIP networks. In: 2009 16th International Conference on Systems, Signals and Image Processing, pp. 1–5. IEEE (2009)
11. Geneiatakis, D., Vrakas, N., Lambrinoudakis, C.: Utilizing bloom filters for detecting flooding attacks against SIP based services. Comput. Secur. **28**(7), 578–591 (2009)
12. Tang, J., Cheng, Y.: Quick detection of stealthy SIP flooding attacks in VoIP networks. In: 2011 IEEE International Conference on Communications (ICC), pp. 1–5. IEEE (2011)
13. Akbar, A., Basha, S.M., Sattar, S.A.: Leveraging the SIP load balancer to detect and mitigate DDos attacks. In: 2015 International Conference on Green Computing and Internet of Things (ICGCIoT), pp. 1204–1208. IEEE (2015)
14. Golait, D., Hubballi, N.: VoIPFD: voice over IP flooding detection. In: 2016 Twenty Second National Conference on Communication (NCC), pp. 1–6. IEEE (2016)
15. Ryu, J.-T., Roh, B.-H., Ryu, K.-Y.: Detection of SIP flooding attacks based on the upper bound of the possible number of SIP messages. KSII Trans. Internet Inf. Syst. **3**(5), 507–526 (2009)
16. Mehić, M., Mikulec, M., Voznak, M., Kapicak, L.: Creating covert channel using SIP. In: Dziech, A., Czyżewski, A. (eds.) International Conference on Multimedia Communications, Services and Security, pp. 182–192. Springer, Cham (2014). doi:10.1007/978-3-319-07569-3

On Enhancing Energy Efficiency via Elastic Cell-Zooming Algorithm in Three-Tier Heterogeneous Wireless Networks

Zhu Xiao, Shuangchun Li, Tong Li, and Dong Wang$^{(\boxtimes)}$

College of Computer Science and Electronic Engineering,
Hunan University, 410082 Changsha, China
{zhxiao,lishuangchun,litong,wangd}@hnu.edu.cn

Abstract. The explosive growth of mobile users has brought great challenges to traditional cellular networks. The deployment of various Small-cell Base Stations (SBSs) provides a flexible way to address the problem of covering blind spots in Macro-cell Base Station (MBS) and reduce the traffic loads from MBS. In this paper, we investigate energy-saving based on various densities of SBSs including picocells and femtocells in multi-tier heterogeneous networks. We propose an elastic cell-zooming algorithm (ECZA) in order to solve the problem of power consumption and traffic loads in the three-tier heterogeneous cellular networks. Besides, to solve the SBSs zooming problem, which is a NP hard problem, we devise the greedy algorithm to find the suboptimal solution. Simulation results show that the proposed scheme can effectively improve the energy efficiency under the constraint of the outage probability of mobile users in the multi-tier HetNets.

Keywords: SBSs · Cell-zooming · Energy efficiency · Outage probability

1 Introduction

Recently, the development of Internet of things and increasing spread of various smart devices make mobile users rapid explosion, which has brought great challenges to existing cellular networks with much lower capacity and coverage. An effective method to solve this problem is to incorporate some Small-cell Base Stations (SBSs), such as Pico-cell Base Stations (PBSs) and Femto-cell Base Stations (FBSs), into the traditional Macro-cell Base Stations (MBSs) and form the heterogeneous networks [1,2]. Deploying various SBSs in the MBSs can reduce the traffic loads from the MBSs and improve service of quality because of the shared bandwidth and the closer distance between SBSs and mobile users [3–5].

Although SBSs have become a hotspot and attracted many academics and research institutions in the recent years, the deployment of SBSs is not well planned, which causes serious energy consumption if there are not an efficient

© Springer International Publishing AG 2017
L. Ma et al. (Eds.): WASA 2017, LNCS 10251, pp. 136–150, 2017.
DOI: 10.1007/978-3-319-60033-8_13

energy-saving scheme to be employed [3]. Meanwhile, the unplanned distributed SBSs bring in much interference [6,7]. Therefore, it is a challenge to propose an effective algorithm to achieve high energy efficiency.

Cell-zooming is a critical technology for the SBSs to save energy and improve the energy efficiency. Recently, many cell-zooming schemes were put forward, such as [8–10]. In [8], Zhisheng Niu et al. proposed the centralized and distributed cell-zooming algorithms, and simulation results showed the proposed method can greatly reduce the energy consumption and develop green cellular networks. In [9], Park et al. proposed a BS-centric load based cell-zooming algorithm with transmit power control in the downlink. The main idea was to use power control part to adjust the transmitting power based on the average distance to adjacent cells, which helped to reduce the overlap of cell coverage and interference to other cells as well. In [10], Balasubramaniam et al. proposed three novel cell zooming techniques to adjust the base station transmission power, and the coverage area of the cell was depended on the location of the farthest user. Simulations showed that nearly 40% reduction in power consumption can be achieved at the base station with cell zooming. However, the above results were only focused on MBSs or SBSs not concerning on the issue for MBSs and SBSs. In [11,12], an approach was proposed to shrink the MBS and enlarge the SBSs in various cellular networks including Macro-cell and Micro-cell Base Stations. Simulation results showed that the proposed algorithm is useful in reducing power consumption, especially in relatively high density and high traffic networks.

Sleep mode is also a valid way to reduce power consumption and improve performance of networks. Because thousands of SBSs deployed in MBS may increase energy consumption when the traffic load is light and SBSs are always in normal operation. Therefore, in recent years, some researches have concentrated on sleep mode for cellular and heterogeneous networks. In [13], two sleep modes for small cells tier, i.e. random sleep mode and load-awareness dynamic sleep mode, were proposed with purpose of reducing energy consumption and improving power efficiency. In [14], a cooperative sleep-mode mechanism implemented by an adaptive sleep-mode mechanism (ASM) algorithm was proposed in the heterogeneous cellular networks. Results suggested that introducing cooperative sleep-mode can improve system energy efficiency by 63%–83% for various traffic densities with a minor cost on compromised system transmission capacity. In [15], a novel sleep mode was proposed via identifying the small cells that are positioned at undesirable interference spots and selecting them for deactivation. The results showed that the proposed sleep mode can increase the gain by up to 34% and 15.6% in terms of data rate and energy efficiency performance, respectively. There are some literatures considered both cell-zooming and sleeping mode in heterogeneous networks, such as [16,17]. In [16], a dynamic cell-zooming and base stations sleeping optimization algorithm was proposed for dense heterogeneous networks including PBSs and MBSs. In this algorithm, it adjusted the coverage area of PBSs and MBSs based on traffic load conditions and allowed lightly loaded MBSs and PBSs switch into sleep state in order to minimize the system power consumption and guarantee the quality of service to end user. In order to minimize energy consumption under the constraint of quality of service, authors in [17] proposed a mechanism based on the traffic demand in two-tier heterogeneous networks, where range expanded SBSs and enhanced inter-cell interference coordination (eICIC) technique were used to cover the sleeping SBSs far from MBS.

In conclusion, cell-zooming and sleep mode as an energy-saving way to be used for cellular and heterogeneous networks. Besides, in heterogeneous networks, cell-zooming is mainly focused on SBSs enlarging their coverage area and MBS shrinking its coverage region to maintain the trade-off between energy consumption and user experience on condition that the density of mobile users and SBSs is large. However, the recent researches about SBSs zooming in and zooming out in the heterogeneous networks are rarely mentioned. Therefore, the work concentrating on how to effectively minimize the total energy consumption of hybrid cellular networks is still an open issue.

In the paper, we consider that energy-saving technologies based on various densities of SBSs have an impact on performance of networks when SBSs is relatively large. Meanwhile, we investigate on the performance when MBS lowers its coverage and only provides service for nearby mobile users and SBSs zoom out or zoom in such as to serve these mobile users that are previously served by MBS. Furthermore, an elastic cell-zooming scheme based on the service of quality of mobile user is proposed to solve the problem of power consumption and traffic loads in the three-tier heterogeneous cellular networks. Besides, the greedy algorithm is proposed to deal with the NP hard problem that how to implement the zooming strategy for SBSs. Finally, Simulation results show that the proposed scheme can effectively improve the energy efficiency with outage probability guaranteed.

The rest of paper is organized as follows. In Sect. 2, energy optimization in three-tier Femto-Pico-Macro heterogeneous networks are detailed. Next, Sect. 2.1 presents an elastic cell-zooming algorithm and the greedy algorithm for given system model. Some numerical results and conclusions are presented in Sects. 4 and 5.

2   Energy Optimization in Three-Tier Femto-Pico-Macro Heterogeneous Networks

2.1   System Model

Consider there are N_f FBSs and N_p PBSs being randomly deployed within the ring R_0 of an MBS, and mobile users distribute at random in the area, as illustrated in Fig. 1. The out circle indicates the normal coverage area of MBS and the red dotted circle denotes the shrunken signal overlay area from the MBS. Mobile users ranging between the red dotted circle and the out circle are serviced by the adjacent FBSs or PBSs. The black dotted circle denotes the coverage area of PBSs or FBSs zooming. The grayed base stations denote the sleep mode. Throughout this paper, MBS changes its coverage area. For

convenience, we refer to the total coverage area of the three-tier networks as
size of the outermost circle, including FBSs and PBSs. Various kinds of BSs
(i.e., MBS, PBSs and FBSs) are connected to the core network by broadband
backhauls and supposed to operate on a licensed band.

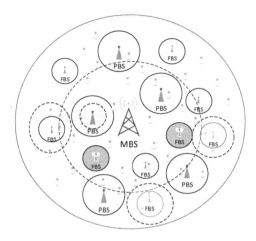

Fig. 1. Illustration of the considered three-tier MBS-PBS-FBS model, where many
PBSs, FBSs and mobile users deployed randomly are given as an example.

2.2   Formulation of Energy Efficiency Optimization

In the proposed model of networks, the CoAP (Constrained Application Protocol) is used as a means of connecting clouds of sensors and smart devices via
mobile users [18]. Besides, the control commands and related information among
BSs are transferred by means of public mobile fog [19,20]. FBSs, PBSs and MBS
obtain the specific message sent by mobile users through mobile fog. So that they
can control the BSs zooming in/out and turning on/off. Meanwhile, we adopt
the shared bandwidth technique for all kinds of base stations.

In the system model, mobile users, PBSs and FBSs are deployed in the original coverage area of MBS randomly, and obey the spatial poisson processes
distribution. Let R_p, R_f denote the radius of coverage area for PBSs and FBSs,
respectively($R_0 >> R_p > R_f$). However, PBSs and FBSs provide service for the
mobile users of their coverage area and the outers because signal power received
from PBSs or FBSs by outer mobile users meets their requirement for service
of quality with improving their transmitting power when the MBS lessens its
coverage area.

Moreover, we define P_m, P_p, P_f as the transmission power of MBS, PBS and
FBS, respectively. However, the power consumption of a base station should
consider the fixed power and dynamic power. We let P_0 denote the static power,

which is a constant power for base station to maintain the essential operation except transmitting power. Therefore, overall power consumption of a base station include the static power (P_0) and the transmitting power (P_m, P_p or P_f). Next, we assume the number of mobile users are a constant, and define N_u as numbers of mobile users. Mobile users can be served by various base stations, which base station mobile users are served depends on service of quality of them'.

In the paper, we consider signal to interference ratio (SIR) as the metric for mobile users to measure service of quality. Besides, we set a threshold value (T) to decide whether a user is serviced by a base station. For a mobile user, if the most SIR exceeds T, this user will be connected to relevant base station, otherwise, this user will not be served. We define β as outage probability of users. The value of β is the number of mobile users not served to total number of users, and let β_0 denote the threshold value about outage probability. Only if β is not more than β_0, the result we obtain is valid.

Finally, we refer to the value of the overall throughput to the total power consumption as the criterion to evaluate system performance. Let C and P denote the overall system throughput and the total power consumption. Therefore, we consider that the optimization problem can be summarized as

$$maximize \qquad \varphi = C/P \tag{1}$$

subject to

$$C = \sum_{i=0}^{i<U} B_i \times \log_2\left(1 + SIR_i\right) \tag{2}$$

$$P = \sum_{i=0}^{i<N_p} P_i + \sum_{j=0}^{j<N_f} P_j + P_m + P_0 \tag{3}$$

$$\beta = P'\left(SIR < T\right), \beta < \beta_0 \tag{4}$$

$$B_i = B/N_u^{service} \tag{5}$$

$$B > B_i \tag{6}$$

$$P_i \geq P_{i_0}, i = 1, 2, ..., N_p, or, 1, 2, ..., N_f, or, 1 \tag{7}$$

The objective function in (1) is to maximize φ by reducing the coverage area of MBS and making SBSs zoom in/out or sleep. Function (2) is to calculate the overall throughput, B_i and SIR_i denote that the bandwidth and SIR obtained by the i-th mobile user. In (3), P represents the total power consumption, P_i, P_j and P_m denote the energy dissipation of the i-th PBS, j-th FBS and MBS, respectively. P_0 denotes the fixed power consumption of FBSs, PBSs and MBS. The constraint in (4) provides the definition of outage probability and ensures that the outage probability is not exceed the given the threshold value (β_0), P', SIR and T represent probability, the received signal power to the interference power and the threshold about service of quality of mobile users, respectively. Function (5) is to count the bandwidth of the i-th mobile user, B denotes the system bandwidth and $N_u{}^{service}$ denotes number of the base station providing service for the i-the user serves mobile users. The constraint in (6) is to guarantee the total bandwidth is not less than bandwidth allocated by user. The next constraint in (7) is power consumption limitations for the PBSs, the FBSs and the MBS. P_{i_0} denotes the fixed power consumption.

In order to effectively solve the optimization problem and achieve the purpose of saving energy and improving energy efficiency. We propose a simple and effective cell-zooming and greedy strategy in three-tier hybrid cellular network to achieve this goal. Next, we introduce the proposed algorithm in detail.

3 Proposed Algorithm

3.1 Elastic Cell-Zooming Algorithm (ECZA)

In conventional cell zooming scheme, a mobile user selects the serving BS in order to maximize its received power. However, most mobile users are served by MBS because the transmitting power of MBS is much larger than PBSs and FBSs. Therefore, if there are thousands of mobile users in the coverage area of MBS, those mobile users obtain less bandwidth from the MBS so that their service of quality are not ideal.

In order to solve above problem, we propose an elastic cell-zooming algorithm (ECZA), where MBS shrinks its coverage area and PBSs and FBSs zoom in/out by adjusting their transmitting power. Moreover, mobile users determine the serving BS according to SIR obtained from MBS, PBSs or FBSs. In addition, it is worth noting that the path loss power cant be neglected in calculating SIR of mobile users. In our proposed algorithm, the path loss power of the serving BS is different from the disturbing BS, the function relationship is shown below [21,22].

$$L = 39.676 + 20 \times \log_{10}d + k \times G \qquad (8)$$

In above function, L denotes the size of the path loss power, d represents the distance between mobile user and BS, G denotes the loss through a wall and k denotes number of walls. The detailed procedure of the proposed cell-zooming algorithm is described as follows.

In step 1, before calculating the SIR of mobile users, initialize the transmitting power of various base stations. The size of transmission power can be obtained by the original relationship between transmission power and coverage area. However, number of mobile users served by each base station is zero.

In step 2, the mobile users choose BS providing the highest SIR for them as the serving BS. Before finding the serving BS, we search all BSs including PBSs, FBSs and MBS and calculate the SIR of every mobile users. The SIR served by the i-th FBS can be obtained as follows:

$$SIR = \frac{P_i}{\sum\limits_{\substack{j=0 \\ j \neq i, j < N_f}} P_j + \sum\limits_{\substack{j=0 \\ j < N_p}} P_j + P_m} \qquad (9)$$

Algorithm 1. Elastic Cell-Zooming Algorithm

Step 1:
    Initialize the transmitting power of BS and the number served by each BS.
Step 2:
2-1: Find a relevant BS providing the maximum SIR for each mobile user.
    Set the threshold value (T) and assign mobile users to BS if SIR is more than T.
2-2: Calculate the outage probability (β) and contrast the size of β and β_0.
    If β is not greater than β_0, go Step 2–3.
    If β is greater than β_0, PBSs and FBSs adopt greedy algorithm, and go Step 2–1.
2-3: Count the number of users served by each base station.
    Calculate the bandwidth of each mobile user allocated from the serving BS.
2-4: Compute the throughput (C) and power consumption (P).
    Obtain the ratio of the overall throughput to the total power consumption (φ)
Step 3:
3-1: Shrink the MBS in proportion to γ to the radius of coverage area (R_i)
    If R_i is not less than the threshold radius of MBS (R_T), go Step 1.
    If R_i is less than R_T, go Step 4.
Step 4:
4-1: Contrast the obtained value (φ) under each condition.
    Find the greatest value (φ) and end the process.

In (9), P_i represents the received signal power from relevant serving base station, the denominator represents the sum of interferences from all FBSs except the i-th FBS, all PBSs and MBS. However, the way to calculate signal power and interference power is different. The interference power includes the wall loss. Then, we obtain the outage probability (β) by SIR of mobile users, when β is greater than β_0, the transmitting power of FBSs or PBSs increases by α dB for SIR less than threshold (T), and decrease by α dB for SIR greater than threshold (T). And repeat Step 2–1 until β is not greater than β_0 or time of zoom in/out achieves the set threshold (T_t). Next, we count the number of mobile users served by each base station and calculate the bandwidth of each mobile user allocated from BS. Finally, we compute the overall throughput (C) and the total power consumption (P) and get the ratio (φ) of C to P.

In Step 3, we shrink MBS in proportion to γ, then some mobile users served originally by MBS may be served by PBSs or FBSs. Next, we continue Step 1 and 2 until the radius of MBS becomes R_T.

In Step 4, we compare all obtained φ and find the greatest one as the result we need.

3.2   Implementing SBSs Zooming In/Out Based on Greedy Algorithm

In order to maximize energy efficiency of function (1) with outage probability guaranteed, we propose an elastic cell-zooming algorithm. As the mobile users reached, base stations which provide service for these mobile users zoom out or zoom in its coverage area according to SIR of mobile users. However, a base station zooms out or zooms in the coverage area for the current mobile user to reach the optimal energy efficiency, which has a significant interference on the other mobile users served by other BSs. Therefore, it is a NP complete problem. SBSs always change its coverage area as the mobile users reached, and the number of mobile users served are different for various SBSs so that we cannot scale the SBSs as a whole. Therefore, we adopt the greedy algorithm to find the suboptimal solution. The detailed process of solving how to zoom about SBSs is described as Algorithm 2.

Algorithm 2. The Greedy Algorithm

1: **for** $N_{u_k} < N_u$ **do**
2:     **while** $N_{u_i} < N_u$ **do**
3:         Find BS_j=max(SIR,N_{u_i}).
4:         Adjust the j-th BS to make it just provide service for the furthest user.
5:     **end while**
6:     Calculate the SIR and the throughput of the k-th user.
7:     Count the total throughput.
8:     Calculate the overall power consumption.
9:     Get the energy efficiency (φ).
10: **end for**

In the algorithm 2, N_{u_i} denotes the i-th mobile user, BS_j denotes the j-th base station, BS may be FBS, PBS or MBS, step 2–5 is used for every mobile user to find the optimal serving BS and ensure the final coverage area of each BS. Besides, it is worth noting that the total throughput of system is calculated after the all BSs zoom in or zoom out. Because the change of a base station affects the SIR of other users served by other BSs. However, the BSs change their coverage area by only considering the quality of service of the current mobile users. Therefore, the proposed algorithm can only find the suboptimal solution.

4   Simulation Results and Discussion

In this section, the system performance with the proposed energy-saving cell zooming scheme in the analytical model, as abstractly described in Fig. 1, is evaluated and compared with two conventional ones. The two ones are set as baselines, (1) we adopt method in [6] where mobile users from MBS are served by the closest PBSs or FBSs when the MBS zooms out; (2) we employ scheme in [7] where MBS shrinks its coverage area and PBSs or FBSs only zooms in to provide service for the mobile users from MBS. For verifying results, we consider various system parameters, such as radius of MBS, the number of mobile users and the density of PBSs and FBSs, to evaluate the performance of system respectively. MATLAB is used in the experimental simulation platform. The setting of key parameters is listed in Table 1.

Table 1. The Setting of key simulation parameters

Parameter	Value
R_0	1000 m
R_p	80 m
R_f	20 m
P_m	46 dBm
P_p	30 dBm
P_f	17 dBm
B	100 MHz
T	10 dB
β_0	5%
T_t	5
G	10 dB
R_T	200 m
γ	100 m
P_{m_0}	36 dBm
P_{p_0}	20 dBm
P_{f_0}	7 dBm
User-location distribution	Spatially random distribution in three-tier cell
SBS-deployment distribution	Spatially random distribution in the ring (R_0)

In the simulation, we use the energy efficiency and outage probability criterion to evaluate the performance of networks in various cell-zooming strategies. We consider a three-tier HetNets with a set of PBSs and FBSs deployed randomly in a single MBS. N_p, N_f and user denote number of PBSs, FBSs and mobile users, respectively. We investigate performance of system in different networks states.

Figure 2 shows energy efficiency of three different cell-zooming schemes vary as the radius of MBS changed when $N_p = 50$, $N_f = 500$, $N_u = 5000$. We can see that energy efficiency of three curves increases with the same speed as the radius of MBS shrunk. Because with radius of MBS reduced, the total power consumption is decreased and the overall throughput increases due to more mobile users served by PBSs or FBSs. Meanwhile, the higher energy efficiency are finally achieved for the method in [7] and the proposed scheme compared to the method in [6]. However, energy efficiency of the proposed algorithm is higher than that of the comparative methods, the reason of which is that method in [6] causes more interference than the proposed algorithm. Besides, much more mobile users are not served in method in [7].

Figure 3 shows the relation between outage probability and the radius of MBS when $N_p = 50$, $N_f = 500$, $N_u = 5000$. It is obvious that the proposed scheme has lowest outage probability because some SBSs zooming in and other SBSs

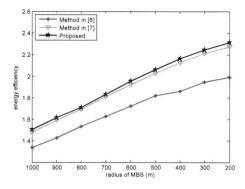

Fig. 2. Energy efficiency of various schemes when $N_p = 50$, $N_f = 500$, $N_u = 5000$.

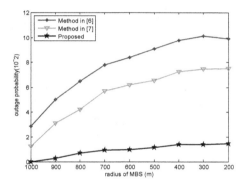

Fig. 3. Outage probability of various schemes when $N_p = 50$, $N_f = 500$, $N_u = 5000$.

zooming out or sleeping in the proposed scheme can effectively reduce interferences from adjacent SBSs and improve SIR of mobile users, which enables more formally MBS associated mobile users to be served by PBSs or FBSs. In Fig. 4, outage probability of three curves increases with different speed as the radius of MBS reduced, this is because more and more mobile users are not served by MBS while PBSs and FBSs cannot provide service for those mobile users from MBS with SIR as the radius of MBS shrunks. Moreover, coverage area of MBS decreases slower when the radius of MBS reduces, which makes the rate of reduction for mobile users and the rate of growth for outage probability tend to be flat. When comparing to the methods in [6,7], the proposed scheme can make more users served by PBSs or FBSs with quality of service guaranteed and effectively decrease the outage probability.

Figure 5 shows that outage probability of the proposed scheme varies with the radius of MBS changed in different numbers of FBSs when $Np = 500$, $N_u = 5000$. We can see that outage probability of various number of FBSs increases with the decreasing radius of MBS, while outage probability curves grow in different

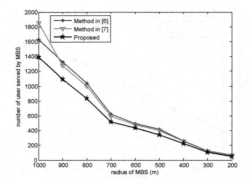

Fig. 4. Numbers of users served by MBS when $N_p = 50$, $N_f = 500$, $N_u = 5000$.

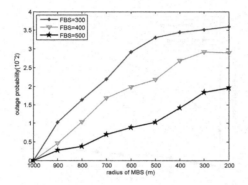

Fig. 5. Outage probability when $N_p = 50$, $N_u = 5000$.

way under various range of the radius of MBS. When the radius of MBS exceeds 600 m, the outage of probability increases with a rapid rise. Meanwhile, it is obvious that outage probability of curve with FBS = 300 is much larger than that in FBS = 500, the reason behind this is that more mobile users are served by FBSs when the number of FBSs increases. Therefore, increasing the number of FBSs can validly reduce outage probability and improve the performance of networks.

Figures 6, 7 and 8 present the relation between the energy efficiency and number of FBSs, PBSs and mobile users. The results are based on the proposed algorithm when the radius of MBS set to is 600 m. In Fig. 6, it can be found out that energy efficiency rises with the increasing of FBSs when number of PBSs is 10. Besides, energy efficiency also increases when the mobile users are to be large. Meanwhile, the rate of growth of energy efficiency exceeds when number of mobile users is less than 5000 than that when mobile users are more than 5000. Therefore, by increasing FBSs can promote the rate of increase for energy efficiency, since the mobile users increased before mobile users are 5000 when the number of FBSs is small. When mobile users exceed 5000, the current FBSs

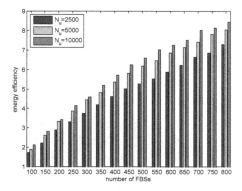

Fig. 6. Energy efficiency with number of FBS in 10 PBSs.

cannot provide enough service for so many mobile users, by increasing number of FBSs can effectively solve the problem.

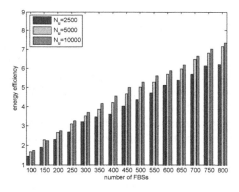

Fig. 7. Energy efficiency with number of FBSs in 30 PBSs.

In Figs. 7 and 8, we consider that the energy efficiency varies with number of FBSs in various mobile users when number of PBSs is 30 and 50, respectively. Based on the results in Figs. 6, 7 and 8, we realize that the energy efficiency decreases when the number of PBSs increases. This is because increasing the number of PBSs brings strong interference for mobile users served by FBSs. Meanwhile, compared to FBSs, increasing the number of PBSs produces more power consumption. Besides, increasing the number of PBSs make it evident that increasing number of FBSs has effects on energy efficiency when number of mobile users is less than 5000. As a result, increasing number of mobile users and FBSs can effectively improve energy efficiency.

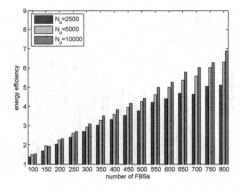

Fig. 8. Energy efficiency with number of FBSs in 50 PBSs.

5   Conclusion

In this paper, we have proposed an elastic cell-zooming scheme for the three-tier heterogeneous cellular networks. And the scheme can optimally adjust the coverage area of FBSs, PBSs and MBS based on the SIR obtained by mobile users. Meanwhile, when a base station does not provide service for any mobile users, this base goes into sleep mode. Besides, we use energy efficiency as a measure of performance to illustrate the problem about the trade-off between throughput and power consumption. And the greedy algorithm is put forward to solve to the problem of how to zoom for SBSs deployed in MBS and find the suboptimal solution. Finally, simulation results show that the proposed mechanism can effectively improve the performance of the networks with the guaranteed quality of service. Specifically, it is suitable for the condition that the mobile users and FBSs are large.

Acknowledgments. This research is supported in part by the National Natural Science Foundation of China (Grants Nos. 61301148 and 61272061), the Hunan Natural Science Foundation of China (Grants No. 2016JJ3041).

References

1. Albrecht, J.F., Ingo, V., Jens, V., Cinzia, S., Simone, R., Gerhard, P.F.: Small-cell self-organizing wireless networks. Proc. IEEE **102**(3), 334–350 (2014)
2. Xiao, Z., Liu, H., Havyarimana, V., Li, T., Wang, D.: Analytical study on multi-Tier 5G heterogeneous networks: coverage performance and energy efficiency. Sensors **16**(11), 1854–1870 (2016)
3. Qingqing, W., Geoffrey, Y.L., Wen, C., Derrick, W.K.N.: Energy-efficient small cell with spectrum-power trading. IEEE Mag. **34**(12), 3394–3408 (2016)
4. Xiao, Z., Li, T., Ding, W., Wang, D., Zhang, J.: Dynamic PCI allocation on avoiding handover confusion via cell status prediction in LTE heterogeneous small cell networks. Wireless Commun. Mob. Comput. **16**(14), 1972–1986 (2016)

5. Condoluci, M., Dohler, M., Araniti, G., Molinaro, A., Zheng, K.: Toward 5G densenets: architectural advances for effective machine-type communications over femtocells. IEEE Commun. Mag. **52**(1), 134–141 (2015)
6. Abdellaziz, W., Abdellatif, K., Essaid, S., Jalel, B., Mohammed, E.K.: Towards improving energy efficiency of mobile in hyper dense LTE small-cells deployments. In: Global Communications Conference (GLOBECOM), Washington, DC, pp. 1–6 (2016)
7. Xiao, Z., Li, Z., Zhang, X., Liu, E., Yi, K.: An efficient interference mitigation approach via quasi-access in two-tier macro-femto heterogeneous networks. Int. J. Commun Syst **28**(5), 901–909 (2016)
8. Niu, Z., Wu, Y., Gong, J., Yang, Z.: Cell zooming for cost-efficient green cellular networks. IEEE Commun. Mag. **48**(11), 74–79 (2010)
9. Jae, H.P., Jung, H.J., Duk, K.K.: A new traffic load based cell zooming algorithm in dense small cell environments. In: Seventh International Conference on Ubiquitous and Future Networks, pp. 332–337. Hotel Okura Sapporo, Sapporo (2015)
10. Balasubramaniam, R., Nagaraj, S., Sarkar, M., Paolini, C.: Cell zooming for power efficient base station operation. In: 9th International Wireless Communications and Mobile Computing Conference (IWCMC), Cagliari, Sardinia, Italy, pp. 556–560 (2013)
11. Khaled, A., Haj, I., Bachir, A., Milad, G., Michel, N.: Reducing power consumption of cellular networks by using various cell types and cell zooming. In: Third International Conference on e-Technologies and Networks for Development (ICeND), pp. 33–38. Faculty of Engineering Lebanese University, Campus of Hadath, Beirut (2014)
12. Chung, Y.L.: An energy-saving small-cell zooming scheme for two-tier hybrid cellular networks. In: International Conference on Information Networking (ICOIN), Siemreab, Cambodia, pp. 148–152 (2015)
13. Xiao, Z., Li, S., Chen, X., Wang, D., Chen, W.: A load-balancing energy consumption minimization scheme in 5G heterogeneous small cell wireless networks under coverage probability analysis. Int. J. Pattern Recogn. Artif. Intell. **32**(7), 21 (2017)
14. Wu, G., Feng, G., Qin, S.: Cooperative sleep-mode and performance modeling for heterogeneous mobile network. In: Wireless Communications and Networking Conference Workshops (WCNCW), Shanghai, China, pp. 6–11 (2013)
15. Aysha, E., Emad, A.: Interference and resource management through sleep mode selection in heterogeneous networks. IEEE Commun. Trans. **65**(1), 257–269 (2017)
16. Hafiz, Y.L., Muhammad, Z.S., Muhamad, I., Amr, M., Khalid, Q.: Towards energy efficient and quality of service aware cell zooming in 5G wireless networks. In: Vehicular Technology Conference (VTC2015-Fall), Boston, USA, pp. 1–5 (2015)
17. Tao, R., Zhang, J., Chu, X.: An energy saving small cell sleeping mechanism with cell expansion in heterogeneous networks. In: Vehicular Technology Conference (VTC Spring), Nanjing, China, pp. 1–5 (2016)
18. Heng, S., Nan, C., Ralph, D.: Combining mobile and fog computing: using CoAP to link mobile device clouds with fog computing. In: International Conference on Data Science and Data Intensive Systems, Paris, France, pp. 564–571 (2015)
19. Alam, M.G.R., Yan, K.T., Choong, S.H.: Multi-agent and reinforcement learning based code offloading in mobile fog. In: International Conference on Information Networking (ICOIN), Kota Kinabalu, Malaysia, pp. 285–290 (2016)
20. Fernando, N., Loke, S.W., Rahayu, W.: Mobile cloud computing: a survey. Future Gener. Comput. Sys. **29**(1), 84–106 (2013)

21. DeLima, C.H.M., Bennis, M., Ghaboosi, K., et al.: Interference management for self-organized femtocells towards green networks. In: 21st International Symposium on Personal. Indoor and Mobile Radio Communications Workshops, Istanbul, Turkey, pp. 352–356 (2010)
22. Alves, H., Bennis, M., Souza, R.D., Latva-Aho, M.: Enhanced performance of heterogeneous networks through full-duplex relaying. EURASIP Wirel. Commun. Netw. 1(1), 1–12 (2012)

Cooperative Downlink Resource Allocation in 5G Wireless Backhaul Network

Yuan Gao[1,2,4(✉)], Hong Ao[2], Quan Zhou[2], Weigui Zhou[2],
Xiangyang Li[4], Yunchuan Sun[3], Su Hu[5], and Yi Li[6]

[1] China Defense Science and Technology Information Center,
Beijing 100142, China
yuangao08@tsinghua.edu.cn
[2] Xichang Satellite Launch Center, Sichuan 615000, China
[3] International Institute of Big Data in Finance, Business School,
Beijing Normal University, Beijing 100875, China
yunch@bnu.edu.cn
[4] Department of Electronic Engineering, Tsinghua University,
Beijing 100084, China
[5] University of Electronic Science and Technology of China,
Sichuan 611731, China
husu@uestc.edu.cn
[6] The High School Affiliated to Renmin University of China,
Beijing 100080, China
liyi@rdfz.cn

Abstract. The 5th wireless communication system will provide higher throughput and more reliable QoS through many key techniques. Cooperation is one possible technology that may provide satisfied performance to users, especially the cell edge users. In this work, we provide the analysis of resource allocation in wireless backhaul networks, through capacity constraint wireless backhaul, the cooperative downlink joint processing is proposed to enhance cell edge performance. We propose the system level simulation and evaluate the cluster performance. Simulation results indicate that the capacity constraint wireless backhaul will bring delay, capacity limit to joint processing method, traditional cooperation scheme will not work well, and our proposed method could gain 13% compared to traditional method.

Keywords: Resource allocation · Capacity constraint · 5G · Wireless backhaul

1 Introduction

The 5th wireless communication system will be released around in 2020, with majorities of new technologies and bring significant improvement to customers [1, 2]. The aim of the 5G wireless communication system is to provide faster speed and flexible QoS [3] to every potential users. There are many possible key techniques, such as large-scale antenna system (LSAS), small cell, flexible deployment and cooperation, etc. However, the deployment of ultra-dense network (UDN) will cause severe

© Springer International Publishing AG 2017
L. Ma et al. (Eds.): WASA 2017, LNCS 10251, pp. 151–160, 2017.
DOI: 10.1007/978-3-319-60033-8_14

interference from adjacent equipment, where cooperation to reduce interference are introduced in the standardization of the 5G network [4, 5].

In the commercial process of the 5G network, cooperation under imperfect condition are considered where the actual performance did not match the theoretical analysis. The cooperation in 5G network will need the high-speed link to transmit cooperation signals, typically using optical fiber. In huge cities such as Beijing and Shanghai, the deployment of optical fiber is quite difficult due to the municipal construction problem, so wireless backhaul becomes one possible solution to adopt cooperation in city area. Both industry and academic scholars are studying the problems caused by cooperation in 5G wireless networks.

In [6, 7], the authors focused on the problem of cognitive in 5G system, by introducing the framework of SON, it is effective to solve the dynamic resource allocation problem in SON network. In [8–10], the flexible power allocation methods are given to achieve higher transmission speed, however, only system level analysis and ideal cooperation parameters are considered. In [11, 12], the authors discussed the antenna configuration problems using LSAS or array antennas to form dynamic beam forming and reduce interferences, then in [13, 14], UWB and mm-Wave in 5G are summarized, where wideband transmission would bring higher transmission speed, but cooperative latency are not introduced. In [15–17], combined resource allocation of time and frequency domain are analyzed and simulated, joint allocation of resources may help squeeze the gainfrom multi-domain obtained by the degree of freedom. To reduce the complexity in cooperation, the authors in [18, 19] proposed the online method and analyzed the approach using game theory, although the method could work in online mode, but the performance is not satisfied. In [20], energy efficiency became the objective function and the author discussed the resource allocation problem to reduce energy consumption, but the delay and throughput are not the primary objective.

Considering the demand of throughput and latency in 5G systems [21, 22], we studied the downlink cooperative scheme in 5G systems using wireless backhaul. We model the capacity and delay constraint wireless backhaul in downlink cooperative processing, and then we propose the novel method to enhance the performance of throughput and reduce the signal processing delay, which is still novel and creative. Therefore, the rest of this work is organized as follows. In Sect. 2, we discussed the scenario and model of the joint processing. In Sect. 3, we present the resource allocation in backhaul networks and then in Sect. 4, simulation and analysis were presented.

2 System Model

In 5G wireless networks, the core network will provide computing resources rather than in base stations in 4G and previous equipment. In Fig. 1, we describe the proposed 5G architecture with wireless backhaul to perform cooperation [23, 24]. Cellular base stations equipped with large-scale antenna systems are providing high-speed transmission service. Wireless backhaul is used to transmit cooperative information such as user data, channel state information (CSI) [25, 26], etc. Due to the demand of multimedia service, the amount of data to be transmitted through joint processing has risen to a new level, where the capacity of wireless backhaul could not afford the load of

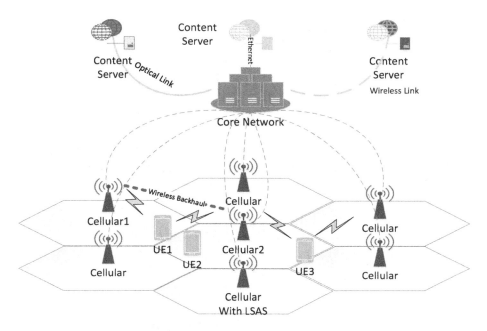

Fig. 1. Network architecture of wireless backhaul network in 5G

multi-users, let alone the need to tackle cell edge interference. Therefore, the architecture brought us the problem of capacity constraint wireless backhaul and transmission delay, and how to deal with this is the key of this work.

We assume that all the users located in this scenariowill receive downlink cooperative signal [27], and the cooperative data are transmitted through wireless backhaul. To make the discussion simple and clear, we take the two base stations as example. In the following discussion, boldface lowercase alphabets are to denote vectors whereas boldface uppercase alphabets denote matrices. $(\cdot)^T$ and $(\cdot)^\dagger$ denote the transpose and conjugate transpose of the matrix arguments. $I(x; y)$ means the mutual information function between x and y. R_+ denotes the nonnegative real domain. I_n denotes the $n \times n$ unitary matrix.

Cellular 1 and 2 are serving User 1 and User 2 through cooperation, the signal model is given in the following equation. In the equations, $y_A(y_B) \sim C^{K \times 1}$ means the received signal of BS A(B), $s \in C^{2K \times 1}$ is the information symbol vector to be transmitted with the kth antenna, s_k is modeled as the required information that will be mapped on subcarrier k. $H_{A(B)} = diag(h_{A(B),k}) \in C^{K \times 2K}$ means the channel matrix that represent the channel state information, andthe diagonal element $h_{A,k}(h_{B,k})$ is the channel response. The noise vector $n_A(n_B) \in C^{K \times 1}$ is a realization of a zero-mean circularly symmetric complexGaussianrandom process: $n_A(n_B) \sim \mathcal{N}C(0, \sigma^2 I_K)$, where σ^2 is noise variance.

$$y_A = H_{A1}x_1 + H_{A2}x_2 + n_A$$
$$\widehat{y_B} = H_{B1}x_1 + H_{B2}x_2 + n_B + z_B$$

$$y = \begin{pmatrix} y_A \\ \widehat{y_B} \end{pmatrix} = \begin{pmatrix} H_{A1} & H_{A2} \\ H_{B1} & H_{B2} \end{pmatrix}\begin{pmatrix} x_1 \\ x_2 \end{pmatrix} + \begin{pmatrix} n_A \\ n_B + z_B \end{pmatrix} \tag{1}$$

$$= \begin{pmatrix} H_A \\ H_B \end{pmatrix}x_s + \begin{pmatrix} n_A \\ n_B + z_B \end{pmatrix} = (H_1\,H_2)\begin{pmatrix} x_1 \\ x_2 \end{pmatrix} + \begin{pmatrix} n_A \\ n_B + z_B \end{pmatrix}$$

The sum rate of the transmission that will reflect the achievable rate could be calculated using the following equation:

$$R_{yy} = E(yy^H) = \begin{pmatrix} H_A \\ H_B \end{pmatrix}Q_s(H_A^H\,H_B^H) + \begin{pmatrix} \sigma^2 I & 0 \\ 0 & \sigma^2 I + \phi_B \end{pmatrix}$$

$$R_{nn} = E(nn^H) = \begin{pmatrix} \sigma^2 I & 0 \\ 0 & \sigma^2 I + \phi_B \end{pmatrix} \tag{2}$$

$$I(x_s; y_A\widehat{y_B}) = H(y_A\widehat{y_B}) - H(y_A\widehat{y_B}\,|\,x_s) = H(y_A\widehat{y_B}) - H(n_A(n_B + z_B))$$

So the mutual information is expressed by combining Eqs. 1 and 2:

$$I(x_s; y_A\widehat{y_B}) = \log\det(\pi e R_{yy}) - \log\det(\pi e R_{nn}) = \log\det(R_{yy}R_{nn}^{-1})$$

$$= \log\det\left(I + \frac{Q_s}{\sigma^2}H_A^H H_A + Q_s H_B^H(\sigma^2 I + \phi_B)^{-1}H_B\right) \tag{3}$$

$$= \log\det\left(I + \frac{Q_s}{\sigma^2}H_A^H H_A + Q_s H_B^H(\sigma^2 A + I)^{-1}A H_B\right)$$

The system will need to transmit cooperative information through backhaul link, so the link model is given using Eq. 4:

$$I(y_B; \widehat{y_B}\,|\,y_A) = H(\widehat{y_B}\,|\,y_A) - H(\widehat{y_B}\,|\,y_B y_A)$$
$$= H(\widehat{y_B}\,|\,y_A) - H(z_B) \tag{4}$$

According to Shannon formula, the achievable backhaul capacity is limited by the link capacity and the delay tolerance of the data traffic, which means if the traffic could not be transmitted within given period, it will be abandoned.

$$I(y_B; \widehat{y_B}\,|\,y_A)$$
$$= H(\widehat{y_B}\,|\,y_A) - H(z_B)$$
$$= \log\det\left(I + \phi_B^{-1}\left(H_B(I + \frac{Q_s}{\sigma^2}H_A^H H_A)^{-1}Q_s H_B^H + \sigma^2 I\right)\right) \tag{5}$$
$$= \log\det\left(I + A\left(H_B(I + \frac{Q_s}{\sigma^2}H_A^H H_A)^{-1}Q_s H_B^H + \sigma^2 I\right)\right)$$

3   Resource Allocation in Wireless Backhaul

Note that the backhaul transmission is under the constraint of link capacity and delay, so the optimization problem could be expressed using the following equation:

$$\max_{A} \ \text{logdet}\left(I + \frac{Q_s}{\sigma^2}H_A^H H_A + Q_s H_B^H(\sigma^2 A + I)^{-1}AH_B\right)$$

$$s.t. \ \log\det\left(I + A\left(H_B(I + \frac{Q_s}{\sigma^2}H_A^H H_A)^{-1}Q_s H_B^H + \sigma^2 I\right)\right) \le R_{BH}$$

(6)

In this problem, we can infer that $R_{y_B|y_A} = U(diag(s_1, s_2, \ldots, s_{M_B}))U^H$ express the rate that base station A could receive the speed of R when transmit the side information to base station B [28], and $\eta_j = \left[\frac{1}{\lambda}\left(\frac{1}{\sigma^2} - \frac{1}{s_j}\right) - \frac{1}{\sigma^2}\right]^+$, where we have λ is such that $\sum_{j=1}^{M_B} \log(1 + \eta_j s_j) = R_{BH}$, so the optimization problem in 6 could be simplified to the following equivalent problem:

It is clear that the objective function about A and Q is concave, but the limitation is not a convex function, so we will make the optimization work by using the compression method when transmit the cooperation signal to adjacent base stations.

$$\max_{A,Q_s} \text{logdet}\left(I + \frac{Q_s}{\sigma^2}H_A^H H_A + Q_s H_B^H(\sigma^2 A + I)^{-1}AH_B\right)$$

$$s.t. \ \log\det\left(I + A\left(H_B(I + \frac{Q_s}{\sigma^2}H_A^H H_A)^{-1}Q_s H_B^H + \sigma^2 I\right)\right) \le R_{BH}$$

$$A \ge 0, \text{tr}(C_1^T Q_s C_1) \le P_1, \text{tr}(C_2^T Q_s C_2) \le P_2$$

$$Q_s = \begin{pmatrix} Q_1 & \\ & Q_2 \end{pmatrix} \ge 0$$

(7)

The objective function could be simplified by using the matrix transform and the redundant information is deleted from information theory point of view, then we have the solvable problem given in Eq. 9, and in this equation, the rate could be expressed by $R_{y_B|y_A} = H_B(I + \frac{Q_s}{\sigma^2}H_A^H H_A)^{-1}Q_s H_B^H + \sigma^2 I$. This problem could be solved

$$\text{logdet}\left(I + \frac{Q_s}{\sigma^2}H_A^H H_A + Q_s H_B^H(\sigma^2 A + I)^{-1}AH_B\right)$$

$$= \log\det\left((I + \frac{Q_s}{\sigma^2}H_A^H H_A\right) + \log\det(I + AR_{y_B|y_A}) - \log\det(I + \sigma^2 A)$$

(8)

$$\max_{A} \ \log\det(I + AR_{y_B|y_A}) - \log\det(I + \sigma^2 A)$$

$$s.t. \ \log\det(I + AR_{y_B|y_A}) \le R_{BH}$$

$$A \ge 0$$

(9)

4 Simulation and Analysis

In this part, we present the analysis using the system level simulation. Because the proposed method are working in offline mode, so the delay of the system is only evaluated through the platform without theoretical analysis. In Table 1, we present the scenario and parameters of the system level simulation platform. Note that the platform is corrected and synchronized with 3GPP Rel-12 specifications, some of the key parameters and models are secured by Qualcomm.

In the simulation, we simulated the 7 base stations scenario, the channel model is 3 GPP dense urban and antenna configuration is 8 by 8 MIMO mode. The adjacent 2 base stations are cooperated together using the wireless backhaul, the link capacity is limited to 6 Gbps and the delay is 45 ms according to the statistical experiment generated by Tsinghua.

First, system throughput are evaluated. In Fig. 2, we compare the cdf of the average throughput using the system level simulation. The x-axis is the throughput in Gbps and the y-axis is the CDF. There are three sets of data; the red dotted curve is the ideal cooperation without capacity constraint, e.g. using optical fiber or high speed wireless

Table 1. Simulation parameters and assumptions according to our SL simulation platform [29].

Name	Value
Channel model	SCME, denseurban
Carrier frequency	2.2 GHz
Tx antenna	8(maximum)
Rx antenna	8(maximum)
Transmit power	38 dBm
BS number	7
Sectors per BS	3
Backhaul capacity	6Gbps
Backhaul delay	45 ms
Users in simulation	3 per cell
Bandwidth	100 MHz
SL to LL mapping	EESM
Inter-site distance	50 m
Pathloss model	L = 128.1 + 37.6log10(R)
Shadowing Std	4 dB
HARQ scheme	CC
AMC Table	16 QAM(R = {1/8, 1/7, 1/6, 1/5, 1/4, 1/3, 2/5, 1/2, 3/5, 2/3, 3/4, 4/5})
UE sig processing	64QAM(R = {1/2, 3/5, 2/3, 3/4, 4/5})
Max re-trans times	MMSE
UE Speed	4
	1 m/s
Channel Estimation	Ideal
Simulation TTIs	2000

link, the green one means our proposed method using the resource allocation in capacity constraint wireless backhaul and the blue curve is the reference cooperation without the optimization of resource allocation in wireless backhaul.

Results indicate the performance metric clearly, the ideal cooperation perform the best because of the backhaul link offer the unlimited resource. When the capacity of backhaul is limited, that means not all the resource could be transmitted successfully, so the reference method suffered about 15% loss. Our proposed method in the system take up the second place, for we compress the cooperation information before transmit using the backhaul link, the redundancy has been reduced to a acceptable level that accord to the link capacity.

In Fig. 3, we discussed the delay of the different method. Legends are the same in Fig. 2. In this figure, we can see that the proposed method and the ideal cooperation are nearly the same, because the proposed method compress the information and reduce the redundancy, then the failure of transmission are limited to accord with the backhaul. Nevertheless, the reference method do not consider the redundancy, so the cooperation are not always successful due to the limitation of delay tolerance. If the queuing data exceed the delay tolerance, such information will be abandoned.

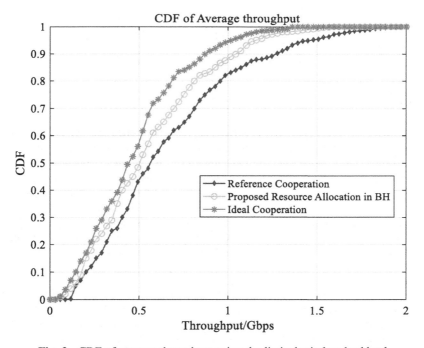

Fig. 2. CDF of average throughput using the limited wireless backhaul

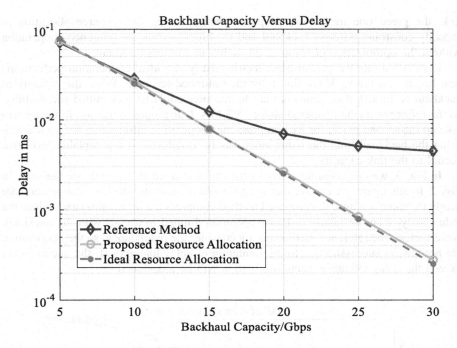

Fig. 3. Delay versus backhaul capacity

5 Conclusion

In this work, we discussed the problem of capacity constraint wireless backhaul resource allocation in 5G wireless networks; we model the performance of capacity and delay and then we propose the compress method in backhaul to enhance system performance. The system level simulation result has been proposed at the end of the work, our proposed method gain 11% of the throughput and 23% of the delay at the most.

Acknowledgement. This work is funded by China's 973 project under grant of 2012CB316002 and China's 863 project under grant of 2013AA013603, National Natural Science Foundation of China(61201192), International Science and Technology Cooperation Program (2012DFG12010); National S&T Major Project (2013ZX03001024-004), Operation Agreement between Tsinghua University and Ericsson, Qualcomm Innovation Fellowship. The work of Su Hu was jointly supported by the MOST Program of International S&T Cooperation (Grant No. 2016YFE0123200), National Natural Science Foundation of China (Grant No. 61471100/61101090/61571082), Science and Technology on Electronic Information Control Laboratory (Grant No. 6142105040103) and Fundamental Research Funds for the Central Universities (Grant No. ZYGX2015J012/ ZYGX2014Z005). We would like to thank all the reviewers for their kind suggestions to this work.

References

1. Haidine, A., Hassani, S.E.: LTE-a pro (4.5G) as pre-phase for 5G deployment: closing the gap between technical requirements and network performance. In: 2016 International Conference on Advanced Communication Systems and Information Security (ACOSIS), Marrakesh, Morocco, pp. 1–7 (2016)
2. Yu, L., et al.: Stochastic load balancing for virtual resource management in datacenters. IEEE Trans. Cloud Comput. **PP**(99), 1 (2016)
3. Jin, R., Zhong, X., Zhou, S.: The access procedure design for low latency in 5G cellular network. In: 2016 IEEE Globecom Workshops (GC Wkshps), Washington, DC, USA, pp. 1–6 (2016)
4. Benfarah, A., Laurenti, N., Tomasin, S.: Resource allocation for downlink of 5G systems with OFDMA under secrecy outage constraints. In: 2016 IEEE Globecom Workshops (GC Wkshps), Washington, DC, USA, pp. 1–6 (2016)
5. Okuyama, T., Suyama, S., Mashino, J., Okumura, Y.: Flexible antenna deployment for 5G distributed Massive MIMO in low SHF bands. In: 2016 10th International Conference on Signal Processing and Communication Systems (ICSPCS), Surfers Paradise, Gold Coaat, Australia, pp. 1–6 (2016)
6. Franco, C.A.S., de Marca, J.R.B., Siqueira, G.L.: A cognitive and cooperative SON framework for 5G mobile radio access networks. In: 2016 IEEE Globecom Workshops (GC Wkshps), Washington, DC, USA, pp. 1–6 (2016)
7. Rimal, B.P., Van, D.P., Maier, M.: Mobile edge computing empowered fiber-wireless access networks in the 5G era. IEEE Commun. Mag. **55**(2), 192–200 (2017)
8. Pedersen, K.I., Niparko, M., Steiner, J., Oszmianski, J., Mudolo, L., Khosravirad, S.R.: System level analysis of dynamic user-centric scheduling for a flexible 5G design. In: 2016 IEEE Global Communications Conference (GLOBECOM), Washington, DC, USA, pp. 1–6 (2016)
9. Al-Falahy, N., Alani, O.Y.: Technologies for 5G networks: challenges and opportunities. In: IT Professional, vol. 19, no. 1, pp. 12–20, January–February 2017
10. Shahab, M.B., Kader, M.F., Shin, S.Y.: On the power allocation of non-orthogonal multiple access for 5G wireless networks. In: 2016 International Conference on Open Source Systems & Technologies (ICOSST), Lahore, Pakistan, pp. 89–94 (2016)
11. Fan, W., et al.: A Step Toward 5G in 2020: Low-cost OTA performance evaluation of massive MIMO base stations. IEEE Antennas Propag. Mag. **59**(1), 38–47 (2017)
12. Hussain, R., Alreshaid, A.T., Podilchak, S.K., Sharawi, M.S.: Compact 4G MIMO antenna integrated with a 5G array for current and future mobile handsets. In: IET Microwaves, Antennas & Propagation, vol. 11, no. 2, pp. 271–279, 29 January 2017
13. Adebomehin, A.A., Walker, S.D.: Ultra-wideband signals for high-resolution cognitive positioning techniques in 5G wireless. In: 2016 IEEE 37th Sarnoff Symposium, Newark, NJ, USA, pp. 1–2 (2016)
14. Aziz, D., Gebert, J., Ambrosy, A., Bakker, H., Halbauer, H.: Architecture approaches for 5G millimetre wave access assisted by 5G low-band using multi-connectivity. In: 2016 IEEE Globecom Workshops (GC Wkshps), Washington, DC, USA, pp. 1–6 (2016)
15. Vishnevsky, V.M., Larionov, A.A., Ivanov, R.E., Dudin, M.: Applying graph-theoretic approach for time-frequency resource allocation in 5G MmWave backhaul network. In: 2016 Advances in Wireless and Optical Communications (RTUWO), Riga, pp. 221–224 (2016)

16. Yang, H., Seet, B.C., Hasan, S.F., Chong, P.H.J., Chung, M.Y.: Radio resource allocation for D2D-enabled massive machine communication in the 5G era. In: 2016 IEEE 14th International Conference on Dependable, Autonomic and Secure Computing, 14th International Conference on Pervasive Intelligence and Computing, 2nd International Conference on Big Data Intelligence and Computing and Cyber Science and Technology Congress(DASC/PiCom/DataCom/CyberSciTech), Auckland, pp. 55–60 (2016)

17. Chen, Z., Li, T., Fan, P., Quek, T.Q.S., Letaief, K.B.: Cooperation in 5G heterogeneous networking: relay scheme combination and resource allocation. IEEE Trans. Commun. **64**(8), 3430–3443 (2016)

18. AlQerm, I., Shihada, B.: A cooperative online learning scheme for resource allocation in 5G systems. In: 2016 IEEE International Conference on Communications (ICC), Kuala Lumpur, pp. 1–7 (2016)

19. Munir, H., Hassan, S.A., Pervaiz, H., Ni, Q.: A game theoretical network-assisted user-centric design for resource allocation in 5G heterogeneous networks. In: 2016 IEEE 83rd Vehicular Technology Conference (VTC Spring), Nanjing, pp. 1–5 (2016)

20. Saeed, A., Katranaras, E., Zoha, A., Imran, A., Imran, M.A., Dianati, M.: Energy efficient resource allocation for 5G heterogeneous networks. In: 2015 IEEE 20th International Workshop on Computer Aided Modelling and Design of Communication Links and Networks (CAMAD), Guildford, pp. 119–123 (2015)

21. Ciou, S.A., Kao, J.C., Lee, C.Y., Chen, K.Y.: Multi-sharing resource allocation for device-to-device communication underlaying 5G mobile networks. In: 2015 IEEE 26th Annual International Symposium on Personal, Indoor, and Mobile Radio Communications (PIMRC), Hong Kong, pp. 1509–1514 (2015)

22. Moya, S.F., Venkatasubramanian, V., Marsch, P., Yaver, A.: D2D mode selection and resource allocation with flexible UL/DL TDD for 5G deployments. In: 2015 IEEE International Conference on Communication Workshop (ICCW), London, pp. 657–663 (2015)

23. Artiga, X., Nunez-Martinez, J., Perez-Neira, A., Vela, G.J.L., Garcia, J.M.F., Ziaragkas, G.: Terrestrial-satellite integration in dynamic 5G backhaul networks. In: 2016 8th Advanced Satellite Multimedia Systems Conference and the 14th Signal Processing for Space Communications Workshop (ASMS/SPSC), Palma de Mallorca, pp. 1–6 (2016)

24. Jaber, M., Imran, M.A., Tafazolli, R., Tukmanov, A.: 5G backhaul challenges and emerging research directions: a survey. In: IEEE Access, vol. 4, pp. 1743–1766 (2016)

25. Pham, A.T., Trinh, P.V., Mai, V.V., Dang, N.T., Truong, C.-T.: Hybrid free-space optics/millimeter-wave architecture for 5G cellular backhaul networks. In: 2015 Opto-Electronics and Communications Conference (OECC), Shanghai, pp. 1–3 (2015)

26. Ahmed, A., Grace, D.: A dual-hop backhaul network architecture for 5G ultra-small cells using millimetre-wave. In: 2015 IEEE International Conference on Ubiquitous Wireless Broadband (ICUWB), Montreal, QC, pp. 1–6 (2015)

27. Weiler, R.J., et al.: Enabling 5G backhaul and access with millimeter-waves. In: 2014 European Conference on Networks and Communications (EuCNC), Bologna, pp. 1–5 (2014)

28. Yu, Y.J., Tsai, W.C., Pang, A.C.: Backhaul traffic minimization under cache-enabled comp transmissions over 5G cellular systems. In: 2016 IEEE Global Communications Conference (GLOBECOM), Washington, DC, USA, pp. 1–7 (2016)

29. Gao, Y., et al.: A novel resource allocation in imperfect D2D cooperation in LTE-Advanced Pro systems. In: 2016 IEEE 7th Annual Information Technology, Electronics and Mobile Communication Conference (IEMCON), Vancouver, BC, pp. 1–5 (2016)

Spectral Partitioning and Fuzzy C-Means Based Clustering Algorithm for Wireless Sensor Networks

Jianji Hu[1], Songtao Guo[1(✉)], Defang Liu[2], and Yuanyuan Yang[3]

[1] College of Electronic and Information Engineering, Southwest University,
Chongqing 400715, China
stguo@swu.edu.in
[2] School of Chemistry and Chemical Engineering,
Southwest University, Chongqing 400715, China
[3] Department of Electrical and Computer Engineering,
Stony Brook University, Stony Brook, NY 11794, USA

Abstract. In wireless sensor networks (WSNs), sensor nodes are usually powered by battery and thus have very limited energy. Saving energy is an important goal in designing a WSN. It is known that clustering is an effective method to prolong network lifetime. However, how to cluster sensor nodes cooperatively and achieve an optimal number of clusters in a WSN still remains an open issue. In this paper, we first propose an analytical model to determine the optimal number of clusters in a wireless sensor network. We then propose a centralized cluster algorithm based on the spectral partitioning method. The advantage of the method is that the partitioned subgraphs have an approximately equal number of vertices while minimizing the number of edges between the two subgraphs. Then, we present a distributed clustering algorithm based on fuzzy C-means method and the selection strategy of cooperative nodes and cluster heads based on fuzzy logic. Finally, simulation results show that the proposed algorithms outperform the hybrid energy-efficient distributed clustering algorithm in terms of energy cost and network lifetime.

Keywords: Clustering · Spectral partitioning · Fuzzy C-means · Cooperative nodes · Wireless sensor networks

1 Introduction

In recent years, wireless sensor networks (WSNs) have been used as an important information gathering paradigm in many applications, such as environmental monitoring, target tracking, battlefield surveillance, home security and health monitoring. A WSN is composed of hundreds or even thousands of sensor nodes to perform distributed sensing tasks. Due to the limited battery capacity and low-cost requirement, sensor nodes are usually equipped with low-end computational module and radio transceiver [1]. As it is infeasible to replace batteries

© Springer International Publishing AG 2017
L. Ma et al. (Eds.): WASA 2017, LNCS 10251, pp. 161–174, 2017.
DOI: 10.1007/978-3-319-60033-8_15

once WSNs are deployed in a harsh environment, an important design principle in WSNs is to minimize energy consumption in sensing, computing and communication.

It has been shown that clustering is an effective scheme in prolonging network lifetime and improving scalability of WSNs [2–4]. Sensor nodes are partitioned into clusters, and each cluster consists of a cluster head (CH) and a number of cluster members. Based on whether sensor nodes can communicate directly with their CH, the clustered WSNs can be classified as single-hop WSNs and multi-hop WSNs. In a multi-hop WSN, the data from some sensor nodes need to be relayed to the CH via multiple hops. The clustered WSNs can also be categorized into homogeneous WSNs and heterogeneous WSNs. A small number of powerful nodes are deployed as cluster heads and the rest of regular nodes act as cluster members. Such a two-layer hybrid network can improve the network lifetime and stability with a marginal increase in the cost of network deployment. Basically, any clustering algorithm involves cluster management which includes determining the suitable number of clusters, selecting the cluster head for each cluster, and transmitting data within clusters and from cluster heads to the sink node [5].

For a clustered WSN, data transmission can be classified into two stages: intra- and inter-cluster communication. One of disadvantages of existing clustering algorithms, such as low-energy adaptive clustering hierarchy (LEACH) [6], hybrid energy-efficient distributed (HEED) [7], centralized LEACH (LEACH-C) [8] and FAR-Zone LEACH (FZ-LEACH) [9], is uneven energy consumption among sensor nodes. Cluster heads tend to consume too much energy due to data gathering and relaying. To improve cluster structure and optimise the selection of cluster heads (CHs), K-means algorithm is very useful in producing clusters for many practical applications including WSN. Several approaches are there based on K-means algorithm [10–15]. However, those K-means based clustering algorithms suffer from some limitations: (i) the initial centroids are chosen just randomly out of the input data set, which leads to local optima and may produce an empty cluster in worst case; (ii) they have very high time complexity and cannot guarantee that the K-means algorithm will converge into best results.

In order to balance the energy consumption between cluster heads and cluster members, we use cooperative nodes located at the edge of clusters and closer to the sink node as relays between cluster heads and the sink node, which can efficiently prolong the lifetime of the network. Furthermore, we utilize spectral partitioning and fuzzy C-means based on midpoint algorithm [16] to produce more balanced cluster compared to K-means. In this paper, we first propose an analytical energy consumption model to determine the optimal number of clusters in a WSN. We then propose a centralized clustering algorithm based on spectral partitioning method. It is shown that the method is robust for graph partitioning, where the network is divided into some clusters based on the characteristics of Laplacian matrix and Fiedler vector. The clusters obtained by the spectral partitioning method have almost same number of cluster members to balance energy consumption among clusters. Furthermore, we present a distributed clustering algorithm based on fuzzy C-means and the selection strategy of cooperative nodes and cluster heads based on fuzzy logic, which optimises CH selection method by considering residual energy. Finally, simulation results verify the performance of the proposed algorithms in terms of network lifetime and node remaining energy.

2   Related Work

In this section, we introduce the existing clustering protocols and overview the fuzzy logic method and the fuzzy C-means (FCM) algorithm.

One of the most classical clustering protocols is LEACH [6], an advantage of which is that it is able to balance the energy consumption among sensor nodes by randomly rotating cluster heads. However, cluster heads located on the edge of a cluster may waste a lot of energy due to the very close distance between cluster heads. The HEED [7] is another well-known clustering algorithm. In this algorithm, residual energy and node proximity to its neighbors are used to select cluster head. In [17], the dynamic cluster head selection method was put forward in order to solve the problem of the unreasonable cluster head selection that may lead to the overlapping coverage and unbalanced energy consumption in the cluster communication. In [18], a novel cluster based routing protocol called LEACH-VH was proposed, in which a new node type called Vice Cluster Head (VH) is introduced in addition to Cluster Head (CH). In [19], the authors introduced a new method using cluster heads with cryptographic keys, for each node, in cluster-based mobile ad hoc networks (MANETs). Furthermore, in [20], for securing CH's data, they proposed a mechanism termed ICMDS (Inter-Cluster Multiple Key Distribution Scheme for Wireless Sensor Networks), which enables the securing of the entire network. In [21], Zhang et al. proposed a femtocells clustering scheme for the femtocell access points (FAPs).

Fuzzy logic has been employed in clustering algorithms to handle the uncertainties in WSNs [10,11,22,23]. In this technique the parameters such as residual energy, distance to sink, node density, load and link quality are considered as input to the fuzzy logic. In [10], an energy aware fuzzy unequal clustering algorithm employs different fuzzy descriptors, i.e., remaining energy, number of neighbor nodes, distance from cluster centroid network traffics, and the distance to the base station, in different environments. In [11], based on the difference in expected residual energy, a fuzzy-logic-based clustering algorithm with an extension to the energy predication was proposed to prolong the lifetime of WSNs by evenly distributing the workload.

The fuzzy C-means (FCM) algorithm was first proposed by Bezdek [24] and has been used in cluster analysis, pattern recognition, image processing. This algorithm is a soft partition technique that assigns a degree of belongingness to a cluster for each sensor node. In [12], the fuzzy C-means (FCM) clustering algorithm was incorporated in the protocol, which was realised on a hardware test-bed with the support of the embedded operating system, TinyOS. In [14], a balanced cluster head selection based on modified k-means was proposed, where more than one CH in a cluster is considered to reduce the time and energy required for re-clustering. In [15], a novel cluster head selection algorithm was proposed based on fuzzy clustering and particle swarm optimization, where fuzzy clustering algorithm is used to initial clustering for sensor nodes according to geographical locations and the cluster head nodes in hierarchical topology are determined based on the improved particle swarm optimization.

3   Network Model and Spectral Classification

In this section, we present the network model, energy model, and introduce briefly Laplacian matrix and spectral classification.

3.1   Network Model

In this paper, we consider a WSN where N sensor nodes are uniformly distributed in an $M \times M$ square area. We model the deployment of sensor nodes as a Poisson distribution [25,26], and use λ to represent the density of the underlying Poisson point process. We assume that the considered sensor network has the following properties and capabilities.

- The network topology keeps unchanged over time, and the base station has unlimited power, computing ability, and locates at the network center.
- Nodes are deployed uniformly and all the nodes are homogeneous.
- Each node is aware of its own position through RSSI localization.
- All sensor nodes are static and their battery cannot be recharged.

The energy of sensor nodes will gradually run out with the information transferring. If the energy of a sensor node is depleted, the node is considered dead. When the number of dead nodes rises to a threshold, the network is considered dead.

3.2   Spectral Partitioning

Spectral clustering algorithms have attracted lots of research attentions recently. Spectral partitioning problem is easy to be solved and implemented by standard linear algebra components, and the spectral clustering algorithms outperform the traditional k-means based clustering algorithms since the latter has some limitations as stated in Sect. 1. Spectral partitioning methods usually involve taking the top eigenvectors of a matrix based on the distance between points (or other properties) and then using them to cluster various points [27]. The second smallest eigenvalue of the Laplacian matrix are associated with connectivity of vertices and the partitioning is achieved by splitting vertices according to their eigenvalues in the corresponding eigenvector.

In this paper, we use an undirected graph $G = (V, E)$ to represent a WSN, where $V = \{v_1, \ldots, v_N\}$ denotes the set of sensor nodes, and $E = \{e_1, \ldots, e_N\}$ indicates the set of wireless links. Let $A_{mtx} = A_{mtx}(G)$ be the adjacency matrix of graph G. In addition, degree matrix $D_{mtx} \in \mathcal{R}^{N \times N}$ of G is a diagonal matrix where d_{ii} is the vertex degree of node i. We can get the Laplacian matrix of graph G by

$$L_{mtx} = D_{mtx} - A_{mtx}. \tag{1}$$

We sort the eigenvalues of $L_{mtx}(G)$ in the order of $\lambda_0 \le \lambda_1 \le \lambda_2 \cdots \le \lambda_{N-1}$. For the second smallest eigenvector v_1, we let V^- denote the set of nodes corresponding to $v_1 < 0$ and V^+ be the set of nodes for $v_1 > 0$. Then we have

$$V^0 = V - V^- - V^+ \tag{2}$$

Then, the set of vertices will be defined by $V = V^+ \bigcup V^-$, where V^+ and V^- are taken as the vertex sets of two new subgraph obtained by spectral graph partitioning, respectively. Spectral graph partitioning is a method of partitioning a graph into two subgraphs such that the subgraphs have an approximately equal number of vertices while minimizing the number of edges between the two subgraphs. In this paper, we use the second smallest eigenvector v_1 of Laplacian matrix $L_{mtx}(G)$ of the graph representing the WSN to determine the optimal bipartitions of a given graph, which will be presented in Subsect. 4.2.

4   Proposed Algorithm

In this section, we propose our clustering algorithms, which consists of three steps: (1) Determining the optimal number of clusters; (2) Achieving distributed clustering; (3) Rotating cluster heads and cooperative nodes.

4.1   Optimal Number of Clusters

It is important to determine the number of clusters, denoted by k, because the amount of inter-cluster communications increases as k increases. On the other hand, the amount of intra-cluster communications grows significantly as k decreases. In the following, we will derive the optimal number of clusters by analyzing the energy model.

Suppose that each cluster area is a square of size $D \times D$. Given the Poisson distribution with density λ, there are λD^2 sensor nodes in each cluster on average. Thus, the number of clusters is $\frac{N}{\lambda D^2}$, and each cluster has on average N/k nodes, i.e., one cluster head and $N/k - 1$ cluster member nodes. After sensor nodes are partitioned into clusters, each cluster member sends the sensed data to its cluster head. The cluster head processes the data and then forwards them to its members that are located near the boundary of the cluster and closer to the sink node while having sufficient residual energy. These members are called as relay nodes. The total energy dissipated in one round of data collection in cluster A can be calculated by

$$E_{cluster} = E_{ch} + \left(\frac{N}{k} - 1 \right) E_{non-ch} \tag{3}$$

$$\approx E_{ch} + \frac{N}{k} E_{non-ch}$$

where E_{ch} denotes the energy consumption of cluster head and E_{non-ch} is the energy consumption of one cluster member. As the cluster head does not transmit the data to another cluster head directly, when the CH transmits an l bit message over distance d_{cn}, by using the similar energy model in [8], E_{ch} can be derived by

$$E_{ch} = \left(\frac{N}{k} - 1\right) * l * E_{elec} + \frac{N}{k} * l * E_{DA}$$
$$+ l * E_{elec} + l * \varepsilon_{fs} * d_{cn}^2 \tag{4}$$

where E_{elec} is the energy dissipated per bit on the transmitter or the receiver circuit, E_{DA} is the processing (data aggregation) cost of a bit transmitted to cooperative node, ε_{fs} indicates the energy loss rate per unit of data transmission of the transmitter for $d_{cn} < d_0$, d_{cn} is the distance from cluster head to cooperative node and d_0 denotes a given distance threshold. Based on Eq. (4), we can get

$$E_{cluster} = E_{ch} + \left(\frac{N}{k}\right) E_{non-ch}$$
$$= \left(\frac{N}{k} - 1\right) * l * E_{elec} + \frac{N}{k} * l * E_{DA} + l * E_{elec} + l * \varepsilon_{fs} * d_{cn}^2$$
$$+ \lambda D^2 \left(l * E_{elec} + \varepsilon_{fs}\frac{M^2}{6k}\right) \tag{5}$$

and the total energy consumption for one round of data collection is

$$E_{total} = k * E_{cluster}$$
$$= \left(\frac{M^2}{D^2}\right) \times \lambda D^2 \left(LE_{elec} + l\varepsilon_{fs}\frac{M^2}{6k}\right)$$
$$+ k \times \left(\left(\frac{N}{k} - 1\right) * l * E_{elec}\right.$$
$$+ \frac{N}{k} * l * E_{DA} + l * E_{elec} + l * \varepsilon_{fs} * d_{cn}) \tag{6}$$

By setting the derivative of E_{total} with respect to k to zero, we can get the optimal number of clusters,

$$k_{opt} = \sqrt{\frac{M^2 N}{6d_{cn}^2}} \tag{7}$$

to reach the minimum value of E_{total}.

4.2   Clustering Algorithm

Centralized Clustering Algorithm. In this part, we propose a centralized clustering algorithm based on the spectral partitioning method to partition the network into a fixed optimal number of clusters. We assume the sink node has full knowledge of the network topology. The sink node employs the spectral partitioning as given in Subsect. 3.2 to divide the sensor nodes into k_{opt} clusters and connect all CHs, where k_{opt} can given by (7) in Subsect. 4.1.

As aforementioned in Subsect. 3.2, we use the second eigenvector of Laplacian matrix, also named as Fiedler vector, of the graph representing the WSN, to determine the optimal bipartitions of a given graph. The process of the spectral partitioning based clustering algorithm consists of two phases, i.e., recursively partitioning the graph into two subgraphs as given in Algorithm 1, and repeatedly applying the same procedures to the subgraphs until the number of subgraphs reaches k_{opt}. According to Algorithm 1, we can get two disjoint graphs G_1 and G_2 and the number of the nodes in G_1 and G_2 is almost same. After spectral partitioning, we can obtain k_{opt} clusters. As shown in Fig. 1, 200 sensor nodes are partitioned into 6 clusters using our proposed spectral partitioning method, which are depicted in 6 colors.

Algorithm 1. Spectral partitioning based clustering algorithm

---

Input:
    The graph $G = (V, E)$;
Output:
    $G_1 = (V_1, E_1)$, $G_2 = (V_2, E_2)$;
 1: compute Laplacian matrix v of graph G by (1);
 2: sort the eigenvalues of $L_{mtx}(G)$ in the order of $\lambda_0 \leq \lambda_1 \leq \lambda_2 \cdots \leq \lambda_{N-1}$;
 3: compute Fiedler eigenvector $v = \{v_i | i = 0, ..., N - 1\}$ corresponding to second
    smallest eigenvalue λ_1;
 4: **for** each node i in G **do**
 5:     **if** $v_i < 0$ **then**
 6:         put node i in partition V_1;
 7:     **else if** $v_i > 0$ **then**
 8:         put node i in partition V_2;
 9:     **else**
10:         denote node i as an isolated node.
11:     **end if**
12: **end for**

Distributed Clustering Algorithm. It is clear that a distributed algorithm would be desirable in WSNs, since it is very difficult for a node to get full knowledge of the overall network. We assume that the sink is aware of the sensing field, but does not need to know the exact locations of sensor nodes. In our proposed distributed algorithm, the sink divides the field into k_{opt} clusters by using fuzzy C-means (FCM), calculates the geographic central point of each cluster area by the midpoint algorithm in [16], and broadcasts the information to all sensor nodes. The sensor nodes in each cluster elect their CH. The sensor node closest to the center of the cluster area is elected as the CH. The CHs then broadcast advertisement messages to sensor nodes to invite them to join their

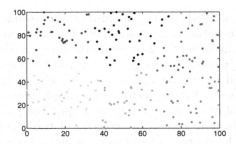

Fig. 1. 6 clusters for 200 nodes obtained by spectral partitioning method.

respective clusters. In the following, we give the main processes of distributed clustering algorithm.

Given a sensing field and the optimal number of clusters, the sink needs to find out the central points of k_{opt} cluster areas. We first divide the whole sensing field into small grids and place a virtual node at the center of each grid to represent the grid. We let V' denote the set of virtual nodes in the network and V'' indicate the set of approximate central points of k_{opt} clusters in the sensing field. After getting the geographic location of the central point of a cluster, the sensor node closest to the central point will become the CH. To elect the CH, we let all nodes within the range of R from the central point be the CH candidates and each candidate broadcasts a CH election message that contains its identifier and location. After a timeout, the candidate with the smallest distance to the central point of the cluster becomes the CH node.

When a CH is elected, the CH broadcasts an advertisement message to other sensor nodes in the sensor field, to invite them to join the cluster. During this phase, each non-CH node joins the cluster with the closest CH node based on the received signal strength of the advertisement message. After that, the sensor node informs the CH node that it will be a member of the cluster by sending a short join message. The process of the distributed algorithm is shown in Algorithm 2.

4.3   Selection of Cooperative Nodes and Cluster Head

In this section, we would like to present how to select cooperative nodes and cluster heads.

Selection of Cooperative Sensor Nodes. The selection of cooperative nodes (CNs) impacts the network lifetime. Thus, it is expected to design an appropriate selection strategy. During the initialization phase, the sink node broadcasts several *BEACON* messages periodically to all sensor nodes at a fixed power level. The nodes near the sink node receive the messages and flood them to the rest of the network.

The best candidate CNs are the sensor nodes that have sufficient residual energy and receive more BEACON messages. When a sensor node v receives a

---

Algorithm 2. Distributed Clustering Algorithm

Input:
  Graph $G = (V, E)$ and V'
Output:
  k clusters;
1: **for** each $j \in V'$ **do**
2:    compute the coefficient u_{ij} for being a member of cluster i, i.e., $u_{ij} = \frac{1}{\sum_1^k (d_{ij}/d_{kj})^{2/(m-1)}}$
3: **end for**
4: **for** $i = 1 \to k_{opt}$ **do**
5:    compute the centroid V'' of cluster i by
     $pos(center_i) = \frac{\sum_{j=1}^n u_{ij}^m pos(node j)}{\sum_{j=1}^k u_{ij}^m}$
6: **end for**
7: **for** $j' \in V$ **do**
8:    compute distance d_{toch} between j' and V'';
9:    **if** $d_{toch} < R$ **then**
10:      j' becomes a CH candidate
11:      j' broadcasts a CH *election* message;
12:    **end if**
13: **end for**
14: CH candidate with the shortest distance to the central (V'') of the cluster becomes Cluster head;
15: **for** $i' = 1 \to k_{opt}$ **do**
16:    broadcast *advertisement* messages to the sensor field
17:    for $j' \in V$ decide cluster to join into;
18: **end for**

BEACON message, it increases the BEACON counter n_b by one and records the signal strength s. Then, the sensor node calculates a probability of being selected as a CN, v_{chance}, based on its residual energy, the counter n_b, and the average signal strength of the received BEACON messages, i.e., v_{chance} can be calculated by

$$v_{chance} = a_1 \frac{E_{res}}{E_{max}} + a_2 n_b + a_3 \frac{\sum s}{n_b} \tag{8}$$

where a_1, a_2 and a_3 are weight coefficients of the residual energy, and the number of received BEACON messages and the average signal strength of received BEACON messages, respectively. E_{res} and E_{max} denote the residual energy and maximum energy of sensor node, respectively.

Subsequently, the node v sends a candidate message containing its identification and the probability value to the cluster head. The nodes with higher probability values are more likely to be elected as CNs. The role of CNs would be rotated among cluster members when the energy level of a CN drops below an energy threshold.

Selection of Cluster Head. Fuzzy logic is very suitable for implementing the heuristic clustering. This is because it does not require the precise and noise-free inputs and can be programmed to fail safely. The model of fuzzy logic control consists of a fuzzier, fuzzy inference engine, and a defuzzier. In this paper, we use fuzzy inference (FIS) to calculate the probability for a node to become a CH. The input variables of fuzzy inference are the residual energy E_{res} and the distance to the central node D_{tocn}, and the output is the probability of the node to be selected as a CH.

The first input variable of fuzzy logic is the distance between the sensor node and the central node, which have three values: close, medium and far. The values of close and far choose the trapezoidal membership function and the function of medium is a triangular membership function. The second one is the residual energy of the sensor node, with the values of low, rather low, medium, rather high and high. The values of low and high corresponds to a trapezoidal membership function, while other values of the variable use a triangular membership function.

Based on the two fuzzy input variables, the corresponding fuzzy mapping rules can be determined. We can derive the fuzzy output of probability by the fuzzy rules. This fuzzy variable has to be transformed into a single crisp number with practical form. This process is called defuzzification and the center of area (COA) can induced by the following defuzzification method

$$output = \frac{\int x * \mu_{chance}(x)dx}{\int xdx}, \tag{9}$$

where $\mu_{chance}(x)$ denotes the membership function of the fuzzy set of probability, and x denotes fuzzy input variable. A node which holds more residual energy and is close to the cooperative sensor node has a higher probability to become a CH.

5   Simulation Results

In this section, we present the simulation results to evaluate the proposed algorithms. In our simulation, sensor nodes are distributed in a $100\,\text{m} * 100\,\text{m}$ area. The sink node is located at a central point $(50, 50)$. We compare our algorithms with HEED algorithm [7] from four respects: the number of rounds until the first node dies, the number of alive sensor nodes over time, the evolution of the remaining energy in the network, and the impact of the initial energy on the performance. This is because similar to our algorithm, HEED algorithm also consider residual energy to select cluster head. We ignore the effect caused by the transmission collisions and the interference in wireless channels.

5.1   Number of Rounds for the First Node Died

It is preferred that all sensor nodes stay alive as long as possible because network performance drops once there is a node to die. Thus it is important to know when the first node dies. The time when the first node dies in the simulations for all compared algorithms can be found in Figs. 2 and 3. Figure 2 shows the performances of these clustering algorithms by increasing the number of sensor nodes, N, from 100 to 300. When there are 200 nodes in the given sensing area, the first node death occurs at the 700-th round by our distributed algorithm, while it is about at the 600-th round by HEED algorithm. It can be seen from Fig. 3 that when the initial energy of sensor nodes is increased from 0.5 to 1.5 and then up to 2.5, the advantage of our algorithms over HEED becomes more evident in terms of prolonging the network lifetime. This is because compared to HEED, our algorithm can obtain the optimal number of clusters based on the network energy model and provide an optimal cluster head selection strategy to minimize energy consumption.

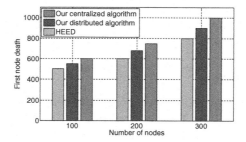

Fig. 2. Impact of the node density.

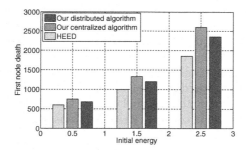

Fig. 3. Impact of the initial energy.

5.2   Node Lifetime

In this subsection, we set the number of sensor nodes to 200, and the initial of each node is $0.5J$. Figure 4 shows the number of nodes alive over time for all compared algorithms. It is clear that our algorithms can improve the network lifetime (the difference between the time that the first node dies and the time that the last node dies) compared to HEED. This is because that our algorithms adopt two strategies to balance the energy consumption among nodes. We first

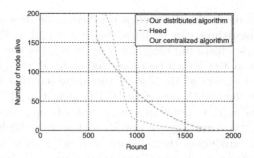

Fig. 4. Number of nodes alive over time

choose cooperative nodes to reduce energy consumption of cluster heads and then we choose cluster heads based on the strategy determined by FIS. The formation of clusters based on the remaining energy of nodes allows the nodes with low energy levels to have a lower probability of to be selected.

5.3   Residual Energy

Figure 5 depicts the total residual energy in the network after a large number of rounds of data collection. We can observe that the network residual energy decreases more rapidly in HEED algorithm than that in our algorithms. We can see that after 1000 rounds of data collection, approximately 95 percent of the total energy is consumed in HEED algorithm. However, but only 82 of total energy is consumed in our centralized algorithm. This improvement is attributed to the consideration of the distance to central nodes and the strategy of cooperative relay, which can efficiently reduce energy consumption in both intra-class and inter-class formation. In fact, the consideration in cluster head selection can ensure the nodes close to the central nodes have higher probability to become cluster heads. The proposed algorithm can also make the nodes distributed uniformly for the different clusters. Besides, our proposed scheme succeeds to rotate the cooperative nodes based on the distance to BS and residual energy. Clearly, cooperative nodes can save the energy consumption of inter-class data transmission.

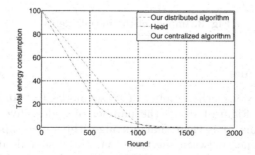

Fig. 5. Residual energy in the network.

6   Conclusions

In this paper, we aim to find an efficient way to prolong the lifetime of wireless sensor networks. In order to reduce the energy consumption of cluster heads, we use cooperative nodes to relay data to the sink node. Based on the energy model, we obtain the optimal number of clusters which can balance the energy consumption of inter-cluster and communication. Furthermore, we propose a centralized algorithm based on spectral partitioning and a distributed algorithm based on fuzzy C-means method to divide the network into clusters. To balance the energy consumption of sensor nodes, we propose an efficient strategy to choose cooperative nodes and cluster heads. It has been shown by simulations that our proposed algorithms achieve a significant performance improvement.

Acknowledgments. This work was supported by the National Natural Science Foundation of China (Nos. 61503309, 61373179, 61373178, 61402381), Natural Science Key Foundation of Chongqing (cstc2015jcyjBX0094), Natural Science Foundation of Chongqing (CSTC2016JCYJA0449).

References

1. Asada, G., Dong, M., Lin, T.S., Newberg, F., Pottie, G., Kaiser, W.J., Marcy, H.O.: Wireless integrated network sensors: low power systems on a chip. In: Proceedings of 24th European Solid-State Circuits Conference, pp. 9–16, September 1998
2. Gong, D., Yang, Y., Pan, Z.: Energy-efficient clustering in lossy wireless sensor networks. J. Parallel Distrib. Comput. **73**, 1323–1336 (2013)
3. Zhang, Z., Ma, M., Yang, Y.: Energy-efficient multi-hop polling in clusters of two-layered heterogeneous sensor networks. IEEE Trans. Comput. **57**, 231–245 (2008)
4. Ma, M., Yang, Y.: Clustering and load balancing in hybrid sensor networks with mobile cluster heads. In: Proceedings of the Third ACM International Conference on Quality of Service in Heterogeneous Wired/Wireless Networks (QShine) (2006)
5. Kumar, D.: Performance analysis of energy efficient clustering protocols for maximising lifetime of wireless sensor networks. Wirel. Sens. Syst. **4**(1), 9–16 (2014)
6. Heinzelman, W., Chandrakasan, A., Balakrishnan, H.: Energy-efficient communication protocol for wireless microsensor networks. In: Proceedings of 33rd Annual Hawaii International Conference on System Sciences, pp. 10–20, January 2000
7. Younis, O., Fahmy, S.: Distributed clustering in ad-hoc sensor networks: a hybrid, energy-efficient approach. In: Proceedings of 23rd Annual Joint Conference of the IEEE Computer and Communications Societies, vol. 1, p. 640, March 2004
8. Heinzelman, W., Chandrakasan, A., Balakrishnan, H.: An application-specific protocol architecture for wireless microsensor networks. Proc. IEEE Trans. Wirel. Commun. **1**(4), 660–670 (2002)
9. Katiyar, V., Chand, N., Gautam, G., Kumar, A.: Improvement in leach protocol for large-scale wireless sensor networks. In: Proceedings of 2011 International Conference on Emerging Trends in Electrical and Computer Technology, pp. 1070–1075, March 2011
10. Bagci, H., Yazici, A.: An energy aware fuzzy unequal clustering algorithm for wireless sensor networks. In: Proceedings of 2010 IEEE International Conference on Fuzzy Systems, pp. 1–8, July 2010

11. Lee, J., Cheng, W.: Fuzzy logic based clustering approach for wireless sensor networks using energy predication. IEEE Sens. J. **12**(9), 2891–2897 (2012)

12. Hoang, D.C., Kumar, R., Panda, S.K.: Realisation of a cluster-based protocol using fuzzy c-means algorithm for wireless sensor networks. IET Wirel. Sens. Syst. **3**(3), 163–171 (2013)

13. Harb, H., Makhoul, A., Couturier, R.: An enhanced k-means and anova-based clustering approach for similarity aggregation in underwater wireless sensor networks. IEEE Sens. J. **15**(10), 5483–5493 (2015)

14. Periyasamy, S., Khara, S., Thangavelu, S.: Balanced cluster head selection based on modified k-means in a distributed wireless sensor network. Int. J. Distrib. Sens. Netw. Article ID **5040475**, 1–11 (2016)

15. Ni, Q., Pan, Q., Du, H., Cao, C., Zhai, Y.: A novel cluster head selection algorithm based on fuzzy clustering and particle swarm optimization. IEEE/ACM Trans. Comput. Biol. Bioinform. **14**(1), 76–84 (2017)

16. Aggarwal, N., Aggarwal, K.: A mid-point based k-mean clustering algorithm for data mining. Int. J. Comput. Sci. Eng. **4**(6), 1174–1180 (2012)

17. Jia, D., Zhu, H., Zou, S., Hu, P.: Dynamic cluster head selection method for wireless sensor network. IEEE Sens. J. **16**(8), 2746–2754 (2016)

18. Mehmood, A., Lloret, J., Noman, M., Song, H.: Improvement of the wireless sensor network lifetime using leach with vice-cluster head. Ad Hoc Sens. Wirel. Netw. **28**(1), 1–17 (2015)

19. Umar, M., Mehmood, A., Song, H.: SeCRoP: secure cluster head centered multihop routing protocol for mobile ad hoc networks. Secur. Commun. Netw. **9**(16), 3378–3387 (2016)

20. Mehmood, A., Umar, M.M., Song, H.: ICMDS: secure inter-cluster multiple-key distribution scheme for wireless sensor networks. Ad Hoc Netw. **55**, 97–106 (2017)

21. Zhang, H., Jiang, D., Li, F., Liu, K., Song, H., Dai, H.: Cluster-based resource allocation for spectrum-sharing femtocell networks. IEEE Access **4**, 8643–8656 (2016)

22. Gupta, I., Riordan, D., Sampalli, S.: Cluster-head election using fuzzy logic for wireless sensor networks. In: Proceedings of 3th Annual Communication Networks and Services Research Conference, pp. 255–260, May 2005

23. Kim, J.M., Park, S.H., Han, Y.J., Chung, T.M.: CHEF: cluster head election mechanism using fuzzy logic in wireless sensor networks. In: Proceedings of 10th International Conference on Advanced Communication Technology, vol. 1, pp. 654–659, February 2008

24. Bezdek, J.C.: Pattern Recognition with Fuzzy Objective Function Algorithms. Springer, Heidelberg (1981). ISBN: 978-1-4757-0452-5

25. Xie, R., Jia, X.: Transmission-efficient clustering method for wireless sensor networks using compressive sensing. IEEE Trans. Parallel Distrib. Syst. **25**(3), 806–815 (2014)

26. Wang, D., Lin, L., Xu, L.: A study of subdividing hexagon-clustered wsn for power saving: analysis and simulation. Ad Hoc Netw. **9**(7), 1302–1311 (2011)

27. Ding, S., Zhang, L., Zhang, Y.: Research on spectral clustering algorithms and prospects. In: Proceedings of 2th International Conference on Computer Engineering and Technology, vol. 6, pp. 149–153, April 2010

Regionalization Compressive Sensing for Optimizing Lifetime of Sensor Networks

Hao Yang[1,2(✉)], Hua Xu[1], and Xiwei Wang[3]

[1] Yancheng Normal University, Yancheng, China
anysuc@163.com
[2] Jiangsu Key Laboratory for Big Data of Psychology and Cognitive Science,
Yancheng, China
[3] Northeastern Illinois University, Chicago, USA

Abstract. Compressive Sensing (CS) has been adopted to address the center problem. However, this technology still has to waste much unnecessary energy. In this paper, we propose a hybrid CS approach through regionalizing the topology of the network to optimize its lifetime. To reduce transmission cost of sensor, the topology of the network is divided into several subareas, and CS is implemented respectively. Subsequently, measurements from each region are transported to the sink for recovery. To further guarantee its availability, we design a suitable measurement matrix to decrease the energy cost, and present an optimization approach to obtain effective routing with low cost. Experiments reveal that the proposed approach is superior to other CS-based methods and the two advanced issues further guarantee its feasibility.

Keywords: Compressive sensing, measurement matrix, route · Wireless sensor network

1 Introduction

Compresssive Sensing (CS) [1] has been effectively utilized to reduce consumption for transmitting data packages [2, 3]. For traditional transmission methods, it is obvious for the center area which is closed to the sink to cost a lot of energy. This is so call the center problem. According to CS theory, it is able to effectively avoid this phenomenon. Meanwhile, a high accurate reconstruction could be obtained. The Fig. 1 reveals the effects of approximation of natural signals. Unfortunately, traditional CS may be not better than no-CS scheme sometimes in practice [4–8], since edge nodes may spend more energy in CS than in no-CS. In detail, they have to transport a fixed number while just few ones for the traditional direct transmission methods.

To address this problem, we propose a CS-based approach based on regionalization in this paper. Its basic idea is to reduce energy cost of inner sensors as many as possible. Moreover, we discuss two advanced issues to further improve the performance of this approach in practical application. Our experiments validate that the performance of our approach is better than that of other CS-based methods through contrasting different parameters of the data package in different scales of the network. Meanwhile, the availabilities of the mentioned issues are verified.

© Springer International Publishing AG 2017
L. Ma et al. (Eds.): WASA 2017, LNCS 10251, pp. 175–184, 2017.
DOI: 10.1007/978-3-319-60033-8_16

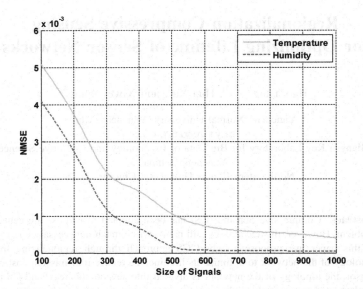

Fig. 1. Comparison of the frontier biggest coefficients and all ones by NMSE. DCT is employed for sparse transform

2 Our Approach

2.1 Problem

A doubt that whether CS always outperforms traditional methods has been noticed. Luo et al. [4] proposed this problem and discussed that traditional CS may be not better than no-CS schemes sometimes. In fact, edge nodes in the network need not relay data from other nodes and thus could employ no-CS method for data transmission for saving unnecessary waste. Caione et al. [6, 7] further verify this idea in Zigbee network. However, these methods still requires that a lot of inner sensors have to cost unnecessary energy.

2.2 Basic Idea

In our work, we propose a hybrid CS(HCS) based on regionalization for data gathering. Its basic idea is that traditional CS is carried out separately in each subarea to save energy costs of the whole network, and then the combination values in subareas will be transported using a simple transmission scheme. Its superiorities are as following:

- Samplings are measured by each subarea, and thus the potential center problem will not appear.
- More nodes are regarded as boundary ones. In this case, energy costs are saving as more as possible.

3 Advanced in Practice

3.1 Measurement Matrix

In our work, we design a suitable measurement matrix to reduce the energy cost of the network. The elements of the measurement matrix ϕ are as follows

$$\phi_{i,j} = \begin{cases} -1, & p_1 \\ 0, & p_2 \\ 1, & p_3 \end{cases}$$

Here, $p_1 + p_2 + p_3 = 1$ and each of them is greater than 0. According our experiments, it is better that both p_1 and p_3 are nearly the same.

3.2 Routing

This paper utilizes and optimizes a Ricci flow-based method in order to obtain an optimal route while saving the relative consumption in the process of construction. In general, a simple Ricci flow-based scheme demands tremendous costs in the process of virtual mapping [9]. In this paper, we propose an optimal method through choosing candidate nodes for virtual transformation beforehand. In detail, we predefine a selection probability to select suitable nodes from the neighbor of the boundaries of subareas. Suppose the selection probability is q whose range is from −1 to 1. Here, $q \in [-1, 0]$ denotes that the elected nodes are in the subareas and $q \in [0, 1]$ denotes that they are out of the subareas. According to our candidate set, the process of transformation will reduce and the energy cost could decrease greatly.

The processing of our optimal method is as follow:

1. Predefine a selection probability to get a candidate set.
2. In the range of the radius of corresponding of sensors.
3. Embed each vertex's related face onto the plane.
4. Find a point that is no more than the range of the radius of corresponding.
5. Map each vertex to its virtual coordinate in this Kelvin model.

4 Evaluations

4.1 Comparison

In this section, our scheme is compared to two CS-based data gathering approaches in previous literatures [6, 7], which are the traditional CS(TCS) and its improved method (ICS). We evaluate the energy consumptions and the number of data transmission for each node in the different dimensions of network. In our experiments, the network consists of various nodes. In details, four groups are employed, which are 100, 300, 500, 1000. Different scales of the network will exhibit the superiority of our approach in the round.

Firstly, we verify the relationship between the number of nodes and energy cost for three schemes. In our experiments, we verify them through a hundred tests and use an average result to avoid the impact of some unknown or uncertain factors. The results are demonstrated in Fig. 2. For TCS, it has to need the most consumption, since the leaf nodes of the network will spend a lot of unnecessary costs. Furthermore, the waste energy will become increasing as the number of nodes in the network enlarges. The reason is that the edge of the network is expanded and the corresponding number of leaf nodes aggrandizes. For ICS, its performance is superior to TCS. It means that the improved strategy is available and feasible. Compared to TCS, its detail advantage is that the energy costs of each leaf node and the related neighbor nodes are saving as many as possible. In addition, the energy spend will reduce more and more when the number of sensors increases, because the probability of leaf nodes becomes large as the boundary of the network enlarges. For our HCS, it outperforms TCS and ICS in total. It verifies that our approach is practical and could be employed in wireless sensor network. More importantly, the increasing tendency of energy cost is gradually smooth. In the other words, the growth rate for HCS is lower than that for other approaches. Hence, it is very suitable for large scale sensor networks.

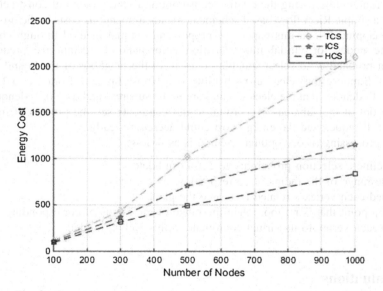

Fig. 2. Comparison of the number of transmission, TCS, ICS, and HCS

Subsequently, we demonstrate that the relation between the number of nodes and the dispersion degree of energy distribution for TCS, ICS and HCS. Here, the dispersion degree of energy distribution is defined as follows:

If the network consists of n nodes and the node i costs e_i, then the dispersion degree of energy distribution is

$$\frac{\sum_{i=1}^{n}(e_i - \text{mean})^2}{\text{mean}}, \text{ where mean is equal to } \frac{\sum_{i=1}^{n} e_i}{n}$$

The experimental results are illustrated in Fig. 3. For TCS, its dispersion degree of energy distribution has no deviation, since all nodes will cost the same energy according to compressive sensing theory. That is, it corresponds to the requirement of balancing energy costs. However, the balance results in a more energy cost in the view of the global network. For ICS, its dispersion degree of energy distribution is out of balance. The reason is that the edge of the network costs lower than the inter network, which lead to the inter nodes become invalid before the leaf ones. From this perspective, it is obvious that the saved energy for the edge of the network is no sense. These existent nodes cannot transmit their reading to the sink. For HCS, its dispersion degree of energy distribution is the largest, because more nodes cost their energy on the basis of the actual situation. The sort of unbalance may be benefit for prolong the lifetime of the network. That is, HCS is more apt for the practical sensor network.

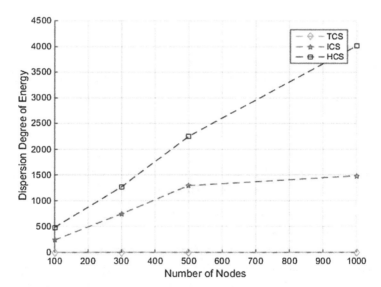

Fig. 3. The relation between the number of nodes and the dispersion degree of energy distribution for TCS, ICS and HCS

4.2 Availability of Measurement Matrix

To validate the availability of our measurement matrix, we verify different relationships, which are the relationship between the probability of nonzero elements and the rate of successfully reconstruction, the relationship between the number of nodes and the length of data package, and the relationship between the absolute value of different of $p_1 - p_3$ and the length of data package, respectively.

Firstly, we show that the relationship between the probability of nonzero elements and the rate of successfully reconstruction based on different sums of $p_1 + p_3$. According to CS theory, the nonzero cannot be reduced unboundedly. In the other words, the probability of nonzero should be maintained in a certain level. Using our measurement matrix, the nonzero number is -1 and 1, therefore the value of p_1 and p_3 should be considered. The summation of them determines the successful rate of recovering the original signal. The Fig. 4 demonstrates the result. When the summation is equal to or more than 0.5, we are able to reconstruct the signal successfully. Nevertheless, the successful rate will drop sharply when the summation is less than the 0.5, since the require mapping in the process of measurement cannot be realized probably.

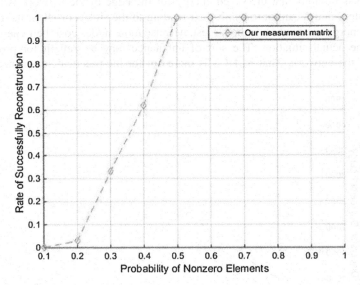

Fig. 4. The relationship between the probability of nonzero elements and the rate of successfully reconstruction based on different sums of $p_1 + p_3$

Furthermore, the relationship between the number of nodes and the length of data package is verified. The length of data package in the process of transmission is an importance metric that measures the energy cost of each sensor in time. According to the above discussion, it is better that the value of summation of measurement parameters is stable. That is, it requires the little change. On this occasion, we suppose that $|p_1 - p_3| = 0$. In addition, we let that the size of measurement is equal to one for simplicity. The results are shown in the Fig. 5.

Afterwards, we consider that the relationship between the absolute value of different of $p_1 - p_3$ and the length of data package. In our experiments, we adopt the scale of the network is 1000. According to the results in the Fig. 6, the length of data package become longer as the absolute value of different of $p_1 - p_3$ is bigger. Furthermore, the speed of increasing for the length of data package is becoming faster. It means that the energy cost of transmission will need more if the different of $p_1 - p_3$ is

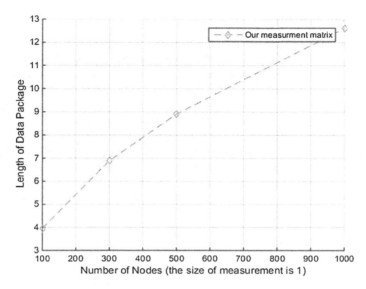

Fig. 5. The relationship between the number of nodes and the length of data package when the size of measurement is 1 and $|p_1 - p_3| = 0$

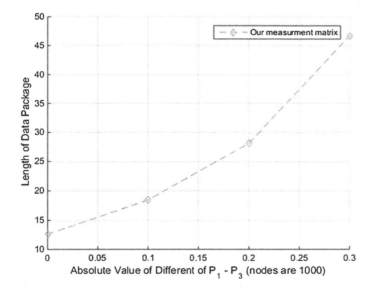

Fig. 6. The relationship between the absolute value of different of $p_1 - p_3$ and the length of data package when the number of nodes is 1000

larger. The reason is that the effect of offset will not valid when both p_1 and p_3 make a great difference. Thus, we should choose similar values for p_1 and p_3 in order to save the energy consumptions in the process of data transmission.

4.3 Feasibility of Route

First of all, we illustrate the relationship between the number of nodes and the successful rate of our optimal solution. As shown in the Fig. 7, when $q \in [0, 1]$, the successful rate is the lowest. It is because lots of required nodes cannot be selected for transforming to virtual coordinators and thus results in the problem of the hole may not be addressed probably. When q belongs to $[-1, 0]$, the successful rate is higher. At this time, more required nodes are mapped and obtained corresponding virtual coordinators. The reason is that the effective nodes for constructing routing are mostly located in each region, nor outside its edge. Both of selection are not comprehensive and not all suitable nodes are choice. More importantly, the successful rate becomes decreasing as the number of nodes increases. Hence, we validate the selection probability $q \in [-1, 1]$. According to experimental results, the successful rate achieves 100% in different scales of networks.

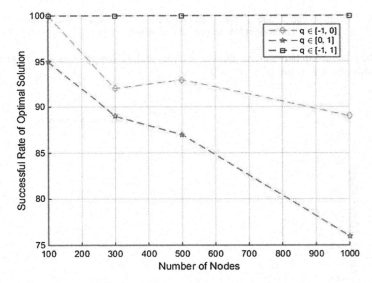

Fig. 7. The relationship between the number of nodes and the successful rate of optimal solution with no energy limited

Secondly, we illustrate the relationship between the number of nodes and energy costs. For simplify, suppose the energy cost is 1 when q belongs to $[-1, 1]$. We compare to the energy consumptions in the case of $q \in [0, 1]$ and $q \in [-1, 0]$. Based on the results in the Fig. 8, the case of $q \in [0, 1]$ costs the most energy, since a lot of nodes are selected to construct route for the network. In case of $q \in [-1, 1]$, the number of selected nodes are more than the case of $q \in [0, 1]$, however, these choice ones are suitable for mapping to virtual coordinators and thus the corresponding cost is lower. For the case of $q \in [-1, 0]$, it spend lower cost than that of case of $q \in [0, 1]$. Because it elects few nodes for virtual transformation.

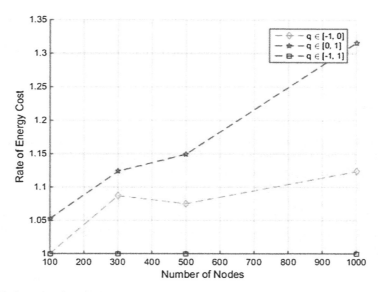

Fig. 8. The relationship between the number of nodes and the rate of energy cost

Finally, we give that the relationship between the number of nodes and the successful rate of optimal solution when the energy cost is fixed. In practice, the energy of each sensor is limited and fixed in a certain range. In this case, we have to prescribe a limit to the cost of the sensor. The experimental results are in the Fig. 9. For the case of $q \in [-1, 1]$, it is capable of obtain the successful rate of optimal solution. For the case

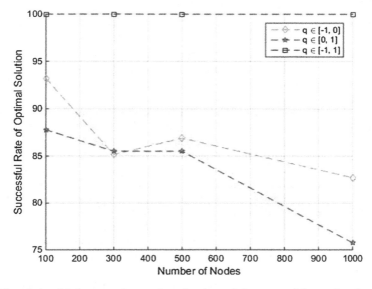

Fig. 9. The relationship between the number of nodes and the successful rate of optimal solution when the energy cost is fixed

of $q \in [0, 1]$ and $q \in [-1, 0]$, the compared results are not certain in various number of nodes. In total, their effects are inferior to the case of $q \in [-1, 1]$. According to the above experiment, we should choose this case to transform nodes to virtual coordinators in actual environment.

5   Conclusion

In this paper, we propose an effective CS-based approach via regionalization, HCS. This method outperforms the previous schemes, including traditional CS and the related optimal methods. The essential advantageous of our mehtod is to limit the number of transmission for as many sensors as possible. To further advance the effectiveness of our approach, two issues about measurement matrix and route are designed. Experiments validate that our approach outperforms other CS-based methods and the designed measurement matrix and the optimal candidate set are benefit for our proposed approach.

Acknowledgments. This work is supported by National Natural Science Foundation of China under Grant Nos. 61402394, 61379064, National Science Foundation of Jiangsu Province of China under Grant No. BK20140462, Natural Science Foundation of the Higher Education Institutions of Jiangsu Province of China under Grant No. 14KJB520040, China Postdoctoral Science Foundation funded project under Grant No. 2016M591922, Jiangsu Planned Projects for Postdoctoral Research Funds under Grant No. 1601162B, Industry university research project in Jiangsu Province under Grant No. 72661632205A, Prospective joint research project of Jiangsu Province under Grant No. BY2016066-04, and sponsored by Qing Lan Project.

References

1. Donoho, D.L.: Compressed sensing. IEEE Trans. Inform. Theory **52**(4), 1289–1306 (2006)
2. Zheng, H., Yang, F., Tian, X., et al.: Data gathering with Compressed sensing in wireless sensor networks: a random walk based approach. IEEE Trans. Parallel Distrib. Syst. **26**(1), 35–44 (2015)
3. Liu, R., Liang, Y., and Zhong, X. Compressed sensing inspired approaches for path reconstruction in wireless sensor networks. In: ACM MobiHoc (2015)
4. Luo, C., Wu, F., Sun, J., Chen, W.C.: Efficient measurement generation and pervasive sparsity for Compressed data gathering. IEEE Trans. Wirel. Commun. **9**(12), 3728–3738 (2010)
5. Yang, H., Tang, K. Hua. X., Zhu, L., Wang, X., Qian, K.: An adaptable CS-based transmission scheme validated on the real-world system. In: INFOCOM (2016)
6. Caione, C., Brunelli, D., Benini, L.: Compressed sensing optimization for signal ensembles in WSNs. IEEE Trans. Ind. Inform. **10**(1), 292–382 (2014)
7. Caione, C., Brunelli, D., Benini, L.: Distributed compressed sampling for lifetime optimization in dense wireless sensor networks. IEEE Trans. Ind. Inform. **8**(1), 30–40 (2012)
8. Yang, H., Huang, L., Xu, H., Liu, A.: Distributed compressed sensing in wireless local area networks. Int. J. Commun Syst **22**(11), 2723–2743 (2014)
9. Yang, H., Tang, K., Yu, J., et al.: Virtual coordinates in hyperbolic space based on Ricci flow for WLANs. Appl. Math. Comput. **243**(6), 537–545 (2014)

IEA: An Intermittent Energy Aware Platform for Ultra-Low Powered Energy Harvesting WSN

Yang Zhang[1,2](✉), Hong Gao[1], Siyao Cheng[1], Zhipeng Cai[3,4], and Jianzhong Li[1]

[1] School of Computer Science and Technology,
Harbin Institute of Technology, Harbin, China
{hitzhangyang,honggao,csy,lijzh}@hit.edu.cn
[2] Key Laboratory of Mechatronics, Heilongjiang University, Harbin, China
zhang_yang@hlju.edu.cn
[3] Department of Computer Science, Georgia State University, Atlanta, USA
[4] College of Computer Science and Technology,
Harbin Engineering University, Harbin, China

Abstract. Energy harvesting (EH) technology largely broadens the range of applications of WSN and extends the life circle thereof. As the energy is unpredictable, the operation of energy harvesting WSN is often intermittent, maybe under the lowest working voltage in most of the time. At this point, the power dissipation may be much larger than that of sleep mode, which will waste energy and prolong the network latency time, whereas the current researches have not attempted to solve the problem. In this paper, we propose a general intermittent energy aware EH-WSN platform (IEA), along with the energy management circuit to switch the power supply automatically without any software, which is capable to decrease the quiescent current below 0.5 uA in undervoltage situation, and takes usage of Ferroelectric RAM to reduce the reboot energy for minimizing the energy dissipation. Besides, integral circuit is firstly used to realize the ultra-low power measurement. Extensive experiments have been performed to verify that the power of IEA in low voltage is at least 55 times lower than that of the current platforms for improving the energy efficiency significantly.

Keywords: Energy harvesting · Intermittent power · Energy measurement · Undervoltage situation

1 Introduction

Wireless sensor network (WSN) collects the physical information in specified area by distributed nodes [1–3], and provides data services such as search, query, and data aggregation [4,5], et al. Comparing with traditional WSN, the energy harvesting WSN has a much longer lifetime because of energy complements from ambient. Subject to various factors, the energy of harvesting WSN, as tiny as hundreds of uW, is often intermittent, and the hardware of WSN constrains its

© Springer International Publishing AG 2017
L. Ma et al. (Eds.): WASA 2017, LNCS 10251, pp. 185–197, 2017.
DOI: 10.1007/978-3-319-60033-8_17

working voltage at least 1.8 V. In severe situations, nodes often can not reach the lowest working voltage and are not capable to work continuously. Therefore, the harvesting WSN nodes must be able to run intermittently.

In order to achieve high efficient use of energy and improve network performance of intermittent WSN, it is essential to solve three problems from hardware level. The first is ultra-low power design. The smaller the energy loss of the node itself, the faster the speed of energy storage, and the network response time is shorter. The second is to reduce the energy consumption of reboot. As the available energy of WSN is very limited, too much reboot energy will seriously affect the network operation. The third is to supply energy information to MCU for determining the routing strategy and planning nodes and network operation.

In most of the time, the voltage of energy harvesting WSN nodes is lower than that of working [6], and we call it as undervoltage situation, resulting in a large amount of current leakage. In Table 1, it is the comparison between the current of representative MCU and RF chips in sleep mode and undervoltage situation. As seen, the dissipated current is increased significantly in undervoltage situation and is uncontrollable. More serious, the current leakage not only wastes the harvested energy, but also increases the boot up energy obviously even leading a failure to boot. In traditional WSN, the consumption is usually ignored since the system boots just once. However, for the intermittent uW magnitude WSN, the consumption is indeed not negligible. Previous studies never attempt to address this problem and there is no related experiments data.

Table 1. Comparison between the current of typical chips in sleep mode and undervoltage mode

Chip	TYPE	Sleep mode	Undervoltage (1.4 V)
PIC18F4523	8-bits MCU	<0.1 uA	31.55 uA
MSP430F1611	16-bits MCU	<0.1 uA	61.75 uA
ATmega128A	8-bits MCU	<1 uA	396.5 uA
STM32F103RB	32-bits MCU	<3 uA	486.7 uA
CC1101	RF transceiver	<0.1 uA	1150.1 uA
CC2540	BLE transceiver	<1 uA	43.73 uA

Traditional WSN is inconsiderable to the problem of intermittent power, therefore, it is possible to schedule network duty-cycle uniformly [7], and optimize the network energy efficiency. However, in the intermittent EH-WSN, the network schedule must take energy as the center, and each of nodes is required to aware the harvested and consumed energy in a certain period. Based on this, nodes decide schedule strategy, and plan the duty-cycle [8,9]. Therefore, it is necessary to measure the harvested and consumed energy accurately. The current researches usually use energy models to predict the available energy in next interval [10], whereas, the energy harvesting is unpredictable [11], existing errors between predicted values and actual values, which results in unpractical of the model. There is hardly any research about energy measurement for ultra low powered EH-WSN till now.

In this paper, we propose a general intermittent energy aware EH-WSN platform (IEA) and the key contributions are as follows:

1. Auto power control. IEA automatically controls power supply of the system according to the voltage of capacitor in hardware. The IEA automatically powers up at the voltage upper to 2.1 V and powers down at the voltage lower than 2.0 V to avoid electric vibration. When the voltage is lower than 2.0 V, the current of IEA is lower than 0.5 uA, which is much lower than that of existing EH-WSN platforms.
2. Accurate energy measurement. IEA uses current sense circuits and integrators to achieve precise measure of energy and the ultra low power. MCU is capable to measure energy harvested and consumed accurately by taking ADC only once, and the measuring error is less than 2%.

Besides, IEA takes MSP430FR6979 as MCU, which uses nonvolatile Ferro-electric RAM memory (FRAM) to store data in undervoltage situation. Comparing with FLASH, the energy consumption of FRAM is 250 times lower than FLASH, and the storing velocity is 100 times faster than the latter. It takes only 0.48 uJ to store 0.5 KB data, significantly reducing data storage and restore energy consumption for intermittent nodes. The design of ultra-low power includes low quiescent current chip selection, hardware and firmware. Experiments show that IEA is comprehensively superior to the existing WSN platforms in aspect of energy saving. The energy consumption is at least 1/55 in undervoltage situation (1.4 V) compared to that of the existing platforms, therefore, the working time of IEA is prolonged in identical energy.

2   Related Works

Considering intermittent power supply, the existing energy harvesting platforms can be divided into two types. The first type not considers intermittent power, but supplies sufficient energy to maintain the voltage of nodes, on which data in the RAM would not lost, without regard to the undervoltage environment and reboot energy consumption. [12–16] have the main structure composed of Solar energy panel, DC-DC converter, rechargeable battery, MCU, and RF Transceiver, thus the harvesting energy is used to power the MCU and RF Transceiver directly. For increasing energy harvesting efficiency, Park C, Chou P H. adopts Multi-Supply and MPPT algorithm [14]. Gorlatova et al. has used MICA2 mote as control module, proposing the UWB-IR physical layer, and uses current sense amplifier to adapt to the harvesting states in real time [16]. This kind of platform depends to stable energy supply, once the system is power down due to insufficient energy, then it is hardly to wakeup without a great mount of energy. In Table 1, the energy consumption of CC1101 chip in undervoltage (1.4 V) is more than 1000 times higher than that in sleep mode, which severely increases the reboot energy and time, failure to use in the area where the power supply is insufficient or unstable.

Another kind of energy harvesting WSN platform is capable to supply intermittently. Smith et al. presents a WISP system for harvesting RF energy [17], but the WISP is neither able to harvest or communicate without RFID reader. Kim et al. designed E-WEHP platform that powered from an ambient digital TV signal where a broadcasting antenna is 6.3 Km away from the proposed wireless energy-harvesting device. E-WEHP needs about 66 s to charge from 1.9 to 3.75 V by harvesting [18]. However, the leakage of the current at undervoltage is not taken in account again, only using diodes and resistors to achieve a simple voltage wake up. Parks, et al. also harvests energy from TV transmitter. To avoid undervoltage state, RF harvesting circuit in this paper adopts S-882Z step-up charge pump to output voltage of 1.8 to 2.4 V. The harvester runs at a location 10.4 Km away from the transmitter and operates with a cycling period of 3 s [19]. Because of conversion loss, the efficiency of DC-DC Convert is hardly up to 100%, thus the DC-DC Convert is not proper for low-power situation.

The above EH-WSN platforms are all overlooked the exceed energy consumption at undervoltage, not considering intermittent power supply and computation, and also can not measure energy precisely. [13,14,16] has merely designed energy harvesting section and tested effects with existing WSN nodes such as MICA2. For measuring characteristics of the harvesting system, [13,14,17] considers MCU and RF chip as resistive load, but the current does not change linearly with the voltage as shown in Table 1. In latest researches, Hassanalieragh et al. proposes a moderate-power system based on solar energy, waking up automatically and measuring harvested and consumed energy [20]. Though the platform takes use of DC-DC converter to achieve auto wake up, its efficiency and accuracy is relatively low. Moreover, the PIC controller for the platform measuring consumes high energy of 10 mW, which is not applicable for the EH-WSN.

3   System Architecture

Because of its importance, we exploit the IEA platform to solve above problems. According to structures, the platform includes three sections, while according to functions of circuit, the platform has eight modules.

As shown in Fig. 1, the platform consists three sections: main board, energy harvesting section, and MCU. The main board (white) contains energy management and measurement, sensors, and communication. MCU board is inserted into the main board only including the minimum system for MCU operation. For energy harvesting, different energy harvesting modules are capable to attach to the left part as required. This structure manages IEA to configure MCU types and energy sources freely for satisfying applications. Eight modules of IEA are signed with red dotted lines, which is shown in Fig. 2.

Fig. 1. Picture of the IEA WSN system.

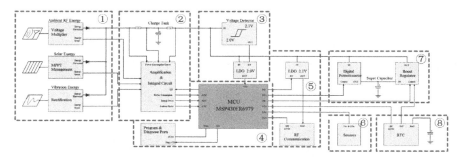

Fig. 2. Hardware structure of the IEA.

1. Energy harvesting module. IEA designs three kinds of modules for energy harvesting, which can be configured as demands to harvest different kinds of energy including solar energy, RF energy, and vibration energy.
2. Energy measurement module is managed to measure the harvested and consumed energy and detects the output voltage of each energy harvesting module.
3. Voltage detection and power supply module. IEA has two modes for working: running mode and undervoltage mode. IEA automatically switches working modes by voltage supply, and controls LDO to power MCU.
4. MCU module takes usage of the Ultra-low-power MSP430FR6979 chip as a controller. For improving network security, the AES hardware encryption module is embedded in chip.
5. Communication module. The SX1211 chip utilized here has reduced the receiving power to 6.6 mW in contrast to the traditional CC1000 chip with power of 33.2 mW.
6. Sensors module is companied by a temperature sensor LM94022 and an acceleration sensor ADXL327, in addition, expansion slots are provided on the system to expand other types of sensors.
7. Super capacitor module. As the capacity of common electrolytic capacitor is not large enough, leading serious waste when the energy is sufficient, the double-stage capacitors structure is properly designed that when energy is sufficient, the super capacitor stores the overflow energy on request of insufficient situation.

8. Real-time clock (RTC) module manages its own energy supply, keeping a time about 5 min even in undervoltage mode. For waking nodes in a certain frequency, RTC controls the super capacitor work under the timing even the ambient energy is deficiency.

4   System Implementation

4.1   Energy Storage

The storage structure of double-stage capacitor consists of electrolytic capacitor C1 and super capacitor C2, as shown in Fig. 3.

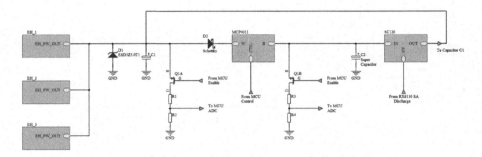

Fig. 3. Circuit for energy storage.

The electric energy from harvesting modules is stored in capacitor C1 directly. When MCU detects sufficient energy, the digital potentiometer MCP4011 starts to charge the Super capacitor C2. The digital potentiometer has to be used because the capacity of C2 is much larger than that of C1. If C1 and C2 were directly connected to each other, C1 would be discharged by C2 in an instant, therefore, it is necessary to use the digital potentiometer to control the charging speed of C2 to prevent power-down due to excessive charging.

When MCU detects insufficient energy, the power in C2 is boosted to 2.5 V by the boost circuit SC120 to keep nodes working. There are two common situations. The first, when MCU performs critical computations and communications, the voltage of C1 is insufficient to complete the operation, then MCU controls C2 to discharge for completing the key operation. The second, C1 can not reach the working voltage for a long time, then RTC module controls C2 to discharge for waking up the system and keeping it running at extreme conditions. The timing of RTC is preset by MCU at runtime.

We have to consider the capacity of C1 carefully. It would cause nodes failure to run large tasks due to insufficient energy if it were too small, in the opposite, too many energy is demanded to charge C1 to reach working voltage, which requires more time and reduces the response frequency of nodes. The energy in capacitance is $E = \frac{CV^2}{2}$, therefore, the value of C1 can be calculated by Eq. 1 based on the minimum working voltage V_{min}, charging voltage V_c, and operating energy E_s.

$$C_{min} \geq \frac{2E_s}{(V_c^2 - V_{min}^2)}. \tag{1}$$

4.2 Voltage Detection and Power Supply

As the harvested voltage maybe over 4.1 V beyond the MCU enduring limitation, IEA takes usage of LDO to supply the system. For system startup, the Initialization program consumes more energy, leading decrease of C1 voltage. However, if we adopted only one voltage detector to control LDO, the voltage of capacitor C1 would vibrate around the threshold that the system could not boot properly. Thus, IEA has a R-S trigger circuit to avoid the situation. The circuit structure, whose function is similar to the Schmitt trigger, is shown in Fig. 4. This section is composed by voltage detectors of U4(2.0 V) and U5(2.1 V), an NAND gate U6, and LDO U2. The R-S trigger, composed of detector and NAND gate, is functioned to control LDO to supply power or not. When the voltage of C1 exceeds the threshold of the voltage detector U5, the R-S trigger outputs at a high level, and the LDO starts to output. On the contrary, when the voltage bellows the threshold of U4, the R-S trigger outputs at a low level leading LDO close down.

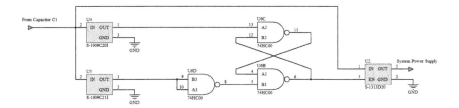

Fig. 4. Circuit for voltage detection and power supply.

4.3 Energy Measurement

It is important for EH-WSN to accurately measure the harvested energy and consumed energy. As the two patterns have totally coincident principle, we describe the measurement of energy consumption. The circuit of energy measurement is shown in Fig. 5. The energy in one second is calculated by $E = \int_0^1 U(t)I(t)dt$. As C1 has a relatively big capacity to manage a stable voltage, we presume the voltage of C1 varying linearly in a period and the value of $U(t)$ can be approximately calculated by average. Hence, we can calculate the energy from the value of $\int_0^1 I(t)dt$, which refers to integral of current. The previous methods exploit the current sense circuit to amplify current signals for obtaining a set of discrete current values, which are added to get points by consecutive sampling of MCU. However, the shortage of the method lies in that MCU has to wake up, leading to great power consumption and CPU time, which is not proper to EH-WSN.

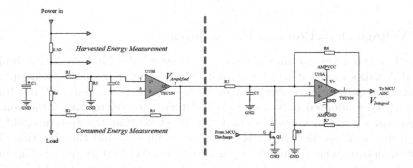

Fig. 5. Circuit for energy measurement.

For measuring $\int_0^1 I(t)dt$ with the lowest energy, we propose to use High-Side current sense amplifier and integrating circuit to solve the problem. The circuit of Fig. 5 includes two sections, wherein the left section is current sense and amplifier circuit, and right section is integral circuit. When current flows through the sense resistor R_s of the left side, it produces a slight voltage drop of $V_{Rs} = I_{Rs} \cdot R_{Rs}$, which is amplified by the first stage amplifier U10-B and outputs to $V_{Amplified}$. To simplify the calculation, we suppose $R_1 = R_2$, $R_3 = R_4$ to get the output value $V_{Amplified} = \frac{R_3}{R_1} V_{Rs}$, which is put into the integral circuit of the right side. In order to simplify the calculation, we suppose $R_5 = R_6$, $R_7 = R_8$, then the value $V_{Integral}$ output to MCU is as shown in formula (2):

$$V_{Integral} = \frac{2}{R_5 C_3} \int V_{Amplified}(t)dt = \frac{2R_3 R_{Rs}}{R_5 C_3 R_1} \int I_{Rs}(t)dt. \qquad (2)$$

Suppose the voltage of capacitor C1 refers to $V_c(t)$, then the consumed energy $E(t)$ at t second is calculated in formula (3):

$$E(t) = \int_{t-1}^{t} U(t)I(t)dt = \frac{V_c(t) + V_c(t-1)}{2} \int_{t-1}^{t} I_{Rs}(t)dt$$
$$= \frac{R_3 R_{Rs}}{R_1 R_5 C_3} \cdot V_{Integral} \cdot (V_c(t) + V_c(t-1)). \qquad (3)$$

Once the resistance is determined MCU is only demanded to measure $V_c(t)$ and $V_{Integral}$ once per second and does a simple multiplication to get the consumed energy (J) in one second, which greatly reduces the calculation amount and wake up time and brings down the power consumption at the same time.

As measuring once time, the field effect transistor Q1 is responsible to discharge the capacitor C to reset the measuring value.

The single path quiescent current of the operational amplifier (OA) TSU104 is only 0.58 uA, far less than the conventional current sense chip, and the measurement power is saved effectively. It worth noting that in order to ensure the Common Mode Range, the MCU is responsible to control the voltage-doubling circuit to supply the OA and ensures the supply voltage is greater than that of capacitor C1. In practical, the energy consumption of modules for measuring depends on the resistance, which requires to balance the relationship of measuring power, measuring range and measuring precision.

5 Evaluation and Experiments

In experiments, firstly, we evaluate the quiescent current of IEA to ensure that the leakage current is effectively decreased in the situation of undervoltage. Secondly, we evaluate modules of energy measuring thereof.

5.1 Quiescent Current Test

The quiescent current of each platform in undervoltage situation is shown in Fig. 6. Here we only measure the quiescent current of the platform (including energy management, MCU and RF circuit), which is irrelevant to the energy harvesting section. In order to eliminate the influence of charge current of capacitors, the filter capacitors of each platform is removed. As seen from Fig. 6, for reducing energy consumption and improving efficiency, IEA platform of this paper consumes much less power under low voltage than that of other energy harvesting platforms. In fact, the current of IEA at 1.4 V is only 0.31 uA, only 1/55 of WISP nodes.

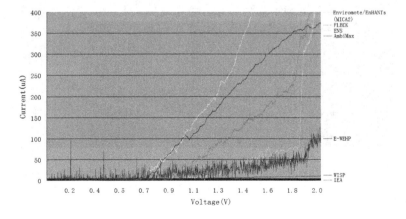

Fig. 6. Comparison of quiescent current of platforms in undervoltage.

5.2   Measurement of Energy Consumption

The energy measurement module includes two parts with identical design, which is harvesting measuring and consumption measuring. In most applications, MCU is able to predict the energy consumption based on the operation, whereas the energy harvesting is usually variable and unpredictable, thus we mainly evaluate the measuring of energy harvesting. As seen from formula (2), the amplification of current depends on the value of resistance. The larger amplification is capable to measure tiny changes of current precisely, but the range is relatively small, while the output value thereof is significantly affected by offset voltage. However, though the range is larger when the amplification is relatively small, it is difficult to distinguish small changes of current. In this test, we refers sampling resistance R_s to $10\,\Omega$, R_1, R_2, R_5, R_6 is $100\,K\Omega$, R_3, R_4, R_7, R_8 is $2\,M\Omega$, C_1 is $2200\,\mu F$, C_2 is $10\,nF$, and C_3 is $10\,\mu F$. The accuracy of resistance is 1%, and the accuracy of capacitance is 5%. According to formula (2), the current amplification factor is 400 times.

The test environment is as follows: using the signal generator (RIGOL DG4102) to generate sine wave to simulate the harvested electric energy, and the voltage is supplied to the IEA platform through the Schottky diode, so as to prevent the current from flowing back. When IEA platform is in receiving mode, an oscilloscope (KEYSIGHT MSOX3024A) is used to measure four signals: input voltage (green), C1 voltage (yellow), current amplified value (pink) and integral output value (blue). In this environment, the sine wave frequency is $10\,Hz$, the amplitude is 2.5 to $3.5\,V$, and the receiving current of IEA platform is $3.20\,mA$. The measuring results of oscilloscope are as shown in Fig. 7.

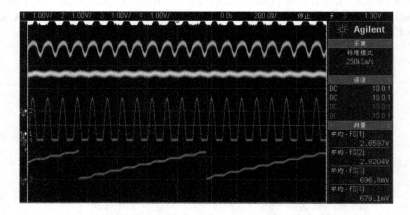

Fig. 7. Harvested energy and signals of measuring modules. The green waves refer to energy harvesting voltage, the yellow is voltage of captaincy C1, the pink is $V_{Amplified}$, and the blue is $V_{Integral}$. (Color figure online)

As can be seen from Fig. 7, the charging current can only appear when the Harvested voltage is higher than the capacitor C1 voltage. The blue waves refer to output results of integrator circuits, and MCU read the results and return it to zero periodically. The measurement results of IEA platform are shown in Table 2.

Table 2. Energy measurement results of IEA platform

	IEA measurement results	Actual value	Error
Average current	3.1775 mA	3.201 mA	−0.7%
Energy acquisition	8.351 mJ	8.514 mJ	−1.9%

IEA platform samples the voltage value and the integral output value in a period of time to calculate energy. As the voltage for calculating energy takes the average value of the two samplings, it may have a large deviation from that of the actual voltage, leading to a larger error for energy measurement. In Table 2, as we seen, the error of energy measurement is −1.9%, whereas the error of current measurement is only −0.7%. Taking into account of components drift, temperature drift, errors from operational amplifier and measurement, the energy measurement error of IEA is within the allowable range.

6   Conclusion

In this paper, we propose a general intermittent energy aware EH-WSN platform (IEA). For improving the intermittent efficiency of energy harvesting WSN, energy management and measurement circuit is developed on the platform to switch the power automatically, which is capable to decrease the quiescent current below 0.5 uA (1/55 of the WISP nodes) in undervoltage situation. Furthermore, the integral circuit is firstly used to realize the accurate energy measurement. based on above, IEA is applicable to occasions that is insufficient or unstable of ambient energy, and in demands of multi-hop communication, such as architecture structure monitoring, and forest carbon sinks, et al. Experiments show that the energy consumption of IEA is superior to the existing WSN platforms comprehensively. IEA is not only an experimental platform, but also is practical in applications and will open up a wide range of opportunities for further studies.

Acknowledgments. This work is supported in part by the Key Program of National Natural Science Foundation of China under Grant No. 61632010, and the National Natural Science Foundation of China under Grant Nos. 61502116, 61370217.

References

1. Vu, C., Cai, Z., Li, Y.: Distributed energy-efficient algorithms for coverage problem in adjustable sensing ranges wireless sensor networks. J. Discrete Math. Algorithms Appl. **1**(03), 299–317 (2009)
2. Li, J., Cheng, S., Gao, H., et al.: Approximate physical world reconstruction algorithms in sensor networks. J. IEEE Trans. Parallel Distrib. Syst. **25**(12), 3099–3110 (2014)
3. Cheng, S., Cai, Z., Li, J., et al.: Extracting kernel dataset from big sensory data in wireless sensor networks. J. IEEE Trans. Knowl. Data Eng. **29**, 813–827 (2016)
4. Li, J., Cheng, S.: (,)-approximate aggregation algorithms in dynamic sensor networks. J. IEEE Trans. Parallel Distrib. Syst. **23**(3), 385–396 (2012)
5. Cheng, S., Cai, Z., Li, J.: Curve query processing in wireless sensor networks. J. IEEE Trans. Veh. Technol. **64**(11), 5198–5209 (2015)
6. Yoshida, M., Kitani, T., Bandai, M., et al.: Probabilistic data collection protocols for energy harvesting wireless sensor networks. J. Int. J. Ad Hoc Ubiquit. Comput. **11**(2), 82–96 (2012)
7. Chen, Q., Cheng, S., Gao, H., et al.: Energy-efficient algorithm for multicasting in duty-cycled sensor networks. J. Sens. **15**(12), 31224–31243 (2015)
8. Shi, T., Cheng, S., Cai, Z., et al.: Exploring connected dominating sets in energy harvest networks. J. IEEE/ACM Trans. Netw. (2017)
9. Shi, T., Cheng, S., Cai, Z., et al.: Adaptive connected dominating set discovering algorithm in energy-harvest sensor networks. In: IEEE INFOCOM 2016-The 35th Annual IEEE International Conference on Computer Communications, pp. 1–9 (2016)
10. Ren, X., Liang, W.: Delay-tolerant data gathering in energy harvesting sensor networks with a mobile sink. In: Global Communications Conference, pp. 93–99 (2012)
11. Hester, J., Scott, T., Sorber, J., et al.: Ekho: realistic and repeatable experimentation for tiny energy-harvesting sensors. In: International Conference on Embedded Networked Sensor Systems, pp. 1–15 (2014)
12. Barnes, M., Conway, C., Mathews, J., et al.: ENS: an energy harvesting wireless sensor network platform. In: International Conference on Systems and Networks Communications, pp. 83–87 (2010)
13. Kyriatzis, V., Samaras, N.S., Stavroulakis, P., et al.: Enviromote: a new solar-harvesting platform prototype for wireless sensor networks/work-in-progress report. In: Personal, Indoor and Mobile Radio Communications, pp. 1–5 (2007)
14. Park, C., Chou, P.H.: AmbiMax: autonomous energy harvesting platform for multi-supply wireless sensor nodes. In: Sensor, Mesh and Ad Hoc Communications and Networks. 168–177 (2006)
15. Sitka, P., Corke, P., Overs, L., Valencia, P., Wark, T.: Fleck - a platform for real-world outdoor sensor networks. In: Proceedings of ISSNIP, vol. 2007, pp. 709–714 (2007)
16. Gorlatova, M., Margolies, R., Sarik, J., et al.: Prototyping energy harvesting active networked tags (EnHANTs). In: International Conference on Computer Communications, pp. 585–589 (2013)
17. Smith, J.R., Sample, A.P., Powledge, P.S., Roy, S., Mamishev, A.: A wirelessly-powered platform for sensing and computation. In: Dourish, P., Friday, A. (eds.) UbiComp 2006. LNCS, vol. 4206, pp. 495–506. Springer, Heidelberg (2006). doi:10.1007/11853565_29

18. Kim, S., Vyas, R., Bito, J., et al.: Ambient RF energy-harvesting technologies for self-sustainable standalone wireless sensor platforms. Proc. IEEE **102**(11), 1649–1666 (2014)
19. Parks, A.N., Sample, A.P., Zhao, Y., Smith, J.R.: A wireless sensing platform utilizing ambient RF energy. In: IEEE Topical Meeting on Wireless Sensors and Sensor Networks (WiSNet 2013) (2013)
20. Hassanalieragh, M., Soyata, T., Nadeau, A., et al.: UR-SolarCap: an open source intelligent auto-wakeup solar energy harvesting system for supercapacitor-based energy buffering. J. IEEE Access **4**, 542–557 (2016)

Scheduling for MU-MIMO Wireless Industrial Sensor Networks

Changqing Xia[1](✉), Xi Jin[1], Jintao Wang[1,2], Linghe Kong[3], and Peng Zeng[1,4]

[1] State Key Laboratory of Robotics, Shenyang Institute of Automation,
Chinese Academy of Sciences, Shenyang, China
{xiachangqing,jinxi,wangjintao,zp}@sia.cn
[2] University of Chinese Academy of Sciences, Beijing, China
[3] Shanghai Jiao Tong University, Shanghai, China
linghe.kong@sjtu.edu.cn
[4] Shenyang Institute of Automation, Guangzhou,
Chinese Academy of Sciences, Guangzhou, China

Abstract. Wireless sensor networks have been widely used in industrial environment. High reliability and real-time requirement are two main characteristics of wireless industrial sensor networks. Each flow can be transmitted to its destination on time by allocation node's transmission slots. However, when transmission conflict occurs, the flow may miss its deadline and generate errors. To address this issue, we introduce MU-MIMO technique into industrial networks and propose a heterogeneous network model. Based on this model, we propose a slot analyzing algorithm (SAA) to guarantee the schedulability of networks. In considering of network cost, SAA also reduces the number of MU-MIMO nodes by slot analyzing. Evaluation results show the effectiveness and efficacy of our approach.

Keywords: WSNs · Scheduling · MU-MIMO · Industrial networks

1 Introduction

Wireless industrial sensor networks are emerging as a new generation of communication infrastructure for industrial process monitoring and control [9,13]. Compared to conventional process control systems, industrial wireless sensor networks have the potential to save costs and enhance reliability. Based on the features of industrial wireless sensor networks, industrial standards such as WirelessHART [3], ISA100 [1] and WIA are used extensively [10].

Since industrial systems demand a high degree of reliability and real-time requirements in communications, traditional wireless sensor networks (or WSNs, for short) cannot be applied directly. We are required to allocate transmission slots and channels for each node before the system works. Lots of studies focus on this issue to improve the schedulability of industrial networks [12,14]. However, the scheduling methods cannot always guarantee the schedulability of networks

© Springer International Publishing AG 2017
L. Ma et al. (Eds.): WASA 2017, LNCS 10251, pp. 198–209, 2017.
DOI: 10.1007/978-3-319-60033-8_18

(when several flows are conflicting at one node, low priority flow may miss its deadline).

To ensure the schedulability of industrial networks, we introduce multi-user multiple-input and multiple-output (or MU-MIMO, for short) technique into wireless industrial sensor networks. For a MU-MIMO node with two antennas, it can receive and send packets simultaneously. The current study makes the following key contributions:

1. To our best knowledge, this is the first study to solve transmission conflict problem in industrial networks with MU-MIMO technique.
2. We first propose a CNSA method to obtain the candidate node set, and then a SAA method has been proposed to improve the schedulability of networks. SAA also reduces sensor nodes in candidate node set by slot analyzing.
3. The simulation results show that our method can guarantee the schedulability of networks with MU-MIMO nodes.

The rest of the paper is organized as follows. Section 2 performs a literature review of previous works. Section 3 presents the system model, which contains network model, fixed priority scheduling policy and MU-MIMO technique. Section 4 proposes the statement of our problem, and we propose our method in Sect. 5. Finally, Sect. 6 provides performance evaluation results and Sect. 7 concludes the paper.

2   Related Works

The first real-time transmission scheduling in wireless industrial networks has been studied in the literature [11], it first formulates the end-to-end real-time transmission scheduling problem based on the characteristics of WirelessHART networks, then the authors proof of NP-hardness of the problem. At last, several scheduling algorithms have been proposed. Based on this study, Refs. [12, 14] study end-to-end delay analysis in WirelessHART networks. Reference [15] analyzes the schedulability of mixed-criticality industrial networks. However, all these studies are based on traditional nodes. The sensor node in these networks can only receive/send one packet at one time slot.

Kong et al. [8] propose a mzig technique to improve the performance of sensor node. Based on mzig, sensor node can receive several packets at the same slot. Reference [6] implements a prototype of CrossZig for the low-power IEEE 802.15.4 in a software-defined radio platform. Chen et al. [4] propose an incast-collision-free data collection protocol, named iCore, to address the many-to-one collision problem in low-duty-cycle WSNs. However, mzig can not receive and send several packets at the same time.

The feasibility of employing MIMO technique in WSNs is envisioned in [16]. To reduce date transmission time for mobile date collection, Ref. [17] introduces MU-MIMO into WSNs. However, only a few studies are focused on MU-MIMO technique in WSNs. Our research, therefore, addresses the schedulability of wireless industrial sensor networks by MU-MIMO technique.

3   System Model

We consider a heterogeneous wireless industrial sensor network consisting of field devices (both MU-MIMO sensor nodes and traditional sensor nodes), one gateway, and one centralized network manager. Our system consists of three aspects. We first propose a network model that is abstracted away from mainstream industrial network standards. Then, we derive FP scheduling in the industrial network. Finally, in order to improve the schedulability of industrial networks, we introduce a MU-MIMO technique.

3.1   Network Model

In this subsection, we propose our network model. Without loss of generality, our model has the same salient features as WirelessHART and WIA, which make it particularly suitable for process industries:

Limiting Network Size. Experiences in process industries have shown the daunting challenges in deploying large-scale WSANs. Typically, 80–100 field devices compose a WirelessHART network with one gateway.

Time Division Multiple Access (TDMA). In industrial wireless sensor networks, time is synchronized and slotted. Because the length of a time slot allows exactly one transmission, TDMA protocols can provide predictable communication latencies and real-time communication.

Route and Spectrum Diversity. To mitigate physical obstacles, broken links, and interference, the messages are routed through multiple paths. Spectrum diversity gives the network access to all 16 channels defined in the IEEE 802.15.4 physical layer and allows per-time slot channel hopping. The combination of spectrum and route diversity allows a packet to be transmitted multiple times, over different channels and different paths, thereby handling the challenges of network dynamics in harsh and variable environments at the cost of redundant transmissions and scheduling complexity [11].

Handling Internal Interference. Industrial networks allow only one transmission in each channel in a time slot across the entire network, thereby avoiding the spatial reuse of channels. Thus, the total number of concurrent transmissions in the entire network at any slot is no greater than the number of available channels [5].

With the above features, the network can be modeled as a graph $G = (V, E, m)$, in which the node set V represents the network devices (all sensor nodes in our model are fixed), E is the set of edges between these devices (transmission links), and m is the number of channels. The number of sensor nodes is N. There are two kinds of sensor nodes in our model: ordinary nodes and MU-MIMO nodes. Each ordinary node in our system is equipped with a half-duplex omnidirectional radio transceiver that can alternate its status between transmitting and receiving. MU-MIMO nodes can receive and transmit packets from several paths (the transmission capacity of MU-MIMO node depends on how many antennas on the node). Each packet transmits though the network under source routing.

3.2   Fixed Priority Scheduling in Industrial Networks

In this subsection, we provide an overview of the fixed priority (or FP, for short) scheduling under wireless industrial sensor networks to analyze system schedulability. FP scheduling is a commonly adopted policy in practice for real-time CPU scheduling, cyber-physical systems, and industrial networks [7]. In FP scheduling policy, each job priority is pre-allocated by network controller, and the transmission is scheduled based on this priority.

In wireless industrial networks, some sensor nodes generate sensory data and transmit it to network destination periodically. Each periodic end-to-end communication between a source and a destination is called a flow. We denote the number of flows as n, the flow set can be denoted as $F = \{F_1, F_2 \ldots F_n\}$. The ith flow F_i is characterized by $\{t_i, d_i, c_i, p_i\}$, where t_i is the period of F_i; d_i is the deadline; c_i is the number of hops from the source to the destination; and pi is the transmission path of F_i. We assume the priority of each flow is the same with its number. That is F_1 has the highest priority in the network. There are two kinds of delay in industrial wireless sensor networks, which can be summarized as follows:

1. Channel contention: each channel is assigned to one transmission across the entire network in the same slot.
2. Transmission conflicts: whenever two transmissions conflict, the transmission that belongs to the lower-priority job must be delayed by the higher-priority one, regardless of how many channels are available. It is important to note that one node can perform only one operation (receiving or transmitting) in each slot.

In real-time system, one task is schedulable when it can be executed completely before its deadline. Hence, the flow could be scheduled when all the packets generated by the flow can arrive destination before their relative deadlines. Then we define the network is schedulable as all flows in a network can be scheduled.

3.3   MU-MIMO in Industrial Networks

Industrial networks as a form of WSNs applications has higher requirements on real-time and reliability, we introduce Multi-user multiple-input and multiple-output (MU-MIMO) technique into industrial networks. MU-MIMO is promising for wireless transmissions since they can improve the average user spectral efficiency [18]. By mounting multiple antennas on a single sensor node, it can receive and transmit simultaneously. The feasibility of employing MU-MIMO technique in wireless sensor networks is envisioned in [17].

Figure 1 is an example of MU-MIMO node deals with transmission conflict. F_1 and F_2 send packets to the same destination simultaneously. We introduce MU-MIMO to solve this issue. The flows can be scheduled by replacing $V3$ with MU-MIMO node. In considering of the power consumption and cost of MU-MIMO node is much higher than normal node, we cannot deploy MU-MIMO node in the entire network.

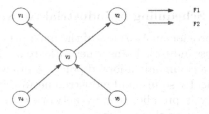

Fig. 1. An example of MU-MIMO Anode deals with transmission conflict.

4   Problem Statement

Given a wireless industrial sensor network $G = (V, E, m)$, the flow set F and the FP scheduling algorithm, our objective is to improve network schedulability by using a few number of MU-MIMO nodes. We first analyze the schedulability of the network. Then if the network cannot be scheduled, we replace several node with MU-MIMO nodes and guarantee the network can be scheduled. The challenges for this issue are listed as follows,

1. When the network is deployed We can easily determine which flow misses its deadline. However, each flow's schedulability is interrelated with others. Then, how can we decide which nodes should be replaced with MU-MIMO nodes?
2. As described in the previous section, the power consumption and cost of MU-MIMO node is much higher than normal node. It's unreasonable and unworthy to deploy a lot of MU-MIMO nodes when the network can be scheduled. Hence, how to meet the requirements of networks with a small number of MU-MIMO nodes is another challenge for this issue.

5   Algorithm

In this section, we study the issue of how to improve network schedulability with the a small number of MU-MIMO nodes. We first screen out the nodes may be replaced with MU-MIMO nodes and define candidate node as follows:

Definition 1 *(Candidate Node). We define candidate node as the node which can occur transmission conflict. As Fig. 1 shown, the path of F_1 and F_2 intersect at $V3$, transmission conflict may occurs at this node. Then $V3$ is a candidate node.*

After obtain the candidate node set, we then determine witch node should be replaced.

5.1   Searching Candidate Node

Industrial network consists by a lots of sensor nodes, we study how to select candidate nodes in this subsection. Transmission conflict occurs at the path overlap of flows. As Fig. 2 shown, there are two types of overlaps (without considering the flow's direction).

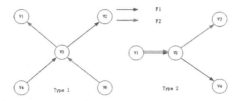

Fig. 2. Transmission conflict.

Lemma 1. *When the paths of flows have overlapping region, the overlap nodes are the candidate of MU-MIMO nodes. We denote the candidate node set as Λ, hence, the node on each flow's path can be denoted as λ_i.*

Proof. Transmission conflict can only occur at the overlapping region obviously. We can solve this issue by MU-MIMO nodes. We have account for the conflicts caused by the first type with Fig. 1. For the transmission conflict caused by the second type, as Fig. 2 shown, there are two nodes ($V1$ and $V2$) on both F_1 and F_2 in the second type of overlap. When the transmission conflict occurs at this part, we can improve the schedulability by replacing both $V1$ and $V2$ with MU-MIMO nodes. Hence, when the paths of flows have overlapping region, the overlap nodes are the candidate of MU-MIMO nodes.

Hence, we propose a Candidate Node Searching Algorithm (or CNSA, for short) to search the set of candidate node as follows,

---

Algorithm 1. Candidate Node Searching Algorithm

Require: F;
Ensure: the candidate node set $\Lambda = \{\lambda_i\}$, $i \in F$;
 1: **for** each flow F_i **do**
 2:    **if** node n_k is the overlap node **then**
 3:       n_k join Λ;
 4:    **end if**
 5: **end for**
 6: **return** Λ;

We search the candidate nodes by traversing the paths of flows in the entire network, if the node is not noly on one flow's path, we join this node into the candidate node set Λ. Obviously, the time complexity of CNSA is $O(F^2)$.

5.2   Reducing Candidate Node Set

After obtaining candidate node set, we reduce the number of nodes in this set to lower network cost. Since not all candidate node could occur transmission conflict, we then analyze the schedulability of industrial networks in one superframe (we can obtain superframe as the lowest common multiple of t_i, $i \in F$).

The flows may be conflicted when they have path overlaps. As Fig. 3 shown, two periodic flows transmit on the network, and they conflict at the second and third slots in the first period. There are two kinds of methods to address transmission conflict. The first method is to adjust slots allocation. However, this is unsuitable for the network which can not be scheduled (in this example, the network cannot be scheduled if the deadline of F_i is 4); The other method is to reallocate slots for each node after replacing conflict nodes with MU-MIMO nodes (in this example, the network can be scheduled when we replace node $V5$ with MU-MIMO node).

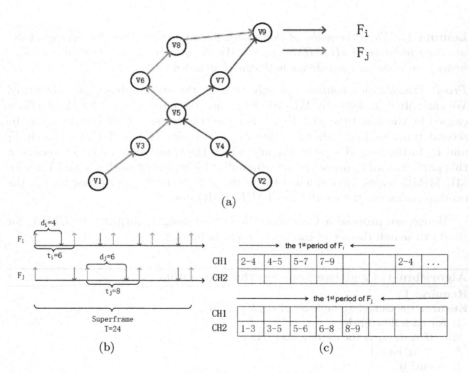

Fig. 3. Conflict analyzing.

Then we propose a Slot Analyzing Algorithm (or SAA, for short) to improve the schedulability of networks by replacing nodes in Λ with MU-MIMO nodes. When the network cannot be scheduled, we need to improve the schedulability by MU-MIMO nodes. Since MU-MIMO nodes support receive/send packets at the same time slot, we first allocate slots for each node without considering transmission conflict (we allocate channel for each translation by FP scheduling policy). Then we replace conflict nodes with MU-MIMO nodes to guarantee network schedulability. Obviously, it is unnecessary and high-cost to replace all the nodes in candidate node set. Hence, SAA reduces the number of MU-MIMO nodes in Λ by slot analyzing. The pseudo code of SAA is as follows,

---

Algorithm 2. Slot Analyzing Algorithm

Require: the characters for each flow F_i; the candidate node set $\Lambda = \{\lambda_i\}$, $i \in F$;
Ensure: the schedulability of networks;
 1: reallocation slots for each nodes.
 2: **for** each flow i **do**
 3:    **if** the flow cannot be scheduled **then**
 4:       find the intersection nodes and reallocate slots for F_i without considering transmission conflict.
 5:    **else**
 6:       retain the original allocation.
 7:    **end if**
 8: **end for**
 9: **for** each node $\lambda_i \in \Lambda$ **do**
10:    **if** λ_i has two or more than two transmissions in the same time slot in one superframe **then**
11:       λ_i need to be replaced;
12:    **else**
13:       remove λ_i out of Λ;
14:    **end if**
15: **end for**
16: **return** Λ;

We reallocation the transmission time slots for each node by the schedulability of each flow (lines 1–8). If the flow cannot be scheduled, we find the intersection nodes and reallocate slots for this flow without considering transmission conflict. Otherwise, we retain the original allocation. Then we analyze transmission slot for each node in Λ (lines 9–16). When the node in Λ has more than one transmission at the same time slot, that is transmission conflict occurs at this node. We need to replace this node with MU-MIMO node. Otherwise, we remove this node out of Λ. At last, we return Λ as the nodes which need to be replaced. Obviously, we can obtain the theorem as follows,

Theorem 1. *The network can be scheduled with SAA when the number of channels is no less than the number of flows $(m \gtrless n)$.*

Proof. When there are k flows conflict at node A, we denote the flow with the highest priority as F_1, and the flow with the lowest priority as F_k. F_1 transmits firstly and cannot be delayed at node A. Otherwise, the other flows must wait to F_1 and may generate delay. For flow $F_i, i \in k$, it will miss its deadline and cannot be scheduled when $c_i + del_i > d_i$, where del is the delay slots. By SAA, we can eliminate delays caused by transmission conflicts. k flows can transmit simultaneously when $m > n$. Since each flow's transmission hops c is not larger than its deadline d. We can guarantee all the flows can be scheduled. Hence, the network can be scheduled with SAA when the number of channels is no less than the number of flows.

6   Experiment

In this section, we conduct experiments to evaluate the performance of our proposed methods. Our approach is compared with the traditional FP algorithm without MU-MIMO nodes. We compare both accept ratio and the number of MU-MIMO nodes. We use accept ratio to represent the schedulability of networks. When all flows can be scheduled, the accept ratio is 1, else is 0. To illustrate the applicability of our method, for each parameter configuration, several test cases are generated randomly.

Our simulations also use the utilization u to control the workload of the entire network. To make flow sets available, we specify the network utilization $U = \sum u_i (U < 1)$, and the UUniFast algorithm [2] is used to generate each flow's utilization u_i ($u_i = \frac{c_i}{t_i}$). The result generated by the UUniFast algorithm follows a uniform distribution and is neither pessimistic nor optimistic for the analysis [2].

As Fig. 4(a) shown, network accept ratio is decreased by FP scheduling policy ($n = 15$, $N = 50$, $m = 16$). That is because the idle resources are reduced when network utilization increased. The latency tolerance of packet is reduced with the idle resources. The network can be scheduled under SAA in any situations by increasing the number of MU-MIMO nodes. Figure 4(b) is the relationship between the number of MU-MIMO nodes and utilization. Obviously, SAA can reduce the number of MU-MIMO nodes on the premise of the network is schedulable. However, neither the number of candidate nodes nor MU-MIMO nodes have an obvious tendency. That is because network utilization not only about the period of flow (t) but also transmission hops (c). We need to regenerate transmission path for each flow to satisfy network utilization. Hence, the number of candidate nodes is up and down. Because of MU-MIMO node is chosen from the candidate node set, the number of MU-MIMO nodes is always less than the number of candidate nodes.

We repeat this simulation for the situation that all flows can be scheduled as Fig. 5 shown. The number of candidate nodes is fixed when we increase network utilization by only adjusting the period of flow (that is because there is only one test in this simulation, and each flow's transmission path does not vary). At the beginning, there is no MU-MIMO node in the network since the network can be scheduled without MU-MIMO nodes. When we increase the network utilization, transmission conflict occurs. To guarantee the schedulability of system, we need more MU-MIMO nodes in this system.

The relationship between accept ratio/the number of MU-MIMO nodes and the number of flows are shown in Fig. 6 ($U = 0.3$, $N = 50$, $m = 16$). The accept

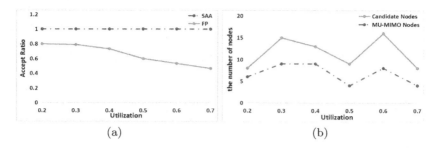

Fig. 4. Relationship between accept ratio/the number of MU-MIMO nodes and network utilization.

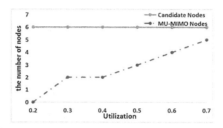

Fig. 5. Relationship between the number of MU-MIMO nodes and network utilization.

ratio is reduced with the number of flows under FP scheduling policy. In addition, both the number of candidate nodes and MU-MIMO nodes are increased with the increasing of flows. The reason is the number of intersections is increased with the number of flows, which occurs more transmission conflicts in the network. The network needs more MU-MIMO nodes to guarantee the schedulability of networks.

Figure 7 are the relationship between accept ratio/the number of MU-MIMO nodes and the number of nodes (U = 0.3, n = 15, m = 16). All these results can illustrate that SAA can guarantee the schedulability of networks. In addition,

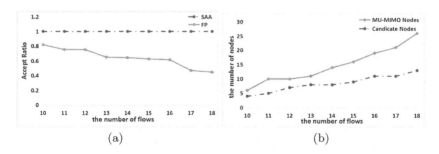

Fig. 6. Relationship between accept ratio/the number of MU-MIMO nodes and the number of flows.

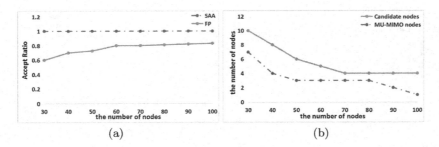

Fig. 7. Relationship between accept ratio/the number of MU-MIMO nodes and the number of flows.

the number of MU-MIMO nodes is no larger than the number of candidate nodes no matter under which conditions.

7   Conclusion

In this paper, we make key contributions to real-time transmission scheduling in wireless industrial sensor networks: (1) we first introduce MU-MIMO technique into industrial networks and analyze the characters of MU-MIMO node in industrial networks; (2) we analyze the transmission paths and obtain the candidate node set; (3) based on the characters of MU-MIMO node, we propose SAA to guarantee the schedulability of networks, in addition, SAA can also reduce the number of candidate nodes. Simulation results show that our scheduling algorithm and analysis have more performance than existing scheduling policy. In the future work, we will study the schedulability of industrial network under the condition of limited number of antennas, and implement it in a real network.

Acknowledgment. This work was partially supported by the National Natural Science Foundation of China (61502474, 61233007 and 61672349) and the Youth Innovation Promotion Association CAS.

References

1. ISA 100. http://www.isa.org/isa100
2. Bini, E., Buttazzo, G.C.: Measuring the performance of schedulability tests. Real-Time Syst. **30**(1–2), 129–154 (2005)
3. Chen, D., Nixon, M., Mok, A.: Why WirelessHART. Springer, Heidelberg (2010)
4. Cheng, L., Gu, Y., Niu, J., Zhu, T., Liu, C., Zhang, Q., Hel, T.: Taming collisions for delay reduction in low-duty-cycle wireless sensor networks. In: 2016-the 35th Annual IEEE International Conference on Computer Communications, IEEE INFOCOM, pp. 1–9. IEEE (2016)
5. Herms, A., Schemmer, S., Lukas, G.: Real-time mesh networks for industrial automation. In: Proceedings of SPS/IPC/DRIVES, Elektrische Automatisierung, Systeme und Komponenten, vol. 7

6. Hithnawi, A., Li, S., Shafagh, H., Gross, J., Duquennoy, S.: Crosszig: combating cross-technology interference in low-power wireless networks. In: 2016 15th ACM/IEEE International Conference on Information Processing in Sensor Networks (IPSN), pp. 1–12. IEEE (2016)
7. Huang, W.H., Chen, J.J.: Self-suspension real-time tasks under fixed-relative-deadline fixed-priority scheduling. In: Proceedings of the 2016 Conference on Design, Automation & Test in Europe, EDA Consortium, pp. 1078–1083 (2016)
8. Kong, L., Liu, X.: mZig: enabling multi-packet reception in ZigBee. In: Proceedings of the 21st Annual International Conference on Mobile Computing and Networking, pp. 552–565. ACM (2015)
9. Lingshuang, X.H.K., Chuanlai, Y., Shenping, X.: Stochastic optimaization model and solution algorithm for blending procedure of process industrial. Inf. Control **45**(1), 40–44 (2016)
10. Liang, W., Zhang, X., Xiao, Y., Wang, F., Zeng, P., Haibin, Y.: Survey and experiments of WIA-PA specification of industrial wireless network. Wireless Commun. Mob. Comput. **11**(8), 1197–1212 (2011)
11. Saifullah, A., Xu, Y., Lu, C., Chen, Y.: Real-time scheduling for wirelessHART networks. In: 2010 IEEE 31st Real-Time Systems Symposium (RTSS), pp. 150–159. IEEE (2010)
12. Saifullah, A., You, X., Chenyang, L., Chen, Y.: End-to-end communication delay analysis in industrial wireless networks. IEEE Trans. Comput. **64**(5), 1361–1374 (2015)
13. Song, J., Han, S., Mok, A., Chen, D., Lucas, M., Nixon, M., Pratt, W.: WirelessHART: applying wireless technology in real-time industrial process control. In: Real-Time and Embedded Technology and Applications Symposium, RTAS 2008, pp. 377–386. IEEE (2008)
14. Wu, C., Sha, M., Gunatilaka, D., Saifullah, A., Lu, C., Chen, Y.: Analysis of EDF scheduling for wireless sensor-actuator networks. In: 2014 IEEE 22nd International Symposium of Quality of Service (IWQoS), pp. 31–40. IEEE (2014)
15. Xia, C., Jin, X., Kong, L., Zeng, P.: Bounding the demand of mixed-criticality industrial wireless sensor networks. IEEE Access (2017)
16. Yuan, Y., He, Z., Chen, M.: Virtual MIMO-based cross-layer design for wireless sensor networks. IEEE Trans. Veh. Technol. **55**(3), 856–864 (2006)
17. Zhao, M., Yang, Y., Wang, C.: Mobile data gathering with load balanced clustering and dual data uploading in wireless sensor networks. IEEE Trans. Mob. Comput. **14**(4), 770–785 (2015)
18. Keke, Z., De Lamare, R.C., Haardt, M.: Multi-branch Tomlinson-Harashima precoding design for MU-MIMO systems: theory and algorithms. IEEE Trans. Commun. **62**(3), 939–951 (2014)

Provably Secure Dual-Mode Publicly Verifiable Computation Protocol in Marine Wireless Sensor Networks

Kai Zhang[1,2], Lifei Wei[3], Xiangxue Li[1,4,5], and Haifeng Qian[1(✉)]

[1] Department of Computer Science and Technology,
East China Normal University, Shanghai, China
zhangkaiecnu@163.com, hfqian@cs.ecnu.edu.cn
[2] The State Key Laboratory of Integrated Services Networks,
Xidian University, Xi'an, China
[3] College of Information Technology, Shanghai Ocean University, Shanghai, China
[4] Westone Cryptologic Research Center, Beijing, China
[5] National Engineering Laboratory for Wireless Security,
Xi'an University of Posts and Telecommunications, Xi'an, China

Abstract. In the marine wireless sensor networks, marine sensors collect multidimensional data such as temperature, salinity, dissolved oxygen and chlorophyll concentration in the ocean using a single hardware unit for further statistical analysis. Once these data are collected, they will be sent to the satellites or vessels for scientific information processing purposes, e.g. computing the mean, the variance and making regression analysis. Verifiable computation (VC) always allows the computationally weak parties to execute computing function operations over outsourced data sets or perform data sets towards outsourced functions to the cloud and still provides an efficient way to verify the returned result, which is an important issue in marine wireless sensor networks. However, the ocean-going voyage vessels always have low computational abilities, in such a way that they may outsource some computations (that need expensive computation costs by themselves) to the data center on the land (e.g. cloud). The computational results cannot be used directly since the cloud may return an incorrect outcome for some profits. Hence, we design a secure publicly VC protocol called $\mathcal{DM-PVC}$, which supports both *public delegation and public verifiability* properties and tackles *outsourced functions and outsourced data sets in a combined way*. We additionally prove the proposed $\mathcal{DM-PVC}$ secure in the random oracle model and evaluate its performance in the end.

Keywords: Marine wireless sensor networks · Dual-Mode · Outsourcing computation · Verifiable computation · Provably secure

1 Introduction

In marine wireless sensor networks (WSNs), marine sensors need to collect multidimensional oceanic data such as temperature, dissolved oxygen, salinity, and

© Springer International Publishing AG 2017
L. Ma et al. (Eds.): WASA 2017, LNCS 10251, pp. 210–219, 2017.
DOI: 10.1007/978-3-319-60033-8_19

the PH value by a single and small hardware unit [1,2], These collected data sets are usually used to monitor the immediate or long-term changes of ocean along with further information processing such as the sum, the mathematical expectation, the variance and more complicated computing functions [3]. For instance, the marine sensors probe the dissolved oxygen of the water per hour and generate a data set including 24 records a day for statistical analysis.

After completing the data collection, the marine sensors send them to a central node (e.g. a base station or a buoy collector) [4]; then the central node will forward them to scientific vessels or satellites through the wireless networks. This aims to carry out further immediate scientific experiments and detect the instantaneous changes of ocean through a variety of computations [5]. But, these ocean-going vessels are not usually equipped with high-quality computation devices. For this reason, they outsource such computations (that needs expensive costs) to the data center on the land (e.g. cloud) [6] and expect to receive correct computational result. Usually, the computational operations performed by the vessels mainly come from two types:

(1) *computing function operations over the outsourced data sets* [7,8];
(2) *inputting the data sets into the outsourced functions* [9,10].

However, the cloud may return an incorrect answer of the computational problem for some profits, thus an efficient solution to check the correctness of result is needed. This motivates the occurrence of verifiable computation (VC) protocol [9,11,12], which allows resource-constrained parties to outsource computations and additionally provides an efficient way to verify the result.

Figure 1 gives a concrete publicly VC example in marine WSNs. Generally speaking, a fleet composed up of a pilot vessel and many non-pilot vessels outsource computations to the cloud, and are willing to verify the result's correctness. Firstly, the pilot vessel does a one-time investment to initialize the VC service, and sends the related system parameters to the cloud, as well as other vessels. Then, any vessel in this fleet can outsource a function and a data

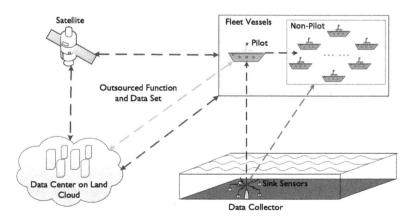

Fig. 1. Publicly verifiable computation protocol in marine wireless sensor networks.

set altogether as inputs to generate a problem description (i.e. **public dele-gation**) [13], hence the computations over the outsourced data and the data sets outsourcing towards the outsourced function can be performed at the same time (i.e. **dual-mode verifiable computation**). Upon receiving the problem description, the cloud executes computations and generates a problem answer back to the delegating vessel. Finally, the vessel or anyone who holds verification information granted by the delegating vessel (i.e. **public verifiability**) can check the correctness of the result [13].

However, we find previous VC protocols cannot be direct applicable to the above example in marine WSNs. On one hand, some only consider either computation delegations over outsourced data sets [7,8] or data sets outsourcing towards outsourced functions [9,10,13]. On the other hand, some [7,9,11,14] only allow the delegating client itself to verify the results (i.e. private verifiability) and fail to support the public delegatable property. To tackle this problem, we aim to design an efficient VC protocol to meet the essential requirements.

Our Results. Our contributions can be summarized as follows:

– We present a *dual-mode publicly verifiable computation* protocol in marine wireless sensor networks: $\mathcal{DM}-\mathcal{PVC}$, which;
  • tackles both *outsourced function* and *outsourced data sets*;
  • supports both *public delegation* and *public verifiability*.
– The $\mathcal{DM}-\mathcal{PVC}$ protocol can additionally be proven *provably secure* in the random oracle model along with its performance evaluation.

Further to say, the $\mathcal{DM}-\mathcal{PVC}$ can be viewed as a hierarchical publicly VC protocol towards only outsourced function. Since the subjective function accepts the outsourced data can be seen as a hierarchical access control procedure.

Organization. Section 2 describes some background knowledge. The designed $\mathcal{DM}-\mathcal{PVC}$ protocol is presented in Sect. 3 and its security analysis is provided in Sect. 4. Section 5 gives the performance evaluation and Sect. 6 concludes this work.

2   Preliminaries

2.1   Notations

We denote by $x, y, z \xleftarrow{\$} S$ that all x, y, z are picked independently and uniformly at random from a set S. By PPT, we denote a probabilistic polynomial-time algorithm. We use $\cdot$ to denote multiplication (or group operation) as well as component-wise multiplication.

2.2   Access Structures

Definition 1. [15] *A (monotone) access structure* $\mathbb{A} = (\mathbf{M}_{\ell \times \ell'}, \rho)$ *for set universe* $\mathcal{U}$ *consists of a matrix consisting of elements over* $\mathbb{Z}_p$ *along with a map* $\rho : [\ell] \to \mathcal{U}$. *We may hold the fact for an attribute set* $\psi \subseteq \mathcal{U}$:

$$\mathbb{A} \, accepts \, \psi \iff 1 \in \mathsf{span}\langle \mathbf{M}_\psi \rangle.$$

Here, $1 = (1, 0, \ldots, 0) \in \mathbb{Z}_p^{\ell'}$ is a row vector; as $\mathbf{M}_j$ represents the j'th row vector of matrix $\mathbf{M}$, a linear span $\mathsf{span}\langle \mathbf{M}_\psi \rangle$ is a collection of vectors $\mathbf{M}_\psi = \{\mathbf{M}_j : \rho(j) \in \psi\}$ over $\mathbb{Z}_p$.

Since any polynomial function can be realized and moreover described by a (monotone) access structure, we hence use the access structures to symbolize the aiming outsourced functions $\mathcal{F}$ throughout this paper.

2.3 Underlying Cryptographic Assumption

Let $\mathbb{G}, \mathbb{G}_T$ be multiplicative groups of prime order p, and g is a generator of group $\mathbb{G}$. An efficient computable map $e : \mathbb{G} \times \mathbb{G} \to \mathbb{G}_T$ is an admissible bilinear map if satisfies:

(1) *Bilinearity.* $g_T = e(g, g)$ where g_T is a generator of group $\mathbb{G}_T$;
(2) *Non-degeneracy.* $e(g, g) \neq 1_{\mathbb{G}_T}$.

2.4 Dual-Mode Public Verifiable Computation

A $\mathcal{DM}-\mathcal{PVC}$ protocol consists of the following four PPT algorithms:

- KeyGen$(\mathsf{F}, \psi, 1^\lambda) \to (\mathrm{PK}_{\mathsf{F},\psi}, \mathrm{EK}_{\mathsf{F},\psi})$: This algorithm takes a function F and an outsourced data set ψ along with a security parameter as input, and outputs a public key PK_{F} and an evaluation key EK_{F}.
- ProbGen$(\mathrm{PK}_{\mathsf{F}}, \omega, \mathsf{G}) \to (\sigma_{\omega,\mathsf{G}}, \mathrm{VK}_{\omega,\mathsf{G}})$: This algorithm takes the public key PK_F to encode an input ω into a problem description $\sigma_{\omega,\mathsf{G}}$ and a verification key $\mathrm{VK}_{\omega,\mathsf{G}}$.
- Compute$(\mathrm{EK}_{\mathsf{F},\psi}, \sigma_{\omega,\mathsf{G}}) \to \sigma_{\mathsf{output}}$: This algorithm inputs the evaluation key $\mathrm{EK}_{\mathsf{F},\psi}$ and the public value $\sigma_{\omega,\mathsf{G}}$, to compute a value σ_{output}.
- Verify$(\mathrm{VK}_{\omega,\mathsf{G}}, \sigma_{\mathsf{output}}) \to \mathsf{output}$: Input the verification key $\mathrm{VK}_{\omega,\mathsf{G}}$ and the worker's input σ_{output}, computes a string $\mathsf{output} \in \{0,1\}^* \cup \{\perp\}^1$.

Correctness. For any security parameter λ, any outsourced function $\mathsf{F} \in \mathcal{F}$ and any outsourced data set $\psi \in \mathcal{U}'$, and for any objective data set $\omega \in \mathcal{U}$ and any subjective function $\mathsf{G} \in \mathcal{F}'$, then

$$\Pr\left[\mathsf{Verify}(\mathrm{VK}_{\omega,\mathsf{G}}, \sigma_{\mathsf{output}}) = \mathsf{F}(\omega, \mathsf{G}) \,\middle|\, \begin{array}{l} (\sigma_{\omega,\mathsf{G}}, \mathrm{VK}_{\omega,\mathsf{G}}) \xleftarrow{\$} \mathsf{ProbGen}(\mathrm{PK}_{\mathsf{F}}, \omega, \mathsf{G}) \\ \sigma_{\mathsf{output}} \xleftarrow{\$} \mathsf{Compute}(\mathrm{EK}_{\mathsf{F},\psi}, \sigma_{\omega,\mathsf{G}}); \end{array} \right] = 1$$

3 Dual-Mode Publicly Verifiable Computation Protocol

Inspired by the work on dual-policy attribute-based encryption (ABE) [16] and the introduced relationship between key-policy ABE and publicly VC [13], we present the first publicly VC protocol towards both outsourced functions and outsourced data sets altogether.

---

[1] The "$\perp$" considers that the verification algorithm reject the worker's answer σ_{output}.

3.1 System Initialization Phase

On input an outsourced function $F \in \mathcal{F}$ with input size n, assume two hash functions $\mathsf{Hash} : \mathbb{Z}_p \to \mathbb{G}$ and $\mathsf{Hash}' : \mathbb{Z}_p \to \mathbb{G}$. The pilot vessel picks $g, \bar{g} \xleftarrow{\$} \mathbb{G}$ and $s, \bar{s}, \alpha, \bar{\alpha} \xleftarrow{\$} \mathbb{G}$. Then generate two key-pairs

$$\mathrm{MPK} := (g, e(g,g)^s, g^\alpha, \mathsf{Hash}, \mathsf{Hash}') \quad \text{and} \quad \mathrm{MSK} := (\gamma, \alpha);$$

$$\overline{\mathrm{MPK}} := (\bar{g}, e(\bar{g},\bar{g})^{\bar{s}}, \bar{g}^{\bar{\alpha}}, \mathsf{Hash}, \mathsf{Hash}') \quad \text{and} \quad \overline{\mathrm{MSK}} := (\bar{\gamma}, \bar{\alpha}).$$

3.2 Evaluation Key Generation Phase

For an access structure $\mathbb{A}' := (N, \pi)$ where $N \in \mathbb{Z}_p^{\ell' \times k'}$ and $\pi : [\ell'] \to [n']$ of an encoded objective outsourced function $F \in \mathcal{F}$, and a subjective outsourced data set $\psi \subset \mathcal{U}'$, pick a random vector $\mathbf{v} \xleftarrow{\$} \mathbb{Z}_p^{k'}$ such that $\mathbf{1v} = \gamma + \alpha r$ for $r \xleftarrow{\$} \mathbb{Z}_p$ and set $\eta_i = N_i \cdot \mathbf{v}, i \in [\ell']$. Output

$$\begin{aligned}
\mathrm{SK}_{F,\psi} : &= \big(K, \ \{K_x\}_{x \in \psi}, \ \{K_i', K_i''\}_{i \in [\ell']} \big) \\
&= \big(g^r, \ \{\mathsf{Hash}(x)^r\}_{x \in \psi}, \ \{g^{\eta_i}\mathsf{Hash}'(\pi(i))^{-r_i}, \ g^{r_i}\}_{i \in [\ell']} \big).
\end{aligned}$$

Similarly, we obtain the corresponding secret key $\mathrm{SK}_{\bar{F},\psi}{}^2$ for the complement function $(\bar{F})$ of the outsourced function F as

$$\begin{aligned}
\overline{\mathrm{SK}}_{\bar{F},\psi} : &= \Big(\bar{K}, \ \{\bar{K}_{\bar{x}}\}_{\bar{x} \in \psi}, \ \{\bar{K}_i, \bar{K}_i'\}_{i \in [\bar{\ell}']} \Big) \\
&= \Big(\bar{g}^{\bar{r}}, \ \{\mathsf{Hash}(\bar{x})^{\bar{r}}\}_{\bar{x} \in \psi}, \ \{\bar{g}^{\bar{\eta}_i}\mathsf{Hash}'(\bar{\pi}(i))^{-\bar{r}_i}, \ \bar{g}^{\bar{r}_i}\}_{i \in [\bar{\ell}']} \Big).
\end{aligned}$$

Hence, output the public key and the evaluation key as

$$\mathrm{PK}_F := (\mathrm{MPK}, \overline{\mathrm{MPK}}) \quad \text{and} \quad \mathrm{EK}_F := (\mathrm{SK}_{F,\psi}, \overline{\mathrm{SK}}_{\bar{F},\psi}).$$

3.3 Problem Generation Phase

On input the objective data set $\omega \subset \mathcal{U}$ and the access structure $\mathbb{A} := (M, \rho)$ where $M \in \mathbb{Z}_p^{\ell \times k}$ and $\rho : [\ell] \to [n]$ of an encoded subjective function $G \in \mathcal{G}$, pick a random vector $\mathbf{u} \xleftarrow{\$} \mathbb{Z}_p^k$ such that $\mathbf{1u} = s$ for $s \xleftarrow{\$} \mathbb{Z}_p$ and set $\lambda_i = M_i \cdot \mathbf{u}, i \in [\ell]$. Sample two equal-length messages $\mathcal{M}, \overline{\mathcal{M}}$ and output

$$\begin{aligned}
\mathrm{CT}_{\omega,G} : &= \big(C, \ C', \ \{C_i\}_{i \in [\ell]}, \ \{C_x''\}_{x \in \omega} \big) \\
&= \big(\mathcal{M} \cdot e(g,g)^s, \ g^s, \ \{g^{\alpha\lambda_i}\mathsf{Hash}(\rho(i))^{-s}\}_{i \in [\ell]}, \ \{\mathsf{Hash}'(x)^s\}_{x \in \omega} \big)
\end{aligned}$$

---

[2] Here, we denote "$\overline{\mathbf{xx}}$" as the related variables belonging to $\overline{\mathrm{SK}}_{\bar{F},\psi}$. Note that $\mathrm{SK}_{F,\psi}$ and $\overline{\mathrm{SK}}_{\bar{F},\psi}$ are pair-wise independent since all related "$\mathbf{xx}$" and "$\overline{\mathbf{xx}}$" are independently and uniformly distributed. Here we omit the descriptions on the sampling process.

and similarly we generate $\overline{\mathrm{CT}}_{\omega,\mathsf{G}}{}^3$ by using $\overline{\mathrm{MPK}}$

$$\overline{\mathrm{CT}}_{\omega,\mathsf{G}} := \left(\bar{C}, \ \bar{C}', \ \{\bar{C}_i\}_{i\in[\ell]}, \ \{\bar{C}''_x\}_{x\in\omega} \right)$$
$$= \left(\overline{\mathcal{M}} \cdot e(\bar{g},\bar{g})^s, \ \bar{g}^s, \ \{\bar{g}^{\alpha\lambda_i}\mathsf{Hash}(\rho(i))^{-s}\}_{i\in[\ell]}, \ \{\mathsf{Hash}'(x)^s\}_{x\in\omega} \right)$$

Hence, output the problem description and the verification key as

$$\sigma_{\omega,\mathsf{G}} := (\mathrm{CT}_{\omega,\mathsf{G}}, \overline{\mathrm{CT}}_{\omega,\mathsf{G}}) \quad \text{and} \quad \mathrm{VK}_{\omega,\mathsf{G}} := (H(\mathcal{M}), H(\overline{\mathcal{M}}))$$

where H is a one-way function.

3.4 Compute Phase

Upon the problem description $\sigma_{\omega,\mathsf{G}}$ and the evaluation key $\mathrm{EK}_{\mathsf{F},\psi}$, compute

$$\mathcal{M}' \leftarrow C \cdot \frac{\displaystyle\prod_{i\in\{i|\rho(i)\in\psi\}} \left(e(C_i, K) \cdot e(C', K_{\rho(j)}) \right)^{u_i}}{\displaystyle\prod_{j\in\{i|\pi(i)\in\omega\}} \left(e(K'_j, C') \cdot e(K''_j, C''_{\pi(j)}) \right)^{v_j}}$$

and

$$\overline{\mathcal{M}}' \leftarrow \bar{C} \cdot \frac{\displaystyle\prod_{i\in\{i|\rho(i)\in\psi\}} \left(e(\bar{C}_i, \bar{K}) \cdot e(\bar{C}', \bar{K}_{\rho(j)}) \right)^{u_i}}{\displaystyle\prod_{j\in\{i|\bar{\pi}(i)\in\omega\}} \left(e(\bar{K}'_j, \bar{C}') \cdot e(\bar{K}''_j, \bar{C}''_{\bar{\pi}(j)}) \right)^{v_j}}.$$

Output the problem solution $\sigma_{\mathrm{output}} := (\mathcal{M}', \overline{\mathcal{M}}')$.

3.5 Verification Phase

On input $\mathrm{VK}_{\omega,\mathsf{G}} := \left(H(\mathcal{M}), H(\overline{\mathcal{M}}) \right)$ and $\sigma_{\mathrm{output}} := (\mathcal{M}', \overline{\mathcal{M}}')$. Output

$$\mathtt{output} := \begin{cases} 0, & \text{if } H(\mathcal{M}') = H(\mathcal{M}) \text{ and } H(\overline{\mathcal{M}}') \neq H(\overline{\mathcal{M}}); \\ 1, & \text{if } H(\overline{\mathcal{M}}') = H(\overline{\mathcal{M}}) \text{ and } H(\mathcal{M}') \neq H(\mathcal{M}); \\ \bot, & \text{otherwise.} \end{cases}$$

4 Security Analysis

4.1 Correctness

Based on the correctness of the dual-policy attribute-based encryption [16] along with our modified transformation between ABE and publicly VC in terms of [13], the correctness follows straightforwardly when both the following two conditions hold: (1) the outsourced function F accepts the data set ω; and (2) the outsourced data set ψ satisfies the function G.

---

[3] Similar to producing $\overline{\mathrm{SK}}_{\overline{\mathsf{F}},\psi}$, we use "$\overline{\mathbf{xx}}$"-type variables to generate $\overline{\mathrm{CT}}_{\omega,\mathsf{G}}$.

Remark 1. The verifiability of $\mathcal{DM}-\mathcal{PVC}$ is mainly against outsourced function since the concept of the complement data sets of ψ does not make sense in practice compared to $\bar{\mathrm{F}}$. Hence, our $\mathcal{DM}-\mathcal{PVC}$ can serve as a hierarchical publicly VC protocol towards just outsourced function, which thinks that subjective function accepts outsourced data set as a hierarchical access control condition.

4.2 Security Proof

Theorem 1 (Main Theorem). *Let $\mathcal{F}$ be a class of boolean functions, and $\bar{\mathcal{F}} = \{\bar{F} \,|\, F \in \mathcal{F}\}$ be a class of the complement function $\bar{F}$ of each function F and the class of the outsourced data set $\mathcal{U}' = \{\psi | \psi \in \mathcal{U}'\}$, and H be any one-way function. Suppose the q-BDHE assumption holds, then the $\mathcal{DM}-\mathcal{PVC}$ protocol in Sect. 3 is secure.*

Due to space, we refer the reader to the full version for the proof.

5   Performance Evaluation

In this section, we give the time and size efficiency analysis for $\mathcal{DM}-\mathcal{PVC}$. Table 1 gives the size calculations and Table 2 lists the dominant time operations (i.e. pairing, exponentiation, multiplication) in group.

Based on NIST recommendation [17], the work [18,19] give a Charm-crypto Benchmark with Python language that is instantiated with a virtual machine running Ubuntu 12.04 with 1 GB memory in VMWare in a MACbook Air ruining Intel i5@1.8 GHz and 4 GB memory. We may employ the asymmetric bilinear group $e : \mathbb{G}_1 \times \mathbb{G}_2 \to \mathbb{G}_T$ instead of symmetric bilinear group $e : \mathbb{G} \times \mathbb{G} \to \mathbb{G}_T$ to

Table 1. Size analysis of our $\mathcal{DM}-\mathcal{PVC}$ protocol

	Description	Sizes
$\mathrm{PK_F}$	Public key	$4|\mathbb{G}| + 2|\mathbb{G}_T|$
$\mathrm{EK_F}$	Evaluation key	$(4\ell + 2n + 2)|\mathbb{G}|$
$\sigma_{\omega,\mathsf{G}}$	Problem description	$(2\ell + 2n + 2)|\mathbb{G}| + 2|\mathbb{G}_T|$
$\mathrm{VK}_{\omega,\mathsf{G}}$	Verification key	$2|\mathbb{G}|$

Table 2. Group operations analysis in each phase of our $\mathcal{DM}-\mathcal{PVC}$ protocol

	Operations
System initialization	$2\mathsf{Pairing} + 2\mathsf{Exp}_{\mathbb{G}_T} + 2\mathsf{Exp}_{\mathbb{G}}$
Evaluation key generation	$(6\ell + 2n)\mathsf{Exp}_{\mathbb{G}} + (2n + 2\ell)\mathsf{Hash} + 2\ell\mathsf{Mul}_{\mathbb{G}}$
Problem generation	$(4\ell + 2)\mathsf{Exp}_{\mathbb{G}} + (2\ell + 2n + 2)\mathsf{Hash} + 2\ell\mathsf{Mul}_{\mathbb{G}}$
Compute	$8n\mathsf{Pairing} + 2n\mathsf{Exp}_{\mathbb{G}_T}$
Verification	$2\mathsf{Hash}$

realize the $\mathcal{DM-PVC}$ protocol, in order to evaluate its enjoyable performance run faster in practice. Assume the size of the data set ψ, ω are n and let ℓ, ℓ' be 10 and the employed elliptic curve [20] is "SS512", we give the actual size evaluation in Fig. 2 and time efficiency simulation in Fig. 3.

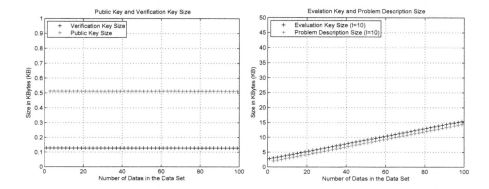

Fig. 2. The size efficiency of the $\mathcal{DM-PVC}$ protocol.

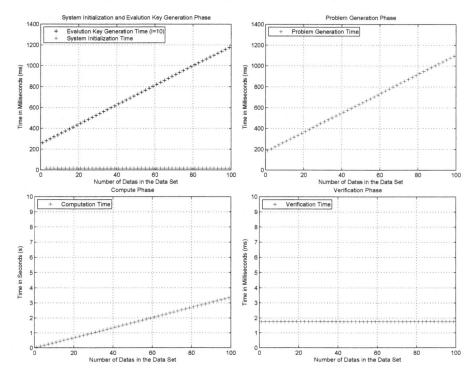

Fig. 3. The time efficiency of the $\mathcal{DM-PVC}$ protocol.

6 Conclusion

In this paper, we proposed a VC protocol in marine WSNs, which supported public delegation and public verifiability over outsourced functions and outsourced data sets in a combined way. We additionally proved the proposed protocol secure and evaluated its performance. However, the clients may outsource multiple functions to the cloud altogether, we leave the $\mathcal{DM}-\mathcal{PVC}$ protocol towards multi-functions as the future work.

Acknowledgement. We thank Ming Zeng and all anonymous reviewers. This work was supported by National Natural Science Foundation of China (61571191, 61572192, 61472142, 61402282, 61472249), the Science and Technology Commission of Shanghai Municipality (13JC1403502, 14YF1404200, 14YF1410400); Open Foundation of State Key Laboratory of Integrated Services Networks (ISN17-11) and International Science & Technology Cooperation & Exchange Projects of Shaanxi Province (2016KW-038).

References

1. D'Este, C., De Souza, P., Sharman, C., Allen, S.: Relocatable, automated cost-benefit analysis for marine sensor network design. Sensors **12**(3), 2874–2898 (2012)
2. Wang, Z., Song, H., Watkins, D.W., Ong, K.G., Xue, P., Yang, Q., Shi, X.: Cyber-physical systems for water sustainability: challenges and opportunities. IEEE Commun. Mag. **53**(5), 216–222 (2015)
3. Zhang, A., Yang, L., Zhang, S., Yu, J., Shu, Y.: Marine vehicle sensor network architecture and protocol designs for ocean observation. Sensors **12**(1), 373–390 (2012)
4. Pengfei, H., Xing, K., Cheng, X., Wei, H., Zhu, H.: Information leaks out: attacks and countermeasures on compressive data gathering in wireless sensor networks. In: International Conference on Computer Communications (INFOCOM), pp. 1258–1266 (2014)
5. Huang, D., Zhao, D., Wei, L., Wang, Z., Yanling, D.: Modeling and analysis in marine big data: advances and challenges. Math. Probl. Eng. **1**–13, 2015 (2015)
6. Mell, P., Grance, T.: The NIST Definition of Cloud Computing. Computer Security Division, Information Technology Laboratory, National Institute of Standards and Technology Gaithersburg (2011)
7. Benabbas, S., Gennaro, R., Vahlis, Y.: Verifiable delegation of computation over large datasets. In: Rogaway, P. (ed.) CRYPTO 2011. LNCS, vol. 6841, pp. 111–131. Springer, Heidelberg (2011). doi:10.1007/978-3-642-22792-9_7
8. Backes, M., Fiore, D., Reischuk, R.M.: Verifiable delegation of computation on outsourced data. In: ACM Sigsac Conference on Computer and Communications Security, pp. 863–874 (2013)
9. Gennaro, R., Gentry, C., Parno, B.: Non-interactive verifiable computing: outsourcing computation to untrusted workers. In: Rabin, T. (ed.) CRYPTO 2010. LNCS, vol. 6223, pp. 465–482. Springer, Heidelberg (2010). doi:10.1007/978-3-642-14623-7_25
10. Fiore, D., Gennaro, R.: Publicly verifiable delegation of large polynomials and matrix computations, with applications. In: ACM Conference on Computer and Communications Security, pp. 501–512 (2012)

11. Applebaum, B., Ishai, Y., Kushilevitz, E.: From secrecy to soundness: efficient verification via secure computation. In: Abramsky, S., Gavoille, C., Kirchner, C., Meyer auf der Heide, F., Spirakis, P.G. (eds.) ICALP 2010. LNCS, vol. 6198, pp. 152–163. Springer, Heidelberg (2010). doi:10.1007/978-3-642-14165-2_14

12. Jiang, Y., Song, H., Wang, R., Ming, G., Sun, J., Sha, L.: Data-centered runtime verification of wireless medical cyber-physical system. IEEE Trans. Industr. Inform. **PP**(99), 1 (2016). doi:10.1109/TII.2016.2573762

13. Parno, B., Raykova, M., Vaikuntanathan, V.: How to delegate and verify in public: verifiable computation from attribute-based encryption. In: Cramer, R. (ed.) TCC 2012. LNCS, vol. 7194, pp. 422–439. Springer, Heidelberg (2012). doi:10.1007/978-3-642-28914-9_24

14. Chung, K.-M., Kalai, Y., Vadhan, S.: Improved delegation of computation using fully homomorphic encryption. In: Rabin, T. (ed.) CRYPTO 2010. LNCS, vol. 6223, pp. 483–501. Springer, Heidelberg (2010). doi:10.1007/978-3-642-14623-7_26

15. Beimel, A.: Secure schemes for secret sharing and key distribution. Ph.D. thesis, Technion-Israel Institute of Technology, Faculty of Computer Science (1996)

16. Attrapadung, N., Imai, H.: Dual-policy attribute based encryption. In: Abdalla, M., Pointcheval, D., Fouque, P.-A., Vergnaud, D. (eds.) ACNS 2009. LNCS, vol. 5536, pp. 168–185. Springer, Heidelberg (2009). doi:10.1007/978-3-642-01957-9_11

17. Giry, D.: Bluekrypt. https://www.keylength.com/en/

18. Akinyele, J.A., Garman, C., Miers, I., Pagano, M.W., Rushanan, M., Green, M., Rubin, A.D.: Charm: a framework for rapidly prototyping cryptosystems. J. Cryptograph. Eng. **3**(2), 111–128 (2013)

19. Zhang, F.: http://student.seas.gwu.edu/~zfwise/crypto. Technical report

20. Miyaji, A., Nakabayashi, M., Takano, S.: New explicit conditions of elliptic curve traces for FR-reduction. IEICE Trans. Fundam. Electron. Commun. Comput. Sci. **84**(5), 1234–1243 (2001)

A Genetic Algorithm Based Mechanism for Scheduling Mobile Sensors in Hybrid WSNs Applications

Yaqiang Zhang[1], Zhangbing Zhou[1,4(✉)], Deng Zhao[1], Yunchuan Sun[3], and Xiao Xue[2]

[1] School of Information Engineering, China University of Geosciences (Beijing), Beijing, China
zhangbing.zhou@gmail.com
[2] College of Computer Science and Technology, Henan Polytechnic University, Jiaozuo, Henan, China
[3] Business School, Beijing Normal University, Beijing, China
[4] Computer Science Department, TELECOM SudParis, Évry, France

Abstract. In hybrid wireless sensor networks (WSNs) sensors can be divided into two categories as static or mobile sensors, where mobile sensors can move to collect the information from static sensors. A challenge in hybrid WSNs is to make the best use of sensor's energy and thus to prolong the network lifetime. To address this challenge, we aim to schedule mobile sensors by applying techniques derived from genetic algorithm in order to balancing the energy consumption of mobile sensors. The network, where static sensors are deployed, are divided into relatively small regions. Thereafter, we adopt our technique to allocate these regions to each mobile sensor, while ensuring the fact that energy consumption of each mobile sensor is relatively close to each other. Experimental evaluation shows that our technique can effectively balance the load of each mobile sensor, and thus, prolong the networks lifetime.

Keywords: Wireless Sensor Networks · Mobile sensors · Energy-balanced · Genetic algorithm

1 Introduction

Hybrid Wireless Sensor Networks (WSNs) have been widely used in many domains, such as the flood or disaster control [6], military surveillance, underwater environment monitoring and so on. And sensors have been looked on as services [8]. Sensors which play an important role in WSNs aim to collect various types of information from their surrounding, and they also have rich properties, such as the communication and movement abilities. Sensors have mostly limited energy, and energy harvesting may not be convenient, or impossible, in certain situations. In this setting, the strategy that can prolong the network lifetime while satisfying the requirement of certain applications is needed.

© Springer International Publishing AG 2017
L. Ma et al. (Eds.): WASA 2017, LNCS 10251, pp. 220–231, 2017.
DOI: 10.1007/978-3-319-60033-8_20

Sensors can be categorized as mobile sensors and static sensors. Intuitively, static sensors aim to collect sensory data from their surrounding environment, while mobile sensors are to gather and aggregate sensory data provided by static sensors. The usage of mobile sensors to collect data can efficiently improve the network ability, and much effort has been proposed to adopt mobile sensors for facilitating sensory data gathering. In [3], mobile sensors collect sensory data provided by static sensors by estimating the value of sensory data through adopting a relatively simple model. The authors in [7] have discuss that mobile sensors collect data based on clusters. Specifically, sensory data in each cluster is divided to be collected. It means that mobile sensors need not to traverse all static sensors. Instead, they only need to pass some positions and gather sensory data that have been collected and assembled. Note that this strategy may accelerate energy consumption of static sensors, since sensory data are required to be assembled after the data gathering phase. In [10] data transmitting between each static sensors is prohibited, and mobile sensors can collect sensory data from static sensors. A mobile sensor contains more energy than that of static sensor, and mobile sensors are undertaking more tasks in WSNs. We define in this paper the lifetime of the network is the time when the first mobile sensor depletes its energy. In order to prolong the lifetime of network, we must concern about the energy consumption of each mobile sensor, and try to ensure that the energy consumption is relatively equivalent for all mobile sensors.

In this article we propose to balance the energy consumption of mobile sensors for prolonging the network lifetime. Sensors in this paper are non-rechargeable unlike in [4]. To support the time-aware domain applications, static sensors sense and gather sensory data, while mobile sensors collect and aggregate sensory data. Generally, more energy should be consumed for the movement of mobile sensors than that for sensory data collection. The main contributions of this article are summarized as follows:

- A non-complete graph is adopted to describe the network region based on region dividing. A graph consist of a set of vertices and a set of edges. The whole WSNs region is divided into many small cells firstly. Then each small cell region is looking on as a vertex, and a appropriate distance between any two cells is looking on as edge of two vertices. Compared with other researches that also have divided the WSNs region, the concept of graph we have introduced can clearly shows the information of a WSNs region and it simplify the question.
- Time constraint is considered for setting the number of mobile sensors. In authenticity, there may have some constraints on time spending when all static sensors have upload their data to mobile sensors once. Setting a suitable number of mobile sensors is paramount. We propose a inequation to calculate a congruous value that satisfy the time constraint.
- An energy balanced scheduling for mobile sensors is proposed. We define each vertex a weight in graph, it represent the number of static sensors contained in a small cell region. Then we use our technique that inspired by some heuristic algorithms like Genetic Algorithm (GA) to schedule routes for each mobile sensor considering energy balance.

The evaluation results show that by applying the technique into the WSNs region, the energy consumption of each mobile sensor is similar, that means no sensors could use out of its energy quickly than others and the network is stable and its lifetime is prolonged.

This paper is organized as follows. Section 2 introduces the region dividing mechanism. Section 3 introduces the routing mechanism for mobile sensors. Section 4 evaluates the procedure developed in this paper, and Sect. 5 makes a conclusion of our work.

2   Networks Region Dividing Mechanism

In this section, we present the first step of our technique, to divide the whole region into pieces and then abstract them into a graph. Dividing can simplify the workload of network. A graph can clearly describe the information in WSNs. Table 1 are some symbols and notations used in subsequent sections. There are three sub-steps in this section.

First step is to divide the monitored region S into many small regions. We consider the region is obstacles free. Sensors are randomly distributed in region S, in some areas it may be dense and other areas it may be sparse. After deployment, sensors position will be fixed and their position information can be get. To

Table 1. Symbol list and notations

Name	Description
S	The WSN region with n static sensors and m mobile sensors, while n is much larger in number than m in real-world application scenarios
r	The communication radius of mobile sensors
g_i	g_i is the small monitored region, where all regions are equal in size
gSide	gSide is the side length of g_i
m	The number of mobile sensors
m_i	The mobile sensor which would work in the c_i (where i $\in$ (0, m])
c_i	The cluster i (where i $\in$ (0, m])
$c_i.gnum$	It contain the number of g_i's for which one mobile sensor is responsible to collect data
Eg_i	The energy consumption of a mobile sensor when gathering data sensed by static sensors in the cluster c_i
Em_i	The energy consumption of a mobile sensor when moving within a cluster c_i
uEm	The energy consumption of a mobile sensor when moving from a g_i to its adjacent g_j
$c_i.EC$	The energy that a mobile sensor consumes when it traverses all small regions in the cluster c_i for collecting data sensed by static sensors. $c_i.EC$ is composed of Em_i and all $g_i.Eg$ where the small region g_i belongs to the cluster c_i

manage the mobile sensors and static sensors we divide the region into small and equal size and shape cells. In each small cell, it may contains more or less some static sensors. It is obvious that each static sensor has its own ID, and with the help of GPS technique, we can know which cell a sensor belongs to. Concerning that the communication radius of mobile sensor is r, the length of small region $gSide$ should be less than $\sqrt{2}r$, so when a mobile sensor moves towards a small rectangular region and stops at the center of the region, it can communicate with all static sensors in this area and collect informations. On the other hand, the length should not be so small, or mobile sensor would consume more energy on traveling. It needs to be emphasized that the region S is relatively a big region, it is necessary to divide S into small regions. If S is a $\sqrt{2}r \times \sqrt{2}r$ region, it only needs one mobile sensor to collect data from the region.

The next step is to abstract the region S into a graph. To simplify the problem we use the concept of graph. A graph G is a set of vertices Ve and a set of edges E, shows the relationship between these vertices. It can be shown as $G = (Ve, E)$. A graph can be divided into complete graph and non-complete graph. In a complete graph every vertex has a relation to every other vertex. To better understand over scenario we model our problem as a non-complete graph in which the cells represent vertices of the graph and a appropriate distance between these cells represents the edges between these vertices. We propose that when a mobile sensor moves from one small cell region to another, it is the best way to stop at the center of the region. It would cover with all the static sensors in the area most possibly. Figure 1 shows that if a mobile sensor does not move to the centre of a small cell region maybe it would not cover with all this region. So we define that the distance between the center of two small cell regions is the corresponding distance of two vertices.

In addition, we assign each vertex a weight which is related to static sensors number contained in cell itself. This concept is very important for our research. It represent the ability on energy consumption. As we have mentioned above,

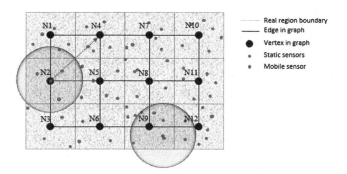

Fig. 1. An example of networks region, the black dot and black line are the graph transform from region, each dot represents the vertex and line represents the edge between vertices, each vertex has a weight in proportional to the number of static sensors. Signal like N1 and N2 and so on are the serial number (SN) of vertex.

static sensors are randomly deployed in the region, each small cell region includes different number of static sensors. We define that the weight of a vertex is the number of static sensors deployed in this cell region. Larger weight values means, the more energy a mobile sensor would consume when visiting the area for gathering information. After above working, now we have put all the information of the region S into a graph. Figure 1 shows an example of graph, it is a noncomplete graph transfer from an rectangle region which we have divided it into 12 pieces of cell region.

3   Mobile Sensors Workload Allocation

In this section, we propose a technique which is to schedule for mobile sensors, and two steps are included in. First step is to determine the number of mobile sensors. Next step is to schedule routes for them using algorithm inspired by genetic algorithm.

3.1   Mobile Sensors Number Mechanism

In this part, we demonstrate how to set the suitable number of mobile sensors. In our work, we use more than one mobile sensor to collect the information gathered by static sensors.

We assume that when a mobile sensor is working, the process of data gathering is instantly completed. That means how long would a mobile sensor complete its work is only related to the number of vertices it would travel around. In order to balance the energy consumption of each mobile sensors and to balance the time consumption, we must allocate each mobile sensor a nearest number of vertices.

When a mobile sensor moves from one vertex to any one of its nearest vertex, the time or energy consumption is same on condition that all mobile sensors have the same speed and they have the same ability in energy consumption. Em_i represent the energy consumption of a mobile sensor during its movement, if Em_i is larger, it means that mobile sensor has spend more time on moving and its total length on moving is larger. The other part of energy consumption is Eg_i, if c_i contains more static sensors, the mobile sensor which is responsible for this cluster would have a larger in Eg_i. Without loss of generality, we assume that Eg_i is in proportional to the number of static sensors in cluster c_i, although there may have minor difference in energy consumption due to the difference in distance between static sensors and a certain mobile sensor. The total energy consumption of m_i is $c_i.EC = Em_i + Eg_i$.

With above conclusion, we propose a method to ensure the amount of mobile sensors so that they can satisfy the time sensitive application:

- T represents the maximum time limitation when all static sensors upload their data to mobile sensors for once. It is manually set, usually we set T concerning about the timeliness of the information, or about timely get the information with the limited memory space.

- N represents the number of vertices in graph.
- v is the speed of mobile sensor.
- t represents the time when a mobile sensor moves between two nearest vertices. We have mentioned above that the mobile sensor must move from one vertex to one of its nearest neighbor, so $t = gSide/v$.
- M represents the number of mobile sensors and it is what we want to ensure.

We can get an inequation which shows the relationship between M and T on condition that T is satisfied:

$$(N/M - 1) * t \leqslant T \tag{1}$$

$$M \geqslant N/(1 + T/t) \tag{2}$$

We set M the minimum integer that greater than M. Up to now we have get the value of M which guarantees the T be satisfied in minimum level. N/M represents the number of vertices that each mobile sensor should pass by.

Further, in some situation, we can not equally divide all vertices in M parts, that means N is not divisible by M. We mention a method (3) to solve this problem. We define that first D mobile sensors must go through a $(C + 1)$ number of vertices, and the other mobile sensors must go through a C number of vertices. C is the quotient of N/M, and D is the remainder of that.

$$N/M = C \cdots D \tag{3}$$

After this step, all N vertices are allocated to M mobile sensors considering the T and time consumption of each mobile sensor.

To have a better understanding, we use an example to clearly show our technique. We set $T = 120\,s$, $N = 54$, and the speed of mobile sensor $v = 5\,m/s$, $gSide = 50\,m$. According to (1) and (2), $M \geqslant 4.15$, so we set $M = 5$. In this region, we deploy 5 mobile sensors to collect data from static sensors. $C = 10$ and $D = 4$, so the allocation of vertices to mobile sensors is $[11, 11, 11, 11, 10]$.

Since we have allocated vertices to each mobile sensor, it still could not ensure time consumption or energy consumption of each mobile sensor is similar, because different route for mobile sensor may cause different length of this route. An ideal situation is that the moving of mobile sensors are either horizontal or vertical, and each vertex would be passed only by once. And that means no repetitive tour between to vertex appears. c_i consists of all g_i's for which one mobile sensor is responsible to collect data. So if there are $c_i.gnum$ small squares contained in a cluster c_i, the length a mobile sensor m_i needs to move should be $(c_i.gnum - 1) \times gSide$, and $Em_i = uEm \times (c_i.gnum - 1)$. To mitigate this issue, we propose that heuristic algorithm could be used to route for each mobile sensor.

3.2   Routing Technique

According to the last section, finding a good route for each mobile sensor ensuring a similar energy consumption and time spending on moving is difficult. In fact, with the expansion of the scale of the vertex, method of exhaustion is not suitable for our issue. We propose that heuristic algorithm could be used to find a feasible solution.

GA is one kind of heuristic algorithm and it is on the basis of evolution theory. It simulates the process of biological evolution, to find the optimal solution. Usually it has four steps: encoding, selection, mutation, and crossover.

Encoding: In this paper, a chromosome represents a route for all mobile sensors, it includes all vertices. Genes that represent the vertex are arranged according to access sequence. The fitness value of a chromosome represents the individual viability in population. We calculate fitness value considering both the total energy consumption on moving and the variance of each mobile sensor's energy consumption on information collection. If one chromosome has the biggest value in fitness in history, it is as the best of the population. Pi represents the probability of survival of a chromosome i according to its fitness value f_i.

$$P_i = f_i / \sum_{i=1}^{N} f_i \tag{4}$$

Selection: We calculate the fitness values of all the chromosomes, the biggest one is reserved and it is added to next generation. Then we use the strategy of roulette, which chooses chromosome according to the proportion of one chromosome's fitness to the sum of fitness of all chromosome. If a chromosome has a bigger f_i, it would more likely to be reserved.

Crossover: Two chromosomes are chosen in population randomly. We mark two chromosomes in same gene position, and then exchange the gene of two chromosomes after the mark point. By doing this the next generation generates two new child chromosomes. As an example in Fig. 2 we choose the 5th position as the mark point and we exchange the gene after it between two chromosomes.

Mutation: There are two mode of mutations. One is randomly choosing a gene (a vertex) from chromosome and move it to another randomly available position. The other is to randomly choosing two points and reposition the vertices between the two points in inverted sequence.

Objective function: When we apply the GA, we must set the objective function F (8). It represents the target of the algorithm. In this paper, we combine two sub objective functions into one. The first one is the total consumption on moving by all the mobile sensors Em (5). The other is the variance of consumption on data gathering of all mobile sensors $V(Eg)$ (7).

$$Em = \sum_{i=1}^{m} Em_i \tag{5}$$

$$\overline{Eg} = \frac{\sum_{i=1}^{m} Eg_i}{m} \tag{6}$$

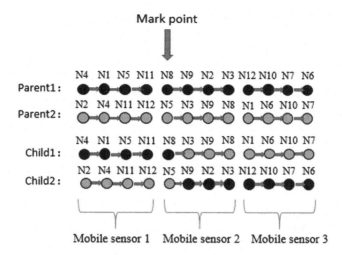

Fig. 2. The process of crossover. In this figure, we have 12 vertices and 3 mobile sensors, we equally divide all vertices into 3 parts, each mobile sensor is allocated 4 vertices.

$$V(Eg) = \frac{\sum\limits_{i=1}^{m}(Eg_i - \overline{Eg})^2}{m} \tag{7}$$

$$F = k1 * Em + k2 * V(Eg) \tag{8}$$

We request the minimum of F, but in fact, we can not usually get the optimal solution. We would like to get the approximately optimal solution. Also we can set the value of $k1$ and $k2$ to influence the result of solution. $k1$ and $k2$ means the importance of two sub objective function. In this paper, we first take into consideration that Em would get the minimum value. On the basis of that, we are as far as possible to ensure the $V(Eg)$ could get the minimum value.

As presented in Algorithm 1, at start of genetic algorithm, it calculates the fitness for all chromosomes in initial population. It chooses the biggest one in fitness to be reserved (line 2). Then it use the strategy of roulette to randomly reserve the next $(n - 1)$ chromosomes (line 4). All new n chromosomes make up a new generation. After that it randomly chooses two chromosomes in new generation by applying the strategy of crossover. Then it gets two new child chromosomes and replace the old two parent chromosomes. Next it applies the strategy of mutation for one randomly chose chromosome (line 7). After above steps, it gets a new generation as the next population. Then it repeats the above steps until it gets a chromosome which has an optimal fitness value.

Algorithm 1. Scheduling algorithm inspired by GA

Require:
 -NG:The number of chromosome in initial generation.
 -L : the total tour length that all mobile sensors have gone.
Ensure:
 -a chromosome with the optimal fitness value.

1: **while** $looptime < maxofiterations$ **do**
2: choose the chromosome that has the current biggest fitness value and add the chromosome to new generation.
3: **for** $i < NG - 1$ **do**
4: randomly choose chromosomes when a chromosome with a high fitness value is more possibility to be chosen.
5: **end for**
6: **for** $i < NG$ **do**
7: use the strategy of crossover and mutation.
8: **end for**
9: return the chromosome with the best fitness value.
10: **end while**

4   Implementation and Evaluation

The prototype has been implemented in a Java program. Experiments are conducted on a desktop with an Intel i5-3470 processor at 3.2 GHz, 8 GB memory, and a 64-bit Windows 10 operation system.

Table 2. Parameter settings

Parameter name	Value
Region size	$450\,m \times 300\,m$
Static sensors number	1000
Communication radius of mobile sensor (r)	50 m
Side length of small region ($gSide$)	50 m
Speed of mobile sensors	5 m/s
Energy consumption on data gathering	1 unit
Energy consumption on moving	20 units

We have conducted experiments to evaluate the performance of our technique. In this section, we respectively named our technique inspired by GA as WGA, to easily describe our experiments. The experiments aim to evaluate the effectiveness in energy balance and time sensitivity of our technique WGA. Table 2 shows the parameter settings of our experiments. The region size is $450\,m \times 300\,m$ with 1000 static sensors in it. We set the energy consumption of mobile sensor when collecting from a static sensor is 1 unit and the consumption on moving from one vertex to its nearest vertex is 20 units. We set $r = 50\,m$ and $gSide = 50\,m$ and the speed of mobile sensor is 5 m/s. V represents the variance of each mobile sensors's energy consumption.

In general, we use V to measure the effect of algorithm, it represents the dispersion degree of energy consumption. If V is small, that means each mobile sensors are similar in energy consumption.

In real applications, people also want to get data from monitored field as soon as possible. We set this experiment to evaluate the performance of our technique WGA. It is assumed that data in monitored region must be collected in 180 s. According to our technique in Sect. 3.1, we work out $m = 3$ according to inequation (1) and (2).

Figure 3 shows that when WGA is applied, with different number of mobile sensors deployed in field, the maximum time a mobile sensor would spend when it finish its work. It is clear that when m is greater than 2, maximum time consumption of mobile sensors are less than 180 s. That means all of mobile sensors would accomplish their work before a deadline when $m > 2$. Figure 4 shows ten times experimental results when V gets to a convergent state. The results of WGA in V are in a lower values and having a fluctuation on a small scale.

In addition, we set the number of mobile sensors from 2 to 6, to show the impact of mobile sensors's number.

Figure 5 shows the variance on energy consumption when applying WGA. From the figure we know that V trend to be stable with the increase of loop time. Each line is stable after a period of time. When m is 2 and 3, the V is similar and less than that of 4, 5 and 6.

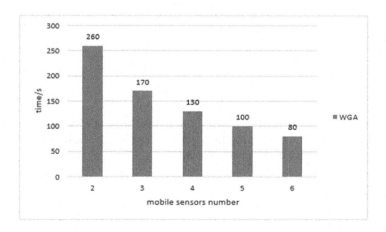

Fig. 3. When m is from 2 to 6 in $450\,m \times 300\,m$ region the maximum time may a mobile sensor consume.

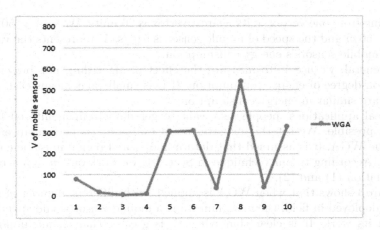

Fig. 4. 10 times results of V by WGA in $450\,m \times 300\,m$ region with 3 mobile sensors.

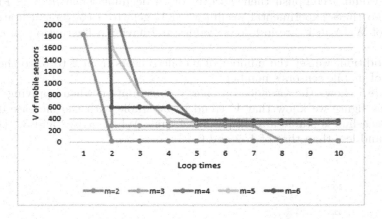

Fig. 5. Diversification of V when applying the WGA in $450\,m \times 300\,m$ region where m is from 2 to 6.

Different number of mobile sensors may cause some differences in result of V. In general, the influence of mobile sensor's number is slight, our techniques are adapted to different mobile sensor scale.

5   Conclusion

The main problem that restricts the development of sensor technique is energy. Scheduling for mobile sensor that makes the most use of its energy and prolongs the lifetime of WSNs is a challenge. Energy factor has been considered in many research fields in sensor networks [1,2,5,9]. In this paper, we focus on the lifetime of WSNs and propose a technique that balance the energy consumption of mobile sensors and prolong the lifetime of network. Firstly we divide the region into many small cells. We abstract the region into a graph then. Each small cell is looked on as a vertex, and mobile sensors are going to collect the data from each vertex. We use the technique inspired by heuristic algorithm to schedule for each mobile sensor considering both the energy consumption of moving and data collection. Experimental results show that our technique can balance the energy consumption of each mobile sensor and the lifetime of network can be prolonged.

References

1. Cheng, S., Cai, Z., Li, J.: Curve query processing in wireless sensor networks. IEEE Trans. Veh. Technol. **64**(11), 5198–5209 (2015)
2. Cheng, S., Cai, Z., Li, J., Gaoo, H.: Extracting kernel dataset from big sensory data in wireless sensor networks. IEEE Trans. Knowl. Data Eng. **29**(4), 813–827 (2017)
3. Gong, X., Wang, X., Guo, J., Wang, A., Xu, D., An, N., Chen, X., Fang, D., Zheng, X.: DEDV: a data collection method for mobile sink based on dynamic estimation of data value in WSN. In: 2016 International Conference on Networking and Network Applications, pp. 77–83 (2016)
4. Han, G., Qian, A., Jiang, J., Sun, N., Liu, L.: A grid-based joint routing and charging algorithm for industrial wireless rechargeable sensor networks. Comput. Netw. **101**(6), 19–28 (2016)
5. He, Z., Cai, Z., Cheng, S., Wang, X.: Approximate aggregation for tracking quantiles and range countings in wireless sensor networks. Theoret. Comput. Sci. **607**(3), 381–390 (2015)
6. Tanumihardja, W.A., Gunawan, E.: On the application of IoT: monitoring of troughs water level using WSN. In: 2015 IEEE Conference on Wireless Sensors, pp. 58–62 (2015)
7. Nikmard, B., Taherizadeh, S.: Using mobile agent in clustering method for energy consumption in wireless sensor network. In: 2010 International Conference on Computer and Communication Technology, pp. 153–158 (2010)
8. Zheng, X., Cai, Z., Li, J., Gao, H.: Scheduling flows with multiple service frequency constraints. IEEE Internet Things **PP**(99), 1 (2016)
9. Zheng, X., Cai, Z., Li, J., Gao, H.: A study on application-aware scheduling in wireless networks. IEEE Trans. Mob. Comput. **PP**(99), 1 (2016)
10. Zhou, Z., Du, C., Shu, L., Hancke, G., Niu, J., Ning, H.: An energy-balanced heuristic for mobile sink scheduling in hybrid WSNs. IEEE Trans. Industr. Inform. **12**(1), 28–40 (2016)

SSD: Signal-Based Signature Distance Estimation and Localization for Sensor Networks

Pengpeng Chen, Yuqing Yin, Shouwan Gao$^{(\boxtimes)}$, and Qiang Niu

School of Computer Science and Technology, China University of Mining and
Technology, Xuzhou, China
{chenp,gaoshouwan}@cumt.edu.cn

Abstract. Node localization is an important supporting technology for
wireless sensor networks (WSN). Existing range-free localization solutions suffer from low accuracy, while range-based methods achieve good
accuracy but costly for ranging hardware. Instead of directly mapping
received signal strength indicator (RSSI) values into physical distances,
we propose a novel signal-based signature distance (SSD) estimation and
localization scheme for WSN. In the proposed scheme, the near-far relationship between nodes is first qualified through comparing of their RSSI,
and then a relative map is constructed based on MDS method. Finally,
we obtain the node positions through procrustes analysis. In order to
verify the effectiveness of the proposed design, we simulate the design in
an irregular network with 200 randomly deployed nodes, and develop a
prototype system with 25 MICAz motes in real outdoor environments.
Results show that our design achieves better positioning performance
and observably reduces localization errors.

Keywords: Range-free localization · Signal-based signature distance ·
Wireless sensor networks

1 Introduction

Wireless sensor network (WSN) is a high and new technology consists of distributed autonomous sensors to monitor the physical world, e.g., indoor human
localization [1], outdoor environment monitoring [2], battlefield surveillance [3],
and so on. In such data-driven WSN, the positioning of nodes itself is very
essential. Besides, some of the routing protocols [4] and data forwarding mechanisms are built on the assumption that nodes' location information is available.
Although node localization plays a role in all those systems, it is a challenging
problem due to extremely limited resources at low-cost and tiny sensor nodes.

There currently exist many excellent localization algorithms in WSN. The
first type is range-based localization, in which the ranging is completed by the
RSSI, time or angle. In practice, the requirement of low system cost often pro-
hibits many range-based methods for localization. The second one is range-free
localization, in which wireless connectivity [5], anchor proximity [6], or localization events detection are adopted for location estimation. These algorithms

© Springer International Publishing AG 2017
L. Ma et al. (Eds.): WASA 2017, LNCS 10251, pp. 232–243, 2017.
DOI: 10.1007/978-3-319-60033-8_21

have low cost but suffer from poor accuracy. Lately, another localization technology is proposed which is based on the channel status information (CSI) [7]. Such methods provide better positioning accuracy, but the CSI is often hard to extract for the general sensor nodes.

Our work is motivated by the finding that the change trend of the received signal strength (RSS) from their neighbors is similar if two nodes are placed near each other. Based on the observation, in this paper we further quantify the near-far relationship between neighboring nodes from two aspects: neighbor pair comparison and RSS difference. After obtaining the relative distance between neighboring nodes, the relative distance among non-neighboring nodes can be calculated by the shortest path algorithm. Thus, we can construct the relative location map of the whole network based on the MDS technology [8]. At last, given at least three anchors, the physical coordinates can be solved by procrustes analysis. Specifically, our main contributions are as follows.

- Different from the traditional hop-based distances, this paper investigates the proximity information embedded in neighborhood RSS, which owns a more accuracy sub-hop resolution.
- The near-far relationships between nodes are carefully qualified based on neighbor pair comparison and single node RSS difference, which have a high correlation with physical distance.
- Extensive simulations and a prototype system are conducted for verifying the effectiveness of the design.

The rest of the paper is organized as follows: Sect. 2 surveys related work. Section 3 explains the motivation behind the paper with empirical data. The main design is introduced in Sect. 4. Section 5 gives the simulation results. Section 6 reports a prototype experiment. Finally, Sect. 7 concludes the paper.

2   Related Work

Generally, the localization approaches can be classified into three categories: range-based [9,10], range-free [6,11–13] and CSI-based [14]. In the following, we will analyze and discuss them one by one.

Range-based methods can be further divided into three types: RSS-based methods, time-based methods, and angle-based methods. These methods generally first estimate distances or angles among nodes and then apply triangulation for location calculation. They could be accurate but costly by adding per-node additional hardware or requiring intensive tuning. Range-free solutions try to estimate node location through a low-cost and smart design. Early solutions mainly employ the proximity information to anchor nodes like Centroid and APIT. Then solutions with wireless connectivity are proposed, such as DV-Hop and Amorphous, which require a small number of anchors for reducing the system cost. Nowadays, works may help solve problems of "holes" [15] in practical irregular deployment with obstacles. However we notice that they do not fully extract the location information available from local neighborhood sensing.

Lately, the CSI-based localization strategies are proposed like SAIL [16] and Tagoram [17]. They utilize physical layer information to compute the propagation delay of the direct path by itself, eliminating the adverse effect of multipath and yielding sub-meter distance estimation accuracy. The adopted wireless technologies are WiFi or RFID. Although CSI is a better choice for physical distance estimation in many scenarios, the CSI is hard to extract for low-cost sensors.

Considering that RSS does provide some useful distance related information beyond indicating connectivity among neighboring nodes, this paper fully extracts the proximity information from the neighbors' RSS and presents a novel method of qualifying the distance among neighbors. The design can effectively improve the system accuracy with little extra cost.

3   Motivation

Our work is motivated by one of outdoor experiments. We have ever conducted a 2D grid network with a 4×4 layout including 16 nodes on a square platform. The grid distance between two nodes is about five meters. Each node records all the RSS values from their neighbors. After obtaining the RSS values, We can see from the relationship between distance and RSS that identical RSS values may correspond to different physical distances, and RSS may vary dramatically for a single distance. Thus, the converting from the RSS to Distance is inaccurate.

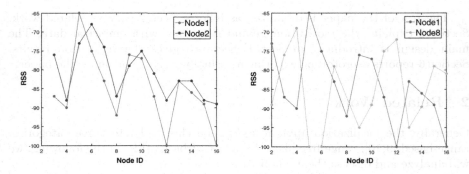

Fig. 1. RSS change trend (Color figure online)

In view of this, we change the observation method of RSS values. From the viewpoint of a single node, we find an interesting phenomenon. In Fig. 1, the red, the blue and the green lines reflect the RSS change trend of node1, node 2 and node 8 respectively. It is known that node 2 is closer than node 8 to node 1. Coincidentally, Fig. 1 tells that node 1 and node 2 have similar change trend, while there exist many inverse trends of RSS vales for Node 1 and Node 8. This phenomenon inspires us to further extract the distance relationship behind the RSS change trend.

4 System Design

This section first presents the main design of qualifying the near-far relationship among nodes. Then we present the construction process of relative map of the whole network, as well as the converting procedure of the physical coordinates.

4.1 Node Distance Quantization

Sequential Distance Estimation. Without loss of generality, we can evaluate the near-far relationship of nodes u_1 and u_2 using the data set $S = (U, V, R)$, where $U = \{u_1, u_2\}$, u_1 and u_2 are the target object for distance quantization; $V = \{v_1(u_1), v_2(u_2), v_3..., v_N\}$, V is a set that consists of all neighbors of u_1, u_2 and simultaneously contains u_1, u_2 themselves. It is not difficult to obtain that there are C_N^2 neighbor pairs for nodes u_1 and u_2, where N is the total number of neighbors of above two nodes. R is a $2 \times N$ matrix, in which R_{ij} represents the received signal strength from node v_j for node u_i.

In order to illustrate our design, we give a simple example in Fig. 2, in which the problem is to evaluate the distance between u_1 and u_2. Table 1 lists the RSS values from all their neighbors. Note that if R_{ij} is set to be Inf, it means that node u_i cannot receive the signal from node v_j. In addition, we set $R_{ii}, i \in \{1, 2\}$ to be zero, which has the strongest signal strength.

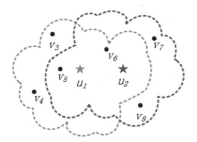

Fig. 2. An example of design

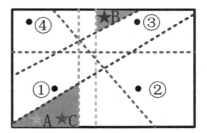

Fig. 3. Nodes with bisectors

Table 1. RSS values from all their neighbors

Object	Neighbor							
	u_1	u_2	v_3	v_4	v_5	v_6	v_7	v_8
u_1	0	-58	-75	-80	-55	-57	Inf	Inf
u_2	-60	0	Inf	Inf	-72	-56	-67	-65

Now we classify the neighbor pairs of nodes u_1 and u_2. By comparing the RSS values, u_1 can judge that it is closer to node v_5 than v_6. We define v_5 and

v_6 as an effective neighbor pair and use N_{eff} to denote the number of effective neighbor pairs. In contrast, u_1 cannot judge whether it is closer to node v_7 than v_8, because it receives nothing from them. We call v_7 and v_8 as an ineffective neighbor pair. Likewise, u_2 cannot judge whether it is closer to node v_3 than v_4. Hence, v_3 and v_4 is also an ineffective neighbor pair. Here N_{inv} is used to represent the number of ineffective neighbor pair. Obviously, the sum of N_{eff} and N_{inv} equals to C_N^2.

Next the distance evaluation between nodes u_1 and u_2 is mainly based on the N_{eff} effective neighbor pairs. For any effective neighbor pair v_j and v_k, they are a concordant pair if $R_{1j} > R_{1k}$ and $R_{2j} > R_{2k}$. Otherwise, if $R_{1j} > R_{1k}$ and $R_{2j} < R_{2k}$ (or $R_{1j} < R_{1k}$ and $R_{2j} > R_{2k}$), v_j and v_k are defined as a discordant pair. In the given example, nodes v_5 and v_7 are a discordant pair, while v_3 and v_5 are a concordant pair. In addition, we use symbols N_{con} and N_{dis} to represent the number of concordant pairs and discordant pairs, respectively.

Based on the above classification and explanations, we quantify the sequential distance between nodes u_1 and u_2 as follows:

Definition 1. *The sequential distance between two neighboring nodes is equal to the ratio between the number of discordant pairs and the number of effective neighbor pairs, namely*

$$d_{seq}(u, v) = N_{dis}/N_{eff};$$
$$\begin{cases} N_{dis} = N_{eff} - N_{con}, \\ N_{eff} = C_N^2 - N_{inv}. \end{cases} \tag{1}$$

Taking u_1 and u_2 in Fig. 2 as an example, we can obtain 11 discordant pairs (v_1, v_2), (v_1, v_6), (v_2, v_5), (v_2, v_6), (v_3, v_7), (v_3, v_8), (v_4, v_7), (v_4, v_8), (v_5, v_6), (v_5, v_7), (v_5, v_8) and 2 ineffective neighboring pars (v_3, v_4), (v_7, v_8). Thus, the relative distance between nodes u_1 and u_2 are $11/(C_8^2 - 2) = 0.42$.

We use the ratio of discordant neighbor pairs for evaluating the node distance. Furthermore, we explore the hidden geometrical relationship behind the formula. Consider any two neighboring nodes and draw a perpendicular bisector to the line joining their locations. This perpendicular bisector divides the localization space into two different regions that are distinguished by their proximity to either neighboring nodes. Similarly, if perpendicular bisectors are drawn for all neighboring pairs (C_N^2), they divide the localization space into many small regions. If nodes u_1 and u_2 are on different sides for many bisectors, they should be far from with each other. Figure 3 illustrates the above mentioned phenomenon. Nodes A and C are close with each other and lie on the same side for most bisectors. However, nodes A and B lie on the different sides for most bisectors and their distance is farther.

SSD Estimation. In the above analysis, we only consider the change trend of RSS. However, the RSS values can also affect the distance between two nodes, especially in the outdoor open-air scenarios. Next, we further introduce the differences of neighbor RSS values into the distance estimation.

For nodes u_1 and u_2, their difference-based distance can be expressed as:

$$d_{diff}(u_1, u_2) = \sum_{i=1}^{N} |R_{1i} - R_{2i}|. \tag{2}$$

Note that in Eq. (2), the RSS differences are used to estimate the distance instead of RSS values, which can in part eliminate the effect of the environment factor and is more robust. Based on sequential distance and difference-based distance, we propose a signal-based signature distance (SSD) for relative distance between one-hop neighboring nodes.

Definition 2. *SSD between a one-hop node pair is equal to the product of the sequential distance and a polynomial based on the difference-based distance, which is shown as follows.*

$$\begin{aligned} SSD(u_1, u_2) &= d_{seq}(u_1, u_2) + d_{seq}(u_1, u_2) * e^{-d_{diff}(u_1, u_2)} \\ &= (1 + e^{-d_{diff}(u_1, u_2)}) * d_{seq}(u_1, u_2). \end{aligned} \tag{3}$$

From Eq. (3), it can be seen that SSD combines the ideas of RSS values (d_{diff}) and RSS change trend (d_{seq}), which makes up for the weakness of using one aspect only and enhances the robustness.

As for unconnected node pairs, we have learned from the design of RSD [18], and now regard the smallest accumulated SSD along the shortest-path of the multi-hop node pair as the estimated relative distance.

4.2 Physical Coordinate Generation

Given the relative distances between any two nodes, we can construct their relative map and further obtain physical coordinates when more than three anchors' positions are known.

Relative Map Construction. This recreation process is exactly the problem that multidimensional scaling (MDS) [8] solves. Intuitively, it is clear that while the $O(n^2)$ distances will be more than enough to determine $O(n)$ coordinates, the result of MDS will be an arbitrarily rotated and flipped version of the true original layout because the inter-point distances make no reference to any absolute co-ordinates.

A symmetric relative distance matrix D can be constructed as:

$$D = \begin{bmatrix} 0 & d_{12} & d_{13} & \cdots & d_{1N} \\ d_{21} & 0 & d_{23} & \cdots & d_{2N} \\ d_{31} & d_{32} & 0 & \cdots & d_{3N} \\ \vdots & \vdots & \vdots & \ddots & \vdots \\ d_{N1} & d_{N2} & d_{N3} & \cdots & 0 \end{bmatrix}$$

MDS assumes that all coordinates are at the origin, so that relative coordinates can be obtained from relative distance information only through linear transformation. First, converting D to its doubly center format B, where $B = -\frac{1}{2}J_N D J_N$, and J_N is a fixed center matrix. Second, assuming that a $N \times 2$ matrix X records all nodes' relative coordinates. Therefore, B can be expressed as the following equation:

$$B = XX^T. \tag{4}$$

Third, by using singular value decomposition, it yields that:

$$B = V\Lambda V^T, \tag{5}$$

where V is an orthogonal matrix whose column vectors are eigenvectors, and Λ is a diagonal matrix composed of eigenvalues. Obviously, X can be solved based on Eqs. (4) and (5).

Procrustes Analysis. Procrustes analysis [19] determines a linear transformation (translation, reflection, orthogonal rotation, and scaling) of the points in the relative-map matrix of anchors to best conform them to the points in the real-position matrix of anchors. As a result, procrustes analysis outcomes a structure S with the following three fields:

(1) c: the translation component;
(2) T: the orthogonal rotation and reflection component;
(3) b: the scale component.

The matrix Y is calculated with the following equation, which represents the estimated physical coordinates among all unknown nodes.

$$Y = S.b * X * S.T + S.c. \tag{6}$$

5   Simulation

In this section, we evaluate the localization performance of our design over several aspects, such as the correlation between relative distance and physical distance, as well as the statistical comparison on maximum, minimum and mean errors with existing localization methods.

5.1   Simulation Configurations

As illustrated in Fig. 4, we model an irregular WSN as a square map without holes, which means that radio signal can reach anywhere in its area of interest. Figure 4(a) presents the network layout. Figure 4(b) shows the connectivity graph of the whole network, where each one-hop link is painted as a line segment. Default simulation configurations are listed in Table 2 for the entire Sect. 5.

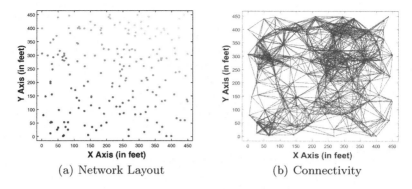

(a) Network Layout   (b) Connectivity

Fig. 4. Simulation setup

Table 2. Default configurations

Parameter	Default values
System scale	$450\,\text{ft} \times 450\,\text{ft}$
Noise model	Logarithmic Attenuation Model
Number of sensor nodes	200, randomly deployed
Number of anchor nodes	40, randomly deployed
Radio range	90 ft
RSS threshold	-114.08

It can be seen from Table 2 that the widely used logarithmic attenuation model [20] is applied for RSS sensing:

$$P_{i,j}(t) = P_t - P_l(d_0) - 10\beta \log(\frac{PD(v_i, v_j)}{d_0}) + X_i(t), \qquad (7)$$

where $P_{i,j}(t)$ stands for the sensing result starting from node v_i to node v_j at time instance t, P_t is the transmit power at a short reference distance d_0, $P_l(d_0)$ is the pass loss, β means the pass loss exponent and $PD(v_i, v_j)$ is the physical distance between the sender and receiver, and $X_i(t)$ is a random noise.

5.2   Distance Correlation

For either traditional hop-based distance or SSD, the correlation coefficient between their values and physical distances is a significant index to judge the validity of regarding them as relative distance.

Figure 5 shows the correlations between hop-based distance, SSD, and the physical distance. As for hop-based distance, one-hop node pairs exhibit an identical value "1" regardless of the corresponding physical distances. Consequently, correlation coefficient ρ is 0. In contrast, as illustrated in Fig. 5(a), a roughly linear correlation exists between SSD value and physical distance, where the

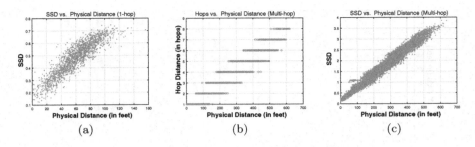

Fig. 5. Distance correlation comparison: Hop vs. SSD

correlation coefficient is $\rho = 0.90$. Thus, SSD can provide a sub-hop resolution that is not available in hop-based methods.

Figure 5(b) and (c) plot all the node pairs (including one-hop and multi-hop node pairs) with their hop distance, SSD and physical distance. Figure 5(b) indicates that only discrete integer hop distances exist among node pairs, but Fig. 5(c) shows that physical distances can be mapped to continuous values, which may nicely void the ambiguity problem in the following localization process. Furthermore, these values of correlation coefficients verify the effectiveness of taking SSD as relative distance rather than hop-based distance.

5.3 Localization Performance

The effectiveness of our design is evaluated by comparing the localization errors with other three classical localization schemes. We use the terminology "DV-Hop" [12] and "MDS-Hop" for the original hop-based approaches, "MDS-RSD" for corresponding method where the relative distance turns to RSD instead of shortest-path hops, and "MDS-SSD" for the newly designed method.

In the simulations, errors are defined as offsets of Euclidean distances between expected nodes' coordinates and real nodes' coordinates. All the statistics reported are averaged over 500 runs, and each run picks anchor nodes randomly.

We increase the number of anchors from 4 to 10 in step of 1 in the network, whereas other system configurations remain invariant. Figure 6(a), (b) and (c)

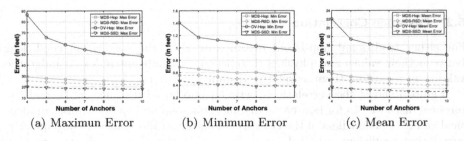

(a) Maximun Error   (b) Minimum Error   (c) Mean Error

Fig. 6. Localization errors with different number of anchors

show the maximum, minimum and mean errors respectively. As expected, localization errors decrease with the increasing of anchor numbers for all methods. From Fig. 6, we can give three remarks.

(i) Two imaginary curves are lower than two solid curves, meaning that relative distances rather than hop distances can help improve the localization accuracy. Just as mentioned above, hop distances are mapped to discrete integers, which enlarges the deviation in localization.

(ii) Our novel introduced SSD method shows the best localization performance as the errors are smallest among three subfigures.

(iii) SSD method achieves approximately 61%, 37%, 29% performance gain by average from DV-Hop, MDS-Hop and MDS-RSD respectively.

6 Experiments

In this section, we report an outdoor test-bed experiment with a regular 2D grid-shaped network.

Experiment Setup. Figure 7(a) shows the experiment scenario with 25 MICAz sensor nodes [21]. They are deployed in a 5×5 grid shape, covering an area of 60×60 square feet. The distance between each row and column is about 15 ft. Every node broadcasts 100 packets with carrier-sensing, which consist of the sender's node ID and a sequence number of the packet.

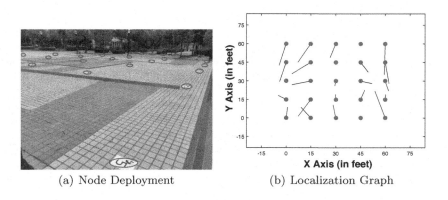

(a) Node Deployment   (b) Localization Graph

Fig. 7. Experiment: regular 2D network (Color figure online)

Localization Performance. Figure 7(b) displays the localization result from the experiment with 4 randomly selected anchors in the network. The blue dots are the real positions of all nodes, and the black line segments are directing to the estimated positions. From the collected data, there exist about 7.9 ft deviations averagely from real positions.

7   Conclusion

This paper firstly investigates the relationship between the RSS change trend and near-far distances, and then introduces a new metric for relative distance named SSD by combining the idea of neighbor pair comparison and single node RSS difference. Secondly, the paper describes the specific process of node localization based on MDS method. Simulations and outdoor experiment are finally carried out to evaluate system effectiveness from several aspects, and results demonstrate that SSD helps improve the localization accuracy.

Acknowledgements. This work was supported in part by the National Natural Science Foundation of China (Grant No. 51674255), the Natural Science Foundation of Jiangsu Province (Grant No. BK20160274), the Department of Science and Technology Project of Jiangsu Province (Grant No. BY2016026-03), the China Postdoctoral Science Special Foundation (Grant No. 2016T90523).

References

1. Zhang, S., Xiao, W., Gong, J.: Mobile sensing and simultaneously node localization in wireless sensor networks for human motion tracking. In: ICARCV 2010, pp. 2313–2318. IEEE Computer Society (2010)
2. Werner-Allen, G., Johnson, J., Ruiz, M., Lees, J.: Monitoring volcanic eruptions with a wireless sensor network. In: Proceeedings of the Second European Workshop on Wireless Sensor Networks, pp. 108–120. IEEE, New York (2005)
3. Hammoudeh, M.: Putting the lab on the map: a wireless sensor network system for border security and surveillance. In: International Conference on Internet of Things and Cloud Computing, p. 4. ACM, New York (2016)
4. Geetha, N., Sankar, A., Pankajavalli, P.B.: Energy efficient routing protocol for wireless sensor networks - an eco-friendly approach. In: 3rd International Conference on Eco-friendly Computing and Communication Systems, pp. 105–109. IEEE, New York (2014)
5. Lederer, S., Wang, Y., Gao, J.: Connectivity-based localization of large scale sensor networks with complex shape. In: InfoCom 2008. IEEE, New York (2008)
6. Sretenović, J.D., Kostić, S.M., Simić, M.I.: Experimental analysis of weight-compensated weighted centroid localization algorithm based on RSSI. In: TELSIKS 2012, pp. 373–376 (2015)
7. Yang, Z., Zhou, Z., Liu, Y.: From RSSI to CSI: indoor localization via channel response. In: ACM Comput. Surv. **46**(2), 25 (2013)
8. Rao, W., Zhu, H., Zhang, L.: An advanced distributed MDS-MAP algorithm for WSNs. In: 2009 International Conference on E-Business and Information System Security, pp. 1–5. IEEE, New York (2009)
9. Shen, G., Zetik, R., Yan, H., Hirsch, O.: Time of arrival estimation for range-based localization in UWB sensor networks. In: IEEE International Conference on Ultra-Wideband, vol. 2, pp. 1–4. IEEE, New York (2010)
10. Chaurasia, S., Payal, A.: Analysis of range-based localization schemes in wireless sensor networks: a statistical approach. In: International Conference on Advanced Communication Technology, pp. 190–195. IEEE, New York (2011)

11. Wu, G., Wang, S., Wang, B., Dong, Y., Yan, S.: A novel range-free localization based on regulated neighborhood distance for wireless ad hoc and sensor networks. Comput. Netw. **56**(16), 3581–3593 (2012)
12. Niculescu, D., Nath, B.: DV based positioning in ad hoc networks. Telecommun. Syst. **22**(1), 267–280 (2003)
13. Zhao, J., Pei, Q., Zhanqi, X.U.: APIT localization algorithms for wireless sensor networks. Comput. Eng. **45**(2), 1855–1858 (2007)
14. Wu, K., Xiao, J., Yi, Y., Chen, D.: CSI-based indoor localization. IEEE Trans. Parallel Distrib. Syst. **24**(7), 1300–1309 (2013)
15. Zhang, S., Zhang, B., Er, M.J., Guan, Z.: A novel node localization algorithm for anisotropic wireless sensor networks with holes based on MDS-MAP and EKF. In: TENCON 2010, pp. 3022–3025. IEEE, New York (2016)
16. Mariakakis, A.T., Sen, S., Lee, J., Kim, K.H.: SAIL: single access point based indoor localization. In: 12th Annual International Conference on Mobile Systems. Applications, and Services, pp. 315–328. ACM, New York (2014)
17. Yang, L., Chen, Y., Li, X.Y.: Tagoram: real-time tracking of mobile RFID tags to high precision using COTS devices. In: 20th Annual International Conference on Mobile Computing and Networking, pp. 237–248. ACM, New York (2014)
18. Zhong, Z., He, T.: RSD: a metric for achieving range-free localization beyond connectivity. In: IEEE Trans. Parallel Distrib. Syst. **22**(11), 1943–1951 (2011). IEEE, New York
19. Wang, Z., Wang, L., Wang, G., Zhang, H.: View recognition based on procrustes shape analysis for gait identification. In: Proceedings of the 33rd Chinese Control Conference, pp. 4905–4909. IEEE, New York (2014)
20. The nsManual, Chapter 18: Radio Propagation Models. http://www.isi.edu/nsnam/ns/doc/index.html
21. Ahmed, S.H., Bouk, S.H., Javaid, N., Sasase, I.: RF propagation analysis of MICAz Mote's antenna with ground effect. In: Multitopic Conference, pp. 270–274. IEEE, New York (2012)

An Adaptive MAC Protocol for Wireless Rechargeable Sensor Networks

Ping Zhong[1], Yiwen Zhang[1], Shuaihua Ma[1], Jianliang Gao[1(✉)],
and Yingwen Chen[2]

[1] School of Information Science and Engineering,
Central South University, Changsha 410083, China
gaojianliang@csu.edu.cn
[2] College of Computer, National University of Defense Technology,
Changsha 410073, China

Abstract. In the existing medium access control (MAC) protocols of rechargeable sensor networks, the maximum charging threshold of sensor nodes generally set to a fixed value based on nodes battery capacity. It leads to the channel occupied due to the long time charging of node so that the data cannot be transmitted on time. In addition, the minimum charging threshold is also set to a fixed value. This will lead to the death of the nodes due to the energy depletion while nodes cannot replenish energy in time. In this paper we put forward an adaptive charging MAC protocol called AC-MAC with double adaptive thresholds to solve the above problems. The nodes can adjust the maximum and minimum charging thresholds based on the number of transmission or receiving packets, the channel idle time and the power of transmission and reception. By analyzing the protocol, it can ensure the minimum energy level of the node, which can effectively extend the network lifetime and reduce the end to end transmission delay.

Keywords: Rechargeable sensor network · Charging thresholds · Energy harvesting · MAC protocol

1 Introduction

Wireless sensor network (WSN) has become an emerging technology combining the world and human beings closely. One of the primary challenges in WSN is the limited operating life of the sensor nodes [1]. The method like replacing batteries to extend the lifetime of network is costly and unstable [2]. Therefore, finding new energy source to replenish the energy of nodes has become an important research issue. After that people use ambient energy such as solar, wind and other ways to charging node, it cannot guarantee the effective data acquisition due to the instability of the natural energy. People try to use man-made resources for energy harvesting, especially the directional radio frequency (RF) technology for energy replenishment in wireless network which has become a kind of new technology [3]. It receives wide attention due to its good energy stability and power controllability.

L. Ma et al. (Eds.): WASA 2017, LNCS 10251, pp. 244–252, 2017.
DOI: 10.1007/978-3-319-60033-8_22

At the same time, we need to set up a reasonable medium access control (MAC) protocol to control the transmission of data and energy in order to coordinate the energy collection and data communication in wireless rechargeable sensor networks. The literature [4–6] proposed polling based MAC protocol that the base station periodically polls each node by sending a polling packet. In [4] the base station according to the data of each node determines whether to charge the battery or not. In [5, 6] when the energy of each node is less than a preset minimum threshold, the node will send charging request to the base station immediately. In addition, the data communication is fixed during this period until the current energy in battery reach to preset maximum threshold. The weakness is the value for maximum threshold is fixed, which it could cause node data transmission delay. In the literature [7], Naderi et al. proposed a RF-MAC protocol based on wireless energy harvesting, in which there has a fixed minimum threshold and an adaptive maximum threshold. If the residual energy of node reaches the preset minimum threshold, it will stop data transmission and began to replenish its energy. However, if the network cannot be timely replenished the energy, it may cause the death of node because of this fixed preset minimal threshold. It affects the network lifetime. This paper presents an adaptive charging MAC protocol (called AC-MAC) for rechargeable sensor networks to solve the above problems. In this protocol, we defined two adaptive charging thresholds. One is an adaptive minimum charging threshold, which node begins to charge once the residual energy of node reaches this value. The other one is an adaptive maximum charging threshold, which means charging process end once the nodes' energy reaches maximum threshold. The nodes adjust the maximum and minimum charging thresholds depends on the network situation, such as the number of transmission or reception packets, the power of transmission or reception, and the channel idle time.

The rest of paper is organized as follows. In Sect. 2, we give the related work. Section 3 introduce the charging model and present the problem description. Section 4 presents the overview of AC-MAC protocol. Protocol optimization and performance analysis presented in Sects. 5 and 6 respectively. Finally, Sect. 7 concludes our work.

2 Related Work

MAC protocols have been put forward to improve energy usage ratio and data transmission efficiency. The [8] presented that the protocols are highly selective and the fitness of any protocol depends solely on the application and design requirements. In this section we will introduce the related medium access control protocols for rechargeable sensor network.

2.1 MAC Protocols for Wireless Sensor Networks with Ambient Energy Harvesting

The sensors in energy harvesting wireless sensor networks (EHWSN) are powered by rechargeable batteries that replenished through energy scavenged from renewable or ambient sources. The MAC protocol of EHWSN aims to maximize the lifetime of

WSN by applying the maximum harvested energy instead of saving the residual energy. In [9], the authors proposed an intelligent solar energy-harvesting system for WSN. In [10], it presents the performance of different MAC protocols based on CSMA and polling techniques for WSN powered by ambient energy harvesting. In [11], the authors proposed an asynchronous, receiver- initiated polling MAC protocol for EHWSN. It dynamically adjusted the number of polling packets to minimize interference. In [12], it proposed a fair MAC protocol based on polling scheme for EHWSN, which adjusts the contention probability in accordance with node itself harvesting rate. In [13], an optimal relay is selected by solved a maximization of minimum value of residual energy.

2.2 MAC Protocols for Sensor Networks with Wireless Energy Transfer

Recently energy harvesting with RF has become an emerging technology instead of ambient natural energy source because of the good stability and controllability of RF [14]. A survey on RF energy harvesting circuits and protocols is presented in [15].

In [16], it proposed two cross-layer approaches depended on device characterization, device-agnostic and device-specific protocols. In [7], the authors for RF energy harvesting sensors proposed a RF-MAC protocol to appropriately balance the channel between energy transfer and communication functions, that means optimizes energy delivery and minimizes the disruption to data communication at same time. In [17], the centralized controller is not only delivering data, but also supplying wireless energy to network nodes. It used a constrained Markov decision process to derive a queueing model so as to obtain the network performance. In [18], the paper proposed a hybrid framework of EHWSN with solar cluster heads and the rest of RF sensor nodes. It used a polynomial-time scheduling algorithm to optimize the joint tour consisting of both wireless charging and data gathering.

3 Charging Model

In wireless sensor network, the energy problem of the nodes affects the performance of the whole network. Each rechargeable sensor nodes are equipped with a same rechargeable battery. The maximum storage capacity of the battery is set as E_{max}. We also set E_{min} to guarantee the normal operation of the node. When the residual current energy $E_{current}$ of node is lower than the minimum energy value E_{min}, the node will stop transmitting because the node lacks of energy. Hence, once the residual energy of node reaches E_{min}, this node will send the request for energy (RFE) packet to the energy transmitters (ETs). The energy transmitter will send a short energy pulse called cleared for energy (CFE) and supplement the energy to the node, where energy is transmitted in the form of packet. The power harvested from one transmitter is calculated as

$$P_r = \eta G_r G_t \left(\frac{\lambda}{4\pi R}\right)^2 P_t \tag{1}$$

Here η is conversion factor of RF to DC, G_r and G_t are antenna gain of reception and transmission respectively, λ is the wave length, R is the distance between node and energy transmitter, P_t is the transmission power.

Assumed node harvested power from multiple transmitters. $P_r(i,m)$ denotes the energy node i harvest from transmitter m. $R(i,m)$ denotes the distance between node i and transmitter m. The $P_r(i,m)$ is calculated as

$$P_r(i,m) = \eta G_r G_t \left(\frac{\lambda}{4\pi R(i,m)}\right)^2 P_t \tag{2}$$

Then we can get the total energy node i harvested from all transmitters N calculated as

$$P_r(i) = \sum_{m=1}^{N} P_r(i,m) \tag{3}$$

The constraint condition of current energy of node after energy replenishment is given at (4), E_r denotes harvested energy, E_{total} denotes current energy after energy replenishment.

$$E_{total} = \begin{cases} E_{\max}, & E_{current} + E_r \geq E_{\max} \\ E_{current} + E_r, & E_{current} + E_r < E_{\max} \end{cases} \tag{4}$$

4   Detailed AC-MAC Protocol Description

The network is assumed a multi-hop sensor networks and the transmission of data and energy occurs in the same frequency band. Data communication and energy supplement share the same channel and access it separately. When the residual energy of the node reaches the minimum threshold, it gives higher priority to the energy supplement than the data transmission for accessing the channel by defining different time slot for data and energy access.

4.1   Adaptive Energy Threshold

In AC-MAC protocol, we define two adaptive energy thresholds $E_{\max thr}$ and $E_{\min thr}$ for effective transmission of data and energy. Maximum charging threshold $E_{\max thr}$ is the upper charging energy thresholds which is less than the system parameter $E_{\max}$. Minimum charging threshold $E_{\min thr}$ is the lower charging energy thresholds which is great than $E_{\min}$.

There are existing two problems during the charging phase. Firstly, if we charge the energy of node to a fixed value or even to $E_{\max}$ and this node already has enough energy to support data transmission. The data still cannot be sent immediately when the current node wants to send data during in the middle of charging because the energy of node still haven't reached the preset fixed value for the moment, which may incur the delay of data transmission or even packet loss due to the long time waiting. Secondly, the current energy of node already reached to preset fixed value but not maximum value and there is no packet to send at this moment, which may result in a waste of energy because of idle channel.

When the traffic is very heavy, the node consumes energy quickly. In other word, it need more energy to support its work. We use an important coefficient of nodes denoted γ to adaptively adjust the node charging energy. The calculated equation is shown in (5) and the adaptive maximum charging threshold is calculated in (6).

$$\gamma = \frac{N_t P_t + N_r P_r}{N_t P_t + N_r P_r + Ct} \tag{5}$$

$$E_{\text{maxthr}} = \gamma(E_{\text{max}} - E_{\text{min}}) + E_{\text{min}} \tag{6}$$

Here, N_t and N_r denote the number of packets have sent and received respectively, P_t and P_r denote transmit power and receiving power. C_t represents the power consumption on data transfer activity that overhead by the nodes whether the beginning or the end. When node consumes more energy on transmitting or receiving, the parameter $E_{\text{max}\,thr}$ will be bigger along with the γ.

Next we are going to discuss the adaptive minimum charging threshold. If the residual energy of node reaches the preset minimum threshold, it will stop data transmission and begin to replenish its energy. However, when the network cannot be replenished energy in a timely, it may cause the death of node because of this fixed preset minimal threshold, which may affect the network lifetime. Hence the adaptive minimum charging threshold $E_{\text{min}\,thr}$ according to the important coefficient calculated as (7).

$$E_{\text{min}\,thr} = (\gamma - 1)^2 E_{\text{max}} + \gamma^2 E_{\text{min}} + 2\gamma(1 - \gamma)\sqrt{E_{\text{max}}E_{\text{min}}} \tag{7}$$

4.2   Adaptive Protocol Operating Procedure

AC-MAC protocol is based on CSMA/CA protocol. When it starts operation, it will calculate adaptive charging threshold $E_{\text{min}\,thr}$ and judge the level of residual energy of nodes. If the current energy of node reaches the $E_{\text{min}\,thr}$, the energy transmission will get the channel access firstly. Then if the channel is idle after waiting for DIFS, the node that needs energy will enter the contention window and select a random backoff time from [0, CW]. It will start backoff timer and if the backoff timer counts to 0, the nodes will send RFE to ETs until receiving the CFE. Then it will send ACK packet that includes the charging duration and the energy transmission begins. If the channel is occupied in the middle of backoff, the backoff timer will be suspended until the channel is idle again and the nodes will keep waiting for DIFS and start backoff timer with the current value, then repeat like above. If the current node energy more than the adaptive minimum charge threshold $E_{\min thr}$, the data communication will first get the channel access. The process of data communication is almost like the energy transmission, in which the only difference is that the data transfer makes use of the RTS-CTS-DATA-ACK mechanism.

4.3   An Example for Adaptive MAC Protocol

As shown in Fig. 1, two nodes N_1 and N_2 are assumed to have residual energy of 2 and 3 Joules respectively. Assuming the energy of N_1 has reached the adaptive minimum charging threshold, meanwhile N_2 needs to send data. N_1 sends out RFE packet requesting for immediate charging and our protocol ensures that N_1 can get the channel access for energy transfer. How much energy should N_1 charge depends on the $E_{\min thr}$. At the same time, N_2 needs to stopping its backoff timer to go into sleeping mode, then ETs will reply with a cleared for energy (CFE) pulse. When N_1 get CFE, it will replay back with ACK packet to the ETs in which it includes the charging duration. Then N_1 is going to turn into charging mode. When N_2 receives CFE, it will calculate how long it should sleep according to the information in CFE. After the end of energy transmission, N_2 is going to access the channel to transmit data.

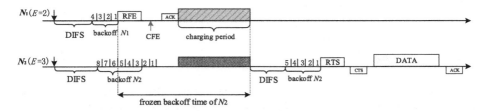

Fig. 1. The operating process of an example under adaptive MAC protocol

5   Performance Evaluation

We use the NS-2 network simulator to evaluate the performance of our adaptive MAC protocol. We compare our adaptive MAC protocol (AC-MAC) with CSMA/CA protocol through the analysis of the network throughput.

In this paper, the network topology is in the plane of a $600 * 200$ m^2. In initial model we defined in total of three sensor nodes, which have two charging nodes and one energy transmitter, they are all in a static state. One of the two charging nodes is used for data transmission and another is used for energy harvesting. Energy transmitter is located at the centric position between these two charging nodes and supplies energy for them. After that we are going to increase the number of the sensor nodes and arrange them in the different position from the transmitter, the data is forwarded to the energy harvesting node by multi-hop network, in which some of the sending nodes can also be as relay nodes for data forwarding.

In the simulation, the preset energy of each node is 100 J with the charging power is 3 w per second. In addition, the charging time is 30 s. The parameters of RF transmission are in Table 1, and the parameters for adaptive MAC protocol presented in Table 2.

Table 1. The parameters of RF transmission

Parameter	Value	Unit
Energy harvesting effiency (η)	0.58	–
Transmitter antenna gain (G_t)	1.0	dbi
Receiver antenna gain (G_r)	1.0	dbi
Frequency (C/λ)	915	MHz

Table 2. The parameters used in AC-MAC

Parameter	Value	Unit
Power consumption of contention	31	mA
Power consumption of transmission	29	mA
Power consumption of sleep	30	uA
Operating voltage	3.0	v
Slot time (energy)	10	μs
Slot time (data)	20	μs
SIFS (energy)	5	μs
SIFS (data)	10	μs

The data rate is increased from 0 to 400 Kbps and the other parameters are kept the default value. As we can see from Figs. 2 and 3, the performance of AC-MAC is better than the CSMA protocol in terms of throughput and transmission delay. Our simulation time is 10000 s. The node can be reduced from E_{max}(100 J) to E_{min}(60 J), the charging process can be carried out during the experiment. As we can see from Fig. 2, the throughput of AC-MAC and CSMA increases linearly when the increase of data rate from 0 to 100 (kbits/s), and the result of AC-MAC is always larger than CSMA. When

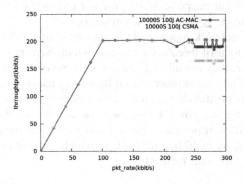

Fig. 2. Performance comparison of throughput between AC-MAC and CSMA

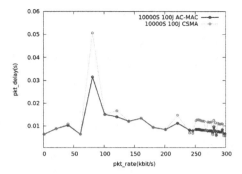

Fig. 3. Performance comparison of delay between AC-MAC and CSMA

the data rate is greater than 100 and less than 200, the throughput of the two protocols are saturated. When it is larger than 200 kbit/s, the throughput of CSMA protocol is significantly decreased.

AC-MAC is still significantly better than CSMA in terms of packet delay. We can see that the trend of AC-MAC and CSMA packet delay is basically consistent. How-ever, AC-MAC can obviously reduce the packet delay of CSMA when the data rate is within a certain range, such as from 50 to 100. The reason is that the adaptive threshold balances the conflict between the charging module and the data transmission. The AC-MAC protocol adaptively adjusts the charging event based on the network environment. Compared with the constant charging parameters of CSMA protocol, it avoids the long time wait at light traffic load and node death at heavy traffic load.

6 Conclusion

In this paper we proposed adaptive minimum and maximum charging thresholds, nodes adjust these thresholds via the number of packets that has been sent and received by nodes, the channel idle time and the power of transmission and reception to prolong the lifetime of the network and the data transmission efficiency. Simulation result reveals that the throughput and transmission delay of AC-MAC protocol are better than the CSMA/CA protocol's performance. The further work we will consider more energy transmitters situation.

Acknowledgments. The work described in this paper was supported by the grant from the National Natural Science Foundation of China (Nos. 61402542 and 61202495).

References

1. Long, J., Dong, M., Ot, K., Liu, A.: Green TDMA scheduling algorithm for prolonging lifetime in wireless sensor networks. IEEE Syst. J. 1–10 (2015)
2. Abdollahzadeh, S., Navimipour, N.J.: Deployment strategies in the wireless sensor network: a comprehensive review. Comput. Commun. **91**, 1–16 (2016)

3. Shaikh, F.K., Zeadally, S.: Energy harvesting in wireless sensor networks: a comprehensive review. Renew. Sustain. Energ. Rev. **55**, 1041–1054 (2016)
4. Misic, V.B., Misic, J.: A polling MAC for wireless sensor networks with RF recharging of sensor nodes. In: 7th Biennial Symposium on Communications (QBSC), pp. 76–80 (2014)
5. Khan, M.S.I., Misic, J., Misic, V.B.: A polling MAC with reliable RF recharging of sensor nodes. In: Wireless Communications and Networking Conference (WCNC), pp. 831–836 (2015)
6. Khan, M.S.I., Misic, J., Misic, V.B.: Impact of network load on the performance of a polling MAC with wireless recharging of nodes. IEEE Trans. Emerg. Topics Comput. **3**(3), 307–316 (2015)
7. Naderi, M.Y., Nintanavongsa, P., Chowdhury, K.R.: RF-MAC: a medium access control protocol for re-chargeable sensor networks powered by wireless energy harvesting. IEEE Trans. Wireless Commun. **13**(7), 3926–3937 (2014)
8. Kosunalp, S.: MAC protocols for energy harvesting wireless sensor networks: survey. ETRI J. **37**(4), 804–812 (2015)
9. Li, Y., Shi, R.H.: An intelligent solar energy-harvesting system for wireless sensor networks. Eurasip J. Wireless Commun. Netw. 1–12 (2015)
10. Eu, Z.A., Tan, H.P., Seah, W.K.G.: Design and performance analysis of MAC schemes for wireless sensor networks powered by ambient energy harvesting. Ad Hoc Netw. **9**(3), 300–323 (2011)
11. Eu, Z.A., Tan, H.P.: Probabilistic polling for multi-hop energy harvesting wireless sensor networks. In: IEEE International Symposium Ad-hoc Sensor Network, pp. 271–275 (2012)
12. Kunikawa, M., Yomo, H., Abe, K., Ito, T.: A fair polling scheme for energy harvesting wireless sensor networks. In: 81st IEEE Vehicular Technology Conference (VTC Spring), pp. 1–5 (2015)
13. Zhang, D.Y., Chen, Z.G., Zhou, H.B., Chen, L., Shen, X.: Energy-balanced cooperative transmission based on relay selection and power control in energy harvesting wireless sensor network. Comput. Netw. **104**, 189–197 (2016)
14. Lu, X., Wang, P., Niyato, D., Kim, D.I., Han, Z.: Wireless networks with RF energy harvesting: a contemporary survey. IEEE Commun. Surv. Tutorials **17**(2), 757–789 (2015)
15. Nintanavongsa, P.: A survey on RF energy harvesting: circuits and protocols. Energy Procedia **56**, 414–422 (2014)
16. Nintanavongsa, P., Doost-Mohammady, R., Felice, M.D., Chowdhury, K.: Device characterization and cross-layer protocol design for RF energy harvesting sensors. Pervasive Mob. Comput. **9**(1), 120–131 (2013)
17. Niyato, D., Wang, P., Kim, D.I.: Performance analysis and optimization of TDMA network with wireless energy transfer. IEEE Trans. Wireless Commun. **13**(8), 4205–4219 (2014)
18. Wang, C., Li, J., Yang, Y., Ye, F.: A hybrid framework combining solar energy harvesting and wireless charging for wireless sensor networks. In: IEEE Infocom, pp. 1–9 (2016)

Fair Multi-influence Maximization in Competitive Social Networks

Ying Yu[1], Jinglan Jia[1], Deying Li[2(✉)], and Yuqing Zhu[3]

[1] School of Mathematics and Statistics,
Central China Normal University, Wuhan, China
[2] School of Information, Renmin University of China, Beijing, China
deyingli@ruc.edu.cn
[3] Department of Computer Science,
California State University, Los Angeles, USA

Abstract. We study multi-influence competing in social networks. First we propose *Timeliness Independent Cascade* (TIC) model - a natural multi-influence propagation model. Second we propose *FairInf* problem: given several companies and their budgets, how to choose their separated seeds such that the overall influence spread is maximized and each individual company's influence spread is fairly distributed. Third, we prove that when seeds for other companies are fixed, a company's influence spread is monotone and submodular, which means greedy algorithm has the ratio of $(1 - 1/e)$. We design a greedy algorithm MG which runs quickly. At last, we conduct extensive experiments on real world social networks of different scales, and evaluate that our algorithm achieves the design goal.

1 Introduction

Social networks are graphs consist of individuals and their relationships. The extreme boom of online social networking sites like Facebook, Twitter, Weibo, etc. has been witnessed in the past decade, and lots of real social network data have been obtained thanks to these online websites. In social networks, the most significant phenomenon is "diffusion", which contains the diffusion of news, innovations, and product adoptions, etc., is a pervasive characteristic of social networks, and people commonly regard such diffusion as influence propagation.

Influence propagation is the basis of *viral marketing* [9,10], which is marketing via "word of mouth" recommendations. How to identify "opinion leaders" to bring large further recommendations, i.e., propagated influence is an essential issue. Formally, the *influence maximization* is the problem of determining k individuals in a social network under certain probabilistic influence model(s), such that the expected influence is maximized.

Single source influence maximization has been studied extensively. In [14] Kempe et al. proposed the two most popular and basic single-influence diffusion models including independent cascade (IC) model and linear threshold (LT) model. Many following studies [7,8,16] focused on the scalable algorithms for

© Springer International Publishing AG 2017
L. Ma et al. (Eds.): WASA 2017, LNCS 10251, pp. 253–265, 2017.
DOI: 10.1007/978-3-319-60033-8_23

single-influence maximization. However, in reality there are often more than one innovations spreading in a social network. Noticing that binary oppositions widely exist in our life, such as ruling party vs. opposition party, truth vs. rumor, people studied the circumstances where two innovations coexist and compete with each other [3,5,13,17]. Nevertheless it is still not general enough, since in many scenarios more than two innovations exist and compete with others trying to maximize their influences respectively. Some models of multiple influence competition have been presented therefore. They are usually the extensions of IC model [1] and LT model [2,18].

There are some multi-influence diffusion models proposed based on LT model recently, however, as another significant model, how to extend IC model to multi-influence competitive scenario is not well studied. Bharathi et al. in [1] proposed their model, however it is oversimplified. In this model, if a node u is active to influence I_1, and successful activates its neighbor v at time t, v will become active to I_1 at time $t + T_{uv}$, where T_{uv} is an independent random variable. This model doesn't fully capture the essence of multiple influences competition. In fact, if another node w active to another influence I_2 successfully activates v after t but before $t + T_{uv}$, v may be active to I_2 instead of I_1. Other IC based models also have similar ignorance (we will give the detailed review in Sect. 2). Note that comparing to LT, IC captures both the competition and timeliness, and fits online social networks more. However on the other side, influence diffusion under IC model in competitive environment is hard to capture and tract. Therefore IC extension under multi-influence competitive scenario needs more attention from both practical significance and theoretical challenge.

Most current related research about competitive influence maximization focus on the game theory aspect [1,2,5,15]. Two issues exist: First, due to the problem complexity, they only gave the strategies for some specific players (we refer influence as player or mover) such as the first mover or the last mover. Second, one common prerequisite of all the games set up in these literatures is that all players are completely aware of the whole social network, which is hard to meet in real scenarios due to two reasons: (1) The player usually doesn't own the social networking platform, e.g., we often see car advertisements on Facebook, but obviously these car companies don't own Facebook. This is troublesome. Nowadays data is everything, it is impossible for the third party platform provider to share the data with these players. (2) Even if the players use web crawlers to collect the data, obtaining the same and integrated network seems to be an impossible mission. Therefore, due to theoretical and practical limits of game theory methods, it is also necessary to study influence maximization strategies for general players considering realistic constraints.

In this paper, to solve the above issues, we first propose a more natural *competitive Timeliness Independent Cascade* (TIC) model for multi-influence diffusion in social networks, and then based on TIC model, we raise a new multi-influence problem *FairInf* that studies how to give companies fair influence spreads according to their budgets. At last, we devise an fast Algorithms MG for *FairInf*, and verify its effectiveness on several real-world networks of different scales and features.

2   Related Work

For single influence propagation, IC and LT models are the most popular diffusion models summarized by Kempe et al. in [14] based on work [10]. The authors in [14] also proved that the influence maximization under both IC and LT models are submodular which leads to a $(1 - 1/e)$ ratio greedy algorithm. Many follow-up research [7,8,16,26] focused on the scalability improvement since the influence computation is too costly. Chen et al. in [7] proposed maximum influence arborescence (MIA) model to compute the influence under IC model and showed that the greedy algorithm on MIA has a very high scalability. Some other literature also study the single influence maximization problem under different application scenarios [4,11,12,22].

Several studies on competitive influence diffusion have emerged recently. [3,5, 6,13,17,23] mainly studied two-influence model. Carnes et al. [5] gave a distance-based model and a wave propagation model both of which are two-influence diffusion models, and showed that in the two influence game the follower can achieve $(1 - 1/e)$ of the maximum influence. Chen et al. [6] presented a single-influence model but negative influence may emerge, they proved the monotony and submodularity of their objective function. He et al. [13] proposed *competitive linear threshold* (CLT) model and focused on *influence blocking maximization* (IBM) problem of how to block the competitor's influence. Li et al. [17] proposed and solved the $\gamma - k$ rumor restriction problem.

In [1,2,15,18,20,24], the authors proposed some general competitive influence diffusion model. Bharathi et al. [1] proposed a new IC based model for the diffusion of multiple innovations, studied the 2 player game and proved that the last mover can obtain $(1 - 1/e)$ of the best response. Kostka et al. [15] classified the node into k states, their basic model is a special case of IC model. They studied a 2 player case and showed that the first mover does not always have the advantage. Pathak et al. [20] presented an extension of LT model for multiple cascades allowing nodes to switch between them. Three LT based competitive models were proposed by Borodin et al. [2], which include the Weight-Proportional Competitive Linear Threshold Model, the Separated-Threshold Model and the Competitive Threshold Model with Forcing. The authors also showed that influence maximization under none of these models is submodular. Zhu et al. [25] studied Competitive - Independent Cascade (C-IC) model and then propose Minimum Cost Seed Set problem (MinSeed) and gave a greedy algorithm with performance guarantee. Lu et al. [18] studied the *Fair Seed Allocation* (FSA) problem from the host perspective under their proposed K-LT model, and proposed a Greedy. This is the most related work, our work differs with it since ours is based on a totally different influence propagation model and with optimization constraints. Also, we propose a near optimal polynomial time solution besides Greedy.

3 IC Model and Monotone Submodular Set Function

According to the definition in [14], an IC influence graph is a weighted graph $G = (V, E, p)$, where V is a set of nodes whose size is n, $E \subseteq V \times V$ is a set of edges whose size is m, and $p : E \to [0, 1]$ is a function that $p_{u,v}$ represents the success probability when node u tries to activate v. The influence propagation in IC model starts with a given set S of active nodes. In every step i, the set of active nodes is S_i (let $S_0 = S$ and $S_{-1} = \emptyset$), which consists of the nodes in S_{i-1} and the nodes activated by the nodes in $S_{i-1} \setminus S_{i-2}$ in step i. Note that each node u only has one chance to activate each of its neighbors v with probability $p_{u,v}$ when u first becomes active, and $p_{u,v}$ is a history independent parameter. The process runs until when $S_{t+1} = S_t$ at a step $t + 1$.

Influence of a given seed set is the expected number of nodes activated by this set. In IC cascade process, fixed p does not fasten the final influence, since each activation from u to v is an event successes with probability $p_{u,v}$. The influence is the expectation over the combination of all the events that a node u activates one of its neighbor v.

A set function f on a given set V is a function from 2^V to $\mathbb{R}$, where 2^V denotes the power set of V and $\mathbb{R}$ is the set of real numbers. We introduce following two basic properties.

- **Monotonicity**: f is *monotone* if $f(X) \le f(Y)$ for any two sets $X \subseteq Y$.
- **Submodularity**: f is *submodular* if for every $X \subseteq Y \subseteq V$ and $z \in V \setminus Y$,
  $f(X \cup \{z\}) - f(X) \ge f(Y \cup \{z\}) - f(Y)$.

4 TIC Model and FairInf Problem

We start to introduce our new multi-influence propagation model. For the sake of conciseness, we will uniformly use influence to represent company from now on.

4.1 TIC Model

In this subsection we introduce our TIC (competitive Timeliness Independent Cascade) model. As usual, the social network is represented as a directed graph $G = (V, E)$. For nodes u and v, if there is a directed edge from u to v, then we call u as v's *in-neighbor* and v as u's *out-neighbor*. Each node has three possible states: *inactive*, *active* or *decided*. Activation is the operation when an *active* or *decided* nodes tries to turn one of its out-neighbors to *active*. For each edge $(u, v) \in E$, it has an independent parameter $p_{u,v}$ that indicates the successful probability if u tries to activate v.

Suppose there are m different influences diffusing in the social network. We use m colors $c_1, ..., c_m$ to denote these m influences. In TIC model, different from existing models, an *active* node does not have a certain color and it may spread multiple influences. For example, suppose u_1 and u_2 are two in-neighbors of node v, if u_1 and u_2 successfully activate v with influence c_1 and c_2 respectively, v

will try to further activate its out-neighbors with both c_1 and c_2. For v, once it receives the first success activation in time t it will turn from *inactive* to *active* in the same time, and begin to activate each out-neighbor w in $t+1$. If this attempt succeeds, v will continue propagating influences to w, else, no future influence can be propagated from v to w. Every node $v \in V$ has a *decision deadline* D_v which is an independent positive integer parameter. v will "remember" all the successful activations it receives before the deadline D_v. Suppose it receives successful activations of c_i for b_i times $(1 \leq i \leq m)$, v will become *decided* to c_i at time D_v with probability $\frac{b_i}{\sum_{i=1}^{m} b_i}$. When v turns to state *decided* with color c^v, it will only spread c^v to its out-neighbors afterwards. If v receives no successful activation before D_v then it will remain *inactive* forever. A seed node of c_i in TIC model is a node s of state *decided* with color c_i at time 0, and the seed set S_i is the set of all c_i's seeds. A seed node can only have one color. The influence propagation of TIC model ends when no further *decided* nodes exists.

4.2   FairInf Problem

Let $\mathbf{S} = \bigcup_{i=1}^{m} S_i$ be the union of all the seed sets belonging to all the influences, and we call $\mathbf{S}$ the *overall seed set*. For each influence i, denote c_i by its color, and it has an integer budget μ_i, $\mu_i \in \mathbb{Z}+$.

Definition 1 *(i-spread). Given the overall seed set $\mathbf{S}$, and S_i, the seed set of color c_i, then i-spread is the expectation of the final number of nodes in color c_i, and it is denoted as*

$$\mathcal{I}_i(S_i, \mathbf{S}).$$

Definition 2 *(Earning-to-Budget Ratio (EBR)). Given $\mathbf{S}$, S_i, and the budget μ_i of influence i, the i-spread $\mathcal{I}_i(S_i, \mathbf{S})$ is the earning. The EBR of influence i is defined as*

$$e_i = \frac{\mathcal{I}_i(S_i, \mathbf{S})}{\mu_i}.$$

Definition 3 *(Fairness). Given all m influences' budgets $\{b_i | 1 \leq i \leq m\}$ and their seed sets $\{S_i | 1 \leq i \leq m\}$, define the Fairness of this seed allocation as*

$$f = \frac{e_{min}}{e_{max}},$$

where e_{min} is the minimum EBR among these influences, i.e., $\min_{1 \leq i \leq m} e_i$, and $e_{max} = \max_{1 \leq i \leq m} e_i$.

Given a TIC graph $G = (V, E)$ and budgets $\{\mu_i\}$ for m influences satisfying that $\sum_{i=1}^{m} \mu_i \leq |V|$, we check following problems.

Problem 1 *(Overall Influence Maximization). To find a set $\mathbf{S}$ satisfying $|\mathbf{S}| = \sum_{i=1}^{m} \mu_i$ that maximizes $\mathcal{I}(\mathbf{S})$, where $\mathcal{I}(\mathbf{S})$ is the expected spread when single influence exists.*

Problem 2 *(Fair Multi-influence Maximization (*FairInf*)).* *Finding m sets S_i satisfying $|\bigcup_{i=1}^{m} S_i| = \sum_{i=1}^{m} \mu_i$ from the agency's (the social network owner) prospective, to maximize total influence $\sum_{i=1}^{m} \mathcal{I}_i(S_i, \mathbf{S})$ first while maximizing the Fairness f as much as possible.*

We explain the connection between Problems 1 and 2. It stands that $\mathcal{I}(\mathbf{S}) = \sum_{i=1}^{m} \mathcal{I}_i(S_i, \mathbf{S})$ ($\mathbf{S} = \bigcup_{i=1}^{m} S_i$), which means that when multiple influences compete each other in a social network, the sum of these influences' spreads with their seed sets is the same as a single influence's spread with the union of these seed sets. This also means that for a given set, arbitrary partitioning this set into several subsets belonging to different influences will not impact this set's overall spread (Please refer details in Sect. 4.4). Hence, to solve *FairInf*, we can begin with solving Problem 1 to obtain $\mathbf{S}$ (first phase), and then allocate nodes in $\mathbf{S}$ to different influences in a fair manner (second phase).

For the first phase, we will prove that $\mathcal{I}(\mathbf{S})$ is monotone and submodular w.r.t. $\mathbf{S}$ in a single influence TIC graph, which implies that simple Greedy has $1 - 1/e$ ratio for Problem 1, and we will also propose another scalable algorithm for this problem. For the second phase, we will firstly find the "constant" feature of each seed in $\mathbf{S}$ that won't be altered no matter which influences other seeds in $\mathbf{S}$ are allocated, and then design algorithms to allocate the seeds to different influences such that the Fairness is maximized.

We would like to discuss more about Fairness here, which is used to judge how EBRs $\{e_i\}$ vary. In fact, criteria like standard deviation or Gini coefficient are more sensitive to EBR variation, but using them as optimization objectives makes the problem much more complex. Instead we will use them to judge our algorithms' performances, and it will be seen that our method works also best in terms of them.

4.3   Properties of TIC Model

In this subsection we will discuss the monotony and submodularity of the influence maximization in TIC social networks. Given two positive numbers $p_1, \widetilde{p_1}$ satisfying that $p_1 \leq \widetilde{p_1}$, we have following lemmas.

Lemma 1. *For any non-negative number δ,*

$$\frac{p_1 + \delta}{\widetilde{p_1} + \delta} \geq \frac{p_1}{\widetilde{p_1}}. \tag{1}$$

Proof 1.

$$(1) \Leftrightarrow \widetilde{p_1}(p_1 + \delta) \geq p_1(\widetilde{p_1} + \delta)$$
$$\Leftrightarrow \delta(\widetilde{p_1} - p_1) \geq 0. \tag{2}$$

(2) is obvious since $p_1 \leq \widetilde{p_1}$, thus Lemma 1 stands.

Lemma 2. *For any non-negative numbers δ_1 and δ_2,*

$$\frac{p_1 + \delta_2}{\widetilde{p_1} + \delta_2} - \frac{p_1}{\widetilde{p_1}} \geq \frac{p_1 + \delta_1 + \delta_2}{\widetilde{p_1} + \delta_1 + \delta_2} - \frac{p_1 + \delta_1}{\widetilde{p_1} + \delta_1}. \tag{3}$$

Proof 2.

$$(3) \Leftrightarrow \frac{\delta_2(\widetilde{p_1} - p_1)}{(\widetilde{p_1} + \delta_2)\widetilde{p}} \geq \frac{\delta_2(\widetilde{p_1} - p_1)}{(\widetilde{p_1} + \delta_1 + \delta_2)(\widetilde{p_1} + \delta_1)}$$
$$\Leftrightarrow (\widetilde{p_1} + \delta_1 + \delta_2)(\widetilde{p_1} + \delta_1) \geq (\widetilde{p_1} + \delta_2)\widetilde{p_1}. \tag{4}$$

Since $\delta_1, \delta_2 \geq 0$, we have $\widetilde{p_1} + \delta_1 + \delta_2 \geq \widetilde{p_1} + \delta_2$ and $\widetilde{p_1} + \delta_1 \geq \widetilde{p_1}$, hence inequation (4) stands, thus Lemma 1 stands.

Theorem 1. *Suppose the seed sets $\{S_j | j \neq i\}$ for other influences are fixed. Then, i-spread $\mathcal{I}_i(S_i, \mathbf{S})$ is a monotone and submodular function w.r.t. S_i.*

Proof 3. *To prove this theorem, we first recall that in TIC model, each u has a sole chance to activate its out-neighbor v. If this attempt succeeds, all the influences can be propagated from u to v, else no influence can be propagated from u to v. Hence, influence propagation in TIC model can be analyzed based on the random graphs like that in IC model. For each edge $(u, v) \in E$, we flip a coin in time 0 of bias $p(u, v)$. If the coin flip indicates an successful activation then we declare (u, v) a live-edge. However, for each node w, it has a deadline D_w, which means that even if there is a path from a seed to w consisting entirely of live-edges, w still may not become active if the influence can not be propagated before D_w, nor become decided at last.*

Definition 4 *(Live-Path).* *We call a path $\langle s, (s, w_1), w_1, (w_1, w_2), ..., (w_{l-1}, w_l), w_l \rangle$ a live-path if each edge (w_{i-1}, w_i) $(w_0 = s)$ is a live-edge, and $i \leq D_{w_i}$ for every node w_i.*

Based on Definition 4, we define c_j-path, which is a live-path where s is a seed of color c_j. Consider the probability space in which each sample point specifies one possible set of outcomes for all the coin flips on the edges, and denote $\mathcal{X}$ one sample point. Our next proof will be based on $\mathcal{X}$, which is also a determined graph. We denote $b_j^{\mathcal{X}}(X, v)$ the number of c_j-paths from X to v based on graph $\mathcal{X}$, and $\sigma_i^{\mathcal{X}}(X, v)$ the i-spread of X on node v, which is the possibility that v finally being decided to c_i, Let $\mathcal{I}_i^{\mathcal{X}}$ be the i-spread based on $\mathcal{X}$. Then

$$\sigma_i^{\mathcal{X}}(X, v) = \frac{b_i^{\mathcal{X}}(X, v)}{\sum_{j=1}^m b_j^{\mathcal{X}}(X, v)}, \quad \mathcal{I}_i^{\mathcal{X}}(X) = \sum_{v \in V} \sigma_i^{\mathcal{X}}(X, v).$$

For the sake of logic correctness, we let $\frac{0}{0} = 0$, which states the fact that if no c_j-path ($\forall j$) reaches v, then v will not be decided at last, i.e., its spread is 0. For any set $X \in S$, $\sum_{j \neq i}^m b_j^{\mathcal{X}}(X, v)$ is a constant since all the seeds with other colors are fixed. Also, for any sets $X \subseteq Y$ and $v \in V$,

$$b_j^{\mathcal{X}}(Y, v) = b_j^{\mathcal{X}}(X, v) + b_j^{\mathcal{X}}(Y \setminus X, v)$$

since the number of c_j-paths only depends on their sources on a fixed graph $\mathcal{X}$, and any two c_j-paths from different sources are different.

(1) We first prove $\mathcal{I}_i^{\mathcal{X}}$'s monotony. By Lemma 1,

$$\sigma_i^{\mathcal{X}}(X \cup \{z\}, v) = \frac{b_i^{\mathcal{X}}(X \cup \{z\})}{\sum_{j=1}^{m} b_j^{v}(X \cup \{z\})}$$

$$= \frac{b_i^{\mathcal{X}}(X, v) + b_i^{\mathcal{X}}(\{z\})}{\sum_{j=1}^{m} b_j^{v}(X, v) + b_i^{\mathcal{X}}(\{z\})}$$

$$\geq \frac{b_i^{\mathcal{X}}(X, v)}{\sum_{j=1}^{m} b_j^{v}(X, v)} = \sigma_i^{\mathcal{X}}(X, v)$$

Hence, $\mathcal{I}_i^{\mathcal{X}}(X \cup \{z\}) \geq \mathcal{I}_i^{\mathcal{X}}(X)$, $\mathcal{I}_i^{\mathcal{X}}$ is monotone.

(2) We prove the submodularity of $\mathcal{I}_i^{\mathcal{X}}$. Suppose $X \subseteq Y \subseteq V$ and $z \in V \setminus Y$. Let $\delta_1 = b_i^{\mathcal{X}}(Y \setminus X, v)$, and $\delta_2 = b_i^{\mathcal{X}}(\{z\}, v)$, then $b_i^{\mathcal{X}}(Y, v) = b_i^{\mathcal{X}}(X, v) + \delta_1$. By Lemma 2 we have

$$\sigma_i^{\mathcal{X}}(X \cup \{z\}, v) - \sigma_i^{\mathcal{X}}(X, v)$$

$$= \frac{b_i^{\mathcal{X}}(X, v) + \delta_2}{\sum_{j=1}^{m} b_j^{v}(X, v) + \delta_2} - \frac{b_i^{\mathcal{X}}(X, v)}{\sum_{j=1}^{m} b_j^{\mathcal{X}}(X, v)}$$

$$\geq \frac{b_i^{\mathcal{X}}(X, v) + \delta_1 + \delta_2}{\sum_{j=1}^{m} b_j^{v}(X, v) + \delta_1 + \delta_2} - \frac{b_i^{\mathcal{X}}(X, v) + \delta_1}{\sum_{j=1}^{m} b_j^{\mathcal{X}}(X, v) + \delta_1}$$

$$= \sigma_i^{\mathcal{X}}(Y \cup \{z\}, v) - \sigma_i^{\mathcal{X}}(Y, v).$$

Hence $\sigma_i^{\mathcal{X}}(X, v)$ is submodular, and $\mathcal{I}_i^{\mathcal{X}}$ is submodular. Finally,

$$\mathcal{I}_i(S_i, \mathbf{S}) = \sum_{sample\ \mathcal{X}} Prob[\mathcal{X}] \cdot \mathcal{I}_i^{\mathcal{X}}(S_i)$$

is monotone and submodular.

Note that Theorem 1 also stands when $\bigcup_{j \neq i} S_j = \emptyset$, i.e., the single influence spread function in TIC social networks is also monotone and submodular.

4.4   Properties of FairInf Problem

Definition 5 *(Individual Spread). Given the fixed overall seed set $\mathbf{S}$, for any seed $s \in \mathbf{S}$, we define its individual spread $\mathcal{I}_{-\mathbf{S}}(s)$ as the expected i-spread when s is the only seed in color c_i among $\mathbf{S}$.*

Note that in Definition 5 there is no i in $\mathcal{I}_{-\mathbf{S}}(s)$, and in fact the individual spread is not related with a specific color c_i, and we give the formula of individual spread here. Recall that $\mathcal{X}$ is a sample graph, and $\forall v \in V$, for any set X, we denote $b^{\mathcal{X}}(X, v)$ the number of all live-paths from X to v based on $\mathcal{X}$. We have:

$$\mathcal{I}_{-\mathbf{S}}(s) = \sum_{\mathcal{X}} Prob[\mathcal{X}] \cdot \sum_{v \in V} \frac{b^{\mathcal{X}}(\{s\}, v)}{b^{\mathcal{X}}(\mathbf{S}, v)}. \tag{5}$$

In (5), $\text{Prob}[\mathcal{X}]$ only depends on the original TIC network, $b^{\mathcal{X}}(\{s\}, v)$ only depends on $\{s\}$ and $b^{\mathcal{X}}(\mathbf{S}, v)$ only depends on $\mathbf{S}$. Hence, $\mathcal{I}_{-\mathbf{S}}(s)$ will not change no matter what color s is and how many colors the other seeds in $\mathbf{S}$ have, thus it is a unchanged value in the competitive TIC networks. This is vital for the correctness of the algorithms we design afterwards. It can be shown that $b^{\mathcal{X}}(S_i, v) = \sum_{s \in S_i} b^{\mathcal{X}}(\{s\}, v)$, hence

$$
\begin{aligned}
\mathcal{I}_i(S_i, \mathbf{S}) &= \sum_{\mathcal{X}} \text{Prob}[\mathcal{X}] \cdot \sum_{v \in V} \frac{b^{\mathcal{X}}(S_i, v)}{b^{\mathcal{X}}(\mathbf{S}, v)} \\
&= \sum_{\mathcal{X}} \text{Prob}[\mathcal{X}] \cdot \sum_{v \in V} \sum_{s \in S_i} \frac{b^{\mathcal{X}}(\{s\}, v)}{b^{\mathcal{X}}(\mathbf{S}, v)} \\
&= \sum_{s \in S_i} \mathcal{I}_{-\mathbf{S}}(s)
\end{aligned}
\tag{6}
$$

5   Myopic Greedy Algorithm for FairInf Problem

In this section, we design is the *Myopic Greedy* (MG) for solving *FairInf* problem: Given selected $\sum_{j=1}^{m} \mu_i$ seeds, how to allocate these seeds to difference influences such that the fairness is maximized.

Theorem 2. *Allocating the seed s to the influence i that has the current lowest EBR e_i is the greedy choice of maximizing Fairness f.*

Proof 4. *Recall that $f = e_{min}/e_{max}$. Without loss of generality, suppose $e_1 \le e_2 \le ... \le e_m$. We prove that for the next seed s to be allocated, c_1 is the current best choice to maximize f. Denote $\{e'_j\}$ the new EBR after allocating s to $\{c_j\}$ respectively. Denote k the minimum integer such that $1 \le k \le m$ and $e_m \le e'_k$. Since $e_m \le e'_m$, such k must exist. Denote the If s is not allocated to c_1 but $c_j(j \ne 1)$:*

(1) $k > 1$. If $j \le k$, then the new fairness f' remains e_1/e_m, else $f' = e_1/e'_k$. However, $e_1/e'_k \le e_1/e_m \le \min\{e'_1, e_2\}/e_m$, the fairness of choosing c_1 in this case.

(2) $k = 1$. $f' = e_1/e'_j$. Since $e_1 \le e_m$ and $e'_j \ge e'_1$, we have $e_1/e'_j \le e_m/e'_1$, the fairness of choosing c_1 in this case.

From above, we see that c_1 is always the best greedy choice of allocating s to maximize f, which is Theorem 2.

In MG algorithm, we first sort the seeds $s_j \in \mathbf{S}$ non-decreasingly by their individual spread $\mathcal{I}_{-\mathbf{S}}(s_j)$, and then one by one allocate them to the influence whose current EBR is the lowest. If more than one such influence exist, then we randomly choose one of them. According to Theorem 2, Algorithm 1 is a greedy heuristic whose objective is f.

The time complexity of MG is $O(\log m \sum_{i=1}^{m} \mu_i)$. Since we have to iteratively allocate $\sum_{i=1}^{m} \mu_i$ seeds to the m influences, and in each iteration we should find the influence with the lowest EBR, which takes $O(\log m)$ time when using min-heap.

Algorithm 1. MG

1: Sort $\{s_j\}$ into $\{\hat{s}_j\}$, such that $\mathcal{I}_{-\mathbf{s}}(\hat{s}_j) \geq \mathcal{I}_{-\mathbf{s}}(\hat{s_{j+1}})$ for $1 \leq j \leq \sum_{i=1}^m \mu_i - 1$;
2: $S_i \leftarrow \emptyset, 1 \leq i \leq m$;
3: **for** $\hat{s}_j$ **do**
4:     $S_{i^*} \leftarrow S_{i^*} \cup \hat{s}_j$, where $i^* = \underset{1 \leq i \leq m}{\arg\min} \frac{\mathcal{I}_i(S_i, \mathbf{S})}{\mu_i}$;
5: **end for**

---

6 Experiment

6.1 Experiment Setup

Datasets. We use three real-world social networks. Douban [19], Epinions [21] and NetHEPT. The basic statistics about our tested networks are plotted in Table 1.

Table 1. Dataset statistics

	Douban	Epinions	NetHEPT
#Nodes	129K	76K	15K
#Edges	1.7M	509K	62K
Avg. outdegree	13.2	13.4	4.12
Max. outdegree	6328	3079	64

Edge Weight and Node Deadline Generation. In TIC model each edge has a weight, just like IC model, it is the propagation probability of this edge. We use WC method *weighted cascade* [14] and *Trivalency* method [7]. For each node $v \in V$, we decide its *decision deadline* D_v by uniformly at random choosing an integer in $[10, 100]$.

6.2 MG Algorithm

In solving *FairInf* problem, the second phase is to allocate the seeds to different influences in a fair manner. We set the following multi-influence competing scenarios to test MG algorithm.

Table 2. Budges of the competition scenarios

m	Equal budges	Unequal budgets
2	$\mu_1 = \mu_2 = 10$	$\mu_1 = 5, \mu_2 = 15$
5	$\mu_1 = \cdots = \mu_5 = 8$	$\mu_1 = 4, \mu_2 = 6, \mu_3 = 8, \mu_4 = 10, \mu_5 = 12$
8	$\mu_1 = \cdots = \mu_8 = 5$	$\mu_1 = \mu_2 = \mu_3 = \mu_4 = 4, \mu_5 = \mu_6 = \mu_7 = \mu_8 = 6$

Competition Scenarios. We choose three values $2, 5$ and 8 for m, the number of influences competing with others. In order to finish our experiments in reasonable times, we pick 40 seeds at most for the three datasets we test. The principle of us designing competition scenarios is to test both equal budgets and unequal budgets to cover more cases. The detailed budget distribution of our designed scenarios are shown in Table 2.

In Table 2, we denote 2(eq) the upper left case, since in this case two influences with equal budgets exist. The upper right case is denoted by 2(neq). It is easy to understand the other cases 5(eq), 5(neq), and so forth. We denote OPT the method of enumerating all the possible seed allocations (of m influences), and OPT takes $m^{\Sigma \mu_i}$ time. We also compare RAN, the random seed allocation. Note that due to OPT's time complexity we only set total 20 seeds in 2(eq) and 2(neq). The results of Fairness f under different cases are plotted in Fig. 1. It can be seen that MG algorithm works very well.

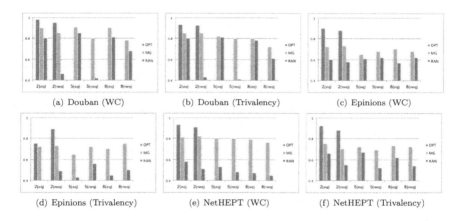

(a) Douban (WC)   (b) Douban (Trivalency)   (c) Epinions (WC)

(d) Epinions (Trivalency)   (e) NetHEPT (WC)   (f) NetHEPT (Trivalency)

Fig. 1. Fairness. (Each subfigure's ordinate is uniformly the Fairness.)

Table 3. Running times of seed allocations on Douban

	2(eq)	5(eq)	8(eq)
MG	8 ms	11 ms	13 ms
RAN	5 ms	7 ms	9 ms

We plot the running times of cases 2(eq), 5(eq) and 8(eq) on Douban in Table 3. MG runs very fast.

7 Conclusion

In this paper we discuss the fair multi-influence maximization problem in social networks. We propose a new TIC model to simulate how multiple influences freely compete with each other. In TIC model, unlike the traditional IC model, we assume that an individual can propagate more than one influence to its neighbors, and each individual may receive multiple influences before it turns decided to one of them. We further notice that in reality the integral social network data is usually lacked, and the companies are often the clients of the networking platform provider, i.e., the agency. Therefore we propose *FairInf* problem from the agency's perspective. We prove that in TIC when other companies' seeds are fixed, a company's influence spread w.r.t. its seeds is monotone and submodular, and this nice property provides a $(1 - 1/e)$ ratio simple Greedy for spread maximization of single influence. We propose a greedy heuristic called MG to solve *FairInf* to allocate the seeds in a fair way. Through experiments, we verify that MG runs efficiently or giving fair influence spreads.

Acknowledgement. This work is partly supported by National Natural Science Foundation of China under grant 11671400.

References

1. Bharathi, S., Kempe, D., Salek, M.: Competitive influence maximization in social networks. In: Deng, X., Graham, F.C. (eds.) WINE 2007. LNCS, vol. 4858, pp. 306–311. Springer, Heidelberg (2007). doi:10.1007/978-3-540-77105-0_31
2. Borodin, A., Filmus, Y., Oren, J.: Threshold models for competitive influence in social networks. In: Saberi, A. (ed.) WINE 2010. LNCS, vol. 6484, pp. 539–550. Springer, Heidelberg (2010). doi:10.1007/978-3-642-17572-5_48
3. Budak, C., Agrawal, D., El Abbadi, A.: Limiting the spread of misinformation in social networks. In: WWW 2011 (2011)
4. Cai, J.L.Z., Yan, M., Li, Y.: Using crowdsourced data in location-based social networks to explore influence maximization. In: IEEE INFOCOM 2016 - The 35th Annual IEEE International Conference on Computer Communications, pp. 1–9, April 2016
5. Carnes, T., Nagarajan, C., Wild, S.M., Van Zuylen, A.: Maximizing influence in a competitive social network: a follower's perspective. In: ICEC 2007 (2007)
6. Chen, W., Collins, A., Cummings, R., Ke, T., Liu, Z., Rincon, D., Sun, X., Wang, Y., Wei, W., Yuan, Y.: Influence maximization in social networks when negative opinions may emerge and propagate. In: SDM 2010, pp. 379–390 (2010)
7. Chen, W., Wang, C., Wang, Y.: Scalable influence maximization for prevalent viral marketing in large-scale social networks. In: KDD 2010, pp. 1029–1038. ACM (2010)
8. Chen, W., Yuan, Y., Zhang, L.: Scalable influence maximization in social networks under the linear threshold model. In: ICDM 2010 (2010)
9. Domingos, P., Richardson, M.: Mining the network value of customers. In: KDD 2001, pp. 57–66. ACM (2001)
10. Goldenberg, J., Libai, B., Muller, E.: Talk of the network: a complex systems look at the underlying process of word-of-mouth. Mark. Lett. **12**, 211–223 (2001)
11. Han, M., Yan, M., Cai, Z., Li, Y.: An exploration of broader influence maximization in timeliness networks with opportunistic selection. J. Netw. Comput. Appl. **63**, 39–49 (2016)

12. Han, M., Yan, M., Cai, Z., Li, Y., Cai, X., Yu, J.: Influence maximization by probing partial communities in dynamic online social networks. Trans. Emerg. Telecommun. Technol. **28**, e3054 (2016)
13. He, X., Song, G., Chen, W., Jiang, Q.: Influence blocking maximization in social networks under the competitive linear threshold model. In: SDM 2012 (2012)
14. Kempe, D., Kleinberg, J., Tardos, É.: Maximizing the spread of influence through a social network. In: KDD 2003, pp. 137–146. ACM (2003)
15. Kostka, J., Oswald, Y.A., Wattenhofer, R.: Word of mouth: rumor dissemination in social networks. In: Shvartsman, A.A., Felber, P. (eds.) SIROCCO 2008. LNCS, vol. 5058, pp. 185–196. Springer, Heidelberg (2008). doi:10.1007/978-3-540-69355-0_16
16. Leskovec, J., Krause, A., Guestrin, C., Faloutsos, C., VanBriesen, J., Glance, N.: Cost-effective outbreak detection in networks. In: KDD 2007 (2007)
17. Li, S., Zhu, Y., Li, D., Kim, D., Huang, H.: Rumor restriction in online social networks. In: IPCCC 2013 (2013)
18. Lu, W., Bonchi, F., Goya, A., Laksmanan, L.V.S.: The bang for the buck: fair competitive viral marketing from the host perspective. In: KDD 2013 (2013)
19. Ma, H., Zhou, D., Liu, C., Lyu, M.R., King, I.: Recommender systems with social regularization. In: WSDM 2011, pp. 287–296 (2011)
20. Pathak, N., Banerjee, A., Srivastava, J.: A generalized linear threshold model for multiple cascades. In: ICDM 2010 (2010)
21. Richardson, M., Agrawal, R., Domingos, P.: Trust management for the semantic web. In: Fensel, D., Sycara, K., Mylopoulos, J. (eds.) ISWC 2003. LNCS, vol. 2870, pp. 351–368. Springer, Heidelberg (2003). doi:10.1007/978-3-540-39718-2_23
22. Shi, T., Cheng, S., Cai, Z., Li, Y., Li, J.: Retrieving the maximal time-bounded positive influence set from social networks. Pers. Ubiquit. Comput. **20**(5), 717–730 (2016)
23. Trpevski, D., Tang, W.K.S., Kocarev, L.: Model for rumor spreading over networks. Phys. Rev. E **81**, 056102 (2010)
24. Zhu, Y., Li, D., Guo, H., Pamula, R.: New competitive influence propagation models in social networks. In: 2014 10th International Conference on Mobile Ad-hoc and Sensor Networks, pp. 257–262, December 2014
25. Zhu, Y., Li, D., Zhang, Z.: Minimum cost seed set for competitive social influence. In: IEEE INFOCOM 2016 - The 35th Annual IEEE International Conference on Computer Communications, pp. 1–9, April 2016
26. Zhu, Y., Wu, W., Bi, Y., Wu, L., Jiang, Y., Xu, W.: Better approximation algorithms for influence maximization in online social networks. J. Comb. Optim. **30**, 97–108 (2015)

Communities Mining and Recommendation for Large-Scale Mobile Social Networks

Ruiguo Yu[1,2], Jianrong Wang[1,2], Tianyi Xu[1,2], Jie Gao[1,2], Kunyu Cao[1,2], and Mei Yu[1,2(✉)]

[1] School of Computer Science and Technology, Tianjin University,
No. 92 Weijin Road, Nankai District, Tianjin, China
{rgyu,wjr,tianyi.xu,gaojie,kunyucao,yumei}@tju.edu.cn
[2] Tianjin Key Laboratory of Advanced Networking,
No. 92 Weijin Road, Nankai District, Tianjin, China

Abstract. Two well-known phenomena are observed in social networks. One is the tendency of users to connect with similar users, leading to the emergence of communities. The other is that certain users belong to multiple communities simultaneously. Understanding these phenomena is the major concern of social network analysis. In this work we focus on overlapping communities detection and personalized recommendation methods. We propose an algorithm with the property which takes closeness and influence of users into account for community detection, and utilizes semantic analysis and statistical analysis for the personalized recommendation. Our contributions include adopting the idea of greedy expansion involved with Clique Theory, extending PageRank to detect communities, and creating recommender from the view of semantics and statistics. In experiments, the algorithm is verified in terms of F1-measure, AP and MAP. The results show that our proposed algorithm can outperform the state-of-the-art methods.

Keywords: Social network analysis · Data mining · Community detection · Personalized recommendation

1 Introduction

With the rapid development of mobile Internet, large-scale mobile social network has become the most popular platform for communication and information propagation [1,2]. As observed, there usually exist multiples ocial communities among user ego-centric networks in complex social networks [3]. Finding and analyzing community structure often provide invaluable help in deeply understanding the structure and function of a network [4]. A large quantity of approaches for detecting community in social networks have been proposed over the years [5–7]. As for social network applications, the situation that some users belong to multiple communities, leading to emergence of overlapping communities, has not been focused on by early researchers. Also, the relationships between users and users, users and topics, users and activities in large-scale mobile social networks would

© Springer International Publishing AG 2017
L. Ma et al. (Eds.): WASA 2017, LNCS 10251, pp. 266–277, 2017.
DOI: 10.1007/978-3-319-60033-8_24

produce massive data, leading to the increase of the difficulties in communities detection and personalized recommendation. Considering this, the problems we solve in this paper are detecting overlapping communities for centric user, which are shown as Fig. 1, and proposing a personalized recommendation method to fulfil the willing of the well-known phenomenon that users like to connect with similar users in large-scale mobile social networks.

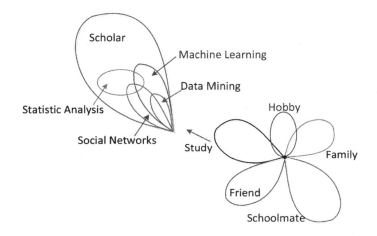

Fig. 1. The overlapping communities

In this paper, we propose an algorithm named Community Mining and Content Recommending (CMCR). Compared with traditional algorithms for both community detection and personalized recommendation, our main contributions of CMCR are summarized as follows.

1. We study an ego-centric network of a certain user rather than the whole network, and define the problems of overlapping communities detection and personalized recommendation within communities, which are very realistic problems that need to be tackled.
2. We propose a novel algorithm based on Clique Theory [8], PageRank, LDA and TF-IDF to solve the problems, which is different from the classic algorithms like RSCM [9], K-means, LDAR [5] and TFIDFR generated from Paper [10].
3. We demonstrate the effectiveness of the proposed method using a real-world dataset. Our experimental results indicate that our algorithm outperforms the existing methods and is easy to be implemented in real time large-scale mobile social networks.

2   Related Work

Fortunato summarizes methods of community detection in graph in Paper [11], and illustrates the features of overlapping communities. He concerns the whole structure of the network but doesn't provide a method to detect communities for a certain user. Paper [12] accomplishes a group behavior research of Twitter users separately using HITS algorithm and CPM (Clique Percolation Method) algorithm. Communities in Twitter are formed based on certain mutual interests. However, community members do not only share contents of their interest but also their personal emotion and life experience etc. Paper [13] introduces a community division algorithm based on information theory. These methods are all based on a fundamental assumption of community structure that community should have tight internal connection and sparse external connection.

However most of the early methods are based on the whole network structure, thus they do not fit for detecting overlapping communities for a certain user. And most of them are one-class classification algorithms. Multi-class classification ones to detect overlapping communities are not developed well.

Paper [4] takes users with high influence and normal users into account differently. First it detects community cores formed by well-known users, and then made an expansion to detect communities, but the cores of a community this algorithm mines are scattered, thus only attached overlapping communities could be detected. Paper [6] introduces a method utilizing random walks on line graph and attraction intensity to discover overlapping communities. This method can efficiently find communities for centric user, but concerning the relations between users would lead to an incomplete community detection.

Paper [9] introduces a cluster method to detect overlapping communities for centric user based on spectrum mapping. However, lacking an efficient strategy to find latent relations among different communities, it would fail to detect complete communities. Paper [14] defines the closeness of users in microblog and distance of communities, then it adopts expanding method to detect users' real social circle. However this algorithm lacks good mechanisms to determine the number of communities and to filter nodes which are isolated. In our approach, when detecting communities, we improve the idea of Paper [9] by a further expansion considering closeness [14], in order to detect a complete social community for a centric user.

As for personalized recommendation, statistical method [10] and probabilistic methods [5,15,16] are both utilized to build user models combining other features in social networks. We adopt a similar idea to proceed personalized recommendation combining the keyword feature and semantic feature together.

3   Social Community Mining and Content Recommending Algorithm

To understand the problem of community detection, some definitions according to Graph Theory about the monodirectional relation called "following" in social networks should be introduced.

Definition 1. First Level Relation Graph G_1:
$G_1 = \{V_1, E_1\}$, $V_1 = \{n | c\ follows\ n\}$, $E_1 = \{(n_1, n_2) | n_1\ follows\ n_2, n_1 \in V_1, n_2 \in V_1\}$.

Definition 2. Second Level Relation Graph G_2:
$G_2 = \{V_2, E_2\}$, $V_2 = \{n|user\ followed\ by\ users\ in\ V_1\} \cup V_1$, $E_2 = \{(n_1, n_2)|n_1\ follows\ n_2, n_1 \in V_2, n_2 \in V_2\}$.

Definition 3. Collective Friends: Define $CF(n_1, n_2)$ as a set of common friends between User n_1 and User n_2.

Definition 4. Closeness: Define $CL(n_1, n_2)$ as the number of Collective Friends between User n_1 and User n_2. $CL(n_1, n_2) = |CF(n_1, n_2)|$.

Definition 5. Closeness Distance: Define $D(community, n)$ as the closeness distance from a certain User n to a certain social Community $community$. as show as Eq. 1. $i \in community, s = |community|$.

$$D(community, n) = \frac{\sum |CF(n, i) \wedge CF(n, c)|}{s \times |CF(n, c)|} \tag{1}$$

In the definitions above, V is the set of vertexes, which represents the set of users. E is the set of edges, which represents the relations. c stands for the centric user and n is an user in microblog.

3.1 Mining Seed Sets

The problem of mining seed sets means to locate some potential foundations for social communities given the users and relations. We introduce an algorithm named K-clique-community Seed Mining (KSM) algorithm to solve that problem. KSM takes the two important theories of Clique Theory [8] into account to implement the mining. The theories are summarized as follows.

1. For any clique with the size s, $s > k$, it forms a community itself.
2. For any two cliques with a overlapping part whose size $\geq k - 2$, they form a community together.

In the theories above, k means the minimum threshold of the size of a community to be mined. Given the users and relations, KSM first locates all the max cliques. With all the cliques detected, the Clique-Overlapping Matrix M is built where M_{ij} stands for the number of public nodes shared by Clique i and j. M_{ii} is the size of Clique i. Then based on the two theories above, the adjacency matrix M' of the undirected graph is computed. The $Seed(c)$ would be the result of a depth-first search of connected subgraph in M'. The pseudocode of KSM algorithm is shown in Algorithm 1.

3.2 Overlapping Communities Detection

The overlapping communities of centric user are detected by expanding $Seed(c)$. We propose two algorithms to do the expansions. The first one with the name Closeness Seed Expansion (CSE) adopts a greedy strategy of considering user with higher closeness to centric user prior.

Algorithm 1. K-clique-community Seed Mining

// input: centric user c, the First Level Relation Graph of centric user G_1,
   parameter k
// output: the set of seeds of social interest circle of specific user $Seeds(c)$
1. $Seeds(c) \leftarrow \varnothing$;
2. search all the max cliques in G_1;
3. build Clique-Overlapping Matrix M according to the result of step 2;
4. for M, subtract the diagonal elements by $k - 1$,
   the else $k - 2$;
5.   for each element e of M
6.   if $e < 0$ $e \leftarrow 0$;
7.   if $e > 1$ $e \leftarrow 1$;
8. $M' \leftarrow M$
9. $Seeds(c) \leftarrow$ depth-first search connected subgraph on M;
10. return $Seeds(c)$;

According to the definitions above, CSE algorithm uses seeds as initial social communities, and makes greedy expansion based on the feature of closeness. Nodes closer enough to a community would be added to it first. Parameter k in K-clique-community is used as standard to filter out the social circle with size not larger than k. The pseudocode of CSE algorithm is shown as Algorithm 2.

The second algorithm to expand the community, called Influence Social Community Expansion (ISCE) algorithm, focuses on the influence of users in the network. To calculate the influence of users, we utilize a similar idea of PageRank to represent the following relations of users. The key point of PageRank is the transition possibility of nodes in Random Walk Model. We decide to redefine that possibility to fit the situations in social networks. First, the similarity between users $Sim(i, j)$ is calculated by cosine similarity of their Message Interest Feature Vector, which is defined in Definition 6, where id stands for the ID of a message, and $cn(u, id)$ means the number of replies that User u replies to Message id, under the assumption that the number a user replies to a message can represent his interest degree to that message.

Definition 6. Message Interest Feature Vector: Define $V(u)$ as message interest feature vector:

$$V(u) = [id_1 = cn(u, id_1), id_2 = cn(u, id_2), ..., id_t = cn(u, id_t)],$$
$$t = |M(u)|, id_i \in M(u) \tag{2}$$

Given the similarities of users, the redefined calculation method of transition possibility of users is shown as Eq. 3. It actually stands for the ratio of information which User i is interested in, from the whole information he gains. The numerator is the quantity of information User i receives from User j. The denominator is the whole quantity of information User i receives.

$$P_{ij} = \frac{M(j) \times Sim(i, j)}{\sum_{n \in V_1} |M(n)||Sim(i, n)|}, i, j \in V_2 \tag{3}$$

Algorithm 2. Closeness Seeds Expansion

//input: c, G_1, $Seeds(c)$, k
//output: $Community(G_1)$
1. $Community(G_1) \leftarrow Seeds(G_1)$;
2. $Candidates(G_1) \leftarrow$ find candidate nodes not included in seeds in G_1;
3. for every node n in $Candidates(G_1)$
4.   calculate $Closeness(n, c)$;
5. sort nodes in $Candidates(G_1)$ by descending order of closeness;
6. for every node n in $Candidates(G_1)$
7. {
8.   for every circle c in $Circles(G_1)$
9.   {
10. $d \leftarrow$ calculate $D(c, n)$;
11.   if $d \geq \delta$
12.   add node n into circle;
13.   }
14.   if n has not been added to any circles
15. $Community(G_1) \leftarrow$ build a new community with n;
16. }
17. for every community c in $Community(G_1)$
18.   if c.size() $\leq k$
19.   delete c from $Community(G_1)$;
20. return $Community(G_1)$;

With the redefinition of transition possibility above, the influence degree of a user could be calculated by Eq. 4 where q is set by experience of PageRank.

$$PR(i) = \frac{1-q}{|V_2|} + q \sum_j PR(j) \times P_{ij}, i, j \in V_2, q = 0.85 i, j \in V_2 \qquad (4)$$

ISCE algorithm puts all candidates in descending sort by influence in the Second Level Relation Graph. Expansion is made by taking the classic modularity function Q as criteria. If the present node can form a good social structure with present social communities, the modularity would increase, then it will be added to an existing community. The pseudocode of ISCE is shown as Algorithm 3. $Community(G_2)$ is the final answer of us to the problem of community detection.

3.3 Microblog Content Recommendation Algorithm

As for the problem about fulfilling the willing that users like to connect with similar users, we propose a personalized recommendation method named Message Content Recommendation Algorithm (MCRA) applied inside each of the communities, which considers the semantic analysis and statistical analysis together to recommend messages to centric user. To illustrate the algorithm, some definitions need to be introduced.

Algorithm 3. Influence Social Circle Expansion

//input: G_2, $Community(G_1)$
//output: $Community(G_2)$
1. $Community(G_2) \leftarrow Community(G_1)$;
2. $Q \leftarrow$ calculate the modularity of G_2 with $Community(G_2)$;
3. calculate influence $PR(i)$ for every node of V_2 by extended PageRank algorithm;
4. $Candidates(G_2) \leftarrow$ find nodes not in any social interest circles in V_2;
5. sort nodes in $Candidates(G_2)$ by descending order of influence;
6. for each node in $Candidates(G_2)$
7.   for each social interest circle in $Community(G_2)$
8.   {
9.   add node into circle;
10. $Q' \leftarrow$ calculate the modularity of the community after adding that node;
11.   if $Q' < Q$
12.   delete node from community;
13.   else
14. $Q \leftarrow Q'$;
15. }
16. return $Community(G_2)$;

Definition 7. Message Semantic Interest $P(M|u)$. The Message Semantic Interest of user is defined as the possibility that User u uses Message M to express his opinion in terms of semantics.

Definition 8. Message Statistical Interest $K(M|u)$. The Message Statistical Interest of user is defined as the possibility that User u uses Message M to express his opinion in terms of statistic.

According to the definitions above, we design a ranking method for candidate messages as shown as Eq. 5.

$$Score(M, u) = \frac{\alpha P(M|u) + \beta K(M|u)}{2} \tag{5}$$

Now the problem is how to compute $P(M|u)$ and $K(M|u)$ for a target user. To compute $P(M|u)$, we use probabilistic method to describe the relationships between users and messages. The messages are represented by "bag of words" model. The idea is that one document exhibits multiple topics, and a topic is made of several words in the form of possibility. Thus the possibility $P(w_i|u)$ of a word w_i being posted by user u is defined as Eq. 6, where t stands for a topic and T is the collection of topics.

$$P(w_i|u) = \sum_{t \in T} P(t|u)P(w_i|t) \tag{6}$$

To compute $P(w_i|u)$ we use Latent Dirichlet Allocation (LDA) to train the model to achieve User-Topic possibility distribution $P(T|u)$ and Topic-Word possibility distribution $P(V|T)$. User-Topic possibility distribution $P(T|u)$ is the vector whose elements are possibilities that a target user u is interested in each topic in topic collection T, as shown in Eq. 7.

$$P(T|u) = \{P(t_0|u), P(t_1|u), \ldots, P(t_n|u)\} \tag{7}$$

In Eq. 7, t_i is the i_{th} topic in T, and $P(t_i|u)$ denotes the possibility that in what degree the messages posted by target user u match the topic t_i.

The Topic-Word possibility distribution $P(V|T)$ is defined as follows. The possibility between Topic t_i and term v_j is $p(v_j|t_i)$, and the possibility of word distribution of Topic t_i is shown as Eq. 8.

$$P(V|t_i) = \{P(v_0|t_i), P(v_1|t_i), \ldots, P(v_{m_0}|t_i)\} \tag{8}$$

Each topic contains numbers of words. And there are numbers of topics in topic collection. Thus the matrix can be formed as Eq. 9.

$$P(V|T) = \begin{pmatrix} p(v_0|t_0) & \cdots & p(v_m|t_0) \\ \vdots & \ddots & \vdots \\ p(v_0|t_n) & \cdots & p(v_m|t_n) \end{pmatrix} \tag{9}$$

$P(M|u)$ could be calculated according to $P(w|u)$ of each word in a message. Generally thinking $P(M|u)$ should be the product of the possibility of each word. However, the length of messages are not quite same, thus leads to an unfair situation because the longer a message is, the smaller the product value tends to be. To avoid this problem, the highest value of $P(w|u)$ among all the values of words in the message will be set as $P(M|u)$ for the whole message in MCRA, as shown as Eq. 10.

$$P(M|u) = max\{P(w_0|u), P(w_1|u), \ldots, P(w_n|u)\} \tag{10}$$

$K(M|u)$ denotes the importance of Message M to User u. To compute $K(M|u)$, the importance degree of each word to the user, i.e. $K(w|u)$, needs to be achieved. We utilize the idea of *TF-IDF* to determine that by calculating its *TF-IDF* weight in the whole corpus. $K(M|u)$ would refer to user-word weight vector formed as shown as Eq. 11, where $w(v_n, u)$ is the weight of v_n in the message collection of target user u.

$$K_u = \{w(v_0, u), w(v_1, u), \ldots, w(v_n, u)\}, \quad v_0, v_1, \cdots \in V_c \tag{11}$$

When calculating $K(M|u)$, the same problem as calculating $P(M|u)$ mentioned above lies ahead, then the same strategy is adopted to calculate $K(M|u)$ as Eq. 12. Notice that if a candidate message contains no word existing in target user's content file, the similarity would be set as the lowest weight in $K(u)$.

$$K_u(M) = \begin{cases} max\{K_u(w_0), \ldots, K_u(w_n)\}, & \exists w_i \in V_{targetusr} \\ min\{w(v_i, u)\}, & v_i \in V_c, \ \forall w_i \notin V_{targetusr} \end{cases} \tag{12}$$

In Eq. 12, $M = \{w_1, w_2, \ldots, w_m\}$, $K_u(w_n)$ is the interest degree that User u likes Word w_n. $w(v_i, u)$ is the interest degree that User u likes to use Word v_i in his own file. $K_u(W)$ is the interest degree that User u tends to post candidate message K.

4   Experiment and Analysis

The efficiency of CMCR is verified on real-world data in terms of F1-measure, Average Position (AP) and Mean Average Position (MAP). The experiment data, which contains messages posted by 128749 users and relations between them, is collected by an application developed by us utilizing the open API of a large-scale mobile social network application named Sina Weibo. RSCM [9], K-means, LDAR [5] and TF-IDFR [10] are selected as baselines.

4.1   Algorithm Parameter Estimation

While detecting overlapping communities, there are two parameters need to be estimated, which are parameter k in KSM algorithm and threshold δ in CSE algorithm. At first, k is assigned as a certain value by experience and δ varies. Then δ would be set as constant and k is alternated. The experiment process is shown as Fig. 2.

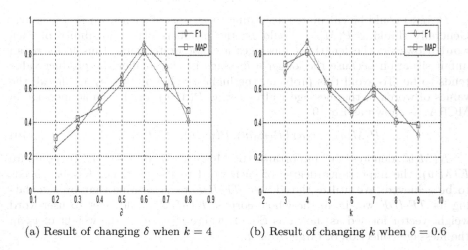

(a) Result of changing δ when $k = 4$ (b) Result of changing k when $\delta = 0.6$

Fig. 2. Parameter estimation

From what can be seen in the result, when $\delta = 0.6$ and $k = 4$, the best performance of the algorithm can be achieved. Thus, δ and k are assigned as above.

In MCRA, EM algorithm is adopted to train the parameters in LDA. After that, the topic number in Target User Topic Model should be estimated based on the recommendation performance. The AP would be chosen as evaluation criteria. The topic numbers are changed from 10 to 200 by virtue of experience, and the interval is 10.

Based on the parameters determined above, CMCR could be implemented.

4.2   Comparison with RSCM and K-Means

To verify the efficiency of the two expansions respectively, the contrast experiment between CMCR and RSCM [9] is conducted on the First Level Relation Graph and the one between CMCR and K-means is conducted on the Second Level Relation Graph. On the Second Level Relation Graph, K-means algorithm directly uses the number of communities detected before as initial numbers of centers. In addition, as K-means algorithm would put every single node into a community, it's reasonable to use the result of the former experiment as restraint and ignore users which are not included. The result is shown in Fig. 3.

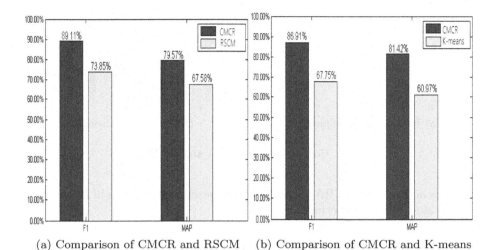

(a) Comparison of CMCR and RSCM   (b) Comparison of CMCR and K-means

Fig. 3. Comparison with RSCM and K-means

The experiment results demonstrate that our proposed algorithm achieves high quality results for the community detection problem, typically outperforming RSCM and K-means.

4.3   Comparison with LDA and TF-IDF

To verify the superior result of MCRA, the basic recommender based on LDA named LDAR [5] and recommending system, which is generated from Paper [10] based on TF-IDF named TF-IDFR are adopted as baseline algorithms.

LDAR is a probabilistic recommendation method inspired by Latent Dirichlet Allocation model, which could be widely used in content recommendation. While TF-IDFR simulates a similarity calculating approach utilizing TF-IDF to build recommending system. All the parameters in MCRA are estimated by methods mentioned above. After making these three recommendation, the evaluation indicators for every method would be recorded when the number of recommending list N is 10, 20, 30, 40, 50, 60, 70 respectively. The performances are compared in Fig. 4.

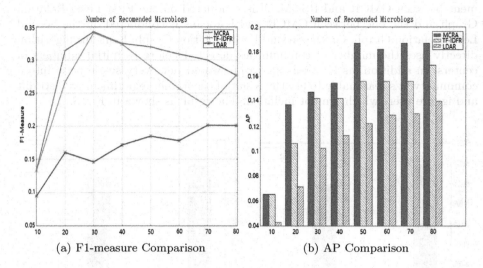

(a) F1-measure Comparison   (b) AP Comparison

Fig. 4. Comparison with LDA and TF-IDF

It can be seen that MCRA outperforms the baseline algorithms in F1-measure and AP almost in all experiment situations.

5   Conclusion and Future Work

In this paper, we propose two problems related to large scale mobile social network analysis. The first one is overlapping community detection and the other one is personalized content recommendation in communities. We propose a novel algorithm as solutions to these two problems. This algorithm detects overlapping communities according to the features of a centric user and recommends messages within the communities detected. In this way, it can efficiently deal with the real time large-scale mobile social networks. The algorithm is verified by contrast experiments, which show that the proposed algorithm can outperform the baseline algorithms in some common criteria. In the future work, more features would be utilized to analyze the social networks and we plan to devise distributed algorithms based on the algorithm for an easy implementation in practice.

References

1. Teutle, A.R.M.: Twitter: network properties analysis. In: 20th Electronics, Communications and Computer (CONIELECOMP), pp. 180–186. IEEE Press, Cholula (2010)

2. Haewoon, K., Changhyun, L., Hosung, B., Sue, M.: What is Twitter, a social network or a news media? In: 19th International Conference on World Wide Web, Raleigh, pp. 591–600. ACM (2010)
3. Akshay, J., Xiaodan, S., Tim, F., Belle, T.: Why we Twitter: understanding microblogging usage and communities. In: 9th WebKDD and 1st SNA-KDD 2007 Workshop on Web Mining and Social Network Analysis, San Jose, pp. 56–65. ACM (2007)
4. Jianshu, W., Ee-Peng, L., Jing, J., Qi, H.: Twitterrank: finding topic-sensitive influential twitterers. In: 3rd International Conference on Web Search and Data Mining, pp. 261–270. ACM, New York (2010)
5. Jianyong, D., Yamin, A.: LDA topic model for microblog recommendation. In: 8th International Conference on Asian Language Processing, Suzhou, pp. 185–188. IEEE (2015)
6. Deng, X., Li, G., Dong, M.: Finding overlapping communities with random walks on line graph and attraction intensity. In: Xu, K., Zhu, H. (eds.) WASA 2015. LNCS, vol. 9204, pp. 94–103. Springer, Cham (2015). doi:10.1007/978-3-319-21837-3_10
7. Yang, J., Leskovec, J.: Overlapping community detection at scale: a nonnegative matrix factorization approach. In: 6th International Conference on Web Search and Data Mining, Rome, pp. 587–596. ACM (2013)
8. William, H., Matthew, C.S., Paul, B., Nagiza, F.S.: On perturbation theory and an algorithm for maximal clique enumeration in uncertain and noisy graphs. In: 1st ACM SIGKDD Workshop on Knowledge Discovery from Uncertain Data, Paris, pp. 48–56, ACM (2009)
9. Hailong, Q., Ting, L., Yanjun, M.: Mining users real social circle in microblog. In: 4th International Conference on Advances in Social Networks Analysis and Mining, Istanbul, pp. 348–352. IEEE (2012)
10. Ba, Q., Li, X., Bai, Z.: A similarity calculating approach simulated from TF-IDF in collaborative filtering recommendation. In: 5th International Conference on Multimedia Information Networking and Security, Beijing, pp. 738–741, IEEE Press (2013)
11. Fortunato, S., Castellano, C.: Community structure in graphs. In: Meyers, R.A. (ed.) 12th Computational Complexity, pp. 490–512. Springer, New York (2012). doi:10.1007/978-1-4614-1800-9_33
12. Zhonghua, Q., Yang, L.: Interactive group suggesting for Twitter. In: 49th Annual Meeting of the Association for Computational Linguistics: Human Language Technologies, Portland, pp. 519–523. ACL (2011)
13. Gergely, P., Imre, D., Illes, F., Tamas, V.: Uncovering the overlapping community structure of complex networks in nature and society. Nature 435(7043), 814–818 (2005)
14. Leon, D., Albert, D., Jordi, D., Alex, A.: Comparing community structure identification. J. Stat. Mech. Theory Exp. 9, P09008 (2005)
15. Kim, Y., Shim, K.: TWILITE: a recommendation system for Twitter using a probabilistic model based on latent Dirichlet allocation. Inf. Syst. 42, 59–77 (2014)
16. Elmongui, H.G., Mansour, R., Morsy, H., Khater, S., El-Sharkasy, A., Ibrahim, R.: TRUPI: Twitter recommendation based on users' personal interests. In: Gelbukh, A. (ed.) CICLing 2015. LNCS, vol. 9042, pp. 272–284. Springer, Cham (2015). doi:10.1007/978-3-319-18117-2_20

Community Verification with Topic Modeling

Feng Wang$^{(\boxtimes)}$ and Ken Orton

School of Mathematical and Natural Sciences,
Arizona State University, Tempe, USA
fwang25@asu.edu

Abstract. Different performance measurement metrics have been proposed to evaluate the performance of community detection algorithms, such as modularity, conductance, etc. However, there is few work which makes sense of a community, that is, explain what does the community do, what is the community's interest. In this paper, we use topic modeling to capture the topics of users in the same community and verify a heuristic community detection algorithm by showing that the users in the communities share strong interests.

Keywords: Community detection · Topic modeling · LDA · Social media

1 Introduction

In his book "Tribes: We Need You to Lead Us", Seth Godin tells us, "For millions of years, human beings have been part of one tribe or another. A group needs only two things to be a tribe: a shared interest and a way to communicate". Today's social media accelerate the form of tribes, which in the context of network theory, communities. Twitter is such an example, where twitter users form communities, either explicitly by specifying their membership or implicitly by forming hidden communities which can be discovered by community detection algorithms. In this paper, we ask the following question, do people on social media form communities because they share common interests?

There exists many community detection algorithms in literature, which can be generally divided into topology-based and topic based method. Topic based method groups individuals who are interested in the same topics in a community, therefore generate communities that are topically similar. Topic based community does not reflect community structure since there might be minimum interaction among users in the same topical community. Topology-based community, as stated in [12], is widely accepted that a community should have more internal connections than external connections. A good community should be internally well-connected and also well-separated from the rest of the network. The goodness of topology-based community is usually measured by structure related metrics, such as modularity, conductance, triangle participation ratio, internal density, transitivity, etc., but it is not clear how to make sense of the

© Springer International Publishing AG 2017
L. Ma et al. (Eds.): WASA 2017, LNCS 10251, pp. 278–288, 2017.
DOI: 10.1007/978-3-319-60033-8_25

identified communities. One straightforward way is to look through tweets from users in the same community to come to a conclusion on what that particular users interests are. However, it is not feasible to find this out for a large amount of users since doing this manually would quickly become tedious. Little effort has been carried out to interpret the topology-based communities.

In this paper, we investigate the problem of whether users associated in a hidden community revealed by topology-based community detection algorithms show topic similarity or not. We use a clique based community detection algorithm called Clique Augmentation Algorithm [1] to discover the hidden community structure, then adopt the topic modeling approach and choose LDA topic model to discover the topic distribution of a twitter user in a community. To be more specific, we train LDA model with wikipedia data, and use the trained model to transform user tweets into vectors of n-dimensional probability distributions. For each user, we use the transformed document vector and compare it to other users using Jensen Shannon distance to measure distances between the probability distributions. Each of these measurements gives us a close approximation of how similar the user tweet documents are according to the topics in the trained model and provide us with a way of interpreting how closely related users might be to each other in their communities. In addition, we can discover unknown relationships and interests among groups of people in social media.

From analysis of our results, looking at the discovered topics within the communities, and the actual tweets from the users within these communities, we found clear cut between the interest of users in the same clique/community and users in random groups. The result shows that the clique augmentation algorithm can detect hidden communities that show strong community theme. It also gives evidence that the assumption that user forms community because they share interest is valid.

The remaining of the paper is organized as following: Sect. 2 gives a brief review of work on community detection and topic modeling. Section 3 introduces the LDA model and the architecture of our system which uses topic modeling to verify twitter communities. Section 4 shows the experimental results and Sect. 5 concludes the paper.

2 Literature Review

Majority of community detection algorithms in literature are topology based. [16] is a survey paper which compares existing community detection algorithms for discovering both disjoint and overlapping communities. They propose good metrics which measure the structural property of the identified communities, such as density, clustering coefficient, conductance, and triangle participation ratio.

There exist a few research on topic-based community detection which generate communities which are topically similar. [22] proposed a generative model to discover communities based on topics, social graph topology, and nature of user interactions. It uses the modularity to measure the goodness of their communities. [8] proposed a Bayesian generative model for community extraction which considers both the network topology and user topic to generate communities that are well-connected and also topically meaningful. The dataset is relatively small with only 151 users and identified 8 communities. [5] proposed and compare several aggregation schemes to train the topic model. [11] proposed an efficient topological-based approach for detecting communities that share common interests on Twitter starting from celebrities representing an interest category. [16] propose performance metrics which measure the similarity between identified communities and the ground-truth communities [13]. They conclude that community detection algorithms with good structural properties are not necessarily yield good performance metrics. Our paper is different since we evaluate communities with the topics users in a community, not with the ground-truth information.

[10] applied LDA topic model to the follow relationship graph of the social network, in order to label the nodes and the edges in the graph with multiple topics. It is different from traditional LDA which is applied on documents to find the topics in the documents. [17] incorporates community discovery into topic analysis in the text-associated graphs to guarantee the topical coherence in the communities so that users in the same communities are closely linked to each other and share common latent topics. The dataset is small and the number of topics are pre-defined. For twitter, they only collected Obama and there are only 1023 users. For DBLP, each user is categorized into data mining, databases, machine learning, and information retrieval. Our paper handles larger dataset without any a priori knowledge of the data. [20] proposed to group the users sharing the same interests by analyzing their textual posts. In addition, they add sentiment-analysis to distinguish users with a positive opinion and negative opinion, called polarities. They apply PCA to find the principle components, called interest center and use k-mean clustering algorithms to cluster the users based on their distance to principle components. This is different from our research since we are not proposing any algorithm for clustering users. [19] proposed a LDA-based model to detect user topics based on their tweets then create the topic graph also called semantic graph where the weight is the topic similarity of two users, then apply existing community detection algorithm to find the community in the topic graph. The evaluation is rather weak since it is not clear how to evaluate their topic based community and the paper only demonstrates the topics in one community.

[21] addressed the problem of friend recommendation and service recommendation with a framework that exploits homophily to establish an integrated network linking a user to interested services and connecting different users with common interests. It mentioned homophily, "A fundamental mechanism that drives the dynamics of networks is the underlying social phenomenon of homophily: people with similar interest tend to connect to each other and people of similar interest are more likely to be friends." Our work is to validate homophile, that is, whether users who form communities on social media share similar interest or not.

3   Topic Modeling

In order to discover the topics a twitter user is interested in, we adopt the approach of topic modeling, a statistical method that analyzes the words in the
original documents to discover the hidden thematic structure in a collection of
documents. The general idea, as stated in [6] is that "the documents themselves
are observed, while the topic structure, the topics, per-document topic distributions, and the per-document per-word topic assignments, is hidden structure.
The central computational problem for topic modeling is to use the observed
documents to infer the hidden topic structure. This can be thought of as revers-
ing the generative process, what is the hidden structure that likely generated the
observed collection?". We choose the well-known statistical topic model, Latent
Dirichlet Allocation (LDA), to reveal the topics in user tweets. In general, a LDA
model contains a list of topics and the distribution of words within those topics.
The model must first be trained with a large collection of documents called a
corpus. When training, we can specify a number of topics that we would like to
discover. The output of this training will then be the topics and the distribution
of words within those topics. The model can then be used with other documents
to discover the distribution of topics within those documents.

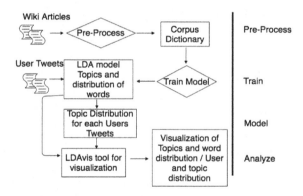

Fig. 1. Topic modeling architecture

Figure 1 illustrates the architecture of our topic modeling on twitter community prototype. It contains four components.

- Preprocess: we preprocess the training data by removing stopwords, urls, and
  short articles.
- Train: we train the LDA model with the wikipedia corpus. This will create
  a list of topics and the distribution of words for each topic. We can then
  use this to discover the topics for a users tweets. We find 100 topics for our
  model. During the training, we can specify the parameters α, β, and K. α
  controls per document topic distribution, a higher alpha value will cause a

document to contain a mixture of more of the topics. β controls per topic word distribution, this means a higher beta value will cause a topic to contain a mixture of more words. K is used to specify the number of topics that we would like to discover.

– Model: we use the model we trained to find the topic distribution of a given users' tweets. All the tweets from a single user are treated as one document. The rich data set of tweets are generally noisy, ambiguous, unstructured, and ungrammatical, so we need to preprocess the tweets. Linguistic processing, remove stop words, urls, hashtag (#), remove non-English languages, and does lemmatization (for example, hire, hiring, hired in user tweet will be changed to hire and marked with noun or verb based on the context).

– Analyze: we determine labels for each topic by looking at the distribution of words for each topic. Then we find the similarity distance between users in the same clique/community. After this we use a tool called LDAvis to visualize our data.

4   Experimental Results

In this section, we our discovery of topological community and their topic similarity. We first describe the dataset used in the experiment. Then show the effectiveness of the trained LDA model. We then compare the topic similarity among users in the same community (called internal topic similarity) with topic similarity among users in different communities (called external topic similarity). We further compare the topic similarity among users in a clique versus users in a community of the same size.

4.1   Data Set

Community: The Twitter users being analyzed are composed of a dataset of 1897 cliques and their respective communities. The cliques and communities were derived from an Arizona Twitter Topology collected in 2013 using a community detection algorithm called Clique Augmentation Algorithm [1]. There are a total of 24,838 unique users in the clique and community dataset. For each unique user, a maximum of 3200 of the most recent Tweets are downloaded from the user's timeline. The average amount of Tweets downloaded for all unique users is 1462. Users with less than 5 Tweets on their timeline are considered inactive and were omitted from the dataset. Omitting these users removes 692 users from the dataset leaving 24,146 unique users. The resulting minimum clique size is 2, average clique size is 5 and maximum clique size is 36. The resulting minimum community size is 3, average community size is 30 and maximum community size is 318. Cliques and their corresponding communities with less than 3 active users were omitted from the dataset, resulting in 1883 cliques and communities left for analysis.

Training data: The corpus used to train an LDA model is the entire collection of articles in the English Wikipedia which was downloaded from [2] in early May

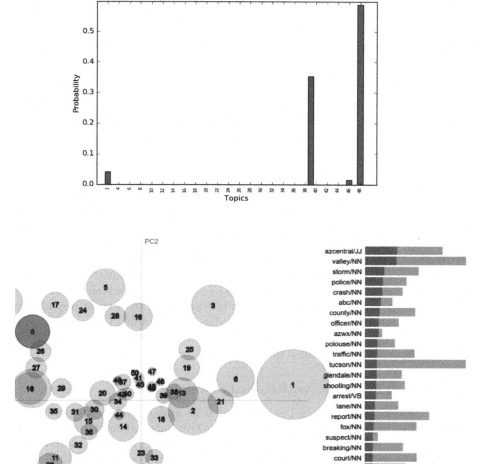

Fig. 2. Distribution of topics of a sample user

of 2016. The collection contains over 5 million articles. The corpus was filtered using a stop word list [4] of non-descriptive and vulgar words. Articles shorter than 50 words were omitted and words in the corpus were tokenized using a lemmatization engine and a part of speech tagger. Words that are less than 2 characters or more than 15 characters in length are omitted from the corpus. A dictionary, containing words and their ids is derived from the corpus. The Wikipedia dictionary is filtered to 170,000 words that occur in no less than 5 and no more than 50% of the articles in the corpus.

User tweets: To understand each user's topics, we download each user's tweets from their timeline. The tweets are then pre-processed by removing hashtag, URL, and at sign. There are total 24,146 unique users in the topology therefore 24,146 tweets documents. Each document is all tweets from one user.

4.2   Model Effectiveness

Figure 2 shows the topic-word distribution of a user who is a bankruptcy lawyer firm. The figure is drawn with LDAVis to demonstrate the effectiveness of the trained model. It can be seen that the word included in this topic are very related and fit the interest of the user as a bankruptcy lawyer.

4.3   Jensen-Shannon Divergence

We use Jensen-Shannon Divergence [15] to measure the similarity of the topic distribution of two users. The Jensen-Shannon Divergence is defined as follows: Given two probability distribution vector P and Q, $JSD(P,Q) = \frac{1}{2}D(P,M) + \frac{1}{2}D(Q,M)$ where $M = \frac{1}{2}(P + Q)$. $D(P,Q)$ is the Kullback-Leibler divergence defined as: $\sum_i P(i)ln\frac{P(i)}{Q(i)}$. $0 \leq JSD(P,Q) \leq ln(2)$. The square root of the Jensen-Shannon divergence is often referred to as Jensen-Shannon distance. In our experiment, for each user, its interest is represented by a topic probability distribution vector calculated by the wikipedia corpus trained LDA model. The smaller the Jensen Shannon Distance between the topic probability distribution of two users is, the more similar the users are.

4.4   Internal Similarity vs. External Similarity

Internal similarity and external similarity can be measured at individual user, clique, and community level. To calculate user-level internal similarity, for each user, we calculate the average JSD between the user and all other users in the same clique or community respectively. To calculate user-level external similarity, for each user, we first choose a number of random users not in the same clique or community as the user, then calculate the average JSD between the user and all other randomly chosen users. In order to compare fairly, we choose the size of the clique or community random users to compare. Clique-level and community-level internal and external similarity is the average of user-level internal or external similarity of all users in the same clique or community respectively.

Figure 3 demonstrates the user-level internal and external topic similarity for a specific user. x-coordinate is the id of users in the same community as the user of interest, y-coordinate is the internal (blue) or external (green) similarity. In this example, there are 44 users in this community. It is clear that randomly chosen user has higher JSD than users in the same community as the user of interest. All user level internal and external similarity show the same pattern. Note that one random user has lower JSD than some of the internal users, this is because this randomly chosen user happens to share strong interest with the user of interest. It is a special case.

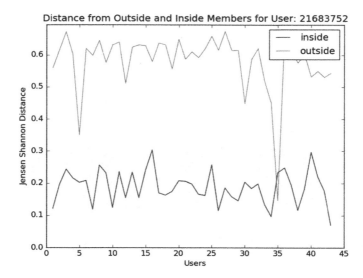

Fig. 3. User level internal similarity vs. external similarity (Color figure online)

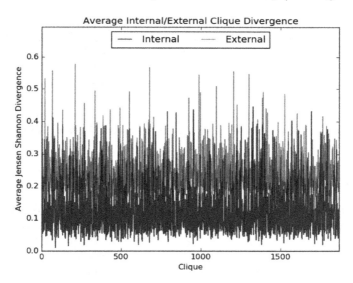

Fig. 4. Clique level internal similarity vs. external similarity

Figure 4 demonstrates the clique-level internal and external topic similarity. x-coordinate is the id of a clique (totally 1883 cliques analyzed), y-coordinate is the internal or external similarity. It is clear that users in the same clique share stronger interest than random users. Another observation is that the majority of cliques have internal similarity below 0.2. This indicates strong interest among users in the same clique. It is also a validation of the effectiveness of our trained topic model.

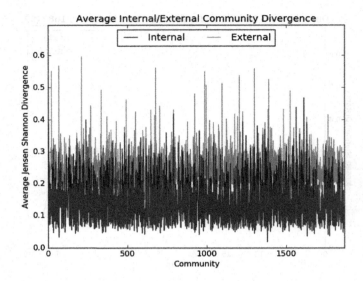

Fig. 5. Community level internal similarity vs. external similarity

Figure 5 compares the community-level internal and external topic similarity. x-axis is the community id (totally 1883 communities analyzed), y-axis is the internal and external topic similarity. Again, as clique-level similarity, it is clear that users in the same community share stronger interest than random users. The majority of communities have internal similarity below 0.2. This validates the Clique Augmentation Algorithm which generates the communities and also is a proof that topology-based hidden communities do show some community themes.

4.5   Clique vs. Community

Figure 6 illustrates the comparison between clique and communities. x-axis is the clique/community id, y-axis is the internal similarity for the clique and the community resultant from the clique. Intuitively, since the size of the community resultant from a clique is larger than the clique, and users chosen into the communities have looser connections than users in the clique, we expect community internal similarity is higher than the clique similarity. Surprising, there is no big difference between these two measurements. It reinforces the performance of the community detection algorithms CAA in terms of finding meaningful communities.

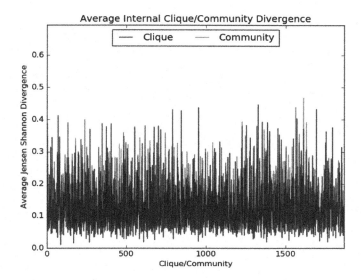

Fig. 6. Clique vs. community

5   Conclusions and Future Work

This paper presents a new methodology to validate communities based on whether they share strong interest or not. It proposes new measurement such as internal and external similarity of clique and community. The result shows that the clique based clique augmentation algorithm can detect hidden communities based on the structure that show strong community theme. It also give evidence that the assumption that user forms community because they share interest is valid. For future work, we would like to investigate more with topic models, such as build models with different topic numbers and train the model with twitter data. Furthermore, It has been pointed out by [23] that traditional LDA does not fit twitter data very well so we will also investigate use other LDA variations. We will also compare different community detection algorithms in terms of their capability of use topic interests.

Acknowledgments. This project is supported by NSF grant CNS #1218212.

References

1. Wagenseller, P., Wang, F.: Community detection algorithm evaluation using size and hashtags (2016). arXiv:1612.03362 [cs.SI]
2. https://dumps.wikimedia.org/enwiki/
3. Fortunato, S.: Community detection in graphs. Phys. Rep. **486**(3–5), 75–174 (2010)
4. http://www.ranks.nl/stopwords
5. Hong, L., Davison, B.D.: Empirical study of topic modeling in Twitter. In: 1st Workshop on Social Media Analytics (SOMA) (2010)

6. Blei, D.M.: Probabilistic topic models. Commun. ACM **55**(4), 77–84 (2012)
7. Java, A., Song, X., Finin, T., Tseng, B.: Why we Twitter: understanding microblogging usage and communities. In: Proceedings of the Joint 9th WEBKDD and 1st SNA-KDD Workshop (2007)
8. Pathak, N., DeLong, C., Banerjee, A., Erickson, K.: Social topic models for community extraction. In: The 2nd SNA-KDD Workshop (2008)
9. Parthasarathy, S., Ruan, Y., Satuluri, V.: Community discovery in social networks: applications, methods and emerging trends. In: Aggarwal, C.C. (ed.) Social Network Data Analytics, pp. 79–113. Springer, New York (2011)
10. Cha, Y., Cho, J.: Social-network analysis using topic models. In: SIGIR (2012)
11. Lim, K.H., Datta, A.: A topological approach for detecting Twitter communities with common interests. In: Atzmueller, M., Chin, A., Helic, D., Hotho, A. (eds.) MSM/MUSE -2012. LNCS, vol. 8329, pp. 23–43. Springer, Heidelberg (2013). doi:10.1007/978-3-642-45392-2_2
12. Ahn, Y.-Y., Bagrow, J.P., Lehmann, S.: Link communities reveal multiscale complexity in networks. Nature **466**(7303), 761–764 (2010)
13. Yang, J., Leskovec, J.: Defining and evaluating network communities based on ground-truth. In: ICDM (2012)
14. Dunbar, R.I.M.: Do online social media cut through the constraints that limit the size of offline social networks? R. Soc. Open Sci. **3**, 150292 (2016)
15. Lin, J.: Divergence measures based on the Shannon entropy. IEEE Trans. Inf. Theory **37**(1), 145–151 (1991)
16. Harenberg, S., Bello, G., Gjeltema, L., Ranshous, S., Harlalka, J., Seay, R., Padmanabhan, K., Samatova, N.: Community detection in large-scale networks: a survey and empirical evaluation. WIREs Comput. Stat. **6**, 426–439 (2014)
17. Yin, Z., Gao, L., Gu, Q., Han, J.: Latent community topic analysis: integration of community discovery with topic modeling. ACM Trans. Intell. Syst. Technol. **3**, 63 (2012)
18. Prat-Pérez, A., Dominguez-Sal, D., Brunat, J.M., Larriba-Pey, J.-L.: Shaping communities out of triangles. In: Proceedings of the 21st ACM International Conference on Information and Knowledge Management, CIKM 2012 (2012)
19. Hannachi, L., Asfari, O., Benblidia, N., Bentayeb, F., Kabachi, N., Boussaid, O.: Community extraction based on topic-driven-model for clustering users tweets. In: Zhou, S., Zhang, S., Karypis, G. (eds.) ADMA 2012. LNCS, vol. 7713, pp. 39–51. Springer, Heidelberg (2012). doi:10.1007/978-3-642-35527-1_4
20. Jaffali, S., Jamoussi, S., Hamadou, A.B.: Grouping like-minded users based on text and sentiment analysis. In: Hwang, D., Jung, J.J., Nguyen, N.-T. (eds.) ICCCI 2014. LNCS, vol. 8733, pp. 83–93. Springer, Cham (2014). doi:10.1007/978-3-319-11289-3_9
21. Yang, S.-H., Long, B., Smola, A., Sadagopan, N., Zheng, Z., Zha, H.: Like like alike: joint friendship and interest propagation in social networks. In: Proceedings of the 20th International Conference on World Wide Web (WWW 2011), pp. 537–546, 2011
22. Sachan, M., Contractor, D., Faruquie, T.A., Venkata Subramaniam, L.: Using content and interactions for discovering communities in social networks. In: Proceedings of the 21st International Conference on World Wide Web, pp. 331–340 (2012)
23. Zhao, W.X., Jiang, J., Weng, J., He, J., Lim, E.-P., Yan, H., Li, X.: Comparing Twitter and traditional media using topic models. In: Clough, P., Foley, C., Gurrin, C., Jones, G.J.F., Kraaij, W., Lee, H., Mudoch, V. (eds.) ECIR 2011. LNCS, vol. 6611, pp. 338–349. Springer, Heidelberg (2011). doi:10.1007/978-3-642-20161-5_34

M2HAV: A Standardized ICN Naming Scheme for Wireless Devices in Internet of Things

Boubakr Nour[1,2], Kashif Sharif[1,2(✉)], Fan Li[1,2(✉)], Hassine Moungla[3], and Yang Liu[4]

[1] School of Computer Science, Beijing Institute of Technology, Beijing, China
{n.boubakr,7620160009,fli}@bit.edu.cn
[2] Beijing Engineering Research Center of High Volume Language Information Processing and Cloud Computing Applications, Beijing, China
[3] Institut Mines-Telecom, Telecom SudParis, Paris, France
hassine.moungla@telecom-sudparis.eu
[4] State Key Laboratory of Networking and Switching Laboratory, Beijing University of Posts and Telecommunication, Beijing, China
liu.yang@bupt.edu.cn

Abstract. The concept Internet of Things in recent years has enabled the connectivity of almost every electronic device using wireless medium, to the Internet. This has created a massive surge in number of heterogeneous wireless devices, with many new challenges regarding content and service naming. The traditional IP-based architectures are now moving towards information/content centric networks. In this paper, we propose a multilayer multi-component hierarchical attribute-value naming scheme for wireless devices. It combines self-certifying names to achieve a standardized naming scheme, which is scalable, efficient, routable, and is secure by design. We use variable-length encoding method to represent hierarchical location names with prefix-labeling. It is highly expressive and customizable using a tree representation, where each level represents a semantic functionality. The qualitative and quantitative analysis show that the proposed scheme is inherently better than many of the available information-centric networking architectures, and is able to reduce the memory and time consumption for name lookup and routing purposes.

Keywords: Information-centric networking · Internet of Things · Naming scheme · Fibonacci encoding

1 Introduction

In the last decade, the world has witnessed a rapid growth of mobiles, data centers, sensors, and smart devices with processing, sensing, and connectivity capabilities [1]. While the human Internet users are in billions, machines and

This work is partially supported by the National Natural Science Foundation of China under Grant Nos. 61370192, 61432015, and 61602038.

© Springer International Publishing AG 2017
L. Ma et al. (Eds.): WASA 2017, LNCS 10251, pp. 289–301, 2017.
DOI: 10.1007/978-3-319-60033-8_26

wireless devices (things) are also becoming active users, producing huge amounts of meaningful information [2]. This evolution has become the Internet of Things (IoT) [3], and has added a number of new challenges [4]. Information-Centric Networking (ICN) [5] has also gained popularity, as users consume content from the network instead of communicating with specific hosts. ICN architecture focuses on content/data as the central entity of the Internet, rather than host-centric networking. The content is the first-class network element in the ICN context, hence it needs to be: globally unique, persistent, secure, location-independent and should have friendly names, which has become a challenge as it is difficult to find one single naming scheme that satisfies all of these properties [6]. Content-Centric Networking (CCN) and many of its variants are instantiations of ICN. In this paper we propose a multi-layer hierarchical naming scheme for content/service and devices in a large-scale IoT network. The existing ICN solutions do not provide a standard naming mechanism for either services or devices, and have not evolved to incorporate IoT into their fold. Due to the nature of information centric networks, using IP address to identify devices/services is not feasible, although the underlying technology could be using low power IP variants. The proposed scheme uses multiple levels with attribute-value pairs to completely identify the name of service and device to represent and control the actions, and extract information from wireless devices. The names are encoded using a variable length universal code, and can be aggregated to increase routing and storage efficiency. This also increases the scalability of overall system, which is shown by implementation and evaluation of the mechanism.

The rest of paper is organized into five sections: Sect. 2 describes the existing ICN architecture solutions and their naming schemes. The proposed design scheme and its components are presented in Sect. 3. In Sect. 4 we evaluate the efficiency of our naming scheme, followed by conclusion in Sect. 5.

2   Related Works

Cheriton and Gritter [7] proposed TRIAD, where they introduced the concept of name-based routing. ICN uses names in order to route data, rather than IP address for finding hosts. There are mainly three categories of naming in ICN [8]: *Hierarchical, Flat,* and *Attribute-Value Based* names, shown in example below:

- Hierarchical Name: */universityname.com/papers/2015/authors/title.type*
- Flat Name: *ni://universityname.com/sha-256; Title*
- Attribute-Value Based Name: *Title<String>: 'PaperTitle'*
  Authors<ListofStrings>: Authors
  Year<Integer>: 2015

Hierarchical naming consists of multiple components to identify the application, services, or resources. It may enhance scalability since name prefix can be aggregated. Flat names for dynamic content are typically obtained through hash algorithms. Therefore, the name is not human-friendly and can hardly be assigned to dynamic content not yet published. Flat naming also has scalability issues since they don't support routing aggregation. In the attribute-value based naming, an attribute has a name, a type, and a set of possible values. Collectively, they represent a single resource and its capabilities.

A number of advanced ICN solution have been proposed with different naming schemes. *Named Data Networking* (NDN) [9] design assumes hierarchically structured opaque names to the network by allowing each application to choose the naming scheme that fits its needs. *MobilityFirst* [10] has self-certifying flat names called Global Unique IDentification (GUID). The GUID and network address are separated from each other and a mapping between them is maintained, making complex routing rules. *Data-Oriented Network Architecture* (DONA) [11] despite preserving the IP addressing and routing, is the first complete ICN architecture. Persistent flat names are used to identify information objects; in particular, names are in the form $P:L$, where P is the ciphered hash of the public key of the content owner, and L uniquely identifies one of the contents with respect to the same owner. *Publish Subscribe Internet Technology* (PURSUIT) project [12], adopts a complete clean-slate approach in designing its ICN architecture. It uses publish/subscribe stack instead of IP protocol stack, along with self-certifying flat names. The new approach means more challenges in IP over/cross ICN environments and transition mechanisms. *Scalable and Adaptive Internet Solutions* (SAIL) [13] inherits aspects both from PURSUIT and NDN, using self-certifying flat names with possible explicit aggregation in the form $ni://A/L$, where A is the authority part, and L is the local part with respect to the authority. *Convergence* [14] uses a number of features from the NDN, by using self-certifying flat names in the form *namespaceID:name*, resembling the $P:L$ pair of DONA. *Content Mediator Architecture for Content-Aware Networks* (COMET) [15] distributes the role of mapping between topological and content information to the Content Mediation Plane. Names in COMET consists of two human-readable parts, i.e. the naming authority, and the content name under it.

Adhatarao et al. [16] perform a qualitative and quantitative comparison for both hierarchical and flat naming schemes in ICN architectures, using several metrics such as name lookup efficiency, aggregate-ability, semantic and manageability. The study shows that hierarchical names have a much higher lookup complexity due the need to parse and lookup for each name component to determine the outgoing interface. Lindgren et al. [17] give a high-level overview of advantages, trade-offs and challenges of information-centric networking for IoT architecture, by discussing the expected benefits for different ICN components: naming, routing, caching, and security. Bari et al. [18] present the core functionalities of ICN architectures by describing the important components in different ICN proposals, highlighting the similarities and differences among them. Their in-depth analysis is done by comparing the routing scalability through name-prefix aggregation, security, data integrity and name semantics in flat, hierarchical and attribute-value based naming, and in-path and off-path name resolution.

In summary, there is no clear consent yet on whether hierarchical or flat names should be used. However, most of the studies recommend using a multilayer naming scheme that combines self-certifying names with a collection of keywords that can be used by different applications (web content, video content, IoT). Also, the naming scheme should support name persistence, security binding, authenticity and global uniqueness.

Most of the wireless IoT communication patterns such as *sensor content retrieval* and *mobile content updates* are by nature following ICN paradigm and benefit from in-network caching, hop-by-hop replication and content-based security. In fact, ICN design suits the large scale wireless IoT device deployment, by improving the performance and energy efficiency.

Waltari and Kangasharju [19] proposed and implemented an ICN architecture for IoT sensor environment with the home-automation system using push-based communication. The architecture uses messages between sensors to get current readings, historical readings, data extraction from CCN repository, and executes actuator instructions. Shang et al. [20] discuss the requirements and challenges for ICN-IoT especially the *Naming* and *Name Resolution* which should be scalable and support millions of wireless *things*. Amadeo et al. [21] discuss the ICN basics and give an overview of existing ICN research projects where none of them have been designed to satisfy the wireless IoT features. Their analysis is focused towards scalability, QoS, security, energy efficiency, mobility, and heterogeneity.

The fundamental challenges that must be considered when defining an ICN-IoT naming scheme are naming of devices, naming of services, size of such names, confidentiality, security, and meta-data, etc.

3   M2HAV Design Scheme

Content names are the primary network element for ICN architecture and it is as important as naming hosts in host-centric networking. Coupled with IoT, the naming scheme should be highly expressive and customizable, and should identify services, content, as well as devices. The heterogeneous device environment (wearable, mobile, sensory, etc.) adds to the challenge of unified naming. Naming devices in IoT is expected to manipulate them (switching a device ON/OFF), and should present an interoperability between different and multi-crossed domains. Moreover, it should support efficient aggregation rules and dynamic content.

In the following subsection, we present a Multilayer Multi-component Hierarchical Attribute-Value (M2HAV) ICN wireless device naming scheme. We use variable-length encoding with prefix-based scheme for the location as well as the attributes. The objective of this scheme is to provide device naming in an IoT setting with next generation ICN architecture.

3.1   Network Reference Model

Internet of Things is designed to establish its base in the world of Internet, where wireless IoT devices can be integrated with other wired or wireless sensors that allow easy accessing, sharing, collecting, and searching for appropriate data. In this work, we use the IoT topology design shown in Fig. 1(a) as a reference model. It involves different sensing and automation applications, and takes into account the routing, security, privacy, mobility, quality of service and heterogeneity of the environment. Based on this, we divide our network into a collection of sub-networks named *ICN-Net* as shown in Fig. 1(b). The *ICN-Net* is defined dynamically, and is bounded by the gateway of the network. It may comprise of two types of wireless IoT devices, namely *AccessThing* (AT) and *EdgeThing* (ET). An AT is a standard *thing* in the topology which can be a sensor or actuator, while an ET acts as a gateway in-between ICN-Nets and/or ISPs. In highly dynamic environments the ET can be mobile, and more than one attached to an ICN-Net for load balancing or in-network caching. ETs are considered as resource-rich devices and ATs as resource-constrained devices.

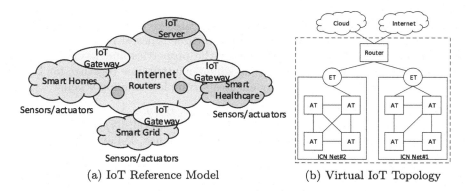

(a) IoT Reference Model   (b) Virtual IoT Topology

Fig. 1. Reference and virtual topologies

3.2 Multilayer Multi-component Naming Design

The proposed top-down naming scheme is illustrated in Fig. 2, where we have defined four levels. The *Root Prefix Level* defines the core network. The *Task Type Level* classifies the data name space in IoT environment into two classes based on the requested *Task* to do; either a *Sensing* (e.g., on-demand sensing data, periodic monitoring) or *Action* (e.g., action triggering, event-triggered alarms). In *Service Type Level* the *Service* to be performed (e.g., temperature sensing, turn *ON/OFF* light) is defined. Finally, the *Location Level* identifies the physical position of a service at the AT/ET level.

Attributes. Each level in the naming scheme has a collection of attribute-value pairs to store and carry different properties about the content/service such as action type, security, owner, etc. Some of them are well-known and

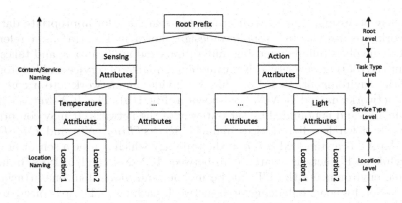

Fig. 2. Multilayer naming design

required, other are optional and may be generated dynamically. Primarily all these Attribute-Value pairs are classified into three types of properties as given below. It is important to understand that the properties and levels in hierarchy are not the same. Properties group different attributes together for better classification, whereas the hierarchy ensures a complete naming scheme.

- Owner: {Signature: ..., PKey: ..., Seq Num: ..., Hash: ...}
- Thing: {Signature: ..., PKey: ..., Seq Num: ..., P-Level: IN/OUT}
- Action: {Action: ON, Type: Standard, S-Level: Auth, P-Level: IN}

The Owner set of properties is used to give more information about the owner of a service or a *thing*, by sharing its signature, public key, etc. The Thing set of properties is related to the identification, location, security, and other related attributes for a physical *thing* itself. The Action set of properties groups the tasks and associated actions, type of actions, etc. We have defined three types of actions in our wireless IoT naming architecture:

- Standard Action: Actions performed by users/applications, e.g.: Turn ON/OFF light, sensing temperature, etc.
- System Action: Actions used by the architecture/system, e.g.: Register/Find, Publish/Subscribe, Authentication Req/Rep, Negotiation, etc.
- Reserved Action: Reserved action for future usage.

The number of attributes used in a particular IoT application is at the discretion of implementer and designer of service. The benefit of Attribute-Value pairs is that, it allows as many different types of information required to be embedded into the message. Moreover, the names and values could be plain text, machine readable, encoded, or encrypted. In this paper we only provide the classification of properties and guideline for attributes. More attributes can be added and/or modified to the following list.

- Well-Known Attributes: *Action*: Action name to be performed on the thing, *Type*: Type of action (standard, system, reserved), *Security Level*: Open or

Authenticated action, *Privacy Level*: Access from IN/OUT of network, *Location*: The location of the thing, *Owner Sign*: The owner of the information
– Optional Attributes: *Sequence No*: To ensure the freshness of data, *Cache Lifetime*: If/how long can the information be stored in repository, *Meta-Data*: For both Owner and the Thing itself e.g. hash, certificates, keywords, content meta, etc.

3.3   Device/Location Naming and Encoding

In this section we propose a device/location naming scheme for fast, unique, compressed, and variable length names. Earlier section discussed location as an attribute of the multilayer multi-component scheme. It is important to clarify that we propose to use the encoded location of device as the name of device too. This method reduces the redundancy of having two different attributes, and makes it easy to identify and route information across the network. Hence, the Location level in Fig. 2 is mainly used for the routing/forwarding process, where aggregation rules can be applied to reduce data in the Forwarding Information Base (FIB).

Location Naming. In order to explain this, we refer to virtual topology and ICN-Net in Fig. 1(b). The whole IoT is a collection of ICN-Nets, which are physically connected to each other. Consider a campus-wide IoT infrastructure of wireless *things*. Virtual ICN-Nets can be created for each classroom/office/lab with at least one ET. These can comprise of sensors/actuators or other AT present in that space. These ICN-Nets can then be grouped at floor level, and then at building level, and further at block level, and ultimately at campus level. This essentially creates a logical hierarchy over the physical network, i.e.

$$campus \rightarrow block \rightarrow building \rightarrow floor \rightarrow room \rightarrow thing$$

We propose that the name and location of device be merged using this scheme. Fundamentally this can be modeled as a tree structure also, which simplifies forwarding and identification at the same time. A detailed tree is shown in Fig. 4. To represent the complete name, the arrows can be replaced with\for simplicity. The fundamental limitation of this scheme is the length of name, as it can be considerably long. Below, we propose an encoding mechanism for these names, so that the length can be kept to minimal levels, thus enhancing scalability and efficiency.

Location Encoding. We propose to use variable-length location encoding with prefix-based scheme. The idea is to assign each label a variable-length number. Instead of encoding the entire location, each node locally encodes its own label into locally unique binary numbers. The size of each label is essentially determined by a specific variable length encoding method that can be different from an *ICN-Net* to another.

Step 1 - Prefix-Based Scheme: The simplest algorithm for prefix-based scheme is a Decimal Classification which can be easily applied on a tree structure. Due to space limitation, we provide the implementation algorithm, and refer to Fig. 4 for implementation example.

Let T be a tree with root r.

Each node $n \in T$ is identified as $key(n).pos(n)$, where

$$key(n).pos(n) = \begin{cases} 1 & \text{if } n = r \\ key(v).pos(v).i & \text{if } n \text{ is } i^{th} \text{ child of node } v \end{cases}$$

Step 2 - Variable-Length Encoding: After using the prefix-based labeling, we apply a variable-length encoding method. We prefer the use of Fibonacci encoding [22] as a universal code which is used as alternative to dense codes for large textual word-based data. It is particularly a good choice for compressing a set of small integers, and fast decoding as well as compressed searches. Furthermore, Fibonacci codes are robust even against insertions and deletions, which means they are robust in terms of correcting errors. If the codes are to be used over a noisy wireless communication channel, their resilience to bit insertions, deletions and to bit-flips is of high importance. Simple Fibonacci sequence can be generated as:

$$F_i = F_{i-1} + F_{i-2}, \text{ for } i \geq 1, \text{ where } F_{-1} = F_0 = 1$$

Using the Fibonacci sequence (excluding the first 0 and 1) a binary code word can be generated. For a number n to be encoded, if $d(0), d(1), ..., d(k-1), d(k)$ represent the digits of the code word representing n, the Fibonacci binary encoding $V(f(n))$ can be obtained as:

$$V(f(n)) = \sum_{i=0}^{k-1} d(i).F(i+2), \text{ and} : d(k-1) = d(k) = 1$$

Where $F(i)$ is the ith Fibonacci number. $d(k)$ is always an appended bit of 1. In essence, the code represents 1 bits for Fibonacci sequence that can be summed to represent n, with a 1 appended at the end. Examples:

$$V(f(4)) = 1011, \quad V(f(7)) = 01011, \quad V(f(32)) = 00101011$$

At the end of this process the lengthy name for a wireless IoT *thing* is converted to small binary value as in Table 2.

4   Analysis and Evaluation

Evaluation of our proposed M2HAV naming scheme is done both qualitatively and quantitatively. In the first part, we have compared our scheme to existing ICN architectures and naming schemes, whereas in the later part we have implemented the location naming algorithms and computed the efficiency of whole process.

4.1 Qualitative Analysis

Table 1 summarizes the comparison of M2HAV with other naming types. The multilayer attribute-value pairs in hierarchy allow complete flexibility to add data integrity, readability aggregation, identification, naming, and security features to the wireless IoT devices and the services/content they provide. Compared to basic hierarchical naming schemes, these features can only be added with extra functionality at the application layer. Attribute-Value paired names, may provide some of these features. Due to space limitation we have omitted the detailed comparison of M2HAV against other ICN architectures, but in summary, M2HAV is a feature rich naming scheme as compared to NDN, DONA, PURSUIT, and NetInf architectures. The major difference is that M2HAV by design has features like device naming, security, in-cache/metadata support, while others have added components to provide some of them.

Table 1. Comparison of M2HAV with different types of names

Properties	M2HAV	Hierarchical	Attribute-value
Name-data integrity	Sign., hash	Sign.	Sign.
Human-readable names	Possible	✓	✓
Name aggregation	✓	✓	✗
Identifying services/content	✓	✗	✓
Naming devices	✓	✗	✗
Short length names	✓	✗	✗
Support privacy/security	✓	✗	✗
Support in-cache	✓	✗	✗
Support meta-data	✓	✗	✓

4.2 Quantitative Evaluation

To show the quantitative efficiency of M2HAV, we have implemented the scheme to carry out an example action task: switching ON the light in the 10th floor, *Room 33* in the *Central Building* in university. The application service flow chart and the action hierarchy are shown in Fig. 3. The application is configured to have three different buildings with ICN-Nets at room level. Names are given to the wireless IoT *things* as proposed in our design. As seen from Fig. 4, the system performs a one time tree construction with prefix labels. Based on these labels, encoding is performed, example of which is shown in Table 2. Dots are used to make encoded names readable. M2HAV has been bench marked against hierarchical naming on an Intel Core i7 2.4 GHz with 8 GB RAM.

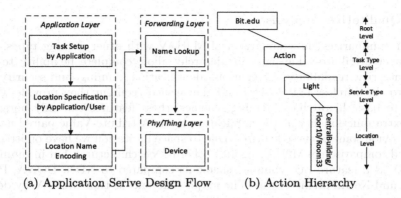

(a) Application Serive Design Flow   (b) Action Hierarchy

Fig. 3. Application and action service

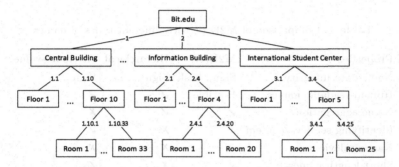

Fig. 4. Virtual ICN-Net topology with prefix-based labeling

Table 2. Encoding process

Location	Prefix label	Encoding location
/Bit.edu/CentralBuilding/Floor1	1.1	11.11
/Bit.edu/CentralBuilding/Floor10/Room33	1.1.10.33	11.11.010011.10101011
/Bit.edu/InformationCenter/Floor4/Room20	2.4.20	011.1011.0101011

Encoding Performance: The application interface for user shows complete alphanumeric names for ease of use, but their length combined with the number of entries in FIB creates a challenge. In our scheme these are encoded to very small bit values which saves the overall size of the FIB. The test scenario has 2585 names of varying lengths. The size of FIB table using hierarchical alphanumeric names is 190960 bytes. On the contrary after encoding the size of FIB is reduced to 62240 bytes, which is a compression ratio of 3:1. By using a Fast Fibonacci Encoding Algorithms the time taken to encode is almost zero. This is mainly due to small integer values of decimal-prefixing in our scheme.

Lookup Performance: Once the FIB has been populated with encoded names, it can be used to perform routing operations. Searching the FIB of a large-scale IoT with thousands of wireless IoT *things* can be time consuming task. Moreover the capability of ETs and other intermediate wireless device may be limited. Although the size of our experimental FIB is small, the difference in searching time is significantly reduced with M2HAV scheme. In Fig. 5 the time to compare and find ten randomly selected names is shown. Figure 5(a) shows the case where names are not sorted in either of the FIB, the time taken to find a match varies. However matching a complete string is always larger than that of few bits. In Fig. 5(b), we use the same data and same lookup operation but with sorted names. A consistent performance is achieved across the board, which is better than that of hierarchical names.

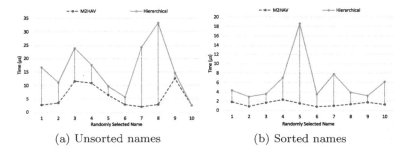

(a) Unsorted names   (b) Sorted names

Fig. 5. Lookup operation in hierarchical and proposed name

5   Conclusion

Information-Centric Network has recently been identified as a potential alternative network paradigm for the Internet of Things. IoT supports a heterogeneous environment with millions of wireless devices. In this paper, we address a major challenge and open issue for naming of wireless devices and services in ICN-IoT architectures. We have proposed a naming scheme design that is composed of multiple layers, for addressing multiple components in attribute-value pairs to identify both service and content/action associated with each device. Since the naming design uses variable-length hierarchy, we have used Fibonacci binary encoding for location naming. The qualitative and quantitative analysis has shown that our scheme is efficient and comprehensive in nature.

References

1. Zheng, X., Cai, Z., Li, J., Gao, H.: A study on application-aware scheduling in wireless networks. IEEE Trans. Mob. Comput. **PP**(99) (2016)

2. Zheng, X., Cai, Z.: Real-time big data delivery in wireless networks: a case study on video delivery. IEEE Trans. Ind. Inform. **PP**(99) (2017)
3. Atzori, L., Iera, A., Morabito, G.: The internet of things: a survey. Comput. Netw. **54**(15), 2787–2805 (2010)
4. Zheng, X., Cai, Z., Yu, J., Wang, C., Li, Y.: Follow but no track: privacy preserved profile publishing in cyber-physical social systems. IEEE Internet Things J. **PP**(99) (2017)
5. Xylomenos, G., Christopher, N., Vasilios, A., Nikos, F., et al.: A survey of information-centric networking research. IEEE Commun. Surv. Tutor. (2013)
6. Zhang, Y., Raychadhuri, D., Grieco, L.A., Baccelli, E., et al.: ICN based architecture for IoT - requirements and challenges. Internet Draft, IETF, August 2015
7. Cheriton, D.R., Gritter, M.: TRIAD: a new next-generation Internet architecture. Computer Science Department, Stanford University (2001)
8. Ahlgren, B., Dannewitz, C., Imbrenda, C., Kutscher, D., Ohlman, B.: A survey of information-centric networking. IEEE Commun. Mag. **50**(7) (2012)
9. Zhang, L., Afanasyev, A., Burke, J., Jacobson, V., Claffy, K., et al.: Named data networking. SIGCOMM Comput. Commun. Rev. **44**(3), 66–73 (2014)
10. Seskar, I., Nagaraja, K., Nelson, S., Raychaudhuri, D.: Mobilityfirst: future internet architecture project. In: Asian Internet Engineering Conference. ACM (2011)
11. Koponen, T., Chawla, M., Chun, B.G., Ermolinskiy, A., Kim, K.H., Shenker, S., Stoica, I.: A data-oriented (and beyond) network architecture. SIGCOMM Comput. Commun. Rev. **37**(4), 181–192 (2007)
12. Fotiou, N., Nikander, P., Trossen, D., Polyzos, G.C.: Developing information networking further: from PSIRP to PURSUIT. In: Tomkos, I., Bouras, C.J., Ellinas, G., Demestichas, P., Sinha, P. (eds.) BROADNETS 2010. LNICSSITE, vol. 66, pp. 1–13. Springer, Heidelberg (2012). doi:10.1007/978-3-642-30376-0_1
13. Brunner, M.: Scalable & Adaptive Internet solutions (SAIL). Future Internet Assembly (2010)
14. Melazzi, N.B., Salsano, S., Detti, A., Tropea, G., Chiariglione, L., Difino, A., et al.: Publish/subscribe over information centric networks: a standardized approach in CONVERGENCE. In: Future Network Mobile Summit, July 2012
15. Garca, G., Beben, A., Ramn, F.J., Maeso, A., Psaras, I., Pavlou, G., et al.: COMET: content mediator architecture for content-aware networks. In: Future Network Mobile Summit, June 2011
16. Adhatarao, S., Chen, J., Arumaithurai, M., Fu, X., Ramakrishnan, K.: Comparison of naming schema in ICN. In: IEEE Local and Metropolitan Area Networks, June 2016
17. Lindgren, A., Abdesslem, F.B., Ahlgren, B., Scheln, O., Malik, A.M.: Design choices for the IoT in information-centric networks. In: IEEE Consumer Communications and Networking Conference, pp. 882–888, January 2016
18. Bari, M.F., Chowdhury, S.R., Ahmed, R., Boutaba, R., Mathieu, B.: A survey of naming and routing in information-centric networks. IEEE Commun. Mag. **50**(12), December 2012
19. Waltari, O., Kangasharju, J.: Content-centric networking in the internet of things. In: IEEE Consumer Communications and Networking Conference, pp. 73–78, January 2016
20. Shang, W., Bannis, A., Liang, T., Wang, Z., Yu, Y., Afanasyev, A., Thompson, J., Burke, J., Zhang, B., Zhang, L.: Named data networking of things. In: IEEE Conference on Internet-of-Things Design and Implementation, pp. 117–128, April 2016

21. Amadeo, M., Campolo, C., Quevedo, J., Corujo, D., Molinaro, A., Iera, A., Aguiar, R.L., Vasilakos, A.V.: Information-centric networking for the internet of things: challenges and opportunities. IEEE Netw. **30**(2), 92–100 (2016)
22. Thomas, J.H.: Variations on the Fibonacci universal code. CoRR (2007)

Multidimensional Trust-Based Anomaly Detection System in Internet of Things

Fangyu Gai, Jiexin Zhang, Peidong Zhu, and Xinwen Jiang[✉]

School of Computer, National University of Defense Technology, Changsha, China
{gaifangyu15,zhangjiexin,pdzhu,xwjiang}@nudt.edu.cn

Abstract. Trust Management (TM) has been playing an important role in dealing with security and privacy issues in the Internet of Things (IoT). Following this trend, we propose a trust-based anomaly detection system which provides a closed loop of trustworthiness computing, decision-making and trust reevaluation. The proposed trust model considers multidimensional trust elements including reputation, Quality of Service (QoS) and social relationship, the result of which is employed to instruct the device to take appropriate security policies against its peers. Moreover, the detected anomaly event will trigger the reevaluation of the peers trustworthiness. To evaluate our system, we consider a shopping mall scenario with a great many of IoT devices, and the simulation results show our system achieves very low false alarm rate under proper trust level threshold.

Keywords: Internet of Things · Trust management · Anomaly detection

1 Introduction

The Internet of Things (IoT) has integrated objects with the Internet resulting in a smart environment where the exchange of data and services is ubiquitous. However, the IoT has been exposed to more risks than the Internet because of the high level of heterogeneity. IoT devices are usually deployed in unsupervised environments, where conventional security mechanisms such as authentication can hardly deal with insider attacks [1]. In particular, malicious nodes owning legitimate tokens can easily tamper with sensitive data without being identified. Additionally, owners may misconfigure their devices, which can cause unpredictable consequences to the whole system.

Trust Management (TM) has become a feasible technique for enhancing user privacy and information security in the IoT environment. The term trust management is first defined by [2], where the earliest trust management system named PolicyMaker is proposed. Since then, a great number of works addressing trust management issues in Mobile Ad hoc Networks (MANETs) and Wireless sensor networks (WSNs) have been proposed, such as CORE [3] and NICE [4].

In recent years, there is a growing trend of trust management research in IoT scenarios, but the solutions are still in fantasy. Unlike other networking

© Springer International Publishing AG 2017
L. Ma et al. (Eds.): WASA 2017, LNCS 10251, pp. 302–313, 2017.
DOI: 10.1007/978-3-319-60033-8_27

systems, the specific characteristics of the IoT have brought new challenges for trust management to fulfill, such as big data trust, user privacy preservation, and user-device trust interaction [5]. Currently, there still lacks a specific study which considering both trust models and trust based decision-making in IoT scenarios.

To fulfill new IoT requirements, we propose a Multidimensional Trust-Based Anomaly Detection (MTBAD) system for the IoT. The proposed system extracts trust information from different dimensions. Specifically, we consider *Reputation*, *QoS* and *Social Relationship* in this paper. According to the specific context, some dimensions can be optional or integrated. After that, trustworthiness will be converted to trust levels using fuzzy approaches, and the results will be used in the device's security policies to assess its peers. In addition, if anomaly inter-actions of nodes are detected, their trust levels will be reevaluated.

The remainder of this paper is organized as follows. Section 2 introduces the related work about trust management in the IoT. Sections 3 and 4 describe the definition of the trust model and the trust-based anomaly detection process respectively. In Sect. 5, we demonstrate the evaluation results of our system experimentally. We conclude in Sect. 6 and point out the directions for future work.

2   Related Work

2.1   Trust Assessment

Trust assessment is also called trust evaluation, which is a computational app-roach of using gathered interaction information to represent whether or to what extent a node can be trusted by others. Chen et al. [6] proposed a trust and rep-utation model TRM-IoT based fuzzy reputation for a specific IoT environment, Wireless Sensor Network (WSN). The trust evaluation metrics include end-to-end packet forwarding ratio, energy consumption, and the package delivery ratio for local and global trust evaluation.

Bao and Chen [7] proposed a trust evaluation model considering multiple trust properties such as honesty, cooperativeness, and community-interest. These properties are used to account for social interaction, and trust is aggregated using both direct observations and indirect recommendations. At the same year, a new paradigm named "Social Internet of Things (SIoT)" was brought by Atzori et al. [8], where social network concept was integrated with the IoT. After that, Nitti et al. [9] proposed two trust models (the subjective model and the objec-tive model) for trustworthiness management. The objective model is derived from P2P communication networks. The trust value of each node is stored and retrieved in a distributed hash table to realize global sharing. The subjective model is deriving from social networks, with each node computing the trust values of its friends based on its own experience and the opinion of its friends.

2.2 Trust Based Decision-Making

Trust based decision-making is the objective of the trust management. The trustworthiness evaluated from the collected trust will help the system make security decisions such as access control, route selection, and anomaly detection. Bao et al. [10] proposed a hierarchical trust management protocol for wireless sensor networks which considers trust attributes derived from communication and social networks to assess the trustworthiness of a sensor node. The authors also analyzed the performance of the proposed trust management protocol by developing a probability model based on stochastic Petri net techniques, and particularly, the protocol was applied to trust-based geographical routing as an application.

Bernabe et al. [11] proposed a flexible access control system for IoT-based trust management, named TACIoT. It provided an end-to-end lightweight authorization mechanism integrated with a novel trust model for IoT devices. Particularly, TACIoT has been successfully implemented and evaluated in a practical testbed for both constrained and non-constrained IoT devices.

3   Trust Models and System Components

3.1   Multidimensional Trust Assessment

Trust involves two roles: a trustor and a trustee. In an IoT environment, a trustor is an object which requests some sort of services while a trustee is an entity who offers the services. Since trust is a complicated concept related to reliability, dependability, belief, confidence and other subjective characters of an entity, it is greatly affected by the trustor's policy. Additionally, it is also influenced by the trustee's competence, performance and quality [12]. Therefore, we propose a multidimensional trust model consisting of three properties namely *Reputation*, *Quality of Service (QoS)*, *Social Relationship*. The details of each property are described as follows.

1. **Reputation** is third-party information and can be considered as feedbacks given by other entities accumulated during past interactions. Let f_{ij}^l be a feedback provided by a entity E_i toward a entity E_j at transaction l. f_{ij}^l can be expressed in a discrete way, i.e., $f_{ij}^l \in \{0, 0.5, 1\}$ for unsatisfied, ordinary and satisfied. Or it can be represented in a continuous range $f_{ij}^l \in [0, 1]$. Therefore, the *Reputation* of E_j considered by E_i can be expressed as the average of all the feedbacks provided by E_i: $R_j = \sum_{l=0}^{n} f_{ij}^l / n$, where n is the number of interactions between E_i and E_j.

2. **QoS** refers to the evaluation of the general quality of service provided by a device including properties about communication delay, packet repetition rate, interaction success rate, etc. These properties are measured by recapping evidence of previous interactions within the peer device being analyzed [11].

3. **Social Relationship** is also considered as part of our trust model. This property is based on the emerging paradigm named *Social Internet of Things (SIoT)* [8], which allows objects to establish social relationships with each

other to boost the discovery, selection, and composition of services. According to this model, five typical relationships are defined: *parental object relationship, co-location/work object relationship, ownership object relationship* and *social object relationship.*

Before an iteration happens, the trustor will first assess the trustworthiness of the trustee based on the evidence about the aforementioned trust properties. Let $T_{ij}(l)$ be the overall trust value of E_i toward E_j. Then it can be calculated as follows:

$$T_{ij}(l) = w_1 T_{ij}^R(l) + w_2 T_{ij}^Q(l) + w_3 T_{ij}^{SR}(l). \tag{1}$$

Accordingly, l means the lth iteration and w_1, w_2 and w_3 represent the weight of each trust property with $w_1 + w_2 + w_3 = 1$. Within each property, T_{ij}^X needs to be updated when E_i interacts with E_j, where $X \in \{Reputation, QoS, SocialRelationship\}$. T_{ij}^X includes *direct trust*, which is according to the trustor's own observation of the trustee, and *recommdation trust* representing opinions about the trustee provided by other entities. When E_i interacts with E_k and $k = j$, $T_{ij}^X(l)$ updates as follows:

$$T_{ij}^X(l) = \alpha T_{ij}^X(l - \delta l) + (1 - \alpha) T_{ij}^{X,direct}(l). \tag{2}$$

Here, $T_{ij}^X(l - \delta l)$ indicates the past trustworthiness of E_i toward E_j and δl is the interval interactions. The parameter $\alpha \in [0, 1]$ is used to balance the weight of the past and the recent trustworthiness. If the context is changing rapidly, then α should be tuned lower (i.e. $\alpha < 0.5$) to pay more attention to the recent trust status, otherwise, α should be tuned higher (i.e. $\alpha > 0.5$).

On the other hand, when E_i interacts with E_k and $k \neq j$, then $T_{ij}^X(l)$ updates as follows:

$$T_{ij}^X(l) = \gamma T_{ij}^X(l - \delta l) + (1 - \gamma)\frac{\sum_{k=1}^{N_i} T_{kj}^{X,recom}(l)}{N_i}. \tag{3}$$

In this case, $T_{ij}^X(l - \delta l)$ is the past trustworthiness of E_i toward E_j while $T_{kj}^{X,recom}(l)$ represents the recommendation trustworthiness, and E_k is the recommender. The parameter $\gamma \in [0, 1]$ is the balancer, which is calculated as follows:

$$\gamma = \frac{1}{1 + \beta T_{ik}(l)} \tag{4}$$

Here another parameter $\beta \in [0, 1]$ is introduced. With β or $T_{ik}(t)$ increases, the impact of the recommendation trust will grow, otherwise it will decrease. The core idea of introducing the parameter β is to protect the trust system from bad-mouthing and ballot-stuffing attacks [13].

3.2   System Components

The proposed MTBAD system consists of two parts: *Trust Models* and *Security Mechanisms*, which are shown in Fig. 1. The *Trust Models* is for trust evaluation, the result of which will be employed by the *Security Mechanisms* for security

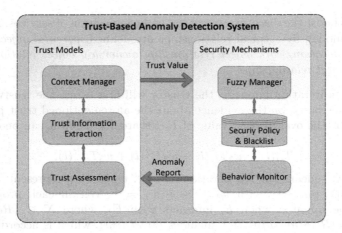

Fig. 1. Scheme of the Multidimensional Trust-Based Anomaly Detection (MTBAD) system

decision-making. We also define and incorporate three basic components to each part. Their responsibilities and interactions are briefly presented as follows:

1. ***Context Manager*** is used to generate dynamical and real-time context information such as time, location, power consumption and device model. This information is transmitted to *Trust Information Extraction Module* to sort data format and employed by the *Trust Assessment* to evaluate the trust value.
2. ***Trust Information Extraction*** is to extract trust evidences by aggregating cross-layer information from IoT devices. It requires some mechanisms to record interaction information such as network delay, packet repetition rate.
3. ***Trust Assessment*** is the core component in the *Trust Models*, where all trust assessment algorithms are implemented. The output of this module will be employed by *Security Mechanisms* for security decision-making.
4. ***Fuzzy Manager*** employs fuzzy approaches. Fuzziness indicates the degree of appropriateness of each dimension being considered as a trust property. Details will be presented in Sect. 4.
5. ***Security Policy & Blacklist*** includes a collection of rules that allow or disallow security-related actions and events about a device. According to the trust level of the trustee, different levels of security policies will bring into effect. Moreover, the blacklist can be shared among trusted entities.
6. ***Behavior Monitor*** is to monitor the trustee's actions during the interactions. Therefore, some detection mechanisms such as [14,15]. When an anomaly event is detected, it will trigger the reevaluation of the peer's trust level.

Due to the ephemeral nature of IoT environment, the deployment of the trust management system should be distributed. The advantage of distributed approach is that it can not only reduce communication overhead but also enhance the collaboration between devices [16]. Nevertheless, the MTBAD system needs more computing resources and power consumptions, which is not suitable to deploy it on non-constrained devices. To balance the tradeoff, we considered the *Fog* computing architecture, [17] which can be considered a semi-distributed system.

4 Trust Based Anomaly Detection

In the proposed model, the trust values of each dimension are evaluated using a fuzzy approach to come up with a crispy trust value. It determines which level of security mechanisms are employed toward the trustee.

4.1 Fuzzy Trust Computation

The fuzzy-based approach is a prospective solution to deal with ambiguous data such as trustworthiness. It offers flexible, adaptive, light-weight and extensive abilities for the system [18]. For this purpose, we introduce fuzzy approaches to our system to evaluate the security level toward a given device.

According to Mamdani Fuzzy Information System [19], the fuzzy mechanism consists of four processes: *Fuzzification, Rule Evaluation, Aggregation* and *Defuzzification*. In Fuzzification step, the linguistic values of each trust dimension are taken as input and then evaluated by membership function $\mu(x)$. The membership function $\mu(x)$ describes the degree of a fuzzy variable x is a member of a group, where a full membership is represented by 1, and no membership by 0. We give an example of the definition of the three linguistic variables in the Table 1, and the membership function is presented in Fig. 2. The parameters can be changed according to the specific environment and more linguistic terms can be assigned such as Very Good, Not Good, Not Bad etc.

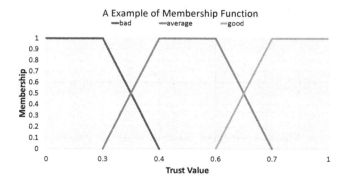

Fig. 2. An example of membership function

Table 1. An example of linguistic values

Linguistic value	Crisp range	Fuzzy numbers
Bad	Below 0.25	(0, 0.25, 0.4)
Average	In range (0.4, 0.6)	(0.3, 0.4, 0.6, 0.7)
Good	Above 0.7	(0.6, 0.7, 1)

The next step is *Rule Evaluation*, which can be expressed as a set of fuzzy rules. The rules are represented in the form If-Then. In our case, the rules are similarly defined as follows:

```
RULE 1: IF QoS is "good"
        AND SocialRelationship is "good"
        THEN TrustLevel is "High";
RULE 2: IF QoS is "bad"
        AND SocialRelationship is "bad"
        OR Reputation is "bad"
        THEN TrustLevel iS "Low";
...
RULE n
```

The terms "High", "Medium" and "Low" are linguistic variables to describe the trust level of the trustor toward the trustee. According to the trust level, the trustor will take appropriate security policies to restrict the behavior of the trustee during the interaction.

4.2 Anomaly Detection Process

The trust model that was described previously is to evaluate trust value before interaction happens while the trust-based anomaly detection is to maintain trust during the interaction. When anomaly behavior is detected, the trust of the trustee will be reevaluated. This process is shown in Fig. 3.

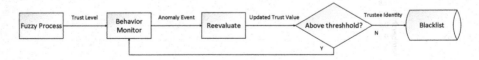

Fig. 3. Trust-based anomaly detection process

We assume that after the fuzzy process, the trust level of entity E_i toward E_j is "high", then the interaction will begin. During the interaction, there are several transactions between the two entities, some of which are normal while others are considered as malicious by the detection mechanisms of E_i. We define that

Table 2. An example of linguistic values

Param description	Value
Area	$400\,\text{m} \times 400\,\text{m}$
Node number	400
Trust level threshold	0.5
Trust level	1–5
Malicious percentage	10%, 20%, 30% and 40%
Interaction frequency	30 times/hour
Duration	200 h

when a malicious transaction is detected, the number of normal and abnormal transactions are α and β, respectively. So according to Bayes' theorem [20], the probability of reducing the trust level $P(x)$ is calculated as follows:

$$P(x|\alpha, \beta) = \frac{P(x, \alpha, \beta)}{P(\alpha, \beta)} = \frac{x^{\alpha}(1 - x)^{\beta}}{\int_0^1 x^{\alpha}(1 - x)^{\beta} dx}. \tag{5}$$

Meanwhile, the *beta function* is defined by:

$$B(\alpha, \beta) = \int_0^1 x^{\alpha-1}(1 - x)^{\beta-1} dx. \tag{6}$$

Therefore, we can take Eq. (6) into Eq. (5), which is:

$$P(x|\alpha, \beta) = \frac{x^{\alpha}(1 - x)^{\beta}}{B(\alpha + 1, \beta + 1)}. \tag{7}$$

From Eq. (7), we can tell that x obeys the beta distribution for $0 \leq x \leq 1$, and shape parameters $\alpha, \beta > 0$. The probability density function of the beta distribution is as follows:

$$f(x|\alpha, \beta) = \frac{x^{\alpha-1}(1 - x)^{\beta-1}}{B(\alpha, \beta)}. \tag{8}$$

So the expected value of x is calculated as follows:

$$E(x|\alpha, \beta) = \frac{\alpha + 1}{\alpha + \beta + 2} \tag{9}$$

Based on Eq. (9), we introduce parameter τ as the trust level threshold, below which the trust level will drop a notch. When the trust level falls to zero, the trustor will add the trustee to the blacklist and forbid all the transactions from the trustee. Note that the blacklist can also be shared among trusted entities to reduce the impact of the malicious devices.

5   Experimental Evaluation

In this section, we considered a real-life IoT scenario—the shopping mall scenario, based on which we implemented several simulations to evaluate the effectiveness of the proposed system. In this scenario, the mall is filled with a great many of IoT devices. The smart objects carried by the customers can communicate with the IoT devices provided by the mall for intelligent service such as indoor instructions, advertisements, commodity recommendations. However, the adversaries may perform DDoS attacks to prevent the devices from providing services, and the unscrupulous businesses may steal the customers' privacy data for illegal purpose.

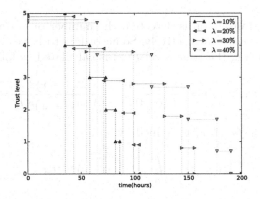

Fig. 4. Trust level evolvement

The default parameters are set based on previous experiments and listed in Table 2. We simulated a 400 m × 400 m area with 400 nodes which can randomly communicate with each other. We consider a malicious node performing abnormal behavior with a probability of 50% and the percentage of malicious nodes λ ranges between 10% and 40%. The initial trust values of all nodes are set to 1 so the trust level of each node will be assessed to the highest level at the beginning. To demonstrate the evolvement of the trust level, we set the levels to 1–5 corresponding "very low", "low", "medium", "high" and "very high". Note that when the trust level falls to 0, it means the node is totally untrust and the node will be added to the blacklist.

Figure 4 demonstrates the trust level evolvement of a malicious node at different malicious circumstances. We note that the trust level of a node drops more quickly when the trust level is lower because lower level means more strict the security mechanisms are. Therefore, malicious interactions are more likely to be detected in this circumstance. In addition, as the percentage of malicious nodes grows, the trust level takes more time falling to next level.

Figure 5 shows the overall false positive and false negative rate of the anomaly detection during the simulation. The *False Negative (FN)* means bad nodes are

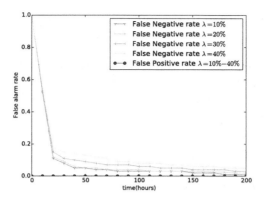

Fig. 5. False alarm rate

misidentified as good ones. We can observe that the *FN* rate initiated at around 0.5 no matter how the malicious percentage varies. This happened because we initially set the highest trust value to every node, so all nodes are considered as good nodes. Afterward, the *FN* rate plummeted to 0.2 approximately, then it slowed down. We also note that the malicious nodes percentage had little effect to the *FN*. On the other hand, the *False Positive (FP)* refers to the system wrongly brings good nodes into the blacklist. It is important to remark that the *FP* rate remained at 0 during the whole experiment. This is due to the fact that as the time progresses, the trust level of good nodes remains at high level. Only constant malicious behaviors can reduce the trust level to level 0, which does not likely to happen in good nodes.

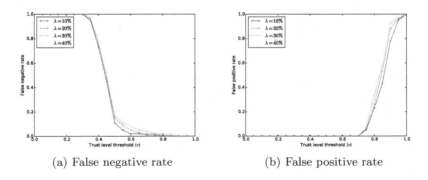

(a) False negative rate   (b) False positive rate

Fig. 6. False alarms with varying malicious nodes percentage

We also explored how the trust level threshold τ affects the false alarm rate with varying malicious nodes percentage, the result of which is depicted in Fig. 6. In Fig. 6(a), the *FN* rate stays at 1 until τ exceeds 3.5. This is because in Eq. (9), when $\alpha = 0$ and $\beta = 1$, the equation approximately equals to 0.33. Consequently, the trust level will not drop only if τ is greater than 0.33. On the contrary, in Fig. 6(b), the *FP* begins to increase after τ is greater than 0.7. This can also be explained using Eq. (9). When $\alpha = 1$ and $\beta = 0$, the equation is approximately equal to 0.66. Accordingly, the good nodes will be falsely identified as malicious nodes only if τ is greater than 0.66. From these two figures, we can observe that the optimal trust level threshold τ is in the range of $[0.5, 0.7]$, at which both the *FN* and the *FP* are lower than 0.1.

6   Conclusions

In this paper, we presented a trust-based system for anomaly detection in IoT environment. We considered a multidimensional trust evaluation model including reputation, QoS, and social relationship, and a trust-based security decision-making mechanism with fuzzy approaches. Through simulations, we evaluated the effectiveness of our system with varying malicious node percentages. The experiment results indicated that our system has very low false alarm rate with proper trust level threshold, and there exists an optimal trust level threshold for minimizing the false alarms.

For future work, we plan to focus on how human behaviors affect the IoT environment and bring human-machine dimension to our trust system.

Acknowledgment. This work is supported by the National Science Foundation of China under Grants Nos. 61272010 and 61572514.

References

1. Liu, Y.B., Gong, X.H., Feng, Y.F.: Trust system based on node behavior detection in Internet of Things. J. Commun. **35**, 8–15 (2014)
2. Blaze, M., Feigenbaum, J., Lacy, J.: Decentralized trust management. In: Proceedings of IEEE Conference on Security and Privacy, vol. 30, no. 1, pp. 164–173 (1996)
3. Michiardi, P., Molva, R.: Core: a collaborative reputation mechanism to enforce node cooperation in mobile ad hoc networks. In: Jerman-Blažič, B., Klobučar, T. (eds.) Advanced Communications and Multimedia Security. ITIFIP, vol. 100, pp. 107–121. Springer, Boston (2002). doi:10.1007/978-0-387-35612-9_9
4. Lee, S., Sherwood, R., Bhattacharjee, B.: Cooperative peer groups in nice. In: Joint Conference of the IEEE Computer and Communications, vol. 2, pp. 1272–1282. IEEE Societies (2003)
5. Yan, Z., Zhang, P., Vasilakos, A.V.: A survey on trust management for Internet of Things. J. Netw. Comput. Appl. **42**(3), 120–134 (2014)
6. Chen, D., Chang, G., Sun, D., Li, J., Jia, J., Wang, X.: TRM-IoT: a trust management model based on fuzzy reputation for Internet of Things. Comput. Sci. Inf. Syst. **8**(4), 1207–1228 (2011)
7. Bao, F., Chen, I.R.: Trust management for the Internet of Things and its application to service composition. In: World of Wireless, Mobile and Multimedia Networks, pp. 1–6 (2012)

8. Atzori, L., Iera, A., Morabito, G., Nitti, M.: The Social Internet of Things (SIoT) - when social networks meet the Internet of Things: concept, architecture and network characterization. Comput. Netw. **56**(16), 3594–3608 (2012)

9. Nitti, M., Girau, R., Atzori, L.: Trustworthiness management in the Social Internet of Things. IEEE Trans. Knowl. Data Eng. **26**(5), 1253–1266 (2014)

10. Bao, F., Chen, I.R., Chang, M.J., Cho, J.H.: Hierarchical trust management for wireless sensor networks and its applications to trust-based routing and intrusion detection. IEEE Trans. Netw. Serv. Manag. **9**(2), 169–183 (2012)

11. Bernabe, J.B., Ramos, J.L.H., Gomez, A.F.S.: TACIoT: multidimensional trust-aware access control system for the Internet of Things. Soft Comput. **20**(5), 1–17 (2016)

12. Yan, Z., Prehofer, C.: Autonomic trust management for a component-based software system. IEEE Trans. Depend. Secur. Comput. **8**(6), 810–823 (2011)

13. Chen, I.R., Bao, F., Guo, J.: Trust-based service management for Social Internet of Things systems. IEEE Trans. Depend. Secur. Comput. **13**, 684–696 (2015)

14. Bao, F., Chen, R., Chang, M., Cho, J.-H.: Trust-based intrusion detection in wireless sensor networks. In: 2011 IEEE International Conference on Communications (ICC), pp. 1–6. IEEE (2011)

15. Raza, S., Wallgren, L., Voigt, T.: SVELTE: real-time intrusion detection in the Internet of Things. Ad Hoc Netw. **11**(8), 2661–2674 (2013)

16. Truong, N.B., Um, T.-W., Lee, G.M.: A reputation and knowledge based trust service platform for trustworthy Social Internet of Things. In: Innovations in Clouds, Internet and Networks (ICIN), Paris, France (2016)

17. Bonomi, F., Milito, R., Zhu, J., Addepalli, S.: Fog computing and its role in the Internet of Things. In: Proceedings of the First Edition of the MCC Workshop on Mobile Cloud Computing, pp. 13–16. ACM (2012)

18. Zadeh, L.A.: Fuzzy logic = computing with words. IEEE Trans. Fuzzy Syst. **4**(2), 3–23 (1996)

19. Mamdani, E.H.: Application of fuzzy algorithms for control of simple dynamic plant. In: Proceedings of the Institution of Electrical Engineers, vol. 121, no. 12, pp. 1585–1588. IET (1974)

20. Pawlak, Z.: Rough sets, decision algorithms and Bayes' theorem. Eur. J. Oper. Res. **136**(1), 181–189 (2002)

Social D2D Communications Based on Fog Computing for IoT Applications

Junjie Yan[1], Dapeng Wu[1(✉)], Honggang Wang[2], Dalei Wu[3], and Ruyan Wang[1]

[1] The School of Communication and Information Engineering,
Chongqing University of Posts and Telecommunications, Chongqing 400065, China
{wudp,wangry}@cqupt.edu.cn, cqupt2013yjj@sina.com
[2] The University of Massachusetts Dartmouth, Dartmouth, MA 02747, USA
hwang1@umassd.edu
[3] The University of Tennessee at Chattanooga, Chattanooga, TN 37403, USA
dalei-wu@utc.edu

Abstract. To satisfy the rapidly growing requirements of wireless data services recently, fog computing which is as an extension of cloud computing is proposed for offloading the Internet of Things (IoT) data services and applications. It depends more on the collaboration of near-located devices, instead of sending the information to remote servers. In this paper, we conceive the idea of utilizing Device-to-Device (D2D) communications as the infrastructures for computation and communication. In particular, D2D communication technology is as one of the most important and innovative revolutions in the development of future cellular networks. In computation part, by analyzing the interest difference of users, a Virtual Fog Community (VFC) is established in this paper. In communication part, by perceiving the importance degrees of users and accordingly employing multi-dimensional network status parameters such as the local and global centralities, the best relay user can be reasonably selected based on the physical and social attributes of users. Simulation results show the proposed mechanism fully exploits the social relationship between users and effectively enhances the network operational efficiency at the cost of relatively low delay.

Keywords: Fog computing · D2D communication · Social attributes · Internet of Things

1   Introduction

As reported by Cisco, around 50 billion intelligent devices would be connected to the Internet for Internet of things (IoT) applications by 2020 [1]. At present, IoT applications include, e.g., smart grids and cities, wireless sensors, internet

---

D. Wu—This work is partially supported by the National Natural Science Foundation of China (61371097, 61271261) and Youth Talents Training Project of Chongqing (CSTC2014KJRC-QNRC40001), Program for Innovation Team Building at Institutions of Higher Education in Chongqing (CXTDX201601020).

© Springer International Publishing AG 2017
L. Ma et al. (Eds.): WASA 2017, LNCS 10251, pp. 314–325, 2017.
DOI: 10.1007/978-3-319-60033-8_28

of vehicles and so on. In such applications, IoT devices (e.g., smart-phones, vehicles) often are utilized as the sink nodes to assist sensing data collection in the manner of end to end communication technology, such as Device-to-Device (D2D) and Machine-to-Machine (M2M) communications [2]. As the IoT devices and its applications increase tremendously, mobile data services are also growing rapidly. As a result, the loads of data centers and base stations grow inevitably.

To solve these problems, Cisco proposed a new computational paradigm, termed as fog computing, that puts a substantial amount of storage, communication, control, configuration, measurement, and management at the edge of a network, rather than establishing channels for the centralized cloud storage and utilization, which extends the traditional cloud computing paradigm to the network edge [3]. The architecture of fog computing is that utilizes a collaborative multitude of end-user clients or near-user edge devices to carry out a substantial amount of communication and computation. Due to the resource utilization of geo-related devices, fog computing has more computation capacity and less communication delay compared with the cloud computing. Therefore, fog computing is often exploited to serve large scale IoT applications [4,5]. What's more, users usually participate in and construct a complex social network by exploiting social attributes of users, such as interests in common, users background and so on. Numerous study results pointed out the "big world, small world" feature of mobile networks [6]. Such social characteristics can be applied by fog computing, and then users can be divided into different social groups, namely, Virtual Fog Community (VFC).

In recent years, social attributes of users are explored in D2D cooperative communication [7]. A series of social relationship structures and social phenomena were analyzed by Refs. [8–12], such as the definition of community and closeness, which further concludes that the stable social structure and social relationship exist in D2D networks. The relationship between content requirements and historical contact information of users was analyzed in Ref. [13]. To effectively reduce the base station load through D2D links, a contact time based D2D resource allocation algorithm was proposed in Ref. [14] to comprehensively consider the encounter time and contact time, by which sociality-aware and sociality-blind resource allocation algorithms are compared. Although the above mentioned references exploited social attributes to analyze D2D data transmission, D2D users are moving in social networks and their trajectories are regular, which were not pointedly analyzed and studied by them.

To solve these problems, in computation part, VFC is proposed based on D2D communications in this paper. In particular, The network structure is firstly detected according to the interest spots difference between users, upon which a physical and social attribute Cooperative Aware Data Forwarding Mechanism (CADFM) is designed in communication part. CADFM extensively considers and reasonably exploits the social relationships between intra-community and inter-community users to select the optimal relay user.

The rest of this paper is organized as follows. A comprehensive outline of the fog computing architecture is proposed based on D2D Communications in Sect. 2

and the user interest difference perceiving and VFC construction methods are further proposed in Sect. 3. Section 4 evaluates the transmission rate between users. Section 5 describes the user importance perceiving mechanism whereas a social and physical attribute cooperatively perceiving D2D data forwarding mechanism is introduced in Sect. 6. Furthermore, the settings of simulation scenarios are given and the performance of the proposed algorithm is analyzed in Sect. 7. Lastly, the conclusion is given in Sect. 8.

2   Network Architecture

Much attention has been paid to cloud radio access network (C-RAN) architecture [15,16]. Based on the previous work on C-RAN architecture, the evolved fog architecture is shown in Fig. 1.

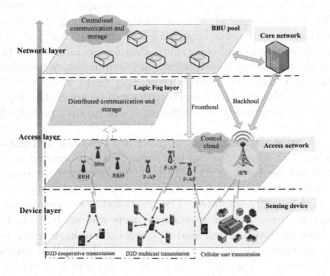

Fig. 1. Fog computing network architecture.

Fog architecture includes three layers: The first layer (device layer) encompasses all the sensing devices, which are responsible for transmitting the sensing data to other sensing devices or its immediate upper layer in the hierarchy; the second layer (access layer) includes evolved access networks and logic fog computing layer. To incorporate fog computing in edge devices, the evolved access network contains the traditional remote radio heads (RRH) and the fog-computing-based access point (F-AP). What's more, logic fog computing layer is introduced to manage some distributed communication and storage functions; the third layer (cloud computing network layer) is the upper-most layer in this architecture. The layer constitutes of multiple high-end servers and data centres which are capable of processing and storing an enormous amount of data.

3   VFC Building

As mentioned above, logic fog computing layer is responsible for local distributed communication by D2D communications. However, users are strongly socially related in D2D networks [17–19]. Therefore, making full use of social attributes can be effective to assist logic fog computing layer in managing the distributed communication. In this section, a logical structure detection method is firstly proposed based on user interest spots difference.

3.1   Interest Difference Perceiving

The user activities are regular and social relationship between them is relatively stable. By exploiting interest spots similarity of users, the network can be divided into logical components, namely VFC. Assuming there are n users in the network, $U = \{u_1, u_2, \cdots, u_n\}$ respectively which can be recorded by BS, and user u_i has m_i interest spots, $M_{u_i} = (a_{u_i}^1, a_{u_i}^2, a_{u_i}^3 \cdots a_{u_i}^{m_i})$ respectively, and interest spots of different users may overlap. The complete set of interest spots can be obtained according to Eq. (1), where $b_i \cap b_j = \emptyset$, $i \neq j; i, j = 1, 2, \cdots, p$.

$$B_i = M_{u_1} \cup M_{u_2} \cup M_{u_3} \cdots \cup M_{u_n} = \{b_1, b_2, b_3, \cdots, b_p\} \tag{1}$$

By comparing the proportions of the appearance times at a given spot to the total appearance times, the interest degree for all spots of user u_i in time t are $F_{u_i}(t) = (f_{u_i}^{b_1}(t), f_{u_i}^{b_2}(t), f_{u_i}^{b_3}(t) \cdots, f_{u_i}^{b_p}(t))$, where constraints hold as shown in Eqs. (2) and (3).

$$0 \leq f_{u_i}^{b_z}(t) \leq 1 (1 \leq z \leq p) \tag{2}$$

$$\sum_{z=1}^{p} f_{u_i}^{b_z} = 1 \tag{3}$$

where $f_{u_i}^{b_z}(t)$ denotes the interest degree for spot b_z of user u_i in time t. Eventually the interest matrix $I = \{F_{u_1}(t), F_{u_2}(t), \cdots F_{u_n}(t)\}^T$ can be obtained.

Definition 1 (User Interest Difference). *At time* t, *the interest of user* u_x *and* u_y *for given spot* b_z, *namely* $f_{u_x}^{b_z}(t)$ *and* $f_{u_x}^{b_z}(t)$ *are different. Their current interest matrices are analyzed and compared to define the interest difference between user* u_x *and* u_y *as shown in Eq. (4), by averaging their interest difference for all spots.*

$$D(u_x, u_y) = \begin{cases} 0 & F_{u_x}(t) = F_{u_y}(t) \\ \sum_{z=1}^{p} \dfrac{\left| f_{u_x}^{b_z}(t) - f_{u_y}^{b_z}(t) \right|}{p} & \text{others} \end{cases} \tag{4}$$

As shown in Eq. (4), $D(u_x, u_y) = 0$ denotes there is no interest difference between user u_x and u_y, whereas $D(u_x, u_y) = 1$ indicates that two users share no interest spots.

3.2   Fog Community Detecting

(1) The establishment of game coalition and objective function

During initialization, If $\max F_{u_i}(t) = f_{u_i}^{b_x}(t)$ at time t. u_x is arranged into fog community b_x. Further, the current fog community set can be defined as $S' = \{s_1, s_2, s_3, \cdots, s_v\}$ $(v \leq p)$, namely the game coalition, where $s_i \cap s_j = \emptyset (i \neq j; i, j = 1, 2, \cdots, p)$ and the coalition participants are $U = \{u_1, u_2, \cdots, u_n\}$ respectively (normally $v \leq n$). Assuming the s_kth $(1 \leq k \leq v)$ fog community has θ_{s_k} users $(1 \leq \theta_{s_k} \leq n)$ and the sum of fog community members is defined by Eq. (5).

$$\sum_{k=1}^{v} \theta_{s_k} = n \tag{5}$$

However, even when users share the same interest spot, their interest may be different. Some users may have the same level of interest for all spots, whereas other users may have stronger interest for one or several spots among all their interest spots. To minimize the interest difference within each fog community, users may reasonably joint or quit given fog communities, namely user transferring.

$$\Omega_{s_k} = \frac{\sum\limits_{u_x=1}^{\theta_{s_k}} \sum\limits_{u_y=1}^{\theta_{s_k}} D(u_x, u_y)}{\theta_{s_k}^2} \tag{6}$$

where Ω_{s_k} represents the interest difference between each other in fog communities s_k. Because the alteration of belonging fog community can cause the change of fog community difference, the user transfer effectiveness is set to the fog community difference. As mentioned above, to reasonably transfer users, the overall interest difference of communities, namely the objective function should be minimized, as shown in Eq. (7).

$$J = \min \sum_{k=1}^{v} \Omega_{s_k} \tag{7}$$

(2) Fog User Transferring

Targeting at the above mentioned problems, the adaptive preference order adjustment method in coalition game is employed to assign the optimal fog communities for each user, namely the user transferring [20], by which the interest difference within each fog community can be minimized and a temporarily stable status of a given fog community can be achieved.

Assuming user u_i is initially arranged into fog community s_k, when u_i prefers the new fog community s_l than the original fog community s_k this situation is denoted by $s_l \succ_{u_i} s_k$. The user transferring constraints are shown in Eq. (8), where the user can be transferred if and only if the interest difference of original fog community s_k does not increase and the interest difference of new fog community s_l decreases.

$$\Omega_{s_l} > \Omega_{s_{l'}} \&\& \Omega_{s_k} \geq \Omega_{(s_k \backslash i)} \tag{8}$$

In Eq. (8), $s_{l'}$ is the new fog community of user u_i and $(s_k \backslash i)$ is the original fog community. By repeating the user transferring constraints on all users until Nash Equilibrium is achieved, the value of objective function can be minimized.

4   Sensing Data Transmission Model

In the underlay mode, D2D communication and cellular communication are both available for users. For instance, if user $u_i, u_j \in U$ are communicating through D2D and sharing the uplink channel of user u, their communication can be interfered by cellular user u. In various network scenarios, physical attributes of users have considerable impacts on the network performance. Assuming P_{u_i} is the transmitting power of D2D user u_i, the channel gain between user u_i and u_j is h_{u_i,u_j}, the received signal of user u_i can be denoted by $P_{u_i} h_{u_i,u_j}$. To be general, channels are assumed to follow Rayleigh distribution, the distance between users u_i and u_j is denoted by d_{u_i,u_j}, and the channel attenuation factor and Gaussian channel coefficient are denoted by ∂ and h_0 respectively. Because the communication between users is under the impact of their distance and channel attenuation, the channel gain between them can be denoted by

$$h_{u_i,u_j} = d_{u_i,u_j}^{-\partial} h_0 \qquad (9)$$

The noise of the received signal is composed of the additive Gaussian white noise N_0, and the same frequency interference noise by cellular user u. Therefore, the noise of the received signal by user u_i can be denoted by $P_u h_{u,u_j} + N_0$. Furthermore, according to the Shannon equation, the transmission rate between D2D users R_{u_i,u_j} can be denoted

$$R_{u_i,u_j} = \log_2(1 + \frac{P_{u_i} h_{u_i,u_j}}{P_u h_{u,u_j} + N_0}) \qquad (10)$$

D2D transmission rate is estimated in this section to further consider the physical attribute for a reasonable relay user selecting. However, only considering the user physical attributes may cause inaccuracy, thus the horizontal and vertical social relationships should be taken into account.

5   User Importance Perceving

The stable social relationship between users can be exploited to enhance the data forwarding efficiency in multi-hop D2D scenarios. By analyzing the proposed local and global centralities, social relationships between users can be evaluated, where the local centrality describes the relationship between directly related users within the same community and the global centrality describes the active degree of a given user for whole fog communities.

5.1 Local Centrality

According to its definition, the local centrality only focuses on users from the same fog community, and only evaluates the directly related users. Therefore, the estimation of connection times should also consider the connection duration and only the connection long enough for the data transmission can be regarded as effective. For user u_i, Eq. (11) describes the encounter between it and user u_j.

$$\delta_{u_i,u_j} = \begin{cases} 1 & \text{user } u_i \text{ and } u_j \text{ had met, } i \neq j \\ 0 & \text{others} \end{cases} \tag{11}$$

To avoid the impact of these invalid short connections, Eq. (12) gives the improved connection determination method by considering the encounter duration.

$$\eta_{u_i,u_j} = \begin{cases} 1 & \text{duration}(u_i u_j) \geq t_{u_i,u_j}, \ i \neq j \\ 0 & \text{others} \end{cases} \tag{12}$$

In Eq. (12), duration(u_i, u_j) denotes the encounter duration of user u_i and u_j, and t_{u_i,u_j} denotes the total transmission delay between user u_i and u_j, which is related to the data transmission rate R_{u_i,u_j} and data size F, as shown in Eq. (13).

$$t_{u_i,u_j} = \frac{F \cdot Ret}{R_{u_i,u_j}} + \frac{d_{u_i,u_j}}{c} \tag{13}$$

In Eq. (13), F denotes the data size and Ret denotes the retransmission times. c is the light speed. Obviously, the directly social relationship exists only if Eqs. (12) and (13) are met. Therefore, the local centrality ξ_{u_i} of user u_i in community s_k can be defined by Eq. (14).

$$\xi_{u_i} = \frac{\sum\limits_{j=i}^{\theta_{s_k}} \delta_{u_i,u_j} \cap \sum\limits_{j=i}^{\theta_{s_k}} \eta_{u_i,u_j}}{\theta_{s_k}} \tag{14}$$

5.2 Global Centrality

A high global centrality signifies a high active degree and a great influence on the whole network. According to the user mobility analysis given by Ref. [21,22], the encounter interval between users can be described by the Pareto distribution. We assume that T_{u_i,u_j} denote the encounter interval between user u_i and u_j. The complementary cumulative distribution function of T_{u_i,u_j} can be calculated by Eq. (15).

$$P_{u_i,u_j}\left\{T_{u_i,u_j} > t\right\} = \left(\frac{\tau_{u_i,u_j}^{\min}}{t}\right)^{\alpha_{u_i,u_j}}, \ t \geq \tau_{u_i,u_j}^{\min} \tag{15}$$

where the $\alpha_{u_i,u_j} > 0$ determines the shape of T_{u_i,u_j}'s probability distribution function, and $\tau_{u_i,u_j}^{\min}$ denotes the minimum possible value of T_{u_i,u_j}.

Thus, the encounter probability between user u_i and u_j during the period Δt can be calculated by Eq. (16).

$$p_{u_i,u_j}(\Delta t) = 1 - \left(\frac{\tau_{u_i,u_j}^{\min}}{\Delta t} \right)^{\alpha_{u_i,u_j}} \tag{16}$$

The global centrality of user u_i can be further denoted by Eq. (17).

$$AL_{u_i}(t) = \frac{1}{n-1} \sum_{j=1, i \neq j}^{n} p_{u_i,u_j}(t) \tag{17}$$

6 Physical and Social Attribute Cooperative Aware Data Forwarding Mechanism

As is mentioned above, the data transmission between users can be divided into the intra-community and inter-community data forwarding. Due to the social relationship difference between physically close neighbor users, the temporarily established links without the social relationship consideration may be invalid short connections, which may cause the low resource utilization. Therefore, the relay user selecting should comprehensively consider the physical attributes along with the social attributes, by which the optimal relay user can be selected for the reasonable intra-community and inter-community data forwarding and to achieve the reliable data delivery.

6.1 Intra-community Data Forwarding

Users from the same community are socially close, encounter each other with high probability and have stable links and long encounter duration. With more directly related users, the local centrality of the given user is higher, which can be regarded as the factor to select the intra-community relay user. Besides, employing the transmission rate between users also contributes to the forwarding efficiency. Therefore, the cooperative intra-community relay user selecting strategy is proposed in this section. The important degrees of relay users can be calculated by Eq. (18), where $u_x(0 \leq x \leq \theta_{s_k}, i \neq x)$ relay user candidates within the communication range of sending user $u_i \in s_k$.

$$Em(i,x) = \alpha \xi_{u_x} + (1-\alpha) R_{u_i,u_x} \tag{18}$$

In Eq. (17), α is the weight factor, which is obviously crucial for the accurate selecting of the optimal relay user. Besides, physical attributes such as the user density and velocity within the given community also affect the intra-community data forwarding. For instance, the user density obviously affects the number of directly related users, and contributes to the local centrality. Besides, in the scenario of high user velocities, data have to be rapidly forwarded to relay users before connections end, which signifies the importance of transmission rates.

In conclusion, the weight factor α should be directly proportional to the user density and inversely proportional to the user velocity, as shown in Eq. (19).

$$\alpha = 1 - \exp(-\frac{\theta_k}{nV_i}) \tag{19}$$

where V_i denotes the movement velocity of user u_i and the user with the maximum $Em(i,x)$ within the communication range of user u_i is selected as the optimal intra-community relay user.

6.2   Inter-community Data Forwarding

For the inter-community data forwarding, user interest varies greatly and the similarity between the sending and receiving users is low, which indicates they may have a short connection duration and even no encounter probability. Therefore, the inter-community data forwarding requires data to be rapidly transmitted to the destination community and, when arriving at community of receiving users, to be forwarded by the user with the highest encounter probability with the receiving user.

When sending and receiving users share no same fog community, the inter-community data forwarding is necessary. Because sending user may not have even remote relationship with the destination community, data must be rapidly forwarded to the destination community to reserve network resources and to enhance the delivery ratio. Assuming users, in the communication range of the sending user, are from the community of receiving users. Because sending and receiving users share no same fog community, the user with the highest encounter probability with the receiving user is selected to forward the data and to minimize the transmission hop count. For relay user candidate u_x, the encounter probability $p_{u_x,u_j}(t)$ between users can be calculated by Eq. (16). If no user within the communication range of the sending user is from the community of receiving users, the user with maximum global centrality $\max(AL_{u_x}(t))$ is selected as the relay user. Again, the relay user from the community of receiving users can be selected among the next-hop relay candidates, until the data eventually arrives at the receiving user.

7   Numerical Results

In this part, we used human mobility trace Infocom06 [23]. To reflect the performance gain of the proposed CADFM, two typical data forwarding mechanisms, Encounter Probability Data Forwarding Mechanism (EPDFM) and Direct Delivery Mechanism (DDM), are compared during the simulation, where EPDFM selects the user with the highest encounter probability to the receiving user as the relay and DDM only forwards data when the receiving user is in the communication range of the sending user.

The successful delivery ratio directly reflects the reliability of data transmission. As shown in Fig. 2, the increased number of users leads to the increased

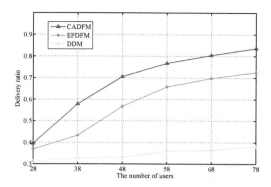

Fig. 2. The successful delivery ratio under various numbers of users.

network user density, which affects the connection times and accordingly the data delivery ratio. Because CADFM employs the reasonable fog community detection and the optimal relay user is selected according to the social attributes of users, the delivery ratio of CADFM is higher than those of EPDFM and DDM. However, the users are always resource limited, thus the active users forward most of data and congestions at these active users prevent the further increase of delivery ratio. According to simulation results, CADFM can achieve 10.2% and 47.6% higher delivery ratios respectively, when compared with EPDFM and DDM.

The average delivery delay under various numbers of users is shown in Fig. 3. The average delivery delays of all three mechanisms are reduced because of the increased number of users and user encounter probability. For DDM, the difficulty of reaching the receiving user is increased due to the growing number of users, thus the average delivery delay is the highest. As shown in Fig. 3, the average delivery delay of CADFM is the lowest, that of EPDFM is higher, because the proposed relay selecting process is based on the centralities and

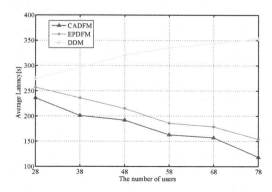

Fig. 3. The average delivery delay under various numbers of users.

encounter probabilities and the data forwarding is more reasonable, accurate and rapid. Simulation results show the proposed CADFM can achieve 14.2% and 45.2% lower average delivery delays respectively, when compared with EPDFM and DDM.

8 Conclusion

In this paper, we proposed a novel approach CADFM for social D2D networks to achieve the efficient data forwarding and reliable data delivery. By analyzing the instantaneous user interest difference, the VFC can be detected for the further realization of the efficient data forwarding. Simulation results show that, compared with traditional fog computing data forwarding mechanisms EPDFM and DDM, the proposed CADFM can achieve the more efficient data forwarding at the cost of a relatively low delivery delay.

References

1. MarketWatch: Cisco delivers vision of fog computing to accelerate value from billions of connected devices. http://www.theiet.org/resources/journals/research/index.cfm. Accessed 2014
2. Bello, O., Zeadally, S.: Intelligent device-to-device communication in the Internet of Things. IEEE Syst. J. **10**(3), 1172–1182 (2016)
3. Bonomi, F., et al.: Fog computing and its role in the Internet of Things. In: Proceedings of Workshop on Mobile Cloud Computing, Helsinki, Finland, pp. 13–16 (2012)
4. Peng, M., Yan, S., Zhang, K., Wang, C.G.: Fog-computing-based radio access networks: issues and challenges. IEEE Netw. **30**(4), 46–53 (2016)
5. TR 45.820: Cellular system support for ultra low complexity and low throughput Internet of Things. V2.1.0, August 2015
6. Wang, W., Li, C.: A core-based community detection algorithm for networks. In: Proceedings of 2012 IEEE 4th International Conference on CASoN, Sao Carlos, Brazil, pp. 20–25 (2012)
7. Zhang, Z.F., Li, Y.X., Yang, J.: Energy efficiency based on joint mobile node grouping and data packet fragmentation in short-range communication system. Int. J. Commun. Syst. **27**(4), 534–550 (2014)
8. Li, Y., Wu, T., Hui, P., Jin, D., Chen, S.: Social-aware D2D communications: qualitative insights and quantitative analysis. IEEE Commun. Mag. **52**(6), 150–158 (2014)
9. Feng, M., Mao, S., Jiang, T.: Joint duplex mode selection, channel allocation, and power control for full-duplex cognitive femtocell networks. Digit. Commun. Netw. **1**(1), 30–44 (2015)
10. Kantarci, B., Mouftah, T.: Trustworthy sensing for public safety in cloud-centric Internet of Things. IEEE Internet Things J. **1**(4), 360–368 (2014)
11. Su, Z., Qi, Q., Xu, Q., Guo, S., Wang, X.: Incentive scheme for cyber physical social systems based on user behaviors. IEEE Trans. Emerg. Top. Comput., September 2017. doi:10.1109/TETC.2017.2671843
12. Su, Z., Hui, Y., Gao, S.: D2D based content delivery with parked vehicles in vehicular social networks. IEEE Wirel. Commun. **23**(4), 90–95 (2016)

13. Zhang, Y., Pan, E.: Social network aware device-to-device communication in wireless networks. IEEE Trans. Wirel. Commun. **14**(1), 177–190 (2014)
14. Wang, L., Liu, L., Cao, X.: Sociality-aware resource allocation for device-to-device communications in cellular networks. IET Commun. **9**(3), 342–349 (2015)
15. Simeone, O., Erkip, E., Shamai, S.: Full-duplex cloud radio access networks: an information-theoretic viewpoint. IEEE Wirel. Commun. Lett. **3**(4), 413–416 (2014)
16. Peng, M., Sun, Y.H., Li, X.L., Mao, Z.D., Wang, C.G.: Full-duplex cloud radio access networks: an information-theoretic viewpoint. IEEE Commun. Surv. Tutor. **18**(3), 2282–2308 (2016)
17. Li, Y., Liao, C., Wang, Y., Wang, C.G.: Energy-efficient optimal relay selection in cooperative cellular networks based on double auction. IEEE Trans. Wirel. Commun. **14**(8), 4093–4104 (2015)
18. Wu, D.P., Wang, Y.Y., Wang, H.G., Yang, B.R., Wang, C.G., Wang, R.Y.: Dynamic coding control in social intermittent connectivity wireless networks. IEEE Trans. Veh. Technol. **65**(9), 7634–7646 (2016)
19. Wu, D.P., Zhang, P.N., Wang, H.G., Wang, C.G., Wang, R.Y.: Node service ability aware packet forwarding mechanism in intermittently connected wireless networks. IEEE Trans. Wirel. Commun. **15**(12), 8169–8181 (2016)
20. Saad, W., Zhu, H., Debbah, M.: Coalitional games for distributed collaborative spectrum sensing in cognitive radio networks. In: Proceedings of the 28th IEEE INFOCOM, Rio de Janeiro, Brazil, pp. 2114–2122 (2009)
21. Karagiannis, T., Boudec, L., Vojnovic, J.: Power law and exponential decay of intercontact times between mobile devices. IEEE Trans. Mob. Comput. **9**(10), 1377–1390 (2010)
22. Chaint, A., Hui, P., Crowcroft, J., Gass, C.: Impact of human mobility on opportunistic forwarding algorithms. IEEE Trans. Mob. Comput. **6**(6), 606–620 (2007)
23. Scott, J., Gass, R., Crowcroft, J., Hui, P., Diot, C., Chaintreau, A.: CRAWDAD data set cambridge/haggle (v. 2006-09-15) (2006)

Defense Against Advanced Persistent Threats with Expert System for Internet of Things

Qing Hu[1,2], Shichao Lv[1,2]($\boxtimes$), Zhiqiang Shi[1,2], Limin Sun[1,2], and Liang Xiao[3]

[1] Beijing Key Laboratory of IOT Information Security,
Institute of Information Engineering, CAS, Beijing, China
{huqing,lvshichao,shizhiqiang,sunlimin}@iie.ac.cn
[2] School of Cyber Security, University of Chinese Academy of Sciences,
Beijing, China
[3] Department of Communication Engineering, Xiamen University, Xiamen, China
lxiao@xmu.edu.cn

Abstract. In this paper, the Advanced Persistent Threats (APTs) defense for Internet of Things (IoT) is analyzed for inaccurate APT detection, i.e., both the miss detection rate and false alarm rate of the APT detection are considered. We formulate an expert system (ES)-based APT detection game, in which an expert will double-check the suspicious behavior or potential APT attackers reported by the autonomous and inaccurate APT detection system. The Nash equilibrium of the APT detection game for IoT with ES is derived, revealing the influence of the APT detection accuracy on the utilities of the IoT system and the attacker. We propose a Q-learning based APT detection method for the IoT system with ES in the dynamic game to obtain the optimal strategy without the knowledge of the attack model. Simulation results show that the proposed APT detection scheme can efficiently use the knowledge of the expert system to improve the defender's utility and increase the security level of the IoT device compared with the benchmark detection scheme.

Keywords: Advanced persistent threats · Internet of Things · Expert system · Game theory · Reinforcement learning

1 Introduction

Combined with the technology of cloud computing, the ability of Internet of Things (IoT) are promoted effectively. A great variety of cloud-enabled IoT applications have sprung up, such as intelligent transportation, smart agriculture, intelligent manufacturing, etc., as shown in Fig. 1. IoT terminals upload data and computation requests to specified cloud devices, and receive computing results from them whenever needed. The cloud may store massive sensitive data that are related to public safety [1–3], with the result that the cloud storage has become a favourite target of APT attackers.

© Springer International Publishing AG 2017
L. Ma et al. (Eds.): WASA 2017, LNCS 10251, pp. 326–337, 2017.
DOI: 10.1007/978-3-319-60033-8_29

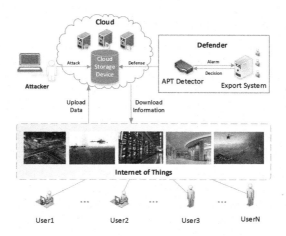

Fig. 1. A typical scenario of IoT combined with cloud. In the various walks of life, IoT systems upload a large amount of data to cloud storages, and defend against APT attackers with autonomous APT detectors and expert systems.

Unlike traditional cyber attackers, APT attackers aim at long-term benefits. They conceal themselves for a long time to steal data secretly or prepare for a mortal damage, which makes it more difficult to defend the IoT systems [4]. The defender analyze massive scanning data to determine whether the device is under attack by APTs or not. The analysis process is called detection and usually performed by an autonomous APT detector, which scan the device constantly and inspect attacks according to built-in rules during a specified period of time. Due to the complexity of APT attack technology, the conclusions of APT detectors are unreliable. The occurrence of inaccurate APT detection forces us to introduce an expert system (ES) to double-check the alarm results and acquire knowledge about the miss detection rate (MDR) and false alarm rate (FAR) of the APT detection.

In this paper, we propose an ES-based APT detection game model to protect the IoT system against APT attacks with an expert system, in which the attacker chooses the duration to intrude while the defender makes a decision on the detection interval without knowing the choice of the opponent. The Nash equilibria (NE) of the ES-based APT detection game is derived to investigate the influence of the APT detection accuracy on the utilities of two players. Furthermore, we study the dynamic game of APT detection strategy based on ES through Q-learning, in which the defender has no knowledge about the attack model. The optimal detection strategy is derived via a trial-and-error method and evaluated via simulations. The results show that, by applying Q-learning, the defender can find the optimal strategy and obtain a higher utility than stochastic method and ϵ-greedy. Besides, the security level is also enhanced.

The major contributions of this paper are summarized as follows:

- We model the interaction between the APT attacker and the IoT system defender with an ES by game theory, considering the inaccurate APT detection, i.e., the miss detection and false alarm.
- We derive the NE of the ES-based APT detection game, and discuss the concrete influence of the MDR and FAR on the utilities of the players.
- We propose an optimal APT detection method for the IoT system with ES by Q-learning algorithm in the dynamic game, and compare its performance with the benchmark detection scheme via simulations.

The rest of this paper is structured as follows. Section 2 reviews related work. Section 3 presents the system model. An ES-based APT detection game with unknown action of the opponent is studied in Sect. 4. Section 5 investigates the dynamic APT game. Simulation results are provided in Sect. 6 and conclusion is given in Sect. 7.

2   Related Work

Game-theoretic methods have been applied to study cyberspace security against APT attackers in recent years. [5] provided a simple and elegant framework FlipIt in which we can formally discuss about the interaction between attackers and defenders in practical scenarios. In [6], a nearly optimal defending strategy was obtained under the limited-resource condition. The two-player FlipIt game model for stealthy takeover was extended by introducing an insider that can trade information to the attacker for a profit in [7], which proposed the first three-player attacker-defender-insider game to model the strategic interactions among the three parties. A game-theoretic model FlipLeakage was proposed in [8] to derive optimal strategies for the defender who could only partially eliminate the attacker's foothold. [9] discussed a three party game theory among a device, a cloud defender and an attacker. By analyzing a three-player game among a mobile device, a smart attacker and a security agent, [10] proposed an offloading strategy to improve the utility of the mobile device and reduce the attack rate of smart attackers. Prospect theory and cumulative prospect theory was applied in [11,12] to study the interactions between a subjective cloud storage defender and a subjective APT attacker. [13,14] investigated APTs defense with theories of evolutionary game and Colonel Blotto game. [15] presented a dynamic game framework against APTs based on two-person zero-sum games across several layers, and provided defense-in-depth strategies.

However, none of these work studied the impacts of the APT detection accuracy on the utilities of the IoT system and the attacker, which is the focus in our work.

3   System Model

In our ES-based APT detection game, there are two players: a skilled APT attacker ($\mathcal{A}$) and an IoT system defender ($\mathcal{D}$) supported by an expert system.

$\mathcal{A}$ aims to access the device illegally for data theft as long as possible before $\mathcal{D}$ detects it, while $\mathcal{D}$ tries its best to prevent the attack and improve the security level of the IoT system.

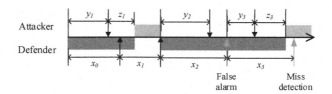

Fig. 2. Illustration of an ES-based APT detection game, in which the defender detects the storage device after interval x_k, the attacker launches APT after interval y_k and the attack duration is z_k, where k is the index of the interaction.

At the beginning of the game, the device is assumed to be safe. After an intentional time y, $\mathcal{A}$ launches an attack, which can take effect within a time period of z, $z > 0$. $\mathcal{D}$ scans the device and gathers information by a APT detector continuously, but has no idea whether the device is compromised until the detector completes a comprehensive analysis in a scheduled period x, which is called a detection interval. $x > 0$ because the analyzing is meaningless when $x = 0$. Once an APT attack is confirmed, $\mathcal{D}$ will restore the device to regain the control right. At the end of the game, if $\mathcal{D}$ does not prevent an attack which is launched already, no matter effectively or not, $\mathcal{A}$ wins a value of C meanwhile $\mathcal{D}$ loses it. C is defined by the importance of the device to both $\mathcal{A}$ and $\mathcal{D}$. The cost of each attack for $\mathcal{A}$ is C_A, and the payoff of unit detection interval for $\mathcal{D}$ is G_D. As rational players, $\mathcal{A}$ and $\mathcal{D}$ choose their optimal strategies over y and x to maximize their individual benefit.

With the assist of the ES, we notice that sometimes the APT detector misjudges the state of the device. Let s_0 and s_1 present the states of the device reported by the detector, and S_0, S_1 are the real states. The MDR p_m and the FAR p_f are defined as

$$p_m = P_r(s_0|S_1) \tag{1}$$
$$p_f = P_r(s_1|S_0) \tag{2}$$

where $P_r(\cdot|\cdot)$ is the conditional probability. By (1) and (2), the probability for the detector to alarm exactly is $P_r(s_1|S_1) = 1 - p_m$ and the probability to report no attacks correctly is $P_r(s_0|S_0) = 1 - p_f$.

The interactions between $\mathcal{A}$ and $\mathcal{D}$ are shown in Fig. 2, where blue bars present S_0 and red bars S_1. Taking false alarm and miss detection into consideration, in the following two cases $\mathcal{D}$ would lose the game:

– If an APT attack takes effect before a detection and be missed out in the detection, $\mathcal{D}$ loses the game.

- When an APT attack is launched before a detection and has not taken effect when $\mathcal{D}$ detects, and if the APT detector do not give a false alarm, the attack would have a chance to work finally.

To sum up, the utility of $\mathcal{D}$ denoted by u_D is composed of three parts: (1) the gain from the fraction of the time during which the device is safe, (2) the gain from the interval waiting to collect more information, and (3) the payment for losing the game. The utility of $\mathcal{D}$ is defined as

$$u_D = \min\left(\frac{y+z}{x}, 1\right) + xG_D - \left(\mathrm{I}(y+z \leqslant x)p_m + \mathrm{I}(y \leqslant x < y+z)(1-p_f)\right)C \quad (3)$$

where $\mathrm{I}(\cdot)$ takes 1 if the event in the parentheses is true and 0 otherwise. By normalization, we have $x \in (0,1]$, $y \in [0,1]$ and $z \in (0,1]$, and we call part 1 security rate.

Similarly, the attacker's utility denoted by u_A includes three aspects: (1) the loss from security time of the device, (2) the cost for launching attack, and (3) the gain from winning the game. The utility of $\mathcal{A}$ is presented by

$$u_A = -\min\left(\frac{y+z}{x}, 1\right) - \mathrm{I}(y < 1)C_A + \left(\mathrm{I}(y+z \leqslant x)p_m + \mathrm{I}(y \leqslant x < y+z)(1-p_f)\right)C \quad (4)$$

Table 1 summarizes the notations used in the paper.

Table 1. Summary of symbols and notation.

Notation	Definition
x/y	Defense/attack interval
z	Duration to complete an attack
p_m/p_f	Rate of miss detection/false alarm of the APT detector
C	Value of the cloud storage device
G_D	Defense gain of the defender
C_A	Attack cost of the attacker
α/β	Mixed-strategy of the defender/attacker

4   ES-Based APT Detection Game with Mixed-Strategy

We particularly focus on the ES-based APT detection game in which both players adopt mixed strategies, because pure-strategy is a special case of mixed-strategy, and the NE of a pure-strategy game is much easier to be predicted than that of a mixed-strategy one.

The mixed-strategy ES-based APT detection game is denoted as $\mathbb{G}$. It is assumed that the detection interval of $\mathcal{D}$ is quantized with $x \in \{m/M\}_{1 \leqslant m \leqslant M}$, when $\mathcal{A}$ quantizes its interval of attack with $y \in \{n/N\}_{0 \leqslant n \leqslant N}$. The detection interval x is determined according to the mixed strategy $\alpha = [\alpha_m]_{1 \leqslant m \leqslant M}$, where

$\alpha_m = P_r(x = m/M)$ is the probability to detect the storage device after x, while the attack interval y is chosen based on the strategy $\boldsymbol{\beta} = [\beta_n]_{0 \leqslant n \leqslant N}$, where $\beta_n = P_r(y = n/N)$ is the probability for $\mathcal{A}$ to launch APT after interval y. By definition, we have $\alpha_m \geqslant 0$, $\beta_n \geqslant 0$, $\sum_{m=1}^{M} \alpha_m = 1$ and $\sum_{n=0}^{N} \beta_n = 1$. For simplicity, we assume that an attacker takes a constant time z to control the device in this game. According to z, we categorize the attackers into two types without loss of generality: the high-level (HL) and the low-level (LL) attacker types. If $z \leqslant \sigma$, $\mathcal{A}$ is HL, and if $z > \sigma$, $\mathcal{A}$ is LL, where σ is the threshold value. Technically, z is relevant to both the ability of $\mathcal{A}$ and the defense level of $\mathcal{D}$.

We define the expected utilities of $\mathcal{D}$ and attacker in ES-based APT detection game $\mathbb{G}$ according to expected utility theory (EUT), and they are given by (5) and (6) as

$$U_D^{EUT}(\boldsymbol{\alpha}, \boldsymbol{\beta}) = \sum_{m=1}^{M} \sum_{n=0}^{N} \alpha_m \beta_n \times u_D(\frac{m}{M}, \frac{n}{N}) \tag{5}$$

$$U_A^{EUT}(\boldsymbol{\alpha}, \boldsymbol{\beta}) = \sum_{m=1}^{M} \sum_{n=0}^{N} \alpha_m \beta_n \times u_A(\frac{m}{M}, \frac{n}{N}) \tag{6}$$

By definition, the NE of the mixed-strategy game $\mathbb{G}$, denoted by $(\boldsymbol{\alpha}^*, \boldsymbol{\beta}^*)$, is given as

$$\begin{cases} \boldsymbol{\alpha}^* = \arg \max_{\boldsymbol{\alpha}} U_D^{EUT}(\boldsymbol{\alpha}, \boldsymbol{\beta}^*) \\ \boldsymbol{\beta}^* = \arg \max_{\boldsymbol{\beta}} U_A^{EUT}(\boldsymbol{\alpha}^*, \boldsymbol{\beta}) \\ \sum_{m=1}^{M} \alpha_m = 1, \boldsymbol{\alpha} \succeq 0 \\ \sum_{n=0}^{N} \beta_n = 1, \boldsymbol{\beta} \succeq 0 \end{cases} \tag{7}$$

Theorem 1. *The NE of game $\mathbb{G}$ with mixed-strategy is given by*

$$\begin{cases} \left[u_D\left(\frac{m}{M}, \frac{n}{N}\right) \right]_{1 \leqslant m \leqslant M, 0 \leqslant n \leqslant N} \left[\beta_i^* \right]_{0 \leqslant i \leqslant N}^T = \lambda_D \mathbf{1}_{N+1} \tag{8a} \\ \left[u_A\left(\frac{m}{M}, \frac{n}{N}\right) \right]_{1 \leqslant m \leqslant M, 0 \leqslant n \leqslant N}^T \left[\alpha_k^* \right]_{1 \leqslant k \leqslant M}^T = \lambda_A \mathbf{1}_M \tag{8b} \\ \sum_{m=1}^{M} \alpha_m^* = 1, \boldsymbol{\alpha} \succeq 0 \tag{8c} \\ \sum_{n=0}^{N} \beta_n^* = 1, \boldsymbol{\beta} \succeq 0 \tag{8d} \\ \lambda_D \geqslant 0, \lambda_A \leqslant 0 \tag{8e} \end{cases}$$

if its solution exists, where $\mathbf{1}_\eta$ represents the η-dimensional all-1 column vector.

Proof. By (5) and (7), the Lagrange function L_D is defined as

$$L_D = U_D^{EUT}(\boldsymbol{\alpha}, \boldsymbol{\beta}^*) - \varphi \left(\sum_{m=1}^{M} \alpha_m - 1 \right) + \sum_{m=1}^{M} \mu_m \alpha_m \qquad (9)$$

And the Karush-Kuhn-Tucker (KKT) conditions are given by

$$\begin{cases} \dfrac{\partial L_D}{\partial \alpha_m} = 0 \\ -\alpha_m \leqslant 0, \mu_m \geqslant 0, \mu_m \alpha_m = 0, 1 \leqslant m \leqslant M \\ \displaystyle\sum_{m=1}^{M} \alpha_m - 1 = 0 \end{cases} \qquad (10)$$

According to (5) and (9), by applying the complementary slackness for (10) we obtain

$$\begin{cases} \displaystyle\sum_{n=0}^{N} u_D \left(\dfrac{i}{M}, \dfrac{n}{N} \right) \beta_n^* = \lambda_D, i \in [1, M] \\ \displaystyle\sum_{m=1}^{M} \alpha_m = 1 \\ \lambda_D \geqslant 0 \end{cases} \qquad (11)$$

and yield (8a). Similarly, (8b) can be obtained.

By discussing a specific situation on $M = 2$, $N = 1$, we have Corollary 1.

Corollary 1. *If $M = 2$, $N = 1$, the ES-based APT detection game $\mathbb{G}$ has a unique NE, which is given by*

$$\alpha_1^* = \frac{u_A(1,1) - u_A(1,0)}{u_A(\frac{1}{2},0) - u_A(\frac{1}{2},1) + u_A(1,1) - u_A(1,0)} \qquad (12)$$

$$\beta_0^* = \frac{u_D(1,1) - u_D(\frac{1}{2},1)}{u_D(\frac{1}{2},0) - u_D(1,0) + u_D(1,1) - u_D(\frac{1}{2},1)} \qquad (13)$$

under the conditions that

$$I_1 : \frac{u_D(\frac{1}{2},0) - u_D(1,0)}{u_D(1,1) - u_D(\frac{1}{2},1)} \geqslant 0 \text{ or } \frac{u_D(1,1) - u_D(\frac{1}{2},1)}{u_D(\frac{1}{2},0) - u_D(1,0)} \geqslant 0 \qquad (14)$$

$$I_2 : \frac{u_A(\frac{1}{2},0) - u_A(\frac{1}{2},1)}{u_A(1,1) - u_A(1,0)} \geqslant 0 \text{ or } \frac{u_A(1,1) - u_A(1,0)}{u_A(\frac{1}{2},0) - u_A(\frac{1}{2},1)} \geqslant 0 \qquad (15)$$

According to Corollary 1, the NE of game $\mathbb{G}$ is given as

$$(\alpha_1^*, \beta_0^*) =$$
$$\left(\frac{z - 1 + (1 - p_m - p_f)C}{z - \min(2z, 1) - C_A + \mathrm{I}(z \leqslant \frac{1}{2})(1 - p_f)C + \mathrm{I}(z > \frac{1}{2})(2 - p_m - 2p_f)C}, \right. \qquad (16)$$
$$\left. \frac{\frac{1}{2}G_D - (1 - p_f)C}{\min(2z, 1) - z - (1 - p_f)C - \mathrm{I}(z > \frac{1}{2})(1 - p_m - p_f)C} \right)$$

We study the influences of MDR and FAR on the performance of game $\mathbb{G}$, against a LL attacker and a HL attacker respectively. According to (16), we set $\sigma = 0.5$, and then the attacker with $z \leqslant 0.5$ is HL and $z > 0.5$ is low-level.

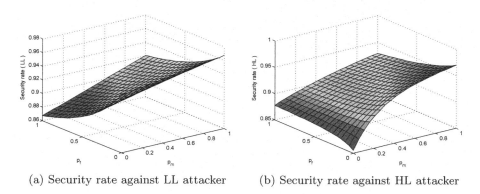

(a) Security rate against LL attacker   (b) Security rate against HL attacker

Fig. 3. Security rate of the ES-based APT detection game $\mathbb{G}$ with mixed-strategy, against LL and HL APT attackers, with $C = 0.2, G_D = 0.15$ and $C_A = 0.46$.

Figure 3 is an illustration of the influences of the MDR and FAR on the security rate of game $\mathbb{G}$. When played with mixed-strategy, the security rate of the game is an expected value. As shown in Fig. 3a, against a LL attacker, the security rate raises with the MDR, while declines with the FAR. For example, the security rate at the point $(p_m, p_f) = (0,0)$ is about 0.94, it increases to 0.96 at $(p_m, p_f) = (0.5, 0)$ but decreases to 0.89 when $(p_m, p_f) = (0, 0.5)$. If the attacker is HL, the situation is quite different, as shown in Fig. 3b. When p_m is less than 0.12, the security rate goes up with both the MDR and FAR, otherwise, it increases with the MDR but decreases with the FAR.

The influences of the inaccurate APT detection on utilities are shown in Figs. 4 and 5. When the attacker is LL, as shown in Fig. 4, the defender's utility decreases with both p_m and p_f, while the attacker's utility raises with the MDR and declines with the FAR. For instance, when (p_m, p_f) goes from (0,0) to (0.5,0), the utility of $\mathcal{D}$ decreases by 1.4% but that of $\mathcal{A}$ increases by 3%, and when (p_m, p_f) goes from (0,0) to (0,0.5), the utility of $\mathcal{D}$ reduces by 0.7% and that of $\mathcal{A}$ lowers by 2.8%. As shown in Fig. 5, where the attacker is HL, the utility of $\mathcal{D}$ declines with both the MDR and FAR when $p_m < 0.2$ and $p_f < 0.2$, but increases with both p_m and p_f otherwise. Smaller p_f makes the defender's utility decrease slower with p_m, especially when $p_f = 0$ the defender's utility does not change with p_m at all. As to $\mathcal{A}$, its utility increases with both p_m and p_f, linearly.

Remark: The expected security rate and utilities of game $\mathbb{G}$ have complicated association with the inaccuracy of APT detection. In this game, $\mathcal{A}$ prefers to attack at a low probability to maintain its utility, and $\mathcal{D}$ adjusts defense strategy according to expert system knowledge about the MDR and FAR of the APT detector to avoid losses.

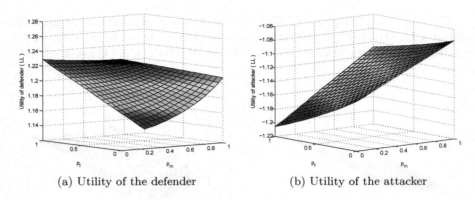

(a) Utility of the defender   (b) Utility of the attacker

Fig. 4. Performance of the ES-based APT detection game $\mathbb{G}$ with mixed-strategy, with $C = 0.2, G_D = 0.15$ and $C_A = 0.46$, when the APT attacker is LL.

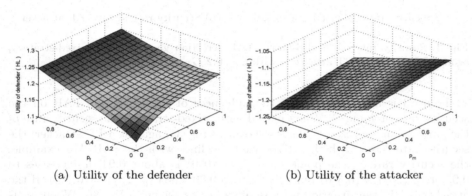

(a) Utility of the defender   (b) Utility of the attacker

Fig. 5. Performance of the ES-based APT detection game $\mathbb{G}$ with mixed-strategy, with $C = 0.2, G_D = 0.15$ and $C_A = 0.46$, when the APT attacker is HL.

5 Dynamic ES-Based APT Detection Game

Q-learning [16] is an off-policy and model-free reinforcement learning algorithm, which enables players to achieve their optimal strategies via trial-and-error without knowledge about the attack model. In the dynamic ES-based APT detection game, the strategy based on Q-learning updates a quality function $Q(s, x)$ to achieve a best payoff. s is the state of system and consists of the action of the opponent and the parameters of the environment. $Q(s, x)$ stands for the expected discounted reward with action x at system state s.

The dynamic mixed-strategy ES-based APT detection game is denoted by $\mathcal{G}$, in which x is the detection interval decided by $\mathcal{D}$. After a duration of x, the APT detector detects the device and reports whether the device is safe. When an intrusion event is reported, the ES will make a further confirmation. According to the suggestion of the ES, $\mathcal{D}$ makes a decision to restore the device whether or not, and then observes its reward.

The system state is the last total attack duration $y_{k-1} + z_{k-1}$ at time k. The Q-function is updated with

$$Q(s_k, x_k) \leftarrow (1 - \gamma)Q(s_k, x_k) + \gamma \left(u_D + \delta \max_{x \in \boldsymbol{x}} Q(s_k, x_k) \right) \qquad (17)$$

Where u_D is the immediate utility of $\mathcal{D}$. The ϵ-greedy algorithm is used to choose the detection interval to maximize the current Q-function as

$$Pr(x_k = \hat{x}) = \begin{cases} 1 - \epsilon, & \hat{x} = \arg\max_{\boldsymbol{x}} Q(s_k, x) \\ \frac{\epsilon}{M-1}, & o.w. \end{cases} \qquad (18)$$

The Q-learning algorithm is summarized in Algorithm 1.

Algorithm 1. Dynamic ES-based APT detection with Q-learning.

Initialize $\gamma = 0.78, \delta = 0.76, \epsilon = 0.1, y_0 + z_0 = 0, Q(s, x) = 0$.
   for $k = 1, 2, 3...$ **do**
      Update the state $s_k = y_{k-1} + z_{k-1}$
      Choose x_k with the ϵ-greedy algorithm
      Detect the device according to strategy x_k
      Observe utility u_D and $y_k + z_k$
      Update $Q(s_k, x_k)$ via (17)
   end for

---

6 Simulation Results

The performance of the APT detection scheme based on Q-learning in the ES-based APT detection dynamic game $\mathcal{G}$ is evaluated by simulations, and the results are shown in Fig. 6. To achieve good performance, we set $\gamma = 0.78, \delta = 0.76$, and $\epsilon = 0.1$, and choose $p_m = 0.2, p_f = 0.36, C = 0.2, G_D = 0.15$ and $C_A = 0.46$ as typical attack and detection parameters. A random strategy process and a ϵ-greedy detection algorithm are used for comparison. The detection interval in greedy algorithm is the one that maximize the immediate utility with the previous attack duration. We assume the attack interval is chosen to maximize the attacker's utility according to last time slot history.

As shown in Fig. 6a, the security rate gets close to 1 after nearly 27 runs and reaches an average value 0.99 when $\mathcal{D}$ chooses detection interval via Q-learning, while the average security rate is 0.91 with ϵ-greedy strategy and 0.87 with random scheme. Figure 6b shows that the method of Q-learning reaches a significantly higher utility than both random strategy and greedy algorithm. The utility of a Q-learning defender converges to an average value 1.12 over 30 runs, while the average value of ϵ-greedy algorithm and random strategy are 0.99 and 0.92.

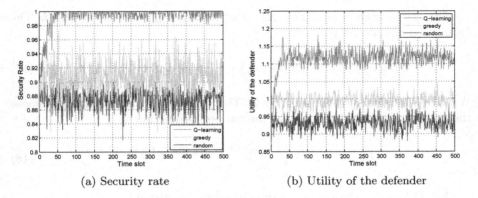

(a) Security rate   (b) Utility of the defender

Fig. 6. Performance of the dynamic ES-based APT detection game $\mathcal{G}$ over 500 runs, with $C = 0.2, G_D = 0.15$ and $C_A = 0.46$.

7   Conclusion

In this paper, we have proposed a static game and a dynamic game for IoT to detect APT based on expert system. The games reveal the effects of the inaccurate detection on the security rate of the IoT system, and the utilities of the players. The NE of the static game is derived, and its existence is demonstrated. The NE shows that, while playing mixed-strategy game, the attacker would not launch attacks frequently, and the defender can adjust detection strategy according to the knowledge of the expert system to increase the security level. Simulation results of the dynamic ES-based APT detection game show that the performance can be improved by the proposed Q-learning scheme, e.g., the security rate increases by 8.8% and the utility of the defender increases by 13.1%, compared with the ϵ-greedy strategy. The expert system has superior performance on APT attack detection, but it would take a period of time to determine. The future work is to further investigate the effect of the expert system on defending against APT for IoT.

Acknowledgments. This work was supported in part by the National Key Research and Development Program of China (2016YFB0800202), Key Research Program of Chinese MIIT under grant No. JCKY2016602B001, National Natural Science Foundation of China under Grants No. U1636120 and 61671396, CCF-Venustech Hongyan Research Initiative (2016-010), and Beijing Municipal Science & Technology Commission Grants No. Z161100002616032.

References

1. Butun, I., Erol-Kantarci, M., Kantarci, B., Song, H.: Cloud-centric multi-level authentication as a service for secure public safety device networks. IEEE Commun. Mag. **54**(4), 47–53 (2016)

2. Mehmood, A., Umar, M.M., Song, H.: ICMDS: secure inter-cluster multiple-key distribution scheme for wireless sensor networks. Ad Hoc Netw. **55**, 97–106 (2017)
3. Song, H., Fink, G.A., Jeschke, S.: Security and Privacy in Cyber-Physical Systems: Foundations, Principles and Applications. Wiley-IEEE Press, Hoboken (2017)
4. Tankard, C.: Advanced persistent threats and how to monitor and deter them. Netw. Secur. **2011**(8), 16–19 (2011)
5. Van Dijk, M., Juels, A., Oprea, A., Rivest, R.L.: Flipit: the game of stealthy takeover. J. Cryptol. **26**(4), 655–713 (2013)
6. Zhang, M., Zheng, Z., Shroff, N.B.: A game theoretic model for defending against stealthy attacks with limited resources. In: Khouzani, M.H.R., Panaousis, E., Theodorakopoulos, G. (eds.) GameSec 2015. LNCS, vol. 9406, pp. 93–112. Springer, Cham (2015). doi:10.1007/978-3-319-25594-1_6
7. Feng, X., Zheng, Z., Hu, P., Cansever, D., Mohapatra, P.: Stealthy attacks meets insider threats: a three-player game model. In: Military Communications Conference (MILCOM), pp. 25–30. IEEE (2015)
8. Farhang, S., Gros3klags, J.: FlipLeakage: a game-theoretic approach to protect against stealthy attackers in the presence of information leakage. In: Zhu, Q., Alpcan, T., Panaousis, E., Tambe, M., Casey, W. (eds.) GameSec 2016. LNCS, vol. 9996, pp. 195–214. Springer, Cham (2016). doi:10.1007/978-3-319-47413-7_12
9. Pawlick, J., Farhang, S., Zhu, Q.: Flip the cloud: cyber-physical signaling games in the presence of advanced persistent threats. In: Khouzani, M.H.R., Panaousis, E., Theodorakopoulos, G. (eds.) GameSec 2015. LNCS, vol. 9406, pp. 289–308. Springer, Cham (2015). doi:10.1007/978-3-319-25594-1_16
10. Xiao, L., Xie, C., Chen, T., Dai, H., Poor, H.V.: A mobile offloading game against smart attacks. IEEE Access **4**, 2281–2291 (2016)
11. Xiao, L., Xu, D., Xie, C., Mandayam, N.B., Poor, H.V.: Cloud storage defense against advanced persistent threats: a prospect theoretic study. IEEE J. Sel. Areas Commun. **35**(3), 534–544 (2017)
12. Xu, D., Xiao, L., Mandayam, N.B., Poor, H.V.: Cumulative prospect theoretic study of a cloud storage defense game against advanced persistent threats. In: IEEE International Conference on Computer Communications (INFOCOM WKSHPS). IEEE (2017)
13. Abass, A., Xiao, L., Mandayam, N.B., Gaijic, Z.: Evolutionary game theoretic analysis of advanced persistent threats against cloud storage. IEEE Access (2017)
14. Min, M., Xiao, L., Xie, C., Hajimirsadeghi, M., Mandayam, N.B.: Defense against advanced persistent threats: a colonel blotto game approach. In: IEEE International Conference on Communications (ICC). IEEE (2017)
15. Rass, S., Zhu, Q.: GADAPT: a sequential game-theoretic framework for designing defense-in-depth strategies against advanced persistent threats. In: Zhu, Q., Alpcan, T., Panaousis, E., Tambe, M., Casey, W. (eds.) GameSec 2016. LNCS, vol. 9996, pp. 314–326. Springer, Cham (2016). doi:10.1007/978-3-319-47413-7_18
16. Watkins, C.J., Dayan, P.: Q-learning. Mach. Learn. **8**(3–4), 279–292 (1992)

QoE Enhancement of Task Scheduling Algorithm for VANET Applications

Nan Ding[1,2(✉)], Shuaihang Nie[1], Huaiwei Si[1], and Huanbo Gao[1]

[1] Dalian University of Technology, Dalian, China
dingnan@dlut.edu.cn
[2] State Key Laboratory of Software Architecture,
Neusoft Corporation, Shenyang, China

Abstract. Providing support for high Quality of Experience for VANETs applications is a significant challenge. Needless inter-core communications in a multi-core processor can affect the real-time response of the tasks. To solve this problem, DRS-V, a data related scheduling algorithm for VANETs (Vehicular Ad Hoc Networks) applications, is proposed in this paper, with considering the multi-task concurrency mechanism in VANETs. According to the tasks and the task parameters in a VANET, a task model is built based on data correlation, to look into correlation between the tasks. Finally, via experiment and simulation, it is verified that DRS-V, compared to load balance algorithm, can shorten the delay caused by inter-core communications.

Keywords: QoE · VANET · Task scheduling · Data-related

1 Introduction

Providing VANETs applications with focus on user Quality of Experience (QoE) constitutes a significant challenge [9]. As scenarios for VANET applications become increasingly complex, the number of the tasks to be processed in VANET is also increasing. To cope with the problem, multi-core technologies are now the effective tools to improve VANET performance.

To ensure the multi-task concurrency mechanism in the multi-core processor system and to improve the response performance, the key is to design an efficient task scheduling algorithm [4,5]. A multi-core processor is capable to handle multiple tasks at the same time and, as a result of that, raises the task throughput, but it also brings about an extra consumption: inter-core communication [2,6]. According to statistics, the response delay caused by inter-core communication during executing tasks is about 3–10 times longer than that caused by intra-core communication [7,8].

For the above purposes and based on the parameters involved in VANET tasks, this paper designs a task model that can describe the data correlation between tasks, and proposes a data related algorithm for scheduling tasks. As verified by experiments, this DRS-V algorithm can allocate more tasks in which data are related into one core, which thus improves the real-time task response since inter-core communications are replaced by the intra-core ones.

L. Ma et al. (Eds.): WASA 2017, LNCS 10251, pp. 338–343, 2017.
DOI: 10.1007/978-3-319-60033-8_30

2 Design of the Data Related Task Model

2.1 Weights of the Task Parameters

Currently, VANET tasks are classified into three types: (1) critical safety; (2) traffic efficiency, and; (3) non-safety [1]. In which, a lot of parameters those intensively used in corresponding task type can be also classified into three types. These parameters corresponding to the three task types can be collected in sets, as follows:

$$X = \{x_1, ..., x_i, ..., x_N\}, Y = \{y_1, ..., y_j, ..., y_M\}, Z = \{z_1, ..., z_k, ..., z_C\} \quad (1)$$

where, x_i, y_j and z_k represent the parameters corresponding to each task type.

In a VANET task, the times of using a parameter, namely the frequency of usage, is different. In this study, statistics of such frequencies is made based on a great number of VANET tasks in different scenarios. Here, we use F to represent frequency. So, the frequency of usage for each parameter is represented by F_{x1}, F_{x2} ,..., F_{y1}, F_{y2},..., F_{z1}, F_{z2},..., respectively. The ratio of the usage times for each parameter to the total times for the parameters of the same type is called as frequency weight (w), which can be expressed as:

$$w_{x_i} = \frac{F_{x_i}}{\sum\limits_{l=1}^{N} F_{x_l}}, w_{y_j} = \frac{F_{y_j}}{\sum\limits_{l=1}^{M} F_{y_l}}, w_{z_k} = \frac{F_{z_k}}{\sum\limits_{l=1}^{C} F_{z_l}} \quad (2)$$

where, $\sum\limits_{i=1}^{N} w_{x_i} = 1$, $\sum\limits_{j=1}^{M} w_{y_j} = 1$ and $\sum\limits_{k=1}^{C} w_{z_k} = 1$. In this study, three $N \times 1$ weight matrixes W_x, W_y and W_z are obtained, which represent the frequency weights of the parameters in the three VANET task types, respectively. They are written as:

$$W_x = \begin{bmatrix} w_{x_1} \\ w_{x_2} \\ \vdots \\ w_{x_N} \end{bmatrix}, W_y = \begin{bmatrix} w_{y_1} \\ w_{y_2} \\ \vdots \\ w_{y_M} \end{bmatrix}, W_z = \begin{bmatrix} w_{z_1} \\ w_{z_2} \\ \vdots \\ w_{z_C} \end{bmatrix} \quad (3)$$

Assume that there are two tasks: P and Q, both of which contain the parameters that belong to X, Y and Z, say, $P, Q \subseteq X \cup Y \cup Z$. Three $1 \times N$ matrixes E_x, E_y and E_z are defined for both P and Q:

$$E_x = \begin{bmatrix} e_1 \ e_2 \ e_3 \cdots e_N \end{bmatrix}, E_y = \begin{bmatrix} e_1 \ e_2 \ e_3 \cdots e_M \end{bmatrix}, E_z = \begin{bmatrix} e_1 \ e_2 \ e_3 \cdots e_C \end{bmatrix} \quad (4)$$

where, $e_g = 1$ or $e_g = 0$, meaning that whether the gth parameter of the type X, Y or Z is contained in the task P or not. In the parameters matrix, the number 1 means that the corresponding parameter is contained in both tasks, while 0 means not.

2.2 Correlation Factor

After the parameter weights being determined, the type-correlation factor of each task can be computed based on the parameter types.

Definition 1. *For task P there are type-correlation factors α_x, α_y and α_z, which mean that the correlation intensity of a type of parameters in VANET. The factors are expressed as:*

$$\alpha_x = E_x W_x, \alpha_y = E_y W_y, \alpha_y = E_y W_y \tag{5}$$

where, α_x, α_y and α_z show how strong or weak the task is correlated to the three parameter types, which, indirectly reflects that which type the task is belonging to.

The range of the type-correlation factor α is [0,1]. When a type-correlation factor is large while the other two are small, it is reasonable to consider that the task belongs to the type corresponding to the large factor.

Definition 2. *For tasks P and Q, there are task-correlation factors $\beta_x(P,Q)$, $\beta_y(P,Q)$ and $\beta_z(P,Q)$, which represent to what degree the data of task P are correlated to those of task Q. These factors can be computed by:*

$$\beta_x(P,Q) = \frac{E_x{}'W_x}{E_x{}''W_x}, \beta_y(P,Q) = \frac{E_y{}'W_y}{E_y{}''W_y}, \beta_z(P,Q) = \frac{E_z{}'W_z}{E_z{}''W_z} \tag{6}$$

where, $E_x{}'$, $E_y{}'$ and $E_z{}'$ mean that whether the common parameters of both P and Q are contained in the three task types or not, say, the intersection of the matrixes E_x, E_y and E_z; and $E_x{}''$, $E_y{}''$ and $E_z{}''$ mean that whether the parameters of P or Q are contained in the three task types or not, say, the union of the matrixes E_x, E_y and E_z.

It can be known from (6) that: $\beta_x(P,Q)$, $\beta_y(P,Q)$ and $\beta_z(P,Q) \in [0,1]$. If the values of $\beta_x(P,Q)$, $\beta_y(P,Q)$ and $\beta_z(P,Q)$ are larger, then the data of task P are more closely correlated to those of task Q.

3 Design of the Data Related Scheduling Algorithm

3.1 The Data Related Task-Relation Model

According to the data related task model as described in Sect. 2, each task has a set of type-correlation factors $A = \{\alpha_x, \alpha_y, \alpha_z\}$. The value of the factor shows that which type the task in the box is the most closely related to. There is a task-correlation factors $B(P,Q) = \{\beta_x(P,Q), \beta_y(P,Q), \beta_z(P,Q)\}$ in each pair of tasks. The three task-correlation factors represent the correlation between the data of the task and those of other tasks. A larger value means that the communication and data transmission between the two tasks are more frequent. Based on this description, we can build the task-correlation table, as shown in Table 1. If a new task is added or canceled, then its correlation should also be added or canceled in the Table 1.

Table 1. Task-correlation factors

Task	X/Y/Z	P_1	P_2	...	P_n
X/Y/Z	-	A_1	A_2	...	A_n
P_1	A_1	-	$B(P_1,P_2)$	...	$B(P_1,P_n)$
P_2	A_2	$B(P_2,P_1)$	-	...	$B(P_2,P_n)$
...	...	...	...	...	...
P_n	A_n	$B(P_n,P_1)$	$B(P_n,P_2)$	...	-

3.2 Design of the Data Related Scheduling Algorithm

In this study, the scheduling of the algorithm is implemented from two aspects: the coarse-grained scheduling and the fine-grained scheduling.

First we implement the coarse-grained scheduling. According to the Table 1, clusters for the tasks of the same type are constructed and represented by CP_x, CP_y and CP_z. Then, tasks can be assigned to corresponding clusters, as follows:

$$CP_x = \{P_i \in Proc | P_i.\alpha_x > \alpha_{th}\} \tag{7}$$

CP_y and CP_z can be similarly obtained. where, $Proc = \{P_1, P_2, P_3, ..., P_n\}(1 \leq i \leq n)$, and α_{th} is a correlation coefficient, which, according to the system performance, is set as $\alpha_{th} \in (0, 1)$.

For a task P_{pre} prepared for allocation, it can be allocated to a cluster according to its type-correlation factor. After that, P_{pre} is scheduled to an executing core that is loaded the least.

If a task is allocated to several clusters, then the fine-grained scheduling will play its role. This scheduling relies mainly on the task-correlation, say, the correlation between P_{pre} and the tasks in the ready queue in the executing core. For a processor that has m cores (in which, core 0 is the scheduling core), there are H tasks in the ready queue in core $i(1 \leq i \leq m - 1)$, which are presented by $Q_1, Q_2, ...,$ and Q_H, respectively. Then, the correlation between P_{pre} and these tasks can be computed by:

$$\beta_{ix}(P_{pre}) = \frac{\sum_{j=1}^{H} \beta_x(P_{pre}, Q_j)}{H} \tag{8}$$

where, $\beta_{ix}(P_{pre})$ falls into the domain of [0, 1]. $\beta_{iy}(P_{pre})$ and $\beta_{iz}(P_{pre})$ can be calculated in the same way. Then we have:

$$\beta_i(P_{pre}) = \frac{\beta_{ix}(P_{pre}) + \beta_{iy}(P_{pre}) + \beta_{iz}(P_{pre})}{3} \tag{9}$$

where, $\beta_i(P_{pre})$ represents the intensity of the task-correlation between P_{pre} and the tasks in core i. Finally, task P_{pre} is scheduled and allocated to the core that it has the strongest correlation with.

4   Experiment and Results

The experiment to test the performance of our designed scheduling algorithm is carried out in an already built environment to simulate the process of both scheduling and executing.

A scheduling queue model is built for the multi-core processor in VANET, in which, the core 0 is taken as the scheduling core while others are taken as executing cores. Scheduling core is running as a scheduler, in charge of updating Table 1 and allocating tasks into executing cores. Executing cores for three types are allocated in accordance with their weights in VANET. Therefore, the number of executing processors for each type can be one, at least, or several.

More details about experiment can't be showed due to space constrains. The experiment results are shown in Fig. 1.

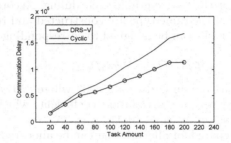

Fig. 1. Communication delay of DRS-V and cyclic with different task amounts

As can be seen from Fig. 1, with increasing the number of the tasks, the delay in communication also increases. This is because the increasing of the tasks will also increase the times of the inter-communications. On the whole level, the delay in our algorithm is smaller than that in the Cyclic algorithm, which suggests that our algorithm is effective to reduce the times of the inter-communications and, therefore, reduce the communication delay.

Seen from the experiments, DRS-V is better than Cyclic in shortening the delay in communication. Besides, as the number (n) of the tasks increases, our algorithm also shows a better optimizing effect. As the number of the tasks keeps increasing, the proportion of decreasing communication gets larger and larger. This is because the increasing of the tasks can enhance the correlation between the data.

Acknowledgement. This work was supported in part by the National Science Foundation of China No. 61471084 and the Open Program of State Key Laboratory of Software Architecture No. SKLSA2016B-02.

References

1. Karagiannis, G., et al.: Vehicular networking: a survey and tutorial on requirements, architectures, challenges, standards and solutions. IEEE Commun. Surv. Tutor. **13**(4), 584–616 (2011)
2. Lin, Y.-H., Tu, C., Shih, C.-S., Hung, S.-H.: Zero-buffer inter-core process communication protocol for heterogeneous multi-core platforms. In: Proceedings of IEEE 15th International Conference on Embedded and Real-Time Computing Systems and Applications (RTCSA 2009), pp. 69–78 (2009)
3. Fan, M., Quan, G.: Harmonic-aware multi-core scheduling for fixed-priority realtime systems. IEEE Trans. Parallel Distrib. Syst. **25**(6), 1476–1488 (2014)
4. Andersson, B.: Global static-priority preemptive multiprocessor scheduling with utilization bound 38%. In: Baker, T.P., Bui, A., Tixeuil, S. (eds.) OPODIS 2008. LNCS, vol. 5401, pp. 73–88. Springer, Heidelberg (2008). doi:10.1007/978-3-540-92221-6_7
5. Han, Q., Wang, T., Quan, G.: Enhanced fault-tolerant fixed-priority scheduling of hard real-time tasks on multi-core platforms. In: 2015 IEEE 21st International Conference on Embedded and Real-Time Computing Systems and Applications, Hong Kong (2015)
6. Wang, T., Niu, L., Ren, S., Quan, G.: Multi-core fixed-priority scheduling of realtime tasks with statistical deadline guarantee. In: 2015 Design, Automation and Test in Europe Conference and Exhibition (DATE), Grenoble, pp. 1335–1340 (2015)
7. Xu, X., Center, N., Wang, L.: Task assignments based on shared memory multi-core communication. In: 2014 2nd International Conference on Systems and Informatics (ICSAI), Shanghai, pp. 324–328 (2014)
8. Wang, Y., Shao, Z., Chan, H.C.B., Liu, D., Guan, Y.: Memory-aware task scheduling with communication overhead minimization for streaming applications on bus-based multiprocessor system-on-chips. IEEE Trans. Parallel Distrib. Syst. **25**(7), 1797–1807 (2014)
9. Xu, C., Zhao, F., Guan, J., Zhang, H., Muntean, G.M.: QoE-driven user-centric VoD services in urban multihomed P2P-based vehicular networks. IEEE Trans. Veh. Technol. **62**(5), 2273–2289 (2013)

Ratee-Based Trust Management System for Internet of Vehicles

Fangyu Gai, Jiexin Zhang, Peidong Zhu$^{(\boxtimes)}$, and Xinwen Jiang

School of Computer, National University of Defense Technology, Changsha, China
{gaifangyu15,zhangjiexin,pdzhu,xwjiang}@nudt.edu.cn

Abstract. There is a growing requirement for effective trust management in Internet of Vehicles (IoV), considering the critical consequences of acting on misleading information spread by malicious nodes. Most existing trust models for IoV are rater-based, where the reputation information of each node is stored in other nodes it has interacted with. This is not suitable for IoV environment due to the ephemeral nature of vehicular networks. To fill this gap, we propose a Ratee-based Trust Management (RTM) system, where each node stores its own reputation information rated by others during past transactions, and a credible CA server is introduced to ensure the integrality and the undeniability of the trust information. Additionally, we built a V2V/V2I trust simulator as an extension to the open source VANET simulator to verify our scheme. Experimental results demonstrate that our scheme achieves faster information propagation and higher transaction success rate than conventional rater-based methods.

Keywords: Internet of Things · Internet of Vehicles · Ratee-based · Trust management

1 Introduction

The Internet of Vehicles (IoV) is a new paradigm brought by the integration of Vehicular Ad-hoc NETworks (VANETs) and Internet of Things (IoT) in the last few years [11]. IoV consists of two types of communications: Vehicle-to-Vehicle (V2V) communication and Vehicle-to-Infrastructure (V2I) communication, which enable tremendous applications ranging from safety to entertainment and commercial services [4]. In addition, vehicles in the network can communicate with each other by switching real-time information about road and traffic conditions, so that they can avoid car accidents and effectively route traffic through dense urban areas.

The motivation of constructing a trust management system for IoV is evident: (1) Malicious nodes may spread misleading information to break the core functionality of the IoV system; (2) There are also many socially uncooperative nodes refusing to provide services to others for selfishness reasons. Considering the dire consequences of false information being sent out by malicious nodes

L. Ma et al. (Eds.): WASA 2017, LNCS 10251, pp. 344–355, 2017.
DOI: 10.1007/978-3-319-60033-8_31

in this scenario, building an effective trust management system for IoV is of paramount importance.

It is challenging to evaluate trust in vehicular networks because it needs past transaction information to compute trust values of the target node. Most of the existing trust management methods for vehicular networks are rater-based methods, where each node stores trust information about the nodes it has interacted with. In vehicular networks, it should not be expected that a node would possibly interact with the same node more than once, so it is difficult for a node to ask for recommendation information. Furthermore, gathering trust information from past transactions is computationally expensive, which introduces another big challenge. Therefore, rater-based methods are not suitable for the ephemeral nature of vehicular networks.

To tackle these problems, we propose a *ratee-based* trust management system. Contract to the rater-based method, in our proposed *ratee-based* model each node stores its own reputation information recorded during the past transactions. When interaction happens, the requester can read trust information from the provider and compute trust value afterward. Some social relationships such as *Parental Object Relationship* (POR), *Social Object Relationship* (SOR), and *Co-Work Object Relationship* (CWOR) defined in [11] will be used in our system for better trust evaluation.

The rest of the paper is organized as follows. Section 2 introduces the related work about social Internet of Vehicles and reputation mechanisms in VANETs. Section 3 describes the details of our system. In Sects. 4 and 5 we demonstrate the simulation results of our system experimentally. We conclude in Sect. 6 and point out the directions for future work.

2   Related Work

The study of trust management in MANETs has reached maturity in the last decade [2,6,8,12]. The estimation of trust values usually relies on two sorts of observations of node behaviors which are first-hand observation and second-hand observation [3]. First-hand observation is the observation about the node's direct experience. It can be collected either passively or actively. While second-hand observation is the observation about other nodes' indirect opinions. It is generally obtained by exchanging first-hand observations with other nodes in the network. First-hand and second-hand observation will be signed different weights according to different scenarios when evaluating trust values.

However, as one of the specific applications in MANETs, VANETs bring new challenges to trust evaluation. Compared to MANETs, VANETs are ephemeral, short-duration wireless networks. The size of VANETs is larger, which may contain millions of vehicles. So the network traffic could be high in the dense area. The topology of VANETs is dynamic since nodes contacting with each other are often with high speed. In [14], The authors propose a list of desired properties that effective trust management should incorporate for VANETs, some of which are important but not carefully concerned.

Only a few trust models have been proposed for trust information sharing in vehicular networks. Huang et al. [5] presented a novel trust architecture named Situation-Aware Trust (SAT) to address the trust management issues. SAT focuses on some specific application situations: an event that affects a particular region with immediate processing needs, or a service that has a clear organizational boundary for its users. In [7], an attack-resistant trust management scheme named ART was proposed for VANETs. The authors claimed that the ART can detect and resist malicious attacks such as Simple Attack, Badmouth Attack, Zigzag Attack, etc. They also evaluated the trustworthiness of both data and mobile nodes in VANETs. Minhas et al. [9] introduced a multifaceted framework to facilitate the effective interaction in VANETs. Their trust models considered various dimensions and combined these elements effectively to assist agents in making transportation decisions.

3   System Model

3.1   Architecture

The Ratee-based Trust Management (RMT) system is composed of four components: *CA Server*, *Cookies*, *Relationship Management* and *Local Trust Management*. The schematic diagram of the RTM architecture is depicted in Fig. 1. The major procedure of one transaction can be described as follows.

For example, vehicle B is asking for congestion information, and vehicle A is willing to provide the information. To show its trustiness, A sends its *Cookies* which accumulate during past interactions along with the congestion information to B. *Cookie* is different from the cookie in HTTP that is to identify users. It is a feedback about a transaction generated by the requester and is used to evaluate trust value to the service provider. After receiving the *Cookies* and congestion

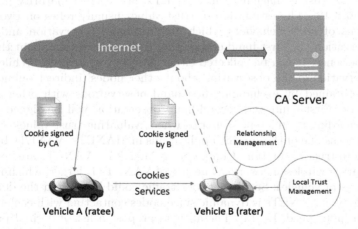

Fig. 1. Overall scheme of ratee-based trust management system

information, B first checks if the *Cookies* are signed by CA, if so, it computes trust value with these *Cookies* to decide whether to trust A or not. If A can be trusted, then the congestion information will be sent to the application, and after that, a *Cookie* which include a feedback about the transaction will be generated, and it will be sent to the CA Server with a sign from B through the Internet. Then after being verified and signed by CA, the *Cookie* will be sent to A when A connects to the Internet. The details of each component are described as follows.

1. *CA Server*: The main problem that storing a node's own reputation information locally is that the reputation information can be easily modified or deleted by the owner. So the basic idea of applying CA is to prevent nodes from tampering with their reputation information, i.e. *Cookies*. Only a *Cookie* with a sign from CA is valid. Before joining the network, users should register their vehicles with the CA server through the Internet. Users should also provide their public keys (generated on their vehicles' unique identities) to the CA for identification, and in turn, users will receive a public key of CA. We assume that CA is attack-resistant by applying IDS and access control technology.

2. *Cookies*: The *Cookie* is defined as trust information in our model. It contains the feedback value of the transaction and other information. Details are shown in Table 1. The feedback value can be expressed either in a binary way, (i.e., the node rates 1 if it is satisfied with the service and 0 otherwise) or in a continuous range $[0,1]$ to evaluate different levels of quality. *Relationship* is also an important attribute when evaluating trust. According to which relationship between the rater and the ratee (SOR, POR or CWOR), the feedback value will be assigned different weights. Nodes extract useful information from *Cookies* to evaluate trust values toward others. *Cookies* are generated toward service provider, and sent to the service provider as its credibility information. They are also stored locally in case that it may contact with the same node in the future so that they can be used as direct evidence.

3. *Relationship Management* (RM): RM is module first proposed in [1]. A node's relationships toward other nodes are recorded in Relationship Management. RM aims to automatically establish relationships toward another node it contacts with. For example, if the vehicle B is produced by the same manufacturer as vehicle A is, the *Relationship Management* of A will establish a POR with B and record this relationship in local storage. When new *Cookies* come, RM will establish the relationship shared between the ratee and the rater by looking up local relationship list.

4. *Local Trust Management* (LTM): In RTM, the trust information is stored in the ratee's local storage. However, to show its credibility, the ratee has to deliver its *Cookies* to the rater to calculate the trustworthiness in the rater's LTM. If the rater has never interacted with the ratee, the trustworthiness only relies on the ratee's *Cookies*. If the rater has stored the *Cookies* generated during past interactions with the ratee, the LTM of the rater has to first calculate the trustworthiness using the rater's *Cookies* as direct experience, and then calculate the trustworthiness using the ratee's *Cookies* as indirect

opinion. In the end, the weighted sum of the direct experience and the indirect opinion will be the final trust value of the ratee.

Table 1. Attributes of *Cookies*

Rater ID	Unique identity of the rater
Ratee ID	Unique identity of the ratee
Relationship	The relationship between the rater and the ratee
Time	When the *Cookie* is generated and the a *Cookie* will become invalid over a certain period of time
Transaction number	The number of transactions between two nodes
Feedback value	The quality of the transaction

3.2 Trust Model

The proposed model is similar to the subjective model proposed by Nitti et al. [10] for SIoT. But their subjective model is not suitable to be applied in SIoV directly. In our trust model, we change the storage from rater-based to ratee-based and modify some factors to adjust the ephemeral nature of vehicular networks. The notations of our model are defined as follows.

In our model, the set of objects is $O = \{o_1, ..., o_i, ..., o_m\}$ with cardinality m, which includes both OBUs and RSUs, because RSUs can be considered as static nodes with high credibility. The vehicular network is described by an undirected graph $G = \{O, E\}$, where $E \subseteq \{O \times O\}$ is the set of edges, each of which represents a social relationship between the set of nodes. Let $S_i = \{o_j \in O : o_i, o_j \in E\}$ be the set of nodes who has a relationship with o_i, and $Q_{ij} = \{o_k \in O : o_k \in S_i \cap S_j\}$ be the set of common friends between o_i and o_j. Let $P^i = \{p_1^i, ...p_j^i, ..., p_n^i\} \subseteq O$ represent the set of objects from whom o_i received *Cookies*, and the cardinality is n.

We identify four major factors to estimate trust value described as follows.

1. *Cookies Number*: The number of *Cookies* received by node o_i, indicated by N_i. In addition, a node o_i is not allowed to receive more than one *Cookies* from node o_j, so it will keep the latest *Cookie* delivered by o_j. This can prevent N_i from unlimited growth, and higher N_i means more credible node o_i is.

2. *Relationship Factor R_{ij}*: R_{ij} indicates a measure of the relationship between node o_i and node o_j, which is a unique characteristic of the SIoT. This factor is related to the relationship value and the number of interactions between two nodes. We sign different values to each relationship respectively, as shown in Table 2. The basic idea of *Relationship Factor* is that as interaction number grows, the closer friends are more reliable. So we define that R_{ij} is calculated as follows:

$$R_{ij} = -1/e^{\varepsilon \times N_{interaction}} + 1 \tag{1}$$

where ε is the relationship value according to Table 2, and $N_{interaction}$ is interaction number between o_i and o_j. As interaction number grows, the value of R_{ij} will infinitely approach to 1 and the growth rate will become slower.

3. *Object Type*: In our model, we only consider two types of objects, OBUs and RSUs. Compared with OBUs, RSUs are static and the quantity is smaller. Furthermore, it is assumed that RSUs are more credible than OBUs, because of the general idea that RSUs are under strict control. So we assign different weights to OBUs and RSUs as 0.5 and 0.8 respectively when counting trust.

4. *Centrality*: The *Centrality* ($Central_{ij}$) of node o_i represents how much node o_j is central to node o_i. This factor helps prevent malicious nodes that build up many relationships to raise their trust value. The defination of $Central_{ij}$ is as follows.

$$Central_{ij} = |Q_{ij}|/(S_i - 1) \tag{2}$$

The general idea is that if two nodes have few friends in common, the impact of o_j to o_i is little, even though o_j has a lot of friends.

Table 2. Parameters for different relationships

Social object relationship	SOR	0.5
Parental object relationship	POR	0.6
Co-work object relationship	CWOR	0.8

3.3 Ratee-Based Trust Management

Different from most existing trust models, our model is ratee-based, where trust information about the quality of a transaction (*Cookies*) from the rater is stored both in the local storage of the ratee and the rater. This is to cope with sparsity because *Cookies* from others is easy to accumulate. If the rater has never interacted with the ratee, the trustworthiness only relies on the ratee's *Cookies* (direct experience). If the rater has stored the *Cookies* generated during past interactions with the ratee, the rater has to first compute the trustworthiness using the rater's *Cookies* as direct experience, and then compute the trustworthiness using the ratee's *Cookies* as indirect opinion. In the end, the weighted sum of the direct experience and the indirect opinion will be the final trust value of the ratee. When a interaction between node o_i and o_j happens, for example, o_i is the requester and o_j is the provider. o_j delivers the set of *Cookies* to o_i to show its credibility.

The trustworthiness of o_i toward o_j (T_{ij}) is computed as follows,

$$T_{ij} = (1 - \alpha - \beta)Central_{ij} + \alpha\varphi_{ij}^{dir} + \beta\phi_{ij}^{ind} \tag{3}$$

where φ_{ij}^{dir} and ϕ_{ij}^{ind} are direct experience toward the provider and indirect opinion from others respectively. α and β are the weights assigned to φ_{ij}^{dir} and $\beta\phi_{ij}^{ind}$

respectively. The computation of φ_{ij}^{dir} is based on the *Cookies* that are feedbacks to o_j and are stored in o_i locally. We assume that the set of *Cookies* are valid (means they are within a certain period of time), and the φ_{ij}^{dir} is computed as follows,

$$\varphi_{ij}^{dir} = \frac{\log(n+1)}{1+\log(n+1)} \times \sum_{k=1}^{n} f_{ij}^k + \frac{R_{ij}}{1+\log(n+1)} \tag{4}$$

where f_{ij}^k represents the kth feedback value from o_i to o_j. The algorithm for direct trust is shown in Algorithm 1.

Algorithm 1. Direct Trust Algorithm

Input: the set of *Cookies* C^i, the number of *Cookies* n, relationship value ε_{ij}
Output: direct trust value φ_{ij}^{dir}
1 $\varphi_{ij}^{dir} = 0$;
2 $sumFeedback = 0$;
3 $R_{ij} = -1/e^{\varepsilon_{ij} \times n} + 1$;
4 **for** $j \leftarrow 1$ **to** n **do**
5 | $sumFeedback += C_j^i.feedbackValue$;
6 $\varphi_{ij}^{dir} = \frac{\log(n+1)}{1+\log(n+1)} \times sumFeedback + \frac{R_{ij}}{1+\log(n+1)}$;

Indirect trust ϕ_{ij}^{ind} is computed based on the *Cookies* received from o_j. The raters of each *Cookie* can be regarded as recommenders to o_i. So the direct trust value from o_i toward each recommenders should be firstly calculated as Algorithm 1. Secondly, the direct trust value from recommenders toward o_j is computed, but the algorithm is not the same as Algorithm 1, because the relationship between recommenders and o_j should not be considered in case the bias of close friends. The ϕ_{ij}^{ind} is computed as follows.

$$\phi_{ij}^{ind} = \sum_{k=1}^{n} \left(\varphi_{kj}^{dir} \right) \bigg/ \sum_{k=1}^{n} \left(\varphi_{ik}^{dir} \right) \tag{5}$$

The algorithm for indirect trust is shown in Algorithm 2.

Parameter α and β are to tune the tradeoff between direct experience vs. indirect opinion when counting T_{ij}. In our model, we allow the weight ratios α and β to be adjusted dynamically by users in response to changing network conditions.

4   Simulations

Due to the dearth of platforms available for simulating trust management in vehicular networks, we built a V2V/V2I trust simulator as an extension to the open source VANET simulator called VANETsim [13]. The map we choose in our

Algorithm 2. Indirect Trust Algorithm

Input: the set of *Cookies* C^j, the number of *Cookies* n, relationship value ε,
relation list L_i of o_i

Output: indirect trust value ϕ_{ij}^{indir}

1   $\phi_{ij}^{indir} = 0;$

2   $sumTrust_{ik} = 0;$

3   $sumTrust_{kj} = 0;$

4   $sumFeedback_{kj} = 0;$

5   **for** $i \leftarrow 1$ **to** n **do**

6   *define* k *is the rater of* $C_i^j;$

7   **if** $C_i^j.raterID$ *in* L_i **then**

8   compute φ_{ik}^{dir} *as Algorithm 1*;

9   **else**

10   *assign a certain value to* φ_{ik}^{dir}

11      $sumTrust_{ik} += \varphi_{ik}^{dir};$

12      $sumFeedback_{kj} += C_i^j.feedbackValue;$

13   $sumTrust_{kj} = \frac{\log(n+1) \times sumFeedback_{kj}}{1+\log(n+1)};$

14   $\phi_{ij}^{indir} = sumTrust_{kj}/sumTrust_{ik};$

---

experiment is Berlin city, and the screenshot of the scenario is shown in Fig. 2, where 1000 vehicles and 100 RSUs are simulated and showed as black dots and green dots respectively. The vehicles are generated randomly with the properties listed in Table 3, and RSUs are distributed evenly aside lanes. Parameter α and β are set to 0.8 and 0.2 respectively to against bad-mouthing attack. At the start of the simulation, 100 of the vehicles are randomly selected to have a certain relationship with each other. Because of the limit of the platform, CA server is not considered in our simulation, so the experiment is based on the belief that the *Cookies* will not be tampered.

Table 3. Properties of vehicles

Min. speed	km/h	100
Max. speed	km/h	200
Acceleration rate	cm/s^2	300
Braking rate	cm/s^2	800
Communication range	m	100
Vehicle length	cm	600
Communication interval	ms	1000

The main advantage of the RTM is the capability with sparsity. Because of the distributed storage of *Cookies*, every piece of interaction information can be used as trust element to estimate trustworthiness. New comers can instantly get

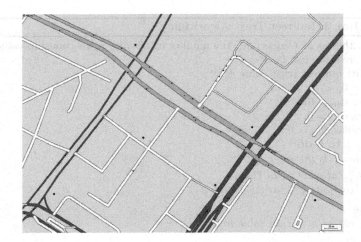

Fig. 2. The simulation of the scenario of Berlin city with 1000 vehicles and 100 RSUs (Color figure online)

services from the network and establish trust with the provider based on their *Cookies*. We run several simulations to evaluate our system comparing with the rater-based trust management, and detailed results and analysis regarding interaction growth and success rate will be presented.

5   Results and Discussion

5.1   Transaction Number Growth

In the simulation, we record the number of interactions between vehicles during 10 h, and the interaction growth in each hour of both methods are calculated. The results are depicted in Fig. 3. In the first hour, the increase of transaction number of both methods are slow and rater-based method is slower. This is because in the initial state of the network, few nodes are related and the interaction information needs time to accumulate to estimate trust. During the rest of the time, the transaction number of rater-based method grows fast and peaks at more than 2000 transactions in the 4th hour, while merely less than 400 transaction growth observed in the rater-based method. It is after the 7th hour that the growth of the rater-based method began to accelerate, but the number is still about 500 less than that of the ratee-based method.

Experimental results illustrate that in ratee-based method, every *Cookie* can be used to estimate trust instantly after generation. With more interactions, the accumulation of *Cookies* will accelerate. In contrast, rater-based method can not guarantee every information produced in interactions will be used in the next time, so the interaction number grows slower than the ratee-based method. After a period of time, the growth of transaction number will fluctuate in a balanced state.

5.2   Transaction Success Rate

We define the malicious nodes as nodes that provide misleading information when providing services and inaccurate feedback *Cookies* when rating services. In this experiment, the percentage of malicious nodes (denoted by mp) is set to 10%, 20%, 30%, and 40% respectively. The purpose of this experiment is to

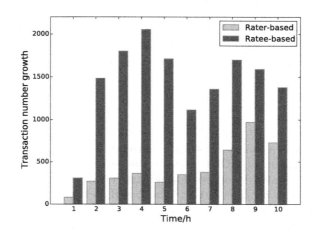

Fig. 3. Transaction number growth in each hour

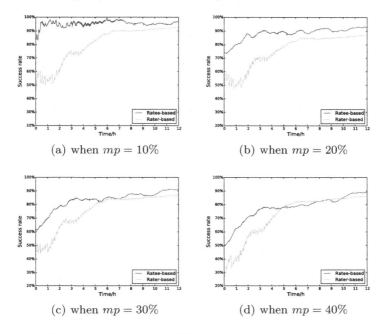

(a) when $mp = 10\%$ (b) when $mp = 20\%$

(c) when $mp = 30\%$ (d) when $mp = 40\%$

Fig. 4. Success rate at different malicious percentage

analyze how transaction success rate of our method grows at different malicious scenarios. Figure 4 shows the results.

Experimental results demonstrate that the ratee-based method has a faster convergence and a higher success rate after convergence. In Fig. 4(a), when $mp = 10\%$ the time of convergence of the ratee-based method is only half an hour, while in the rater-based method, the time is more than 6 h. We note that as mp grows, the success rate of both ratee-based and rater-based methods decrease since the estimation of trust value is profoundly influenced by malicious feedback. Furthermore, the retee-based method is more sensitive to malicious nodes, because when a good node gets enough feedback from malicious nodes, it is difficult for the node to get more *Cookies* from others to recover its reputation until bad *Cookies* expire.

6   Conclusions

In this paper, we focus on the trust issue in the social IoV by proposing a Ratee-based Trust Management (RTM) system, where each node stores its own reputation information rated by others during past transactions. In RTM, each node estimates the service provider's trust value based on the social relationship with the provider, and the provider's *Cookies*, which are generated during past interactions. By establishing the social relationship shared between the requester and the provider, the trustworthiness of the provider is more accurate. We validated our system by implementing a trust simulator as an extension to an open source VANET simulator. Experimental results demonstrate that compared with the rater-based method, the proposed ratee-based method has a faster convergence and higher transaction success rate. As for future work, we will introduce intrusion detect technologies into our system to prevent the network from external attacks.

Acknowledgments. This work is supported by the National Science Foundation of China under Grants Nos. 61272010 and 61572514.

References

1. Atzori, L., Iera, A., Morabito, G.: Siot: giving a social structure to the internet of things. IEEE Commun. Lett. **15**(11), 1193–1195 (2011)
2. Buchegger, S., Boudec, J.Y.L.: Performance analysis of the CONFIDANT protocol. In: ACM Interational Symposium on Mobile Ad Hoc NETWORKING and Computing, MOBIHOC 2002, Lausanne, Switzerland, 9–11 June 2002, pp. 226–236 (2002)
3. Buchegger, S., Le Boudec, J.-Y.: A robust reputation system for mobile ad-hoc networks. Technical report (2003)
4. Gerla, M., Lee, E.K., Pau, G., Lee, U.: Internet of vehicles: from intelligent grid to autonomous cars and vehicular clouds. In: IEEE World Forum on Internet of Things, pp. 241–246 (2014)

5. Huang, D., Hong, X., Gerla, M.: Situation-aware trust architecture for vehicular networks. IEEE Commun. Mag. **48**(11), 128–135 (2010)
6. Li, W., Joshi, A., Finin, T.: Coping with node misbehaviors in ad hoc networks: a multi-dimensional trust management approach. In: 2010 Eleventh International Conference on Mobile Data Management (MDM), pp. 85–94. IEEE (2010)
7. Li, W., Song, H.: ART: an attack-resistant trust management scheme for securing vehicular ad hoc networks. IEEE Trans. Intell. Transp. Syst. **17**(4), 1–10 (2016)
8. Michiardi, P., Molva, R.: Core: a collaborative reputation mechanism to enforce node cooperation in mobile ad hoc networks. In: Jerman-Blažič, B., Klobučar, T. (eds.) Advanced Communications and Multimedia Security. ITIFIP, vol. 100, pp. 107–121. Springer, Boston, MA (2002). doi:10.1007/978-0-387-35612-9_9
9. Minhas, U.F., Zhang, J., Tran, T., Cohen, R.: Intelligent agents in mobile vehicular ad-hoc networks: leveraging trust modeling based on direct experience with incentives for honesty. In: IEEE/WIC/ACM International Conference on Intelligent Agent Technology, IAT 2010, Toronto, Canada, 31 August–September, pp. 243–247 (2010)
10. Nitti, M., Girau, R., Atzori, L.: Trustworthiness management in the social internet of things. IEEE Trans. Knowl. Data Eng. **26**(5), 1253–1266 (2014)
11. Nitti, M., Girau, R., Floris, A., Atzori, L.: On adding the social dimension to the internet of vehicles: friendship and middleware. In: IEEE International Black Sea Conference on Communications and NETWORKING, pp. 134–138 (2014)
12. Patwardhan, A., Joshi, A., Finin, T., Yesha, Y.: A data intensive reputation management scheme for vehicular ad hoc networks. In: Annual International Conference on Mobile and Ubiquitous Systems, pp. 1–8 (2006)
13. Tomandl, A., Herrmann, D., Fuchs, K.P., Federrath, H.: VANETsim: an open source simulator for security and privacy concepts in VANETs. In: International Conference on High PERFORMANCE Computing and Simulation, pp. 543–550 (2014)
14. Zhang, J.: A survey on trust management for VANETs. In: 2011 IEEE International Conference on Advanced Information Networking and Applications (AINA), pp. 105–112. IEEE (2011)

Achieving Secure and Seamless IP Communications for Group-Oriented Software Defined Vehicular Networks

Chengzhe Lai[1]([✉]), Rongxing Lu[2], and Dong Zheng[1]

[1] National Engineering Laboratory for Wireless Security,
Xi'an University of Posts and Telecommunications, Xi'an 710121, China
`lcz_xupt@163.com`
[2] Faculty of Computer Science, University of New Brunswick,
Fredericton, Canada
`RLU1@unb.ca`

Abstract. Supporting secure and efficient mobility management in heterogeneous vehicular networking is a challenge issue. Most of traditional mobility management schemes suffer from long handover delay and lack mobility support for roaming across various access networks. As a promising new network paradigm, software-defined networks (SDN)-based vehicular networks enables flexible ubiquitous connection and real-time network management with the software controller. However, the existing works still cannot support the emerging group-oriented vehicular environment, such as platoon scenario. Especially, Internet Protocol security (IPsec) and Internet Key Exchange version 2 (IKEv2), which are considered to be used to secure IPv6 Network Mobility (NEMO), face challenge in terms of performance when implementing in the group-oriented vehicular environment. To address these issues, in this paper, a new SDN-enabled VANET-Cellular integrated network architecture is proposed by following the SDN concept, which is based on the Open-Flow (OF) protocol. Then, we introduce a unified secure and seamless IP communications framework for group-oriented heterogeneous vehicular environment. We try to address two major challenges: i.e., (1) how to securely and flexibly set up the platoon, and (2) how to control the handover signalling overload (mainly introduced by group access authentication and IPsec establishment), and reduce handover latency when a large number of platoon members need to securely access the Internet.

Keywords: Software defined vehicular networks · Network Mobility (NEMO) · IPv6 · Security · IPsec

1 Introduction

With the rapid development of information and communication technologies (ICT), equipping vehicles with wireless communication capabilities is expected to be the next frontier for automotive revolution [9]. Especially, the connectivity

© Springer International Publishing AG 2017
L. Ma et al. (Eds.): WASA 2017, LNCS 10251, pp. 356–368, 2017.
DOI: 10.1007/978-3-319-60033-8_32

to the Internet has become an essential part of on-board communication [10]. Currently, IEEE has developed IEEE 802.11p as the main communications standard for vehicular networking, while the emerging 5G cellular networks represent practical and convenient marketing solutions to enable ubiquitous and reliable connections to vehicles.

The media-rich Internet contents delivery for vehicles requires high-rate Internet access but the existing wireless technologies, such as Long Term Evolution (LTE), LTE-Advanced (LTE-A), and Wi-Fi, become the bottleneck because of the explosive growth of data traffic and shortage of spectrum. The 5G wireless systems, with improved data rates, capacity, latency, and QoS is expected to be the promising solution in the near future. Recently, several standards forums and organizations, including the 3rd Generation Partnership Project (3GPP), Huawei, Datang Telecom Technology & Industry Group, etc., have engaged in cellular-assisted V2X communication technology (LTE-V) standard development, which is one of the most potential technology in 5G era.

To ensure more efficient Internet access, the mobility management for IP-based vehicular networks, i.e., the issue of seamless handover, is of great importance for guaranteeing service continuity and quality-of-service (QoS), when vehicles are handed off to another network. At present, vehicular communications standards are developed by different organizations, which means the applied vehicular communication modules are also different. The operating system and hardware are bundled together when they are produced by respective manufacturers. This will increase the complexity of the network, and plenty of network resources may be wasted, leading to low quality of experience (QoE) for vehicle users. In addition, different network operators have their own management policies, which will also increase the difficulty of network management.

As a promising new network paradigm, software-defined networks (SDN)-based vehicular networks [8] enables flexible ubiquitous connection, fast rerouting, and real-time network management with the software controller. One of the main features of SDN is the separation of the control plane and data plane, and centralization of control functions. With a programmable SDN controller, network operators can easily configure new network devices and quickly deploy new applications. With SDN, vehicle users are able to access network services anywhere and anytime regardless of the network type (e.g., Wi-Fi, 3G, LTE, LTE-A) as long as these networks belong to the same operator or there are agreements between operators. Furthermore, security and privacy-related policies are also manageable [1].

To provide seamless handover in heterogeneous networks, 3GPP has discussed basic interworking architectures which is based on mobile IP techniques. Currently, mobile IPv6 (MIPv6) [11] is a widely accepted standard to support global mobility for Mobile Hosts (MHs). However, there are still some important issues failed to resolve in terms of performance and security. In this article, we first review the state of art in mobility management for vehicular networks. Furthermore, we pay attention to another noteworthy issue, i.e., secure IP communications in SDN-based vehicular networks, especially in the group-oriented vehicular environment. At present, Internet Protocol security (IPsec) and Internet Key Exchange version 2 (IKEv2) are considered to be used to secure IPv6 Network Mobility (NEMO). However, this technique faces challenge in terms of performance when implementing in the group-oriented vehicular environment. To address this issue and provide secure IP communications, a new SDN-enabled VANET-Cellular integrated network architecture is proposed by following the SDN concept, which is based on the OpenFlow (OF) protocol. Then, we introduce a unified secure and seamless IP communications framework for group-oriented heterogeneous vehicular environment.

The remainder of this paper is organized as follows. We present the SDN-enabled VANET-Cellular integrated network architecture (SDNVCNET) and introduce the new function of network elements in Sect. 2. We then discuss two major challenges in group-oriented heterogeneous vehicular environment, including secure group setup and seamless IP communications. Furthermore, we propose a unified secure and seamless IP communications framework for group-oriented heterogeneous vehicular environment in Sect. 3. Finally, we conclude this paper in Sect. 4.

2   Network Architecture

Figure 1 shows the SDN-enabled VANET-Cellular integrated network architecture (SDNVCNET). To support SDNVCNET, appropriate SDN protocols, such as OpenFlow and Simple Network Management Protocol (SNMP), will be added to base stations, wireless access points, and other network entities through an external standardized application programming interface (API). OpenFlow is in charge of data path control, and SNMP can be used for IPsec establishment in this article. As the SDN controller is just a program running on a server, it can be placed anywhere in the SDNVCNET.

The SDNVCNET is designed based on the exiting 3GPP LTE/EPC architecture. The access network can mainly be divided into cellular and Non-3GPP access network. To support MIPv6, the base stations (i.e., eNodeBs) or other wireless access points function as mobile access gateways (MAGs) to provide vehicles with wireless access to Internet. Besides access networks, there is a core network. In the core network, the mobility management control (MM-C) plane substitutes the mobility management entity (MME) and communicates with the OpenFlow Controller using API. In our architecture, MM-C is responsible for vehicle authentication and authorization, and intra-3GPP mobility management. Different from MME, the MM-C will not be responsible for the serving gateway (S-GW) and packet data network gateway (P-GW) selection. The S-GW can be separated into S-GW control (SGW-C) plane and S-GW data (SGW-D) plane. SGW-C is responsible for GTP tunnel and IPsec establishment. SGW-D represents an advanced OpenFlow switch (OF-switch) that is able to encapsulate/decapsulate GTP packets. This switch applies the rules received from the OpenFlow Controller. Its responsibility is just packet forwarding between the eNodeBs and P-GW. P-GW still has the same function as in the 3GPP

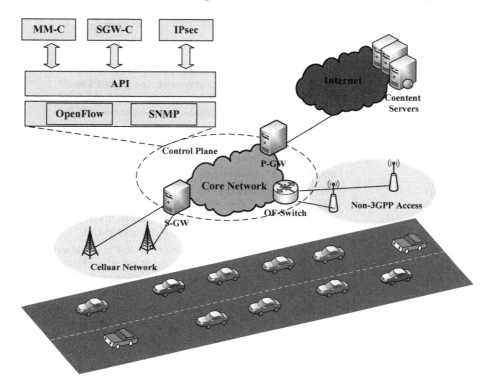

Fig. 1. SDN-enabled VANET-Cellular integrated network architecture

standard and is responsible to act as an "anchor" of mobility between 3GPP and Non-3GPP technologies. Therefore, it plays a role in local mobility anchor (LMA).

In SDNVCNET, vehicles employing LTE-V technology and equipping built-in cellular module can connect to the 3GPP E-UTRAN via the eNodeB. LTE-V can be further divided into two work modes, i.e., LTE-V-Cell for centralized network and LTE-V-Direct for decentralized network. The former is the extension of the existing cellular technology, and designed mainly for the traditional Internet service. The latter introduces the LTE device-to-device (D2D) and realize the vehicle-to-vehicle (V2V) communication. Therefore, the introduction of LTE-V-Direct can meet the requirements of low latency and high reliability among connected vehicles. Moreover, vehicles equipping other wireless communication module can also access the core network via Non-3GPP access network. To provide secure and efficient data transmission, we define the concept of secure mobile gateways. Different from the traditional fixed gateway, a secure mobile gateway refers to the dual-interfaced vehicle that relays data from other vehicle sources to the SDNVCNET backhaul network and makes sure the security during data transmission. The main network elements and function description is summarized in Table 1.

Table 1. Summarizing table of main network elements

Network elements	Function
MM-C	MM-C belongs to the control plane and substitutes MME. MM-C communicates with the OpenFlow Controller using API. It is responsible for vehicle authentication and authorization, and intra-3GPP mobility management
SGW-C	SGW-C belongs to the control plane. SGW-C is separated from S-GW and responsible for GTP tunnel and IPsec establishment
SGW-D	SGW-D is separated from S-GW and represents an advanced OF-switch. SGW-D applies the rules received from OpenFlow Controller. Its responsibility is just packet forwarding between eNodeBs and P-GW
P-GW	P-GW reserves the same function as 3GPP standard and is responsible to act as an "anchor" of mobility between 3GPP and Non-3GPP technologies. In fact, it plays a role in LMA
Dual-interfaced vehicle	Dual-interfaced vehicle is a secure mobile gateway that is different from traditional fixed gateway. It relays data from other vehicle sources to the SDNVCNET backhaul network and makes sure the security during data transmission

3 Secure and Seamless IP Communications for Group-Oriented Vehicular Environment

Platooning is one of emerging automotive intelligent transportation systems (ITS) applications [12]. In a platoon situation, the platoon leader can be aware of the kinematic state of the platoon members in real time for monitoring purposes. There two major challenges for such a group-oriented vehicular environment, i.e., (1) how securely and flexibly set up the platoon, and (2) how to control the handover signalling overload (mainly introduced by group access authentication and IPsec establishment), and reduce handover latency when a large number of platoon members need to securely access the Internet.

3.1 Secure Group Setup

In the platoon situation, a group of vehicles sharing a similar itinerary over a period of time form a vehicle fleet train, coordinated by a platoon leader. The platoon leader may coordinate with platoon members for group maneuvering, such as platoon joining/leaving/group speed. In this situation, the platoon-based driving pattern facilitates the potential cooperative communication applications, for example, data sharing or forwarding, and may significantly improve the performance of vehicular networking. However, the members of the platoon may

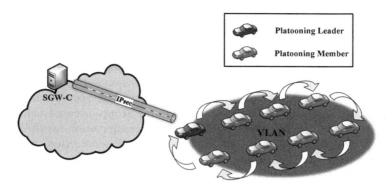

Fig. 2. Group-oriented vehicular environment

change quite dynamically, and vehicles may join or leave the platoon at any time. Therefore, how to securely create and maintain a group is a challenge issue.

As shown in Fig. 2, all of vehicles in the platoon form a vehicular local area network (VLAN). In the VLAN, all members need to negotiate a key to ensure securely group communication. Although the platoon leader can act as the group founder and key distribution server in the VLAN, such a canalized method may tend to be both expensive and unexpectedly complex and is not suitable for dynamic peer group settings. Therefore, the distributed key agreement technique is required. Contributory group key agreement protocols can generate group keys based on contributions of all group members and this technique can be the building block of secure group setup. We have proposed a contributory key agreement-based framework (SPGS) [7] by adopting the scheme [5].

The SPGS can support the following operations in the platoon situation, including *Platoon Joining*: a new platoon member can be added to the group with privacy-preserving attribute matching; *Platoon Leaving*: a platoon member can be removed from the group; *Platoon Merging*: an emerging group of vehicles want to be added to the group; *Platoon Partition*: a subgroup is split from the group; *Key Refresh*: the group key should be updated duly.

Once a platoon is securely established and maintained, all members can cooperatively access the Internet for various communication applications in this platoon-based driving pattern. Accordingly, another critical challenge is emerging, i.e., secure and efficient mobility management for IP communications in group-oriented vehicular environment.

3.2 Secure and Seamless IP Communications

It is well known that in the mobility management for IP-based vehicular networks, the issue of seamless handover is of great importance for guaranteeing service continuity and QoS, when a automobile is handed off to another network. In addition, in heterogeneous networks, the access authentication is the crucial procedure for ensuring secure communication. Unfortunately, most of mobile IPv6 protocols operate only in layer 3 (L3) and do not consider the authentication process, yet the authentication procedure is essential and induces large latency during handover. Therefore, the handover method must take into account network characteristics and support effective performance regarding delay and packet loss during handover. Meanwhile, as the candidate secure scheme for IP communications, original IPsec is not suitable for group-oriented vehicle environment because of the large communication and computation overhead.

When a group of vehicles want to access the Internet, they firstly need to securely access the E-UTRAN and should send their access authentication requests toward the core network successively over a short period, or even at the same time. Furthermore, they must establish the secure tunnels with the core network by utilizing IPsec. These operations will lead to communication and computation burden in the different nodes of the network, across the communication path, which includes

Radio Network Overload: Radio network overload takes place in some applications because of mass concurrent access authentication requests. In addition, IPsec establishment process also induces large communication overhead. The network should be optimized to enable a mass of vehicles in a particular area to access the network and transmit data almost simultaneously.

Core Network Overload: Access authentication and IPsec establishment signalling overload in the core network is caused by a high number of vehicles trying almost simultaneously: (1) to attach to the network or (2) to activate/modify/deactivate a connection.

3.2.1   Group-Oriented Access Authentication

According to the discussion in the above section, group-oriented access authentication on alleviating security-related signaling overload is desired. Unfortunately, the recent authentication and key agreement (AKA) protocols dedicated for 3GPP cellular network, known as EPS-AKA; or for non-3GPP access networks (e.g., WLAN or WiMAX), known as EAP-AKA cannot provide group authentication mechanism [6]. If a group of vehicles in a platoon need to access the network almost simultaneously, the traditional authentication protocols (e.g., EPS-AKA or EAP-AKA) will suffer from high signalling overhead, leading to authentication signaling congestion and decreasing the QoS of the network. The reason is that every vehicle must perform a full AKA authentication procedure with the core network, respectively.

By utilizing the identity-based aggregate signature (IBGS) technique [3], the group-oriented access authentication can be proposed. In an aggregate signature scheme, multiple signatures can be aggregated into a compact "aggregate signature" even if these signatures are on (many) different documents and were produced by (many) different signers. Particularly, in IBGS, the verifier does not need to obtain and/or store various signer public keys to verify; instead, the verifier only needs a description of who signed what, along with two constant-length "tags": i.e., the short aggregate signature and the single public key of a Private Key Generator (PKG). Therefore, IBGS is suitable for vehicular networks.

When each vehicle registers with the core network, it contacts the PKG, provides its identity, and then receives its private key. Only the authenticated vehicle user can get the private keys from the PKG. The PKG can be integrated with the authentication server, which has pre-established secure channels with the MM-C plane by using the NDS/IP security mechanism. By adopting the IBGS, the platoon leader can collect all signatures of members in the same group and aggregate them to a new signature SIG_{agg}. Then, the platoon leader sends SIG_{agg} to the network and all members in the group can be authenticated at the same time. Moreover, the independent session key can be negotiated between the core network and each platoon member. Therefore, this scheme can relief the authentication signalling overload occurring at the network nodes significantly.

3.2.2 Secure and Seamless IP Communications Framework

As discussed above, original IPsec is not suitable for group-oriented vehicle environment. Therefore, we appropriately modify the packet structure in IPsec tunnel mode, as shown in Fig. 3.

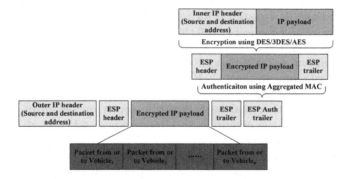

Fig. 3. Modified packet structure in IPsec tunnel mode

In the proposed framework (Fig. 2), all of vehicles in the platoon have formed a VLAN, which is a private network. In VLAN, each platoon member has an inner IP address and unique identity (UID) that form a private addressing identifier (PAI). As everyone knows, in the Internet addressing architecture, a private network is a network that uses private IP address space, following the standards set by RFC 1918 for IPv4, and RFC 4193 for IPv6. Private IP address spaces were originally defined in an effort to delay IPv4 address exhaustion, but they are also a feature of IPv6 addresses for security purpose. Therefore, PAIs do not need to be allocated by any specific organization and platoon members can use these addresses without approval from a regional Internet registry. However, IP packets addressed from them cannot be transmitted through the public Internet, and if VLAN needs to connect to the Internet, it must do so via a network address translator (NAT) gateway, i.e., the platoon leader in our framework. That is, the platoon leader should have a public IP address for Internet access.

When platoon members want to send or receive data to/from Internet, they first need communicate with the platoon leader. At that moment, the platoon leader plays a role in secure mobile gateways to provide secure and efficient data transmission for other platoon members. Taking an example of sending data, each platoon member generates their own packet with inner IP header, i.e., PAI. Then, they send the encrypted packets to the platoon leader by using the group key (DES/3DES/AES). The platoon leader collects all encrypted packets of platoon members and assembles them in sequence to form an entire IP payload, as in Fig. 3. The IP payload is then encapsulated into a new IP packet with a new outer IP header. For authenticating the IP packet, an ESP Auth trailer needs to be added to the IP packet. To reduce the authentication overhead, the aggregate message authentication code technique can be applied.

When IP layer (L3) handover occurs, both the access authentication and IPsec tunnel establishment should be optimized simultaneously. We can adopt the proposed group access authentication running within IKEv2 between the platoon leader and the SGW-C plane for authentication and key agreement. At the same time, L3 handover process should be performed. In this article, the SDN concept of logically centralized control can be implemented in PMIPv6 through OpenFlow. For instance, in reference [4], the controller resides in the backbone network and connects to all the gateways and the anchor. The gateways implement the OpenFlow protocol, upon which the controller communicates with them. An OpenFlow mobile access gateway (OMAG) notifies the controller about a automobile attachment through PMIPv6 control message in the OpenFlow protocol, and the controller performs all the PMIPv6 related mobility control signaling with the anchor and authentication server on behalf of the OMAG. Theoretically, most of the extension and improvement schemes of PMIPv6 can be applied in our framework.

The complete procedure of a platoon handing off from Non-3GPP access network to eNodeB is presented in Fig. 4, which can be divided broadly into two phases: Phase 1: Secure Group Setup and Packets Aggregation and Phase 2: Group-oriented L2/L3 Joint Handover and Secure Tunnel Establishment. In Phase 1, the secure group setup is performed by using contributory group key agreement, and all platoon members share a group key (GK). After that, all vehicles are driving in the form of platoon. When they want to access the Internet, each platoon member generates their own encrypted packet C_i and the corresponding signature σ_i, and sends them to the platoon leader. By adopting the IBGS, the platoon leader can collect all signatures of members in the same group and aggregate them to a new signature SIG_{agg} for next access authentication. In Phase 2, when IP layer (L3) handover occurs, the pre-authentication mechanism should be adopted for reducing the handover latency, i.e., the group access authentication is performed prior to L2 and L3 handover. In addition, the PMIPv6-based L3 handover procedure needs to be carried out. As introduced in [2], every time IPsec requests the IKEv2 daemon running on top of OF controller

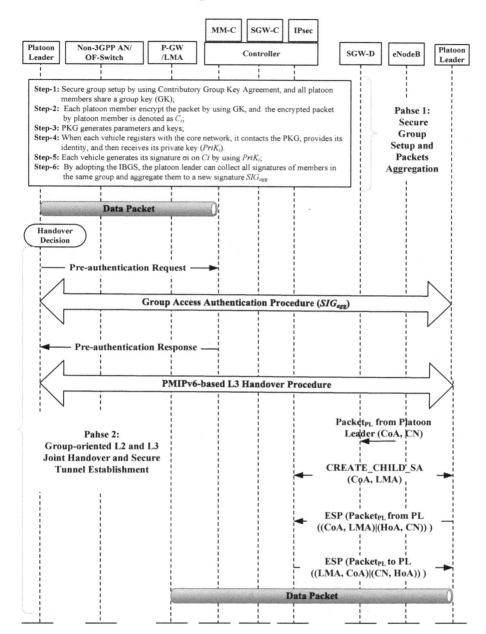

Fig. 4. The procedure of a platoon handing off from Non-3GPP access network to eNodeB

for a new SA. In order to protect the required IKEv2 negotiation, a dedicated security association for IKEv2 messages has to be established before. This association is called "IKE Security Association" (IKE_ SA), which is established in the first and non protected exchange called "IKE SA Initiation (IKE_SA_INIT). This is the initial mobility and security bootstrap. Next, IKEv2 negotiation for creating IPsec associations to protect data traffic during handover is presented in Fig. 4. The procedure of a platoon handing off from eNodeB to Non-3GPP access network is basically same as the procedure in Fig. 4 since the proposed framework is unified.

3.3   Performance Evaluation

In this section, we evaluate the performance of the proposed framework in terms of the average handover signalling cost and average handover latency. The proposed framework enables the platoon leader to aggregate a collection of each member's signatures in the same group. In addition, we appropriately modified the packet structure in IPsec tunnel mode, which can reduce the overhead of ESP Auth trailer by adopting the aggregate message authentication code. When IP layer (L3) handover occurs, the pre-authentication mechanism is adopted for reducing the handover latency, i.e., the group access authentication is performed prior to L2 and L3 handover. Therefore, it largely reduces the average handover signalling cost and average handover latency.

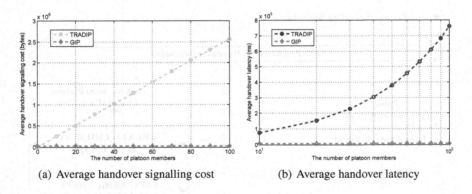

(a) Average handover signalling cost   (b) Average handover latency

Fig. 5. Performance comparison between TRADIP and GIP

In the following, for the comparison with our proposed framework, we consider two types of existing IP-based handover authentication schemes, one is traditional scheme, denoted by TRADIP, where each vehicle needs to perform a complete authentication procedure with the access networks, respectively, and L2 and L3 handover are separated; the other one is our proposed scheme, denoted by GIP. We assume that there are n vehicles forming in the platoon. Parts of the parameter values are referred to the papers [2,6]. The total signaling cost C_{HO} can be calculated as $C_{HO} = C_{ho} + C_{AUTH} + C_{IPsec}$, where C_{ho} is average cost needed for L3 handover, C_{AUTH} is average cost needed for access authentication and C_{IPsec} is average cost needed for IPsec establishment. The average length of the signature is set to be 160 bits.

The total handover latency T_{HO} can be calculated as $T_{HO} = T_{ho} + T_{L2HO} + T_{AUTH} + T_{IPsec}$, where T_{ho} is average required time for L3 handover and T_{L2HO} is average time needed for L2 handover; T_{AUTH} is average time needed for access authentication and T_{IPsec} is IPsec establishment time. The average time needed for L2 handover is set to be 20 ms. The average time needed for L3 handover is set to be 52 ms in the proposed framework and 1000 ms in traditional schemes.

Figure 5 shows the comparison between TRADIP and GIP in terms of average handover signalling cost and average handover latency.

4 Conclusion

In this paper, we have investigated the secure and seamless IP communications in the SDN-enabled VANET-Cellular integrated network architecture (SDNVC-NET), especially for supporting the emerging group-oriented vehicular environment, such as platoon scenario. We first presented a new SDN-enabled VANET-Cellular integrated network architecture by following the SDN concept, which is based on the OF protocol. Then, we proposed a unified secure and seamless IP communications framework for group-oriented heterogeneous vehicular environment, which aims to address two major challenges: i.e., (1) how to securely and flexibly set up the platoon, and (2) how to control the handover signalling overload (mainly introduced by group access authentication and IPsec establishment), and reduce handover latency when a large number of platoon members need to securely access the Internet. For the challenge 1, the secure group setup is performed by using contributory group key agreement, and all platoon members share a group key (GK). By adopting the IBGS, the platoon leader can collect all signatures of members in the same group and aggregate them to a new signature SIG_{agg} for next access authentication. For the challenge 2, we appropriately modified the packet structure in IPsec tunnel mode, which can reduce the overhead of ESP Auth trailer by adopting the aggregate message authentication code. When IP layer (L3) handover occurs, the pre-authentication mechanism is adopted for reducing the handover latency, i.e., the group access authentication is performed prior to L2 and L3 handover. In addition, the most of PMIPv6-based L3 handover procedure can be applied to our framework.

Acknowledgments. Our research is supported by the National Natural Science Foundation of China Research Grant (61502386, 61472472), and the International Science and Technology Cooperation and Exchange Plan in Shaanxi Province of China (2015KW-010).

References

1. Duan, X., Wang, X.: Authentication handover and privacy protection in 5G hetnets using software-defined networking. IEEE Commun. Mag. **53**(4), 28–35 (2015)

2. Fernandez, P., Santa, J., Bernal, F., Gomez-Skarmeta, A.: Securing vehicular IPv6 communications. IEEE Trans. Dependable Secure Comput. **13**(1), 46–58 (2016)
3. Gentry, C., Ramzan, Z.: Identity-based aggregate signatures. In: Yung, M., Dodis, Y., Kiayias, A., Malkin, T. (eds.) PKC 2006. LNCS, vol. 3958, pp. 257–273. Springer, Heidelberg (2006). doi:10.1007/11745853_17
4. Kim, M.S., Lee, S.K.: Enhanced network mobility management for vehicular networks. IEEE Trans. Intell. Transp. Syst. **17**(5), 1329–1340 (2016)
5. Kim, Y., Perrig, A., Tsudik, G.: Simple and fault-tolerant key agreement for dynamic collaborative groups. In: Proceedings of ACM CCS, pp. 235–244 (2000)
6. Lai, C., Lu, R., Zheng, D., Li, H.: Toward secure large-scale machine-to-machine comm unications in 3GPP networks: challenges and solutions. IEEE Commun. Mag. **53**(12), 12–19 (2015)
7. Lai, C., Lu, R., Zheng, D.: SPGS: a secure and privacy-preserving group setup framework for platoon-based vehicular cyber-physical systems. Secur. Commun. Netw. **9**(16), 3854–3867 (2016)
8. Liu, K., Ng, J.K.Y., Lee, V.C.S., Sang, H.S.: Cooperative data scheduling in hybrid vehicular ad hoc networks: VANET as a software defined network. IEEE/ACM Trans. Netw. **24**(3), 1759–1773 (2016)
9. Lu, N., Cheng, N., Zhang, N., Shen, X.: Connected vehicles: solutions and challenges. IEEE Internet Things J. **1**(4), 289–299 (2014)
10. Luan, T.H., Ling, X., Shen, X.: MAC in motion: impact of mobility on the MAC of drive-thru internet. IEEE Trans. Mob. Comput. **11**(2), 305–319 (2012)
11. Perkins, C.E., Johnson, D.B.: Mobility Support in IPv6. RFC 3775 (2001)
12. Vinel, A., Lan, L., Lyamin, N.: Vehicle-to-vehicle communication in C-ACC/platooning scenarios. IEEE Commun. Mag. **53**(8), 192–197 (2015)

An Efficient Distributed Randomized Data Replication Algorithm in VANETs

Junyu Zhu[1,2], Chuanhe Huang[1,2(✉)], Xiying Fan[1,2], and Bin Fu[3]

[1] State Key Lab of Software Engineering,
Computer School, Wuhan University, Wuhan 430072, China
[2] Collaborative Innovation Center of Geospatial Technology,
Wuhan University, Wuhan 430072, China
huangch@whu.edu.cn
[3] Department of Computer Science,
The University of Texas Rio Grande Valley, Edinburg, TX 78539, USA
bin.fu@utrgv.edu

Abstract. Motivated by message delivery in vehicular ad hoc networks, we study distributed data replication algorithms for information delivery in a special completely connected network. To improve the efficiency of data dissemination, the number of message copies that can be spread is controlled and a distributed randomized data replication algorithm is proposed. The key idea is to let the data carrier distribute the data dissemination tasks to multiple nodes to speed up the dissemination process. We show how the network converges and prove that the network can enter into a balanced status in a small number of stages. Most of the theoretical results described in this paper are to study the complexity of network convergence. Simulation results show that the proposed algorithm can disseminate data to a specific area with low delay.

Keywords: Data replication · Randomized · Complexity of convergence · VANET

1 Introduction

Vehicular ad hoc networks (VANETs) have become an important area of research with potential applications in various domains such as safety, navigational applications, in-vehicle infotainment etc. [1]. Lots of researches have been done on safety and comfort purposes of VANETs. Efficient data dissemination is essential for such applications, which require that data can be delivered with high success rate and low delay. Data replication has been recognized as an effective approach for data dissemination in VANETs [2]. Data replication enables multiple copies of the same data carried by different nodes to be transmitted to most

C. Huang—This work is supported by the National Science Foundation of China (Nos. 61373040, 61173137), by National Science Foundation Early Career Award 0845376 and Bensten Fellowship of the University of Texas - Rio Grande Valley.

© Springer International Publishing AG 2017
L. Ma et al. (Eds.): WASA 2017, LNCS 10251, pp. 369–380, 2017.
DOI: 10.1007/978-3-319-60033-8_33

of the nodes in the network. Thus, useful data will be distributed to a specific area in a quick manner [3].

Moreover, as emerging large-scale ad hoc networks are characterized by the lack of centralized access to information and control, distributed coordination and consensus problems are fundamental problems in ad hoc network applications [4]. Motivated by these problems, distributed algorithms are designed, in which agents can reach consensus on a common decision or achieve a global objective collectively [5]. The problems also arise in a number of applications including information delivery in vehicular ad hoc networks. This paper focuses on the randomized average consensus problem as well as studies the data replication algorithms [6].

1.1 Primary Motivations

Dynamic data replication in distributed network systems can accelerate information spread in a specific area. However, some algorithms, such as epidemic and gossip algorithms, could cause significant network overhead by essentially passing around redundant information multiple times. The redundant messages can also cause congestion issues. Aiming at the problem, this paper proposes a data replication scheme, in which the number of message copies is bounded, to reduce unnecessary transmissions. Data replication algorithms also improve upon the convergence speed of message transmission by increasing the diversity of pairwise exchanges. As load balancing is an important goal in ad hoc networks, we hope every node in the network can carry an approximately equal number of message copies. In this way, the data delivery and network computing burden will be distributed among the nodes and communication can be managed in a very quick and efficient way.

1.2 Main Contributions

To overcome the drawbacks of the data replication algorithms, we propose two conceptions: bounded number of copies and balanced network status. In this paper, according to the network traffic density, based on graph theory, we divide the VANET topology into three types of graphs: linear graph, arbitrary graph and complete graph. In this paper, we propose a distributed randomized algorithm for one certain type of graph, complete graph. We measure the complexity of convergence by the number of communication stages in a distributed computing environment. In each stage, every node is involved in at most one message transmission. If a network can enter into a balanced status in a small number of stages, it can improve the efficiency of message passing. Following the algorithms, the paper provides mathematical analysis of the proposed randomized algorithm. It shows how the network converges.

The rest of this paper is organized as follows. Section 2 overviews the related work. Section 3 describes some definitions used in the paper. In Sect. 4, we propose a randomized algorithm for complete graph in VANET. Section 5 gives some theoretical analysis of the proposed algorithm. Section 6 presents the simulation results. Finally, Sect. 7 concludes the paper.

2   Related Work

In this section, we give an overview of the related work. First, we review on the data replication algorithms in vehicular network, then discuss existing studies about randomized average consensus problem.

As broadcast is the basic mechanism of VANET communication, flooding is the most common method in data dissemination. While it can achieve the maximum coverage and rapid data dissemination, flooding can cause broadcast storm. In epidemic routing [7], two nodes exchanged the data that they didn't hold whenever they met. Yang et al. [8] first challenged the accuracy of the innovative assumption that is widely adopted in delay performance analysis of network-coding-based epidemic routing in delay-tolerant networks. Some algorithms delivered data packets with control on the replication rules. Balasubramanian et al. [9] proposed RAPID. RAPID explicitly calculated the effect of replication on the routing metric while considered resource constraints. To exploit constrained network capacity with data replication, Wu et al. [10] proposed a capacity-constrained replication scheme for data delivery. The authors explored the residual network capacity for data replication and designed a distributed algorithm. [11] designed the data dissemination to a desired number of receivers in VANET scheme, which was inspired by processor scheduling treating roads as processors to optimize the workload assignment.

Randomized average consensus gossiping is an asynchronous protocol where a node contacts a neighbor randomly within its connectivity radius, and exchanges a state variable to produce a computation update. Wu and Rabbat [12] proposed and analyzed a family of broadcast gossip algorithms for strongly connected directed graphs, which were guaranteed to converge to the average consensus. In [13], the authors analyzed the averaging problem under the gossip constraint for an arbitrary network graph. [14] proved that the random consensus value was the average of initial node measurements and that it could be made arbitrarily close to this value in mean squared error sense under a balanced connectivity model. Fabio and Sandro [15] allowed to reach consensus in a point which may be different from the average of the initial states. Nedic and Liu [16] proposed an algorithm for finite time distributed averaging in the case of a ring network of agents, subject to a gossip constraint on communications. Falsone et al. [17] investigated the properties of the weighted-averaging dynamic for consensus problem and established new convergence rate results related to the diameters of weakly spanning trees contained in the given graphs.

3   Definitions and Models

An ϵ-balanced status (See Definition 3) will be obtained after a series of average operations. We define some concepts in this section.

When a node carries message M and it controls at most a copies of message M to be distributed over a network, it must have $a \geq 1$, and each node with nonzero value is at least one. The total number of message copies is bounded by parameter n.

We need to define the concept of potential in order to analyze the number of stages for the system to enter into a balanced status, and need the following lemma.

Definition 1. *For a set of vehicles, their connected graph is an undirected graph $G(V, E)$ such that each node represents a vehicle and an edge between two nodes indicates that the corresponding vehicles are within the distance of communication. We consider $G(V, E)$ constructed in a high traffic density, such as a parking lot. Assume every two vehicle nodes are within each other's communication range under such condition. $G(V, E)$ is treated as a Complete Graph.*

Definition 2. *Let M be a message. Let $G(V, E)$ be the connected graph for a set of vehicles. If each node i has a parameter n_i to control the number of copies of message M that i can replicate, then $G(V, E)$ associated with n_i becomes a graph with a bounded number of message copies.*

Definition 3. *Let $G(V, E)$ be a connected graph. Each node of G is assigned a nonnegative number n_i. The nodes of G are ϵ-balanced in the corresponding bounded message graph if the following conditions are satisfied:*

- *Each node of G with $n_i > 0$ satisfies $n_i \geq 1$.*
- *For every two nodes with $n_i, n_j > 0$, $|n_i - n_j| \leq \epsilon$, and*
- *There is no edge between nodes of values n_i and n_j in G, respectively, such that $n_i \geq 2$ and $n_j = 0$.*

Definition 4. *Let R be the set of real numbers and N be the set of nonnegative integers. Define the following concepts:*

- *A real average function $A(.,.)$ is a mapping $R \times R \to R \times R$, such that for two numbers $a \leq b$, $A(a, b) = (\frac{a+b}{2}, \frac{a+b}{2})$ if $a + b \geq 2$, or $A(a, b) = (a, b)$ if $a + b < 2$.*
- *An integer average function $A(.,.)$ is a mapping $N \times N \to N \times N$ such that for two numbers $a \leq b$, $A(a, b) = (k, k)$ if $a + b = 2k \geq 2$, $A(a, b) = (k, k + 1)$ if $a + b = 2k + 1 \geq 2$, or $A(a, b) = (a, b)$ if $a + b < 2$.*
- *For a list $L : a_1, a_2, \cdots, a_m$ of numbers, define the potential of L to be $P(L) = a_1^2 + a_2^2 + \cdots + a_m^2$.*
- *Let $A(.,.)$ be an average function and $S_A(\langle a, b \rangle) = 2(b - d)(b - c)$. Assume that $a_1, a_2, \cdots, a_n$ is a list of numbers. It is transformed into another list $a_1', a_2', \cdots, a_n'$ by a series of average operations. Define its sum of product to be $S(H) = \sum_{(a,b) \in H} S_A(a, b) = P(L) - P(L')$, where H is the set of tuples (a, b) that take average operations. It is considered as the change of the potential after taking an average operation.*

Definition 5. *A stage of communication is an average operation among a set of independent edges in the connected graph. Pairs of nodes in the network to exchange messages in parallel are allowed.*

We use the number of *stages* to characterize the complexity to enter into ϵ-balanced status.

4 Complete Connected Graph

We consider the case that the connected graph of a set of nodes is a complete graph, in which every two nodes are within each other's communication rage. Our results show fast speed to achieve ϵ-balanced status by applying randomized algorithms.

4.1 Distributed Randomized Algorithm for Complete Graph

In this section, we present a distributed randomized algorithm (see Algorithm 1). It is very simple and easy to implement in practice.

Assume each vehicle node has a value to indicate the data distribution task, trying to achieve a general consensus in the shortest possible time. As we know, nodes within each other's communication range can exchange their information. In the case of complete connected graph, there might be many vehicles in one vehicle's communication range. When the vehicle who carries message receives more than one communication requests, it chooses the vehicle with the largest gap to take average operation and computes the pairwise average, which then becomes the new value for both nodes. It will stop iterating this pairwise averaging process until the network enters into ϵ-balanced status.

Algorithm 1. *randomized algorithm for complete graph*

Input: bounded message graph G (see Definition 2).
Output: bounded message graph G'.
Let $a = 1$;
Stage a:
    Each vehicle flip a coin;
    Each vehicle with coin side 1 randomly selects a vehicle and send request;
    Each vehicle with coin side 0 selects the request with the largest gap;
    Take average with the selected vehicle;
    Enter Stage $a + 1$ and let $a = a + 1$;

The analysis of our randomized algorithm uses the well-known Chernoff bounds, which are described below. All proofs of this paper are self-contained except the following famous theorems in probability theory and the existence of a polynomial time algorithm for linear programming.

Theorem 1 [18]. *Let $X_1, \ldots, X_n$ be n independent random 0-1 variables, where X_i takes 1 with probability p_i. Let $X = \sum_{i=1}^{n} X_i$, and $\mu = E[X]$. Then for any $\delta > 0$,*

1. $\Pr(X < (1 - \delta)\mu) < e^{-\frac{1}{2}\mu\delta^2}$, and
2. $\Pr(X > (1 + \delta)\mu) < \left[\frac{e^\delta}{(1+\delta)^{(1+\delta)}}\right]^\mu$.

We follow the proof of Theorem 1 to make the following versions (Theorem 2, Theorems 3, and Corollary 1) of Chernoff bounds for our algorithm analysis.

Theorem 2. *Let $X_1, \ldots, X_n$ be n independent random 0-1 variables, where X_i takes 1 with probability at least p for $i = 1, \ldots, n$. Let $X = \sum_{i=1}^{n} X_i$, and $\mu = E[X]$. Then for any $\delta > 0$, $\Pr(X < (1 - \delta)pn) < e^{-\frac{1}{2}\delta^2 pn}$.*

Theorem 3. *Let $X_1, \ldots, X_n$ be n independent random 0-1 variables, where X_i takes 1 with probability at most p for $i = 1, \ldots, n$. Let $X = \sum_{i=1}^{n} X_i$. Then for any $\delta > 0$, $\Pr(X > (1 + \delta)pn) < \left[\frac{e^\delta}{(1+\delta)^{(1+\delta)}}\right]^{pn}$.*

Define $g_1(\delta) = e^{-\frac{1}{2}\delta^2}$ and $g_2(\delta) = \frac{e^\delta}{(1+\delta)^{(1+\delta)}}$. Define $g(\delta) = \max(g_1(\delta), g_2(\delta))$. We note that $g_1(\delta)$ and $g_2(\delta)$ are always strictly less than 1 for all $\delta > 0$. It is trivial for $g_1(\delta)$. For $g_2(\delta)$, this can be verified by checking that the function $f(x) = (1 + x)\ln(1 + x) - x$ is increasing and $f(0) = 0$. This is because $f'(x) = \ln(1 + x)$ which is strictly greater than 0 for all $x > 0$.

Corollary 1 [19]. *Let $X_1, \ldots, X_n$ be n independent random 0-1 variables and $X = \sum_{i=1}^{n} X_i$.*

(1) If X_i takes 1 with probability at most p for $i = 1, \ldots, n$, then for any $\frac{1}{3} > \epsilon > 0$, $\Pr(X > pn + \epsilon n) < e^{-\frac{1}{3}n\epsilon^2}$.
(2) If X_i takes 1 with probability at least p for $i = 1, \ldots, n$, then for any $\epsilon > 0$, $\Pr(X < pn - \epsilon n) < e^{-\frac{1}{2}n\epsilon^2}$.

5 Analysis of the Proposed Randomized Algorithm

In this section, we present a detailed analysis of the proposed randomized distributed algorithm. We will show how a list of numbers shrinks its gap after a series of random average operations.

Lemma 1. *Let $r(.)$ be a function from $S \to S$ that $r(x)$ generates a random element in S. Assume that A and B are two subsets of S. Assume that $|A| \leq |B|$, and $R(A) = \{x : x \in A, r(x) \in B\}$, $H(A) = \{r(x) : x \in A, r(x) \in B\}$. Then with a probability at most*

$$g(\epsilon)^{\frac{|A||B|}{|S|}} + ((1 - \gamma))^{(2\gamma - 1)(1 - \epsilon) \cdot \frac{|B|}{|S|} \cdot |A|},$$

we have

$$|H(A)| \leq (1 - \gamma)(1 - \epsilon) \cdot \frac{|B|}{|S|} \cdot |A|,$$

where γ is a constant in $(0, 1)$. Furthermore, if $|B| \geq \delta|S|$ for some fixed $\delta \in (0, 1)$, then the failure probability is at most $2(1 - a)^{|A|}$ for some fixed $a \in (0, 1)$.

Proof. Let $m = |R(A)|$. For each element in A, with probability $\frac{|B|}{|S|}$, it sends a request to an element in B. By Chernoff bound, we have $m < (1 - \epsilon) \cdot \frac{|B|}{|S|} \cdot |A|$ with a small probability

$$\zeta_1 \leq g(\epsilon)^{\frac{|A||B|}{|S|}}. \tag{1}$$

For each $x \in A$, define $r(x)$ to be the element that x sends.
Let γ have $e(1 - \gamma) \leq 1$ and $\gamma \in (0, 1)$.
Let $n = |B|$. The probability that $|H(A)| \leq (1 - \gamma)m$ is

$$\zeta_2 \leq \binom{n}{(1 - \gamma)m} \cdot (\frac{(1 - \gamma)m}{n})^m \tag{2}$$

$$\leq \frac{n^{(1-\gamma)m} e^{(1-\gamma)m}}{((1 - \gamma)m)^{(1-\gamma)m}} \cdot (\frac{(1 - \gamma)m}{n})^m \tag{3}$$

$$\leq e^{(1-\gamma)m} (\frac{(1 - \gamma)m}{n})^{\gamma m} \tag{4}$$

$$\leq (\frac{e(1 - \gamma)m}{n})^{(1-\gamma)m} (\frac{(1 - \gamma)m}{n})^{(2\gamma-1)m} \tag{5}$$

$$\leq (\frac{(1 - \gamma)m}{n})^{(2\gamma-1)m} \tag{6}$$

$$\leq ((1 - \gamma))^{(2\gamma-1)m}. \tag{7}$$

From above analysis, the total failure probability is at most $\zeta_1 + \zeta_2 \leq g(\epsilon)^{\frac{|A||B|}{|S|}} + ((1 - \gamma))^{(2\gamma-1)(1-\epsilon)\cdot\frac{|B|}{|S|}\cdot|A|}$ by inequalities (1) and (7). This proves the lemma.

Definition 6. *Let $L = a_1, \cdots, a_k$ be a list of real numbers. Define* $\mathrm{gap}(L)$ *to be* $\max_{1 \leq i,j \leq k} |a_i - a_j|$.

Definition 7. *Let $\alpha > 0$, and $K = a_1, \cdots, a_k$ be a list of real numbers. Assumed K is transformed into another list $K' = a'_1, \cdots, a'_k$ after a series of average operations. If $\mathrm{gap}(K') \leq (1 - \alpha)\mathrm{gap}(K)$, then K' is called α-shrink of K.*

Definition 8. *Let c, d, δ be parameters. A series of c stages is α-successful if the gap of a list of numbers is shrinked by a factor of at least α. The failure probability of an α shrink of the list is denoted by δ.*

Lemma 2. *Let c be a parameter. All stages are partitioned into multiple groups of c stages $G_1, G_2, \cdots, G_k$. Then there are k independent $0, 1$ random variables r_i for each group G_i such that*

1. $\mathrm{Prob}(G_i \text{ is } \alpha\text{-successful}) \geq \mathrm{Prob}(r_i = 1)$
2. $\mathrm{Prob}(r_i = 1) \geq 1 - \delta$.
3. $\mathrm{Prob}(\text{there are at least } t \text{ } G_i \text{ to be } \alpha\text{-successful}) \geq \mathrm{Prob}(r_1 + r_2 + \cdots + r_k \geq t)$.

Proof. First, let $S_1, S_2, ..., S_m \in \{1, 2, \cdots, m\}$ denote the m random numbers in the range $\{1, 2, \cdots, m\}$. Let $a_i \in \{0, 1\}$ denote the status that whether a vehicle is receiving or sending requests.

Then, we have the 0,1 string $W_j = a_1 S_1, a_2 S_2, ..., a_m S_m$, which denotes an average operation among the m vehicles.

Let $D_i = W_1 ... W_z$, $z = O(\log m)$. It means after $O(\log m)$ stages, the string D_i will get an α shrink. There are $O(\log n)$ stages of D_i which will get an α shrink.

Each G_i corresponds to a random sequence D_i. Let T be the total number of random paths for group G_i.

Let $D_1, D_2, \cdots, D_T$ be an rearrangement of all the random paths such that $D_1, \cdots D_{H_i}$ are all α-successful sorted by lexicographic order. In the same way, $D_{H_{i+1}+1}, \cdots, D_T$ are also sorted by lexicographic order. For each random sequence D_i to be α-successful, make it correspond to an integer in $[1, T]$. Assume that G_i is α-successful for H_i random paths with $H_i \geq T \cdot (1 - \delta)$. Without loss of generality, each α-successful sequence corresponds to a unique integer in the range $[1, H_i]$. Then G_i is α-successful if and only if r_i is an event with a random number s_i in $[1, T]$ with $s \leq T \cdot (1 - \delta)$.

It is proved by an induction on the number of groups k. It is trivial for the case $k = 1$. Assume that it is true for k. Consider the case $k + 1$. For each random sequence $D_1 D_2 \cdots D_k$, we consider the extension $D_1 D_2 \cdots D_k D$ for a random sequence D for G_{k+1}. The number of cases of D that G_{k+1} is α-successful for D random paths is $H_{k+1} \geq T \cdot (1 - \delta)$. Then G_{k+1} is α-successful if and only if r_{k+1} is an event with a random number s_{k+1} in $[1, T]$ with $s_{k+1} \leq T \cdot (1 - \delta)$.

6   Performance Evaluation

In this section, we first introduce the simulation environment, then present the compared algorithms, performance metrics and finally give the simulation results.

6.1   Simulation Setup

To evaluate the performance of the proposed algorithm, we have conducted extensive simulations. In simulation, the following default settings are used. Compromised to the complexity of simulations, we select a bounded 3 km*4 km regional area for our simulations. Each road segment has two lanes with the bidirectional traffic. For each simulation run, different number of vehicle nodes are involved in the message delivery. The number varies from 100 to 500. The mobility of vehicles is generated by VANET-Mobisim [20], in which the destination of each transmission is randomly selected. The coverage of V2V communications is set to be 300 m. Transmission frame duration is set as 1ms. The number of allowed maximum data copies varies from 200 to 800.

6.2   Compared Algorithms

We compare the proposed algorithm with the following data dissemination algorithms.

- Epidemic: It is flooding-based in nature, as nodes continuously replicate and transmit messages to newly discovered relays that do not possess a data copy.
- Randomized flooding or Gossiping (random-flood): Similar to epidemic routing, but a message only gets copied with some probability.
- Bounded copied in arbitrary graph (arbitrary): Vehicles randomly choose the vehicle to take average.
- Bounded copied in linear graph (linear): Vehicles randomly choose the vehicle to take average.
- Bounded copied in complete graph (randomized): A vehicle randomly selects another vehicle within its communication range and sends request. The vehicle selects the request with the largest gap among all the requests it has received.

6.3   Performance Metrics

We choose the total number of average operations as a measure of overhead and choose the dissemination delay and the actual number of vehicles reached as measures of effectiveness.

The following performance metrics will be taken into account for purpose of algorithms evaluation in the simulation experiments.

Number of stages: Average operations that characterize the complexity to enter into a balanced status among a set of nodes whose communication are based on their connected graph.

Dissemination delay: It denotes the average time between the sending and receiving times for packets received. In this paper, it indicates the time for the network to enter into a balanced status.

6.4   Simulation Results

In this section, we will evaluate the effect of the number and velocity of vehicles on the performance of different algorithms.

(1) The effect of the number of vehicles on routing performance

Figures 1 and 2 respectively depict the number of stages and dissemination delay as the number of vehicles changes from 100 to 500. As is evident by these figures, the distributed randomized algorithm performs significantly fewer transmissions than other compared algorithms. Assume that traffic loads are low with enough network capacity, in terms of dissemination delay, as epidemic has close-to-optimal delays under these conditions, the proposed distributed randomized algorithm manages to achieve delays that are quite close to those of flooding-based schemes. Meanwhile, if traffic starts increasing, it actually outperforms all schemes in terms of delay.

(2) Effect of different velocities on the performance of different algorithms

As the number of message copies varies from 800 to 200, Figs. 3 and 4 compare the number of communication stage and dissemination delay of all the compared algorithms.

As can be seen from Fig. 3, when the number of allowed maximum copies decreases all the way from 800 to 200, the averaging time for the network to enter into a balanced status decreases in all the compared algorithms. It is obvious that the proposed randomized algorithm consumes fewer communications than other algorithms. Figure 4 shows that proposed randomized algorithm performs better dissemination delay when there are more message copies in the network.

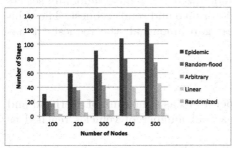

Fig. 1. Stages VS. number of nodes   **Fig. 2.** Delay VS. number of nodes

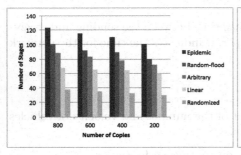
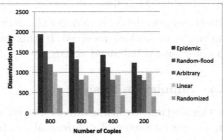

Fig. 3. Stages VS. number of copies   **Fig. 4.** Delay VS. number of copies

7   Conclusion

To facilitate message delivery in ad hoc networks, we study distributed data replication algorithms in a connected network. We use graph theory to describe network topology, then propose a distributed randomized data replication algorithm for complete graph. We show how the network converges after a series of random average operations. Most of the results in the paper are to study the network convergence speed. Extensive simulations show that the performance of the proposed algorithm is superior to the other approaches.

Acknowledgements. The authors are very grateful to the anonymous reviewers for their helpful comments on an earlier version of this paper.

References

1. Mukherjee, J.C., Gupta, A., Sreenivas, R.C.: Event notification in VANET with capacitated roadside units. IEEE Trans. Intell. Transp. Syst. **17**(7), 1867–1879 (2016)
2. He, J., Cai, L., Cheng, P., Pan, J.: Delay minimization for data dissemination in large-scale VANETs with buses and taxis. IEEE Trans. Mob. Comput. **15**(8), 1939–1950 (2016)
3. Yan, T., Zhang, W., Wang, G., Zhang, Y.: Access points planning in urban area for data dissemination to drivers. IEEE Trans. Veh. Technol. **63**(1), 390–402 (2014)
4. Bi, Y., Shan, H., Shen, X., Wang, N., Zhao, H.: A multi-hop broadcast protocol for emergency message dissemination in urban vehicular ad hoc networks. IEEE Trans. Intell. Transp. Syst. **17**(3), 735–750 (2016)
5. Cunha, F.D., Villas, L., Boukerche, A., Maia, M., Viana, A., Mini, R.A.F., Loureiro, A.A.F.: Data communication in VANETs: protocols, applications and challenges. Ad Hoc Netw. **44**, 90–103 (2016)
6. Janech, J., Lieskovsky, A., Krsak, E.: Comparison of strategies for data replication in VANET environment. In: International Conference on Advanced Information Networking and Applications Workshops, pp. 575–580 (2012)
7. Zhao, C., Yao, S., Zhang, W., Yang, Y.: A framework for modeling delay performance of network coding based epidemic routing. In: 2015 IEEE International Conference on Communications (ICC), pp. 3400–3405 (2015)
8. Yang, Y., Zhao, C., Yao, S., Zhang, W., Ge, X., Mao, G.: Delay performance of network-coding-based epidemic routing. IEEE Trans. Veh. Technol. **65**(5), 3676–3684 (2016)
9. Balasubramanian, A., Levine, B.N., Venkataramani, A.: Replication routing in DTNs: a resource allocation approach. IEEE/ACM Trans. Netw. **18**(2), 596–609 (2010)
10. Wu, Y., Zhu, Y., Zhu, H., Li, B.: CCR: capacity-constrained replication for data delivery in vehicular networks. In: Proceedings of IEEE INFOCOM 2013, pp. 2580–2588 (2013)
11. Yan, T., Zhang, W., Wang, G.: DOVE: data dissemination to a desired number of receivers in VANET. IEEE Trans. Veh. Technol. **63**(4), 1903–1916 (2014)
12. Wu, S., Rabbat, M.G.: Broadcast gossip algorithms for consensus on strongly connected digraphs. IEEE Trans. Sig. Process. **61**(16), 3959–3971 (2013)
13. Nedic, A., Ozdaglar, A.: Convergence rate for consensus with delays. J. Glob. Optim. **47**(3), 437–456 (2010)
14. Aysal, T.C., Yildiz, M.E., Sarwate, A.D., Scaglione, A.: Broadcast gossip algorithms for consensus. IEEE Trans. Sig. Process. **57**(7), 2748–2761 (2009)
15. Fabio, F., Zampieri, S.: Randomized consensus algorithms over large scale networks. IEEE J. Sel. Areas Commun. **26**(4), 634–649 (2008)

16. Nedic, A., Liu, J.: On convergence rate of weighted-averaging dynamics for consensus problems. IEEE Trans. Autom. Control **62**(2), 766–781 (2017)
17. Falsone, A., Margellos, K., Garatti, S., Prandini, M.: Finite time distributed averaging over gossip-constrained ring networks. IEEE Trans. Control Netw. Syst. (2017)
18. Motwani, R., Raghavan, P.: Randomized Algorithms. Cambridge University Press, Cambridge (2000)
19. Ming, L., Ma, B., Wang, L.: On the closest string and substring problems. J. ACM **49**(2), 157–171 (2002)
20. Haerri, J., Fiore, M., Filali, F.: Vehicular mobility simulation with VanetMobiSim. Simulation **87**(4), 275–300 (2011)

Preserving Privacy in Social Networks Against Label Pair Attacks

Chenyang Liu, Dan Yin$^{(\boxtimes)}$, Hao Li, Wei Wang, and Wu Yang

Information Security Research Center,
Harbin Engineering University, Harbin 150001, China
{chenyliu,yindan,lhao,w_wei,yangwu}@hrbeu.edu.cn

Abstract. With the popularity of social networks, publishing social network data is necessary for research purposes, which causes privacy leakage undoubtedly. Therefore, many methods are proposed to deal with different attack models. This paper focuses on a novel privacy attack model and refers it as a label pair attack. In the label pair attacks, the adversary can re-identify a pair of friends by using the labels of two vertices connected by an edge. We present a new anonymity concept, called Label Pair k^2-anonymity which ensures that there exists at least $k - 1$ other vertices such that each of the $k - 1$ vertices also has an incident edge of the same label pair and reduces the probability of a vertex being re-identified to less than $1/k$. The experimental results demonstrate that the approach can preserve the privacy and utility of social networks effectively.

Keywords: Privacy preserving · Social network · Label pair

1 Introduction

More and more social network datasets are published for different purposes, such as research purposes with the advance on mobile and Internet technology. Specially, the mobile social network is popular among people. It provides a platform for sharing interests, hobbies, status and activity information. So the publication of social network datasets may lead the privacy leakage easily. This problem has raised people's attention, many works [1, 5–7, 20, 22, 23] have proposed various protection means to protect individual privacy from attack. The social networks are modeled as a graph in which each vertex represents a user, each edge represents the social relationship and the label indicates the feature of one user.

There are a variety of attacks nowadays, such as friendship attacks, mutual friend attacks, neighborhood attacks and structural attacks. Some works solve the social structure problem only, and some works solve the problem of social networks with users' labels. We consider the two aspects of the structure and labels. Whereafter, we propose a new attack named label pair attacks. The attacks frequently happen in mobile social networks. The adversary can use the vertex labels of two individuals and friendship to identify users. And the labels and friendship of users are easily obtained, the adversary can easily launch the attack. However, the methods referred in papers [2, 11, 13, 14, 18] can protect privacy from common attacks, while they cannot protect

© Springer International Publishing AG 2017
L. Ma et al. (Eds.): WASA 2017, LNCS 10251, pp. 381–392, 2017.
DOI: 10.1007/978-3-319-60033-8_34

privacy from the label pair attacks. Thus it can be seen that the problem should be solved as soon as possible.

In this paper, we introduce a new relationship attack model based on the vertex label pair of an edge. An adversary can acquire the label of an individual from the social network website or application easily, such as Facebook, Twitter. Furthermore, the adversary can also know whether two individuals have a friendship relation. The label pairs which will be mentioned later are made of the labels of two individuals who are friends. So the adversary can use the label pairs to issue a label attack from the published social networks on the purpose of recognizing victims' identity. As a concrete example, Fig. 1(a) is an original social network, every vertex represents a user, such as Mary, Bob, Ed. Meanwhile, we can obtain the profession label of each user, such as Doctor, Teacher. Then we remove all users' names and reserve the profession labels as shown in Fig. 1(b). Obviously, an adversary cannot re-identify anyone from the social network with anonymous vertices with the only label information. But if the adversary knows Mary's label is Doctor, Bob's label is Teacher and they have a friendship relation, he can easily identify Mary and Bob through the label pair (Doctor, Teacher) in Fig. 1(b). Only if an adversary grasps the background knowledge about friendship relation and the label information, he can launch the attack to identify individuals and obtain various privacy information.

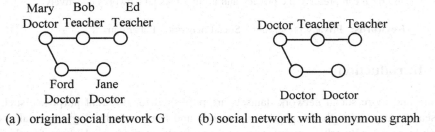

(a) original social network G   (b) social network with anonymous graph

Fig. 1. An example of the label pair attacks.

To avoid the label pair attacks, a new type of privacy-preserving method called LP k^2-anonymity is introduced in this paper. For every vertex v with an edge of label pair (l_1, l_2), there will be at least $k - 1$ other vertices having an edge of the same label pair. It can be guaranteed that the probability of a vertex being identified is not greater than $1/k$. We propose algorithms to achieve LP k^2-anonymity for the graphs of original social networks. Our approach mainly includes two steps. First, we adopt a method named LGA (Label Generalization Anonymization) to group the vertices and generalize the labels of vertices. Then we anonymize the graph by LGAN (Label Group ANonymization). The algorithm can effectively protect the individual privacy from the label pair attacks, meanwhile preserve the vertex set. Above all, the algorithm is designed to preserve as much utility as possible.

Contributions. Our contributions are summarized as follows:

1. This paper is the first to propose the new type attack model named label pair attacks. And we take measures to tackle the problem of the label pair attacks.
2. To deal with the problem, we introduce Label Pair k^2-anonymity concept, namely LP k^2-anonymity, which can prevent users with labels from being re-identified when the adversary launches the label attack.
3. Two algorithms are devised to achieve the purpose to anonymize. The first algorithm is to group the vertices and generalize the labels of vertices named LGA (Label Generalization Anonymization). Another algorithm named LGAN (Label Group ANonymization) is to anonymize the social networks by edge addition and edge deletion. We do not add noise vertices or delete vertices to preserve the vertex set and adopt the specific order which is illustrated in Sect. 4 to protect dataset utility.
4. The empirical results on the real datasets show that our algorithms perform well in anonymizing the social networks.

The rest of paper is organized as follows. We introduce the related work about the problem of anonymizing social networks in Sect. 2. We define the problem and propose the practical solution in Sects. 3 and 4. Finally, we conduct the experiments on real data sets and conclude in Sects. 5 and 6.

2 Related Work

Privacy preservation in publishing social networks is a new challenge that has drawn more and more people's attention. Recently, some works [15] propose to encrypt for the data to protect privacy and other works propose to achieve k-anonymity based on various adversary knowledge. Many approaches [5, 10] have been proposed to guarantee privacy. Liu and Terzi [8] propose the k-degree anonymization, for any node v, there exists at least $k - 1$ other nodes in the graph having the same degree as node v. Sun et al. [11] propose a new type anonymity concept, called k-NMF anonymity against mutual friend attacks. Zou et al. [16] propose the k-automorphism model, which converts the original network into a k-automorphic network. Tai et al. [2] present a friendship attack, in which the adversary uses the degree of each vertex and friendship relation to identify users. Zhang et al. [21] combine k-anonymity and randomization together to protect data privacy.

What is said above is not referred the data with labels. There are labels of vertices and labels on the edges. Liu et al. [9] treat weights on the edges as sensitive labels and propose a method to preserve shortest paths between most pairs of vertices in the graph. And some studies usually generalize labels [3, 4, 12] to protect privacy. Generalization involves replacing (or recording) a value with a less specific but semantically consistent value. Zhou and Pei [18] adopt this way in social networks. They propose a practical solution to battle neighborhood attack, the solution considers modeling social networks as labeled graphs and also can be used to answer aggregate network queries with high accuracy. Yuan et al. [13] introduce a framework which provides privacy protection based on the users' requests. It combines the label generalization protection and the structure protection techniques to satisfy three levels' requests. Song et al. propose a privacy protection scheme that only prevents the disclosure of identity of users but also the disclosure of sensitive labels. Yuan et al. [14] define a k-degree-l-diversity anonymity model that consider the protection of structural information as well as sensitive labels of individuals and further propose a novel anonymization method based on adding noise vertices.

3 Preliminaries and Problem Definition

In this paper, we model a social network as an undirected graph $G = (V, E, L)$ where V is a set of nodes which represents the individuals, $E \subseteq V \times V$ is a set of edges representing the relationship of users, and L is a set of labels. In this work, we assume that the adversary uses friendship relations and labels of users as background knowledge to reveal the identities of users. First, we should form a generalization tree (GTree) using the label set L. For example, if the locations of users are used as labels of vertices in a social network, L contains not only the specific locations such as Beijing, Washington, New York, California, Berlin, London, but also general categories like China, America, Germany, England. We assume that there exists a symbol $* \in L$ which is the most general category generalizing all labels. For two labels $m, n \in L$, if m is more general than n, we write $m \prec n$. For example, America $\prec$ New York. And when we form the generalization tree (GTree), we had better form it by the number of leafs in descending order. We put nodes which have descendants in front of the nodes having fewer on the purpose of reducing cost and protect the utility of data. These concepts are clarified by the following definitions:

Definition 1 Label Pair Attack. Given a social network $G = (V, E, L)$ and the anonymized network $G' = (V', E', L')$ for publishing. For a vertex $v \in V$ and all edges connecting with it, the adversary can get the label pair (m, n) corresponding one edge. The adversary can take advantage of the label pair to identify victims.

An adversary re-identifies the v with high confidence if the number of candidate vertices is too small. Hence, we set a threshold k to make sure that the number of candidate vertices is no less than k for each vertex $v \in V$. We define LP k^2-anonymity as follows.

Definition 2 LP k^2-Anonymity. If a graph $G' = (V', E', L')$ is LP k^2 anonymous, for each vertex with an edge of label pair (m, n) in G', there exists at least $k - 1$ other vertices having an edge of the same label pair.

Consider the graphs in Fig. 2 as an example. Each vertex in the graphs represents a user, the edge between two vertices represents the fact that the two users are friends. And the labels annotated to the vertices show the profession of the user. For convenience, we make letter T represent the profession of teacher and D represent the profession of doctor. The Fig. 2(a) is a simple example. There are three vertices and each vertex has the label pair (D, D). Therefore, the graph is $LP\,3^2$ anonymous. The Fig. 2(b) is $LP2^2$ anonymous. Because vertices {1, 4} have the label pairs (D, T) and

(D, D), vertices {2, 3, 5} have the label (T, D) and vertices {2, 3} have the label pair (T, T). Similarly, in the Fig. 2(c), vertices {1, 3, 5} have the label pairs (T, D) and (T, T), vertices {2, 4, 6} own the label pair (D, T) and vertices {2, 6, 7} own the label pair (D, D). Hence, it is $LP\,3^2$ anonymous.

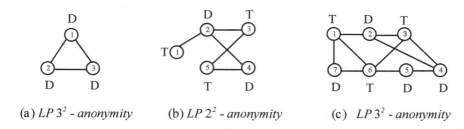

(a) $LP\,3^2$ - *anonymity*   (b) $LP\,2^2$ - *anonymity*   (c) $LP\,3^2$ - *anonymity*

Fig. 2. Examples of LPk^2 - *anonymity* graphs

Definition 3 Generalization Cost. In our approach, we need to generalize vertex labels. The generalization cost is

$$GenCost(l_u, l_t) = \frac{|h_{l_t} - h_{l_u}|}{|GTree|} \qquad (1)$$

l_u represents the original label of vertex u. l_t represents the target label of vertex u. h_{l_t} represents the height of label l_t in the generalization tree. h_{l_u} represents the height of label l_u in the generalization tree. $|GTree|$ represents the total height of the generalization tree.

Definition 4 Anonymity Cost. The cost of anonymizing $G = (V, E, L)$ to $G' = (V', E', L')$ is

$$Cost(G, G') = |E' \backslash E| + |E \backslash E'| + \sum_{v_1}^{v_m} GenCost(l_u, l_t) \qquad (2)$$

Suppose there are m vertices in a graph.

4   LP k^2-Anonymity Approach

In this section, we devise two effective algorithms, one is LGA (Label Generalization Anonymization) for grouping the vertices and generalizing the labels of vertices. Another is used for anonymizing the social network graph by adding and deleting edges called LGAN (Label Group ANonymization). The two algorithms share the same purpose that is to preserve the utility while satisfying the LP k^2-anonymity.

4.1 Label Generalization Anonymization (LGA) Algorithm

In this section, we organize vertices into groups and generalize vertices' labels by Algorithm LGA. We require there exist at least k vertices in each group. And generalizing vertices' labels makes all the vertices in each group have the same label.

To get the goal as described above, first we should sort the vertices sequence f in a specific order. Take the order of subtrees into account. At first, we consider the first subtree. We scan the labels of vertices in the graph in a breadth-first way, and sort them by the order in which the vertices have the same label or have the label of sibling relationship. Then we handle the vertices with the labels in the following subtrees in the same way. And these vertices which are handled newly will be added into f. The process is finished until all the subtrees are considered, that is all vertices are sorted.

Suppose the sequence is $f = (v_1, v_2, v_3 \ldots v_m)$. Then we group the vertices into $GP_1, GP_2 \ldots GP_n$ and make sure that there exist at least k vertices in each group, there are m vertices in the graph. These m vertices should be divided into multiple groups. First, we put k vertices into GP, if $|GP| \geq k$, we should analyze v_{k+1} and v_k two vertices' label relationship. If they have the same label or have the label of sibling relationship, we put v_{k+1} into GP. Otherwise, we start another group. We mark $GR = \{GP_1, GP_2 \ldots GP_n\}$. Then we choose a target label for vertices in each group. The selection rule is made according to the smallest generalization cost in Eq. (1) introduced in Sect. 2.

Example 1. We take an example of LP 2^2-anonymity. First, we form a generalization tree for the social network graph which is shown in Fig. 4(a). The generalization tree is displayed in Fig. 3. The vertices in Fig. 4(a) are sorted as $f = \{3, 2, 4, 6, 1, 5, 7, 8\}$. We group them into three groups. $GP_1 = \{3, 2, 4, 6\}$, $GP_2 = \{1, 5\}$,

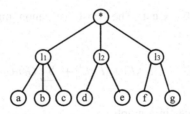

Fig. 3. An example of a generalization tree (GTree)

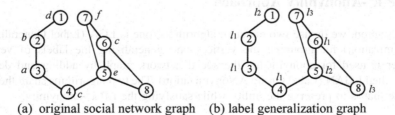

(a) original social network graph   (b) label generalization graph

Fig. 4. Examples of generalizing labels

$GP_3 = \{7, 8\}$, $GR = \{GP_1, GP_2, GP_3\}$. We choose a target label l_1 for GP_1, l_2 for GP_2, l_3 for GP_3 and generalize the labels of vertices to be their target labels. The generalization result is shown as Fig. 4(b).

4.2   Algorithm Label Group Anonymization (LGAN)

We propose an algorithm named LGAN to add edges or delete edges of the vertices after grouping. First, for every vertex in each group, we examine whether there are not less than $k - 1$ other vertices owning the same label pair of (m, n) between groups. The group which satisfies the condition is removed from the set GR. The left groups in the set GR will be processed. The average degree of vertices in each group is calculated. The group with the highest average degree is selected firstly, and the process of adding edges or deleting edges is performed to ensure that each label pair (m, n) in the group is either zero or not less than k. We use table $VerTbl[x][y]$ to store the number of vertices in x with edges connecting to the vertices in y, x represents the vertices whose labels are m and y represents the vertices whose labels are n. $EdgTbl[x][y]$ stores the number of edges connecting vertices in x·and y, and x represents the vertices whose labels are m and y represents the vertices whose labels are n. We ensure that two groups have enough edges by adding edges or deleting edges. For each label (m, n), if $0 < VerTbl[x][y] < k$ or $0 < VerTbl[y][x] < k$, we get the cost of edge addition, i.e., $k - min(VerTbl[x][y], VerTbl[y][x])$ and the cost of edge deletion, i.e., $EdgTbl[x][y]$. If the cost of edge deletion is no more than the cost of edge addition, we delete the edges between group x and group y. Then we set $VerTbl[x][y]$, $VerTbl[y][x]$, $EdgTbl[x][y]$, $EdgTbl[y][x]$ as zero. Otherwise, we add edges between group x and group y according the following strategy:

(1)   vertex u (or v) in group x has no connection with v (or u) in group y;
(2)   the shortest path between every two candidate vertices is the minimal one in the original graph.

After the group is handled, we remove the group from the set GR. We iterate this step until the set GR is empty.

Example 2. After Example 1, we get the graph of Fig. 4(b). On the basis of Fig. 4(b), we add edges or delete edges between groups. In Fig. 4(b), for every vertex in GP_3, there are not less than $k - 1$ other vertices owning the same label pair of (m, n) between groups. The group is removed from the set GR directly. We consider the left groups GP_1, $GP\text{-}_2$. Vertex 6 in GP_1 can be uniquely identified by the label pair (l_1, l_3). Similar, vertex 5 in GP_2 can be uniquely identified by the label pair (l_2, l_3). We calculate the average of the vertices in each group, we can know the average degree of GP_1 is 2.25, and the average degree of GP_2 is 2.5. As a consequence, we give priority to deal with the vertex 5 in GP_2. LGAN deletes an edge (5, 7) as shown in Fig. 5(a). Then, we remove GP_2 from the set GR. To protect vertex 6, an edge (4, 8) is chosen to add. Then, we remove GP_1 from the set GR. The set GR is empty that means the social network graph in Fig. 4(a) is already anonymized completely. Finally, the Fig. 5(a) is the LP 2^2 anonymous resulting graph.

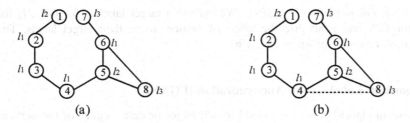

Fig. 5. An example of LP 2^2-anonymity graphs

5   Experimental Evaluation

In the section, we introduce the datasets and evaluate our algorithm. All the experiments are conducted in a virtual machine on a PC computer. The PC is with a 2.50 GHz Intel (R) Core(TM) i7-6500U CPU and 4.0 GB memory. The virtual machine runs Fedora release 23 system with 1.5 GB memory. The program is implemented in C.

5.1   Data Sets

We conduct our experiments on two real datasets. One dataset is a co-authorship data in network science [24]. We construct a social network from the data and extract author names as labels. Each vertex in the graph represents an author, and two vertices are linked by an edge if the two corresponding authors co-authored at least one paper in the data set. There are 1461 vertices and 2742 edges in the co-authorship graph after removing the isolated vertices and the average degree is about 3.76. Another is from the e-print arXiv. We derive a graph describing the citations between papers from Arxiv HEP-TH (high energy physics theory) [25]. If one paper cites another paper, an undirected edge will connect both corresponding vertices. The graph includes 12130 vertices and 76043 edges after removing the isolated vertices. The average degree of vertices is about 12.54.

5.2   Data Utility

We evaluate the performances the LGA and LGAN algorithm by measuring the degree distribution, average clustering coefficient, average path length, the numbers of edge changes and running time.

Degree Distribution. Figure 6 shows the degree distributions of the original graphs and the anonymized graphs. It can be seen the degree distributions of anonymized graphs are similar with the original graphs.

Average Clustering Coefficient (CC). Figure 7 compares the average clustering coefficients of the original graphs and the anonymized graphs. The basic trend is that the CC values on two datasets decrease when k increases. Specially, when k value is 3, the CC value of the HEP-TH dataset increases a little.

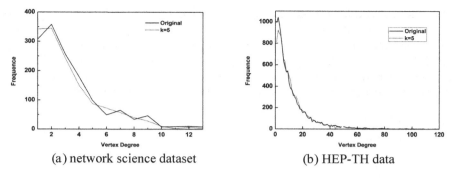

Fig. 6. Degree distribution

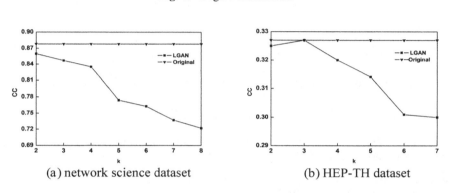

Fig. 7. Average clustering coefficient

Average Path Length (APL). The average path lengths on two datasets for the original graphs and the anonymized graphs are shown in Fig. 8. The APL of the graph anonymized is very close to the APL of the original graphs, especially when k value is small.

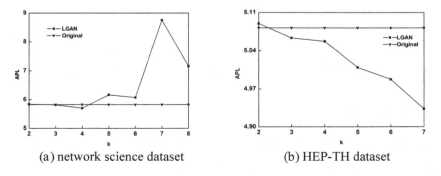

Fig. 8. Average path lengths

Percentages of Edges Changed. We consider the edge changes in our algorithm. Figure 9 shows the edge changes on the original graphs. The changes include the ratios of edges added and edges deleted. In our algorithm, we change the fewest edges. In the HEP-TH dataset, the vertex degree is smaller relatively than the dataset in the same size. For better experimental results, we make many vertices own the same label by generalizing labels. Also k value is set little when we perform the experiment.

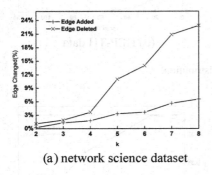
(a) network science dataset

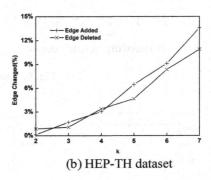
(b) HEP-TH dataset

Fig. 9. Percentages of edges added and deleted

From the above evaluation, it can be seen our algorithm can preserve the utility of the original graph effectively.

Running Time. Figure 10 shows the runtime on the network science dataset with respect to different k values. We can know the runtime increases when the k value increases from the figure.

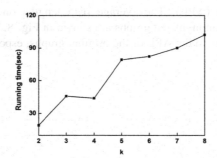

Fig. 10. The runtime on network science dataset

6   Conclusions

In this paper, we have proposed a new concept LP k^2-anonymity to protect individual privacy against a new type attack, called label pair attack. For LP k^2-anonymity, we provide a new method to anonymize the social graphs by algorithm LGA and LGAN.

In order to preserve the original graphs, we generalize the vertex labels as fewer as possible and only add necessary edges to construct a new graph without adding the noisy vertices in our algorithms. We also give a detail analysis of the data utility. The experimental results on two real data sets demonstrate that our approaches can preserve much of the utility of the original graph.

Acknowledgement. This work is supported by National Natural Science Foundation of China under Grant 61572459, 61672180 and 61602129. The paper is funded by the International Exchange Program of Harbin Engineering University for Innovation-oriented Talents Cultivation.

References

1. Cai, Z., He, Z., Guan, X., Li, Y.: Collective data-sanitization for preventing sensitive information inference attacks in social networks, p. 1 (2016)
2. Tai, C.H., Yu, P.S., Yang, D.N., Chen, M.S.: Privacy preserving social network publication against friendship attacks. In: Proceedings of KDD, San Diego, CA, pp. 1262–1270 (2011)
3. Campan, A., Truta, T., Cooper, N.: P-sensitive k-anonymity with generalization constraints. Trans. Data Priv. **2**, 65–89 (2010)
4. Fung, B.C.M., Wang, K., Yu, P.S.: Top-down specialization for information and privacy preservation. In: International Conference on Data Engineering, pp. 205–216 (2005)
5. He, Z., Cai, Z., Han, Q., Tong, W., Sun, L., Li, Y.: An energy efficient privacy-preserving content sharing scheme in mobile social networks. Pers. Ubiquit. Comput. **20**(5), 833–846 (2016)
6. He, Z., Cai, Z., Sun, Y., Li, Y., Cheng, X.: Customized privacy preserving for inherent data and latent data. Pers. Ubiquit. Comput. **21**(1), 1–12 (2016)
7. Hay, M., Miklau, G., Jensen, D., Towsley, D., Weis, P.: Resisting structural re-identification in anonymized social networks. VLDB J. **19**(6), 797–823 (2010)
8. Liu, K., Terzi, E.: Towards identity anonymization on graphs. In: Proceedings of SIGMOD, Vancouver, BC, pp. 93–106 (2008)
9. Liu, L., Wang, J., Liu, J., Zhang, J.: Privacy preserving in social networks against sensitive edge disclosure (2008)
10. Liu, X., Yang, X.: Protecting sensitive relationships against inference attacks in social networks. In: Lee, S.-g., Peng, Z., Zhou, X., Moon, Y.-S., Unland, R., Yoo, J. (eds.) DASFAA 2012. LNCS, vol. 7238, pp. 335–350. Springer, Heidelberg (2012). doi:10.1007/978-3-642-29038-1_25
11. Sun, C., Yu, P., Kong, X., Fu, Y.: Privacy preserving social network publication against mutual friend attacks. Trans. Data Priv. **7**, 71–97 (2013)
12. Wang, K., Yu, P.S., Chakraborty, S.: Bottom-up generalization: a data mining solution to privacy protection. In: ICDM, pp. 249–256 (2004)
13. Yuan, M., Chen, L., Yu, P.: Personalized privacy protection in social networks. VLDB **4**, 141–150 (2010)
14. Yuan, M., Chen, L., Yu, P., Yu, T.: Protecting sensitive labels in social network data anonymization. IEEE Trans. Knowl. Data Eng. **25**, 633–647 (2013)
15. Zheng, X., Cai, Z., Li, J.Z., Gao, H.: Location-privacy-aware review publication mechanism for local business service systems. In: The 36th Annual IEEE International Conference on Computer Communications (2017)

16. Zou, L., Chen, L., Zsu, M.T.: K-automorphism: a general framework for privacy preserving network publication. Proc. VLDB Endow. **2**(1), 946–957 (2009)
17. Zhang, L., Cai, Z., Wang, X.: Fakemask: a novel privacy preserving approach for smartphones. IEEE Trans. Netw. Serv. Manag. **13**(2), 1 (2016)
18. Zhou, B., Pei, J.: Preserving privacy in social networks against neighborhood attacks. In: ICDE, pp. 506–515 (2008)
19. Zhou, B., Pei, J., Luk, W.S.: A brief survey on anonymization techniques for privacy preserving publishing of social network data. ACM SIGKDD Explor. Newsl. **10**(2), 12–22 (2008)
20. Zheng, X., Cai, Z., Yu, J.Z, Wang, C.K., Li, Y.S.: Follow but no track privacy preserved profile publishing in cyber-physical social systems. IEEE Internet Things (2017)
21. Zhang, J., Sun, J., Zhang, R., Zhang, Y., Hu, X.: Privacy-preserving social media data publishing (2017)
22. Zhang, L., Zhang, W.: Edge anonymity in social network graphs. In: International Conference on Computational Science and Engineering, pp. 1–8 (2009)
23. Zhang, L., Wang, X., Lu, J., Li, P., Cai, Z.: An efficient privacy preserving data aggregation approach for mobile sensing. Secur. Commun. Netw. **9**(16), 3844–3853 (2016)
24. The Web Environment at U-M. http://www-personal.umich.edu
25. Stanford Network Analysis Project. https://snap.stanford.edu

Preserving Local Differential Privacy in Online Social Networks

Tianchong Gao[1(✉)], Feng Li[1(✉)], Yu Chen[2], and XuKai Zou[1]

[1] Indiana University-Purdue University Indianapolis, Indianapolis, IN, USA
{tgao,fengli}@iupui.edu, xkzou@cs.iupui.edu
[2] Binghamton University, Binghamton, NY, USA
ychen@binghamton.edu

Abstract. Following the trend of Online Social Networks (OSNs) data sharing and publishing, researchers raise their concern about the privacy problem. Differential privacy is such a mechanism to anonymize sensitive data. It deploys graph abstraction models, such as the Hierarchical Random Graph (HRG) model, to extract graph features. However, the injected noise amount, determined by the sensitivity, is usually proportion to the size of the whole network. Therefore, achieving global differential privacy may harm the utility of the releasing graphs.

In this paper, we define the notion of group-based local differential privacy. In particular, by splitting the network into 1-neighborhood graphs and applying HRG-based methods, our scheme reduces the noise scale on local graphs when achieving differential privacy. By deploying the grouping algorithm, our scheme focuses on anonymizing similar users. The experiment results show that our scheme could preserve more utility than the global scheme under the same privacy level.

Keywords: Social network data publishing · Anonymization · Differential privacy · Local topological features

1 Introduction

Recently, Online Social Networks (OSNs) have exploded in popularity. The OSN providers, like Facebook and Twitter, own vast amount of personal data and relationship information of their users. The data is often released to third-parties for the purpose of producing knowledge of human social relationships, feeding advertisements to recommendation target, and evaluating effectiveness of applications. However, publishing OSNs without sufficient anonymization work results in privacy leakage which will cause panic to the users of social media.

Thus, various anonymization techniques have been proposed to preserve the privacy of published OSNs. The simplest technique is the naive ID removal [1] which is proved to be vulnerable to de-anonymization attacks [2]. K-anonymity based techniques are suitable to anonymize relational data [3,4], however, they are only designed to anonymize some specific structural semantics, and can often be overcome by other structural semantics.

© Springer International Publishing AG 2017
L. Ma et al. (Eds.): WASA 2017, LNCS 10251, pp. 393–405, 2017.
DOI: 10.1007/978-3-319-60033-8_35

Fortunately, differential privacy based techniques, which theoretically provide a strong privacy guarantee, are proposed to solve the vulnerability [5,6]. *Sala et al.* employed the dK-2 series feature extraction model in [7] while *Xiao et al.* purposed a similar work with the Hierarchical Random Graph (HRG) model in [8]. Their algorithms achieve global ϵ-differential privacy over the entire dataset with different graph abstraction models. However, network data is very sensitive to the changes in network structure. Although these global differential privacy techniques are rich in preserving privacy, the regenerated graph lacks enough utility for network analysis. In [7], $\mathcal{O}(\sqrt{n})$ noise was injected into the dK-2 series. The work in [8] performs better that it needs $\mathcal{O}(\log n)$ noise for the HRG model. Here n means the number of vertices in the whole graph since these schemes calculate the noise based on the global sensitivity.

How to balance the anonymization technique's privacy level with its negative utility impact is always a question for privacy-preserving data publishing. In this paper, the first step towards achieving such balance is splitting the whole graph into some subgraphs. The main advantage of the segmentation is that it reduces the desired noise scale of differential privacy, so the notion of local differential privacy preserves more graph utility than global differential privacy under the same privacy parameter ϵ. Notice that the subgraph model, 1-neighborhood graph, is realistic because it captures the information of the direct relationships between the target user and its neighbors, which is the most important prior knowledge for de-anonymization. After that, the HRG model is deployed to extract the features under a differential privacy manner. The segmentation work reducing the graph size also helps to reduce the HRG output space size. Therefore, each HRG has higher posterior probability and regenerating a perturbed graph from it loses less information.

The grouping algorithm is also introduced based on the similarity of HRG models to enhance the anonymization power. Specifically, the HRGs with overlap in their output space are grouped together to form a representative HRG, which is used to smooth other ones inside the group. Since all sanitized subgraphs in a group are regenerated from one HRG, the adversary will not able to differentiate the target even with the help of prior knowledge. In conclusion, the proposed scheme abandons the attempt to hide one user's friendship into the whole OSN, but hides the relationship inside the relationships between all his/her friends, the similar users and their friends. Then the proposed scheme can preserve more data utility than previous schemes while the privacy level is higher than the pure local ϵ-differential privacy criteria.

The major technical contributions are the following: (1) The notion of local differential privacy, which could preserve more information when the privacy level is the same as global differential privacy, is defined. (2) The nodes with similar local features are grouped. By carefully designing the heuristic method, we show the grouping algorithm could enhance the privacy level without loss of too much information. (3) An uniform framework is designed to publish the perturbed networks which satisfying the group-based local ϵ-differential privacy.

Finally, the evaluation work on two different OSN datasets, Facebook and Enron email network, is completed. The results show that under the same differential privacy criteria, the proposed scheme can preserve more structural information like the degree distribution and the clustering coefficient than the previous scheme.

2   Preliminaries

In this paper, an OSN graph is modeled as an undirected graph $G = (V, E)$, where V is the set of vertices and E is the set of edges. $|V|$ is the cardinality of the set V.

1-Neighborhood Graph. For each node v in V, we define its 1-neighborhood graph as the graph containing all the neighbors of v and the node v itself. The 1-neighborhood graph of v is denoted as $G(v) = (V(v), E(v))$, where $V(v) = v \cup \{u | e_{v,u} \in E\}$ and $E(v) = \{e_{w,u} | w, u \in V(v) \wedge e_{w,u} \in E\}$. The node v is marked as the central node of the subgraph while the other nodes are outer nodes.

2.1   Hierarchical Random Graph Model

Because the connection probability between two vertices depends on their degrees, the HRG model is captured by statical collection. Specifically, the HRG model is a dendrogram $\mathcal{T}$, which is a rooted binary tree with $|V|$ leaf nodes corresponding to $|V|$ vertices in the graph G. Each node on the tree except the leaf node has a number on it which shows the probability of connection between its left part and right part. Assuming r is one of the interior nodes of the dendrogram $\mathcal{T}$, then the probability is denoted as p_r.

Let L_r and R_r denote the left and right subtrees rooted at r respectively. n_{L_r} and n_{R_r} are the numbers of leaf nodes in L_r and R_r. Let E_r be the total number of edges between the two group of nodes L_r and R_r. Then, the posterior probability for the subtrees rooted at r is $p_r = E_r / (n_{L_r} n_{R_r})$. The posterior probability of the whole HRG model $\mathcal{T}$ to represent G is given by:

$$p(\mathcal{T}) = \prod_{r \in \mathcal{T}} p_r^{E_r} (1 - p_r)^{n_{L_r} n_{R_r} - E_r} \qquad (1)$$

Example 1. Figure 2 gives an example of two possible dendrograms of B's 1-hop neighborhood graph in Fig. 1(c). The p_r in each root node is first calculated. For instance, in the dendrogram $\mathcal{T}_{B2}$, the root node of subtrees $\{A, C\}$ and $\{B, E\}$ has a probability $1/2$ because there are two edges between the two sets of nodes, we have $E_r = 2$ so $p_r = 2/(2*2) = 1/2$. Then we get the posterior probability of the two HRGs. $p(\mathcal{T}_{B1}) = (1/3)(2/3)^2 \approx 0.148$ while $p(\mathcal{T}_{B2}) = (1/2)^2(1/2)^2 \approx 0.006$. $p(\mathcal{T}_{B1})$ is greater than $p(\mathcal{T}_{B2})$, so $\mathcal{T}_{B1}$ has more probability of representing $G(\mathrm{B})$. Furthermore, since the size of 1-hop neighborhood graph is often small, there are few candidate dendrograms. If ignoring the sequential change of leaf nodes, $G(\mathrm{B})$ just has 2 possible structures of HRG as shown in Fig. 2, and $\mathcal{T}_{B1}$ is the more plausible of these two.

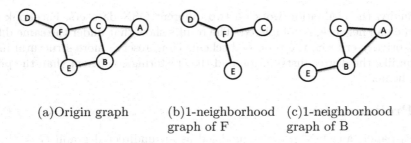

(a)Origin graph   (b)1-neighborhood   (c)1-neighborhood
                   graph of F   graph of B

Fig. 1. An example of the 1-neighborhood graph

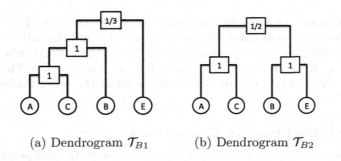

(a) Dendrogram $\mathcal{T}_{B1}$ (b) Dendrogram $\mathcal{T}_{B2}$

Fig. 2. Some dendrograms generated from B's 1-neighborhood graph

2.2 Differential Privacy

Differential privacy is designed to protect the privacy between neighboring databases which differ in only one element. It means that the adversary could not distinguish whether one of the elements changes based on the releasing result. In the model of OSNs, the adversary is not able to be sure if two users are linked in the original network.

Definition 1 (NEIGHBOR DATABASE). *Given a database D_1, its neighbor database D_2 differs from D_1 in at most one element.*

In this paper, the neighbor database/graph refers to a OSN with one edge added or deleted.

Definition 2 (SENSITIVITY). *The sensitivity ($\triangle f$) of a function f is the maximum distance of any two neighbor databases in the ℓ_1 norm.*

$$\Delta f = \max_{D_1, D_2} ||f(D_1) - f(D_2)||, \tag{2}$$

Definition 3 (ϵ-DIFFERENTIAL PRIVACY). *A randomized algorithm $\mathcal{A}$ achieves ϵ-differential private if for all neighbor datasets D_1 and D_2 and all $S \subseteq Range(\mathcal{A})$*

$$\Pr[\mathcal{A}(D_1) \in S] \leq e^{\epsilon} \times \Pr[\mathcal{A}(D_2) \in S] \tag{3}$$

Equation (3) calculates the probability that two neighbor databases have the same result under the same algorithm. Based on the definition, researchers designed the exponential mechanism to achieve ϵ-differential privacy when the query's result is an output space instead of a real value. It resamples the original output space OS with a new probability sequence. In particular, it assigns exponential probabilities with respect to the sensitivity ($\triangle f$) and the desired security parameters ϵ so that the final output space is smoothed [8].

Theorem 1 (EXPONENTIAL MECHANISM). *For a function $f\colon (G, OS)$ $\rightarrow \mathbb{R}$, the randomized algorithm $\mathcal{A}$ that samples an output O from OS with the probability proportional to* $\exp\left(\frac{\epsilon \cdot f(G, OS)}{2\triangle f}\right)$ *achieves ϵ-differential privacy.*

3 Scheme

To preserve link privacy, previous research advocated differential privacy [7,8], where the output changes at a small probability (less than e^ϵ) with the modification of one of its tuple. It is a rigorous privacy guarantee and it may create a significant negative impact on utility because the necessary noise amount is proportional to the whole graph size, which is a significant number in OSN analysis.

Instead of hiding every link in the network with the same probability, the proposed scheme reduces the scale of the network. The notion of local is defined as the 1-neighborhood graph comparing with the notion of global which means the whole graph. Also the grouping algorithm is deployed in the proposed scheme to form a confidential group, then the users hide among other users with similar structural information, but not all users in the network.

In this paper, the concept of group-based local ϵ-differential privacy is defined, which can preserve privacy with less information loss.

Definition 4 (GROUP-BASED   LOCAL ϵ-DIFFERENTIAL PRIVACY). *For a group of at least k nodes, a randomized algorithm $\mathcal{A}$ extracts local features. $\mathcal{A}$ achieves group-based local ϵ-differential privacy if for all neighbor graphs D_1 and D_2 with one edge adding/deleting the result probability $\Pr[\mathcal{A}(D) \in S]$ satisfies the Eq. (3).*

Given an information network, the goal is to publish an anonymized network that preserves the structural utility as much as possible while satisfying group-based local ϵ-differential privacy. This is achieved via:

1. finding the approximate maximum independent set,
2. getting the 1-neighborhood graph of each node in the set,
3. extracting the HRGs to each node's subgraph under the criteria of differential privacy,
4. grouping the HRGs and sampling one representative for each group,
5. regenerating the 1-neighborhood graph and pasting the sanitized one to the whole graph.

Algorithm 1. Extract differential private HRG profile

Input: $G(v)$: the subgraph, m: profile size, ϵ: privacy parameter
Output: HRG profile $\{T^1...T^m\}$
 1: $\triangle f \leftarrow f(G)$ ▷ calculate the local sensitivity according to the size of graph $G(v)$
 2: choose a random starting dendrogram T_0
 3: $\{T^1...T^m\} \leftarrow T_0$
 4: **while** step number i < maximum iteration time **do**
 5:     randomly pick an internal node r
 6:     pick a neighbor dendrogram T'_i of T_{i-1}^1 by randomly choosing a configuration
        of r's subtrees
 7:     $T_i^1 \leftarrow T'_i$ with the probability min $\left(1, \dfrac{\exp\left(\frac{\epsilon}{2\triangle f} p(T'_i)\right)}{\exp\left(\frac{\epsilon}{2\triangle f} p(T_{i-1}^1)\right)}\right)$
 8:     ...
 9:     $T_i^m \leftarrow T'_i$ with the probability min $\left(1, \dfrac{\exp\left(\frac{\epsilon}{2\triangle f} p(T'_i)\right)}{\exp\left(\frac{\epsilon}{2\triangle f} p(T_{i-1}^m)\right)}\right)$
10:     **if** equilibrium of $p(T_i^1)$ is researched **then**
11:         **break**
12:     **end if**
13: **end while**

3.1   Maximum Independent Set

Since the proposed scheme splits the whole network G to many 1-neighborhood graphs and perturbs these subgraphs as described in Sect. 3.4, a set of subgraphs is carefully chosen that could sanitize together without any mutual influence. The most basic prerequisite is that any two central nodes of two subgraphs are not adjacent. Hence, an approximation algorithm [9] is deployed to search the maximum independent set of graph G.

3.2   HRG Extraction

The HRG model is deployed to capture the local features because it is easy to integrate local ϵ-differential privacy into the dendrogram and a new graph could be regenerated from the sanitized dendrogram. In this section, we first introduce the work to extract HRG model, then derive the amount of noise necessary to achieve a given local ϵ-privacy level.

The number of possible dendrograms is $|T| = (2|V|-3)!!$ for a network with $|V|$ vertices [8], where !! is the semi-factorial symbol. Although the size of the whole output space OS is largely reduced by segmentation, extracting OS is still expensive for large subgraphs. In Algorithm 1, a Markov chain Monte Carlo (MCMC) process is deployed to control the time complexity and give an approximate result.

T_i^m is defined as the dendrogram with the m-th highest posterior probability in the i-th step. The purpose of Algorithm 1 is to publish a profile $\{T^1...T^m\}$ having m candidate dendrograms with the highest probability of the input graph. Specifically, Algorithm 1 first chooses an initial dendrogram T_0. Assuming T_{i-1}^1 is the most possible dendrogram of the last step, then in the new step the MCMC

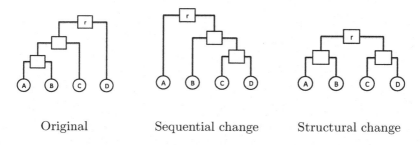

Original   Sequential change   Structural change

Fig. 3. Two neighbor configuration samples of r's subtree

process randomly chooses a root node r in $\mathcal{T}_{i-1}^1$ and then configure a neighbor HRG of $\mathcal{T}_{i-1}^1$ called $\mathcal{T}_i'$. There are $A_4^4 * 2 = 48$ candidate neighbors of a four-leaf-node subtree and two of the neighbor examples is shown in Fig. 3. The dendrograms in the profile are replaced by $\mathcal{T}_i'$ at the acceptance ratio $\frac{p(\mathcal{T}'_i)}{p(\mathcal{T}_{i-1})}$, otherwise it remains $\mathcal{T}_{i-1}$. When equilibrium of $p(\mathcal{T}^1)$ is reached, the set of m possible dendrograms will be stored.

According to Theorem 1, if the desired result is to achieve ϵ-differential privacy, there should be another sample process after drawing the original output space. In Algorithm 1, the MCMC process picks the HRG profile and simulate the exponential mechanism at the same time. The exponential mechanism requires a resampling of the output space OS with the probability $\exp\left(\frac{\epsilon \cdot f(G,OS)}{2\triangle f}\right)$. So the acceptance ratio is changed from $\frac{p(\mathcal{T}'_i)}{p(\mathcal{T}_{i-1})}$ to $\frac{\exp\left(\frac{\epsilon}{2\triangle f}p(\mathcal{T}'_i)\right)}{\exp\left(\frac{\epsilon}{2\triangle f}p(\mathcal{T}_{i-1})\right)}$.

The local sensitivity $\triangle f$ must be analyzed to finish the acceptance ratio equation. When the ϵ-differential privacy is in the link privacy area, the neighbor of a graph is a graph with just one edge changes according to Definition 4. It is assumed that the edge is missing without a loss of generality. So the sensitivity could be denoted as:

$$\triangle f = \max\left(p(\mathcal{T}(E_r)) - p(\mathcal{T}(E_r - 1))\right)$$

$$\log(\triangle f) = \max\left(n_{Lr}n_{Rr}\left(h\left(\frac{E_r}{n_{Lr}n_{Rr}}\right) - h\left(\frac{E_r - 1}{n_{Lr}n_{Rr}}\right)\right)\right) \quad (4)$$

where $h(p) = -p\log(p) - (1-p)\log(1-p)$. $\triangle f$ monotonically increases when $n_{Lr} * n_{Rr}$ increase. Detailed analysis is omitted for space constraints, $\triangle f$ gets the maximum value when n_{Lr} and n_{Rr} have the same value equal to half of the total vertices number $\frac{|V|}{2}$.

$$\triangle f = \frac{|V|^2}{4} * \left(1 + \frac{1}{\frac{|V|^2}{4} - 1}\right)^{\frac{|V|^2}{4} - 1}$$

$$\log(\triangle f) = \log\left(\frac{|V|^2}{4}\right) + \left(\frac{|V|^2}{4} - 1\right)\log\left(1 + \frac{1}{\frac{|V|^2}{4} - 1}\right) \quad (5)$$

$$\left(\frac{|V|^2}{4} - 1\right) \log \left(1 + \frac{1}{\frac{|V|^2}{4} - 1}\right) = \log \left(1 + \frac{1}{y}\right)^y < \log e$$

$$\log(\triangle f) \leqslant \log \left(\frac{|V|^2}{4}\right) + 1$$

Hence, $\log \left(\frac{|V|^2}{4}\right) + 1$ can be used as the sensitivity when calculating the log-based posterior probability of HRG model. The amplitude of noise increases when $|V|$ increases, where $|V|$ is the total number of nodes in the graph. Splitting the graph greatly reduces the size of the 1-neighborhood graph from $|V|$ to $|V(v)|$. Prior studies have demonstrated that in large network graphs, the maximum value of $|V(v)|$ is upper bounded by $\mathcal{O}(\sqrt{|V|})$ [10]. Furthermore, the proposed algorithm adds sufficient noise to different HRGs according to different $|V(v)|$ but not the maximum value. If the desired privacy criteria ϵ is the same, there is more utility preserved under the local ϵ-differential privacy compared with the global ϵ-differential privacy.

3.3   HRGs Grouping and Sampling

Here the proposed scheme deploys the grouping algorithm to enhance the privacy power. Although the user could not hide behind the whole graph, it hides in a group with other users having similar structural information. The general procedure here is to group the similar HRGs together and make them indistinguishable.

Intuitively, the HRGs extracted from the same 1-neighborhood graph should be grouped together. Based on this starting point, the procedure of HRGs grouping can also be viewed as the procedure of central node grouping. Since the number of leaf nodes in a HRG dendrogram is equal to the number of nodes in the original graph, only the subgraphs with the same size may have overlap in their output HRG space OS. Hence, for a given graph $G = (V, E)$, we group nodes $\{v\} \in V$ according to the metric $|V(v)|$, number of nodes in its 1-hop neighborhood graph.

Although the group formulation procedure groups the subgraphs with the same sizes together, not all groups have a size greater than or equal to our desired size k. Therefore, the small groups are merged if they have the most similar $|V(v)|$ to make sure each group has an appropriate size which is at least k. Then, the sampling space OS is grouped together, each group contains at least $k * m$ candidate HRGs.

To achieve the group-based local ϵ-differential privacy, each group chooses a representative HRG from the group's output space OS. It is sampled from the HRG group according to its probability $\exp \left(\frac{\epsilon}{2\triangle f} p(T)\right)$.

In the dendrogram extraction algorithm in Sect. 3.2, the proposed scheme introduces noise proportional to ϵ to make each node's subgraph similar to all its possible neighbors. Not like the particular group-mates in the grouping algorithm, differential privacy uses a manner to create neighbors, or building synthetic group-mates. In the group sampling algorithm in this section, the proposed scheme also finds $k - 1$ particular group-mates for each subgraph, and makes these group-mates extremely similar to each other. Hence, an attacker will not be able to identify the target node from a confidential group of at least k members even with the help of the releasing graph and prior knowledge of the 1-neighborhood relationship.

3.4   Subgraph Regeneration and Connection

In the last part of the proposed scheme, the subgraphs are restored from HRGs and the entire perturbed graph $\tilde{G}$ is published. Firstly, the sanitized 1-neighborhood graph is generated according to the group representative HRG. It is shown in the Subgraph Regeneration procedure in Algorithm 2. For each internal node r, the algorithm randomly generates E_r edges between the two node groups L_r and R_r.

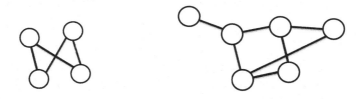

(a)Sanitized subgraph from $\mathcal{T}_{B2}$ (b)Graph $\tilde{G}$ with perturbed $G(B)$

Fig. 4. One possible change on B's 1-neighborhood graph

Algorithm 2. Subgraph regeneration and connection

Input: G: the whole graph,
     $\{\mathcal{T}^1...\mathcal{T}^{\lfloor \frac{|V|}{k} \rfloor}\}$: representative HRGs for each group
Output: A perturbed graph $\tilde{G}$
1: **for** each node $v \in V$ **do**
2:    $\mathcal{T} \leftarrow$ v's representative HRG
3:    **procedure** SUBGRAPH REGENERATION$(v,\mathcal{T})$
4:        **for** each internal node r $\in \mathcal{T}$ **do**
5:            $E_r \leftarrow p_r * n_{Lr} * n_{Rr}$ $\triangleright$ p_r is recorded in $\mathcal{T}$
6:            find the two groups L_r and R_r
7:            randomly place E_r edges between nodes from L_r and nodes from R_r
8:        **end for**
9:    **end procedure**
10:   random choose $|V(v)| - 1$ nodes in $\tilde{G}(v)$ $\triangleright$ v has $|V(v)| - 1$ neighbors in G
11:   $\tilde{G} \leftarrow G + \tilde{G}(v)$ $\triangleright$ paste the perturbed subgraph according to the neighbors
12:   $\tilde{G} \leftarrow \tilde{G} - G(v)$ $\triangleright$ cut v's original 1-neighborhood graph
13: **end for**
14: **return** $\tilde{G}$ $\triangleright$ The 1-neighborhood graph of every node in the independent set has been replaced

---

Secondly, the sanitized subgraph replaces the original 1-neighborhood graph. Specifically, for each node v, the sanitized graph randomly chooses $|V(v)|$-1 nodes as v's neighbor. The perturbed graph could easily be pasted on the whole graph G when the neighbor nodes' label is changed to its corresponding label in the original graph. However, the connecting algorithm is forced to deal with the subgraphs having at least $|V(v)|$-1 nodes. A small graph is not appropriate to replace a large subgraph because it does not have enough outer nodes.

Figure 4 shows an example of subgraph regeneration and connection. The original subgraph is $G(B)$ in Fig. 1(c), and the sanitized subgraph is based on T_{B2} in Fig. 2(b). The dendrogram T_{B2} requires to have two pairs of linked nodes, and they are randomly connected with two edges. Figure 4(a) is one possible sanitized subgraph rather than the original $G(B)$. Then Algorithm 2 randomly chooses three nodes in the sanitized subgraph to be the node A, C, and E in the original graph. Using the three nodes, the sanitized subgraph is pasted on the whole graph. Finally, for simplicity and anonymization purposes, the sanitized subgraphs do not contain the labels, as well as the final releasing graph $\tilde{G}$.

4 Evaluation

In this section, the anonymization scheme is evaluated over two real-world datasets, namely Facebook and Enron [11]. The statistics of these datasets are given in Table 1. Because $|V(v)|$ is smaller than $|V|$ in the datasets, the noise of local differential privacy scheme is largely reduced.

Table 1. Network dataset statistics

Dataset	# of nodes	# of edges	Max subgraph size
Facebook	4039	88234	1045
Enron	33692	183831	1383

4.1 Experimental Settings

ϵ is a privacy parameter to measure the ability of hiding existing edges. The smaller ϵ is, the better the privacy protection is [8]. In this paper, a strict criteria is set where $\epsilon = 0.1$ to test the utility performance of the local privacy scheme. The minimum group size is set to 10, corresponding to the size of networks. Each subgraph has 3 candidate HRGs, so the representative HRG is sampled from the profile with at least 30 HRGs.

For comparison purposes, one state-of-the-art technique is implemented as reference. It is the basic global differential privacy algorithm with HRG models in [8] under the same privacy criteria. The evaluation is based on the python implementation of the work in [12]. In the following figures, the result of previous global differential privacy HRG scheme is marked as 'reference', the result of proposed scheme is marked as 'LDP' (local differential privacy).

4.2   Evaluation Result

Degree Distribution. The degree of a node in a network is the number of edges the node has to other nodes. Figure 5 shows the degree distribution of the two different datasets. For better presentation, a base-10 log scale is used for the X axis because these schemes have different results in the low degree space.

Taking the Facebook result as an example, all the results have similar average degree but different distributions. The standard deviation of degree is 52.4, 7.0, 48.0 corresponding to the original graph, the reference result, the result of LDP scheme. And there is no node degree lower than 23 in the reference result while other results have low degree nodes. The LDP scheme follow the trend that there are less nodes when the degree becomes higher at the origin. However, the global differential privacy scheme has a new trend that the degree centralizes in a small range.

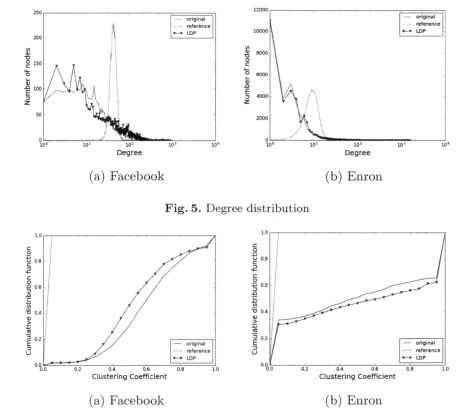

(a) Facebook   (b) Enron

Fig. 5. Degree distribution

(a) Facebook   (b) Enron

Fig. 6. Clustering coefficient distribution

Clustering. Clustering coefficient is a measure of how nodes in a graph tend to cluster together. While other models like dk2 [7] may break the features of cluster, HRG model is believed to protect some clustering information because it is a procedure of grouping close nodes together to build the dendrogram. Figure 6 shows the clustering coefficient distribution of the two datasets.

The global differential privacy scheme reduces the clustering coefficient to a low level. In the Enron dataset result, 33.6%, 99.8%, and 30.2% nodes have clustering coefficient lower than 0.03 corresponding to the original graph, the reference result, and the result of LDP scheme. The highest clustering coefficient under the global differential privacy scheme is 0.17, while the original dataset and the LDP scheme have 34.2% and 37.8% nodes with clustering coefficient higher than 0.95. These nodes are the critical users in the Enron dataset and our local differential privacy scheme could preserve some of them. In the two datasets, our local schemes can preserve more clustering distribution information than the global differential scheme.

5 Conclusion

In this paper, the problem of publishing OSN data that provides specified level of differential privacy guarantee while preserving as much structural information as possible was studied. The group-based local differential privacy criteria was identified and a uniform framework was proposed based on HRG models to generate a perturbed social network under that criteria. A realistic model, 1-neighborhood graph, was adapted to capture the local features and reduce the total amount of noise. The proposed scheme also contained a grouping algorithm to enhance the privacy level. The empirical study indicated that the proposed scheme does less damage to graph utility compared with previous global privacy mechanisms.

References

1. Narayanan, A., Shmatikov, V.: De-anonymizing social networks. In: 2009 30th IEEE Symposium on Security and Privacy, pp. 173–187. IEEE (2009)
2. Ji, S., Li, W., Mittal, P., Hu, X., Beyah, R.: SecGraph: a uniform and open-source evaluation system for graph data anonymization and de-anonymization. In: Proceedings of USENIX Security Symposium (2015)
3. Zhou, B., Pei, J.: Preserving privacy in social networks against neighborhood attacks. In: IEEE 24th International Conference on Data Engineering, ICDE 2008, pp. 506–515. IEEE (2008)
4. Zou, L., Chen, L., Tamer Özsu, M.: K-automorphism: a general framework for privacy preserving network publication. Proc. VLDB Endowment **2**(1), 946–957 (2009)
5. Dwork, C.: Differential privacy. In: van Tilborg, H.C.A., Jajodia, S. (eds.) Encyclopedia of Cryptography and Security, pp. 338–340. Springer, New York (2011)
6. Chen, R., Acs, G., Castelluccia, C.: Differentially private sequential data publication via variable-length n-grams. In: Proceedings of the 2012 ACM Conference on Computer and Communications Security, pp. 638–649. ACM (2012)

7. Sala, A., Zhao, X., Wilson, C., Zheng, H., Zhao, B.Y.: Sharing graphs using differentially private graph models. In: Proceedings of the 2011 ACM SIGCOMM Conference on Internet Measurement Conference, pp. 81–98. ACM (2011)
8. Xiao, Q., Chen, R., Tan, K.-L.: Differentially private network data release via structural inference. In: Proceedings of the 20th ACM SIGKDD International Conference on Knowledge Discovery and Data Mining, pp. 911–920. ACM (2014)
9. Boppana, R., Halldórsson, M.M.: Approximating maximum independent sets by excluding subgraphs. BIT Numer. Math. **32**(2), 180–196 (1992)
10. Kwak, H., Lee, C., Park, H., Moon, S.: What is Twitter, a social network or a news media? In: Proceedings of the 19th International Conference on World Wide Web, pp. 591–600. ACM (2010)
11. Leskovec, J., Krevl, A.: SNAP datasets: Stanford large network dataset collection, June 2014
12. Clauset, A., Moore, C., Newman, M.E.J.: Structural inference of hierarchies in networks. In: Airoldi, E., Blei, D.M., Fienberg, S.E., Goldenberg, A., Xing, E.P., Zheng, A.X. (eds.) ICML 2006. LNCS, vol. 4503, pp. 1–13. Springer, Heidelberg (2007). doi:10.1007/978-3-540-73133-7_1

Pricing Privacy Leakage in Location-Based Services

Fenghua Li[1,2], Jiawen Liu[3], Liang Fang[1,4],
Ben Niu[1], Kui Geng[1(✉)], and Hui Li[5]

[1] State Key Laboratory of Information Security,
Institute of Information Engineering, Chinese Academy of Sciences, Beijing, China
{lfh,niuben,gengkui}@iie.ac.cn, Fangliang_iie@163.com
[2] School of Cyber Security, University of Chinese Academy of Sciences,
Beijing, China
[3] Central University of Financial and Economics, Beijing, China
liujiawen11@outlook.com
[4] School of CyberSpace Security,
Beijing University of Posts and Telecommunications, Beijing, China
[5] National Key Laboratory of Integrated Networks Services,
Xidian University, Xi'an, China
lihui@mail.xidian.edu.cn

Abstract. Quantifying location privacy is an interesting and hot topic in Location-Based Services (LBSs). However, existing schemes only consider the privacy leakage to the untrusted LBS servers, leaving out the leakage during the transportation phase. In this paper, we propose a privacy-preserving scheme to help the LBS user to select optimal privacy strategy with considering the aforementioned problem for the first time. In order to measure the efficacy of different kinds of Privacy-Preserving Mechanisms (PPMs) including cryptographic and non-cryptographic types, we first quantify the revenue of two kinds of aforementioned PPMs by considering the privacy loss and privacy leakage probability on the channel and LBS server, as well as the accumulated leakage previously, simultaneously. Then, we take the consumption of different PPMs into account, to compute the investment. Evaluation results illustrate the effectiveness and efficiency of our proposed scheme.

1 Introduction

With the proliferation of mobile devices, Location-Based Services (LBSs) play an increasingly significant role in our daily life and bring us more conveniences. We can utilize smart devices to obtain various applications to enrich our life, such as Google maps, Foursquare, Yelp!, etc. In order to enjoy the convenience provided by the LBS service providers, mobile users have to submit their location data to untrusted servers of LBSs through unreliable channels. During the process, any untrusted parts are capable of inferring mobile users' their private information (e.g., ID, occupation, home address, behavior pattern, interests, etc.) through obtaining these data [5,7,14]. Therefore, we need to pay more attention on it.

© Springer International Publishing AG 2017
L. Ma et al. (Eds.): WASA 2017, LNCS 10251, pp. 406–418, 2017.
DOI: 10.1007/978-3-319-60033-8_36

During the past decade years, a lot of schemes have been proposed to solve such privacy issues in LBSs. Existing works can be classified into two main categories, cryptographic schemes [2] and non-cryptographic based schemes including obfuscation-based mechanisms [3], dummy-based mechanisms [9,11] and anonymization-based mechanisms [18,19]. By utilizing methods above, some systems have been designed to achieve different optimal points in the trade-offs between the service quality or energy consumption and the privacy degree [17]. In the meantime, some researchers aim at quantifying the privacy. For example, Shokri *et al.* proposed a set of measurements to quantify mobile user's privacy in LBSs [16], in web search service [6] and in the database [15], respectively.

However, most of existing schemes leave out three essential problems. Firstly, users' location information has to go through unreliable channels and arrive at an untrusted server. This leads to the risk of information leakage to both eavesdroppers and untrusted server, thus causes severe damage to users. Yet current methods either aim only to protect the information from the untrusted server and ignore the transportation, or guard only against the eavesdroppers. Secondly, the influence of a single leakage is closely related to the accumulated leakage before this single item, while most of existing methods ignore the previous leakage. Thirdly, their quantification methods are incomprehensible for public.

In this paper, we propose a scheme to help mobile users selecting the most appropriate privacy-preserving strategy based on existing PPMs, where service providers are generally untrusted, and the channels are unreliable. Specifically, we price mobile users' privacy leakage, which is used to measure the benefit of each privacy strategy. This leakage is measured from two aspects through an easy-to-understand way: (1) both the leakage during the transportation phase and on the untrusted servers are considered, (2) the previous information leakage is also taken into account. Then, their consumptions are quantified as users' investments. Based on consumption and privacy leakage quantified above, we finally compute the Return on Investment (ROI) for different kinds of PPMs, which can be viewed as the overall evaluation value of each privacy strategy to help user select a proper one.

The contributions of this paper are summarized as follows:

– We borrow the concept of ROI from microeconomics to evaluate the benefits obtained from different kinds of PPMs in LBSs, which is a very suitable concept here in measuring benefits of adopting these PPMs. The benefit is measured by considering several factors, including the privacy benefits and costs of applying different privacy strategies. Additionally, our model can measure different types of PPMs, including the cryptographic approaches and non-cryptographic solutions in a same range.
– Since leaking different location in different phases and conditions will cause different privacy loss, we consider three aspect in privacy loss: (1) the accumulated leakage before every single location activity, (2) the leakage during both the transportation phase and (3) to the untrusted LBS server. This can properly measure the amount of information leaked to adversaries.

– We provide performance analysis of our proposed scheme and demonstrate its effectiveness in balancing the trade-off between privacy and consumptions.

The rest of this paper is organized as follows. Section 2 reviews current related work. Section 3 gives some preliminaries including motivation and basic concepts. Section 4 describes our scheme in detail. Section 5 presents evaluation of our results from experiments. Finally, the conclusion is drawn in Sect. 6.

2   Related Work

2.1   Location Privacy Preserving Systems

Most researchers aime at constructing privacy preserving systems or mechanisms to solve specific issues. They will also define the privacy in their papers, in order to demonstrate the effectiveness of their schemes.

Mechanisms are designed to solve specific problems. Li *et al.* [7] provided a transparent privacy control under different context. They quantified their privacy by assigning different levels to different locations. Niu *et al.* [10] adopted a different protocol in their designed system for uploading and aggregating data anonymously. They prove their guarantees on location privacy in face of side information, using the zero-knowledge. Bindschaedler and Shokri [3] generated synthetic trace to cope with the location inference attacks, where they quantify their privacy as statistical dissimilarity between the synthetic trace and its seed. Zhang *et al.* [19] redesigned the *k-anonymity*, to provide location privacy for privacy-sensitive users and simulated other privacy-indifferent users. Methods above have three problems: (1) their proposed PPMs are designed to solve one certain problem in LBS, which aren't applicable to other problems, (2) their quantification methods were biased in favor of their own PPM, some even assigned subjectively, (3) most of them are designed only against the untrusted or half-trusted server, by assuming the transportation will be safe as long as using the cryptographic methods.

System are designed to solve some comprehensive problems. Fawaz *et al.* [4] analyzed the location access control from more than 400 location-aware apps and proposed an effective location access control tool in the same time maintaining the app's function. Bilogrevic *et al.* [1] constructed a system, firstly predicting the motivation behind users' location sharing through machine learning. Then they construct the relation between the utility and privacy, utility and motivation separately. Finally, they obfuscate the check-in information in a proper degree according to this trade off relation. However, they have a common drawback that only one PPM can be chose in their system, namely, ways to protect the privacy are very limited and their quantification methods are incompletely.

2.2   Quantifying Location Privacy

Shokri *et al.* [16] measured location privacy by formalizing the adversary's performance, considering the prior information available to the attacker, and various attacks that can be performed. They quantified the privacy as the success probability of adversaries in their location-inference attacks. Gervais *et al.* [6] proposed generic quantitative method for evaluating users' web-search privacy. They used machine-learning algorithms to learn the link-ability between user queries and quantify privacy of users with respect to linkage attacks. Olteanu *et al.* [12] quantified the effect of co-location information on location privacy, considering an adversary who has access to these data. They quantified their location privacy by the expected error of the adversary when performing a localization attack.

Most of the methods above had three defects: (1) their quantification methods are incapable of measuring different types of PPMs in the same dimensions, (2) most of them either do not consider the effect of the previously leakage to current leakage, or leave out the privacy leakage on the transportation, (3) all of their quantification methods are incomprehensible for public.

3 Preliminaries

3.1 Basic Concepts

Location Privacy Strategy (LPS) refers to a particular location PPM with its parameter. In this paper, we use a set $LPS = \{lps_1, lps_2, \cdots\}$ to represent all the PPMs with their parameters, where lps_i is a tuple $\langle ppm_i, \langle para, \cdots \rangle \rangle$, ppm_i indicates a PPM and $\langle para, \cdots \rangle$ indicates ppm_i's parameters configuration. For instance, *k-anonymity* (k=10) mechanism is represented as $lps_1 = \langle k\text{-}anonymity, \langle 10 \rangle \rangle$.

Privacy Leakage Probability refers to the probability the real location information can be reconstructed by an adversary, after this adversary obtained the observed location.

Privacy Loss refers to the amount of users' personal information that can be analyzed and inferred by adversary utilizing this leaked real location.

ROI refers to the ratio of the return to investment. Specifically, the reduction of the privacy risk can be viewed as the return of privacy strategy, and the consumption of adopting that strategy is defined as the investment.

Privacy Leakage refers to the expected privacy loss, which is decided by the privacy loss and privacy leakage probability.

Location Activity refers to a specific event, where user issued a specific query containing a specific location during a certain time period to LBS server. This is formalized in Sect. 3.2.

3.2 User and Adversary

We consider a scenario where users move in an area partitioned into M discrete regions $G = \{g_1, \ldots, g_j, \ldots, g_M\}$. A location activity is represented by $loc_{i,j,l}$, which means user u_i has been the location g_j during time period t_l. The profile of mobile user u_i can be denoted as: $profile_i = \{\langle g_1, n_{i,1} \rangle, \langle g_2, n_{i,2} \rangle, \cdots\}$, where $n_{i,j}$ means the times that user u_i move in region g_j. Apparently, a $\langle g_j, n_{i,j} \rangle$ is composed of several *loc*s.

Generally, the channel is untrusted, adversaries can easily eavesdrop the communication channels and obtain these protected information. As LBS users are sporadic, the knowledge that the adversary can accumulate by continuous eavesdropping is users' issuing probability distribution over different regions. We assume that the LBS servers are untrusted but honest. That is to say the server will follow the protocol to provide service to users using their location information, but may attempt to learn more information than allowed, more specifically, to reconstruct users' integral location profiles.

3.3   Motivation

Figure 1 illustrates the general architecture and processes of current LBSs. To enjoy the convenience provided by LBS applications, mobile user *Alice* needs to pay electricity fee to keep her smartphone alive and another part of money for her data plan to suffer the internet. She really wonders these costs can be worthwhile for enjoying the service while protecting her privacy. However, existing metrics in privacy protection is obscure. It is necessary to make it be easy-to-understanding by public. Since money is always considered as a directly way to represent the benefit, it makes sense to introduce ROI into our measurement. On the other hand, quantification methods always emphasizing on some specific topics, such as privacy preservation to the untrusted LBS server, and ignore the privacy leakage on the transportation phase. Therefore, it is interesting and meaningful to design a comprehensive model to measure user's privacy. As shown in Fig. 1, within *Alice*'s phone (the left dotted rectangle), different PPMs brings various resource consumptions, which mean the cost that we need to pay for our privacy protection, it plays an important role in deciding whether this PPM is economical. Out of her phone (the right dotted rectangle), *Alice* suffers from two unsafe points, the untrusted LBS servers and the unreliable communication channels. The key problem in such two points is to price the privacy leakage, which is vital to compute privacy leakage revenue after adopting a specific PPM. Therefore, we need to comprehensively study the privacy loss and the privacy leakage probability over different phase.

Generally, the privacy leakage probability varies in different phases and PPMs. If users adopt *k-anonymity* [8] to protect their locations, these will be leaked to the eavesdropper and the untrusted LBS server in same probability. However, if users adopt an cryptographic method such as RSA algorithm to

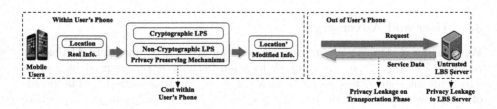

Fig. 1. Our motivation

encrypt their locations, the probabilities for the eavesdroppers and untrusted servers to guess the real locations are obviously different.

It is also hard to measure the privacy loss, because it is affected by different phases and different amount of previous leakage (i.e., adversary's knowledge). To be specific, if adversaries already get 8 *locs* of a particular user, they might not know a lot of this person. However, if adversaries can get the 9th *loc*, they may re-identify this user in a very high probability. Apparently, the 9th *loc* can obviously cause larger privacy loss than previous 8 *locs*. In other words, adversaries can re-identify user to different extent by combining different previous leaked information with current information.

3.4 Our Basic Idea

Based on observation above, concept of ROI is borrowed from microeconomics to design a metric reflecting the profits brought by different privacy strategies. The key problem is to formalize the ROI in a proper manner to measure the PPMs of cryptographic and non-cryptographic privacy-preserving schemes in a same range. We price the return after applying a specific location privacy strategy, as well as the investment. Then the ratio of the return to the investment can clearly represent the ROI of this strategy. Finally, the location privacy strategy with the highest ROI is our recommended strategy. When our metrics are used, users only need to input there current location and we can automatically output the most suitable privacy strategy to them.

4 Our Proposed Scheme

4.1 System Overview

Figure 2 shows the structure of our scheme, and illustrates how to compute the ROI of a specific location privacy strategy *lps* for a certain location activity $loc_{i,j,l}$. The steps are summarized as follows:

(i) In Sect. 4.2, we quantify the privacy leakage probability as $Pr(lps_i)_{trans}$ and $Pr(lps_i)_{server}$ separately for every $lps_i \in LPS$. Note that these probabilities are only related to the LPSs.

(ii) Next, in Sect. 4.2, we formalize the privacy loss in the two phases separately for different location activity as $loss(loc_{i,j,l})_{server}$ and $loss(loc_{i,j,l})_{trans}$. These are related to different location activity and different previous leakage, and have to be calculated every time.

(iii) Utilizing the leakage probabilities and the privacy losses in two phases, we calculate the *return* of applying a specific *lps* in the third part of the Sect. 4.2. The $Pr(lps_i)_{trans}$ and $loss(loc_{i,j,l})_{trans}$ are used to compute the privacy leakage in transportation, and $Pr(lps_i)_{server}$ and $loss(loc_{i,j,l})_{server}$ are used to compute the privacy leakage in LBS server. Then, the change of the total privacy leakage before and after the adoption of lps_i is *return*.

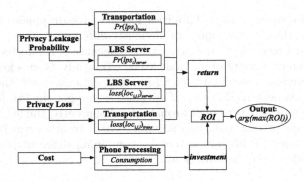

Fig. 2. Scheme overview

(iv) Then the resource consumptions of every *lps* are monitored in advance, which is used to compute the investment of the adoption of LPS in Sect. 4.3.
(v) Based on the the *return* and *investment* above, the ROI is calculated to measure the profit rate of every *lps* in Sect. 4.4. We finally output the best strategy for mobile users.

4.2 Return

In this section, firstly, we define the leakage probability as Pr. This measures the probability of leaking the location information to the attacker. Then we define the privacy loss as *loss*, to measure the amount of privacy loss after the real location information being leaked to adversaries. Finally, we design leakage (*leakage*) as expectation loss to measure privacy loss in the whole LBS process.

$$leakage = \sum Pr * loss.$$

Intuitively, after applying a specific LPS, information leakage will reduce. So, we define the amount of this leakage decreased after protection as the *return*:

$$return = \Delta leakage = leakage_{before} - leakage_{after},$$

where triangle symbol is used for difference, $leakage_{before}$ and $leakage_{after}$ means the *leakage* before and after applying the privacy strategy.

Privacy Leakage Probability (Pr). We assume a strong attacker has the ability to obtain the modified message. Then leakage probability is the probability that the attacker can successfully reconstruct the real location from the modified location. This is based only on different LPSs, as well as different phases.

Cryptographic LPSs: We use subset $LPS_{en} \subsetneq LPS$ to represent the cryptographic LPSs.

In the phase of transportation, attackers can get the encrypted location. He needs to reconstruct the private key in order to reconstruct the real location.

We use the probability of successfully reconstruct the private key to define the leakage probability of LPS_{en}. This is detailed as follows. The LPS_{en} can be divided into two categories, the 1st is the LPSs that generalized their extraction of root into the intractability of factoring large numbers and the 2nd is these that generalized their attack process into intractability of extracting discrete logarithms (EDL) over finite groups. The way to solve and reconstruct the plaintext is to factor the large number (FLN), whose complexity is $\sqrt{large\ number}$, and extract discrete logarithms (EDL) over finite groups whose complexity is $para_i$. Since the probability of reconstructing the private key is nearly to zero, we define there leakage probability as: $Pr(lps_i)_{trans} = 0$.

In the phase of LBS server, since untrusted servers have the corresponding private key to decrypt, the probability of reconstructing the real location is apparently 1. Namely, $Pr(lps_i)_{server} = 1$, $lps_i \in LPS_{en}$. Moreover, some cryptographic LPSs are homomorphic, the leakage probability here will be the same as the transportation, namely the $Pr(lps_i)_{server} = Pr(lps_i)_{trans}$.

Non-cryptographic LPSs: We use subset $LPS_{non-en} \subsetneqq LPS$ to represent the non-cryptographic LPSs in LBS including the dummy, obfuscation and anonymization. Because the untrusted server also has no way to figure out the real location from the modified location information, these LPSs have the same effect in the phase of transportation and LBS server. This means they have the same leakage probability in the two phases. Taking the *k-anonymity* to illustrate, with parameter $para_i = k$, we can have $Pr(\langle k\text{-}anonymity, k\rangle)_{trans} = Pr(\langle k\text{-}anonymity, k\rangle)_{server} = \frac{1}{k}$.

Privacy Loss (*loss*). We use location profiles defined in Sect. 3.2 composed of several location activity (*loc*) to represent users' privacy. Obviously, a single leakage to adversary can be harmless, while accumulated leakage can cause severe damage. When adversary has already obtained some *loc*s of a user, the leakage of the next *loc* may cause larger privacy loss than previous. That is to say, different *loc*s leaked in different phases under different adversary knowledges can cause different privacy losses. As a result, we first define the total loss $LOSS$, then the loss of a single location activity $loc_{i,j,l}$ can be calculated as:

$$loss(loc_{i,j,l}) = \Delta LOSS. \tag{1}$$

It means the difference of the total loss before and after leaking $loc_{i,j,l}$ to attacker.

From Sect. 3.1, we can learn that $LOSS$ is the amount of privacy leakage when all accurate location has been revealed to adversary. To be more secure we assume a strong adversary that the real location activities are revealed as long as been eavesdropped. Then, there will be a user's profile $profile'_i$ collected by the adversary: $profile'_i = \{\langle g_1, n'_{i,1}\rangle, \langle g_2, n'_{i,2}\rangle, \cdots\}$.

Then, we can use similarity between the user u_i's $profile'_i$ obtained by the adversary and his/her original profile $profile_i$ to represent the total loss $LOSS$:

$$LOSS(profile'_i) = \sum_j \frac{n_{i,j}}{\sum_j n_{i,j}} * sim(\langle g_j, n_{i,j}\rangle, \langle g_j, n'_{i,j}\rangle). \tag{2}$$

To be more accurately, considering the time effect, we can divide the tuple $\langle g_j, n_{i,j} \rangle$ by time periods. Then we will have a time sequence for every location: $\langle g_j, n_{i,j} \rangle = \langle (t_1, n_{i,j,1}), (t_2, n_{i,j,2}), \cdots \rangle$ where $(t_l, n_{i,j,l})$ is the number of $loc_{i,j,l}$ in a certain time periods t_l. In the same way, the adversary can also construct a similar time sequence for every eavesdropped location: $\langle g_j, n'_{i,j} \rangle = \langle (t_1, n'_{i,j,1}), (t_2, n'_{i,j,2}), \cdots \rangle$. We can calculate their similarity by the adjusted cosine similarity as:

$$\frac{\sum_l (n'_{i,j,l} - \overline{n'_{i,j}})(n_{i,j,l} - \overline{n_{i,j}})}{\sqrt{\sum_l (n'_{i,j,l} - \overline{n'_{i,j}})^2} + \sqrt{\sum_l (n_{i,j,l} - \overline{n'_{i,j}})^2}}. \tag{3}$$

Then, using the total loss before and after leaking a specific location activity $loc_{i,j,l}$, we can calculate the privacy loss of a single leakage as:

$$loss(loc_{i,j,l}) = LOSS(profile'_i + loc_{i,j,l}) - LOSS(profile'_i),$$

where $profile'_i + g_j$ is the $profile'_i$ after the g_j leaked to adversary.

Return. After adopting a specific LPS lps_i to protect a specific location g_i, we can firstly calculate the *leakage*:

$$leakage(lps_i, loc_{i,j,l}) = \sum_{tans,server} Pr(lps_i) * loss(loc_{i,j,l}).$$

Apparently, before adopting the lps_i, the leakage of getting the LBS using the unprotected location g_i is:

$$leakage(\cdot, loc_{i,j,l}) = \sum_{tans,server} Pr(\cdot) * loss(loc_{i,j,l}).$$

where the leakage probability of an unprotected location is 1, namely $Pr(\cdot) = 1$.

Then the return denoted as $return(lps_i, loc_{i,j,l})$ means using this lps_i to protect the location activity $loc_{i,j,l}$ can easily be calculated as:

$$leakage(\cdot, loc_{i,j,l}) - leakage(lps_i, loc_{i,j,l}).$$

4.3   Investment

There will be different cost when applying different LPSs with different parameter configuration. Their costs can justifiably be viewed as investments, including the power consumption $E(lps_i)$ (energy) and data consumption $D(lps_i)$. Then converting these consumptions into money by multiple their tariff, we can define investment as the sum of all these cost:

$$investment(lps_i, loc_{i,j,l}) = E + D.$$

4.4   ROI

Using the return and investment calculated above, ROI is calculated as:

$$ROI(lps_i, loc_{i,j,l}) = \frac{return(lps_i, loc_{i,j,l})}{investment(lps_i, loc_{i,j,l})}.$$

This concept can easily be understood by anyone who even know nothing about privacy protection. People can learn about why they must use these PPMs to protect their location and what they can obtain by using these PPMs.

5   Performance Evaluations

5.1   Setup

Profile Generation. Users' real profiles that we use belong to 100 randomly chosen mobile users from dataset [13]. Each $profile_i$ contains the issuing times within different locations of a user every 120 min for 8 h. The area within which the user move is divided into 40 regions forming a 5×8 grid. In order to have a strongest adversary, we feed the adversary with users' accurate history location.

Table 1. User's original profile and profile observed by adversary

	$Profile_i$				$Profile'_i$			
Time period	t_1	t_2	$\cdots$	t_4	t_1	t_2	$\cdots$	t_4
g_1	18	16	$\cdots$	10	16	2	$\cdots$	1
g_2	10	7	$\cdots$	7	6	2	$\cdots$	0
$\cdots$	$\cdots$	$\cdots$	$\cdots$	$\cdots$	$\cdots$	$\cdots$	$\cdots$	$\cdots$
g_{40}	18	25	16	23	4	19	12	5

Privacy Loss Measurement. Figure 3(a) showed the privacy loss of different location in our the time periods.

In our instance, we randomly chose a location activity (g_3, t_2) as user's current activity and computed its privacy loss. This event is represented as $loc_{i,3,2}$. The profile observed by the eavesdropper is constructed in Table 1, denoted as $profile'_{i,ea}$, and observed by the server is denoted as $profile'_{i,se}$. $LOSS_{before,ea} = 0.41463$, $LOSS_{after,ea} = 0.415038$, $LOSS_{before,se} = 0.99964766$, $LOSS_{before,se} = 1$. Then we can have the loss of $loc_{i,3,2}$ on the transportation as: $loss(loc_{i,3,2})_{trans} = 0.000408$, and loss on the server $loss(loc_{i,3,2})_{server} = 0.0003523$.

Return. We use the k-$anonymity$ with parameter $k = 5 \sim 20$ [8] to instance the non-cryptographic LPSs and the paillier [2] with key_length = 2048-bit and 512-bit to instance the cryptographic LPSs. $returns$ of the two LPSs under different parameters are showed in Fig. 3(b). The red points represent $return$ of paillier under 512-bit and 2048-bit key_length. Red points have nearly the same value.

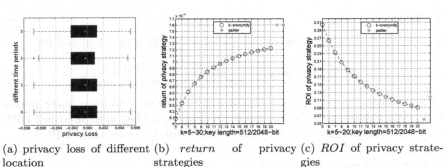

(a) privacy loss of different location (b) *return* of privacy strategies (c) *ROI* of privacy strategies

Fig. 3. *Return* and *ROI* and *privacy loss* of *k-anonymity* and paillier with their parameters (Color figure online)

ROI. Under 'WiFi', the original data is 2KB, we monitored the energy consumption and data consumption of the *k-anonymity* with the parameter $k = 5 \sim 20$ and the paillier with key_length = 2048-bit and 512-bit. We collected ten groups of data for 1000 times and average them, showed in Table 2. Using these consumptions, we compute their investments under current fee standards as: $investment(lps_i, loc_{i,j,l}) = E * 5.88 * 10^{-7} + D * 2 * 10^{-4} = 2.005 * 10^{-3}$. Finally the ROI is computed as: $ROI(\langle k - anonymity, 10 \rangle, loc_{i,3,2}) = \frac{return(\langle k-anonymity,10 \rangle, loc_{i,3,2})}{investment(lps_i, loc_{i,j,l})} = 0.314$. The rest of ROIs are presented in Fig. 3(c). The first red point in Fig. 3(c) is the ROI of paillier under key_length = 512-bit, the second one is under key_length = 2048-bit.

Table 2. Consumption of privacy strategies

	k-anonymity (para = k)					Paillier (para = key_length)	
Parameter value	5	6	7	⋯	20	512-bit	2048-bit
D (in *mAh*)	1.83	1.84	3.72	⋯	3.64	7.42	81.86
E (in *KB*)	10	12	14	⋯	40	64	32

5.2   Results

The result tallied with the fact that $k - anonymity$ with $k = 5$ has the highest ROI. From the ROIs of different privacy strategies above, we can draw some conclusions. Even though some LPSs (such as paillier) have the overwhelm advantage over others (such as *k-anonymity*) intuitively, yet their ROIs are not necessary higher. This is resulted from our consideration of both the privacy leakage on the transportation and LBS servers, as well as the consumption in our scheme.

6   Conclusions

In this paper, we priced mobile user's privacy with our proposed Return on Investment (ROI), which is a new and easily-to-understand definition in LBSs. We considered two possible ways to reveal user's privacy, including the privacy loss during the transportation phase and to the untrusted LBS servers. We also quantified the LBS user's consumption within the smart phone. Based on these information, we inferred and formalized the ROI. The evaluation results showed that our newly-defined ROI can effectively measure different kinds of PPMs in the same range.

Acknowledgement. This work was supported by the General Program of National Natural Science Foundation of China (61672515), the National Key Research and Development Program of China (2016YFB0800303) and the National Natural Science Foundation of China (61502489).

References

1. Bilogrevic, I., Huguenin, K., Mihaila, S., Shokri, R., Hubaux, J.P.: Predicting users' motivations behind location check-ins and utility implications of privacy protection mechanisms. In: Proceedings of ISOC NDSS (2015)
2. Bilogrevic, I., Jadliwala, M., Kalkan, K., Hubaux, J.-P., Aad, I.: Privacy in mobile computing for location-sharing-based services. In: Fischer-Hübner, S., Hopper, N. (eds.) PETS 2011. LNCS, vol. 6794, pp. 77–96. Springer, Heidelberg (2011). doi:10. 1007/978-3-642-22263-4_5
3. Bindschaedler, V., Shokri, R.: Synthesizing plausible privacy-preserving location traces. In: Proceedings of IEEE S&P (2016)
4. Fawaz, K., Feng, H., Shin, K.G.: Anatomization and protection of mobile apps' location privacy threats. In: Proceedings of USENIX Association USENIX Security (2015)
5. Fechner, T., Kray, C.: Attacking location privacy: exploring human strategies. In: Proceedings of ACM UbiComp (2012)
6. Gervais, A., Shokri, R., Singla, A., Capkun, S., Lenders, V.: Quantifying web-search privacy. In: Proceedings of ACM CCS (2014)
7. Li, H., Zhu, H., Du, S., Liang, X., Shen, X.: Privacy leakage of location sharing in mobile social networks: attacks and defense. IEEE Trans. Dependable Secure Comput. (2016)
8. Niu, B., Li, Q., Zhu, X., Cao, G., Li, H.: Achieving k-anonymity in privacy-aware location-based services. In: Proceedings of IEEE INFOCOM (2014)
9. Niu, B., Li, Q., Zhu, X., Cao, G., Li, H.: Enhancing privacy through caching in location-based services. In: Proceedings of IEEE INFOCOM (2015)
10. Niu, B., Zhu, X., Lei, X., Zhang, W., Li, H.: Eps: encounter-based privacy-preserving scheme for location-based services. In: Proceedings of IEEE Globecom (2013)
11. Niu, B., Zhu, X., Li, W., Li, H.: Epcloak: an efficient and privacy-preserving spatial cloaking scheme for lbss. In: Proceedings of IEEE MASS (2014)
12. Olteanu, A.M., Huguenin, K., Shokri, R., Humbert, M., Hubaux, J.P.: Quantifying interdependent privacy risks with location data. IEEE Trans. Mob. Comput. **10**(1109), 1536–1233 (2016)

13. Piorkowski, M., Sarafijanovoc-Djukic, N., Grossglauser, M.: A parsimonious model of mobile partitioned networks with clustering. In: Proceedings of COMSNETS (2009). http://www.comsnets.org
14. Rizoiu, M.A., Xie, L., Caetano, T., Cebrian, M.: Evolution of privacy loss in wikipedia. In: Proceedings of ACM WSDM (2015)
15. Sankar, L., Rajagopalan, S.R., Poor, H.V.: Utility-privacy tradeoffs in databases: an information-theoretic approach. IEEE Trans. Inf. Forensics Secur. 8(6), 838–852 (2013)
16. Shokri, R., Theodorakopoulos, G., Boudec, J.Y.L., Hubaux, J.P.: Quantifying location privacy. In: Proceedings of IEEE S&P (2011)
17. Shokri, R., Theodorakopoulos, G., Troncoso, C., Hubaux, J.P., Le Boudec, J.Y.: Protecting location privacy: optimal strategy against localization attacks. In: Proceedings of IEEE CCS (2012)
18. Zhang, S., Yang, H., Singh, L.: Anonymizing query logs by differential privacy. In: Proceedings ACM SIGIR (2016)
19. Zhang, Y., Tong, W., Zhong, S.: On designing satisfaction-ratio-aware truthful incentive mechanisms for k-anonymity location privacy. IEEE Trans. Inf. Forensics Secur. 11(11), 2528–2541 (2016)

MAIS: Multiple Activity Identification System Using Channel State Information of WiFi Signals

Chunhai Feng[✉], Sheheryar Arshad, and Yonghe Liu

University of Texas at Arlington, Arlington, TX, USA
{chunhai.feng,sheheryar.arshad}@mavs.uta.edu, yonghe@cse.uta.edu

Abstract. An extensive set of papers have employed channel state information of WiFi signals to perform human activity identification. Given the satisfactory performance, WiFi signals provide a device free, low cost, and non-intrusive alternative to traditional approaches including sensor based and camera based monitoring systems. Unfortunately, most existing papers have focused on the scenario where only a single subject presents. In this paper, we propose a novel human activity identification scheme termed Multiple Activity Identification System (MAIS), targeting at identifying multiple activities of different subjects in the same environment. In designing MAIS, we identify several challenges in identifying activities of multiple subjects and present corresponding solutions, including noise filtering, two-step detection of start/end point of activities, and kNN (k-Nearest Neighbors) algorithm to predict the number of people and the exact activities they are performing. Our experiments show that MAIS achieves an accuracy of 98.04% for anomaly detection, 97.21% for predicting the number of people, and 93.12% for predicting the activities they perform. To the best of our knowledge, this is the first system that achieves high accuracy identifying multiple activities performed by multiple people.

Keywords: Multiple activity identification · Wireless communications · Channel state information

1 Introduction

Given the ubiquitous presence of WiFi signals, numerous research efforts have been devoted to fully unfold their potentials in real life applications. Among them, channel state information (CSI) of WiFi signals have recently been extensively exploited in various scenarios. These include indoor navigation [15], gesture recognition [7], and human body activity identification [6]. For instance, house monitoring in case of an intrusion and emergency care for elders are very common contexts of use in modern society. Obviously, many traditional approaches, exemplified by computer vision [2] and wearable devices [3], can be employed for these applications. However, they usually require specific hardware and targeted deployments. In contrary, device free detection using WiFi signals piggybacks on existing infrastructure and hence serves as a low cost, non-intrusive alternative.

© Springer International Publishing AG 2017
L. Ma et al. (Eds.): WASA 2017, LNCS 10251, pp. 419–432, 2017.
DOI: 10.1007/978-3-319-60033-8_37

Employing the CSI collecting tool provided in [4], many previous researches [9, 14] have attempted activity detection in both stationary and dynamic circumstances. The disturbance of CSI among different subcarriers caused by human movements, both amplitude and phase information, can be used for anomaly detection. By extracting specific features and combining with classic machine learning algorithms, many proposed systems have achieved desirable performance. However, almost all existing CSI based activity identification systems *focus on the scenario where only a single subject presents*. These systems obviously have significant limitations as scenarios with multiple subjects are more common [10]. Additionally, many of these systems employ either a simple threshold [9] or outlier detection [5] without the capability of extracting the start and end points of each activity.

In this paper, we propose a novel human activity identification scheme termed MAIS, short for Multiple Activity Identification System. Different from existing schemes, MAIS targets at *identifying multiple activities of different subjects in the same environment*, using only commercially off the shelf WiFi devices. In designing MAIS, we have to overcome several challenges. First, reflections of wireless signals by multiple subjects owing to multipath effects are more complicated than those by a single subject, further complicating the identification of activities. Second, an efficient algorithm for extracting the start and end point of each activity automatically is needed. Existing work, based on empirical thresholds requiring large amount of preparatory experiments or outlier detection, is not accurate and adaptive enough in multiple subjects cases. And finally, choosing the correct number of features is critical for identifying multiple activities from different subjects as only limited metrics can represent the characteristics of signals.

To address these challenges, we first apply selected filters to smooth the amplitudes of signals, helping enlarge the feature dataset to be extracted by machine learning algorithms. We also execute linear transformation on the phase information in order to mitigate the significant impact of random noise. In order to identify the start and ending point of activities, we first apply outlier filtering and differential algorithms to the variance of signals among different subcarriers. We then calculate the largest eigenvalues from both amplitude and calibrated phase correlation matrix in order to remove any false detection. Finally, we introduce the kNN (k-Nearest Neighbors) algorithm to predict the number of people and the exact activities they are performing. Extensive experiments with one to three people and various combinations of activities are performed to evaluate the performance of MAIS. We show that MAIS achieves an accuracy of 98.04% for anomaly detection. With a number of features obtained from different filters, MAIS achieves an average accuracy of 97.21% for predicting the number of people and 93.12% for predicting the activities they perform. To the best of our knowledge, this is the first system that achieves high accuracy identifying multiple activities performed by multiple people.

In the rest of paper, we review related work in Sect. 2. Section 3 gives a brief introduction of channel state information. Section 4 provides an overview of the system framework, followed by detailed explanation of each component. Experiments and evaluations of MAIS are provided in Sect. 5. Finally we conclude in Sect. 6.

2   Related Works

An extensive range of work for activity detection have been performed in both the literature and industry. Based on employed hardwares, they can generally be divided into the following three groups.

Sensors Based: Sensors based activity detection have long drawn strong interests from researchers. They generally require sensors to be deployed on objects in the monitored environments. For example, in [11], a set of "tape and forget" sensors are deployed inside a house in order to recognize activities of interests for medical professionals. In others, sensors may be required to be carried by human subjects. For instance, in [3] the authors identify activities based on the data collected from wearable sensors under unsupervised settings. While these systems can achieve appealing accuracy, the installation and maintenance may incur extra costs with possible accompanied inconvenience with wearable devices.

Camera Based: Activity detection based on computer vision has been the subject of extensive research. In [2], the authors deploy four cameras at the ceiling corners in order to capture different scenes for tracking the users. Similarly, a smart video system [1] is built to monitor the behaviors of pedestrians and suspicious activities around public transportation areas. Although vision systems are a mature way to track users' behaviors, additional hardware is needed and privacy concerns in domestic scenarios need to be addressed.

Wireless Based: Many previous papers [5,9,14] have utilized wireless signals for human activity detection. In [12] the authors propose two mathematical models to establish the relationship between channel state information and a specific human activity. A system called WiLocuscis is constructed in [16] in order to present human walking trajectories by detecting a number of moving behaviors in sequence. E-eyes [14] constructs signal profiles and compares them with known activities with location information. Nevertheless, all of these systems only consider the scenario of one subject, which is not true in most scenarios. For example, a national survey [10] concludes that the average number of people per household in US is 2.54 in 2015.

3   Overview of Channel State Information

Denote the transmitted and received WiFi signals as $T(f,t)$ and $R(f,t)$ in frequency domain. We have

$$R(f,t) = H(f,t) \times T(f,t) + S(f,t), \tag{1}$$

where $H(f,t)$ is the CSI estimation of subcarrier with the central frequency of f and time of t. Assume noise $S(f,t)$ follows the Circularly-symmetric and zero mean complex normal distribution as $S \sim N_c(0, \Gamma)$, $H(f,t)$ can be approximated as

$$\widehat{H(f,t)} = \frac{R(f,t)}{T(f,t)}. \tag{2}$$

In order to get the amplitude and phase information, $\widehat{H(f,t)}$ can also be represented as

$$\widehat{H(f,t)} = ||\widehat{H(f,t)}||e^{j\angle\widehat{H(f,t)}}, \tag{3}$$

where $||\widehat{H(f,t)}||$ and $\angle\widehat{H(f,t)}$ indicate the amplitude and phase respectively.

4   System Design of MAIS

In this section, we provide a brief introduction of MAIS. As shown in Fig. 1, there are three fundamental modules, data processing, activity detection, and activities classification, in MAIS. Data processing is designed for smoothing the amplitude and calibrating the phase, while activity detection module detects the start and end data point of activities. By extracting a variety of features and taking advantage of kNN, MAIS is able to predict the number of people and the activities they are performing.

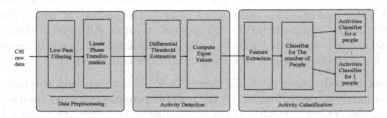

Fig. 1. System overview

4.1   Data Processing

Leveraging minor modifications on the firmware of commodity 802.11n Network Interface Cards (NIC) [4], we can get a group of 30 CSI reports from the subcarriers. In other words, CSI measurements of each packet are divided into 30 subcarriers with each subcarrier providing one sample for each data point. However, both the amplitude and phase information obtained from the raw CSI measurement are extremely noisy. Therefore, different filtering and calibration algorithms are applied on the raw data in order to eliminate the impact of random noise and phase shift.

Amplitude Filtering: Many factors, such as environmental changes and thermal noises within devices, can lead to uncertain fluctuations of the amplitude.

As shown in Fig. 2a, the raw amplitude information is too noisy to be further analyzed. In order to smooth the raw amplitude and remove the outliers, different filters are applied so that different features can be obtained from each filtered set.

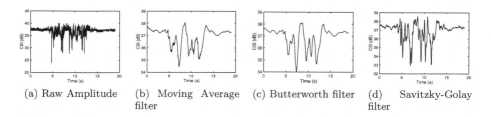

(a) Raw Amplitude   (b) Moving Average filter   (c) Butterworth filter   (d) Savitzky-Golay filter

Fig. 2. Performance of different filters on the same dataset

As shown in Fig. 2, in this paper, we explore three types of low frequency filters. All these filters achieve satisfactory performance compared with noisy raw data. Savitzky-Golay filter keeps most of the features of the signal while the filtered signal still fluctuates dramatically compared with the other two filters. Processed signal of Moving Average filter is not as smooth as Butterworth filter, while it still keeps most of the features of raw signal. Most importantly, Butterworth filter achieves the best performance, achieving desirable smoothness while retaining vital features. In this paper, all these three filtered signals will be used for feature extraction in order to increase the dimensions of feature dataset.

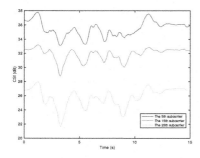

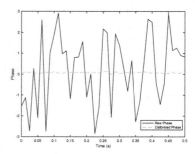

Fig. 3. Amplitude fluctuation in different subcarriers

Fig. 4. Comparison between the raw and calibrated phase

In addition, we also find that the signals of all 30 subcarriers for the same activity actually share similar patterns. In Fig. 3, the disturbances of different subcarriers caused by the same walking activity are likely the same. Therefore, we conclude that samples from all 30 subcarriers can be utilized for training and testing purpose, which will be further discussed in Subsect. 4.3.

Phase Calibration: In order to achieve satisfactory performance for multiple activities detection, MAIS also takes advantage of phase information. Due to channel frequency offset and synchronization issues between the transmitter and receiver, the raw phase signal is even noisier as compared to the amplitude. We perform a linear transformation [13] to eliminate the random noise and uncertain shifts.

Assume that the measured phase of subcarrier k, $\angle \widehat{H_k}$, can be represented as

$$\angle \widehat{H_k} = \angle H_k + 2\pi \frac{n_k}{N} \Delta t + \beta + Z, \tag{4}$$

where $\angle H_k$ is the original phase, n_k is the subcarrier index, N is the size of FFT, Δt is the time shift, β and Z are unknown noise shift and random noise respectively. In order to eliminate β and Z, the sanitized phase can be approximately estimated as

$$\angle \widetilde{H_k} = \angle \widehat{H_k} - an_k - b, \tag{5}$$

where $a = (\angle \widehat{H_K} - \angle \widehat{H_1})/(n_K - n_1)$, $b = (\sum_{k=1}^{K} \angle \widehat{H_k})/K$ and K is the total number of subcarriers.

As shown in Fig. 4, this linear transformation algorithm removes the random phase shift as expected. The calibrated phases are distributed stably in the time domain, which is greatly helpful for feature extraction.

4.2 Activity Detection

It is well known that the disturbances among different subcarriers can be considered as an indicator of activity detection. In this paper, we design a two-steps algorithm by taking advantage of such signal fluctuations in order to extract the start and end point of each activity. Figure 5a depicts an example of signal variance in the time domain. Evidently the variance of stationary environments is generally much more stable than that with movement.

Step One: In order to remove the outliers that may cause misdetection as shown in Fig. 5a, we firstly compare the value at the m_{th} point with the difference between the prior and posterior points and set it as the average value of these two points if it is determined as an outlier. Denote the raw variance of 30 subcarriers amplitudes as V. We have

$$V(m) = \begin{cases} (V(m-1) + V(m+1))/2, & \text{if } V(m) > \delta_v \\ V(m), & \text{otherwise} \end{cases} \tag{6}$$

where $\delta_v = \lambda |V(m+1) - V(m-1)|$ represents an indicator of outlier and λ is an empirical coefficient. Figure 5b presents the signal where outliers of stationary environment are removed. Note that the outliers with the presence of human activity do not affect the determination of activity since it only helps to exaggerate the variance.

Next, in order to detect the presence of activity, the signal is split into different time slots. In the i_{th} slot, denote the increasingly ordered variance as

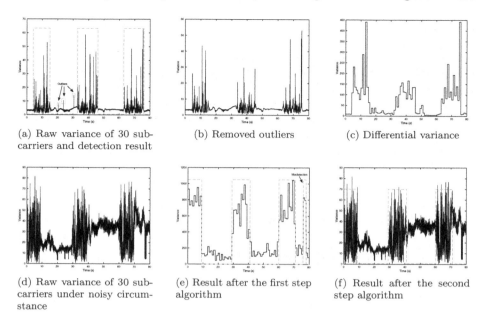

(a) Raw variance of 30 subcarriers and detection result

(b) Removed outliers

(c) Differential variance

(d) Raw variance of 30 subcarriers under noisy circumstance

(e) Result after the first step algorithm

(f) Result after the second step algorithm

Fig. 5. Performance of activity detection algorithm

$V'(j)$, where $j = 1, 2, \ldots, R_s$ and R_s is the sampling rate of CSI. In other words, $V'(1) < V'(2) < \ldots < V'(R_s)$. Then the differences between the largest half and the lowest half of values are calculated as

$$D_i = \sum_{j=1}^{R_s/2} (V'(j + R_s/2) - V'(j)). \tag{7}$$

The differential result corresponding to Fig. 5a is shown in Fig. 5c, we can easily see that there are three activities in this dataset. By comparing D_i with a self adaptive threshold δ_D, we can get an initial result that determines whether there is an activity in this slot

$$I_i = \begin{cases} 1, \text{ if } D_i > \delta_D \\ 0, \text{ otherwise} \end{cases} \tag{8}$$

where I is the indicator of the presence of activity, $\delta_D = (\sum_{i=1}^{L/R_s} D_i)/(L/R_s)$ and L here represents the total length of the dataset. Generally it can detect the activity correctly as shown in Fig. 5a. However, in certain cases with extremely noisy environment and multiple people activities, detection error can occur. Figure 5e shows an example where the first step algorithm misdetects an activity. Owing to this, we design a second step algorithm to double check the results and remove rare misdetections.

Step Two: Considering that the noises caused by multiple activities are much stronger than that by single people scenario, it is necessary to take a second step so that MAIS can remove the misdetections in the first step. The signal fluctuations of consecutive packets can be considered as highly correlated in stationary cases while the presence of human activity can cause temporal abruptions between successive points. Based on this observation, we propose to construct correlation matrices of both amplitude and calibrated phase within a certain window. Let the size of window be W. The CSI measurements in this window can be represented as

$$H(i) = [H_1(i), H_2(i), \ldots, H_K(i)],$$

where $i = 1, 2, \ldots, W$ and K is the total number of subcarriers. The covariance matrices of amplitude and phase then can be expressed as

$$\mathbf{A} = \begin{bmatrix} cov(|H(1)|, |H(1)|) & \cdots & cov(|H(1)|, |H(W)|) \\ \vdots & \ddots & \vdots \\ cov(|H(W)|, |H(1)|) & \cdots & cov(|H(W)|, |H(W)|) \end{bmatrix}$$

and

$$\mathbf{P} = \begin{bmatrix} cov(\angle\widetilde{H(1)}, \angle\widetilde{H(1)}) & \cdots & cov(\angle\widetilde{H(1)}, \angle\widetilde{H(W)}) \\ \vdots & \ddots & \vdots \\ cov(\angle\widetilde{H(W)}, \angle\widetilde{H(1)}) & \cdots & cov(\angle\widetilde{H(W)}, \angle\widetilde{H(W)}) \end{bmatrix}.$$

Afterwards, the largest normalized eigenvalues of $\mathbf{A}$ and $\mathbf{P}$ can be denoted as $\alpha_A = max(norm(eigen(\mathbf{A})))$ and $\alpha_P = max(norm(eigen(\mathbf{P})))$ respectively. After extensive experiments, we find that α_A and α_P tend to be smaller with the presence of human activity. As depicted in Fig. 6, stationary cases can be clearly separated from those with movements. Moreover, this threshold is independent from different environmental setups since eigenvalues are power independent. Therefore, this method greatly improves the accuracy based on the result of **Step One**.

4.3   Activity Classification

After we determine the start and end point of each activity, similar patterns of the same activity are found among different subcarriers. As we have discussed in Sect. 4.1, both the filtered amplitude and calibrated phase of CSI provide meaningful information for classifying activities. In this paper, the k-Nearest Neighbors algorithm (kNN) [8] is applied to train and test the CSI measurements in order to classify the detected activities.

In addition, CFR power, namely $|H(f,t)|^2$, is utilized to measure the amplitude information considering that it fluctuates with the lengths of multipaths.

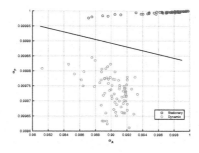

Fig. 6. Eigenvalues comparison between stationary and dynamic cases

Assume CFR can be represented as the sum of dynamic CFR and static CFR. That is

$$H(f,t) = e^{-j2\pi\Delta ft}(H_d(f,t) + H_s(f,t)), \tag{9}$$

where $H_d(f,t)$ and $H_s(f,t)$ represent dynamic CFR and static CFR respectively. Given that dynamic CFR can also be represented as the sum of CFRs of paths that varies because of human activity,

$$H(f,t) = e^{-j2\pi\Delta ft}(\sum_{m \in P_d} a_m(f,t)e^{-j2\pi d_m(t)/\lambda} + H_s(f,t)), \tag{10}$$

where P_d is the set of paths that change due to human movement, $d_m(t)$ is the length of the m_{th} path at time t, $a_m(f,t)$ is the amplitude and λ is the wave length at frequency f. It is well known that CFR amplitude varies because of the change of paths reflected by humans, which is also known as multipath effect.

By utilizing Euler's formula in Eq. 10, CFR power can be inferred as

$$\begin{aligned}
|H(f,t)|^2 = &\sum_{m \in P_d} 2|H_s(f,t)a_m(f,t)|cos(\frac{2\pi d_m}{\lambda}) \\
&+ \sum_{\substack{m,n \in P_d \\ m \neq n}} 2|a_m(f,t)a_n(f,t)|cos(\frac{2\pi(d_m - d_n)}{\lambda}). \\
&+ \sum_{m \in P_d} |a_m(f,t)|^2 + |H_s(f,t)|^2
\end{aligned} \tag{11}$$

Compared with amplitude, CFR power can be considered as an indicator of the speed of paths length change caused by multiple people activities [12]. After extensive experiments, six metrics of CFR power are chosen in this paper. They are the standard deviation, median absolute deviation, max, mean, first and third quartile of the filtered CFR power respectively.

On the other hand, features of the calibrated phases are also extracted. The same metrics on CFR power are applied in order to get enough phase information, which means it will generate 6 features from the phase. With the 18 features from CFR power, thus we can get a group of 24 features for each sample in total.

The kNN classifier is one of the classic machine learning algorithms based on non-parametric density estimation techniques. It categorizes the data points according to their distance to neighbors and classifies the new point based on the majority of nearest neighbor classes. Fine kNN is one of the extensions of kNN that finely detailed distinctions between classes, where a sample is simply classified to its nearest neighbor.

Let's denote the feature vector of the i_{th} sample as $x_i = \{f_1, f_2, \ldots, f_{24}\}$ and the corresponding label as ω_i, where $i = 1, 2, \ldots, N$ and f_j ($j = 1, 2, \ldots, 24$) depicts the j_{th} feature above. In other words, the training data set can be expressed as $T = (x_i, \omega_i)$ with uncertain distribution. Based on the training set, a local sub-space $R(x) \subseteq \Re^d$ at estimation point x is then constructed by kNN, which can be denoted as

$$R(x) = \{\widehat{x} | D(x, \widehat{x}) \leq d_k\}, \tag{12}$$

where d_k is k_{th} order of $\{d(x, \widehat{x})\}_1^N$ and $D(x, \widehat{x})$ is the distance between x and $\widehat{x}$. Assuming the number of samples labeled as ω in space $R(x)$ is $k[\omega]$, the posterior probability becomes

$$P(\omega | x) = \frac{p(x | \omega) p(\omega)}{p(x)} = \frac{k[\omega]}{k}, \tag{13}$$

where k is the total number of sample points in $R(x)$.

Given a specific estimation point x, the decision function is calculated by finding the class with the highest $k[\omega]$. It can be expresses as

$$g(x) = \begin{cases} 1 & \text{if } k[\omega = 1] \geq k[\omega \neq 1] \\ 2 & \text{if } k[\omega = 2] \geq k[\omega \neq 2] \\ \vdots & \\ n & \text{if } k[\omega = n] \geq k[\omega \neq n] \end{cases} . \tag{14}$$

where n is the total number of classes.

Since all subcarriers are used for classification, we can obtain 30 predicted labels for each activity. The intuitive way to predict the final result is by majority vote. In other words, assume that the predicted result of one activity is $g = [g(1), g(2), \ldots, g(30)]$. The final predicted label by MAIS is

$$L = \max_{j \in [1, 2, \ldots, n]} \left(\frac{\sum_{i=1}^{30} (g(i) == j)}{30} \right). \tag{15}$$

By implementing kNN, we first classify the activities based on the number of people. Then each activity is further classified in each category in order to predict the exact types of activities being performed.

5   Experiments and Evaluation

In this section, we present the evaluation performance of MAIS by implementing different experiments on commercial WiFi devices.

5.1   Experimental Setup

We implement MAIS with two commercial off-the-shelf WiFi devices. One of them is Linksys EA4500 Dual Band router that acts as an access point, while the other is a Sony laptop equipped with Intel WiFi Link 5300 802.11n NIC. Both of the devices are configured to work on 2.4 GHz frequency band with 20 MHz bandwidth channels. By following the instructions in [4], we are able to modify the driver and record CSI for each packet. Besides, all the experiment data is collected with a packet transmission rate of 80 pkts/s. In summary, we can get a group of 30 subcarriers CSI information for each packet.

5.2   Data Collection

All the data are collected in our lab, whose size is 6×8 m and decorated with normal furniture, such as tables and cubicles. A total number of 933 samples are collected in order to evaluate the system performance of MAIS. Considering MAIS utilizes information provided by all 30 subcarriers to train and classify activities, it implies the actual size of dataset is 27990 in total.

In this paper, we conduct experiments with not only a single person but also multiple people. Different number of people, from 1 to 3, are required to perform three different activities that consist of running, walking and hands movement respectively. Since the number of combination possibilities for multiple people dramatically increases, we choose three different combinations for each category in order to make the experiment feasible. Table 1 depicts all the activities performed and corresponding datasets collected in this paper.

Table 1. Summary of dataset

Number of people	Activities	Number of samples
1	R	120
	W	120
	H	117
2	W & W	102
	R & W	96
	W & H	96
3	W & W & H	102
	R & W & H	84
	W & W & W	96

*R, W, H represent run, walk and hand movement respectively.

5.3   Evaluation

All the collected data are processed in MATLAB 2016a, where MAIS is implemented. We evaluate the performance of our system in three aspects as detailed below.

Accuracy of Detecting the Presence of Activities: Two metrics are taken in order to evaluate the performance of activity detection. They are True Positive (TP) and False Positive (FP) respectively. The former metric indicates the expected accuracy while the later one represents the false alarm probability of this system. The goal is obviously to increase the former rate while decreasing the later one. However, it is usually highly challenging to achieve both at the same time in reality. Our technique is to achieve high TP rate while keeping FP at a relatively low level.

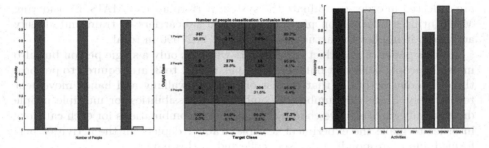

Fig. 7. Accuracy of activity detection

Fig. 8. Accuracy of classifying the number of people

Fig. 9. Accuracy of classifying the type of activities

Figure 7 shows the accuracy of activity detection in terms of the number of people. Evidently MAIS achieves promising result in all cases. For a single person, MAIS can detect the activity with an accuracy rate of 98.32%. Similar results are found for multiple people, it achieves 97.62% and 98.11% accuracy rate with two and three people respectively. On the other hand, the false alarm rate is only 1.12%, 1.36% and 2.52% for three cases respectively. In general, MAIS achieves an accuracy rate of 98.04% and a false alarm rate of 1.65% on average.

Accuracy of Classifying the Number of People: In order to classify activities based on the number of people, we first try to analyze the difference of activities performed by different number of people. After extracting different features from each activity and utilizing kNN as discussed in the last section, MAIS is able to classify the activities into different categories with high accuracy.

Figure 8 plots the accuracy MAIS achieves for predicting the number of people. In each category, different activities are performed by different number of volunteers. For instance, both the combination of running & walking and the combination of walking & walking are supposed to be classified in the category of two people. It can be found that most of the activities are correctly classified by MAIS. In particular, it classifies the activities based on the number of people with 100%, 94.9% and 96.2% respectively. Overall, MAIS achieves an average accuracy rate of 97.2% for predicting the number of people.

Accuracy of Classifying the Type of Activities: In order to evaluate the performance of MAIS, a different number of volunteers are required to perform activities at the same time. Activities performed by individuals are Run (R), Walk (W) and H (Hand Movement). We also ask two volunteers to act three different combinations of activities simultaneously, which are Walk & Hand Movement (WH), Walk & Walk (WW) and Run & Walk (RW). Additionally, here are also three combinations of activities that are performed by three people at the same time. They are Run & Walk & Hand Movement (RWH), Walk & Walk & Walk (WWW) and Walk & Walk & Hand Movement (WWH).

Figure 9 depicts the accuracy results that MAIS achieves for classifying different activity combinations. Overall, all the activities are correctly predicted with an accuracy higher than 85%. In particular, all the accuracies of single people activities are over 95%. It achieves 97.5%, 95.0% and 96.49% for R, W and H respectively. Meanwhile, MAIS achieves an average accuracy rate of 91.09% and 91.20% for two and three people activities respectively. It is observed that the accuracy of different people activities improves with the size of samples and explains that why our system obtained somewhat lower accuracy for two people activities than three people activities classification. We plan to research these details in our future work. In conclusion, MAIS achieves an accuracy of 93.12% for all activities in average.

6   Conclusion and Future Work

Different from existing work using WiFi signals to detect activities of a single person, we present a novel human activity identification scheme termed MAIS, targeting at identifying multiple activities of different subjects in the same environment. By implementing the tool and modifying the driver on Intel 5300 NIC, we are able to obtain the CSI from commercial off-the-shelf WiFi devices. We present various components of the system including noise filtering, activity detection and activity/subject identification. Extensive experiments show that MAIS achieves an accuracy of 97.21% for predicting the number of people and 93.12% for classifying the types of activities. We are currently establishing experimental environment to test MAIS for identifying simultaneous activities of a large number of people.

References

1. Bodor, R., Jackson, B., Papanikolopoulos, N.: Vision-based human tracking and activity recognition. In: Proceedings of the 11th Mediterranean Conference on Control and Automation, vol. 1. Citeseer (2003)

2. Duong, T.V., Bui, H.H., Phung, D.Q., Venkatesh, S.: Activity recognition and abnormality detection with the switching hidden semi-markov model. In: 2005 IEEE Computer Society Conference on Computer Vision and Pattern Recognition (CVPR 2005), vol. 1, pp. 838–845. IEEE (2005)
3. Ermes, M., Pärkkä, J., Mäntyjärvi, J., Korhonen, I.: Detection of daily activities and sports with wearable sensors in controlled and uncontrolled conditions. IEEE Trans. Inf Technol. Biomed. **12**(1), 20–26 (2008)
4. Halperin, D., Hu, W., Sheth, A., Wetherall, D.: Tool release: gathering 802.11 n traces with channel state information. ACM SIGCOMM Comput. Commun. Rev. **41**(1), 53–53 (2011)
5. Han, C., Wu, K., Wang, Y., Ni, L.M.: Wifall: Device-free fall detection by wireless networks. In: IEEE INFOCOM 2014-IEEE Conference on Computer Communications, pp. 271–279. IEEE (2014)
6. Huang, X., Dai, M.: Indoor device-free activity recognition based on radio signal. IEEE Trans. Veh. Technol. (2016)
7. Kellogg, B., Talla, V., Gollakota, S.: Bringing gesture recognition to all devices. In: 11th USENIX Symposium on Networked Systems Design and Implementation (NSDI 2014), pp. 303–316 (2014)
8. Li, C., Zhang, S., Zhang, H., Pang, L., Lam, K., Hui, C., Zhang, S.: Using the k-nearest neighbor algorithm for the classification of lymph node metastasis in gastric cancer. Comput. Math. Methods Med. **2012**, Article no. 876545 (2012)
9. Sheheryar, A., Chunhai, F., Yonghe, L., Yupeng, H., Ruiyun, Y., Siwang, Z., Heng, L.: Wi-chase: a Wifi based human activity recognition system for sensorless environments. In: 2017 IEEE 18th International Symposium on A World of Wireless, Mobile and Multimedia Networks (WoWMoM). IEEE (to appear)
10. Statista: Average size of households in the u.s. 1960–2015. https://www.statista.com/statistics/183648/average-size-of-households-in-the-us/
11. Tapia, E.M., Intille, S.S., Larson, K.: Activity recognition in the home using simple and ubiquitous sensors. In: Ferscha, A., Mattern, F. (eds.) Pervasive 2004. LNCS, vol. 3001, pp. 158–175. Springer, Heidelberg (2004). doi:10.1007/978-3-540-24646-6_10
12. Wang, W., Liu, A.X., Shahzad, M., Ling, K., Lu, S.: Understanding and modeling of Wifi signal based human activity recognition. In: Proceedings of the 21st Annual International Conference on Mobile Computing and Networking, pp. 65–76. ACM (2015)
13. Wang, X., Gao, L., Mao, S.: PhaseFi: phase fingerprinting for indoor localization with a deep learning approach. In: 2015 IEEE Global Communications Conference (GLOBECOM), pp. 1–6. IEEE (2015)
14. Wang, Y., Liu, J., Chen, Y., Gruteser, M., Yang, J., Liu, H.: E-eyes: device-free location-oriented activity identification using fine-grained Wifi signatures. In: Proceedings of the 20th Annual International Conference on Mobile Computing and Networking, pp. 617–628. ACM (2014)
15. Wu, K., Xiao, J., Yi, Y., Gao, M., Ni, L.M.: Fila: fine-grained indoor localization. In: INFOCOM, 2012 Proceedings IEEE, pp. 2210–2218. IEEE (2012)
16. Yang, G.: WiLocus: CSI based human tracking system in indoor environment. In: 2016 Eighth International Conference on Measuring Technology and Mechatronics Automation (ICMTMA), pp. 915–918. IEEE (2016)

Differentially Private Frequent Itemset Mining from Smart Devices in Local Setting

Xinyuan Zhang, Liusheng Huang$^{(\boxtimes)}$, Peng Fang, Shaowei Wang, Zhenyu Zhu, and Hongli Xu

School of Computer Science and Technology, University of Science and Technology of China, Hefei 230027, Anhui, China
{dwz,fape,wangsw,zzy7758}@mail.ustc.edu.cn,
{lshuang,xuhongli}@ustc.edu.cn

Abstract. Frequent itemset mining has become an important approach of smart devices to upgrade service level for users, but comes with risks to privacy. And privacy leakage will result in serious consequence. Accordingly, it is highly desirable to mine frequent itemset while protecting users' privacy. Moreover, users may not trust anyone else (including the miner) and are willing to share their information only if it has been perturbed appropriately before leaving their smart devices. Local differential privacy resolves this problem by only aggregating randomized itemsets from each user, with providing plausible deniability; meanwhile the miner can still obtain relatively accurate frequent patterns. Moreover users might have diverse privacy requirements on different items. These facts have led to the personalized differentially private frequent itemset mining, which preserves privacy with stochastic responses. Motivated by this, we propose a novel personalized local privacy preservation scheme for smart devices, which retains desirable accurate results while providing rigorous privacy guarantees.

Keywords: Local differential privacy · Smart devices · Personalized · Frequent itemset mining · Stochastic response

1 Introduction

Nowadays, with the rapid development of smart devices, it becomes ubiquitous to optimize resources and provide better service through mining frequent patterns from aggregated users' information. The aim of frequent itemsets mining (FIM) is to extract the sets of items which often occur together. Smart devices connected with the miner by a wireless network, including smart phones, grids, homes and vehicles, are changing the way we live. The frequent itemsets mined from collected users' data of smart devices has been an invaluable asset to hardware designers and application developers. For instance, smart homes can analyze residents' living habits using the data collected by sensors, further customize corresponding service schemes for users coming from different regions. Residents'

L. Ma et al. (Eds.): WASA 2017, LNCS 10251, pp. 433–444, 2017.
DOI: 10.1007/978-3-319-60033-8_38

individual electricity usage should be solicited and extracted commonplace patterns in smart power grids. Towards to provide more proper service, the hospital needs to aggregate patients' medical records and genetic information from sensors. Apple Inc. makes use of the collected data to mine frequent usage patterns, and then concentrates on promoting popular ones.

Nevertheless, the process of collecting and mining users' information brings unprecedented privacy threats [9]. The leakage of personal privacy may lead to serious consequences and extensive damages. Privacy concerns have become an inevitable impediment to the widespread participation of contributing sensitive information to the data miner [7]. Users wouldn't like to share their private data with the collector unless their privacy requirements have been satisfied. In addition, the operator (e.g. Apple Inc, Samsung, Amazon) will obtain more accurate frequent itemsets with the number of contributed users increasing. In other words, if the data miner doesn't provide sufficient privacy guarantees, it will not mine or extract relatively accurate results because lacking of adequately large number of data contributors. Based on this, it's very important to devise a rigorous privacy preservation scheme of the frequent itemsets mining task for participants.

A majority of existing methods are proposed based on the condition where data miners are trusted (e.g. Netflix, Google). Most of them apply the notion of differential privacy (DP) [2] to protect contributed users' privacy. DP is the state of the art privacy definition which aims to resolve the privacy problem in the process of FIM. It has been demonstrated that differential privacy can provide strict privacy guarantees, no matter how much background knowledge and computational power an adversary has. However, the privacy concerns in mining data from smart devices pertain to another new privacy notion named local ϵ-differential privacy (LDP) [6]. The locality means that a user's private data have been sanitized and protected properly yet before leaving his/her smart device such as a mobile phone. Besides, a trustable third-party is no longer a necessity in local setting. In particular, the data a user holds may be merely one single itemset instead of a database in centralized differential privacy. Therefore, both Laplace mechanism [5] and exponential mechanism [5] will introduce too much noise to gain reliable mining results, and the two common mechanisms of differential privacy can't be resorted to protect users' privacy locally.

Furthermore, a user may have diverse privacy expectations among the set of his/her attributes in practice. For example, some attributes are more sensitive than others and need to be perturbed with high privacy level; certain ones seem that will not reveal users' privacy which can be contributed public fully. On the other hand, users are likely to have different privacy requirements on the same attribute. Thus, a data miner adopting differential privacy has restrained choices. One possibility is to set a global privacy budget enough small to satisfy each user's requirement. In this way, it will introduce so much noise that data utility is influenced seriously. Otherwise, specifying a larger privacy budget may result in excluding a significant part of users from data mining [4]. This option will also compromise data utility. In addressing the above issues, we need to design a FIM from smart devices scheme based on LDP which takes various privacy levels of each user into account. The scheme conforms to LDP requirements meanwhile retaining reasonable data utility.

In this paper, we propose a differentially private frequent itemset mining scheme for smart devices in local setting. Enforcing local differential privacy on FIM tasks in this scheme, we can maintain data utility to obtain accurate mining results and preserve privacy simultaneously. Specifically, this paper makes the following contributions:

- We formulate the privacy preservation issue of frequent itemset mining from users' smart devices. In response to participants' personalized privacy requirements, we design a novel personalized differential privacy scheme. The scheme provides a better trade-off between privacy and utility.
- We propose a multiple randomized response (MRR) mechanism. In this mechanism, we divide the set of items into diverse parts according to their privacy concern levels and apply different randomized perturbation approaches to attain the complementation of these mechanism.
- We conduct experiments to evaluate the performance of our proposed mechanism. The simulation results not only show that the scheme provides a better trade-off between data privacy and utility, but also reveals that the accuracy of frequent itemsets is improved with the privacy budget of participants increasing.

The rest of this paper is organized as follows. Section 2 introduces preliminary knowledge about local differential privacy definition, frequent itemset mining and two randomized response mechanism. Section 3 introduces our proposed MRR mechanism. Section 4 describes the private frequent itemset mining scheme. Section 5 shows the experimental results of our mechanism with comparison to the existing other approaches. Section 6 reviews the related work. In the end, Sect. 7 concludes our work.

2   Preliminaries

In this section, we first formulate the problem of frequent itemset mining, and the notion of local ϵ-differential privacy. Then, we briefly introduce two mechanisms that conforms to LDP requirements, i.e., the *k-ary randomized response* (*k*-RR) [11] mechanism and the randomized aggregatable privacy-preserving ordinal response (RAPPOR) [3] mechanism.

2.1   Frequent Itemset Mining

We model a database D as a set of tuples from a universe $\mathcal{D}$, where each tuple represents the private information contributed by smart devices owners. In our setting, the database in frequent itemset mining is called a *transaction database*.

Definition 1 (Transaction database). *A transaction database is a set of transactions $d =< t_1, \ldots, t_m >$, where each transaction is a subset of $\mathcal{I}$ whose length is n.*

Let $X = \{i_1, \ldots, i_q\}$ be a set of items, i.e., an itemset. If the number of transactions in an item surpasses a specified threshold, we call the itemset a frequent itemset with respect to the threshold τ. The support of itemset X, denoted by $\sigma(X)$, is the number of transactions in D which contains X as a subset.

Definition 2 (Frequent itemset). *For any itemset X, if its support $\sigma(X)$ is larger than or equal to a specified threshold τ, the itemset X is called a frequent itemset with respect to the threshold τ.*

For ease of presenation, we denote a itemset including k items by k-itemset, and frequent itemsets with respect to the threshold τ by frequent itemsets in the rest of this paper. The term of "Frequent Itemset Mining" is basically a mining which extracts the frequent itemsets from given database D.

2.2   Local Differential Privacy

Local differential privacy (LDP) [2] is a rigorous privacy notion in local setting, which provides a stronger privacy guarantee than the centralized differential privacy. In this scheme, each data contributor perturbs his/her personal information employing a stochastic mechanism before releasing a private version of his/her original one to a data miner. That is, users can protect their data from anyone else (including data miners) and a trustable data curator is no longer needed. Thus, LDP is quite appropriate for preserving contributors' privacy in FIM tasks.

LDP requires that an adversary with arbitrary background knowledge cannot distinguish the perturbed information and its original. In other words, the data recipient should receive the same information with a high probability no matter what a user has. Moreover, in LDP, users may hold just a single data element to contribute, instead of a database. Formally, local differential privacy is given below.

Definition 3 (Local Differential Privacy [2]). *For a user u_i, a randomized $\mathcal{F}$ algorithm satisfies ϵ-local differential privacy, if for all pairs of transaction t and $t' \in D$, and for all $M \subseteq Range(\mathcal{F})$,*

$$Pr[\mathcal{F}(t) \in M] \leq \exp(\epsilon) \cdot Pr[\mathcal{F}(t') \in M], \tag{1}$$

where ϵ denotes privacy budget, and D represents the domain of privacy data.

Recall that LDP is enforced on a single data rather than a database, it can provide more rigorous privacy guarantee than traditional differential privacy. However, since the universe size $|D|$ is usually very large, LDP introduces so much noise to perturb private data. Hence, it's very important to design a mechanism to achieve a reasonable trade-off between privacy and utility under LDP.

2.3   The k-ary Randomized Response

The k-ary randomized response (k-RR) mechanism [11] Q^k is a locally differentially private mechanism whose noisy output alphabets $\mathcal{O}$ is the original input domain $\mathcal{I}$ (i.e., $\mathcal{I} = \mathcal{O}$). The conditional probabilities are given by

$$Q^k(y|x) = \begin{cases} \frac{e^\epsilon}{e^\epsilon + k - 1}, & if \quad y = x \\ \frac{1}{e^\epsilon + k - 1}. & if \quad y \neq x \end{cases} \tag{2}$$

Actually k-RR can be considered as an extension of the idea of replying true answers with a limited probability which was proposed by Warner (W-RR) [1] in 1965. That is, W-RR is equivalent to the k-RR mechanism when $k = 2$. In the work proposed by Kairouz *et al.*, we know the k-RR mechanism has been proved to be optimal in the low privacy regime for many information theoretic utility functions [10].

2.4   The Randomized Aggregatable Privacy-Preserving Ordinal Response

The randomized aggregatable privacy-preserving ordinal response (RAPPOR) mechanism [3] Q^r is a technology to protect the privacy of users and enable the aggregation of user data over time. RAPPOR uses two rounds of binary randomized response to satisfy the requirement of local differential privacy. Firstly, RAPPOR initializes a binary vector B of zeros, then maps the input of a user to a position in B and sets the position to 0. In the first round, for each bit B_i in B, the output B_i' is given by:

$$Q^r(B_i'|B_i) = \begin{cases} \frac{e^{\epsilon/2}}{e^{\epsilon/2}+1}, & if \quad B_i' = B_i \\ \frac{1}{e^{\epsilon/2}+1}. & if \quad B_i' = 1 - B_i \end{cases} \tag{3}$$

Further, every bit in B' is independent with each other. In our context, we just use the simplified version of RAPPOR (i.e. One-time RAPPOR) without the second round for ease of presentation, denoted by k-RAPPOR here. In the paper proposed by Erlingsson *et al.*, we know that this randomized response scheme achieves ϵ-local differential privacy. k-RAPPOR is a optimal privacy-preserving mechanism in high privacy regime [10].

3   The Randomized Response Mechanism

In this section, we first introduce the representation of users' data for frequent itemset mining tasks, and then present a novel multiple randomized response (MRR) mechanism that enables the category-based privacy expectations control. In the end, we theoretically demonstrate the proposed mechanism satisfies ϵ-local differential privacy.

3.1   Data Representation

In order to extract beneficial patterns from users' data, we need to normalize each attribute in their data to apply to the existing data mining algorithms (e.g. Apriori).

For each categorical attribute (including binary attribute), map each attribute-value pair to a new binary item, i.e., create k binary attributes for a original one if it has k attribute-value pairs. But for a continuous attribute, we require a discretization of its domain. Firstly, divide the continuous attribute range into finite intervals, then map each interval to a binary attribute. Let k_i be the number of the binary attribute with regard to the ith attribute of original data and k denote the set of $k_i, i = 1, \ldots, l$.

In this way, users' raw private data is denoted as a vector m_r of size $n = k_1 + \ldots + k_l$. The jth item in m_r is valued between 0 and 1, meaning that a user does or does not have the relevant attribute. In particularly, assuming several binary attributes belong to a original one (e.g. categorical or continuous attribute), there is just one attribute valued from 1, and others are 0.

Moreover, to satisfy users' different privacy requirements among the set of attributes, we define a binary vector of privacy concern levels p_l that consists of $p_l(1), \ldots, p_l(l)$. For each bit i in p_l, $p_l(i)$ represents the user-specified privacy concern level for attribute i, which is taken value in the set {"Public", "High", "Low"}. For ease of presentation, we use '0' to denote "Public", '1' and '2' to indicate "High" and "Low" respectively. For instance, when we have p_l = {public, high, public, low, high, low}, p_l can be denoted by the binary vector {0, 1, 0, 2, 1, 2}.

3.2   The Proposed Multiple Randomized Response

As mentioned in Sect. 2, k-RAPPOR is optimal in high privacy regime and suboptimal in low privacy regime. However, k-RR is opposite to k-RAPPOR, i.e., k-RR is optimal in low privacy regime and suboptimal in high privacy regime.

Motivated by this, we propose MRR, a novel mechanism for locally differentially private frequent itemset mining based on k-RAPPOR and k-RR. The MRR mechanism targets on maintaining the quality of attribute aggregates on sanitized data associated with high and low attributes while releasing all raw data only connected with public attribute. Furthermore, it's obvious to use smaller privacy budget ϵ_s to protect the high attributes, but preserving the low attributes with bigger privacy budget ϵ_b.

The general idea of our proposed MRR is to divide privacy budget into two parts ϵ_s and ϵ_b according to users' privacy concern levels, then apply k-RR with ϵ_b and k-RAPPOR with ϵ_s to perturb the low and high attributes respectively. Specially, the MRR mechansim is performed on local smart devices as Algorithm 1 with parameters $(m_r, k, p_l, \epsilon_s, \epsilon_b)$.

Algorithm 1. Multiple Randomized Response Algorithm

Input: a private binary itemset $m_r \in \{0,1\}^n$
Input: an item-category vector K and a privacy concern levels vector PL
Input: two privacy budgets ϵ_s, ϵ_b associated with "High Privacy" and "Low Privacy" respectively
Output: a perturbed itemset $m_p \in \{0,1\}^n$ which satisfies local ϵ-differential privacy.
1: initialize a binary vector $m_p = 0 \in \{0,1\}^n$ and a variable $t = 0$
2: **for** each item k_i in K **do**
3:    **if** $PL(i) == 0$ **then**
4:       **for** $j = 0$ to k_i **do**
5:          $m_p(t) = m_r(t)$
6:          $t = t + 1$
7:       **end for**
8:    **else if** $PL(i) == 1$ **then**
9:       **for** $j = 0$ to k_i **do**
10:          $m_p(t) = \begin{cases} m_r(t), & \text{with probability } \frac{e^{\epsilon_s/2}}{e^{\epsilon_s/2}+1} \\ 1 - m_r(t), & \text{with probability } \frac{1}{e^{\epsilon_s/2}+1} \end{cases}$
11:          $t = t + 1$
12:       **end for**
13:    **else if** $PL(i) == 2$ **then**
14:       select j if $m_r(j) == 1$ from t to $t + k_i$
15:          $j' = \begin{cases} j, & \text{with probability } \frac{e^{\epsilon_b}}{e^{\epsilon_b}+k_i-1} \\ UniformRandom([1, k_i] \backslash \{j\}), & \text{with probability } \frac{k_i-1}{e^{\epsilon_b}+k_i-1} \end{cases}$
16:       $m_p(j) = 1$
17:       $t = t + k_i$
18:    **end if**
19: **end for**
20: **return** m_p

The MRR mechanism protects privacy through introducing uncertainty using the randomized response technique, thus provides a strong privacy assurance for users. MRR is performed on each user's smart device independently, and it satisfies Definition 3. Due to space limitation, we omit the proof of Theorem 1 here.

Theorem 1. *For each user u_i with privacy concern levels k_i, the multiple randomized response mechanism satisfies local $\epsilon = \sum_{k=1}^{n} \epsilon_{ik}$-differential privacy requirement in Definition 3.*

4   Private Frequent Itemset Mining

In this section, we are considering the problem of mining frequent k-itemset from noisy dataset. We will propose the noisy version of the method to construct private itemset support.

In order to derive frequent itemsets from users' perturbed data, the central miner needs to estimate the support σ of each candidate itemset. Therefore, how to estimate the value of σ is the crux of our proposed scheme. Considering that every piece of received data has been perturbed before leaving smart devices, the miner can't obtain the support of a candidate itemset directly. Therefore, we must estimate the value of σ for the next work.

We propose a high-precision estimation method of private support here. Other than the original method, our tactic is to obtain the probability p to decide that the support of a candidate itemset is added one or zero. Assuming that the candidate itemset is $X = \{i_1, \ldots, i_q\}$, where $i_j = [x, y]$, x, y denote x^{th} attribute and y^{th} value of the attribute respectively. Without loss of generality, let the collected data bits $1, \ldots, n$ be set, i.e., $m_p^* = \{m_p(1) = 1, \ldots, m_p(k_1) = 0, \ldots, m_p(n - k_l + 1) = 1, \ldots, m_p(n) = 0\}$. Let $B = \{b_1 b_2 \ldots b_q\}$ denote the index of X in the private data m_p. Then, we can deduce the following equation based on the Bayes' theorem:

$$
\begin{aligned}
&P(i_1 i_2 \ldots i_q | m_p^*(1) m_p^*(2) \ldots m_p^*(n)) \\
&= P(i_1 i_2 \ldots i_q | m_p^*(b_1) m_p^*(b_2) \ldots m_p^*(b_q)) \\
&= \frac{P(i_1 i_2 \ldots i_q) \cdot P(m_p^*(b_1) m_p^*(b_2) \ldots m_p^*(b_q) | i_1 i_2 \ldots i_q)}{P(m_p^*(b_1) m_p^*(b_2) \ldots m_p^*(b_q))}.
\end{aligned}
\tag{4}
$$

Through the total probability theorem, we have the following equation:

$$
\begin{aligned}
&P(m_p^*(b_1) m_p^*(b_2) \ldots m_p^*(b_q)) \\
&= \sum_{v_1=0}^{1} \cdots \sum_{v_q=0}^{1} P(m_p(1) m_p(2) \ldots m_p(q)) \\
&\cdot P(m_p(1) m_p(2) \ldots m_p(b_q) | m_r(1) = v_1, m_r(2) = v_2, \ldots, m_r(q) = v_q).
\end{aligned}
\tag{5}
$$

Equations (4) and (5) shows we can employ users' private data to estimate the value of σ, further extract frequent itemsets.

However, we cannot obtain the initial prior probability of attribute value. First of all, we assume that all attributes are independent of each other. Then, we can use the conclusion in [7] to estimate the original frequency of each attribute value. Let F_{ij} denote the jth value of ith attribute, we can deduce the following equation:

$$
F_{ij} = O_{ij} + \frac{\sum_{k=1}^{C_{ij}^1}(1-b) - \sum_{k=C_{ij}^1}^{C_{ij}} b}{a - b} + \frac{\sum_{k=1}^{M_{ij}^1}(1-c) - \sum_{k=M_{ij}^1}^{M_{ij}} d}{c - d},
\tag{6}
$$

where O_{ij}, C_{ij} and M_{ij} represent the numbers of "Public", "High" and "Low" among noisy data respectively, and $a = \frac{\epsilon_s}{1+\epsilon_s}, c = \frac{\epsilon_b}{k-1+\epsilon_s}, b = 1 - a, d = 1 - c$.

By applying our proposed decoding method to every collected perturbed data, we obtain the support of each candidate itemset. Then the frequent k-itemsets can be extracted from users' private data using the reconstructed support.

5   Experiments

In this section, we experimentally evaluate the performance of our privacy preservation for mining frequent itemset from users' sensitive data, and verify our proposed frequent itemset mining with local differential privacy scheme over two different synthetic datasets.

The first dataset *norm-user* we use consists of users' personal data whose attribute value complies with a norm distribution. The second data *exp-user* dataset contains users' sensitive information of which attribute value display exponential decay. The number of attributes of each user is a moderate number 15, the number of participants is 1000. The synthetic normal distribution has mean 4 and standard deviation 0.1. The simulated exponential distribution has standard deviation 4.

Our main goal of this experimental study is to validate that by taking personal multiple privacy budgets into account, our mechanism can usually obtain more accurate FIM results, compared to k-RAPPOR and k-RR mechanism proposed in [11] and [10] respectively. To compare the performance of algorithms, we employ F score as the measure of utility here.

Definition 4 (F score). *Let R_p be the set of frequent itemsets generated by a differentially private itemset mining algorithm, and R_c be the set of correct frequent itemsets, then*

$$precision = \frac{|R_p \cap R_c|}{R_p}, recall = \frac{|R_p \cap R_c|}{R_p}$$

and the F score is defined as follows

$$Fscore = 2 * \frac{precision * recall}{precison + recall}.$$

For ease of presentation, the size of all attributes value domain is a uniform number 8 in the experiments of each group. The small privacy budget we employ ranges from 1.0 to 3.0, and the big privacy budget ranges from 3.0 to 5.0. In these simulations, the privacy concern levels p_l is assigned with $\{0, \ldots, 1, \ldots, 2\}$ where the numbers of three parts are the same.

We conduct three simulations on two kinds of datasets severally to compare the performance between the three mechanism comprehensively. The first experiment performing our proposed algorithm is denoted by MMR here, the second one performs k-RAPPOR algorithm, is signified by k-RAPPOR and the last one perfoms k-RR algorithm, is denoted by k-RR. In the normal setting, the threshold we use is set to 0.3, and it is set to 0.2 in the second setting. We verify the performance of our proposed scheme when the length of frequent itemsets 1 one and 2 respectively.

We conduct 12 simulation experiments in total, and these simulations are divided into four groups which are denoted by *norm-1*, *norm-2*, *exp-1*, *exp-2* respectively. As can be observed in Fig. 1, *norm-1* refers to the left subfigure, and

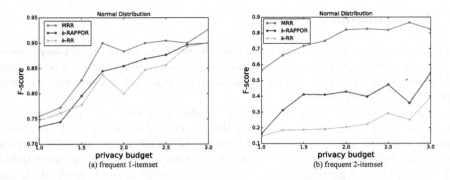

Fig. 1. The simulation results of frequent itemset mining with LDP under normal distribution.

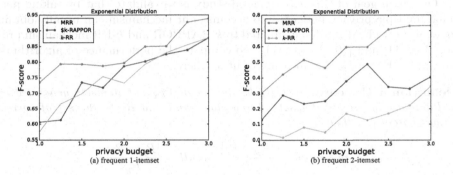

Fig. 2. The simulation results of frequent itemset mining with LDP under expoential distribution.

norm-2 refers to the right one. These two simulations are conducted to mining the frequent 1-itemset and 2-itemset. In Fig. 2, we use the two subfigures to corresponding to the two simulations *exp*-1 and *exp*-2. They are run to compare the performance differences between our proposed mechanism and others.

It can be observed that the personalized multiple randomized response mechanism we propose substantially outperforms the other two mechanisms. And the simulation results also show that there is obvious divergence between our MRR mechanism and k-RAPPOR or k-RR when mining frequent 2-itemsets. That is to say, the data utility has been significantly improved under the MRR mechanism, compared to the other two mechanisms.

All the experimental results demonstrate that in FIM tasks, the avenues of applying the complementation of k-RR and k-RAPPOR under different privacy domains with personalized privacy concern levels to data privacy cloaking. Using the privacy preservation scheme for FIM from smart devices, as a result of being able to specify their privacy concern levels, users tend to share their sensitive information with the data miner. Besides the miner don't need to choose an enough small privacy budget to every participant. The results together show that our proposed MRR mechanism is very approximate for privacy preservation for frequent itemset mining from smart devices.

6   Related Work

Privacy concerns about mining information from smart devices have been proposed in plenty of literatures (e.g. in [9]). The aim of privacy preservation is to protect users' sensitive data from others, while collecting and analyzing private information. The work on privacy preserving data mining can be divided into two categories: centralized privacy preservation and local privacy preservation.

Centralized privacy preservation (e.g. in [12]) aggregates users' non-private data firstly and then forces corresponding algorithms to protect users' information. Although these approaches provide differential privacy guarantees, they can't ensure the data curator is absolutely trustable. A user's privacy may be violated when the data curator colludes with others. Besides, the uniform privacy budget might also impede the data miner obtains more accurate results.

LDP perturbs users' original data locally before the data leaving smart devices for data mining [3,7,11]. Aggarwal et al. [8] proposed that it's possible for an adversary to predict sensitive fields in records by association rules learned from the dataset. Therefore, it can't provide sufficient privacy guarantee to employ anonymity to protect users' sensitive information (e.g. [15]). However, local ϵ-differential privacy can solve the problem mentioned above. Sun et al. [14] proposed that applies the k-ary randomized response technique to perturb users' data locally, and then shares the private data with the data miner. Though the method can meet the requirement of local differential privacy, it may make the data miner cannot obtain accurate results because of introducing too much noise.

In this paper, we consider that different users may have diverse privacy concerns the set of attributes and propose our multiple randomized response mechanism. In the mechanism, we combine the k-RAPPOR [3] mechanism and the k-RR [11] mechanism to improve the utility of data mining results while providing personal privacy preservation. Our mechanism allocates diverse privacy budgets to attributes according to a user's privacy concern level, and applies k-RAPPOR to high private attributes and k-RR to low private ones. In this way, we can make use of the respective advantages of k-RAPPOR and k-RR to obtain more accurate frequent itemsets.

7   Conclusion

We have introduced a personalized local privacy-preserving scheme for frequent itemset mining. The scheme combines the strength of differential privacy with the added flexibility of user-specific privacy concern levels. And we have also proposed a novel mechanism which is comprised of the k-ary randomized response and the randomized aggregatable privacy-preserving ordinal response, it can achieve local ϵ-differential privacy while providing data utility efficiently. From a theoretical and empirical perspective, our proposed mechanism provides a more disirable trade-off between privacy preservation and data utility for frequent itemset mining than the k-RR mechanism and the k-RAPPOR mechanism. Our theoretical and experimental results demonstrate that our scheme is a very effective scheme. And we believe that our work belongs to an important step to better privacy protection in frequent itemset mining from smart devices.

Acknowledgements. This paper is supported by the National Science Foundation of China under Nos. 61472385 and U1301256, the sgcc project under XXB17201400056.

References

1. Warner, S.L.: Randomized response: a survey technique for eliminating evasive. J. Am. Stat. Assoc. **60**, 63–69 (1965)
2. Dwork, C.: Differential privacy. In: Bugliesi, M., Preneel, B., Sassone, V., Wegener, I. (eds.) ICALP 2006. LNCS, vol. 4052, pp. 1–12. Springer, Heidelberg (2006). doi:10.1007/11787006_1
3. Erlingsson, Ú., Pihur, V., Korolova, A.: Rappor: randomized aggregatable privacy-preserving ordinal response. In: CCS. ACM (2014)
4. Jorgensen, Z., Yu, T., Cormode, G.: Conservative or liberal personalized differential privacy. In: ICDE. IEEE (2015)
5. Dwork, C.: Differential privacy: a survey of results. In: Agrawal, M., Du, D., Duan, Z., Li, A. (eds.) TAMC 2008. LNCS, vol. 4978, pp. 1–19. Springer, Heidelberg (2008). doi:10.1007/978-3-540-79228-4_1
6. Prasad, K.S., Lee, H.K., Nissim, K., et al.: What can we learn privately? In: IEEE Symposium on Foundations of Computer Science 2008, pp. 531–540 (2008)
7. Wang, S., Huang, L., Tian, M., et al.: Personalized privacy-preserving data aggregation for histogram estimation. In: GLOBECOM. IEEE (2015)
8. Aggarwal, C.C., Pei, J., Zhang, B.: On privacy preservation against adversarial data mining. In: KDD. ACM (2006)
9. Kantarcioglu, M., Jin, J., Clifton, C.: When do data mining results violate privacy? In: KDD. ACM (2004)
10. Kairouz, P., Bonawitz, K., Ramage, D.: Discrete distribution estimation under local privacy. In: ICML. IEEE (2016)
11. Kairouz, P., Oh, S., Viswanath, P.: Extremal mechanisms for local differential privacy. In: Advances in Neural Information Processing Systems, pp. 2879–2887 (2014)
12. Lee, J., Clifton, C., Christopher, W.: Top-k frequent itemsets via differential private FP-trees. In: SIGKDD. ACM (2014)
13. Shi, E., Chan, T.H., Rieffel, E., Chow, R., Song, D.: On differentially private frequent itemset mining. In: VLDB 2012, pp. 25–36 (2012)
14. Sun, C., Fu, Y., Zhou, J., Gao, H.: Personalized privacy-preserving frequent itemset mining using randomized response. Sci. World J. (2014)
15. Atzori, M., Bonchi, F., Giannotti, F., Pedreschi, D.: Anonymity preserving pattern discovery. In: VLDB 2008, pp. 703–727 (2008)

3P Framework: Customizable Permission Architecture for Mobile Applications

Sujit Biswas[1,2], Kashif Sharif[1,2(✉)], Fan Li[1,2(✉)], and Yang Liu[3]

[1] School of Computer Science, Beijing Institute of Technology, Beijing, China
{sujitedu,7620160009,fli}@bit.edu.cn
[2] Beijing Engineering Research Center of High Volume Language Information
Processing and Cloud Computing Applications, Beijing, China
[3] State Key Laboratory of Networking and Switching Technology,
Beijing University of Posts and Telecommunications, Beijing, China
liu.yang@bupt.edu.cn

Abstract. Mobile applications & smart devices have drastically changed our routine tasks, and have become an integral part of modern society. Along with the numerous benefits we get, major challenges like privacy and safety have become complicated than before. The permission based system for mobile applications is designed to empower the user to decide which resources and information they want the application to access. Most of these permissions are granted during installation of application, but our study shows that the users make weak decisions in protecting their information. Majority of the users, even with technical backgrounds, blindly grant all permissions requested by the application even if they are not necessary for the application to run. In order to give more control to the user, and to enable them to make informed decisions regarding permission, we have proposed a Privacy Permission Policy Framework in this paper. This framework enables the user to have greater control over the permission granting while installing the mobile applications. The implementation and testing of the framework also enabled us to run forensic analysis and understand the scope of permissions requested, based on which this framework can advise the user to select minimum required permissions for the application to work. This makes the users' privacy more secure, and grants full control over the process.

Keywords: Privacy behaviors · Mobile app privacy · Android security · Users privacy consciousness

1 Introduction

Smart phones have dramatically changed the mobile world within a very short period. The global smart phone users exceeded 2.1 billion in 2016, and smart

This work is partially supported by the National Natural Science Foundation of China under Grant Nos. 61370192, 61432015, and 61602038.

© Springer International Publishing AG 2017
L. Ma et al. (Eds.): WASA 2017, LNCS 10251, pp. 445–456, 2017.
DOI: 10.1007/978-3-319-60033-8_39

phone penetration in China will cross 60% by 2020 [1,2]. A tremendous growth in the number of mobile apps, and app distribution platforms has also been observed. Applications are used for various daily life purposes including communication, mobile payments, entertainment, navigation, etc. In essence a smart phone contains a summary of complete daily life of a person. The on-line stores to obtain application *apks* for android are uncountable. Although this has helped in increasing the application development and ease of access, but at the same time, it has created numerous new challenges, among which user security and safety is a dominating one.

Android's existing security is built upon a permission based mechanism which restricts access of third-party Android applications to critical resources on a device (e.g., wi-fi, camera, etc.), change phone settings, read or write data (e.g. text message, contacts). App developers can use these permissions according to the requirements and services in their applications. Unfortunately, malicious and unscrupulous apps may also take benefit of these mechanisms for illegal purposes [3–6]. Moreover, some developers lack of privacy awareness [7], due to which, developers over-claim the permissions necessary to run the application. In existing security system of Android users see those required permissions of an application as a warning during installation or at runtime. In majority of cases, the user of application struggles to understand at installation, what the permission actually will do. In this paper, we propose a comprehensive smartphone permission policy framework, which sits between the kernel and the application *apks*, and intercepts the permission process. This creates a comprehensive solution to control which permissions are being granted for the device resources and user data. In order to better understand the awareness level of users regarding permission process of applications, we have also conducted a survey. Based on its recommendations, this framework assists users to fully control which permissions are to be granted.

The rest of paper is organized as: Sect. 2 discusses related work regarding the studies done about user awareness of security and privacy threats. In Sect. 3 we present results collected from survey to determine the correlation between users' educational background and the app permission awareness. Section 4 describes the Privacy Permission Policy Framework in detail, followed by implementation and analysis in Sect. 5. Conclusion is drawn in Sect. 6.

2   Related Works

Chin et al. [8] conducted a user study involving 60 smart phone users to gain understanding into user perceptions of smart phone security and installation habits. Their survey collects information about users such as; (a) users are more concerned about privacy on their smart phones than their laptops, (b) users are apprehensive about performing privacy-sensitive and financial tasks on their smart phones than their laptops (c) users worry about physical theft and data loss, malicious applications, and wireless network attackers. The conclude that users need to be more vigilant about security, and should use applications that protect from intrusions, security breaches, and malware. They also suggest that users need to be educated more about the safety and security of devices and data. Felt et al. [9] ran a survey on 3115 users and suggested a ranking of the risks of 54 smart phone application permissions. Lin et al. [10] framed mobile privacy in the form of people's expectations and concluded implication for employing crowdsourcing as a privacy evaluation technique. Balebako et al. [7] surveyed on 228 app developers to quantify privacy and security behaviors, suggested tools and opportunities to reduce the barriers for app developers to implement privacy and security best practices. In addition a number of papers address the perception of users with regards to user confidence in security, the complexity of permissions, and permission management [11–15]. Moreover there is a large collection of mobile applications [16–20], that are available to change the privacy settings, permissions, and other aspects. Majority of these tools are designed to change settings after the application has been installed, which is an *after the fact* situation.

Improvement and awareness of security situation is a continuous process. As the technologies improve & evolve, and become available for mass public usage, it becomes important to educate and make the user aware of the risks and concerns of safety and privacy.

3   Users' Privacy Awareness Analysis

The primary objective of *user privacy awareness* analysis is to understand the behavior of people at the time of installing an application on their smartphone. Once the user has granted permission for the application to access resources on the phone, the app can legitimately access or modify the information for it's purpose. We have conducted a structured survey of 252 multinational smartphone users. The online/offline survey questionnaire was designed to collect information regarding the decision process at app installation time: i.e. how users take decisions about permissions, and how much they are conscious about privacy and security. In addition the survey was focused towards people who have engineering background. The survey has 90% participants who are studying in different engineering disciplines and most of them are scholars studying in China from different countries. A follow-up survey was done on 30 participants, where they provided open-ended explanations of their feelings about smart phone security behavior.

Demographics: Participant ages range from 11 to 40 years (76.1% were 21–30, 12.5% between 31–40 years) while 35.9% were female and 64.1% were male. We classified participants basically in two categories, i.e. Engineers (all engineering students & professionals) and Others (other professionals like medical, administrator, etc.). In the survey sample, 69.5% were engineer and 30.5% belonged to other professionals. The predominant group of 78.1% were students and 15.6% were professionals. Within the students 76.4% were engineering students.

Table 1. Summary of responses regarding smartphone security and privacy

No	Knowledge	Engineers		Others	
		Yes	No	Yes	No
1	Read information before installation	30.5%	39.1%	13.3%	17.1%
2	Heard about permissions	85.4%	14.6%	79.5%	20.5%
3	Used security software	46.1%	53.9%	33.3%	66.7%
4	Have idea about effects of permissions	42.7%	57.3%	33.3%	66.7%
5	Noticed any privacy risk before	49.4%	50.6%	35.9%	64.1%
6	Knows that all photos tag geo location by default	43.8%	56.2%	28.2%	71.8%
7	Effect of malicious apps/permission on email, credit card, private data	80.9%	19.1%	53.8%	46.2%
8	Apps can be used for other purpose than declared	49.4%	50.6%	35.9%	64.1%

Survey Results: The percentage of users who expressed their perception on security related issues at time of app installation or later is presented in Table 1. It is observed that most of the people (39.10% out of 69.60%, 17.10% out of 30.40% engineering & non engineering respectively) do not read about apps privacy/permission information before installation. Surprisingly 14.60% engineers didn't know about permissions while 20.50% from other disciplines expressed lack of knowledge about permissions related to apps. 57.3% engineers who heard about permissions, but had no idea about the effects of permitting. It is very interesting to note that 80.90% of engineers do have concerns regarding malicious apps stealing their private data like email, credit card etc. Most of the responder (engineers 50.60% and 64.10% others) do not have any idea that one application can be used for other purposes than what it declares to do. In summary, as shown in Fig. 1, only 39.68% responders claim to have knowledge about permissions effect. About 19.05% users never read information while 30.30% rarely read about information and instructions at installation time. Only 42.06% of responders claimed to have used safety software for privacy or security. About 56% engineers have no idea about the effect of permissions on smart phone whereas non-engineers percentage in this regard is about 69%.

Based on the survey results, we form the following hypotheses about the privacy and security behavior of smart phone users.

Hypothesis (H1): *Technological education and privacy knowledge relationship is positive but weakly correlated.*

We examined this hypothesis based on the participants' opinion and calculated their correlation which has been shown in Table 2. The correlations between educational background and answer of question number 1 to 8 are very weak. This observation supports the hypothesis that educational background has no significant effect on: (*a*) reading warnings during installation, (*b*) hearing about

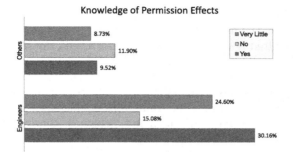

Fig. 1. Privacy consciousness statistics

permission and its effect on security (c) knowledge about the effect of malicious apps on personal data, or (d) utilization of apps.

During the follow-up interviews with selected participants, similar observation was made. Users are often surprised about the permissions requested, data collected by apps, and the recipients of such data. We also observed that users do not understand privacy notices. In essence most of the users have little or no idea about permissions, privacy & security practices, and don't read applications documentation to fully understand the risk. Hence it becomes impossible to consciously arrive at a permission decision. Most of the users accept all permissions requests, because of their desire to use the application for it's advertised purpose.

Table 2. Correlation matrix for questions in survey

	Engr	1	2	3	4	5	6	7	8
Engr	1								
1	0.008	1							
2	0.093	.345**	1						
3	0.105	0.119	0.018	1					
4	0.029	.254**	.262**	0.106	1				
5	.287**	.176*	0.137	0.035	0.129	1			
6	.218*	.198*	.213*	0.046	.189*	0.101	1		
7	0.169	0.035	.312**	0.046	.213*	.205*	0.168	1	
8	0.146	0.167	0.089	0.065	.307**	.320**	.224*	.243**	1

**Correlation is significant at the 0.01 level (2-tailed).
*Correlation is significant at the 0.05 level (2-tailed).

4   Privacy Permission Policy (3P) Framework

In light of the survey results and review of literature, we propose a new framework for ensuring privacy and permission control for different types of smart phone users. This Privacy Permission Policy (3P) framework takes smart decisions about warning the users of all permissions requested and assist in choosing the minimum required permissions based on user needs. As shown in Fig. 2, the framework is essentially a middleware, which takes into account the preferences & behavior of the user, detailed permissions requested in the application *apk*, and ensures that only those permissions are granted which will not go beyond the intended use of application. The framework enables user to pick and choose which permissions to grant and which not, which is contrary to majority of the installation processes. Current installers only show the users a subset of requested permissions, and denying them usually results in rejection of application installation. Hence the user has no choice to either accept all, or not use the application.

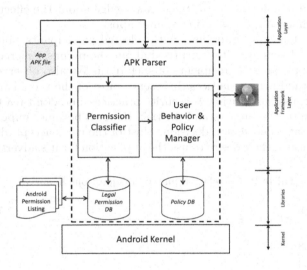

Fig. 2. 3P framework

Our frame work has three major modules, which work with each other and interact with the user to customize the permission process. These are explained in the following subsections.

APK Parser: This module is responsible of parsing the *.apk* file to extract the permissions from *AndroidManifest.xml* file. This customized parser looks for all the different types of permissions requested and then feeds them to the classifier module for further analysis. In case the parser is unable to locate the manifest file, or the format is not understandable, the application is immediately rejected and marked as a security threat.

Permission Classifier: This module plays a major role in the whole installation process, as it is responsible for identifying and classifying the permissions into different categories. The permissions can primarily be classified into three categories. Android SDK provides a list of permissions which are available to application developers, for gaining access to different resources/information available on the smart device. In addition the application developers provide information on application distribution stores, regarding which permissions they will be requesting/requiring to use the application. In light of this, the permission classifier categorizes the list based on manifest file as: (a) Requested and listed in app description, (b) Requested but not listed in app description, and (c) Requested but not listed and are not part of the standard list of permissions available with SDK (details in Sect. 5).

The permission classifier maintains a Legal Permission Database, which extracts information from the available and regularly updated permission lists for Android SDK online [21]. It also maintains a historical listing and changes in it.

User Behavior and Policy Manager: This is another core module of the customized installer, as it has a multi facet job. It is responsible for interacting with the user, categorization of apps, maintain/enforce the permission policy for installation of the app. Fundamentally this module classifies the application into different categories and then limits the permissions required for a specific category. It is a tricky task to categories the large number of applications that are available online, but Google Play store fundamentally divides all apps into Games and Applications. Games are further divided into 17 subcategories, and Applications into 30 subcategories, as of writing of this paper. It is mainly for searching, but we make use of this classification in order to limit the permission requirement[1].

This module interacts with the user to check which subcategory the application falls in, and shows them the minimum required permissions for that category. For Example, the applications in Photography category do not need to have access to *account_manager* or *read_contacts* permission. Hence the minimum default permissions are set based on apps services, purpose, and users' requirements. In addition the users do have the option to custom select the permissions as they seem fit.

The information is stored in the policy database, and it is updated to learn the behavior of the user. For instance, if the user specifically grants a permission that is not the default for the category, next time the user installs a similar application (or the same) it is highlighted. The user interface shows the user options to select minimum default recommended, accept what the application has requested, or customize completely for advanced users.

---

[1] Change is categories at Google Play Store does not effect implementation of this research. Other application categorizations can also be as effectively used as this one.

5   Implementation and Analysis

The 3P Framework as a whole is implemented at the Application Framework layer of the Android 5.1.1 OS, with API 25 for permissions. The Legal Permission Database and Policy Database are implemented as libraries. As shown in Fig. 2, the *.apk* file may come through the application layer or directly selected from the local memory by the user. After permission classification is done, the minimum required permissions are granted and applications are installed. We have used our framework to install three applications: i.e. Facebook (v76.0.0.0.27), WeChat (v6.5.4), QQi (International v5.1.2) obtained from Google Play store. In this section we describe the permission classification, forensic analysis, and installation with minimum required permissions.

The objective of this exercise is to understand the process of permission requests and users' capability to select which to allow and which not to. Hence the intention is not to highlight security vulnerabilities in these apps, but rather to empower the user to select the permission while still being able to use the application.

5.1   Permission Classification Analysis

The permission Classifier module classifies the permission requested by the application into three categories, as described in earlier sections. It is important to note the difference among the three. The first category is legitimate, but the second is of concern, as the user is not aware or notified about the permissions required. Moreover many of the installation platforms group the permission broadly, which hides the detail and depth of permissions requested from the user. Lastly the third category is surprising to even exist. There could be a number of reasons for them to be present, including multi-platform compatibility, version revisions, internal application working, etc. But as they are listed in manifest file, it is important to be aware of their existence.

Table 3 summarizes parsed permissions from the *apk* files of the above mentioned applications for Android. The listed permissions are taken from the Android SDK reference. This table shows permissions which were listed in the app description and requested, not listed but requested, and not requested at all. We can see that Facebook requests 30 permissions in total, but only 11 are listed in the Google Play description of it[2]. Keeping in view that Facebook is a rich social platform, the number of permissions required is large, but listing them explicitly for the information of user is important. WeChat is an even comprehensive application with micro-banking and other capabilities. It requests 40 permissions from the user, out of which 15 are listed on the Google Play description page for it. QQi which is the international version of the QQ application, and is primarily a communication app, requests 44 permissions and only 18 of them are listed on the Google Play description page.

---

[2] All observations regarding number of permissions is based on the information available at the time of writing this paper. This information is subject to change at anytime.

Table 3. Permissions requested by mobile apps. L: Listed, NL: Not Listed, R: Requested, NR: Not Requested

Permission	Facebook	WeChat	QQi
ACCESS_COARSE_LOCATION	L, R	L, R	L, R
ACCESS_FINE_LOCATION	L, R	L, R	L, R
ACCESS_NETWORK_STATE	L, R	L, R	L, R
ACCESS_WIFI_STATE	L, R	L, R	L, R
AUTHENTICATE_ACCOUNTS	L, R	NL, R	L, R
BATTERY_STATS	NL, R	NR	NR
BLUETOOTH	NR	NL, R	L, R
BLUETOOTH_ADMIN	NR	NL, R	L, R
BODY_SENSORS	NR	L, R	NR
BROADCAST_STICKY	NL, R	NL, R	NL, R
CALL_PHONE	NR	NR	NL, R
CAMERA	L, R	L, R	L, R
CHANGE_CONFIGURATION	NR	NR	NL, R
CHANGE_NETWORK_STATE	NL, R	NR	L, R
CHANGE_WIFI_MULTICUST_STATE	NR	NR	NL, R
CHANGE_WIFI_STATE	NL, R	L, R	L, R
DISABLE_KEYGUARD	NR	NR	NL, R
DOWNLOAD_WITHOUT_NOTIFICATION	NR	NL, R	NR
FLASHLIGHT	NR	NR	NL, R
GET_ACCOUNTS	NL, R	NL, R	L, R
GET_PACKAGE_SIZE	NR	NL, R	NR
GET_TASKS	NL, R	NL, R	NL, R
INSTALL_SHORTCUT	NR	NL, R	NL, R
INTERNET	L, R	L, R	L, R
KILL_BACKGROUND_PROCESSES	NR	NR	NL, R
MANAGE_ACCOUNTS	NL, R	NL, R	NL, R
MODIFY_AUDIO_SETTINGS	NR	L, R	NL, R
NFC	NR	L, R	L, R
PERSISTENT_ACTIVITY	NR	NR	NL, R
READ_CALENDER	L, R	NR	NL, R
READ_CONTACTS	NL, R	L, R	L, R
READ_EXTERNAL_STORAGE	L, R	NR	NR
READ_LOGS	NR	NR	NL, R
READ_PHONE_STATE	NL, R	NL, R	NL, R
READ_PROFILE	NL, R	NL, R	NR
READ_SETTINGS	NR	NR	NL, R
READ_SMS	NL, R	NR	NL, R
READ_SYNC_SETTINGS	NL, R	NL, R	NR
RECEIVE_BOOT_COMPLETED	NL, R	NL, R	NL, R
RECORD_AUDIO	NL, R	L, R	L, R
RESTART_PACKAGES	NR	NR	NL, R
SEND_SMS	NR	NR	NL, R
SET_ALARM	NR	NL, R	NR
SYSTEM_ALERT_WINDOW	NL, R	NL, R	NL, R
UNINSTALL_SHORTCUT	NR	NL, R	NR
USE_CREDENTIALS	NR	NL, R	NR
USE_FINGERPRINT	NR	NL, R	NR
VIBRATE	NL, R	NL, R	L, R
WAKE_LOCK	NL, R	NL, R	L, R
WRITE_APP_BADGE	NR	NL, R	NR
WRITE_CALENDER	L, R	NR	NL, R
WRITE_CONTACTS	NL, R	NL, R	NL, R
WRITE_EXTERNAL_STORAGE	L, R	NR	L, R
WRITE_SETTINGS	NR	NL, R	NL, R
WRITE_SYNC_SETTINGS	NL, R	NL, R	NL, R

In addition the above permissions, the parser module detected unknown permissions, for example: *facebook.pages.app.provider.access*, *smartdevice. permission.broadcast*, *tencent.mm. location.permission.send_view*, to name a few. Most of these permissions seem to be remnants of older version of the applications or cross-platform development. For example *nokia.pushnotification* and *htc.launcher* are most probably hardware specific permissions that are required by customized Android OS on these devices. Nonetheless, these permissions are in fact hidden from the user, and by default accepted for the application to be installed.

5.2   Post-installation Analysis

Once the Permission Classifier has categorized all the permissions requested they are forwarded to User Behavior and Policy Manager. To evaluate basic permission set against the working of application, we allowed only the basic minimum permissions listed in Google API as well as declared in the application description. For Facebook, only 11 listed permissions were granted and application was installed. The application installed successfully and launched normally, which proves that it is not necessary for the user to accept all the permissions in order to install the application. Similarly, for WeChat 15 basic permissions were granted and app was installed. For QQi, 18 permissions were granted and application was installed. It is very important to note that after successful launch of weChat, prompt was given for other permissions, which were required to use some of the features of the application. This is acceptable behavior as, it clearly informs the user of permission related to the service they are about to use.

In addition, an important factor that masks the visibility of requested permissions from the users is the UI of operating system, especially if it customized by the hardware vendor. In our implementation, we tested the framework on three different hardware, i.e. XiaoMi, LG, and Huawei. For Facebook installation the total number of permissions requested as shown by XiaoMi were 34, while LG showed 22, and Huawei 28. This is mainly attributed how the different flavors of Android customization groups and perceives the requested permissions. This extends to a potential future work of our system. After installation of the application, if the app requests new permissions, they need to be intercepted and user needs to be notified if any bulk permissions are being granted.

6   Conclusion

Privacy of mobile application users is a major security concern. Android based applications access different device resources and personal information by seeking permissions from the user. Although this system is designed to inform the user of what they are allowing on their device, but in reality the user has no real knowledge of what permissions do, or which permissions they are granting. In this paper, we presented results from a survey of smartphone users, with an emphasis on how technical education is related to permissions/privacy knowledge. We found that although the correlation is positive, but has no real significance. This drives the need to have permission frameworks, which can assist and truly inform the user of which permissions they are granting. We have proposed and implemented a Privacy Permission Policy (3P) framework, which essentially helps the user and gives them more control over granting application access at installation. We also have found that, not only the applications request a number of unnecessary permissions, but have permissions that are not listed in Android API 25. Our framework enables the user to custom select these permissions, so that they are more secure.

References

1. Statista: Number of Smartphone Users Worldwide from 2014 to 2020. https://www.statista.com/statistics/330695/number-of-smartphone-users-worldwide/
2. Statista: Share of Mobile Phone Users that Use a Smartphone in China from 2013 to 2019. https://www.statista.com/statistics/257045/smartphone-user-penetration-in-china/
3. Felt, A.P., Finifter, M., Chin, E., Hanna, S., Wagner, D.: A survey of mobile malware in the wild. In: ACM Workshop on Security and Privacy in Smartphones and Mobile Devices (SPSM), pp. 3–14 (2011)
4. Thurm, S., Kanel, Y.I.: Your apps are watching you. Wallstreet J. (2010)
5. Zhang, L., Cai, Z., Wang, X.: FakeMask: a novel privacy preserving approach for smartphones. IEEE Trans. Netw. Serv. Manag. **13**(2), 335–348 (2016)
6. He, Z., Cai, Z., Li, Y.: Customized privacy preserving for classification based applications. In: Proceedings of the ACM Workshop on Privacy-Aware Mobile Computing, pp. 37–42. ACM (2016)
7. Balebako, R., Marsh, A., Lin, J., Hong, J., Cranor, L.F.: The privacy and security behaviors of smartphone app developers. In: Workshop on Usable Security UsEC, February 2014
8. Chin, E., Felt, A.P., Sekar, V., Wagner, D.: Measuring user confidence in smartphone security and privacy. In: Proceedings of Symposium on Usable Privacy and Security SOUPS. ACM, July 2012
9. Felt, A.P., Egelman, S., Wagner, D.: I'Ve got 99 problems, but vibration ain't one: a survey of smartphone users' concerns. In: ACM Workshop on Security and Privacy in Smartphones and Mobile Devices (SPSM), pp. 33–44 (2012)
10. Lin, J., Amini, S., Hong, J.I., Sadeh, N., Lindqvist, J., Zhang, J.: Expectation and purpose: understanding users' mental models of mobile app privacy through crowdsourcing. In: Proceedings of the ACM Conference on Ubiquitous Computing (UbiComp), pp. 501–510. ACM, September 2012
11. Benenson, Z., Kroll-Peters, O., Krupp, M.: Attitudes to IT security when using a smartphone. In: Federated Conference on Computer Science and Information Systems (FedCSIS), pp. 1179–1183, September 2012
12. Mylonas, A., Kastania, A., Gritzalis, D.: Delegate the smartphone user? Security awareness in smartphone platforms. Comput. Secur. **34**, 47–66 (2013)
13. Fife, E., Orjuela, J.: The privacy calculus: mobile apps and user perceptions of privacy and security. Int. J. Eng. Bus. Manag. **5**(1) (2012)

14. Balebako, R., Jung, J., Lu, W., Cranor, L.F., Nguyen, C.: Little brothers watching you: raising awareness of data leaks on smartphones. In: Proceedings of the Symposium on Usable Privacy and Security SOUPS. ACM (2013)
15. Kelley, P.G., Consolvo, S., Cranor, L.F., Jung, J., Sadeh, N., Wetherall, D.: A conundrum of permissions: installing applications on an Android smartphone. In: Blyth, J., Dietrich, S., Camp, L.J. (eds.) FC 2012. LNCS, vol. 7398, pp. 68–79. Springer, Heidelberg (2012). doi:10.1007/978-3-642-34638-5_6
16. Beresford, A.R., Rice, A., Skehin, N., Sohan, R.: MockDroid: trading privacy for application functionality on smartphones. In: Proceedings of the Workshop on Mobile Computing Systems and Applications, pp. 49–54. ACM (2011)
17. Hornyack, P., Han, S., Jung, J., Schechter, S., Wetherall, D.: These aren't the droids you're looking for: retrofitting Android to protect data from imperious applications. In: Proceedings of the ACM Conference on Computer and Communications Security, pp. 639–652. ACM (2011)
18. Zhou, Y., Zhang, X., Jiang, X., Freeh, V.W.: Taming information-stealing smartphone applications (on Android). In: McCune, J.M., Balacheff, B., Perrig, A., Sadeghi, A.-R., Sasse, A., Beres, Y. (eds.) Trust 2011. LNCS, vol. 6740, pp. 93–107. Springer, Heidelberg (2011). doi:10.1007/978-3-642-21599-5_7
19. Au, K.W.Y., Zhou, Y.F., Huang, Z., Lie, D.: PScout: analyzing the Android permission specification. In: Proceedings of the ACM Conference on Computer and Communications Security, pp. 217–228. ACM (2012)
20. Mueller, K., Butler, K.: Flex-P: flexible Android permissions. In: IEEE Symposium on Security and Privacy, May 2011
21. Android, S.D.K.: Android Manifest Permission API 25. https://developer.android.com/reference/android/Manifest.permission.html

A Bitcoin Based Incentive Mechanism for Distributed P2P Applications

Yunhua He[1,2], Hong Li[2,3]($\boxtimes$), Xiuzhen Cheng[2], Yan Liu[5], and Limin Sun[3,4]

[1] The School of Computer Science,
North China University of Technology, Beijing, China
heyunhua@ncut.edu.cn
[2] The Department of Computer Science,
George Washington University, Washington, DC, USA
lihong@iie.ac.cn
[3] Beijing Key Laboratory of IOT Information Security Technology,
IIE, CAS, Beijing, China
[4] University of Chinese Academy of Sciences, Beijing, China
[5] The School of Software and Microelectronics, Peking University, Beijing, China

Abstract. The effectiveness of distributed Peer-to-Peer (P2P) applications heavily relies on the cooperation of mobile users. Each user should receive a satisfying reward to compensate its resource consumption for cooperation. However, suitable incentive mechanisms that can meet the diverse requirements of users in dynamic and distributed P2P environments are still missing. Therefore in this paper, we propose a Bitcoin based incentive mechanism for distributed P2P applications that applies the basic idea of Bitcoin to incentivize users for cooperation. In this mechanism, users who help with a successful delivery get rewarded. Through a game theoretical analysis and evaluation study, we demonstrate the effectiveness and security strength of our proposed incentive mechanism.

1 Introduction

Peer-to-Peer (P2P) applications [7,13] are featured by *distributed architectures* that partition tasks or work loads between peers without a trusted authority. Example P2P applications include mobile data offloading that allows mobile users to cooperatively deliver cellular network data by exploiting complementary network technologies (WiFi, femtocell, etc.), delay-tolerant networking where nodes opportunistically forward messages for others by following a store-carry-forward mechanism, and mobile crowdsensing in which users collaboratively upload data for the purpose of reducing energy consumption and mobile data cost.

The effectiveness of data transfer, packet forwarding, or data collection in the P2P applications relies on the cooperation of mobile users. Selfish users may be reluctant to cooperate in data transmissions for the concerns on energy and bandwidth consumption. Thus, they should be provided with enough rewards for cooperation. Many incentive mechanisms have been proposed and implemented, including the reputation systems, Tit-for-Tat schemes, and credit based

© Springer International Publishing AG 2017
L. Ma et al. (Eds.): WASA 2017, LNCS 10251, pp. 457–468, 2017.
DOI: 10.1007/978-3-319-60033-8_40

approaches. Reputation systems [16, 19] can help identify uncooperative users by computing users' reputation scores, but such systems generally lack the considerations on collusion attacks and on how to define the reputation of a new user. Tit-for-Tat schemes [15] stimulate mobile users to cooperate by exchanging equal services among them, but these schemes are restricted to applications with long session durations. Credit based approaches [4–6] could be the most promising due to their explicit and flexible incentive methods; nevertheless, most credit based incentive schemes either rely on a central trusted authority or do not give an explicit digital currency system that is provably secure, leading to possible system collapses.

Bitcoin is a decentralized digital currency that is provably secure. It has recently gained a noticeable popularity, and its current market capitalization is over $16 billion. The security of Bitcoin depends on a majority of the computing power instead of a central authority [17], thus eliminating the risks of one taking control over the system, generating inflation, or completely shutting down the system. In this paper, we exploit Bitcoin transactions to incentivize users to cooperate in P2P applications.

The basic idea of our incentive scheme is to employ Bitcoin transactions to reward those intermediate nodes that contribute to a successful delivery from the sender to the receiver. If an intermediate node helps transmit the data, the next-hop node sends it a signed acknowledgement which is used as a proof of getting the rewards. The miners in the Bitcoin system are in charge of verifying whether there is a successful delivery, and examining the validity of the signed acknowledgements. This brings another concern: if a miner can see the content of a signed acknowledgement, she can disguise as a cooperative intermediate node to get the payment. To overcome this problem, we extend the Bitcoin transaction syntax [8, 14] to support a secure validation of the acknowledgement by using commutative encryptions [12]. We also propose a pricing strategy to defend the possible attacks resulted from selfish users and to prevent their collusions. The major contributions of the paper are summarized as follows:

- We design a Bitcoin-based incentive mechanism that can meet the diverse requirements of users in dynamic and distributed P2P environments.
- We introduce a secure validation method to keep the to-be-verified content secret from the miners in the Bitcoin system, and a pricing strategy to prevent selfish users from exhibiting selfish actions and to defend the collusion attacks resulted from them.
- We further employ a game theoretical analysis and simulation study to demonstrate the security and efficiency of our incentive mechanism.

The remainder of the paper is structured as follows. Section 2 outlines the related work. In Sect. 3, we introduce the threat model and assumptions employed in this paper. Our incentive scheme is detailed in Sect. 4, followed by a comprehensive security analysis and evaluation in Sect. 5. The paper is concluded in Sect. 6.

2   Related Work

The incentive schemes for P2P applications fall into three categories: Reputation, Tit-for-Tat, and Credit. In a reputation system [16], each user is given a score interpreted as the probability of an entity behaving honestly, such a system can be utilized to identify misbehaving users. Reputation systems generally suffer from the following drawbacks: (i) the possibility of selfish users colluding with each other to maximize their welfare is generally ignored; and (ii) they are known to be vulnerable to Sybil attacks [9] and whitewashing attacks [21].

Tit-for-Tat based schemes [15] stimulate mobile users to cooperate by exchanging equal services based on what contributions they have done for others. Tit-for-Tat schemes are restricted to applications with long session durations that can provide many opportunities for reciprocation between pairs of users [18]. Another challenge of Tit-for-Tat is its hardness to meet the different service requirements of the users.

In Credit based systems [10,11,20,21], a central authority assigns certain virtual money to each user. When a user needs others' help (for example, to forward a message), it should pay the helper certain amount of virtual money. Zhong et al. [21] proposed a cheat-proof, credit-based system for stimulating cooperation among selfish nodes in mobile ad hoc networks. The scheme assumes that a routing path between the sender and the receiver is determined before data transmission occurs. Zhu et al. [22] proposed a layered incentive scheme for dynamic routing in DTNs. This mechanism emphasizes the generation and verification of the secure layered messages but does not involve a detailed pricing strategy. Chen and Chan [4] presented a pricing strategy running on top of a given DTN routing module. We notice that all the credit based incentive schemes rely on central trusted authorities that do not exist in P2P applications. Furthermore, no explicit virtual digital currency system that is provably secure was proposed by any credit based system.

3   Threat Model and Assumptions

A typical architecture of P2P applications consists of senders, intermediate nodes, and receivers. Senders transmit certain files, messages, or the sensed data to the receivers with the help of the intermediate nodes. The numbers of senders and receivers are different in different P2P applications. For example, there are 1 sender and n receivers in mobile data offloading, while in the context of DTN there are only 1 sender and 1 receiver. In this paper, we consider a simple case with 1 sender and 1 receiver. Our incentive scheme can be easily extended to the more complex cases with multiple senders and receivers.

Data transmissions in P2P applications rely on the cooperation between intermediate nodes. To incentivize the cooperations, senders give certain rewards to the nodes that help transmit the data. In this work, we assume that nodes are *selfish* but would take a rational decision to maximize their profit. Specially, each node may launch the following attacks:

- *Refusing to Pay:* A sender can refuse to pay back the intermediate nodes when the data are successfully delivered to the receiver.
- *Denying Attack:* The intermediate nodes or the receiver can deny that they have received the data from other nodes, which could prevent others from getting rewarded.
- *Extending/Shortenning the Path:* The intermediate node can extend or shorten the path to get more reward from the sender.
- *Collusion Attack:* Nodes can collude with each other to maximize their profit. In this work, we only consider the collusion among intermediate nodes or between an intermediate node and the receiver. We shall address the case where the sender colludes with the receiver in our future work by considering reputation based inventive systems.

4   Bitcoin Based Incentive Mechanism

In our model, we employ the idea of credit based incentives to motivate intermediate nodes to cooperate. In a credit based scheme, incentive can be considered as a transaction. When discussing a transaction, we should figure out the following questions: (1) who pays who; (2) how to pay the bill; and (3) how much the payer should pay.

4.1   Who Pays Who?

When a sender wants to transmit a certain message to a receiver, there exist three different options to pay back the intermediate nodes. The first option is to let the receiver give rewards to all the intermediate nodes; but this approach allows malicious nodes to get high rewards by sending many fake messages. The second option is to give the rewards by both the sender and the receiver, which could suffer the same problem as the first option since the sender can collude with the intermediate nodes. The third option is for the sender to pay back the intermediate nodes when it figures out that the message is successfully delivered to the receiver, which is adopted by this work.

Another relevant question we need to answer is who should get the rewards. In this study, we choose to award only those nodes that contribute to a successful delivery, which means that an intermediate node cannot get a reward if the receiver does not receive the message correctly. To identify the intermediate nodes who help forward the message, the node in the next hop is required to send a signed acknowledgement back. Because a node is considered *cooperative* if and only if the node has a signed acknowledgement from its successor, it is important for an intermediate node to stimulate its successor by paying certain money to its successor for sending the signed acknowledgement.

4.2   How to Pay the Bill?

As mentioned before, intermediate nodes should be motivated to cooperate in a dynamic and distributed environment. In particular, a sender knows the receiver, but it does not know the route to the receiver. The sender should give rewards to the intermediate nodes who help transmit the message. Cooperative nodes can be divided into two types: *negative cooperative nodes* who help transmit the data but the receiver fails to receive the data, and *positive cooperative nodes* who help transmit the data and the receiver does successfully receive the data. In our consideration, the sender only pays back the positive cooperative nodes.

In our model, the sender employs the Bitcoin system to pay back the positive cooperative nodes. The workflow of the payment consists of three steps. In the first step, the sender publicizes a transmission task and makes a certain deposit that is used to pay back the positive cooperative nodes. In the second step, the sender transmits data to the receiver by opportunistic connections. In the last step, the positive cooperative nodes get their payments. Suppose that a sender A sends a message m to a receiver E, and B, C, D are the positive cooperative nodes who help A transmit the data to E. The workflow of the payment is elaborated as follows.

(1) Publishing a Transmission Task: A announces a task $A \rightarrow E : m$ and generates two random numbers R_1 and R_2 that should be kept secret. Then A makes a deposit to commit that it will give the rewards to the positive cooperative nodes if the message is successfully delivered; otherwise A would get the deposit back. The transcript of the transaction [1,3] is shown in Fig. 1.

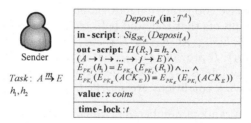

Fig. 1. A publishes a task and makes a deposit.

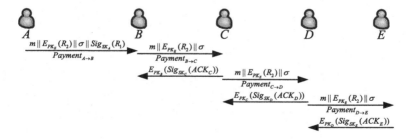

Fig. 2. A transmits the data to E.

(2) Data Transmission: The process of the data transmission from A to E is illustrated in Fig. 2. A first sends the message $m||E_{PK_E}(R_2)||\sigma||Sig_{SK_A}(R_1)$ to

B, and constructs a transaction $Payment_{A \to B}$. Then, B, C, and D help A transmit the message $m||E_{PK_E}(R_2)||\sigma$ to the receiver E, and construct transactions $Payment_{B \to C}$, $Payment_{C \to D}$, and $Payment_{D \to E}$, respectively. C, D, and E send the signed encrypted acknowledgement back to B, C, and D, respectively. The Bitcoin transactions in the data transmission are illustrated in Fig. 3.

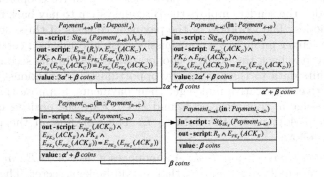

Fig. 3. Transactions in a multihop message transmission.

(3) Obtaining the Payments: After the data is successfully delivered to the receiver, all the positive cooperative nodes should get the rewards by providing the miners with the proofs that they did help transmit the data. Specifically, B provides $\{E_{PK_B}(R_1), E_{PK_B}(ACK_C), PK_A, PK_C\}$; C provides $\{E_{PK_C}(ACK_C),$ $E_{PK_C}(ACK_D), PK_D\}$; D provides $\{E_{PK_D}(ACK_D), E_{PK_D}(ACK_E), PK_E\}$; and E provides $\{R_2, E_{PK_E}(ACK_E)\}$. The transactions are considered to be valid if and only if the following conditions are satisfied:

- E can provide the random number R_2, which is verified by $H(R_2) = h_2$;
- There is a route from A to E, and the route can be determined by the transaction chain from A to E.
- B can provide the random number R_1, which can be verified by

$$E_{PK_B}(h_1) = E_{PK_A}(E_{PK_B}(R_1));$$

- B, C, D can provide the correct acknowledgements, which are verified by

$$E_{PK_B}(E_{PK_C}(ACK_C)) = E_{PK_C}(E_{PK_B}(ACK_C)),$$
$$E_{PK_C}(E_{PK_D}(ACK_D)) = E_{PK_D}(E_{PK_C}(ACK_D)),$$
$$E_{PK_D}(E_{PK_E}(ACK_E)) = E_{PK_E}(E_{PK_D}(ACK_E)).$$

4.3 How Much Should the Payers Pay?

By setting a suitable pricing strategy, we can guarantee the security of our incentive mechanism against the selfish behaviors of the users and the collusion attacks. To be more specific, a sender should determine the payment to the positive cooperative nodes for their help to transmit its data, and each positive cooperative node needs to determine the payment to its successor for sending the signed acknowledgement. Instead of considering the two components separately, we consider the final payment to the positive cooperative nodes and the receiver. Without loss of generality, we assume that A sends m to E via $P = (P_1, P_2, \cdots, P_n)$, the list of positive cooperative nodes who help the transmission. Then, the final payment to node i can be computed by

$$
p_i = \begin{cases} \alpha/2^{n-1}, & \text{if } i \in P, \\ \beta, & \text{if } i = E, \\ 0, & \text{otherwise.} \end{cases} \quad and \quad \begin{cases} \alpha > 2^{n-1}c_{\max}, \\ \beta > c_E, \\ \alpha < \beta/q^2. \end{cases}
$$

Note that in our implementation, A first makes a deposit; after determining the number of positive cooperative nodes, A determines the actual amount of coins given to them. For example, in the case of multiple positive cooperative nodes shown in Fig. 1, A first makes a deposit of $\alpha + \beta$ coins. After all the positive cooperative nodes have been identified (Fig. 3), A sets $\alpha' = \alpha/2^{3-1} = \alpha/4$.

5   Security Analysis and Performance Evaluation

5.1   Data-Transmission Game Analysis Model

To study the security of our incentive mechanism, we employ a static game to analyze the cooperative behaviors of the intermediate nodes. Through the Nash equilibrium results of the game, we can obtain the best strategies of the players under different pricing strategies. The model of the data-transmission game analysis is described as follows.

Players. This game has $n + 1$ players, the positive cooperative nodes $P = (P_1, P_2, \cdots, P_n)$ and the receiver E.

Strategies. Each player i has two possible actions: play honestly or play selfishly. If player i plays honestly, it follows the protocol; otherwise, it plays selfishly, either behaves selfishly itself or colludes with its neighbors. We denote the strategy of node i by s_i. Then s_i is either $Honest$ or $Selfish$.

Utilities. Player i can get its utility by deducting its cost from its received payment. Without colluding with its neighbors, the utility of u_i is computed by

$$
u_i = \begin{cases} \alpha/2^{n-1} - c_i, & i \in P \text{ and } s_i = Honest, \\ \beta - c_E, & i = E \text{ and } s_i = Honest, \\ 0, & i \in P \text{ and } s_i = Selfish, \\ 0, & i = E \text{ and } s_i = Selfish. \end{cases}
$$

where c_i is the cost of i for transmitting the data, sending a signed acknowledgement, and providing the validation information, c_E is the cost of the receiver E for sending a signed acknowledgement and providing the validation information.

When player i colludes with others, it is more complicated because the utility should consider the success probability of the collusion attack. Here we present some definitions for the security analysis of our incentive scheme.

Definition 1. *An incentive mechanism is receiver-collusion-resistant if the receiver and any group of its colluding neighbors cannot increase the expected sum of their utilities by using any strategy profile other than the one in which everybody plays honestly.*

Definition 2. *An incentive mechanism is intermediate-node-collusion-resistant, if any group of colluding intermediate nodes cannot increase the expected sum of their utilities by using any strategy profile other than the one in which everybody plays honestly.*

Definition 3. *An incentive mechanism is secure if $s_i = Honest$ is the best response strategy for each player and the game is receiver-collusion-resistant and intermediate-node-collusion-resistant.*

5.2 Security Analysis Without Collusion Attacks

Theorem 1. *In the data-transmission game, $s_i = Honest$ is the best response strategy for player i if $\alpha > 2^{n-1}c_i$ and $\beta > c_E$.*

Proof. When player i plays honestly, we have

$$u_i = \begin{cases} \alpha/2^{n-1} - c_i, & i \in P, \\ \beta - c_E, & i = E. \end{cases}$$

If player i does not respond honestly, we have $u_i' = 0$ in this case. As $\alpha > 2^{n-1}c_i$, $u_i' = 0 < \alpha/2^{n-1} - c_i = u_i$; thus P_i's utility is reduced by playing selfishly. Therefore, if $\alpha > 2^{n-1}c_i$ and $\beta > c_E$, $s_i = Honest$ is the best response strategy for the payer i.

5.3 Security Analysis with Collusion Attacks

We first consider the case when E colludes with its neighbors; then we analyze the case when an intermediate node colludes with its neighbors.

Theorem 2. *Our incentive mechanism is receiver-collusion-resistant if $\alpha < \beta/q^2$, where q is the probability that two arbitrary nodes encounter each other.*

Proof. We first consider the case with one conspired node; then we extend to the case of multiple conspired nodes.
  Case 1. Suppose $G = \{E, E_1\}$ is a collusion group. G forges a bogus path with one positive cooperative node, i.e., $A \to E_1 \to E$. Let $E(u_G)$ denote the expected sum of the utility of G. Our goal is to show that $E(u_G) \leq u_E$.
  If E_1 gets R_1, E and E_1 can get the payment from A, which means that E_1 has encountered both E and A (with a probability of q^2). The expected sum of the payment of G is $p_G = q^2(\alpha + \beta) + (1 - q^2)\beta = q^2\alpha + \beta$. Considering the cost of E_1 to provide the validation information and to communicate with E, we have the expected sum of the utility of G to be $u_G = q^2\alpha + \beta - \beta - c_E = q^2\alpha - c_E$. Thus we obtain $u_G = q^2\alpha - c_E < \beta - c_E = u_E$.

Case 2. Suppose $G = \{E, E_1, \cdots, E_n\}$ is a collusion group. G forges a bogus path with multiple positive cooperative nodes, i.e., $A \to E_1 \to \cdots \to E_n \to E$. Let $E(u_G)$ denote the expected sum of the utility of G. Our goal is to show that $E(u_G) \leq u_E$.

When $(A, E_1), (E_1, E2), \cdots, (E_n, E)$ encounter each other, G gets the payment. The expected sum of the payment of G is

$$p_G = q^{n+1}(n\alpha/2^{n-1} + \beta) + (1 - q^{n+1})\beta$$
$$= q^{n+1}n\alpha/2^{n-1} + \beta.$$

Deducting the cost of G, we have the expected sum of the utility of G:

$$u_G = q^{n+1}n\alpha/2^{n-1} + \beta - n\beta - c_E.$$

As $\alpha < \beta/q^2$, we have

$$u_G = q^{n+1}n\alpha/2^{n-1} + \beta - n\beta - c_E$$
$$< \frac{q^{n+1}n\beta}{2^{n-1}q^2} - n\beta + \beta - c_E$$
$$= (q^{n-1}/2^{n-1} - 1)n\beta + \beta - c_E$$
$$< \beta - c_E = u_E.$$

Therefore, if $\alpha < \beta/q^2$, our incentive mechanism is receiver-collusion-resistant.

Theorem 3. *Our incentive mechanism is intermediate-node-collusion-resistant.*

Proof. An intermediate node can collude with its neighbors to extend or shorten the path.

Case 1. An intermediate node colludes with its neighbors to extend the path. We first Consider the case with one positive cooperative node $A \to B \to E$. Let $G = \{B, B_1, \cdots, B_n\}$ be the collusion group. G extends the path to $A \to B \to B_1 \to \cdots \to B_n \to E$. Let $E(u_G)$ denote the expected sum of utility of G. Our goal is to show that $E(u_G) \leq u_B$, where u_B is the utility of B to play honestly. As B indeed helped A transmit data to E, it can get all the needed validation information from A and E, which means that B can always launch a successful collusion attack. According to our pricing scheme, we have

$$E(u_G) = (n + 1)\alpha/2^n - c_B;$$
$$u_B = \alpha - c_B.$$

Let $f(x) = (x+1)/2^x$, $x \geq 1$. We have $f'(x) = 2^{-x}(1 - (1+x)x) < 0$. Thus, $f(x)$ is a monotonically decreasing function. Accordingly we have $f(n) < f(n-1) < \ldots < f(1)$. It is easy to see that

$$E(u_G) = (n + 1)\alpha/2^n - c_B < \alpha - c_B = u_B.$$

Now we consider the case with multiple positive cooperative nodes. Let $u_B = \alpha' - c_B$. We can deduce that

$$E(u_G) = (n+1)\alpha'/2^n - c_B < \alpha' - c_B = u_B.$$

Case 2. An intermediate node colludes with its neighbors to shorten the path $A \to P_1 \to \cdots \to P_i \to P_{i+1} \to \cdots \to P_n \to E$. Let $G = \{P_i, P_{i+1}\}$ be a collusion group. Then G shortens the path to $A \to P_1 \to \cdots \to P_i \to P_{i+2} \to \cdots \to P_n \to E$. Let $E(u_G)$ denote the expected sum of the utility of G. Our goal is to show that $E(u_G) \leq u_{P_i} + u_{P_{i+1}}$, where u_{P_i} and $u_{P_{i+1}}$ are respectively the utilities of P_i and P_{i+1} to play honestly. As P_i and P_{i+1} indeed helped transmit the data, they can get all the needed validation information. Thus they can launch a successful collusion attack. According to our pricing scheme, we have

$$E(u_G) = \alpha/2^{n-2} - c_{P_i} - c_{P_{i+1}};$$
$$u_{P_i} = \alpha/2^{n-1} - c_{P_i};$$
$$u_{P_{i+1}} = \alpha/2^{n-1} - c_{P_{i+1}}.$$

It is easy to see that $E(u_G) = u_{P_i} + u_{P_{i+1}}$.

Therefore, our incentive mechanism is intermediate-node-collusion-resistant.

The three theorems together prove the following theorem.

Theorem 4. *Our incentive mechanism is secure if $\alpha > 2^{n-1}c_{\max}$, $\beta > c_E$, and $\alpha < \beta/q^2$.*

5.4   Performance Evaluation

We employ a laptop computer with an Intel Core i7-2640M Processor to implement a prototype of our system using the Crypto++5.62 library and consider a path of 5 hops, to evaluate the overhead of our incentive mechanism. The OS of the laptop is Windows 10 Pro 64. The length of a message payload is 1024 bytes, and the message digest function is MD-5. We consider three commutative encryption schemes: ElGamal with a modulus of 1024 bits, RSA with a modulus of 1024 bits, and RSA with a modulus of 3072 bits.

Table 1. CPU processing time

Commutative encryption	Sender (ms)	Intermediate nodes (ms)	Receiver (ms)	Miner (ms)
ElGamal 1024	28	17	13	17
RSA 1024	11	5	4	7
RSA 3072	63	39	21	12

CPU Processing Time. In our incentive system, the major processing overhead is the R2 encryption operation, the message and R1 signing operations, and the transaction generating operation by the sender, the ACK signing and encryption operation (or the R1 decryption operation) and the transaction generating operation by each intermediate node, the message verification operation, the R2 decryption operation, and the ACK signing and encryption operation by the receiver, and the verification operation by the miners. The columns of Table 1 report the CPU processing time of the sender, an intermediate node (average), the receiver, and a miner. We observe that RSA has a much smaller overhead. Therefore if reducing overhead is the major objective, RSA is a better implementation choice.

Bandwidth and Storage. Compared with the opportunistic routing protocols introduced in [2] but without any incentive mechanism, the major increased message overhead includes the encrypted R2, the signed R1, and the signed and encrypted ACK. For ElGamal and RSA with a modulus of 1024 bits, the encrypted R2 takes about 128 bytes, the signed R1 takes about 128 bytes, the signed and encrypted ACK takes about 128 bytes; for RSA 3074 bits, the encrypted R2 takes about 384 bytes, the signed R1 takes about 384 bytes, and the signed and encrypted ACK takes about 384 bytes. The storage requirement for the Bitcoin transactions is analyzed as follows. For RSA 1024 and ElGamal 1024, each transaction requires at least 1 byte for the previous transaction reference, 128 bytes for the in-script, 1 byte for the Bitcoin value, and 128 bytes for out-script; adding up together we get 258 bytes for a minimum-sized Bitcoin transaction. For RSA 3074, each transaction requires 384 bytes for the in-script and 384 byes for the out-script, resulting in a 770-byte minimum-sized Bicoin transaction.

6   Conclusion

In this paper, we propose a Bitcoin based incentive mechanism that can meet the diverse requirements in a dynamic and distributed P2P environment. In our incentive mechanism, intermediate nodes who contribute to a successful delivery can obtain rewards from Bitcoin transactions. The transactions are verified by the miners in a secure way by using commutative encryptions. A pricing strategy is proposed to guarantee the security of our incentive mechanism. We also employ a static game model to demonstrate the security strength of our incentive mechanism.

Acknowledgment. This work was supported by the National Natural Science Foundations of China (61472418, 61672415, U1636120), the National Defense Science and Technology Innovation Foundation of the Chinese Academy of Sciences (CXJJ-16Z234) and the Science and Technology Innovation Service Capacity Building Project (PXM2017-014212-000002).

References

1. Andrychowicz, M., Dziembowski, S., Malinowski, D., Mazurek, L.: Secure multi-party computations on bitcoin. In: S&P, pp. 443–458. IEEE (2014)

2. Batabyal, S., Bhaumik, P.: Mobility models, traces and impact of mobility on opportunistic routing algorithms: a survey. IEEE Commun. Surv. Tuts. **17**(3), 1679–1707 (2015)
3. Bentov, I., Kumaresan, R.: How to use bitcoin to design fair protocols. In: Garay, J.A., Gennaro, R. (eds.) CRYPTO 2014. LNCS, vol. 8617, pp. 421–439. Springer, Heidelberg (2014). doi:10.1007/978-3-662-44381-1_24
4. Chen, B., Chan, M.C.: Mobicent: a credit-based incentive system for disruption tolerant network. In: INFOCOM, pp. 1–9. IEEE (2010)
5. Duan, Z., Li, W., Cai, Z.: Distributed auctions for task assignment and scheduling in mobile crowdsensing systems. In: ICDCS (2017)
6. Duan, Z., Yan, M., Cai, Z., Wang, X.: Truthful incentive mechanisms for social cost minimization in mobile crowdsourcing systems. Sensors **16**(4), 1–14 (2016)
7. Han, B., Hui, P., Kumar, V.A., Marathe, M.V., Shao, J., Srinivasan, A.: Mobile data offloading through opportunistic communications and social participation. IEEE Trans. Mob. Comput. **11**(5), 821–834 (2012)
8. Kumaresan, R., Moran, T., Bentov, I.: How to use bitcoin to play decentralized poker. In: CCS, pp. 195–206 (2015)
9. Li, H., He, Y., Cheng, X., Zhu, H., Sun, L.: Security and privacy in localization for underwater sensor networks. IEEE Commun. Mag. **53**(11), 56–62 (2015)
10. Li, W., Cheng, X., Bie, R., Zhao, F.: An extensible and flexible truthful auction framework for heterogeneous spectrum markets. IEEE Trans. Cogn. Commun. Netw. **2**(4), 427–441 (2016)
11. Li, W., Wang, S., Cheng, X.: Truthful multi-attribute auction with discriminatory pricing in cognitive radio networks. In: ACM MobiCom Workshop CRAB (2013)
12. Lian, S., Liu, Z., Ren, Z.: Commutative encryption and watermarking in video compression. IEEE Trans. Circ. Syst. Video Technol. **17**(6), 774–778 (2007)
13. Liu, W., Li, H., Chen, Y., Zhu, H.: Lares: latency-reduced neighbour discovery for contagious diseases prevention. Int. J. Ad. Ubiq. Co. **16**(1), 3–13 (2014)
14. Luu, L., Teutsch, J., Kulkarni, R., Saxena, P.: Demystifying incentives in the consensus computer. In: CCS, pp. 706–719 (2015)
15. Mei, A., Stefa, J.: Give2get: forwarding in social mobile wireless networks of selfish individuals. IEEE Trans. Depend. Secure **9**(4), 569–582 (2012)
16. Mousa, H., Mokhtar, S.B., Hasan, O., Younes, O., Hadhoud, M., Brunie, L.: Trust management and reputation systems in mobile participatory sensing applications: a survey. Comput. Netw. **90**, 49–73 (2015)
17. Nakamoto, S.: Bitcoin: a peer-to-peer electronic cash system, pp. 1–28 (2008). https://bitcoin.org/bitcoin.pdf
18. Ning, T., Yang, Z., Xie, X., Wu, H.: Incentive-aware data dissemination in delay-tolerant mobile networks. In: SECON, pp. 539–547. IEEE (2011)
19. Tarable, A., Nordio, A., Leonardi, E., Marsan, M.: The importance of being earnest in crowdsourcing systems. In: INFOCOM, pp. 2821–2829 (2015)
20. Wang, Y., Cai, Z., Yin, G., Gao, Y.: An incentive mechanism with privacy protection in mobile crowdsourcing systems. Comput. Netw. **102**, 157–171 (2016)
21. Zhong, S., Chen, J., Yang, Y.R.: Sprite: a simple, cheat-proof, credit-based system for mobile ad-hoc networks. In: INFOCOM, pp. 1987–1997. IEEE (2003)
22. Zhu, H., Lin, X., Lu, R., Shen, X.S.: A secure incentive scheme for delay tolerant networks. In: ChinaCom, pp. 23–28. IEEE (2008)

An Attribute-Based Secure and Scalable Scheme for Data Communications in Smart Grids

Chunqiang Hu[1,4(✉)], Yan Huo[2], Liran Ma[3], Hang Liu[4], Shaojiang Deng[5], and Liping Feng[6]

[1] School of Software Engineering, Chongqing University, Chongqing, China
hcq0394@163.com
[2] School of Electronics and Information Engineering, Beijing Jiaotong University, Beijing, China
yhuo@bjtu.edu.cn
[3] Department of Computer Science, Texas Christian University, Fort Worth, USA
l.ma@tcu.edu
[4] Department of Electrical Engineering and Computer Science, The Catholic University of America, Washington, Dc, USA
liu1999@ieee.org
[5] School of Computer Science, Chongqing University, Chongqing, China
[6] Department of Computer Science and Technology, Xinzhou Teachers University, Xinzhou, China

Abstract. The concept of Smart Grid gains tremendous attention amongst researchers and utility providers in recent years. One of the challenges is to establish a secure communication architecture among smart meters, utility companies, and third-party service providers, whilst address the prevalent security and privacy concerns. In this paper, we propose a communication architecture for smart grids, and design a scheme to secure the data communications among smart meters, utility companies, and third-party service providers by employing Decentralized Ciphertext-Policy Attribute Based Encryption (CP_ABE) to store the data in ciphertext format, hence ensuring data security. The architecture we proposed is high scalable since the decentralized feature. Also, our architecture achieves an role-based access control by employing an access control LSSS matrix that describes the attributes required to access the data. We analyze the proposed scheme, and argue that it provides message authenticity and collusion resistance, and is efficient and feasible.

Keywords: Smart meters · Smart grids · Secure communication mechanisms · LSSS · Bilinear maps · Attribute-based cryptosystem

1 Introduction

In smart grids, advanced technologies such as sensing, control, digital communications, and networking, are merged into the power transmission and distribution

© Springer International Publishing AG 2017
L. Ma et al. (Eds.): WASA 2017, LNCS 10251, pp. 469–482, 2017.
DOI: 10.1007/978-3-319-60033-8_41

systems to effectively and intelligently control and monitor the power grid. The smart grid will bring new features into the power grid: renewable-based generation, demand-response, wide area protection, smart metering, etc. [1]. During the periods of peak energy consumption, utility companies can send alerts to notify consumers the current price and may further ask consumers to reduce their power consumption by temporarily turning off some devices [2]. On the other hand, for safe operations, certain critical control actions should be sent from the control center to smart meters and expect immediate executions. Furthermore, wide area protection schemes are being deployed to prevent cascaded failures and provide better interconnections. Despite the attractive features provided by Smart Grid technologies, it still presents challenges, especially in cyber security and privacy [3].

In order to authenticate the utility companies (control centers or other parties involved in the system) whenever messages or control commands are sent to smart meters, multicast authentication schemes such as Biba, and OTS [1,4] were proposed. Data aggregation schemes based on homomorphic encryption, secret sharing [5,6], and other technologies [7–10], were proposed to aggregate consumers' data and to protect customers' privacy; However, the above schemes are still possible to extract users' usage patterns from the data uploaded by smart meters every 15 min. Similarly, third-party service providers may need to collect electricity usage records of smart devices. The customer's data have tremendous value. It is the customers's decision whether to disclose electricity usage of a smart devices or not, and customers should have the right to decide who has the accessibility to their data.

Recently, a data repository is proposed [6,11] to store all customers' data and distribute them to the third-party service providers under the supervision of a fine-grained access control model. It is desirable to have a data repository that store the massive data generated by the smart meters due to the fact that the computation and storage power of the smart meters are more limited. In such a case, it is the data repository's responsibility to enforce the access control policies and distribute customers' data under their willing or based on related regulations and laws, which certainly put tremendous burden to the data repository server since the compromise of the data repository server reveals all the data. To mitigate the burden of data repository, we can store encrypted data and even the data repository itself has no access to the data, we propose a communication architecture for smart grids based on Decentralized Ciphertext-Policy Attribute-based Encryption [12] to store data in ciphertext format, achieve a role-based access control and easily support the multicast of the customers' data.

In our proposed scheme, every entity has a globally verifiable identifier (GID) and a set of attributes that describe its identity. Smart meters can encrypt a data item and control the access of the data by specifying an access structure. Encrypted data are stored on data repository along with the corresponding access structure that indicates who has the access to the data. All the data stored are encrypted, which indicates that the data remains private even if the data repository server is compromised. Furthermore, since the access of a data item is described by an access structure specified by the sender, a Role Based Access Control (RBAC) is achieved, and we don't need further software based access control and we significantly reduce the trust we put on the data repository.

The contribution of this paper can be summarized as:

– We propose a secure and scalable communication model involving multiple authorities (key generation centers), smart meters, data consumers, and data repository for Smart Grid systems. Our scheme emphasize customers' control on their privacy, which is their energy consumption data. And authorities in our architecture are fully decentralized, which is more secure and scalable.
– We employ Decentralized CP_ABE to provide role based access control to the data generated by smart meters, and analyze the efficiency and feasibility of our proposed scheme. In particular, we discuss the security of the proposed scheme from different views like resistant against collusion attacks, message authenticity and so on.
– We evaluate the performance of the proposed scheme in terms of communication cost, computation cost, and storage overhead.

The remainder of this paper is structured as follows. In Sect. 2, we discuss the related work. In Sect. 3, we introduce the system model and outline the required preliminaries. Section 4 propose a secure communication scheme to ensure access control for the sensitive data. Section 5 gives the correctness and security analysis, followed by the conclusions in Sect. 6.

2   Related Work

Shamir [13] suggested the identity-based signature scheme. But it was Boneh and Franklin who proposed the first usable identity based encryption (IBE) mechanism [14], which is provably secure in the random oracle model. Later, several IBE schemes [15,16] are proposed to work without random oracles, but under a weaker Selective-ID model [15].

One of the primary original motivations for Attribute-Based Encryption (ABE) is to design an error-tolerant (or Fuzzy) identity-based encryption scheme [17] that could use biometric identities. A more general idea called key-policy attribute-based encryption (KP_ABE) was proposed by Goyal *et al.* [18] to embed a general secret sharing scheme for a monotonic access tree instead of the Shamir secret sharing scheme used in [17]. In KP_ABE, data is associated with a set of descriptive attributes and a users' key has a monotonic tree-access structure. As long as the data's attributes pass through the users' tree-access structure, the user can decrypt the ciphertext.

In smart grids, potential security problems in networking lie in the subjects of sensor networks [19], wireless networks [20], and the Internet. Liu *et al.* [21] investigated cyber security and privacy in smart grids, pointing out further study areas to enhance the security level of the grids. For wired networks, multiple networking security technologies can be utilized to secure the smart grids. Zhongwei *et al.* [22] claimed that Ethernet Passive Optical Networks (EPON) would be a promising solution for smart grid broadband access networks, and proposed a secure communication protocol for the EPON by using identity-based cryptography, which generates a public key from an arbitrary data string, and binds the corresponding private key with the information. This work lacks a performance analysis in terms of package overhead and scalability, and does not discuss how to setup a key distribution center. In this paper, we emphasize customers' control on their own data by specifying an access structure for each data item and encrypt the data with the Decentralized CP_ABE [12] scheme, which is more scalable and realistic than CP_ABE schemes [23,24]. Our scheme can be expanded to facilitate anonymity, data aggregation, and message authentication based on identity-based signature, and so on.

3   System Model and Preliminaries

In this section, we present our system model and the required preliminary knowledge.

3.1   System Model

We consider a Smart Grid communication architecture depicted in Fig. 1. There are four major entities in this system: Attribute Authorities, Smart meters, Data Repository, and Data Consumer. Data Consumer mainly refers to Utility Companies (UC) and Third-Party Service Providers (TPSP). In the following subsections, we summarize the major functions of each entity.

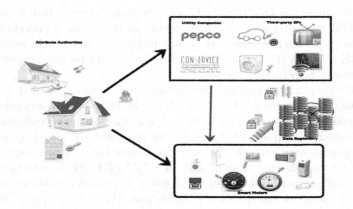

Fig. 1. A communication architecture in smart grid systems.

Attribute Authorities (AAs). The AAs are used to generate and distribute keys for smart meters and data consumers. Keys play an essential role in our architecture since only with a proper set of keys, the data receiver can decrypt the data encrypted under an access structure, which describes the combination of attributes required to access the data. Each Attribute Authority processes its own set of attributes. For example, an AA in Los Angles, CA may issue attribute "Los Angles, CA" to a third-party air conditioner service provider. And there is an AA in Washington DC that issue this third-party air conditioner service provider attribute "Air Conditioner Service Provider". A third-party service provider with keys to attributes { "Air Conditioner Service Provider", "Los Angles"} will be able to decrypt the date with the access structure ("Air Conditioner Service Provider" AND ("Los Angles, CA" OR "Washington, DC")). One have to notice that in reality, there are multiple attribute authorities around the world and they may have no idea of each other's existence. To request a key for attribute "Los Angles, CA", the third-party service provider should send his globally verifiable identifier (GID) to the AA in Los Angles, CA. And then, after the verification of the requester's identity, the AA will generate the corresponding key, which will associated with the requester's (in most of the case, the requester in our paper refers to the Data Consumer, which will be introduced later) GID to prevent collusion attack. The verification of requester's identity can be done in other proper channel, which is beyond the discussion of this paper. For example, the requester can go to AA's office with the proofs that they are qualified for the attributes requested. Due to the fact that the AAs are distributed, our architecture is highly scalable.

Smart Meters. Smart meters are the key elements in the power system. In our architecture, smart meters mainly encrypt customer's home energy consumption data and upload it to the data repository. Customers can configure the smart meter and specify data consumer's access to the data. According to customer's settings, the smart meter will construct an access structure, for example: ("Air Conditioner Service Provider" AND ("Los Angles, CA" OR "Washington, DC")), encrypt the data with the access structure, which actually is a LSSS matrix [25]), and then upload the encrypted data to the data repository.

Data Consumers. Data Consumers refer to Utility Companies (UC) and Third-Party Service Providers (TPSP). A UC can send consumption related instructions and emergency/error notifications to smart meters and collect sub-hourly power usage reports. It can also interact with smart meters in regulating power consumption levels. For example, to reduce power loads during peak hours, a UC can instruct smart meters to limit their usage. It can then be up to the smart meters to regulate their household devices. This approach hides individual devices from the UC and protects user privacy. A TPSP could be a device manufacture that may need to upgrade the software of a device.

Data consumers have its own GID and acquire the keys to attributes from different AAs. GID will be "bound" to the keys issued by AAs to prevent collusion attack, which will be explained in Subsect. 5.2.

Data Repositories. The Data Repository is used to store the encrypted data uploaded by smart meters. The data repository is only responsible for correctly store the data and response to data consumer's request. It can have several data storage centers. Processing can be done by one or more data processors, which can provide efficient search and help to organize the data in databases. Any technologies that facilitates a efficient storage can be adopted as long as data are stored correctly.

3.2 Preliminaries

We now introduce preliminaries for the cryptographic primitives used in this paper.

Bilinear Maps. Let $\mathbb{G}_1$ and $\mathbb{G}_2$ be two bilinear groups of prime order p, and g be a generator of $\mathbb{G}_1$. Our proposed scheme makes use of a bilinear map: $e : \mathbb{G}_1 \times \mathbb{G}_1 \to \mathbb{G}_2$ with the following properties:

1. *Bilinear:* A mapping $e : \mathbb{G}_1 \times \mathbb{G}_1 \to \mathbb{G}_2$ is bilinear if and only if for all $P, Q \in \mathbb{G}_1$ and all $a, b \in \mathbb{Z}_p$, there is $e(P^a, Q^b) = e(P, Q)^{ab}$. Here $\mathbb{Z}_p = \{0, 1, \ldots, p-1\}$ is a Galois field of order p.
2. *Non-degeneracy:* The generator g satisfies $e(g, g) \neq 1$.
3. *Computability:* There is an efficient algorithm to compute $e(P, Q)$ for any $P, Q \in \mathbb{G}_1$.

Access Structure. Let $\{P_1, \ldots, P_n\}$ be a set of parties. A collection $\mathbb{A} \subseteq 2^{\{P_1, \ldots, P_n\}}$ is monotone if $\forall B, C$: if $B \in \mathbb{A}$ and $B \subseteq C$, then $C \in \mathbb{A}$. An access structure [25] (respectively, monotone access structure) is a collection (respectively, monotone collection) $\mathbb{A}$ of non-empty subsets of $\{P_1, \ldots, P_n\}$, i.e., $\mathbb{A} \subseteq 2^{\{P_1, \ldots, P_n\}} \backslash \{\}$. The sets in $\mathbb{A}$ are called the authorized sets, and the sets not in $\mathbb{A}$ are called the unauthorized sets.

In our architecture, attributes will play the role of parties and we will only consider monotone access structures. However, more general access structures can be realized, though inefficiently, by letting the negation of an attribute be a separate attribute (this doubles the total number of attributes).

Linear Secret-Sharing Schemes: Instead of use Shamir Secret-Sharing and polynomial interpolation reconstruction, we use linear secret-sharing schemes (LSSS) [25].

Linear Secret-Sharing Schemes: A secret sharing scheme Π over a set of parties $\mathcal{P}$ is called linear (over $\mathbb{Z}_p$) if

1. *The shares for each party form a vector over $\mathbb{Z}_p$.*
2. *There exists a matrix A called the share-generating matrix for Π. The matrix A has ℓ rows and n columns. For all $x = 1, \ldots, \ell$, the xth row of A is labeled by a party $\rho(x)$ (ρ is a function from $\{1, \ldots, \ell\}$ to $\mathcal{P}$). When we consider the column vector $v = (s, r_2, \ldots, r_n)$, where $s \in \mathbb{Z}_p$ is the secret to be shared and $r_2, \ldots, r_n \in \mathbb{Z}_p$ are randomly chosen, then Av is the vector of ℓ shares of the secret s according to Π. The share $(Av)_x$ belongs to party $\rho(x)$.*

Linear Reconstruction Property: suppose that Π is an LSSS for access structure A. Let S denote an authorized set, and define $I \subseteq \{1, ..., \ell\}$ as $I = \{x | \rho(x) \in S\}$. Then the vector $(1, 0, ..., 0)$ is in the span of rows of A indexed by I, and there exist constant $s\{\omega_x \in \mathbb{Z}_p\} x \in I$ such that, for any valid shares $\{\lambda\} x$ of a secret s according to Π, we have: $\sum_{x \in I} \omega_x \lambda_x = s$. These constants $\{\omega_x\}$ can be found in polynomial time with respect to the size of the share-generating matrix A [25].

4 Secure Communication Scheme

We propose a secure and flexible communication scheme, which is based on decentralized CP_ABE [12], to secure the messages when Data Consumer communicates with Smart Meters and Data Repository to get the power usage and other information. For example, a smart meter may specify the following access structure, which is a boolean formula, for a data item: ("Air Conditioner Service Provider" AND ("Los Angles, CA" OR "Washington, DC")), which indicates that only the air conditioner service providers in Los Angles, CA or Washington, DC have the access to this data. Thus an air conditioner maintenance company located in Washington DC with a set of attributes {Washington DC, Air Conditioner Service Provider} has an access to the data mentioned above. Note that all the data stored in data repository are encrypted. Also note that the access right of a data item is described by an LSSS Matrix, converted from boolean formulas that specified by the customer's smart meter, indicating that Role Based Access Control (RBAC) is achieved.

Our scheme consists of five Algorithms. Algorithms 1 and 2 are the system initialization and authority setup separately. System initialization is a global setup that only perform once. Authority setup can be run every time a new authority joins the system. Algorithm 3 is executed by attribute authorities to generate private keys for the data consumers based on the attributes acquired. Note that Algorithm 3 is performed by an authority. If a data consumer wants to obtain keys of attributes from different authorities, each and every authority will run Algorithm 3 to generate keys for the data consumer. The encryption procedure is detailed in Algorithm 4 to encrypt a message/data M whose access control is specified by an LSSS matrix A (We will firstly convert the boolean formula T to LSSS matrix A). This algorithm is performed mainly by smart meters to encrypt their data before uploading to the data repository. Algorithm 5 implements decryption and authentication, which should be executed by data consumers to get the plaintext data based on their attributes since they receive only encrypted data from data repository.

The following procedure illustrates how a data consumer obtains the data intended to him: A smart meter encrypts the data of its household devices using Algorithm 4, and then sends the encrypted data to a data repository at a regular interval. When the data consumer possessing keys for attribute set S wants to read the plaintext data, the following steps need to be performed:

1. The attribute authority executes Algorithm 3 to compute private keys for corresponding attributes $K_{i,GID} = g_i^{\alpha_i} H(GID)^{y_i}$ for the data consumer;

Algorithm 1. System Initialization

1: Select a bilinear group G of order $N = p_1 p_2 p_3$.
2: Select a generator g_1 of G_{p_1}.
3: A Hash function $H : \{0,1\}^* \to G$ that maps global identities GID to elements of G. The function H is modeled as a random oracle.
4: Publish GP $= \{N, g_1\}$ and H.

Algorithm 2. Authority Setup (GP)

Inputs: GP

1: **for** Each attribute i belongs to the authority **do**
2:     chooses two random exponents $\alpha_i, y_i \in \mathbb{Z}_N$.
3:     calculates $\{e(g_1, g_1)^{\alpha_i}, g_1^{y_i}\}$
4: **end for**
5: Publishes $PK_j = \{e(g_1, g_1)^{\alpha_i}, g_1^{y_i} \forall i\}$ as its public key.
6: Keeps $SK = \{\alpha_i, y_i \forall i\}$ as its secret key.

Algorithm 3. Key Generation *(GID, {i}, SK, GP)*

Inputs: GID, {i}(the attributes requested by data consumer), SK, GP.

1: **for** Each attribute i request by the data consumer **do**
2:     Calculate the key for attribute i.

$$K_{i,GID} = g_i^{\alpha_i} H(GID)^{y_i} \tag{1}$$

3: **end for**

---

2. The data repository sends the encrypted data CT to the data consumer as requested;
3. Upon receiving CT, the data consumer executes Algorithm 5 to decrypt CT and verify whether the message (plaintext) has been modified or not.

For the smart meter to encrypt the data, the smart meter will construct an access tree based on customer's specification and configuration. An access tree will be transformed into a boolean formula [26]. The boolean formula T will then be taken as an input of the function *BooleanFormula2LSSS* $(root(T), v, c, A, \rho())$. And the output will be the LSSS matrix with function $\rho()$ mapping its rows to attributes. Here is an example that demonstrates how the transformation works:

As it showed in Fig. 2, consider the formula *A AND (D OR (B AND C))*. The root *AND* node of this tree is labeled (1). Its left child, the leaf node corresponding to A, is labeled $(1,1)$. Its right child, the *OR* node, is labeled $(0,-1)$. The left child of the *OR* node corresponds to D and is labeled $(0,-1)$. Its right child is an *AND* node and is labeled $(0,-1)$. The left child of the *AND* node,

---

Algorithm 4. Encryption *(M, T, GP, {PK})*

Inputs: plaintext message M; the boolean formula T, global parameter GP, and the public keys for the attributes involved $\{PK\}$.

1: T is the boolean formula as an access tree, where interior nodes are AND and OR gates and the leaf nodes correspond to attributes.
2: Let v = (1), which represents the root of T.
3: Let c = 1, which is a counter that used during the converting process.
4: A is the LSSS matrix, initialized to null; $\rho()$ is the function that mapping its rows to attributes.
5: BooleanFormula2LSSS(root(T),v, c, A, $\rho()$);
6: Pads shorter ones in A with 0's at the end form a $n \times \ell$ matrix.
7: Chooses a random $s \in \mathbb{Z}_N$.
8: Chooses a random vector $v_r \in \mathbb{Z}_N^\ell$ with s as the first entry.
9: Let $\lambda_x = A_x \cdot v_r$, where A_x is row x of A
10: Chooses a random vector $\omega \in \mathbb{Z}_N^\ell$ with 0 as the first entry.
11: Let $\omega_x = A_x \cdot \omega$, where A_x is row x of A
12: Computes the first part of ciphertext $C_0 = Me(g_1,g_1)^s$;
13: **for** each row A_x in A **do**
14:     Chooses a random $r_x \in \mathbb{Z}_N$
15:     Computes the cihpertext as:

$$C_{1,x} = e(g_1,g_1)^{\lambda_x} e(g_1,g_1)^{\alpha_{\rho(x)} r_x}, \tag{2}$$
$$C_{2,x} = g_1^{r_x}, \quad C_{3,x} = g_1^{y_{\rho(x)} r_x} g_1^{\omega_x}$$

16: **end for**
17: The ciphertext $CT = (C_0, C_{1,i}, C_{2,i}, C_{3,i} \forall i$ as rows of $A)$
18: Computes $MA = e(H(M|e(g_1,g_1)^s), g_1)$ as message authentication
19: The message CK consists of $\{A, \rho(), CT, MA\}$
20:
21: **function** (BooleanFormula2LSSS $(node, v, c, A, \rho())$)
22:     **if** *node* is an AND gate **then**
23:         pads v with 0's (if necessary) to make it length of c;
24:         labels the left child with the vector $v|1$; // | means concatenation;
25:         labels the right child with the vector $(0, ..., 0)| - 1$, where $(0,...,0)$ denotes the zero vector of length c;
26:         $c = c + 1$;
27:     **else if** *node* is an OR gate **then**
28:         labels the left child and the right child with the vector v;
29:     **end if**
30:     **for** *node*'s children node as n_c **do**
31:         **if** n_c is an attribute **then**
32:             A.push(v); // add v to the end of matrix A
33:             adds the mapping $\rho(v) = n_c$;
34:         **else if**
35:             **then** BooleanFormula2LSSS($n_c, v, c, A, \rho()$)
36:         **end if**
37:     **end for**
38: **end function**

Algorithm 5. Decryption $(CK, \{K_{i,GID}\}, \text{GP}, (A, \rho))$

Inputs: A ciphertext CT, the secret keys $\{K_{i,GID}\}$, GP, (A, ρ), MA.

1: Calculates $H(GID)$;
2: **if** the decryptor has the secret keys $\{K_{\rho(x),GID}\}$ for a subset of rows A_x of A such that $(1,0,...,0)$ is in the span of these rows **then**
3:     **for** each such x **do**

$$\frac{C_{1,x} \cdot e(H(GID), C_{3,x})}{e(K_{\rho(x)}, GID), C_{2,x}} = e(g_1, g_1)^{\lambda_x} e(H(GID), g_1)^{\omega_x} \tag{3}$$

4:     **end for**
5: **else Return** $\perp$;
6: **end if**
7: Chooses a constants $c_x \in \mathbb{Z}_N$ such that

$$\sum_x c_x A_x = (1, 0, ..., 0) \tag{4}$$

8: Compute:

$$\prod_x (e(g_1, g_1)^{\lambda_x} e(H(GID), g_1)^{\omega_x})^{c_x} = e(g_1, g_1)^s \tag{5}$$

//Recall that $\lambda_x = A_x \cdot v_r$ and $\omega_x = A_x \cdot \omega$, where $v_r \cdot (1, 0, ..., 0) = s$ and $\omega \cdot (1, 0, ..., 0) = 0$
9:

$$M' = \frac{C_0}{e(g_1, g_1)^s} \tag{6}$$

10: **if** $e(H(M'|e(g_1, g_1)^s), g_1) = MA$ **then**
11:     M' = M, the message is valid;
12: **end if**

---

which corresponds to B, is labeled $(0, -1, 1)$, and the right child, corresponding to C, is labeled $(0, 0, -1)$.

Note that the decryption process employs the keys for attributes set S to match the LSSS matrix A carried by CT. The LSSS matrices in your scheme was in $\mathbb{Z}_N$, where $N = p_1 p_2 p_3$ is a product of three distinct primes. The S is matched if the rows of the access matrix A labeled by elements in S have the vector $(1, 0, ..., 0)$ in their span modulo N. And for the unmatched set S, the corresponding rows of A do not include the vector $(1, 0, ..., 0)$ in their span modulo the individual prime factors of N. In Fig. 2, {A, D} and {A, B, C} are matched sets and for example, {B, C, D} is a unmatched set.

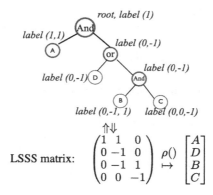

Fig. 2. An example of boolean access structure and its LSSS matrix

5 Correctness and Security Analysis

In this section, we prove the correctness and security of the scheme, analyze its security from the aspects of collusion resistance, authenticity and defend against other attacks. Due to the space limited, the performance evaluation is omitted here, we will evaluate our scheme performance in terms of storage overhead and time complexity in the extended version.

5.1 The Correctness of the Proposed Scheme

In this subsection, we show that the scheme is indeed feasible, correct and secure.

If there are indeed n attributes involved in the encryption, the LSSS matrix will have n rows. The Ciphertext length grow linearly with the amount of attributes involved, so does the key size, encryption and decryption time. For a cryptography scheme that has linear computational cost, it is feasible.

In Algorithm 5, if the decryptor found a matched subset that has $(1, 0, ..., 0)$ in the span, for each row in this subset, Eq. (3) will be performed. Later c_x in Eq. (4) will be found in time polynomial in the size of the LSSS matrix [25]. With Eqs. (5) and (6), we have

$$
\begin{aligned}
M' &= \frac{C_0}{\prod_x (e(g_1, g_1)^{\lambda_x} e(H(GID), g_1)^{\omega_x})^{c_x}} = \frac{C_0}{e(g_1, g_1)^{\sum_x \lambda_x c_x} e(H(GID), g_1)^{\sum_x \omega_x c_x}} \\
&= \frac{C_0}{e(g_1, g_1)^{\sum_x (A_x v_r) c_x} e(H(GID), g_1)^{\sum_x (A_x \omega) c_x}} \\
&= \frac{C_0}{e(g_1, g_1)^{v_r \sum_x (A_x c_x)} e(H(GID), g_1)^{\omega \sum_x (A_x c_x)}} \\
&= \frac{C_0}{e(g_1, g_1)^{v_r \cdot (1,0,...,0)} e(H(GID), g_1)^{\omega \cdot (1,0,...,0)}} = \frac{C_0}{e(g_1, g_1)^s}
\end{aligned}
$$

If $e(H(M'|e(g_1, g_1)^s), g_1) = MA$, then the massage decrypt correctly.

5.2   Security Strength

In this subsection, we analyze the security strength of the proposed scheme by examining how it can counter possible major attack.

Collusion Attack Resistance. The key challenge in building a attribute based encryption scheme is to prevent users (data consumers) from colluding each other. For example, if the data has an access structure ("Air Conditioner Service Provider" AND ("Los Angles, CA" OR "Washington, DC"), we don't want it to be accessible to a pair of unauthorized users, where one has {"Los Angles, CA"} and the other has {"Air Conditioner Service Provider"}. Neither user is actually an authorized user to this data.

The global identity, GID in our proposed scheme is the key component to defend against collusion attack. The decryption algorithm Algorithm 5 will recover a target group element of the form $e(g_1, g_1)^{\lambda_x} \cdot e(g_1, H(GID))^{\omega_x}$ (which is the Eq. (3). This group element first contains a secret share λ_x of a secret s in the exponent, and these shares can be combined to recover the message. At the same time, these will each be blinded by a share ω_x which is a share of 0 in the exponent with base $e(g_1, H(GID))$. The decryption algorithm should reconstruct the secret s and unblind it (which means to cancel the $H(GID)$) in parallel. If two users with different global identifiers GID, GID' attempt to collude, the cancellation (which is the Eq. (5) will not work since the ω_x shares will have different bases.

6   Conclusion and Future Work.

In this paper, we present an efficient attribute-based encryption scheme, which is a one-to-many encryption method. In other words, the message is meant to be read by a group of users that satisfy certain access control rules in the Smart Grid.

Our future research lies in the following directions: design a decentralized CP_ABE scheme with constant size of ciphertext length to reduce the storage and communication cost. Examine more attacks on the architecture we proposed and defend those attacks. Cooperate our current scheme with other broadcast authentication schemes and signature schemes to make a more comprehensive and applicable architecture.

Acknowledgement. We are very grateful to all reviewers who have helped improve the quality of this paper. This research was partially supported by the National Science Foundation of the US under grants CNS-1624485, and the National Natural Science Foundation of China under grants 61471028 and 61672119, and the Fundamental Research Funds for the Central Universities (Grant No. 2016JBZ003).

References

1. Li, Q., Cao, G.: Multicast authentication in the smart grid with one-time signature. IEEE Trans. Smart Grid **2**(4), 686–696 (2011)

2. Ipakchi, A., Albuyeh, F.: Grid of the future. IEEE Power Energy Magazine **7**(2), 52–62 (2009)
3. Liu, Y., Ning, P., Reiter, M.K.: False data injection attacks against state estimation in electric power grids. ACM Trans. Inf. Syst. Secur. (TISSEC) **14**(1), 13:1–13:33 (2011)
4. Hu, C., Cheng, X., Tian, Z., Yu, J., Akkaya, K., Sun, L.: An attribute-based sign-cryption scheme to secure attribute-defined multicast communications. In: Thurais-ingham, B., Wang, X.F., Yegneswaran, V. (eds.) SecureComm 2015. LNICSSITE, vol. 164, pp. 418–437. Springer, Cham (2015). doi:10.1007/978-3-319-28865-9_23
5. Chunqiang, H., Liao, X., Cheng, X.: Verifiable multi-secret sharing based on LFSR sequences. Theoret. Comput. Sci. **445**, 52–62 (2012)
6. Hu, C., Li, W., Cheng, X., Yu, J., Wang, S., Bie, R.: A secure and verifiable access control scheme for big data storage in clouds. IEEE Trans. Big Data (2017). doi:10.1109/TBDATA.2016.2621106
7. Rongxing, L., Xiaohui Liang, X., Li, X.L., Shen, X.: EPPA: an efficient and privacy-preserving aggregation scheme for secure smart grid communications. IEEE Trans. Parallel Distrib. Syst. **23**(9), 1621–1631 (2012)
8. Li, D., Aung, Z., Williams, J.R., Sanchez, A.: Efficient authentication scheme for data aggregation in smart grid with fault tolerance and fault diagnosis. In: 2012 IEEE PES Innovative Smart Grid Technologies (ISGT), pp. 1–8. IEEE (2012)
9. Cai, A., He, Z., Guan, X., Li, Y.: Collective data-sanitization for preventing sen-sitive information inference attacks in social networks. IEEE Trans. Dependable Secure Comput. (2016). doi:10.1109/TDSC.2016.2613521
10. Zhang, L., Cai, Z., Wang, X.: Fakemask: a novel privacy preserving approach for smartphones. IEEE Trans. Netw. Serv. Manag. **13**(2), 335–348 (2016)
11. Ruj, S., Nayak, A., Stojmenovic, I.: A security architecture for data aggregation and access control in smart grids. arxiv preprint arXiv:1111.2619 (2011)
12. Lewko, A., Waters, B.: Decentralizing attribute-based encryption. In: Paterson, K.G. (ed.) EUROCRYPT 2011. LNCS, vol. 6632, pp. 568–588. Springer, Heidelberg (2011). doi:10.1007/978-3-642-20465-4_31
13. Shamir, A.: Identity-based cryptosystems and signature schemes. In: Blakley, G.R., Chaum, D. (eds.) CRYPTO 1984. LNCS, vol. 196, pp. 47–53. Springer, Heidelberg (1985). doi:10.1007/3-540-39568-7_5
14. Boneh, D., Franklin, M.: Identity-based encryption from the weil pairing. In: Kilian, J. (ed.) CRYPTO 2001. LNCS, vol. 2139, pp. 213–229. Springer, Heidelberg (2001). doi:10.1007/3-540-44647-8_13
15. Canetti, R., Halevi, S., Katz, J.: A forward-secure public-key encryption scheme. In: Biham, E. (ed.) EUROCRYPT 2003. LNCS, vol. 2656, pp. 255–271. Springer, Heidelberg (2003). doi:10.1007/3-540-39200-9_16
16. Boneh, D., Boyen, X.: Efficient selective-ID secure identity-based encryption without random oracles. In: Cachin, C., Camenisch, J.L. (eds.) EUROCRYPT 2004. LNCS, vol. 3027, pp. 223–238. Springer, Heidelberg (2004). doi:10.1007/978-3-540-24676-3_14
17. Sahai, A., Waters, B.: Fuzzy identity-based encryption. In: Cramer, R. (ed.) EURO-CRYPT 2005. LNCS, vol. 3494, pp. 457–473. Springer, Heidelberg (2005). doi:10.1007/11426639_27
18. Goyal, V., Pandey, O., Sahai, A., Waters, B.: Attribute-based encryption for fine-grained access control of encrypted data. In: Proceedings of the 13th ACM Con-ference on Computer and Communications Security, pp. 89–98. ACM (2006)
19. Zheng, X., Cai, Z., Li, J., Gao, H.: Location-privacy-aware review publication mech-anism for local business service systems. In: INFOCOM. IEEE (2017)

20. Hu, C., Huo, Y.: Efficient privacy-preserving dot-product computation for mobile big data. IET Commun. **11**(5), 704–712 (2017)
21. Liu, J., Xiao, Y., Li, S., Liang, W., Chen, P.C.L.: Cyber security and privacy issues in smart grids. IEEE Commun. Surv. Tutor. **14**(4), 981–997 (2012)
22. Zhongwei, S., Sitian, H., Yaning, M., Fengjie, S.: Security mechanism for smart distribution grid using ethernet passive optical network. In: 2010 2nd International Conference on Advanced Computer Control (ICACC), vol. 3, pp. 246–250. IEEE (2010)
23. Chunqiang, H., Zhang, N., Li, H., Cheng, X., Liao, X.: Body area network security: a fuzzy attribute-based signcryption scheme. IEEE J. Sel. Areas Commun. **31**(9), 37–46 (2013)
24. Chunqiang, H., Li, H., Huo, Y., Xiang, T., Liao, X.: Secure and efficient data communication protocol for wireless body area networks. IEEE Trans. Multi-Scale Comput. Syst. **2**(2), 94–107 (2016)
25. Beimel, A.: Secure schemes for secret sharing and key distribution. Ph.D. thesis, Israel Institute of Technology, Technion, Haifa, Israel (1996)
26. Bethencourt, J., Sahai, A., Waters, B.: Ciphertext-policy attribute-based encryption. In: 2007 IEEE Symposium on Security and Privacy, SP 2007, pp. 321–334. IEEE (2007)

Space Power Synthesis-Based Cooperative Jamming for Unknown Channel State Information

Xin Fan[1](✉), Liang Huang[1], Yan Huo[1], Chunqiang Hu[2], Yuqi Tian[1], and Jin Qian[3]

[1] School of Electronics and Information Engineering,
Beijing Jiaotong University, Beijing, China
fanxin@bjtu.edu.cn

[2] Key Laboratory of Dependable Service Computing in Cyber Physical Society,
Chongqing University, Chongqing, China

[3] Taizhou University, Taizhou, China

Abstract. Recently, the physical layer security technologies based on artificial noise and beamforming has been getting in focus. Although those schemes provide an idea to design security policies for wireless networks, most existing works mainly concentrate on the secrecy capacity analysis for known Channel State Information (CSI) of eavesdroppers, as well as the corresponding power allocation and algorithm optimization. Since the eavesdroppers may hide their own personal state information and steal confidential message in the wireless networks, we investigate the space power synthesis for multiple jamming signal in this work, so as to achieve the cooperative jamming in the case of unknown CSI. According to the superposition principle of various electromagnetic waves in space, the multiple jammers-based anti-eavesdropping model is formulated. Taking into account the free space fading, we study the total impact caused by the jammers with different locations in a limited region, and present the corresponding schemes to minimize the synthetic jamming power of all jammers at the legitimate user. Numerical simulation results demonstrate that our solutions to the cooperative jamming problem can make the strength of the synthesized interference power at the legitimate user be the lowest value in a confined region. Based on this, we can improve the system secrecy capacity when the CSI of eavesdropper is unknown.

Keywords: Power synthesis · Cooperative jamming · Channel state information · Security capacity · Physical layer security

1 Introduction

In wireless networks, the spectrum utilization, transmission rate and so on are very important [1–3], but the security of communication can not be ignored. Security has attracted widespread concerns due to the presence of the

© Springer International Publishing AG 2017
L. Ma et al. (Eds.): WASA 2017, LNCS 10251, pp. 483–495, 2017.
DOI: 10.1007/978-3-319-60033-8_42

eavesdropper. Traditionally, the existing works solved this issue by using crypto-graphic approaches when they assumed that the physical (PHY) layer provides a reliable communication [4]. However, the cryptographic approaches may fail to protect the messages on the one hand due to the increasingly powerful comput-ing capacity of the eavesdroppers. On the other, the hypothesis of the reliable wireless link is hard to achieve because of the openness and broadcasting. Thus, it is not sufficient to ensure information security only exploiting the encryption communication. To deal with this, the PHY layer security [5], as a complement technology to the existing security schemes, is proposed without compromising the existing cryptographic-technique-based security protection.

PHY layer security approaches aim to protect the transmission security via preventing the eavesdroppers from correctly decoding the intercepted signals [4,6]. In addition to increasing throughput [7,8], secrecy capacity has also been taken seriously, which is defined as the maximum rate difference between the legitimate transmitter-receiver channel and the transmitter-eavesdropper chan-nel [9]. A great amount of effort has been put to improve the secrecy capacity in existing research, among which the main solution is to generate noise signals that can be eliminated at the legitimate receiver but cannot be eliminated at the eavesdroppers so as to degrade the transmitter-eavesdropper channel [10]. However, most of the existing works for the friendly jamming strategies are pre-sented based on the known channel state information (CSI) of eavesdroppers. In fact, legitimate nodes in wireless networks have difficulties in obtaining any information of eavesdroppers because of the passive receiving mode. Therefore, the assumption in above security schemes is impractical.

Considering the unknown CSI of eavesdroppers, we investigate the space power synthesis in this paper, so as to achieve hidden communication via the PHY layer. In general, a variety of friendly jamming signals with different trans-mission parameters are superimposed in wireless network space, which results in the enhancement or weakening of the jamming signals. Therefore, in order to null the interference for the legitimate receivers as well as ensure adequate interference for eavesdroppers during the cooperative jamming, it is important to find the enhancing or the weakening points in the space. The contribution of our work can be summarized as below.

- Considering the different interference threshold for the legitimate users and the eavesdroppers, a novel cooperative jamming strategy based on the space power synthesis is proposed in the case of unknown CSI of eavesdroppers.
- We formulate the signal power synthetic problem based on the analysis of electromagnetic waves emitted by different antennas in wireless space.
- For different physical locations of the jammers, a series of solutions for the problem is investigated from the aspects of the number of the jammers, the initial phase current, and the transmission parameters of each jammer.

The remainder of this paper is organized as follows. The related work is summarized in Sect. 2, followed by the system model and the corresponding problem formulation in Sect. 3. For the various physical location and different transmitted parameters of the jammers, Sects. 4 and 5 present the existence and uniqueness of solution for the cooperative jamming system model, respectively. Next, we demonstrate the synthetic power graphs from the aspect of various transmission parameters and locations of the jammers through several numerical simulations in Sect. 6. Finally, our conclusion is presented in Sect. 7.

2   Related Work

According to the earliest work on the concept of secrecy capacity, Wyner presented a trade-off curve between transmission rate and equivocation of data in [9] for the novel wiretap channel model. He claimed that the transmission in this situation is accomplished in perfect secrecy if the equivocation is equal to the entropy of the data source. Back in 2005, Negi and Goel first proposed a method in [11] which was to use artificial noise to degrade the eavesdropper's channel while not affecting legitimate users. They suggested that the primary objective of this was to maximize the system secrecy capacity.

To achieve the optimal PHY layer security via friendly jamming, there are some studies focusing on the design of cooperative jamming process, artificial noise generation and performance analyses in basic network models [10,12,13]. After that, a series of latest researches on the topic were absorbed in the complex optimization problems of the secrecy capacity for various wireless environment. In [14], Oggier calculated the perfect secrecy capacity of the MIMO wiretap channel, where the number of antennas is arbitrary for the entities in the network. To find the optimal solution for the power constraints wireless networks, Li et al. in [15] maximized the secrecy capacity based on the geometric programming, and extended their work to the cognitive Internet of Things to design a novel cooperative jamming scheme to encourage the helper by employing energy harvesting technology [16]. The similar work in [17] investigated cooperative secure communications in consideration of clean relaying process. Moreover, in [18], authors intended to design a jamming noise transmit strategy for the secondary users in the cognitive radio networks to maximize the secrecy rate. However, those existing works required knowing CSI between the legitimate transmitter and the eavesdroppers. The reason of the assumption is that the optimization needs to exploit the received Signal-to-Interference-plus-Noise-Ratio (SINR) at eavesdroppers to calculate the wiretap channel capacity via Shannon Theorem.

Obviously, the above assumption of the known CSI to compute secure capacity is impractical. The eavesdroppers in wireless network are often in the passive receiving state and do not actively transmit signals, so that they cannot be aware by the legitimate users. Therefore, the traditional friendly jamming schemes on optimize secrecy capacity are no longer applicable. In [19], Vilela et al. presented a more practical method, in which the authors considered path-loss and fading effects of the wiretap channel to obtain the statistical CSI. As an extension of this work, [20] minimized the unsecured area in considering the eavesdroppers statistical mode. Moreover, Li et al. in [21] also introduced the channel uncertainty into the optimization of secrecy capacity, and attempted to analyze the effect of channel state on secure communication performance.

Nevertheless, the study on cooperative jamming scheme in unknown CSI of eavesdroppers is still a crux for PHY layer security. Thus, differing from the aforementioned jamming strategies, we intend to employ space power synthesis to design the secure communication in that case. To the best of our knowledge, this work we put forward in the paper provides a pioneering direction that has not been studied in the PHY layer security issue based on cooperative jamming.

3   System Model and Problem Formulation

3.1   System Model

Considering a free-space path propagation model in Fig. 1, a transmitter Tx wants to communicate with the legitimate receiver Rx in a confined region. However, one or more illegal receivers in the region, Ev, attempt to eavesdrop that information. In order to prevent the eavesdropping behavior, the legitimate users intend to select N nodes as jammers, $Jm_i, i = 1, 2, \cdots, N$, to broadcast jamming signals during the data transmission. In that case, eavesdroppers cannot decode or even receive the secrecy signals.

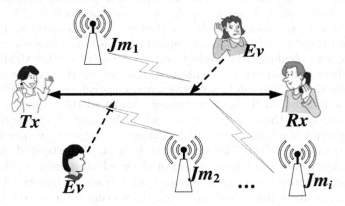

Fig. 1. The cooperative jamming model with multiple jammers.

The goal of our model is to increase the SINR of the legitimate receiver and decrease that of the the eavesdropper. In other words, we should minimize the synthetic power of the jamming signals emitted by $Jm_i, i = 1, 2, \cdots, N$ at Rx, as well as to ensure a certain interference temperature in the confined region. Therefore, the secrecy capacity in that case of unknown eavesdroppers' CSI can be improved because the synthetic jamming power at the legitimate receiver is much lower than elsewhere of the region.

3.2   Problem Formulation

Assuming that current of the ith antenna with length L is I_i, we can derive the far electric field strength of emitted signal from n antennas to the target based on the principle of antenna and electromagnetic wave, i.e.,

$$E_\theta = \sum_{i=1}^{n} \frac{f_i(\theta, \phi) I_i L \eta}{2\lambda r_i} e^{j(\beta r_i + \varphi_i)} e^{j\omega t}, \tag{1}$$

where $f_i(\theta, \phi)$ is defined as the directivity function of the ith antenna, φ_i represents the initial phase, and λ denotes the wavelength of transmitted signal. r_i is the distance from the the antenna to the target, and η and β are the parameters for the wave impedance of the medium and the phase constant. Besides, ω and t denote frequency and time.

Without loss of generality, all the antennas have the same length $L = \frac{\lambda}{4}$ as well as the same signal wavelength. The wave impedance of the medium $\eta = 120\pi$, and the directivity of an antenna is only in two-dimensional space, i.e. $\theta = \frac{\pi}{2}$ and $f_i(\theta, \phi) = \sin \theta = 1$. Thus, (1) can be simplified as below.

$$E = \sum_{i=1}^{n} A_i e^{j(\beta r_i + \varphi_i)} e^{j\omega t} \tag{2}$$

where $A_i = \frac{15\pi I_i}{r_i}$ is the amplitude of ith jamming signal.

According to the Poynting theorem and Maxwell equation, the synthetic power density is

$$P_r = \frac{1}{2} \text{Re}\, (\boldsymbol{E} \times \boldsymbol{H}^*) = \frac{E^2}{2\eta} \tag{3}$$

where $H = \frac{E}{\eta}$, is the superposition magnetic field strength.

Obviously, the synthetic power density of the target is proportional to the square of the amplitude of the synthetic electric field strength, i.e.

$$P_r \propto |E|^2 \tag{4}$$

Therefore, the size of the electric field is related to several factors, including the number of jammers n, the antenna current for each jammer I_i, the distance from the antenna to the target r_i, and the initial phase φ_i.

So far we have built the power synthesis-based cooperative jamming model to increase secrecy capacity in the case of unknown eavesdroppers' CSI. Next, we need to analyze the effect of these factors on P_r, so as to minimize the synthetic power at Rx.

4   The Existence of Fundamental Solution

Ideally, we expect the minimum synthetic power at Rx to be zero but not elsewhere. It goes without saying that this goal cannot be achieved by a single jammer with single antenna. To further study the proportional relationship in (4), we present the following lemma for the system with two jammers.

Lemma 1. *Considering a cooperative jamming system with two friendly jammers, the synthetic power density is proportional to the square of two signal superimposed amplitude, i.e.*

$$P_r \propto A^2 = A_1^2 + A_2^2 + 2A_1 A_2 \cos(\triangle\phi) \tag{5}$$

where $\triangle\phi = \varphi_2 - \varphi_1 + \beta(r_2 - r_1)$ is the corresponding phase difference.

Proof. According to (2), the synthetic electric field intensity for the two jammers system is

$$E = \frac{15\pi I_1}{r_1} e^{j(\beta r_1 + \varphi_1)} e^{j\omega t} + \frac{15\pi I_2}{r_2} e^{j(\beta r_2 + \varphi_2)} e^{j\omega t},$$

which can be decomposed into a real part and an imaginary part via Euler formula, i.e.

$$E = \mathrm{Re}(E) + j\mathrm{Im}(E), \tag{6}$$

By using the Rotation Vector algorithm, (6) can be derived as

$$E = A\cos(\omega t + \varphi) + jA\sin(\omega t + \varphi) = Ae^{j(wt+\varphi)} \tag{7}$$

where A is the two signal superimposed amplitude, and φ is the corresponding superimposed phase. Due to the proportion between P_r and $|E|^2$ as shown in (4), formula (5) holds and Lemma 1 has been proved.

Using the mathematical induction, the synthetic power in the scenario of multiple jammers should also be proportional to the square of multiple signal superimposed amplitude. Due to Lemma 1, it is important to find the suitable jammers with optimal initial emitted phases and currents when the location of Rx is certain, so as to solve the optimization problem.

As previously described, the synthetic power at Rx should be null. In that case, the initial emitted phases and currents should satisfy two conditions.

$$\text{Phase condition:} \qquad \triangle\phi = (2k+1)\pi \quad k \in Z \tag{8}$$

$$\text{Amplitude condition:} \quad \frac{I_1}{r_1} = \frac{I_2}{r_2} \tag{9}$$

As a result of this, we learn that the synthetic power density can be nulled at Rx as long as the phase and amplitude conditions hold.

5   The Uniqueness of Solution

As explained in Sect. 4, we learn that there exists at least one solution, which can make the synthetic power density be zero at Rx. However, it is still a problem whether to exist other zero points in the rest of the confined region. The analysis in this section is to prove the uniqueness of the solution.

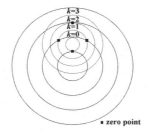

Fig. 2. Zero points location diagram.

Here, we still follow the phase and amplitude conditions in (8) and (9) for the two jammers system. Thus, the distance r_1 and r_2 is computed by

$$\begin{cases} r_1 = \frac{(2k+1)\pi+\varphi_1-\varphi_2}{\beta(I_2-I_1)} I_1 \\ r_2 = \frac{(2k+1)\pi+\varphi_1-\varphi_2}{\beta(I_2-I_1)} I_2 \end{cases} \quad (k \in Z) \tag{10}$$

If we take the locations of every jammer as the center of each circle with the corresponding radius $r_i, (i = 1, 2)$, as shown in Fig. 2, the intersection of the two circles is the position of the zero point. Obviously, the two circles for each k may have two intersections, i.e. two zero points. Note that there are two identical intersections when the two circles are tangent.

From this perspective, our goal is to make the solution unique. According to the various positional relationship between jammers and the legitimate receiver, we provide different analyses as below.

5.1 *Rx* Is Collinear with Two Jammers

For the collinear scenario, we should consider two different relative position, which are the externally-tangent and internally-tangent. Assume that $d_{i,j}, i, j \in \{Rx, Jm_1, Jm_2\}$ is the distance between node i and node j. Here, we provide Lemmas 2 and 3 to illustrate the uniqueness of solution in this case.

Lemma 2. *When there exists a externally-tangent point of two jammers with r_1 and r_2 based on (8), we cannot find other intersection points along with the increase of k, if and only if*

$$\lambda > \lambda_{\text{ext}} = d_{Jm_1,Jm_2} + d_{Rx,Jm_1} - d_{Rx,Jm_2} \tag{11}$$

where $d_{Rx,Jm_2} > d_{Rx,Jm_1}$.

Proof. Assuming $d_{Rx,Jm_2} > d_{Rx,Jm_1}$, the phase and amplitude conditions in (8) and (9) can be rewrote as below.

$$I_2 = \frac{d_{Rx,Jm_2}}{d_{Rx,Jm_1}} I_1 \tag{12}$$

$$\triangle\phi = \varphi_2 - \varphi_1 + \beta(d_{Rx,Jm_2} - d_{Rx,Jm_1}) = (2k+1)\pi \tag{13}$$

where $d_{Rx,Jm_2} = \frac{(2k+1)\pi+\varphi_1-\varphi_2}{\beta(I_2-I_1)}I_2$ and $d_{Rx,Jm_1} = \frac{(2k+1)\pi+\varphi_1-\varphi_2}{\beta(I_2-I_1)}I_1$.

Obviously, due to the externally-tangent point of two jammers, two circles will be far away (no intersection) when decrease of k, as shown in Fig. 2. Yet, with k increasing (e.g. $\triangle\phi = (2k+3)\pi$), there is also no intersection, if the distance difference between r_1 and r_2 satisfies

$$|r_2 - r_1| = r_2 - r_1 = \frac{2\pi}{\beta} + (d_{Rx,Jm_2} - d_{Rx,Jm_1}) > d_{Jm_1,Jm_2}$$

where r_2 is larger than r_1 because of $d_{Rx,Jm_2} > d_{Rx,Jm_1}$. Accordingly, we can derive the condition of (11), and Lemma 2 has been proved.

Lemma 3. *When there exists a internally-tangent point of two jammers with r_1 and r_2 based on (8), we cannot find other intersection points along with the decrease of k, if and only if*

$$\lambda > \lambda_{\text{int}} = d_{Rx,Jm_2} - d_{Rx,Jm_1} - \frac{I_2 - I_1}{I_1 + I_2}d_{Jm_1,Jm_2} \tag{14}$$

where $d_{Rx,Jm_2} > d_{Rx,Jm_1}$.

Proof. Similar to the proof of Lemma 2, when there exists a internally-tangent point of *jammers* at Rx, the distance relationship among Rx and two jammers is defined as below.

$$d_{Rx,Jm_2} - d_{Rx,Jm_1} = d_{Jm_1,Jm_2}$$

Also, when k decreases, i.e. $\triangle\phi = (2k-1)\pi$, the sum of r_1 and r_2 satisfies

$$r_1 + r_2 = \frac{(2k-1)\pi + \varphi_1 - \varphi_2}{\beta}\frac{I_1 + I_2}{I_2 - I_1} < d_{Jm_1,Jm_2}$$

Thus, we can derive the condition of (14). In that case, the circle with r_1 is in the other circle with r_2, and there is no intersection between two circles.

Accordingly, we can achieve the unique solution by adjusting different restrictions on λ in the case of collinear scenario.

5.2 Rx Is Not Collinear with Two Jammers

In this scenario, it is impossible to have two circles tangent at Rx, which means we cannot achieve the unique solution by using two jammers. Nevertheless, we can still ensure that there are only two zero points, so as to select two groups of jammers to achieve the only zero point in the confined region.

Lemma 4. *Under the premise of satisfying (8) and (9), we can find two intersection points at most along with the changing k, if and only if*

$$\lambda > \max(\lambda_{\text{ext}}, \lambda_{\text{int}}) \tag{15}$$

Proof. Here, we still consider the scenario of $d_{Rx,Jm_2} > d_{Rx,Jm_1}$. According to Lemmas 2 and 3, two circles no longer intersect when k increases if satisfying (11), while there is not any intersection when k decreases if following (14). Therefore, λ should be set to the largest one of the two inequalities.

According to Lemma 4, we have to select another two jammers that have two intersection points. For the purpose of ensuring one zero point in the confined region, we can deliberately set a coincident zero point for the two groups of intersection points. In that case, the jamming system of the two groups of jammers (actually four jammers) have a unique solution at Rx.

5.3   A Special Case

Additionally, Rx may be located on the perpendicular bisector of two jammers, i.e. $d_{Rx,Jm_1} = d_{Rx,Jm_2}$. In that case, the synthetic power at Rx can be nulled as long as the two jammers satisfy (8) and (9).

However, the synthetic power of all points on the perpendicular bisector is zero. For the purpose of the uniqueness of the solution, we also exploit two groups of jammers, which is similar to the above subsection. In this way, the only zero point is the intersection of two perpendicular bisectors of these jammers.

5.4   Other Cases for Unique Solution

Although the above analyses have provided the unique zero point in the case of two jammers (or two groups of jammers) with different locations, there are still other cases for the only zero point. Taking three jammers scenario for example, we can also obtain only one solution for the system by the Rotation Vector algorithm. Here, we only present the corresponding conclusion in this case.

$$\begin{cases} A_3^2 = A_1^2 + A_2^2 + 2A_1 A_2 \cos \varphi_{2,1} \\ \varphi_3 + \beta d_{Rx,Jm_3} - \varphi = (2k+1)\pi \end{cases}$$

where $\varphi = \arctan \frac{A_1 \sin(\beta d_{Rx,Jm_1} + \varphi_1) + A_2 \sin(\beta d_{Rx,Jm_2} + \varphi_2)}{A_1 \cos(\beta d_{Rx,Jm_1} + \varphi_1) + A_2 \cos(\beta d_{Rx,Jm_2} + \varphi_2)}$, d_{Rx,Jm_3} represents the distance between Rx and jammer 3, and $\varphi_{2,1} = \varphi_2 - \varphi_1 + \beta(d_{Rx,Jm_2} - d_{Rx,Jm_1})$.

As long as the parameters of these three jammers satisfy the conditions described above, we can obtain the unique zero point. Moreover, we can derive similar conditions for other cases, which are omitted here.

6   Numerical Simulation

In this section, we discuss several characteristics of synthetic jamming power in the different scenarios. Here, nodes (including legitimate users and jammers) in the confined region $(2000 \times 2000\,\text{m}^2)$ have different locations, while the eavesdroppers are scattered in the region except for the location of legitimate receive. For the different cases as described in the previous section, we provide heat map which represents the synthetic power of every location. Accordingly, the effect of jammers on the synthetic power is illustrated in the following figures, in which the zero points have been marked by arrow.

Considering the collinear scenario, Fig. 3 presents the results when Rx locates between two jammers but not on the their perpendicular bisector. Obviously, there is more than one zero point if the parameters of two jammers do not satisfy Lemma 2. Similarly, Fig. 4 shows an example for the case where the Rx locates on the extension of two jammers. In that case, there is only one zero point when Lemma 3 holds.

However, the wavelength λ of jamming signals is too large to hard to design. Moreover, according to the hypothesis of far-field intensity in our work, the conclusion of two jammers should satisfy the condition $r_i > d_f$, where the far-field distance d_f can be computed by Fraunhofer area. In that case, the large

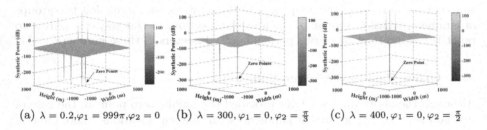

(a) $\lambda = 0.2, \varphi_1 = 999\pi, \varphi_2 = 0$ (b) $\lambda = 300, \varphi_1 = 0, \varphi_2 = \frac{\pi}{3}$ (c) $\lambda = 400, \varphi_1 = 0, \varphi_2 = \frac{\pi}{2}$

Fig. 3. The effect of different λ of jammers on the synthetic jamming power. The simulation parameters are set as follow. Rx, Jm_1, Jm_2 are located at $(0, 0)$, $(0, 150)$, $(0, -250)$, respectively. Besides, $I_1 = 3\,\text{A}$, $I_2 = 5\,\text{A}$.

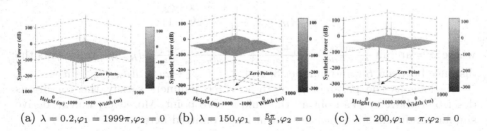

(a) $\lambda = 0.2, \varphi_1 = 1999\pi, \varphi_2 = 0$ (b) $\lambda = 150, \varphi_1 = \frac{5\pi}{3}, \varphi_2 = 0$ (c) $\lambda = 200, \varphi_1 = \pi, \varphi_2 = 0$

Fig. 4. The effect of different λ of jammers on the synthetic jamming power. The simulation parameters are set as follow. Rx, Jm_1, Jm_2 are located at $(0, 450)$, $(0, 150)$, $(0, -50)$, respectively. Besides, $I_1 = 3\,\text{A}$, $I_2 = 5\,\text{A}$.

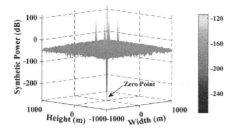 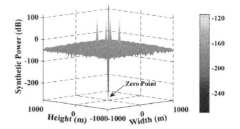

Fig. 5. Synthetic jamming power of four jammers distribution diagram. The simulation parameters are set as follow. Rx, Jm_1, Jm_2, Jm_3, and Jm_4 are located at $(0, 0)$, $(144, -192)$, $(-256, -192)$, $(-144, 192)$, $(256, 192)$, respectively. Besides, $\lambda = 0.4$ m, $I_1 = I_3 = 3$ A, $I_2 = I_4 = 4$ A, $\varphi_1 = \varphi_3 = 0$, $\varphi_2 = \varphi_4 = pi$.

Fig. 6. Synthetic jamming power of three jammers distribution diagram. The simulation parameters are set as follow. Rx, Jm_1, Jm_2, and Jm_3 are located at $(0, 0)$, $(0, 500)$, $(0, -500)$, $(300, 0)$, respectively. Besides, $\lambda = 0.3$ m, $I_1 = I_2 = 3$ A, $\varphi_1 = \varphi_2 = 0$.

near-field area of every jammer caused by the huge λ (e.g. $\lambda = 400$ m in Fig. 3(c)) no longer meets the two jammer's conclusions. Consequently, the synthetic power by three or four jammers should be paid more attention.

Figure 5 depicts the case of non-collinear scenario. Here, Rx is not collinear with two jammers and is not on their perpendicular bisector. Through adjusting the parameters of four jammers, we can obtain the only zero point at Rx. Moreover, the simulation of three jammers is provided in Fig. 6, which can also get the same result.

7 Conclusion and Future Work

This paper presents a novel approach to study jamming for secure communications. Comparing with traditional way, we utilize the space power synthesis to introduce the differential interference between the legitimate receiver and the eavesdroppers. The characteristics for jamming signals are studied to maximize the system secrecy capacity. Without knowing the CSI of the eavesdroppers, our strategy present a new cooperative jamming optimization criterion based on space power synthesis, which can null the synthetic jamming power at Rx but not elsewhere in a confine region. As a future work, we will focus on the further studies on MIMO system with unknown eavesdroppers' CSI. Moreover, we also intent to research the power allocation algorithms based on our system to maximize the system secrecy capacity subject to the global power constraint.

Acknowledgments. We are very grateful to all reviewers who have helped improve the quality of this paper. This work was supported by the National Natural Science Foundation of China (Grant Nos. 61471028 and 61572070) and the Fundamental Research Funds for the Central Universities (Grant No. 2016JBZ003).

References

1. Cai, Z., Duan, Y., Bourgeois, A.G.: Delay efficient opportunistic routing in asynchronous multi-channel cognitive radio networks. J. Combin. Optim. **29**(4), 815–835 (2015)
2. Duan, Y., Liu, G., Cai, Z.: Opportunistic channel-hopping based effective rendezvous establishment in cognitive radio networks. In: Wang, X., Zheng, R., Jing, T., Xing, K. (eds.) WASA 2012. LNCS, vol. 7405, pp. 324–336. Springer, Heidelberg (2012). doi:10.1007/978-3-642-31869-6_28
3. Yu, L., Sapra, K., Shen, H., Ye, L.: Cooperative end-to-end traffic redundancy elimination for reducing cloud bandwidth cost. In: IEEE International Conference on Network Protocols, pp. 1–10 (2012)
4. Mukherjee, A., Fakoorian, S.A.A., Huang, J., Swindlehurst, A.L.: Principles of physical layer security in multiuser wireless networks: a survey. IEEE Commun. Surv. Tutor. **16**(3), 1550–1573 (2014). Thrid
5. Jiang, K., Jing, T., Li, Z., Huo, Y., Zhang, F.: Analysis of secrecy performance in fading multiple access wiretap channel with SIC receiver. In: IEEE INFOCOM 2017 - The 36th Annual IEEE International Conference on Computer Communications, pp. 1–9, May 2016
6. Shiu, Y.S., Chang, S.Y., Wu, H.C., Huang, S.C.H., Chen, H.H.: Physical layer security in wireless networks: a tutorial. IEEE Wirel. Commun. **18**(2), 66–74 (2011)
7. Jing, T., Shi, H., Huo, Y., Ma, L., Cai, Z.: A novel channel assignment scheme for multi-radio multi-channel wireless mesh networks. In: Cheng, Y., Eun, D.Y., Qin, Z., Song, M., Xing, K. (eds.) WASA 2011. LNCS, vol. 6843, pp. 261–270. Springer, Heidelberg (2011). doi:10.1007/978-3-642-23490-3_24
8. Guan, X., Li, A., Cai, Z., Ohtsuki, T.: Coalition graph game for robust routing in cooperative cognitive radio networks. Mobile Netw. Appl. **20**(2), 147–156 (2015)
9. Ozarow, L.H., Wyner, A.D.: Wire-tap channel ii. AT T Bell Lab. Tech. J. **63**(10), 2135–2157 (1984)
10. Tekin, E., Yener, A.: The general Gaussian multiple-access and two-way wiretap channels: achievable rates and cooperative jamming. IEEE Trans. Inf. Theory **54**(6), 2735–2751 (2008)
11. Negi, R., Goel, S.: Secret communication using artificial noise. In: 2005 IEEE 62nd Vehicular Technology Conference on VTC-2005-Fall, 2005, vol. 3, pp. 1906–1910, September 2005
12. Weingarten, H., Steinberg, Y., Shamai, S.S.: The capacity region of the gaussian multiple-input multiple-output broadcast channel. IEEE Trans. Inf. Theory **52**(9), 3936–3964 (2006)
13. Shen, W., Ning, P., He, X., Dai, H.: Ally friendly jamming: how to jam your enemy and maintain your own wireless connectivity at the same time. In: 2013 IEEE Symposium on Security and Privacy, pp. 174–188, May 2013
14. Oggier, F., Hassibi, B.: The secrecy capacity of the mimo wiretap channel. IEEE Trans. Inf. Theory **57**(8), 4961–4972 (2011)
15. Li, Z., Jing, T., Cheng, X., Huo, Y., Zhou, W., Chen, D.: Cooperative jamming for secure communications in MIMO cooperative cognitive radio networks. In: 2015 IEEE International Conference on Communications (ICC), pp. 7609–7614, June 2015
16. Li, Z., Jing, T., Huo, Y., Qian, J.: Worst-case jamming for secure communications in multi-antenna cooperative cognitive radio networks with energy harvesting. In: 2015 International Conference on Identification, Information, and Knowledge in the Internet of Things (IIKI), pp. 110–115, October 2015

17. Lin, P.H., Gabry, F., Thobaben, R., Jorswieck, E.A., Skoglund, M.: Multi-phase smart relaying and cooperative jamming in secure cognitive radio networks. IEEE Trans. Cogn. Commun. Netw. **2**(1), 38–52 (2016)
18. Nguyen, V.D., Duong, T.Q., Dobre, O.A., Shin, O.S.: Joint information and jamming beamforming for secrecy rate maximization in cognitive radio networks. IEEE Trans. Inf. Forensics Secur. **11**(11), 2609–2623 (2016)
19. Vilela, J.P., Bloch, M., Barros, J., McLaughlin, S.W.: Wireless secrecy regions with friendly jamming. IEEE Trans. Inf. Forensics Secur. **6**(2), 256–266 (2011)
20. Li, H., Wang, X., Hou, W.: Security enhancement in cooperative jamming using compromised secrecy region minimization. In: 2013 13th Canadian Workshop on Information Theory, pp. 214–218, June 2013
21. Li, Z., Jing, T., Ma, L., Huo, Y., Qian, J.: Worst-case cooperative jamming for secure communications in CIoT networks. Sensors **16**(3), 339 (2016)

Breakdown by Rumors: Vulnerability of D2D Communications from Online Social Networks

Tianyi Pan[✉], Md Abdul Alim, Xiang Li, and My T. Thai

University of Florida, Gainesville, FL 32611, USA
{tianyi,alim,xixiang,mythai}@cise.ufl.edu

Abstract. In this paper, we study how rumors in Online Social Networks (OSNs) may impact the performance of device-to-device (D2D) communication. As D2D is a new technology, people may choose not to use it when believed in rumors of its negative impacts. Thus, the cellular network with underlaying D2D is vulnerable to OSNs as rumors in OSNs may decrement the throughput of the cellular network in popular content delivery scenarios. To analyze the vulnerability, we introduce the problem of finding the most critical nodes in the OSN such that the throughput of a content delivery scenario is minimized when a rumor starts from those nodes. We then propose an efficient solution to the critical nodes detection problem. The severity of such vulnerability is supported by extensive experiments in various simulation settings, from which we observe up to 40% reduction in network throughput.

Keywords: D2D communication · Online Social Networks · Vulnerability

1 Introduction

D2D communication is a promising approach to cope with the rapidly increasing demand of mobile data [1], in which user equipments (UEs) directly communicate with each other while bypassing the cellular network's base stations (BSs). For the cellular network, utilizing D2D communication can therefore offload its mobile data traffic and significantly boost the overall performance [2–4].

However, as a new technology, D2D communication will be likely to face doubts from various perspectives, such as efficiency, safety, etc. When users lacking the knowledge of D2D, exaggerated disadvantages of D2D can also be generated and spread as rumors, either randomly by some normal users, or intentionally by malicious individuals. With OSN as the medium, rumors can propagate conveniently and affect a large portion of the users in the network [5] and cause the users to opt-out of D2D, thus increase the burden of the BS and degrade the overall throughput. Therefore, the cellular network is vulnerable to the rumors spreading in its interconnected OSN. An example is depicted in Fig. 1.

© Springer International Publishing AG 2017
L. Ma et al. (Eds.): WASA 2017, LNCS 10251, pp. 496–508, 2017.
DOI: 10.1007/978-3-319-60033-8_43

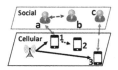
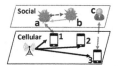
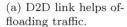

(a) D2D link helps offloading traffic.   (b) Throughput drops due to rumor.

Fig. 1. Rumor impacts network throughput

Fig. 2. The cellular network

To assess the vulnerability of the cellular network from an interdependent OSN, we propose the TMIN (Throughput Minimization in INterdependent D2D/OSN) problem that asks for a set of k nodes in the OSN, such that when a rumor starts from those nodes, the throughput in the cellular network for a popular content delivery scenario is minimized. In order to consider the vulnerability in the *worst* case, we assume the rumor starts early and all OSN users believed in the rumor will disable D2D on their devices *before* the content delivery starts. The throughput of the content delivery scenario in the cellular network is then calculated based on the (possibly) reduced number of D2D devices. The main challenge of TMIN is that the data transmission problem in the cellular network and the information propagation problem in the OSN must be jointly considered in order to accurately depict the impact or rumors to D2D communication. With high complexity from both problems, it is difficult to optimally solve TMIN.

To cope with the challenges, we propose Rumor the Critical Framework (RCF) that connects the two networks by evaluating the criticality of UEs in content delivery and mapping the values to the OSN, and then efficiently solve the Influence Maximization (IM) problem in the OSN, considering node criticality.

In summary, our contributions are as follows:

- We analyze the vulnerability of a cellular network with underlaying D2D from an interdependent OSN, by solving the problem TMIN of finding the most critical nodes in the OSN to the throughput in the cellular network.
- We propose RCF that can near optimally solve TMIN efficiently.
- We experimentally evaluate the vulnerability in various simulation settings with realistic cellular network parameters and real-world OSN data.

Related Work. Recently, the use of D2D communication to improve spectrum efficiency and system capacity has received much interest [2–4,6–8]. In order to construct stable D2D links, the social aspect can be utilized [6,7]. However, none of the existing works can capture how information diffusion in OSNs affects D2D communication underlaid cellular networks.

In OSNs, the NP-Complete IM problem [9] is widely studied. Since the seminal work by Kempe et al. [9], a plethora of works for IM have been proposed [10–14]. The state-of-the-art works [12–14] follow the RIS approach proposed in [12]. The existing works usually focus on the OSNs, without considering how the information can influence D2D communication.

Organization. The rest of the paper is organized as follows. In Sect. 2, we describe the model of interest and formally define the TMIN problem. We propose our solution RCF to TMIN in Sect. 3. The experiment results are illustrated in Sect. 4. We conclude the paper in Sect. 5.

2   System Model

2.1   The Cellular Network

We study a cellular system as illustrated in Fig. 2. It has a single BS B and a set $\mathcal{D}$ of UEs. We denote the cellular network as $G^c = (V^c, E^c)$, where $V^c = \mathcal{D} \cup \{B\}$ and E^c denotes all cellular/D2D links. A subset of UEs $V^d \subseteq \mathcal{D}$ enables D2D. Denote $G^d = (V^d, E^d)$ as the network induced in G^c by V^d. A link $(i,j) \in E^d$ exists if and only if UEs $i, j \in V^d$ are within D2D communication range. A subset $R \subseteq \mathcal{D}$ of UEs request the same content. $R = R^c \cup R^d$ where $R^c = R \backslash V^d$ and $R^d = R \cap V^d$. The set of UEs $V^r = V^d \backslash R^d$ are the relay devices. For a node i, denote $N(i)$ as the neighborhood of i.

Cellular Resources. In this paper, we consider the resource sharing model discussed in [3,4,8]. In the model, the D2D and cellular links use disjoint portion of the licensed band. Denote the total bandwidth of the BS as W. If a resource allocation scheme allocates W^c of the band to cellular links, the bandwidth for D2D links is then $W - W^c$. Therefore, interference only exists among D2D links. Additionally, there is no further division in the frequency domain, so that cellular/D2D links will use the full bandwidth W^c/W^d.

Data Rates. Based on the resource sharing model, a cellular link (B, i) receives no interference from D2D links and uses the full bandwidth. We can express its data rate $r(B, i)$ under distance-dependent path loss and multipath Rayleigh fading as in (1), where $\gamma_{B,i}$ is its Signal to Noise Ratio (SNR). In $\gamma_{B,i}$, p_B is the transmit power of the BS; d_{Bi} is the distance between B, i; α is the path loss exponent; m_0 is the fading component and N_0 is the additive white Gaussian noise.

$$r(B, i) = W^c \log_2(1 + \gamma(B, i)) \tag{1}$$

$$\gamma_{B,i} = \frac{p_B d_{Bi}^{-\alpha} |m_0|^2}{N_0} \tag{2}$$

$$r(j, k) = W^d \log_2(1 + \gamma(j, k)) \tag{3}$$

$$\gamma(j, k) = \frac{p_j d_{jk}^{-\alpha} |m_0|^2}{\sum_{(j',k') \in \mathcal{L}} p_{j'} d_{j'k}^{-\alpha} |m_0|^2 + N_0} \tag{4}$$

For a D2D link (j, k), we must include interference from other D2D links when calculating data rate $r(j, k)$. Denote $\mathcal{L}$ as the set of D2D links that transmit at the same time with (j, k), we can calculate $r(j, k)$ using (3). $\gamma(j, k)$ is the Signal to Interference and Noise Ratio (SINR) and $p_j, p_{j'}$ are the transmit powers for UEs j, j' respectively.

The model can be extended to handle multiples BSs by adding intercell interference to the denominator part of (2) and (4). We can also model device mobility as multiple snapshots of static cellular networks.

2.2   The Online Social Network

We abstract the OSN to be a weighted directed graph G^s with a node set V^s and a directed link set E^s, where a node $v \in V^s$ represents a user. A link $(u, v) \in E^s$ exists if and only if node v follows node u in the OSN. Also, each (u, v) is associated with a weight $p(u, v) \in [0, 1]$ for information propagation.

Information Propagation. To characterize how rumor propagates in the OSN, we will focus on the Independent Cascading (IC) model [9] in this paper. However, our results can be easily extended to the Linear Threshold (LT) model.

In the IC Model, initially no nodes believe the rumor, we term this as the unactivated status. Given a seed set S, the rumor propagates in rounds. In round 0, only the nodes $v \in S$ are activated (believed in the rumor). In round $t \geq 1$, all nodes activated at round $t - 1$ will try to activate their neighbors. An activated node u will remain activated. It has probability $p(u, v)$ to activate each unactivated neighbor v at the next round and it cannot activate any neighbors afterwards. The process stops when no more nodes can be activated. When a problem considers differentiated gain of influencing the nodes, we denote the expected gain over all influenced nodes by S as $\mathbb{I}^c(S)$.

Interconnection Between OSN and the Cellular Network. The owners of the UEs $\mathcal{D}$ in the cellular network may be users in an OSN, as illustrated in Fig. 1. As our focus is on the impact of OSNs to D2D communication, we construct a link e^{vi} only if a UE $i \in V^d$ has a corresponding user $v \in V^s$. The collection of all such edges is denoted as E^{ds}. We assume that each UE can be related to at most one OSN user and each OSN user owns at most one UE. Otherwise, dummy nodes can be used to recover the one-to-one correspondence. If $e^{vi} \in E^{ds}$ and $i \in V^d$, when v believed in the rumor, UE i will no longer be in V^d and cannot be included in any D2D links. Now we are ready to define the TMIN problem. Solving TMIN reveals the top-k nodes in the OSN that are critical to the cellular network.

Definition 1 (TMIN). *Consider a cellular system with BS B, devices $\mathcal{D}$, content requesters $R \subset \mathcal{D}$ and the cellular network $G^c = (V^c, E^c)$. Also, consider the OSN $G^s = (V^s, E^s)$ and the correspondence among devices in V^d and users in V^s depicted by the edge set E^{ds}. The information propagation is described using the IC model with probability p_{uv} for each $(u, v) \in E^s$. TMIN asks for a seed set in G^s with size at most k to minimize the throughput T in G^c.*

3   Solution to TMIN

3.1   The Overview

Intuitively, the goal for TMIN is to find the most critical nodes in the OSN as seed nodes for the rumor, in order to impact the cellular network throughput the most. However, the OSN alone contains no information about the cellular network. Therefore, we must utilize the cellular network to provide information to the OSN and guide its critical nodes selection. In RCF, we first calculate the criticality of all UEs in the cellular network using Algorithm 2, based on the solutions for a throughput minimization problem defined in the cellular network. Then, we cast the criticality values of the devices to their corresponding users in the OSN and introduce an efficient targeted IM algorithm (Algorithm 3) to find the top-k critical nodes in the OSN. The framework RCF is described in Algorithm 1, while the two subroutines, Algorithms 2 and 3 are discussed in Sects. 3.2 and 3.3, respectively.

Algorithm 1. RCF

Input: Cellular Network snapshots $G^c = (V^c, E^c)$, Social network $G^s = (V^s, E^s), k$
Output: Seed set $S \subseteq V^s$
    Calculate criticality values $\mathcal{C} = \{cr_i, |\forall i \in v^d\}$ using Algorithm 2 with budgets $k, k+1, \cdots, |V^d|$ and project them to corresponding nodes in V^s.
    Solve the seed set $\bar{S}$ by Algorithm 3.

3.2   Criticality Evaluation Scheme

As the goal of the cellular network is to maximize its throughput, the criticality of the devices must be related to their contribution in throughput reduction. To characterize criticality, we start from the problem of finding the top-u critical nodes in the cellular network: those whose switching from D2D to cellular mode can minimize the maximum network throughput. With a fixed u, we are able to obtain the top-u critical nodes, yet with this piece of information alone we can only assign criticality value 1 for the top-u nodes and 0 for all the remaining. Such criticality values can be misleading as the values may change drastically with other u values. Therefore, it is necessary to consider the top-u critical nodes for various values of u and integrate the pieces of information, in order to have a complete view of how critical the devices are.

In the following, we first propose an approach to find the top-u critical nodes in the cellular network, via solving a bi-level mixed integer linear program (MILP). Then, based on the solution of the MILP, we discuss Algorithm 2, Node Criticality Evaluation (NCE), to determine node criticality.

Find the Critical Nodes in the Cellular Network. Under the system model discussed in Sect. 2.1, the cellular network can be modeled as a flow network. The capacity and flow of a cellular/D2D link is its maximum data rate and actual data rate, respectively. However, special care is required in the construction, for linearizing the calculation of data rate, and modeling devices switching from cellular to D2D mode, which will be discussed respectively as follows.

Data Rate Estimation. In practice, calculating data rate often requires nonlinear formulas considering interference management and resource allocation. However, adding nonlinear constraints to a formulation can greatly increase its complexity. To avoid this, we describe an approach to estimate data rate. As the main purpose of studying TMIN is to demonstrate how cellular network throughput can be impacted by rumors in OSNs, the estimated data rates suffice.

To estimate data rates, we first discuss the collision management for D2D and cellular links. To avoid collision, links sharing the same band cannot transmit concurrently if they are in the same access domain. We denote such links as an Interference Set. The interference set for a link $e = (i,j)$, $I(e)$, can be defined as $I_e = \{(i',j')|d_{ii'} \leq \beta d_0\}$ where β is a tunable parameter and d_0 is the maximum D2D communication distance. With the interference sets for all links, we can obtain the set of links that are allowed to transmit at the same time, $L(e)$, given one active link e. $L(e)$ is constructed as follows. First we set $L(e) = \{e\}$. Then we iteratively select a link into $L(e)$ if it causes the largest drop in data rate among links that are not in the interference sets of links in $L(e)$. Assume each device has a fixed transmission power, the SINR for each D2D link can therefore be obtained using (4). Based on (3), the data rate is proportional to the bandwidth, which is a variable. For notation convenience, we calculate $c(e)$ using (3), assuming unit bandwidth. Therefore, the maximum data rate of link e can be expressed by $W^d \times c(e)$, recall that W^d is the bandwidth assigned to D2D links. Similarly, we can use (1), (2) to obtain the maximum data rate for a cellular link e', which is $W^c \times c(e')$. The actual data rate $f(e)$ is modeled as a linear variable upper bounded by the maximum data rate.

Network Modification. To create a flow network with a single source and a single sink, we introduce additional components, including a global sink node v^t as well as the links $(i,v^t), \forall i \in R$ and (v^t, B). A link among those has infinite capacity and an empty interference set. Next, we model nodes switching from D2D mode to cellular mode. Two types of devices may switch their modes. The first type is the relay devices V^r. When such devices turn to cellular mode, we can remove them from the network as they neither request any data nor contribute to D2D transmission. The second type is the receiver devices R^d. When such devices switch their modes, they still request data from the BS. So we must remove all D2D links associated with those devices, but keep their cellular links. To model a switch as a link removal, we split each node $i \in V^d$ into two nodes i^-, i^+. The incoming D2D links are connected to i^- and all outgoing links are connected to i^+. Denote $E^{d'} = \{(i^+, j^-)|(i,j) \in V^d\}$ as the set of all D2D links. For the cellular link (B,i), we replace it with (B,i^-) if $i \in V^r$ and (B,i^+) if $i \in R^d$. Let $E^l = \{(B,i)|i \in v^c\backslash v^d\} \cup \{(B,i^-)|i \in V^r\} \cup \{(B,i^+)|i \in R^d\}$ as the set of all cellular links. Nodes i^-, i^+ are connected by link $e_i = (i^-, i^+)$, which has an empty interference set and infinite capacity. Let $E^m = \{e_i|i \in V^d\}$. Denote the modified graph as $G^{c'} = (V^{c'}, E^{c'})$ where $V^{c'} = (V^c \backslash V^d) \cup \{i^-, i^+ | i \in V^d\} \cup \{B, v^t\}$ and $E^{c'} = E^l \cup E^{d'} \cup E^m \cup \{(v^t, B)\} \cup \{(i, v^t) | i \in R\}$.

We can easily verify that switching a node i from D2D to cellular in G^c is equivalent to removing link (i^-, i^+) in $G^{c'}$.

$$\mathcal{P} : \min T(\mathbf{z}) \qquad (5)$$

$$s.t. \sum_{e \in E^m} z_e \leq u \qquad (6)$$

$$z_e \in \{0, 1\}, \forall e \in E^m$$

$$T(\mathbf{z}) = \max f_{v^t B} \qquad (7)$$

$$s.t. \sum_{i \in N^-(j)} f_{ij} - \sum_{k \in N^+(j)} f_{jk} = 0, \forall j \in V^{c'} \qquad (8)$$

$$\sum_{e' \in I(e)} \frac{f_{e'}}{W^c \times c(e')} \leq 1, \forall e \in E^l \qquad (9)$$

$$\sum_{e' \in I(e)} \frac{f_{e'}}{W^d \times c(e')} \leq 1, \forall e \in E^{d'} \qquad (10)$$

$$f_e \leq c(e)(1 - z_e), \quad \forall e \in E^m \qquad (11)$$

$$W^c + W^d \leq W \qquad (12)$$

$$f_e \geq 0, \quad \forall e \in E^{c'}, W^c, W^d \geq 0$$

$$\mathcal{P}^d : \min W \times l + \sum_{e \in E^m} c(e)(r_e - \delta_e)$$

$$s.t. \sum_{e \in E^m} z_e \leq u$$

$$\delta_e \leq z_e, \forall e \in E^m \qquad (13)$$

$$\delta_e \leq r_e, \forall e \in E^m \qquad (14)$$

$$\delta_e \geq r_e - (1 - z_e), \forall e \in E^m \qquad (15)$$

$$p_B - p_{v^t} \geq 1 \qquad (16)$$

$$p_{v^t} - p_i \geq 0, \forall i \in R \qquad (17)$$

$$p_j - p_i + \sum_{e \in I(i,j)} \frac{q_e^c}{c(i,j)} \geq 0, \forall (i,j) \in E^l \qquad (18)$$

$$p_j - p_i + \sum_{e \in I(i,j)} \frac{q_e^d}{c(i,j)} \geq 0, \forall (i,j) \in E^{d'} \qquad (19)$$

$$p_j - p_i + r_e \geq 0, \forall e = (i,j) \in E^m \qquad (20)$$

$$l - \sum_{e \in E^l} q_e^c \geq 0, \ l - \sum_{e \in E^d} q_e^d \geq 0$$

$$z_e \in \{0, 1\}, r_e \geq 0, \delta_e \geq 0, \forall e \in E^m$$

$$q_e^c \geq 0, \forall e \in E^l, \ q_e^d \geq 0, \forall e \in E^{d'}, l \geq 0$$

Fig. 3. The primal program   **Fig. 4.** The dual program

With the data rate model and the modified network $G^{c'}$, we formulate the problem as a bi-level MILP $\mathcal{P}$ in Fig. 3. The objectives (5) (outer stage) and (7) (inner stage) guarantees the problem to be a minimization of the maximum throughput T. Constraint (6) restrict the solution to be top-u critical nodes. The binary variable z_e reaches 1 if link e is removed. Therefore, at most u links in E^m, i.e. at most u devices in V^d can be removed. Constraint (8) is the flow balance constraint. The traffic received by a device must be equal to what it transmits. Collision management in the cellular network are considered in (9) and (10), by which we ensure that only one link among all links in an interference set can transmit at any point of time. Also, since the traffic f_e must be non-negative, (9) and (10) upperbound the traffic on any link by its data rate. Constraint (11) model the case that no flow can be assigned to a removed edge. Notice that we omit all links with infinite capacity for the capacity constraints. Constraint (12) limits the total bandwidth being used by cellular and D2D communications.

As $\mathcal{P}$ cannot be solved directly due to its bi-level structure, we reformulate it as a single-level MILP $\mathcal{P}^d$ by dualization and linearization techniques. The solution of $\mathcal{P}^d$ is attainable via existing MILP solvers.

Dualization of the Inner Stage. By dualization, we can transform the inner stage to a equivalent minimization problem, so that the original minimax bi-level formulation is equivalent to a minimization problem in only one stage. Denote p, q_c, q_d, r, l as the dual variables corresponds to constraints (8)–(12), respectively. The reformulated program after dualization is denoted as $\mathcal{P}^d$ in Fig. 4.

Linearization. The original dual objective contains a quadratic term $\sum_{e \in E^m} c(e) r_e (1 - z_e)$, which largely increases complexity. To achieve a linear formulation, we substitute $r_e z_e$ with δ_e and add constraints (13) to (15). The equivalence after the step is proved in Lemma 1.

Lemma 1. *Constraints* (13) *to* (15) *guarantee* $\delta_e = r_e z_e, \forall e \in E^m$.

Proof. First, we claim that the range of any r_e is $[0,1]$. Based on the objective, both l and r_e should be minimized. As the only constraint that potentially requests an r_e value be higher than 0 is inequality (20), the value of r_e can be written as $\max\{0, p_i - p_j\}$ for $e = (i,j) \in E^m$. Based on constraints (16) to (19), the largest value for any $p_i - p_j$ is 1, otherwise the l value will be unnecessarily large and the solution is not optimal. Therefore, $0 \leq r_e \leq 1$ for all $e \in E^m$. By constraints (13) to (15), when $z_e = 0$, $\delta_e = 0 = z_e r_e$; when $z_e = 1$, $\delta_e = r_e = z_e r_e$ (as $r_e \leq 1 = z_e$). As z_e is binary, we have $\delta_e = z_e r_e$ in all cases.

The NCE Algorithm. By the discussion at the beginning of Sect. 3.2, we can use the solutions of $\mathcal{P}^d$ to support criticality evaluation as in Algorithm 2. The program $\mathcal{P}^d$ is solved under a set $\mathcal{U} = \{u_1, u_2, ... u_w\}$ of budgets. Denote the solutions as $\mathbf{z}^1, ..., \mathbf{z}^w$, we define the criticality of node i as $cr_i = \sum_{p=1,...,w} z_{e_i}^p$. The definition of cr_i is aligned with the concept of being critical. A device i that appears in more $\mathcal{P}^d$ solutions has higher criticality than another device j that contributes to less $\mathcal{P}^d$ solutions. Intuitively, all users with no devices in the considered cellular network have 0 criticality.

Algorithm 2. Node critical-ity Evaluation(NCE)	**Algorithm 3. Targeted-IM**
Input: $G^c = (V^c, E^c)$, List of budgets $\mathcal{U} = \{u_1, u_2, ..., u_w\}$	**Input:** Social network $G^s = (V^s, E^s, \mathcal{C})$, k, $\epsilon > 0$, $\delta \in (0,1)$, γ
Output: $\mathcal{C} = \{cr_i | \forall i \in V^d\}$	**Output:** Seed set $S \subseteq V^s$
Initialize $cr_i = 0, \forall i \in V^d$	$\mathcal{R} = \emptyset$, $N_R = \gamma, N_R^0 = 1$
for all $u_p \in \mathcal{U}$ **do**	**while** $\deg_{\mathcal{R}}(\bar{S}) < \gamma$ **do**
Solve $\mathcal{P}^d$ with budget u_p.	Generate N_R^0 RR sets $\tilde{R}$ by BSA in [14]
Denote the solution as $\mathbf{z}$.	$\mathcal{R} = \mathcal{R} \cup \{\tilde{R}\}$
$cr_i += z_{e_i}, \forall i \in V^d$.	$\bar{S} = GreedyMC(\mathcal{R}, k)$
end for	$N_R^0 = N_R, N_R = 2N_R$
	end while

We assume the availability of the full knowledge of the cellular network. In reality, BSs may observe some frequently reappearing location patterns or mobility traces of the UEs in the form of snapshots, or static networks. Then, the criticality of the devices can be calculated by using Algorithm 2 in all snapshots. However, how the snapshots are obtained is out of the scope of this paper, as our aim is to understand the vulnerability in the worst case.

3.3   Targeted IM Algorithm

With Algorithm 2, we can quantitatively evaluate the criticality of all nodes in the OSN. Due to the way the criticality values are assigned, when more nodes with large criticality values in the OSN are influenced, we can expect a more severe throughput reduction in the cellular network. Therefore, the problem of finding the top-k critical nodes in the OSN can be interpreted as the targeted-IM problem of finding k seed nodes to maximize the total criticality of all influenced nodes. In the following, we propose an efficient Targeted-IM algorithm based on the reverse influence sampling (RIS) technique.

Brief Review of the RIS Technique [12]. RIS first samples Reverse Reachable (RR) sets and then apply a greedy maximum coverage (MC) algorithm to obtain the seed set. An RR set $\tilde{R}$ consists of the set of nodes that can reach an origin node $o_{\tilde{R}}$ in a sample graph $\tilde{G}$. With enough RR sets, one can estimate the influence of each seed set S, by relating S and the RR sets to a coverage instance, in which an RR set corresponds to an element and a node corresponds to a set. An element is covered if and only if the node exists in the RR set. Approximately, the influence spread of a seed set is positively correlated to the number of covered RR sets over the total number of RR sets, greedily solving the MC can output a seed set with near-optimal influence spread.

In our scenario, as the nodes are of different criticality values, the probability of starting a random RR set from node is $\frac{cr_v}{\Omega}$, proportional to its criticality. Denote $\deg_{\mathcal{R}}(S)$ as the number of RR sets in $\mathcal{R}$ covered by seed set S.

To limit the number of RR sets, we set exponential check points during its generation. At each check point, we greedily solve the weighted MC problem [15] and examine if $\deg_{\mathcal{R}}(\bar{S})$ exceeds a threshold, where $\bar{S}$ is the greedy MC solution. If so, we stop and output $\bar{S}$ as the seed set. The Targeted-IM algorithm is presented in Algorithm 3. With an improved threshold, the time complexity of Targeted-IM is a constant smaller than the state-of-art algorithm BCT [14].

In the following, we present the approximation ratio and time complexity of Algorithm 3. Due to space limit, the proofs are omitted here and can be found in [16].

Theorem 1. *With $\epsilon > 0$, $0 < \delta < 1$, the seed set $\bar{S}$ calculated by Algorithm 3 satisfies $\mathbb{I}^c(\bar{S}) \geq (1 - \frac{1}{e} - \epsilon)\mathbb{I}^c(S^*)$ with probability at least $1 - \delta$.*

Theorem 2. *The expected running time of Algorithm 3 is $O(\gamma |E^s|)$.*

4   Experiments

4.1   Setup

Cellular Network. As the real data sets are limited due to our requirements, we use synthetic data for the cellular network. We consider a square cell with the BS at the lower-left corner and 50 data requesters generated at random locations, with 30/20 devices in D2D/cellular mode respectively. To enable D2D communication, we also generate 60 D2D relay devices at random locations within the area. All the wireless parameters are summarized in Table 1.

OSN. To model information propagation in the OSN, we use real-world Facebook network topology from [17], with 4039 nodes and 88234 edges. The influence on an edge was assigned randomly from a uniform distribution.

Table 1. Wireless network parameters

Notation	Description	Notation	Description
Cell dimension	50 x 50 m^2	D2D distance	15 m
Network bandwidth	0.1 MHz	Channel model	Multipath Rayleigh fading
Path loss exponent	3	Noise spectral density	−174 dBm/Hz
BS transmit power	100 W	D2D transmit power	10 W

Interdependency. For the interconnection between the two networks, we consider two scenarios, namely stadium and shopping mall. In the stadium scenario, the UEs are not likely to be socially connected. In the mall scenario, however, as the shoppers normally resides closer than the game goers, the UEs are more likely to be connected in the OSN, compared with the stadium scenario.

We use the following procedure to create the interconnections. For each D2D node $i \in V^d$, we randomly choose a $v \in V^s$ and construct e^{vi}. Then, with probability p_1, we choose a random $i' \in N(i)$ and $v' \in N(v)$ and construct $e^{v'i'}$. With probability p_2, we construct $e^{\bar{v}\bar{i}}$ for a random $\bar{i} \in N(i')$ and $\bar{v} \in N(v')$, when $e^{v'i'}$ is constructed. To differentiate the scenarios, we apply higher p_1, p_2 values for mall. In our experiments we have set $p_1 = 0.7$ and $p_2 = 0.4$ for stadium, and $p_1 = 0.9$ and $p_2 = 0.6$ for mall.

Algorithms. To illustrate the efficacy of RCF, especially Algorithm 2, we compare it with two approaches. The first uses degree centrality as criticality and the second randomly assigns criticality. Then, both approaches run the same targeted IM algorithm embedded in RCF to obtain the critical nodes in the OSN.

4.2 Vulnerability of the Cellular Network

We first observe how the throughput can be impacted by varying seed set size. For both scenarios, the throughput (Figs. 5, 6) of the cellular network had substantial decreases after rumor propagation. The decrements are higher when increasing the number of seeds. With RCF, the damage to throughput is severer than other approaches, indicating RCF can better reveal the critical nodes. The gap between RCF and the other methods increases significantly as more seed nodes can be selected. It is worth noticing that the random approach can also lead to noticeable decrease in throughput. Therefore, the interdependent cellular/social networks is vulnerable even to randomly originated rumors.

Next, we examine how social connectivity impacts the throughput. Intuitively, denser social connections leads to larger influence of rumors and a more vulnerable cellular network. The measure we use is the relative throughput decrease Q_k. Denote the throughput after rumor propagation with k seed nodes as T_k, we define $Q_k = \frac{T_0 - T_k}{T_0} \times 100\%$.

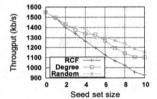

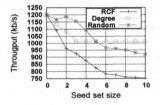

Fig. 5. Throughput - stadium   **Fig. 6.** Throughput - mall

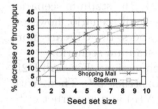

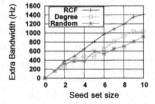

Fig. 7. Impact of social connectivity   **Fig. 8.** Extra bandwidth requirement

As can be seen from Fig. 7, Q_k for the mall scenario increases faster in most cases, which demonstrates that the social connections aid rumor propagation and increase the vulnerability. The slow increase in Q_k for the mall scenario after seed set size 8 is due to saturation that all D2D users are already influenced.

Then, we show in Fig. 8 the additional bandwidth cost to recover the throughput to the level before rumor propagation, in the stadium scenario. Consistent with our previous findings, the critical nodes found by RCF result in the largest bandwidth requirement. After rumor propagation, the extra bandwidth required can be up to 1400 Hz, which indicates that supporting all the requirements after rumor propagation can be costly and thus a heavy burden to the BSs.

5   Conclusion

In this paper, we investigated the vulnerability of D2D communication from interdependent OSN. To evaluate the vulnerability, we proposed the problem TMIN to find the most critical nodes in the OSN and its solution RCF. We quantitatively demonstrated how vulnerable the cellular networks could be by experiments when rumors can propagate in the interdependent OSN.

Acknowledgement. This work is partially supported by NSF CNS-1443905 and NSF EFRI-1441231.

References

1. Cisco Visual Networking Index Cisco. Global mobile data traffic forecast update, 2015–2020. White paper (2016)
2. Klaus, D., Rinne, M., Wijting, C., Ribeiro, C.B., Hugl, K.: Device-to-device communication as an underlay to LTE-advanced networks. IEEE Commun. Mag. **47**(12), 42–49 (2009)
3. Yu, C.-H., Doppler, K., Ribeiro, C.B., Tirkkonen, O.: Resource sharing optimization for device-to-device communication underlaying cellular networks. IEEE Trans. Wirel. Commun. **10**(8), 2752–2763 (2011)
4. Lei, L., Zhong, Z., Lin, C., Shen, X.: Operator controlled device-to-device communications in LTE-advanced networks. IEEE Wirel. Commun. **19**(3), 96 (2012)
5. Nguyen, N.P., Yan, G., Thai, M.T., Eidenbenz, S.: Containment of misinformation spread in online social networks. In: Proceedings of the 4th Annual ACM Web Science Conference, pp. 213–222. ACM (2012)
6. Chen, X., Proulx, B., Gong, X., Zhang, J.: Exploiting social ties for cooperative D2D communications: a mobile social networking case. IEEE/ACM Trans. Netw. **23**(5), 1471–1484 (2015)
7. Zhang, Y., Pan, E., Song, L., Saad, W., Dawy, Z., Han, Z.: Social network aware device-to-device communication in wireless networks. IEEE Trans. Wirel. Commun. **14**(1), 177–190 (2015)
8. Li, Y., Jin, D., Hui, P., Han, Z.: Optimal base station scheduling for device-to-device communication underlaying cellular networks. IEEE J. Sel. Areas Commun. **34**(1), 27–40 (2016)
9. Kempe, D., Kleinberg, J., Tardos, E.: Maximizing the spread of influence through a social network. In: Proceedings of the Ninth ACM SIGKDD International Conference on Knowledge Discovery and Data Mining, pp. 137–146. ACM (2003)
10. Leskovec, J., Krause, A., Guestrin, C., Faloutsos, C., VanBriesen, J., Glance, N.: Cost-effective outbreak detection in networks. In: Proceedings of the 13th ACM SIGKDD International Conference on Knowledge Discovery and Data Mining, pp. 420–429. ACM (2007)

11. Chen, W., Wang, Y., Yang, S.: Efficient influence maximization in social networks. In: Proceedings of the 15th ACM SIGKDD International Conference on Knowledge Discovery and Data Mining, pp. 199–208. ACM (2009)
12. Borgs, C., Brautbar, M., Chayes, C., Lucier, B.: Maximizing social influence in nearly optimal time. In: Proceedings of the Twenty-Fifth Annual ACM-SIAM Symposium on Discrete Algorithms, pp. 946–957. SIAM (2014)
13. Tang, Y., Shi, Y., Xiao, X.: Influence maximization in near-linear time: a martingale approach. In: Proceedings of the 2015 ACM SIGMOD International Conference on Management of Data, pp. 1539–1554. ACM (2015)
14. Nguyen, H.T., Thai, M.T., Dinh, T.N.: Cost-aware targeted viral marketing in billion-scale networks. In: 2016 IEEE Conference on Computer Communications (INFOCOM). IEEE (2016)
15. Vazirani, V.V.: Approximation Algorithms. Springer Science & Business Media, Heidelberg (2013)
16. Pan, T., Alim, M.A., Li, X., Thai, M.T.: Vulnerability of D2D communications from interconnected social networks. arxiv preprint arXiv:1702.02040 (2017)
17. McAuley, J.J., Leskovec, J.: Learning to discover social circles in ego networks. In: NIPS, vol. 2012, pp. 548–56 (2012)

Security Enhancement via Dynamic Fountain Code for Wireless Multicast

Qinghe Du[1,3(✉)], Wanyu Li[1], and Houbing Song[2]

[1] Department of Information and Communications Engineering,
Xi'an Jiaotong University, Xi'an, China
duqinghe@mail.xjtu.edu.cn
[2] Department of Electrical, Computer, Software, and Systems Engineering,
Embry-Riddle Aeronautical University, Daytona Beach, FL 32114, USA
h.song@ieee.org
[3] Shaanxi Smart Networks and Ubiquitous Access Research Center, Shaanxi, China

Abstract. Harnessing the broadcast nature of wireless channels towards efficient multicast faces very challenging security issues, because reliability assurance for each multicast receiver often result vast frequent retransmissions, thus increasing the chance for eavesdropping. This paper proposes a dynamic fountain code design for security enhancement in wireless multicast against passive eavesdropping. The main features of the proposed scheme include two folds: (i) adaptive encoding structure based on legitimate receivers' feedback, which aims at degrading the signal quality at the eavesdropper; (ii) benefit the legitimate receivers' reception as maximally as possible, thus increasing the transmission efficiency compared with the conventional non-adaptive designs. Simulation results are presented to demonstrate that the proposed scheme can effectively decreasing intercepting probability while achieving the higher transmission efficiency, thus facilitating wireless connections in support of multicast services.

Keywords: Adaptive fountain code · Multicast · Security · Eavesdropper · Intercept probability · Transmission efficiency

1 Introduction

Nowadays, computing, control, sensing, and networking have been deeply integrated for ubiquitous information exchange and applications, while the network and system components must be efficient, interoperable, and safe [1–11]. Mobile

The research work reported in this paper is supported by the National Natural Science Foundation of China under the Grant Nos. 61461136001 and 61671371, the National Science and Technology Major Project of China under Grant No. 2016ZX03001012-004, Science and Technology Program of Shaanxi Province under the Grant No. 2016KW-032, and Fundamental Research Funds for the Central Universities.

L. Ma et al. (Eds.): WASA 2017, LNCS 10251, pp. 509–521, 2017.
DOI: 10.1007/978-3-319-60033-8_44

multicast is one of the most important networking scenario for common information dissemination, where multicast messages can be transmitted to the entire multicast group via shared media and/or paths [1,5–10]. Consequently, mobile multicast gains many applications, such as remote teleconferencing and highway mobile traffic updating. However, assuring security from eavesdroppers evidently is evidently one of the major challenges in mobile multicast, especially for wireless multicast which transmit the data over the completely open broadcast-natured wireless channels.

There have been diverse approaches, including not only encryption by also physical-layer designs [3], to enhance the wireless security. Physical-layer security approaches thoroughly design the channel coding and transmission signals to turn the superiority of channel quality over eavesdroppers into security assurance. But in realistic systems, the information of eavesdroppers' channels is typically unknown to the legitimate transmitter. Moreover, the time-varying nature of wireless channels makes the legitimate user's channel quality can always dominate the eavesdroppers. Thus, security enhancement without being aware of eavesdroppers' channel information becomes extremely important [3,4].

The fountain code [12] is a powerful technique for reliable efficient multicast in terms of its high efficiency gained by the rate-less feature [13] and excellent scalability inherited from error-correction coding. Recently, the research community realizes that the fountain code also offers capability of security protection, which attracts considerable research attention [14–16]. Specifically, at the transmitter, the entire information block is partitioned into a block of information packets each with equal length. Then, the fountain-code-aided transmitter keeps generating and multicasting coded packets, which are bit-wise XOR over randomly selected information packets, until all multicast users give feedback indicating completion of decoding for recovery of the entire coded block [12,17]. Then, via designs maximally benefiting the physical-layer transmission for the legitimate user, which in fact statistically degrading the quality overheard by the eavesdropper, the legitimate user can accumulate sufficient number of coded packets to compete decoding before the eavesdropper does with a high probability [14].

While applying fountain code to enhance security opens a promising research direction [14,15], the specific secure fountain code design for wireless multicast services has been neither sufficiently understood nor thoroughly studied. Particularly, [14,15] concentrated on unicast transmissions, which is hard to bring insight for users with independent channel fading. Therefore, there are the urgent needs in developing specific yet practical fountain codes for security protection in wireless networks.

To address the aforementioned problems, this paper develops a novel fountain-encoding mechanism for mobile multicast services which dynamically changes the encoding for all multicast users based on the feedback messages from them. Specifically, the transmitter conducts the adaptive fountain-encoding design, which aims at maximally improving the decoding rates at multicast receivers, such that the legitimate users compete decoding before the eavesdropper. The simulation results show that the intercept probability of the proposed scheme is significantly decreased as compared with traditional non-adaptive fountain-coding schemes, while the transmission efficiency is also improved.

The remainder of this paper is organized as follows. Section 2 presents the system model and describes the general encoding principles as well as the decoding process of fountain codes. Section 3 interprets the proposed scheme in details. Then, Sect. 4 presents the simulation setup and simulation results among the proposed scheme and the traditional ones. Finally, this paper is concluded in Sect. 5.

2   System Model

2.1   System Description

This section first presents the system model of mobile multicast services in a wireless network, which typically has a cellular structure. As depicted in Fig. 1, a base station (BS), i.e., the transmitter, is located in the center of the cell and multicast users denoted are randomly distributed in different locations in the cell. Meanwhile, the malicious eavesdropper locates at the cell. Each users position is independent and identically distributed. The position for the ith user is jointly determined by the distance from BS denoted as d_i and the angle between user-BS and horizontal axis denoted as θ_i. The distance between the ith and jth user denoted as $d_{i,j}$ is expressed as

$$(d_{i,j})^2 = d_i^2 + d_j^2 - 2d_i d_j \cos(\theta_i - \theta_j). \tag{1}$$

During each slot, BS broadcasts fountain packet to all multicast users in different locations. The wireless link between any two nodes includes the large-scale fading, small-scale fading and additive Gauss white noise (AWGN) in the receiver. The large-scale fading caused by path loss is modeled as

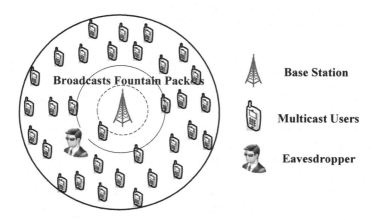

Fig. 1. System model for wireless multicast network.

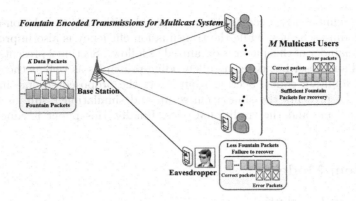

Fig. 2. Fountain-encoded transmission model for multicast system

$$PL(d_{i,j}) = d_{i,j}^{-\eta} \tag{2}$$

where η represents the path loss exponent. Besides, the small-scale fading induced by multi-path fading is modeled as the block flat Rayleigh fading. That is to say, the channel coefficients remain constant during one slot and changes independently during different slots. The channel coefficient h_{ij} is assumed as a circularly symmetric complex Gaussian random variable, namely, $h_{i,j} \sim \mathcal{CN}(0,1)$. The additive Gaussian white noise is introduced at the receiver with variance N_0. For the ith user, the symbol it receives during T_s slot is expressed as

$$y_i^{T_s} = \sqrt{P_s d_{s,i}^{-\eta}} h_{s,i} x_{f_{T_s}} + n_i. \tag{3}$$

where P_s denotes the transmit power of BS; $d_{S,i}$ represents the distance between the BS and the ith user; $h_{S,i}$ denotes the Rayleigh fading channel coefficients for the transmission link between BS and the ith user; n_i denotes the received noise for the ith user; $x_{f_{T_s}}$ represents the fountain packet transmitted by BS during T_S slot. Consequently, the received SNR for the ith user can be defined as

$$\gamma_i^{T_s} = \frac{P_s |h_{s,i}|^2 d_{s,i}^{-\eta}}{N_0}. \tag{4}$$

Once $d_{S,i}$ is fixed, $\gamma_i^{T_s}$ obeys the exponential distribution with the parameter of $\lambda_i = (N_0 d_{s,i}^\eta)/P_s$.

In Fig. 2, by introducing fountain code at the BS, fountain-encoded transmission model for multicast system is demonstrated in details. First, BS completes the encoding process from data packets to fountain packet and broadcasts it to all users. Meantime, the eavesdropper attempts to overhear the transmitted fountain packet. Then the fountain packets are delivered by BS at each time slot. Hence, all users (including the eavesdropper) intend to obtain a sufficient number of fountain packets to finally recover the original files. Once all multicast users receive sufficiently many fountain packets and finishes decoding, they will send feedback information to BS to terminate the process of encoding and transmission. At this time, security of multicast services transmission will be guaranteed if the eavesdropper does not receive enough fountain packets to complete the decoding of original data packets.

2.2 The Encoding Principles and Decoding Process

In order to elicit the proposed scheme design, here it is necessary to previously describe the encoding principles and decoding process of fountain codes. The general principles [17] of generating a fountain packet in the fountain encoder of transmitter are conceptually described Algorithm 1.

Accordingly, the decoder in the receiver recovers the data packets based on the following rule [18]:

(a) If there is at least one fountain packet that comprising of one data packet, then this data packet can be recovered immediately since it is a copy of the fountain packet.
(b) The recovered data packet is exclusive-ored into the remaining fountain packets that consist of that data packet.
(c) The recovered data packet is removed from these fountain packets and the degree of each such fountain packets is decreased by one.

Algorithm 1. General Principles of Fountain Packet Encoding

1: *Degree Selection of Fountain Packet*
   Randomly choose the degree (defined as d) of fountain packet from a degree distribution. Generally speaking, different fountain codes obey the different degree distributions.
2: *Data Packet Selection of Fountain Packet*
   Choose uniformly at random d distinct data packets as neighbors of the fountain packet.
3: *Exclusive-Or Operation*
   The value of the fountain packet is the exclusive-or of the d neighbors.

---

3 Fountain-Code-Aided Transmission Design

This section illustrates the implementation mechanism of the proposed scheme in details, as depicted in Fig. 3. Specifically, the innovative points of the proposed scheme are mainly reflected in two aspects: the transmission mechanism for BS in multicast networks described in Sect. 2.1 as well as an adaptive fountain-encoding scheme in BS. The following two subsections respectively address the detailed principles and procedures for the proposed scheme.

3.1 Transmission Mechanism for BS

Fig. 3 depicts the transmission procedures for BS during the time slot for transmitting one fountain packet. Notably, before introducing the fountain encoder, BS first divides the large data file into K data packets whose length are equal. According to the proposed adaptive fountain-encoded design illustrated in

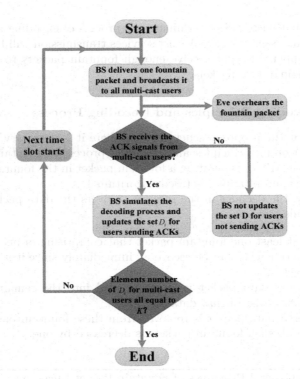

Fig. 3. The transmission flow chart for BS during one transmitting slot.

Sect. 3.2, BS completes the fountain encoding process from several data packets to one fountain packet. Then after performing the CRC encoding at the data link layer as well as the channel encoding at physical layer, BS broadcasts the encoded fountain packet to all multicast users over wireless channels. Meanwhile, the eavesdropper (Eve) attempts to wiretap the transmitted fountain packet. Due to the differences of the channel conditions among multicast users, some users fail to receive the fountain packet. The multicast users successfully receiving the fountain packet send ACK signals back to BS. After receiving the ACKs, BS "simulates" the decoding process and updates the index set of decoded data packets denoted as D_i for corresponding users which send ACKs back to BS. Finally, if the element number of set D_i for all users equal to K (K denotes the original number of data packets), BS stops encoding and broadcasting fountain packets. Contrarily, if the element number of set D_i for at least one user is less than K, BS continues to complete fountain encoding process for next time slot and repeats these procedures discussed above.

It is worth noting that certain users which succeed in receiving fountain packet during each slot only send ACK signals back to BS while BS "simulates" the decoding operation and updates the set D_i for them. Such transmission mechanism yields lower feedback overhead for multicast channels than other existing ones.

Algorithm 2. Adaptive Fountain-Encoding Procedures

1: BS records the rowers for full-0-lines and full-1-lines and respectively stores them in matrix ln_0 and ln_1.

2: Determine whether the matrix ln_1 is empty.
   If ln_1 is not empty
      Encoding rules are as follows:
      $a)$ Randomly choose **one** element from ln_1 denoted as S_c.
      $b)$ Take out **all** elements from ln_0 denoted as $S_{0,1}, S_{0,2}, ..., S_{0,t}$.
      $c)$ The encoded fountain packet is the exclusive-or of: $x_{f_{T_s}} = S_c \oplus S_{0,1} \oplus S_{0,2} \oplus ... \oplus S_{0,t}$,
   where $x_{f_{T_s}}$ denotes the encoded fountain packet during T_S-th slot.
   else   Switch to Step 3.

3: Determine whether the length of ln_0 is smaller than $K/4$.
   If length$(ln\_0) \leqslant K/4$
      Encoding rules are as follows:
      $a)$ Compute the sum of each row as P_line. Find the maximum value in P_line and records the corresponding rowers as S_max.
      $b)$ Traverse K lines to search for several lines whose rowers are denoted as $S_{r,1}, S_{r,2}, ..., S_{r,n}$ to meet the following conditions:
      • Denote the matrix constructed from $S_{r,1}, S_{r,2}, ..., S_{r,n}$ by P_temp.
      • The summation over each column of P_temp is less than 2.
      $c)$ The encoded fountain packet is the exclusive-or of: $x_{f_{T_s}} = S_{max} \oplus S_{r,1} \oplus S_{r,2} \oplus ... \oplus S_{r,n}$,
   where $x_{f_{T_s}}$ denotes the encoded fountain packet during T_S-th slot.
   else   Switch to Step 4.

4: Encoding rules are as follows:
      $a)$ Remove the full-0-lines from P and obtain the matrix P_temp.
      $b)$ Compute the sum of each row as P_line. Find the maximum value in P_line and records the corresponding rowers stored in S_min.
      $c)$ Choose as many elements as possible from S_min indexed by $S_{r,1}, S_{r,2}, ..., S_{r,m}$ to meet the following requirements:
      • Denote the matrix constructed from $S_{r,1}, S_{r,2}, ..., S_{r,m}$ by P_temp.
      •The sum of each column for P_temp must be less than 2.
      $d)$ The encoded fountain packet $x_{f_{T_s}}$ is then $x_{f_{T_s}} = S_{min} \oplus S_{r,1} \oplus S_{r,2} \oplus ... \oplus S_{r,m}$.

3.2   Adaptive Fountain-Encoding Scheme

After addressing the transmission mechanism for BS, this part focuses on the adaptive fountain-encoding steps in BS which is the core innovation of the proposed scheme. Without loss of generality, here takes a certain transmitting slot as an example.

Before introducing the adaptive fountain-encoding steps one by one, BS records the decoding indicator of data packets for all multicast users until current time slot and defines the "encoding structure matrix" as $P_{K \times M}$ where K and M respectively denotes the number of data packets as well as multicast users. Here sets initial matrix $P = P^0$ in which all the elements of P are 1 initially. As an element of matrix $P_{K \times M}$, p_{ij} is a decoding indicator where $p_{ij} = 1$ denotes the jth multicast user succeeds in decoding the ith data packet and $p_{ij} = 0$ denotes the jth multicast user fails to decode the ith data packet. In addition, the index set of original data packets is assumed as $\{S_1, S_2, ..., S_K\}$. Accordingly, the rowers of P are also described as $\{S_1, S_2, ..., S_K\}$.

Through the judging and processing of P, the adaptive fountain-encoding procedures are designed in Algorithm 2. During each time slot, BS first records the rowers of full-0-lines and full-1-lines and respectively stores them in matrix ln_0 and ln_1. Then BS should judge whether ln_1 is empty. When ln_0 is not empty, the main encoding idea is that the encoded fountain packet is the exclusive-or of all decoded data packets as well as one un-decoded data packet, which indicates a novel insight into secure delivery: Eve fails to intercept as long as it has an un-decoded data packet involved in the set of decoded data packets for multicast users. Contrarily, BS should continue to judge whether the length of ln_0 is smaller than $K/4$ when ln_1 is empty.

Similarly, if the length of ln_0 is not more than $K/4$, BS computes the sum of each row as P_line and then records the maximum value as well as the corresponding rowers in P_line. BS traverses K lines to search for several lines to form a new matrix whose sum of each column must be less than 2. This encoding concept is to guarantee that the data packet corresponding to the most serious packet loss attempts to retransmit and by traversing the matrix P to select several line so as to improve the transmission efficiency. When the length of ln_0 is larger than $K/4$, the encoding keys embodies in traversing searching for enough data packets to simultaneously decode for multicast users when most users complete the transmission for all original data packets. In this way, the decoding rates for those few users can be effectively raised.

4   Simulation Evaluation

4.1   Simulation Setup

The simulation environment is established in a cellular cell with radius $R = 1$ where BS locates in the center and M multicast users are randomly distributed in the cell. Moreover, the assumption that there is no users locating within a circle with radius of 0.01 is considered in the simulation. BS and multicast users all adopt the single antenna. As to the multicast channels discussed in Sect. 2.1, the path loss exponent η is set to 2.6 and Rayleigh fading yields the complex Gaussian distribution with zero mean and variance 1. In the simulation, system SNR is defined as $\rho = P_s/N_0$ which ranges from 10 dB to 35 dB as one varying factor. Another varying factor is the number of multicast users changing from $M = 2$ to $M = 100$. Since the position of Eve is unfixed, without loss of generality, here Eve is assumed to locate on the circumference of a radius of 1, namely, the distance between BS and Eve is 1. It is worth noting that the original number of data packets defined as K is assumed as $K = 128$. For simplicity, the packet error rate (PER) in the presence of additive white Gaussian noise (AGWN) is approximated as [19]:

$$\text{PER}_n(\gamma) \approx \begin{cases} 1, & if\ 0 < \gamma < \gamma_{pn} \\ a_n \exp(-g_n\gamma), & if\ \gamma \geqslant \gamma_{pn} \end{cases} \tag{5}$$

where n is the mode index, γ denotes the received SNR, and the mode-dependent parameters a_n, g_n, γ_{pn} are obtained by fitting (5) to the exact PER. According to [20], the fitting parameters for different transmission modes are provided in Tables I and II respectively. In the simulation, it adopts 16-QAM modulation and the coding rate is set to 9/16. By referring to the Tables II in [20], the fitting parameters are listed as follows:

$$a_n = 50.1222, g_n = 0.6644, \gamma_{pn} = 7.7021. \tag{6}$$

From (5) and (6), it is easy to get the mapping from the received SNR to channel PER under fading channels.

In addition, three performance indexes are clarified to evaluate and characterize the performance for the proposed scheme as well as the counterparts:

(a) **Intercept Probability for Eve**: Upon BS stopping encoding and transmitting fountain packets, Eve records its number of decoded data packet denoted as Num_Eve. If $Num\_Eve < K$, Eve successfully intercepts the original confidential file; otherwise, Eve fails to intercept. Hence, the intercept probability can be defined as the ratio between the number of successful eavesdropping and the total number of transmitting original confidential file after sufficient transmission attempts.

(b) **Transmission Efficiency of BS**: Upon stopping encoding and transmitting fountain packets, BS records the number of fountain packets it has transmitted which is denoted as Num_BS. The transmission efficiency of BS is defined as the average of K/Num_BS after a sufficient number of transmission attempts.

Finally, the following two schemes are recommended as baseline schemes for comparison:

(a) LT codes [18] is a rate-less fountain codes. As discussed in Algorithm 1, LT codes adopt the degree distribution of

$$\rho(d) \begin{cases} 1/K, d = 1 \\ 1/d(d-1), d = 2, 3, ..., K \end{cases} \tag{7}$$

where K denotes the number of original data packets in transmitter. The selection of degree distribution is randomly and the selection of rand d distinct data packets is uniformly.

(b) As discussed in [5], in order to maximize the average number of successfully decoded data packets, the optimal fountain-packet degree is defined by

$$d^*(K, \theta) = \left\lceil \frac{K + 1 - \theta}{\theta} \right\rceil \tag{8}$$

where K and θ respectively denotes the number of data packets and undecoded data packets. $\lceil \delta \rceil$ denotes the least integer number that is larger than or equal to δ. Similar to LT codes, the selection of rand d distinct data packets is also uniformly.

4.2 Simulation Results

This section compares the performances for the proposed scheme with two baselines. The comparisons are presented in terms of the intercept probability for Eve and the transmission efficiency of BS.

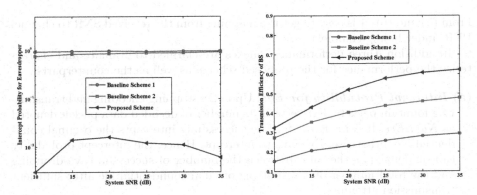

Fig. 4. Performance comparison between the proposed and baseline schemes, where the number of multicast users is set to 100 and system SNR varies from 10 to 35 dB. (a) Intercept probability versus SNR; (b) Transmission efficiency versus SNR

In Fig. 4, it is assumed that the number of multicast users is set to 100 and transmission attempts are conducted by 10^4. These figures demonstrate the performance comparisons between the proposed scheme and two baseline schemes with system SNR varying from 10 dB to 35 dB.

From Fig. 4(a), it is concluded that the intercept probability for the proposed scheme is far lower than those of two baselines and it fluctuates near 10^{-2} when system SNR varies. This is due to the fact that the proposed fountain-encoding scheme targets at adjusts the encoding rules while non-adaptive schemes adopts fixed encoding rules. In Fig. 4(b), the transmission efficiency of BS climbs when system SNR increases in the proposed scheme, which significantly superior to two benchmarks. Remarkably, the improvement of transmission efficiency indicates another advantage towards the proposed scheme.

In Figs. 5 and 6, it is assumed that system SNR is set to 20 dB and transmission attempts are conducted by 10^4. These figures depict the performance comparisons between the proposed scheme and two baseline schemes with increasing number of multicast users. In Fig. 5, the intercept probability of the proposed scheme remains 0 when the number of multicast users is less than 10 whereas it remains higher than 0.1 for two baselines. When the number of multicast users raises above 10, all curves go up with a larger number of users. Among these, the proposed curve is the lowest one suggesting that the proposed scheme yields higher security than baselines. Figure 6 shows that all curves drop sharply and the transmission efficiency of the proposed curve is obviously higher than others when number of users varies from 2 to 10. Moreover, the transmission efficiency of BS roughly remains constant 64% as the number of multicast users raises above 10 for the proposed scheme, which significantly superior to the baselines.

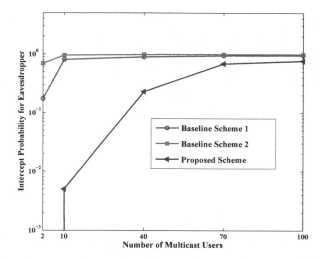

Fig. 5. Comparison of Eve's recovering proportion between the proposed scheme and baseline schemes, where the system SNR is set to 20 dB and the number of multicast users varies from 2 to 100.

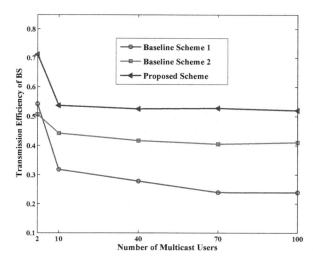

Fig. 6. Transmission efficiency comparison between the proposed scheme and baseline schemes, where the system SNR is set to 20 dB and the number of multicast users varies from 2 to 100.

5   Conclusions

This paper proposed a novel fountain-encoding scheme achieve data security for multicast services over wireless networks, which can adaptively design the encoding pattern for multicast transmissions so as to reduce the probability of being intercepted by the eavesdropper. By receiving the ACK signals fed back from multicast users, BS simulates the decoding processes towards these corresponding users and real-time updates the index set of decoded data packets. Based on these updated messages, BS conducts the adaptive fountain-encoding design which makes for improving the decoding rates of multicast users. In this way, multicast receiver can complete decoding earlier than the eavesdropper does. Simulation results show that the proposed scheme outperforms the traditional non-adaptive encoding schemes with lower intercept probability and higher transmission efficiency.

References

1. Forman, H., Zahorjan, J.: The challenges of mobile computing. IEEE Comput. **27**(4), 38–47 (1994)
2. Hui, Y., Su, Z., Guo, S.: Utility based data computing scheme to provide sensing service in internet of things. IEEE Trans. Emerg. Top. Comput., June 2017. doi:10.1109/TETC.2017.2674023
3. Bloch, J., Barros, M.: Physical-Layer Security, From Information Theory to Security Engineering. Cambridge University Press, Cambridge (2011)
4. Hussain, M., Du, Q., Sun, L., Ren, P.: Security enhancement for video transmission via noise aggregation in immersive systems. Multimed. Tools Appl. **75**(9), 5345–5357 (2016)
5. Zhang, X., Du, Q.: Adaptive low-complexity erasure-correcting code based protocols for QoS-driven mobile multicast services over wireless networks. IEEE Trans. Veh. Technol. **55**(5), 1633–1647 (2006)
6. Cai, Z., Lin, G., Xue, G.: Improved approximation algorithms for the capacitated multicast routing problem. In: Proceedings of the 11th International Computing and Combinatorics Conference (COCOON 2005) (2005)
7. Du, Q., Zhang, X.: Statistical QoS provisionings for wireless unicast/multicast of multi-layer video streams. IEEE J. Sel. Areas Commun. **28**(3), 420–433 (2010)
8. Zheng, X., Li, J., Gao, H., Cai, Z.: Capacity of wireless networks with multiple types of multicast sessions. In: The 15th ACM International Symposium on Mobile Ad Hoc Networking and Computing (MOBIHOC 2014) (2014)
9. Cai, Z., Chen, Z., Lin, G.: A 3.4713-approximation algorithm for the capacitated multicast tree routing problem. Theor. Comput. Sci. **410**(52), 5415–5424 (2009)
10. Cai, Z., Goebel, R., Lin, G.: Size-constrained tree partitioning: approximating the multicast k-tree routing problem. Theor. Comput. Sci. **412**(3), 240–245 (2011)
11. Su, Z., Xu, Q., Hui, Y., Wen, M., Guo, S.: A game theoretic approach to parked vehicle assisted content delivery in vehicular ad hoc networks. IEEE Trans. Veh. Technol. doi:10.1109/TVT.2016.2630300
12. MacKay, D.J.C.: Fountain codes. IEEE Proc. Commun. **152**(6), 1062–1068 (2005)
13. Liu, X., Lim, T.J.: Fountain codes over fading relay channels. IEEE Trans. Wireless Commun. **8**(6), 3278–3287 (2009)
14. Niu, H., Iwai, M., Sezaki, K., et al.: Exploiting fountain codes for secure wireless delivery. IEEE Commun. Lett. **18**(5), 777–780 (2014)
15. Sun, L., Ren, P., Du, Q., Wang, Y.: Fountain-coding aided strategy for secure cooperative transmission in industrial wireless sensor networks. IEEE Trans. Ind. Inform. **12**(1), 291–300 (2016)

16. Du, Q., Sun, L., Song, H., Ren, P.: Security enhancement for wireless multimedia communications by fountain code. IEEE COMSOC MMTC E-Lett. **11**(2), 47–51 (2016)
17. Byers, J.W., Luby, M., Mitzenmacher, M.: A digital fountain approach to asynchronous reliable multicast. IEEE J. Sel. Areas Commun. **20**(8), 1528–1540 (2002)
18. Luby, M.: LT codes. In: Proceedings of the IEEE 43rd Annual Symposium on Foundation of Computer Science, pp. 271–280, November 2002
19. Liu, Q., Zhou, S., Giannakis, G.B.: Queuing with adaptive modulation and coding over wireless links: cross-layer analysis and design. IEEE Trans. Wireless Commun. **4**, 1142–1153 (2005)
20. Liu, Q., Zhou, S., Giannakis, G.B.: Cross-layer combining of adaptive modulation and coding with truncated ARQ over wireless links. IEEE Trans. Wireless Commun. **2**(5), 1746–1775 (2004)

Accurate Indoor Localization with Multiple Feature Fusion

Yalong Xiao[1], Jianxin Wang[2], Shigeng Zhang[2(✉)], Haodong Wang[2,3],
and Jiannong Cao[4]

[1] College of Literature and Journalism, Central South University, Changsha, China
ylxiao@mail.csu.edu.cn
[2] School of Information Science and Engineering, Central South University,
Changsha, China
{jxwang,sgzhang}@mail.csu.edu.cn, hwang@eecs.csuohio.edu
[3] Department of Electrical Engineering and Computer Science,
Cleveland State University, Cleveland, USA
[4] Department of Computing, The Hong Kong Polytechnic University,
Hung Hom, Kowloon, Hong Kong
csjcao@comp.polyu.edu.hk

Abstract. In recent years, many fingerprint-based localization
approaches have been proposed, in which different features (e.g., received
signal strength (RSS) and channel state information (CSI)) were used as
the fingerprints to distinguish different positions. Although CSI-based
approaches usually achieve higher accuracy than RSSI-based approaches,
we find that the localization results of different approaches usually compensate with each other, and by fusing different features we can get
more accurate localization results than using only single feature. In this
paper, we propose a localization method that fusing different features by
combining results of different localization approaches to achieve higher
accuracy. We first select three most possible candidate positions from
all the candidate positions generated by different approaches according
to a newly defined metric called confidence degree, and then use the
weighted average of them as the position estimation. When there are
more than three candidate positions, we use a minimal-triangle principle
to break the tie and select three out of them. Our experiments show that
the proposed approach achieves median error of 0.5 m and 1.1 m respectively in two typical indoor environments, significantly better than that
of approaches using only single feature.

Keywords: Indoor localization · Channel state information · Multiple
features

1 Introduction

With the rapid development of information technology and widespread popularity of mobile intelligent terminals, location-based services (LBSs) have been

© Springer International Publishing AG 2017
L. Ma et al. (Eds.): WASA 2017, LNCS 10251, pp. 522–533, 2017.
DOI: 10.1007/978-3-319-60033-8_45

widely used in many fields including travel guidance, mobile advertising, and urban computing. Many LBSs require to know the positions of target objects in indoor environments. However, the widely used Global Positioning System (GPS) suffers from severe degradation in localization accuracy and reliability in indoor environments because of the occlusion and complex electromagnetic interferences. Therefore, the research and implementation of indoor positioning systems that can provide real-time and high-precision localization services has attracted many research attentions in recent years [1,2].

Because of the pervasive penetration of wireless local area networks (WLANs) and Wi-Fi enabled mobile terminals, the fingerprint based indoor positioning technology [3] has attracted many research attentions in both academic and industry communities. Most existing works utilize received signal strength (RSS) [4,5] or channel state information (CSI) [5,6] as the fingerprint of a particular position. Unlike RSS that is an aggregated value of the all subcarriers' amplitudes, CSI estimates the channel on each subcarrier in the frequency domain. Thus it can depict the multipath propagation to some extent and provide more stable and fine-grained signature in differentiating different positions [7].

Although the overall positioning performance of the CSI-based method is usually better than that of RSS-based approaches [6,8], we find that it is not the case that for every position CSI-based approaches generate more accurate results than RSS-based approaches. We perform a preliminary experiment to show this. We conduct the RSS and CSI measurements in a typical computer lab as shown in Fig. 2(a). For the testing spot located at (2.5, 3.5), we feed our measurements to Horus [9] and FIFS [6] scheme. The corresponding localization errors are 0.63 m and 1.52 m, respectively. Obviously, the result suggests that, it is Horus (an RSS-based approach) rather than FIFS (a CSI-based approach) generates more accurate position estimation for the testing spot.

The above observation inspired us to design new localization algorithms to achieve higher localization accuracy by fusing different features. In particular, we combine the results of Horus [9], FIFS [6] and D-CSI [10], which use different features as fingerprints of positions, to achieve higher accuracy than using each single feature. D-CSI [10] is a new positioning approach which uses the distribution of CSI amplitude as location fingerprints. It achieves higher accuracy than FIFS because it uses distribution of CSI amplitude as position fingerprints, which contains both spacial-diversity and frequency-diversity of the signal, while FIFS only simply adds up all the subcarriers' amplitudes and uses it as position fingerprints.

In this paper, we propose a hybrid method with multiple feature fusion(MFF) to counteract the positioning error of single feature based approaches. Firstly, we get a set of reference points called alternative reference points by running Horus, FIFS, and D-CSI, respectively. These approaches uses three different features as position fingerprints, namely RSS, He, and Hp. Secondly, we select three most possible candidate positions from the generated reference points of the three approaches. When there are more than three reference points, we use a minimal-triangle principle to select three out of them. Finally, we calculate a weighted centroid of the three reference points and take it as the target location. Experiments show that the proposed localization approach achieves median error of 0.5 m and 1.1 m in two typical indoor environments, significantly less than that of the best single-feature based approach whose corresponding error is 0.7 m and 1.3 m, respectively.

The rest of this paper is organized as follows. Section 2 reviews related work. In Sect. 3 the proposed method is described in detail with analysis. The simulation results are given and discussed in Sect. 4. Finally, Sect. 5 concludes this paper.

2   Related Work

Indoor localization has attracted a growing research attention and various techniques have been proposed, including Wi-Fi [4,9,11], Bluetooth [12], radio-frequency identification(RFID) [13], FM radio [14], acoustic signals [15], magnetic field [16], UWB [17] and light [18]. Among these signals, the use of Wi-Fi signal has attracted continuous attention due to the pervasive deployment of WLANs and Wi-Fi enabled mobile devices. Many efforts have been done to improve accuracy of WLAN based localization approaches.

The indoor localization system RADAR [4] is a pioneer work in WLAN fingerprinting, which used the K-nearest neighbor method to get the location of a person and achieved a median error of about 5 m. Horus [9] used a maximum likelihood based approach to infer the target position and achieves higher accuracy than RADAR. Besides these two typical RSS-based fingerprint location approaches, there are many improvements over them. More RSS-based indoor localization approaches can be found in the literature review [1].

The signals of WLAN based localization contain RSSI and CSI. Compared to using RSSI as fingerprints, channel state information is considered as a finer grained signature to improve the localization accuracy. Xiao et al. [6] proposed an FIFS system that uses the aggregated CSI amplitude values over all the sub-carriers and leverages the spatial diversity to improve the performance of the RSS-based method. The location fingerprint, which is aggregated over the all sub-carriers, is a coarse metric and may not effectively distinguish the locations. Sen et al. [19] proposed a PinLoc system that utilizes the per-subcarrier frequency response as the features of a location, and relies on the machine learning algorithms to classify a device measurement to one of the trained locations. It leverages the frequency diversity, but does not consider the spatial diversity. Wang et al. [20] presented DeepFi which is a deep learning based indoor fingerprinting scheme using CSI information. Although these techniques achieve a high localization precision, they require intensive computations and more training samples to localize the mobile users via machine learning or deep learning.

3   Algorithm Description

The CSI-based approaches usually achieve higher accuracy than the RSS-based approaches, but we find that the former may have lower accuracy than the latter in some positions. Therefore, the localization accuracy can be improved by integrating the methods that are based on different physical measurement.

3.1 Algorithm Framework

There are two phases in fingerprint-based positioning system: the training phase and the positioning phase. Figure 1 shows the framework of the proposed multiple feature fusion (MFF) algorithm. In the training phase, we acquire physical measurements of wireless signals for calibration points, including both RSS and CSI. Then the features of He [6] and Hp [10] are extracted from the CSIs, together with the RSS as the location feature. Finally, we use the position information and the location feature of the calibration points to construct the fingerprint databases of RSS, He and Hp, respectively.

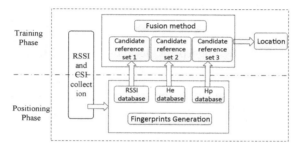

Fig. 1. System architecture

In the positioning phase, RSS and CSI values are firstly collected at an unknown location. They are sent to the positioning engine and processed using the method as in the training phase to extract the fingerprint. For each fingerprint feature, MFF finds three candidate reference points whose fingerprints are mostly close to the fingerprint of the unknown position. Specifically, we feed out the RSS, He and Hp to Horus, FIFS and D-CSI, respectively, to calculate the candidate position set for each approach. Three most possible candidate points are then selected from these positions according to a newly defined metric called confidence degree. Finally, the weighted centroid of the three selected candidate points are calculated and used as the position estimation.

3.2 Algorithm Details

The framework of MFF is given in Algorithm 5. Assume that there are N APs and M reference points in the region. The positions of the reference points are denoted as $L = \{L_1, L_2, \cdots, L_M\}$. The algorithm contains 4 steps and the detailed operations in each step will be described as follows.

Step 1: Establish the RSSI, He and Hp fingerprint database

Given the coordinates of the reference points and corresponding RSS and CSI values, we build the RSS, He and Hp fingerprint database. Taking RSS as an

---

Algorithm 1. The algorithm of MFF

Input: The RSS and CSI values of the test point. The coordinates, RSS and CSI values of the calibration points.

Output: The coordinates of the test point

1: According to the coordinate, RSS and CSI values of the calibration points to build RSS, He and Hp fingerprint database //Step 1
2: According to RSS and CSI values collected at the test point and the fingerprint databases built in step 1, using the Euclidean distance or KL distance as the similarity metric, calculate candidate calibration point set under the various features of the fingerprint. //Step 2
3: Merge the candidate reference points and calculate the degree of each candidate calibration point.//Step 3
4: Depending on the size of each calibration point degree obtained in step 3, optimize the final location of the test point.//Step 4
5: **return** The coordinates of the test point

---

example, the process of the fingerprint database construction is as the follows. We denote the RSS vector of the M reference points as $F\_RSS = [F\_RSS_1, F\_RSS_2, \cdots, F\_RSS_M]$. The RSS vector of the ith reference point is $F\_RSS_i = [RSS_1^i, RSS_2^i, \cdots, RSS_N^i]$, where RSS_N^i represents the RSS of the ith reference point from the Nth AP. Then, F_RSS and L constitute the RSS fingerprint database.

Step 2: Calculating of candidate reference points

We denote $T\_RSSI = [RSS_1, RSS_2, \cdots, RSS_N]$ to be the RSS obtained by the mobile device at an unknown location. Then the distance between the point and the reference point is $D_i = sqrt(\sum_{j=1}^{N} |RSS_j - RSS_j^i|^2)$, where $i=1,2,\cdots,M$. A smaller D_i represents a shorter distance between the unknown position and the reference point. We sort D_i in the ascending order and select the first three reference points as the candidate positions for RSS, denoted by $Node\_RSS = [n\_RSS_1, n\_RSS_2, n\_RSS_3]$. In the same way, we can get the candidate reference points for He and Hp and denote the corresponding point se as $Node\_he$ and $Node\_hp$, respectively.

Step 3: Result fusion

We put all points in $Node\_RSSI$, $Node\_he$ and $Node\_hp$ into a position set called $Node\_all$ and calculate the degree of each candidate point as follows. For each candidate point, we draw a circle with radius R (whose optimal value will be determined in the Sect. 4) and count the number of reference points in $Node\_all$ that fall in the circle. The number is defined as the confidence degree of that candidate point. When calculating the degree, if the reference point is at the area boundary, its degree is increased by 0.5 to compensate for the boundary effect. After calculating degree for all points in $Node\_all$, we sort them in descending order according to their degree, and denote the sorted set as $sort\_D$.

Step 4: Position calculation

The final position calculation and optimization is shown in Algorithm 2.

Algorithm 2. Optimization of the final location of the test point.

Input: $Node\_all$, $sort\_D$, R, $offset$
Output: The coordinates of the target point
1: **if** the number of reference points with degree $sort\_D(1)$ is one **then**
2:     **if** the number of reference points with degree $sort\_D(2)$ is greater than 2 **then**
3:         Finding all reference points of degree $sort\_D(2)$. A candidate set consists of any two of the reference points of degree $sort\_D(2)$ and one reference point of degree $sort\_D(1)$.
4:     **else**
5:         Selecting the reference points with degrees $sort\_D(1)$, $sort\_D(2)$ and $sort\_D(3)$ as candidate sets.
6: **else**
7:     **if** The number of reference points with degree $sort\_D(1)$ is two **then**
8:         Finding all reference points with degrees $sort\_D(2)$. A candidate set consists of any one of the reference points of degree $sort\_D(2)$ and two reference points of degree $sort\_D(1)$.
9:     **else**
10:         The $R + offset$ will be used as the radius and recalculate the degree of each reference point according to the procedure in step 3, then repeat the operation of steps 1 to 7.
11:         **if** The number of reference points of degree $sort\_D(1)$ is greater than two **then**
12:             Find all the reference points of $sort\_D(1)$, triple three combinations as the candidate sets.
13: According to all the candidate sets, calculate the perimeter of the triangle enclosed by the reference point in the set, select the set of reference points with the shortest perimeter, and find the center of the triangle as the coordinate of the point to be measured.
14: **return** result

3.3 Algorithm Analysis

Assume that the reference points are evenly distributed in a grid pattern with grid space a. When R is less than a, the degree of each reference point will be zero because no other reference point will fall within the circle. When $a \leq R < \sqrt{2}a$, the candidate reference point adjacent to the reference point will fall into the circle. When $\sqrt{2}a \leq R < 2a$, the candidate reference point that is either adjacent to the reference point or diagonally opposite the rectangle will fall into the circle. Therefore, based on the above analysis, in the next section of performance analysis, we compare the positioning error of the MFF under the different R.

In Algorithm 2, another parameter $offset$ is set for the following reasons. When there are more than 3 reference points with the same degree, they cannot be distinguished to be used as the one of candidates reference set. It is necessary to increase the length of the radius, filter out those reference points with no further increase, and then select the reference point set which is close to the point to be measured. Combining the above analysis of R, $offset$ sets the following principles. When $a \leq R < \sqrt{2}a$, $offset$ should be set $\sqrt{2}a \leq R+offset<2a$; when $\sqrt{2}a \leq R<2a$, $offset$ should be set $2a \leq R+offset<\sqrt{5}a$; when $2a \leq R<\sqrt{5}a$, $offset$ should be set $\sqrt{5}a \leq R+offset<3a$.

The algorithm proposed in this chapter can improve the positioning accuracy, mainly for the following two reasons. One is the set of reference points is under three fingerprint features. As a single feature has limitations in positioning, a set of reference points obtained by merging multiple features can make up for its shortcomings. The second is to use a moderate reference point set. The higher the degree of the reference point is, the closer it is to the test point.

4   Experiment Results

For the method proposed in this paper, we have collected the signal value of the corresponding locations. This section first introduces the experimental set up and the data acquisition process. Then we compare the performance of the fusion location algorithm with different radius R, as well as the performance of the location method with the single feature fingerprint.

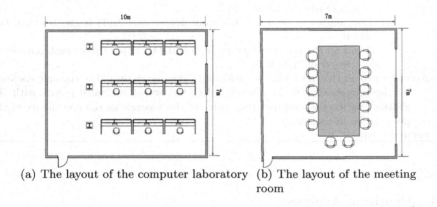

(a) The layout of the computer laboratory (b) The layout of the meeting room

Fig. 2. The layout of two environments

4.1   Experiment Scenarios

In our experiment, the training spots are evenly distributed in the entire room and the test spots are randomly chosen. TL-WR742N routers work as the transmitters, while a Dell E6410 equipped with an Intel Wi-Fi Link 5300 NIC is used as the mobile device. We also modify the driver as in [6] to collect the raw CSI values. We evaluate the system in two typical indoor environments: a computer laboratory and a meeting room.

(1) Computer laboratory

The floor plan of the computer laboratory is shown in Fig. 2(a). Four APs are deployed at the four corners. In the training phase, the RSSI and the CSI values are collected at 42 locations with 1.2 m spacing for constructing the fingerprint database. During the test, we randomly select 30 locations as the test positions. At each spot, we collect the raw CSI values of 60 packets. We collect 20 RSSI samples at each position and select the RSSI that appears the most times as the fingerprint of the corresponding location.

(2) Meeting room

The floor plan of the meeting room is shown in Fig. 2(b) and the four APs are also placed on the four corners. We collect 49 different calibration positions which are 1 m apart in this scenario. 10 test locations are randomly selected. At each location, we also collect the RSSI and the CSI data of 60 packets. We also collect 20 RSSI samples at each position and select the RSSI that appears the most times as the fingerprint of the corresponding position.

4.2 Optimal Radius

We first consider the influence of system parameter R. R is a system parameter which is used in calculating each candidate reference point degree. The setting of R has a great influence on the size of the reference point degree, and affects the selection of the reference point, which determines the positioning performance. Through the experiments, we determine the R that makes the positioning performance of the fusion localization algorithm the best.

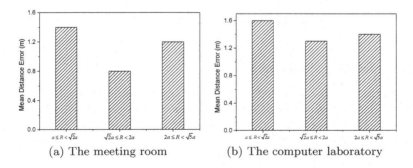

(a) The meeting room   (b) The computer laboratory

Fig. 3. The mean distance error of MFF under the different indoor environments

Figure 3 shows the mean distance error of the fusion localization method along with R in the two experimental scenarios. When $a \leq R < \sqrt{2}a$, the positioning error can reach the minimum. When R is too large, the reference points that should not be selected may be used to determine the test spot. In extreme cases, when R is the length of the entire region boundary, all reference points will be three for a group to be the candidate reference point sets of the test spot, so it can not make full use of the feature that filter the points by calculating the size of degree, thus affecting the positioning accuracy.

In addition, when R is too small, it will make the degree of the reference points with no difference, so it cannot distinguish which reference point should be selected for calculating the position of the test spot. In the extreme case, as R is too large, it can not make full use of the feature that filter the reference points by the confidence degree, thus affecting the positioning accuracy. So R is too large or too small, the positioning effect will have a negative impact.

Figure 4 shows the cumulative distribution functions of errors under the different R. As shown in the figure, when $\sqrt{2}a \leq R < 2a$, the positioning errors of more than 80% test points are less than 1.2 m, but when $2a \leq R < \sqrt{5}a$ and $a \leq R < \sqrt{2}a$, in the case of having the same number of test points, the positioning errors range is expanded to 1.5 m and 2 m. The same trend is seen in Fig. 4(b). Based on our results in two experimental scenarios, MFF can achieve better positioning performance when R is set to $\sqrt{2}a \leq R < 2a$.

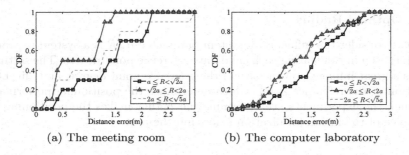

(a) The meeting room   (b) The computer laboratory

Fig. 4. The CDF of MFF under the different R

4.3   Localization Performance

In this section, we conduct the performance comparison between MFF and the existed works that used a single feature, such as Horus, FIFS and D-CSI. We consider the radius varying from $\sqrt{2}a$ to $2a$. We give the mean distance error and the cumulative distribution function of localization error of the four localization schemes in two representative scenarios.

(1) Mean distance error

Figure 5 gives the mean distance error obtained by the proposed algorithm MFF, Horus, FIFS and D-CSI. As shown in the figure, in the meeting room, MFF achieves the median accuracy of 0.8 m, which outperforms D-CSI, FIFS, and Horus by more than 0.1 m, 0.5 m and 0.7 m, and the gain is about 11%, 38%, 47%, respectively. Moreover, in the computer laboratory scenario, where there exists

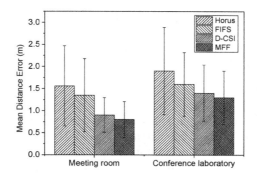

Fig. 5. Mean distance error

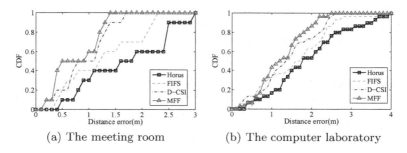

(a) The meeting room   (b) The computer laboratory

Fig. 6. The CDF of MFF under the different indoor environments

abundant multipath, the mean accuracy of our approach is 1.3 m, which is about 7%, 18.5% and 31% gain than D-CSI, FIFS and Horus, respectively.

In addition, the standard deviation of the localization error of each method is given in Fig. 5. From the two experimental scenarios, we find that Horus has the largest standard deviation, which shows that there is a big error difference among the test spots. MFF has the minimum standard deviation. This shows that the difference of the localization error becomes smaller and more stable after fusing the RSSI, He and Hp features. Therefore, MFF is suitable for applications that require the smaller jitter of localization results.

(2) The cumulative distribution function of localization error

Figure 6 plots the CDFs of the localization errors in the meeting room and the computer laboratory, respectively. As shown in Fig. 6(a), for over 80% of the test spots, the errors of MFF are less than 1.1 m. However, D-CSI, FIFS and Horus has the localization errors of 1.2 m, 2.1 m and 2.4 m under the same experimental conditions. All of the MFF test spots have an error under 1.3 m, while only about 85%, 60% and 40% of the D-CSI, FIFS and Horus test spots have the same localization accuracy.

As shown in Fig. 6(b), in this more complex wireless signal environment, our scheme and D-CSI have a distance error of 1.4 m for 50% of the test spots.

Meanwhile, the median error of FIFS and Horus is 1.6 m. However, for over 80% of the test spots, the error of MFF is 0.5 m lower than D-CSI, the error of FIFS is 0.3 m lower than Horus.

5 Conclusion

This paper proposes a multiple feature based indoor localization scheme that uses RSSI and CSI information extracted from the commercial off-the-shelf Wi-Fi NICs. Firstly, we get the summation of the received signals(He) and the distribution of the subcarriers(Hp) from the CSI value. Then, a set of candidate reference points is obtained using the localization method of each fingerprint feature. Finally, according to the degree of each reference and the principle of triangle minimization, we find the best three reference points and take the centroid as the target location. The proposed method is evaluated in two typical indoor environments and is compared with the existing work. The results show that our scheme achieves the better performance under the different scenarios.

Acknowledgment. This work is partially supported by the National Natural Science Foundation of China under Grant Nos. 61402056 and 61402541, the Hunan Provincial Natural Science Foundation of China under Grant No. 2017JJ3413, the NSFC/RGC Joint research Scheme under Grant No. N_PolyU519/12, ANR/RGC Joint Research Scheme under Grant No. A-PolyU505/12, and the CERNET Innovation Project under Grant No. NGII20160309.

References

1. He, S., Gary Chan, S.-H.: Wi-Fi fingerprint-based indoor positioning: recent advances and comparisons. IEEE Commun. Surv. Tutor. **18**(1), 466–490 (2015)
2. Zhang, S., Liu, X., Wang, J., Cao, J., Min, G.: Accurate range-free localization for anisotropic wireless sensor networks. ACM Trans. Sens. Netw. (TOSN) **11**(3), 51 (2015)
3. Gentile, C., Alsindi, N., Raulefs, R., Teolis, C.: Geolocation Techniques: Principles and Applications. Springer Science & Business Media, New York (2012)
4. Bahl, P., Padmanabhan, V.N.: RADAR: an in-building RF-based user location and tracking system. In: Proceedings of the 19th Annual Joint Conference of IEEE Computer and Communications Societies (INFOCOM), Tel Aviv, Israel, pp. 775–784, (2000)
5. Yang, Z., Zhou, Z., Liu, Y.: From RSSI to CSI: indoor localization via channel response. ACM Comput. Surv. **46**(2), 25 (2013)
6. Xiao, J., Wu, K., Yi, Y., Ni, L.M.: FIFS: fine-grained indoor fingerprinting system. In: Proceedings of the 21st International Conference on Computer Communication and Networks (ICCCN), Munich, Germany, pp. 1–7 (2012)
7. Wen, Y., Tian, X., Wang, X., Lu, S.: Fundamental limits of RSS fingerprinting based indoor localization. In: Proceedings of the 34th Annual Joint Conference of IEEE Computer and Communications Societies (Infocom), Hong Kong, China, pp. 2479–2487 (2015)

8. Wu, K., Xiao, J., Yi, Y., Chen, D., Luo, X., Ni, L.M.: CSI-based indoor localization. IEEE Trans. Parallel Distrib. Syst. **24**(7), 1300–1309 (2013)
9. Youssef, M., Agrawala, A.: The horus WLAN location determination system. In: Proceedings of the 3rd International Conference on Mobile Systems, Applications, and Services (Mobisys), Seattle, USA, pp. 205–218 (2003)
10. Xiao, Y., Wang, J., Zhang, S., Wang, H., Cao, J.: Exploiting distribution of channel state information for accurate wireless indoor localization. Technical report, School of Information Science and Engineering, Central South University, China. (2016)
11. Alsindi, N., Chaloupka, Z., AlKhanbashi, N., Aweya, J.: An empirical evaluation of a probabilistic rf signature for wlan location fingerprinting. IEEE Trans. Wirel. Commun. **13**(6), 3257–3268 (2014)
12. Zhao, X., Xiao, Z., Markham, A., Trigoni, N., Ren, Y.: Does BTLE measure up against WiFi? A comparison of indoor location performance. In: Proceedings of the 20th European Wireless Conference (EW), Barcelona, Spain, pp. 1–6 (2014)
13. Yang, L., Chen, Y., Li, X.-Y., Xiao, C., Li, M., Liu, Y.: Tagoram: real-time tracking of mobile RFID tags to high precision using COTS devices. In: Proceedings of the 20th Annual International Conference on Mobile Computing and Networking (MobiCom), Maui, USA, pp. 237–248 (2014)
14. Yoon, S., Lee, K., Rhee, I.: FM-based indoor localization via automatic fingerprint DB construction and matching. In: Proceeding of the 11th Annual International Conference on Mobile Systems. Applications, and Services (MobiSys), Taipei, Taiwan, pp. 207–220 (2013)
15. Huang, W., Xiong, Y., Li, X.-Y., Lin, H., Mao, X., Yang, P., Liu, Y.: Shake and walk: acoustic direction finding and fine-grained indoor localization using smartphones. In: Proceedings of the 33rd Annual Joint Conference of IEEE Computer and Communications Societies (INFOCOM), Toronto, Canada, pp. 370–378 (2014)
16. Xie, H., Gu, T., Tao, X., Ye, H., Lv, J.: MaLoc: a practical magnetic fingerprinting approach to indoor localization using smartphones. In: Proceedings of the ACM International Joint Conference on Pervasive and Ubiquitous Computing (UbiComp), Seattle, USA, pp. 243–253 (2014)
17. Taponecco, L., D'Amico, A.A., Mengali, U.: Joint TOA and AOA estimation for UWB localization applications. IEEE Trans. Wirel. Commun. **10**(7), 2207–2217 (2011)
18. Yang, Z., Wang, Z., Zhang, J., Huang, C., Zhang, Q.: Wearables can afford: light-weight indoor positioning with visible light. In: Proceedings of the 13th Annual International Conference on Mobile Systems, Applications, and Services (MobiSys), Florence Italy, pp. 317–330 (2015)
19. Sen, S., Radunovic, B., Choudhury, R.R., Minka, T.: You are facing the Mona Lisa: spot localization using PHY layer information. In: Proceedings of the 10th Annual International Conference on Mobile Systems, Applications, and Services (Mobisys), Low Wood Bay, United Kingdom, pp. 183–196 (2012)
20. Wang, X., Gao, L., Mao, S., Pandey, S.: CSI-based fingerprinting for indoor localization: a deep learning approach. IEEE Trans. Veh. Technol. **66**(1), 763–776 (2017)

A Power-Efficient Scheme for Outdoor Localization

Kang Yao[1], Hongwei Du[1], Qiang Ye[2(✉)], and Wen Xu[3]

[1] Shenzhen Key Laboratory of Internet Information Collaboration,
Department of Computer Science and Technology,
Harbin Institute of Technology Shenzhen Graduate School, Shenzhen, China
finderyao@gmail.com, hongwei.du@ieee.org
[2] School of Mathematical and Computational Sciences,
University of Prince Edward Island, Charlottetown, Canada
qye@upei.ca
[3] Department of Mathematics and Computer Science,
Texas Woman's University, Denton, USA
wxu1@twu.edu

Abstract. With the extensive use of smart phones, location-based services are becoming prevalent. Global Positioning System (GPS) is a widely-adopted localization method. However, it drains the battery of smart phones quickly and it is vulnerable to weak GPS signals. GSM-based localization is more robust, but it only leads to low localization precision, which cannot meet the requirements of many location-based services. With the pervasive deployment of WiFi, WiFi-based localization has become a promising indoor localization method. Nevertheless, simply applying indoor localization methods to outdoor metropolitan environments does not work well. In this paper, we present a hybrid outdoor localization scheme, which leverages WiFi signals and the built-in sensors in smart phones to achieve high localization precision and low power consumption. Our experimental results show that the proposed hybrid scheme outperforms the widely-adopted GPS method in terms of localization precision and power consumption.

Keywords: Outdoor localization · Power efficiency · Fingerprinting

1 Introduction

Location-based service has become increasingly important in our daily life. The Global Position System (GPS) [1] has been the de facto localization method for outdoor environments. However, GPS is vulnerable to the lack of line of sight to satellites. In addition, it drains power supply quickly. A variety of different localization schemes have been proposed to tackle these problems. Here are a few example systems: cellular-based systems [2,10], infrared-based systems [3], ultrasonic-based systems [4] and radio frequency (RF) based systems [5–7].

© Springer International Publishing AG 2017
L. Ma et al. (Eds.): WASA 2017, LNCS 10251, pp. 534–545, 2017.
DOI: 10.1007/978-3-319-60033-8_46

Among these schemes, RF-based systems (e.g. WiFi fingerprinting localization) that use wireless data network (e.g. 802.11 [11]) to estimate user location have gained much attention, especially in the domain of indoor applications. Compared with other localization methods, WiFi fingerprinting localization does not require extra hardware and is easy to be deployed. Devices such as smart phones can easily collect RSSI information of WiFi access points, which is critical to localizing moving objects. Technically, this approach treats fingerprints as patterns instead of estimating positions with signal-strength-based distances. By matching a detected fingerprint obtained on the go to the fingerprints stored in an offline database that is constructed during the training stage, the location corresponding to the fingerprint that leads to the minimum difference is selected as the estimated position.

In this paper, we present an efficient hybrid outdoor localization scheme utilizing WiFi fingerprinting, sensor information and even GPS statistics. Our goal is to provide a power-efficient localization system whose accuracy is not worse than GPS. Specifically, an offline fingerprint database is first constructed through crowdsourcing [9]. To reduce the computational cost of the matching phase, we proposed the map tile mechanism, which helps determine constrained matching space with sensor readings. Technically, instead of simply fusing sensor data and WiFi fingerprint with some kind of fusion algorithm, our method integrates motion information into fingerprint database and takes it into account while the matching operation is executed. Then, only the fingeprints in constrained area are involved in the matching stage, resulting in a more accurate location at a low computational cost. In addition, in the process of matching, our method considers not only the WiFi status, but also the GPS statistics recorded during the crowdsourcing training phase. Our experimental results show that the proposed hybrid method outperforms GPS in terms of accuracy and power efficiency in the areas with densely-constructed buildings.

The major contributions of our research can be summrized as follows:

1. We make use of sensor readings to confine matching space in map tiles. That is, only the fingerprint data in a specific area constrained by sensor information will participate in localization calculation. And a caching mechanism is adopted on the client side, avoiding frequent localization requests.
2. Not only WiFi signal status but also GPS health information is recorded in crowdsourced fingerprint data. We take these statistics into consideration and use them as an influence factor while calculating final estimation, mitigating large outliers consequently.
3. A prototype system is implemented and several experiments are conducted in real-life environments using off-the-shelf devices. The experimental results indicate that our method is feasible and efficient.

The rest of this paper is organized as follows. In Sect. 2, we have a brief overview of previous research work. Section 3 presents our preliminary measurements and observations. Section 4 describes the details of our hybrid method, followed with the experiments and performance evaluation in Sect. 5. Finally, Sect. 6 concludes the paper.

2   Related Work

Localization methods without GPS has been active for many years since wireless sensor networks (WSN). They are mainly divided into two categories: range-based method and range-free method. Here, we provide a brief overview of them.

2.1   Range-Based Method

In general, range-based methods rely on related distance, which can be obtained through measuring methods like ToF/ToA [18], TDoA [19] or propagation model generated from RSSI value [20]. [12–15] build optimal models based on physical distances to solve localization problems. Since these methods are highly dependent on surrounding environment, they are prone to errors induced by obstacles. Other distance measuring technique like dead reckoning could assist user tracking, but produces accumulative errors over time.

2.2   Range-Free Method

Fingerprint localization is the most commonly used range-free method, especially in the area of indoor localization. Classical fingerprint methods in outdoor localization include visual fingerprint-based localization, motion fingerprint-based systems and signal fingerprint-based ones.

Visual Fingerprint-Based Localization. Image-processing techniques equipped in smartphones make it possible to get user location through image matching. Google Goggles is a typical application that can identify specific landmarks in images. [23] provide corresponding visual-based localization systems. However, challenges of matching speed in content-based image retrieval (CBIR) exist and camera operations cost too much battery energy of smartphones. Besides, visual-based localization method is coarse-grained in the regard of positioning accuracy.

Motion Fingerprint-Based Localization. Motion fingerprint-based localization usually detect user's motion data to get location. User movement data is collected from built-in sensors such as gyroscope and accelerometer. CompAcc [24] figures out user's moving pattern or trail to match with pre-generated motion signatures. Due to the noise produced by sensors, errors accumulate with time going on.

Signal Fingerprint-Based Localization. The extensively deployed WiFi infrastructure contributes to signal-based fingerprint method, especially in the area of indoor localization. Some outdoor applications include [21,22]. WiFi fingerprinting localization method generally consists of two phases: offline training phase and online fingerprint matching phase. During the training phase, correlations between fix locations and Received Signal Strength (RSS) patterns from various Access Points (APs) are constructed to form a fingerprint database. In the matching phase, to locate the device, matching algorithm searches database for a fingerprint with minimum difference, in which the labeled location is the estimated as user location. In fact, fingerprints can be expressed in two forms: deterministic form (e.g., Radar [5]) and probabilistic form (e.g., Horus [8]). The deterministic form means calculating pattern difference based on Euclidean distance. As for probabilistic type, it can perfectly store the state about signal strength distribution at a fix location. But in mobile localization environment, probabilistic method needs to take more time to collect enough samples to fit the signals fluctuating state, thus generating time delay. In the view of effect, signal-based fingerprint localization has the potential to obtain fine-grained results. Nevertheless, owing to the heavy training work and the complexity of outdoor environment, it is not realistic to migrate this method from indoor scenarios to outdoor environment directly.

3   Preliminary

In this section, we investigate several characteristics in traditional outdoor localization method including GPS and typical WiFi signal fingerprinting algorithms based on real experiments. It is demonstrated that some crucial problems, which have exist extensively to be dealt with, definitely affect the accuracy or energy cost in outdoor localization.

3.1   Problem Statement

Denote a fingerprint as $f = [r_i, i = 1, \cdots, n]$, in which r_i represents the RSS value of the AP $A_i \in A$, the access points set of n APs appearing in f. For two fingerprints f and f', the dissimilarity can be calculated based on RSS difference $\sigma_i = |r_i - r'_i|$ at each A_i. Since two fingerprints may not contain absolutely identical set of APs. For APs appearing in fingerprint f, if it is not included in f', we set the missing value as -100. Then the dissimilarity between f and f' is calculated as

$$\eta(f, f') = \sqrt{\sum_{i=1}^{p} \sigma_i^2} \tag{1}$$

where $p = |A \cup A'|$.

By comparing the query fingerprint f with all samples stored in the fingerprint database $\mathcal{F}$, the sample with minimum dissimilarity can be found.

$$f^* = \arg\min_{f_i \in \mathcal{F}} \eta(f, f_i) \tag{2}$$

Then the corresponding location $L(f^*)$ of f^* is considered as user location. And $\epsilon = \|L(f) - L(f^*)\|$ is used to denote locating errors. However, in our issue, the question is more complicated, some modified work has to be done based on the following observations.

3.2 Observations

High Power Consumption. Typical outdoor localization method like GPS is an energy-hungry technology that consumes too much battery resource. And frequent network requests is another main cause among factors. For GPS, electric energy has to be provided continuously to serve the GPS antenna, which is working on searching satellites and communicating with them at a slow data transfering speed. As for frequent network requests, it happens in the process of swapping data between user clients and servers. In a nutshell, the above two reasons lead to high battery energy cost.

Locating Outliers. In GPS localization, the performance of positioning accuracy is highly dependent on environments. GPS signals quality gets worse and generates locating outliers in some interfering areas such as around buildings or in forests. In our preliminary experiments, Fig. 1 shows that GPS positioning outlier happens when device holder is near buildings.

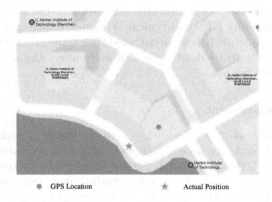

Fig. 1. Locating outlier happens in GPS interfering area.

Computational Cost Caused by Global Mechanism. Few previous research work considers avoiding global matching overhead in fingerprint database, which leads to much computational consumption. Typical matching method means that the algorithm needs to search the whole fingerprint database to get the estimated location. With fingerprinting database growing larger, much computational cost and time delay emerge. Though some previous research like clustering method [8], was proposed to reduce the computational cost. Updated fingerprint changes by crowdsourcing still cause extra computational overhead.

4 Power-Efficient Localization

As illustrated in Fig. 2, the proposed system includes several parts as shown. Roughly speaking, first, in the so-called training phase, fingerprint data containing GPS status and corresponding WiFi signal state is collected through crowdsourcing technique, forming fingerprint database in server-side. Then, pre-processing work like map tile mechanism will be accomplished. In the formal online localization phase, user device calculates dissimilarity between detected signals pattern and the samples in some certain fingerprint map tiles, which is stored in local cache and constrained by sensor information. Finally, the location of fingerprint with minimum distance is estimated as the current location of device. In the following content, we present the details of this scheme.

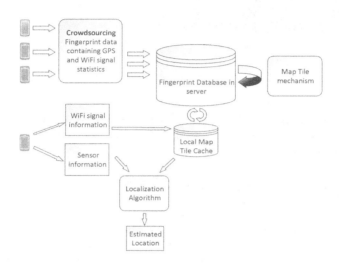

Fig. 2. System architecture

4.1 Map Tiles Cache Mechanism

As discussed in observations, frequent network requests in typical positioning scheme generate high power consumption, and even lead to long response time if network congestion emerges. Though some offline application such as Big Planet Tracks was proposed to tackle this problem. Our cache mechanism based on map tiles makes use of geographic features to divide map into a great many map tiles and maintains a local database cache.

As Fig. 3 shows, this area is partitioned into n map tiles, with each side length of w meters. Uploaded fingerprint data is allocated into different map tiles according to its location (longitude and latitude). In addition, only m map tiles, for example 4 tiles in the above figure, is maintained in local database of user client. When user device senses surrounding WiFi signal information, it is must first guaranteed that user roughly locates in the map tiles in local database through our sensor-assisted method, which is detailed in next section. If this coarse position is absent from local fingerprint database, it means that local data cache is outdated, with prefetching operation following to update cache from server. Assume that the number of positioning requests is r in total,

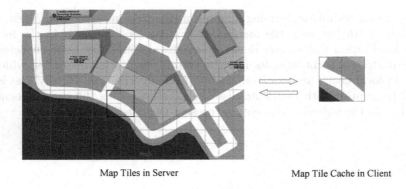

Map Tiles in Server   Map Tile Cache in Client

Fig. 3. Map tile cache mechanism

typical fingerprint mechanism needs r network requests. In our map tile cache mechanism, this number can be reduced to just r/m, achieving the energy-saving and efficient purpose.

4.2   Sensor-Assisted Matching Method

Global matching is consuming and unnecessary if measured query fingerprint consisting of RSS features has to be compare with all fingerprints in database. In this sense, it is necessary to decrease matching space and do matching operation in a small space constrained through sensor information such as direction and travel distance.

As illustrated in Fig. 4, assume that the previous location is P, based on which current location can be calculated. Special to note is that the initial location is obtained by GPS. Distance and direction from the previous location to current position are assumed as l and θ respectively. In fact, the distance l and direction θ can be estimated by dead reckoning method utilizing built-in inertial sensors like accelerometer, gyroscope, and compass. [16] indicates that the accuracy of count steps in dead reckoning can reach 98%. By multiplying with user's step length, the footsteps could then be converted to physical displacement, namely distance l. In addition, the direction θ is obtained using gyroscope and compass, which is detailed in [16]. As a result of noisy sensors and heterogenous devices, distance l and direction θ cannot be 100% accurately calculated. We introduce two variables Δl and $\Delta\theta$ as fault-tolerant range to cope with this problem. With the above variables determined, an annular region $ABCD$ in which current position locates forms. Before working out estimated current location, we must figure out which crowdsourcing fingerprint points in local cache are locating in this constrained area. Here, we offer a solution based on Haversine formula [17].

Given the start point longitude and latitude (φ, λ), distance d and bearing θ from the start point, we can calculate the destination point (φ', λ') through the following formula

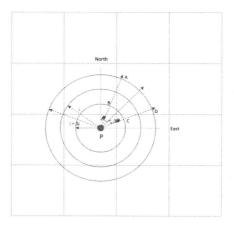

Fig. 4. Sensor-assisted matching in local map tile cache

$$\begin{cases} \varphi' = arcsin(\sin\varphi \cdot \cos\delta + \cos\varphi \cdot \sin\delta \cdot \cos\theta) \\ \lambda' = \lambda + arctan(\sin\theta \cdot \sin\delta \cdot \cos\varphi / \cos\delta - \sin\varphi \cdot \sin\varphi') \end{cases} \quad (3)$$

where δ is the angular distance l/R, with R denotes the earth's radius.

With the above formula, we can obtain a set $\mathcal{F} = \{f_i, i = 1, \cdots, n\}$, a subset of local fingerprint database cache, in which the location $L_i(f_i)$ of every fingerprint f_i locates in the constrained area ABCD.

4.3   Localization

Since the observations indicate that probabilistic fingerprinting algorithm demands enough time to collect samples while locating current position, we adopt modified deterministic framework here. Each fingerprint sample f in $\mathcal{F}$ is chosen to be compared with query fingerprint signal f'. And the most similar K points participate in estimating the final result of current location $\hat{L}$ through Weighted K-nearest neighbor method.

$$\hat{L} = \sum_{i=1}^{K} \frac{w_i}{\sum_{j=1}^{K} w_j} L_i \quad (4)$$

where all weights w_i are nonnegative and correlated with stored GPS signal state (number of satellites n, signal noise ratio snr) and dissimilarity in RSS.

Since discrimination capability exists in different APs, the discrimination factor depends on the distance between AP and user device. From the Log-Distance Path Loss model $P_d = P_0 - 10\gamma \log \frac{d}{d_0}$, we specify the discrimination factor of the i-th AP with formula

$$\rho_i = \frac{1}{d_i} = 10^{\frac{r_i - P_0}{10\gamma}} \quad (5)$$

where P_0 denotes the RSS value received at a distance d_0. γ is the path loss exponent, and P_d is the RSS sensed in a distance of d. Afterwards, an normalized form ρ_i^N from $\sum_{i=1}^{p} \rho_i$ is embed into the formula 6. Then, the modified dissimilarity in RSS between query fingerprint and stored one is

$$h(f, f') = \sqrt{\sum_{i=1}^{p} (\rho_i^N \cdot \sigma_i)^2} \tag{6}$$

In addition, the satellite signal health plays a role in ultimate synthesized discrimination. In our research, we incorporate GPS statistics into synthesized influence factor. GPS health is chiefly concerned with effective satellites number n and corresponding signal-to-noise ratio snr, and it is expressed with formula

$$\psi = \frac{\sum_{j=1}^{n} snr_j}{10n} \tag{7}$$

which means that the bigger ψ is, the stored location of this sample fingerprint is more reliable.

Integrating all these factors into unified one, the ultimate synthesized dissimilarity metric is formulated as

$$\eta = \frac{h(f, f')}{\psi} \cdot \frac{p}{q} \tag{8}$$

where $p = |A \cup A'|$ and $q = |A \cap A'|$. Specifically, q denotes the number of common APs in stored fingerprint f and query one f'. With p/q involved, dissimilarity of two fingerprints with fewer common APs will be amplified. Finally, the absolute weight is obtained by

$$w_i = \frac{1}{\eta} \tag{9}$$

which is used to calculate the current location in formula 4.

5   Experiments and Evaluation

5.1   Experiments

A real system is implemented on Samsung Galaxy Grand Prime running Android Operating System. Our experiment is conducted along the road around the Academic Building A in Harbin Institute of Technology Shenzhen Graduate School. First, the map area is divided into many map square tiles, with each side length w. In our research, w is set to 15 m. Then crowdsourcing fingerprint data is collected at random positions along the road. In fact, at each position of about 150 sampling points, average state including GPS statistics and signals information of 10 samples is recorded as the fingerprint data. And device handheld posture is unified to get rid of human body effects in the whole experiment process. As

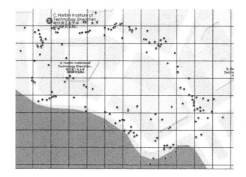

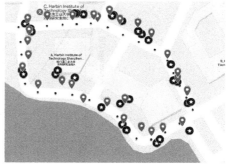

Fig. 5. Crowdsourcing data distribution in map tiles

Fig. 6. Distribution of pre-calibrated points, GPS positioning results and Our hybrid results, represented by black dots, gray icons and black star icons respectively.

the Fig. 5 illustrates, part of our real fingerprint data in database is allocated into corresponding map tile after training phase.

In online matching process, estimated locations are computed with the assistance of formula 3, where we specify earth radius R at ground level as about 6375.024 km according our approximate latitude and altitude. Actually, we did this at 30 pre-calibrated points along the road for ten times. And meanwhile, battery energy percentages in both phones for GPS localization and our hybrid method are recorded every 10 min to get power-consuming log.

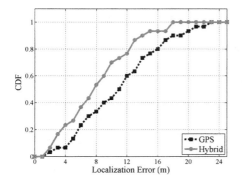

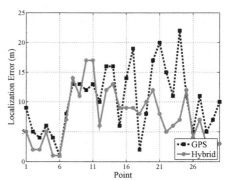

Fig. 7. Localization errors of GPS and our hybrid method

Fig. 8. Localization error at each point

5.2 Evaluation

As Fig. 6 shows, calibrated coordinates, GPS positioning and our hybrid localization results are plotted into Google map according to their coordinates. We

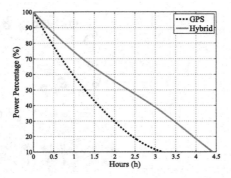

Fig. 9. Power consumption

compare the real locations at 30 pre-calibrated points with GPS results and ours respectively. Figure 7 shows the error cumulative distribution of GPS results and ours. Our calculation results indicates that our method results in an average error of 7.57 m while the number is 10.3 for GPS. Besides, the error at each point is shown in Fig. 8. At point 17, 21 and 24, errors from hybrid method are much smaller than that in GPS, meaning that our method can mitigate large outliers to some extent. About energy cost, Fig. 9 demonstrates that our hybrid method enhances the battery life for 1.5 h roughly, achieving energy-saving purpose.

6 Conclusion

In this paper, we summarize the problems with typical localization methods. These problems motivated us to design the proposed hybrid outdoor localization scheme, which is based on GPS statistics, sensor information and map tile mechanism. Our experimental results indicate that the proposed scheme slightly outperforms GPS localization in terms of positioning precision. From the perspective of power consumption, the proposed scheme is more efficient than GPS localization.

Acknowledgement. This work was supported by National Natural Science Foundation of China (No. 61370216).

References

1. Kaplan, E., Hegarty, C.: Understanding GPS: Principles and Applications. Artech House, Norwood (2005)
2. Ibrahim, M., Youssef M.: CellSense: a probabilistic RSSI-based GSM positioning system. In: 2010 IEEE Global Telecommunications Conference (GLOBECOM 2010), pp. 1–5. IEEE (2010)
3. Azuma, R.: Tracking requirements for augmented reality. Commun. ACM **36**(7), 50–51 (1993)

4. Priyantha, N.B., Chakraborty, A., Balakrishnan, H.: The cricket location-support system. In: Proceedings of the 6th Annual International Conference on Mobile Computing and Networking, pp. 32–43. ACM (2000)
5. Pahl, P., Radar, P.V.: An in-building RF-based user location and tracking system. IEEE Commun. Societies **2**, 775–784 (2000)
6. Wang, Y., et al.: RSSI-based bluetooth indoor localization. In: 2015 11th International Conference on Moile Ad-hoc and Sensor Networks (MSN). IEEE (2015)
7. Youssef, M.A., Agrawala, A., Shankar, A.U., et al.: A probabilistic clustering-based indoor location determination system (2002)
8. Youssef, M., Agrawala, A.: The horus WLAN location determination system. In: Proceedings of the 3rd International Conference on Mobile Systems, Applications, and Services, pp. 205–218. ACM (2005)
9. Howe, J.: The rise of crowdsourcing. Wired Mag. **14**(6), 1–4 (2006)
10. Ibrahim, M., Youssef, M.: CellSense: an accurate energy-efficient GSM positioning system. IEEE Trans. Veh. Technol. **61**(1), 286–296 (2012)
11. IEEE 802.11, part11: Wireless LAN medium access control (MAC) and physicallayer (PHY) specifications (2012)
12. Ye, Q., et al.: A matrix-completion approach to mobile network localization. In: Proceedings of the 15th ACM International Symposium on Mobile ad Hoc Networking and Computing. ACM (2014)
13. Cheng, J., et al.: DISCO: a distributed localization scheme for mobile networks. In: 2015 IEEE 35th International Conference on Distributed Computing Systems (ICDCS). IEEE (2015)
14. Cheng, J., et al.: MIL: a mobile indoor localization scheme based on matrix completion. In: 2016 IEEE International Conference on Communications (ICC). IEEE (2016)
15. Kharidia, S.A., et al.: HILL: a hybrid indoor localization scheme. In: Proceedings of MSN 2014, Hawaii, USA, 19–21 December 2014 (2014)
16. Wu, C., et al.: Footprints elicit the truth: improving global positioning accuracy via local mobility. In: 2013 IEEE Proceedings of the INFOCOM. IEEE (2013)
17. Robusto, C.C.: The cosine-haversine formula. Am. Math. Mon. **64**(1), 38–40 (1957)
18. Liu, K., Liu, X., Li, X.: Guoguo: enabling fine-grained indoor localization via smartphone. In: Proceeding of the 11th Annual International Conference on Mobile Systems, Applications, and Services. ACM (2013)
19. Luo, J., Shukla, H.V., Hubaux., J.-P.: Non-interactive location surveying for sensor networks with mobility-differentiated ToA. In: 25th IEEE International Conference on Computer Communications, Proceedings IEEE INFOCOM 2006, vols. 1–7, no. LCA-CONF-2005-027. IEEE (2006)
20. Chintalapudi, K., Padmanabha Iyer, A., Padmanabhan, V.N.: Indoor localization without the pain. In: Proceedings of the Sixteenth Annual International Conference on Mobile Computing and Networking. ACM (2010)
21. LaMarca, A., Chawathe, Y., Consolvo, S., Hightower, J., Smith, I., Scott, J., Sohn, T., Howard, J., Hughes, J., Potter, F., Tabert, J., Powledge, P., Borriello, G., Schilit, B.: Place lab: device positioning using radio beacons in the wild. In: Gellersen, H.-W., Want, R., Schmidt, A. (eds.) Pervasive 2005. LNCS, vol. 3468, pp. 116–133. Springer, Heidelberg (2005). doi:10.1007/11428572_8
22. PlaceEngine. http://www.placeengine.com/en
23. Schroth, G., et al.: Mobile visual location recognition. IEEE Signal Process. Mag. **28**(4), 77–89 (2011)
24. Constandache, I., Choudhury, R.R., Rhee, I.: Towards mobile phone localization without war-driving. In: 2010 IEEE Proceedings of the INFOCOM. IEEE (2010)

Design and Realization of an Indoor Positioning Algorithm Based on Differential Positioning Method

Wei-qing Huang[1,2,3], Chang Ding[2,3], Si-ye Wang[1,2,3(✉)],
Junyu Lin[2(✉)], Shao-yi Zhu[2,3], and Yue Cui[2,3]

[1] School of Computer and Information Technology,
Beijing Jiaotong University, Beijing, China
huangweiqing@iie.ac.cn
[2] Institute of Information Engineering,
Chinese Academy of Sciences, Beijing, China
{dingchang,wangsiye,linjunyu,zhushaoyi,
cuiyue}@iie.ac.cn
[3] School of Cyber Security,
University of Chinese Academy of Sciences, Beijing, China

Abstract. Nowadays, with the rapid development of location based services, the indoor positioning technology has become a hot research topic. In order to eliminate interference factors of indoor wireless signal propagation and improve the accuracy adaptability of indoor location, we design and implement an indoor location algorithm based on differential signal strength method. We reduce the effect of the fluctuation of wireless signal and improve the signal stability by using the first order difference method to deal with the collected signal strength parameters. According to small scale multipath effects of wireless signals are approximately equal in the same environment, we combine difference localization theory and plane geometric method to get the indoor target's position. Our positioning algorithm can adapt to various indoor location technology and has good compatibility.

Keywords: Indoor localization · Differential positioning algorithm · RFID · Bluetooth · RSSI

1 Introduction

In recent years, with the development of mobile network and intelligent terminal, the demand of indoor location based services grows fast. Obtaining the target's position information has very important significance in many fields. People stay in the indoor environment about 87% of the time, so the indoor positioning technology has got widely concerned. Achieving the accurate indoor positioning results offers a broad prospects in logistics management, emergency rescue, device testing, disaster prevention and many other fields [1–3].

Because of the complicated transmission environment and various designs of room construction, the transmission consumption of signals will be unstable with the

© Springer International Publishing AG 2017
L. Ma et al. (Eds.): WASA 2017, LNCS 10251, pp. 546–558, 2017.
DOI: 10.1007/978-3-319-60033-8_47

environment changing. When there are barriers indoor, the transmission of signal will be effected by diffraction, refraction and scattering. So the amplitude, phase and signal strength will change a lot. Usually people take RSSI(Receive Signal Strength Indicator) into the module of wireless signal transmission to estimate signal broadcast distance, and then compute the location of target. Because of small scale shadow fading which is caused by signal multipath transmission, RSSI will not go down linearly as the transmission distance increase. And the location accuracy will be limited. How to reduce the propagation error of wireless signal and lower the signal transmission multipath effect influence is the key to improve indoor localization accuracy [4].

The main contributions of our paper are as follows:

- According to small scale multipath effects of wireless signals being approximately equal in the same environment, we combine difference localization theory and plane geometric method to design and implement an indoor location algorithm.
- The algorithm effectively reduces the indoor wireless signal propagation multipath effect and other interference factors and improve the accuracy of indoor location. The test results show our positioning algorithm's calculation error is less than 0.65 m even in a very complex indoor environment.
- Our algorithm adapts to various indoor location technology such as RFID, Bluetooth and so on. It has good compatibility. Using this algorithm can effectively reduce the density and cost of hardware deployment.

The structure of this paper is as follows:

In the second part, we introduce some current indoor location algorithms and analyze their features.

In the third part, we introduce the wireless signal indoor propagation model and analyze the transmission error caused by the multipath effect.

In the fourth part, we put forward to the multipath effect error reduction method.

In the fifth part, we introduce the theory of our differential positioning algorithm. And the implementation and calculation method of our differential positioning algorithm.

In the sixth part, we test our positioning algorithm's locating results. And we compare our algorithm with other two positioning algorithms to evaluate our algorithm's location accuracy.

Finally, we summarize the full text and talk about the direction of the future work.

2 Related Work

Common indoor location algorithm can be divided into two categories: one is based on fingerprint matching and the other is based on distance measuring. The algorithm based on fingerprint matching first sample in the location environment and set up a fingerprint database in this environment after data processing. Then at real-time positioning stage, we use the collected data to match the samples and get the coordinates. The RFID location algorithm LANDMARC belongs to this type of location algorithm, it uses RSSI to value and reduce the requirements of reader receiving synchronization mechanism [5]. Meanwhile, it reduces the performance requirements of the reader hardware and has better applicability. However, this algorithm introduces the concept of the reference labels, it increases the complexity and cost of the positioning system.

The algorithms based on distance measuring mainly build from the transformation model of indoor wireless signal. In the process of real-time location, we can get the real-time distance according to the signal parameters, then use appropriate algorithm to get the real-time coordinates by real-time distance. At present, this type of indoor location algorithms mainly includes angle of arrival (AOA), time of arrival (TOA), time difference of arrival (TDOA), weighted central localization (WCL) and so on [6]. When the system is based on TOA/TDOA positioning algorithm, it requires devices to change the received signal strength value into the distance information according to path loss model. Then put the distance information into TOA/TDOA solving model to calculate the result. This kind of method will make large error and need lots of processing time [7]. The comparison of some indoor localization algorithms is in Table 1 [8, 9].

Table 1. Summary of indoor localization algorithm

Name	Accuracy	Real-time capability	Device require	Adaptive capacity	Cost
AOA	Better	Poor	Higher	Poor	Higher
TOA	Better	Poor	Higher	Poor	Higher
TDOA	Better	Poor	Higher	Poor	Higher
WCL	Better	Poor	Lower	Better	Lower
Sub-triangle	Poor	Poor	Lower	Better	Lower
LANDMARC	Better	Better	Lower	Better	Higher

3 Wireless Signal Indoor Propagation Model and Transmission Error Analysis

Without the electromagnetic interference, the transmission loss of electromagnetic waves in indoor environment is in accordance with the log-normal shadowing model:

$$PL(d_0) = 10n \log_{10} \left[G_t G_r \lambda^2 / (4\pi)^2 d_0^2 \right]. \tag{1}$$

$PL(d_0)$ is the power density loss of received signal when the distance is d_0; G_t denotes the gain of transmitting antenna; G_r denotes the gain of the receiving antenna; λ is the wavelength of transmitted signal; d_0 is the recommended distance, which usually is 1 m; n is the environmental factor. In the case of propagation distance of d, the loss of radio signal strength can be calculated as:

$$PL(d) = PL(d_0) + 10n \log_{10}[d/d_0] + X_\sigma. \tag{2}$$

$PL(d)$ is the power density loss of received signal when the distance is d; $X\sigma$ is the normal distribution function which standard deviation is 4 to 10.

$$\Pr(d) = Pt - PL(d). \tag{3}$$

Pr(d) is the power of received signal; Pt denotes the power intensity of the transmitted signal. Combine the (2) and (3), we calculate the received signal strength in (4). $\Pr(d_0)$ is the power strength of the received signal when the test distance is d_0.

$$\Pr(d) = \Pr(d_0) - 10\mathrm{n}\log 10(d/d_0) - X_\sigma. \tag{4}$$

From (4), we can conclude that the power strength of the received signal decreases with the distance increasing in ideal status, and the trend accords with logarithmic curve. In our experiments, we utilize the received signal strength indication (RSSI), which can reflect the energy strength of the signal in different distance to indicate the power intensity of the signal. However, the RSSI value fluctuates significantly in real indoor environments. The main factor restricts the indoor wireless signal strength stability and reliability is that the signal strength measurement value is the superposition of multipath transmission effect. According to the simplification of the multipath effect, the signal strength that the receiver gets consists of two parts or more. The receiver can't distinguish the signal propagation paths. Due to the complex indoor environment and dense multipath effect, it makes the signal's transmission stability and reliability poorer.

4 Indoor Wireless Signal Multipath Transmission Interference Reduction Methods

The differential positioning technology has been widely applied to outdoor positioning study, which utilizes the difference between two measured values of two targets from one measuring station, or the difference between two measured values of one target from two measuring stations, or the difference between twice measured values of one target from one measuring station. It can eliminate the common data items and thus reduces common error and common parameters. Using outdoor differential positioning method for reference, the common error and interference of indoor wireless signals can also be effectively reduced. As shown in Fig. 1, wireless signal receivers R1 and R2

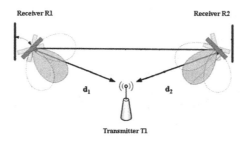

Fig. 1. Schematic of multiple receivers of wireless signals

receive signals from transmitter T1, the distance between R1 and transmitter is d1, the distance between R2 and transmitter is d2, and the distance between R1 and R2 is d.

According to the indoor wireless signal attenuation model, the signal strength received by R_1 and R_2 are:

$$\Pr(d_1) = \Pr(d_0) - 10n \log 10(d_1/d_0) - X_{\sigma 1}. \tag{5}$$

$$\Pr(d_2) = \Pr(d_0) - 10n \log 10(d_2/d_0) - X_{\sigma 2}. \tag{6}$$

To avoid the signal attenuation error induced by multipath effect, we use first order differential method to combine (5) with (6). The result is as follow:

$$\Pr(d_1) - \Pr(d_2) = 10n \log \frac{d_2}{d_1} + X_{\sigma 2} - X_{\sigma 1}. \tag{7}$$

As shown in Fig. 2, when the distance between receiver R_1 and R_2 is decreasing, R_1 and R_2 can be considered to be in the same environmental conditions, and the multipath effect interference is approximately equal within small scale condition. Therefore, their common items (normal distribution parameters) can be mutually eliminated.

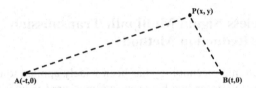

Fig. 2. Schematic of distance ratio

$$\Pr(d_1) - \Pr(d_2) = 10n \log \frac{d_2}{d_1}. \tag{8}$$

From (8) we can obtain the ratio of d_1 and d_2:

$$\frac{d_2}{d_1} = 10^{\frac{P(d1) - P(d2)}{10n}}. \tag{9}$$

According to (9), the power strength of signals can be collected by receivers, the environmental factor is a constant value. So the differential calculation method avoids the multipath error which is induced by direct switch between power strength of wireless signals and distances. It eliminates the error caused by common parameter items.

5   Differential Positioning Algorithm

5.1   Positioning Target Movement Trajectory

As shown in Fig. 2, given two different points A, B on a plane, the central perpendicular of segment AB is set as the Y-axis, thus the coordinates of point A is $(-t,0)$, and the coordinates of point B is $(t, 0)$, and the point $P(x, y)$ satisfies $PA/PB = \lambda$ in the same plane.

It can be obtained from planar Euclidean distance formula:

$$\sqrt{\frac{[(x+t)]^2+y^2}{[(x-t)]^2+y^2}}. \tag{10}$$

When $\lambda \neq 1$, the formula can be simplified to:

$$\left(x - \frac{\lambda^2*t+t}{\lambda^2-1}\right)^2 + y^2 = r^2. \tag{11}$$

The trajectory of point P satisfies the circle trajectory equation, as shown in Fig. 3.

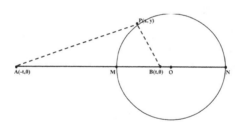

Fig. 3. Schematic of target movement trajectory

The coordinates of the target trajectory circle center is $\left(\frac{\lambda^2*t+t}{\lambda^2-1}, 0\right)$. According to the trajectory equation, points M, N are the inner point and outer point of the line segment AB split by constant ratio λ, thus the segment MN is the diameter of circle trajectory. Then we can get the length of MN using (12) and (13).

$$\begin{cases} \dfrac{d_{AM}}{d_{BM}} = \lambda \\ d_{AM} + d_{BM} = d_{AB} \end{cases}. \tag{12}$$

$$\begin{cases} \dfrac{d_{AN}}{d_{BN}} = \lambda \\ \\ d_{AN} + d_{BN} = d_{AB} \end{cases}. \tag{13}$$

The radius of the target trajectory circle r is dMN/2. So the radius can be calculated in (14).

$$r = \frac{d_{MN}}{2} = \left[\frac{\lambda}{\lambda^2 - 1}\right] d_{AB}.$$ (14)

According to the conclusion of (14), the position of indoor target satisfies the requirement that the ratio of distances to the two receivers is a constant value.

$$\lambda = 10^{\frac{P(d1)-P(d2)}{10n}}$$

Meanwhile, as the positions of signal receiver R1 and R2 are changing, which means d1 $\neq$ d2 and Pr(d1) $\neq$ Pr(d2), the position of the positioning target satisfies the circle trajectory. The length of AB is the signal receiver's displacement, apparently it in (15). In order to determine the accurate position of target, we solve the intersection coordinates by simultaneous circular trajectory equations.

$$\begin{cases} \left(x1 - \frac{\lambda1^2 * t + t}{\lambda1^2 - 1}\right)^2 + y1^2 = r1^2 \\ \left(x2 - \frac{\lambda2^2 * t + t}{\lambda2^2 - 1}\right)^2 + y2^2 = r2^2 \\ \quad \cdots \\ \left(xn - \frac{\lambda3^2 * t + t}{\lambda3^2 - 1}\right)^2 + yn^2 = rn^2 \end{cases}$$ (15)

As shown in Fig. 4, multiple circle equations can be obtained using multiple signal receivers. Combine (9), (14) and (15), the position coordinates of positioning target can be calculated.

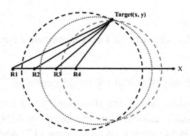

Fig. 4. Schematic of multiple circular trajectory positioning

5.2   The Realization of the Differential Positioning Algorithm

Data Acquisition and Pre-treatment. First, we define quaternion series data pattern and normalize the pattern of collected data. Then form the data in a standard data pattern including time, strength value, ID and displacement.

$$R_{(i,j)} = \langle TimeStamp, RSSI, ID, Position \rangle$$

Due to the work instability of the transmitter and receiver, there exist certain fluctuation and variation of received signal strength at the same position. In order to reduce the effect of the fluctuation of wireless signal with real-time, we utilize single exponential smoothing method to process the collected signal strength parameters. If we collect n signal strength data in the period of time T, the corresponding signal strength parameter is:

$$RSSI_i = \{RSSI_1, RSSI_2, \ldots RSSI_n\}$$

According to the single exponential smoothing algorithm principal, the calculation formula is as follow:

$$RSSI_t = \alpha \sum_{n=0}^{t} (1 - \alpha)^n RSSI_{t-n}. \tag{16}$$

In the single exponential smoothing algorithm, all former observed values affect the current smoothing value, but the effect is decreasing progressively. Therefore, the signal strength parameters after the single exponential smoothing processing can guarantee both the integrity and instantaneity of data. The single exponential smoothing method can effectively reduce the fluctuation of wireless signal and received signal errors in time domain.

Using processed signal strength data, we calculate the difference value of signal strength between adjacent positions by movement antenna matrix. And then we calculate the distance ratio in (17) to get the target's position circular trajectory.

$$\lambda = 10^{\frac{R_{i,j}(RSSI) - R_{i,j+1}(RSSI)}{10n}}. \tag{17}$$

Target Position Determination. Normally, the position of the target can be determined by solving the intersection point and common domain of multiple circles. But the process of solving multiple circle equations is so complicated and the sensor deployment in real application is difficult. In order to reduce the calculation complexity and enhance the algorithm efficiency, we apply Monte Carlo method to simulate and use fuzzy map strategy to obtain the coordinates of the target position. We divide the plane by 10 cm*10 cm unit area and establish plane rectangular coordinate system [12].

The coordinates of the target circular trajectory is (Xoi, Yoi). The judge condition of whether each unit area is included by the generated target circular trajectory is as follow:

$$d_i = \sqrt{(X_i - X_{oi})^2 + (Y_i - Y_{oi})^2} \le R_i. \tag{18}$$

Mark the unit area as 1 which means it is contained by the target circular trajectory. And mark the unit area as 0 for not contained by the target circular trajectory.

$$T_i = \begin{cases} 0, when\ d_i > R_i \\ 1, when\ d_i \leq R_i \end{cases}. \tag{19}$$

The unit area marked 1 consist a fuzzy map. As for the targets to be positioned, each movement cycle of receiver has a corresponding a fuzzy map. As shown in (20), the candidate unit area can be obtained by counting the intersection amount of multiple fuzzy maps.

$$S(T_i) = \sum_{i=1}^{n} T_i. \tag{20}$$

After counting the intersection amount of multiple fuzzy maps in every unit area, we can get the indoor position heat map as shown in Fig. 5, the deeper color area means that the higher possibility of the target position. Solve the intersection coordinate of fuzzy maps can obtain the most likely position of the target.

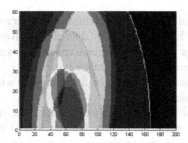

Fig. 5. Schematic of fuzzy map analysis (Color figure online)

When solving the coordinates of target, considering the two weights of W1i and W2i, in which W1i is the containing density of circular trajectory. As shown in (21), Sk (Ti) is the number of unit area Ti contained by circular trajectory during the Kth movement process of the receiver. The number of unit area contained by circular trajectory is more, the containing density is larger, and the weight value Wli is bigger.

$$W_{1i} = \frac{\sum_{k=1}^{k} S_k(T_i)}{\sum_{k=1}^{k} \sum_{i=1}^{n} S_k(T_i)}. \tag{21}$$

The weight W2i is the density of the selected unit area, na is the number of the candidate unit area selected from the whole positioning domain, and nci is the number of the candidate unit area connected with the candidate unit area Ti. According to (22), the density of candidate unit area connected with Ti is larger, the weight W2i is bigger.

$$W_{2i} = \frac{n_{ci}}{\sum_{i=1}^{n_a} n_{ci}}. \tag{22}$$

Considering both W1i and W2i, the total weight Wi can be calculated as follow:

$$W_i = W_{1i} \times W_{2i}. \tag{23}$$

Based on the respective weight of each candidate unit area, the position of ultimate target can be calculated by (24):

$$(\mathrm{x}, \mathrm{y}) = \sum_{i=1}^{n_a} W_i(x_i, y_i). \tag{24}$$

6 Device Deployment and Algorithm Testing

6.1 Positioning Algorithm Test Equipment

To verify the practicability and the accuracy of our localization algorithm, we use different types of wireless hardware to test and analyze the results. We select the Arduino open source hardware platform and NORDIC nRF51422 processor chip as the Bluetooth communication module to test the algorithm. Also, we choose Impinj R420 device to test the localization algorithm's applicability for the RFID equipment.

We stick the signal receiver on the motor guide rail. The guide rail moves at a fixed speed and pause every second to receive signal parameters.

6.2 Algorithm Test Method and Results Analysis

As shown in Fig. 6, we choose two test place in the laboratory area. Test area 1 is open and has little environment interference. And Test area 2 has many interference factors. Each test area covers more than 150 square meters. We place the positioning target randomly in the test area. Signal receiver move with the guide rail at a fixed rate to collect the wireless signal strength data. Based on the experience data, we set the environment factor as 1.8.

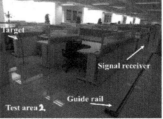

Fig. 6. Positioning algorithm test area1 and area 2

We use standard errors (RMSE) to describe position errors. The calculation formula is shown in Eq. (25), where (x, y) is the target's real coordinates and (x1, y1) is the algorithm's position results.

$$RMSE = E\left[(x - x_1)^2 + (y - y_1)^2\right]^{1/2}. \tag{25}$$

To evaluate our algorithm's position effect, we respectively get 30 times of experiment data in Test area 1 and 2. Then we compare the position results with the real position to get the algorithm's error. Bluetooth and RFID devices positioning error results are shown in Fig. 7.

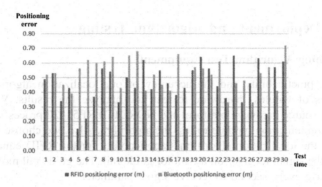

Fig. 7. Algorithm's positioning error results

From the experiment, we collect the positioning error data of the algorithm in both test areas. The experiment results are shown in Table 2.

Table 2. Summary data of positining algorithm error

Positioning device	Max error	Min error	Average error	Variance
RFID	0.65	0.15	0.46	0.13
Bluetooth	0.72	0.15	0.51	0.12

The experiment results indicate that our positioning algorithm has a high localization accuracy about 0.5 m in the indoor environment. And even in the complex area, the positioning accuracy of our algorithm is still fine. Besides that, the test results show that our algorithm also has good performance in stability.

To prove the positioning performance of our algorithm, we compare our algorithm with trilateration positioning algorithm and LANDMARC positioning algorithm using both RFID and Bluetooth devices in the teat area 2 of which environment is more complex. The experiment results are shown in the Fig. 8.

From the comparing experiment, we collect the positioning performance data of the three algorithms. The experiment data of three algorithms using RFID device are shown in Table 3. The experiment data of three algorithms using Bluetooth devices are shown in Table 4.

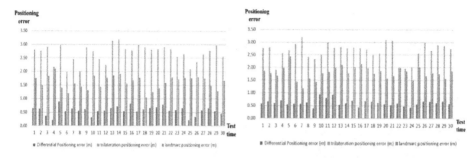

Fig. 8. Algorithm's positioning error comparing results in RFID and Bluetooth

Table 3. Summary data of positioning algorithm performance (RFID)

Algorithm name	Max error	Min error	Average error	Variance
Differential positioning	0.90	0.21	0.57	0.16
Trilateration positioning	3.19	1.98	2.67	0.32
LANDMARC positioning	2.10	1.05	1.61	0.24

Table 4. Summary data of positioning algorithm performance (Bluetooth)

Algorithm name	Max error	Min error	Average error	Variance
Differential positioning	0.94	0.40	0.62	0.12
Trilateration positioning	3.20	1.90	2.65	0.33
LANDMARC positioning	2.43	1.19	1.79	0.25

The experiment results show that our algorithm can get more accurate and stable indoor positioning results in the same environment. Our algorithm positioning average error is less than 0.65 m in the indoor environment. Our algorithm positioning average error is about 20% of the trilateration positioning algorithm and about 30% of the LANDMARC positioning algorithm.

7 Conclusion and Future Work

This paper puts forward an indoor positioning algorithm based on difference localization theory and plane geometric method. Using RFID and Bluetooth device, we collect indoor positioning parameter data in the real environment and calculate the target's coordinates. According to the test results, our algorithm can well reduce the multipath transmission effect in real indoor environment and get more accurate results.

According to the actual requirement and the characteristics of the algorithm, the main direction of future work is to achieve the higher accuracy of our algorithm. We plan to use probability parameter to replace the signal strength parameter. Using the Gaussian distribution model computes the probability of the target position. Furthermore, based on the previous research achievements, we plan to design a system architecture which can access both indoor positioning data and the geographic data. In this way, we can combine indoor positioning results with the real geographical information, which makes positioning results have higher practical application value.

References

1. Yang, Z., Zhou, Z., Liu, Y.: From RSSI to CSI: indoor localization via channel response, ACM Comput. Surv. **46**(2) 2014
2. Pu, Q., Gupta, S., Gollakota, S., Patel, S.: Whole-home gesture recognition using wireless signals. In: Proceedings of ACM MobiCom (2013)
3. Wang, Y., Liu, J., Chen, Y., Gruteser, M., Yang, J., Liu, H.: E-eyes: in-home device-free activity identification using fine-grained WiFi signatures. In: Proceedings of ACM MobiCom (2014)
4. Wang, J., Vasisht, D., Katabi, D.: RF-IDraw: virtual touch screen in the air using RF signals. In: Proceedings of ACM SIGCOMM (2014)
5. Ni, L.M., Liu, Y., Lau, Y.C., Patil, A.P.: LANDMARC: indoor location sensing using active RFID. Wirel. Netw. **10**(6), 701–710 (2004)
6. Hihnel, D., Burgard, W., Fox, D.: Mapping and localization with RFID technology. In: Proceedings of IEEE International Conference on Robotics and Automation. Barcelona, Spain, pp. 1015–1020 (2004)
7. Hori, T., Wada, T., Ota, Y.: A multi-sensing-range method for position estimation of passive RFID tags. In: Proceedings of IEEE International Conference on Wireless and Mobile Computing, Networking and Communication. Avignon, France, pp. 208–238. (2008)
8. Werb, J., Lanzl, C.: Designing a positioning system for finding things and people indoors. IEEE Spectr. **35**(9), 71–78 (1998)
9. Hightower, J., Want, R., Borrlello, G.: SpotON: an indoor 3D location sensing technology based on RF signal strength. Department of Computer Science and Engineering, University of Washington, Seattle, USA (2000)
10. Yang, L., Chen, Y., Li, X., Xiao, C., Li, M., Liu, Y.: Tagoram: real-time tracking of mobile RFID tags to millimeter-level accuracy using cots devices, ACM MobiCom (2014 to appear)
11. Wilson, J., Patwari, N.: See-through walls: Motion tracking using variance-based radio tomography networks. IEEE Trans. Mob. Comput. **10**, 612–621 (2011)
12. Luo, Y., Jiang, J., Wang, S., Jing, X., Ding, C., Zhang, Z., Zhang, Y.: The research on filtering and cleaning for RFID streaming data based on finite state machine. J. Softw. **8**, 1713–1728 (2014)

A Study on the Second Order Statistics of κ-μ Fading Channels

Changfang Chen[1,2(✉)], Minglei Shu[1,2], Yinglong Wang[1,2], and Nuo Wei[1,2]

[1] Shandong Computer Science Center (National Supercomputer Center in Jinan),
Jinan 250014, China
chenchangfang012@163.com
[2] Shandong Provincial Key Laboratory of Computer Networks,
Jinan 250014, China

Abstract. In this paper, the second order statistics of the κ-μ fading channel model are studied. Based on the joint probability density function (PDF) of the envelope and its time derivative of the κ-μ fading signal, the closed-form expressions are obtained for the level crossing rate (LCR) and the average duration of fades (ADF) of the proposed model. These equations can also be applied to analyze the temporal statistical behavior of the Rice, Rayleigh, and Nakagami-m models. Based on the Rice's sum of sinusoids, a simple and efficient deterministic simulation model is presented, which enables the emulation of the κ-μ fading channel models with the desired statistics. The κ-μ model provides an enhanced fit to the measurement data obtained from the mobile human body to body communication channels within indoor environments at 2.45 GHz.

Keywords: κ-μ fading channels · Second order statistics · Level crossing rate · Average duration of fades · Deterministic channel modeling

1 Introduction

A large number of channel models have been proposed that well describe the statistics of the mobile radio signal. It is known that the long term signal variation follows the Lognormal distribution whereas the short term signal variation is characterized by several distributions such as Rice, Rayleigh, Nakagami-q, Weibull and Nakagami-m. However, the flexibility of these models is limited, and they are not adequate for adaptation to the statistics of the real-world mobile radio channels [1]. Much research has focused on extending existing fading models so as to obtain more flexible scenarios [2,3]. The κ-μ fading distribution is proposed as a general multipath model representing the small-scale variation of a fading signal under line-of-sight (LOS) conditions, and it provides more flexibility to model the severe fading conditions [4,5]. Besides, this model includes some

This work was supported by the National Natural Science Foundation of China under Grant 61603224 and Grant 61304008.

L. Ma et al. (Eds.): WASA 2017, LNCS 10251, pp. 559–571, 2017.
DOI: 10.1007/978-3-319-60033-8_48

classical fading distributions as particular cases, such as One-Sided Gaussian, Rayleigh, Rice, and Nakagami-m. In [6], the κ-μ distribution is applied to the analysis of the statistics in body to body communication channels for fire and rescue personnel.

The level crossing rate and average duration of fades are two important second-order statistics associated with envelope fading in wireless communications [7–13]. They characterize the correlation properties of the fading channels and the dynamic temporal behavior of envelope fluctuations. Specifically, the LCR describes how often the signal envelope crosses a certain threshold level and the ADF indicates the mean time that the received envelope is below the same threshold. In [8,9], exact closed-form expressions for the LCR and ADF are derived over Nakagami-m and Weibull fading channels, respectively. Youssef et al. [10] studies the second order statistics of the Nakagami-q fading channel model, and expressions for the LCR and ADF are derived. A more general model is analyzed in [11], closed-form expressions are obtained for the η-μ fading channels envolving the level crossing rate, average duration of fades, and phase crossing rate. Cheng et al. [12] investigates the LCR and ADF of non-isotropic scattering vehicle-to-vehicle (V2V) Ricean fading channels, which can be expressed in terms of some important parameters, e.g., the shape of the scattering region, angle spread, and mean angles. In [13], the characteristic function based approach is developed to obtain the envelope LCR and ADF of the Rician shadowed model because the PDF-based approach is intractable.

By using the common approach for calculating the LCR and ADF of a random process, we can obtain the second order statistics of the κ-μ distribution in this paper. To this end, the joint distribution of the envelope and its time derivative of the received signal is first derived, and exact closed-form expressions for the level crossing rate and average duration of fades are obtained for the κ-μ fading channels. Furthermore, an efficient deterministic simulation model is presented, which enables the implementation of the κ-μ model on a computer. Finally, the obtained analytical statistics are compared against measurement data, which enables the κ-μ fading model to be suitable to describe the statistics of real-world mobile radio channels.

The paper is organized as follows. In Sect. 2, the κ-μ fading channel model and its first order statistical properties of the amplitude and phase processes are presented. In Sect. 3, the joint distribution of the envelope and its time derivative of the κ-μ fading signal is first derived, and the second order statistics, i.e., the LCR and ADF, of the proposed model are obtained. The deterministic simulation model of the κ-μ distribution is given in Sect. 4, where the derived statistical results are compared with the simulation and measurement data. Finally, we come to the conclusion of the paper in Sect. 5.

2   The κ-μ Fading Channel and Its First Order Statistics

The κ-μ distribution assumes that the signal composes of clusters of multipath waves propagating in a nonhomogeneous manner. Within each cluster, the intra-cluster scattered waves have the random phases and similar temporal delays, but the intercluster delay-time spreads are relatively larger. Moreover, it is assumed identical power for the scattered waves, and arbitrary power for the dominant components. From the physical model of the κ-μ distribution, the envelope R can be written in terms of the in-phase and quadrature components as follows [14]

$$R^2 = \sum_{i=1}^{\mu}(X_i + p_i)^2 + \sum_{i=1}^{\mu}(Y_i + q_i)^2 \tag{1}$$

where X_i and Y_i are mutually independent Gaussian processes with mean $E[X_i] = E[Y_i] = 0$, and variance $E[X_i^2] = E[Y_i^2] = \sigma^2$, and p_i and q_i are real numbers, which represent the mean values of the in-phase and quadrature components of cluster i. Here, μ denotes the number of multipath clusters, which is a positive integer number, and it can also be further extended to the real case expressed by

$$\mu = \frac{(1 + 2\kappa)}{(1 + \kappa)^2} \frac{E^2[R^2]}{Var[R^2]} \tag{2}$$

where Var denotes the variance operator, and κ is the ratio between the total power of the dominant components and the total power of the scattered waves. For κ-μ fading distribution with the mean-root-square (rms) value $\hat{r} = \sqrt{E[R^2]}$ of R, the envelope probability density function $p_R(r)$ is expressed as follows

$$f_R(r) = \frac{2\mu(1 + \kappa)^{\frac{\mu+1}{2}}r^\mu}{\kappa^{\frac{\mu-1}{2}}\hat{r}^{\mu+1}} \exp\left(-\mu\kappa - \mu(1 + \kappa)\frac{r^2}{\hat{r}^2}\right) I_{\mu-1}\left(\frac{2\mu\sqrt{\kappa(1 + \kappa)}r}{\hat{r}}\right) \tag{3}$$

where $I_\nu(\cdot)$ is the modified Bessel function of the first kind with order ν [15]. Figure 1 plots the probability density functions of the κ-μ distribution for a fixed μ ($\mu = 0.5$) and varying κ. In Fig. 1, when $\kappa = 0$ and $\mu = 0.5$, it coincides with Nakagami-m distribution with $m = 0.5$, where m is the Nakagami-m parameter, and thus also the One-Sided Gaussian distribution.

The phase PDF $f_\Theta(\theta)$ is not a closed form, which can be obtained by integrating the joint phase-envelope PDF with respect to r, i.e.,

$$
\begin{aligned}
f_\Theta(\theta) &= \int_0^\infty f_{R,\Theta}(r,\theta)dr \\
&= \int_0^\infty \frac{\mu^2(1 + \kappa)^{\frac{\mu}{2}+1}r^{\mu+1}|sin(2\theta)|^{\frac{\mu}{2}-1}I_{\frac{\mu}{2}-1}\left(\left|\frac{cr}{\hat{r}}cos\theta cos\phi\right|\right)I_{\frac{\mu}{2}-1}\left(\left|\frac{cr}{\hat{r}}sin\theta sin\phi\right|\right)}{2\kappa^{\frac{\mu}{2}-1}\hat{r}^{\mu+2}|sin(2\phi)|^{\frac{\mu}{2}-1}cosh\left(\frac{cr}{\hat{r}}cos\theta cos\phi\right)cosh\left(\frac{cr}{\hat{r}}sin\theta sin\phi\right)} \\
&\quad \cdot \exp\left(-\frac{\mu(1 + \kappa)}{\hat{r}^2}r^2 - \mu\kappa + \frac{cr}{\hat{r}}cos(\theta - \phi)\right)dr
\end{aligned}
\tag{4}
$$

where $c = 2\mu\sqrt{\kappa(1 + \kappa)}$. For $\mu = 4$, $\phi = \pi/4$ and varying κ, Fig. 2 shows the phase probability density function of the κ-μ distribution. For $\kappa = 0$, it reduces to the PDF of the Nakagami-m distribution, as expected. Moreover, for a given μ, with the increase of κ, Nakagami-m-like curves finally become the Rice-like ones with the peak tending to concentrate at $\pi/4$.

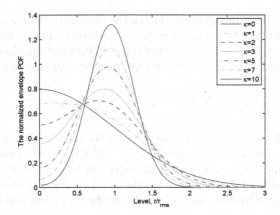

Fig. 1. The normalized envelope PDF of the κ-μ fading model ($\mu = 0.5$)

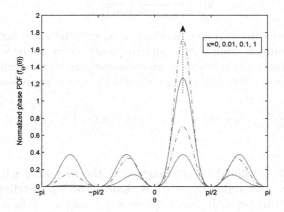

Fig. 2. Phase PDF of the κ-μ fading model ($\mu = 4$, $\phi = \pi/4$, and κ varying).

3   Second Order Statistics

The level crossing rate and average duration of fades are of great significance
in the design and analysis of the mobile radio systems. These quantities can be
used for the selection of the adaptive symbol rates, packet length and time slot
duration [16], and they are also useful for Markov modeling of fading channels
[17] and velocity estimation of mobile units [18]. Based on the traditional PDF-
based approach, the expression for the LCR of the process $R(t)$, denoted by
$N_R(r)$, can be evaluated by the following integral

$$N_R(r) = \int_0^\infty \dot{r} p_{R\dot{R}}(r, \dot{r}) d\dot{r} \tag{5}$$

where $p_{R\dot{R}}(r, \dot{r})$ is the joint probability density function (JPDF) of $R(t)$ and its derivative $\dot{R}(t)$. Let

$$X^2 = \sum_{i=1}^{\mu}(X_i + p_i)^2$$

$$Y^2 = \sum_{i=1}^{\mu}(Y_i + q_i)^2$$

(6)

The derivative of X with respect to time is

$$\dot{X} = \frac{\sum_{i=1}^{\mu}(X_i + p_i)E[\dot{X}_i]}{X}$$

(7)

Since X_i, $i = 1, 2, \ldots, \mu$, are Gaussian processes, the variates $\dot{X}_i$, $i = 1, 2, \ldots, \mu$ are Gaussian distributed with zero mean and variance $\dot{\sigma}^2 = 2(\pi f_{max}\sigma)^2$, where f_{max} is the maximum Doppler frequency. In view of the linear form in (7), given the individual envelopes X_i, $i = 1, 2, \ldots, \mu$, $\dot{X}$ follows the zero-mean Gaussian distribution with variance $\dot{\sigma}^2$, and thus its PDF is

$$f_{\dot{X}}(\dot{x}) = \frac{1}{\sqrt{2\pi}\dot{\sigma}} \exp\left(-\frac{\dot{x}^2}{2\dot{\sigma}^2}\right)$$

(8)

Define

$$\kappa = \frac{p^2 + q^2}{2\mu\sigma^2}$$

$$\sigma^2 = \frac{\hat{r}^2}{2\mu(1 + \kappa)}$$

(9)

where $p^2 = \sum_{i=1}^{\mu}p_i^2$, and $q^2 = \sum_{i=1}^{\mu}q_i^2$. Defining phase parameter as $\phi = \arg(p + jq)$, then it follows that

$$p = \sqrt{\frac{\kappa}{1 + \kappa}}\hat{r}\cos(\phi)$$

$$q = \sqrt{\frac{\kappa}{1 + \kappa}}\hat{r}\sin(\phi)$$

(10)

Let $Z = X^2$, and it follows the non-central chi-squared distribution with degrees of freedom μ, so its PDF is computed as follows

$$f_Z(z) = \frac{z^{\frac{\mu-2}{4}}}{2\sigma^2|p|^{\frac{\mu}{2}-1}} \exp\left(-\frac{z + p^2}{2\sigma^2}\right) I_{\frac{\mu}{2}-1}\left(\frac{\sqrt{z}|p|}{\sigma^2}\right)$$

(11)

Since X can be written as $X = sgn(X) \times |X|$, where $sgn(\cdot)$ denotes the sign function. Note that $|X| = \sqrt{Z}$, we can obtain the PDF of $f_{|X|}(x)$

$$f_{|X|}(x) = \frac{x^{\frac{\mu}{2}}}{\sigma^2|p|^{\frac{\mu}{2}-1}} \exp\left(-\frac{x^2 + p^2}{2\sigma^2}\right) I_{\frac{\mu}{2}-1}\left(\frac{|p|x}{\sigma^2}\right)$$

(12)

Using the method in [19], the PDF of X can be derived from the PDF of $|X|$

$$f_X(x) = \frac{|x|^{\frac{\mu}{2}}}{2\sigma^2 |p|^{\frac{\mu}{2}-1} \cosh\left(\frac{px}{\sigma^2}\right)} \exp\left(-\frac{(x-p)^2}{2\sigma^2}\right) I_{\frac{\mu}{2}-1}\left(\frac{|px|}{\sigma^2}\right) \tag{13}$$

Following the same procedure, we can obtain the PDFs $f_Y(y)$, $f_{\dot{Y}}(\dot{y})$ of Y, $\dot{Y}$, respectively. Since $X(Y)$ is independent $\dot{X}(\dot{Y})$, and X is independent Y, it follows that X, Y, $\dot{X}$, and $\dot{Y}$ are mutually independent. So we can obtain the JPDF of X, Y, $\dot{X}$, and $\dot{Y}$ as follows

$$f_{XY\dot{X}\dot{Y}}(x,y,\dot{x},\dot{y}) = \frac{1}{2\pi\dot{\sigma}^2} \exp\left(-\frac{\dot{x}^2+\dot{y}^2}{2\dot{\sigma}^2}\right) \frac{|xy|^{\frac{\mu}{2}} I_{\frac{\mu}{2}-1}\left(\frac{|px|}{\sigma^2}\right) I_{\frac{\mu}{2}-1}\left(\frac{|qy|}{\sigma^2}\right)}{4\sigma^4 |pq|^{\frac{\mu}{2}-1} \cosh\left(\frac{px}{\sigma^2}\right) \cosh\left(\frac{qy}{\sigma^2}\right)}$$
$$\cdot \exp\left(-\frac{(x-p)^2+(y-q)^2}{2\sigma^2}\right)$$
$$\tag{14}$$

Using the standard procedure of transformation of variates, we obtain that $f_{R,\dot{R},\Theta,\dot{\Theta}}(r,\dot{r},\theta,\dot{\theta}) = |J| f_{XY\dot{X}\dot{Y}}(x,y,\dot{x},\dot{y})$, where $|J| = r^2$ is the Jacobian of the transformation. Expressing x and y in terms of r and θ yields the following JPDF $f_{R,\dot{R},\Theta,\dot{\Theta}}(r,\dot{r},\theta,\dot{\theta})$

$$f_{R,\dot{R},\Theta,\dot{\Theta}}(r,\dot{r},\theta,\dot{\theta})$$
$$= \frac{r^2}{2\pi\dot{\sigma}^2} \exp\left(-\frac{\dot{r}^2+r^2\dot{\theta}^2}{2\dot{\sigma}^2}\right) \frac{|r^2\sin\theta\cos\theta|^{\frac{\mu}{2}} I_{\frac{\mu}{2}-1}\left(\frac{|pr\cos\theta|}{\sigma^2}\right) I_{\frac{\mu}{2}-1}\left(\frac{|qr\sin\theta|}{\sigma^2}\right)}{4\sigma^4 |pq|^{\frac{\mu}{2}-1} \cosh\left(\frac{pr\cos\theta}{\sigma^2}\right) \cosh\left(\frac{qr\sin\theta}{\sigma^2}\right)} \tag{15}$$
$$\cdot \exp\left(-\frac{r^2+p^2+q^2-2pr\cos\theta-2qr\sin\theta}{2\sigma^2}\right)$$

where $0 \leq r < \infty$, $-\infty < \dot{r} < \infty$, $-\pi \leq \theta < \pi$, and $-\infty < \dot{\theta} < \infty$. Thus, the JPDF $f_{R,\dot{R}}(r,\dot{r})$ of the process R and $\dot{R}$ can be computed as

$$f_{R,\dot{R}}(r,\dot{r}) = \int_{-\infty}^{\infty} \int_0^{2\pi} f_{R,\dot{R},\Theta,\dot{\Theta}}(r,\dot{r},\theta,\dot{\theta}) d\dot{\theta} d\theta$$
$$= \frac{1}{\sqrt{2\pi}\dot{\sigma}} \frac{\mu^2(1+\kappa)^{\frac{\mu}{2}+1} r^\mu}{2\kappa^{\frac{\mu}{2}-1} \hat{r}^{\mu+2}} \exp\left(-\frac{\dot{r}^2}{2\dot{\sigma}^2}\right) \exp\left(-\frac{\mu(1+\kappa)}{\hat{r}^2} r^2 - \mu\kappa\right)$$
$$\cdot \int_0^{2\pi} \frac{I_{\frac{\mu}{2}-1}\left(\left|\frac{cr}{\hat{r}}\cos\theta\cos\phi\right|\right) I_{\frac{\mu}{2}-1}\left(\left|\frac{cr}{\hat{r}}\sin\theta\sin\phi\right|\right)}{\cosh\left(\frac{cr}{\hat{r}}\cos\theta\cos\phi\right) \cosh\left(\frac{cr}{\hat{r}}\sin\theta\sin\phi\right)}$$
$$\cdot \frac{|\sin(2\theta)|^{\frac{\mu}{2}} \exp\left(\frac{cr}{\hat{r}}\cos(\theta-\phi)\right)}{|\sin(2\phi)|^{\frac{\mu}{2}-1}} d\theta \tag{16}$$

By carrying the integration of $f_{R,\Theta}(r,\theta)$ with respect to θ, the PDF of r can be obtained

$$f_R(r) = \int_0^{2\pi} f_{R,\Theta}(r,\theta)d\theta$$
$$= \frac{\mu^2(1+\kappa)^{\frac{\mu}{2}+1}r^{\mu+1}}{2\kappa^{\frac{\mu}{2}-1}\hat{r}^{\mu+2}}\exp\left(-\frac{\mu(1+\kappa)}{\hat{r}^2}r^2-\mu\kappa\right)\cdot G_1 \tag{17}$$

where

$$G_1 = \int_0^{2\pi} \frac{I_{\frac{\mu}{2}-1}\left(\left|\frac{cr}{\hat{r}}\cos\theta\cos\phi\right|\right)I_{\frac{\mu}{2}-1}\left(\left|\frac{cr}{\hat{r}}\sin\theta\sin\phi\right|\right)}{\cosh\left(\frac{cr}{\hat{r}}\cos\theta\cos\phi\right)\cosh\left(\frac{cr}{\hat{r}}\sin\theta\sin\phi\right)}$$
$$\cdot\frac{|\sin(2\theta)|^{\frac{\mu}{2}}\exp\left(\frac{cr}{\hat{r}}\cos(\theta-\phi)\right)}{|\sin(2\phi)|^{\frac{\mu}{2}-1}}d\theta \tag{18}$$

Comparing (17) with the envelope PDF in (3), it follows that

$$G_1 = \frac{4\hat{r}}{\mu r\sqrt{\kappa(1+\kappa)}}I_{\mu-1}\left(\frac{2\mu\sqrt{\kappa(1+\kappa)}r}{\hat{r}}\right) \tag{19}$$

Using this result for substitution, we obtain

$$f_{R,\dot{R}}(r,\dot{r}) = \frac{2\mu(1+\kappa)^{\frac{\mu+1}{2}}r^{\mu}}{\sqrt{2\pi}\dot{\sigma}\kappa^{\frac{\mu-1}{2}}\hat{r}^{\mu+1}}\exp\left(-\frac{\dot{r}^2}{2\dot{\sigma}^2}\right)\exp\left(-\frac{\mu(1+\kappa)}{\hat{r}^2}r^2-\mu\kappa\right)$$
$$\cdot I_{\mu-1}\left(\frac{2\mu\sqrt{\kappa(1+\kappa)}r}{\hat{r}}\right) \tag{20}$$

Note that $f_{R,\dot{R}}(r,\dot{r}) = f_R(r)f_{\dot{R}}(\dot{r})$, which leads to the conclusion that R and $\dot{R}$ are statistically independent. This result is the same as that obtained for the corresponding cases of Rice, Rayleigh, and Nakagami-m fading channels.

From (5), the LCR $N_R(r)$ of the κ-μ distribution can be evaluated as

$$N_R(r) = \frac{\sqrt{2\pi}\mu f_{max}(1+\kappa)^{\frac{\mu}{2}}r^{\mu}}{\kappa^{\frac{\mu-1}{2}}\hat{r}^{\mu}}\exp\left(-\frac{\mu(1+\kappa)}{\hat{r}^2}r^2-\mu\kappa\right)I_{\mu-1}\left(\frac{2\mu\sqrt{\kappa(1+\kappa)}r}{\hat{r}}\right) \tag{21}$$

As a particular case, the Rician LCR can be obtained from (21) by setting $\mu = 1$. As $\kappa \to 0$, (21) deteriorates into the Nakagami-m LCR, and for $\kappa = 0$, $\mu = 1$, the Rayleigh LCR is obtained.

Another statistical quantity to characterize the correlations of the fading channels is the ADF. The ADF $T_R(r)$ is the expected value of time intervals over which the signal envelope R is below a given threshold r, and it is defined as

$$T_R(r) = \frac{P_R(r)}{N_R(r)} \tag{22}$$

where $P_R(r)$ is the probability that the process $R(t)$ is found below the level r, which can be computed by

$$
\begin{aligned}
P_R(r) &= \int_0^r f_R(z)dz \\
&= 1 - \frac{1}{a^{\mu-1}} \int_b^\infty x^\mu \exp\left(-\frac{a^2 + x^2}{2}\right) I_{\mu-1}(ax)dx \\
&= 1 - Q_\mu(a, b)
\end{aligned}
\tag{23}
$$

where $x = \sqrt{2\mu(1+\kappa)}z/\hat{r}$, $a = \sqrt{2\mu\kappa}$, and $b = \sqrt{2\mu(1+\kappa)}r/\hat{r}$. Thus, it follows that

$$
T_R(r) = \frac{1 - Q_\mu(a, b)}{N_R(r)}
\tag{24}
$$

where $Q(\cdot, \cdot)$ is the generalised Marcum Q function.

4   Simulation Results

In this section, the deterministic channel model is used to simulate the κ-μ distribution based on the sum of sinusoids. According to the physical model of the κ-μ distribution, it is needed to generate 2μ uncorrelated Gaussian random processes $z_{i,l}$, $i = 1, 2$, $l = 1, 2, \ldots, \mu$, where $z_{i,l}$ are approximated by

$$
z_{i,l}(t) = \sum_{n=1}^{N_{i,l}} c_{i,n,l} \cos(2\pi f_{i,n,l}t + \theta_{i,n,l})
\tag{25}
$$

The parameters $c_{i,n,l}$, $f_{i,n,l}$ and $\theta_{i,n,l}$ represent the gains, discrete Doppler frequencies, and phases, and $N_{i,l}$ is the number of sinusoids for generating $z_{i,l}(t)$. And several methods have been proposed to compute these parameters in [20]. Here, the Method of Exact Doppler Spread (MEDS) is used, and thus the phases in (25) are realizations of a random variable uniformly distributed over $(0, 2\pi]$, and $c_{i,n,l}$ and $f_{i,n,l}$ are computed by

$$
\begin{aligned}
c_{i,n,l} &= \sigma\sqrt{\frac{2}{N_{i,l}}} \\
f_{i,n,l} &= f_{max} \sin(\Phi_{i,n,l})
\end{aligned}
\tag{26}
$$

where

$$
\Phi_{i,n,l} = \frac{(2n-1)\pi}{4N_{i,l}}
\tag{27}
$$

It can be easily shown that by choosing the above parameters the deterministic process $z_{i,l}(t)$ in (25) has the mean value 0 and variance σ^2. When $1 \leq n \leq N_{i,l}$, it follows that $\pi/4N_{i,l} \leq \Phi_{i,n,l} \leq (2N_{i,l} - 1)\pi/4N_{i,l}$, thus $0 < \Phi_{i,n,l} < \pi/2$.

From (26), it can be seen that the discrete frequencies $f_{i,n,l}$ are monotonously increasing with the increase of n over the interval $(0, f_{max})$. To guarantee $f_{i,n,l} \neq f_{k,m,s}$, the following condition must be satisfied

$$\frac{N_{i,l}}{N_{k,s}} \neq \frac{2n-1}{2m-1} \qquad (28)$$

where $n = 1, 2, \ldots, N_{i,l}$, $m = 1, 2, \ldots, N_{k,s}$, $i, k = 1, 2$, and $l, s = 1, 2, \ldots, \mu$. (28) indicates that the quotient of $N_{i,l}$ and $N_{k,s}$ can not be equal to the ratio of two odd numbers. In practice, we can choose the numbers of sinusoids $N_{i,l}$ such that (28) is not satisfied for only a few pairs of (n, m) because in this case the cross-correlation of any pair are very small which can be neglected. Here, the values of $N_{i,l}$ are selected to be $N_{11} = 22$, $N_{12} = 23$, $N_{13} = 25$, $N_{14} = 26$, $N_{21} = 28$, $N_{22} = 29$, $N_{23} = 31$ and $N_{24} = 32$.

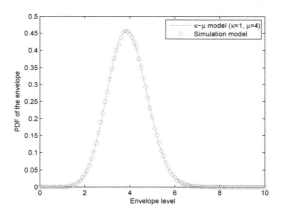

Fig. 3. κ-μ probability density function.

Figure 3 illustrates the simulated envelope PDFs obtained from the output of the channel simulator and theoretical results. The corresponding parameters are chosen as follows: $\sigma = 1$, $f_{max} = 2.45 * 10^9$, $\kappa = 1$, $\mu = 4$, and the mean values of in-phase and quadrature components of the multipath waves of cluster p_i and q_i are given by

$$p_{i,l} = \sqrt{\frac{\eta_{i,l}\kappa}{1+\kappa}} \hat{r} \cos(\phi)$$
$$q_{k,s} = \sqrt{\frac{\eta_{k,s}\kappa}{1+\kappa}} \hat{r} \sin(\phi) \qquad (29)$$

where $\eta_{11} = 0.335$, $\eta_{12} = 0.203$, $\eta_{13} = 0.411$, $\eta_{14} = 0.051$, $\eta_{21} = 0.126$, $\eta_{22} = 0.126$, $\eta_{23} = 0.063$ and $\eta_{24} = 0.685$. It can be shown that MEDS can provide good approximation to the desired first order statistics of the reference model.

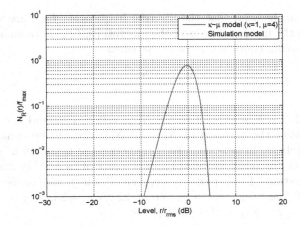

Fig. 4. Normalized level-crossing rate $N_R(r)/f_{max}$ for κ-μ distribution: analytical results (blue solid line) and simulation results (red dot line). (Color figure online)

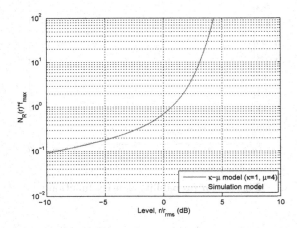

Fig. 5. Normalized average duration of fades $T_R(r) \cdot f_{max}$ for κ-μ distribution: analytical results (blue solid line) and simulation results (red dot line). (Color figure online)

Moreover, Figs. 4 and 5 plot the normalized LCR and ADF of the analytical κ-μ fading model and the simulation model for comparison. The trapezoidal method in [21] is used to compute the integrals involved in the analytical expressions of the LCR and ADF. It can be observed that the simulated LCR and ADF are in good coincidence with the analytical results for all the threshold levels in these figures.

Figure 6 shows some empirical data obtained from the mobile human body to body channels where the transmitter and receiver are positioned on the back and right-shoulder of different persons within an indoor environment at 2.45 GHz [6].

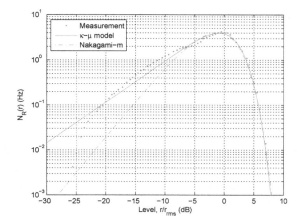

Fig. 6. Comparison of the κ-μ LCR ($\kappa = 1.2$, $\mu = 1.4$, $f_m = 5\,\text{Hz}$), Nakagami-m LCR ($m = 2.1$, $f_m = 2.25\,\text{Hz}$), and measurements.

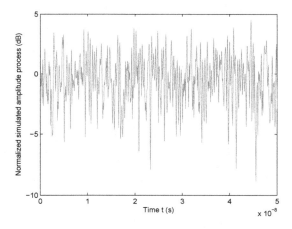

Fig. 7. A waveform example of the normalized simulated deterministic process $R(t)$.

The results show that the analytical LCR of the κ-μ model offers a better match to the measured results, which validates the advantage of the κ-μ model over the Nakagami-m model. Although in some cases Rice and Nakagami distributions are in good agreement with the measured data, the κ-μ model increases the flexibility of the model and enables better fitting of measurement data. Figure 7 plots a waveform example of the simulated envelope process of the κ-μ distribution with the same parameters.

5   Conclusions

In this paper, exact closed-form expressions are obtained for the level crossing rate and the average duration of fades of the κ-μ fading channels. The derived results can be validated by the particular cases, such as Rayleigh, Rice and Nakagami-m distributions. Based on the sum of sinusoids, the deterministic channel model is presented to simulate the κ-μ fading channels. The simulator is validated by comparing the simulated envelope PDF and the LCR and ADF against the corresponding analytical and measurement results. The analytical results offer a better match to the corresponding measurement data, and thus this model can be applied to characterize the statistical behavior of real-world mobile fading channels, such as human body to body communication channels.

References

1. Yacoub, M.D.: The κ-μ distribution and the η-μ distribution. IEEE Antennas Propag. Mag. **49**(1), 68–81 (2007)
2. Cotton, S.L.: A statistical model for shadowed body-centric communications channels: theory and validation. IEEE Trans. Antennas Propag. **62**(3), 1416–1424 (2014)
3. Papazafeiropoulos, A.K., Kotsopoulos, S.A.: η-λ-μ: a general fading distribution. In: IEEE Global Telecommunications Conference, Honolulu, Hawai, USA, pp. 1–5, 30 November–4 December 2009
4. Paris, J.F.: Statistical characterization of κ-μ shadowed fading. IEEE Trans. Veh. Technol. **63**(2), 518–526 (2014)
5. Rabelo, G.S., Dias, U.S., Yacoub, M.D.: The κ-μ extreme distribution: characterizing severe fading conditions. In: The SBMO/IEEE MTT-S International Microwave and Optoelectronics Conference (IMOC), Belem, Brazil, pp. 244–248, 3–6 November 2009
6. Cotton, S.L., Scanlon, W.G., Guy, J.: The κ-μ distribution applied to the analysis of fading in body to body communication channels for fire and rescue personnel. IEEE Antennas Wirel. Propag. Lett. **7**(99), 66–69 (2008)
7. Cotton, S.L., Scanlon, W.G.: Higher order statistics for lognormal small-scale fading in mobile radio channels. IEEE Antennas Wirel. Propag. Lett. **6**, 540–543 (2007)
8. Yacoub, M.D., Bautista, J.E.V., Guedes, L.: On higher order statistics of the Nakagami-m distribution. IEEE Trans. Veh. Technol. **48**(2), 790–794 (1999)
9. Sagias, N.C., Zogas, D.A., Karagiannidis, G.K., Tombras, G.S.: Channel capacity and second-order statistics in Weibull fading. IEEE Commun. Lett. **8**(6), 377–379 (2004)
10. Youssef, N., Wang, C.-X., Pätzold, M.: A study on the second order statistics of Nakagami-Hoyt mobile fading channels. IEEE Trans. Veh. Technol. **54**(4), 1259–1365 (2005)
11. Da Costa, D.B., Santos Filho, J.C.S., Yacoub, M.D., Fraidenraich, G.: Second-order statistics of η-μ fading channels: theory and applications. IEEE Trans. Wirel. Commun. **7**(3), 819–824 (2008)
12. Cheng, X., Wang, C.-X., Ai, B., Aggoune, H.: Envelope level crossing rate and average fade duration of nonisotropic vehicle-to-vehicle Ricean fading channels. IEEE Trans. Intell. Transp. Syst. **15**(1), 62–72 (2014)

13. Abdi, A., Lau, W.C., Alouini, M.-S.: A new simple model for land mobile satellite channels: first- and second-order statistics. IEEE Trans. Wirel. Commun. **2**(3), 519–528 (2003)
14. Dias, U.S., Yacoub, M.D.: The κ-μ phase-envelope joint distribution. IEEE Trans. Commun. **58**(1), 40–45 (2010)
15. Olver, F.W.J., Lozier, D.W., Boisvert, R.F., Clark, C.W.: NIST Handbook of Mathematical Functions. Cambridge University Press, Cambridge (2010)
16. Chau, Y.A., Huang, K.Y.T.: Burst-error analysis of dual-hop fading channels based on the second-order channel statistics. IEEE Trans. Veh. Technol. **59**(6), 3108–3115 (2010)
17. Zheng, K., Liu, F., Lei, L., Lin, C., Jiang, Y.: Stochastic performance analysis of a wireless finite-state Markov channel. IEEE Trans. Wirel. Commun. **12**(2), 782–793 (2013)
18. Tepedelenlioglu, C., Abdi, A., Giannakis, G.B., Kaveh, M.: Estimation of Doppler spread and signal stength in mobile communications with applications to handoff and adaptive transmission. Wirel. Commun. Mob. Comput. **1**(2), 221–242 (2001)
19. Yacoub, M.D., Fraidenraich, G., Santos Filho, J.C.S.: Nakagami-m phase-envelope joint distribution. Electron. Lett. **41**(5), 259–261 (2005)
20. Wang, C.-X., Päatzold, M., Yuan, D.: Accurate and efficient simulation of multiple uncorrelated Rayleigh fading waveforms. IEEE Trans. Wirel. Commun. **6**(3), 833–839 (2007)
21. Press, W.H., Flannery, B.P., Teukolsky, S.A., Vetterling, W.T.: Numerical Recipes in C, The Art of Scientific Computing. Cambridge University Press, Cambridge (1990)

Effective Influence Maximization Based on the Combination of Multiple Selectors

Jiaxing Shang[1,2($\boxtimes$)], Hongchun Wu[1,2], Shangbo Zhou[1,2], Lianchen Liu[3], and Hongbin Tang[1,2]

[1] College of Computer Science, Chongiqng University, Chongqing, China
[2] Key Laboratory of Dependable Service Computing in Cyber Physical Society, Ministry of Education, Chongqing University, Chongqing, China
{shangjx,wuhc,shbzhou}@cqu.edu.cn, bin_tang78@163.com
[3] Department of Automation, Tsinghua University, Beijing, China
liulianchen@tsinghua.edu.cn

Abstract. Influence maximization is an extensively studied optimization problem aiming at finding the best k seed nodes in a network such that they can influence the maximum number of individuals. Traditional heuristic or shortest path based methods either cannot provide any performance guarantee or require huge amount of memory usage, making themselves ineffective in real world applications. In this paper, we propose MSIM: a multi-selector framework which combines the intelligence of different existing algorithms. Our framework consists of three layers: (i) the selector layer; (ii) the combiner layer, and (iii) the evaluator layer. The first layer contains different selectors and each selector can be arbitrary existing influence maximization algorithm. The second layer contains several combiners and combines the output of the first layer in different ways. The third layer evaluates the candidates elected by the second layer to find the best seed nodes in an iterative manner. Experimental results on five real world datasets show that our framework always effectively finds better seed nodes than other state-of-the-art algorithms. Our work provides a new perspective to the study of influence maximization.

Keywords: Influence maximization · Multi-selector framework · Social network analysis · Data mining · Information networks

1 Introduction

Among the many research topics in social networks, influence maximization (IM) is an extensively studied problem in recent years. This problem orients from the question of how to find the "best" initial seeds so that a piece of information or product can be most widely propagated?

Kempe et al. [1] gave the first formal mathematical definition of the influence maximization problem: given a network $G(V, E)$, influence maximization aims to find a subset S of $k = |S|$ vertices such that the diffusion orients from S can cause the maximum cascade of influence, i.e., $S^* = \arg_S \max \sigma(S)$, where

© Springer International Publishing AG 2017
L. Ma et al. (Eds.): WASA 2017, LNCS 10251, pp. 572–583, 2017.
DOI: 10.1007/978-3-319-60033-8_49

$\sigma(S)$ is an objective function evaluating the influence spread, which is defined as the expected number of successfully influenced users in the network after the diffusion stopped. Kempe et al. proved that under two general diffusion models (linear threshold model and independent cascade model), this problem is NP hard, and the objective function is submodular. Based on the mathematical properties of submodular functions [2], Kempe et al. proposed a "hill-climbing" greedy algorithm to solve this problem and proved that the greedy algorithm provides a factor of $(1 - 1/e - \varepsilon)$ performance guarantee to the optimal solution under both the two models. In real experiments, the solution provided by the greedy algorithm is quite close to the optimal solution. However the greedy algorithm requires tens of thousands of Monte-Carlo simulations to approximate the objective function, which severely hinders its time efficiency on real world applications.

To solve the time efficiency problem of traditional greedy algorithm, a spectral of algorithms were proposed by researchers in recent years. Some works make use of submodularity, such as the CELF algorithm proposed by Leskovec et al. [3]. Another way to reduce the time complexity is to simply select top k nodes based on some heuristic metrics [4–6], such as the degree centrally, betweenness centrality, node potential, et al. However, since the heuristic methods take no consideration of diffusion models, they usually give poor solutions. Some research works achieve a balance between time efficiency and quality of solution by assuming that the influence can spread on the network only through shortest paths [7–9], such that the objective function can be approximately computed. However, these algorithms may require huge memory usage in order to maintain the shortest paths.

To overcome the disadvantages of traditional influence maximization algorithms, in this paper, we proposed **MSIM**: a **M**ulti-**S**elector framework for effective **I**nfluence **M**aximization by combining the intelligence of different individual algorithms. Our framework consists of three layers: (i) the selector layer; (ii) the combiner layer, and (iii) the evaluator layer. The first layer contains different selectors and each selector can be arbitrary existing influence maximization algorithm. The second layer contains several combiners and combines the output of the first layer in different ways so that the intelligence of multiple individual algorithms can be fully utilized. The third layer evaluates the candidates provided by the combiners to find the best seed nodes. Experimental results on real world datasets show that our framework always effectively finds "good" seed nodes as compared to other state-of-the-art algorithms.

The rest of this paper is organized as follows. Section 2 reviews the literature on influence maximization. Section 3 elaborates the preliminaries of the problem to be addressed. Section 4 introduces our MSIM framework. Section 5 presents the evaluation framework together with the results. Section 6 concludes this paper.

2 Related Works

In recent years a lot of research works have been published to tackle the influence maximization problem.

Leskovec et al. [3] take advantage of submodularity property to improve the time efficiency of the greedy algorithm and proposed the CELF (Cost-Effective Lazy Forward) algorithm. Inspired by similar idea, Goyal et al. [10] proposed the CELF++ algorithm which is about 30 $\sim$ 50% faster than the CELF algorithm. Although the two algorithms are much faster than the traditional greedy algorithm, they still cannot handle large-scale networks.

Another simple idea is to select the top k nodes based on some predefined centrality metrics (e.g., degree centrality, betweenness centrality, et al.). In [4] Chen et al. proposed an algorithm named SD (Single Discount) by considering the effect of already selected nodes on current candidates. Wang and Feng [5] proposed an algorithm named TW (Targeted Wise) based on node potential. The algorithm of Kundu et al. [6] selects top k nodes based on their diffusion degree, which considered both degree and influence probability of a node. In general, these algorithms are much faster than traditional submodularity-based algorithms, but they cannot provide accurate results due to the lack of consideration about diffusion models.

There are also influence path-based algorithms which generally assume that influence can spread along the network only through some special paths. Kimura and Saito [7] firstly proposed SP1M (Shortest Path 1 Model), a shortest path-based influence maximization algorithm which only considers the shortest and the second shortest paths. Chen et al. [8] proposed MIA (Maximum Influence Arborescence), an algorithm which uses local graph structure—arborescence—to approximate the influence spread. Kim et al. [9] proposed another influence path-based algorithm IPA (Independent Path Algorithm) which made the assumption that different influence paths were independent of each other.

Besides the above introduced methods, there are also many other influence maximization methods, such as the community based algorithms [11], the competitive influence maximization algorithms [12], et al.

3 Preliminaries

3.1 Network Preliminaries

Without loss of generality, we define a directed weighted graph[1] $G = (V, E)$, where V is the set of vertices and E is the set of edges. G has adjacency matrix A, where:

$$A_{ij} = \begin{cases} a_{ij} & \text{if } i \text{ and } j \text{ are connected} \\ 0 & \text{otherwise} \end{cases} \tag{1}$$

where $a_{ij} > 0$ is the weight of the directed edge connecting nodes i and j.

---

[1] Our framework is also applicable to undirected or unweighted networks.

3.2 Diffusion Model

When studying the influence maximization problem, we have to consider the specific diffusion models [13] defining how influence is propagated. Currently the most widely used models are IC (Independent Cascade) model and LT (Linear Threshold) model [1]. In the two models, each node is in one of two states: *active* or *inactive*. Active nodes are those who have adopted the product and will propagate the product to their neighbors. Inactive nodes are those who have not heard of the product or have heard of but rejected to adopt it. Initially all nodes are inactive, then k nodes are selected to be activated and propagation starts from the k seed nodes.

IC Model: In this model, at step t, for an active node u, it will try to activate each of its inactive neighbor v, and succeed with probability p_{uv}. Node u has only one chance to activate v, whether succeed or not, u will make no attempt to activate v in the future. If v was successfully activated, then from step $t+1$, v will be active and try to activate its inactive neighbors. If no more node is activated at step T, the diffusion process will stop.

LT Model: In this model, the activation of node v depends on the set of its active neighbors. For each directed edge from u to v, there is a weight b_{uv} indicating the influence of u on v. For each node v, the constraint $\Sigma_{u \in N^-(v)} b_{uv} \leq 1$ must be satisfied, where $N^-(v) = \{u | a_{uv} > 0\}$ is the in-neighbor set of v. Node v has an activation threshold θ_v, which is between 0 and 1. Once the condition $\Sigma_{u \in A^-(v)} b_{uv} \geq \theta_v$ is satisfied, v will become active. Here $A^-(v)$ is the active in-neighbor of v. When no more nodes can be activated, the diffusion process will stop.

3.3 Problem Definition

The influence maximization problem is defined as follows:

Definition 1 *(Influence Maximization* [1]). Given a network and a diffusion model, the influence maximization problem aims to find a subset S of k nodes ($|S| = k$), such that the expected number of overall activated nodes $\sigma(S)$ is maximized:

$$S^* = \arg_S \max \sigma(S) \tag{2}$$

Kempe et al. [1] proved that under IC and LT models, the influence maximization problem defined in Definition 1 is NP-hard and the objective function $\sigma(S)$ is submodular. A set function $f : 2^V \rightarrow R$ is submodular if for all $v \in V, S \subseteq T \subseteq V$, it has the following property:

$$f(S \cup \{v\}) - f(S) \geq f(T \cup \{v\}) - f(T) \tag{3}$$

Based on the submodualrity, Kempe et al. further proposed a "hill-climbing" greedy algorithm which starts with an empty seed set $S = \Phi$, and then iteratively add one node that can bring the maximum marginal gain of influence spread to S, until $|S| = k$. They proved that the algorithm provided a factor of $(1-1/e-\varepsilon)$ guarantee to the optimal solution, as shown in Theorem 1.

Theorem 1 (Kempe et al. [1]). *For influence maximization problem defined in Definition 1, the seed set generated by the hill-climbing greedy algorithm provides a factor of $(1 - 1/e - \varepsilon)$ approximation to the optimal solution, i.e., $f(S) \geq (1 - 1/e - \varepsilon)f(S^*)$, where S^* is the optimal solution.*

Theorem 2 (Chen et al. [4]). *The time complexity of the hill-climbing greedy algorithm is $O(knRm)$, where k is the number of seed nodes, n is the number of network nodes, m is the number of network edges, and R is the number of Monte-Carlo simulations for computing $\sigma(S)$.*

From Theorem 2 we see that the time complexity of the simple greedy algorithm proposed by Kempe et al. [1] is very high, motivating a lot of research works to tackle its time efficiency issue.

4   Multi-selector Framework

4.1   Framework

The MSIM (multi-selector influence maximization) framework proposed in this paper is shown in Fig. 1. The intuition behind this framework is the observation

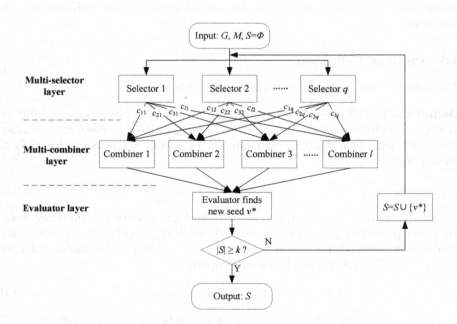

Fig. 1. The multi-selector framework

of drawbacks in traditional algorithms. For example, some heuristic algorithms like degree or potential based ones can successfully find the first few seed nodes (e.g., $k < 10$), but their results go worse when the number of seed nodes becomes larger. On the contrary, some other algorithms such as the influence path based ones will show their superiority over heuristic algorithms only when the number of seed nodes is not small (e.g., $k > 30$). This phenomenon has been reported in the previous work of Shang et al. [11].

Based on our observations, in this paper we come up with the idea: since single algorithm cannot find the satisfactory solutions, we may combine the results of multiple "weak selectors[2]" (individual algorithms) to generate more accurate solutions.

From Fig. 1 we see that the MSIM framework takes the graph G, the diffusion model M, and an empty seed set $S = \Phi$ as input. The output is a set with $|S| = k$ seed nodes. The framework mainly consists of three layers: (i) the multi-selector layer; (ii) the multi-combiner layer, and (iii) the evaluator layer. In the following subsections we will give detailed description about each layer and illustrate how to put into practice our idea of combining "weak selectors".

(i) The multi-selector layer: The multi-selector layer consists of multiple selectors, and each selector represents an individual influence maximization algorithm, which can be chosen to have high time efficiency. Each selector has the form as shown in Fig. 2. Given the input G, M, S, the selector will incrementally find several new seed nodes based on the current seed set S and output a new pair set PS defined as

$$PS = \{(v_i, p_i)|v_i \in V, p_i \geq 0, \sum_i p_i = 1\} \qquad (4)$$

where v_i is the new proposed seed node and p_i is the wegiht indicating the selector's confidence about v_i being selected as a new seed node. The number of proposed seed nodes, i.e., $|PS|$ is determined by the selector itself, but the constraint $p_i \geq 0, \Sigma_i p_i = 1$ should be satisfied. It means that at each step any selector is expected to select only one new seed node.

The output for all the selectors as be represented by a matrix

$$\mathbf{B} = \begin{pmatrix} b_{11} & b_{12} & \cdots & b_{1n} \\ b_{21} & b_{22} & \cdots & b_{2n} \\ \vdots & \vdots & \ddots & \vdots \\ b_{q1} & b_{q2} & \cdots & b_{qn} \end{pmatrix} \qquad (5)$$

G, M, S → | Selector | → G, M, S, PS

Fig. 2. The structure of selector

---

[2] We call individual algorithms selectors since their main purpose is to select the seed nodes.

where q is the number of selectors, and $n = |V|$ is the number of nodes. We define $b_{ij} = 0$ for any node j not in selector i's output list. It is easy to see that we have $\Sigma_j b_{ij} = 1$.

(ii) The multi-combiner layer: As shown in Fig. 1, the multi-combiner layer contains multiple combiners and each combiner is connected to several selectors. By connecting the selectors, we may combine the result of different algorithms and using multiple combiners allows us to combine the selectors' results in different manners. The weight c_{ij} indicates the importance of selector j's output on combiner i. The weights can be expressed with the matrix

$$\mathbf{C} = \begin{pmatrix} c_{11} & c_{12} & \cdots & c_{1q} \\ c_{21} & c_{22} & \cdots & c_{2q} \\ \vdots & \vdots & \ddots & \vdots \\ c_{l1} & c_{l2} & \cdots & c_{lq} \end{pmatrix} \tag{6}$$

where l and q are the number of selectors and combiners, respectively. For each combiner j, it satisfies $\Sigma_{j=1}^q c_{ij} = 1$, i.e., the sum of elements for each row in $\mathbf{C}$ add up to 1. Similar to the selectors, the output of a combiner contains a pair set $PS = \{v_i, p_i\}$. For combiner i, the weight of its output node v is defined as

$$d_{iv} = \sum_{j=1}^q c_{ij} b_{jv} \tag{7}$$

It can be proved that for each combiner i, we have $\Sigma_{v \in V} d_{iv} = 1$, so that the output of each combiner is normalized, and the matrices $\mathbf{B}, \mathbf{C}, \mathbf{D}$ satisfies

$$\mathbf{D} = \mathbf{CB} \tag{8}$$

The output nodes of the combiners are treated as the candidates for new seed nodes.

(iii) The Evaluator Layer: the evaluator receive the candidates from the combiners and evaluate their contribution. The node v^* with the maximum marginal gain of influence spread with respect to the current seed set S will be selected as the new seed node. Then the new seed v^* will be added to S and returned to the multi-selector layer to find the next seed. In order to improve the time efficiency, for each combiner i, the evaluator will only evaluate top κ candidate nodes with the highest d_{iv} value.

4.2   Discussion About the Framework

Our MSIM framework has several interesting properties.

First, the matrix $\mathbf{C}$, i.e., the weight of links connecting the selectors and the combiners can significantly affect the final results. If we choose the i-th row to be all one, and the other rows to be all zero, then the framework will degenerate to the single algorithm with respect to the i-th selector. This means that our framework can be used to interpret any existing influence maximization algorithms. If $q = l$ and $\mathbf{C}$ is a unit matrix $\mathbf{I}$, then the framework will work in a "voting" manner, i.e., the evaluator directly evaluate the output of each selector to find the best new seed node.

Second, our framework can be easily parallelized with almost no extra operations. For example, we can put the selectors, combiners and the evaluator on different computers, or even on the cloud. The parallelizability of our framework benefits from the loose coupling between different layers in the framework.

Third, the MSIM framework is highly flexible. Designers may choose any number of selectors and combiners, use arbitrary types of connections to generate an accurate solution. They can even use their own evaluators.

4.3 Algorithm

Our algorithm is based on the MSIM framework as shown in Fig. 1. We use three selectors: Degree, CoFIM [11] and IMM [14].

The connection matrix between selectors and combiners is a 3 by 3 unit matrix $(\mathbf{I})^{3 \times 3}$. Each selector output 2 nodes in one step and we set the weights of the two nodes as $p_{v_1} = 0.6$ and $p_{v_2} = 0.4$ respectively. The parameter $\kappa = 2$, i.e., the evaluator will evaluate the top 2 candidate nodes for each combiner. We use Monte-Carlo evaluator, i.e., we run MC simulations to approximate the influence contribution for each candidate.

5   Experimental Evaluation

5.1   Dataset

We first evaluate the performance of our framework on five real world datasets, which provide a spectral of application areas and ranges from medium to larger sizes. Two medium-sized datasets (NetHEPT and NetPHY) are downloaded from the website[3] provided by Chen et al. [4], while the other three larger datasets are obtained from the SNAP website[4] maintained by Jure Leskovec.

NetHEPT: This dataset contains the collaboration relationships among authors in the area High Energy Physics Theory. If an author i co-authors at least one paper with author j, then an undirected edge will be created between i and j.

NetPHY: The NetPHY dataset also comes from the arXiv platform, including the collaboration relationships among authors in the area of Physics. The network includes 37K nodes and 174K edges.

Epinions: The Epinions dataset contains the who-trust-whom data from a consumer review site Epinions.com, where customers can submit online reviews on the products and other users may choose whether or not to trust the review, forming the trust relationships.

---

[3] http://research.microsoft.com/enus/people/weic/graphdata.zip.
[4] http://snap.stanford.edu/data/.

Amazon: The Amazon dataset provides the data from the online shopping platform Amazon (http://www.amazon.com). If a product i is frequently co purchased with product j, then an undirected edge is created between i and j.

DBLP: The DBLP online library is a large collection of papers in computer science. The dataset provides a co-authorship network among research workers. If two authors have collaborated on at least one paper, an undirected edge is created between them.

For simplicity, we treat all the edges as undirected ones. Table 1 summaries the statistical properties of these datasets.

Table 1. Summary of five real world datasets

Dataset	NetHEPT	NetPHY	Epinions	Amazon	DBLP
# Ndoes	15K	37K	76K	335K	317K
# Edges	31K	174K	406K	926K	1M
Max. degree	64	178	3,044	290	343
Avg. degree	4.12	9.38	10.69	4.34	6.62

5.2   Baseline Algorithms

We compare the performance of our MSIM framework with five baseline algorithms, which include three state-of-the-art algorithms having been successfully applied on large-scale networks and two node centrality based heuristic algorithms. We do not include the traditional greedy algorithm due to its extremely low time efficiency in handling large-scale networks.

- **CoFIM**: The CoFIM (Community-based Framework for Influence Maximization) is a community-based influence maximization algorithm proposed by Shang et al. [11]. The authors divided the influence diffusion process into two phases and the propagation is restricted within communities in the second phase. Due to the high performance of this algorithm on real-world datasets, we select it as one of our selectors in the MSIM framework. We set the parameter $\gamma = 3$ for the CoFIM algorithm.
- **IMM**: The IMM (Influence Maximization via Martingales) algorithm proposed by Tang et al. [14] is an extension of their previously proposed TIM+ [15] algorithm. By taking advantage of martingales (a classic statistical tool), IMM algorithm is able to provide a worst-case guarantees to the optimal solution with low computational costs. We set the parameter $\varepsilon = 0.1$ for the IMM algorithm.
- **IPA**: The IPA (Independent Path Algorithm) is an influence path based algorithm proposed by Kim et al. [9]. The algorithm assumes that influence only propagate through paths whose influence probability is larger than a

given threshold θ and different influence paths are independent of each other. Based on this assumption, the influence spread can be efficiently computed in a parallel manner. We set the parameter $\theta = 1/320$ as recommended by the authors in their paper.

- **SD**: The SD (Single Discount) algorithm is a node centrality-based algorithm proposed by Chen et al. [4]. In each iteration the algorithm selects the node with the highest degree and add it to the seed set. Meanwhile, once a node is selected, the degree of each of its neighbors will be reduced (discounted) by 1.
- **Degree**: The simple degree based algorithm selects top k nodes with the highest degree.

5.3 Experimental Procedure

We build our experiments as follows:

Diffusion Model: The diffusion model used in this paper is the weighted cascade (WC) model, an extension to the independent cascade model where the propagation probability from u to v is $p_{uv} = 1/k_v$, relying only on the degree of v.

Experimental Environment: The experiments are carried out on a computer with 3.5 GHz Intel Xeon E3-1246 v3 CPU and 32 GB memory.

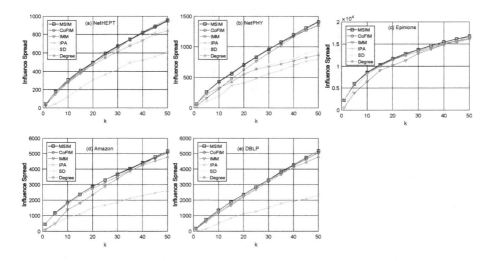

Fig. 3. The influence spread on five real world datasets

5.4 Experimental Results

We compare the influence spread of different algorithms on five real world datasets, as shown in Fig. 3. Given seed set S, influence spread is defined as the

number of expected active nodes after the diffusion process stopped. It is used
to evaluate the effectiveness of influence maximization algorithms. We obtain
the influence spread value by running 10,000 Monte-Carlo simulations. The IPA
algorithm performs worst on all the networks except for the Epinions dataset.
The node centrality based algorithms (SD and Degree) are effective only with
small k, as shown in Fig. 3(a) and (b). On the contrary, the IMM algorithm
performs well when k is large. However, when k is small, it becomes ineffective
and its performance is even inferior to the simple heuristic algorithms, as shown
in Fig. 3(b), (c) and (d). For example, on the Epinions dataset, when $k \leq 35$,
the influence spread value of the IMM algorithm is lower than all the other
algorithms. Among all the baseline algorithms, CoFIM exhibits the best overall
performance, but it still suffers at the point $k = 50$. Compared to the baseline
algorithms, our MSIM algorithm, by combining the intelligence of different individual algorithms (Degree, CoFIM, and IMM), shows great superiority over the
other algorithms with all values of k. This can be further illustrated in Fig. 4,
which shows how many times different algorithms show their best performance
in selecting top k ($1 \leq k \leq 50$) seeds. In sum, the results on real world datasets
validate the effectiveness of the MSIM framework.

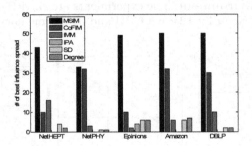

Fig. 4. The times of best influence spread of different algorithms

6   Conclusion

In this paper, we propose a multi-selector framework to effectively solve the
influence maximization problem by combining the intelligence of different existing algorithms. The effectiveness of our framework is evaluated on five real world
datasets and the results of our algorithm show great superiority over other state-
of-the-art algorithms in terms of influence spread. Our work provides a new
perspective to the study of influence maximization.

Acknowledgements. This work was supported by the Fundamental Research Funds
for the Central Universities of China (Nos. 106112016CDJXY180003 , 0216001104621).

References

1. Kempe, D., Kleinberg, J., Tardos, É.: Maximizing the spread of influence through a social network. In: Proceedings of the Ninth ACM SIGKDD International Conference on Knowledge Discovery and Data Mining, ACM (2003)
2. Nemhauser, G.L., Wolsey, L.A., Fisher, M.L.: An analysis of approximations for maximizing submodular set functions-I. Math. Program. 14(1), 265–294 (1978)
3. Leskovec, J., Krause, A., Guestrin, C., Faloutsos, C., Van-Briesen, J., Glance, N.: Cost-effective outbreak detection in networks. In: Proceedings of the 13th ACM SIGKDD International Conference on Knowledge Discovery and Data Mmining, ACM (2007)
4. Chen, W., Wang, Y., Yang, S.: Efficient inuence maximization in social networks. In: Proceedings of the 15th ACM SIGKDD International Conference on Knowledge Discovery and Data Mining. ACM (2009)
5. Wang, Y., Feng, X.: A potential-based node selection strategy for influence maximization in a social network. In: Huang, R., Yang, Q., Pei, J., Gama, J., Meng, X., Li, X. (eds.) ADMA 2009. LNCS, vol. 5678, pp. 350–361. Springer, Heidelberg (2009). doi:10.1007/978-3-642-03348-3_34
6. Kundu, S., Murthy, C.A., Pal, S.K.: A new centrality measure for influence maximization in social networks. In: Kuznetsov, S.O., Mandal, D.P., Kundu, M.K., Pal, S.K. (eds.) PReMI 2011. LNCS, vol. 6744, pp. 242–247. Springer, Heidelberg (2011). doi:10.1007/978-3-642-21786-9_40
7. Kimura, M., Saito, K.: Tractable models for information diffusion in social networks. In: Fürnkranz, J., Scheffer, T., Spiliopoulou, M. (eds.) PKDD 2006. LNCS, vol. 4213, pp. 259–271. Springer, Heidelberg (2006). doi:10.1007/11871637_27
8. Chen, W., Wang, C., Wang, Y.: Scalable influence maximization for prevalent viral marketing in large-scale social networks. In: Proceedings of the 16th ACM SIGKDD International Conference on Knowledge Discovery and Data Mining, ACM (2010)
9. Kim, J., Kim, S.-K., Hwanjo, Y.: Scalable and parallelizable processing of influence maximization for large-scale social networks. In: 2013 IEEE 29th International Conference on Data Engineering, IEEE (2013)
10. Goyal, A., Wei, L., Lakshmanan, L.V.: Celf++: optimizing the greedy algorithm for influence maximization in social networks. In: Proceedings of the 20th International Conference Companion on World Wide Web. ACM (2011)
11. Shang, J., Zhou, S., Li, X., Liu, L., Hongchun, W.: CoFIM: a community-based framework for influence maximization on large-scale networks. Knowl.-Based Syst. 117, 88–100 (2017)
12. Chen, W., Collins, A., Cummings, R., et al.: Influence maximization in social networks when negative opinions may emerge and propagate. SDM 11, 379–390 (2011)
13. Mahajan, V., Muller, E., Bass, F.M.: New product diffusion models in marketing: a review and directions for research. In: Nakićenović, N., Grübler, A. (eds.) Diffusion of Technologies and Social Behavior, pp. 125–177. Springer, Heidelberg (1991). doi:10.1007/978-3-662-02700-4_6
14. Tang, Y., Shi, Y., Xiao, X.: Influence maximization in near-linear time: a martingale approach. In: Proceedings of the 2015 ACM SIGMOD International Conference on Management of Data, ACM, 1539–1554 (2015)
15. Tang, Y., Xiao, X., Shi, Y.: Influence maximization: near-optimal time complexity meets practical efficiency. In: Proceedings of the 2014 ACM SIGMOD International Conference on Management of Data, pp. 75–86. ACM (2014)

A Simpler Method to Obtain a PTAS for Connected k-Path Vertex Cover in Unit Disk Graph

Zhao Zhang[1(✉)], Xiaohui Huang[2(✉)], and Lina Chen[1]

[1] College of Mathematics Physics and Information Engineering,
Zhejiang Normal University, Jinhua 321004, Zhejiang, China
`hxhzz@sina.com`
[2] Library and Information Center, Zhejiang Normal University,
Jinhua 321004, Zhejiang, China
`xdhqjt@sina.com`

Abstract. Given a connected graph $G = (V, E)$, a connected k-path vertex cover (CVCP_k) is a vertex set $C \subseteq V$ which contains at least one vertex from every path of G on k vertices and the subgraph of G induced by C is connected. This paper presents a new PTAS for Min-CVCP_k on unit disk graphs. Compared with previous PTAS given by Liu *et al.*, Our method not only simplifies the algorithm but also simplifies the analysis by a large amount.

Keywords: Connected k-path vertex cover · Unit disk graph · PTAS · Approximation algorithm

1 Introduction

Given a connected graph $G = (V, E)$ with vertex set V and edge set E, a *k-path vertex cover* (abbreviated as VCP_k) is a vertex subset $C \subseteq V$ such that every k-path has at least one vertex in C, where a *k-path* is a path on k-vertices. Or equivalently, C is a VCP_k of G if and only if $G - C$ does not contain any k-path. The *minimum VCP_k problem* (Min-VCP_k) is to find a VCP_k of the smallest size.

In recent years, studies on VCP_k have attracted a lot of attentions because of its background in network security. In [8], Novotny proposed the *k-generalized Canvas scheme* which guarantees data integrity sent in a network under the assumption that at least one vertex is not captured on each k-path. Hence each k-path has at least one protected vertex, and the protected vertices form a VCP_k. Since a protected vertex is more costly than a regular vertex, it is desirable to find a smallest VCP_k.

Connectivity is a major concern in many applications in wireless sensor networks (WSNs). For example, when constructing a virtual backbone in a WSN, in order that information can be shared by the whole network, it is often required that backbone nodes induce a connected graph [11]. The same consideration

© Springer International Publishing AG 2017
L. Ma et al. (Eds.): WASA 2017, LNCS 10251, pp. 584–592, 2017.
DOI: 10.1007/978-3-319-60033-8_50

motivates the concept of *connected k-path vertex cover* (abbreviated as $CVCP_k$), that is, a VCP_k which induces a connected graph.

A homogeneous wireless sensor network is usually modeled as a *unit disk graph* (UDG), in which very vertex of the graph corresponds to a node on the plane and two vertices are adjacent in the graph if and only if the Euclidean distance between their corresponding nodes is at most one.

In [7], Liu *et al.* presented a PTAS for Min-$CVCP_k$ on unit disk graphs. That is, for any real positive number ε, their algorithm computes in polynomial time a $CVCP_k$ whose size is at most $(1 + \varepsilon)$ times that of an optimal solution. In this paper, we present a simpler method to obtain a PTAS.

1.1 Related Work

There are a lot of studies on Min-VCP_k from 2011, particularly for $k = 3$, including graph theoretical point of view [2], FPT algorithm [3], and approximation algorithm [10], etc. Since the focus of this paper is on the algorithmic aspect of connected VCP_k, we only mention known results on Min-$CVCP_k$ in the following.

Liu *et al.* [7] were the first to consider Min-VCP_k with a connectivity requirement. They gave a PTAS for Min-$CVCP_k$ on unit disk graphs using the Partition and Shifting method. Their algorithm is an adaptation of the method in [4,14] which gave a PTAS for the minimum connected dominating set problem. Injecting a c-local assumption into such a strategy, Wang *et al.* [12,13] obtained a PTAS for the minimum *weight* $CVCP_k$ problem. In all these algorithms, a constant approximation algorithm is a prerequisite. In particular, the constant approximation algorithm for Min-$CVCP_k$ used in [7] has performance ratio k^2.

In [5], Li *et al.* gave a linear-time algorithm for Min-$CVCP_k$ on trees, and they further showed that the performance ratio of Min-$CVCP_k$ on a general graph can be improved to k if the graph has girth at least k, where the girth of a graph is the length of a shortest cycle. In particular, Min-$CVCP_3$ has performance ratio at most 3.

1.2 Our Contribution

In this paper, we present a simpler method to obtain a PTAS for Min-$CVCP_k$ on unit disk graphs, *which no longer requires a constant approximation*. Furthermore, the analysis is also much simpler than that in [7], and the time needed is less. The highest outline of our method is also Partition and Shifting.

The idea of Partition is to divide the region under consideration into smaller blocks, each block having a constant side-length; solve the problem in each block optimally or approximately; then assemble these local solutions into a feasible solution to the original problem. To control the loss after assembling, Shifting strategy is used.

In all previous works [4,7,14], each block is divided into an inner part and a boundary part, and the output is the union of locally optimal solutions for inner parts and the set of nodes of a constant approximation falling into the boundary parts. The purpose of using those boundary nodes is to *connect*.

Contrary to such a strategy, our method will *expand* every block. We shall show that a moderate expansion is sufficient to guarantee that the union of locally optimal solutions is a connected vertex set (no more vertices are needed for connection), thus eliminating the need of a constant approximation. Furthermore, the definition of a locally optimal solution is also simpler than previous ones. As a result, there is no need to deal with inner parts and boundary parts separately, which leads to a simplification of analysis. Such a method also reduces the size needed for a block, and thus leads to a reduction on computation time.

This paper is organized as follows. In Sect. 2, we introduce some terminologies and briefly introduce the method used in previous papers. In Sect. 3, the new algorithm is provided as well as its performance analysis. Section 4 concludes the paper.

2   Preliminaries

In this paper, we shall provide a new method to obtain a PTAS for Min-CVCP$_k$ on unit disk graphs, where k is a constant. It is assumed that the unit disk G is given with its geometric representation, that is, we are given the set of nodes on the plane which induce G. In the following, terminology node is used as a geometric version of a vertex. For a vertex set C, the subgraph of G induced by C is denoted as $G[C]$.

The partition and shifting method is as follows. In the partition phase, the region containing all nodes is divided into smaller blocks of constant side length, and local solutions on each block are assembled into a feasible solution to the original problem. Then, shifting method is used to obtain a series of partitions. Finally, a best solution is chosen among all solutions to these partitions. In general, if a problem has a ρ-approximation on every block, then for any real number $\varepsilon > 0$, after applying the shifting method, the original problem has approximation ratio $\rho + \varepsilon$.

Adding connectivity requirement adds a lot of challenge, because connectivity is a global property. In [4], Cheng *et al.* studied the minimum connected dominating set problem (CDS) in unit disk graphs, and gave the first PTAS. To deal with the connectivity requirement, Cheng *et al.* adapted the Partition and Shifting method as follows. Each block is divided into an inner region and a boundary region, with the inner region and the boundary region having an overlap. A locally optimal solution is obtained for each inner region. However, the union of these locally optimal solutions, say D, might not be connected. So, the algorithm further makes use of a constant approximation algorithm for the original problem. Suppose D_0 is the output of the constant approximation algorithm. Those vertices in D_0 which fall into the boundary regions are added into D, for the purpose of connection. Zhang *et al.* [14] refined their analysis to produce a PTAS for CDS in unit ball graphs in higher dimensional space. Liu's PTAS for CVCP$_k$ [7] also employs the same strategy. In all of these algorithms, a constant approximation algorithm is a prerequisite.

3   The Algorithm

In this section, we propose the new algorithm with its theoretical analysis.

3.1   Partition

Suppose all vertices of the graph is contained in a square region of size $L \times L$. Let q be a constant which is an integer related with error ε. Such a q will be determined later. For convenience of statement, suppose L is divisible by q. Enlarge the square into a larger square by adding a boundary of width q to the left and adding a boundary of width q to the bottom (see Fig. 1). Denote the enlarged square as Q. Divide Q into *blocks* of size $q \times q$. For each block b of Q, enlarge it to an *extended-block* $\hat{b}$ by adding a boundary of width k to each of its four sides. Call the extended region as the boundary region of $\hat{b}$, and call the union of boundary regions of all extended-blocks as boundary region of the partition of Q.

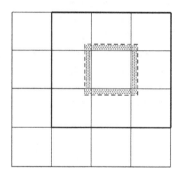

Fig. 1. An illustration of a partition. The blackened square contains all nodes, and Q is obtained from the blackened square by adding a boundary to the left and to the bottom. The dashed square is an extended-block and the dotted area is its boundary region.

   Suppose, without loss of generality, that the above square Q has its left-bottom corner at the origin $(0,0)$, and denote such a partition as $P(0)$. For each $a = 0, 1, \ldots, q-1$, let $P(a)$ be the partition obtained from $P(0)$ by shifting the left-bottom corner to coordinate (a, a).

3.2   Locally Optimal Solution on an Extended-Block

The algorithm is based on finding locally optimal solutions on extended-blocks, where the meaning of a locally optimal solution is defined as follows.

Definition 1. For a block b, denote by $V_{\hat{b}}$ the set of nodes falling into $\hat{b}$, and let $G_{\hat{b}}$ be the subgraphs of G induced by $V_{\hat{b}}$. A vertex subset $C \subseteq V_{\hat{b}}$ is said to be a *locally feasible solution of extended-block* $\hat{b}$ if the restriction of C on each connected component of $G_{\hat{b}}$ is an $CVCP_k$ of that component. Vertex set C is a *locally optimal solution* if C is a locally feasible solution with the minimum size.

The following lemma shows that a locally optimal solution can be found in polynomial time (recall that we have assumed that both k and q are constants).

Lemma 1. *For each extended-block $\hat{b}$, a locally optimal solution can be found in time $O(1.66^k n_{\hat{b}}^{O((k-1)\gamma)} poly(n_{\hat{b}}))$, where $\gamma = 2(q+2k)^2/\sqrt{3} + 2(q+2k) + 1$ and $n_{\hat{b}}$ is the number of nodes falling into $\hat{b}$.*

Proof. Suppose C is a locally optimal solution of $\hat{b}$. Then $G_{\hat{b}} - C$ is P_k-free. By Lemma 2.3 of [15], $V_{\hat{b}} - C$ can be partitioned into at most $k - 1$ independent sets. By Zassenhaus-Groemer-Oler inequality (see [6] or [9]), and by the observation that $\hat{b}$ is a square of side length $q + 2k$, we see that every independent set contained in $\hat{b}$ contains at most γ nodes. Hence $|V_{\hat{b}} - C| \leq (k-1)\gamma$.

To find out C, it suffices to enumerate every node set of $\hat{b}$ containing at most $(k-1)\gamma$ nodes, check whether the remaining nodes form a locally feasible solution, and choose the smallest one. Since there are at most $n_{\hat{b}}^{O((k-1)\gamma)}$ node sets to be considered, and since the feasibility can be checked in time $O(1.66^k \cdot poly(n_{\hat{b}}))$ (finding a path of length k can be done in time $O(1.66^k \cdot poly(n_{\hat{b}}))$ by the algorithm in [1] and checking connectivity can be done in time $O(n_{\hat{b}}^2)$). The time complexity follows.

3.3   Algorithm

The algorithm is described in Algorithm 1.

Algorithm 1. Algorithm for Min-$CVCP_k$ on a unit disk graph.

Input: A connected unit disk graph G with its geometric representation, a constant k, and an error bound ε.
Output: A vertex set C which is a $CVCP_k$ of G.
  1: Let $q \leftarrow \lceil 8k^2/\varepsilon \rceil$.
  2: **for** $a = 0, \ldots, q-1$ **do**
  3:    **for** each extended-block $\hat{b}$ of partition $P(a)$ **do**
  4:       Find a locally optimal solution $C_a(\hat{b})$.
  5:    **end for**
  6:    $C_a \leftarrow \bigcup_{\hat{b}} C_a(\hat{b})$.
  7: **end for**
  8: $a_0 \leftarrow \arg\min\{|C_a| : a = 0, 1, \ldots, q-1\}$
  9: Output C_{a_0}.

3.4   Analysis

First, we consider the correctness of the algorithm.

Lemma 2. *For each $a = 0, 1, \ldots, q - 1$, the vertex set C_a computed by Algorithm 1 is a $CVCP_k$ of G.*

Proof. First, we show that C_a is a VCP_k of G. If this is not true, then there is a k-path P in $G - C_a$. Suppose, without loss of generality, that P has a node u in block b. Then any node of P has Euclidean distance at most $k - 1$ from u. Hence P is completely contained in the extended-block $\hat{b}$. It follows that there is a node of P belonging to the locally optimal solution $C_a(\hat{b}) \subseteq C_a$, a contradiction.

Next, we show that $G[C_a]$ is connected. Suppose this is not true. Consider two connected components of $G[C_a]$ which are nearest to each other in G, say G_1 and G_2. Let $P = u_0 u_1 \ldots u_t$ be a shortest path in G connecting G_1 and G_2, where $u_0 \in V(G_1)$ and $u_t \in V(G_2)$. By the shortest assumption of the path, $P' = u_1 \ldots u_{t-1}$ is a path in $G - C_a$. If $t \geq k + 1$, then P' is a path in $G - C_a$ on at least k vertices, contradicting that C_a is a VCP_k of G. Hence $t \leq k$. Suppose u_0 is in block b, then path P is completely contained in the extended-block $\hat{b}$. Hence u_0 and u_t are in a same connected component of $G_{\hat{b}}$. By the definition of locally optimal solution, u_0 and u_t belong to a same connected component of $G[C_a(\hat{b})]$, contradicting that G_1 and G_2 are different connected components of $G[C_a]$. ∎

By a similar argument as in Lemma 2, we have the following lemma.

Lemma 3. *Suppose G is a connected graph and C is a VCP_k of G which is not connected. Then by adding at most $k - 1$ vertices will merge at least two connected components of $G[C]$.*

Suppose C^* is an optimal solution to $CVCP_k$. Let $B_a(C^*)$ be the set of nodes of C^* falling into the boundary region of partition $P(a)$.

Lemma 4. *For each $a = 0, 1, \ldots, q - 1$, $|C_a| \leq |C^*| + 4k|B_a(C^*)|$.*

Proof. Let $C^*(\hat{b})$ be the set of nodes of C^* falling into $\hat{b}$. Clearly, $C^*(\hat{b})$ is a VCP_k of $G_{\hat{b}}$.

Suppose there is a connected component H of graph $G_{\hat{b}}$ such that the restriction of $C^*(\hat{b})$ on H has l connected components $H_1, \ldots, H_l$ with $l \geq 2$. By Lemma 3, adding at most $(k - 1)(l - 1)$ vertices can change the restriction of $C^*(\hat{b})$ on H into a $CVCP_k$ of H. Notice that every H_i contains some boundary node of H because $G[C^*]$ is connected. Furthermore, such boundary nodes are distinct since they belong to distinct connected components. Hence l is upper bounded by the number of boundary nodes in H. Doing the same operation on every connected component of $G_{\hat{b}}$, the node set $C^*(\hat{b})$ can be changed into a locally feasible solution $C'(\hat{b})$ such that

$$|C'(\hat{b})| \leq |C^*(\hat{b})| + (k - 1)|B_a(C^*, \hat{b})|,$$

where $B_a(C^*, \hat{b})$ is the set of nodes of C^* falling into the boundary region of $\hat{b}$ of partition $P(a)$.

Since $C_a(\hat{b})$ is a locally optimal solution of $\hat{b}$, we have

$$|C_a(\hat{b})| \leq |C'(\hat{b})| \leq |C^*(\hat{b})| + (k-1)|B_a(C^*, \hat{b})|.$$

Summing the above inequality over all extended-blocks $\hat{b}$,

$$|C_a| \leq \sum_{\hat{b}} |C_a(\hat{b})| \leq \sum_{\hat{b}} |C^*(\hat{b})| + (k-1) \sum_{\hat{b}} |B_a(C^*, \hat{b})|.$$

Notice that if a node of C^* is counted more than once in the righthand side of the above inequality, then this node must be in the boundary region $B_a(C^*)$. Furthermore, a node falls into at most four boundary regions of extended-blocks. Hence

$$|C_a) \leq (|C^*| + 4|B_a(C^*)|) + 4(k-1)|B_a(C^*)| = |C^*| + 4k|B_a(C^*)|.$$

The lemma is proved.

Now, we are ready to prove that Algorithm 1 is a PTAS for Min-CVCP$_k$.

Theorem 1. *Algorithm 1 finds a CVCP$_k$ of G in time $O(n^{O(1/\varepsilon^2)})$ which approximates the optimal value within a factor of $(1 + \varepsilon)$.*

Proof. Summing the inequality in Lemma 4 for a rangeing over 0 to $q - 1$, we have

$$\sum_{a=0}^{q-1} |C_a| \leq q|C^*| + 4k \sum_{a=0}^{q-1} |B_a(C^*)|.$$

Since every node of C^* belongs to at most $2k$ boundary regions of different partitions,

$$\sum_{a=0}^{q-1} |B_a(C^*)| \leq 2k|C^*|.$$

Since $|C_{a_0}| = \min\{|C_a|: a = 0, 1, \ldots, q-1\}$, we have

$$q|C_{a_0}| \leq q|C^*| + 8k^2|C^*|.$$

The performance ratio follows from the choice of $q = \lceil 8k^2/\varepsilon \rceil$.

The time complexity is a result of Lemma 1, by the choice of q and recalling that k is a constant.

4   Conclusion and Discussion

In this paper, we presented a simpler PTAS algorithm for Min-CVCP$_k$. Compared with previous method in [7], our algorithm no longer needs a constant approximation. Furthermore, our analysis is also much simpler than the one in [7]. The simplification can also be seen from the choice of the block size q. In [7], q is chosen to be $\lceil 40(k-1)k^3/\varepsilon \rceil$, while in our algorithm $q = \lceil 8k^2/\varepsilon \rceil$. Such a decrease on q also reduces the time needed to compute a solution.

The idea of expanding blocks can also be used to simplify the methods used in [4,14] to compute a connected dominating set (CDS) on unit disk graphs. Notice that for this problem, the restriction of an optimal dominating set on an extended block $\hat{b}$ is not necessarily a dominating set of $G_{\hat{b}}$ (some node in $\hat{b}$ might be dominated by a node outside of $\hat{b}$). So, one has to define a locally optimal solution on a shrunk block, which is obtained from an extended block by shrunken the boundary by one unit. This adds a little complexity to the analysis. However, it still can be proved that the union of locally optimal solutions is guaranteed to be connected, and thus eliminating the need of a constant approximation. It can be expected that the idea in this paper can be further applied to other geometric covering problems with connectivity requirement.

Acknowledgment. This research is supported by NSFC (11531011, 61222201, 61502431).

References

1. Björklund, A., Husfeldt, T., Kaski, P., Koivisto, A.M.: Narrow sieves for parameterized paths and packings, arXiv:1007.1161
2. Brešar, B., Kardoš, F., Katrenič, J., Semaniš, G.: Minimum k-path vertex cover. Discret. Appl. Math. **159**, 1189–1195 (2011)
3. Chang, M., Chen, L., Hung, L., Rossmanith, P., Su, P.: Fixed-parameter algorithms for vertex cover P_3. Discret. Optim. **19**, 12–22 (2016)
4. Cheng, X., Huang, X., Li, D., Wu, W., Du, D.: A polynomial-time approximation scheme for the minimum-connected dominating set in ad hoc wireless networks. Networks **42**(4), 202–208 (2003)
5. Li, X., Zhang, Z., Huang, X.: Approximation algorithms for minimum (weight) connected k-path vertex cover. Discret. Appl. Math. **205**, 101–108 (2016)
6. Liu, Q., Li, X., Wu, L., Du, H., Zhang, Z., Wu, W., Hu, X., Xu, Y.: A new proof for Zassenhaus-Groemer-Oler inequality. Discret. Math. Algorithms Appl. **4**(2), 1250014 (2012)
7. Liu, X., Lu, H., Wang, W., Wu, W.: PTAS for the minimum k-path connected vertex cover problem in unit disk graphs. J. Glob. Optim. **56**, 449–458 (2013)
8. Novotný, M.: Design and analysis of a generalized canvas protocol. In: Samarati, P., Tunstall, M., Posegga, J., Markantonakis, K., Sauveron, D. (eds.) WISTP 2010. LNCS, vol. 6033, pp. 106–121. Springer, Heidelberg (2010). doi:10.1007/978-3-642-12368-9_8
9. Oler, N.: An inequality in the geometry of numbers. Acta Math. **105**, 19–48 (1961)
10. Tu, J., Zhou, W.: A factor 2 approximation algorithm for the vertex cover P_3 problem. Inf. Process. Lett. **111**, 683–686 (2011)

11. Wan, P., Alzoubi, K., Frieder, O.: Distributed construction of connected dominating set in wireless ad hoc networks. ACM Springer Mob. Netw. Appl. **9**(2), 141–149 (2004). A preliminary version of this paper appeared in IEEE INFOCOM 2002
12. Wang, L., Zhang, X., Zhang, Z., Broersma, H.: A PTAS for the minimum weight connected vertex cover P_3 problem on unit disk graphs. Theoret. Comput. Sci. **571**, 58–66 (2015)
13. Wang, L., Du, W., Zhang, Z., Zhang, X.: A PTAS for minimum weighted connected vertex cover P_3 problem in 3-dimensional wireless sensor networks. J. Comb. Optim. **33**, 106–122 (2017)
14. Zhang, Z., Gao, X., Wu, W., Du, D.: A PTAS for minimum connected dominating set in 3-dimensional wireless sensor networks. J. Glob. Optim. **45**(3), 451–458 (2009)
15. Zhang, Z., Li, X., Shi, Y., Nie, H., Zhu, Y.: PTAS for minimum k-path vertex cover in ball graph. Inf. Process. Lett. **119**, 9–13 (2017)

Maximum-Weighted λ-Colorable Subgraph: Revisiting and Applications

Peng-Jun Wan[1,2,4(✉)], Huaqiang Yuan[1,4], Xufei Mao[1,4], Jiliang Wang[3,4], and Zhu Wang[3,4]

[1] School of Computer Science, Dongguan University of Technology, Dongguan, People's Republic of China
`wan@cs.iit.edu`
[2] Department of Computer Science, Illinois Institute of Technology, Chicago, USA
[3] School of Software, Tsinghua University, Beijing, People's Republic of China
[4] Department of Mathematics, Computer Science, and Statistics, State University of New York at Oneonta, Oneonta, USA

Abstract. Given a vertex-weighted graph G and a positive integer λ, a subset F of the vertices is said to be λ-colorable if F can be partitioned into at most λ independent subsets. This problem of seeking a λ-colorable F with maximum total weight is known as **Maximum-Weighted λ-Colorable Subgraph (λ-MWCS)**. This problem is a generalization of the classical problem **Maximum-Weighted Independent Set (MWIS)** and has broader applications in wireless networks. All existing approximation algorithms for λ-**MWCS** have approximation bound strictly increasing with λ. It remains open whether the problem can be approximated with the same factor as the problem **MWIS**. In this paper, we present new approximation algorithms for λ-**MWCS**. For certain range of λ, the approximation bounds of our algorithms are the same as those for **MWIS**, and for a larger range of λ, the approximation bounds of our algorithms are strictly smaller than the best-known ones in the literature. In addition, we give an exact polynomial-time algorithm for λ-**MWCS** in co-comparability graphs. We also present a number of applications of our algorithms in wireless networking.

Keywords: Coloring · Channel assignment · Approximation algorithm

1 Introduction

Consider an undirected graph $G = (V, E)$ and a positive integer λ. A subset I of V is said to be *independent* if any pair of vertices in I are non-adjacent. A subset F of the vertices is said to be λ-*colorable* if F can be partitioned into at most λ independent subsets (or equivalently, the subgraph of G induced by F is λ-colorable). Suppose that each vertex v has a positive weight $w(v)$. The weight of each subset $F \subseteq V$ is defined to be $w(F) := \sum_{v \in F} w(v)$. The problem of seeking a λ-colorable subset F of V with maximum weight is known as **Maximum-Weighted λ-Colorable Subgraph (λ-MWCS)** [3,12,13]. The

© Springer International Publishing AG 2017
L. Ma et al. (Eds.): WASA 2017, LNCS 10251, pp. 593–604, 2017.
DOI: 10.1007/978-3-319-60033-8_51

special case of this problem with $\lambda = 1$ is the classical problem **Maximum-Weighted Independent Set** (**MWIS**). In general, the problem λ-**MWCS** may be strictly harder than **MWIS**. Indeed, when restricted the class of split graphs, Yannakakis and Gavril [12] showed that this problem is NP-hard, but the problem **MWIS** can be solved in polynomial time. On the other hand, by a result in [3], the existence of a μ-approximation algorithm for **MWIS** always implies a greedy $1 / \left[1 - (1 - 1/(\mu\lambda))^\lambda \right]$-approximation algorithm for λ-**MWCS**, which repeatedly takes an μ-approximate weighted independent set in the remaining graph for λ times. Note that the approximation bound $1 / \left[1 - (1 - 1/(\lambda\mu))^\lambda \right]$ strictly increases with λ.

Various approximation algorithms for **MWIS** have been developed in [1,9, 13]. For each $v \in V$, $N(v)$ denotes the set of neighbors of v in G. Let $\prec$ be an ordering of V. For any $u, v \in V$, both $v \prec u$ and $u \succ v$ represent that v appears before u in the ordering $\prec$. For any $v \in V$ and any $U \subseteq V$, we use $U_{\prec v}$ (respectively, $U_{\succ v}$) to denote the set of $u \in U$ satisfying that $u \prec v$ (respectively, $u \succ v$); in addition, $U_{\preceq v}$ denotes $\{v\} \cup U_{\prec v}$, and $U_{\succeq v}$ denotes $\{v\} \cup U_{\succ v}$. The *backward local independence number* (BLIN) of G in $\prec$ is defined to be the maximum number of non-adjacent vertices in $N(v) \cap V_{\prec v}$ for all $v \in V$. An *orientation* of G is a digraph obtained from G by imposing an orientation on each edge of G. Suppose that D is an orientation of G. For each $v \in V$, $N_D^{in}(v)$ (resp., $N_D^{out}(v)$) denotes the set of in-neighbors (resp., out-neighbors) of v in D. The *inward local independence number* (ILIN) of D is defined to be the maximum number of non-adjacent vertices in $N_D^{in}(v)$ for all $v \in V$. Then, the following algorithmic results have be established:

– Given an ordering of V with BLIN β, there is a β-approximation algorithm for **MWIS** [1,13].
– Given an orientation of G with ILIN γ, there is a 2γ-approximation algorithm for **MWIS** [9].

By plugging the above approximation algorithms for MWIS into the greedy approximation framework for λ-**MWCS** proposed in [3], the following algorithmic results can be obtained:

– Given an ordering of V with BLIN β, there is an $1 / \left[1 - (1 - 1/(\beta\lambda))^\lambda \right]$-approximation algorithm for λ-**MWCS**.
– Given an orientation of G with ILIN γ, there is an $1 / \left[1 - (1 - 1/(2\gamma\lambda))^\lambda \right]$-approximation algorithm for λ-**MWCS**.

Moreover, given an ordering with BLIN β, Ye and Borodin [13] extends β-approximation algorithm for **MWIS** directly to a $\left(\beta + 1 - \frac{1}{\lambda} \right)$-approximation algorithm for λ-**MWCS**. While the approximation bound is relatively larger, the algorithm is simpler and more efficient in implementation. All those approximation bounds are greater than the respective approximation bounds for **MWIS**. A natural open question is whether and when the same approximation bound for **MWIS** can be achieved for λ-**MWCS**. A more general open question is whether and when a better approximation bound may be achieved than those best-known approximation bounds.

Motivated by the above two open questions, this paper develops two new approximation algorithms for λ-**MWCS**.

- Given an ordering of V with BLIN β, the algorithm developed in Sect. 3 is not only simpler than that proposed in [13], but also achieves a strictly better approximation bound

$$\max\left\{\beta, \left(1 - \frac{1}{\lambda}\right)\beta + 1\right\}.$$

  In particular, if $\lambda \leq \beta$, the approximation bound is β, which is also the best-known approximation bound for the problem **MWIS**. If $\lambda < 2\beta$, this approximation bound is strictly smaller than the best-known approximation bound $1/\left[1 - (1 - 1/(\beta\lambda))^\lambda\right]$.

- Given an orientation with ILIN γ, the algorithm developed in Sect. 4 achieve an approximation bound

$$\max\left\{2\gamma, 2\gamma\left(1 - \frac{1}{\lambda}\right) + 1\right\}.$$

  Again if $\lambda \leq 2\gamma$, the approximation bound is 2γ, which is also the best-known approximation bound for the problem **MWIS**. If $\lambda < 4\gamma$, this approximation bound is strictly smaller than the best-known approximation bound $1/\left[1 - (1 - 1/(2\gamma\lambda))^\lambda\right]$.

The above two algorithms are not only of theoretical interest, but have significant implications for the practical applications where λ is not too large compared to the BLIN or ILIN.

An ordering $\prec$ of V is said to be *cocomparable* if the following transitivity of independence is satisfied: for any triple of vertices $v \prec v' \prec v''$ with $vv' \notin E$ and $v'v'' \notin E$, we have $vv'' \notin E$. If there is a cocomparable ordering of V, then G is called a *cocomparability graph*. When restricted to comparability graphs, the problem **MWIS** is solvable in polynomial time (e.g., [9]), and consequently the greedy approximation framework for λ-**MWCS** proposed in [3] can achieve an approximation bound $1/\left[1 - (1 - 1/(\lambda))^\lambda\right]$. In Sect. 5, we give an exact polynomial-time algorithm for λ-**MWCS** in cocomparability graphs. This algorithm generalizes the classic result by Frank [6] on the unweighted variant of λ-**MWCS** in cocomparability graphs.

The remainder of this paper is organized as follows. In Sect. 2 we introduce two basic algorithmic ingredients to be used in the two subsequent sections. In Sect. 3, we develop an ordering-based selection algorithm. In Sect. 4, we present an orientation-based selection algorithm. In Sect. 5, we give an exact polynomial-time algorithm when the graph G is a co-comparability graphs. In Sect. 5, we apply these algorithms to the problem of seeking a maximum-weighted wireless communication requests which can transmit at the same time over multiple channels.

2   Preliminaries

Motivated by the NP-completeness of the feasibility test, we introduce a tractable and strong type of feasibility. Let $\prec$ be an ordering of V. A set $F \subseteq V$ is said to be *inductively feasible* in $\prec$ if for each $v \in F$, $|N(v) \cap F_{\prec v}| < \lambda$. An inductively feasible set F is always λ-colorable; indeed, a coloring of F can be greedily produced as follows:

- The first vertex v in F receives the first color.
- For each subsequent vertex $v \in F$ in the ordering $\prec$, it receives the first color which is not used by any vertex in $N(v) \cap F_{\prec v}$. This is always possible because the number of colors that have been assigned to $N(v) \cap F_{\prec v}$ is at most $|N(v) \cap F_{\prec v}| < \lambda$.

Such coloring is referred to as the *greedy coloring* of F in $\prec$.

For any subset $S \subseteq V$, an inductively feasible subset F of S can be computed as follows:

- Initially, F is empty.
- For each $v \in S$ in the ordering $\prec$, v is added to F if and only if $|N(v) \cap F_{\prec v}| < \lambda$.

The set F computed in this greedy manner is referred to as the *maximal inductively feasible subset* of S in $\prec$. It is maximal in the sense that for each $v \in S \setminus F$, $|N(v) \cap F_{\prec v}| \geq \lambda$. However, how to select the "candidate" subset S is very essential. In fact, when $S = V$ or $S = \emptyset$ at the two opposite extremes, the maximal inductively feasible subset of S in $\prec$ is almost surely to have poor performance in general. This motivates us to utilize variants of the local-ratio scheme [1–3,5,9,13], which is equivalent to the primal-dual scheme [4], for selecting candidate set S properly.

Given an ordering $\prec$ of V, the local-ratio scheme computes a candidate set S in the following *greedy* manner:

- S is initially empty.
- For each $v \in V$ in the *reverse* order of $\prec$, a *discounted* weight $\overline{w}(v)$ of v is computed by

$$\overline{w}(v) = w(v) - \frac{1}{\lambda} \overline{w}(N(v) \cap S);$$

and if $\overline{w}(v) > 0$, v is added to S.

The final set S computed in this greedy manner is referred to as the *greedy candidate subset* of V in $\prec$. For each $v \in V$, its original weight and its discounted weight have the following relation:

$$w(v) = \overline{w}(v) + \frac{1}{\lambda} \overline{w}(N(v) \cap S_{\succ v}).$$

In addition, the maximal inductively compatible subset F of S in $\prec$ has the following property

Lemma 1. *The maximal inductively feasible subset F of S in $\prec$ satisfies that $w(F) \geq \overline{w}(S)$.*

Proof. By the greedy selection of F, for each $v \in S \backslash F$, $|N(v) \cap F_{\prec v}| \geq \lambda$. Thus,

$$
\begin{aligned}
w(F) &= \sum_{v \in F} w(v) = \sum_{v \in F} \overline{w}(v) + \frac{1}{\lambda} \sum_{v \in F} \overline{w}(N(v) \cap S_{\succ v}) \\
&= \sum_{v \in F} \overline{w}(v) + \frac{1}{\lambda} \sum_{v \in F} \sum_{u \in N(v) \cap S_{\succ v}} \overline{w}(u) = \overline{w}(F) + \frac{1}{\lambda} \sum_{v \in S} \overline{w}(v) |N(v) \cap F_{\prec v}| \\
&\geq \overline{w}(F) + \frac{1}{\lambda} \sum_{v \in S \backslash F} \overline{w}(v) |N(v) \cap F_{\prec v}| \geq \overline{w}(F) + \sum_{v \in S \backslash F} \overline{w}(v) = \overline{w}(S).
\end{aligned}
$$

So, the lemma holds.

Next, we proceed to compute an ordering $\prec$ such that the discounted weight of the greedy candidate subset S in $\prec$ is close to the original weight of an optimal solution.

3   Ordering-Based Selection

Suppose that $\prec$ is an ordering of V with BLIN β. Denote

$$
\beta_\lambda := \max \left\{ \beta, \beta \left(1 - \frac{1}{\lambda}\right) + 1 \right\}.
$$

Then, the discounted weight of the greedy candidate subset S in $\prec$ and the weight of a maximum-weight feasible subset O are related as follows.

Lemma 2. *The greedy candidate subset S of V in $\prec$ satisfies that $\overline{w}(S) \geq w(O)/\beta_\lambda$.*

Proof. Consider any $v \in V$. We show that

$$
|O \cap \{v\}| + \frac{1}{\lambda} |N(v) \cap O_{\prec v}| \leq \beta_\lambda.
$$

We consider two cases.

Case 1: $v \notin O$. Then

$$
|O \cap \{v\}| + \frac{1}{\lambda} |N(v) \cap O_{\prec v}| = \frac{1}{\lambda} |N(v) \cap O_{\prec v}| \leq \frac{1}{\lambda} \lambda \beta = \beta \leq \beta_\lambda.
$$

Case 2: $v \in O$. Then

$$
\begin{aligned}
&|O \cap \{v\}| + \frac{1}{\lambda} |N(v) \cap O_{\prec v}| \\
&= 1 + \frac{1}{\lambda} |N(v) \cap O_{\prec v}| \leq 1 + \frac{1}{\lambda} (\lambda - 1) \beta = \beta \left(1 - \frac{1}{\lambda}\right) + 1 \leq \beta_\lambda.
\end{aligned}
$$

Using the relations between the original weights and the discounted weights, we have

$$w(O) = \sum_{v \in O} w(v)$$

$$= \sum_{v \in O} \overline{w}(v) + \frac{1}{\lambda} \sum_{v \in O} \overline{w}(N(v) \cap S_{\succ v})$$

$$\geq \sum_{v \in S \cap O} \overline{w}(v) + \frac{1}{\lambda} \sum_{v \in O} \overline{w}(N(v) \cap S_{\succ v})$$

$$= \sum_{v \in S \cap O} \overline{w}(v) + \frac{1}{\lambda} \sum_{u \in O} \overline{w}(N(u) \cap S_{\succ v})$$

$$= \sum_{v \in S \cap O} \overline{w}(v) + \frac{1}{\lambda} \sum_{v \in S} \overline{w}(v) |N(v) \cap O_{\prec v}|$$

$$= \sum_{v \in S} \overline{w}(v) \left[|O \cap \{v\}| + \frac{1}{\lambda} |N(v) \cap O_{\prec v}| \right]$$

$$\leq \beta_\lambda \sum_{v \in S} \overline{w}(v) = \beta_\lambda \overline{w}(S).$$

So, the lemma holds.

Motivated by the above lemma and Lemma 1, we propose the following ordering-based approximation algorithm, which runs in three steps:

1. Compute the greedy candidate subset S of V in $\prec$.
2. Compute the maximal inductively feasible subset F of S in $\prec$.
3. Compute the greedy coloring of F in $\prec$.

All the three steps are greedy in nature and have very simple implementations. The approximation bound of this algorithm follows immediately from Lemmas 1 and 2.

Theorem 1. *F has an approximate bound β_λ.*

Note that when $\lambda \leq \beta$, $\beta_\lambda = \beta$. For $\lambda > \beta$, $\beta_\lambda = \beta \left(1 - \frac{1}{\lambda}\right) + 1$ and we compare it against the best-known approximation bound. The comparison is a based on the following algebraic inequalities.

Lemma 3. *For any positive integer μ, if $1 < \lambda < 2\mu$, then*

$$\left[1 - \left(1 - \frac{1}{\mu\lambda}\right)^\lambda \right]^{-1} > \mu \left(1 - \frac{1}{\lambda}\right) + 1;$$

if $\lambda \geq 2\mu$ then

$$\left[1 - \left(1 - \frac{1}{\mu\lambda}\right)^\lambda \right]^{-1} < \mu \left(1 - \frac{1}{\lambda}\right) + 1.$$

The proof of the above lemma is quite lengthy, and is omitted in this paper. From the above lemma, we conclude that when $\lambda < 2\mu$, β_λ is smaller than the best-known approximation bound $\left[1 - \left(1 - \frac{1}{\beta_\lambda} \right)^\lambda \right]^{-1}$.

4   Orientation-Based Selection

Suppose that D is an orientation of G with ILIN γ. In this section, we present an approximation algorithm for λ-**MWCS** with approximation bound

$$(2\gamma)_\lambda := \max \left\{ 2\gamma, 2\gamma \left(1 - \frac{1}{\lambda} \right) + 1 \right\}.$$

Consider a non-zero "opportunistic" vector $x \in [0,1]^V$. For any non-empty subset U of V, a vertex $v \in U$ is said to be a surplus vertex in U with respect to x and D if

$$x \left(N_D^{in}(v) \cap U \right) \geq x \left(N_D^{out}(v) \cap U \right).$$

It was proved in [8] that there exists at least one a surplus vertex in U with respect to x and D. Based on this fact, an ordering of V can be computed by a simple *greedy* strategy as follows.

– Initialize U to V.
– For $i = |V|$ down to 1, let v_i be a surplus bid in U with respect to x and delete v_i from U.

Then, the ordering $\langle v_1, v_2, \cdots, v_{|V|} \rangle$ is referred to as a *surplus-preserving ordering* of V with respect to x and D. It has the following property.

Lemma 4. *Suppose that $\prec$ is a surplus-preserving ordering of V with respect to D and some non-zero $x \in [0,1]^V$. Then, the greedy candidate subset S in $\prec$ satisfies that*

$$\overline{w}(S) \geq \frac{\sum_{v \in V} w(v) x(v)}{\max_{v \in V} \left(x(v) + \frac{2}{\lambda} x \left(N_D^{in}(v) \right) \right)}.$$

Proof. Since $\prec$ is a surplus-preserving ordering of V with respect to x and D, for any $v \in V$ we have

$$x \left(N(v) \cap V_{\prec v} \right) \leq 2x \left(N_D^{in}(v) \cap V_{\prec v} \right) \leq 2x \left(N_D^{in}(v) \right).$$

Using the relations between the original weights and the discounted weights, we have

$$\sum_{u \in V} w(v) x(v)$$

$$= \sum_{v \in V} \overline{w}(v) x(v) + \frac{1}{\lambda} \sum_{v \in V} x(v) \sum_{u \in N(v) \cap S_{\succ v}} \overline{w}(u)$$

$$\leq \sum_{v\in S} \overline{w}(v)\, x(v) + \frac{1}{\lambda}\sum_{v\in V} x(v) \sum_{u\in N(v)\cap S_{\succ v}} \overline{w}(u)$$

$$= \sum_{v\in S} \overline{w}(v)\, x(v) + \frac{1}{\lambda}\sum_{u\in S} \overline{w}(u) \sum_{v\in N(u)\cap V_{\prec u}} x(v)$$

$$= \sum_{v\in S} \overline{w}(v)\, x(v) + \sum_{v\in S} \overline{w}(v)\, x\left(N(v)\cap V_{\prec v}\right)$$

$$= \sum_{v\in S} \overline{w}(v)\left(x(v) + \frac{1}{\lambda} x\left(N(v)\cap V_{\prec v}\right)\right)$$

$$\leq \sum_{v\in S} \overline{w}(v)\left(x(v) + \frac{2}{\lambda} x\left(N_D^{in}(v)\right)\right)$$

$$\leq \max_{v\in V}\left(x(v) + \frac{2}{\lambda} x\left(N_D^{in}(v)\right)\right) \sum_{v\in S}\overline{w}(v)$$

$$= \overline{w}(S)\max_{v\in V}\left(x(v) + \frac{2}{\lambda} x\left(N_D^{in}(v)\right)\right).$$

Therefore, the lemma holds.

Note that a non-zero $x\in[0,1]^V$ maximizing the value

$$\frac{\sum_{v\in V} w(v)\, x(v)}{\max_{v\in V}\left(x(v) + \frac{2}{\lambda} x\left(N_D^{in}(v)\right)\right)}$$

is achieved by an optimal solution to the following linear program (LP):

$$\begin{aligned} \max\ & \sum_{v\in V} w(v)\, x(v) \\ \text{s.t.}\ & x(v) + \frac{2}{\lambda} x\left(N_D^{in}(v)\right) \leq 1, \forall v\in V \\ & x(v) \geq 0, \forall v\in V \end{aligned} \qquad (1)$$

The value of the above LP and the weight of a maximum-weight feasible subset O are related as follows.

Lemma 5. *The value of the LP in Eq. (1) is at least $w(O)/(2\gamma)_\lambda$.*

Proof. Consider any link $v\in V$. We show that

$$|\{v\}\cap O| + \frac{2}{\lambda}\left|N_D^{in}(v)\cap O\right| \leq (2\gamma)_\lambda.$$

We consider two cases.

Case 1: $v\notin O$. Then

$$|O\cap\{v\}| + \frac{2}{\lambda}\left|N_D^{in}(v)\cap O\right| = \frac{2}{\lambda}\left|N_D^{in}(v)\cap O\right| \leq \frac{2}{\lambda}\lambda\gamma \leq 2\gamma \leq (2\gamma)_\lambda.$$

Case 2: $v\in O$. Then

$$|O\cap\{v\}| + \frac{2}{\lambda}\left|N_D^{in}(v)\cap O\right| = 1 + \frac{2}{\lambda}(\lambda-1)\gamma = 2\left(1-\frac{1}{\lambda}\right)\gamma + 1 \leq (2\gamma)_\lambda.$$

Let y be the function on V defined by

$$y(v) = \begin{cases} \frac{1}{(2\gamma)_\lambda}, & \text{if } v \in O; \\ 0, & \text{if } v \notin O. \end{cases}$$

Then, for each $v \in V$,

$$x(v) + \frac{2}{\lambda} x \left(N_D^{in}(v) \right)$$

$$= \frac{1}{(2\gamma)_\lambda} \left[|\{v\} \cap O| + \frac{2}{\lambda} \left| N_D^{in}(v) \cap O \right| \right] \leq \frac{1}{(2\gamma)_\lambda} (2\gamma)_\lambda = 1.$$

Thus, y is a feasible solution to the LP in Eq. (1), and consequently the value of the LP in Eq. (1) is at least

$$\sum_{v \in V} w(v) y(v) = \frac{1}{(2\gamma)_\lambda} \sum_{v \in O} w(v) = \frac{1}{(2\gamma)_\lambda} w(O).$$

So, the lemma holds.

The above two lemmas together with Lemma 1 motivates us to propose the following orientation-based approximation algorithm, which runs in five steps

1. Compute an optimal solution x to the LP in Eq. (1).
2. Compute a surplus-preserving ordering $\prec$ of V with respect to D and x.
3. Compute the greedy candidate subset S of V in $\prec$.
4. Compute the maximal inductively feasible subset F of S in $\prec$.
5. Compute the greedy coloring of F in $\prec$.

The approximation bound of the output F follows immediately from the above two lemmas and Lemma 1.

Theorem 2. *The F has an approximation bound $(2\gamma)_\lambda$.*

Again when $\lambda \leq 2\gamma$, $(2\gamma)_\lambda = 2\gamma$. For $\lambda > 2\gamma$,

$$(2\gamma)_\lambda = 2\gamma \left(1 - \frac{1}{\lambda} \right) + 1.$$

By Lemma 3, when $\lambda < 4\gamma$, $(2\gamma)_\lambda$ is smaller than the best-known approximation bound $\left[1 - \left(1 - \frac{1}{2\gamma\lambda} \right)^\lambda \right]^{-1}$.

5   Exact Algorithm in Cocomparability Graphs

Suppose that $G = (V, E)$ is cocomparability graph with a cocomparability ordering $\langle v_1, v_2, \cdots, v_n \rangle$ of its vertices. In this section, we present a polynomial-time algorithm which computes a maximum-weighted λ-colorable subset F of V by a reduction to minimum-cost flow.

We first construct a flow network D. Each vertex $v_i \in V$ is replaced by two replicas x_i and y_i. Then the vertex set of D consists of all these $2n$ replicas, a source vertex s, and a sink vertex t. The arc set of D consists of the $3n$ arcs

$$\{(x_i, y_i) : 1 \le i \le n\} \cup \{(s, x_i) : 1 \le i \le n\} \cup \{(y_i, t) : 1 \le i \le n\}$$

and the $n(n-1)/2 - |E|$ arcs

$$\{(y_i, x_j) : 1 \le i < j \le n, v_i v_j \notin E\}.$$

All arcs have unit capacity. In addition, each arc (x_i, y_i) has a cost $-w(v_i)$, and each other arc has zero cost. There is an one-to-one correspondence between the s-t paths in D and the independent sets in G:

- For each path P, let I be the set of vertices in V who replications appear in the path P. Then, I is independent, and is referred to the independent set *induced by* P. In addition, the length (i.e., cost) of the path P is equal to $-w(I)$.
- For each independent set I in G sorted in the cocomparable order $v_{i_1}, v_{i_2}, \cdots, v_{i_l}$, the sequence of vertices $s, x_{i_1}, y_{i_1}, x_{i_2}, y_{i_2}, \cdots, x_{i_l}, y_{i_l}, t$ form an s-t path P in D. Then, the length (i.e., cost) of P is equal to $-w(I)$.

Since all arcs in D have unit capacity, the above correspondence implies that the minimum cost of all s-t flows of value at most λ in D is equal to the additive inverse of the maximum weight of all λ-colorable subsets of vertices in G. Based on this relation, a maximum-weighted λ-colorable subset of vertices in G can be computed as follows.

- Compute an integral minimum-cost flow s–t flow f of value at most k in D, and decompose f into s–t paths flows using the standard flow decomposition method. Since each arc has unit capacity, each path in the path flow decomposition carries exactly one unit of flow. Thus, the number of paths is at most k.
- For each path P, let I be the independent set induced by P. The collection of all these at most k independent sets is returned as the output.

6 Applications

Consider a set A of point-to-point wireless communication requests. All requests in A are assumed to be node-disjoint and can access a common set of λ channels. A subset of A is said to be feasible if they can transmit at the same time over the λ channels. Suppose each request has a positive weight. We would like to select a maximum weighted feasible subset of A. Under a protocol interference model, the conflict relations among A is represented by a graph G on A, in which there is an edge two requests a and b in A if and only if they have conflict. Then, a subset of A is feasible if and only if it is λ-colorable in G.

The protocol interference model is classified into two communication modes:

- Unidirectional mode: For each request $a \in A$, the communication occurs in a single direction from its sender to its receiver, and the sender has an interference range, and the interference range of a is the interference range of its sender. Two requests in A conflict with each other if and only if the receiver of at least one request lies in the interference range of the other.
- Bidirectional mode: For each request $a \in A$, the communication occurs in both directions between its two endpoints, and each of its endpoint has an interference range. The interference range of a is the union of the interference ranges of its two endpoints. Two requests in A conflict with each other if and only if at least one request has an endpoint lying in the interference range of the other.

In the plane geometric variant, the interference range of an endpoint u of a request a is assumed to be a disk centered at u, whose radius is also knows as the interference radius. The following special orientations of the conflict graph and orderings of the requests have been discovered in the literature:

- Unidirectional mode: An orientation of the conflict graph introduced in [8] has ILIN at most

$$\left\lceil \pi / \arcsin \frac{c-1}{2c} \right\rceil - 1$$

  under the assumption that the interference radius of each request is at least c times the distance between its sender and its receiver for some constant $c > 1$.
- Bidirectional mode: An orientation of the conflict graph defined in [10] has ILIN at most 8, and an ordering of the requests given in [8] has BLIN at most 23. In case of symmetric interference radii (i.e., the two endpoints of each request have equal interference radii), an ordering of the requests introduced in [10] has BLIN at most 8. In the bidirectional mode with uniform interference radii (i.e., all endpoints of all requests have equal interference radii), an ordering of the requests described in [7] has BLIN at most 6.

By adopting those orientations of the conflict graphs or the orderings of the requests, the approximation algorithms developed in Sects. 4 and 3 achieve constant approximation bounds when applied to the conflict graph G. The derivation of these approximation bounds are straightforward and are omitted in this paper. In addition, it is also easy to identify the range of λ over which these approximation bounds do not increase with λ, or are smaller than those achieved by the greedy approximation framework proposed in [3].

When all links have uniform interference radii, the links can be partitioned into a small constant number μ of groups such that the conflict graph of each group is a co-comparability graph [11]. By applying the algorithm presented in Sect. 5 to the conflict graph of each group, a maximum-weighted feasible subset of each group can be computed in polynomial time. Then, among those μ feasible subsets, the one with the largest weight is returned as the output. Such divide-and-conquer scheme achieves the approximation bound μ, which does not depend on the number λ of channels at all.

Acknowledgements. This work was supported in part by the National Natural Science Foundation of P.R. China under grants 61529202, 61572131, 61572277, and 61379177, by the National Science Foundation of USA under grants CNS-1219109, CNS-1454770, and EECS-1247944, and by SUNY Oneonta Faculty Development Funds.

References

1. Akcoglu, K., Aspnes, J., DasGupta, B., Kao, M.-Y.: Opportunity cost algorithms for combinatorial auctions. In: Kontoghiorghes, E.J., Rustem, B., Siokos, S. (eds.) Computational Methods in Decision-Making, Economics and Finance. Applied Optimization, vol. 74, pp. 455–479. Springer, Heidelberg (2002)
2. Bar-Noy, A., Bar-Yehuda, R., Freund, A., Naor, J., Schieber, B.: A unified approach to approximating resource allocation and scheduling. JACM **48**–**5**, 1069–1090 (2001)
3. Bar-Noy, A., Guha, S., Naor, J., Schieber, B.: Approximating the throughput of multiple machines in real-time scheduling. SIAM J. Comput. **31**–**2**, 331–352 (2001)
4. Bar-Yehuda, R., Rawttz, D.: On the equivalence between the primal-dual schema and the local ratio technique. SIAM J. Disc. Math. **19**, 762–797 (2005)
5. Bar-Yehuda, R., Rawttz, D.: Using fractional primal-dual to schedule split intervals with demands. J. Discret. Optim. **3**(4), 275–287 (2006)
6. Frank, A.: On chain and antichain families of a partially ordered set. J. Comb. Theory Ser. B **29**, 176–184 (1980)
7. Joo, C., Lin, X., Shroff, N.B.: Understanding the capacity region of the greedy maximal scheduling algorithm in multi-hop wireless networks. In: Proceedings of IEEE INFOCOM (2008)
8. Wan, P.-J.: Multiflows in multihop wireless networks. In: Proceedings of ACM MOBIHOC, pp. 85–94 (2009)
9. Wan, P.-J., Jia, X., Dai, G., Du, H., Frieder, O.: Fast and simple approximation algorithms for maximum weighted independent set of links. In: IEEE INFOCOM, pp. 1653–1661 (2014)
10. Wan, P.-J., Ma, C., Wang, Z., Xu, B., Li, M., Jia, X.: Weighted wireless link scheduling without information of positions and interference/communication radii. In: Proceedings of IEEE INFOCOM (2011)
11. Wan, P.-J., Wang, L., Huang, A., Li, M., Yao, F.: Approximate capacity subregions of uniform multihop wireless networks. In: IEEE INFOCOM (2010)
12. Yannakakis, M., Gavril, F.: The maximum k-colorable subgraph problem for chordal graphs. Inf. Process. Lett. **24**(2), 133–137 (1987)
13. Ye, Y., Borodin, A.: Elimination graphs. ACM Trans. Algorithms **8**(2), 14:1–14:23 (2012)

Wireless Image Relay: Prioritized QoE Scheduling with Simplified Space-Time Coding Mode Selection

Shuan He and Wei Wang$^{(\boxtimes)}$

Department of Computer Science,
San Diego State University, California 92182, USA
she@rohan.sdsu.edu, wwang@mail.sdsu.edu

Abstract. To address the challenge of improving Quality of Experience (QoE) of mobile users in the next generation of wireless networks, we propose an optimal multimedia relay scheme by jointly considering application multimedia content distribution and mobile devices' antenna chain selection diversity in this paper. Benefiting from the feedback channel information and Multi-Input-Multi-Output (MIMO) diversity gain in relay systems, the multimedia content compression-truncation and antenna selection schemes would be dynamically adjusted with the feedback channel information, potentially improving the multimedia QoE and the wireless communication energy efficiency performances. In the proposed relay transmission scheme, the Quadtree fractal image compression method is used for content preparation and the Alamouti space-time coding technique is applied for diverse data transmission. Simulation results demonstrated that with the new dynamic multimedia content compression and antenna-chain selection scheme, the relayed multimedia QoE performance is significantly improved and energy resource efficiency also outperforms the traditional schemes.

Keywords: Quality of Experience (QoE) · Quadtree fractal compression · MIMO

1 Introduction

How to improve mobile user's Quality of Experience (QoE) becomes an essential challenge in wireless multimedia communications, since the QoE-driven multimedia services are dominating the wireless network traffic [1–4]. Social media-based image content sharing contributed a lot to the mobile media traffic. Benefited from the wireless network infrastructure and facilities, the dramatically increased usage of mobile devices such as smartphones leads to an exponential growth in mobile multimedia traffic [5], supported by a plethora of research advancements such as Device-to-Device (D2D) communications, small cell 5G systems, and massive Multiple-Input and Multiple-Output (MIMO) [6–8]. Parallel to the

© Springer International Publishing AG 2017
L. Ma et al. (Eds.): WASA 2017, LNCS 10251, pp. 605–616, 2017.
DOI: 10.1007/978-3-319-60033-8_52

research advancement at physical layer, source coding issues of images (i.e. compression) are also widely addressed at application layer to improve the quality of multimedia transmission and resource efficiency [9–11].

In this paper we propose a new approach for energy efficient wireless image relay, leveraging both application layer image content prioritization in compression and physical channel MIMO diversity. Alamouti firstly proposed a two-branch transmit diversity scheme in [12], which has the same diversity order as maximal-ratio receiver combining (MRRC) without requiring any bandwidth expansion. Authors in [13] proposed a cross layer strategy by considering application and physical layer diversities that allow Adaptive Channel Selection (ACS) over MIMO. The ACS-MIMO strategy had demonstrated improved multimedia quality in wireless video transmissions. Taking advantage of MIMO technology, a QoE-guaranteed wireless multimedia service pattern was studied in a relay based two-hop transmission scenario [14]. In addition, the resource allocation and energy efficiency schemes have also been widely considered in literature addressing the QoE problem using MIMO strategy. Authors in [15] built an energy-efficiency model in the MIMO-OFDM multimedia communication system with statistical service quality constraint. With little extra resource consumption, an efficiency feedback MIMO resource allocation scheme was proposed in cognitive radio network [16].

At application layer, typical state of the art image compression systems use either Discrete Cosine Transform (DCT) or Discrete Wavelet Transform (DWT) techniques in transform domain. For instance, the well-known JPEG image compression standards uses DCT compression scheme. The DWT scheme is widely used in JPEG2000 and Set Partitioning in Hierarchical Trees (SPIHT) [17]. Aforementioned techniques have shown the capability to achieve highly compression ratios and transmission efficiency in wireless communication systems, although the computational complexity is relatively high. Fractal image compression technology using Quadtree decomposition technique can achieve higher image compression ratio and rate-quality performance without complex transforms [18]. It has the advantages such as easy to implement and being suitable for low power mobile devices. The fractal compression concept is used as the source coding approach in this paper. Separating positions and values by identifying Quadtree structures (representing large flat areas) and tree leaves (representing fine details), we utilize Quadtree decomposition and Huffman entropy coding for image bit-packing before MIMO transmission.

As shown in Fig. 1, we propose a wireless relay scheme jointly considering image compression and antenna selection to address the multimedia QoE issue in energy constraint wireless communications. Transmitting (Tx), relay and receiving (Rx) devices are all assumed to be equipped with multiple antennas in our work. We refer to the Alamouti space time coding scheme addressing the antennas selection issue at the physical layer. The Quadtree fractal compression method is studied at application layer to prioritize the image contents.

The rest of this paper is outlined as follows. The system model is described in Sect. 2. The methodology details of the proposed transmission scheme are

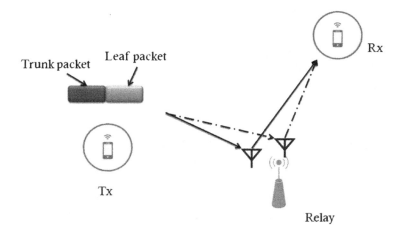

Fig. 1. Transmitting device, relay and receiver all equip two antennas in our proposed system. This figure shows that the relay uses two antennas to receive and send, but Tx and Rx only activate one antenna in transmission.

discussed in Sect. 3. Section 4 presents the numerical simulation and results. Finally we conclude our work in Sect. 5. The key notations and nomenclature used in this paper are summarized in Table 1.

2   System Model and Analysis

The objective of our work is to improve the QoE of receiver in the relay-based wireless networks. We propose the mathematical model by jointly considering the image content compression and antenna chain selection among mobile devices. By considering the fractal image compression method, image content is compressed into two types of packets: the trunks describing the positions and leafs describing the values, as shown in Fig. 1.

S_{trunk} and S_{leaf} denote the corresponding resource allocation sets for trunk and leaf packets, which include pairs of the image compression strategy and antenna chains selection. More specifically, $S_{trunk} = \{(L_{trunk}, M_{Tx-Rx})\}$ and $S_{leaf} = \{(L_{leaf}, M_{Tx-Rx})\}$. So our system model is addressed as an energy constrained QoE maximization problem with optimal choices of resource allocation set.

$$\{S_{trunk}, S_{leaf}\} = \arg\max\{QoE\} \tag{1}$$

s.t

$$E_{Tx} + E_{Relay} + E_{Rx} \leq E_{\max} \tag{2}$$

The constraint of energy resource is highlighted in our model, since the energy budget is the vital factor for mobile devices in wireless transmission. In general, trunk packet has higher reduction of decoded Root-Mean-Square-Error (RMSE)

Table 1. Summary of key notations

Symbol	Notes
$E_{Tx}, E_{Rx}, E_{Relay}$	Energy consumption at transmitting, receiving, and relay devices
$E_{\max}$	Total energy constraint
QoE	Notation for quality of experience of receiver
p_{A-B}	The packet error rate between device A and B
BER	Bit error rate of the physical channel
P_t	Transmitting power of device
P_c	Receiving/circuit power
T_A	The number of active antenna(s) on device A
L_o, L_{trunk}, L_{leaf}	Length of packet overhead/trunk/leaf packet

than leaf packet, and with smaller packet length. In other words, the truck packets are smaller, but more important in image coding. The rationale behind the content diversity strategy is that important packets (i.e., trunk packets), which will distinctly affect the quality of image transmission, should be transmitted with high priority when the resource is strictly limited.

Equipped with the MIMO at physical layer, each mobile device activates one or two antennas to transmit data based on the importance of packets and its available energy resources. Let M_{Tx-Rx} denote the antenna chain selection strategy between Tx and Rx. *To simplify the notations for all possible antenna chains*, we define S_{space} as

$$M_{Tx-Rx} \in S_{space} \tag{3}$$

$$S_{space} = \{0000, 0001, ...1110, 1111\} \tag{4}$$

We consider one relay in our work. Thus, for Tx, Rx and relay, they can choose to activate one or two antennas for transmitting/receiving. There are totally $2 * 2 * 2 * 2 = 16$ strategies (in terms of choosing antenna chain) to transmit packets from transmitting device to the receiver. As shown in Eq. 4, we use four binary digits to simplify the mode description of all strategies. Let '0000' represent the simplest antenna chain selection, which implies there is only one antenna be activated on all mobile devices. The '0110' mode implies that a single active antenna on Tx/Rx and two active antennas on relay (as illustrated in Fig. 1). Lastly, '1111' represents every device on the selected antenna chain has two active antennas.

On the right hand side of Eq. 1, the QoE of receiver could be defined as the RMSE summation of trunk and leaf packets, multiplied by the probability that they are being successfully transmitted.

$$QoE = D_{trunk}(1 - p_{Tx\_Relay})(1 - p_{Relay\_Rx}) + \\ D_{leaf}(1 - p_{Tx\_Relay})(1 - p_{Relay\_Rx}) \tag{5}$$

where D_{trunk} and D_{leaf} represent the RMSE reduction of trunk and leaf packet, respectively. The RMSE reduction of each packet will be counted at receiver only if it is successfully delivered from Tx to relay, and then to Rx. The packet error rate p_{A-B} is determined by the channel Bit Error Rate (BER). Assuming a random error model, it is calculated as

$$p = 1 - (1 - BER)^L \tag{6}$$

where L is the length of packet. According to [12], the channel BER will be significantly reduced when applying the space time coding mode during transmission.

One overhead of utilizing multiple antennas scheme is the extra energy consumption. Next, we will model our energy consumption in the wireless relay transmission. We assume T_i denotes the number of active antennas, the total energy consumption of the transmitting device can be interpreted as following:

$$E_{Tx} = P_t \frac{L_o + L_{trunk} + L_{leaf}}{R} + P_c \frac{L_o + L_{trunk} + L_{leaf}}{R} T_{Tx} \tag{7}$$

It includes two parts, transmitting power for sending data and the incurred circuit power consumption during the transmitting process. Following the same logic, we define the energy consumption at Rx and relay sides.

$$E_{Rx} = P_c \frac{L_o + L_{trunk} + L_{leaf}}{R} T_{Rx} \tag{8}$$

$$E_{Relay} = P_c \frac{L_o + L_{trunk} + L_{leaf}}{R} T_{Relay} + \tag{9}$$
$$P_t \frac{L_o + L_{trunk} + L_{leaf}}{R} T_{Relay} + P_c \frac{L_o + L_{trunk} + L_{leaf}}{R} T_{Relay}$$

It is worth noting that if two antennas are activated for transmission on the device, the transmitting power P_t should be evenly allocated on each antenna. From above equations we can conclude that there are two factors impacting energy consumption in wireless relays. One is resource allocation such as power and antenna-chain selection. The other is the proportion of trunk and leaf packets of image content. The proper fraction of trunk packets also plays an important role in multimedia quality. In following sections we will discuss how to improve the QoE of receiver in details.

3 Unifying Application Content Prioritization and Physical Antenna Selection

3.1 The Image Content Diversity at Application Layer

The redundancy and similarity among different regions of images make compression feasible. By taking the fractal compression method, i.e., Quadtree approach, we divide a square image into four blocks with different sizes based on the preset criterion (such as a minimum constraint in terms of compression quality). Fractal compression saves huge transmission resources due to its high compression ratio. One contribution of this paper is that we address the challenge of designing and arranging the multimedia data for image compression and content bit packing in a scalable manner using Quadtree approach, such that some bits can be traded off to meet the energy constraints with minimum loss in quality. The data packets of one image are partitioned into two types of packets: trunk and leaf. Trunk packets have higher RMSE reduction (also implies the multimedia quality) than leaf packets, and with smaller length (comparing with leaf ones). In addition, the Quadtree scheme we used in this paper is directly applied in spatial domain rather than transform domain, which has low computing overheads avoiding complex wavelet or cosine transforms [19].

3.2 Antenna Chain Selection and Packets Compression Strategies in Different Physical Channel and Energy Budget Scenarios

As we can notice form Eqs. (5) and (6), QoE of receiver is mainly determined by the RMSE reductions of packets (trunk and leaf) and the BER of the physical channel. The energy consumption also plays a vital role to affect the QoE, since the battery size is strictly limited in mobile device. In the following, two different transmission cases are discussed in details.

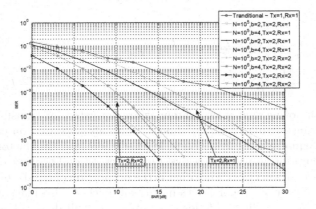

Fig. 2. Illustration of the comparisons of BER performance in different antenna chains: the traditional scheme with $Tx = 1, Rx = 1$, and the new scheme under Alamouti method ($Tx = 2, Rx = 1$ and $Tx = 2, Rx = 2$).

CASE I: Highly BER in Severe Physical Channel. Being exposed in a severe situation with lower Signal-to-Noise Ratio (SNR) and high BERs, mobile device has to depend on relay and antenna selection to make up the highly packet loss rate. The space-time block coding technique is considered in this paper to model the multiple antennas scenario. As shown in Fig. 2, N denotes the number of symbol pairs to be transmitted. b is the constellation size of the selected modulation scheme. Tx and Rx denote the number of antennas for transmitter and receiver, respectively, in a way similar to symbols defined in [20]. Comparing with the traditional approach '0000' with single transmitting and receiving antenna, the BER decreases significantly when taking '1010' (two antennas send and one antenna receives) and '1111' (two antennas send and two antennas receive) mode. In Fig. 2, the transmitting powers in MIMO and traditional (single antenna) methods are the same. It is worth pointing out that the extra cost for implementing the multiple antennas scheme on mobile devices is to equip a more complex antenna circuit array. But it should be easily pay off since the worse physical condition is, the better performance multi-antenna scheme gets.

CASE II: Strict Energy Budget in Wireless Relays. By considering D2D relay communication in the new generation of wireless networks, energy budget is strictly limited by the battery's capacity equipped on the mobile device. The Quadtree fractal compression method is designed to meet the trade-off between energy constraint and multimedia quality. Each image can be compressed into two groups with different lengths, one is important trunk packet group and the other is unimportant leaf packet group. The total length of trunk and leaf packets keeps constant. Our method in strict energy budget case is to change the portion of trunk packet for adjusting the energy limitation in transmission. As mentioned before, trunk packet contains the most important information of images (higher RMSE reduction per bit), which should be considered to transmit first when the resources are limited. Even trunk packets only take a small portion of the whole image, the final accumulated reduced RMSE will be significantly improved.

In addition, in our proposed transmission method, the multi-antenna scheme is only activated for transmitting trunk packets, to ensure the high quality image data could be transmitted in low BER conditions. Leaf packets were transmitted in '0000' (i.e. single antenna) mode to save energy. By choosing the proper trunk proportion in image compression, we can achieve the best RMSE reduction per unit energy consumption. More details about this part are shown in the simulation section.

3.3 Algorithm and Discussion

Algorithm 1 illustrates the process of the proposed image transmission scheme in this paper. The compression strategy and multi-antenna selection decision are decided based on the near real-time physical channel information. Transmission begins with a feedback channel (similar to a pilot "handshake"), shown in step 4–5. In order to output the optimal transmission strategy, we evaluate the RMSE performance for each (L_{trunk}^i, M_{A-B}^j) pair based on the feedback channel information. The RMSE gain for each image compression and multiple-antenna selection strategy is calculated in step 11, the optimal L_{trunk}^i and M_{A-B}^j that get the best RMSE performance for each image is also calculated and stored in this step. Finally, the output of our algorithm should be the optimal transmission scheme which attains the maximum RMSE reduction, i.e. the $RMSE_{\max}$.

In Algorithm 1, we assume the physical environment keeps consistent during the short period of time of a single wireless packet transmission. So the output (L^i_{trunk}, M^j_{A-B}) should be global optimal. For stable environment with minimum fading, the channel feedback can be evaluated for every image transmission. In this way, we will get the optimal (L^i_{trunk}, M^j_{A-B}) for every specific image with less computation overhead.

Algorithm 1: Optimal transmission-relay scheme which jointly considering the image compression, multi-antenna selection, and physical information

```
1.  Input of algorithm:
    Symbol rate R and channel information (SNR).
    Energy budget of mobile devices Emax and number of images Nimage.
    Transmitting and circuit power Pt and Pc.
    RMSE reductions of trunk and leaf packets.
2.  Output: The optimal relay scheme for images.
3.  Initialize parameters: Econ = 0, RMSEmax = 0.
4.  Tx transmits the whole image as a trunk packet to Rx.
5.  Tx get the feedback (physical channel information) from Rx.
6.  Gradually increasing the trunk proportion of image Li_trunk.
7.  Choosing the antenna pair Mj_A-B from '0000' ~ '1111'.
8.  For k = 1: Nimage
9.   If Econ ≤ Emax
10.   Calculate the accumulated energy consumption Econ
         based on equation (7) ~ (9) for each (Li_trunk, Mj_A-B).
11.   Calculate the accumulated RMSE at receiver side
         based on equation (5) and (6).
         If the RMSE reduction gain is bigger than RMSEmax,
         store current relay scheme and
         replace the RMSEmax as current RMSE reduction gain.
12.   Else end
13.  End For
14.  Output the relay scheme which gets the RMSEmax
```

4   Numerical Simulations and Results

In this section, we perform numerical simulations to evaluate the system performance with the image content diversity and space-time coding. Let symbol rate R equal 20 MHz. Let transmitting power P_t and circuit power P_c equal to 50 mw and 30 mw, respectively. The "Cameraman" and "Lena" grayscale images are chosen as image sources for the simulation. There are 20 images in maximum to be transmitted in the wireless relay network setting. The length of each basic test image is 27250 bits. Image resolutions could be scaled in 128×128, 256×256, and 512×512 pixels.

First, we evaluate QoE gain in different physical channel conditions with '1010' mode. In Fig. 3, we show the receiver's RMSE at a good BER level (the default BER for single antenna mode is 10^{-4}). As we can notice from the result, system gets the best performance (blue line) when trunk packet takes larger portion of the image (nearly 50%) in good physical channel conditions. The RMSE reduction is almost twice of the black line when the energy is enough for transmitting all the images. The smallest trunk portion case gets the worst performance in terms of multimedia quality (black line). The gain of RMSE reduction keeps the trend of going down with the decreasing of trunk packet's proportion in image compression.

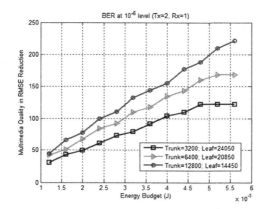

Fig. 3. Illustration of RMSE reduction performance in good physical channel scenario, bigger trunk packet gets better multimedia quality performance. (Color figure online)

The BER at 10^{-6} level is the best case in this study. The BER could be much worse in real wireless communications for various reasons such as the signal interference, multipath fading and channel noise. In Fig. 4 (left), we show the RMSE performance of system in the BER of 10^{-5} level. It turns out that the overall RMSE reduction gain decreases when physical channel gets worse. The RMSE reduction is less than the half of it is in the previous case (i.e. the best case). Furthermore, the largest trunk proportion no longer gets the best performance when channel BER gets higher. Smaller portion of trunk packet start to show advantages in multimedia relay quality gain. In Fig. 4 (right), we evaluate the system performance in a much worse channel. The result reveals that the smallest trunk (takes 10% of the image) performs the best in such a severe physical environment. Short trunk packet and MIMO are the best transmission scheme combinations when facing the severe physical environment with high BERs.

Another factor that leads to the results shown in Fig. 4 is the high packet error rate. According to Eq. (6), packet error rate p dramatically increases along the increasing length of packet. Under the same bit error rate, longer packet causes higher packet error rate, which further leads to lower reduction of RMSE consequently. In the following simulation, we demonstrate that there exists a threshold for the length of trunk packet in a specific channel condition. Smaller trunk packets cannot always lead to good multimedia QoE performance. The

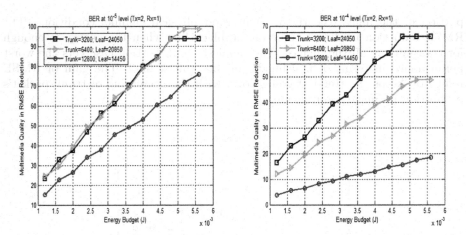

Fig. 4. RMSE performance of different trunk-leaf proportion in the BER at 10^{-5} level and 10^{-4} level.

rationale behind the threshold is that the trunk portion has to carry certain amount of important content of the image, otherwise the reduction of RMSE could not accumulate to a significant amount during the transmission process.

We take three different trunk portions into simulation. The percentages of trunk packets are 6%, 23%, and 59%, respectively. The BER represents bit level error rate under space time coding mode, i.e. error rate after applying space time coding. Simulation results of this scenario are shown in Fig. 5 (left). We can notice from the figure that extremely small trunk (6%) gets worse performance comparing with trunk of 23%, even in very bad channel condition. The rationale is that, like the aforementioned example, very small trunk will lose some crucial content information in the image compression. On the contrary, the RMSE reduction of 59% trunk reaches 270 in the good BER, which is close to the RMSE reduction upperbound (we assume the system attains the maximum RMSE reduction gain when we compress the whole image as a single trunk packet and transmit it in ideal channel with zero BER).

Finally we evaluate the wireless image relay energy efficiency in traditional transmission scheme and in Alamouti scheme. We compress each image with very tiny portion of trunk and a big portion of leaf packets in the simulation (1% for trunk). Simulation results of this scenario are shown in Fig. 5 (right). The extra energy consumption of '1111' mode (i.e. the 2:2:2:2 mode) is due to activating an additional antenna on each side when transmitting data. Due to the improved QoE gain, the multimedia quality per Joule energy consumption performs the best when we choose the '1111' mode activating more antennas in relay.

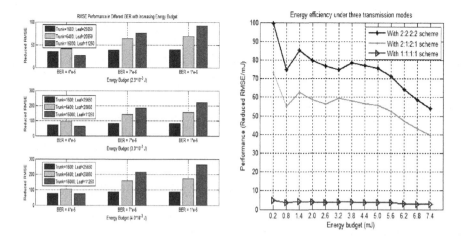

Fig. 5. Illustration of multimedia gain and energy efficiency in different conditions and transmission modes.

5   Conclusion

In this work, a novel wireless relay scheme which jointly considering image compression and space time coding mode is proposed to address the multimedia QoE challenge in energy constraint relay communication scenarios. First, the Quadtree fractal approach is utilized to compress image into prioritized trunk packet and leaf packet based on the preset quality criterion. Compares with leaf packet, trunk packet holds more important information of image with smaller length, which makes it with high priority in energy constraint situations. Then the space time coding method is utilized to improve QoE by allocating more antennas to important truck packets in relay. Last, based on the feedback channel information, the proposed algorithm adopts dynamic image compression and antenna selection scheme. Simulation results demonstrated that the proposed wireless relay scheme significantly improve QoE gain and energy efficiency with severe physical channel errors or strict energy constraints.

Acknowledgments. This research was support in part by National Science Foundation Grants No. 1463768 on energy efficient wireless multimedia communications.

References

1. Vleeschauwer, D., De Viswanathan, H., Beck, A., Benno, S., Li, G., Miller, R.: Optimization of HTTP adaptive streaming over mobile cellular networks. In: IEEE INFOCOM, pp. 898–997, Turin (2013)
2. Wen, Y., Zhu, X., Rodrigues, J., Chen, C.: Cloud mobile media: reflections and outlook. IEEE Trans. Multimedia **16**, 885–902 (2014)

3. Fisher, Y., Menlove, S.: Fractal encoding with HV partitions. In: Fisher, Y. (ed.) Theory and Application to Digital Images, pp. 119–136. Springer, Heidelberg (1994)
4. He, S., Wang, W.: User-centric QoE-driven power and rate allocation for multimedia rebroadcasting in 5G wireless systems. In: IEEE Vehicular Technology Conference (VTC), Workshop on User-Centric Networking for 5G and Beyond, Nanjing (2016)
5. Cisco, Visual Networking Index, white paper. www.Cisco.com
6. Wu, Y., Liu, W., Wang, S., Guo, W., Chu, X.: Network coding in device-to-device (D2D) communications underlaying cellular networks. In: IEEE International Conference on Communications (ICC), London (2015)
7. Cheng, W., Zhang, X., Zhang, H.: QoS-aware power allocations for maximizing effective capacity over virtual-MIMO wireless networks. IEEE JSAC **31**, 2043–2057 (2013)
8. Agiwal, M., Roy, A., Saxena, N.: Next generation 5G wireless networks: a comprehensive survey. IEEE Commun. Surv. Tutor. **99**, 1617–1655 (2016)
9. Wang, W., Peng, D., Wang, H., Sharif, H.: An adaptive approach for image encryption and secure transmission over multirate wireless sensor networks. Wirel. Commun. Mob. Comput. J. **9**, 383–393 (2009)
10. Mahasukhon, P., Sharif, H., Hempel, M., Zhou, T., Wang, W., Chen, H.H.: IEEE 802.11b based ad hoc networking and its performance in mobile channels. IET Commun. **3**, 689–699 (2009)
11. Wang, W., Peng, D., Wang, H., Sharif, H., Chen, H.H.: Energy-constrained quality optimization for secure image transmission in wireless sensor networks. Adv. Multimedia **2007**, 9 p., Article no. 25187 (2007). doi:10.1155/2007/25187
12. Alamouti, S.: A simple transmitter diversity scheme for wireless communications. IEEE J. Select. Areas Commun. **16**, 145 (1998)
13. Song, D., Chen, C.W.: Scalable H.264/AVC video transmission over MIMO wireless systems with adaptive channel selection based on partial channel information. IEEE Trans. Circuits Syst. Video Technol. **17**, 1218–1226 (2007)
14. Park, J., Lee, S.: MIMO beamforming for QoS enhancement via analog digital and hybrid relaying. IEEE Trans. Broadcast. **56**, 494–503 (2010)
15. Ge, X., Huang, X., Wang, Y., Chen, M., Li, Q., Han, T., Wang, C.X.: Energy efficiency optimization for MIMO-OFDM mobile multimedia communication systems with QoS constraints. IEEE Trans. Veh. Technol. **63**, 2127–2138 (2014)
16. Chen, X., Yuen, C.: Efficient resource allocation in rateless coded MU-MIMO cognitive radio network with QoS provisioning and limited feedback. IEEE Trans. Veh. Tech. **62**, 395–399 (2013)
17. Raid, A.M., Khedr, W.M., El-dosuky, M.A., Ahmed, W.: JPEG image compression using discrete cosine transform - a survey. Int. J. Comput. Sci. Eng. Surv. (IJCSES) **5**, 39–47 (2014)
18. Pandey, S., Seth, M.: Hybrid fractal image compression using quadtree decomposition with Huffman coding. Int. J. Sci. Res. (IJSR) **3**, 943–948 (2014)
19. Balaji, V., Wang, W.: Spatial domain image packet prioritization for energy-constrained wireless communications. In: IEEE Global Communications Conference (GLOBECOM), Workshop on Quality of Experience for Multimedia Communications, Washington DC (2016)
20. Alamouti Code. www.mathworks.com/matlabcentral/fileexchange/41811-comparison-of-alamouti--mrc-schemes-over-rayleigh-channelv

Software Defined Routing System

Xianming Gao$^{(\boxtimes)}$, Baosheng Wang, and Wenping Deng

School of Computer, National University of Defense Technology,
Changsha 410073, China
nudt_gxm@163.com

Abstract. Traditional distributed routing protocol just can calculate the shortest forwarding path based on restricted routing metric (e.g. least hops, lowest cost, etc.). Due to partial-view and selfishness of local strategy, the routing calculation results usually are not optimal. Software defined network(SDN), as the representative of centralized control mechanism, can obtain real-time network status, perform routing calculation from global network view, and install routing strategies, hence to promote network toward optimal target. Drawing further on this, this paper firstly puts forwards Software Defined Routing System (SDRS), by introducing centralized control mechanism into routing system on basis of distributed paths generated by distributed routing protocol. Centralized controller can calculate centralized paths and selectively deploy centralized paths into network according to orchestration strategy. SDRS not only preserves the properties of flexible survivability and fast self-healing in distributed routing protocol, but also keeps global optimal ability of centralized controller. Finally, we implement SDRS prototype, and our experimental results reveal that SDRS can obtain the same routing convergence performance with distributed routing protocol and a better self-healing ability than pure centralized framework.

Keywords: Routing system · Control mechanism · Distribution/ centralization · Flexible survivability · Fast self-healing

1 Introduction

Distributed routing protocol runs in network layer of TCP/IP model, to provide reachable transmission channels for end-to-end communication [1]. It firstly synchronizes network status among distributed network nodes by flooding way, and then calculates the shortest routing path to destination network according to beforehand rules (e.g. minimum hops, minimum costs, etc.). Therefore, it has ability of flexible survivability and fast self-healing, which is the fundamental reason for its massive success in the Internet. For instances, when network has a single point of failure, it can quickly install routing strategies into node to re-establish new path for end-to-end communication by perceiving changes of network status and flooding update messages to each node. Distributed routing protocol is essential for current Internet, yet it also faces lots of challenges: (1) incomplete information of partial-view, which making distributed routing protocol just attain knowledge about link-status topology, rather than all of network status [2]; (2) selfishness of local strategy, leading to a situation that part of nodes or links are occupied by a large amount of routing paths while other

© Springer International Publishing AG 2017
L. Ma et al. (Eds.): WASA 2017, LNCS 10251, pp. 617–628, 2017.
DOI: 10.1007/978-3-319-60033-8_53

resources being in idle status [2]. At the same time, calculation rule for forwarding paths is also beforehand arranged, rather than a reconfigure value.

The centralized control architecture (e.g., Software Defined Network) is able to attain real-time network status and calculate the optimal routing strategies, promoting network toward optimal target [3]. Meanwhile, centralized control architecture supports for dynamical configuration and management through the openness of control interface of routing protocol, to obtain orchestration ability of routing system [15–18]. This way provides a solution to ossification of calculation rules in existing routing schemes in the foreseeable future. Unfortunately, centralized control architecture generally has bad system robustness and long delay of network status synchronization, thus it hardly has ability of flexible survivability and fast self-healing [4, 5]. As a result, centralized control architecture usually is deployed in medium-sized and small area networks (e.g. data-center network, campus network, enterprise network, etc.), which hardly deployed in WANs.

We firstly propose Software Defined Routing System (SDRS), by introducing centralized control framework into routing system on basis of distributed paths generated by distributed routing protocol. It provides a flexible routing mechanism with integration of centralization and distribution, organically integrates distributed routing protocol and centralized control framework. It consists of two types of routing control elements including distributed routing protocol and centralized controller to calculate routing strategy together. Distributed routing protocol is responsible for calculation of reachable distributed paths, while centralized controller calculates centralized paths based on real-time link-status topology coming from distributed routing protocol, further selects centralized paths on basis of orchestration strategy, and finally deploys them into network. At last, we implement a SDRS prototype, and verify feasibility and validity of SDRS in terms of routing convergence time, path maintenance time, acquisition time of link-status topology, and management performance. Our main contributions are as follows: (1) integration of centralized and distributed control, not only making SDRS obtain features of full-view, global routing strategy and opening control in centralized control model, but also remedying disadvantages of each control model (e.g. centralized control model can efficiently enhance fast re-routing ability of distributed routing protocol; while distributed routing protocol can solve low efficiency problem in path maintenance of centralized control model); and (2) highly flexible survivability mechanism, creatively using distributed routing protocol to release centralized routing paths by making full use of the ability of flexible survivability and fast self-healing in distributed routing protocol, and to avoid severe impact on network forwarding function when centralized controller releasing centralized paths by itself.

The remainder of this paper is organized as follow. Section 2 describe existing research works about routing control mechanism. Section 3 presents how SDRS framework integrates distributed routing protocol and centralized mechanism. In Sect. 4, we propose centralized path maintenance mechanism by using distributed routing protocol, and further present how it works. Meanwhile, we establish SDRS prototype to verify its feasibility and validity in Sect. 5. At last we conclude and describe our future work in Sect. 6.

2 Related Works

Now, there are two typical control mechanisms including distributed framework and centralized framework for routing system. Routing system attracts more attractions from research communities and equipment vendors as the development of SDN.

Besides, research communities start to integrate two control mechanisms and propose some schemes [6–9]. I2RS (Interface to Routing System) is the most typical solution, which using centralized controller to optimize routing strategy [8, 9]. However, routing strategies are still generated by distributed routing protocol. Centralized controller just works and selects the best routing strategy when these are several routing strategies for the same destination network. Under this context, I2RS just optimizes routing system on basis of distributed framework. Thus it cannot efficiently work to promote network toward optimal target.

3 SDRS Framework

Due to typical disadvantages including incomplete information of partial-view, selfishness of local strategy in distributed routing protocol, we propose Software Defined Routing System, namely SDRS, by introducing centralized control mechanism into distributed routing system. These two routing control models establish forwarding paths for end-to-end communication together, as shown in Fig. 1. SDRS consists of centralized controller and distributed network nodes: centralized controller is mainly responsible for calculation and installation of routing strategies of centralized paths; and nodes run distributed routing protocol to calculate routing strategies of distributed

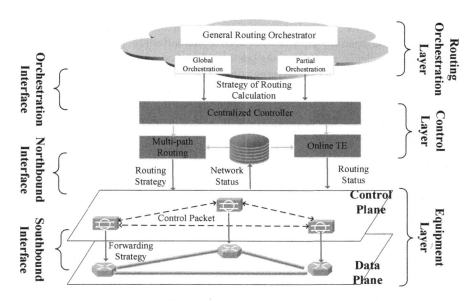

Fig. 1. SDRS framework

path. These two types of routing strategies are used to transmit data-flow together, and paths to the same destination network include centralized paths and distributed paths.

SDRS Framework includes three layers: routing orchestration layer, control layer and equipment layer. Routing orchestration layer allows administrators to orchestrate service ability of routing mechanism (e.g. maximum of hop steps, maximum amount of centralized paths to the same destination network, etc.) by invoking control interface of routing protocol, to enhance flexibility and reconfiguration of SDRS. Control layer is regarded as decision-maker of routing strategies by using real-time link-status topology coming from distributed routing protocol. In equipment layer, control plane runs distributed routing protocol which not only calculates distributed paths, but also is responsible for notification of changes of link-status topology to centralized controller and path maintenance of centralized paths established by centralized controller; data plane forwards packets according routing strategies coming from two control mechanisms. Meanwhile, SDRS uses three communication interfaces including orchestration interface, northbound interface, and southbound interface to achieve message exchange between two adjacent layers. For instances, orchestration interface locates between orchestration layer and control layer; northbound interface is responsible for message exchange between control layer and equipment; southbound interface locates between control plane and data plane in equipment layer.

SDRS establishes a closed-loop control system by integrating distributed routing protocol with centralized controller. On one hand, real-time link-status topology from distributed routing system is as the input for centralized controller. On the other hand, routing strategies of centralized paths calculated by centralized controller in return make influence on distributed routing protocol. SDRS includes self-determination routing way and coordination routing way to achieve routing control system. In self-determination routing way, distributed routing protocol can calculate centralized paths all by itself without aid of centralized controller, to provide fundamental communication service for network transmission. Coordination routing, compared with self-determination routing, provide enhanced communication service. In summary, centralized controller is mainly responsible for calculation of centralized paths on basis of real-time link-status topology coming from distributed routing protocol, and distributed routing protocol is responsible for path maintenance of centralized paths when centralized paths should be released. Coordination routing way can improve network performance when network is being in stable status, namely an enhanced version of self-determination. Self-determination can take over data-flow transmission without centralized controller, when network is being a changeable status.

SDRS introduces centralized controller into distributed routing protocol, which not only can reserve advantages of distributed routing protocol, but also can enhance the ability of flexible survivability and fast self-healing. We explain above attributes in terms of below two aspects.

- Centralized paths are released by distributed routing protocol, because distributed routing protocol can quickly perceive changes of link-status topology. When a single point of failure in centralized paths or routing loop between centralized paths and new created distributed paths occurs, SDRS quickly releases centralized paths to avoid severe influence on network. SDRS, compared with SDN, uses distributed routing protocol to remedy disadvantages of centralized control framework in terms of low robustness and low reliability.

- Enhancement of ability of flexible survivability and fast self-healing of routing system is another feature of SDRS. SDRS uses centralized paths calculated by centralized controller and distributed paths calculated by distributed routing protocol to transmit data-flow in parallel. Thus, when one distributed path has a single point of failure, survival centralized paths continue transmitting data-flow to avoid communication interrupted by rerouting of distributed routing protocol, of which is the same with fast rerouting mechanism [10].

4 Path Maintenance Mechanism

When link-status topology changes, distributed routing protocol can complete release and re-calculation of distributed paths by itself. In order to avoid inefficiency of release task of centralized paths by centralized controller, SDRS uses distributed routing protocol to release centralized paths. On one hand, when distributed path has a failure, centralized paths without crossing with distributed paths aren't released, to ensure data-flow transmission via survival centralized paths, and to avoid communication interrupted by path re-calculation. On the other hand, when centralized path has a single point of failure, distributed routing protocol just releases failed centralized paths, rather than all of centralized paths to the same destination network. This section describes centralized path maintenance mechanism in terms of change of distributed path status and change of centralized path status.

4.1 Change of Centralized Path Status

Different from change of distribution path status, the establishment of new neighbor relationship just causes the re-establishment of centralized paths installed by centralized controller. The release of centralized path is performed by distributed routing protocol, which can greatly enhance flexible survivability of routing system. Thus, change of centralized path status is just caused by centralized path failure.

When centralized path has a single point of failure, centralized path maintenance mechanism is performed by distributed routing protocol. This can efficiently avoid a severe problem that centralized controller perceives changes of network topology slowly. However, the traditional distributed routing protocol does not support for centralized path maintenance. A new approach is then introduced to maintain centralized paths to solve centralized path failure. It extends a new type of link state message, Enhanced Link Status Advertisement (ELSA), based on the traditional distributed routing protocol. When network node detects centralized path failure by detecting interface status, it firstly encapsulates the information of centralized path into ELSA message, and then floods it to all other nodes in network. After other nodes receive ELSA messages, they releases the corresponding centralized paths based on ELSA messages.

The centralized path maintenance mechanism includes two parts: (1) generation and flood of ELSA message, which generating ELSA message containing of the information of centralized path when a failure of centralized path is detected and flooding ELSA messages to all other nodes; (2) ELSA message processing and routing update, which receiving ELSA message and performing routing update based on ELSA message, so as to achieve the purpose of centralized path maintenance.

Take Fig. 2 for example, there is a centralized path (A-C-D-F) from node A to node F, and routing table in each node is as shown in Fig. 2(a). At some time, link (D-F) has a single point of failure, node D firstly perceives the invalid of neighbor relationship

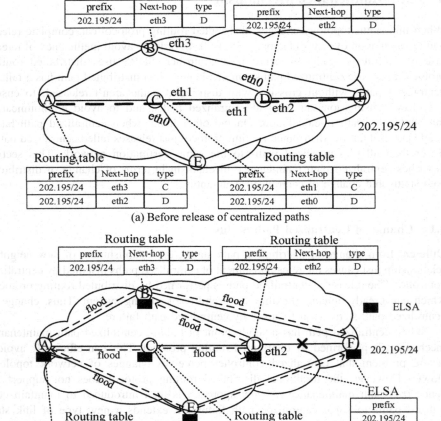

(a) Before release of centralized paths

(b) After release of centralized path

Fig. 2. Path maintenance of centralized path

between node D and node F. And it then searches routing table by using index {next-hop = eth2, type = centralized} and finds corresponding routing entry. Finally, it generates ELSA including path information {prefix = 202.195/16, sequence = 1, version = 44} and floods it to other neighbor nodes. When other nodes receives ELSA messages, it searches routing table by using {prefix = 202.195/16, sequence = 1, version = 44} and deletes matched routing entries as shown in Fig. 2(b).

4.2 Change of Distributed Path Status

The reasons for change of distributed path status include distributed path failure (e.g. node failure, link failure, etc.) and establishment of new neighbor (e.g. join of new node, recovery of failed node, etc.). We describe distributed path maintenance mechanism as follows.

When network node detects distributed path failure by detecting interface status, it checks whether or not the corresponding routing strategy of centralized paths: if not, it just maintains distributed paths; otherwise, it firstly encapsulates the information of centralized path into ELSA message, and then floods it to all other nodes in network. After other nodes receive ELSA messages, they releases the corresponding centralized paths based on ELSA messages.

5 Experiment and Analysis

In order to verify validity of SDRS, we make experiments in terms of routing convergence time, path maintenance time, acquisition time of link-status topology, and management performance. Firstly, we select ten typical network topology from Internet Topology Zoo [11] as shown in Table 1. The information of network topology includes topology name, number of nodes, and number of links. Besides, we use open-source applications to implement a SDRS prototype based on a cluster of commodity servers. For network node, Click modular router supporting for fast re-development is responsible for data plane [12], and OSPF protocol provided by Quagga protocol suite

Table 1. Ten typical network topology

Name	Seq.	Year	Number of nodes	Number of links
CERNET	1	2010	35	49
Abilene	2	2005	11	14
Renater	3	2005	35	46
Asia pacific	4	2010	15	21
Canerie	5	2010	24	31
Ernet	6	2010	16	18
Janet	7	2011	22	33
Garr	8	2011	36	45
Grnet	9	2010	33	37
Pionier	10	2011	27	32

is used to establish control plane [13]. For centralized controller, we develop its functions. And there are ten network nodes, one centralized controller and two hosts in SDRS prototype. At last, we further use CORE network simulator to establish thirteen virtual machines by container technology, deploy our nodes and centralized controller into different virtual machines, and evaluate basic performance of SDRS [14].

5.1   Routing Convergence Time

In order to testify that SDRS has a good routing convergence performance, we make an experiment on routing convergence performance of distributed routing system and SDRS under different network diameters, as shown in Fig. 3.

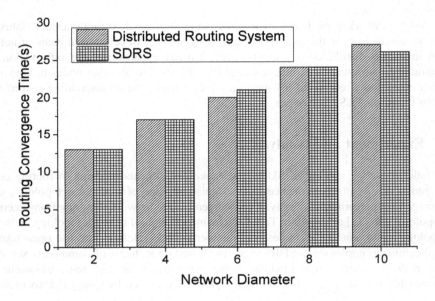

Fig. 3. Routing convergence time

The routing convergence time in SDRS is nearly equal to that in distributed routing system. For example, when the value of network diameter is 2, 4, and 8, the routing convergence time is correspondingly 13 s, 17 s, and 24 s. On one hand, SDRS can uses distributed routing protocol to calculate distributed paths for end-to-end communications, even though centralized controller in SDRS doesn't complete installation of centralized paths. On the other hand, as the value of network diameter increases, routing convergence time doesn't markedly increase as well, because OSPF protocol uses "first flooding and then calculating" way to achieve routing convergence, which just resulting into the increase of transmission time of link-status message with the increase of network diameter.

5.2 Path Maintenance Time

SDRS uses distributed routing protocol to maintain centralized paths, while pure centralized framework (e.g. SDN) just revokes centralized paths by using centralized controller. So we evaluate these two mechanisms of path maintenance and calculate ratio of path maintenance time, as shown in Fig. 4.

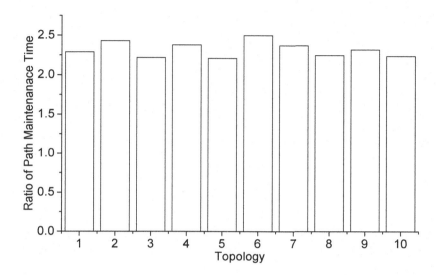

Fig. 4. Path maintenance time

Path maintenance time in pure centralized framework is two or more times as much as that in SDRS system, because the change message of link-statue in pure centralized framework is firstly notified to centralized controller and the latter then revokes routing strategies of centralized paths; while nodes in SDRS can quickly generates release message of centralized paths and floods messages to other nodes when perceiving changes of centralized path. Thus, our experimental results show that path maintenance time in SDRS is better than that in pure centralized frameworks.

5.3 Acquisition Time of Link-Status Topology

Acquisition time of link-status topology refers to synchronization time of link-status topology when centralized controller firstly connecting to network. Only when SDRS completes the synchronization of link-status topology between routing strategy layer and equipment layer, it can start to calculate centralized path. So we evaluate acquisition time of link-status topology by using ten typical topologies as shown in Fig. 5.

Acquisition time of link-status topology is closely with the number of nodes, rather than the number of links. And it's an exact linear relationship between the number of nodes and acquisition time of link-status topology. For example, Garr with thirty-six

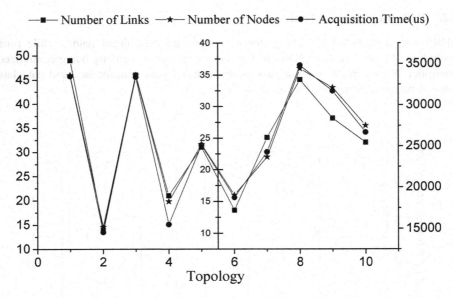

Fig. 5. Acquisition time

nodes takes about 0.35 s to complete the acquisition of link-status topology. We can see that centralized controller can attain the information of network topology in some seconds.

5.4 Management Performance

We also evaluate management performance of SDRS prototype in terms of installation time of distributed routing strategy, installation time of centralized routing strategy, installation time of orchestration strategy, and keep-alive time, as shown in Table 2.

SDRS can complete installation of routing strategies in about 2 ms. And installation time of centralized routing strategy is longer than installation time of distributed routing strategy, because centralized routing strategy coming from routing strategy layer is installed data plane via control plane while distributed routing strategy is directly installed by control plane.

Table 2. Control and management time

Name	Time
Installation time of distributed routing strategy	0.32 ms
Installation time of centralized routing strategy	1.24 ms
Installation time of orchestration strategy	0.31 ms
Keep-alive time	0.31 ms

6 Conclusion and Next Works

Traditional distributed routing protocol faces with some challenges in terms of incomplete information of partial-view, selfishness of local strategy. Software defined network (SDN), as the representative of centralized control mechanism, brings a new solution to above problems. In light of this, this paper firstly puts forwards software defined routing system (SDRS) by introducing centralized control framework into distributed routing system. SDRS felicitously integrates centralized control framework with distributed routing protocol, to make full use of their advantages and remedy their disadvantages. At last, we implement a SDRS prototype to verify its feasibility and validity.

In the future, we will mainly focus on the following aspects:

- Atom operation of routing strategy. One centralized path installed by centralized controller usually consists of several routing strategies and these routing strategies are installed into different nodes. On one hand, routing strategies installed for one centralized path should be revoked when the installation of one routing strategy belonging to this centralized path fails. On the other hand, centralized controller should install routing strategies in order to avoid packet loss.
- Synchronization of centralized path status. When centralized controller reconnects to network again, part of centralized paths still continue running in network. If centralized controller does not synchronize path status with distributed routing protocol, it may result in non-consistent of path status. As a result, centralized controller should firstly synchronize the information of centralized paths in the network, when reconnecting to network again.
- Incremental deployment ability. SDRS prototype needs to expand OSPF protocol to support for centralized path maintenance. It hardly can be deployed in current router equipment. We will make lots of efforts to achieve SDRS by using control interface of routing protocol, which doesn't need to modify distributed routing protocol.

Acknowledgement. This work is supported by National Natural Science Foundation of China (NSFC) project grant No. 61373039, and National Basic Research Program of China (973) grant No. 2012CB315906.

References

1. Xu, D., Chiang, M., Rexford, J.: Corrections to link-state routing with hop-by-hop forwarding can achieve optimal traffic engineering. IEEE/ACM Trans. Netw. (TON) **23**(5), 1702–1703 (2015)
2. Fortz, B., Thorup, M.: Internet traffic engineering by optimizing OSPF weights. In: Proceedings of Nineteenth Joint Conference of the IEEE Computer and Communications Societies, INFOCOM 2000, pp. 519–528 (2001)
3. Akyildiz, I.F., Lee, A., Wang, P., et al.: A roadmap for traffic engineering in SDN-OpenFlow networks. Comput. Netw. **71**, 1–30 (2014)

4. Jammal, M., Singh, T., Shami, A., et al.: Software defined networking: state of the art and research challenges. Comput. Netw. **72**, 74–98 (2014)
5. Zhang, H., Yan, J.: Performance of SDN routing in comparison with legacy routing protocols. In: International Conference on Cyber-Enabled Distributed Computing and Knowledge Discovery, pp. 491–494 (2015)
6. Bennesby, R., Mota, E., Fonseca, P., et al.: Innovating on interdomain routing with an inter-SDN component. In: 2014 IEEE 28th International Conference on Advanced Information Networking and Applications, pp. 131–138. IEEE (2014)
7. Kotronis, V., Gämperli, A., Dimitropoulos, X.: Routing centralization across domains via SDN: a model and emulation framework for BGP evolution. Comput. Netw. **92**, 227–239 (2015)
8. Hares, S., White, R.: Software-defined networks and the interface to the routing system (I2RS). IEEE Internet Comput. **17**(4), 84–88 (2013)
9. Sgambelluri, A., Paolucci, F., Cugini, F., et al.: Generalized SDN control for access/metro/core integration in the framework of the interface to the routing system (I2RS). In: IEEE GLOBECOM Workshops, pp. 1216–1220 (2013)
10. Shand, M., Bryant, S.: IP fast reroute framework. LoopFree Altern. **4**(4), 206–207 (2010). IETF RFC 5286
11. Knight, S., Nguyen, H.X., Falkner, N., et al.: The internet topology zoo. IEEE J. Sel. Areas Commun. **29**(9), 1765–1775 (2011)
12. Kohler, E., Morris, R., Chen, B., et al.: The click modular router. ACM Trans. Comput. Syst. **18**(3), 263–297 (2001)
13. Jakma, P., Lamparter, D.: Introduction to the quagga routing suite. IEEE Netw. **28**(2), 42–48 (2014)
14. Ahrenholz, J., Danilov, C., Henderson, T.R., et al.: CORE: a real-time network emulator. In: Military Communications Conference, MILCOM 2008, pp. 1–7. IEEE (2008)

Towards Efficient Multimedia Data Disseminating in Mobile Opportunistic Networks

Peng Liu, Yue Ding, Jia Xu, and Tingting Fu$^{(\boxtimes)}$

School of Computer Science and Technology,
Hangzhou Dianzi University, Hangzhou 310018, China
`ftt@hdu.edu.cn`

Abstract. When there arises tremendous needs for large size file transmissions in Mobile Opportunistic Networks, such as multimedia advertisement distribution in vehicular ad-hoc networks, or video sharing in mobile social networks, the storage space of relay nodes is becoming the bottleneck of achieving higher performance. E.g., an intermediate node with better delivery utility may refuse to relay a data file copy due to insufficiency of its storage space. Traditional methods without considering the data size are not likely to work efficiently in this scenario. In this paper, we model this routing challenge as a multiple knapsacks problem and propose a distributed algorithm to solve it. The algorithm is executed locally when two nodes encounter within the existing network structure. From the experiment on the real data trace, we show that our scheme achieves better performance than the competitors in terms of delay and delivery ratio.

1 Introduction

Camera enabled devices are popular nowadays both in Vehicular Ad-hoc Networks and Mobile Social Networks with the wide use of smartphones and car dashcameras. It is common that a user may want to share a video clip with his friends or a vehicle needs to distribute emergency videos to other vehicles. If there is the support of the backbone network, the users are able to download data via access points (APs) or 4G networks through wireless means. The efficiency between APs and downloaders is the main concern of those work. However, regarding Mobile Opportunistic Networks, in many cases, the backbone network doesn't even exist. Therefore, the data forwarding is carried out as a store-forward manner through opportunistic contacts between nodes. According to traditional research assumptions, data size is omitted so that each relay can response to infinite number of requestors. Therefore, the routing algorithm that works on a single pair of source-destination nodes also works on multiple pairs. In terms of multimedia data, when there are a lot of source nodes doing transmission simultaneously, the storage of an intermediate node may be filled by many requests of forwardings. The insufficient space of the storage in relay nodes will potentially cause extra delay. For example, as indicated in Fig. 1(a), suppose each node can only accommodate just one video clip. When Relay R_1 meets the

© Springer International Publishing AG 2017
L. Ma et al. (Eds.): WASA 2017, LNCS 10251, pp. 629–640, 2017.
DOI: 10.1007/978-3-319-60033-8_54

relay node R_2, if do not consider the storage limitation, it should forward the video clip a to R_2. However, it is not possible when R_2 can only hold one video clip. Therefore, two nodes exchange their video clip as shown in Fig. 1(b). Thus, according to the figure, node R_1 with b and R_2 with a is better than node R_1 with a and R_2 with b, but not as good as a and b are both with R_2. When there are a lot of data files with different size and we consider the delivery metric of different relay nodes to different destinations, the conflict is common when the routing strategy is actually first-come first served. According to [8], the probability of successful delivery exponentially decreases when the data size increases. Also, it is difficult to collect information and apply the centralized scheduling in a Mobile Opportunistic Network. Distinguished from existing work, in this paper, we seek to improve the forwarding efficiency without additional resource.

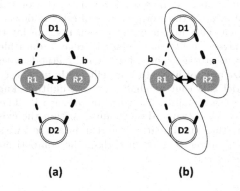

(a)   **(b)**

Fig. 1. An example to show the challenge in proposed scenario. The relay node R_1 tries to send a video clip a to the destinations D_1 while the relay node R_2 tries to send a video clip b to the destinations D_2. Each relay can only hold one video clip. The thick dashed lines indicated better encountering opportunity of two nodes.

To reduce delivery delay and improve probability of successful data delivery, in opportunistic networks, data replication is often adopted. However, apparently, it will bring more storage overhead and severe burden to the whole network, which will worsen the situation and greatly increase the cost. Therefore, in this paper, we will focus on a single copy based forwarding strategy and try to make best use of each individual storage of the nodes. In some work, data is fragmented into small pieces and sent via multiple path for a better probability to reach the destinations. But in opportunistic networks, since the topology of the network is highly dynamic, to ensure the quality of service and guaranteed delay, a data file should be sent in whole during node-to-node transmission in our scenario. Our contribution is threefold:

1. We consider the single copy forwarding for multimedia data files in a Mobile Opportunistic Network.

2. We model the problem as a multiple knapsacks problem and give a greedy based solution.
3. We further consider the limited communication bandwidth during nodes meet, model it as a 0–1 knapsack problem on top of the results of the above multiple knapsacks solution.

2   Related Work

Data forwarding is one of the hot research areas in Mobile Opportunistic Networks. The key challenge is how to select appropriate relays such that data can be forwarded to destinations with short latency and forwarding cost, where mobile nodes carry and forward messages upon intermittent contacts. Single copy based methods are firstly applied to reduce the resource requirements [11]. However, most of them are based on the assumption that there is no limitation of storage space in nodes and bandwidth during data exchanging. When consider the multimedia data which is very large in volume compared with small messages, the storage constraint will bring a lot of unexpected problems.

Large data file dissemination is a new paradigm in opportunistic networks. SADF [6] is an automatic data packet dividing algorithm. To improve the delivery ratio, it cuts the large file into small segments according to the network quality and duration of contacts. It enables large files to be transmitted in the network but it does not touch the problem of efficient relaying after partition. METhoD [10] implements a platform for distributing multimedia contents in the delay tolerant networks. It dose not give solution on how to prevent memory overflow but adding a lot of external storage to help the big data application. Abdelmoumen et al. [1] analyzes the adverse effect brought by the insufficient of nodes' storage. By adding some fixed nodes with large storage space, the problem can be solve to some extent. However, in many cases the data file is not allowed to be divided. Also, additional infrastructure is costly. Zhao et al. [13] turns the problem of global optimizing of forwarding utility into the local optimizing of forwarding utility upon nodes encounter. The proposed cooperative forwarding is model as a 0–1 knapsack problem and solved by a greedy algorithm. Large volume content disseminating in VANETs is considered in [7]. The authors try to find a static routing path between the source and the destination.

Many real world network applications can be modeled as Knapsack problems and solved by approximate algorithms. In this paper, a multiple knapsacks [3] problem is modeled extended from 0–1 knapsack problem. Generally speaking, a set of n items and m bins are given (knapsacks) such that each item i has a profit $p(i)$ and a size $s(i)$, and each bin j has a capacity $c(j)$. The goal is to find a allocation of items such that they have a maximum profit packing in the bins.

3   System Model and Preliminaries

In this section, we present the system model and preliminaries. For simplicity and without loss of generality, we assume every inter-nodes transmission is successful and none of the nodes is selfish. Then the solution will focus on how to arrange data files between two nodes upon their encountering. The objective of this paper is to develop an efficient single copy data forwarding scheme for multimedia data files. The first performance metric is the total amount of data bits that have been successfully transmitted. Because data files contain different volume of data, the amount of data bits is a better metric than the number of data copies. The second performance metric is the delivery delay which is the average dissemination duration of all source-destination pairs.

3.1 System Model

We consider a network with N users (nodes) in the Mobile Opportunistic Network, where they opportunistically encounter each other along the time scale. Some of the nodes among them raise requests of delivering multimedia data files to other destination nodes. Each source has only one destination and a single copy of the data file is allowed to be transported from the source to the destination at a time. Duplicated copies are not adopted because it may lead to severe Denial of Forward in the network. We call a set of source node and destination node a source-destination pair. A node could be source as well as destination at the same time. Each node i is associated with a probability vector $(u_i^1, u_i^2, ..., u_i^N)$, where u_i^j indicates the contact strength between node i and j. Here, we adopt the total number of contacts during a period as the metric to evaluate the contact strength. Therefore, the higher the contact strength between a node to the destination, the more possibility of successful delivery through that node, named as delivery possibility. When two nodes encounter, they may exchange data files according to the delivery possibility. The metric is widely used in the Opportunistic Networks [2,4] and has been proved very efficient. Since the contacts are not evenly distributed along the time scale, we propose **recent delivery possibility** (Definition 2) based on the **full delivery possibility** (Definition 1). The prior one considers the most recent contact status between nodes which is similar to locality principle, while the latter one focuses on the average situation. Since the contact is opportunistically happening between nodes, it is not simple to tell which metric is better while the t of **recent delivery possibility** is adjustable. We will evaluate different metrics in our experiments and analyze the results.

Definition 1. The **full delivery possibility** is the total number of encounters between the node and the destination in the entire evaluation period T.

Definition 2. The **recent delivery possibility** is the number of encounters between the node and the destination in a given recent time duration t.

3.2 Priority of Data Files

The priority of the data is not considered in the related work. No data is dropped on purpose or refused to relay because there are enough resources. In the proposed scenario, when the storage can only hold one data file, the rest of them have to be dropped or denied. Then there needs a scheme to keep the fairness and efficiency of the data files. Assigning each data file a priority is a popular solution. The priority could based on many aspects such as the priority of the sender and the receiver, the significance of the data itself, the elapsed time of the data file, etc. Many of the schemes could be very complex and hare to manage.

Since one of the main goals of the paper is to maximize the amount of successfully transmitted data, we assign the priority of a data file associated with its data size. In another word, the larger the size is, the higher the priority is. Since any decision is only between two encountered nodes, there is no need to maintain global priority, which greatly reduces the overhead. No priority information is necessary to be kept, two nodes can handle this in a distributed and realtime manner.

3.3 Basic Idea

When two nodes encounter, each of them may contain several multimedia data files. For each node, a data file has a different probability of being delivered to the destination. It is like there are two knapsacks and we try to put items in them to achieve maximal value under the constraint of storage. Besides that, the duration of each encountering is limited so that not all desired data files can be exchanged so that we need also consider the communication constraint. We model the scenario as a multiple knapsacks problem [3] where we try to achieve the maximal delivery possibility of all data files. When two nodes meet, the first step is to gather all data files together. Then the second step is that all the data files be re-arranged according to their delivery possibility in different nodes as a multiple knapsacks problem. However, it is not that simple. When the re-arrangement is applied the spare space may not be enough for the movement of these data files. The another limitation is the capacity of the channel, due to the bandwidth and the contact duration, there exists a bound for maximal amount data could be transmitted. We will also provide solution for these constraints.

4 Multiple Knapsacks Based Forwarding Scheme

4.1 Problem Statement

Suppose the capacity of two encountered node i and j is c_i and c_j respectively. The size of data file k is s_k. The delivery possibility of k on node i is $u_i^{dest}(k)$. Assume two encountered nodes have n data files in total. Then, the multiple knapsacks problem can be formulated as:

$$\max \sum\nolimits_{k=1}^{n} u_m^{dest}(k), \ m = i \ or \ j$$

$$s.t. \max \sum\nolimits_{k=1}^{n} s_k \leq c_i \text{ where } k \text{ is on } i \tag{1}$$

$$\max \sum\nolimits_{k=1}^{n} s_k \leq c_j \text{ where } k \text{ is on } j \tag{2}$$

The conditions 1 and 2 are the constraints of the storage limitation on node i and j respectively. We apply the algorithm in Ref. [3] to get the result. Based on this model, we propose the forwarding algorithm as follow.

Algorithm 1. Multiple Knapsack based multimedia forwarding method

---

Input: Data file list from both nodes (including size, destination information),
    capacity size of two nodes
Output: an arrangement of data files in both nodes
1: **FOR** the two encountering node i and j **DO**
2:    **IF** i or j is a destination to any current data files **THEN**
3:       forward the data files to i or j;
4:    **ELSE IF** get the list of rest data files **THEN**
5:       solve the arrangement as a multiple knapsacks problem;
6:       exchange the data files according to above result.
7:    **END IF**
8: **END FOR**

4.2   Forwarding Time Window

Since the contact duration varies from time to time, many multimedia data files can not be transmitted within one contact. While we do not allow the split of data files, only those data files can be transmitted within the contact will be forwarded. To make it simple, we use term **forwarding time window (FTW)** as defined in Definition 3 to represent the capacity of the contact. There are two ways to estimate **FTW** between two nodes via offline and online methods respectively. First method is to use history records. Second method is to negotiate between two nodes. Note that the channel is a bidirectional one so that **FTW** only stands for one way capacity. Because of the constraint of FTW, Algorithm 1 may not have enough time to finish exchanging data files. Therefore, we must then achieve the optimal forwarding exchange under the additional FTW constraint. As shown in Fig. 2, Node i and j have total storage capacity of 6 each. When node j has a better delivery possibility to data file a and d while node i has a better one to data file b, the capacity of FTW (which is 5) is enough for the data files exchange. Then the Algorithm 1 can achieve its performance.

Definition 3. The **forwarding time window** stands for the maximal amount of data bits that can be transferred one way during a contact. It depends on many facts such as communication bandwidth, contact duration, etc.

When the capacity of FTW is 4 as seen in Fig. 3, only d and b can be rearranged. Data file a has to stay with node i.
When the capacity of FTW is 1 as seen in Fig. 4, only a and b can be rearranged. Data file d has to stay with node i. Suppose the capacity of FTW is noted as c_{FTW}, we have the new equation.

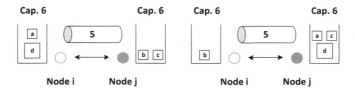

Fig. 2. An example to show forwarding time window with capacity 5 where the size of a, b, c is 1 and the size of d is 4.

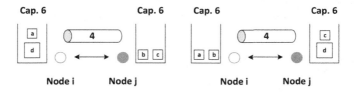

Fig. 3. An example to show forwarding time window with capacity 4 where the size of a, b, c is 1 and the size of d is 4.

$$\max \sum\nolimits_{k=1}^{n} u_m^{dest}(k), \ m = i \ or \ j$$

$$s.t. \max \sum\nolimits_{k=1}^{n} s_k \leq c_i \text{ where } k \text{ is on } i \tag{3}$$

$$\max \sum\nolimits_{k=1}^{n} s_k \leq c_j \text{ where } k \text{ is on } j \tag{4}$$

$$\max \sum\nolimits_{k=1}^{n} s_k \leq c_{FTW} \text{ where } k \text{ is forwarded}$$

$$\text{from } i \ to \ j \ or \ viceverse \tag{5}$$

Equation 5 guarantees the exchanged data won't exceed the communication capacity between two nodes. We use Algorithm 2 to solve the multiple knapsacks problem with the FTW constraint. Finally, the problem will be solve by solving sub problems in a dimensionality reduction manner.

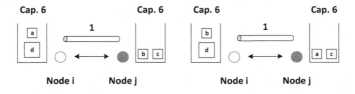

Fig. 4. An example to show forwarding time window with capacity 1 where the size of a, b, c is 1 and the size of d is 4.

Algorithm 2. Multiple Knapsack based multimedia forwarding method with FTW constraint

---

Input: Data file list from both nodes (including size, destination information),
capacity size of two nodes
size of the FTW
Output: an arrangement of data files in both nodes
1: **FOR** the two encountering node i and j **DO**
2:    **IF** i or j is a destination to any current data files **THEN**
3:      forward the data files to i or j;
4:    **ELSE IF** get the list of rest data files **THEN**
5:      solve the arrangement as a multiple knapsacks problem;
6:      **FOR** the data files in each direction **DO**
7:        model the problem as a 0-1 knapsack problem where the one way data files are the items and the capacity of the FTW is the knapsack
8:      **END FOR**
9:      exchange the data files according to above result.
10:   **END IF**
11: **END FOR**

---

5   Simulation

To evaluate the performance, we compare our algorithms with a single copy forwarding strategy proposed in [4,13] using the real trace data. Two main metrics are *Delivery delay* and *Delivery ratio* respectively, according to the objects of the paper. The first one is the average value of all the source-destination pairs. The second one is not the ratio of the number of received files but the amount of received bits. We first present the experiment settings followed by the analysis of three cases. Finally, we summarize the simulation results and discuss the interest findings.

5.1   Simulation Settings

We run the simulation on the real trace Infocom 06 [9] in which contacts between people during a conference are recorded. As shown in Table 1, there are 78 nodes moving in the area and have opportunistic contacts. The duration of the data collecting is 4 days. The basic number of source-destination pairs is 50. The common data file size is 6 and the storage space is 50. Those source-destination pairs are randomly picked in the node set. Each sender will initiate a data file with the size around 3 to 10. Also, each node will be assigned a storage space between 25 to 75. The FTW is calculated using the history records.

Four algorithms are evaluated. *MultiKnap-Full* represents the multiple knapsacks based forwarding algorithm which is proposed in this paper. It forwards data files according to the **full delivery possibility**. *MultiKnap-Recent* is the same algorithm that is running on the **recent delivery possibility**. The rest algorithms are a combination of [4,13], and use the **full delivery possibility** and the **recent delivery possibility** respectively. When two nodes meet, each of them will evaluate and pull data files from the other node. To achieve the maxima of incremental benefit, they model it as a 0–1 knapsack problem and solve it using a greedy algorithm. We call them *GreedyKnap-Full* and *GreedyKnap-Recent* respectively. For methods using **recent delivery possibility**, they will only use the number of contacts in the current day for reference. Each simulation is repeated for 200 times and record the average value.

Three sets of experiment are conducted to observe the effect of three facts, which is closely related to large data file transmission. First is the number of concurrent forwardings, second is the storage capacity of nodes, the last is the size of data files.

Table 1. Simulation parameters

Parameter	Value
Total nodes	78
Number of contacts	227, 657
Experiment duration	4 days
Number of source-destination pairs	50
Basic data file size	6
Basic storage space	50

5.2 Simulation Result

5.2.1 Number of Concurrent Forwardings

We set the criterion of source-destination pairs as 50, therefore most of nodes are included in forwarding data files. Then we slightly decrease and increase the number of source-destination pairs to see how it will affect the performance.

As shown in Fig. 5(a), the proposed *MultiKnap-Recent* method achieves the lest delay where there is a 15% improvement compared with the runner-up *GreedyKnap-Recent* method. The *GreedyKnap-Full* method gets the worst delay, about 25% more than that of the *MultiKnap-Recent* method. The forwarding metric based on recent contact performs better than the total history contact which follows the locality principle. However, it is difficult to find the optimal parameter for the recent time period which is out of the scope of this paper. The result joggles because the source-destination pairs are randomly selected, according to the nature of opportunistic contact, it will seriously affect the delay. Furthermore, we observe that these methods are less sensitive to the number of nodes.

As shown in Fig. 5(b), we evaluate the delivery ratio by how many bits have been received by the destinations not the number of data files. With the increasing of the number of source-destination pairs, the delivery ratio drops in all 4 methods. However, our proposed methods can achieve better ratio than the greedy methods since the solution to multiple knapsacks can optimize the total value (size) of the data files.

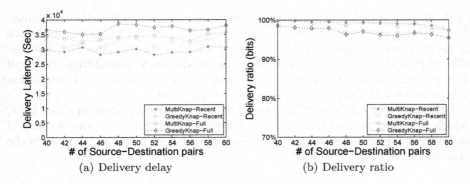

(a) Delivery delay

(b) Delivery ratio

Fig. 5. Results of different number of source-destination pairs

5.2.2 Storage Capacity of Nodes

We then fix the number of source-destination pairs and adjust the storage capacity of nodes.

As shown in Fig. 6(a), when the storage space is very limited, all 4 methods surfer from a very large delay. As the storage space increases from 50% to 100%, our proposed *MultiKnap-Recent* method reduces the delay quickly. Although other 3 methods also reduce the delay, but the rate is slower than the *MultiKnap-Recent* method. When the storage space is large enough such that a single node can accommodate the forwarding requests from multiple senders, each method gets approaching to others. Although the *MultiKnap-Recent* method still achieves the best but the result of using multiple knapsacks algorithm is not apparent any more.

It is no doubt the delivery ratio goes up when the capacity increases. Our two methods have a better growth rate than the greedy methods as can be seen in Fig. 6(b).

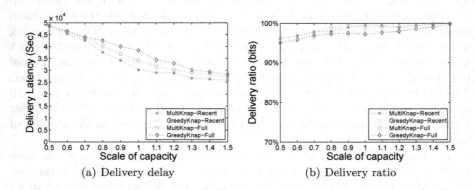

(a) Delivery delay

(b) Delivery ratio

Fig. 6. Results of different scale of capacity size

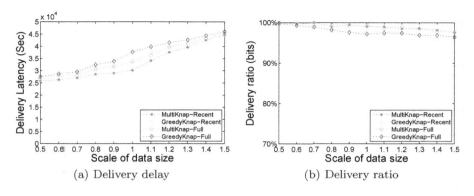

(a) Delivery delay   (b) Delivery ratio

Fig. 7. Results of different scale of data file size

5.2.3   Size of Data Files

Figure 7(a) demonstrates the result when the size of data file increases from 50% to 150%.

The larger the size of the data file, the less the number of data files a single node can keep. Therefore, without the optimal arrangement of the forwarding selection, the *GreedyKnap-Full* and *GreedyKnap-Recent* methods will soon lead to a bad performance. The multiple knapsacks based method can slow down this process so that it is 23% better than the greedy knapsack method when the ratio of data file is 100%. However, when the size of data files is too large for any scheduling, all methods turn to get a worse delay. Figure 7(b) is similar to that of Fig. 5(b), the *MultiKnap-Recent* method achieves better delivery rate than other methods.

5.3   Summary of Simulation

After investigating into the real trace data, we draw a conclusion that the proposed *MultiKnap-Recent* method can achieve not only best delay performance under all simulation settings, but also a better delivery ratio. The multiple knapsacks based methods can guarantee the maximal delivery possibility of most portion of data files, especially those large data files. However, the performance is not as good as expected. Two reasons lie behind. First is the opportunistic nature of the network, therefore, any different source-destination pair will get different delay. Second is the interference between forwardings, i.e., any current decisions may affect other forwardings or future forwardings. A local optimal does not mean global optimal, e.g., after allocating the free space to a data file, a node may meet another data file with better delivery possibility in the near future.

6   Conclusion

In this paper, we consider multimedia data delivery in the opportunistic networks. To solve the contradiction between limited storage capacity and big multimedia data size, we propose the multiple knapsacks based solution which can achieve the local optimal in a distributed manner. It first applies full arrangement of multimedia data when two nodes meet as a multiple knapsacks problem. Then the contact duration is considered so that the arrangement has to follow the constraint of communication capacity. Simulation is conducted using real trace data. The results show our scheme achieves better performance both in delivery delay and ratio than the greedy knapsack based competitors. In the future work, we will try to explore deploying fixed infrastructures such as Throwbox [5] or Home [12], to help the scheduling of forwardings.

Acknowledgments. This work is supported by the Natural Science Foundation of China (61601157), Chinese Scholarship Council (201208330096).

References

1. Abdelmoumen, M., Frikha, M., Chahed, T.: Performance of delay tolerant mobile networks and its improvement using mobile relay nodes under buffer constraint. In: ISNCC, pp. 1–6. IEEE (2015)
2. Ayub, Q., Rashid, S., Zahid, M.S.M., Abdullah, A.H.: Contact quality based forwarding strategy for delay tolerant network. J. Netw. Comput. Appl. **39**, 302–309 (2014)
3. Chekuri, C., Khanna, S.: A PTAS for the multiple knapsack problem. In: Proceedings of the Eleventh Annual ACM-SIAM Symposium on Discrete Algorithms, pp. 213–222. ACM Press, New York, 9–11 January 2000
4. Erramilli, V., Crovella, M., Chaintreau, A., Diot, C.: Delegation forwarding. In: MobiHoc, pp. 251–260. ACM (2008)
5. Fan, B., Leng, S., Shao, C., Zhang, Y., Yang, K.: Joint optimization of throwbox deployment and storage allocation in mobile social networks. In: ICC, pp. 1213–1218. IEEE (2015)
6. Feng, L., Zhang, Y., Li, H.: Large file transmission using self-adaptive data fragmentation in opportunistic networks. In: CSNT, pp. 1051–1055 (2015)
7. Hu, M., Zhong, Z., Ni, M., Bajocchi, A.: Design and analysis of a beacon-less routing protocol for large volume content dissemination in vehicular ad hoc networks. SENSORS **16**(11), 1–27 (2016)
8. Lu, Z., Sun, X., Porta, T.F.L.: Cooperative data offloading in opportunistic mobile networks. CoRR abs/1606.03493 (2016)
9. Scott, J., Gass, R., Crowcroft, J., Hui, P., Diot, C., Chaintreau, A.: Crawdad trace cambridge/haggle/imote/infocom. v.2009-05-29, May 2009
10. Siby, S., Galati, A., Bourchas, T., Olivares, M., Gross, T.R., Mangold, S.: METhoD: a framework for the emulation of a delay tolerant network scenario for media-content distribution in under-served regions. In: ICCCN, pp. 1–9. IEEE (2015)
11. Spyropoulos, T., Psounis, K., Raghavendra, C.S.: Efficient routing in intermittently connected mobile networks: the single-copy case. IEEE/ACM Trans. Netw. **16**(1), 63–76 (2008)
12. Wu, J., Xiao, M., Huang, L.: Homing spread: community home-based multi-copy routing in mobile social networks. In: INFOCOM, pp. 2319–2327. IEEE (2013)
13. Zhao, G., Chen, M., Zuo, Q.: Data dissemination based on system utility in cooperative delay tolerant networks. J. Comput. Res. Dev. **50**, 1217–1226 (2013)

Job Scheduling Under Differential Pricing: Hardness and Approximation Algorithms

Qiuyuan Huang[3], Jing Zhao[2(✉)], Haohua Du[2], Jiahui Hou[2],
and Xiang-Yang Li[1(✉)]

[1] University of Science and Technology of China, Hefei, China
xiangyangli@ustc.edu.cn
[2] Illinois Institute of Technology, Chicago, USA
jing.john.zhao@gmail.com
[3] University of Florida, Gainesville, USA

Abstract. To induce a favorable energy demand pattern, generalized pricing models were proposed to achieve better aggregated energy consumption pattern. In this work we study how to schedule jobs under two differential pricing models, namely the combined pricing of day ahead pricing (DAP) and inclining block rate (IBR) both in the micro scope and macro scope. In the micro scope we study *offline* job scheduling with a goal to minimize the electricity cost of consumers when the electricity price and job profile are known beforehand. In the macro scope we study the aggregated effect on the cost of power generation when each entity (*e.g.*, a household or a factory) schedules their jobs autonomously. We first prove that the job scheduling problems are either APX-hard or NP-hard under two combined price models of DAP and IBR. We then present efficient methods with bounded approximation ratio and show that our scheduling achieves comparable electricity cost saving.

1 Introduction

Demand Side Management (DSM) [1,20] tries to impact the pattern of energy consumption. DSM encourages customers to shift their energy consumption from peak hours to less busy hours or to hours with sufficient renewable resources by rewarding them with a lower bill. To achieve this, DSM uses differential electricity pricing instead of the flat rate pricing used in traditional power grid. A underlying assumption of all differential pricing schemes is that end users will schedule its electricity demand (composed of a set of jobs) to minimize the total electricity payment while satisfying the requirement of each job.

In general, two kinds of differential electricity pricing are used in practice [1,20]: (1) *time varying electricity pricing*: electricity pricing that depends on the time of electricity usage; (2) *amount dependent electricity pricing*: electricity pricing that depends on the amount of electricity usage. Depending on when the

---

The research of Li is partially supported by China National Funds for Distinguished Young Scientists with No. 61625205, Key Research Program of Frontier Sciences, CAS, Nos. QYZDY-SSW-JSC002, NSF CMMI 1436786, and NSF CNS 1526638.

© Springer International Publishing AG 2017
L. Ma et al. (Eds.): WASA 2017, LNCS 10251, pp. 641–652, 2017.
DOI: 10.1007/978-3-319-60033-8_55

electricity price is announced, time varying electricity pricing can further be classified as *time of use pricing* (TOUP), *day ahead pricing* (DAP) and *real time pricing* (RTP) [1]. In amount dependent electricity pricing, on the other hand, electricity rate is different with regard to different amount of electricity consumption: the more you consume, the higher the rate is. In the electricity market, mostly used amount based differential pricing is Inclining Block Rate (IBR) [11]. In IBR, if the energy consumption is higher than some threshold, a lower electricity rate will be charged.

Previous researches concerning DSM can generally be grouped into two categories: (1) researches in the micro scope, which study the scheduling of the jobs carried out by machines to minimize the electricity cost for a household or a factory given certain electricity pricing [2–9,21]; (2) researches in the macro scope, which study the pricing strategy [16–19], or joint scheduling of power generation and consumption [21,22] to lower the power generation cost. Among these researches, there exist works that study combined RTP and IBR [10,11,15,24]. The generalized models bring more flexibility into pricing compared with pure RTP or IBR. Such flexibility helps to achieve better aggregated energy consumption pattern [11] that may lower the cost on the power generation. These works generally focus on how to predict the electricity price in RTP and provide scheduling algorithms to address the uncertainties in price and load.

However, existing literature lacks a comprehensive study concerning the combination of DAP and IBR both in the micro scope and macro scope. There is report [25] showing that some companies, such as Ameren in Illinois, change their pricing strategy from RTP to DAP as required by customers. Compared with combined pricing of RTP and IBR, combined pricing of DAP and IBR remove the uncertainty in electricity price. We believe that *offline scheduling* with sure knowledge of electricity price and appliance usage information, which can be controlled by customers, will be more suitable for combined pricing of DAP and IBR compared with previously proposed algorithms [10,11,15,24] with price uncertainty assumption. The works by Clark and Lampe [26] and Bina and Ahmadi [27] are closest to our proposed research, which also studied combined pricing of RTP and DAP for household appliance scheduling. These works, however, either only focus on reducing peak average ratio (PAR) or load prediction. Computation efficiency as well as the power generation cost are not considered or evaluated.

In this work, we study the combined pricing of DAP and IBR both in the micro scope and macro scope. In the micro scope, we assume that an end-user has a set of jobs need to be run within a certain constraint, such as time-window to run each job and the total electricity demand to finish the job. We study how to schedule a set of jobs under this generalized pricing model to minimize the electricity cost for consumers. For job scheduling, we are first concerned with the complexity of the scheduling algorithm. The reasons are as follows: (1) for household appliance scheduling, there is research [23] showing that the power generation as well as the power consumption cost will be lower, if customers join family plans and schedule their appliances together, which may involve the scheduling of a large number of appliances; (2) for industrial load scheduling, the number of machines could be very large. We also design efficient scheduling method with approximable performance. In the macro scope, we study the aggregated effect on the cost of power generation when the jobs are distributively scheduled in each household and factory. In the macro scope, we take both renewable resources and traditional power generators, such as generator using fuels into consideration.

The contribution of this paper is summarized as follows. We show the hardness of offline job scheduling under two combined price models of DAP and IBR: in the first price model we show minimizing the total electricity payment is APX-Hard and cannot be approximated by a ratio of $1 + \frac{\min_{i=1}^{m}(b_i - a_i)}{\sum_{i=1}^{m} a_i}$, in the second price model, we show that the problem is NP hard. We propose efficient algorithms with bounded approximation ratio, which are dependent on the relationship between the energy consumption of jobs and the thresholds of the IBR. We show that the proposed scheduling algorithm achieves comparable electricity cost saving with respect to the optimal scheduling. We did a thorough evaluation of the scheduling both on the power consumption end and power generation end using simulations on real world data sets. Our experiments (results omitted due to space limit) show that our scheduling algorithms achieve over 10% reduction on household appliance energy consumption, over 20% reduction on industrial energy consumption and over 30% reduction on power generation cost. In addition, our extensive evaluation results show that our algorithm may achieve a 7% reduction on carbon dioxide emission. Also, our algorithms only use less than 2% of the time of a mixed integer based solution.

2   System Models

We focus on the scheduling of demand (composed of a set of n jobs, denoted as $J = \{1, 2, 3, \cdots, j, \cdots, n\}$) from a single entity. We assume that all jobs J have to be scheduled within a given period of time H. H will be further divided into frames with equal length h, where different frames have different price settings. For example, H could be a day, and h could be an hour. Next, we will introduce the job model and price model that we use respectively.

Job Model. Assume that each job j has a constant instantaneous energy consumption d_j and a constant duration γ_j. Notice that here we do not consider the case that a job can have different duration and instantaneous energy consumption by using different voltages. Thus the energy consumption of job j can be computed by $q_j = d_j * \gamma_j$. There are generally two kinds of jobs: jobs that could only be assigned to fixed frames (lighting, television, etc.) and jobs that could be assigned to arbitrary frames (charging, washing, etc.). We call jobs of the second kind *schedulable* jobs. Suppose h is the duration of a frame. In this work, we only consider the scheduling of schedulable jobs with $\gamma_j \leq h$, i.e. the short jobs which can be done within one frame. The short jobs we consider is non-interruptible.

However this job model could be easily extended to support interruptible jobs. We can divide interruptible jobs into small job unit and consider each job unit a non-interruptible job. The problem is thus to find a schedule which assigns jobs to different frames such that $\sum_{i \in H} p_i(L_i)$ is minimized, where L_i denotes the energy consumed in frame i and $p_i(L_i)$ is the price charged of L_i.

Price Model. The pricing models we consider are generalizations of TOU and IBR. Let m be the number of frames and c_i be the threshold of frame i.

In the first model, $\forall i \in [1, m]$, the cost of energy consumed in frame i is given by $p_i(L_i)$, as follows:

$$\textbf{Price model I:} \, p_i(L_i) = \begin{cases} a_i * L_i, \text{if } 0 \le L_i \le c_i \\ b_i * L_i, \text{if } L_i > c_i \end{cases}$$

In this pricing model, each frame has a certain energy consumption threshold c_i. If the energy consumed in frame i is lower than c_i, the price per unit for all the consumed energy is a_i. Otherwise, the price per unit of all the consumed energy will be b_i. Different frames may have different coefficients a_i, b_i and c_i. Note that for this pricing model, there is a payment discontinuity at the energy consumption L_i.

The second pricing model is similar to the first one and the cost of energy consumed in frame i is given by:

$$\textbf{Price model II:} \, p_i(L_i) = \begin{cases} a_i * L_i, \text{if } 0 \le L_i \le c_i \\ b_i * (L_i - c_i) + a_i * c_i, \text{if } L_i > c_i \end{cases}$$

The second model is introduced by Mohsenian-Rad and Leon-Garcia [11]. The only difference between the first model and the second model is that in the second model only the portion above the threshold has to pay a higher price. Suppose $a_{min} = \min\limits_{1 \le i \le m} a_i$, $a_{max} = \max\limits_{1 \le i \le m} a_i$, $b_{min} = \min\limits_{1 \le i \le m} b_i$ and $b_{max} = \max\limits_{1 \le i \le m} b_i$. We require that $a_{max} < b_{min}$. If $a_{max} \ge b_{min}$, the optimal solution clearly will not schedule jobs to the frame i with $a_i > b_{min}$. It is obvious that these models generalize IBR and TOU: the models are reduced to IBR, if $\forall 1 \le i, j \le m, a_i = a_j \bigwedge b_i = b_j$. The models are reduced to TOU, if $\forall 1 \le i \le m, a_i = b_i$.

Suppose I is the set of frames and J is the set of jobs. The job scheduling problem we study is defined as:

Definition 1. *Given a set of jobs J and a set of time-frames H that jobs can be scheduled to, for each job $j \in J$, assign job j to a frame in H such that $\sum_{i \in H} p_i(L_i)$ is minimized, where $L_i = \sum_{j \text{ is assigned to } i} q_j$.*

3   Problem Approximation Hardness

Our objective is to schedule all jobs to the frames such that the overall price charged for these jobs is minimized. It is straight forward that we can assign all jobs to the frame with the minimum pricing-coefficient b_{min}. Then we have an approximation factor of $\frac{b_{min}}{a_{min}}$. This naive approximation factor holds for the problem under both price models. In the following parts of this section we will analyze the hardness of the problem under different price models, respectively.

3.1   APX-Hardness Under Price Model I

In this section, we will prove the APX-Hardness (approximation hardness) of the assignment problem under the first price model when there are at least two frames. For APX-Hardness, we want to show what is the lower bound of the approximation ratio, i.e., the cost achieved by approximation algorithm against the optimal solution, that a polynomial algorithm could achieve. We use c_i denote the threshold of frame i and q_j to denote the energy consumption of job j. In this problem, we mainly consider the scheduling of short schedulable jobs. Thus the jobs we referred to here are schedulable jobs and the threshold c_i we considered here is the original threshold subtracted by the energy consumption of the unschedulable jobs in that frame. Let m be the number of frames and n be the number of schedulable jobs.

Suppose $\sum_{1 \leq i \leq m} c_i = L$. We will construct a set of jobs J with a total power consumption demand $\sum_{1 \leq j \leq n} q_j = (1 + \delta)L$, where δ is a given parameter. We prove that the problem is APX-Hard even in the following special subcases: (1) $\delta = 0$; (2) $\delta < 0$; (3) $\delta > 0$. The three cases correspond to the cases when the total energy consumption equals, is smaller than or greater than the sum of the thresholds respectively. By these three subcases, we would like to show the problem is generally hard to approximated. We will also prove that when $\delta > 0$ and $\frac{1}{\delta}$ is smaller than some constant C, we can achieve an approximation ratio of $1 + \frac{3C}{2}$ in polynomial time.

APX Hardness When $\delta = 0$. The proof of APX hardness uses the reduction from the subset sum problem. Recall that the decision subset sum problem (SS) is that given a set of integers $I = \{I_1, I_2, \cdots, I_n\}$, decides whether there is a subset S of I such that $\sum_{i \in S} I_i = \frac{1}{2} \sum_{j=1}^{n} I_j$. This is known to be a NP-hard problem. Given a set of jobs with power consumption demand $\{q_1, q_2, \cdots, q_n\}$, we construct a subset problem instance I with values $I = \{q_1, q_2, ..., q_n\}$. We say that $I \in SS$ if the decision subset sum problem of I is yes. Otherwise we say $I \notin SS$.

Theorem 1. *Consider the job scheduling problem with $\sum_{1 \leq i \leq m} c_i = \sum_{1 \leq j \leq n} q_j$. The JS problem under price model I is APX-Hard even if there are only two frames with pricing-coefficients (a_1, b_1) and (a_2, b_2) respectively. The best approximation ratio we can get is* $\min \left(\frac{a_1 + b_2}{a_1 + a_2}, \frac{a_2 + b_1}{a_1 + a_2} \right)$.

Proof. We will prove the approximation hardness of the problem as well as the lower bound of the problem using gap preserving techniques [12]. We will describe a reduction from the subset sum problem to our job scheduling problem (JS).

Consider a subset problem instance I with a set of integers $\{q_1, q_2, \cdots, q_n\}$. Suppose $L = \sum_{1 \leq i \leq n} q_i$. We construct a polynomial transformation function τ from an instance of SS to an instance I of our job scheduling problem JS. In $\tau(I)$, we create two time frames f_1 and f_2 with equal thresholds c_1 and c_2 being $\frac{L}{2}$. We use a_i and b_i to denote the low price and high price of frame i. To make the scheduling non-trivial, here $a_{max} = \max_i a_i \leq b_{min} = \min_j b_j$. Let $J = \{1, 2, ..., n\}$ be the set of jobs and the energy consumption of each job j in J is q_j, the integer q_j in I. We use $JS(\tau(I))$ to denote the minimum payment of all valid scheduling of jobs in $\tau(I)$ after the schedule. For a set of jobs S, we use L_S denote the total energy consumption demand of jobs in S. Let $w = (a_1 + a_2) * L/2$, which clearly is a lower bound on the payment by any job scheduling method to schedule jobs in $\tau(I)$.

We will prove the following claim:

$$\begin{cases} I \in SS \Rightarrow JS(\tau(I)) = w \\ I \notin SS \Rightarrow JS(\tau(I)) > \min\left(\frac{a_1+b_2}{a_1+a_2}, \frac{a_2+b_1}{a_1+a_2}\right) * w, \end{cases} \quad (1)$$

If $I \in SS$, we can divide the jobs of J into two subsets S_1 and S_2 such that the sum of energy consumption in S_1 is equal to that of S_2. Then we can assign the corresponding jobs in S_1 and S_2 to the two frames respectively. Under this scheduling, the cost of the energy consumption is optimized and we have $JS(\tau(I)) = w = (a_1 + a_2) * \frac{L}{2}$.

If $I \notin SS$, we can not divide the jobs in J into two subsets with equal total energy consumption. To schedule those jobs, we still need to divide those jobs into two sets S_1 and S_2. Without loss of generality, assume S_1 is the set with a smaller total energy consumption, thus, $L_{S_1} < \frac{L}{2} < L_{S_2}$. We first assume that the jobs of S_i is assigned to f_i. Thus, we have $JS(\tau(I)) = a_1 * L_{S_1} + b_2 * L_{S_2}$. As $a_1 \leq b_2$, the larger L_{S_1} is, the smaller $JS(\tau(I))$ is. Then we have $JS(\tau(I)) = a_1 * L_{S_1} + b_2 * L_{S_2} > a_1 * \frac{L}{2} + b_2 * \frac{L}{2} = \frac{a_1+b_2}{a_1+a_2} * w$. When the jobs of S_1 is assigned to f_2 (and the jobs of S_2 is assigned to f_1), we similarly conclude that $JS(\tau(I)) > \frac{a_2+b_1}{a_1+a_2} * w$. Consequently, we conclude that $JS(\tau(I)) > \min\left(\frac{a_1+b_2}{a_1+a_2}, \frac{a_2+b_1}{a_1+a_2}\right) w$. The above analysis shows that if there is an algorithm for JS problem with approximation ratio less than $\min\left(\frac{a_1+b_2}{a_1+a_2}, \frac{a_2+b_1}{a_1+a_2}\right)$ under the price model I, then we can use this algorithm to solve the SS problem in polynomial time. As we know that SS problem is NP-hard, thus, it is NP-hard to design polynomial time algorithms for JS problem with approximation ratio better than $\min\left(\frac{a_1+b_2}{a_1+a_2}, \frac{a_2+b_1}{a_1+a_2}\right)$.

Theorem 2. *Consider the job scheduling problem with $\sum_{1 \leq i \leq m} c_i = \sum_{1 \leq j \leq n} q_j$. Assume that there are m time-frames, where the pricing-coefficients of the i-th frame are (a_i, b_i) with threshold c_i, i.e., the payment of electricity x is $a_i x$ if $x \leq c_i$, and $b_i x$ otherwise. The job assignment problem under price model I is APX-Hard. The best approximation ratio by a polynomial time algorithm is $1 + \frac{\min_{i=1}^{m}(b_i - a_i)}{\sum_{i=1}^{m} a_i}$.*

Theorem 1 gives a lower bound on the approximation ratio of the problem. However, the transformed problem we derive from the subset sum problem is a very special case of the job scheduling problem, *i.e.*, the total energy consumption of the jobs equals the threshold of the frames. Now we analyze the approximation ratio of the job scheduling problem in more general cases: (1) total energy consumption of the jobs is below the threshold of the frames and (2) total energy consumption of the jobs is above the threshold of the frames.

APX Hardness When $\delta < 0$, $\delta > 0$. We first consider the job scheduling case where all the jobs have a total electricity demand $\sum_{1 \leq j \leq n} q_j$ that is *at most* $(1 - \delta) \sum_{1 \leq i \leq m} c_i$ for a postive constant $\delta > 0$. In this case, intuitively we can schedule all the jobs such that, at any time-frame i, the total demand L_i from all allocated jobs in this frame is at most the threshold c_i for extra-charge. To prove the low bound on approximation ratio, we will construct a job scheduling such that, when we cannot equally partition the jobs, one time-frame will result in sufficiently large over-payment.

Theorem 3. *Assume that $(1 - \delta) \sum_{1 \leq i \leq m} c_i = \sum_{1 \leq j \leq n} q_j$ with a value $\delta < 0$. The job assignment problem under price model I is APX-Hard even if there are only three frames. The approximation ratio by any polynomial time method is* at least $1 + \frac{\min_{i=1}^{m}(b_i - a_i)}{\sum_{i=1}^{m} a_i}$.

We then consider the case when the total demand from all the jobs is larger than the summation of the thresholds of all frames.

Theorem 4. *The job assignment problem under price model I is APX-Hard even if there are only three frames and $(1 + \delta) \sum_{1 \leq i \leq m} c_i = \sum_{1 \leq j \leq n} q_j$ with $\delta > 0$. The best approximation ratio we can get is* at least $1 + \frac{\min_{i=1}^{m}(b_i - a_i)}{\sum_{i=1}^{m} a_i}$.

$\frac{1}{\delta}$ is Larger than 0 and Smaller than Some Constant C

Theorem 5. *If the total energy consumption of the jobs is greater than $(1 + \frac{1}{C})L$, where C is some positive constant, we can achieve an approximation ratio of $1 + \frac{3C}{2}$.*

In this case, we can derive an algorithm based on the GAP problem with approximation ratio related to C.

Lemma 1. *There exists an optimal solution where there is only one frame in which the energy consumption is larger than the threshold. The optimal price is given by $CPT = \sum_{i \in [1,m]} a_i L_i + b_k x + (b_k - a_k) L_k$, where k is the frame that has the minimum $b_k x + (b_k - a_k) L_k$, and x is the energy consumed by jobs that can't be assigned to any frame without violating the threshold.*

3.2   NP Hardness Under Price Model II

Theorem 6. *The job assignment problem under Price Model II is NP-hard.*

Algorithm 1. Scheduling jobs in pricing model I

1: $H^{'} = \{\}$; set $c_{m+1} = 0$
2: sort frames in the non-decreasing order of a_i
3: **for** $i = 1$ to m **do**
4:     add frame i to $H^{'}$; SE=MKP$\{J, H^{'}\}$
5:     **if** the total energy consumption of unscheduled jobs are less than c_{i+1} **then**
6:         assign those jobs to frame i+1; add those assignments to SE
7:         return SE
8:     **end if**
9: **end for**
10: **if** There are jobs unscheduled **then**
11:     find the frame $k^{'}$ with minimum $(b_{k'} - a_{k'})L_{k'} + xb_{k'}$
12:     assign all the remaining jobs to the frame; add the assignment to SE
13:     return SE
14: **end if**

---

4   Approximation Algorithms

In this section, we will propose an approximation algorithm for the job scheduling problem under each price model. We will also derive the approximation bound for the algorithms under different cases. The algorithms we derive is based on the algorithm for the multiple knapsack problem (MKP), a special case of the general assignment problem (GAP) [13]. The GAP is to assign a set of items to a set of bins such that the total weight of the items is minimized or maximized. Each bin j has a capacity. Each item has a different weight in different bin. In MKP, the items have the same profit and size for all bins. There exists a polynomial-time approximation scheme (PTAS) for the MKP problem [14]. We use MAX-MKP to denote the maximization version of the MKP problem.

Theorem 7 [14]. *For MKP, packing the bins one by one using a $(1 - \epsilon)$-approximation single knapsack algorithm gives a $\frac{1}{2+\epsilon}$ approximation, where $\epsilon > 0$ can be arbitrarily small.*

4.1   Algorithm Under Price Model I

Scheduling Algorithm. We will use a α-approximation MAX-MKP algorithm to construct our algorithm, where α is a constant quantifying the ratio of worst case total weight achieved by the approximation algorithm against the optimal solution. As the aim of MAX-MKP is to maximize the value of the item packed, α should be some positive smaller than 1. We denote the algorithm to solve MKP by MKP(J,H), where J is the set of jobs and H is set of frames. The output of MKP(J,H) is a set of assignments $SE = \{(j,i) \mid j \in J, i \in H\}$. Our algorithm is basically divided into two parts: the first part is to assign as many jobs to the frames without violating the threshold as possible; the second part is to find one suitable frame to assign the rest of the jobs.

Table 1. Approximation ratios for model 1

Cases	Our algorithm	Lower bound
$r = 0$	$min\{\frac{b_{min}}{a_{min}}, \frac{a_{max}}{a_{min}} - \frac{1}{m} + (1 - \alpha + \frac{1}{m})\frac{b_{max}}{a_{min}}\}$	$\frac{a_{min}}{2a_{max}} + \frac{b_{min}}{2a_{max}}$
$r > 0$	$\frac{(1+\eta)b_{min}}{a_{max}+\eta b_{min}}$	$\frac{a_{min}}{2a_{max}} + \frac{b_{min}}{2a_{max}}$

The algorithm is mainly done in two steps: first schedule as many jobs as possible to the frames without violating the threshold; second find a frame with lowest $(b_k - a_k)L_k + xb_k$ as described in Lemma 1 and schedule all the jobs to it.

Analysis. Consider a job set J. Suppose the maximum energy consumption of J could be scheduled under the threshold by the optimal solution is L. Suppose the total energy consumption of all the jobs is $(1 + \eta)L$. There will be only two cases $\eta = 0$ and $\eta > 0$. $\eta < 0$ is impossible as the total energy consumption should not be smaller than L. The approximation ratio of our algorithm and the lower bound of the approximation ratio of the problem is shown in Table 1. The lower bound follows the proofs in previous section.

Suppose the energy consumption that could be scheduled under the thresholds by the MKP algorithm is L'. Let L'_i be the energy consumption of the jobs scheduled in frame i by the MKP algorithm. Let L_i be the energy consumption scheduled under the threshold in frame i by some optimal solution.

Theorem 8. *If $\eta = 0$, the approximation ratio reached by our algorithm for price model I is $min\{\frac{b_{min}}{a_{min}}, \frac{a_{max}}{a_{min}} - \frac{1}{m} + (1 - \alpha + \frac{1}{m})\frac{b_{max}}{a_{min}}\}$. Here α could be as large as $1 - \epsilon$.*

Theorem 9. *If $\eta > 0$ the approximation ratio of our algorithm for price model II is $\frac{(1+\eta)a_{min}}{a_{min}+\eta b_{min}}$.*

From the approximation bound, we can see that when $\eta > 0$, our approximation algorithm may achieve better approximation ratio as it is lower bounded by b_{min} and a_{min}, which is close to the theoretical bound of the problem. when $\eta = 0$, our approximation algorithm may perform worse as $\frac{b_{max}}{a_{min}}$ could be large.

4.2 Algorithm Under Price Model II

Scheduling Algorithm. For the problem under price mode II, we will also build an algorithm based on the α-approximation MKP algorithm used in the previous section.

The only difference between the algorithm under price model 2 and price model 1 is that in price model 2, the algorithm does not assign all the remaining jobs to the same frame. The reason is that in price model II, only the part above the threshold has to pay the higher price. After running MKP, some frames may have residue capacity. When the job is assigned to these frames, only a portion of their energy consumption has to pay the higher price.

Algorithm 2. Scheduling jobs in pricing model II

1: $H^{'} = \{\}$; sort frames in the non-decreasing order of a_i
2: **for** i=1 to m **do**
3:     add frame i to $H^{'}$; set $c_{m+1} = 0$; SE=MKP$\{J,H^{'}\}$
4:     **if** the energy consumption of unscheduled jobs is less than c_{i+1} **then**
5:         assign those jobs to frame $i + 1$; add those assignments to SE
6:         return SE
7:     **end if**
8: **end for**
9: **if** There are jobs unscheduled **then**
10:     **for** each frame i **do**
11:         the residue capacity of frame i is calculated as $r_i = c_i - L_i$
12:     **end for**
13:     **for** each unscheduled job j **do**
14:         find the frame $k^{'}$ with minimum $b_{k'}(w_j - r_{k'}) + a_{k'}r_{k'}$
15:         assign j to frame $k^{'}$; $r_{k'} = r_{k'} - w_j$
16:         If $r_{k'} < 0$ let $r_{k'} = 0$.
17:         add the assignment to SE
18:     **end for**
19:     return SE
20: **end if**

Table 2. Approximation ratios for model 2

Cases	Our algorithm	Lower bound
$\eta = 0$	$\frac{\alpha a_{max}}{a_{min}} + \frac{(1-\alpha)b_{min}}{a_{min}}$	$1 + \epsilon$
$\eta > 0$	$\frac{\alpha a_{max}+(1+\eta-\alpha)b_{min}}{a_{min}(1+\eta)}$	$1 + \epsilon$

Analysis. Given a job set, suppose the maximum energy consumption could be scheduled under the threshold by the optimal solution is L. Suppose the total energy consumption of all the jobs is $(1 + \eta)L$. Similar to the discussion of price model I, we will also discuss the algorithm in two cases: $\eta = 0$ and $\eta > 0$. The comparison of the approximation ratio acquired by our algorithm and that of the lower bound of the algorithm is given by Table 2.

Theorem 10. *If $\eta = 0$, the approximation ratio reached by our algorithm under price model II is $\frac{\alpha a_{max}}{a_{min}} + \frac{(1-\alpha)b_{min}}{a_{min}}$.*

Theorem 11. *If $\eta > 0$, the approximation ratio achieved by our algorithm for price model II is $\frac{\alpha a_{max}+(1+\eta-\alpha)b_{min}}{a_{min}(1+\eta)}$.*

5   Conclusion

We studied the job scheduling in smart grid. We proved that the hardness of these problems, proposed two approximation algorithms, and analyzed the approximation ratios in different cases. Our experiments on real-world data traces show that our algorithm can significantly reduce the energy cost both for the consumers and power generators. A future work is to study the scheduling problem of long jobs, IBR with multiple steps and jobs with different scheduable interval.

References

1. Hossain, E., Han, Z., Poor, H.V.: Demand-side managment for smart grid: opportunities and challenges. In: Smart Grid Communications and Networking (2012)
2. Kim, T.T., Poor, H.V.: Scheduling power consumption with price uncertainty. IEEE Trans. Smart Grid **2**(3), 519–527 (2011)
3. Shinwari, M., Youssef, A., Hamouda, W.: A water-filling based scheduling algorithm for the smart grid. IEEE Trans. Smart Grid **3**(2), 710–719 (2012)
4. Mohsenian-Rad, A.-H., Wong, V.W., Jatskevich, J., Schober, R.: Optimal and autoncmous incentive-based energy consumption scheduling algorithm for smart grid. In: IEEE PES Conference Innovative Smart Grid Technologies (2010)
5. Carons, S., Kesidis, G: Incentive-based energy consumption scheduling algorithms for the smart grid. Technical report (2010)
6. Xiong, G., Chen, C. Kishore, S., Yener, A.: Smart (in-home) power scheduling for demand response on smart grid. In: IEEE Innovative Smart Grid Technologies (ISGT) (2011)
7. Pedrasa, M.A.A., Spooner, T.D., MacGill, I.F.: Coordinated scheduling of residential distributed energy resource to optimized smart home energy services. IEEE Trans. Smart Grid **1**(2), 134–143 (2010)
8. Tang, S., Li, X.-Y., Huang, Q., Wu, D.: Smoothing the energy consumption: peak demand reduction in smart grid. In: IEEE INFOCOM (2013)
9. Yi, P., Dong, X., Iwayemi, A., Zhou, C., Li, S.: Real-time opportunistic scheduling for residential demand response. IEEE Trans. Smart Grid **4**(1), 227–234 (2013)
10. Samadi, P., Mohsenian-Rad, H., Wong, V.W.S., Schober, R.: Tackling the load uncertainty challenges for energy consumption scheduling in smart grid. Energy Policy (2008)
11. Mohsenian-Rad, A.-H., Leon-Garcia, A.: Optimal residential load control with price prediction in real-time electricity pricing environments. IEEE Trans. Smart Grid **1**(2), 120–133 (2010)
12. Arora, S., Lund, C.: Hardness of approximations. In: Approximation Algorithms for NP-Hard Problems (1996)
13. Kuhn, H.W.: The hungarian method for the assignment problem. Naval Res. Logist. Q. **2**(1–2), 83–97 (1955)
14. Chekuri, C., Khanna, S.: A PTAS for the multiple knapsack problem. In: ACM SODA (2000)
15. Khan, M.A., Javaid, N., Mahmood, A., Khan, Z.A., Alrajeh, N.: A generic demand-side management model for smart grid. Int. J. Energy Res. **39**(7), 954–964 (2015)
16. Ferreira, R., Barroso, L.A., Lino, P.R., Carvalho, M.M., Valenzuela, P.: Time-of-use tariff design under uncertainty in price-elasticities of electricity demand: a stochastic optimization approach. IEEE Trans. Smart Grid **4**(4), 2285–2295 (2013)
17. Ma, J., Deng, J., Song, L., Han, Z.: Incentive mechanism for demand side managemert in smart grid using auction. IEEE Trans. Smart Grid **5**(3), 1379–1388 (2014)
18. Zhong, H., Xie, L., Xia, Q.: Coupon incentive-based demand response: theory and case study. IEEE Trans. Smart Grid **28**(2), 1266–1276 (2013)

19. Li, C., Tang, S., Cao, Y., Xu, Y., Li, Y., Li, J., Zhang, R.: A new stepwise power tariff model and its application for residential consumers in regulated electricity markets. IEEE Trans. Power Syst. **28**(1), 300–308 (2013)
20. Aghaei, J., Alizadeh, M.: Demand response in smart electricity grids equipped with renewable energy sources: a review. Renew. Sustain. Energy Rev. **18**, 64–72 (2013)
21. Wang, D., Ge, S., Jia, H., Wang, C., Zhou, Y., Lu, N., Kong, X.: A demand response and battery storage coordination algorithm for providing microgrid tie-line smoothing services. IEEE Trans. Sustain. Energy **5**(2), 476–486 (2014)
22. Paterakis, N.G., Erdinc, O., Bakirtzis, A.G., Catalao, J.: Load-following reserves procurement considering flexible demand-side resources under high wind power penetration. IEEE Trans. Power Syst. **30**(3), 1337–1350 (2015)
23. Huang, Q., Li, X., Zhao, J., Wu, D., Li, X.Y.: Social networking reduces peak power consumption in smart grid. IEEE Trans. Smart Grid **6**(3), 1403–1413 (2015)
24. Zhao, Z., Lee, W.C., Shin, Y., Wu, D., Song, K.B.: An optimal power scheduling method for demand response in home energy management system. IEEE Trans. Smart Grid **4**(3), 1391–1400 (2013)
25. Scallet, M.: Day Ahead vs Real Time Pricing, May 2009. http://powersmartpricing. blogspot.com/2009/05/day-ahead-vs-real-time-pricing.html
26. Clark, M., Lampe, L.: Electrical grid peak reduction with efficient and flexible automated demand response scheduling. In: Proceeding of the IEEE 28th Canadian Conference on Electrical and Computer Engineering (2015)
27. Bina, M.T., Ahmadi, D.: Aggregate domestic demand modelling for the next day direct load control applications. IET Gen. Trans. Distrib. **8**(7), 1306–1317 (2015)

Distributing Negative Messages in VANET Based on Meet-Table and Cloud Computing

Baohua Huang[1,2] and Wei Cheng[2(✉)]

[1] School of Computer and Electronic Information,
Guangxi University, Nanning 530004, Guangxi, China
bhhuang66@gxu.edu.cn
[2] Department of Computer Science, Virginia Commonwealth University,
Richmond, VA 23220, USA
wcheng3@vcu.edu

Abstract. A negative message defines the negative attributes of a vehicle. CRL (Certificate Revocation List) and black list are typical negative messages. Securely and efficiently distributing negative messages is essential to protect VANET (Vehicular Ad hoc Network) from attacks. We formally define coverage percentage as the availability of negative message, and accurate coverage percentage represents the efficiency of distributing negative messages. These two metrics jointly evaluate the performance of a negative message distributing method. Meet-Table in a vehicle or a RSU (Road Side Unit) records the encountered vehicles. A scheme based on Meet-Table and Cloud Computing is proposed to accurately distributing negative messages in VANET in this paper. An algorithm for distributing negative messages, and an algorithm for redistributing negative messages when its objective vehicle enters a new area are proposed within the scheme. Security analysis shows that the proposed scheme is secure against fake and holding on negative messages, DDoS (Distributed Denial of Service), and confusing Meet-Table attacks. Simulation results show that the proposed scheme, comparing to the RSU broadcasting and epidemic model, is the only one that achieve high coverage percentage and high accurate coverage percentage simultaneously.

Keywords: VANET · Meet-Table · Accurate coverage percentage · RSU broadcasting · Epidemic model

1 Introduction

VANET (Vehicular Ad hoc Network) has many applications. The most significant and attractive application is improving safety [1]. The traditional safety related information includes speed limit, work zone notification, curve warning, accident information, etc. With the development of VANET, dangerous and untrustworthy vehicle identification information can also play important role in safety. We call this type of information negative messages, as it is used to describe the negative sides of a vehicle. Negative messages include but are not limited to dangerous driving, untrustworthy certificate, black list, etc. Comparing to other information in VANET, a negative message has two significant properties: (1) It is used to describe a definite vehicle; and (2) it is really

© Springer International Publishing AG 2017
L. Ma et al. (Eds.): WASA 2017, LNCS 10251, pp. 653–664, 2017.
DOI: 10.1007/978-3-319-60033-8_56

cared by the vehicles that may encounter it. Accordingly, negative messages needn't to be distributed to all vehicles in VANET, instead, it should be distributed to a subset of vehicles that may encounter the vehicle that generates the negative messages.

Information management in VANET has been extensively studied [2], and there are a few works about distributing CRL (Certificate Revocation List) in VANET [3, 4], but as far as we know, there is no work clearly presents the concept of negative message. In [3], VII (The Vehicle Infrastructure Integration) tries to distribute CRL to vehicle through RSU broadcasting. This method required very large number of RSU and high cost. In [4], Haas et al. try to propagate CRL in an epidemic fashion. Epidemic method can distribute CRL to all vehicles with less number of RSU and less time, but it requires large storage and communication capacity in VANET. In our previous work, we propose Meet-Table to optimize CRL propagation in VANET [5]. In this paper, we propose the concept of negative message in VANET, and present a scheme for distributing negative message based on Meet-Table and cloud computing.

In the proposed scheme, every RSU or vehicle has a Meet-Table recording the vehicles encountered it. And all the RSUs' Meet-Tables are sent to the cloud for storing and aggregation. The cloud service uses NoSQL database to manipulate Meet-Table and negative messages in a highly scalable and efficient way. Because humans' movement follow simple reproducible patterns [6] and the trajectories of vehicles are part of humans' movement, trajectories of vehicles are certainly reproducible. In other words, a vehicle may encounter the same set of RSUs and vehicles every day. Therefore, with the help of Meet-Table, we can efficiently distribute a vehicle's negative message through the encountered RSUs and vehicles.

Our major contributions include the followings:

(1) We propose the concept of negative message in VANET and formally define it and its coverage percentage and accurate coverage percentage.
(2) We propose a scheme for distributing negative message in VANET based on Meet-Table and Cloud Computing.
(3) We analyze security of the proposed scheme and evaluate its performance through simulations.

2 Definition of Negative Message

A negative message uniquely binds with a vehicle. As the negative message is not usable for all vehicles in the VANET, it has a set of the vehicles that care about it.

Definition-1: A negative message is a negative description of a vehicle. Formally, negative message

$$\mathrm{m} \stackrel{\mathrm{def}}{=} <o, d, C > \tag{1}$$

In formula 1, m is negative message, and it's a 3-tuple consisted by v, d and C; o is the objective vehicle of m; d is data in the message describing o; C is a set of vehicles that concern the message m.

In VANET, we should process negative message m in a way that: (1) can push m to all vehicle $v \in C$ as soon as possible; (2) for every vehicle $v \in C$, can get m with high availability. General message dissemination methods in VANET try to distribute data to all vehicles. These methods are not very much efficient, and are not very suitable for negative message. For example, broadcasting CRL in a national wide VANET is not only unfeasible but also unnecessary [5]. For evaluating the method processing negative message, we define coverage percentage and accurate coverage percentage in the followings.

Definition-2: The coverage percentage of a negative message is the percent of vehicles possessing the message in vehicles concerning the message. Formally, coverage percentage

$$r_c = \frac{|B \cap C|}{|C|} = \frac{\sum_{b \in B} \begin{cases} 1, b \in C \\ 0, b \notin C \end{cases}}{|C|} \tag{2}$$

Definition-3: The accurate coverage percentage of a negative message is the percent of vehicles concerning the message in vehicles possessing the message. Formally, accurate coverage percentage

$$r_{ac} = \frac{|B \cap C|}{|B|} = \frac{\sum_{b \in B} \begin{cases} 1, b \in C \\ 0, b \notin C \end{cases}}{|B|} \tag{3}$$

In Eqs. 2 and 3, B is the set of vehicles that possess the negative message, C is a set of vehicles that concern the message. In fact, the coverage percentage of a negative message represents the availability of the message, and the accurate coverage percentage of the message represents the efficiency of the distribution method. Naturally, we can give the evaluation criteria of distribution method of negative message.

Evaluation-Criteria-1: A good negative message distributing method should have both high coverage percentage and high accurate coverage percentage.

3 Scheme of Distributing Negative Message in VANET Based on Meet-Table and Cloud Computing

3.1 Accurately Distributing Negative Message Based on Meet-Table

According to Evaluation-Criteria-1, the most ideal model of disseminating negative message m in VANET is to make C, the set of vehicles concerning m, equals to B, the set of vehicles possessing m. In VANET, if we know C, which is the set of vehicles caring negative message m, we can accurately distribute m to vehicles in C. In fact, vehicles in C are these vehicles that may encounter the objective vehicle of m. According to the reproducible moving patterns of human [6], we can assume that these vehicles pass by the same RSU may encounter one another. So, we can record vehicles passed a RSU or vehicle with table, called Meet-Table. Formally, Meet-Table of w, a RSU or a vehicle, can be defined as

$$T_w = \{p_i | 1 \leqq i \leqq n_{T_w}\} \tag{4}$$

$$p_i \overset{\text{def}}{=} \langle v, t, c \rangle, \text{ v passed w} \tag{5}$$

In Eq. 4 and formula 5, T_w is the Meet-Table generated by w; n_{T_w} is the number of elements in T_w; p_i is the ith recorder in T_w, and it's a 3-tuple consisted of v, t, and c; v is a vehicle passed w c times by time t.

For negative message m, if $\exists p_i \in T_w, p_i.v = m.o$, then m should be distributed through w.

3.2   Putting Global Meet-Table into Cloud

For Meet-Tables are distributed in RSUs, we need to construct a global Meet-Table for negative message distribution. Because negative messages are often released by authorized entities, and the size of global Meet-Table of VANET is huge, we can use Cloud Computing to process the global Meet-Table and distribute negative message. Formally, the global Meet-Table can be defined as

$$G = \{g_i | 1 \leqq i \leqq [n_G]\} \tag{6}$$

$$g_i \overset{\text{def}}{=} \langle v, U \rangle, \forall u \in U, \text{v passed u} \tag{7}$$

In Eq. 6 and formula 7, G is the global Meet-Table; n_G is the number of elements in G. g_i is the ith recorder of G, and it's a 2-tuple. v is the vehicle passed all RSUs in U. In VANET, size of G may be huge, and its recorders have variable lengths, so it should be processed with NoSQL database [7] in Cloud Computing environment.

3.3   Architecture of the Scheme Based on Meet-Table and Cloud Computing

With the help of Meet-Table and Cloud Computing, we can efficiently distribute negative messages in VANET. The architecture of the whole scheme based on Meet-Table and Cloud Computing is showed in Fig. 1.

There is a Cloud Service running on the Internet to process global Meet-Table and help to distribute negative messages. It utilizes high scalability and virtualization of Cloud Computing [8, 9] and NoSQL Database to serve global Meet-Table processing and negative messages distributing.

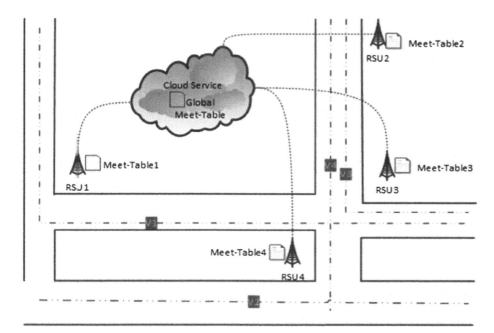

Fig. 1. Architecture of scheme based on Meet-Table and Cloud Computing

RSUs are built at the roadsides. They are connected to the Internet through wired or wireless communication channels, e.g. 5G [10]. Every RSU can record the vehicles pass it into its Meet-Table. The Meet-Table of a RSU can be send to Cloud Service in a planned schedule. When a RSU receives a negative message from the Cloud Service, it broadcasts the message to encountered vehicles.

A vehicle travels along its ways. When it passes a RSU on the roadside, it can be recorded by the RSU. At the same time, it can accept messages broadcasting from the RSU. If it comes across other vehicles, it can record them into its Meet-Table, and broadcast the messages gotten from RSUs to them.

3.4   Negative Message Distribution Algorithm

A negative message describes a negative attribute of its objective vehicle. It is often distributed by an authorized entity. For example, CRL is a typical negative message issued by CA (Certificate Authority). In the proposed scheme, the algorithm for distributing negative message is presented in Alg-Distribute. It is invoked by the entity that wants to distribute the message m, and executed by the Cloud Service, RSUs and vehicles in an asynchronous and distributed model.

```
Name: Alg-Distribute; Input: G, m
```

```
 1:   Let  G_m = {g_i|g_i ∈ G, g_i.v = m.o}
 2:   For each  g_i ∈ G_m
 3:     For each  u ∈ g_i.U
 4:       Push m to u
 5:       For each v, which is passing u
 6:         u broadcasts m to v
 7:         For each vv, which comes across v
 8:           v broadcasts m to vv
 9:         End for
10:       End for
11:     End for
12: End for
```

3.5 Negative Message Redistribution Algorithm

When a RSU u encounters a vehicle v that never encountered before, the RSU must redistribute negative message to keep high coverage percentage and accurate coverage percentage of the message. The negative message redistribution algorithm is presented in Alg-Redistribute. It is invoked by RSUs, and executed by RSUs and vehicles in an asynchronous and distributed model. Every RSU executes its own Alg-redistribute procedure respectively. The Cloud Service provides interface for query negative message of a vehicle.

```
Name: Alg-Redistribute; Input: v, T_u
```

```
 1:   For each  p_i ∈ T_u
 2:     If  p_i.v = v then
 3:       Break
 4:     Else
 5:       Put v into T_u
 6:       Query m, m.o=v from Cloud Service
 7:       If  m ≠ ∅ then
 8:         For each vv, which is passing u
 9:           u broadcasts m to vv
10:           For each vvv, which comes across vv
11:             vv broadcasts m to vvv
12:           End for
13:         End for
14:       End if
15:     End if
16: End for
```

4 Security Analysis

4.1 Attack Model

In the proposed scheme, we assume that authorized entity, Cloud Service, most RSUs, and most vehicles are trustworthy. Under this assumption, we can profile the major attacks that can be conducted on the scheme.

(1) Fake negative message attack. An attacker tries to distribute untrue negative message of a target vehicle to disturb communication and operation of the victim.
(2) Holding on negative message attack. An attacker tries to let vehicles received negative messages from RSUs don't broadcast the negative message to other vehicles encountered.
(3) Confusing Meet-Table attack. An attacker tries to build confusing Meet-Table by driving vehicle to pass lots of RSUs that are not necessary to pass in a normal human travel model.
(4) DoS (Denial of Service) attack. An attacker tries to jam broadcasting of RSUs, to block negative messages pushed from cloud service, to stop Cloud Service, to broadcast huge number of garbage messages, etc.

4.2 Security of the Scheme

From the architecture and the algorithms described above, we know that the proposed scheme executes in a distributed and asynchronous model, so the scheme has some potential anti-attack properties. In addition, utilizing the matured Cloud Computing technology, the Cloud Service is scale free and hard to attack.

For fake negative message attack, there are lots of anti-attack measurements. For example, Cloud Service can authenticate the sender; and negative message may be signed with signature for verification in RSUs and vehicles.

If a vehicle is controlled by attacker, it may not broadcast negative message received from RSUs and other vehicles to the vehicles it encounters. This holding negative message attack can hardly affect the propagation of negative message in VANET, for comparing to other uncontrolled vehicles, the number of vehicles controlled by attacker is very less.

Attacker can drive vehicle passing RSUs to build confusing Meet-Table, but it is very cost and easy to detect. This physical attack is hardly to take place in a large scale. In addition the movement pattern of the attacker's vehicle is very different from the ordinary human's reproducible pattern [6], it's can be easily detected and cleared from the global Meet-Table.

Generally, DoS, especially DDoS (Distributed DoS) is hard to defeat if opposite has enough resources [11]. In the proposed scheme, DoS, even DDos is hard to achieve its goal. If attacker wants to jam broadcasting of a RSU, he must present at the site of the RSU, so he can only attack very limited RSUs. For the matured protection technology of Cloud Computing, it's hard for attacker both to block negative message pushed from Cloud Service and to stop Cloud Service. Attacker can broad cast huge number of garbage message to a limited part of VANET and affect a limited area of it, but he can't affect the whole VANET, even the main part of it, for it is distributed, executes asynchronously, and has numerous RSUs and vehicles.

In summary, the scheme is secure to face attacks if it is implemented carefully, for it is distributed, executes asynchronously, has numerous entities, and based on Cloud Computing technology.

5 Performance Evaluation

5.1 Simulation Dataset

Simulation of VANET can use dataset of realistic traces of vehicles [12] or generated traces based on map [4, 13]. Realistic traces dataset of numerous vehicles is very hard to get. The dataset used in [12] is realistic Taxi GPS traces from Shenzhen and Beijing, China, and San Francisco, USA. The total number of vehicles in this dataset is only about 13000, and it contains only Taxi, no other types of vehicles. In addition, the time length of this dataset is no more than three days.

To evaluate the performance of the proposed scheme, we generated a dataset to simulate all vehicles in San Francisco, USA. The dataset was created based on parameters shown in Table 1.

On the generated dataset, the percent of vehicles and RSUs a vehicle met versus time are shown in Fig. 2(a) and (b) respectively.

Table 1. Parameters for generating simulation dataset

Parameter	Value	Note
Number of vehicles	471388	Total number of vehicles in [14]
Number of RSUs	1193	Refer to the no. of signalized intersections in [14]
Intersections	7200	Estimated no. of intersections in [14]
Length of road	1741 (km)	Total length of road in [14]
Area	121 (km^2)	Area – land in [14]
Mean travel time	0.5 (h)	Mean travel time to work in [14]
Speed	38.6 (km/h)	Average speed of commuter traffic speeds in [15]
maxV2I	100 m	Max communication distance of vehicle to RSU
maxV2V	10 m	Max communication distance of vehicle to vehicle

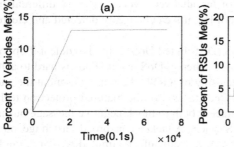
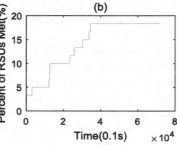

Fig. 2. Time vs. vehicle met vehicles and RSUs

5.2   Simulation Results

In order to compare performance of the proposed scheme with RSU broadcasting and epidemic model, we simulate three methods on the generated dataset. The simulation results are shown in Figs. 3, 4 and 5.

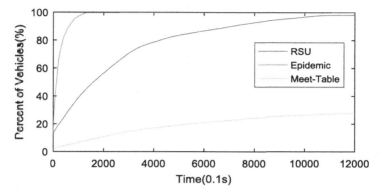

Fig. 3. Time vs. percent of vehicles possessing message

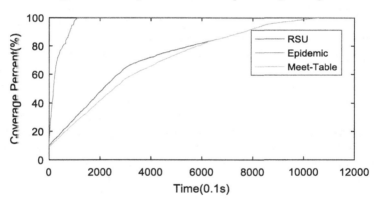

Fig. 4. Time vs. coverage percentage

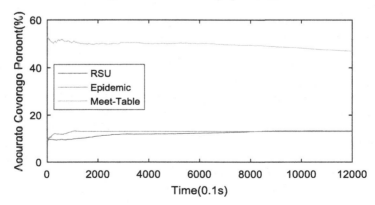

Fig. 5. Time vs. accurate coverage percentage

Table 2 Summaries the simulation results. According to Table 2 and Evaluation-Criteria-1, the Meet-Table based scheme is the best method for distributing negative message in VANET.

Table 2. Summary of simulation results

Value name	Method		
	Epidemic model	RSU broadcasting	Meet-Table based scheme
Percent of vehicles possessing message	Much high	High	Low
Coverage percentage	Much high	High	High
Accurate coverage percentage	Low	Low	High

6 Related Works

To enhance the safety of traffic is the major goal of VANET. In order to archive this goal, VANET must gather, process, and disseminate information, such as road condition, position of obstacle, speed limit, road accidents, etc. [2]. With the development of VANET, especially when self-driving cars really run on the road, security of VANET will be the key of safe traffic. Secure VANET requires ID authentication, message integrity, communication confidentiality, availability, and access control [16]. In order to satisfy these requirements, lots of solutions have been proposed. In these solutions, public key cryptography, trust management, black list, etc. are employed. Therefore, secure VANET needs to process messages about security in a secure and efficient way. As elsewhere, certificates used in VANET must be revoked in circumstances, such as compromising or losing of private key, illegal using of certificate etc. [17]. CA (Certificate Authority) can issue CRL and store it on LDAP (Lightweight Directory Access Protocol) server for retrieving [18]. A vehicle can also use OCSP (Online Certificate Status Protocol) to request CRL [19]. Instead of directly accessing Internet, vehicle in VANET often access Internet through infrastructure domain, so both to retrieve CRL from LDAP server and to request CRL using OCSP is not applicable.

VII (The Vehicle Infrastructure Integration) tries to distribute CRL to vehicle through RSU broadcasting [3]. This method required very large number of RSU and high cost. In [4], Haas et al. try to propagate CRL in an epidemic fashion. Epidemic method can distribute CRL to all vehicles with less number of RSU and less time, but it requires large storage and communication capacity in VANET.

In [6] mobile phone users' trajectory proves that humans follow simple reproducible patterns. According to the research results in [12, 20, 21], VANET is a Small world. In [22], a query processing algorithm that can determine the scope of each query is used to help vehicle to avoid returning overwhelmed large amount results. These works give us the clue to accurately distribute message in VANET. Our previous work proposes Meet-Table to optimize CRL propagation in VANET [5].

7 Conclusion

We propose the concept of negative message in VANET and formally define it and its coverage percentage and accurate coverage percentage to represent availability of the message and the efficiency of the distribution method, respectively. Based on the definitions, we present the evaluation criteria of distribution method to point out that a distribution method with high coverage percentage and accurate coverage percentage at the same time is critical. We propose a scheme base on Meet-Table and Cloud Computing to accurately distribute negative messages in VANET with the distribution and redistribution algorithms presented in detail. Security analysis shows the scheme is secure against several attacks. Performance simulation results demonstrate that, comparing with RSU broadcasting and epidemic model, the proposed scheme achieve high coverage percentage and high accurate coverage percentage at the same time.

In the future work, we will study the proposed scheme in a system with real Cloud Computing and NoSQL database support.

Acknowledgments. This work was supported by National Natural Science Foundation of China under Grant No. 61262072.

References

1. Zhu, H., Li, M., Fu, L., et al.: Impact of traffic influxes: revealing exponential intercontact time in urban VANETs. IEEE Trans. Parallel Distrib. Syst. **22**(8), 1258–1266 (2011)
2. Kakkasageri, M.S., Manvi, S.S.: Information management in vehicular ad hoc networks: a review. J. Netw. Comput. Appl. **39**(3), 334–350 (2014)
3. Farradyne, P.: Vehicle Infrastructure Integration-VII Architecture and Functional Requirements, v1.1. http://ral.ucar.edu/projects/vii.old/vii/docs/VIIArchandFuncRequirements.pdf
4. Haas, J.J., Hu, Y.-C., Laberteaux, K.P.: Efficient certificate revocation list organization and distribution. IEEE J. Sel. Areas Commun. **29**(3), 595–604 (2011)
5. Huang, B., Mo, J., Lu, Q., Cheng, W.: Optimizing propagation network of certificate revocation in VANET with meet-table. In: Wang, G., Ray, I., Alcaraz Calero, J.M., Thampi, S.M. (eds.) SpaCCS 2016. LNCS, vol. 10067, pp. 147–154. Springer, Cham (2016). doi:10.1007/978-3-319-49145-5_15
6. Gonzalez, M.C., Hidalgo, C.A., Barabasi, A.-L.: Understanding individual human mobility patterns. Nature **453**(7196), 779–782 (2008)
7. Tian, X., Huang, B., Wu, M.: A transparent middleware for encrypting data in MongoDB. In: 2014 IEEE Workshop on Electronics, Computer and Applications (IWECA 2014), Ottawa, Canada, pp. 906–909 (2014)
8. Yu, L., Shen, H., Sapra, K., et al.: CoRE: cooperative end-to-end traffic redundancy elimination for reducing cloud bandwidth cost. IEEE Trans. Parallel Distrib. Syst. **28**(2), 446–46 (2017)
9. Yu, L., Cai, Z.: Dynamic scaling of virtualized networks with bandwidth guarantees in cloud datacenters. In: The 35th Annual IEEE International Conference on Computer Communications (INFOCOM), San Francisco, USA, pp. 1–9 (2016)
10. Ndashimye, E., Ray, S.K., Sarkar, N.I., et al.: Vehicle-to-infrastructure communication over multi-tier heterogeneous networks: a survey. Comput. Netw. **112**, 144–166 (2017)

11. Bouali, T., Senouci, S.-M., Sedjelmaci, H.: A distributed detection and prevention scheme from malicious nodes in vehicular networks. Int. J. Commun. Syst. **29**(10), 1683–1704 (2016)

12. Ding, J., Gao, J., Xiong, H.: Understanding and modelling information dissemination patterns in vehicle-to-vehicle networks. In: 23rd SIGSPATIAL International Conference on Advances in Geographic Information Systems, New York, NY, USA, pp. 1–10 (2015)

13. Naumov, V., Baumann, R., Gross, T.: An evaluation of inter-vehicle ad hoc networks based on realistic vehicular traces. In: 7th ACM International Symposium on Mobile Ad Hoc Networking and Computing, Florence, Italy, pp. 595–604 (2006)

14. SFMTA: San Francisco Transportation Fact Sheet. https://www.sfmta.com/sites/default/files/2013%20SAN%20FRANCISCO%20TRANSPORTATION%20FACT%20SHEET.pdf

15. Reisman, W.: Commute speeds have slowed down for San Francisco drivers. http://archives.sfexaminer.com/sanfrancisco/commute-speeds-have-slowed-down-for-san-francisco-drivers/Content?oid=2187521

16. Engoulou, R.G., Bellaïche, M., Pierre, S., et al.: VANET security surveys. Comput. Commun. **44**(2), 1–13 (2014)

17. Chokhani, S.: Toward a national public key infrastructure. IEEE Commun. Mag. **9**, 70–74 (1994)

18. Yeh, Y.-S., Lai, W.-S., Cheng, C.-J.: Applying lightweight directory access protocol service on session certification authority. Comput. Netw. **38**(5), 675–692 (2002)

19. Hormann, T.P., Wrona, K., Holtmanns, S.: Evaluation of certificate validation mechanisms. Comput. Commun. **29**(3), 291–305 (2006)

20. Cunha, F.D., Vianna, A.C., Mini, R.A.F., et al.: Are vehicular networks small world? In: IEEE Conference on Computer Communications Workshops, ON, Canada, pp. 195–196 (2014)

21. Zhang, H., Lia, J.: Modeling and dynamical topology properties of VANET based on complex networks theory. AIP Adv. **5**, 1–11 (2015)

22. Wang, X., Guo, L., Ai, C., Li, J., Cai, Z.: An urban area-oriented traffic information query strategy in VANETs. In: Ren, K., Liu, X., Liang, W., Xu, M., Jia, X., Xing, K. (eds.) WASA 2013. LNCS, vol. 7992, pp. 313–324. Springer, Heidelberg (2013). doi:10.1007/978-3-642-39701-1_26

CacheRascal: Defending the Flush-Reload Side-Channel Attack in PaaS Clouds

Weijuan Zhang[1,2,3,4], Xiaoqi Jia[1,2,3,4(✉)], Jianwei Tai[2,3,4],
and Mingsheng Wang[1,2]

[1] State Key Laboratory of Information Security,
Institute of Information Engineering, CAS, Beijing, China
{zhangweijuan,jiaxiaoqi,wangmingsheng}@iie.ac.cn
[2] School of Cyber Security, University of Chinese Academy of Sciences,
Beijing, China
taijianwei@iie.ac.cn
[3] Key Laboratory of Network Assessment Technology, CAS, Beijing, China
[4] Beijing Key Laboratory of Network Security and Protection Technology,
Beijing, China

Abstract. The phenomenon that different instances in the cloud reside on the same physical machine is defined as co-residence. Co-residence introduces the risk of side-channel attacks, which utilize the shared resources to gain useful information. Flush-Reload attack is one of the cache-based side-channel attacks that are usually used to extract the victim process's sensitive information such as private keys. We propose a defense scheme called CacheRascal to mitigate the Flush-Reload attack in the PaaS clouds. CacheRascal can automatically detect the execution of security-critical modules and initiate protection through cache confusion within 1 ms. It does not need to make any changes to the existing PaaS clouds and is easy to deploy. The experiment results show that our defense scheme effectively obfuscates the cache and incurs performance overhead of less than 2%.

Keywords: PaaS cloud · Co-resident · Flush-Reload · Side-channel · Cache

1 Introduction

Since the Platform-as-a-Service (PaaS) cloud offers a well deployed environment for the customers to develop, run, and manage applications, saving the effort to build and maintain the complicated environments associated with the applications, PaaS is becoming more and more popular. Cloud platform usually serves multiple tenants and offers the chance for different customers' instances[1] residing on the same physical machine, which means co-residence [1]. Co-residence introduces a new threat that malicious instance can utilize the shared resources to

---

[1] Here "instance" refers to a service unit provided to the tenants by the cloud providers, e.g., a container or a virtual machine.

© Springer International Publishing AG 2017
L. Ma et al. (Eds.): WASA 2017, LNCS 10251, pp. 665–677, 2017.
DOI: 10.1007/978-3-319-60033-8_57

launch co-resident attacks such as denial of service attack or sensitive information extraction. PaaS cloud has relatively smaller service unit than Infrastructure-as-a-Service (IaaS) cloud, so there is more chance for the PaaS cloud instances to achieve co-residence.

There have been numerous researches on the co-resident problem in IaaS clouds, from the co-resident threat, the co-resident attacks to the defense of co-resident attacks. In recent years, researchers begin to focus on the co-resident problem on the PaaS clouds. Varadarajan et al. [2] briefly discussed the placement vulnerabilities of the PaaS clouds in their work; Zhang et al. [3] studied three popular PaaS clouds Amazon Elastic Beanstalk, IBM Bluemix and OpenShift to identify the co-residence threat in their placement policies; Zhang et al. [4] presented an attack framework for conducting cache-based side-channel attacks on commercial PaaS clouds and uses the Flush-Reload attack [5] to trace a victim's execution.

Flush-Reload attack is one of the cache-based side-channel attacks. It can be used to extract the coarse-grained information, such as the inputs passed to a program [6], or fine-grained information, such as the number of items in a shopping cart, the password reset link [4], the private key in decryption [7], etc. Flush-Reload attack mainly utilizes the shared memory, e.g., the libraries or executables, to monitor the co-resident instances. When the PaaS cloud is isolated by virtual machines (with memory de-duplication enabled), containers or users [4], the instances have the chance to share memory. Thus contributes to the Flush-Reload attack.

In this paper, we propose a secure scheme *CacheRascal* to defend against the Flush-Reload attack in the PaaS cloud. Our scheme can automatically detect the execution of *security-critical modules* and immediately start to protect them. It does not need to make any changes to the existing PaaS clouds and is convenient for the cloud providers to deploy. To the best of our knowledge, this is the first work that focus on the defense of the co-resident attacks on the PaaS clouds.

The main contributions of our paper are: (1) We proposed the scheme CacheRascal to defend against Flush-Reload attacks in PaaS clouds. CacheRascal consists of the *auto-detect module* and the *protect module*. In the *auto-detect module*, CacheRascal monitors the execution of the *security-critical modules* regularly. Once a *security-critical module* is detected executing, CacheRascal executes the *protect module* to defeat Flush-Reload attacks. (2) We utilized cache confusion in the protect stage to confuse the attacker. To minimize the performance influence on the protected programs, we use cache loading rather than cleansing to obfuscate the monitor results of the cache. (3) We implemented a prototype of the defense scheme for the Docker [8] container-based PaaS clouds and tested its availability. The prototype can automatically detect Flush-Reload attacks and start protection within 1 ms. (4) We tested the security effectiveness and performance overhead of the prototype. The results show that, CacheRascal can confuse the cache effectively and introduces negligible overhead.

2   Background

2.1   The Flush-Reload Side-Channel Attack

The Flush-Reload side-channel attack was first defined by Yarom and Falkner [7]. They launched the attack through monitor the state of the shared last-level cache (LLC) on a multi-core system and extracted RSA [9] private keys in GnuPG. Later, Zhang et al. [4] extended the Flush-Reload attack to spy on the code paths of the processes running in the PaaS clouds. Here we give a brief explanation of the Flush-Reload attack proposed by Yarom and Falkner [7].

In Flush-Reload attacks, malicious instance generally utilizes the LLC as the side-channel to monitor the co-resident instances. Most modern CPUs have multiple levels of caches. For the multi-core CPUs, each core has its own caches and all the cores share a relatively lager one. Take the Intel Core i5-3470 processor as an example. The Intel Core i5-3470 processor is a quad-core processor, each core has separate L1i (32 KB), L1d (32 KB) and L2 (256 KB) caches and all the cores share the LLC cache (6 MB). Each cacheline in the Core i5-3470 processor is 64 bytes. Cache reduces the average cost to access data from the main memory. Through the time of reading a chunk of memory the attacker can judge whether the memory is in the cache or not.

Suppose the two processes, the *attack process* and the *victim process*, execute the same program, only one copy of the shared program is needed in the physical memory. The *attack process* can tell which memory line the *victim process* is visiting by monitoring the shared memory over time. There are three steps in the attack:

Flush: The *attack process* evicts the monitored memory line from the cache hierarchy (e.g., using the *clflush* instruction).

Interval: The *attack process* waits for a period of time, long enough for the *victim process* to visit the same memory line.

Reload: The *attack process* reloads the memory line again and measures the time to load it.

If the *victim process* has visited the memory line during the interval, the memory line was loaded into the cache before the *attack process* visiting it. Then the *attack process* can reload the memory line from the cache directly, the reload time will be short. Otherwise, the reload time will be longer. From the memory reload time the *attack process* can infer the code paths of the *victim process*.

2.2   Memory Sharing

Memory sharing is the base of the Flush-Reload attacks. Zhang et al. [4] mentioned four isolation mechanisms in the PaaS clouds, the user-based isolation, the runtime-based isolation, the VM-based isolation and the container-based isolation. For the runtime-based and user-based PaaS clouds, since all the instances run within the same operating system (OS), they have many chances to share memory. For the VM-based PaaS clouds, if the hypervisor enables *memory de-duplication*, it will coalesce the pages with identical contents. These pages could belong to different VMs. For the container-based PaaS clouds, the libraries and some executables are shared among all the containers. In summary, the memory sharing phenomenon is common in the PaaS clouds and thus brings the threat of Flush-Reload attacks.

In this paper, we implement a prototype of the defense scheme against the Flush-Reload attacks in a Docker container virtual environment. The reason we choose Docker container-based PaaS clouds as a representation is that Docker container has became the most popular technology in PaaS services nowadays. Its has several advantages such as light-weighted, easy to deploy, appropriate resource constraint, etc. Thus make it more suitable for the PaaS clouds and more and more PaaS clouds (e.g., Amazon, Google Cloud Platform, Microsoft Auzre, etc.) introduce Docker container technology. However, the defense scheme proposed in this paper is not only confined to the container-based PaaS clouds, it could also be applied to the other cloud architectures.

3   The Flush-Reload Attack Scenario in the PaaS Cloud

In this paper, we first state a Flush-Reload attack scenario in Docker container-based virtual environment and then propose the defense scheme. In our attack scenario, the malicious instance try to extract the RSA private key of the GnuPG-4.1.12 running in a co-resident instance. We deploy the Docker environment on a local machine with a quad-core Intel(R) Core(TM) i5-3470 processor. We create two containers from the same image with GnuPG installed to ensure the sharing of all the libraries and programs. In one of the containers we run the *victim process* to launch RSA decryption using the GnuPG program and in another instance we run the *attack process*.

As described by Yarom [7], the goal of the attacker is to extract a secret exponent used in the decryption. To compute the decryption function, GnuPG-4.1.12 uses the square-and-multiply exponentiation algorithm [10] which computes the modular exponentiation $x = b^e \bmod m$ using the binary representation of e (Fig. 1), i.e., $e = 2^{n-1}e_{n-1} + ... + 2^0 e_0$. It can be observed that the sequence of function calls square, multiply and modulo reduce correspond directly with the bits of the exponent. We use S, M and R stand for the function square, multiply and modulo reduce. The sequence of the function call S-R-M-R represents the bit value 1 and the sequence of function call S-R without M-R represents the bit value 0.

The first stage of the attack is to extract the sequence of function calls. To trace the operations of the *victim process*, the *attack process* probes the cache regularly. In each test slot it probes one memory line of the code in each of the square, multiply and modulo reduce function and marks the memory reload time. So in each test slot we get a three-dimensional time vector. We adopt the multi-class support vector machine (SVM) [11] to classify the function calls, which has been mentioned by Zhang et al. [12]. The reason why we use the SVM

```
function exponent (b, e, m)

begin
    x ← 1

    for  i ← |e| −1  downto  0  do

        x ← x²                    (S)
        x ← x mod m               (R)
        if ( eᵢ = 1 ) then
            x = xb                (M)
            x = x mod m           (R)
        endif
    done
    return  x
end
```

$$x \leftarrow x^2 \quad \text{(S)}$$
$$x \leftarrow x \bmod m \quad \text{(R)}$$
$$x = xb \quad \text{(M)}$$
$$x = x \bmod m \quad \text{(R)}$$

Fig. 1. The square-and-multiply algorithm.

classifier to classify the results is that we found in some cases, more than one cache hit are detected within one test slot. Under this circumstance, using a single threshold to distinguish function calls is not so accurate.

To collect the training set of the SVM, the attacker should know the accurate function call along with each test slot. This requires communication between containers. We solve this problem by making the victim container to share a folder with the malicious container. Then we modify the GnuPG program to make it write a file under the shared folder regularly. When the GnuPG enters the functions square, multiply and modulo reduce, corresponding letter "S", "M" or "R" is written into the file. When the process leaves the functions, the letter "X" is written into the file. In each test slot, the *attack process* read the file to get the right operation after probing the cache. So from the attacker's point of view, the operations are classified into four classes–"S", "M", "R" and "X". Each test slot gets a time vector labeled with an operation.

We only focus on the first stage of the attack since the accuracy of detecting function call sequence can significantly influence resuming the secret key in the following steps. And the well mix of the function call sequence reflects the effectiveness of our defense scheme.

4   Design and Implementation

4.1   Design Goal

We aim at implementing a Flush-Reload attack defense scheme that suits existing PaaS cloud platforms. The scheme should be easily adopted by the cloud providers and integrated into the modern cloud architectures. To make the scheme more practical, the scheme should follow these design goals: (1) The scheme should show effectiveness in defending the Flush-Reload attacks. (2) The scheme should not need to modify existing cloud platform, instances or applications. We want to implement a light-weighted protect scheme that is easy to deploy and does not influence the use of the original clouds. (3) The scheme should not introduce too much performance overhead. A heavy overhead, in a sense, is also a kind of attack.

4.2 Architecture

If the cloud provider want to protect the instances running on a CPU, he should create a *protect instance* and bind it to a core of the target CPU. Then the *protect instance* shares the LLC with the other instances running on the same CPU. The CacheRascal is deployed in the *protect instance*. CacheRascal consists of the *auto-detect module* and the *protect module*. When the *auto-detect module* detects the call of the *security-critical modules*, the protect module will be executed to protect the related *security-critical module*. Multiple *protect instances* could be created if the server has multi-processors. Figure 2 shows the architecture within a single CPU and Fig. 3 shows the workflow of CacheRascal. The workflow is as follows:

Step 1: Choose *security-critical modules*. At the beginning, we choose the *security-critical modules* which needed to be protected, e.g., the libgcrypt library, the php-fpm library, the encryption programs, etc. All these modules consist a module pool, which is the target of protection.

Step 2: Map the *security-critical modules*. In the protect instance, CacheRascal maps all the *security-critical modules* in the pool to its address space. Since co-resident instances share memory pages, CacheRascal only needs to map the modules within the protect instance.

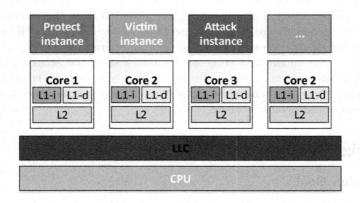

Fig. 2. The architecture of the defense scheme.

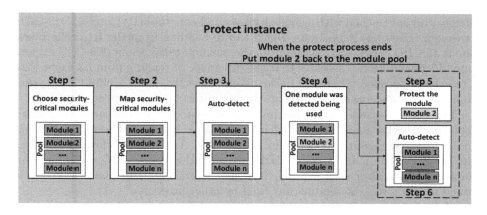

Fig. 3. The workflow of CacheRascal.

Step 3: Auto-detect. The *auto-detect module* uses the Flush-Reload technique to monitor the use of the *security-critical modules*. In each round of test, CacheRascal probes all the modules and mark the reload time. Of course, a *threshold* should be determined in advance to distinguish whether the memory is in the cache or not. We set 100 rounds of test as a group. There is an interval between two group of tests to reduce the performance overhead. In each test group, if a certain proportion of the reload time about one module was below the threshold, the module is detected being used.

Step 4: One module was detected being used. If module 2 was detected being used, CacheRascal will execute the *protect module* to obfuscate the cache used by module 2. Module 2 will be removed from the module pool temporarily. Simultaneously, CacheRascal goes on detecting the module pool (**Step 6**).

Step 5: Protect the *security-critical module*. When the *protect module* starts, it maps the target *security-critical module* and loads the module into the cache regularly, thus mix the probe results of the *attack process*. We set a fixed number of times in the *protect module* to iteratively load the module. After the iteration, module 2 will be put back to the pool.

4.3   Implementation

The Auto-Detect Module. For the *auto-detect module* there are mainly three aspects to focus on. The first is the design of the test slot. We choose the instructions that are frequently used in a module to monitor. There is no need to monitor too many instructions since the purpose of the detect process is to tell whether one module is being used. An interval is added between two group of tests to reduce overhead. The time interval could influence the sensitivity of detecting the usage of *security-critical modules*.

The second focused aspect is the threshold to judge cache hit. We test the average instruction loading time of loading from the L1 cache and the physical memory on our testbed with a single-socket quad-core Intel(R) Core(TM) i5-3470 processor. Each test repeats for 10000 times. Loading from the L1 cache takes about 45 CPU cycles and loading from the memory takes about 304 CPU cycles. Intel documentation [13] states that the difference of reading from L3 cache and L1 cache is between 22 and 39 cycles. We set the threshold as 150 CPU cycles combines the test results and the statement in the Intel documentation.

The third focused point is the appropriate percentage (the cache hit probability in the detection) to decide whether a module is detected being used. With too high percentage, no module can be detected. And with too low percentage, the *detect module* may has false alarm due to various noises. We use 5% in our implementation after a set of tests. That means, if 5 cache hit was detected in a round of 100 tests, the module was used by other processes.

The Protect Module. The implementation of the protect module needs to consider the cache confusion method and the iteration times. We choose memory loading to mix the cache state to reduce the caused performance overhead. When entered protect state, CacheRascal iteratively loads the *security-critical module*. If a memory load happens before the reload operation of the *attack process*, the reload time will sure be short. Since when an instruction is visited, a whole cacheline (64 KB) will be loaded into the cache, the *protect module* visits an instruction every 64 KB. The number of iterations influences the protect time as well as the performance overhead. We set the number of iterations as 5000 in our implementation after a set of tests. After the iteration, the detected *security-critical module* is put back to the module pool.

5 Evaluation

In this section, we test the security effectiveness and the performance overhead of CacheRascal in defending Flush-Reload attack. Our testbed was equipped with a single-socket quad-core Intel(R) Core(TM) i5-3470 processor with an operating frequency of 3.20 GHz. The machine is Dell OptiPlex with the main memory of 10 GB. The virtual environment is build on Ubuntu 14.04 with Docker-1.9.1. All the containers also has the environment of Ubuntu 14.04. We start three containers from the same image with the GnuPG-4.1.12 program installed. One of them runs the GnuPG decryption program (victim instance), one of them launches the Flush-Reload attack program (attack instance) and the other one runs CacheRascal (protect instance).

5.1 Security Evaluation

Sensitivity of Detection. We first test the sensitivity of CacheRascal in detecting the use of *security-critical modules*. The sensitivity is reflected by the detection latency, which is defined as the period from the time the victim instance starts to execute security-critical operations to the time the operations are detected. We varied the percentage that determines whether the *security-critical module* is detected being used (1%, 5%, 10%, 50%) and the interval between two group of test slots to see the differences. We get the results (Table 1) that, the high percentage above 50% will lead to no execution being detected and the low percentage 1% will lead to execution being detected all the time even without security-critical operations. We choose the appropriate threshold 5% in our flowing tests. Table 1 also shows that CacheRascal can identify the attack on the order of microseconds and shorter interval can effectively reduce the detection latency.

Effectiveness of the Protection. To show the effectiveness of our defense scheme, we choose the multi-class SVM with a radial basis kernel function to give a quantitative evaluation. In each experiment, the SVM is trained with the labeled 8000 Flush-Reload results and then tested on an additional 4000 Flush-Reload results. Table 2 shows the results with/without protection. As we can see, with CacheRascal disabled, the SVM classifies the testing results with accuracy over 90%, which is well enough to resume the private keys in the following steps as mentioned in [14]. While with CacheRascal enabled, the results of the M, R, X are well mixed, which introduces enough noise and make it hard to resume the keys.

Table 1. Detection latency (microseconds) of CacheRascal with varied intervals and percentage thresholds. The result is the average of ten time tests.

Percentage	Interval (Microsecond)		
	100	500	1000
1%	-	-	-
5%	74.1	529.4	627.4
10%	88.1	357.4	833.4
50%	-	-	-

5.2 Performance Evaluation

In this section we evaluate the performance overhead under various circumstances (Fig. 4). The baseline is the time the GPG program needed to decrypt a 4G encrypted file. Each test is repeated for 20 times. We set the *auto-detect module's* interval as 500 microseconds and the percentage threshold as 5%. The suffix "−5000", "−10000", "−20000" means the *security-critical module* is loaded repeatedly for 5000, 10000 or 20000 times in the *protect module*. The results show that CacheRascal alone decreases the GPG performance by less than 2%, which is quite low when compared with the performance degradation caused by the Flush-Reload cache side-channel attack (9.8%). At the circumstance that

Table 2. Confusion matrix of SVM classification in tests.

(a) Without protection				
Success rate	S	M	R	X
S	0.972	0.002	0.013	0.013
M	0.175	0.818	0.001	0.006
R	0.000	0.000	1.000	0.000
X	0.028	0.001	0.006	0.965
(b) With protection				
Success rate	S	M	R	X
S	0.943	0.039	0.013	0.005
M	0.425	0.360	0.215	0.000
R	0.656	0.190	0.148	0.006
X	0.996	0.002	0.001	0.001

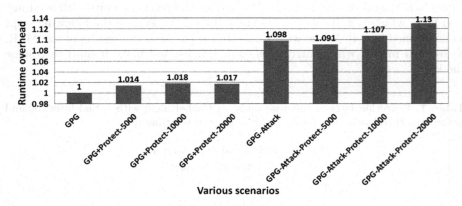

Fig. 4. Runtime overhead. Labels on top of the bars represent the ratio compared with single GPG run.

CacheRascal runs together with the *attack process*, the highest overhead caused by CacheRascal is less than 3% compared with the scenario "GPG-Attack". As the cache load iterations increases, the overhead slightly increases.

6   Related Work

The Flush-Reload attack was first described by Bangerter et al. [15] to trace the victim's access to the S-Boxes in AES. They only considered the attack on a time-shared core. Later Yarom and Falkner [7] exposes the use of a shared LLC and demonstrates that the technique can be used in multi-core and in virtualized environments. Yuval Yarom and Katrina Falkner named the attack as "Flush-Reload attack". Further it was demonstrated in various security sensitive modules [16–18] and different virtualized platforms with different variants

[4,19–21]. It can also be used to extract the coarse-grained information of the everyday applications [6]. Recently, Zhang et al. [22] implemented the attack on the ARM architecture and considered implementing it on the android devices.

There have been numerous previous researches on the defense of cache based side-channel attacks. They are mainly divided into two categories: the *cache partitioning* and *cache confusion*. *Cache partitioning* is the most straightforward method to eliminate cache side-channels. This can be done at the hardware level [23–25] or the software level [26,27]. Though *cache partitioning* can eliminate the Flush-Reload attacks however, it reduce the resource utilization to a great extent. Researchers have also tried to prevent attackers from getting useful information from the cache by *Cache confusion*. This includes cache prefetches [28], cache cleansing [14] and memory-to-cache mappings randomization [25,29]. The implementation of all these approaches need to modify the existing cloud infrastructures.

None of these approaches mentioned above focus on the defense of cache based side-channel attacks on PaaS clouds while we aim to propose a security scheme based on cache loading to prevent the PaaS instances from suffering Flush-Reload attacks without modifying the existing cloud architecture.

7   Conclusion

In this paper we present a cache confusion-based defense scheme that does not need to modify the hypervisor or instances to mitigate Flush-Reload attacks in the PaaS clouds. The scheme automatically detects the execution of security-critical modules and launch protection immediately to confuse the cache status. We implemented a prototype for the Docker container-based PaaS clouds. We demonstrated the security effectiveness and negligible performance overhead of our prototype. The evaluation results also show high detect sensitivity. To the best of our knowledge, this is the first scheme that focus on the Flush-Reload attacks in the PaaS clouds.

Acknowledgement. This paper was supported by National Natural Science Foundation of China (NSFC) under Grant No. 61100228 and the project Core Electronic Devices, High-end Generic Chips and Basic Software (No. 2015ZX01029101-001).

References

1. Ristenpart, T., Tromer, E., Shacham, H., Savage, S.: Hey, you, get off of my cloud: exploring information leakage in third-party compute clouds. In: Proceedings of the 16th ACM Conference on Computer and Communications Security, pp. 199–212. ACM (2009)
2. Varadarajan, V., Zhang, Y., Ristenpart, T., Swift, M.: A placement vulnerability study in multi-tenant public clouds. In: 24th USENIX Security Symposium (USENIX Security 15), pp. 913–928 (2015)

3. Zhang, W., Jia, X., Wang, C., Zhang, S., Huang, Q., Wang, M., Liu, P.: A comprehensive study of co-residence threat in multi-tenant public PaaS clouds. In: Lam, K.-Y., Chi, C.-H., Qing, S. (eds.) ICICS 2016. LNCS, vol. 9977, pp. 361–375. Springer, Cham (2016). doi:10.1007/978-3-319-50011-9_28

4. Zhang, Y., Juels, A., Reiter, M.K., Ristenpart, T.: Cross-tenant side-channel attacks in PaaS clouds. In: Proceedings of the 2014 ACM SIGSAC Conference on Computer and Communications Security, pp. 990–1003 (2014)

5. Bangerter, E.: Cache gamesc bringing access-based cache attacks on AES to practice. In: Workshop COSADE, vol. 2010, no. 1, pp. 490–505 (2011)

6. Side-channel attacks on everyday applications: Distinguishing inputs with flush+reload. http://www.blackhat.com/docs/us-16/materials/us-16-Hornby-Side-Channel-Attacks-On-Everyday-Applications-wp.pdf (2016). Accessed 1 Jan 2017

7. Yarom, Y., Falkner, K.: Flush+ reload: a high resolution, low noise, L3 cache side-channel attack. In: 23rd USENIX Security Symposium (USENIX Security 14), pp. 719–732 (2014)

8. Docker. https://www.docker.io/. Accessed 23 Apr 2016

9. Rivest, R.L., Shamir, A., Adleman, L.: A method for obtaining digital signatures and public-key cryptosystems. Commun. ACM 21(2), 120–126 (1978)

10. Gordon, D.M.: A survey of fast exponentiation methods. J. Algorithms 27(1), 129–146 (1998)

11. Chang, C.-C., Lin, C.-J.: LIBSVM: a library for support vector machines. ACM Trans. Intell. Syst. Technol. (TIST) 2(3), 27 (2011)

12. Zhang, Y., Juels, A., Reiter, M.K., Ristenpart, T.: Cross-VM side channels and their use to extract private keys. In: Proceedings of the 2012 ACM Conference on Computer and Communications Security, pp. 305–316. ACM (2012)

13. CORPORATION, I.: Intel 64 and ia-32 architecture optimization reference manual (2012)

14. Zhang, Y., Reiter, M.K.: Düppel: retrofitting commodity operating systems to mitigate cache side channels in the cloud. In: Proceedings of the 2013 ACM SIGSAC Conference on Computer & Communications Security, pp. 827–838. ACM (2013)

15. Gullasch, D., Bangerter, E., Krenn, S.: Cache games-bringing access-based cache attacks on AES to practice. In: 2011 IEEE Symposium on Security and Privacy, pp. 490–505. IEEE (2011)

16. Benger, N., Pol, J., Smart, N.P., Yarom, Y.: Ooh Aah.. Just a Little Bit: a small amount of side channel can go a long way. In: Batina, L., Robshaw, M. (eds.) CHES 2014. LNCS, vol. 8731, pp. 75–92. Springer, Heidelberg (2014). doi:10.1007/978-3-662-44709-3_5

17. Yarom, Y., Benger, N.: Recovering OPENSSL ECDSA nonces using the flush+ reload cache side-channel attack. IACR Cryptol. ePrint Arch. 2014, 140 (2014)

18. Bruinderink, L.G., Hülsing, A., Lange, T., Yarom, Y.: Flush, gauss, and reload-a cache attack on the bliss lattice-based signature scheme. Exchange 6(18), 24 (2016)

19. Gruss, D., Maurice, C., Wagner, K., Mangard, S.: Flush+ flush: a fast and stealthy cache attack. arXiv preprint arXiv:1511.04594 (2015)

20. Gruss, D., Spreitzer, R., Mangard, S.: Cache template attacks: automating attacks on inclusive last-level caches. In: 24th USENIX Security Symposium (USENIX Security 15), pp. 897–912 (2015)

21. Irazoqui, G., Inci, M.S., Eisenbarth, T., Sunar, B.: Wait a minute! a fast, cross-VM attack on AES. In: Stavrou, A., Bos, H., Portokalidis, G. (eds.) RAID 2014. LNCS, vol. 8688, pp. 299–319. Springer, Cham (2014). doi:10.1007/978-3-319-11379-1_15

22. Zhang, X., Xiao, Y., Zhang, Y.: Return-oriented flush-reload side channels on arm and their implications for android devices. In: Proceedings of the 2016 ACM SIGSAC Conference on Computer and Communications Security, pp. 858–870, ACM (2016)
23. Domnitser, L., Jaleel, A., Loew, J., Abu-Ghazaleh, N., Ponomarev, D.: Non-monopolizable caches: low-complexity mitigation of cache side channel attacks. ACM Trans. Architecture Code Optim. (TACO) **8**(4), 35 (2012)
24. Liu, F., Ge, Q., Yarom, Y., Mckeen, F., Rozas, C., Heiser, G., Lee, R.B.: Catalyst: defeating last-level cache side channel attacks in cloud computing. In: 2016 IEEE International Symposium on High Performance Computer Architecture (HPCA), pp. 406–418. IEEE (2016)
25. Wang, Z., Lee, R.B.: New cache designs for thwarting software cache-based side channel attacks. In: ACM SIGARCH Computer Architecture News, vol. 35, pp. 494–505. ACM (2007)
26. Kim, T., Peinado, M., Mainar-Ruiz, G.: Stealthmem: system-level protection against cache-based side channel attacks in the cloud. In: Presented as Part of the 21st USENIX Security Symposium (USENIX Security 12), pp. 189–204 (2012)
27. Shi, J., Song, X., Chen, H., Zang, B.: Limiting cache-based side-channel in multi-tenant cloud using dynamic page coloring. In: 2011 IEEE/IFIP 41st International Conference on Dependable Systems and Networks Workshops (DSN-W), pp. 194–199. IEEE (2011)
28. Liu, F., Lee, R.B.: Random fill cache architecture. In: 2014 47th Annual IEEE/ACM International Symposium on Microarchitecture, pp. 203–215. IEEE (2014)
29. Wang, Z., Lee, R.B.: A novel cache architecture with enhanced performance and security. In: 2008 41st IEEE/ACM International Symposium on Microarchitecture, pp. 83–93. IEEE (2008)

Measuring the Declared SDK Versions and Their Consistency with API Calls in Android Apps

Daoyuan Wu[✉], Ximing Liu, Jiayun Xu, David Lo, and Debin Gao

School of Information Systems, Singapore Management University,
Singapore, Singapore
{dywu.2015,xmliu.2015,jyxu.2015,davidlo,dbgao}@smu.edu.sg

Abstract. Android has been the most popular smartphone system, with multiple platform versions (e.g., KITKAT and Lollipop) active in the market. To manage the application's compatibility with one or more platform versions, Android allows apps to declare the supported platform SDK versions in their manifest files. In this paper, we make a first effort to study this modern software mechanism. Our objective is to measure the current practice of the declared SDK versions (which we term as DSDK versions afterwards) in real apps, and the consistency between the DSDK versions and their app API calls. To this end, we perform a three-dimensional analysis. First, we parse Android documents to obtain a mapping between each API and their corresponding platform versions. We then analyze the DSDK-API consistency for over 24K apps, among which we pre-exclude 1.3K apps that provide different app binaries for different Android versions through Google Play analysis. Besides shedding light on the current DSDK practice, our study quantitatively measures the two side effects of inappropriate DSDK versions: (i) around 1.8K apps have API calls that do not exist in some declared SDK versions, which causes runtime crash bugs on those platform versions; (ii) over 400 apps, due to claiming the outdated targeted DSDK versions, are potentially exploitable by remote code execution. These results indicate the importance and difficulty of declaring correct DSDK, and our work can help developers fulfill this goal.

Keywords: Android bug detection · Android app security

1 Introduction

Recent years have witnessed the extraordinary success of Android, a smartphone operating system owned by Google. At the end of 2013, Android became the most sold phone and tablet OS. As of 2015, Android evolved into the largest installed base of all operating systems. Along with the fast-evolving Android, its fragmentation problem becomes more and more serious. Although new devices

---

X. Liu, J. Xu—These two author names are in alphabetical order.

© Springer International Publishing AG 2017
L. Ma et al. (Eds.): WASA 2017, LNCS 10251, pp. 678–690, 2017.
DOI: 10.1007/978-3-319-60033-8_58

ship with the recent Android versions, there are still huge amounts of existing devices running old Android versions [1].

To better manage the application's compatibility with multiple platform versions, Android allows apps to declare the supported platform SDK versions in their manifest files. We term these declared SDK versions as DSDK versions. The DSDK mechanism is a modern software mechanism that to the best of our knowledge, few systems are equipped with such mechanism until Android. Nevertheless, so far the DSDK receives little attention and few understandings are known about the effectiveness of the DSDK mechanism.

In this paper, we make a first attempt to systematically study the DSDK mechanism. In particular, our objective is to measure the current practice of DSDK versions in real apps, and the consistency between DSDK versions and their apps' API calls. To this end, we perform a three-dimensional analysis that analyzes Google Play, Android documents, and each individual app. We use a large dataset that contains over 24K apps crawled from Google Play in July 2015. Our study sheds light on the current DSDK practice and quantitatively measures the two side effects of inappropriate DSDK versions.

We summarize the contributions of this paper as follows:

- (*New problem*) We study a modern software mechanism, i.e., allowing apps to declare the supported platform SDK versions. In particular, we are the first to measure the declared SDK versions and their consistency with API calls in Android apps.
- (*New understanding*) We give the first demystification of the DSDK mechanism and its two side effects of inappropriate DSDK versions.
- (*Hybrid approach*) We propose a three-dimensional analysis method that operates at both Google Play, Android document, and Android app levels.
- (*Insightful results*) We have three major findings, including (i) around 17% apps do not claim the targeted DSDK versions or declare them wrongly, (ii) around 1.8K apps under-set the minimum DSDK versions, causing them crash when running on lower Android versions, and (iii) over 400 apps under-claim the targeted DSDK versions, making them potentially exploitable by remote code execution.

2   Demystifying the Declared SDK Versions and Their Two Side Effects

In this section, we first demystify the declared platform SDK versions in Android apps, and then explain their two side effects if inappropriate DSDK versions are being used.

2.1 Declared SDK Versions in Android Apps

```
<uses-sdk  android:minSdkVersion="integer"
           android:targetSdkVersion="integer"
           android:maxSdkVersion="integer" />
```

Listing 1.1. The syntax for declaring the platform SDK versions in Android apps.

Listing 1.1 illustrates how to declare the supported platform SDK versions in Android apps by defining the `<uses-sdk>` element in apps' manifest files (i.e., `AndroidManifest.xml`). These DSDK versions are for the runtime Android system to check apps' compatibility, which is different from the compiling-time SDK for compiling source codes. The value of each DSDK version is an integer, which represents the API level of the corresponding SDK. For example, if a developer wants to declare the SDK version 5.0, he/she sets its value as 21 (the API level of Android 5.0 is 21). Since each API level has a precise mapping of the corresponding SDK version [2], we do not use another term, *declared API level*, to represent the same meaning of DSDK throughout this paper.

We explain the three DSDK attributes as follows:

- The `minSdkVersion` integer specifies the minimum platform API level required for the app to run. The Android system refuses to install an app if its `minSdkVersion` value is greater than the system's API level. Note that if an app does not declare this attribute, the system by default assigns the value of "1", which means that the app can be installed in all versions of Android.
- The `targetSdkVersion` integer designates the platform API level that the app targets at. An important *implication* of this attribute is that Android adopts the back-compatible API behaviors of the declared target SDK version, even when an app is running on a higher version of the Android platform. Android makes such compromised design because it aims to guarantee the same app behaviors as developers expect, even when apps run on newer platforms. It is worth noting that if this attribute is not set, the default value equals to the value of `minSdkVersion`.
- The `maxSdkVersion` integer specifies the maximum platform API level on which an app can run. However, this attribute is *not* recommended and already *deprecated* since Android 2.1 (API level 7). That said, modern Android no longer checks or enforces this attribute during the app installation or re-validation. The only effect is that Google Play continues to use this attribute as a filter when it presents users a list of applications available for download. Not that if this attribute is not set, it implies no any restriction on the maximum platform API level.

2.2 Two Side Effects of Inappropriate DSDK Versions

Figure 1 illustrates the two side effects of inappropriate DSDK versions. We first explain the symbols used in this figure, and then describe the two side effects in the subsequent paragraphs. As shown in Fig. 1, we can obtain $minSDK$, $targetSDK$, and $maxSDK$ from an app manifest file. Based on the API calls of an app, we can calculate the minimum and maximum API levels it requires, i.e., $minLevel$ and $maxLevel$. Eventually, the app will be deployed to a range of Android platforms between $minSDK$ and $maxSDK$.

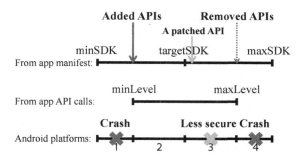

Fig. 1. Illustrating the two side effects of inappropriate DSDK versions. (Color figure online)

Side Effect I: Causing Runtime Crash Bugs. The blue part of Fig. 1 shows two scenarios in which inappropriate DSDK versions can cause app crash. The first scenario is $minLevel > minSDK$, which means a new API is introduced after the $minSDK$. Consequently, when an app runs on the Android platforms between $minSDK$ and $minLevel$ (marked as the block 1 in Fig. 1), it will crash. We verified this case by using the `VpnService.Builder.addDisallowedApplication()` API, which was introduced at Android 5.0 at the API level 21. We called this API at the MopEye app [3] and ran MopEye on an Android 4.4 device. When the app executed the `addDisallowedApplication()` API, it crashed with the `java.lang.NoSuchMethodError` exception.

The second crash scenario is $maxSDK > maxLevel$, which means an old API is removed at the $maxLevel$. Similar to the first scenario, the app will crash when it runs on the Android platforms between $maxLevel$ and $maxSDK$.

Side Effect II: Making Apps Less Secure. The red part of Fig. 1 shows the scenario in which inappropriate DSDK versions cause apps fail to be patched that they originally should be able to. Suppose an app calls an API (e.g., `addJavascriptInterface()` [4]) that is vulnerable before the $targetSDK$. However, if the `targetSdkVersion` of the app is lower than the patched API level, Android will still take the compatibility behaviors, i.e., the non-patched API behavior in this case, even when the app runs on the patched platforms (between $targetSDK$ and $maxLevel$). Some such vulnerable app examples are available in https://sites.google.com/site/androidrce/.

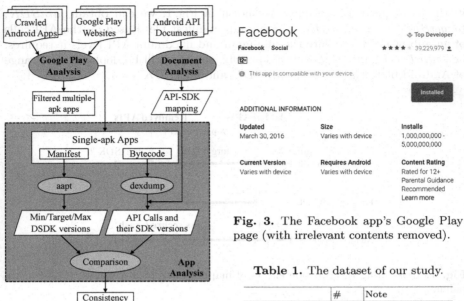

Fig. 2. The overview of our methodology.

Fig. 3. The Facebook app's Google Play page (with irrelevant contents removed).

Table 1. The dataset of our study.

	#	Note
All crawled apps	24,426	The initial dataset
Multiple-apk apps	1,301	Filtered apps
Single-apk apps	23,125	The final dataset

3 Methodology

In this section, we present an overview of our methodology and its three major components.

3.1 Overview

Figure 2 illustrates the overall design of our method. It performs the analysis at three levels. First, we crawl and analyze each app's Google Play page to filter *multiple-apk* apps that provide different app binaries (i.e., *apks*) for different Android platforms. Since each apk of these apps is tailored for a particular Android version, its declared platform SDK version is no longer important. We therefore exclude these multiple-apk apps for further analysis. Second, we parse Android API documents to build a complete mapping between each API and their corresponding platform versions. We call this mapping the *API-SDK mapping*.

In the final app analysis phase, we first extract apps' declared SDK versions and API calls, then leverage the existing API-SDK mapping to infer the range of SDK versions from API calls, and finally compare these two SDK versions (i.e., the declared SDK versions and the SDK versions inferred from API calls).

The output is the (in)consistency results between declared SDK versions and API calls, which can be further leveraged to detect bugs and vulnerabilities.

3.2 Google Play Analysis

Design and Implementation. The main objective of running Google Play analysis is to filter multiple-apk apps. We explain this step using a representative Google Play page, the Facebook app's page as shown in Fig. 3. We can notice that three attributes ("Size", "Current Version", and "Requires Android") all have the same value of "Varies with device". This indicates that Facebook employs the multiple-apk approach to handle the app compatibility over different versions of Android platforms. The apps that do not have the value of "Varies with device" are thus the single-apk apps.

To implement the Google Play analysis, we write Python scripts based on our previous codes [5,6] and Selenium, a web browser automation tool. We use Selenium's Firefox driver to load each app's Google Play page, and extract the attribute values we are interested by parsing the page's HTML source.

Dataset. Table 1 lists the dataset used in this paper. We have crawled 24,426 apps from Google Play in July 2015. We run Google Play analysis for all these apps, among which we identify and filter 1,301 multiple-apk apps. Therefore, the remaining 23,125 single-apk apps assemble our final dataset, which will be further analyzed in Sect. 3.4. Unless stated otherwise, we refer to our dataset as these 23,125 apps in this paper.

3.3 Android Document Analysis

Method. To build the API-SDK mapping, we analyze Android SDK documents based on a previous work [7]. Specifically, we first build a list of all Android APIs and the corresponding platform versions they were introduced to by parsing a SDK document called `api-versions.xml`. This file covers both initial APIs (those introduced in the first Android version) and other newly added APIs in subsequent Android versions. We further count the API change (e.g., deprecated and removed APIs) by analyzing the HTML files in the `api_diff` directory.

After running the document analysis for 23 Android versions (from 1.0 to 6.0), we recorded a total of 30,083 APIs, out of which 794 APIs were afterwards deprecated and 190 APIs were finally removed. However, we found that the lists of deprecated and removed APIs are not fully accurate, probably due to the mistakes made by Google developers when they wrote SDK documents. For example, the `removeAccount(Account, Callback, Handler)` API in the `AccountManager` class was recorded as "removed in SDK version 22" in the documents, but actually it is still available in the SDK version 23. This result implies that such a document-based analysis employed by the previous work [7] requires further improvement. As a future work, we will explore to retrieve the API-SDK mapping directly from each SDK `jar` file. In this paper, since the list

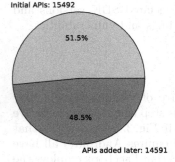

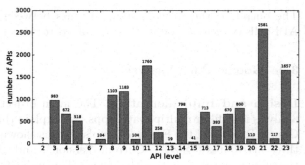

Fig. 4. The comparison between initial and added APIs.

Fig. 5. The distribution of added Android APIs.

of added APIs is accurate, we use only this part of results for the subsequent DSDK analysis in Sect. 4.

Results. We now present the results of document analysis. Figure 4 shows the comparison between the initial Android APIs and those subsequently added APIs. We can see that almost half of all APIs were added afterwards. This indicates that Android evolves dramatically along the whole process. In Fig. 5, we further plot the distribution of those subsequently added APIs since API level 2. Android 5.0 (API level 21) changed most, with 2,581 new API introduced. The following two most changed versions are Android 3.0 (API level 11) and Android 6.0 (API level 23), with 1,760 and 1,657 new APIs, respectively.

3.4   Android App Analysis

Retrieving Declared SDK Versions. We leverage aapt (Android Asset Packaging Tool) to retrieve DSDK versions *directly* from each app without extracting the manifest file. This method is more robust than the traditional apktool-based manifest extraction employed in many other works. Indeed, our aapt-based approach can successfully analyze all 23,125 apps, whereas a recent work [8] shows that apktool fails six times in the analysis of top 1K apps.

In the course of implementation, we observed and handled two kinds of special cases. First, some apps define minSdkVersion multiple times, for which we only extract the first value. Second, we apply the by-default rules (see Sect. 2.1) for the non-defined minSdkVersion and targetSdkVersion. More specifically, we set the value of minSdkVersion to 1 if it is not defined, and set the value of targetSdkVersion (if it is not defined) using the minSdkVersion value.

Extracting API Calls and Their SDK Versions. To extract API calls from apps' bytecodes, we first translate the compressed bytecodes into readable texts by using the dexdump tool. We then use a set of Linux bash commands to extract each app's method calls from their dexdump outputs.

With the extracted API calls, we use the API-SDK mapping to compute their corresponding SDK versions (i.e., `minLevel` and `maxLevel`, as explained in Fig. 1). To compute the `minLevel`, we calculate a maximum value of all API calls' added SDK versions. Similarly, to compute the `maxLevel`, we calculate a minimum value of all API calls' removed SDK versions. If an API is never removed, we set its removed SDK version to a large flag value (e.g., 100,000).

During the experiments, we find that it is necessary to exclude library codes' API calls from host apps' own API calls. Libraries such as Android Support Library provide the stub implementation of higher-version APIs on lower-version platforms to ensure the backward-compatibility of higher-version APIs. If an app is running on a higher-version platform, the library directly calls the corresponding API. Otherwise, the library calls the stub implementation, which actually does nothing but would not crash the app. Since we currently do not differentiate such control-flow information, we exclude library codes for the consistency analysis.

Comparing Consistency. With the DSDK and API level information, it is easy to compare their consistency. We compute the following three kinds of inconsistency (as previously mentioned in Sect. 2.2):

- `minSdkVersion` < `minLevel`: the `minSdkVersion` is set too low and the app would crash when it runs on platform versions between `minSdkVersion` and `minLevel`.
- `targetSdkVersion` < `maxLevel`: the `targetSdkVersion` is set too low and the app could be updated to the version of `maxLevel`. If the `maxLevel` is infinite, the `targetSdkVersion` could be adjusted to the latest Android version.
- `maxSdkVersion` > `maxLevel`: the `maxSdkVersion` is set too large and the app would crash when it runs on platform versions between `maxLevel` and `maxSdkVersion`.

4   Evaluation

Our evaluation aims to answer the following three research questions:

RQ1: What are the *characteristics* of the DSDK versions in real-world apps?
RQ2: What are the *characteristics* of the API calls in real-world apps?
RQ3: Could we identify the *inconsistency* between DSDK versions and API calls in real apps? In particular, could we discover crash bugs and potential security vulnerabilities?

4.1   RQ1: Characteristics of the Declared SDK Versions

In this section, we report a total of four findings regarding the RQ1.

Finding 1: Not all apps define the `minSdkVersion` and `targetSdkVersion` attributes, and 16.5% apps do not claim the `targetSdkVersion` attributes. From Table 2, we can see that rare apps (about 0.22%) do not

Table 2. The number and percentage of non-defined `DSDK` attributes in our dataset.

	# Non-defined	% Non-defined
`minSdkVersion`	51	0.22%
`targetSdkVersion`	3,826	16.54%
`maxSdkVersion`	23,109	99.93%

define the `minSdkVersion`, while a noticeable portion of apps (over 15%) do not define the `targetSdkVersion`. Out of these apps, 48 apps declare neither the `minSdkVersion`, nor the `targetSdkVersion`. Consequently, the values of both `minSdkVersion` and `targetSdkVersion` will be assigned to "1" by the system. We also notice that almost all apps (over 99%) do not define the `maxSdkVersion`. This result is reasonable because, as we described in Sect. 2.1, the `maxSdkVersion` attribute is strongly suggested *not* to define.

Finding 2: There are 53 outlier `targetSdkVersion` values. We also find out some declared `targetSdkVersion` are outlier values. One app defines its `targetSdkVersion` as 0, which is lower than the `minSdkVersion`. Others' `targetSdkVersion` are larger than the newest SDK version (API level 23 at that time). Some apps declare `targetSdkVersion` as 24, 25, 26 or larger, however, these SDK versions have not been released yet in year 2015. Even more surprisingly, one app sets the `targetSdkVersion` value to "10000". In general, `targetSdkVersion` should be always greater than or equal to the `minSdkVersion`, but 34 apps have negative `targetSdkVersion`- `minSdkVersion` value.

Finding 3: The minimal platform versions most apps support are Android 2.3 and 2.2, whereas the most targeted platform versions are Android 4.4 and 5.0. In Figs. 6 and 7, we plot the distribution of `minSdkVersion` and `targetSdkVersion`, respectively. We can see that most apps (around 85%) have `minSdkVersion` lower than or equal to level 11 (i.e., Android 3.0), which means that they can run on the majority of Android devices in the market [1]. Moreover, the minimal platform versions most apps support are Android 2.3 and 2.2. Figure 7 shows that more than 89% apps test their apps on platform versions larger than Android 4.0, and the most targeted platform versions are Android 4.4 and 5.0.

Finding 4: The mean version difference between `targetSdkVersion` and `minSdkVersion` is 8. We define a new metric called `lagSdkVersion` to measure the version difference between `targetSdkVersion` and `minSdkVersion`, as shown in Eq. 1.

$$\text{lagSdkVersion} = \text{targetSdkVersion} - \text{minSdkVersion} \qquad (1)$$

After removing negative `targetSdkVersion` values and outliers, we draw the CDF (Cumulative Distribution Function) plot of `lagSdkVersion` in Fig. 8.

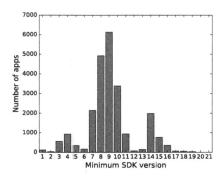

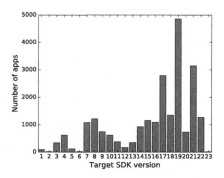

Fig. 6. Distribution of `minSdkVersion`.   **Fig. 7.** Distribution of `targetSdkVersion`.

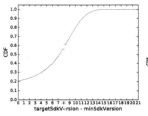

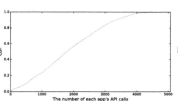

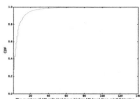

Fig. 8. CDF plot of `lagSdkVersion`.

Fig. 9. CDF plot of the number of each app's API calls.

Fig. 10. CDF plot of each app's number of API calls that have higher API level than `minSdkVersion`.

It shows that more than 20% apps have equal `targetSdkVersion` and `minSdkVersion`. Furthermore, the majority of apps (more than 95% apps) have a `lagSdkVersion` less than 12.

4.2 RQ2: Characteristics of the API Calls

In this section, we briefly present two more findings related to the RQ2. It is worth noting that here we consider all API calls that include the API calls in libraries.

Finding 5: Around 500 apps call less than 50 APIs, making them lightweight apps. On the other hand, half of apps call over 1.8K APIs. We find that 446 apps call less than 50 APIs. The majority of them are about user interface improvement, such as system theme and wallpaper apps. These apps are regarded as lightweight ones that have less dependency on the SDK versions. Additionally, many other apps contain several thousand API calls. We plot the distribution of apps by API call numbers in Fig. 9.

Finding 6: Library codes contribute more higher-version API calls than apps' own codes. Libraries such as Android support library provide

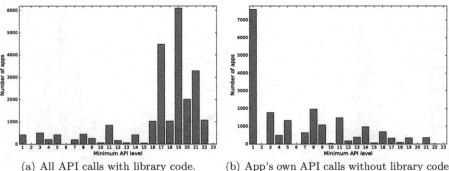

(a) All API calls with library code.   (b) App's own API calls without library code.

Fig. 11. The distribution of `minLevel` that is calculated from API calls w/o library.

backward-compatible versions of Android framework APIs, as well as the features that are only available through the library APIs. Each support library is backward-compatible to a specific API level, which allows an app that contains higher-version APIs run correctly on a lower version of Android system. Figure 11(a) shows that distribution of the `minLevel` of API calls with the library code, whereas Fig. 11(b) presents the distribution of the `minLevel` of API calls without the library code. By analyzing and de-compiling the support library, we found that they can redirect the APIs calls in a higher-version SDK to some similar APIs which are already in a lower SDK or to an empty function.

4.3   RQ3: Inconsistency Results

In this section, we report two important findings regarding the RQ3.

Finding 7: Around 1.8K apps under-set the `minSdkVersion` value, causing them would crash when they run on lower Android versions. We find that 1,750 apps have over five API calls, the levels of which are larger than the declared `minSdkVersion`. In 692 apps, more than ten API calls have higher API level than `minSdkVersion`. In Fig. 10, we draw the CDF plot of the number of API calls that have higher API level than `minSdkVersion`. Based on this figure, we find that several apps have more than 50 API calls whose API level is higher than `minSdkVersion`.

Finding 8: Around 400 apps fail to update their `targetSdkVersion` values, making them potentially exploitable by remote code execution. The `addJavascriptInterface()` API [4] has a serious security issue. By exploiting this API, attackers are able to inject malicious codes, which may obtain any information from SD card. Google later fixed this bug on Android 4.2 and afterward. However, as mentioned in the side effect II, if an app has the `targetSdkVersion` lower than 17 and calls this API, the system will still call the vulnerable API even when running in Android 4.2 and afterward. In our dataset, we find that 909 apps call the `addJavascriptInterface()` API. Among these apps, 413 apps are vulnerable, which may cause privacy information leakage. In particular, out of these 413 apps, 238 apps do not define the `targetSdkVersion` attribute (i.e., `targetSdkVersion` is null).

5 Threats to Validity

In this section, we discuss a couple of threats to the validity of our study.

First, we have not performed the control-flow analysis to determine whether an API call will be invoked only when running on certain Android versions. During the experiments, we noticed that many library codes take `if-else` blocks to call higher-version APIs on when the app is running on the corresponding versions. To mitigate its impact to our analysis, we currently exclude the library codes for consistency analysis (Sect. 3.4), and use a threshold value to minimize the potential version-related `if-else` blocks in app codes (Sect. 4.3).

Apps may employ Java reflection to call private Android APIs [9] that are not included in the SDK but contained in Android framework. Similarly, developers may use native codes to access Android APIs. Currently we have not handled these two cases and leave them as our future work.

Our assumption in Sect. 3.1 that multiple-apk apps do not have compatibility issues may not be always true. In particular, developers may provide only one apk for several Android platforms to share. In this case, those shared apks are similar to single-apk apps.

6 Related Work

Our paper is mainly related to prior works that also study Android APIs or SDKs. The work performed by McDonnell et al. [7] is the closest to our paper. They studied the Android API evolution and how client apps follow Android API changes, which is different from our focus on the consistency between apps' DSDK and API calls. In the methodology part, we followed their document analysis method for extracting the API-SDK mapping. But in the future we plan to directly analyze Android SDKs instead of documents for more accurate mapping extraction. Other related works have studied the coefficient between apps' API change and their success [10], the deprecated API usage in Java-based systems [11], and the inaccessible APIs in Android framework and their usage in third-party apps [12]. Two recent works [13,14] also focused on the fragmentation issues in Android. Compared to all these works, our study is the first systematic work on DSDK versions and their consistency with API calls.

7 Conclusion and Future Work

In this paper, we made a first effort to systematically study the declared SDK versions in Android apps, a modern software mechanism that has received little attention. We measured the current practice of the declared SDK versions or DSDK versions in a large dataset of apps, and the consistency between the DSDK versions and their app API calls. To facilitate the analysis, we proposed a three-dimensional analysis method that operates at both Google Play, Android document, and Android app levels. We have obtained some interesting and novel findings, including (i) around 17% apps do not claim the targeted DSDK versions or declare them wrongly, (ii) around 1.8K apps under-set the minimum DSDK versions, causing them would crash when running on lower Android versions, and (iii) over 400 apps under-claim the targeted DSDK versions, making them potentially exploitable by remote code execution. In the future, we plan to contact the authors of the apps to inform them about the detected issues and collect their feedback, release a publicly available tool to let app developers detect and fix issues, and improve our approach to further mitigate the threats to validity (e.g., by designing and incorporating a suitable control-flow analysis technique).

References

1. Android: Dashboards. https://developer.android.com/about/dashboards/
2. Android: Platform codenames, versions, and API levels. https://source.android. com/source/build-numbers.html
3. Wu, D., Li, W., Chang, R., Gao, D.: MopEye: monitoring per-app network performance with zero measurement traffic. In: CoNEXT Student Workshop (2015)
4. Drake, J.: On the WebView addJavascriptInterface saga (2014). http://www. droidsec.org/news/2014/02/26/on-the-webview-addjsif-saga.html
5. Wu, D., Chang, R.K.C.: Analyzing android browser apps for:// vulnerabilities. In: Chow, S.S.M., Camenisch, J., Hui, L.C.K., Yiu, S.M. (eds.) ISC 2014. LNCS, vol. 8783, pp. 345–363. Springer, Cham (2014). doi:10.1007/978-3-319-13257-0_20
6. Wu, D., Chang, R.K.C.: Indirect file leaks in mobile applications. In: Proceedings of IEEE Mobile Security Technologies (MoST) (2015)
7. McDonnell, T., Ray, B., Kim, M.: An empirical study of API stability and adoption in the android ecosystem. In: Proceedings of IEEE ICSM (2013)
8. Wu, D., Luo, X., Chang, R.K.C.: A sink-driven approach to detecting exposed component vulnerabilities in android apps. CoRR abs/1405.6282 (2014)
9. Andrew: Hacking the "private" Android API. http://andrewoid.blogspot.com/ 2008/12/hacking-android-api.html
10. Linares-Vásquez, M., Bavota, G., Bernal-Cárdenas, C., Penta, M.D., Oliveto, R., Poshyvanyk, D.: API change and fault proneness: a threat to the success of android apps. In: Proceedings of ACM FSE (2013)
11. Brito, G., Hora, A., Valente, M.T., Robbes, R.: Do developers deprecate APIs with replacement messages? A large-scale analysis on Java systems. In: Proceedings of IEEE SANER (2016)
12. Li, L., Bissyandé, T.F., Traon, Y.L., Klein, J.: Accessing inaccessible android APIs: an empirical study. In: Proceedings of IEEE ICSME (2016)
13. Mutchler, P., Safaei, Y., Doupe, A., Mitchell, J.: Target fragmentation in android apps. In: Proceedings of IEEE Mobile Security Technologies (MoST) (2016)
14. Wei, L., Liu, Y., Cheung, S.C.: Taming android fragmentation: characterizing and detecting compatibility issues for android apps. In: Proceedings of ACM ASE (2016)

Employing Smartwatch for Enhanced Password Authentication

Bing Chang[1,2,3], Ximing Liu[4], Yingjiu Li[4], Pingjian Wang[1,2,3],
Wen-Tao Zhu[1,2(✉)], and Zhan Wang[5]

[1] State Key Laboratory of Information Security,
Institute of Information Engineering, Chinese Academy of Sciences, Beijing, China
wtzhu@ieee.org
[2] Data Assurance and Communication Security Research Center,
Chinese Academy of Sciences, Beijing, China
[3] School of Cyber Security, University of Chinese Academy of Sciences,
Beijing, China
[4] School of Information Systems, Singapore Management University,
Singapore, Singapore
[5] RealTime Invent, Inc, Beijing, China

Abstract. This paper presents an enhanced password authentication scheme by systematically exploiting the motion sensors in a smartwatch. We extract unique features from the sensor data when a smartwatch bearer types his/her password (or PIN), and train certain machine learning classifiers using these features. We then implement smartwatch-aided password authentication using the classifiers. Our scheme is user-friendly since it does not require users to perform any additional actions when typing passwords or PINs other than wearing smartwatches. We conduct a user study involving 51 participants on the developed prototype so as to evaluate its feasibility and performance. Experimental results show that the best classifier for our system is the Bagged Decision Trees, for which the accuracy is 4.58% FRR and 0.12% FAR on the QWERTY keyboard, and 6.13% FRR and 0.16% FAR on the numeric keypad.

Keywords: Wearable devices · User authentication · Sensor · Machine learning

1 Introduction

A smartwatch is a computerized wristwatch with functionalities beyond time-keeping. The use of smartwatch has become a rising trend in today's consumer electronics. Equipped with rich sensors, smartwatches can be used in many applications such as monitoring heart rate, steps taken and calories burned. In recent studies, smartwatch sensor data are exploited to conduct keystroke inference attacks. When a user types on a keyboard or PIN pad wearing a smartwatch, an attacker may access the user's smartwatch sensor data and infer what

© Springer International Publishing AG 2017
L. Ma et al. (Eds.): WASA 2017, LNCS 10251, pp. 691–703, 2017.
DOI: 10.1007/978-3-319-60033-8_59

the user types from the sensor data, thus compromising user's security or privacy [7,8,15,16]. While prior studies reveal that smartwatch sensor data can be exploited for launching attacks, we further reveal that such data contain unique features of users' typing behaviors beyond what users type, and thus can be exploited to enhance password authentication against known password attacks and keystroke imitation attacks. An enhance password authentication system is still reliable even if an adversary knows a user's password and can imitate the user's keystroke dynamics.

In particular, we extract unique features from smartwatch sensor data when a smartwatch bearer types his/her password (or PIN), and train certain machine learning classifiers using these features. We then design a smartwatch-aided password authentication scheme using the trained classifiers. We show that our scheme can defend against the keystroke imitation attack proposed in [9]. Even if an adversary obtains users' passwords and imitates users' keystroke dynamics, our system can still differentiate imitators from legitimate users by analyzing smartwatch sensor data during password entry.

Our scheme is user-friendly since it does not require users to perform any additional actions when typing passwords or PINs other than wearing their smartwatches. The performance of our scheme is evaluated in an IRB-approved user study with 51 participants. Five widely used classification algorithms are evaluated in which the best performer turns out to be the Bagged Decision Trees. Rigorous experiments on the accuracy of our scheme are conducted in our user study, yielding 4.58% FRR and 0.12 FAR on the QWERTY keyboard, and 6.13% FRR and 0.16% FAR on the numeric keypad. It is also shown that the keystroke imitation attack has insignificant impact to the accuracy of our scheme.

2 Background

2.1 Smartwatch and Sensor Dynamics

There are various sensors on smartwatches to collect information about users, including accelerometer, gyroscope, heart rate sensor, and microphone. We choose Moto 360 sport, which is powered by Android Wear OS, for our evaluation purpose. We collect data from accelerometer and gyroscope for the purpose of user authentication. The built-in motion sensor is an InvenSense MPU 6051 Six-Axis (Gyroscope + Accelerometer) MEMS motion tracking device, which can measure the accelerations and angular velocities of movement in x-, y- and z-axis regardless of the orientation of watch. Accelerometer and gyroscope in smartwatches have been extensively used in user behavioral characterization, including sensor-based keystroke inference [7,8,15,16]. The basic idea is that the sensor data provide necessary information which can be used to accurately recognize the hand movements performed by users wearing smartwatches. Instead of using such sensor data for keystroke inference, we use them for user authentication.

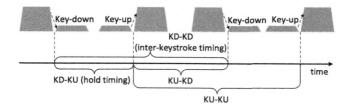

Fig. 1. Keystroke timings used in keystroke dynamics techniques.

2.2 Keystroke Dynamics

Keystroke dynamics refers to the timing information associated with key-press events. Two types of key-press events are usually used in modeling keystroke dynamics, including (a) key-down event (KD): a user presses a key and (b) key-up event (KU): a user releases a key. One or more possible keystroke timings associated with consecutive key-press events, e.g., KD-KU time and KD-KD time, are considered as keystroke dynamics features in [6] and shown in Fig. 1. Keystroke dynamics features have been used to identify and authenticate users on both hardware keyboards [1,5,17] and software keyboards [13,14]. However, Meng et al. [9] revealed that a training interface can be set up to help attackers imitate users' keystroke dynamics, which makes it unsafe to use keystroke dynamics for user authentication. Because keystroke dynamics contains only the timing information about users' keystroke, it is possible for an attacker to imitate a user's keystroke via a training interface. To address this problem, we model a user's typing behavior using both acceleration data and angular velocity data from the user's smartwatch. It is difficult for an attacker to imitate a user's typing behavior in our model without accessing the victims' smartwatch sensor data.

3 Assumptions

It is assumed that a user (the victim) wears a smartwatch such as Apple Watch or Moto 360 Sport, while he/she types passwords and PINs. The smartwatch is equipped with accelerometer and gyroscope which collect the motion information of the victim's wrist. If the victim uses one hand to type, the smartwatch is worn on the same hand. As smartwatches are widely used, it is not uncommon to make such assumption in daily life. We focus on two types of keyboards in this paper, including QWERTY keyboards and numeric keyboards, which can be used on PCs, mobile devices, Point of Sale (POS) terminals and Automatic Teller Machines (ATMs).

An attacker intends to login to a user/victim's account after the attacker obtains the victim's username and password/PIN. The attacker may observe or record the victim's entry of passwords or PINs. However, it is assumed that the attacker cannot obtain any sensor data about the victim's typing of passwords/PINs from the victim's smartwatch; instead, the attacker has the following capabilities. First, the attacker may obtain the victim's username and password (e.g., by shoulder-surfing attack or key logger). Second, the attacker may obtain the victim's keystroke timing data and imitate the victim's keystroke as shown in [9]. In attacks, the attacker may wear a same kind of smartwatch and access to a same kind of keyboard as the victim's.

4   Scheme Design

4.1   Overview

The main goal of our design is to demonstrate that using smartwatches can help enhance the security of password authentication systems. Password authentication systems suffer from password observation attacks such as shoulder surfing and key logger in which attackers may obtain users' passwords. We design and implement a system which can distinguish legitimate users from illegitimate users by processing the sensor data from the smartwatches worn on legitimate users' wrists. Even if an attacker types in the same password as a victim, the attacker's hand motion is different from the user's. The accelerometer and gyroscope in a smartwatch can be used to track its wearer's hand motion during password input. As smartwatches are widely used nowadays, our system does not require any additional actions when typing passwords/PINs other than wearing smartwatches, making our system user-friendly. Our system can be employed as long as a smartwatch is worn on the user's wrist when the user types a password/PIN on a keyboard, or keypad of any device such as PC, ATM, and mobile phone.

Our system takes as input the password and the raw sensor data (e.g., acceleration, angular velocity) from the smartwatch worn on a user's wrist. The password and the raw sensor data are sent to our server for verification. The password is for the conventional password authentication while the raw sensor data are processed to further verify the user. Our system consists of two phases, the training phase and the detection phase. During the training phase, the password is registered for the conventional password authentication and the raw sensor data are recorded. The raw sensor data are then processed according to our feature extraction method which translates all the recorded sensor data into features suitable for our classifier. After the features are extracted, we train the classifier with these features. During the detection phase, the system verifies the password first. If the typed password is correct, it extracts features from the sensor data and inputs the extracted features into the classifier so as to verify the user. The classifier matches the features extracted from the sensor data against all the known user profiles to identify whether the password is typed by the legitimate user. A user is authenticated only if both the password is correct and the typing pattern matches the user's profile.

As the conventional password authentication has been rigorously investigated, we focus on how to use machine learning techniques to process the sensor data of smartwatches and match users' profiles. We collect the sensor data when users type passwords on QWERTY keyboards or PINs on numeric keypads. QWERTY keyboards and numeric keypads are mainstream devices for inputting passwords and PINs nowadays, respectively. As long as a user types passwords or PINs with the hand wearing the smartwatch, the sensor data can help authenticate the user. We extract unique features from the sensor data and train certain classifiers using the features as user profiles. The classifiers are used to authenticate users.

4.2 Data Collection

Our system collects the accelerometer and gyroscope data within a time window from a smartwatch worn on a user's wrist. The time window begins when the user begins to type a password or PIN, and ends once the user presses "Enter" to finish the input. The data from accelerometer and gyroscope are streams of timestamped real values along three axes. For a given timestamp, t, the accelerometer data are in the form of $a(t) = (a_x, a_y, a_z)$ while the gyroscope data are in the form of $\omega(t) = (\omega_x, \omega_y, \omega_z)$. Note that the accelerometer data are affected by the earth gravity, so when the smartwatch is lying flat on the desk, the accelerometer data show that there is an acceleration of $9.8 \, \mathrm{m/s^2}$ along the z-axis. We can install an app in each smartwatch used in our experiment to collect the sensor data. The app is given the permission to access the accelerometer and gyroscope of the smartwatch. The app is also given the permission to communicate with the password input interface and obtain the timing information when the user begins typing and when the user finishes typing. According to the timing information, the app collects the sensor data and sends the data to our server which is used to authenticate users. We collect the sensor data in both the training phase and the detection phase. In the training phase, we collect enough data to train certain classifiers. Assuming it takes 6 s for a user to type in a password or PIN, it will take 10 min to type in the password 100 times, which is enough for training. In the detection phase, the app collects the sensor data when the user types the password or PIN and send the data to our server to verify whether the user is legitimate.

4.3 Feature Extraction

The raw data from accelerometer and gyroscope are streams of timestamped real values along three axes. We extract temporal features from these data for authentication purpose. We summarize the features that we extract from the sensor data streams in Table 1 [3]. The detail of these features have been documented previously in report [2]. Since there are three axes for both sensors, we obtain a vector of 36 elements after extracting the features from a sensor data stream. Our server extracts the aforementioned features for certain classifier in both the training phase and the detection phase. In the training phase, all the extracted features are used to train the classifier, while in the detection phase, the features are used to authenticate the user according to the classifier.

4.4 Supervised Learning and Detection

In the training phase, after the system extracts all the features, it trains the classifier using the features. In Sect. 5, we evaluate five widely used classifica-

Table 1. Extracted features.

Feature	Description
Mean strength	Arithmetic mean of the signal strength
Standard deviation	Standard deviation of the signal strength
Average deviation	Average deviation from mean
Skewness	Measure of asymmetry about mean
Kurtosis	Measure of the flatness or spikiness of a distribution
RMS	Square root of arithmetic mean of squares of the signal strength

tion algorithms, including Support Vector Machine (SVM), k-Nearest Neighbor (k-NN), Bagged Decision Trees (Matlab's Treebagger model), Naive Bayes classifier and Discriminant Analysis classifier. We discover that the Bagged Decision Trees outperforms the other classifiers in Sect. 5. In the detection phase, a feature vector is extracted from the sensor data of a user's smartwatch, and fed into a trained classifier which generates the authentication result: whether the user is legitimate or illegitimate.

5   Evaluation

5.1   Experimental Setup

To collect the sensor data when a user wearing a smartwatch types in a password or PIN, we setup a data collection system which consists of four components, a keyboard, a laptop, a mobile phone and a smartwatch. Figure 2(a) illustrates our data collection system. A user just needs to wear a smartwatch and type in passwords on the laptop using the keyboard. The sensor data will be recorded automatically on the mobile phone.

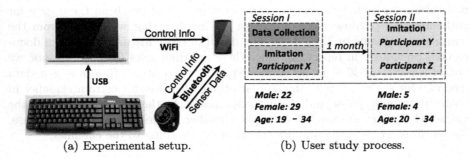

(a) Experimental setup.   (b) User study process.

Fig. 2. Overview of our experiment.

Keyboard. We use a DELL SK-8115 keyboard for data collection. Users type passwords on the QWERTY keyboard and type PINs on the numeric keypad.

Laptop. The laptop is a MacBook Pro with an Intel i7 2.7 GHz processor with 8 GiB RAM, running an Ubuntu 14.04 64-bit virtual machine. We obtain the source code of the data collection system from the authors of [9] and rebuild their system. We modify their system for our experiments. The main functions of the modified system include providing tasks for users to type, judging whether users' inputs are correct and sending control information to the mobile phone via WiFi connection. The user interface is a web page for users to type in passwords or PINs according to a prompt. When the system shows the prompt, it sends out a "start" message to the mobile phone at the same time. Once receiving the message, the mobile phone also sends a "start" message to the smartwatch, which begins to record the sensor data. When the user presses "Enter" to finish the input, the system sends a "finish" message to the mobile phone and triggers it to send a "finish" message immediately to the smartwatch. The smartwatch finishes its recording of the sensor data and sends the data to the phone. If the input password is incorrect or the user presses "Backspace", the user's input is erased and the system sends a "restart" message to the phone and in turn to the smartwatch which restarts the recording of the sensor data.

Mobile Phone. The mobile phone is a Nexus 6 powered by Android 6.0. We install an app in this phone to communicate with the laptop and the smartwatch, as well as store the sensor data obtained from the smartwatch. The app receives the control information from the laptop through WiFi connection and communicates with the smartwatch through Bluetooth connection. After the user finishes typing each password or PIN, the accelerometer data and gyroscope data from the smartwatch are stored in two files respectively. Each file is a list of the sensor data entries which contain the timestamps and the values of three axes.

Smartwatch. The smartwatch is a Moto 360 Sport, which runs on the Android Wear platform. We install an app in this smartwatch to collect the sensor data. When the app receives a "start" message from the phone, the app starts recording accelerometer and gyroscope readings. During data collection, the sensor data are stored locally. When the app receives a "finish" message, the sensor data are transferred to the phone via Bluetooth. Note that the sampling frequency (50 Hz) is the highest on Moto 360 sport and we specify the *SENSOR_DELAY_FASTEST* flag at the sensor listener registration time to accomplish this.

5.2   User Study

Figure 2(b) shows the process of our user study[1]. We collect testing data from 51 participants in our university (students and staff), including 22 males and 29 females with ages between 19 and 34 (45 of them are between 20 and 27

---

[1] The user study was approved by the Institutional Review Board of our university. Data collected from the participants were anonymized and protected according to the corresponding IRB submission documents.

years old). 26 of them are major in computer science and all of them are skilled keyboard users. Our user study involves two sessions, and each of them takes about 60 min. Every participant takes part in Session I and we choose 9 of them (5 males and 4 females) to take part in Session II. Each participant is paid with 10 dollars after completing each session.

Data Collection. In the data collection phase of Session I, we collect the sensor data when each participant types a predefined QWERTY keyboard password and a predefined keypad password. The QWERTY keyboard password is used to simulate that a user types a password on a standard keyboard while the keypad password is used to simulate that a user types a PIN on a keypad of ATM or POS terminal. The participants are required to wear smartwatches on their right wrists, and type in QWERTY passwords with both hands while type in PINs with the right hands. The participants are also required to keep standing when they type PINs, since people usually type PINs on ATMs or POS terminals standing. We choose the QWERTY keyboard password and the keypad password as "ths.ouR2" and "924673", respectively in our experiment. The password "ths.ouR2" is a strong password used in previous work [9] while "924673" is a randomly generated PIN. The participants are required to type each password 100 times.

Keystroke Imitation Attack. In order to find some participants who are good at keystroke imitation and test whether our system can resist the imitation attack proposed in [9], we arrange an imitation phase in both Session I and Session II. We rebuild the system proposed in [9] and require that each participant uses this system to imitate a previous participant's keystroke dynamics. After the participant finishes each input, the system shows an interface (Fig. 3) and a score to indicate the differences between this input and the target typing pattern. Note that in Fig. 3, the circles mean the hold timings and the bars mean the inter-keystroke timings. A participant can adjust his/her typing according to the interface. In the imitation phase of Session I, we aim to find some participants who are good at imitation, so each participant is required to imitate a previous participant's typing pattern of "ths.ouR2". We find 9 best imitators according to the imitation performance and they are invited to take part in Session II. In Session II, the participants are required to imitate other two participants' typing

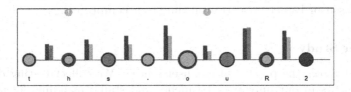

Fig. 3. The interface of the imitation system (Fig. 3 in [9]). The circles mean the hold timings and the bars mean the inter-keystroke timings. The blue circles and bars are the target's timing information. Imitators can adjust their typing according to the differences between their timing information and the target's. (Color figure online)

patterns of "ths.ouR2" and "924673". Similar to the conclusion drawn in [9], we discover that it is unable to distinguish these imitators from the victims according to the keystroke dynamics only, but we aim to find out whether it is possible to distinguish them by analyzing the sensor data taken from smartwatches.

5.3   Performance Analysis

Data Processing. To show the performance of our system on both QWERTY keyboard and numeric keypad, we process the sensor data collected when the 51 participants type "ths.ouR2" and "924673". The participants are required to type in the same password as we aim to find out whether the sensor data can help differentiate them. After deleting the invalid data caused by system error, we extract the features according to Sect. 4.3 and obtain 4,789 feature vectors for the QWERTY keyboard and 4,868 feature vectors for the numeric keyboard. For each participant, we have approximately 93 feature vectors, including the mean values of the three axis of the accelerometer. We delete some outliers based on the accelerometer data as follows. We first calculate the mean value M and the standard deviation D of the mean strengths, and then calculate the difference between M and each mean strength. If the difference is larger than three times of D, we delete the corresponding feature vector. In addition, if the D values of some participants are three times higher than others, we also delete these data to improve the quality of the collected data. In total, we delete 759 out of 4,789 feature vectors for the QWERTY keyboard and 609 out of 4,868 feature vectors for the numeric keypad. To access the performance, we use FAR (false acceptance rate), which indicates the fraction of imposter access attempts identified as valid users, and FRR (false rejection rate), which indicates the fraction of valid user attempts identified as impostors.

Performance of Different Classifiers. We evaluate the performance of five classifiers, including Support Vector Machine (SVM), k-Nearest Neighbor (k-NN), Bagged Decision Trees (Matlab's Treebagger model), Naive Bayes classifier and Discriminant Analysis classifier. For training and testing of these classifiers, we *randomly* select 50% of the feature vectors for each participant as a training set while the remaining 50% as a testing set. To prevent any bias in our experiments, we randomize the training and testing sets 10 times and compute the average accuracy. Our experimental results are shown in Tables 2 and 3. In the tables, "keyboard (improved)" and "keypad (improved)" mean the improved data set derived by removing outliers from the original data set. The results show that the Bagged Decision Trees outperforms the other classifiers and its accuracy is 4.58% FRR and 0.12% FAR on the QWERTY keyboard, and 6.13% FRR and 0.16% FAR on the numeric keypad.

Impact of Different Sensors. To understand the impact of different sensors, we also test our system using the data from one sensor only. Figure 4 shows the evaluation results with the Bagged Decision Trees. In all cases, using accelerometer only can reach almost the same accuracy as using both sensors, while using

Table 2. FRR in different scenarios (BDT: Bagged Decision Trees; DAC: Discriminant Analysis Classifier).

	keyboard (improved)	keypad (improved)	imitation I (keyboard)	imitation I (keypad)	imitation II (keyboard)	imitation II (keypad)
SVM	18.15%	11.79%	14.81%	5.46%	14.00%	6.64%
k-NN	28.03%	20.02%	22.10%	9.23%	20.99%	8.80%
BDT	4.58%	6.13%	1.93%	1.51%	2.03%	3.41%
Naive Bayes	8.79%	11.03%	12.02%	6.97%	11.42%	9.34%
DAC	6.08%	6.09%	1.72%	1.51%	1.47%	3.95%

Table 3. FAR in different scenarios (BDT: Bagged Decision Trees; DAC: Discriminant Analysis Classifier).

	keyboard (improved)	keypad (improved)	imitation I (keyboard)	imitation I (keypad)	imitation II (keyboard)	imitation II (keypad)
SVM	0.43%	0.28%	1.5%	0.47%	1.3%	0.63%
k-NN	0.67%	0.48%	2.2%	0.83%	1.9%	0.80%
BDT	0.12%	0.16%	0.21%	0.15%	0.24%	0.47%
Naive Bayes	0.21%	0.26%	1.2%	0.78%	0.78%	1.0%
DAC	0.14%	0.14%	0.17%	0.15%	0.08%	0.04%

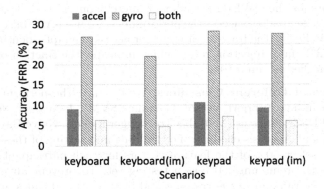

Fig. 4. The accuracy (FRR) when using only one sensor.

gyroscope only results in lower accuracy. Nonetheless, using both sensors can improve the accuracy by about 3% compared to using accelerometer only. As a result, we use both sensors in our system.

5.4   Defending Against Keystroke Imitation Attack

To test whether our system can defend against the keystroke imitation attack proposed in [9], we process the sensor data when nine selected participants imitate others. Note that the selected participants are the best imitators among the 51 participants selected in Session I. In Session II, they are requested to imitate other two participants' typing patterns on QWERTY keyboard and numeric keypad. We have reproduced the results of [9] with these nine participants. After trained with the system proposed in [9], the selected participants can imitate the target typing patterns in a success rate higher than 90%. To test whether our system can differentiate original users from imitators, we first extract the features from the sensor data collected from the original users and from the imitators, respectively. We then *randomly* select 50% of the feature vectors from each person to train the classifiers. The other 50% of the feature vectors are used as the testing set. The results are shown in Tables 2 and 3. In the first round of imitation, the results show that the accuracy of the Bagged Decision Trees is 1.93% FRR and 0.21 FAR on the standard keyboard, and 1.51% FRR and 0.15% FAR on the numeric keypad. In the second round of imitation, the accuracy of the Bagged Decision Trees is 2.03% FRR and 0.24 FAR on the standard keyboard, and 3.41% FRR and 0.47% FAR on the numeric keypad. The keystroke imitation attack has little impact on our system.

6 Related Work

Sensor Information Leaks on Smartwatches. Previous research has studied sensor information leaks on smartwatches [7, 8, 15, 16]. Wang et al. [16] propose a linguistic model based system to infer user typed words on a standard keyboard using accelerometer and gyroscope data in smartwatches. Their system is unable to deal with non-contextual inputs, such as passwords and PIN sequences, since the system relies on a linguistic model. Liu et al. [7] make use of the sensors in smartwatches, including accelerometer and microphone, to infer users' inputs on keyboards or POS terminals. Their approach is based on machine-learning techniques and training of hand movements between keystrokes. Maiti et al. [8] also make use of the sensors in smartwatches to infer users' input, and present a protection framework to regulate sensor access. Wang et al. [15] propose a training-free and contextual-free system to infer users' input by exploiting the sensors in wearable devices, including accelerometers, gyroscopes and magnetometers. Their system does not require any training or contextual information.

Keystroke Dynamics. Tremendous efforts have been made on using keystroke dynamics as biometrics (e.g., [10–12]). However, Meng et al. [9] propose a feedback and training interface, called *Mimesis*, which can help one person imitate another through incremental adjustment of typing patterns. If an attacker can obtain the information of a victim's typing pattern, the attacker can imitate the victim with the help of *Mimesis*. This makes keystroke dynamics based authentication systems insecure. Giuffrida et al. [4] propose sensor-enhanced keystroke dynamics to authenticate users typing on mobile devices. They use motion sensor data to characterize users typing behavior and use machine learning techniques to perform user authentication. However, their system works on mobile devices only. When users type passwords on standard keyboards or PINs on keypads, their system does not work. In comparison, our solution is more generic, since the smartwatch is worn on the user's wrist. Wherever the user types, our system can obtain the sensor data which reflect the motions of the user's wrist, and thus authenticate the user by analyzing the sensor data.

7 Conclusion

In this paper, we propose to use smartwatches to track the motion of users' wrists when they type passwords on standard keyboards or numeric keypads. In particular, we present a novel enhanced password authentication scheme by systematically exploiting the motion sensors in the users' smartwatches. The experimental results show that the best classifier for our system achieves an accuracy of 4.58% FRR and 0.12% FAR on the QWERTY keyboard, and 6.13% FRR and 0.16% FAR on the numeric keypad. Our work paves the way for authenticating users using smartwatch sensor data and machine learning techniques.

Acknowledgment. This work is supported by the Singapore National Research Foundation under NCR Award Number NRF2014NCR-NCR001-012. This work is partially supported by Youth Innovation Promotion Association, CAS.

References

1. Clarke, N.L., Furnell, S., Lines, B., Reynolds, P.L.: Keystroke dynamics on a mobile handset: a feasibility study. Inf. Manag. Comput. Secur. **11**(4), 161–166 (2003)
2. Das, A., Borisov, N., Caesar, M.: Exploring ways to mitigate sensor-based smartphone fingerprinting. CoRR, abs/1503.01874 (2015)
3. Das, A., Borisov, N., Caesar, M.: Tracking mobile web users through motion sensors: attacks and defenses. In: Proceedings of the 23rd NDSS (2016)
4. Giuffrida, C., Majdanik, K., Conti, M., Bos, H.: I sensed it was you: authenticating mobile users with sensor-enhanced keystroke dynamics. In: Dietrich, S. (ed.) DIMVA 2014. LNCS, vol. 8550, pp. 92–111. Springer, Cham (2014). doi:10.1007/978-3-319-08509-8_6
5. Karatzouni, S., Clarke, N.: Keystroke analysis for thumb-based keyboards on mobile devices. In: Venter, H., Eloff, M., Labuschagne, L., Eloff, J., Solms, R. (eds.) SEC 2007. IIFIP, vol. 232, pp. 253–263. Springer, Boston, MA (2007). doi:10.1007/978-0-387-72367-9_22
6. Killourhy, K., Maxion, R.: Why did my detector do *That*?!. In: Jha, S., Sommer, R., Kreibich, C. (eds.) RAID 2010. LNCS, vol. 6307, pp. 256–276. Springer, Heidelberg (2010). doi:10.1007/978-3-642-15512-3_14
7. Liu, X., Zhou, Z., Diao, W., Li, Z., Zhang, K.: When good becomes evil: keystroke inference with smartwatch. In: Proceedings of the 22nd ACM SIGSAC Conference on Computer and Communications Security, pp. 1273–1285. ACM (2015)
8. Maiti, A., Armbruster, O., Jadliwala, M., He, J.: Smartwatch-based keystroke inference attacks and context-aware protection mechanisms. In: Proceedings of the 11th ACM Asia Conference on Computer and Communications Security (2016)

9. Meng, T.C., Gupta, P., Gao, D.: I can be you: questioning the use of keystroke dynamics as biometrics. In: Proceedings of the 20th NDSS (2013)
10. Monrose, F., Rubin, A.: Authentication via keystroke dynamics. In: Proceedings of the 4th ACM Conference on Computer and Communications Security (1997)
11. Monrose, F., Rubin, A.D.: Keystroke dynamics as a biometric for authentication. Future Gen. Comput. Syst. **16**(4), 351–359 (2000)
12. Peacock, A., Ke, X., Wilkerson, M.: Typing patterns: a key to user identification. IEEE Secur. Privacy **2**(5), 40–47 (2004)
13. Tasia, C.-J., Chang, T.-Y., Cheng, P.-C., Lin, J.-H.: Two novel biometric features in keystroke dynamics authentication systems for touch screen devices. Secur. Commun. Netw. **7**(4), 750–758 (2014)
14. Trojahn, M., Ortmeier, F.: Biometric authentication through a virtual keyboard for smartphones. Int. J. Comput. Sci. Inf. Technol. **4**(5), 1 (2012)
15. Wang, C., Guo, X., Wang, Y., Chen, Y., Liu, B.: Friend or foe?: your wearable devices reveal your personal pin. In: Proceedings of the 11th ACM Asia Conference on Computer and Communications Security, pp. 189–200. ACM (2016)
16. Wang, H., Lai, T.T.T., Roy Choudhury, R.: Mole: motion leaks through smartwatch sensors. In: Proceedings of the 21st Annual International Conference on Mobile Computing and Networking, pp. 155–166. ACM (2015)
17. Zahid, S., Shahzad, M., Khayam, S.A., Farooq, M.: Keystroke-based user identification on smart phones. In: Kirda, E., Jha, S., Balzarotti, D. (eds.) RAID 2009. LNCS, vol. 5758, pp. 224–243. Springer, Heidelberg (2009). doi:10.1007/978-3-642-04342-0_12

AIS: An Inaudible Guider in Your Smartphone

Xing Zhou, Liusheng Huang, Yang Xu, and Wei Yang(✉)

School of Computer Science and Technology,
University of Science and Technology of China, Hefei, Anhui, China
{zhou999,smallant}@email.ustc.edu.cn, {lshuang,qubit}@ustc.edu.cn

Abstract. In the problem of indoor localization, acoustic schemes exhibit their superiority over radio ways for lower propagation speed of sound in the air. Recent studies upon acoustic positioning and tracking proposed a couple of solutions at millimetre level. Enlightened by the outstanding work of relevant scholars, we propose an acoustic-based interactive system (AIS) for commercial-off-the-shelf (COTS) smartphones, which senses users' moving states and routes by estimating the Doppler effect of received ultra sound signals using off-the-shelf smartphones. The ultra sound stems from surrounding fixed speakers. We test the performance of AIS with commercial smartphones and speakers in two cases. In the results of our experiments, we can achieve 1.1% false positive rate and 8.9% false negative rate for trajectory identification.

Keywords: Acoustic signals · Doppler effect · Chirp signal · Smart devices · Ultra sound

1 Introduction

Indoor localization service plays an important role in many cyber-physical applications. For example, shopping malls can analyze the routes of customers, to see how many people look at a certain display and get interested in it [2]. On the other hand, shoppers may want to receive more information of the goods they like, when they stand by the goods. Similarly, visitors in museums also expect real-time indoor localization service to explain their points of interest. Moreover, it is desirable for the service not to require any customized devices for people. Since almost everyone has a smartphone, a localization system based on smartphone is at the first choice.

By now, most smartphones provide dual track microphones and support 44.1 kHz sampling rate. According to the Nyquist's Theorem, current smartphone is able to receive acoustic signals up to 22.05 kHz. Experiments in [1] show that acoustic signals in 19.5 ∼ 22 kHz band can be recorded by most smart devices. That means smartphones' microphones can be used as weak ultra sound sensors. On the other side, many researchers have already leveraged ultra sound into tracking system on smartphones [3,10]. Their tracking techniques based on ultra sound can be extended to build a localization system.

© Springer International Publishing AG 2017
L. Ma et al. (Eds.): WASA 2017, LNCS 10251, pp. 704–715, 2017.
DOI: 10.1007/978-3-319-60033-8_60

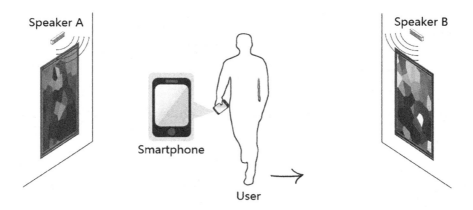

Fig. 1. A common scenario for AIS in museum.

In this paper, we propose an acoustic-based interactive system (AIS) which takes different responses according to the trajectories of users. Figure 1 demonstrates a common scenario using our system. In Fig. 1, there is a person taking a mobile device walking around in a portrait museum. A loudspeaker is installed beside every exhibition. These speakers emit a lasting modulated ultra sound. When the person wants to view the right portrait, he walks to it and stops in a close distance. AIS can detect this approach and then show extra information which could be an audio clip or an introduction video of that portrait. When the person leaves from the portrait, AIS will detect his departure and close the show of extra information. If he just passes a portrait without stopping, AIS takes no action but make records.

To translate the above high-level ideas into a working system, we develop a trajectory detection module and a data transmission module. The trajectory detection module estimates speed using Doppler effect and then identifies three trajectories. For data transmission, we embed a unique index into chirp signals in ultra sound. Each index is associated with a certain speaker. Since each speaker is beside a portrait, there is a one-to-one mapping between an index and a portrait. AIS will send the received index to a remote sever storing related datum and fetch what it needs. Last but not least, we divide adjacent speakers into different channel to avoid aliasing.

Our main contributions are summarized as follows: (1) An acoustic-based interactive system combing acoustic tracking with acoustic transmission. (2) An accurate Doppler effect based trajectory detection module employing undersampling technique. (3) A channel selection strategy based on RMS measurement.

2   Overview

Figure 2 shows an overview of AIS. On the left side, speakers emits a combination of a sine signal and a chirp signal. The process of this acoustic signal consists in three parts:

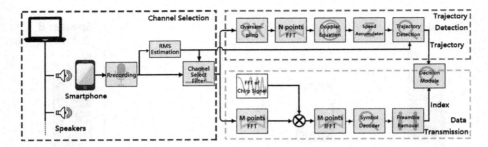

Fig. 2. An overview of AIS

Trajectory Detection. In our observation, there are three major trajectories during viewing an exhibit: approach, departure and passing. By applying short-term Fourier Transform (STFT) on the sine signal, we can get frequency shift and then speed. The integral of speed shows how relative distance changes when a mobile device moves around. Those trajectories have different tendencies on the change of relative distance and can be easily distinguished. Under this circumstance, we design an algorithm to efficiently work out trajectories in Sect 3.2.

Data Transmission. We employ chirp signal, originally used in radar applications, as our carrier for its robustness. If an approach is detected, AIS will decode the received chirp signals into a unique index. Then it will send this index to a remote server to get related information. [1] shows that chirp signal can achieve reliable long range communication ranging up to 25 m at maximum. It also shows that traditional digital modulation schemes, e.g., phase/frequency shift keying (PSK/FSK) which are used for electromagnetic wave communication, are limited in aerial acoustic communications for smart devices. We make our simple communication scheme by calculating correlation of chirp signal.

Channel Selection. In our design, adjacent speakers must be in different channel to avoid interference. Thus speakers in the same channel are separated by other speakers. By setting speakers to a proper volume, sound signals emitted by them can hardly affect each other. To select the valid channel, we use root mean square (RMS) as something like sound power. Our system works only on the channel with largest RMS. We also use RMS to determine wether it's close enough for approach trajectory. In this case, it's necessary to set a calibration procedure for different smartphones may get different RMS in the same environment.

We implement and evaluate AIS with off-the-shelf android phones and speakers. In the test, we achieve a high accuracy of 1.1% false positive and 8.9% false negative for trajectories identification.

3   Trajectory Detection

3.1   Estimating Speed Using Doppler Effect

Doppler effect (or the Doppler shift) occurs if there is a relative speed between an observer and its wave source. Since speakers keep fixed, frequency shifts are only caused by the movement of mobile device. Let F denote the frequency of the sine signal, ΔF denote the frequency shift of the received sine signal, c denote propagation speed of sound in the air, and Δv denote the relative speed between a sound source and a mobile device. Then we can get the speed of a mobile device from the following equation:

$$\Delta v = \frac{\Delta F}{F} c \tag{1}$$

A receiver calculates frequency shift by applying STFT. Let F_s and n_s denote frequency band and the amount of samples for STFT analysis. Here we introduce a conception called *velocity resolution*. Velocity resolution (Δv_{res}) represents the minimum difference between two STFT analyses that can be measured. In our solution, Δv_{res} is determined by the following equation:

$$\Delta v_{res} = \frac{F_b}{n_s F} c \tag{2}$$

According to android developer reference, a standard android smartphone's microphone supports a sampling rate up to 48 kHz. We choose a common sampling rate of 44.1 kHz for both speakers and receivers. Its Nyquist rate is 22.05 kHz which means sounds of higher frequency will not be detected. Assume n_s is 4096 and F is 20 kHz. c is about 346 m/s in dry air at 26°C. We can obtain that Δv_{res} is about 18.6 cm/s. For an adult, the average walking speed and acceleration is around 1 m/s and 1 m/s^2. The change of speed in 0.1 s is often larger than 18.6 cm/s. Thus we need to improve Δv_{res}.

It's obvious that smaller Δv_{res} gets better performance. Hence we should set the value of F and n_s as large as possible and find a narrower frequency band for STFT. Since the value of F ranges from 18 kHz to 22.05 kHz. The variance of F has less influence to Δv_{res}. Keeping a small n_s contributes to less power consumption. So we manage to decrease F_b by combining undersampling together with an overlap technique. The acoustic signals are firstly handled by a high-frequency bandpass filter to remove low frequencies noise. For a $n\times$ undersampling, one data point in every n points will be remained for further calculation. This will translate high-frequency bandpass signal to low-frequency low-pass signals without distortion in spectrum. However, $n\times$ undersampling need $n\times$ samples to achieve the same performance. We use an overlap technique to reuse previous sampling data. If n_s is 4096, a $8\times$ undersampling keeps 512 samples and one STFT analysis will handle these samples with past 3584 samples. Then the overlapping ratio is 87.5%. Figure 3 indicates that compared with directly applying Doppler equation, using undersampling can get more details on speed.

In Table 1, we list several frequency bands supported by undersampling with a sampling rate of 44.1 kHz. Among them, $7\times$ undersampling is a ideal choice for a sinesoid signal of 20 kHz. We get a Δv_{res} of 2.67 cm/s which is sufficient for our system.

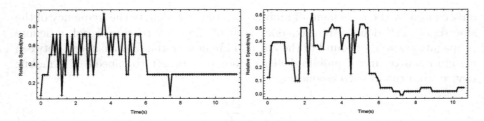

Fig. 3. Relative speed calculated by direct using Doppler equation (left) and undersampling techniques (right). It shows a user approaches to a speaker.

Table 1. Some frequency bands supported by $n\times$ undersampling for sampling rate 44.1 kHz. Inaudible frequency bands are underlined.

n	F_s^* (kHz)	Frequency band (kHz)	Δv_{res} (cm/s)
7	3.15	$12.6 \sim 15.75$, $\underline{18.9 \sim 22.05}$	2.67
8	2.76	$11.03 \sim 13.78$, $16.54 \sim 19.29$	2.33
9	2.45	$14.7 \sim 17.15$, $\underline{19.6 \sim 22.05}$	2.07
10	2.205	$13.23 \sim 15.44$, $\underline{17.64 \sim 19.85}$	1.86

3.2 Classifying Trajectories

Enlightened by Zhang's work [11], we propose three kinds of trajectories: approach, departure and passing. Figure 4 shows the three movement patterns.

In these trajectories, only approach can activate AIS to analyse chirp signals. Departure will stop the current action. Passing won't get any response. So we need to tell these three trajectories from each other. By integrating their speed, it's easy to see that the integral of approach or departure is a positive number or a negative number. The integral of passing is a small value around zero. However, the integral of absolute value of speed for passing is a large value, which distinguish it from standstill. So if the integral result is a positive or negative number and is larger than a threshold d_0, then it must be approach or departure. If its absolute value is smaller than d_0, it can be viewed as passing. We also define that a user stops walking if his moving length is smaller than a threshold d_s within t_s.

The whole classification procedure is summarized as follows: (1) At the very beginning, our system starts to calculate the current speed for every 4096 samples received, until shut down. Meanwhile, a RMS value used to measure sound power is also being estimated. (2) After every calculation, it will calculate the integral of speed d and the integral of speed's absolute value d_{abs} of the past several seconds. (3) If d keeps lower than a threshold d_s, we consider the user has stopped and begin the analysis (Abs(x) returns the absolute value of x):

- If $d > d_0$ and $RMS > r$ (threshold for RMS), AIS outputs an approach.
- If $Abs(d) > d_0$, $d < 0$ and $RMS < r$, AIS outputs an departure.
- If $Abs(d) < d_0$, $d_{abs} > d_s$ and $RMS < r$, AIS outputs an passing.

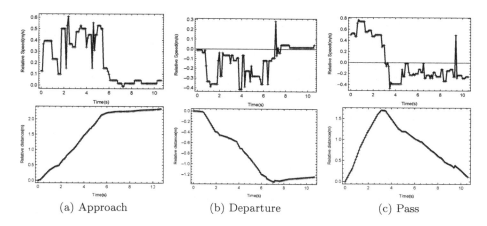

Fig. 4. Three kinds of trajectories' velocity and distance graphs.

Doppler Shift VS. Acceleration. Although we use integral in classifications, what we get is not walking length but the distance to the speaker. If we use acceleration to calculate walking distance, there will be a problem when users move like a round. Also, using acceleration cannot get the right direction, for devices may rotate or spin. In the end, we need to make twice integral to get walking length, which results in larger accumulative error.

4   Acoustic Data Transmission

For data transmission, we adopt chirp binary orthogonal keying (BOK) from [1] as our modulation scheme for aerial acoustic communication. Chirp signal is a kind of wave whose frequency varies over time. Up chirp and down chirp mean increasing and decreasing frequencies, respectively. Figure 5(a) and (b) show time-domain forms of up and down chirp. Due to unsynchronization and different sampling rate, sound signal experience both phase and frequency distortion after transmission. Thus PSK and FSK need extra cost to eliminate deviations. Chirp signal has good auto and cross correlation characteristic as show in Fig. 5(c) and (d), for the up and down chirp are nearly orthogonal. We can employ this characteristic to build our coding system.

A pair of chirp signals sweeping from f_1 to f_2 Hz are defined as:

$$s_1(t) = cos(2\pi f_1 t + \mu t^2/2 + \phi_0) \tag{3}$$

$$s_2(t) = cos(2\pi f_2 t - \mu t^2/2 + \phi_0), \quad 0 \leq t \leq T, \tag{4}$$

where ϕ_0 is an arbitrary initial phase and T is the duration time of one symbol.

The main thought of chirp BOK is taking up and down chirp signal as two different symbols in the modulation scheme. Receiver calculates correlations by convolving received signal $r(t)$ with time-reversed versions of $s_1(t)$ and $s_2(t)$ which is:

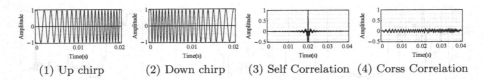

(1) Up chirp   (2) Down chirp   (3) Self Correlation (4) Corss Correlation

Fig. 5. An example of an up chirp and a down chirp, sweeping from 500 to 1500 Hz with 20 ms symbol duration.

$$c_{1,2} = \int r(\tau)s_{1,2}(T - \tau)d\tau \tag{5}$$

If $c_1 > c_2$, the receiver will take received signal as 1 otherwise 0.

Considering less computing consumption, the complexity ($O(n^2)$) of convolution is too high. This processing can be simplified by using FFT($O(n \log n)$):

$$c_{1,2} = \mathcal{F}^{-1}\{\mathcal{F}\{r(t)\}\mathcal{F}\{s_{1,2}(T - t)\}\}, \tag{6}$$

where $\mathcal{F}$ and $\mathcal{F}^{-1}$ denote FFT and inverse FFT (IFFT).

We test this scheme with an AL-931 speaker as the sender and MX5 smartphone as the receiver. The sender emit a lasting sound signal where up and down chirp signals take turns. And the receiver calculates correlation for both symbols so long as it received enough data samples. Figure 6 shows the result of our test. Red frames pick out peaks correlation values in their segment.

In our expected scenarios, a unique 16 bit index will be encoded in to chirp signals. That will take 320 ms to transmit for 20 ms a cycle. To tell the beginning of this index, we put a preamble in front of every index. This preamble is a 16 bit chirp signal with down chirp in head and tail and up chirp filling the rest.

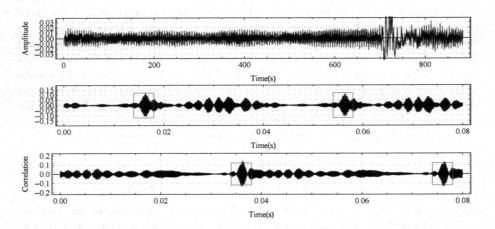

Fig. 6. Correlation calculated with original up and down chirp signals. Peaks marked by red frames represent received 1 or 0. (Color figure online)

5   Channel Selection

If we want AIS to provide a localization service, we need to set adjacent speakers into different frequency bands, namely channels, to avoid aliasing. The channel with the largest RMS value is chosen as the current working channel. To obtain RMS of a channel, we firstly handle the sound wave data with a band-pass filter to get rid of noise and other ultra sounds. Then we take a SFFT and get a set of amplitudes. These amplitudes represent the strength of sound at that frequency. We take amplitudes from the targeted channel and solve out their RMS value which represents the sound power of that channel.

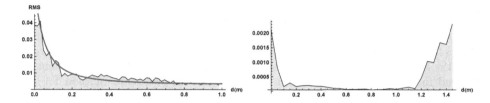

Fig. 7. Left graph shows RMS decreases along with distance. Right one shows RMS distribution between two speakers.

For adjacent speakers, they emit ultra sound in different channels. The left graph of Fig. 7 shows sound power of one channel decreases along with distance. That means closer speaker will have bigger RMS due to the attenuation of sound. For speakers in the same channel, they must be set at a farther distance. The right one in Fig. 7 shows distribution of sound power between two speakers. This indicates that speakers in the same channel can work together when keeping a proper distance.

In Sect 3.2, we define that AIS outputs departure when $Abs(d) > 0$, $d < 0$ and $RMS < r$. For multiple speakers, departure will never be found because AIS often changes channel when $RMS < r$. So we change our rules that AIS should output departure if the previous trajectory is approach when it enters a new channel. For passing, the new condition is if RMS has had a peak and channel gets changed.

6   Evaluation

In this section, we assess the performance of our system. Through several experiments, we prove the effectiveness of our proposed trajectory detection, data transmission and channel selection modules.

For each experiment, we use four kinds of commercial off-the shelf smart devices, MX5,nexus 7, HUAWEI 6p, Dozen. They all run android and support dual track microphone. We use two AL-931 speakers as our sound sources. The sampling rate of sound sender and receiver are set as 44.1 kHz.

Before the experiment, we set a calibration procedure. Due to the different frequency selectivity of microphones, the same speaker could give different RMSs for different smartphones at the same distance. In Sect. 3.2, we set a threshold r in trajectory detection. So it's necessary to calibrate this r value. Users only need to stand in front of a standard speaker for a while. AIS will take the average RMS value during the standing as r. In the same way, we can determine the value of d_0 as well and we set $d_s = d_0$.

6.1 Trajectory Detection Evaluation

We collect 30 traces from 3 subjects for each category of the trajectories. For approach, subjects stand 3 m away from the speaker, walk towards it with their normal gaits and stop in the end. For departure, subjects take the inverse action. For passing, subjects walk through the whole area without stopping. Figure 9(a) shows the result of this experiment. In general, our method achieves an accuracy of 1.1% false positive and 8.9% false negative in lab controlled environment as showed in Fig. 8 (a). We don't list the error rate of data transmission for it's nearly 0%.

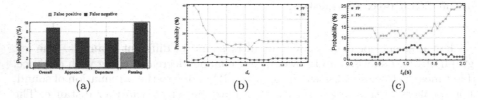

(a)   (b)   (c)

Fig. 8. (a) Result of single speaker experiment. (b) Influence of d_s on FP and FN. (c) Influence of t_s on FP and FN.

Parameters that affects the result includes d_0, r, d_s and t_s. We have confirmed d_0, d_s and r in the previous calibration. So the variety of d_s and t_s is the key to high accuracy. Figure 8(b) and (c) depict how FP and FN changes along with d_s and t_s. In Fig. 8 (b), false negative keeps high at beginning and is stabilized in the end because low d_s make less identified trajectories and high d_s allows all legal trajectories. In Fig. 8(c), false positive and false negative are both steady at first. Then false positive turns out lower and false negative get higher while t_s grows. The growth of false negative owes to large t_s which keeps most checks of trajectory out. We can see that keeping d_s not too low and t_s not too high is favorable to the final result.

6.2 Multiple Speakers Performance

To test the performance of our multiple speakers strategy, we set two AL-931 speakers at 3 m away from each other. Let's denote them as speaker A and

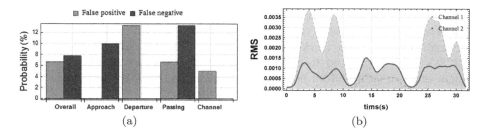

Fig. 9. (a) Result of multiple speakers experiment. (b) RMS for two channels. (Color figure online)

speaker B. Subjects firstly walk towards A and stop to read a note in front of them, simulating the scene of read pushed message on the phone. Then they leave A and walk through B to finish one test. One test includes approach, departure and passing. Each Subject repeats the test 10 times. We also collect 30 traces for each category of the trajectory. Figure 9(a) demonstrates the result for the multiple speakers experiment. The overall false positive and false negative is 6.67% and 7.78%. We can see that the false negative of departure and channel selection is both zero. This is because of the new rule that departure occurs only when channel selection happens.

Figure 9(b) shows a fraction of the variety of RMS during tracing. The sound of channel 2 emitted by speaker B has a higher frequency than channel 1. Due to the frequency selectivity of speaker B, the second blue peak is much lower than expected causing the false positive of channel selection.

7 Related Work

In-door localization system has a considerable development during a long period. Commercial off-the-shelf system for in-door localization is one of the hot points. Some scholars implement their tracking system with radio wave. Wu et al. [9] use wireless signals to estimate walking direction. mTrack [8] takes advantage of 60 Ghz milimeter wave (mmWave) radios to track the trajectory of a writing object.

Compared with wireless signal, acoustic signal has shorter wave length and is easier to be handled in mobile phones. FingerIO [5] employs the phase of a cyclic OFDM acoustic signal and sound reflection to locate the position of finger tip. In [7], the authors propose Low-Latency Acoustic Phase (LLAP) scheme which analyses the In-phase and the Quadrature components of the reflected base band signal, to get relative distance between finger tip and speaker. Their works are mainly about near-field gesture but still enlightening to us.

BeepBeep [6] measures speed through elapsed time between the two time-of-arrival (ETOA) information of acoustic signals. It also builds a tracking system with this ranging scheme. AAMouse [10] also use Doppler effect to get speed and set two speakers to achieve a two dimension tracking. High-precision Acoustic

Tracker (CAT) [3] aims to replace a traditional mouse, by developing distributed Frequency Modulated Continuous Waveform (FMCW) to achieve mm-level tracking accuracy. These tracking systems deal well within several meters. However, it's too complicated to extend their system with new speakers. For our design, one can easily add a new speaker as long as keeping a proper distance and setting the correct channel.

For acoustic transmission, Dhwani [4] is a peer-to-peer NFC-like system based on mobile phones. It works in limited range and audible sound. Our design mainly refers to [1]. It comes up with a chirp BOK modulation scheme and that scheme can deliver information at approximately 16 bps up to 25 m with 97% success rate.

8   Conclusion

This paper proposes AIS, an acoustic-based interactive system which can be easily extended with new speakers. We build a single tracker with trajectory detection and data transmission module. When cooperating with multiple speakers, AIS selects working channels by measuring the largest RMS value. Our experiments prove the exhibit factors affecting the overall result and effectiveness of our design.

References

1. Lee, H., Kim, T.H., Choi, J.W., Choi, S.: Chirp signal-based aerial acoustic communication for smart devices. In: 2015 IEEE Conference on Computer Communications (INFOCOM), pp. 2407–2415 (2015)
2. Link, J., Smith, P., Viol, N., Wehrle, K.: Footpath: accurate map-based indoor navigation using smartphones. In: 2011 International Conference on Indoor Positioning and Indoor Navigation, IPIN 2011, Guimaraes, Portugal, 21–23 September 2011, pp. 1–8 (2011). http://dx.doi.org/10.1109/IPIN.2011.6071934
3. Mao, W., He, J., Qiu, L.: CAT: high-precision acoustic motion tracking. In: Proceedings of the 22nd Annual International Conference on Mobile Computing and Networking, MobiCom 2016, New York City, NY, USA, 3–7 October 2016, pp. 69–81 (2016). http://doi.acm.org/10.1145/2973750.2973755
4. Nandakumar, R., Chintalapudi, K.K., Padmanabhan, V., Venkatesan, R.: Dhwani: secure peer-to-peer acoustic NFC. SIGCOMM Comput. Commun. Rev. 43(4), 63–74 (2013)
5. Nandakumar, R., Iyer, V., Tan, D., Gollakota, S.: Fingerio: using active sonar for fine-grained finger tracking. In: Proceedings of the 2016 CHI Conference on Human Factors in Computing Systems, San Jose, CA, USA, 7–12 May 2016, pp. 1515–1525 (2016). http://doi.acm.org/10.1145/2858036.2858580
6. Peng, C., Shen, G., Zhang, Y., Li, Y., Tan, K.: Beepbeep: a high accuracy acoustic ranging system using COTS mobile devices. In: Proceedings of the 5th International Conference on Embedded Networked Sensor Systems, SenSys 2007, Sydney, NSW, Australia, 6–9 November 2007, pp. 1–14 (2007). http://doi.acm.org/10.1145/1322263.1322265

7. Wang, W., Liu, A.X., Sun, K.: Device-free gesture tracking using acoustic signals. In: Proceedings of the 22nd Annual International Conference on Mobile Computing and Networking, MobiCom 2016, New York City, NY, USA, October 3–7, 2016, pp. 82–94 (2016). http://doi.acm.org/10.1145/2973750.2973764

8. Wei, T., Zhang, X.: mtrack: high-precision passive tracking using millimeter wave radios. In: Proceedings of the 21st Annual International Conference on Mobile Computing and Networking, MobiCom 2015, Paris, France, 7–11 September 2015, pp. 117–129 (2015). http://doi.acm.org/10.1145/2789168.2790113

9. Wu, D., Zhang, D., Xu, C., Wang, Y., Wang, H.: Widir: walking direction estimation using wireless signals. In: Proceedings of the 2016 ACM International Joint Conference on Pervasive and Ubiquitous Computing, UbiComp 2016, NY, USA, pp. 351–362 (2016). http://doi.acm.org/10.1145/2971648.2971658

10. Yun, S., Chen, Y., Qiu, L.: Turning a mobile device into a mouse in the air. In: Proceedings of the 13th Annual International Conference on Mobile Systems, Applications, and Services, MobiSys 2015, Florence, Italy, 19–22 May 2015, pp. 15–29 (2015). http://doi.acm.org/10.1145/2742647.2742662

11. Zhang, H., Du, W., Zhou, P., Li, M., Mohapatra, P.: Dopenc: acoustic-based encounter profiling using smartphones. In: Proceedings of the 22nd Annual International Conference on Mobile Computing and Networking, MobiCom 2016, NY, USA, pp. 294–307 (2016). http://doi.acm.org/10.1145/2973750.2973775

A Case Study of Usable Security: Usability Testing of Android Privacy Enhancing Keyboard

Zhen Ling[1(✉)], Melanie Borgeest[2], Chuta Sano[3], Sirong Lin[3], Mogahid Fadl[4],
Wei Yu[5], Xinwen Fu[3], and Wei Zhao[6]

[1] Southeast University, Nanjing, China
zhenling@seu.edu.cn
[2] University at Albany - SUNY, Albany, NY 12222, USA
mborgeest@albany.edu
[3] University of Massachusetts Lowell, Lowell, MA 01854, USA
Chuta_Sano@student.uml.edu, {slin,xinwenfu}@cs.uml.edu
[4] Wartburg College, Waverly, IA 50677, USA
mogahid.fadl@wartburg.edu
[5] Towson University, Towson, MD 21252, USA
wyu@towson.edu
[6] University of Macau, Macau, China
weizhao@umac.mo

Abstract. We invent a novel context aware privacy enhancing keyboard
(PEK) for touch-enabled devices to keep users safe from various password inference attacks. When a user inputs normal text like an email or
a message, PEK shows a normal QWERTY keyboard. However, every
time a user of a touch-enabled device presses a password input box on
the screen, we will randomly shuffle the positions of the characters on
the keyboard and show this randomized keyboard to the user. PEK was
released on the Google Play in 2014, but the number of installations is
below our expectation now. For the purpose of usable security and privacy, we design a two-stage usability test and perform extensive experiments to evaluate the user experience of PEK and discover the reason
behind the lukewarmness of using PEK. We implement two new features
so as to improve PEK based on the feedback of usability tests.

Keywords: Usability testing · Android · Keyboard · Privacy · Touch
screen · PEK

1 Introduction

Touch-screen enabled devices have become a burgeoning attack target. Many
attacks target sensitive information such as passwords entered on mobile devices
by exploiting the soft keyboard. In residue-based attacks [1,10,20,22], oily or
heat residues left on the touch screen indicate which keys are tapped. By measuring the heat residue left on the touched positions, even the order of tapped
keys may be determined. In computer vision-based attacks [3–5,8,16,18,19],

© Springer International Publishing AG 2017
L. Ma et al. (Eds.): WASA 2017, LNCS 10251, pp. 716–728, 2017.
DOI: 10.1007/978-3-319-60033-8_61

the interaction between the hand and the keyboard is exploited. For example, the hand movement and finger position indicates which keys are being touched [7,18,19,21]. In sensor-based attacks [2,6,9,12,13,15,17], the malware senses a device's motion difference via its accelerometer (acceleration) and gyroscope (orientation) when different keys are touched and the device moves slightly.

To fight against these attacks listed above, we invent a novel context aware privacy enhancing keyboard (PEK) for touch-enabled device. The attacks introduced above can work because the keyboard keys are always at the same position. With PEK, every time a user of a touch-enabled device presses a password input box on the screen, we will randomly shuffle the positions of the characters on the keyboard and show this randomized keyboard to the user. That is, the user can derive a randomly shuffled keyboard every time while tapping their passwords on the screen. We maintain PEK's usability through its context aware feature: a randomized keyboard only shows up when a user inputs a password or pin. When a user inputs normal text like an email or a message, PEK shows a normal QWERTY keyboard or a system default keyboard. **We are the first to design a generic randomized keyboard for Android** while the idea of randomizing the key layout was proposed before for other applications with dedicated keypads [14]. PEK can be chosen as the default keyboard for Android so that it can be used for any app.

We released PEK as a free Android app to Google Play in August 2014 after our presentation at Black Hat USA [19]. It has been downloaded 2352 times at the time of writing. We released 7 versions of PEK, correcting bugs and improving the interface. PEK 1.0 is based on an Android code example. PEK 2.x.x is based on OpenWnn [11] although we fixed bugs and adapted it to later versions of Android. The current version of PEK is 3.1.0.0.

Since the number of PEK installations is below our expectation, for the purpose of usable security and privacy, we designed a two-stage usability test to evaluate the user experience of PEK and find out the reason behind the lukewarmness of using PEK. The first usability test was a pilot usability test. A major finding from the pilot test is the complicated installation and configuration processes discourage users from using PEK although installation and configuration instructions are given. We then performed the main usability test including a web survey and a focus group usability test. The web survey used Amazon Mechanical Turk. A major finding from the web survey and focus group study is that more people show interest in using PEK if a randomness toggle button is provided. With the button, users may enable or disable the random keyboard on the fly. Based on the usability test, we implemented a PEK app that allows a user to configure and enable PEK through an app on the launcher screen. We also add a randomness toggle button to the randomized keyboard.

The rest of this paper is organized as follows. We introduce the design and implementation of the third party keyboard of PEK in Sect. 2. The methodology of the usability test is presented in Sect. 3. The results of the usability test are given in Sect. 4. We conclude this paper in Sect. 5.

2   Privacy Enhancing Keyboard

In this section, we present the basic idea of the privacy enhancing keyboard. Given the limited space allowed in the paper, we do not include the technique details of PEK implementation. An extended version of technical report is available on demand.

To mitigate various attacks including residue-based attacks, computer vision-based attacks, and sensor-based attacks, we randomly shuffle the positions of keys of a software keyboard on a touch screen in order to show the user a randomized keyboard each time they input a password. As a result, profiles for particular keys cannot be established via vibration or orientation information through an accelerometer. Finger oily or thermal residue left on the screen does not imply particular keys. Vision based attacks also fail since a touched position by a finger does not refer to a fixed key.

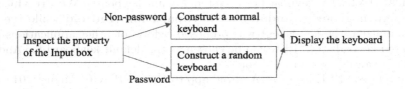

Fig. 1. Workflow of PEK constructing a keyboard

Figure 1 shows the basic idea and the workflow of PEK constructing a keyboard when a user touches an input box. First, we inspect the property of the input box to determine whether or not the input box is a password input box. If the input box is a password input box, we parse the property of the keys from a XML file that stores the layout of the keyboard, and change the label and value of the keys so as to shuffle the positions of the keys. If the input box is not a password input box, a QWERTY keyboard is shown.

We implemented two versions of PEK. One version is a third party keyboard implemented through an Android service that runs in the background. A third party keyboard is installed in the format of an Android app. A user has to find the system input setting menu in her phone in order to enable PEK. However, the location of the input setting menu is different in distinct phones. Before PEK 3.0, we provided a generic introduction to the input setting process and pretty much count on users to find the input setting menu. A note is we are also able to revise the source code of the Android system default keyboard and recompile it with the entire Android project. Apparently such a strategy implementing PEK is not practical for users. The second version of PEK is a 10-digit keypad for the unlock screen. To implement the randomized keypad, we have to revise the Android system source code, override the method "createKeyFromXml()" in the code file "PasswordEntryKeyboard.java" and recompile the entire Android project. Since a user has the option of choosing a conventional keyboard for the unlock screen and recompilation of the entire Android project is not feasible for broad adoption, our usability study below focuses on the PEK - a third party keyboard and the term PEK refers to the third party keyboard particularly.

3   Usability Testing Methodology

In this section, we present our two-stage usability study of PEK: the pilot study and the main study, which are similar although the main study involves more participants, questions, and other measurements. In a usability study, in general there are not too many participants in the interview and focus group study. However, face-to-face interaction with participants provides us lots of detailed information/insights about users' view to our research questions. A web survey engages more subjects and produces quantitative and statistic results. That's the main difference between qualitative research (e.g., interview, focus group) and quantitative research methods. We used multiple methods to gather users' information from different perspectives.

3.1   Pilot Usability Test

There are two sessions in the pilot usability test that forms and improves the main usability test conducted after the completion of the pilot usability test. The first session is composed of a pre-survey with 10 questions, an interview with 5 open ended questions, and a post survey with 4 questions. Both the pre-survey and post-survey have multiple-choice questions so that the answers are easily interpreted and classified. Two to three days after the first one, the second session is conducted and includes an interview with 10 open ended questions. The interview involves recording the participants' answers and there is a portion of the interview, which was timed to see how long participants took to install and configure PEK. Three major issues are addressed during the pilot test.

- *PQ1:* After the release of PEK, there are some complaints on the Google Play Store page for PEK that specified that the configuration process was difficult. Hence, we want to find out the answers to the following questions. How easily can smart device users install and configure PEK onto their smart devices? Does the installation and configuration process discourage users from using PEK?
- *PQ2:* Perhaps the underlying reason why smart device users are not broadly employing PEK is simply because they are not interested in protecting their information and/or they are uneducated about security on their smart devices. Therefore, we ask: are smart device users in general concerned with the security on their phones?
- *PQ3:* When PEK is enabled and the user selects a password input box, the keyboard is randomized, therefore, it takes users longer to find the characters compared to when using a regular QWERTY keyboard. Do users think the extra input time needed when using PEK is worth protecting their passwords and/or pins?

3.2   Main Usability Test

The main usability test consists of a web survey and a focus group usability test based upon the findings in the pilot usability test. The web survey is hosted on the Qualtrics platform on Amazon Mechanical Turk and does not require any tasks from participants except completing the survey. Each participant is compensated a dollar for following directions and answering the survey honestly and correctly. The focus group usability test involves an interview. The participants are asked to install and configure PEK on their own devices and answer several questions. Four major issues are addressed during the main test.

- *MQ1:* What are the most frequent activities performed by smart device users on their personal devices? If the results showed one of the most frequent activities performed by smart device users involved sensitive information, they could be apart of PEK's target audience.
- *MQ2:* Do smart device users utilize any default security precautions already provided on their smart devices? This question relates to the one from the pilot usability test and whether or not typical smart device users are concerned with the security measures on their personal devices.
- *MQ3:* Do users consider that their smart devices are properly protected from outsider attacks?
- *MQ4:* Would smart device users consider implementing more security measures on their devices?

4   Usability Testing Results and Interpretation

This section presents results from the pilot usability test and main usability test performed between May and July 2016.

4.1   Answers for Pilot Usability Test

In the pilot usability test, there are 2 male participants who have Android mobile smart phones. During the interview, participants have to install and configure PEK on their own devices. They are timed for how long it takes them to successfully configure PEK and for the randomized keyboard to show up successfully when they try to input a password and/or pin.

Answers to Question PQ1: Users are able to find PEK on Google Play and install PEK without difficulty. However, when it comes to configuring PEK, some issues arise. Table 1 illustrates the time of installation and configuration during the pilot usability test. The configuration time is obviously longer. Along with the longer times, we note that both participants are not able to configure PEK by themselves; both of them need additional instructions from the researcher to configure the application. The participants **look for a PEK application icon** on their devices but find none. When they try to login to one of their accounts, such as an email, they are confused when the randomized keyboard does not show up when they hit a password field. The participants are frustrated during

Table 1. Installation and configuration time of PEK

Participants	Installation time (seconds)	Configuration time (seconds)
Participant 1	29.01	45.79
Participant 2	15.00	125.00

the configuration process. If the researcher does not aid them during the process, both of the participants most likely would have given up trying to configure PEK.

Answers to Question PQ2: Both participants admit that they would not use PEK on a regular basis on their own personal devices. Neither participant has information on their personal device that they consider sensitive. Nor do either of them have any other security enhancements enabled on their smart devices. The only security precaution Participant 1 admits undertaking is not using applications or services that request important data or sensitive data on their mobile phone; they prefer doing those types of activities in their home on their laptop or on their desktop. However both participants acknowledge that they might not be apart of PEK's target audience since both of them considered themselves educated about mobile security and how to prevent related attacks.

Answers to Question PQ3: Participant 1 during the second session after two to three days, does not consider the tradeoff between his time spent entering, for example, his pin to open his phone, worth protecting whatever personal information that is contained on his mobile phone. Participant 1 predicts that a user could never get better at entering a password and/or pin using PEK since the keyboard is randomized each time and no key is in the same place. Unlike a regular QWERTY keyboard, which a user can memorize and use easily, PEK cannot be learned. It is also challenging to multi-task when using PEK. For instance, if a user is on the move and trying to login to their phone, it is more difficult to login when using PEK than a regular QWERTY keyboard. Another difficulty that Participant 1 encounters is their mobile phone go to asleep when they attempt to enter their password using PEK to unlock their phone and the user has to enter their password all over again; this leaves Participant 1 frustrated at his time lost by using PEK. Unlike Participant 1, Participant 2 reckons his time lost by entering passwords using PEK is worth protecting the information stored on his mobile phone. Participant 2 compares PEK to someone using their hand to cover their screen while inputting their password with their other hand; except that PEK is more practical and dependable than a user's hand covering their screen.

Two observations can be made from the pilot usability test.

1. The configuration of PEK is difficult for both participants during the pilot usability test. Neither could complete configuration without aid. To remedy this, it is desirable to have more instructions on the Google Play Store to assist users and an icon for users to open when PEK is installed. Both the

participants look for a PEK icon on their mobile phone's interface when the application finishes downloading, however, PEK does not have an icon.
2. Participant 1 mentions difficulty using PEK when attempting to access their mobile phone quickly and while multitasking. We decide to create a separate button on the privacy-enhanced keyboard to allow the user to easily disable PEK. Thus, if a user needs to quickly unlock their mobile phone, they are able to disable PEK to enter their password and/or pin and avoid the extra input time needed to use PEK. It is preferred that PEK is the default keyboard when a user clicks on a password field. Then, if the user wants to use the regular QWERTY keyboard, they can easily hit a button on the privacy-enhanced keyboard to disable it and use the QWERTY keyboard instead.

4.2   Main Usability Test - Web Survey

The main usability test has 2 participants in the focus group usability test and 266 participants, including 132 females and 134 males, in the web survey. The ages of the participants range from 18 years old to above the age of 50. 136 participants use Android devices, which PEK is compatible with, and 123 participants use Apple devices. The other 7 participants choose the "Other, please specify" option during the web survey. We have 21 questions and obtain 266 responses. There is a combination of multiple choice questions and open-ended questions.

Answers to Question MQ1: The purpose behind this research question is to find out whether any of the most frequent activities performed by mobile smart device users involve users' personal information that may be considered sensitive. Smart device users that do bank mobilely, shop online, and/or social network may enter sensitive personal information that could be susceptible to being stolen. Figure 2 shows statistics from the web survey. Internet use is the top answer at 8.0%. Comparably, 5.4% of the web survey takers shop online, 5.7% bank mobilely, and 7.1% use social networking sites. Any of these actions could result in personal information being leaked and an account being hacked. The web survey takers that do perform any of the actions we listed above could be apart of PEK's target audience if they are interested in protecting their information that bank applications or online shopping applications require to use.

Answers to Question MQ2: If smart device users do not implement other security precautions that are already provided on their mobile devices, it is likely they would not utilize PEK. The amount of smart device users who employ other security precautions on their mobile smart devices was not significant. However, this may be a result of most smart device users being unaware of potential attacks that can be performed on their smart devices. Figure 3 shows the distribution of security precautions that the web survey takers implement on their own personal mobile smart devices. At 20.55%, automatic screen lock after a certain amount of time was the top answer amongst web survey takers. The results of these particular questions lead to more questions about smart device users. Are smart device users generally unconcerned with security or are

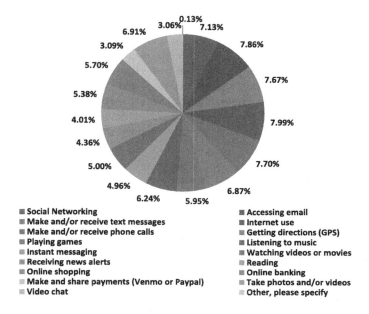

Fig. 2. Answers to question MQ1

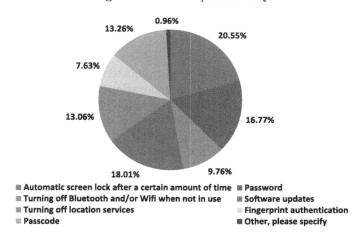

Fig. 3. Distribution of security precautions

they just uninformed about the lack of security on their mobile devices and the potentiality of malicious attacks?

The question is purposefully worded to discover the opinions of the web survey takers and whether they consider their own personal smart devices properly protected against outsider attacks. This can further lead us to determine whether smart device users are simply uneducated about attacks to their devices or they just are not concerned with security. The answers to this question varied by the degree to which the web survey takers were concerned with security. The top answer was "Probably yes" at 36.59%, followed by "Maybe" at 29.27%, then "Probably not" at 20.05%. How users rate the degree of protection on their personal mobile devices may differ a lot from how they are actually protected. The high level of certainty the web survey takers display about their smart devices being protected is a little worrisome. Every smart device user should feel doubt when it comes to how well protected their smart devices are. Figure 4 portrays the distribution of answers web survey takers chose when asked this question.

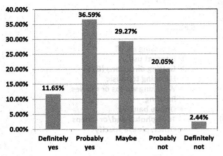 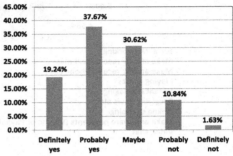

Fig. 4. Distribution of answers to question MQ3

Fig. 5. Distribution of answers to question MQ4

Answers to Question MQ4: Surprisingly, depicted in the web survey results, users are willing to consider implementing more security features to their mobile smart devices. Although this differs from users actually implementing more security features, it is a start. Figure 5 illustrates the distribution of the answers resulting from the web survey; 37.67% of the web survey takers answered "Probably yes", followed by 30.62% of survey takers answering "Maybe", then 10.84% of the survey takers said "Definitely yes". This portion of web survey takers could be potential users of PEK as long as the user experience and promise of security is ensured.

4.3   Main Usability Test - Focus Group Usability Test

Apart from the web survey, a focus group usability test is conducted with 2 participants. This test is a recorded interview with 19 questions, all open ended. There is one session and both participants were interviewed at the same time. Similar questions are asked during this group usability test as during the web survey. Both the participants use mobile Android smart phones.

(a) *What three activities do you primarily do on your mobile phone?* Participant A lists using the alarm, reading the news and listening to music as the activities they perform the most on their Android smart phone. Participant B says sending/receiving texts, taking photos and using social network applications as their top three activities they perform on their mobile smart device. Participant A most likely would not have a use for PEK. Participant B may be a more likely candidate for PEK and have more use for it than Participant A. However, neither lists any activities that were prominently chosen by the web survey takers on the web survey.

(b) *What kind of security have you implemented on your mobile phone?* Both Participant A and Participant B have the same exact answer for this question, "Nope." Neither has any default security installed on their mobile phones.

(c) *Are you satisfied with the level of security on your mobile phone?* Again, both Participant A and Participant B have the same answer for this question, a simple "Yes."

(d) *Would you ever consider adding more security features to your mobile phone?* Surprisingly both participants are somewhat open to considering implementing more security features to their mobile phones. Perhaps it is out of pure laziness that they do not have any security installed on their mobile devices, or they are sure to not perform any actions that require sensitive data on their mobile phones.

(e) *At this point during the interview we have both participants install and configure PEK.*

(f) *Would you recommend this application to a friend?* Participant A says yes they would recommend it to a friend who is concerned with security and who might be in public a lot. Participant B says as well that they would recommend PEK to a friend if and when a friend asks them about adding more security to their mobile phone.

(g) *Do either of you have any suggestions about improving the application?* Participant B's first impression of PEK is, "It can be used, but I will not use it." Participant A complains about the keys on PEK, how the larger popup disappears too quickly. For example, when you hit the key "U" on PEK, a popup will emerge from the key "U" and display a larger version of the letter, and that is for any letter when typing on PEK. Participant A recommends getting rid of this feature since he considers it annoying.

4.4   Improvements in PEK 3.x

In the pilot usability test, we learn that both two participants take long time to configure PEK, since they cannot find the PEK icon on their smartphones. To mitigate this problem, we put an icon of the PEK on the Android home screen as shown in Fig. 6. A user can tap the icon and configure the settings of PEK as shown in Fig. 7. Then, the user can click the "Open Android Input Settings" and set PEK as a keyboard available for users.

In addition, the participants suggest creating a new button for turning on/off the randomization of the PEK. Because PEK cannot be learned and it is inconvenient to use PEK in some circumstances. To this end, we implementa random toggle button on the PEK as shown in Fig. 8. Then, users can decide to save time using a regular keyboard to input the password or protect their password using PEK.

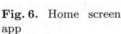

Fig. 6. Home screen app

Fig. 7. PEK setting

Fig. 8. Toggle button

5   Conclusion

This paper conducts a full-scale usability testing of a generic Android privacy enhancing keyboard (PEK) that can prevent various attacks against touch-enabled devices from inferring user pins or passwords. We perform both the pilot usability test and main usability test in order to identify how to improve PEK for broad adoption. Based on the results of the usability study, we implement two new features in PEK 3.x, a home screen app to easily activate PEK and a toggle button to enable/disable randomness of PEK. The usability test also demonstrates the worrisome phenomena that many users blindly trust their phones for security or are not concerned with the possible breaches. This phenomena demonstrates the human factor that contributes to the vulnerabilities of the cyber space. For future work, we plan to continue to improve PEK and perform another round of usability test in order to find out if the improved PEK attracts more adoption and better rating.

Acknowledgments. This work was supported in part by National Natural Science Foundation of China under grants 61502100, 61532013, 61402104, 61572130, 61602111, 61632008, and 61320106007, by US NSF grants 1461060, 1642124, 1547428, and CNS 1350145, by University System of Maryland Fund, by Jiangsu Provincial Natural Science Foundation of China under grants BK20150637 and BK20140648, by Jiangsu

Provincial Key Technology R&D Program under grants BE2014603, by Jiangsu Provincial Key Laboratory of Network and Information Security under grants BM2003201, by Key Laboratory of Computer Network and Information Integration of Ministry of Education of China under grants 93K-9 and by Collaborative Innovation Center of Novel Software Technology and Industrialization. Any opinions, findings, conclusions, and recommendations in this paper are those of the authors and do not necessarily reflect the views of the funding agencies.

References

1. Aviv, A.J., Gibson, K., Mossop, E., Blaze, M., Smith, J.M.: Smudge attacks on smartphone touch screens. In: Proceedings of Workshop on Offensive Technology WOOT (2010)
2. Aviv, A.J., Sapp, B., Blaze, M., Smith, J.M.: Practicality of accelerometer side channels on smartphones. In: Proceedings of the 28th Annual Computer Security Applications Conference (ACSAC) (2012)
3. Backes, M., Chen, T., D1rmuth, M., Lensch, H.P.A., Welk, M.: Tempest in a teapot: compromising reflections revisited. In: Proceedings of the 30th IEEE Symposium on Security and Privacy (S&P) (2009)
4. Backes, M., Duermuth, M., Unruh, D.: Compromising reflections - or - how to read LCD monitors around the corner. In: Proceedings of the 29th IEEE Symposium on Security and Privacy (S&P) (2008)
5. Balzarotti, D., Cova, M., Vigna, G.: Clearshot: eavesdropping on keyboard input from video. In: Proceedings of the 29th IEEE Symposium on Security and Privacy (S&P) (2008)
6. Cai, L., Chen, H.: TouchLogger: inferring keystrokes on touch screen from smartphone motion. In: Proceedings of the 6th USENIX Workshop on Hot Topics in Security (HotSec) (2011)
7. Cai, Z., He, Z., Guan, X., Li, Y.: Collective data-sanitization for preventing sensitive information inference attacks in social networks. IEEE Trans. Dependable Secur. Comput. (2016)
8. Maggi, F., Volpatto, A., Gasparini, S., Boracchi, G., Zanero, S.: A fast eavesdropping attack against touchscreens. In: Proceedings of the 7th International Conference Information Assurance and Security (IAS) (2011)
9. Miluzzoy, E., Varshavskyy, A., Balakrishnany, S., Choudhury, R.R.: Tapprints: your finger taps have fingerprints. In: Proceedings of the 10th International Conference on Mobile Systems, Applications, and Services (MobiSys) (2012)
10. Mowery, K., Meiklejohn, S., Savage, S.: Heat of the moment: characterizing the efficacy of thermal camera-based attacks. In: Proceedings of Workshop on Offensive Technologies (WOOT) (2011)
11. OMRON SOFTWARE Co., Ltd., Openwnn (2012). https://sourceforge.net/u/lluct/me722-cm/ci/890e9a90d9a7fe5f0243b9392eaa787d1381e987/tree/packages/inputmethods/OpenWnn/
12. Owusu, E., Han, J., Das, S., Perrig, A., Zhang, J.: ACCessory: keystroke inference using accelerometers on smartphones. In: Proceedings of the Thirteenth Workshop on Mobile Computing Systems and Applications (HotMobile). ACM, February 2012
13. Ping, D., Sun, X., Mao, B.: Textlogger: inferring longer inputs on touch screen using motion sensors. In: Proceedings of the 7th ACM Conference on Security and Privacy in Wireless and Mobile Networks (WiSec) (2015)

14. Shin, H.-S.: Device and method for inputting password using random keypad. United States Patent No. 7, 698, 563 (2010)
15. Simon, L., Anderson, R.: Pin skimmer: inferring pins through the camera and microphone. In: Proceedings of the 4th ACM Workshop on Security and Privacy in Smartphones and Mobile Devices (SPSM) (2013)
16. Sun, J., Jin, X., Chen, Y., Zhang, J., Zhang, R., Zhang, Y.: VISIBLE: video-assisted keystroke inference from tablet backside motion. In: Proceedings of the 23rd ISOC Network and Distributed System Security Symposium (NDSS) (2016)
17. Xu, Z., Bai, K., Zhu, S.: Taplogger: inferring user inputs on smartphone touch-screens using on-board motion sensors. In: Proceedings of The ACM Conference on Wireless Network Security (WiSec) (2012)
18. Yue, Q., Ling, Z., Fu, X., Liu, B., Ren, K., Zhao, W.: Blind recognition of touched keys on mobile devices. In: Proceedings of the 21st ACM Conference on Computer and Communications Security (CCS) (2014)
19. Yue, Q., Ling, Z., Fu, X., Liu, B., Yu, W., Zhao, W.: My google glass sees your passwords! In: Proceedings of the Black Hat USA (2014)
20. Zalewski, M.: Cracking safes with thermal imaging (2005). http://lcamtuf.coredump.cx/tsafe/
21. Zhang, L., Cai, Z., Wang, X.: Fakemask: a novel privacy preserving approach for smartphones. IEEE Trans. Netw. Serv. Manag. 13(2), 335–348 (2016)
22. Zhang, Y., Xia, P., Luo, J., Ling, Z., Liu, B., Fu, X.: Fingerprint attack against touch-enabled devices. In: Proceedings of the 2nd Workshop on Security and Privacy in Smartphones and Mobile Devices (SPSM) (2012)

Detecting Flooding DDoS Under Flash Crowds Based on Mondrian Forest

Degang Sun, Kun Yang, Zhixin Shi$^{(\boxtimes)}$, and Yan Wang

Institute of Information Engineering, Chinese Academy of Sciences, Beijing, China
shizhixin@iie.ac.cn

Abstract. Flooding Distributed Denial of Service (DDoS) attacks could cause huge damages to Internet, which has much similarity with Flash Crowds (FC). Traditional Machine learning methods usually have a better performance for offline processing, however, they cannot process huge volume data which cannot be loaded in memory at one time and can't auto-update model in time. In this paper, a streaming detection mechanism based on Online Random Forest-Mondrian Forest is proposed to solve this problem. Firstly, a deep analysis has been done on client's characteristics of DDoS and FC to find anomaly traffic behaviors in network layer. Based on the analysis, a new feature set has been concluded to describe the client behavior of DDoS and FC. Then a streaming detecting mechanism employed with online Random Forest based on the new feature set has been proposed. To evaluate this method, a comparison with the traditional offline batch process method-Random Forest has been done on two public real-world datasets. The results show that even though this method has a bit lower accuracy around 93% on Test Data, it can be trained like a streaming way which doesn't need load all data in memory at one time and can update itself automatically with time, which is more applicable for Big Data situations.

Keywords: Flooding DDoS · Flash crowds · Real-time Detection · Online random forest · User behavior analysis

1 Introduction

Flooding Distributed Denial of Service (DDoS) attacks have been wreaking havoc on Internet and show no signs of fading [1]. Especially, it simulates the normal users and hidden under Flash Crowds (FC) [2], which has much similarity with Flooding DDoS, such as server status, network status and traffic status [3], they always lead to existing defending systems helplessness. To avoid the confusion of concept, this paper uses FC to represent Flash Crowds, Flash Events, and uses DDoS to represent Flooding DDoS Attacks entirely.

Considerable literatures have been published on detecting and defending DDoS. However, there are few literatures on discriminating DDoS and FC. The existing Machine Learning Methods are mainly used on offline situations but there are still some defects, such as: incapable to be used in huge volume data

© Springer International Publishing AG 2017
L. Ma et al. (Eds.): WASA 2017, LNCS 10251, pp. 729–740, 2017.
DOI: 10.1007/978-3-319-60033-8_62

and incapable of increment learning. The significant characteristic of DDoS and FC is the production of huge traffic burst in a sudden time, but the traditional Machine Learning Methods need the loading of all data into memory at one time and need repeated learning, which lead to the high complexity of computation and cannot be used in huge volume traffic. Motivated to guard against this case, we propose an online streaming detection mechanism based on behavior analysis to discriminate DDoS and FC.

Major contributions of this paper are summarized as below:

(1) Conclusion of a new feature sets after analyzing the behavior of Bots in DDoS and legitimate users in FC, which can be used to profile the behavior of each Bot or legitimate client.
(2) Design of a streaming detection mechanism employed with online Random Forest based on the new feature set, which not only discriminate DDoS and FC, but also auto-update itself without manual intervention.

The paper has been structured as follows: Sect. 2 reviews current available literatures. Section 3 shows the conclusion of a new feature set with explanation of our idea in details. Section 4 shows the experiments to evaluate the new features and our proposed idea, with comparison to the traditional methods and the summary of the result. Section 5 is the conclusion of our work.

2   Related Work

According to our understanding of the field, we simply divide the existing methods to two categories: Turing Test and Anomaly Behavior Analysis.

Turing Test: DDoS are usually launched by Botnets while FC derive from legitimate clients, consequently, the problem of differentiating DDoS attacks and FC can be translated into how to identify the client is one human or a Bot. According to the client's responses, then distinguish the client is a normal user or not [4], that are Turing Test, which are the main and pervasive methods for distinguishing DDoS and FC. The common Turing test are graphical puzzles, which display a slightly blurred or distorted picture or some puzzle and ask the user to type in the depicted symbols. This task is easy for humans, yet very hard for computers. CAPTCHAs (Completely Automated Public Turing test to tell Computers and Humans Apart) [4] and AYAHs (Are You A Human) [5] are the most commonly used methods.

Anomaly Behavior Analysis: Generally speaking, an inappropriate and exaggerated image of hackers existed usually, which are extremely smart and can easily compromise and control lots of computers. Nevertheless, it is simply not true, due to many factors constraining the number of active Bots hackers can be used to launch attacks simultaneously, such as widely used anti-virus software, software patching, or power off of host computers [6]. Rajab et al. [7] discovered that the number of active Bots launched attacks simultaneously is usually at the hundreds or a few thousands level. Jung et al. [2] firstly concluded few characteristics used for discriminating DDoS and FC after analyzing various FC traces.

Xie and Yu [8] proposed a novel method to detect anomaly events based on the hidden Markov model. But the input parameters are difficult to achieve through training. Theerasak et al. [9] proposed a discriminating method based on the packet arrival patterns. Pearson's correlation coefficient was used to measure the packet patterns. However, defining the packet pattern are difficult. Bhatia et al. [10] proposed a technique combine the analysis of both network traffic features and server load characteristics to distinguish DDoS and FC. However, the computational complexity is very higher. Yu et al. [6] employed flow similarities to discriminate DDoS and FC and achieved a better effect. The author mainly used fixed thresholds needed craft design and professional field knowledge, so this would be little deficiencies. Saravanan et al. [11] combined multi-parameters with weights to discriminate DDoS and FC, but those weights were fixed and could not be updated automatically. Somani et al. [12] surveyed new environments for DDoS.

Online Machine Learning [13] is a common technique used in areas of machine learning where it is computationally infeasible to train over the entire dataset, requiring the need of out-of-core algorithms. It is also used in situations where it is necessary for the algorithm to dynamically adapt to new patterns in the data, or when the data itself is generated as a function of time, e.g. stock price prediction, commerce and social networking industry.

Online Random Forest is a popular online machine learning method due in part to their accuracy, scalability, and robustness in real-world classification tasks [14]. Existing online random forests (ORF-Saffari [14] and ORF-Denil [15]) start with an empty tree and grow the tree incrementally. Existing online random forests, however, require more training data than their batch counterpart to achieve comparable predictive performance.

As far as we kown, Turing Test are the most pervasive and promising methods to distinguish DDoS and FC. However, with the rapid development of Reverse Turing Test, which means Turing Test will not completely defend DDoS and distinguish DDoS and FC any more. On the other hand, existing anomaly analysis are too sensitive to detection thresholds needed to be elaborately designed, moreover the selfadaption and automaticity of those methods usually are not very well. To guard against this case, in this work, we propose an online detection mechanism employed online Random Forest to solve the problem.

3   Proposed Method

In this paper, we describe network traffic as a form like Fig. 1, x-axis represents time interval ($\Delta t_j, j = 1, 2, ...$), while y-axis represents the packet size ($p_i, i = 1, 2, ...$) sent by each client. ($\delta t_k, k = 1, 2, ...$) represents the packets arrival time between two packets sent by each client. In each interval Δt_j, it may contain DDoS and FC at the same time, or it contains one traffic type-DDoS or FC.

Due to DDoS mainly rely on Botnets and Bots are controlled by preprogramed codes, it leads the packets arrival time between two packets (δt_k) sent by each Bot will be unchanged too much and the packet size (p_i) follows the

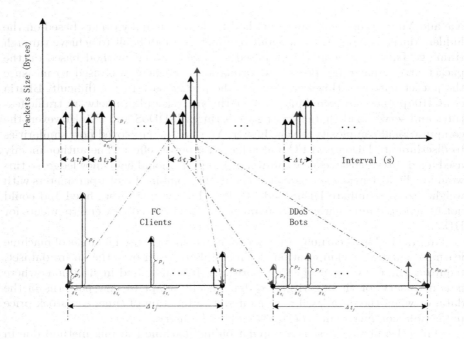

Fig. 1. The characteristics of DDoS and FC.

same pattern, it also has a stable packet size, while those patterns are totally different to FC caused by legitimate users, which sent packets are random, so the δt_i and p_i are changeable. On the other hand, in order to attain expected effect, Bots have to send packets as many as they can. So a few traffic anomalies have been caused, which plays a major role in distinguishing DDoS and FC. In order to represent the behavior of each Bot or client, we proposed a concept called Behavior Vector, which is made up of clients characteristics, such as packets size, packet arrival time difference, and label the behavior class: normal or abnormal, according to the priori knowledge, which is used to profile user behavior. Behavior Vector can be represented as follows:

$$BehaviorVector = (TS, srcIP, dstIP, nPkts, uPktsSize, stdPktsSize,$$
$$uArrivalTime, stdArrivalTime, behaviorClass)$$

In which, the first three features are used to locate the attack time and the Bot attended in the attack, the latter five features and one class label are truly used as input for our idea.

The notations used in this paper can be seen detailedly in Table 1.

Based on the Behavior features, in this paper, we design a streaming detection mechanism employed with online Random Forest-Mondrian Forest (MF) [16]. The algorithm can be seen in Algorithm 1. Along with time, the detection model keep training on the arrival traffic data, and auto-update itself constantly to

Table 1. Notations

Δt: An interval, which is the smallest processing unit to calculate features for behavior vector
ΔT: An online process interval, which is the batch size in online processing phase
TS: The accurate time
$srcIP$: Source IP
$dstIP$: Destination IP
$nPkts$: The number of sent packets by each IP or client in each interval-Δt
$uPktsSize$: The average packet size sent by each source IP in each interval-Δt
$stdPktsSize$: The standard deviation of packet size sent by each source IP In each interval-Δt
$uArrivalTime$: The average packet arrival time difference of sent packets by each source IP in each interval-Δt
$stdArrivalTime$: The standard deviation of packet arrival time difference of sent packets by each source IP in each interval-Δt
$behaviorClass$: The class of behavior vector-DDoS_Flow or FC_Flow

make a better performance. The auto-update process can be seen in Fig. 2. At the begining, in Δt_1, we achieve the $Model\_1$, and when Δt_2 arrived, the $Model_1$ will updated itself, then we get $Model_2$, and the $Model_i$ will updated itself constantly with time.

MF is a novel class of Online Random Forests [14], which can be trained incrementally in an efficient manner [16]. Balaji et al. [16] proved that MF significantly outperforms existing online random forests interms of training time as well as number of training instances required to achieve a particular test accuracy. And MF achieves competitive test accuracy to batch random forests trained on the same fraction of the data. The authors also show that the computational complexity of MF is linear in the number of dimensions (since rectangles are represented explicitly) which could be expensive for high dimensional data.

In this paper, we continue to use the denfinition and notions of Mondrian Forest proposed by the authors [16]. A Mondrian forest classifier is constructed much like a random forest: Given training data $D_{1:N}$, sample an independent collection $T_1, T_2, ..., T_M$ of so-called Mondrian trees. The authors gave the definition of the prediction made by each Mondrian tree T_m, which is a distribution $p_{T_m}(y|x, D_{1:N})$ over the class label y for a test point x. So the Mondrian Forest's prediction is the average $\frac{1}{M}\Sigma_{m=1}^m p_{T_m}(y|x, D_{1:N})$ of the individual tree predictions.

Balaji et al. also listed the online learning process, the training examples are presented one after another in a sequence of trials, while Mondrian forests excel in this setting: at iteration $N + 1$, each Mondrian tree $T \sim MT(\lambda, D_{1:N})$ is updated to incorporate the next labeled example (x_{N+1}, y_{N+1}) by sampling an extended tree T' from a distribution $MT_x(\lambda, T, D_{N+1})$. Using properties of the Mondrian process, we can choose a probability distribution MTx such that $T' = T$ on $D_{1:N}$ and T' is distributed according to $MT(\lambda, T, D_{N+1})$, i.e.,

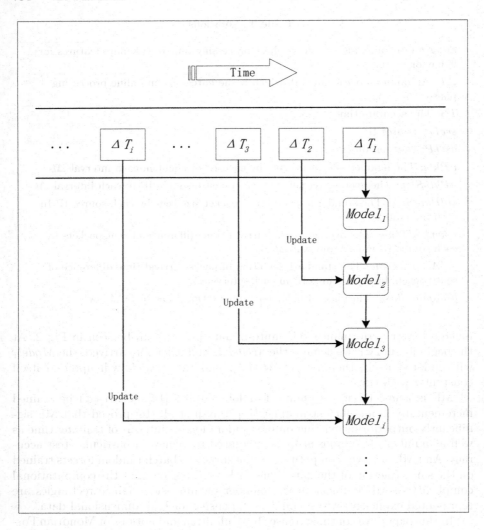

Fig. 2. The auto-updated process.

$$T \sim MT(\lambda, D_{1:N})$$
$$T'|T, D_{1:N+1} \sim MT_x(\lambda, T, D_{N+1})$$
$$implies \quad T' \sim MT_x(\lambda, T, D_{N+1})$$

As a result, the authors showed that the distribution of Mondrian trees trained on a dataset in an incremental fashion is the same as that of Mondrian trees trained on the same dataset in a batch fashion, irrespective of the order in which the data points are observed.

Based on the above advantages of Mondrian Forest, we choose it as a basic component for our online detection system.

Algorithm 1. Proposed Distinction Mechanism

Input:
    Traffic contain DDoS and FC.
Output:
    The filtered traffic: only legitimate traffic without DDoS
1: Calcuate bahavior features in every interval Δt, label the class: $DDoS\_Flow$ or FC_Flow, then form Behavior Vector.
2: Train model in Real-time on Behavior Vector data By online Machine Learning Method-Mondrian Forest. And auto-update model constantly.
3: Use the trained model to test new traffic.
4: Discriminate whether the new traffic is $DDoS\_Flow$ or not. If it is $DDoS\_Flow$, then filter, else, pass.
5: Go to Step 2.

---

4 Experiments

Dataset: In this section, we do experiments to estimate the method proposed on two public real-world datasets: CAIDA "DDoS Attack 2007" Dataset (CAIDA 2007 Dataset) [17] used as the DDoS data and World Cup 1998 Dataset (WC 1988 Dataset) [18] used as the FC data.

In our experiments, we select 10 s DDoS data-2007-08-05 05:30:00 to 2007-08-05 05:30:10-from CAIDA 2007 dataset, which can be seen in Fig. 3. It shows that the sent packet rate is about 18000 packets per second and there are a few noises in the 10 s. Due to no additional information can achieved from the CAIDA 2007 dataset, the reason of noises produced is not clear. While select 10 min FC data-1998-06-10 16:00:00 to 1998-06-10 16:10:00, which can be seen in Fig. 3. The client request rate is about 1900 requests per second. From Fig. 3,

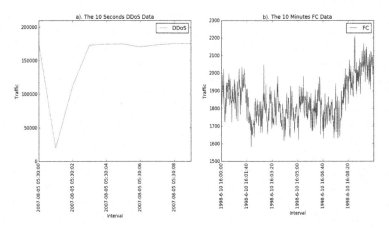

Fig. 3. (a). The 10 s DDoS data with the interval-1 s from 2007-08-05 05:30:00 to 2007-08-05 05:30:10 (b). The 10 min FC data with the interval-1 s from 1998-06-10 16:00:00 to 1998-06-10 16:10:00

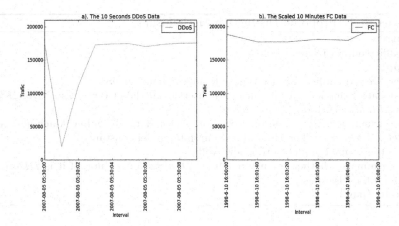

Fig. 4. (a). The 10 s DDoS data with the interval-1 s from 2007-08-05 05:30:00 to 2007-08-05 05:30:10 (b). The scaled 10 min FC data with the intervel-100 s from 1998-06-10 16:00:00 to 1998-06-10 16:10:00.

we could find there are different traffic existed in each interval, the packets sent rate is about 180000 packets per second in DDoS, while the client request rate is about 1900 requests per second in FC, both of them are completely different, this phenomenon caused by effects came from bandwidth, so we should reduce the effects.

In this paper, we assure that different datasets could produce as same traffic volume as possible in each interval through scaling the interval to minimize the effects caused by bandwidth. After analyzing the different datasets, we choose the scale interval rate 1:100, which means the traffic produced in 1s DDoS interval almost equals the one produced in 100 FCs intervals. After this processing, we achieved the scaled traffic in each new interval in Fig. 4. It can be found that the average traffic of both datasets is the same basically around 17500 to 18500 packets sent per second, which could minimize the bandwidth effect came from different datasets.

Thereafter, we make calculation on the scaled interval to achieve the required behavior features and label for the behavior Class-DDoS_Flow or FC_Flow in each interval to form Behavior Vector, more details can be seen in Sect. 3. And we mix the vectors by random sampling and normalization to wipe out the effects of different scale of each feature. We apply these mixed and normalized data as input data for model training and evaluation.

In order to make further evaluation of our new features and proposed idea, we should make analysis on new test data. So we choose another 10 s DDoS data-2007-08-05 05:34:00 to 2007-08-05 05:34:10-from CAIDA2007 and 10 min FC data-1998-07-03 16:00:00 to 1998-07-03 16:10:00-from WorldCup98 to analyze. All the procedure of processing is the same as previous one, the only difference is the scale rate. After analyzing the new datasets, we choose the scale interval rate 1:80, which means the traffic produced in 1 DDoS interval almost equals the one produced in 80 FCs intervals. After this processing, we achieved the scaled traffic in each new interval in Fig. 5. It can be found that the average traffic of both datasets is the same, which is basically around 15500 to 17000 packets sent per second and could minimize the effect caused by different datasets bandwidth.

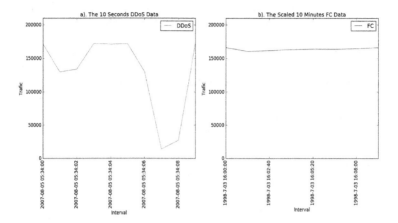

Fig. 5. (a). The 10 s DDoS data with the interval-1 s from 2007-08-05 05:34:00 to 2007-08-05 05:34:10 (b). The scaled 10 min FC data with the intervel-100 s from 1998-07-03 16:00:00 to 1998-07-03 16:10:00.

Finally, we obtained the input data for the latter process, the whole Train set and Test set, details can be seen in Table 2. For Train set, the whole number of samples is 103313, there are 47648 samples for FC and 55665 samples for DDoS. As for Test set, total number of samples is 106732, there are 54167 samples for FC and 52565 samples for DDoS.

Table 2. Train set and test set.

	Data set	
Class	Train set	Test set
DDoS_Flow	55665	52565
FC_Flow	47648	54167
Total	103313	106732

Evaluation of Proposed Idea: In this section, we employ Online Random Forest-Mondrian Forest to evaluate our method on the mixed and normalized data as above. And Confusion Matrix, Accuracy, False Positive Rate (FPR) and False Negative Rate (FNR) are all applied together as evaluation standards.

In this section, the number of trees in forests is 10, then we training model by Mondrian Forest, the batch size in each Interval ΔT is 5000, which split the Train set to $(103312/5000 = 20.662)$ 20 batch Interval ΔT, while the last batch size is less than 5000 samples, and we make test on the whole Train set and Test set at the same time on every model updated at each batch Interval ΔT.

The results can be seen in Fig. 6 and we could find obviously that the predicted Accuracy on the whole Train set and Test set is increasing gradually along with time, while FNR is decreasing at the same time, which means the model keep updating itself constantly with time. For FPR, there are a little bit difference on the whole Train set and Test set, it gradually decreases on the whole Train set with time, while remains stable on the whole Test set, which means that there are some differences existed between Train set and Test set. It may have some new samples in Test set but doesnt exist in Train set, therefore, the model cannot have a good effect on Test set about FPR.

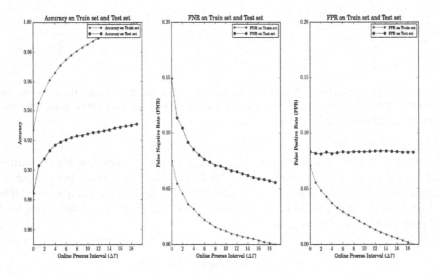

Fig. 6. Accuracy, FNR, FPR on train set and test set.

Upon completion of training on the whole Train set, we could achieve the final model, saying that the average number of leaves in tree is 15072.6, the average number of non-leaves is 15071.6, the average of tree depth is 25.5, while the number of the Train set is 103313. The distinctive results can be seen in Table 3. With the new features and Mondrian Forest, we could distinguish DDoS and FC with 100% Accuracy, 0% FPR and FNR on Train set, while more than 93% Accuracy, around 8.245% FPR and 5.538% FNR on Test set. Even though there decreased a bit of Accuracy on Test set, but as a whole, the online detection mechanism employed with Mondrian Forest still has a good performance.

In order to make further evaluation, we compare it with offline method: Random Forest, which takes the whole Train set to t model and test the model

Table 3. Distinguished results with Mondrian forest on online situation.

Methods		Mondrian forest			
DataSet		Train set		Test set	
Confusion matrix	DDoS FC	DDoS	FC	DDoS	FC
		55665	0	49654	2911
		0	47648	4466	49701
Accuracy		100%		93.088%	
False Positive Rate (FPR)		0%		8.245%	
False Negative Rate (FNR)		0%		5.538%	

Table 4. Distinguished results with random forest on offline situation.

Methods		Random forest			
DataSet		Train set		Test set	
Confusion matrix	DDoS FC	DDoS	FC	DDoS	FC
		55665	0	51566	999
		0	47648	26	54141
Accuracy		100%		99.040%	
False Positive Rate (FPR)		0%		0.048%	
False Negative Rate (FNR)		0%		1.901%	

on Train set and Test set. The result can be seen in Table 4, which shows that it could distinguish DDoS and FC with 100% Accuracy, 0% FPR and 0% FNR on Train set and it is the same as Mondrian Forest, while more than 99% Accuracy, around 0.048% FPR and 1.901% FNR on Test set. It is better than Mondrian Forest.

Even though the traditional Random Forest is a little better than Mondrian Forest, it should be loaded with all data into memory at one time and cannot auto update itself with time. If there is huge volume data beyond the memory size, it cannot be used. On the contrary, Mondrian Forest have a slightly lower Accuracy than Random Forest, but it can detect in online way and update model automatically, which is more important for the situations that train data cannot be loaded in memory at a time, such as Big Data, Cloud situations. So we believe that the online detection mechanism employed with Mondrian Forest can play a more important role in the long term.

5   Conclusion

In this paper, we conclude a new feature set to form Behavior Vector based on analysis of the client behavior in DDoS and FC, which can be used to profile each client in DDoS and FC. Based on Behavior Vector, we design an online detection mechanism employed with online Random Forest-Mondrian Forest to discriminate DDoS under FC. We make experiments on two public real-world datasets to evaluate the proposed method, the results indicate that it cannot automatically update the detected model along with time and without manual intervention, but can achieve a better performance slightly less than offline Random Forest, which is very applicable for Big Data situations. Therefore, we strongly believe that our idea may act as a complementary mechanism for the existing defending system.

References

1. Mansfield-Devine, S.: The growth and evolution of ddos. Netw. Secur. **2015**(10), 13–20 (2015)
2. Jung, J., Krishnamurthy, B., Rabinovich, M.: Flash crowds and denial of service attacks: characterization and implications for CDNS and web sites. In: Proceedings of the 11th international conference on World Wide Web, pp. 293–304. ACM (2002)
3. Prasad, K.M., Reddy, A.R.M., Rao, K.V.: Discriminating DDoS attack traffic from flash crowds on internet threat monitors (ITM) using entropy variations. Afr. J. Comput. ICT **6**(3) (2013)
4. Von Ahn, L., Blum, M., Langford, J.: Telling humans and computers apart automatically. Commun. ACM **47**(2), 56–60 (2004)
5. AYAHs: website:ayahs. http://areyouahuman.com
6. Yu, S., Guo, S., Stojmenovic, I.: Fool me if you can: mimicking attacks and anti-attacks in cyberspace. IEEE Trans. Comput. **64**(1), 139–151 (2015)
7. Rajab, M.A., Zarfoss, J., Monrose, F., Terzis, A.: My botnet is bigger than yours (maybe, better than yours): why size estimates remain challenging. In: Hotbots, p. 5 (2012)
8. Xie, Y., Yu, S.Z.: A large-scale hidden semi-markov model for anomaly detection on user browsing behaviors. IEEE/ACM Trans. Netw. (TON) **17**(1), 54–65 (2009)
9. Thapngam, T., Yu, S., Zhou, W., Beliakov, G.: Discriminating DDoS attack traffic from flash crowd through packet arrival patterns. In: 2011 IEEE Conference on Computer Communications Workshops (INFOCOM WKSHPS), pp. 952–957. IEEE (2011)
10. Bhatia, S., Mohay, G., Tickle, A., Ahmed, E.: Parametric differences between a real-world distributed denial-of-service attack and a flash event. In: 2011 Sixth International Conference on Availability, Reliability and Security (ARES), pp. 210–217. IEEE (2011)
11. Saravanan, R., Shanmuganathan, S., Palanichamy, Y.: Behavior-based detection of application layer distributed denial of service attacks during flash events. Turk. J. Electr. Eng. Comput. Sci. **24**(2), 510–523 (2016)
12. Somani, G., Gaur, M.S., Sanghi, D., Conti, M., Buyya, R.: Ddos attacks in cloud computing: Issues, taxonomy, and future directions. arXiv preprint arXiv:1512.08187 (2015)
13. Bottou, L., Gun, Y.L.: Online learning for very large data sets. Appl. Stochast. Models Bus. Ind. **21**(2), 137–151 (2005)
14. Saffari, A., Leistner, C., Santner, J., Godec, M., Bischof, H.: On-line random forests. In: IEEE International Conference on Computer Vision Workshops, pp. 1393–1400 (2009)
15. Denil, M., Matheson, D., Freitas, N.D.: Consistency of online random forests. Eprint Arxiv, pp. 1256–1264 (2013)
16. Lakshminarayanan, B., Roy, D.M., Teh, Y.W.: Mondrian forests: efficient online random forests. Adv. Neural Inf. Process. Syst. **4**, 3140–3148 (2015)
17. DDoS: Caida ddos attack 2007 dataset (2007). http://www.caida.org/data/passive/ddos-20070804_dataset.xml
18. FlashCrowds: World cup 1998 dataset (1998). http://ita.ee.lbl.gov/html/contrib/WorldCup.html

A 3-Layer Method for Analysis of Cooperative Behaviors of Physical Devices in Cyber-Physical Systems

Gang Ren[1,2(✉)], Pan Deng[1,2], and Chao Yang[1,2]

[1] Institute of Software, Chinese Academy of Sciences, Beijing 100190, China
{rengang2013,dengpan,yangchao}@iscas.ac.cn
[2] University of Chinese Academy of Sciences, Beijing 100190, China

Abstract. With wide application of wireless sensor technology, more and more physical devices are being connected to Cyber-Physical Systems (CPSs). On the other hand, CPS applications have made their way into the domain of Safety-Critical Systems (SCSs), where there is a higher requirement for temporal correctness of cooperative behaviors of physical devices. Therefore, it has been becoming a challenging task for practicing engineers to ensure temporal correctness of cooperative behaviors. In practice, practicing engineers mainly depend on graphic modeling methods or formal modeling methods to analyse cooperative behaviors. However, since different methods have their own features, a single method can't ensure temporal correctness of cooperative behaviors very well. To address this issue, in this paper, a 3-layer method, consisting of the graphic modeling layer, the formal specification layer, and the formal verification layer, is proposed. This method combines the advantages of graphic methods and formal methods and can provide a more thorough analysis for cooperative behaviors. Moreover, due to adoption of 3-layer architecture, this method has a good extensibility in structure. The usability of the proposed method is illustrated by a practical application scenario.

Keywords: Cyber-Physical Systems · Cooperative behaviors · Graphic model · Formal model · Formal verification

1 Introduction

CPSs consist of a variety of physical devices such as sensors, RFID tags, actuators, appliances and industrial equipments. A CPS application usually involves multiple physical devices, and these devices fulfil a given task by communicating and cooperating with each other [1–3]. On one hand, with wide application of wireless sensor technology, cooperative behaviors of physical devices have been becoming more and more complex. On the other hand, we have seen CPS applications making their way into the domain of SCSs [4–6], where there is a higher requirement for temporal correctness of cooperative behaviors. As a result, it

© Springer International Publishing AG 2017
L. Ma et al. (Eds.): WASA 2017, LNCS 10251, pp. 741–754, 2017.
DOI: 10.1007/978-3-319-60033-8_63

has been becoming a challenging task for practicing engineers to ensure temporal correctness of cooperative behaviors in the context of CPSs.

Generally speaking, the temporal correctness means that cooperative behaviors can satisfy the expected temporal properties. Specifically, these properties can be divided into two kinds: structure property and business property. Structure property expresses objective requirements to cooperative behaviors. It can be further classified as deadlock property and equivalence property. Deadlock property states whether cooperative behaviors are free from deadlocks. Equivalence property represents whether different models of a system are consistent. In contrast, business property expresses subjective requirements to cooperative behaviors and illustrates whether execution order of cooperative behaviors satisfies specific business regulations.

In practice, practicing engineers mainly depend on graphic modeling methods or formal modeling methods to analyse cooperative behaviors [7–9]. Graphic methods use graphic models to describe cooperative behaviors. They have the intuitive presentation capability and allow better communication between practicing engineers and further elicit cooperative behaviors. But they lack the definite description capability, and different people may have different understandings toward a same model. On the contrary, formal methods are a kind of mathematical method, which can definitely describe a system and theoretically anticipate all possible situations. But, they are not very intuitive and have a higher communication cost. Overall, different methods have their own features and a single method can't ensure the temporal correctness of cooperative behaviors very well [10,11].

To address this issue, in this paper, we attempt to combine different analysis methods for CPS applications and systems. The main contributions of this paper are listed below.

(1) A 3-layer method is proposed for analysis of cooperative behaviors, that combines the advantages of graphic methods and formal methods and can provide a more thorough analysis for cooperative behaviors.
(2) Three sets of transformation rules between different models are presented that provide the theoretical basis for transformation of different models of cooperative behaviors.
(3) We apply the proposed method to a practical application scenario in the field of intelligent transport systems and illustrate the usability of the proposed method.

The remainders of this paper proceed as follows. Section 2 introduces architecture of the proposed method. A traffic accident rescue scenario is introduced to illustrate how to create graphic models of cooperative behaviors in Sect. 3. The formal specification of cooperative behaviors is depicted in Sect. 4. In Sect. 5, verification of structure property and business property is addressed. Section 6 discusses the related work on ensemble methods. In the end, we draw some conclusions about this paper and propose the possible research direction in the future.

2   Architecture of 3-Layer Method

The proposed 3-layer method consists of three layers, namely graphic modeling layer, formal specification layer, and formal verification layer. The UML sequence diagram and statechart diagram [12] are two promising tools for describing dynamic aspects of a system. The sequence diagram can describe cooperative behaviors among all device objects of a system according to the temporal order whereas the statechart diagram tends to depict cooperative behaviors of a device object in detail. In the first layer, we employ the sequence diagram to create graphic model of cooperative behaviors from the system perspective and the statechart diagram to create graphic model from the device perspective, respectively.

In the second layer, graphic models of the first layer are transformed into formal models. This layer has three effects: First, it provides uniform semantics for different graphic models, helping to eliminate misunderstandings towards graphic models. Second, it offers formal models, which is a prerequisite for formal verification, to the formal verification layer. Third, it can cancel coupling between the graphic modeling layer and the formal verification layer and improve extensibility of our model. When adding a new tool to its former or latter layer, we only need to consider relationship of the new tool with the formal specification layer. The π-calculus [13] is a famous process algebra and suitable for describing various concurrent systems. Moreover, it is familiar with many practicing engineers. For these reasons, we accommodate π-calculus as formal specification language. The method for translation from graphic model into π-calculus model is introduced in Sect. 4. Here, we develop two translators, called SD2PI and SC2PI to do this translation process.

In the third layer, formal models of the second layer are verified against structure properties and business properties. MWB [14] is the main analysis tool for π-calculus models and supports verification of deadlock and equivalence properties. So, we choose it as the verification tool for structure properties. However, it doesn't support verification of user-defined business properties. Hence, we choose another verification tool, SPIN, to verify business properties. SPIN [15] is a model checker for verification of a finite-state system and supports verification of user-defined business properties. Moreover, a counterexample will be fed back if the system violates the desired properties. But, it only accepts a program written by Promela. So we need to translate the π-calculus model into a Promela program, additionally. We define the translation rules from the π-calculus model into a Promela program that will be introduced in detail in Sect. 5. Here, a translator, called PI2SPIN, is developed to automate generation of Promela program from π-calculus model.

Overall, this method is a method with 3 layers structure, that facilitates the coupling of graphical representation and formal verification and has good extensibility.

3   Modeling Graphic Model for Cooperative Behaviors

3.1   Scenario of Traffic Accident Rescue

Traffic accident rescue is a typical CPSs paradigm in the field of intelligent transport systems [16]. This scenario involves four types of devices: Road Monitor (RM), Control Center (CC), Fire Engine (FB) and Chemical Biological Incident Response Force (CBIRF). RM is in charge of monitoring roads. Once a traffic accident occurs, RM will inform CC, which is responsible for scheduling rescue vehicles such as FB and CBIRF. On receipt of a rescue request from RM, CC will forward it into the relevant FB and CBIRF, which will decide to either accept or reject this request according to their statuses. Once FB and CBIRF accept the request, they will rush to accident site as soon as possible. In general, the order of rescue does not matter in terms of rescue effect. But in some rare cases, it will become very critical for rescue effect. For example, if accident vehicles loads up dangerous chemical materials, it will reduce rescue effect, even may cause a second explosion if FB starts its rescue before CBIRF. We will apply the proposed method to analysis and verification of this scenario throughout this paper.

3.2   Creating System Model for Cooperative Behaviors

The sequence diagram includes two main entities: object and message. Here, we employ object to represent physical device, and message to represent cooperative behaviors among physical devices. According to this idea, we create the system model of the rescue scenario shown in Fig. 1, where there are 4 device objects, namely RM, CC, FE and $CBIRF$. The 4 devices are placed from left to right and exchanging messages between them are portrayed from top to bottom in light of time order. The cooperative process starts with that RM sends message *Request* to CC. Then 2 concurrent messages from CC to FE and $CBIRF$ are modeled as a rectangular frame with the keyword *parallel*. Afterwards, the alternative messages from FE and $CBIRF$ to CC, which represent that emergency vehicles either accept or reject the request, are modeled as 2 rectangular frame with the keyword *opt*. Finally message *Over* is sent from CC to RM.

3.3   Creating Device Model for Cooperative Behaviours

Unlike creating system model that put all devices into one sequence diagram, we create an independent device model for every device. A statechart diagram has two basic entities: state and transition. Here, we use the transition to represent cooperative behaviour and the state represent to device state after execution of cooperative behavior.

Figure 2 shows device model of the rescue scenario *System*, which is a concurrent state consisting of 4 sub-states, RM, CC, FE and $CBIRF$. The device model of CC is shown in Fig. 3, which is also a concurrent state and comprises 3 sub-states, CC_{fe}, CC_{cbirf} and CC_{syn}. Figure 4 shows the device model of RM,

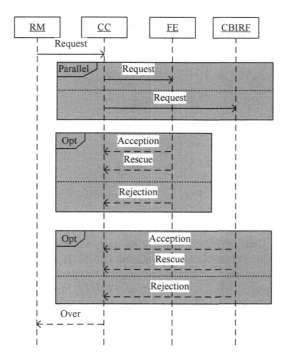

Fig. 1. System model of the rescue scenario

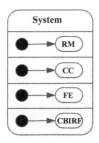

Fig. 2. Device model of the rescue scenario

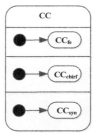

Fig. 3. Device model of CC

which includes two simple states, RM and RM_1. The arrow between the two states is a notation for a transition. On sending of the message *Request*, the state RM is exited and the state RM_1 is reached. The RM waits for a response in state RM_1. Upon receipt of the message *Over*, the process terminates. The device models of CC_{fe} and CC_{cbirf} are shown in Figs. 5 and 6 respectively. Once receiving the message *Request*, they exit their initial states and enter their next states in which they forward *Request* into relative rescue devices.

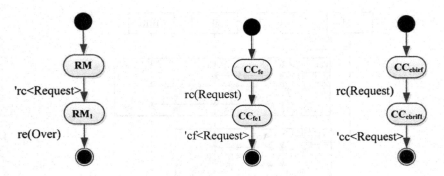

Fig. 4. Device model of *RM*   **Fig. 5.** Device model of *CC_fe*   **Fig. 6.** Device model of *CC_cbirf*

The device models of *FE* and *CBIRF* are shown in Figs. 8 and 9 respectively, in each of which there are 3 states and 4 transitions. Initial states are state *FE* and *CBIRF* and the 2 pairs of alternative transitions represent messages *Acception* or *Rejection* from device *FE* and *CBIRF* to *CC*. Figure 7 describes the device model of *CC_syn*, which consists of 10 states and 13 transitions. Out

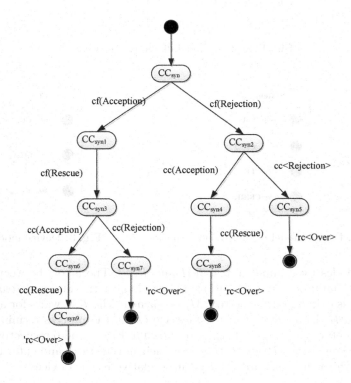

Fig. 7. Device model of *CC_syn*

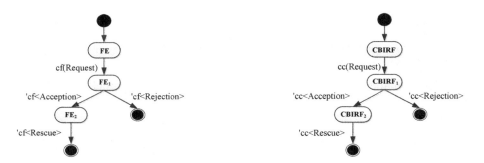

Fig. 8. Device model of FE **Fig. 9.** Device model of $CBIRF$

of 13 transitions, 3 pairs of them are alternative transitions. Initially, it stays state CC_{syn} and waits for a message from emergency vehicle EF over channel cf. Message *Acception* and *Rejection* are modeled as a pair of alternative transitions. Once receiving all messages from emergency vehicles, message *Over* is sent and the device process terminates.

4 Creating Formal Model for Cooperative Behaviors

4.1 From System Model to π-Calculus Model

The key of transform of the system model to the π-calculus model is to find mapping relationships between elements of sequence diagram and that of π-calculus. From the discussions of the above section, we have known that sequence diagram has two entities, namely object and message. The message can also be further divided into concurrent message and alternative message. The π-calculus comprises two main elements, names and actions. The name is used mainly to represent concepts of process, channel, and message. The action include input action $x(y)$, output action $\overline{x}\langle y\rangle$, choice action "$+$" and concurrent action "$|$". The π-calculus processes can communicate with each other depending on sending message via channels. Below, we define the rules for transformation of system model to π-calculus model.

Rule 1. *Each device of the system model is transformed into a same name process of π-calculus model.*

Rule 2. *Sending of a message is transformed into an output action $\overline{x}\langle y\rangle$ of π-calculus model.*

Rule 3. *Receipt of a message is transformed into an input action $x(y)$ of π-calculus model.*

Rule 4. *Concurrent messages are transformed into concurrent action "$|$" of π-calculus model.*

Rule 5. *Alternative messages are transformed into choice action "+" of π-calculus model.*

Rule 6. *All π-calculus processes are combined with concurrent action "|", composing the whole π-calculus model.*

According the above rules, we can obtain the system formal model of the rescue scenario as follows.

(1) System

$$System = RM|CC|FE|CBIRF \tag{1}$$

(2) RM

$$RM = \overline{rc}\langle Request\rangle.rc(Over).0 \tag{2}$$

(3) CC

$$CC = CC_{fe}|CC_{cbirf}|CC_{syn} \tag{3}$$

$$CC_{fe} = rc(Request).\overline{cf}\langle Request\rangle.0 \tag{4}$$

$$CC_{cbirf} = rc(Request).\overline{cc}\langle Request\rangle.0 \tag{5}$$

$CC_{syn} = cf(Acception).(cf(Rescue).cc(Acception).cc(Rescue).\overline{rc}\langle Over\rangle.0 + cf(Res$

$cue).cc(Rejection).\overline{rc}\langle Over\rangle.0) + cf(Rejection).(cc(Acception).cc(Rescue).\overline{rc}\langle Over\rangle.$

$$0 + cc(Rejection).\overline{rc}\langle Over\rangle.0) \tag{6}$$

(4) *FE*

$$FE = cf(Request).(\overline{cf}\langle Acception\rangle.\overline{cf}\langle Rescue\rangle + \overline{cf}\langle Rejection\rangle).0 \tag{7}$$

(5) *CBIRF*

$$CBIRF = cc(Request).(\overline{cc}\langle Acception\rangle.\overline{cc}\langle Arrival\rangle + \overline{cc}\langle Rejection\rangle).0 \tag{8}$$

4.2   From Device Model to π-Calculus Model

Unlike the transformation of system model to π-calculus model, where the device of system model and π-calculus process is one-to-one relationship, to transform the system model to π-calculus model, we consider that a state in the statechart diagram is transformed into a process in π-calculus. In other words, the relationship of state of statechart diagram and π-calculus process is one-to-one. The detail rules are listed as follow.

Rule 1. *A concurrent state of a device model is transformed into a concurrent π-calculus process, and sub-states of the concurrent state are transformed sub-processes of the π-calculus process.*

Rule 2. *A simple state followed by a simple transition of a device model is transformed into a π-calculus process, consisting of a prefix action and a new process. The prefix action represents the simple transition and the new process represents remaining states.*

Rule 3. *A simple state followed by an alternative transition is transformed into an unique process in π-calculus, consisting of two sub-processes combined with choice operator "$+$".*

According to these rules, we can obtain π-calculus models of the device models (Figs. 2, 3, 4, 5 and 6) as follows. Note that suffix "state" is added to the process'name to distinguish from the system model.

(1) *System*

$$System\_state = RM\_state | CC\_state | FE\_state | CBIRF\_state \tag{9}$$

(2) *RM*

$$RM\_state = \overline{rc}\langle Request \rangle.RM\_state_1 \tag{10}$$

$$RM\_state_1 = rc(Over).0 \tag{11}$$

(3) *CC*

$$CC\_state = CC\_state_{fe} | CC\_state_{cbirf} | CC\_state_{syn} \tag{12}$$

(4) CC_state_{fe}

$$CC\_state_{fe} = rc(Request).CC\_state_{fe1} \tag{13}$$

$$CC\_state_{fe1} = \overline{cf}\langle Request \rangle.0 \tag{14}$$

(5) CC_state_{cbirf}

$$CC\_state_{cbirf} = rc(Request).CC\_state_{cbirf1} \tag{15}$$

$$CC\_state_{cbirf1} = \overline{cc}\langle Request \rangle.0 \tag{16}$$

(6) CC_{syn}

$$CC\_state_{syn} = cf(Acception).CC\_state_{syn1} + cf(Rejection).CC\_state_{syn2} \tag{17}$$

$$CC\_state_{syn1} = cf(Rescue).CC\_state_{syn3} \tag{18}$$

$$CC\_state_{syn2} = cc(Acception).CC\_state_{syn4} + cc(Rejection).CC\_state_{syn5} \tag{19}$$

$$CC\_state_{syn3} = cc(Acception).CC\_state_{syn6} + cc(Rejection).CC\_state_{syn7} \tag{20}$$

$$CC\_state_{syn4} = cc(Rescue).CC\_state_{syn8} \tag{21}$$

$$CC\_state_{syn5} = \overline{rc}\langle Over \rangle.0 \tag{22}$$

$$CC\_state_{syn6} = cc(Rescue).CC\_state_{syn9} \tag{23}$$

$$CC\_state_{syn7} = \overline{rc}\langle Over \rangle.0 \tag{24}$$

$$CC\_state_{syn8} = \overline{rc}\langle Over \rangle.0 \tag{25}$$

$$CC\_state_{syn9} = \overline{rc}\langle Over \rangle.0 \tag{26}$$

(7) *FE*

$$FE\_state = cf(Request).FE\_state_1 \tag{27}$$

$$FE\_state_1 = \overline{cf}\langle Acception\rangle.FE\_state_2 + \overline{cf}\langle Rejection\rangle.0 \tag{28}$$

$$FE\_state_2 = \overline{cf}\langle Rescue\rangle.0 \tag{29}$$

(8) *CBIRF*

$$CBIRF\_state = cc(Request).CBIRF\_state_1 \tag{30}$$

$$CBIRF\_state_1 = \overline{cc}\langle Acception\rangle.CBIRF\_state_2 + \overline{cc}\langle Rejection\rangle.0 \tag{31}$$

$$CBIRF\_state_2 = \overline{cc}\langle Rescue\rangle.0 \tag{32}$$

5   Verification of Structure Property and Business Property

5.1   Verification of Business Property Using SPIN

Because SPIN can only accept a Promela program as verification model, the key issue that use spin to verify the business attributes is to transform the π model into a Promela program. Promela is a formal description language for modeling finite state systems. It is similar to the C language, allowing the dynamic creation of concurrent processes, through the definition of the message channel can be synchronized and asynchronous communication. The Promela program consists of three objects, namely data objects, processes and message channels. The key issue of transform a π-calculus formal model into a Promela program is to find their mapping relations. Below, we define s set of rules for transformation from π-calculus model to a Promela program:

Rule 1. *System process of π-calculus model is translated into the main process of PROMELA, and its concurrent sub-processes are translated into processes of the main module running in parallel.*

Rule 2. *A device process of π-calculus model is translated into a process in PROMELA, in which, there is a Variable state which represents the transition of device state.*

Rule 3. *A channel of a π-calculus device process is translated into a channel of the same name in PROMELA. The input action and output action over this channel in π-calculus corresponds to the taking and pressing statements in PROMELA.*

According to the above rules, we obtain a PROMELA program that has 384 lines in total, consisting of 1 main module and 4 sub-modules.

The second step is to define the business properties to be verified using Linear Temporal Logic (LTL) [17] formulas, that is a temporal logic language and can specified how the truth of a formula changes dynamically as time proceeds. Here, we choose two business properties as follows:

Property 1. *The device CC can reply RM with Over only after receiving the response from all rescuing devices.*

$$G!((re = Over) \& (eh = Request))$$

Property 2. *The vehicle CBIRF must arrive at accident site before rescue of the vehicle FE.*

$$G((cc! = Rescue) U (cf = Rescue))$$

The last step is to verify the cooperative behaviors against the desired business properties. The version of SPIN is 6.1.0. It took approximately 3 s to finish the verification of these formulas. The results show that Property 1 can be satisfied and Property 2 not. A counterexample of Property 2 is fed back. That illustrates that the FE may start its rescue before $CBIRF$ in this scenario.

From the above example, we can conclude that as long as we use the LTL language to define the expected business logic, our method can automatically find out the potential defects of cooperative behavior and give the counterexample that helps locate error.

Table 1. Results of deadlock verification

Device process	Trace number	Number of maximum commitments	Number of total commitments	Time elapsed for deadlock verification
System	29	12	303	2.367
System_state	37	13	399	7.386
RM	1	2	2	0.001
RM_state	1	2	2	0.001
CC	10	7	69	0.018
CC_state	17	8	121	0.048
FE	2	3	5	0.002
FE_state	2	3	5	0.003
CBIRF	2	3	5	0.001
CBIRF_state	2	3	5	0.002

5.2 Verification of Structure Property Using MWB

As discussed in Sect. 2, the proposed method takes MWB as the tool of verification of structure property. Its version is 3.1. First, we directly import the π-calculus models into MWB, and then use the MWB command *deadlock* to verify deadlock property of all the device processes. The results are listed in Table 1. We can see that the most complex process is *System_state*. It has 37 possible execution traces in total. The number of the maximum commitments of these traces is 13. These traces comprises 399 commitments totally. It took 7.386 s to perform this command.

Table 2. Results of equivalence verification

Device process of system model	Device process of device model	Size of simulation steps	Time elapsed for equivalence verification
System	System_state	8644	384.437
RM	RM_state	3	0.001
CC	CC_state	298	0.155
FE	FE_state	4	0.001
CBIRF	CBIRF_state	4	0.001

Next, we use the MWB command *eq* to verify equivalence property between the system model and the device model of every device process. The results are listed in Table 2. We can see that the verification process of the pair of *System* and *System_state* is the most time-consuming. The MWB took 8644 simulation steps and 384.437 s to fulfil its verification process.

From the above results, we can see that the proposed method can examine the deadlock property of cooperative behaviors by simulation. Moreover, it can verify the equivalence property for the system model and device model, that can provide a more thorough analysis for cooperative behaviors of physical devices in CPSs.

6   Related Work on Ensemble Methods

Currently, there has been some research on combination of different methods and tools for analysis of a system. For instance, a method of combination of π-calculus with MWB was discussed in [18]. This method adopts π-calculus to specify cooperative behaviors, and employs MWB to verify structure properties. Another method, which combines π-calculus with NuSMV [19], was proposed in [20]. This method supports specification of cooperative behaviors using π-calculus and verification of business properties using NuSMV. However, comparing to the 3-layer method proposed in this paper, the two methods have only 2 layers, i.g., formal specification layer and verification layer, and no graphic modeling layer. As a result, they lacks the graphic modeling capability.

A 3-layer method was proposed in [21]. The Authors takes the Simulink [22] as modeling tool of the graphic layer, the Hybrid CSP [23] as specification language of the formal specification layer, and the Hybrid Hoare Logic prover [24] as verification tool of the formal verification layer. Another 3-layer method proposed in [25], which adopts the statechart diagram as the graphic modeling tool, π-calculus as the formal specification tool and NuSMV as the model checker. Overall, both methods adopt the 3-layer architecture and have capabilities of both graphic modeling and formal verification. But their graphic layers have only one tool, and can't provide multi-perspective models. In addition, they lack capability of equivalence property verification in the formal verification layer as they can't create multi-perspective models in the graphic layer.

Comparing to the above methods, the proposed method is novel in the sense that:

First, for the function of graphic analysis, it can create both system model and device model for cooperative behaviors in the graphic layer, which are more comprehensive than a single model and contribute to a more thorough analysis.

Second, for the function of formal verification, the proposed method not only supports equivalence property verification but can also support business verification. Specially, it can check the consistency between between two different perspective models of a system, helping to a more thorough analysis for cooperative behavior.

7   Conclusion

In this paper, a novel 3-layer analytical method is proposed for cooperative behaviors of physical devices in CPSs. Functionally, this method combines the advantages of graphic methods and formal methods and provides a more thorough analysis of cooperative behaviors. Structurally, due to adoption of 3-layer architecture, this method is extensible and new analysis tools can be added easily. The usability of the proposed method is illustrated by a practical application scenario.

In the future, we will further add more cooperative semantics of physical devices into our method, and apply it to analysis of more complex scenario.

Acknowledgment. This work was supported by the National Science Foundation of China (No. 61100066).

The authors would like express sincere gratitude to all the authors of the references in this paper.

The authors also extend their thanks to all anonymous referees for providing valuable comments and constructive criticisms on this paper.

References

1. Yao, J.G., Xu, X., Liu, X.: MixCPS: mixed time/event-triggered architecture of cyber physical systems. Proc. IEEE **104**(5), 923–937 (2016)
2. Bendjima, M., Feham, M.: Architecture of an MAS-based intelligent communication in a WSN. Int. J. Distrib. Sens. Netw. **11**(10), 145–154 (2015)
3. Sun, Y., Zhang, S., Xu, H., Lin, S.: Cooperative communications for wireless Ad Hoc and sensor networks in 2013. Int. J. Distrib. Sens. Netw. **10**(3), 1–2 (2014)
4. Knight, J.C.: Safety critical systems: challenges and directions. In: Proceedings of International Conference on Software Engineering, Orlando, FL, USA, pp. 547–550, May 2002
5. Riazul, S.M., Daehan, K., Humaun, M., Hossain, M.: The internet of things for health care: a comprehensive survey. IEEE Access **3**, 678–708 (2015)
6. Alam, K.M., Saini, M., El Saddik, A.: Toward social internet of vehicles: concept, architecture, and applications. IEEE Access **3**, 343–357 (2015)

7. Ng, K.M., Reaz, M.B.I., Ali, M.A.: A review on the applications of Petri nets in modeling, analysis, and control of urban traffic. IEEE Trans. Intell. Transp. Syst. **14**(2), 858–870 (2013)
8. Ren, G., Pan, D., Chao, Y., Jianwei, Z., Qingsong, H.: A formal approach for modeling and verication of distributed systems. In: Proceedings of CLOUDCOMP 2015, Daejeon, South Korea, 18–20 October 2015 (2015)
9. Ren, G., Deng, P., Zhang, J., Hua, Q., Li, J., Qiu, Y.: Formal semantics of UML sequence diagram for safety-critical systems. J. Comput. Inf. Syst. **11**(23), 1–8 (2015)
10. Fantechi, A., Flammini, F., Gnesi, S.: Formal methods for intelligent transportation systems. In: Margaria, T., Steffen, B. (eds.) ISoLA 2012. LNCS, vol. 7610, pp. 187–189. Springer, Heidelberg (2012). doi:10.1007/978-3-642-34032-1_19
11. Russo, A.G., Ladenberger, L.: A formal approach to safety verification of railway signaling systems. In: 2012 Proceedings - Annual Reliability and Maintainability Symposium (RAMS), p. 4. IEEE (2012)
12. OMG unified modeling language (omg uml). Report, OMG (2015)
13. Parrow, J.: An introduction to the π-calculus. In: Bergstra Ponse Smolka Handbook of Process Algebra Elsevier S, vol. 179, no. 1, pp. 479–543 (2000)
14. Bundgaard, M.: A brief introduction to mobility workbench (MWB). Report, Department of Theoretical Computer Science, IT University of Copenhagen (2005)
15. Holzmann, G.: The SPIN Model Checker: Primer and Reference Manual. DBLP, Boston (2004)
16. Liu, J., Wan, J., Wang, Q., Deng, P., Zhou, K.: A survey on position-based routing for vehicular Ad Hoc networks. Telecommun. Syst. **62**(1), 15–30 (2016)
17. Clarke, E.M., Grumberg, O., Peled, D.A.: Model Checking. MIT Press, Cambridge (2000)
18. Yuan, M., Huang, Z., Zhao, J., Li, X.: Modeling and verification of automatic multi-business transactions. In: Proceedings of SEKE, pp. 274–279 (2009)
19. Cimatti, A., Clarke, E., Giunchiglia, E., Giunchiglia, F., Pistore, M., Roveri, M., Sebastiani, R., Tacchella, A.: NuSMV 2: an opensource tool for symbolic model checking. In: Brinksma, E., Larsen, K.G. (eds.) CAV 2002. LNCS, vol. 2404, pp. 359–364. Springer, Heidelberg (2002). doi:10.1007/3-540-45657-0_29
20. Deng, P., Ren, G., Yuan, W.: An integrated framework of formal methods for interaction behaviors among industrial equipments. Microprocess. Microsyst. **39**(8), 1296–1304 (2015)
21. Zou, L., Zhany, N., Wang, S., Franzle, M., Qin, S.: Verifying simulink diagrams via a hybrid hoare logic prover. In: 2013 Proceedings of the International Conference on Embedded Software (EMSOFT), pp. 1–10 (2013)
22. Simulink User's Guide. http://www.mathworks.com/help/pdf_doc/simulink/sl_using.pdf. Accessed 24 July 2016
23. Liu, J., Lv, J., Quan, Z., Zhan, N., Zhao, H., Zhou, C., Zou, L.: A calculus for hybrid CSP. In: Ueda, K. (ed.) APLAS 2010. LNCS, vol. 6461, pp. 1–15. Springer, Heidelberg (2010). doi:10.1007/978-3-642-17164-2_1
24. Zou, L., Lv, J., Wang, S., Zhan, N., Tang, T., Yuan, L., Liu, Y.: Verifying Chinese train control system under a combined scenario by theorem proving. In: Cohen, E., Rybalchenko, A. (eds.) VSTTE 2013. LNCS, vol. 8164, pp. 262–280. Springer, Heidelberg (2014). doi:10.1007/978-3-642-54108-7_14
25. Lam, V.S.W., Padget, J.: Symbolic model checking of UML statechart diagrams with an integrated approach. In: Proceedings of 11th IEEE International Conference and Workshop on the Engineering of Computer-Based Systems, Los Alamitos, CA, USA, pp. 337–346, May 2004

A User Incentive-Based Scheme Against Dishonest Reporting in Privacy-Preserving Mobile Crowdsensing Systems

Xinyu Yang[1], Cong Zhao[1(✉)], Wei Yu[2], Xianghua Yao[3], and Xinwen Fu[4]

[1] Department of Computer Science and Technology, Xi'an Jiaotong University,
Xi'an, People's Republic of China
yxyphd@mail.xjtu.edu.cn, zhaocong@stu.xjtu.edu.cn
[2] Department of Computer and Information Sciences,
Towson University, Towson, USA
wyu@towson.edu
[3] School of Electronics and Information Engineering,
Xi'an Jiaotong University, Xi'an, People's Republic of China
txyao@mail.xjtu.edu.cn
[4] Department of Computer Science, University of Massachusetts Lowell, Lowell, USA
xinwenfu@cs.uml.edu

Abstract. Proliferating Mobile Crowdsensing Systems (MCSs) is a promising paradigm to realize large-scale sensing targets in an agile and economical manner. Privacy protection mechanisms, which alleviate mobile user's concern on participating MCS tasks, also introduce the issue of data quality to the MCS server. In privacy-preserving MCSs, dishonest reporting of mobile sensing data from task participants could severely affect the MCS sensing accuracy. In this paper, we develop a user incentive-based scheme against dishonest reporting in privacy-preserving MCSs. Our proposed scheme is capable of improving the MCS sensing accuracy by encouraging users to honestly upload obtained sensing information for a higher serving profit. The performance of our scheme is evaluated via extensive real-world trace-driven simulations. Our experimental results show that our scheme can effectively ensure MCS sensing accuracy while encouraging honest reporting.

Keywords: Mobile Crowdsensing System · Data quality · User incentive

1 Introduction

As a promising sensing paradigm in the big data era, Mobile Crowdsensing Systems (MCSs) [1,2] aim at realizing large-scale sensing targets, including environment monitoring [3], online urban sensing [4], mobile social networking [5,6], and other Internet of Things applications [7,8], by leveraging pervasively distributed personal mobile smart devices. Mobile smart devices with enriched sensing capabilities are capable of providing fine-grained and economically cheap sensing

© Springer International Publishing AG 2017
L. Ma et al. (Eds.): WASA 2017, LNCS 10251, pp. 755–767, 2017.
DOI: 10.1007/978-3-319-60033-8_64

services [9,10]. Considering the proliferation of MCS applications with improving security intensities [11,12], the potential privacy leakage raised by the use of personal mobile devices has been hindering the development of MCSs [13,14]. Realizing the importance of user privacy protection in MCSs, considerable research efforts have been devoted to preserving mobile user's privacy, including real identity [15], geological location [16,17], contributed data [18], among others.

Nonetheless, in privacy-preserving MCSs, it is difficult to relate a mobile user to its MCS task reports if the identity of real user is obscured. Thus, the quality of sensing data reported by mobile users is difficult to achieve due to the lack of accountable information. In addition, self-interested mobile users are more likely to report non-objective information in MCS tasks, considering that the cost of such dishonest behavior is negligible, while the benefits may be substantial and monetary. How to ensure the sensing data quality in privacy-preserving MCSs is essential for MCS in real-world practice.

In this paper, we present a user incentive-based scheme against potential dishonest reporting in privacy-preserving MCSs, which guarantees the quality of sensing data by rewarding honest users who upload objective sensing reports. Our contributions are summarized as follows: First, we develop an online method for the MCS server to simultaneously compute the sensing truth and estimate the quality of user-reported data without the use of any historical information. Our method is feasible in privacy-preserving MCSs, since it only requires the sensing observations of all participants of the assigned MCS task. Second, based on the developed data quality estimation method and user profit model, we present a user incentive-based method to encourage MCS participants to report objective information for higher profit. Our method can autonomously adjust the actual profit of each participant according to its impact on the entire system. In doing so, our method can ensure that honest participants are rewarded while dishonest participants are reprimanded. Third, we carry out a thorough evaluation on the performance of our proposed scheme based on extensive real-world trace-driven simulations. Simulation results demonstrate that our scheme can realize effective user incentives to guarantee the sensing accuracy of MCSs against dishonest reporting in privacy-preserving MCSs.

The remainder of the paper is organized as follows: In Sect. 2, we present the system model and describe the user incentive problem in privacy-preserving MCSs. In Sect. 3, we present our scheme in detail. In Sect. 4, we present our experimental design and the results of our performance evaluation. Finally, we conclude the paper in Sect. 5.

2   System Model and Problem Formalization

In this section, we first introduce the system model. As shown in Fig. 1, a general MCS consists of a cloud server s and a set of registered mobile users $\mathcal{P}$, where $|\mathcal{P}| \geqslant 2$. All users in $\mathcal{P}$ can communicate with s via either WiFi access points, or cellular base stations. For the privacy-preserving requirement, each user in $\mathcal{P}$ has a pseudo-identity $i \in \{1, 2, \ldots, i, \ldots, N\}$ (where $N = |\mathcal{P}|$), which enables anonymous communications between i and s (will be explained later).

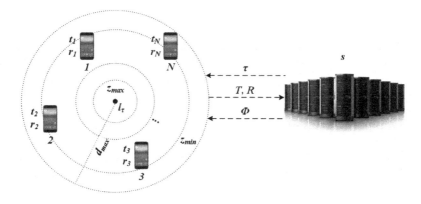

Fig. 1. A system model

For a specific MCS task τ, s publishes an announcement that clarifies the required sensing observation o_τ (e.g., what data is required), and the desired sensing location l_τ (e.g., where the data should be sensed). An user $i \in \mathcal{P}$ within the effective sensing area (e.g., the circular area with l_τ as the center, and d_{max} as the radius) can participate in τ according to their interests.

For each task participant $i \in \mathcal{E} = \{1, 2, \ldots, M\}$ ($\mathcal{E} \subseteq \mathcal{P}$), i determines its serving time t_i for τ based on its serving confidence c_i, and local status $\boldsymbol{x_i}$ (containing i's geological zone z_i and unit serving price p_i), which will be discussed later. Then, during the serving time t_i, a participant i conducts required sensing obligation and records corresponding observation o_i under s's instruction. When τ is finished, each $i \in \mathcal{E}$ uploads its sensing report $\boldsymbol{r_i}$, which contains o_i, c_i and $\boldsymbol{x_i}$, to s. According to $\mathcal{T} = \{t_1, t_2, \ldots, t_M\}$ and $\mathcal{R} = \{\boldsymbol{r_1}, \boldsymbol{r_2}, \ldots, \boldsymbol{r_M}\}$, s pays corresponding monetary credits $\varPhi = \{\phi_1, \phi_2, \ldots, \phi_M\}$ to $\mathcal{E}$.

We now explicitly define the user incentive problem in privacy-preserving MCSs. To begin with, we clarify the privacy-preserving settings in MCSs. We consider the protection of user privacy with respect to both real identities and precise geological locations. First, via anonymous communications based on pseudo-identities that are dynamically adjusted, the cloud server s will not maintain any derivative relation between sensing reports and their generators. For any user i, no information about its real identity will be disclosed because of participating in MCS tasks[1]. Second, instead of precise GPS coordinates, s is only interested in the rough geological locations of MCS task participants. As illustrated in Fig. 1, the effective sensing area is divided into several geological zones (i.e., from z_{min} to z_{max}, approaching the desired sensing location l_τ). As a user i only uploads its geological zone z_i as a part of its local status, the cloud server s cannot obtain the precise spatial-temporal tracks of MCS task participants.

---

[1] As this can be achieved according to anonymous communications described in [19–22], we provide no further discussion.

In order to provide incentives to users to participate in the sensing efforts in MCSs, it is reasonable for the cloud server s to pay the maximum credits to MCS task participants as a stimulation. Nonetheless, to guarantee MCS sensing accuracy, the actual profit that a participant can obtain by serving a certain task must be determined by the quality of its reported data and its serving costs. In privacy-preserving MCSs, the estimation of reported data quality is challenging for the reasons outlined as follows. First, the lack of relation between real identities and reported data of users obstructs the accountability of historical user behaviors. Second, it is highly possible that self-interested users report dishonestly for higher profits, especially in the non-accountable privacy-preserving scenario. Therefore, to achieve effective user incentives that encourage mobile users to upload quality reports in privacy-preserving MCS tasks, the cloud server s needs to address the following three problems: (i) How to estimate the quality of reported data without knowing user historical behaviors, (ii) How to maximize a participant's profit for stimulation according to the quality of its report, and (ii) How to realize effective user incentives against potential dishonest reporting.

3   Our Approach

In this section, we design our approach to address the aforementioned three problems.

3.1   Online Quality Estimation of User-Reported Data

In the following, we address the issue of how to estimate the quality of the sensing data reported, using only the information related to the current MCS task. Considering the fact that there is no available ground truth of an MCS task τ, meanwhile there is no referable historical information of task participants, s needs to compute τ's sensing truth o_τ according to all reported sensing observations $\mathcal{O} = \{o_1, o_2, \ldots, o_M\}$, which is treated as the criterion to estimate the quality of user-reported data.

To compute o_τ for the estimation of reported data quality, we construct Algorithm 1 based on the sensing truth discovery process in our prior work [23]. Here, it is worth noting the difference between Algorithm 1 and the truth discovery process in [23]: since the work of [23] did not focus on the privacy-preserving scenario, its weighted truth discovery process has access to the historical reputation of each participant, which reflects the prior credibility of its sensing observation. Nonetheless, our Algorithm 1 computes the sensing truth only based on observations of the current task. In addition, the primary purpose of truth discovery in [23] is to evaluate each participant's contribution to the MCS task, while the purpose of our Algorithm 1 is to estimate the quality of reported observations.

3.2   User Profit Definition and Maximization

In this subsection, we formally define the computation of user profits for serving MCS tasks. Meanwhile, we further demonstrate that any participant of an MCS task can obtain its maximum profit only when it behaves honestly and uploads an objective sensing report.

Intuitively, for each participant $i \in \mathcal{M}$ of task τ, its serving profit ϕ_i is determined by considering its serving time t_i ($t_i \geqslant 0$), serving confidence c_i ($0 < c_i \leqslant 1$), reported observation o_i, and local status $\boldsymbol{x_i} = (z_i, p_i)$ (i.e., geological zone z_i ($z_{min} \leqslant z_i \leqslant z_{max}$), and unit serving price p_i ($0 < p_i \leqslant 1$)). Here, c_i indicates the expected quality of i's observation o_i, and p_i indicates i's synthesized unit cost with respect to battery and network traffic for serving τ.

Algorithm 1. Data Quality Estimation based on Truth Discovery

---

Input:
$\mathcal{O}$: observations of $\forall i \in \mathcal{M}$;
ϵ: convergence threshold of truth discovery;
Output:
$\mathcal{Q}$: data quality of $\forall i \in \mathcal{M}$.

---

1 Compute the standard deviation of $\mathcal{O}$: $std_{\mathcal{O}}$;
2 Initialize the discovered truth o_τ as a random value;
3 Initialize $\forall w_i \in \mathcal{W} = 0$ as the initial weight of $\forall o_i \in \mathcal{O}$;
4 Initialize $\forall q_i \in \mathcal{Q} = 0$ as the initial data quality of $\forall i \in \mathcal{M}$;
5 **repeat**
6   **for** $\forall i \in \mathcal{M}$ **do**
7        $w_i = \log(\dfrac{\sum_{j \in \mathcal{M}} \frac{(o_j - o_\tau)^2}{std_{\mathcal{O}}}}{\frac{(o_i - o_\tau)^2}{std_{\mathcal{O}}}})$;
8     $o'_\tau = o_\tau$;
9     $o_\tau = \dfrac{\sum_{j \in \mathcal{M}} w_j o_j}{\sum_{j \in \mathcal{M}} w_j}$;
10 **until** $|o_\tau - o'_\tau| < \epsilon$;
11 **for** $\forall q_i \in \mathcal{Q}$ **do**
12     $q_i = 1 - \dfrac{|o_i - o_\tau|}{o_\tau}$;
13 **return** $\mathcal{Q}$;

Specifically, participant i can compute its expected serving profit $\hat{\phi}_i$ as:

$$\hat{\phi}_i = c_i t_i - p_i \frac{z_i}{z_{max}} t_i^2. \tag{1}$$

Similarly, the cloud server i can derive i's actual serving profit ϕ_i as:

$$\phi_i = q_i t_i - p_i \frac{z_i}{z_{max}} t_i^2. \tag{2}$$

where q_i can be estimated according to Algorithm 1 based on $\mathcal{O}$.

From a practical perspective, we assume that, for each MCS task τ, participant i can locally determine t_i, c_i, and o_i all by itself, whereas z_i and p_i are extracted by mobile device firmware as its local status x_i. In this case, it is easy to obtain that $\hat{\phi}_{imax} = \frac{z_{max}c_i^2}{4p_iz_i}$ when participant i determines to serve τ for $\hat{t}_{imax} = \frac{z_{max}c_i}{2p_iz_i}$. Because x_i is always objectively reported, there is $\phi_{imax} = \hat{\phi}_{imax}$ only when $q_i = c_i$. Therefore, if participant i uploads a more objective c_i that was closer to q_i, and serves for $\hat{t}_{imax}$, he or she should obtain an actual profit ϕ_i, which is closer to $\hat{\phi}_{imax}$. According to Subsect. 3.1, for each MCS participant, an effective way to enhance the quality of reported data in privacy-preserving MCSs is to honestly report objective sensing observations.

3.3   User Incentive-Based Scheme Against Dishonest Reporting

Based on our data quality estimation mechanism and user serving profit model, we now design a user Incentive-based scheme Against Dishonest Reporting (IADR) for cloud servers of privacy-preserving MCSs.

According to Subsect. 3.2, each participant $i \in \mathcal{M}$ of task τ can determine t_i, c_i, and o_i in its sensing report r_i. In fact, participants may report dishonestly for potentially higher profits, considering their self-interested nature. To encourage participants to upload objective reports, the cloud server s is responsible for rewarding participants for quality data and reprimand those who are dishonest. Nonetheless, this is difficult to realize based solely on our data quality estimation method and user serving profit model.

From the perspective of the cloud server s, local report determinations of all participants can be formalized as a non-cooperative game, considering the fact that each $i \in \mathcal{M}$ does not know about the decisions of the other participants. Thus, inspired by the BMT algorithm in [24], we developed the IADR scheme for cloud server s to autonomously enhance/downgrade the serving profit of each participant according to its actual impact on the total profit of all participants. Specifically, IADR consists of two components: (i) *Zone-Distinguished Quality Estimation* and (ii) *Impact-Driven Profit Determination*.

Zone-Distinguished Quality Estimation. When receiving all $r_i \in \mathcal{R}$ of a single MCS task τ, it is reasonable for cloud server s to separately estimate the quality of the reported data of different geological zones, considering the fact that sensing observations at different distances from the desired sensing location are likely to be different. The quality of each observation is estimated considering all other observations from its same zone.

Impact-Driven Profit Determination. After obtaining all $q_i \in \mathcal{Q}$, s needs to determine the final serving profit ϕ_i for each $i \in \mathcal{M}$ based on $\mathcal{T}$, $\mathcal{R}$ and $\mathcal{Q}$. Specifically, our impact-driven profit determination process is shown in Algorithm 2: if a participant has a positive effect on τ, it deserves a bonus reward; otherwise it will be reprimanded.

Algorithm 2. Impact-Driven Profit Determination

Input:
$\mathcal{T}$: serving time of $\forall i \in \mathcal{M}$;
$\mathcal{R}$: sensing reports of $\forall i \in \mathcal{M}$, where $r_i = (o_i, c_i, z_i, p_i)$;
$\mathcal{Q}$: data qualities of $\forall i \in \mathcal{M}$;
Output:
Φ: final profits of $\forall i \in \mathcal{M}$.

1 **for** $\forall i \in \mathcal{M}$ **do**
2 $\quad$ calculate $\phi_i = q_i t_i - p_i \frac{z_i}{z_{max}} t_i^2$;
3 **for** $\forall i \in \mathcal{M}$ **do**
4 $\quad$ **for** $\forall j \in \mathcal{M}/i$ **do**
5 $\quad\quad$ calculate $\phi'_j = \frac{z_{max} q_j^2}{4 p_j z_j}$;
6 $\quad$ calculate $\delta_i = \sum_{j \in \mathcal{M}/i} \phi_j - \sum_{j \in \mathcal{M}/i} \phi'_j$;
7 $\quad$ $\phi_i = \phi_i + \delta_i$;
8 **return** Φ;

4 Performance Evaluation

In this section, we demonstrate the effectiveness of IADR in confronting dishonest reporting through extensive simulations. In the following, we first describe the evaluation methodology and then present evaluation results.

4.1 Evaluation Methodology

To evaluate the effectiveness of IADR, our evaluation adopted a real-world outdoor temperature dataset crowdsensed by taxis in Rome, Italy [25]. The used dataset contains 4485 entries, which are opportunistically uploaded by 366 taxis within 24 h. Each entry contains a temperature sensing observation, its generator, sensing time, and the GPS coordinates of the sensing location.

According to the dataset, we constructed an MCS with one cloud server and 366 mobile users on the OMNeT++4.6 simulator. A fixed effective sensing area was divided into 5 geological zones (i.e., $z_{min} = 1$, $z_{max} = 5$), and GPS coordinates in all data entries were mapped into corresponding geological zones. For each round of simulation, the cloud server spontaneously announced MCS tasks, and each user participated in the tasks and uploaded sensing reports according to corresponding data entries. Each round of simulation lasted for 86400 simulation seconds.

In terms of parameter settings, we set unit serving price p of all users as 0.5 for the sake of simplicity, and set the truth discovery convergence threshold $\epsilon = 0.1$ for controlling accuracy. For benign participants who follow the system regulations, the serving confidence c is set as the estimated data quality in the last MCS task q'. They serve each task for $\hat{t}_{max}$ before uploading objective sensing report r. Nonetheless, for potential dishonest participants, they may upload non-objective sensing observation o or/and serving confidence c.

In our simulations, we formulated two patterns of dishonest reporting from participants: (i) only a single factor in the report is non-objective (i.e., random o_i ($2\,°C \leqslant o_i \leqslant 24\,°C$), random c_i ($0 < c_i \leqslant 1$), or higher c_i ($c_i = 1$)), and (ii) there are multiple non-objective factors in the report (i.e., random o_i and random c_i, or random o_i and higher c_i). Without introducing any dishonest reporting into the system deliberately, we ran a round of simulation, in which all participants followed system regulations as our baseline scenario. Then, we designed two sets of experiments to analyze the impacts of dishonest reporting on MCS's sensing accuracy and participant's serving profit, respectively. We further discussed whether IADR can realize effective user incentive against dishonest reporting based on the results.

4.2   Impact of Dishonest Reporting on MCS's Sensing Accuracy

Considering the fact that the primary requirement of MCS is to achieve accurate sensing, we investigate the impacts of different ratios of dishonest reporting (i.e., the ratio of dishonest reporting to total reports) on MCS's sensing accuracy in this set of experiments. Specifically, we conducted two groups of simulations, where all participants were set to perform dishonest reporting at rates of 10% and 15% in all MCS tasks, respectively. One thing should be noted is that our settings should be reasonably considering the ratio of malicious behaviors in existing mechanisms (e.g., 10% in [26] and 4% in [27]). All discovered sensing truths during simulations were collected, and their cumulative distributions are shown in Figs. 2 and 3.

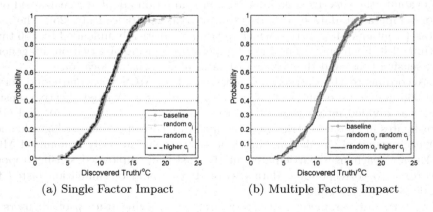

(a) Single Factor Impact   (b) Multiple Factors Impact

Fig. 2. Impact of general dishonest reporting (10%) on discovered truth

According to Fig. 2, we can observe that: with a 10% general dishonest reporting ratio, neither the report with single non-objective factor, nor the report with multiple non-objective factors obviously affects the cumulative distribution of discovered sensing truth. In detail, the average discovered sensing truth of the 'baseline' scenario is 11.28 °C, and that of other scenarios are: (i) random o_i: 11.39 °C, (ii) random c_i: 11.26 °C, (iii) higher c_i: 11.28 °C, (iv) random o_i and random c_i: 11.54 °C, (v) random o_i and higher c_i: 11.39 °C. The maximum deviation of the average sensing truth is 2.30%, which is nearly negligible, especially considering that 10% of the total reporting are non-objective.

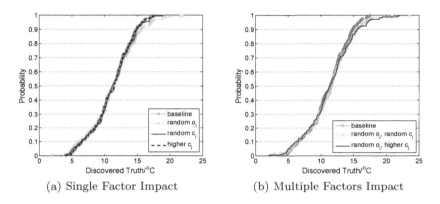

(a) Single Factor Impact   (b) Multiple Factors Impact

Fig. 3. Impact of general dishonest reporting (15%) on discovered truth

According to Fig. 3, the evaluation results with a 15% general dishonest reporting ratio is similar: the cumulative distribution of discovered sensing truth is not significantly affected by either single non-objective factor or multiple non-objective factors, and the maximum deviation of the average sensing truth is 2.04%, which is also negligible.

To summarize, the evaluation results indicate that IADR can effectively guarantee the MCS sensing accuracy in MCSs with dishonest reporting.

4.3   Impact of Dishonest Reporting on User Profit

Considering the fact that the essential reason for mobile users to participate in MCS tasks is to obtain profit for sensing services offered, we investigate the impact of a user's dishonest reporting on its own serving profit in this set of experiments. Specifically, we conducted three groups of simulations, where the user (i) participates in the most number of MCS tasks (i.e., the TopC user), (ii) obtains the most serving profit (i.e., the TopP user), and (iii) obtains less serving profit (i.e., the LessP user), in the baseline scenario was set to perform dishonest reporting in all MCS tasks, respectively. It should be reasonable for us to evaluate these representative users for a thorough understanding on IADR's performance. The variations of the total serving profit of these users along an entire simulation round were collected, which are depicted in Figs. 4, 5, and 6.

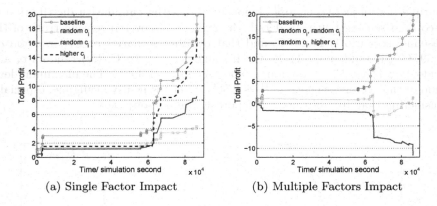

(a) Single Factor Impact   (b) Multiple Factors Impact

Fig. 4. Impact of TopC user's dishonest reporting on its total profit

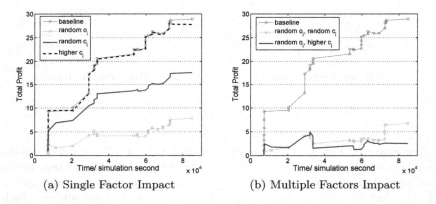

(a) Single Factor Impact   (b) Multiple Factors Impact

Fig. 5. Impact of TopP user's dishonest reporting on its total profit

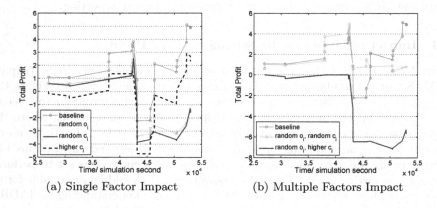

(a) Single Factor Impact   (b) Multiple Factors Impact

Fig. 6. Impact of LessP user's dishonest reporting on its total profit

According to Fig. 4, we can observe that the total profit of the TopC user is severely downgraded as long as it reports non-objective factor/factors. In detail, in the 'baseline' scenario, its total profit at the end of the simulation round is 19.87, and that of other scenarios are: (i) random o_i: 4.32 (-78.26%), (ii) random c_i: 8.49 (-57.27%), (iii) higher c_i: 17.58 (-11.52%), (iv) random o_i and random c_i: 1.33 (-93.31%), (v) random o_i and higher c_i: -11.63 (-158.53%). Although that the TopC user is one of the most active users in the MCS, its serving profit is still dominated by the quality of its reports.

According to Fig. 5, we can see that as long as the TopP user performs non-objective reporting, its total profit will be severely downgraded. Considering the fact that the TopP user is one of those who provides the most quality sensing reports in the MCS, objective reporting is demonstrated to be effective in enhancing a user's serving profit.

According to Fig. 6, the total profit of the LessP user is also severely downgraded if it uploads non-objective reports. In addition, since the LessP user can represent the majority of MCS participants (e.g., mediocre ones), the simulation results indicate that, with the adoption of IADR, the LessP user cannot obtain higher profit by uploading non-objective reports.

To summarize, our results demonstrate that IADR achieves effective user incentive against dishonest reporting in MCSs.

5   Conclusion

In this paper, we developed a user incentive-based scheme against dishonest reporting in privacy-preserving MCSs, which encourages mobile users to honestly report sensing information. To be specific, we first developed an online mechanism for the MCS server to estimate the quality of reported data. We then constructed a serving profit model, which would maximize the profit of honest users. Further, we developed a mechanism for the MCS server to autonomously reward honest users, while reprimanding those who are dishonest. To demonstrate the effectiveness of our proposed scheme, we performed an extensive performance evaluation using real-world crowdsensing data. Our experimental results demonstrated that our scheme can ensure MCS sensing accuracy when there exists harsh dishonest reporting, meanwhile it can effectively reprimand users who report dishonest sensing information.

References

1. Guo, B., Wang, Z., Yu, Z., Wang, Y., Yen, N., Huang, R., Zhou, X.: Mobile crowd sensing and computing: the review of an emerging human-powered sensing paradigm. ACM CSUR **48**(1), 7 (2015)
2. Duan, Z., Li, W., Cai, Z.: Distributed auctions for task assignment and scheduling in mobile crowdsensing systems. In: Proceedings of IEEE ICDCS (2017)
3. Capezzuto, L., Abbamonte, L., De Vito, S., Massera, E.: A maker friendly mobile and social sensing approach to urban air quality monitoring. In: Proceedings of IEEE Sensors, pp. 12–16 (2014)

4. Gao, R., Zhao, M., Ye, T., Ye, F., Wang, Y., Bian, K., Wang, T., Li, X.: Jigsaw: indoor floor plan reconstruction via mobile crowdsensing. In: Proceedings of ACM Mobicom, pp. 249–260 (2014)
5. Bakht, M., Trower, M., Kravets, R.: Searchlight: won't you be my neighbor? In: Proceedings of ACM Mobicom, pp. 185–196 (2012)
6. Li, J., Cai, Z., Yan, M., Li, Y.: Using crowdsourced data in location-based social networks to explore influence maximization. In: Proceedings of IEEE Infocom (2016)
7. Lin, J., Yu, W., Zhang, N., Yang, X., Zhang, H., Zhao, W.: A survey on internet of things: architecture, enabling technologies, security and privacy, and applications. IEEE Internet-of-Things (IoT) J. (2017)
8. Ren, X., Yang, X., Lin, J., Yu, W.: On binary decomposition based privacy-preserving aggregation schemes in real-time monitoring systems. IEEE Trans. Parallel Distrib. Syst. **27**(10), 2967–2983 (2016)
9. Yurur, O., Liu, C., Sheng, Z., Leung, V.: Context-awareness for mobile sensing: a survey and future directions. IEEE Commun. Surv. Tuts. **18**(1), 68–93 (2016)
10. Duan, Z., Yan, M., Cai, Z., Wang, X., Han, M., Li, Y.: Truthful incentive mechanisms for social cost minimization in mobile crowdsourcing systems. Sensors **16**(4), 481 (2016)
11. Zhao, C., Yang, S., Yang, X., McCann, J.: Rapid, user-transparent, and trustworthy device pairing for D2D-enabled mobile crowdsourcing. IEEE Trans. Mob. Comput. (99), 1 (2016)
12. Na, R., Gao, L., Zhu, H., Jia, W., Li, X., Hu, Q.: Toward optimal dos-resistant authentication in crowdsensing networks via evolutionary game. In: Proceedings of IEEE ICDCS, pp. 364–373 (2016)
13. He, D., Chan, S., Guizani, M.: User privacy and data trustworthiness in mobile crowd sensing. IEEE Wirel. Commun. **22**(1), 28–34 (2015)
14. Wang, Y., Cai, Z., Ying, G., Gao, Y., Tong, X., Wu, G.: An incentive mechanism with privacy protection in mobile crowdsourcing systems. Comput. Netw. **102**, 157–171 (2016)
15. Wang, X., Cheng, W., Mohapatra, P., Abdelzaher, T.: Enabling reputation and trust in privacy-preserving mobile sensing. IEEE Trans. Mob. Comput. **13**(12), 2777–2790 (2014)
16. Wang, W., Zhang, Q.: Location privacy preservation in collaborative spectrum sensing. In: Proceedings of IEEE Infocom, pp. 729–737 (2012)
17. To, H., Ghinita, G., Shahabi, C.: A framework for protecting worker location privacy in spatial crowdsourcing. Proc. VLDB Endow. **7**(10), 919–930 (2014)
18. Li, Q., Cao, G.: Providing efficient privacy-aware incentives for mobile sensing. In: Proceedings of IEEE ICDCS, pp. 208–217 (2014)
19. Ling, Z., Yang, M., Lou, J., Fu, X., Yu, W.: De-anonymizing and countermeasures in anonymous communication networks. IEEE Commun. Mag. **53**(4), 60–66 (2015)
20. Pingley, A., Yu, W., Zhang, N., Fu, X., Zhao, W.: Cap: a context-aware privacy protection system for location-based services. In: Proceedings of IEEE ICDCS, pp. 49–57 (2009)
21. Yu, W., Fu, X., Graham, S., Xuan, D., Zhao, W.: DSSS-based flow marking technique for invisible traceback. In: Proceedings of IEEE S&P, pp. 18–32 (2007)
22. Ling, Z., Luo, J., Yu, W., Fu, X., Xuan, D., Jia, W.: A new cell-counting-based attack against Tor. IEEE/ACM Trans. Netw. **20**(4), 1245–1261 (2012)
23. Zhao, C., Yang, X., Yu, W., Yao, X., Lin, J., Li, X.: Cheating-resilient incentive scheme for mobile crowdsensing systems. In: Proceedings of IEEE CCNC, pp. 1–6 (2017)

24. Yang, S., Adeel, U., McCann, J.: Backpressure meets taxes: faithful data collection in stochastic mobile phone sensing systems. In: Proceedings of IEEE Infocom, pp. 1490–1498 (2015)
25. Alswailim, M.A,. Hassanein, H.S., Zulkernine, M.: CRAWDAD dataset queensu/crowd_temperature (v.2015-11-20) (2015). http://crawdad.org/queensu/crowd_temperature/20151120
26. Li, X., Zhou, F., Yang, X.: Scalable feedback aggregating (SFA) overlay for large-scale P2P trust management. IEEE Trans. Parallel Distrib. Syst. **23**(10), 1944–1957 (2012)
27. Shen, H., Lin, Y., Sapra, K., Li, Z.: Enhancing collusion resilience in reputation systems. IEEE Trans. Parallel Distrib. Syst. **27**(8), 2274–2287 (2016)

You Can Charge over the Road: Optimizing Charging Tour in Urban Area

Xunpeng Rao[1], Panlong Yang[1,2(✉)], and YuboYan[1,2]

[1] PLA University of Science and Technology, Nanjing, China
raoxunpeng@gmail.com, panlongyang@gmail.com, yanyub@gmail.com
[2] University of Science and Technology of China, Hefei, China

Abstract. Wireless energy transfer has provided a promising technology to extend the lifetime of wireless rechargeable sensor network. Most of previous studies focus on scheduling chargers or deploying stationary charging stations to replenish energy for rechargeable sensors. These methods could not be applicable when real deployment is concerned, because the roadway needs to be fully respected for mobile chargers in typical urban area. In dealing with this difficulty, we investigate the problem of scheduling mobile chargers with mobility constraints in the scenario of a city graph. First of all, we aim at optimizing the traveling path for chargers to minimize the traveling cost. Consequently, we convert our scheduling problem into edge coverage problem, which is quite different from the point coverage problem. Then classical problem CARP (Capacitated Arc Routing Problem), which has been proved NP-hard, is applied to solve aforementioned problem. To this end, a simple but efficient genetic algorithm cooperated with decoding algorithm Split is proposed. Finally, we evaluate the impacts of different parameters on our algorithm and get the near optimal solution.

Keywords: Wireless rechargeable sensor network · Capacitated Arc Routing Problem · Genetic algorithm

1 Introduction

1.1 Backgrounds and Motivation

With the extensive development of wireless sensor network, it had been applied in urban road monitor system [2,4]. The wireless public transportation monitoring network, which can efficiently promote improved transportation efficiency, has been studied in [1]. Considering the characteristics of traffic monitoring and the urban traffic architectures, numerous routing protocols have been proposed to optimize the energy conservation and extend the network life [6]. Specially, the concerns in energy efficiency had attracted more attentions. Many solutions, *e.g.*, [7,8] focus on the optimal energy-efficient route by taking routing cost and remaining energy of nodes into consideration simultaneously. Considering the balance between energy consumption and time delay, [5] proposed an optimal

© Springer International Publishing AG 2017
L. Ma et al. (Eds.): WASA 2017, LNCS 10251, pp. 768–779, 2017.
DOI: 10.1007/978-3-319-60033-8_65

energy-efficient routing scheme. In summary, most of existing work in urban traffic-monitoring network usually aim to pursue the minimum energy consumption or the maximum network lifetime. Due to the sensors limited power, innovative techniques that prolong the network lifetime are highly required.

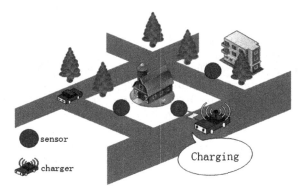

Fig. 1. The scenario of roadside wireless rechargeable traffic sensing network.

As mentioned in [9], wireless energy transfer technologies [10] have become a promising method to extend the lifetime of wireless rechargeable sensor network. Most of existing studies [11,12,16] focus on how to schedule mobile chargers to replenish energy for rechargeable sensors, such as maximizing network lifetime, minimizing charging delay or traveling path. For example in [15], the chargers travel along their predefined paths to charge sensors. As depicted in Figs. 1 and 2, which are similar to [15], the vehicles have to move along the streets belong to topological graph. In that, the recharging with practical considerations of deployment constraints of sensor nodes in urban area should be concerned. We notice that the charging distance between charger and receiver is the main factor that needed to be fully considered for charging efficiency, which has been shown in [10]. Therefore, it is essential for mobile chargers to optimize the charging distance between node and charger carefully. Meanwhile, the mobility constraint caused by roadway should be respected. However, most of existing studies [13,26] regard the recharging for a sensor node as visiting or covering a point. Therefore, the points coverage problems, that all points are required to be covered by chargers over a cycle path, are usually been converted into Traveling Sales Problem. The common feature of above studies is ignoring the mobility constraints caused by geography. These methods are impractical when the mobility constraints cannot be ignored, *e.g.*, city graph. Also, the paths selection problem in the [15] is converted into set cover problem which is unsuitable for scheduling chargers. To the best of our knowledge, there are not any studies focus on handling this kind of scheduling problem with mobility constraints. Motivated by this kind of insufficient in scheduling with mobility constraints, we investigate the problem of scheduling mobile chargers to service nodes with mobility constraints caused by city topological graph. In Fig. 1, some of streets are installed with sensor nodes which could monitor the traffic situation. The mobile chargers start from a service station to replenish energy for sensor nodes with wireless energy transfer technologies. After visiting the arranged sensor nodes, it would return to the service station. In the streets, the mobile charger is regarded as a car which should obey the traffic rules. In our problem, we consider how to schedule the mobile charger for sensor nodes deployed on the street. In our concern, the recharging sensors are deployed along the street. For efficient and effective coverage, the mobile charger should go along the entire street segmentation. To this end, the streets equipped with sensors should be regarded as edges in graph perspective. Then the edge coverage problem is incorporated for further study. A preliminary study [3] has been presented, while for this version, we convert our scheduling problem into Capacitated Arc Routing Problem, which has been proved NP-hard. The classical genetic algorithm cooperated with a decoding algorithm is proposed to handle out the problem. Finally, we conduct extensive evaluations, and the results show the improved performance of the genetic algorithm.

1.2 Contributions

In summary, our contributions could be summarized as follows:

- We investigate the scheduling problem for mobile chargers with mobility constraints which has not been studied before. It can be a supplement contribution for scheduling in wireless rechargeable sensor network.

Table 1. Annotations for frequently used symbols

Symbol	Definition
$G = (V, E)$	The city graph
$V = \{v_1, v_2 ..., v_n\}$	The set of crossroads
E	The set of edges
d_{ij}	The distance between crossroad i and j
$S = \{s_1, s_2, ..., s_m\}$	The set of sensor nodes
$E^0 = \{e_1, e_2, ..., e_m\}$	The set of nodes' initial energy
D	The maximum charging distance
p_k^c	Charging power of node k
r_k	The charging distance for node k
$\mathbb{T} = \{t_1, t_2, ..., t_m\}$	The set of recharging time for all nodes
$Q = \{q_k | 1 \le k \le m\}$	The set of recharging cost for all nodes
RC	The total recharging cost
$\mathcal{R} = \{R_1, R_2, ..., R_{|\mathcal{R}|}\}$	The set of traveling path
MC	The moving cost
x_i	The symbol indicates node i is visited or not

- We formulate our problem and convert it into Capacitated Arc Routing Problem. We handle this problem by classical genetic algorithm cooperated with a decoding algorithm Split.
- We made extensive experiments to evaluate the impacts of different parameters on algorithm, and get the near-optimal solution.

1.3 Paper Organization

The remainder of this paper is organized as follows. In Sect. 2, we introduce our proposed network model and recharging model, cost model. In Sect. 3, we formulate our problem and convert it into Capacitated Arc Routing Problem. A genetic algorithm is proposed to solve it. We conduct extensive simulations and show our results with comprehensive analyses in Sect. 4. Finally, we conclude our work in Sect. 5 (Table 1).

2   System Model

2.1   Network Model

We start our scenario with a city graph $G = (V, E)$, where V is the set of vertexes (i.e., crossroads), $V = \{v_1, v_2..., v_n\}$, and E is the set of edges (i.e., streets). Practically, we assume that all of streets are two-way streets. The length d_{ij} between neighbouring crossroad i and j is Euclidean distance, which is given by

$$d_{ij} = ||(v_i, v_j)||_2.$$

As shown in Fig. 1, for sensing the streets traffic, the sensor nodes are deployed at roadsides. The set of sensor nodes is denoted by $S = \{s_1, s_2, ..., s_m\}$. In our model, we assume that each street can only be installed with one sensor node. That is to say, we have $m \leqslant |E|$. All the sensor nodes construct a wireless sensor network that can sensing the traffic for each street in this city.

The initial residue energy of nodes is denoted by $E^0 = \{e_1, e_2, ..., e_m\}$. For long-time continuing energy replenishment, a mobile charger with a battery of capacity E_c (we call charging ability) is scheduled to service sensor nodes by wireless power transfer technologies. The mobile charger starts to service the nodes from a service station. The charger have to travel along the traffic routes and observe traffic regulation. After visiting all sensor nodes, it will return to the service station for recharging or refueling. Similar to [13], we also assume that the nodes' residue energy level is invariable over a charging cycle.

2.2   Recharging Model

Inspired by [14], we know that the charging efficiency would be affected by charging distance between charger and rechargeable device. As depicted in Fig. 2, we take the charging distance into consideration in the recharging model. Denote D the threshold of charging distance, which is the maximum charging distance for nodes. Charger can service nodes if charger is within the charging range determined by a threshold. To minimize energy lost, the mobile charger transmits power to a node at the location which is the closest point to that node. The minimum charging distance is denoted by r_k for node k ($1 \leqslant k \leqslant m$). Inspired by the experiments in [23], the charing power p_k^c of node k by charger can be quantified by an empirical model as follows:

$$p_k = (-0.0958r_k^2 - 0.0377r_k + 1) \cdot P_o$$

where the P_o is output power from charger. The charging power for all nodes can be denoted by $P = \{p_k | 1 \leq k \leq m\}$. We assume that the all nodes require being charged to full energy E_{max}. Then the charging time at node k can be given by:

$$t_k = \frac{E_{\max} - e_k}{p_k}.$$

Denote $\mathbb{T} = \{t_1, t_2, ..., t_m\}$ the recharging time for all sensor nodes.

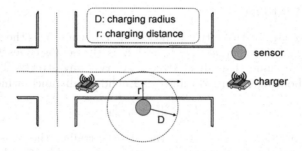

Fig. 2. The recharging model

2.3   Cost Model

In this subsection, we would introduce the recharging cost and moving cost. As mentioned in Sect. 2.2, the charging power received on nodes would be affected by charging distance, which means that the recharging cost for each node is different. For node k, the recharging cost of charger can be given by $q_k = p_k \cdot t_k$. Therefore, the required recharging cost for all nodes can be denoted by $Q = \{q_k | 1 \leq k \leq m\}$, and RC is the sum of each node's required recharging cost, which is

$$RC = \sum_{k=1}^{m} q_k.$$

Another cost is moving cost with respect to the moving distance. We assume that the mobile charger moves with a constant moving speed. The traveling path of mobile charger is assumed with $\mathcal{R} = \{R_1, R_2, ..., R_{|\mathcal{R}|}\}$ which consists of edges in graph G, $i.e.$, $\mathcal{R} \subseteq E$. Also, the symbol R_i could be used to denote the traveling cost in R_i. Then the total moving cost denoted by MC can be given by:

$$MC = D(\pi, R_1) + \sum_{i=1}^{|\mathcal{R}|-1} [R_i + D(R_i, R_{i+1})] + R_{|\mathcal{R}|} + D(R_{|\mathcal{R}|}, \pi)$$

where the $D(R_i, R_{i+1})$ is the moving distance from R_i to R_{i+1} and π is the service station.

3   Problem Formulation and Solution

3.1   Problem Formulation

With the models we have discussed in Sect. 2, we need to find an optimal traveling path for mobile charger to minimize the moving cost. Denote x_i at the state that the node i is visited by charger or not, which is given by:

$$x_i = \begin{cases} 1 & visited \\ 0 & not\,visited \end{cases}$$

Then our problem can be formulated as follows:

$$\min\ MC$$
$$s.t.\ \sum_{i=1}^{m} x_i = m;$$
$$RC < K \cdot E_c;$$

where the K is the number of mobile chargers. Then our problem is how to schedule the mobile chargers with the objective of minimizing moving cost. In this paper, our problem could be formulated into a famous Arc Routing Problem (ARP) with two cases:

(1) $m = |E|$. It means all streets are installed with one node. That is to say, all edge in graph G should be visited, which we call Chinese Postman Problem (CPP) [18];
(2) $0 < m < |E|$. It means only some of edges in G should be visited. And we call it Rural Postman Problem (RPP) [19], which has been proved NP-hard.

3.2   Problem Analysis

Given a graph $G = (V, E)$, in the first case, CPP is an edge coverage problem in a graph with minimum distance. For ease of conversion, the postman is regarded as the mobile charger and visiting an edge is considered as recharging a that the node in the edge should be charged by charger. This problem can be reduced into Eulerian Tour problem [20] if the graph is Eulerian graph. It has been proved that typical CPP could be solved in polynomial time. An algorithm with computation complexity $O(|V|^3)$ proposed by Edmonds and Johnson [21] can be used.

In the second case, RPP need constrained combinatorial computation, where the selected visiting edges are the subset of all edges in the graph. Taking the charging ability into consideration, it is also known as CARP (Capacitated Arc Routing Problem) [24] which has been proved NP-hard. That is to say, only the edges in subset $E' \subseteq E$ are allowed to visit. This case is more practical than the first one. For this problem, an efficient heuristic algorithm called GA (Genetic Algorithm) can be used to handle. Considering the limited charging ability, the case of multi-chargers should be concerned. Then a decoding algorithm called Split [22] could be used for a partitioning method of dividing the service edges into several parts. Each part can be serviced with one mobile charger.

3.3 Algorithm and Solution

Inspired by heuristic algorithm in Traveling Sales Problem, we use the Genetic Algorithm to handle it. As shown in Algorithm 1, it consists of two functions which represent two kinds of algorithms. The first function indicates the genetic algorithm iteration procedures. The below function is an algorithm named Split, which can be used to decode the iteration results. *Select* is the operation of natural selection, and $CrMu$ is the operation of crossover and variation in genetic algorithm. In the crossover operation procedure, we used the general operation of interstitial chiasma. About the variation operation, we select two genes to exchange randomly. From line 15 to 38, the Split can divide all arcs into the several traveling cycle paths with minimum number of chargers. In this function, it output two arrays which are traveling cost array V and the array $Pred$ that can be used to recover the all traveling paths. Given a feasible solution, Split can acquire the minimum traveling cycle paths and chargers with the time complexity $O(n^2)$.

4   Simulation

4.1   Experimental Setups

Given a city graph $G = (V, E)$ in an area of $45\,\text{km} \times 30\,\text{km}$, we use MATLAB to generate $n = |V| = 90$ locations of intersections V and the streets E between some intersections randomly. The city graph is shown in Fig. 3. Similar to existing works [11], the charging output power P_o is set by $5w$. The battery capacity of sensor is $10.8\,\text{kJ}$ [25].

4.2   Evaluation Results and Analyses

The simulation results are shown in Figs. 4, 5 and 6. These figures show the relationship between the number of sensor nodes and traveling cost or charging ability E_c of charger.

Firstly, in Fig. 4, we explore the impacts of the increased number of nodes and charging ability E_c on number of chargers and traveling cost. In Fig. 4(a), we can

---

Algorithm 1. Genetic Algorithm for Capacitated Arc Routing Problem

---

Require: $AdjMat, MAXGEN, Sink, E_c$
Ensure:
1: **function** GA($AdjMat, Chrom, MAXGEN, Sink$)
2:     **while** $num < MAXGEN$ **do**
3:         $FitnV \leftarrow$ SPLIT($Chrom, Sink, E_c, AdjMat$)
4:         $SelCh \leftarrow Select(Chrom, FitnV)$
5:         $Selch \leftarrow CrMu(Selch, P_{cro}, P_{mut})$
6:         $SelFitnV \leftarrow$ SPLIT($Selch, Sink, E_c, AdjMat$)
7:         **if** $SelFitnV < min(FitnV)$ **then**
8:             $Chrom \leftarrow Chrom + Selch;$
9:         **end if**
10:        $num \leftarrow num + 1$
11:     **end while**
12:     **return** $SelCh$
13: **end function**
14:
15: **function** SPLIT($Chrom, Sink, E_c, AdjMat$)
16:     **for** $i = 1 \rightarrow n$ **do**
17:         $load \leftarrow 0$
18:         $cost \leftarrow 0$
19:         $j \leftarrow i$
20:         **while** $j <= n$ **and** $load <= E_c$ **do**
21:             $load \leftarrow load + q[j]$
22:             **if** $i == j]$ **then**
23:                 $cost \leftarrow AdjMat[Sink, Chrom[j]] + \omega(Chrom[j]) + AdjMat[Chrom[j], Sink]$
24:             **else**
25:                 $cost \leftarrow cost - AdjMat[Chrom[j-1], Sink] + djMat[Chrom[j-1], Chrom[j]] + \omega(Chrom[j]) + AdjMat[Chrom[j], Sink]$
26:             **end if**
27:             **if** $load <= E_c$ **then**
28:                 $VNew \leftarrow V[i-1] + cost;$
29:                 **if** $VNew < V[j]$ **then**
30:                     $V[j] \leftarrow VNew;$
31:                     $Pred[j] \leftarrow i - 1;$
32:                 **end if**
33:                 $j \leftarrow j + 1;$
34:             **end if**
35:         **end while**
36:     **end for**
37:     **return** $result$
38: **end function**

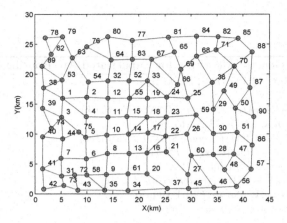

Fig. 3. City roadmap for simulation

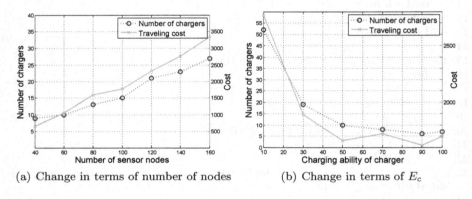

(a) Change in terms of number of nodes   (b) Change in terms of E_c

Fig. 4. The changes of number of chargers and traveling cost.

see that the number of chargers and traveling cost increase with the increased number of sensor nodes. And Fig. 4(b) shows that the number of chargers and traveling cost decrease with the increased charging ability E_c. Considering the constraints of charging ability E_c, it is obvious that more sensor nodes need more chargers. Similarly, more sensor nodes mean more traveling cost. Meanwhile, the number of chargers and traveling cost can be reduced by increasing the charging ability E_c. It means that the way to reduce the number of chargers and traveling cost is to enhance the charging ability of charger.

In addition, we consider that the location of service station may affect the number of chargers. Two experiments are conducted, that the results are shown in Fig. 5. Three cases of service station locations are taken into consideration, that are city center, city and suburb. In Fig. 5, it shows that the number of chargers would not be affected with different service stations in terms of the increased number of nodes or charging ability E_c. From these two figures, we

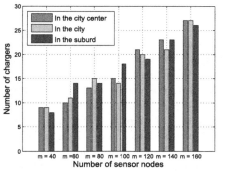

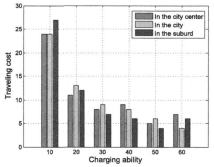

(a) Chargers' number in terms of number of nodes

(b) Chargers' number in terms of E_c

Fig. 5. The changes of number of chargers with different service stations.

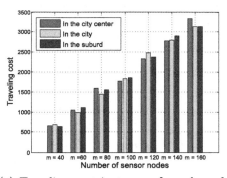

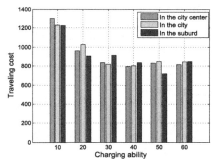

(a) Traveling cost in terms of number of nodes

(b) Traveling cost in terms of E_c

Fig. 6. The changes of traveling cost with different service stations.

can get that the number of chargers wouldn't be affected by the location of service station.

Lastly, we investigate the impact of different locations of service station on traveling cost with the increased number of nodes or charging ability E_c. In Fig. 6, it can see that the traveling cost would not be affected by different service stations with the increased number of nodes or charging ability E_c. Otherwise, we can see that the traveling cost would decrease firstly and then maintain unchanged. Because, in the decreasing stage, the traveling cost is determined by the chargers's total traveling cost. In the maintaining stage, the traveling cost is determined by the locations of nodes and service station.

By combining the same phenomenon between Figs. 5 and 6, we can see that the number of chargers and traveling cost is insensitive to the location of service station.

5   Conclusion

In this paper, we investigate the problem of scheduling mobile chargers with mobility constraints. The chargers start from and end with the service station, which are scheduled to charged sensor nodes following the city topological graph. With the objective of minimizing the traveling cost, we aim at optimizing the traveling path for chargers. And we convert our scheduling problem into a class Capacitated Arc Routing Problem, which has been proved NP-hard. Then a simple but efficient genetic algorithm is proposed to handle it. Furthermore, a decoding algorithm named Split is cooperated to acquire the exact solution. Finally, we evaluate the impact of different parameters on our algorithm. And we can see that the number of chargers and traveling cost are insensitive to the location of service station.

Acknowledgments. This research is partially supported by NSF of Jiangsu For Distinguished Young Scientist: BK20150030, NSFC with Nos. 61632010, 61232018, 61371118, China National Funds for Distinguished Young Scientists with Nos. 61625205, Key Research Program of Frontier Sciences, CAS, Nos. QYZDY-SSW-JSC002, 61402009, 61672038, 61520106007 and NSF ECCS-1247944, NSF CMMI 1436786, and NSF CNS 1526638.

References

1. Wang, X., Guo, L., Ai, C., Li, J., Cai, Z.: An urban area-oriented traffic information query strategy in VANETs. In: Ren, K., Liu, X., Liang, W., Xu, M., Jia, X., Xing, K. (eds.) WASA 2013. LNCS, vol. 7992, pp. 313–324. Springer, Heidelberg (2013). doi:10.1007/978-3-642-39701-1_26
2. Huang, Y., et al.: Multicast capacity analysis for social-proximity urban bus-assisted VANETs. In: IEEE International Conference on Communications, pp. 6138–6142. IEEE (2013)
3. Rao, X., Yang, P., et al.: Poster abstract: optimizing tours for mobile chargers with roadside segment coverage. ACM International Conference on Internet-of-Things Design and Implementation (2017)
4. Guan, X., Huang, Y., Cai, Z., et al.: Intersection-based forwarding protocol for vehicular ad hoc networks. Telecommun. Syst. **62**(1), 1–10 (2016)
5. Zhou, J., Chen, C.L.P., Chen, L.: A small-scale traffic monitoring system in urban wireless sensor networks. In: IEEE International Conference on Systems, Man, and Cybernetics, pp. 4929–4934. IEEE (2013)
6. Alkaraki, J.N., Kamal, A.E.: Routing techniques in wireless sensor networks: a survey. IEEE Wirel. Commun. **11**(6), 6–28 (2004)
7. Gan, L., Liu, J., Jin, X.: Agent-based, energy efficient routing in sensor networks. In: International Joint Conference on Autonomous Agents and Multiagent Systems, pp. 472–479. IEEE Xplore (2004)
8. Heo, J., Hong, J., Cho, Y.: EARQ: energy aware routing for real-time and reliable communication in wireless industrial sensor networks. IEEE Trans. Industr. Inf. **5**(1), 3–11 (2009)
9. Yang, Y., Wang, C.: Wireless Rechargeable Sensor Networks. Springer, Berlin (2015)

10. Kurs, A., Karalis, A., Moffatt, R., et al.: Wireless power transfer via strongly coupled magnetic resonances. Science **317**(5834), 83–86 (2007)
11. Shi, Y., Xie, L., Hou, Y.T., et al.: On renewable sensor networks with wireless energy transfer. Proc. IEEE INFOCOM **1**(3), 1350–1358 (2011)
12. Fu, L., Cheng, P., Gu, Y., et al.: Minimizing charging delay in wireless rechargeable sensor networks. In: 2013 Proceedings IEEE INFOCOM, pp. 2922–2930. IEEE (2013)
13. Chen, L., Lin, S., Huang, H.: Charge me if you can: charging path optimization and scheduling in mobile networks. The, ACM International Symposium, pp. 101–110. ACM (2016)
14. Kurs, A., Moffatt, R., Soljacic, M.: Simultaneous mid-range power transfer to multiple devices. Appl. Phys. Lett. **96**(4), 044102 (2010)
15. Zhang, S., Qian, Z., Wu, J., et al.: Optimizing itinerary selection and charging association for mobile chargers. **PP**(99), 1 (2016)
16. He, S., Chen, J., Jiang, F., et al.: Energy provisioning in wireless rechargeable sensor networks. IEEE Trans. Mob. Comput. **12**(10), 1931–1942 (2013)
17. Kwan, M.K.: Graphic programming using odd or even points. Chin. Math **1**, 263–266 (1962)
18. Orloff, C.S.: A fundamental problem in vehicle routing. Networks **4**(1), 35–64 (1974)
19. Eiselt, H.A., Laporte, G.: A historical perspective on arc routing. In: Dror, M. (ed.) Arc Routing, pp. 11–19. Springer, New York (2000)
20. Edmonds, J., Johnson, E.L.: Matching, Euler tours and the Chinese postman. Math. Program. **5**(1), 88–124 (1973)
21. Lacomme, P., Prins, C., Ramdane-Cherif, W.: Competitive memetic algorithms for arc routing problems. Ann. Oper. Res. **131**(1), 159–185 (2004)
22. Dai, H., Liu, Y., Chen, G., et al.: Safe charging for wireless power transfer. In: Proceedings of IEEE INFOCOM, pp. 1105–1113 (2014)
23. Xie, L., Shi, Y., Hou, Y.T., et al.: Multi-node wireless energy charging in sensor networks. IEEE/ACM Trans. Netw. **23**(2), 1 (2014)
24. Golden, B.L., Wong, R.T.: Capacitated arc routing problems. Networks **11**(3), 305–315 (1981)
25. Linden, D.: Handbook of batteries. Fuel Energy Abstr. **36**(36), 265–265 (2002)
26. Zhao, J., Dai, X., Wang, X.: Scheduling with collaborative mobile chargers inter-WSNs. Int. J. Distrib. Sens. Netw. **2015**, 1–7 (2015)

A HCI Motion Recognition System Based on Channel State Information with Fine Granularity

Hao Yang[1,2(✉)], Licai Zhu[1], and Weipeng Lv[1]

[1] Yancheng Normal University, Yancheng, China
anysuc@163.com
[2] Jiangsu Key Laboratory for Big Data of Psychology and Cognitive Science, Yancheng, China

Abstract. Interactive applications, such as somatic games, attract various researches on developing robust human-computer interfaces (HCI) to improve user experiences. Inspired by recent advances in RF-based human sensing, we seek to extract motion-induced Doppler effects using Channel State Information (CSI) provided on commercial WiFi devices. Our work is motivated from the observation that the direction of motion will lead to different frequency shift, which could be extracted and used to isolate the detailed directions from ambiguous trajectory. In this paper, we prototype *WiSome*, a contactless somatic game with off-the-shelf WiFi, which is able to accurately recognize the player's movements with different directions without training. Extensive experiments validate that *WiSome* is superior to the previous methods, which could reach to an overall recognition accuracy of 95.4%.

Keywords: Channel State Information · Human-computer interface · Motion recognition

1 Introduction

Researchers have found that interactive soft sports (*e.g.* somatic games) can improve the fitness, health and social involvement of players [1]. In this case, various human-computer interfaces (HCI) arise in the industries (*e.g.* Kinect Sports) and academia [2]. Most interfaces rely on contactless technologies, such as computer vision, inertial sensors, sonic technology. Due to unsatisfactory exercise conditions in contemporary life (*e.g.* fragmented time and space) [3–6], a more ubiquitous HCI with fewer environment constraints is essential to interactive somatic games.

This paper explores to promote the state-of-the-art WiFi based HCI by utilizing Doppler effect of incident signals. Its essential consideration is to extract motions deduced from the changes of incident signals with fine granularity. In detail, Doppler shift of Channel State Information (CSI) from PHY layer is adopted to recognize different directions of movements. In our work, the detailed motion directions will be identified through extracting frequency shift from the preprocessed data. Moreover, the sensing plane which moving in is further subdivided compared to the previous method. As a proof-of-concept, we propose *WiSome*, a somatic-game with off-the-shelf commercial

© Springer International Publishing AG 2017
L. Ma et al. (Eds.): WASA 2017, LNCS 10251, pp. 780–790, 2017.
DOI: 10.1007/978-3-319-60033-8_66

WiFi devices as shown in Fig. 1. We demonstrate its performance in extensive experiments. *WiSome* is able to satisfactorily distinguish different movement directions. On the contrary, most previous methods can only differentiate coarse categories. Furthermore, the performance of *WiSome* is comparable to popular classifiers, such as kNN and SVM. Our work is similar with [7] while more accurate recognization. Extensive experiments validate that *WiSome* achieves the recognition accuracy of 95.4%.

Fig. 1. Human-computer interaction interface of *WiSome*

Our main contributions are summarized as follows:

- *Analyzing fine-grained directions of movements via physical layer on off-the-shelf wireless infrastructure in a non-invasive and contactless manner*: To the best of our knowledge, *WiSome* provides the first solution to accurately recognize the directions of human motion with fine granularity on COTS wireless devices. Compared to the previous gesture recognition methods, our solution is able to isolate the detailed direction from straight directions. Furthermore, it can identify the directions of motions separately from oblique directions.
- *Recognizing motion directions by extracting Doppler shifts of CSI signals derived from human movements*: Our solution is benefited by the observation that the frequency of the radio signals will lead to shift based on Doppler effect, which can be used to isolate the detailed directions. To adequately extract the frequency shift from raw CSI, *WiSome* includes three modules, data preprocessing, doppler extracting and movement recognizing.
- *Different motions are recognized by WiSome without prior training under the WiFi environment*: To validate the effectiveness of *WiSome*, various indoor settings of experiments are considered. By exploiting the complete information of Doppler shifts for motion recognition, it outperforms the existing approaches.

2 Methodology

2.1 System Overview

WiSome is a contactless interactive somatic-game with fine granularity under commercial devices in WiFi. Its main technical challenge is to promptly and precisely recognize the human motion direction from raw CSI signals by extracting Doppler frequency shift.

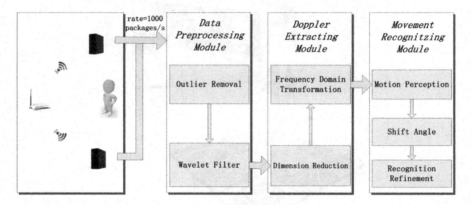

Fig. 2. The framework of our system

As shown in Fig. 2, *WiSome* includes three modules as following:

- *Data Preprocessing Module* processes the raw signals by removing outlier, filtering waveform so as to present the effect of Doppler shift clearly.
- *Doppler Extracting Module* extracts sufficient information of Doppler effect from CSI by reducing the dimension of CSI and transforming frequency domain.
- *Movement Recognizing Module* identifies motion directions of the player by perceiving motion, shifting angle and refining result.

2.2 Data Preprocessing Module

Outlier Removal. Raw received CSI always contain a variety of outliers, such as several abrupt changes, which are apparently not induced by the player's actions. Therefore, we need to remove them from amplitudes and phases of CSI, because they will interfere the effects of Doppler shifts. Figure 3 shows the sequential waveform of one subcarrier. In the figure, some abrupt salutations of both amplitude and phase could be found in the wave profile.

With *WiSome*, Local outlier factor [8] is employed to find anomalous data points. To remove the anomalous point, the local reach density (LRD) of the collected CSI signals

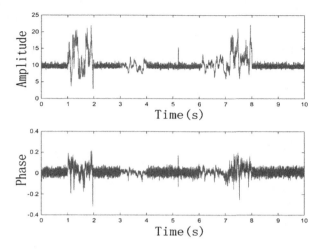

Fig. 3. Before data processing

needs to be measured. This step can avoid disadvantageous affect of occasional saltation of raw CSI. Otherwise, part of outliers may not be filtered and will affect the subsequent processings shown in the Fig. 4.

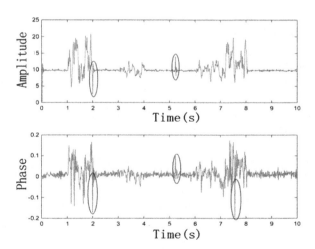

Fig. 4. After data processing *without* outlier removal

Wavelet Filter. Subsequently, the noise of CSI signals should be wiped off. In general, their frequency is located in the high end of the spectrum and the uctuation of signal waveforms induced by motion is in the low frequency of the spectrum. However, the Doppler frequency shift of human moving is not always apparent. Moreover, segment motion need to be divided clearly from the series of CSI for accurate recognition. With *WiSome*, the wavelet filter is employed to not only smooth away noises but also preserve extremely sharp transitions. The Fig. 5 demonstrates the effect of data processing. It is obvious that the signal becomes more recognizable.

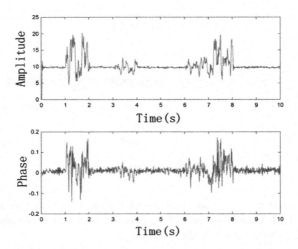

Fig. 5. After data processing *with* outlier removal

2.3   Doppler Extracting Module

Dimension Reduction. After obtaining the multiplication of CSI, we reduce the dimensionality of the result for motion inference. In our work, we collect CSI signal adopting Intel 5300 NIC with 3 receiver antennas, and each data package includes thirty subcarries. That is, the dimension of multiplication is also thirty. Figure 6 illustrates their waveforms as a whole.

For clearly manifestation of the motion inuence, a certain amount of data transmission should be needed. Moreover, the quantity of signals will further increased because of interpolation. Hence, it is necessary to decrease their dimension.

In reality, two characters of subcarries should be noticed. One is that the signals for each subcarrier are relative in aninterval sequence. And the other is that some subcarriers are also associated at several moments. For avoiding destructing the topology of subcarriers while indicating major power variations caused by human motions, *WiSome* utilizes Locally linear embedding (LLE) [9] to reduce the dimensionality of CSI. LLE is a nonlinear dimensionality reduction algorithm and can visualize low dimensional projections of the original data. Different from density modeling methods (*e.g.* PCA) and mixtures of factor analyzers, it is capable of providing a consistent set of global coordinates which embed the observations across the entire manifold, and guaranteing the essential structure of the profile.

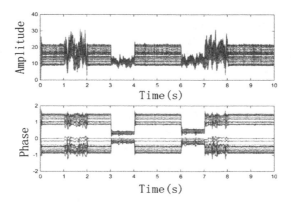

Fig. 6. Waveforms in thirty dimensions

Frequency Domain Transformation. Subsequently, we obtain the corresponding spectrogram of the instantaneous frequency employing short-time Fourier transform (STFT) to extract the effect of Doppler frequency shift. According to our experiments, amplitudes of CSI are almost stable and phases of CSI will not jump evidently in a time slot about 0.18 s, thus we utilize this interval as the time window of STFT.

2.4   Movement Recognizing Module

Motion Perception. For *WiSome*, the player may be static for a while to wait or ascertain the direction symbols (*e.g.* arrow). The motions during the waiting time are not useful in this period. We should detect motion before perceiving the player's motions. More importantly, the lightweight detection should be achieved in order to percept actions as soon as possible. *Wisome* employ the effect size [10] to reach it.

Shift Angle. When the player stretches or retreats his/her leg, the power of spectrogram from the received signal will fluctuate in a divided fragment because of Doppler effect. *WiSome* uses the ratio of accumulative absolute values of the frequency collected from two receivers to distinguish different directions. To present the angle of the Doppler shift, the anticosine of the signal is calculated. For every sampling, uncertain noises induced by various causes obstruct the accuracy of detection, thus *WiSome* adopts two steps to recognize the directions of movements.

We first consider four coarse-grained cases to differentiate the player's motions, which are presented in the counterclockwise order: **case 1** *vertical direction* ("|"), up and down; **case 2** *backslash direction* ("\"), left-up and right-down; **case 3** *horizontal direction* ("-"), left and right; **case 4** *slash direction* ("/"), left-down and right-up. Their theoretical anticosine values are 45, 0, 90 and 135, separately. For robustness empirically, *WiSome* amends the predefined thresholds and sets a tolerance of 20. The recognition results of this step are demonstrated in Fig. 7.

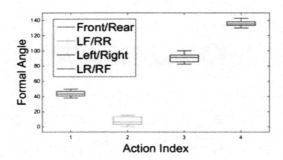

Fig. 7. Differentiation cognition

Recognition Refinement. On this basis, *WiSome* refines fine-grained movement directions of the player. The above four cases are differentiated as eight directions through the orders of positive and negative ratio shifts. According to the above phases, *WiSome* is able to cognise fine-grained movements.

3 Performance Evaluation

3.1 Experiment Settings

We implement our evaluation in diverse offices with different indoor environments. Two mini-computers as two receivers are employed in monitor mode on Channel 157 at 5.785 GHz, which are 3.6 GHz CPU and 4 GB ROM. The operation system is Ubuntu 12.04. They have three omni-directional antennas and the distance of the receiving antennas is one wavelength. The transmitter is TP-Link TL-WR742 N. The devices of *WiSome* are deployed as Fig. 8.

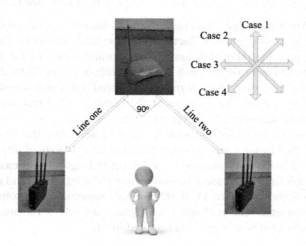

Fig. 8. Profile of *WiSome*

For evaluation, a dancing pad with pressure sensors is utilized to record the real directions of the player's movements. There are eight directions for *WiSome*, which are up ("↑"), left-up ("↖"), left ("←"), left-down ("↙"), down ("↓"), right-down ("↘"), right ("→"), right-up ("↗") separately. In experiments, the player are required to act sufficiently, and there are 5000 records in total.

To equitably illustrate the superiority of *WiSome*, we compare two learning-based methods, kNN-*WiSome*, svm-*WiSome*. They use the same procedures similar to *WiSome*, yet they train samples for eight directions in advance.

3.2   Evaluation

Performance for *WiSome*. Taking all directions into considered, the overall accuracy of detection with *WiSome* reaches to 95.4%. Both 8 × 8 matrices indicate recognition results of *WiSome* in Fig. 9. Their rows denote real directions and their columns denote recognition results. After extensive experiments, *WiSome* could obtain a stable high accuracy for different directions.

Furthermore, the performance of detecting vertical or horizontal direction (case 1 and case 3) is better than the one of recognizing slash or back slash (case 2 and case 4). For instance, the result exhibits that the accuracy of *WiSome* for segment motion could achieve more than 96% for the former, while lower than 93% for the latter in most cases. In addition, the errors just appear in the related directions. For instance, if the real direction is left, the two mistakes are left-up and left-down, it is impossible to be regarded as right or other directions.

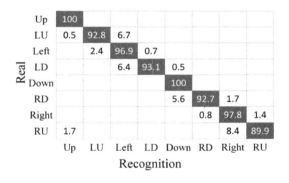

Fig. 9. The accuracy of *WiSome*

Comparison to Training Scheme. To evaluate the performance of our non-training method, we compare *WiSome* to two classical supervised learning schemes, kNN and SVM. kNN-*WiSome* adopts kNN to train eight movement directions. Due to interpolation, the number of samples for each motion is not very small. To accelerate the searching process, *K* Dimensional Tree is utilized to calculate the nearest neighbours of the signals. The reason is that it is suitable for the reduced dimension data of doppler extracting module.

SVM-*WiSome* utilizes One-versus-One SVM (OVOSVM) to classify directions. To generate each sub-classifiers, two types of samples induced by two motions are selected. One type is labeled as positive (record "1") and the other one is negative (record "−1"). In this way, twenty-eight sub-classiers are built. In the process of recognition, the samples will be classied by each of them. Though more sub-classiers have to be trained, this method still takes less time than One-versus-Rest SVM (OVRSVM), because OVRSVM has to use all samples for each training even through it only trains eight sub-classiers. Through universal pairwise comparisons, OVOSVM avoids the biased result. We accumulate the total scores of all sub-classiers and select a category which corresponds to the highest score.

The Figs. 10 and 11 show that the accuracies of recognition for the supervised methods: kNN-*WiSome* is 95.9%, svm-*WiSome* is 95.5%. That is, these schemes are just partly better than *WiSome* and their superiorities are nearly trivial. Hence, we can say that *WiSome* is capable to precisely recognize the directions compared to the training approach.

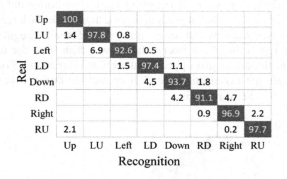

Fig. 10. The accuracy of kNN-*WiSome*

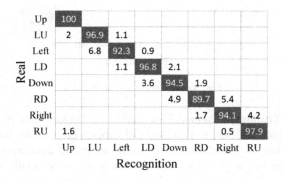

Fig. 11. The accuracy of SVM-*WiSome*

Moreover, it is noticed that both supervised methods attain mild accuracy for each classification. Their accuracies in some oblique directions are higher than that of *WiSome* because they adequately trains different samples before recognition, however, the over-fitting problem in training method also obstructs their performances.

4 Discussion

4.1 External Interference by Other People

WiSome can sense and extract the variance of signal frequency according to Doppler effect. In reality, there exists several Non-Line of Sight (NLOS) paths in the process of wireless propagation, which are derived from the behaviors of other persons around the player through diffusing, reecting and scattering. It results in a more complex composition of the received CSI. The extraction of frequency shift is also blemished. These external interference, more or less, will inuence the performance of *WiSome*. We argue that is a common issue for most of wireless signal-based systems. Some intuitive solutions can partially circumvent this problem. For instance, the transmitting and receiving antennas are deployed in a suitable position, and the directional antenna can be used for the transmitter. For further promoting the performance, their distances can be recalibrated based on experimental measurements.

4.2 Simultaneous Motions by Two Legs

Segment motion or continuous motion deduced by the player could be recognized accurately by *WiSome*. A potential assumption is that the player move one of his/her leg for every motion. The frequency shift can be attributed to only one cause. For some reasons (*e.g.* the occasional distraction), both legs of the player are probably utilized. To address it, conjugate multiplication of the signals from two link should be implemented twice. If the difference of two results is large, it means simultaneous motion by two legs, whereas the player only move one of his/her legs.

4.3 Motion in 3D Space

Our *WiSome* is a somatic game through moving the player's lower limbs. The employed devices and the player are in the same horizontal plane for enhancing the effectiveness of classification. A better experience requests collaborative motions by the player's arms and legs. We leave this issue of recognizing motion in 3D space for the future work.

5 Conclusion

In this paper, we propose a somatic game prototype, *WiSome*, in WiFi. We firstly extract the frequency shifts of the CSI based on Doppler effect in the process of actions. Then, movement directions are recognized from spectrogram of Doppler shifts. Various experiments validate that it attains an overall recognition accuracy of 95.4%. Since *WiSome* achieves delightful performances with only off-the-shelf WiFi devices, we regard it as a hopeful advance for human-computer interface in commercial WiFi and enhance our belief in future wireless contactless applications.

Acknowledgments. This work is supported by National Natural Science Foundation of China under Grant Nos. 61402394, 61379064, National Science Foundation of Jiangsu Province of China under Grant No. BK20140462, Natural Science Foundation of the Higher Education Institutions of Jiangsu Province of China under Grant No. 14KJB520040, China Postdoctoral Science Foundation funded project under Grant No. 2016M591922, Jiangsu Planned Projects for Postdoctoral Research Funds under Grant No. 1601162B, Industry university research project in Jiangsu Province under Grant No.72661632205A, Prospective joint research project of Jiangsu Province under Grant No. BY2016066-04, and sponsored by Qing Lan Project.

References

1. Staiano, A.E., Calvert, S.L.: Exergames for physical education courses: physical, social, and cognitive benefits. Child. Dev. Perspect. **5**(2), 93–98 (2011)
2. MengChieh, C., ShihPing, C., YuChen, C., Hao-Hua, C., ChiaHui, C.C., FeiHsiu, H., JuChun, K.: Playful bottle: a mobile social persuasion system to motivate healthy water intake. In: Proceedings of ACM Ubicomp (2009)
3. Abdelnasser, H., Youssef, M., Harras, K.A.: Wigest: a ubiquitous wifi-based gesture recognitionsystem. In: Proceedings of IEEE INFOCOM (2015)
4. Ali, K., Xiao, L.A., Wei, W., Shahzad, M.: Keystroke recognition using wifi signals. In: Proceedings of ACM MobiCom (2015)
5. Joshi, K., Bharadia, D., Kotaru, M., Katti, S.: WiDeo: Fine-grained device-free motion tracing using RF backscatter. In: Proceedings of USENIX NSDI (2015)
6. Sheng, T., Jie, Y.: Wifinger: leveraging commodity wifi for fine-grained finger gesture recognition. In: Proceedings of ACM MobiCom (2015)
7. Qian, K., Wu, C., Zhou, Z., Zheng, Y., Yang, Z., Liu, Y.: Inferring motion direction using commodity wi-fi for interactive exergames. In: SIGCHI (2017)
8. Breunig, M.M., Kriegel, H.-P., Ng, R.T., Sander, J.: LOF: identifying density-based local outliers. ACM SIGMOD Record **29**(2), 93–104 (2011)
9. Roweis, S.T., Saul, L.K.: Nonlinear dimensionality reduction by locally linear embedding. Science **290**(5500), 2323–2326 (2000)
10. Yang, H., Xu, H., Tang, K.: WiHumo: a Real-time lightweight indoor human motion detection. Int. J. Sens. Netw. (2017, in press)

Broadband Communications for High Speed Trains via NDN Wireless Mesh Network

Fan Wu, Wang Yang[(✉)], Runtong Chen, and Xinfang Xie

School of Information Science and Engineering,
Central South University, Changsha 410083, China
{wfwufan,yangwang,runtongchen,xinfangxie}@csu.edu.cn

Abstract. With increasing investment and deployment of high speed trains (HST), a critical demand of high bandwidth and the better user experience under high speed mobility arises. Although, TCP/IP has been studied in a static, walking and lower mobility environment, it can not work well at high speed (>50 m/s) cases. The reason is cellular networks use TCP/IP (eg. Mobile-IP) protocol that consumer node requires to connecting to producer node when the consumer handover to anther node. In this paper, we proposed NDN wireless mesh network architecture for HST networking (NDN-Mesh-T), which combined advantages of WMN and NDN architectures. We attempt to solve the reliability and handoff delay problems, which supports high bandwidth and lower latency Internet access in HST scenario. We proposed direction-aware forwarding to keep the same direction of running train, which further improve reliability and bandwidth. The simulation results show that the proposed scheme can significantly improve the packet loss ratio up to 67% comparing to IP. In addition, the proposed can reduce number of node deployments, hanoff delay and data redundancy.

Keywords: Named Data Networking · Wireless communications · High speed trains · Mobility · Handoff

1 Introduction

With the fast development of high speed trains (HST) [1,2], the average train moving speed has reached nearly 300 km/h in china CRH train. As the train speed increased, the consumer requires high bandwidth mobile networking face with new challenges. The public cellular network solutions are usually based on the use of several cellular networks deployed over landmasses. Cellular networks adopts 2G/3G/4G networks provide fast data access based on TCP/IP to achieve wireless transmission. To improve TCP/IP mobility problems, some research works have been investigated [3,4]. These schemes add extra protocols to maintain the mobility of IP (e.g. Mobile IP [5]). The extra protocol will lead to the mobile communications more complexity and lack of flexibility. Due to these reasons, it is difficult to directly apply TCP/IP to HST networking.

© Springer International Publishing AG 2017
L. Ma et al. (Eds.): WASA 2017, LNCS 10251, pp. 791–803, 2017.
DOI: 10.1007/978-3-319-60033-8_67

This is the reason why the train speed improved so fast, and the HST mobile communications has not efficiently resolved.

Named Data Networking [6] is an innovative network architecture. NDN is an approach to evolve the Internet infrastructure to directly support this use by introducing uniquely named data as a core Internet principle. NDN fundamentally shifts the network communication model from host-centric to data-centric. Data becomes independent from location, application, storage, and means of transportation, enabling in-network caching and replication. The consumer only concerns about information itself by using the content centric communication mode. NDN can handle consumer mobility [7], security issues more efficiently than the current Internet architecture. However, there are still some open problems for research in wireless network [8], since original NDN is designed aiming at a whole Internet architecture, rather than HST architecture. Therefore, we consider a radical innovation architecture to solve the current high mobility problems in HST networking.

Wireless Mesh Networks (WMN) [9] backbone infrastructures are proposed as a cost effective technology to provide city-wide Internet access, and general consist of mesh portal point (MPP) and mesh access point(MAP). Since the WMN provides Multi-hop network and transmission information via IP to access Internet, WMN can not efficiently solve the high mobility problems over IP for HST. NDN can efficiently solve the problems and supports WMN work well in HST. Due to the rapid deployment and easy maintenance of WMN, we consider combined advantages of WMN and NDN architectures for HST networking.

In HST, how to efficiently improve the reliability of mobile communications even during high mobility. Such as throughput, latency, frequent handover, consumer mobility. To solve these challenges, innovation high speed trains communication architecture which combined WMN and NDN architectures named NDN-Mesh-T is proposed.

The remainder of the paper is organized as follows. Section 2 introduces the problem description. Section 3 reviews the related work. Section 4 proposes a system architecture. Section 5 proposes a direction-aware forwarding strategy. Section 6 describes the simulation environment and results. Section 7 concludes the paper.

2   Problem Description

In TCP/IP networks, Mobile IP is created to enable users to maintain the same IP address while traveling to different networks, ensuring that roaming individuals can continue to communicate without a session or connection being dropped. However, Mobile IP requires mobile node registers its current location with the Foreign Agent (FA) and Home Agent (HA) during registration. This registration process may lead to data latency that decreases the application quality of service. In addition, Mobile-IP requires HA to tunnel the packets to FA (triangular routing) when it receives them from the mobile node, which increases extra delay. Especially, thousand of consumers will handoff at almost the same time, when the high speed train move to FA. If frequent handoff of train, the data latency will occur at FA as well as HA, which further reduce the user experience. Mobile IP handoff and data delivery process as shown in Fig. 1. The deep-seated reason of poor mobility is that IP networks must be clear about the two endpoints of data transmission, establish and maintain a continuous connection for the endpoints. To address the problem, we proposed NDN-Mesh-T architecture, which combined advantages of WMN and NDN architectures.

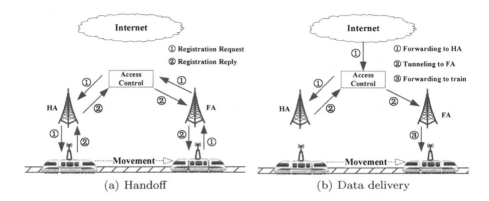

Fig. 1. Mobile IP handoff and data delivery

In NDN, once the Interest reaches a node that has the requested data, the return *Data* packet follows in reverse the path taken by the Interest to get back to the requesting consumer. If Interest forwarding to the opposite direction of running train, the return *Data* packet will chase the train. Therefore, the consumer needs to resend the Interest at the next node to pull the data to the current node. At the same time, to ensure that the train at the current node within the coverage area of consumer to receive Data. The experimental results show that the data hit rate and the data return delay time and packet loss rate are greatly increased with the increase of train speed.

In this paper, we propose NDN-Mesh-T architecture as a solution to address these challenges.

3 Related Work

In recent years, some research works have been investigated on how to apply the NDN architecture to wireless networks [10–14]. Some congestion control schemes are proposed to improve the throughput of NDN [15–17]. Ming et al. [18] analyzes the weakness of Mobile IP in railway wireless network and proposes an architecture that leverages NDN to deal with frequent handoff problem. Amadeo et al. [19] proposed bind forwarding and provider-aware forwarding for wireless ad hoc network. Yu et al. [20] provides the Neighborhood-Aware Interest Forwarding scheme based on its *Data* retrieval rate for a given name prefix and its distance to the consumer, which reduces the bandwidth usage induced by indiscriminate interest flooding in NDN forwarding. In NDN, some mobility support schemes are proposed [7,21–23], but these schemes mainly applicable to low-speed (<50 m/s) environment. There is no scheme to effectively reduce frequent handoff delay and improve the network throughput at high speed train environment, which lead to reduce user experience. To the best of our knowledge, we are the first to take both frequent handoff performance and high bandwidth into consideration for high speed environment in NDN-Mesh-T architecture.

4   System Architecture

To address the mobility problem in HST environment, we consider the WMN and NDN network to construction HST network architecture. As shown in Fig. 2, the HST networking architecture includes three network entities:

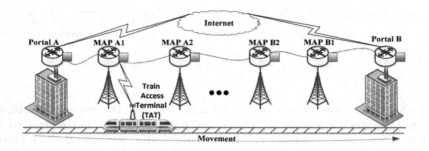

Fig. 2. NDN-Mesh-T communication architecture.

- *Mesh Portal Point (MPP):* The MPP form a mesh of self-configuring, self-healing links among themselves. With gateway/bridge functionality, MPP can be connected to the Internet.
- *Mesh Access Point (MAP):* MAP also has the necessary functions for mesh networking, and thus can also work as a router in HST. MAP meshing provides peer-to-peer networks among MAP devices. P2P communication anytime anywhere is an efficient solution for information sharing. In this architecture, MAP nodes constitute the actual network to perform routing and configuration functionalities as well as providing end-user applications to consumers. Consumers can access the network through MAP as well as directly meshing with other mesh nodes.
- *Train Access Terminal (TAT):* TAT also has the necessary functions for mesh networking as well as MAP. TAT transmissions information to MAP, which further improve handoff latency.

A WMN is dynamically self-organized and self-configured, with the nodes in the network automatically establishing and maintaining mesh connectivity among themselves, which provides flexibility and reliability of mesh network architecture for HST networking. However, in high speed environment, WMN can not efficiently to address the problems: triangular routing, NAT traversal, and address management. MAP and TAT nodes consist of ad hoc network, which further decreased handoff delay and improved the user experience.

In the HST architecture as shown in Fig. 2, all network devices (including MPP, MAP and TAT) are equipped with the protocols of NDN. NDN routes and forwards *Data* and *Interest* packets based on names without IP addresses, which eliminates some problems cased by IP addresses in the IP architecture: triangular routing, NAT traversal, and address management. There is no triangular routing problem since the NDN uses names to route packets. There is no NAT traversal problem since NDN does away with addresses, when consumer frequent handoff in HST networking. Moreover, address assignment and management is no longer required in NDN when consumer handoff to different networks.

In the proposed, combined advantages of WMN and NDN architectures. This architecture has some advantages comparing to IP networks as following:

Consumer Mobility. The NDN architecture is naturally supports consumer mobility. The extra overhead is resent an *Interest* package, when the consumer moving to a new network node.

Frequent Handover. In our proposed architecture, the consumer does not require any changes on content names and reconfiguration in HST network, when the consumer has frequent mobility. We use the MAP to forward the Interest to MPP for access Internet, which has improved the network reliability and decreased handoff latency.

Content Caching. Content caching is fundamentally important to support the data delivery model of NDN at low cost. NDN provides high benefits to dynamic contents in case of multicast or retransmission due to packet loss. It significantly reduces the network data dissemination latency in HST. We consider caching content in NDN-Mesh-T local router (MAP), which further reduces the overhead at the producer side and decreases the data delay during the handover process. In-network caching can be efficiently improved the data delivery latency.

5   Direction-Aware Forwarding Strategy

To further improve the performance of HST networking, we proposed direction awareness forwarding strategy (DAF) in order to keep the same direction of Interest forwarding with running train. We describe the detail of NDN-Mesh-T data communication process in HST, which consists of three parts: define direction, interest forwarding and data delivery.

5.1 Define Direction

In HST networking, consumers has different MAPs, which can forwarding *Interest* and *data* packets. We assume that *Interest* forwarding direction flag is *DF*. If $DF = 1$, the same direction between *Interest* forwarding with running train. If $DF = -1$, the direction of *Interest* forwarding is opposite direction of running train. The consumers get the direction of running train from the train devices. We settings the current direction is $DF = 1$, when consumers get the direction of running train.

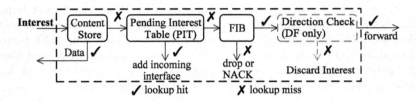

Fig. 3. NDN Interest forwarding process in proposed.

5.2 Interest Forwarding

In NDN, communication is receiver-driven. NDN uses two fundamental types of packets: *Interest* and *Data* packets. Interest packets are originally released into the network by consumers nodes willing to access a particular content, addressing it via its content name. *Data* packets include the content itself with the addition of a cryptographic signature. An NDN router is composed by three main elements: (1) Forward Information Base (FIB), (2) Pending Interest Table (PIT) and (3) Content Store (CS). When an *Interest* packet arrives, an NDN router will match on its CS, PIT and FIB. When a *Data* packet arrives, an NDN router first checks the PIT entry for matching data and forwards the data to matching interface. If a *data* packet with no matching PIT entries arrives, it is treated as unsolicited and discarded. NDN routers forward *Interest* packets toward data producers based on the names carried in the packets, and forward *Data* packets to consumers based on the PIT state information set up by the *Interests* at each hop.

To address direction-aware of *Interest* forwarding, we add *DF* flag bit in *Interest* packet and FIB table. As shown in Fig. 3, NDN Interest forwarding process in NDN-Mesh-T architecture. Consumers send *Interest* packet to MAP for access Internet, *Data* packet will be pulled to the MAP node. If the consumer did not receive the data package from the MAP, then the MAP forwarding the *Interest* packet to subsequent MAPs. In the first send *Interest* packet, FIB table will add an entry with *Interest* forwarding direction (*DF*) value. In the following *Interest* forwarding should be checked the *DF* flag at first, if the *DF* value is the same, thus the Interest will be forwarded to the direction of running train. The *Interest* packet will be discard, when the *DF* values is different. Until the

Interest packet reaches a producer location or cache hit on intermediate MAP. Even if both directions of *Interest* package forwarding are improved for transport reliability. However, in high speed environment, if *Interest* forwarded to opposite direction of running train, *Data* packet will follow the train run. Moreover, if the consumer handoff to the next MAP, the data packet only reached the MAP, where first receive the *Interest* packet. The results lead to unnecessary bandwidth consumption and increase network redundancy in HST networking. We consider *Interest* forwarding direction keep the same with running train, which reduces the network redundancy and data latency.

5.3   Data Delivery

NDN architecture is naturally and effectively supports consumer mobility without extra operation. *Data* packets will return by the interest forwarding reverse path back to consumer. In train running direction, *Data* packets will be cached along the path in local MAP. If consumer send Interest is satisfied in local MAP (connecting MAP node), which direct return *Data* packet for consumer, as shown in Fig. 4(a). If cache miss in local MAP, only send Interest to next MAP, as shown in Fig. 4(b). Once the consumer retransmission of the *Interest* request in next-hop MAP, returns data packets directly from the local MAP or next-hop MAP. In opposite direction of the train running, *Data* packets are chasing the train running, until the Data packets meets the *Interest* request in the same MAP. In this case, *Data* packets will be lost seriously and increase data latency, especially in high speed environment. We proposed an *Interest* forwarding direction-aware to keep the same direction with train running, which further improve the user experience.

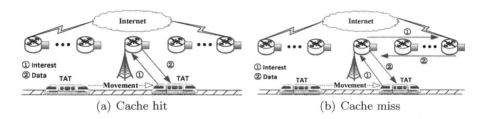

(a) Cache hit   (b) Cache miss

Fig. 4. NDN-Mesh-T data delivery.

6   Evaluation

In this section, we implemented the NDN-Mesh-T architecture and evaluated the performance in ndnSIM [24], which is extended to support high speed network and the direction-aware forwarding strategy proposed in this paper.

6.1 Simulation Settings

In NDN-Mesh-T network, all network nodes are enabled with caching functionality and the Leave Copy Everywhere (LCE) policy is used, which means that all network nodes may cache Data packets. In order to work in high speed environment, we use the log-distance propagation model for channel-induced losses. We consider different number of MAP nodes, the nominal coverage radius is 175 m for each node. The main simulation parameters are summarized in Table 1.

Table 1. Simulation parameters

Parameter	Value
Data payload	600 bytes
CS size	10000 packets
Propagation model	Log distance
Nominal radio range	175 m
Technology	IEEE 802.11b
Number of MAP nodes	11, 21, 31, 41
Mobility model	Constant velocity
Speed of consumer	10–100 m/s

6.2 Simulation Results

To explain the performance of our proposed scheme, we have done a comparative analysis in the following:

NDN-Mesh-T vs IP. To evaluate the proposed architecture, we compare the performance of packet loss ratio (PLR) under different speed. In this experiment, we setting 5 number of MAP nodes in NDN-Mesh-T and IP network architecture, DAF forwarding and IP-OLSR routing strategy. In Fig. 5, the result shows that the PLR of IP is increased fast than DAF by the increased of speed. DAF reduces PLR by up to 67% compare to IP, when the consumer running at 100 m/s. The reason is that mobile IP should address NAT traversal and address management as consumer move fast.

Impact of Forwarding Strategies. We consider direction-aware forwarding strategy to keep the same direction of *Interest* forwarding with running train. In Fig. 6, we evaluate the impacts of the different forwarding strategies on different MAP nodes. Despite the NDN multicast forwarding strategy PLR lower than the proposed DAF strategy, but we cut down half number of *Interest* packets and reduce data redundancy in the opposite direction. If *Interst* packets forwarding to the opposite direction of running train, Data packets will cached in MAP nodes even though consumer received the data packets from the direction of running train, which increased data redundancy and bandwidth consumption.

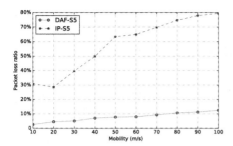

Fig. 5. NDN-Mesh-T vs IP network

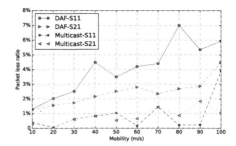

Fig. 6. Direction-aware forwarding vs NDN multicast forwarding

Moreover, the PLR only increase 7% at the most, even though the consumer moving at 100 m/s.

Impact of Speed. In high speed environment, we consider the impact of forwarding direction and numbers of MAP nodes in different speeds. DAF indicates that *Interest* packets forwarding to the same direction of running and DAF-Opposite forwarding *Interest* packet to the opposite direction of running train. In Fig. 7, the proposed DAF lower PLR than the DAF-Opposite, since the Interest packet forwarding to the same direction of running train, which means consumer will receive *Data* packets in next-hop MAP on the direction of running train. The Interests may be satisfied by the intermediate MAP nodes rather than the content providers, which further reduce packet loss ratio due to the cache functions in the NDN-Mesh-T architecture. With the increase of the number of the MAP nodes, DAF reduces PLR by up to 25% at the speed increased 100 m/s, as shown Figs. 7 and 8. It also can be observed that the DAF lower PLR for 41 MAP nodes than 11 MAP nodes, since the NDN-Mesh-T network can cached more data packet when increase the number of MAP nodes.

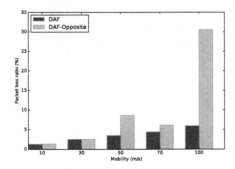

Fig. 7. 11 MAP nodes   Fig. 8. 41 MAP nodes

Overlap Areas of Two MAP Nodes. Mobile IP increased overlap areas of two MAP nodes for high speed train environment, which lead to number of MAP nodes deployed and costs increased. The MAP nominal radio range is 175 m, we consider decrease the overlap areas to reduce number of MAP nodes. In Figs. 9 and 10, we reduce the overlap areas of two MAP nodes from 100 m to 5 m, the results shown that the DAF lower PLR than DAF-Opposite. The reason is that NDN can naturally support consumer seamless handoff and *Interest* packet spend time on select which MAP node to connection in overlap areas. In this scenario, DAF maintains lower PLR while reducing number of MAP nodes by approximately 20%.

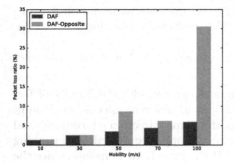

Fig. 9. Overlap areas is 100 m

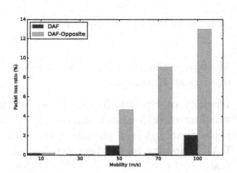

Fig. 10. Overlap areas is 5 m

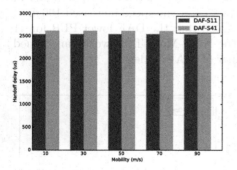

Fig. 11. Handoff delay

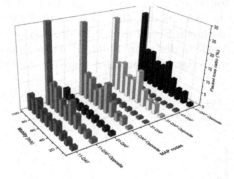

Fig. 12. Results display in 3D

Impact of Handoff Delay. There is no measuring method to calculate the handoff delay in wireless NDN network. In order to calculate the handoff delay, we consider a simple measuring method. We calculate the time interval that consumer send the last *Interest* packet to the MAP and receive the first *Data* packet from the next-hop MAP when consumer handoff. In fact, the time interval will be higher than real handoff delay due to *Data* packet may lead to latency. We calculate average handoff delay in different number of MAP nodes at different speed. In Fig. 11, we find out that we reduce handoff delay around three orders of magnitude compare to Mobile IP [25]. It also can be observed that all handoff delay almost the same in the same consumer even in high speed environment. The experimental results show that the proposed scheme significantly reduces handoff delay and data latency. Figure 12 shown that the packet loss ratio performance with different impacts of speed, number of MAP nodes and forwarding strategies. DAF significantly reduces packet loss ratio at higher speeds, which further improves the user experience in HST environment.

7 Conclusions

HST is developing very quickly in the world, particularly in Asia and the European. However, TCP/IP network challenges brought by high speed trains. For this application background, we try to use the NDN wireless Mesh network architecture to solve some key points on wireless communications for HST scenarios. We propose NDN-Mesh-T architecture that utilize NDN architecture to handle with the frequent handover when consumer moving. We consider the advantage of wireless mesh networks to support NDN development in HST. The proposed NDN-Mesh-T combined advantages of WMN and NDN architectures, which improve significantly frequent handoff and data latency. To further improve the performance of HST networking, we proposed DAF in order to keep the same direction of Interest forwarding with running train. The results shown that DAF packet loss ratio slightly higher than NDN multicast forwarding strategy, and we cut down half number of *Interest* packets and reduce data redundancy in the opposite direction. In addition, we reduce the overlap areas of two MAP nodes, which decreased the number of node deployments. In future work, we plan to conduct theoretical analysis and real experiments to evaluate the proposed schemes in real-world HST environment.

Acknowledgment. This work was supported by the National Natural Science Foundation of China under grant (No. 61309025), International Science and Technology Cooperation Program of China under grant (No. 2013DFB10070), and the National Key Technology R&D Program under grant (No. 2015BAH05F02) and the Fundamental Research Funds for the Central Universities (No. 2017zzts146).

References

1. Masson, É., Berbineau, M., Lefebvre, S.: Broadband internet access on board high speed trains, a technological survey. In: Kassab, M., Berbineau, M., Vinel, A., Jonsson, M., Garcia, F., Soler, J. (eds.) Nets4Cars/Nets4Trains/Nets4Aircraft 2015. LNCS, vol. 9066, pp. 165–176. Springer, Cham (2015). doi:10.1007/978-3-319-17765-6_15
2. Li, L., Xu, K., Wang, D., Peng, C., Xiao, Q., Mijumbi, R.: A measurement study on TCP behaviors in HSPA+ networks on high-speed rails. In: IEEE Conference on Computer Communications (INFOCOM), pp. 2731–2739 (2015)

3. Wang, X., Qian, H.: A mobility handover scheme for IPv6-based vehicular ad hoc networks. Wirel. Pers. Commun. **70**(4), 1841–1857 (2013)

4. Wozniak, J.: Mobility management solutions for current IP and future networks. Telecommun. Syst. **61**(2), 257–275 (2016)

5. Magnano, A., Fei, X., Boukerche, A., Loureiro, A.A.F.: A novel predictive handover protocol for mobile IP in vehicular networks. IEEE Trans. Veh. Technol. **65**(10), 8476–8495 (2016)

6. Zhang, L., Afanasyev, A., Burke, J., Jacobson, V., Crowley, P., Papadopoulos, C., Wang, L., Zhang, B., et al.: Named data networking. ACM SIGCOMM Comput. Commun. Rev. **44**(3), 66–73 (2014)

7. Zhang, Y., Afanasyev, A., Burke, J., Zhang, L.: A survey of mobility support in named data networking. In: Proceedings of the Third Workshop on Name-Oriented Mobility: Architecture, Algorithms and Applications (NOM 2016) (2016)

8. Moon, C., Han, S., Woo, H., Kim, D.: Named data networking for infrastructure wireless networks. In: IEEE International Conference on Consumer Electronics (ICCE), pp. 343–344 (2016)

9. Vural, S., Wei, D., Moessner, K.: Survey of experimental evaluation studies for wireless mesh network deployments in urban areas towards ubiquitous internet. IEEE Commun. Surv. Tutor. **15**(1), 223–239 (2013)

10. Amadeo, M., Campolo, C., Molinaro, A., Ruggeri, G.: Content-centric wireless networking: a survey. Comput. Netw. **72**, 1–13 (2014)

11. Liu, X., Li, Z., Yang, P., Dong, Y.: Information-centric mobile ad hoc networks and content routing: a survey. Ad Hoc Netw. **56**, 1–14 (2016)

12. Amadeo, M., Molinaro, A., Ruggeri, G.: E-CHANET: Routing, forwarding and transport in information-centric multihop wireless networks. Comput. Commun. **36**(7), 792–803 (2013)

13. Anastasiades, C., Weber, J., Braun, T.: Dynamic unicast: information-centric multi-hop routing for mobile ad-hoc networks. Comput. Netw. **107**, 208–219 (2016)

14. Silva, F.A., Boukerche, A., Silva, T.R.M.B., Ruiz, L.B., Cerqueira, E., Loureiro, A.A.F.: Vehicular networks: a new challenge for content-delivery-based applications. ACM SIGCOMM Comput. Commun. Rev. **49**(1), 1–29 (2016)

15. Schneider, K., Yi, C., Zhang, B., Zhang, L.: A practical congestion control scheme for named data networking. In: The 3rd ACM Conference on Information-Centric Networking (ICN), Kyoto, Japan, pp. 21–30, September 2016

16. Ren, Y., Li, J., Shi, S., Li, L., Wang, G.: An explicit congestion control algorithm for named data networking. In: IEEE Conference on Computer Communications Workshops (INFOCOM), San Francisco, USA, pp. 294–299, April 2016

17. Ren, Y., Li, J., Shi, S., Li, L., Wang, G., Zhang, B.: Congestion control in named data networking - a survey. Comput. Commun. **86**, 1–11 (2016)

18. Ming, Z., Wang, H., Xu, M., Pan, D.: Efficient handover in railway networking via named data. Int. J. Mach. Learn. Cybernet. **6**(1), 167–173 (2015)

19. Amadeo, M., Campolo, C., Molinaro, A.: Forwarding strategies in named data wireless ad hoc networks: design and evaluation. J. Netw. Comput. Appl. **50**, 148–158 (2015)

20. Yu, Y., Dilmaghani, R.B., Calo, S.B., Sanadidi, M.Y., Gerla, M.: Interest propagation in named data manets. In: International Conference on Computing, Networking and Communications, ICNC 2013, San Diego, CA, USA, 28–31 January, pp. 1118–1122 (2013)

21. Augé, J., Carofiglio, G., Grassi, G., Muscariello, L., Pau, G., Zeng, X.: Anchor-less producer mobility in ICN. In: the 2nd International Conference on Information-Centric Networking (ICN), San Francisco, USA, pp. 189–190, September 2015

22. Azgin, A., Ravindran, R., Wang, G.: Mobility study for named data networking in wireless access networks. In: IEEE International Conference on Communications, ICC 2014, Sydney, Australia, 10–14 June, pp. 3252–3257 (2014)
23. Zhang, Y., Zhang, H., Zhang, L.: Kite: a mobility support scheme for NDN. In: 1st International Conference on Information-Centric Networking (ICN), Paris, France, 24–26 September, pp. 179–180 (2014)
24. Mastorakis, S., Afanasyev, A., Moiseenko, I., Zhang, L.: ndnSIM 2: an updated NDN simulator for NS-3. Technical report NDN-0028, Revision 2, NDN (2016)
25. Lee, J.S., Koh, S.J., Kim, S.H.: Analysis of handoff delay for mobile IPv6. In: IEEE 60th Vehicular Technology Conference, VTC2004-Fall, vol. 4, pp. 2967–2969 (2004)

Phishing Website Detection Based on Effective CSS Features of Web Pages

Jian Mao[1(✉)], Wenqian Tian[1], Pei Li[1], Tao Wei[3], and Zhenkai Liang[2]

[1] School of Electronic and Information Engineering,
Beihang University, Beijing, China
maojian@buaa.edu.cn
[2] School of Computing, National University of Singapore,
Singapore, Singapore
[3] Baidu USA LLC, Sunnyvale, CA, USA

Abstract. In a web-based phishing attack, an attacker sets up scam web pages to deceive users to input their sensitive information. The appearance of web pages plays an important role in deceiving users, and thus is a critical metric for detecting phishing web sites. In this paper, we propose a robust phishing page detection mechanism based on web pages' visual similarity. To measure the similarity of the suspicious pages and victim pages accurately, we extract features from the Cascading Style Sheet (CSS) of web pages, and select the effective feature sets for similarity rating. We prototyped our approach in the Google Chrome browser and used it to analyze suspicious web pages. The proof of concept implementation verifies the effectiveness of our algorithm with a low performance overhead.

1 Introduction

In a web-based phishing attack, an attacker sets up scam web pages to deceive users to input their sensitive information, such as passwords, credit card numbers, and social security numbers. The attacker usually sends emails or publishes web links on social networks that trick users to visit the scam pages. Phishing attacks are on the rise. According to a PhishMe report [1], the number of phishing emails has exceeded six million in the first quarter of 2016, more than 6-fold increase compared to the last quarter of 2015.

Phishing detection techniques based on URL analysis are extensively studied and widely used in web browsers. For example, in the work [7,22], the authors developed Bayesian anti-phishing toolbars combined with black/white-list databases of phishing sites. Meanwhile, additional features of a web page are suggested to be included in anti-phishing mechanisms [10,11,24], e.g., registration dates, life time, or lock sign of SSL-enabled web sites, etc. However, all these features are not the key features in deceiving users. Therefore, attackers can afford to change them without affecting the effectiveness of phishing attacks.

As phishing pages usually maintain the similar visual appearance as their target pages, solutions based on page content similarity are developed [21,32].

© Springer International Publishing AG 2017
L. Ma et al. (Eds.): WASA 2017, LNCS 10251, pp. 804–815, 2017.
DOI: 10.1007/978-3-319-60033-8_68

With the help of search engines, they compare the similarity of texts on pages between the current web page and other known web pages. However, attackers can add noises to their web page texts by embedding invisible web contents to bypass these solutions. Other solutions [26,29,30] compare images of rendered pages to evaluate their visual similarity. However, these approaches are not efficient due to the effort needed to render the page. In addition, the effectiveness of the detection is significantly influenced by the differences of browser rendering mechanisms. In our earlier investigation [17], we note that page contents and page layouts are fundamental features that determine web pages' appearance, and uses the Cascading Style Sheets (CSS) of web pages to represent these features. However, not all page elements and CSS style rules are of the same importance in deceiving the users. The insignificant elements and style rules can be leveraged by attackers to bypass detection.

In this paper, we propose a new technique to efficiently and accurately detect phishing web pages according to the similarity of pages' visual features. As the visual appearance of a web page is jointly determined by its elements and its CSS rules, our approach first evaluates the role these elements and rules play on the final appearance to users, and selects the *effective* features as the basis of our approach. In this way, our decision will not be affected by CSS elements that have little influence on the visual appearance. Based on these effective CSS features, we develop a new algorithm to effectively aggregate these features and detect phishing pages.

We implemented our approach as a prototype tool, called PhishingAlarm, as an extension to the Google Chrome browser. We evaluated it using more than 7000 phishing pages collected from phishtank.com. The experiment results show the advantages of PhishingAlarm over existing solutions in accuracy and performance.

In summary, we made the following contributions in this paper:

- We propose a robust solution to identify phishing pages according to the visual features of web pages, which is difficult to be evaded by attackers.
- We develop techniques to select the effective CSS features on a web page, and propose an efficient method for page similarity detection according to these CSS features.
- We prototyped our approach and evaluated it using a large set of phishing pages. The results illustrate that our approach is efficient and effective.

2   Overview

In this section, we introduce the basis of CSS and give an overview of our approach.

2.1   Cascading Style Sheets

Cascading Style Sheets (CSS) is the standard technique to represent the layout of web pages. CSS includes a series of rules that specify the visual properties of web pages' elements. The browsers retrieve the CSS specification of the web pages currently visited by the users and render the web pages according to the rules specified in the CSS documents.

A CSS rule consists of two parts, a *selector* and a series of *declarations*. The *selector* is a pattern to specify HTML elements and the *declaration* includes two components, *property* and *value*. CSS rules are organized in the following formats.

```
Selector₁ {Property₁-1: Value₁-1;Property₁-2: Value₁-2; ...};
Selector₂ {Property₂-1: Value₂-1;Property₂-2: Value₂-2; ...}; ...
```

CSS rules have several types of selectors, e.g., *tag* selectors, *id* selectors, *.class* selectors and *other* selectors (for example, some attribute selectors). In a CSS rule, the properties specify the attributes of the specific elements, e.g., *color, font-size, font-family, border, margin, padding* for the *paragraph* element. And the visual appearance of an element is specified by the value of the corresponding property. For instance, a developer can specify the red color by setting the value of the color property as "#ff0000".

When rendering a web page, for each element on the page, the browser looks up its matching style rules, and applies them to decide its visual features, such as the location on the page, the color of text, etc. CSS rules that do not have matching page elements will not affect the page appearance. We call the set of CSS rules that are actually affecting the web page appearance *effective CSS rules*.

2.2   Phishing Page Detection Based on Effective CSS Features

Aiming to robustly detect phishing pages based on their visual features, our solution has three main steps with the following respective objectives: extracting and representing effective CSS features, computing similarity scores, and detecting phishing pages. PhishingAlarm achieves the above objectives in three steps.

Step I – Extracting and Representing Effective CSS Features. In this step, given a suspicious page P_s, we extract its CSS structure $CSS(P_s)$ and page elements $Ele(P_s)$. Based on the interaction between $CSS(P_s)$ and $Ele(P_s)$, we identify the set of effective CSS features $ECSS(P_s)$, and use it to represent the page's visual features.

Step II – Measuring Similarity Between the Suspicious Page and the Target Pages. Based on the effective CSS features of the suspicious page and potential target pages, we design metrics to measure their complexity scores and similarity score accordingly.

Step III – Deciding Phishing Pages. In this step, we check whether the pages' similarity score is over a preset threshold ϵ. By the similarity score and a list of target web sites, our approach decides whether the suspicious page is a phishing page.

In the next section, we focus on the key techniques, extracting effective CSS features and measuring page similarity.

3   Measuring Page Similarity Using Effective CSS Features

Not all page elements and CSS rules have the same influence on page appearance. For example, the size of page elements can reflect the influence of the combination of CSS rules and page elements. We should only focus on the features that have actual influence on the page. The idea is to exclude CSS rules that do not have matching page elements, and page elements with minor or no visual presence. Page elements matching any of the following cases are excluded from the similarity computing, as well as the CSS rules that only matches these elements.

Case I: the area of element is too small, occupying only a few pixels.
Case II: the *visibility* property of element is *hidden*.
Case III: the *display* property of element is *none*.

To facilitate page similarity measurement, the extracted effective CSS rules are presented in a normalized format that is indexed by the properties in CSS, which is called comparison units [17].

The *similarity score* and the related concepts that we use to evaluate the pages' similarity are defined as follows.

Given the CSS rule set of a web page X, CSS(X), let $\{p_j\}_{1 \leq j \leq N_P}$ represent the property set in CSS(X), where N_P is the number of the properties in CSS(X). For $1 \leq j \leq N_P$, let $\{v_j^k\}_{1 \leq k \leq N_V^j}$ represent the value set of the property p_j, where N_V^j is the number of optional values of the property p_j. For $1 \leq j \leq N_P, 1 \leq k \leq N_V^j$, let $\{s_l^{jk}\}_{1 \leq l \leq N_S^{jk}}$ represent the set of selectors that have property p_j with value v_k, where N_S^{jk} is the number of the chosen selectors. And we use I_l^{jk} ($j \in [1..N_p], k \in [1..N_V^j], l \in [1..N_S^{jk}]$) represent the area of selector s_l^{jk} (the l-th selector that has property p_j with value v_k), in the web page X.

The *Complexity Score* of a web page is a score to describe how complicated the layout of web page is.

Definition 1 (*Complexity Score*). *Given the comparison-unit representation of a web page* X, *the complexity of the web page* X *is*

$$C(X) = \sum_{j=1}^{N_P} \sum_{k=1}^{N_V^j} \sum_{l=1}^{N_S^{jk}} I_l^{jk} \tag{1}$$

Given two CSS rule sets of two web pages, CSS(X) and CSS(Y), let $\{p_j\}_{1 \leq j \leq M_P}$ represent the common property set in CSS(X) and CSS(Y), where M_P is the number of the matched properties. For $1 \leq j \leq M_P$, let $\{v_j^k\}_{1 \leq k \leq M_V^j}$ represent the value set of the property p_j in the common property set, where

M_V^j is the number of common values of the property p_j. For $1 \leq j \leq M_P, 1 \leq k \leq M_V^j$, let $\{s_r^{jk}\}_{1 \leq r \leq M_{S_x}^{jk}}$ represent the set of selectors in CSS (X) that have property p_j with value v_k and $\{s_t^{jk}\}_{1 \leq t \leq M_{S_y}^{jk}}$ represent the set of selectors in CSS (Y) that have property p_j with value v_k, where $M_{S_x}^{jk}$, $M_{S_y}^{jk}$ are the number of the chosen selectors respectively. $I_r^{jk}(X)$ ($j \in [1..M_p], k \in [1..M_V^j], r \in [1..M_{S_x}^{jk}]$) and $I_t^{jk}(Y)$ ($j \in [1..M_p], k \in [1..M_V^j], t \in [1..M_{S_y}^{jk}]$) represent the area of selector s_r^{jk} and s_t^{jk} in web page X and Y respectively.

The *Match Score* is a metric that measures how much visual appearance two pages have in common.

Definition 2 (Match Score). *Given two web pages X and Y, the Match Score of X and Y labeled as $M(X,Y)$ is*

$$M(X,Y) = \sum_{j=1}^{M_P} \sum_{k=1}^{M_V^j} min(\sum_{r=1}^{M_{S_x}^{jk}} I_r^{jk}(X), \sum_{t=1}^{M_{S_y}^{jk}} I_t^{jk}(Y)) \tag{2}$$

The *Similarity Score* is a metric that measures how similar one page is to another.

Definition 3 (Similarity Score). *Given two web pages X and Y, the Similarity Score of X and Y labeled as $S(X,Y)$ is*

$$S(X,Y) = \frac{M(X,Y)}{C(X) + C(Y) - M(X,Y)} \tag{3}$$

To evaluate the similarity of two web pages according to the definitions above, we propose an algorithm that takes the visual characteristics of two pages as input and outputs their visual similarity score. The visual characteristics of website include the CSS rules in every stylesheets and the structure of web page, which is defined as the DOM tree of the page's body. Shown in Algorithm 1, it first extracts the visual characteristics from a suspicious page and a legitimate page, identifies the effective CSS rules, and computes the similar rate of the two web pages.

4   Implementation

We have implemented our algorithm into a Google Chrome browser extension, called PhishingAlarm. As shown in Fig. 1, PhishingAlarm consists of three modules: *Pre-Processor, Similarity Checker* and *Target List*.

The Pre-Processor contains three components: *CSS Extractor, DOM Extractor* and *Visual Characteristics Filter*. CSS Extractor extracts internal CSS rules directly from the code of web page, and downloads CSS rules in external stylesheets from online servers. DOM Extractor is in charge of copying the

```
 1  let P be a suspicious web-page;
 2  let L be the corresponding target web-page;
 3  let ε be a preset similarity threshold
 4  let CompUnit() be the comparison-unit of web page.
 5  let FilUnit() be the filtered comparison-unit of web page.
 6  Phase I:Extracting and Filtering.
 7  Function Extract()is
        input    : a suspicious page P
        output   : the filtered comparison-unit of P, FilUnit(P)
 8      get the CSS text of P, CSS(P);
 9      compute CompUnit(P);
10      /* convert CSS(P) into comparison-unit                              */
11      compute FilUnit(P);
12      /* delete unnecessary CSS from CompUnit(P)                          */
13      Return FilUnit(P)

14  Phase II: Similarity Computing.
15  Function Similarity(A,B)is
        input    : FilUnit(P), FilUnit(L)
16      /* FilUnit(L) is pre-provided                                       */
        output   : similarity score S(P, L)
17      compute the complexity score of the P, C(P);
18      compute the complexity score of page L, C(L);
19      compute the match score of page L and P, M(P, L);
20      compute the similarity score between page L and P, S(P, L);
21      Return S(P, L)

22  Phase III:Making Decision.
23  Function Decision(S(P,L))is
        input    : S(P, L)
        output   : the classification result of P
24      if S(P, L) > ε then
25          the page A is similar to the target page B;
26          display "warning" and the similarity score S(P, L);
27      else
28          display similarity score Sim(A, B)
```

Algorithm 1: Visual Similarity Based Phishing Detection Scheme

structure of page's body, and acquires the area as well as the value of *display* and *visibility* property of each page element. Then Visual Characteristics Filter uses information from both two extractors to exclude CSS rules that have no significant visual influence. Finally, all the rest of CSS rules will be converted into the comparison unit representation and sent to the similarity checker.

Target List stores the comparison units and the URLs of a set of legitimate websites. We include legitimate web pages that are most likely to be attacked by phishing attackers into the target list.

Similarity Checker includes a *Similarity Calculator*, which computes the similarity value between two pages, and a *Decision Maker*, which decides whether the suspicious page is phishing or not. Similarity Calculator computes the similarity value between suspicious page and legitimate pages from Target List, one pair at a time. The results are sent to Decision Maker. If any of similarity value is beyond the pre-set threshold, the suspicious page is classified as phishing.

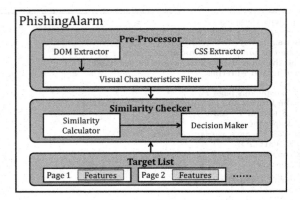

Fig. 1. Overall architecture of PhishingAlarm

5   Evaluation and Analysis

We collected a large number of phishing samples to train the similarity threshold and tested the correctness of PhishingAlarm using real-world phishing web pages.

5.1   Experiment Sample

we collected 9307 verified phishing websites from PhishTank.com as the experiment sample set, which consists of phishing pages targeting Paypal, eBay, Apple, and other popular website. We used 6192 pages from them as the sample set for similarity threshold training, and 3115 of them as the sample set for correctness assessment. To check whether these pages are appropriate for our experiment, we used manual operation combined with page element extraction to check through every page in the sample sets. Within the training set, 4934 of the pages were unable to visit or have an visual appearance of blank page. 2826 pages of evaluation set had the same problem as well. Therefore, these web pages were excluded from our experiment. Besides, we also collected 246 legitimate pages to test the false positive rate of PhishingAlarm.

5.2   Similarity Threshold Training

We selected 547 pages from training sample set and computed the similarity value between them and their corresponding target pages. The results are illustrated in Table 1(a). 66.91% of the phishing samples have a similarity value over 0.8 and less than 1% of them have a similarity value under 0.1.

For the rest 715 pages in the training sample set, PhishingAlarm computes the similarity value between the phishing samples and non-targeted websites. For instance, for a phishing page imitating AOL, we use PhishingAlarm to calculate the similarity rate between it and a non-AOL page. The experiment results are shown in Table 1(b).

Table 1. (a) Similarity between phishing pages and their targets (b) Similarity between phishing pages and non-targets

Similarity p	Number	Ratio
$0 \leq p < 0.1$	5	0.92%
$0.1 \leq p < 0.2$	105	19.20%
$0.2 \leq p < 0.6$	29	5.30%
$0.6 \leq p < 0.8$	42	7.67%
$0.8 \leq p < 1$	366	66.91%

(a)

Similarity p	Number	Ratio
$p = 0$	102	14.27%
$0 \leq p < 0.03$	76	10.62%
$0.03 \leq p < 0.06$	29	4.06%
$0.06 \leq p < 0.08$	486	67.97%
$0.08 \leq p < 0.1$	18	2.52%
$p > 0.1$	4	0.56%

(b)

Furthermore, we manually analyzed the five pages with similarity value less than 0.1 from Table 1(a). Three of them are visually different from their reported target pages and can be easily distinguished by users. Intuitively, a proper threshold should keep the number of misclassified pages as low as possible. According to our experiment result, the value 0.1 satisfies this condition well, so we select 0.1 as the similarity threshold for PhishingAlarm.

5.3   Result Analysis

Metrics. We use three basic metrics to describe the detection results of PhishingAlarm. The precision rate and recall rate measure the percentage of web pages correctly classified as phishing pages.

$$Precision = \frac{TP}{TP + FP} \tag{4}$$

$$Recall = \frac{TP}{TP + FN} \tag{5}$$

True positive (TP) and false negative (FN) are the number of correctly and incorrectly classified phishing pages respectively. False positive (FP) is the number of legitimate pages misclassified as phishing pages. Besides, we use F1-measure as a metric to evaluate our approach as well.

$$F1 = 2 * \frac{Precision * Recall}{Precision + Recall} \tag{6}$$

To evaluate the effectiveness of PhishingAlarm, we used pages from evaluation set to conduct a real-time detection. 283 out of 289 phishing sites were correctly detected by PhishingAlarm, while six of them successfully bypassed it. According to our manual analysis, three of these six misclassified phishing pages are obviously different from the visual appearance of their target pages, and can be easily recognized by users. From the experiment results, the TP of PhishingAlarm is 283 and FN is 6. We also use PhishingAlarm to check the 246 legitimate websites and none of them were classified as phishing: as a result, the FP is 0.

Based on the data above, the *precision* rate of PhishingAlarm is 100% and *recall* is 97.92%. According to the equation (6), the *F1* score is 98.95%.

Table 2 illustrates the three metrics of PhishingAlarm and six other approaches (CANTINA [32], CANTINA+ [28], Corbetta et al. [8], Belabed et al. [3], Zhang et al. [31] and CASTLE [21]). CASTLE has a higher recall than PhishingAlarm, but PhishingAlarm achieves the highest precision. Both of them have an F1 score as 0.99, higher than five other approaches.

Table 2. The precision, recall, and F1 score of PhishingAlarm and other approaches

Approaches	Precision	Recall	F1
CANTINA [32]	94.2%	97.0%	0.956
CANTINA+ [28]	97.5%	93.47%	0.963
Corbetta et al. [8]	95.3%	73.08%	0.827
Belabed et al. [3]	96.6%	98.0%	0.973
Zhang et al. [31]	91.0%	91.90%	0.915
CASTLE [21]	99.5%	98.50%	0.990
PhishingAlarm	100%	97.92%	0.990

6 Related Work

Phishing Detection by Content Analysis. Medvet et al. proposed a scheme [18] to detect phishing pages by comparing the pages using their visual features. They select text pieces, images and overall visual appearance as the basic properties to compare the similarity of two pages. Chen et al. [5] present another visually similar web page detection algorithm according to Getstalt theory, in which they process the webpage as an indivisible entity. Zhang et al. propose *CANTINA* [32] to detect phishing pages based on "term frequency-inverse document frequency (TF-IDF)". SpoofGuard [6] takes *domain name, URL, link* and *image* as the critical features to check suspicious pages.

Content-based approaches generally extract content features of web pages to identify suspicious websites. GoldPhish [9] captures an image of the page, employs optical character recognition (OCR) to convert the image into text (especially the company logo), leverages the Google PageRank algorithm to obtain the top ranked domains from a search engine and compares them with the current page. Pan and Ding [23] utilize textual clues from the DOM tree of websites to detect anomalies in DOM objects and HTTP transactions in the page based on the fact that phishing pages activate more abnormal behaviors compared to honest pages. Zhang et al. [31] extract spatial layout characteristics as rectangle blocks from a given page and compute spatial layout similarity between the current page and the real one based on spatial characteristic matching algorithms. Furthermore, they leverage an R-tree index algorithm to query similar-looking web pages in a spatial feature library and thus determine whether a web page is imitating another one. Wardman et al. [25] propose a set of file matching algorithms to calculate file similarity between two pages and filter out potential phishing web pages. Abbasi et al. [2] detect phishing websites by exploiting genre information. Their solution associates fraud cues with the different purposes between legitimate and phishing websites and demonstrates through genre composition and design structure.

Moghimi and Varjani [19] discover a rule-based scheme used two novel feature sets to detect phishing in internet banking. One feature set is used to evaluate the identity of page resources and the other is utilized to identify the access protocol. Bottazzi et al. [4] proposed a framework in Android mobile devices for phishing detection, which includes a machine learning detection engine for key protection from new phishing activities.

Phishing Detection by URL and Structure Features. URL-based detection techniques analyze URL features of web pages to filter out suspicious malicious websites. Ma et al. [15,16] use online learning and statistical methods to discover the tell-tale lexical and host-based properties of malicious website URLs. Khonji et al. [13] present a modified variant of a website classification technique to filter phishing URLs in e-mails. Their previous work lexically analyzes URL tokens to increase prediction accuracy [12]. Mohammad et al. [20] extract 17 features of websites (e.g. URL length, specific URL symbols, domain name, domain year, etc.) and manually set a rule for each feature to determine whether a link is malicious.

Support vector machine (SVM) is employed to webpages classification. Lee et al. [14] exploit a linear chain CRF model to study users' web browsing behaviors faced phishing situations and then make behavioral prediction for context-aware phishing detection. Experiments were made to show good performance for prediction and blocking of phishing threats from user behaviors. Wu et al. [27] present an automated lightweight anti-phishing method for mobile phones, MobiFish. In this scheme, actual identity is compared to the claimed identity of webpages and applications.

7 Conclusion

Phishing is a critical social engineering attack technique for attackers to obtain victim users' sensitive information, e.g., username with passwords, credit card numbers, social security numbers, etc. In this paper, we propose a robust phishing detection approach, PhishingAlarm, based on CSS features of web pates. We develop techniques to identify effective CSS features and algorithms to efficiently evaluate page similarity. We prototyped PhishingAlarm as an extension to the Google Chrome browser and demonstrated its effectiveness in evaluation.

Acknowledgment. This work was supported in part by the National Natural Science Foundation of China (No. 61402029), the National Natural Science Foundation of China (No. 61370190 and No. 61379002), Singapore Ministry of Education under NUS grant R-252-000-539-112.

References

1. PhishMe Q1 2016 malware review (2016). https://phishme.com/project/phishme-q1-2016-malware-review/
2. Abbasi, A., Zahedi, F.M., Zeng, D.: Enhancing predictive analytics for anti-phishing by exploiting website genre information. J. Manag. Inf. Syst. **31**(4), 109–157 (2015)
3. Belabed, A., Aimeur, E., Chikh, A.: A personalized whitelist approach for phishing webpage detection. In: 7th International Conference on Availability, Reliability and Security (ARES), Prague, pp. 249–254. IEEE, August 2012
4. Bottazzi, G., Casalicchio, E., Cingolani, D., Marturana, F., Piu, M.: MP-shield: a framework for phishing detection in mobile devices. In: Proceedings - 15th IEEE International Conference on Computer and Information Technology, CIT 2015, 14th IEEE International Conference on Ubiquitous Computing and Communications, IUCC 2015, 13th IEEE International Conference on Dependable, Autonomic and SE, pp. 1977–1983 (2015)
5. Chen, T.-C., Dick, S., Miller, J.: Detecting visually similar web pages: application to phishing detection. ACM Trans. Internet Technol. **10**(2), 1–38 (2010)
6. Chou, N., Ledesma, R., Teraguchi, Y., Boneh, D., Mitchell, J.C.: Client-side defense against web-based identity theft. In: Proceedings of the 11th Annual Network and Distributed System Security Symposium (NDSS) (2004)
7. C.Inc.: Couldmark toolbar, August 2015. http://www.cloudmark.com/desktop/ie-toolbar
8. Corbetta, J., Invernizzi, L., Kruegel, C., Vigna, G.: Eyes of a human, eyes of a program: leveraging different views of the web for analysis and detection. In: Stavrou, A., Bos, H., Portokalidis, G. (eds.) RAID 2014. LNCS, vol. 8688, pp. 130–149. Springer, Cham (2014). doi:10.1007/978-3-319-11379-1_7
9. Dunlop, M., Groat, S., Shelly, D.: Goldphish: using images for content-based phishing analysis. In: 5th International Conference on Internet Monitoring and Protection (ICIMP), Barcelona, pp. 123–128. IEEE, May 2010
10. Fette, I., Sadeh, N., Tomasic, A.: Learning to detect phishing emails. In: Proceedings of the International World Wide Web Conference (WWW), May 2007
11. iTrustPage. http://www.cs.toronto.edu/ronda/itrustpage/
12. Khonji, M., Iraqi, Y., Jones, A.: Lexical URL analysis for discriminating phishing and legitimate websites. In: 8th Annual Collaboration, Electronic Messaging, Anti-Abuse and Spam Conference, pp. 109–115. ACM, New York (2011)
13. Khonji, M., Iraqi, Y., Jones, A.: Enhancing phishing e-mail classifiers: a lexical URL analysis approach. Int. J. Inf. Secur. Res. (IJISR) **2**(1/2), 40 (2012)
14. Lee, L.-H., Lee, K.-C., Juan, Y.-C., Chen, H.-H., Tseng, Y.-H.: Users' behavioral prediction for phishing detection. In: Proceedings of the 23rd International Conference on World Wide Web, no. 1, pp. 337–338 (2014)
15. Ma, J., Saul, L. K., Savage, S., Voelker, G.M.: Beyond blacklists: learning to detect malicious web sites from suspicious URLs. In: 15th ACM SIGKDD International Conference on Knowledge Discovery and Data Mining, pp. 1245–1254. ACM, New York (2009)
16. Ma, J., Saul, L.K., Savage, S., Voelker, G.M.: Identifying suspicious URLs: an application of large-scale online learning. In: 26th Annual International Conference on Machine Learning, pp. 681–688. ACM, New York (2009)
17. Mao, J., Li, P., Li, K., Wei, T., Liang, Z.: BaitAlarm: detecting phishing sites using similarity in fundamental visual features. In: Proceedings of the 5th International Conference on Intelligent Networking and Collaborative Systems (2013)

18. Medvet, E., Kirda, E., Kruegel, C.: Visual-similarity-based phishing detection. In: Proceedings of SecureComm 2008. ACM, September 2008
19. Moghimi, M., Varjani, A.Y.: New rule-based phishing detection method. Expert Syst. Appl. **53**, 231–242 (2016)
20. Mohammad, R., Thabtah, F., McCluskey, L.: An assessment of features related to phishing websites using an automated technique. In: International Conference for Internet Technology and Secured Transactions, London, pp. 492–497. IEEE, December 2012
21. Nourian, A., Ishtiaq, S., Maheswaran, M.: CASTLE: a social framework for collaborative anti-phishing databases. In: 2009 5th International Conference on Collaborative Computing: Networking, Applications and Worksharing, Washington, DC, pp. 1–10 (2009)
22. Likarish, P., Jung, E., Dunbar, D., Hansen, T.E., Hourcade, J.P.: B-apt: Bayesian anti-phishing toolbar. In: Proceedings of IEEE International Conference on Communications, ICC 2008. IEEE Press, May 2008
23. Pan, Y., Ding, X.: Anomaly based web phishing page detection. In: 22nd Annual Computer Security Applications Conference, Miami Beach, FL, pp. 381–392. IEEE, December 2006
24. Ronda, T., Saroiu, S., Wolman, A.: iTrustPage: a user-assisted anti-phishing tool. In: Proceedings of Eurosys 2008. ACM, April 2008
25. Wardman, B., Stallings, T., Warner, G., Skjellum, A.: High-performance content-based phishing attack detection. In: eCrime Researchers Summit, San Diego, CA, pp. 1–9. IEEE, November 2011
26. Wenyin, L., Xiaotie, D.: Detecting phishing web pages with visual similarity assessment based on earth mover's distance. IEEE Trans. Dependable Secure Comput. **3**(4), 301–311 (2006)
27. Wu, L., Du, X., Wu, J.: MobiFish: a lightweight anti-phishing scheme for mobile phones. In: Proceedings - International Conference on Computer Communications and Networks, ICCCN (2014)
28. Xiang, G., Hong, J., Rose, C.P., Cranor, L.: CANTINA+: a feature-rich machine learning framework for detecting phishing web sites. ACM Trans. Inf. Syst. Secur. (TISSEC) **14**(2), 21 (2011)
29. Xiaotie, D., Guanglin, H., Fu, A.Y.: An antiphishing strategy based on visual similarity assessment. Internet Comput. **10**(2), 58–65 (2006)
30. Cao, Y., Han, W., Le, Y.: Anti-phishing based on automated individual white-list. In: Proceedings of the 4th ACM Workshop on Digital Identity Management, pp. 51–60 (2008)
31. Zhang, W., Lu, H., Xu, B., Yang, H.: Web phishing detection based on page spatial layout similarity. Informatica **37**(3), 231–244 (2013)
32. Zhang, Y., Hong, J., Cranor, L.: Cantina: a content-based approach to detecting phishing web sites. In: Proceedings of the International World Wide Web Conference (WWW), May 2007

A Neural Network Model Based Adaptive Flight Control System

Jiaqi Liang[✉], Wenwen Du, Kai Xing, and Chunlin Zhong

University of Science and Technology of China,
Heifei, People's Republic of China
liangjiaqi1993@gmail.com, 1455112695@qq.com, kxing@ustc.edu.cn,
chlzhong@mail.ustc.edu.cn

Abstract. The study of neural network controller has become increasingly mature as plenty of simulations were conducted to verify the theoretical analysis. In this paper, a neural network model based flight control system is proposed. This model is capable of sensing interference caused by change of the mathematical model of aircraft, so that it can start or stop the learning process automatically. The flight controller equipped with this model can adjust the learning step due to the intensity of interference during the learning process. Furthermore, the convergence time of control error is shortened to a ultra low level. Comparative experiments on aircraft confirm that the proposed neural network model has high adaptability, which illustrates its good performance under different aircraft models.

Keywords: Neural network model · Self-adaptive learning · Flight control system

1 Introduction

There are continuously increasing interests in applying neural network to the identification and control of practical systems, which are characterized by nonlinearity, uncertainly, communication constraints, and complexity. Neural network has been proven to be a promising algorithm to model the unknown uncertainties for the approximation ability over a compact domain. Many useful control methods have been proposed in the development of adaptive neural network control. For example, Ge et al. [6] deal with the problem of known control direction by combining the Nussbaum gain function with adaptive backstepping neural network control. [17] introduces the adaptive dynamic surface technique.

In recent years, neural network model based flight control system has aroused interests from a wide variety of researchers. Commonly used controllers can be classified into traditional flight controller [1], robust controller [15], expert controller [3] and neural network controller [18], etc. However, the study of intelligent control stops at the level of theories, and validations of intelligent control theories are mainly based on the simulation.

© Springer International Publishing AG 2017
L. Ma et al. (Eds.): WASA 2017, LNCS 10251, pp. 816–828, 2017.
DOI: 10.1007/978-3-319-60033-8_69

In this paper, the neural network controller is designed on the neural network model. The model can start or stop learning process automatically, and adjust learning rate in real time. Compared with traditional models, the control error of neural network model can be converged. In the real application scenario, there is few work validating the model through hardware experiments. In this paper, the aircraft based comparative experiments are conducted to verify the neural network model, which illustrates its good performance under different aircraft models.

The major contributions of this paper are identified as below:

- We propose an neural network model, which can detect the interference caused by aircraft model and start or stop the learning process automatically.
- The neural network model can adjust learning step value according to the intensity of interference in the learning process.
- The aircraft control system can adapt itself to the change of aircraft model and the uncertainty interference of the external environment.
- Our flight control system combines theories with hardware experiments successfully.

The rest of the paper is organized as follows: Sect. 2 presents the related works. The model and algorithm of the improved neural network are introduced in Sect. 3. Section 4 further introduces the neural network application in flight control. Section 5 provides our experiment results and discussion, followed by the conclusion in Sect. 6.

2   Related Work

In the following, we briefly overview the structure characteristics of various kinds of controllers and summarize the most related researches introduced in the related works.

Since the excellent universal approximation ability of the neural network was proven in [13], the neural network has become an active research topic in the control domain. Further adaptive neural network control has attracted much attention and shown to be particularly useful the control of highly uncertain, nonlinear, and complex systems [14]. What's more, a lot of adaptive neural network control approaches have been proposed based on Lyapunov stability theory and the backstepping technique [5].

Neural network requires relatively less information about dynamics of the system [2,20]. It also has been maturely proved to be effective in addressing the control problem of nonlinear systems with unknown dynamics [9] in recent years.

In the control designment of uncertain nonlinear systems, neural network has already been widely employed. For example, [19] analyzes the neural control for longitudinal dynamics of a generic hypersonic aircraft in presence of unknown dynamics and actuator fault. And [16] proposes the neural network control of a flexible robotic manipulator using the lumped spring-mass model.

In recent years, the neural network has aroused great attention in control field with its advantages, which can approximate any complex nonlinear system. Neural network based complex and uncertain system has high adaptive and self-learning ability, which let it has strong robustness and fault tolerance. The neural network controller has been applied on the ship roll reduction in [4], and the hypersonic in [18]. In [10,11], authors introduce an active demand-side management and robotic systems respectively. In [12], neural network is applied for the tip tracking of a flexible manipulator. A novel neural network tracking controller is designed in [7] in order to handle the system uncertainties. In [8], the utilization of neural network control is presented to efficiently compensate for the modeling errors a flexible multline system.

3   Model and Algorithm of the Neural Network Controller

3.1   The Modification of Neural Network Model

In this paper, the dynamic multilayer forward neural network model is adopted. And it can be used to control the model of single-input-single-output system, as shown in Fig. 1.

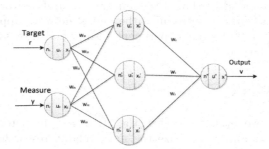

Fig. 1. Structure of the improved neural network

There are two neurons in the input layer to receive external information from the single-variable control system: one accepts the target value and the other accepts the control value. The output of input layer neurons are transmitted to the hidden layer by connection weights for comprehensive treatment. Then, the output of the hidden layer are transmitted to output layer by connection weights. Finally, the neuron of output layer implements the outcome of the whole network control model.

At time t, n_j is defined as the total input value of the nth neuron of the neural network. The value of n_j is the sum of the connected output of each branch $x_1, x_2, ..., x_n$ multiplied by weight $w_{1j}, w_{2j}, ..., w_{nj}$ respectively. The input of the neuron n_j and the current state are regarded as independent variables, and the next state value u_j can be generated by the state function $g(\cdot)$, which determines the transition from state n to state u in neuron, and $g(\cdot)$ is defined in input layer as follows:

$$u_i(k) = g_i(n_i(k)) = n_i(k) \tag{1}$$

For the hidden layer, the neural network model is used to simulate the control of the traditional neural network, and the three neurons in the hidden layer are used as the proportional, integral and differential control unit. The output of hidden layer neurons are as follows:

$$u_1'(k) = g_1'(n_1'(k)) = n_1'(k) \tag{2}$$

$$u_2'(k) = g_2'(n_2'(k)) = u_2'(k-1) + n_2'(k) \tag{3}$$

$$u_3'(k) = g_3'(n_3'(k)) = n_3'(k) - n_3'(k-1) \tag{4}$$

And the output of output layer neuron is as follows:

$$u''(k) = g''(n'(k)) = n''(k) \tag{5}$$

x_j is the output value of the neuron j, which can be decided by its output function $f(\cdot)$. The state of the neuron u_j are regarded as an independent variable, and the output value of the neuron can be generated by the output function.

Threshold function is used as the output function, given by:

$$f(x) = \begin{cases} 1, & x > 1 \\ x, & -1 \le x \le 1 \\ -1, & x < -1 \end{cases} \tag{6}$$

3.2 Forward Algorithm of the Neural Network Model

The forward algorithm of the neural network is initialized by two input values, then the total output can be decided by current weight values, state function and the output function.

The input layer has two neurons. At any sampling time k, the output values are:

$$x_i(k) = \begin{cases} 1, & u_j(k) > 1 \\ u_i(k), & -1 \le u_j(k) \le +1 \\ -1, & u_j(k) < -1 \end{cases} \tag{7}$$

where $i = 1, 2; j = 1, 2, 3$.

Hidden layer has three neurons, the output values of hidden layer neurons are:

$$x_j'(k) = \begin{cases} 1, & u_j'(k) > 1 \\ u_j'(k), & -1 \le u_j'(k) \le 1 \\ -1, & u_j'(k) < -1 \end{cases} \tag{8}$$

where $j = 1, 2, 3$; w_{ij} represent the connection weights of the input layer to hidden layer. The variables with superscript $'$ belong to the hidden layer.

There is only one neuron in output layer, the output value of the output layer neuron is:

$$x''(k) = \begin{cases} 1, & u''(k) > 1 \\ u''(k), & -1 \leq u''(k) \leq 1 \\ -1, & u''(k) < -1 \end{cases} \tag{9}$$

And the output of the improved neural network is equal to the value of the output layer, therefore:

$$v(k) = x''(k) \tag{10}$$

where $v(k)$ represents the actual value.

3.3   Back Propagation Algorithm of the Neural Network Model

Back propagation algorithm is the error back propagation learning algorithm, which can change the weight value and has the function of learning and memorizing. Back propagation algorithm is used to minimize the square deviation between the actual output and the ideal output of the network at corresponding time. The expression is shown as:

$$E = \frac{1}{l} \sum_{k=1}^{l} \left(v'(k) - v(k) \right)^2 \tag{11}$$

where l represents the sample point and $v'(k)$ represents the target value.

Gradient descent algorithm is used to adjust the weights. When the model is trained and learned by n_0 times, the weights of each layer's iterative equation are

$$W(n_0 + 1) = W(n_0) - \eta \frac{\partial E}{\partial W} \tag{12}$$

4   The Neural Network Application in Flight Control

Aircraft is a complex control system which requires precise control over attitude, horizontal position and height. Although traditional flight control method performed well under certain conditions, its performance under poor external environment is terrible. Because of the benefits of neural network such as good adaptability, self-learning and decision-making ability, neural network is very suitable for complex control system.

4.1 Neural Network Attitude Control Model

Attitude control refers to the control over yaw-pitch-roll attitude angles. It consists of angular loop control and angular velocity loop control. The control block diagram is shown in the Fig. 2.

For angle loop controller, the input training data is given by the attitude angle of the target value and the actual value solved through IMU, and its output is regarded as the target value.

For angular velocity loop controller, the input training data is obtained from the target value of angel loop and the angular velocity values measured by gyro, and its output is regarded as the whole output of system.

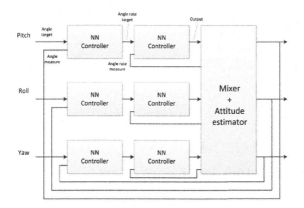

Fig. 2. Control block diagram

There are 6 neural network controllers in the whole control system, the learning process of which are independent from each other. Thus the stability of the whole system is guaranteed.

For every neural network controller, the error function is defined as:

$$E = \frac{1}{N} \sum \left(target - measure\right)^2 \tag{13}$$

where N is the sample size.

The aim of neural network controller is to minimize E. The controller uses structure introduced in Sect. 3, as shown in the Fig. 3.

Due to the uncertainty of the flight control system, the back propagation algorithm of the neural network controller needs to be modified as follows:

Input Layer to Hidden Layer

$$w_{ij}(k) = w_{ij}(k-1) - \eta_{ij} \cdot \frac{\partial E}{\partial w_{ij}} \tag{14}$$

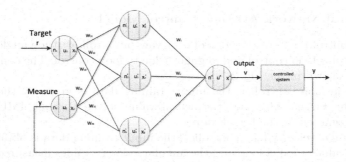

Fig. 3. Neural network controller system

$$\frac{\partial E}{\partial w_{ij}} = \frac{\partial E}{\partial v} \cdot \frac{\partial v}{\partial x''} \cdot \frac{\partial x''}{\partial u''} \cdot \frac{\partial u''}{\partial n''} \cdot \frac{\partial n''}{\partial x'_j} \cdot \frac{\partial x'_j}{\partial u'_j} \cdot \frac{\partial u'_j}{\partial n'_j} \cdot \frac{\partial n'_j}{\partial w_{ij}} \tag{15}$$

$\frac{\partial u'_j}{\partial n'_j}$ can not be directly determined, so use the differential function:

$$\frac{\partial u'_j}{\partial n'_j} = \frac{u'_j(k) - u'_j(k-1)}{n'_j(k) - n'_j(k-1)} \tag{16}$$

when $n'_j(k)$ is equal to $n'_j(k-1)$, we define $\frac{\partial u'_j}{\partial n'_j} = 0$.

Hidder Layer to Output Layer

$$w_i(k) = w_i(k-1) - \eta_i \frac{\partial E}{\partial w_i} \tag{17}$$

$$E = \frac{1}{l} \sum_{k=1}^{l} (r(k) - y(k))^2 \tag{18}$$

$$\frac{\partial E}{\partial w_i} = \frac{\partial E}{\partial e} \cdot \frac{\partial e}{\partial y} \cdot \frac{\partial y}{\partial v} \cdot \frac{\partial v}{\partial x''} \cdot \frac{\partial x''}{\partial u''} \cdot \frac{\partial u}{\partial w_i} \tag{19}$$

Because of the instability of the control system, the value of $\frac{\partial y}{\partial v}$ can not be directly determined, the differential function $\frac{\partial y}{\partial v}$ is replaced with:

$$\frac{\partial y}{\partial v} = \frac{y(k) - y(k-1)}{v(k) - v(k-1)} \tag{20}$$

When $v(k)$ is close to $v(k-1)$, in order to eliminate outliers, the neural network learning rules are defined as follows:

$$\frac{\partial y}{\partial v} = sgn\left(\frac{y(k) - y(k-1)}{v(k) - v(k-1)}\right) \tag{21}$$

This method, which eliminates outliers but restrains the rate of error reduction at the same time, is not suitable for flight control system. Therefore we define the differential function as follows:

When $v(k)$ equals to $v(k-1)$, we define $\frac{\partial y}{\partial v} = 0$.

4.2   The Initialization of Weights

In order to determine the weights of neural network model of the initial parameter manually, PID parameter tuning is used in the neural network controller, which makes neural network controller hard to achieve good control effect by using initial weights. Under normal circumstance:

$$W_{11} = W_{12} = W_{13} = 1,$$
$$W_{21} = W_{22} = W_{23} = -1; \tag{22}$$

where W_1, W_2, W_3 need to be tuned manually.

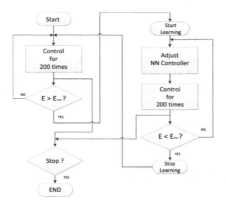

Fig. 4. Learning flow chart

4.3   Automatically Start or Stop of Learning in Neural Network Controller

As shown in the Fig. 4, the system is stable after the neural network model is initialized, but it needs to achieve a new stable state because the aircraft model changes along with environment. Therefore the neural network controller ought to determine when to start learning process automatically. The learning process is stopped after the system becomes stable until the model changes next time. The controller error is calculated as:

$$E = \frac{1}{N} \sum (target - measure)^2 \tag{23}$$

The start condition is:

$$E > E_{max} \tag{24}$$

and the stop condition is:

$$E < E_{min} \tag{25}$$

The value of E_{min} and E_{max} are the min and max control thresholds, which are based on massive statistical data of flight.

4.4 Learning Rate Adjustment in Neural Network Controller

The neural network controller's control error must converge in order to ensure the long-term stability of system. So certain conditions of learning rate must be satisfied:

$$0 < \eta < \frac{1}{\varepsilon^2} \tag{26}$$

where ε can be assigned according to the Lyapunov stability principle:

$$\varepsilon = \frac{1}{2\sqrt{E}} \cdot \frac{\partial E}{\partial y} \cdot \frac{\partial y}{\partial v} \cdot \frac{\partial v}{\partial w} = \frac{1}{2\sqrt{E}} \cdot \frac{\partial E}{\partial w} \tag{27}$$

where w is the adjusted weight.

When the learning process starts, the learning rate is set as a large value η_0. With the increasing of times, the learning rate η declines, and η satisfies the function (17). In order to decline the learning rate under $\frac{1}{\varepsilon^2}$ in time, index decline algorithm is used:

$$\eta = \frac{\eta}{k} \tag{28}$$

5 Experiment Results and Discussion

In this section, two group of comparative experiments are conducted to verify the control effect of the neural network controller. In order to verify the adaptability of the neural network control system under inaccurate and abrupt situation, the observation of aircraft flight control system's control error is adopted. Then the experiment results are analyzed and discussed according to the comparison diagrams.

The sample size for each learning process is 200 times, the control time is 60 s and the control error set is 0.1.

5.1 Validation of Adaptability for the Aircraft Model Using Neural Network Controller

In order to observe the changes of control error during flight, the experiments use the contrast test of traditional flight control system model and the neural network control system model. The group of experiments using traditional control system model is adopted as the control group. In the fist part of the experiments, three kinds experiments are designed. The first experiment is: Unmanned air drone does not carry any weight for flight test. The second is: The body is equipped with weights of 200 g before the unmanned air drone take off. The third is: Carrying the weights of 200 g to a unmanned air drone that has reached a steady state. In the second part of the experiment uses the neural network system model to repeat the above experiments. After the experiments are done,

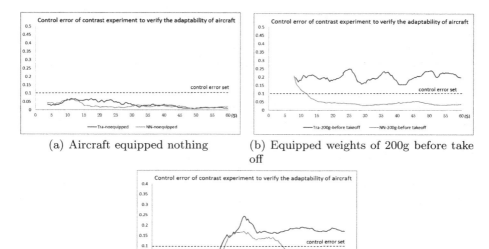

(a) Aircraft equipped nothing

(b) Equipped weights of 200g before take off

(c) Equipped weights of 200g after take off

Fig. 5. Control error of contrast experiment to verify the adaptability of aircraft

the control error of one flight control system model is compared with the other. Then the comparison diagrams are plotted.

It can be seen from Fig. 5(a) that when there are no weights on the aircraft, no matter what flight control system are used, the control error are still under the control error set.

According to Fig. 5(b) the control effect of aircraft with different flight control system model makes a considerable difference. The model of aircraft changes when it takes off, so the aircraft using neural network flight control system starts self-learning. Intuitively, the control error decreases continually until under the control error set, then system will stay in a state of equilibrium. But the aircraft using traditional flight control system will be in a terrible situation that the curve are twists and turns and the values of control error are all over the control error set. Thus it can be seen that the neural network flight control system has an effective adjustment for the change of models.

From Fig. 5(c) it can be seen that the two models' control error are both under the control error set at first. The model changes when weights of 200 g are suddenly put onto the aircraft at 20 s. According to the curve we can know that the control error of aircraft using traditional flight control system rise, but the other curve's value goes down under the value of set.

From the experiments above it can be seen that the changes can't be detected by traditional control system model and it is not suitable for real-time reaction dealing with sudden model change, but the neural network flight control system has the adaptability for the change of models.

5.2   The Influence of Different Initial Learning Rates

The effect of initial learning rate on the convergence of control error E is obvious. There are three sets of initial learning rate in this part of experiments and the control error is recorded.

As shown in the Fig. 6(a), when the initial learning rate is 0.01, the control error of the aircraft can converge in a short time under control error set. When the initial learning rate is 0.001, the control error convergence time is significantly longer.

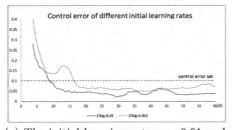

(a) The initial learning rates are 0.01 and 0.001

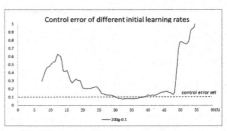

(b) The initial learning rates is 0.1

Fig. 6. Control error of different initial learning rates

From Fig. 6(b) it can be seen that when the initial learning rate is 0.1, the control error can converge in a very short time, but the control error significantly increases and divergence happens at 13 s. The reason is that the abnormal mutation of control error leads to divergence when the learning rate is large. Although a large initial learning rate can reduce the convergence time, it may also lead to local divergence in the face of the abnormal mutation value of the control error.

6   Conclusions

In this paper, we proposed a neural network model, which can detect the interference caused by aircraft model to start or stop the learning process automatically. Our model can also adjust learning step value according to the interference during learning process. Compared with other traditional models, the control error of aircraft can be converged in our neural network model. The experimental results show that the neural network model based controller has high adaptability. Besides, the new aircraft flight control system can adapt itself to uncertainty interference from external environment, which provides good scalability for future aircraft model.

References

1. Chang, W.D., Shih, S.P.: PID controller design of nonlinear systems using an improved particle swarm optimization approach. Commun. Nonlinear Sci. Numer. Simul. **15**(11), 3632–3639 (2010)
2. Cheng, L., Hou, Z.G., Tan, M., Lin, Y., Zhang, W.: Neural-network-based adaptive leader-following control for multiagent systems with uncertainties. IEEE Trans. Neural Netw. **21**(8), 1351–1358 (2010)
3. Dequan, S., Guili, G., Zhiwei, G., Peng, X.: Application of expert fuzzy pid method for temperature control of heating furnace. Procedia Eng. **29**, 257–261 (2012)
4. Fang, M.C., Zhuo, Y.Z., Lee, Z.Y.: The application of the self-tuning neural network PID controller on the ship roll reduction in random waves. Ocean Eng. **37**(7), 529–538 (2010)
5. Ge, S.S., Hang, C.C., Lee, T.H., Zhang, T.: Stable Adaptive Neural Network Control, vol. 13. Springer Science & Business Media, Heidelberg (2013)
6. Ge, S.S., Hong, F., Lee, T.H.: Adaptive neural control of nonlinear time-delay systems with unknown virtual control coefficients. IEEE Trans. Syst. Man Cybern. Part B (Cybern.) **34**(1), 499–516 (2004)
7. Gutierrez, L.B., Lewis, F.L., Lowe, J.A.: Implementation of a neural network tracking controller for a single flexible link: comparison with PD and PID controllers. IEEE Trans. Industr. Electron. **45**(2), 307–318 (1998)
8. Isogai, M., Arai, F., Fukuda, T.: Modeling and vibration control with neural network for flexible multi-link structures. In: Proceedings of 1999 IEEE International Conference on Robotics and Automation, vol. 2, pp. 1096–1101. IEEE (1999)
9. Lewis, F., Jagannathan, S., Yesildirak, A.: Neural Network Control of Robot Manipulators and Non-linear Systems. CRC Press, Boca Raton (1998)
10. Lian, R.J.: Adaptive self-organizing fuzzy sliding-mode radial basis-function neural-network controller for robotic systems. IEEE Trans. Industr. Electron. **61**(3), 1493–1503 (2014)
11. Matallanas, E., Castillo-Cagigal, M., Gutiérrez, A., Monasterio-Huelin, F., Caamaño-Martín, E., Masa, D., Jiménez-Leube, J.: Neural network controller for active demand-side management with PV energy in the residential sector. Appl. Energy **91**(1), 90–97 (2012)
12. Öke, G., İstefanopulos, Y.: End-effector trajectory control in a two-link flexible manipulator through reference joint angle values modification by neural networks. J. Vib. Control **12**(2), 101–117 (2006)
13. Park, J., Sandberg, I.W.: Universal approximation using radial-basis-function networks. Neural Comput. **3**(2), 246–257 (1991)
14. Polycarpou, M.M., Mears, M.J.: Stable adaptive tracking of uncertain systems using nonlinearly parametrized on-line approximators. Int. J. Control **70**(3), 363–384 (1998)
15. Shah, R., Mithulananthan, N., Lee, K.Y.: Large-scale PV plant with a robust controller considering power oscillation damping. IEEE Trans. Energy Convers. **28**(1), 106–116 (2013)
16. Sun, C., He, W., Hong, J.: Neural network control of a flexible robotic manipulator using the lumped spring-mass model. IEEE Trans. Syst. Man Cybern.: Syst. (2016)
17. Wang, D., Huang, J.: Neural network-based adaptive dynamic surface control for a class of uncertain nonlinear systems in strict-feedback form. IEEE Trans. Neural Netw. **16**(1), 195–202 (2005)

18. Xu, B., Sun, F., Yang, C., Gao, D., Ren, J.: Adaptive discrete-time controller design with neural network for hypersonic flight vehicle via back-stepping. Int. J. Control **84**(9), 1543–1552 (2011)
19. Xu, B., Zhang, Q., Pan, Y.: Neural network based dynamic surface control of hypersonic flight dynamics using small-gain theorem. Neurocomputing **173**, 690–699 (2016)
20. Zhang, H., Qin, C., Luo, Y.: Neural-network-based constrained optimal control scheme for discrete-time switched nonlinear system using dual heuristic programming. IEEE Trans. Autom. Sci. Eng. **11**(3), 839–849 (2014)

Supporting Producer Mobility via Named Data Networking in Space-Terrestrial Integrated Networks

Di Liu[1,2], Chuanhe Huang[1,2(✉)], Xi Chen[1,2], and Xiaohua Jia[1,3]

[1] State Key Lab of Software Engineering, Computer School,
Wuhan University, Wuhan, China
huangch@whu.edu.cn
[2] Collaborative Innovation Center of Geospatial Technology, Wuhan, China
[3] Department of Computer Science, City University of Hong Kong,
Hong Kong, China

Abstract. As a promising future network architecture, Named Data Networking (NDN) can provide content consumer mobility support naturally, but the content producer mobility support is remaining a challenging problem. Most previous researches just consider this problem in terrestrial scenarios, which has stable infrastructures to achieve node mobility management. In this paper, we consider it in a Future Space-Terrestrial Integrated Networks (FSTINs) scenario without handover management infrastructure. Specifically, we propose a tracing-based producer mobility management scheme and an addressing-assisted forwarding method via NDN architecture. In order to calculate the route of space segment, we formally describe Multi-Layered Satellite Networks (MLSNs) via a Time Varying Graph (TVG) model and define the foremost path calculating problem, as well as an algorithm that can work in both dense (connected) and sparse (delay/disruption tolerant) scenarios. Performance evaluation results demonstrate that the proposed scheme can support fast handover and efficient forwarding in the FSTIN scenario.

Keywords: Mobility management · Space-Terrestrial Integrated Network · NDN forwarding

1 Introduction

In the upcoming "Space 2.0" era [1], there are much more space nodes equipped with powerful communication links and they can serve as either data producers/consumers or relay nodes. It makes efficient Space-Terrestrial integrated communication possible. One possible scenario is shown in Fig. 1 and it can be referred as Future Space-Terrestrial Integrated Networks (**FSTINs**) [2–4].

This work was supported by the National Science Foundation of China (Nos. 61373040 and 61572370).

© Springer International Publishing AG 2017
L. Ma et al. (Eds.): WASA 2017, LNCS 10251, pp. 829–841, 2017.
DOI: 10.1007/978-3-319-60033-8_70

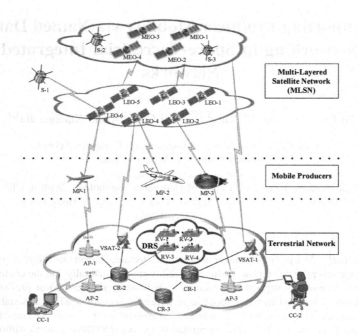

Fig. 1. A Space-Terrestrial Integrated Network (STIN) scenario

In such a scenario, mobility is the norm rather than the exception. The current TCP/IP architecture is not competent and we need location-independent communication model [5]. A common criticism is the so-called location-identity conflation problem. Despite the enormous body of work on dealing with device mobility so as to achieve location-independent communication, most known approaches fundamentally take one of just three different approaches [5–9]: (1) indirection routing; (2) name resolution; (3) name-based routing. Among them, name-based routing tries to solve this problem from a new perspective by changing the mobility problem from "delivering packets to a Mobile Node (MN)" to "retrieving data produced by MNs".

Named Data Networking (NDN) [10] is a promising Future Internet architecture that changes the network communication model from point-to-point packet delivery to named data retrieval without concerning the exact locations where data reside in. As a newly proposed network architecture, NDN has drawn much attention from networking researchers and has been applied in several fields, such as vehicular networking [11], video streaming [12] etc.

The NDN architecture naturally supports consumer mobility through its stateful forwarding plane and the receiver-driven paradigm. But the content producer mobility problem remains an active research topic [5–8]. Producer mobility leads to frequent routing update and low routing aggregation due to the locator/identifier binding properties. The quantitative comparison results [5] suggest that name-based routing may be augmented with addressing-assisted approaches to handle content producer mobility for highly dynamic scenarios, such as FSTINs.

In tracing-based mobility solutions [6, 8], whenever a Mobile Producer (MP) changes its Attachment Point (AP), it needs to inform its *Rendezvous* (RV) to create a "breadcrumb trail" that can be followed by *Interest* to reach it. This process can be referred as Attachment Update (AU) and it does not need to perform any location registration or update operation [13]. Existing solutions just consider these situations that AUs occur between non-moving APs that reside in terrestrial network, e.g. MP-1 moves from AP-2 to AP-1, as illustrate in Fig. 2 (green dashed line).

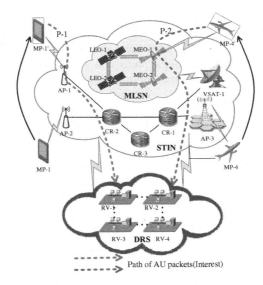

Fig. 2. Illustration of producer mobility in FSTIN (Color figure online)

In such an AU, the forwarding path (P-1) on which the AU packet will be routed could be considered as a known condition, just as most existing solutions. But such an assumption will not hold, if the current AP is also a space node. As in the AU that after MP-4' AP was changed from AP-3 to MEO-1, P-2 would across the Multi-Layered Satellite Networks (MLSNs) where the MEO-1 resides in. In MLSNs, all links are switch frequently, how such special *Interest* packets should be routed is remaining a challenging problem, that is, time-varying route calculation (See Sect. 4.1 for details).

In this paper, we focus on Space-Terrestrial Integrated Mobility Supporting in NDN. The main contributions are summarized as follows:

(a) We propose a tracing-based producer mobility management scheme with *Distributed Rendezvous System* (DRS), so as to achieve Space-Terrestrial Integrated Mobility Supporting in NDN.

(b) We propose a Space-Terrestrial Integrated forwarding method via NDN, to help
achieve globally "anywhere-anytime" communication.

(c) We formally describe MLSNs via a Time Varying Graph (TVG) model and define
the foremost path calculation problem, as well as a corresponding algorithm that
can adaptively work in both dense (connected) and sparse (delay/disruption tolerant) scenarios.

2 The Basic Design of the Mobility Management Scheme

This section presents a tracing-based producer mobility management scheme via NDN
for highly dynamic scenarios. In particular, we focus on Space-Terrestrial Integrated
scenarios, e.g., as shown in Fig. 1. We partly borrow the ideas of [8, 9]. RVs are used
to guarantee the global reachability of MPs and all RVs form a Distributed Rendezvous
System(DRS). Each object has a unique prefix and with a hierarchical name following
it. The data's order of magnitude may be too high to processing them separately in
Forwarding Information Base (FIB). We just store a soft-state in tFIB [9]. For
long-term relocation of data producers, they need to re-publish data by using the prefix
of its current RV, so as to avoid long-term path stretching.

We define a special traceable *Interest* packet–AU packet (AUP), the specific
structure is shown in Fig. 3.

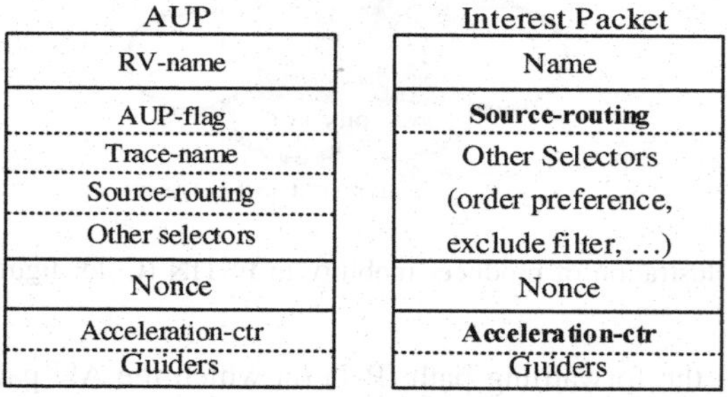

Fig. 3. The AUP and modified interest packet structure

"RV-name" is used to lead AUP Advancing toward its corresponding RV.
"AUP-flag" is used to indicate whether the packet is an AUP or not. The specific
processes are described in Sect. 3. "Trace-name" indicates which *Interest* will be
traced, and it should be exactly same with the *Data* name. It is worth noting that here
"Data name" is not restrict to a piece of content, it could be an aggregation one.
"Source-routing" field is used to carry the route which the AUP will follow if exists.
"Acceleration-ctr" field is optional. A typical MP mobility management process is
shown in Fig. 4.

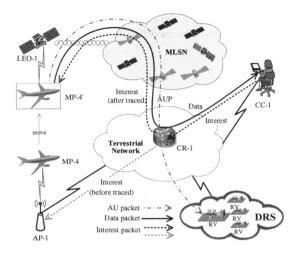

Fig. 4. Illustration of MP' mobility management process

The steps are as follows:

Step 1. MP-4 sends one or more AUPs to its RV after its AP has been changed from AP-1 to LEO-1 (satellite).

Step 2. The following *Interest* packet will still be forwarded towards AP-1. Until this moment, Content Consumer(CC-1) has not aware of this mobility event.

Step 3. The *Interest* packets will trace the AUP at one Content Router (CR), e.g., CR-1.

Step 4. The following *Interests* will be forwarded towards MP-4 along the traced path, as well as the unsatisfied *Interests* which have been sent out before traced.

Step 5. MP-4 sends *Data* packet (s) back to CC-1 along the reverse path of *Interests*.

It is worth noting that RVs do not need to participate in producer/consumer communications, and they just act as the rendezvous of AUPs and the unsatisfied *Interests*.

Then, we need addressing the problem that how AUP could be forwarded in the space segment, especially in MLSNs.

3 Space-Terrestrial Integrated Forwarding

This section presents the addressing-assisted forwarding method in NDN. In MLSNs, all links are time-related and there has no stable infrastructure. The CRs will need to update their FIBs frequently, if we directly use pure name-based forwarding. We allocate each satellite a globally reachable name prefix and then calculate the source route of the space segment. After that, the source route will be attached in selector field, so as to assist forwarding process. The modified forwarding process is shown in Fig. 5.

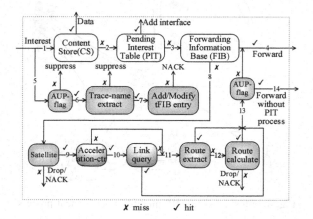

Fig. 5. The modified forwarding process

Process 1–4 just keep the same with the process that in original NDN architecture. Process 5 is used to judging whether the packet is an *Interest* or an AUP. If hit, then suppress, else process 6 extract the "Trace name" that has been attached in the selector fields which will be used in the next process. Process 7 generates the correspondence between "Trace-name" and "Interface", the former is the globally reachable prefix (addressing-assisted) and the latter is the interface through which the *Data* packet(s) can be sent back. After that, the added or modified tFIB entry could be used to guide the following forwarding process and the corresponding *Interests* will toward to the current AP and finally reach the MP.

It is worth noting that after process 7 has been done, the AUP will be suppressed due to the fact that the AUP has been forwarded and toward to its RV through standard process, e.g., process 1 to 4. Our method will not increase the communication burden of CR in terrestrial networks and the additional computation cost is very slight. In most cases, these *Interest* packets are regular ones and the additional cost is one logical judgment, as in process 5.

In MLSNs, the return value of process 3 is "miss" for most packets due to the above analyses. We propose the addressing-assisted forwarding processes. In process 8, if the node is not a satellite, then returns a "NACK" message, else goes to process 11 to extract attached source route, if process 11 return "hit", then go to process 13, else go to process 12 and calculate the source route. If process 13 returns "miss", that is, the packet is an *Interest*, then goes to process 4, else goes to process 14 and forwards the AUP without adding an entry in Pending Interest Table (PIT) so as to reduce entries.

4   The Routing of MLSNs

In MLSNs, links switches frequently which results in time-varying network topology whose characteristics are in accordance with Temporal Networks [14]. In this section, we characterize the time-varying characteristics of MLSNs via a TVG model [15] and then solve the dynamic routing problem from the perspective of edge changes.

4.1   Problem Statement and Definitions

Assume that the time is divided into discrete and equal time slots, such as $\mathcal{T} = \{t_1, \ldots, t_n\}$. Let $V = \{v_1, \ldots, v_n\}$ be the set of all individual nodes in the network (which represents the set of satellites or other cyclical nodes if needed), then $G = \{V, E\}$ is the traditional static graph, but it cannot represent the information of time dimension. We further define $\mathcal{G} = (G, V, \mathcal{T}, \rho, \zeta)$, a TVG of G, in which, $\mathcal{T} \subseteq \mathbb{T}$ is the cycle of $\mathcal{G}$ and MLSNs; $\rho : E \times \mathcal{T} \to \{0, 1\}$ is called presence function, and indicates whether a given edge is available at a given time t; $\zeta : E \times \mathcal{T} \to \mathbb{T}$ is called latency function, and indicates the time for one MTU takes to cross a given edge if starting at a given t (the latency of an edge could vary with time); $\mathcal{L} \in \mathbb{N}^+$ represents the time-labeling of one edge, then $\mathcal{L}_{i+1} - \mathcal{L}_i \geq 2\zeta$ according to the "active-time" constraint of edges. $\mathcal{G}_{\mathcal{L}} = (V, E(\mathcal{L}))$ represents the $\mathcal{L}^{th}$ static instance. In where, $E(\mathcal{L})$ represents the edges with label $\mathcal{L}$ (which could be empty) in G. $|n|$ represents the number of vertices, $|m|$ represents the number of edges and $|\mathcal{L}|$ represents the number of labels. Then, the number of time edges in $\mathcal{G}$ is $|m_{\mathcal{L}}| = |m| \times |\mathcal{L}|$. If $\rho[t_a, t_b](e) = 1$ then for $\forall t \in [t_a, t_b]$ and $\forall e \in E$, $\rho(e) \equiv 1$. We use $\mathcal{G}' = \mathcal{G}_{[t_a, t_b]}$ to represent the subgraph of $\mathcal{G}$ in $\mathcal{T}' = \mathcal{T} \cap [t_a, t_b]$.

Definition 1. P is a time-related route in $\mathcal{G}$, iff there is an edge sequence $\{e_1, e_2, \ldots, e_k\}$ in G, for $\forall i < k, \{\rho(e_i, t_i) = 1 \wedge t_{i+1} \geq t_i + \zeta(e_i, t_i) \wedge \rho_{[t_i, t_i + \zeta(e_i, t_i))}(e_i) = 1\}$.

Where, t_1 is the depart time and t_k is the arrival time of P, denoted as $d(P)$ and $a(P)$ respectively. Notice that, the actual arrival time is $t_k + \zeta_k$ due to the presence of transmission delay.

Property. P can be used for data transmission.

Proof. For $\forall i < k$, e_i can allow one MTU across it due to the defined *latency* function. And the restrict condition $\{\rho(e_i, t_i) = 1 \wedge \rho_{[t_i, t_i + \zeta(e_i, t_i))}(e_i) = 1\}$ can guarantee the availability of $\forall e_i \in P$, as well as its capacity, and the restrict condition $\{\rho(e_i, t_i) = 1 \wedge t_{i+1} \geq t_i = 1\}$ can guarantee that all edges are arranged strictly in non-descending time, that is, we cannot use such a time edge to transmit data which only present in past time.   ∎

Define $\mathcal{P}$ as the set of P in $\mathcal{G}$ and $\mathcal{P}_{(u,v)} \subseteq \mathcal{P}$ as the set of P which departs from u and arrives at v. We define it as *direct path* if P resides in one $\mathcal{G}_\mathcal{L}$, otherwise *indirect path*. The propagation delay of P is defined as:

$$\zeta(P) = \sum_{1 \le i \le k} \zeta(e_i) \tag{1}$$

It is worth noting that the availability of $P(u, v)$ does not mean that there must be a $P(v, u)$, due to the fact that the paths and edges are both time-related. As illustrated in Fig. 6, there exists a path $P(u, v) = \{(ua, 1), (av, 4)\}$, but $P(v, u) = \phi$. "[1,2]" and "[4,6]" denote the active time of corresponding edges.

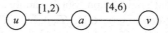

Fig. 6. Illustration of time-related paths

Definition 2. $P(u, v)$ is a *foremost path* at time t, iff (2), (3), (4) holds.

$$d(P) \ge t \tag{2}$$

$$a(P) = \min\{a(P')|P' \in \mathcal{P}\} \tag{3}$$

$$\zeta(P) = \min\{\zeta(P')|P' \in \mathcal{P}\} \tag{4}$$

If there is no *direct path* in any $\mathcal{G}_\mathcal{L}$, e.g., in sparse scenarios, then the *indirect path* is the foremost one whose $a(P)$ is the earliest, due to the fact that (4) is a weak constraint. But for dense scenarios, there may has one or more direct paths, then (4) is a strong constraint which makes the problem more challenging.

4.2   The Dynamic Algorithm Based on TVG

We now describe the algorithm which can efficiently calculate the foremost path that starts from source node $s \in V$ to destination node $v \in V\backslash\{s\}$ and can adapt both sparse and dense scenarios automatically. Assume each node corresponds to one satellite and the edges represent interactions between them over time. Every satellite can know the time-varying corresponding satellites of all RVs via the CP method [16].

Algorithm.

1: //Initialization
2: $t \leftarrow t_{start}$, $L'_{max} \leftarrow TTL + t_{start} + 1$
3: **for each** $v \in V \setminus \{s\}$ **do**
4:     $p[v] \leftarrow \phi$
5:     $a[v] \leftarrow \infty$
6:     $d[v] \leftarrow \infty$
7: **end for**
8: $d[s] \leftarrow 0$
9: Initialize queue Q
10: In-queue (Q, s)
11: //Calculate the precursor time nodes and $\zeta(P)$
12: **while** $d \notin Q$ and $t \neq L'_{max}$ **do**
13:         **for each** $u \in Q$ **do**
14:             Out-queue (Q)
15:         **for each** $(u, v) \in E(t)$ **do**
16:             **if** $p[v] = \emptyset$ **then**
17:                 $p[v] \leftarrow u$
18:                 $a[v] \leftarrow t$
19:                 $d[v] = d[u] + \zeta(u, v)$
20:             **else if** $a[v] = t$ **then**
21:                     Relax $(u, v, d[v])$
22:             **end if**
23:             In-queue (Q, v)
24:         **end if**
25:         **end for**
26:     **end for**
27:     $t{+}{+}$
28: **end while**

Theorem. The algorithm can correctly output the *foremost path–* $P(u, v)$, on given the required inputs.

Proof. To ensure the correctness of this algorithm, there must has $d[v] = \zeta(s, v)$ for each node $v \in Q$, at the start of each iteration of the **while** loop between line 12 and 28. That is, we must proof that (5) always holds when $\forall u \in V$ is added to queue Q.

$$d[u] = \zeta(s, u) \tag{5}$$

At time t_{start}, $d[s] = \zeta(s, s) = 0$ must hold due to the fact that $Q = \{s\}$. Then, in each iteration, let u be the first node that (5) will not holds when it is added to queue Q at time t. We must have $u \neq s$ and $Q \neq \phi$. There must be one or more paths from s to u and contains $p(s, u)$, for otherwise $d[u] = \zeta(s, u) = \infty$ by the non-path property, which would violate our assumption.

We suppose further that there has another path p' from s to u, which satisfies $a(P') < a(P)$, that is, $d'[u] < d[u]$. Then, at time $t' < t$, there must have another time-edge (w, u, t') which satisfies $w \in Q, u \notin Q$. So, the algorithm will add u to queue Q at $t' < t$, which would violate our initial assumption.

We conclude that there must have $d[u] = \zeta(s, u)$ when node v is added to queue Q, and that this equality is maintained at all times thereafter.

At termination, there has $Q = \phi$, which indicates that all nodes are in-queue and out-queue once. Consequently, there must have $d[u] = \zeta(s, u)$ for all nodes $u \in Q$ which can ensure the correctness of the algorithm.   ∎

Consider the worst case, all nodes will be added to queue Q, until the $\mathcal{L}'_{max}$ th iteration. So the *while loop* between line 12 and 28 will be executed $O(\mathcal{L}'_{max})$ times. The algorithm will traverse $O(n)$ nodes in each iteration. The complexity of relax and queue management is $O(n \log n)$ based on a modified Fibonacci heap structure. The complexity of one iteration is $O(n^2 \log n (1 + 2 + \ldots + \mathcal{L}'_{max})) = O(n^2 (\log n)(\mathcal{L}'_{max})^2)$. The additional accumulation factor is $O(m_{\mathcal{L}})$ due to the fact that each time-edge is just be accessed once. In summary, the overall time complexity is $O(n(\log n)(\mathcal{L}'_{max})^3 + m_{\mathcal{L}})$.

Consider the actual route calculating, if $\mathcal{G}_{\mathcal{L}}$ is connected at time t, that is, there has direct path, the time complexity is $O(n(\log n) + m)$. On the contrary, $\mathcal{G}_{\mathcal{L}}$ is not connected (DTN), then we can control $\mathcal{L}'_{max}$ to an small natural number through the *TTL* value in line 2. By doing this, the algorithm could converge after several iterations. The route calculation is performed for each packet which has a time constraint, algorithm could process a subgraph $\mathcal{G}' = \mathcal{G}_{[ta,tb]}$ and then the time complexity is $O(n(\log n) + m\mathcal{L})$.

5   Performance Evaluation

5.1   Scenario Description

We construct the terrestrial segment as illustrated in Fig. 1 and set one RV. We set the MLSN according to the "Iridium NEXT" project which starts in 2016 [17]. The link rate is set to 10 Mbps. The specific constellation parameters are shown in Table 1.

Table 1. Constellation parameters

Satellite type	Satellite number	Orbit period	Orbit altitude	Orbit inclination	RAAN	True anomaly
MEO [18]	2×5	360 min	10390 km	45°/135°	Interval 72°	–
LEO [17]	6×11	100 min	780 km	86.4°	Interval 45°	Interval 60°

5.2   Average Handover Latency

We define the handover latency as the time duration which begins from the time when link handover begins to the time when the mobile producer can receive the first Interest packet from a new AP.

We adopt 10 aircrafts serve as MPs and 100 CCs distributed in the scenario. Then, we evaluate the average handover latency by varying the network load rate from 0.1 to 1.0. The results are shown in Fig. 7(a). It can be observed clearly that the average handover latency of space to terrestrial is the lowest. We also notice that, the acceleration strategy leads to a slight increase of latency (about 1.4%–4.1%) in these handovers that from space to terrestrial. The reason may be that there exists a strategy computation time. And the average handover latency increases from 14% to 26% when the network load rate changes from 0.1 to 1. The acceleration strategy can reduce the average handover latency about 10%–16% while the network load rate is varying from 0.1 to 1.0 in these handovers from terrestrial to space.

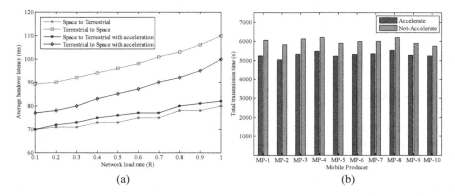

Fig. 7. (a) Average handover latency *vs* network load rate; (b) total transmission time of different strategies

5.3   Forwarding Performance

We store 1000 different *contents* in each MP, the average size of these *contents* is 1 Mbyte. Allocate 10 CCs to fetch back these *contents* from the corresponding MP. Then, we evaluate the forwarding performance. The results are shown in Fig. 7(b). It can be observed clearly that the total transmission time of different MP have slightly difference. But the acceleration strategy can obtain speedup ratios from 9% to 13.4% and the average speedup ratio of 10 MPs is 11.5%.

We vary the network load rate from 0.1 to 0.8, and evaluate the average transmission time under two different strategies: accelerate and not-accelerate. The results are shown in Fig. 8(a). We can observe that while R $\leq$ 0.5, the average transmission time increases slowly. Then, we vary the network load rate from 0.1 to 0.8 and evaluate the PIT aggregation performance from the aggregation percentage point of view.

We use K to denote the aggregation number of PIT, and the results are shown in Fig. 8(b). We can observe that the network load rate slightly affects K. Most packages are benefited from PIT aggregation; The Non-aggregation rate is 15% to 28%. And there are only 6% to 8% entries where $K = 4$. The reason is that we only allocate three interfaces to these CRs in terrestrial networks.

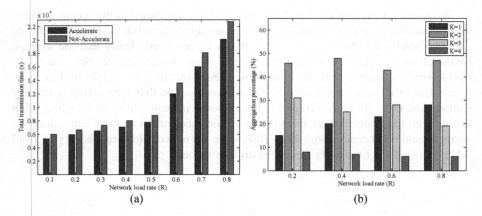

Fig. 8. (a) Total transmission time *vs* network load rate. (b) PIT aggregation percentage *vs* network load rate

6 Conclusion

In this paper, we propose a space-terrestrial integrated mobility support method based on NDN architecture for the purpose of assisting space-terrestrial integrated cooperative communication in FSTIN scenarios. We first describe the FSTIN scenario and analyze the producer mobility problem in it, and then design a tracing-based producer mobility management scheme to reduce the FIB update operations in CRs, as well as an addressing-assisted forwarding method which can leverage NDN's stateful forwarding plane. Moreover, we formally describe MLSNs via a TVG model and define the foremost path calculating problem, as well as an efficient algorithm. Finally, we perform extensive evaluations to verify the handover latency and forwarding efficiency of the scheme.

References

1. Sacchi, C., Bhasin, K., Kadowaki, N., Vong, F.: Toward the "space 2.0" Era [Guest Editorial]. IEEE Commun. Mag. **53**(3), 16–17 (2015)
2. Guta, M., Ververidis, C., Drougas, A., Andrikopoulos, I., Siris, V., Polyzos, G., Baudoin, C.: Satellite-terrestrial integration scenarios for future information-centric networks. In: 30th AIAA International Communications Satellite System Conference, 15043. AIAA (2012)
3. Li, D., Shen, X., Gong, J., Zhang, J., Lu, J.: On construction of China's space information network. Geomatics Inf. Sci. Wuhan Univ. **40**(06), 711–715 (2015)
4. Min, S.: An idea of China's space-based integrated information network. Spacecraft Eng. **22**(05), 1–14 (2013)
5. Gao, Z.Y., Venkataramani, A., Kurose, J., Heimlicher, S.: Towards a quantitative comparison of location-independent network architectures. ACM SIGCOMM Comput. Commun. Rev. **44**(04), 259–270 (2014)

6. Zhang, Y., Afanasyev, A., Burke, J., Zhang, L.: A survey of mobility support in named data networking. In: Workshop on Name-Oriented Mobility: Architecture, Algorithms and Applications, pp. 83–88. ACM (2016)
7. Kim, D.H., Kim, J.H., Kim, Y.S., Yoon, H.S., Yeom, I.: Mobility support in content centric networks. In: Proceedings of the Second Edition of the ICN Workshop on Information-Centric Networking, pp. 13–18. ACM (2012)
8. Zhang, Y., Zhang, H., Zhang, L.: Kite: a mobility support scheme for NDN. In: Proceedings of the 1st International Conference on Information-Centric Networking, pp. 179–180. ACM (2014)
9. Aug´e, J., Carofiglio, G., Grassi, G., Muscariello, L., Pau, G.: Anchorless producer mobility in ICN. In: Proceedings of the 2nd International Conference on Information-Centric Networking, pp. 189–190. ACM (2015)
10. Zhang, L., Afanasyev, A., Burke, J., Jacobson, V., Crowley, P., Papadopoulos, C.: Named data networking. ACM SIGCOMM Comput. Commun. Rev. **44**(04), 66–73 (2014)
11. Grassi, G., Pesavento, D., Pau, G., Zhang, L., Fdida, S.: Navigo: interest forwarding by geolocations in vehicular named data networking. In: IEEE 16th International Symposium on a World of Wireless, Mobile and Multimedia Networks, pp. 1–10. IEEE (2015)
12. Gusev, P., Burke, J.: NDN-RTC: real-time videoconferencing over named data networking. In: Proceedings of the 2nd International Conference on Information-Centric Networking, pp. 117–126 (2015)
13. Soliman, H., Castelluccia, C., Elmalki, K., Bellier, L.: Hierarchical mobile IPv6 (HMIPv6) mobility management. IETF RFC 5380 (2008)
14. Holme, P., Saramäki, J.: Temporal networks. Phys. Rep. **519**(3), 97–125 (2012)
15. Casteigts, A., Flocchini, P., Quattrociocchi, W., Santoro, N.: Time-varying graphs and dynamic networks. Int. J. Parallel Emergent Distrib. Syst. **27**(5), 387–408 (2012)
16. Fraire, J.A., Finochietto, J.M.: Design challenges in contact plans for disruption-tolerant satellite networks. IEEE Commun. Mag. **53**(5), 163–169 (2015)
17. GunterI.: ridium-NEXT. http://space.skyrocket.de/doc_sdat/iridium-next.htm
18. Liu, H., Sun, F.: Routing for predictable multi-layered satellite networks. Sci. China Inf. Sci. **56**(11), 1–18 (2013)

Development and Performance Evaluation of Filterbank Multicarrier Systems

Su Hu[1(✉)], Yixuan Huang[1], Chuanxue Jin[1], Qu Luo[1], Jin Zhang[1],
Yuan Gao[2,3(✉)], and Xiangyang Li[3]

[1] University of Electronic Science and Technology of China,
Chengdu 611731, China
husu@uestc.edu.cn
[2] Department of Electronic Engineering,
Tsinghua University, Beijing 100084, China
yuangao08@tsinghua.edu.cn
[3] China Defense Science and Technology Information Center,
Beijing 100142, China

Abstract. As an alternative to OFDM systems with Cyclic Prefix (CP), filter bank multicarrier (FBMC) transmission technique leads to an enhanced physical layer conventional communication network and it is an enabling technology for the new concepts and, particularly, cognitive radio. Due to the feature of good time-frequency localization, there is no need for FBMC systems adding any guard interval, definitely leading to higher spectral efficiency compared with CP-OFDM. FBMC has the potential to fulfill the requirements of the new concepts, but a major research effort is necessary for full exploitation and optimization in all aspects of the radio context. In this paper, a testbench based on National Instrument universal software radio peripheral has been developed for FBMC systems. Meanwhile, systematic performances, including synchronization, channel estimation and bit error rate are evaluated.

Keywords: Filter bank multicarrier (FBMC) · NI-USRP · Testbench

1 Introduction

Nowadays, both industry and academia are working towards the 5G mobile communication systems. As future wireless communication scenarios always involve a very harsh communication environment, it has been questioned if OFDM is still the best choice for all cases. The recent research trend has been looking into other alternative modulation schemes. As an alternative modulation scheme to conventional OFDM with cyclic prefix (CP), filter bank multicarrier (FBMC) systems employ offset quadrature amplitude modulation (OQAM), is one of competitive candidates for 5G applications [1]. Due to the absence of CP, FBMC achieves very high spectrum efficiency [2]. The properly designed pulse shaping filter enables FBMC a more localized time-frequency response, which leads to a lower out-of-band leakage and enhances the robustness to synchronization errors.

In recent years, many researchers have done lots of work on key technologies of FBMC, such as MIMO, channel estimation and equalization and so on. However, these

© Springer International Publishing AG 2017
L. Ma et al. (Eds.): WASA 2017, LNCS 10251, pp. 842–853, 2017.
DOI: 10.1007/978-3-319-60033-8_71

studies mostly limited to theoretical research. Thanks for the NI collaboration, researchers can setup a simple prototype easily for their technologies. Through prototyping, it is easy to verify that their research whether meet the actual industrial applications or not.

Open source is applied in a series of radio programs, and the study seeks to become amateur radio hardware products. In [3], authors have presented a full duplex prototype of OFDM Physical layer receiver based on NI USRP 2922 board and GNU Radio software. On the other hand, with the escalation of technology and the cooperation NI collaboration with the industry's leading top companies, USRP has developed into a major prototype implemented platform in the latest wireless protocol study, such as the NI collaboration with Nokia Communications develop 5G millimeter wave demonstration system, NI and Sweden Lund University to develop 5G Massive MIMO test bench [4].

In this paper, NI USRP devices (USRP RIO 2953R) are considered as hardware nodes through LabVIEW software programming to demonstrate wireless communication links. Meanwhile, FBMC systems hardware testbench is set up. In order to better reflect the evolution of mobile communications, the FBMC testbench is based on 3GPP LTE structure. Furthermore, we selected several indicators to make comparison with OFDM. The Bits Error Ratio (BER) performance and Power Spectral Density (PSD) of FBMC is analyzed in the experiment and compared with BER and PSD for OFDM. By comparison, one can see that FBMC on the spectral efficiency is hesitant than OFDM.

The paper is organized as follows: Sect. 2 presents the system model of FBMC and the implementation structure based on IFFT/FFT transforms. In Sect. 3, we present a FBMC frame structure, synchronization, channel estimation method followed by zero-forcing (ZF) equalization technique. NI USRP SDR platform is also introduced exhaustively, and experimental results are presented and discussed in Sect. 4. In the end, this paper is summarized in Sect. 5.

2 FBMC System Model

Consider an equivalent FBMC baseband model with M subcarriers, where the subcarrier spacing is $1/T$ with T being the complex symbol interval. The equivalent continuous-time FBMC signal is expressed as [5]:

$$s(t) = \sum_{n=-\infty}^{+\infty} \sum_{m=0}^{N-1} \left[a_{m,n}^R g_{m,2n}(t) + a_{m,n}^I g_{m,2n+1}(t) \right], \tag{1}$$

where $a_{m,n}^R$ and $a_{m,n}^I$ denote the real and imaginary parts of the transmission data $a_{m,n}$. $g_{m,n}(t)$ is the base function coordinates at time-frequency grid (m, n).

$$g_{m,n}(t) = e^{j\frac{\pi}{2}(m+n)} e^{j2\pi m v_0 t} g(t - n\tau_0), \tag{2}$$

where v_0 represents the interval between subcarriers, τ_0 is the time offset of the real and imaginary parts between adjacent symbols. T is the symbol period of OFDM system without CP and F represents subcarrier spacing, and $T = 2\tau_0 = 1/F = 1/v_0$.

Equation (2) is substituted into Eq. (1) can be obtained:

$$s(t) = \sum_{n=-\infty}^{+\infty} \sum_{m=0}^{N-1} e^{j\frac{\pi}{2}(m+2n)} e^{j2\pi m v_0 t} + \left[a_{m,n}^R g(t - 2n\tau_0) + j a_{m,n}^I g(t - 2n\tau_0 - \tau_0) \right]. \quad (3)$$

Assuming a distortion-free channel, perfect reconstruction of real symbols is obtained owing to the following real orthogonality condition:

$$\Re\{\langle g_{m,n} \mid g_{p,q} \rangle\} = \Re\left\{ \int g_{m,n}(t) g_{p,q}^*(t) dt \right\} = \delta_{m,p} \delta_{n,q}, \quad (4)$$

where, $\delta_{m,p} = 1$ if $m = p$, and $\delta_{m,p} = 0$ if $m \neq p$. For concision purpose we set $\langle g \rangle_{m,n}^{p,q} = -j\langle g_{m,n} \mid g_{p,q} \rangle$, with $\langle g_{m,n} \mid g_{p,q} \rangle$, a pure imaginary term for $(m,n) \neq (p,q)$.

The orthogonality between different sub-lattices is automatically guarantied and is independent of the prototype function as long as this function is even. In this paper, we use an implementation method by direct discretization of the continuous time model without considering the perfect reconstruction (PR) condition [6]. The FBMC modulator is easily implemented by an IFFT block in the transmitter side, whereas the FBMC demodulator can be implemented by an FFT block (Fig. 1).

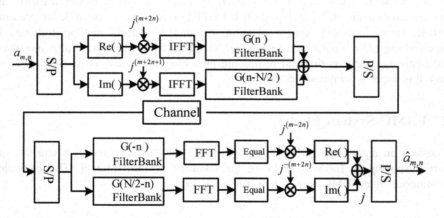

Fig. 1. The implementation diagram based on IFFT/FFT operation

3 Key Technical Methods

3.1 Frame Structure Design

As shown in Fig. 2, in this experiment, a FBMC frame is constituted by one training sequence, one preamble and five FBMC symbols. The training sequence is used to estimate time and frequency synchronization, and the preamble sequence is used to estimate channel state information. The length of each training sequence or symbol is 1024. That is, there are 1024 subcarriers in a symbol. When using 800 subcarriers to

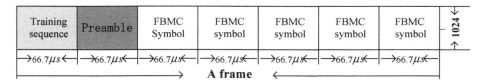

Fig. 2. SISO-FBMC frame structure

carry information of them and the modulation is 4QAM, thus, each FBMC symbol can transmit 1600 bits. The subcarrier spacing is 15 kHz while the sampling rate is 15.36 M/s. Therefore, the number of samples in a complete FBMC frame is 7168.

Because the FBMC system is also a multicarrier technology, when there is the system symbol timing offset (STO) and carrier frequency deviation between subcarriers, thus orthogonality will be destroyed, and system performance affect seriously. Therefore, time and frequency synchronization have to be considered in the FBMC Testbench. Block diagram of frame synchronization is shown in Fig. 3.

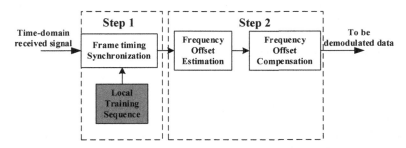

Fig. 3. Block diagram of frame synchronization in receiver

3.2 Frame Synchronization

Common synchronization error detection algorithm comprises secondary synchronization (such as training sequence) and blind synchronization method. Several preamble autocorrelation-based methods for frame synchronization were tested [7–9]. In [10], authors present a timing synchronization and frequency synchronization algorithm based on CAZAC sequence. In this paper, two identical zero correlation zone (ZCZ) synchronization sequences are used in order to operate easily. In the receiver, STO is estimated by maxing the similarity within two blocks of the sliding window, as shown in Fig. 4.

Firstly, in the transmitter, the training sequences can be created as:

$$c_u(n) = e^{-j\frac{\pi u n(n+1)}{63}}, \ n = 0, 1, \cdots, N-1 \tag{5}$$

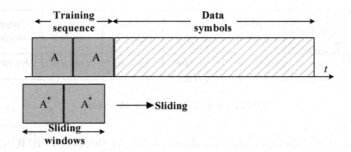

Fig. 4. STO estimation based on repetitive training sequence method

where u is the root index, according to the district ID value, generally is taken 25/29/34. The local training sequence is composed of two identical synchronization sequences whose length is 512.

In the receiver, firstly we need to cache sufficient length data collecting from the receiving antenna, and cut out a frame data. Let intercepted data do correlation operation with local training sequence, and then take the square of the result, as the following formula:

$$Cor(\tau) = \left| \sum_{n=0}^{N-1} \left[Seq_{recv}(\tau+n) \cdot Seq_{local}^*(n) \right] \right|^2, \tag{6}$$

where $Seq_{recv}(\tau)$ represents a received signal intercepted, $Seq_{local}(\tau)$ is the local training sequence, N is the length of the sliding window, i.e. the length of local training sequence, $N = 1024$. Next, repeat the above operation until the end of the frame. Comparing with all the values of $Cor(\tau)$, and finding out the maximum value, the index corresponding to the maximum τ is the synchronous starting position.

And then using the same training symbols, carrier frequency offset (CFO) can be also estimated. Suppose the value of CFO is ε, if the STO is estimated perfectly, it will incur phase difference $\pi\varepsilon$ between two adjacent sampling points. Assuming a rotational phase angle is uniform distribution, the CFO is obtained by the following method:

$$\hat{\phi} = \frac{1}{N/2} \sum_{n=0}^{N/2-1} \left[Seq_{recv}^*(n+N/2) \cdot Seq_{recv}(n) \right]$$

$$\hat{\varepsilon} = \frac{N}{2\pi(N/2)} \arg\{\hat{\phi}\}, \tag{7}$$

wherein, $\hat{\phi}$ is the estimated phase shift, $\hat{\varepsilon}$ is estimated frequency offset. $\arg\{X\}$ is the complex argument, $(X)^*$ is plural conjugate operation of X, and $N = 1024$.

3.3   Channel Estimation

Channel estimation is mainly to estimate the channel that signal through. It is essential to estimate channel accurately for a completed communication link. In this paper, we use a modified channel estimation method called Inference Cancellation Method (ICM) [11]. The pilot may be generated as follows:

$$z[n] = \begin{cases} -1, 1 & (n \bmod 2 \neq 0) \\ 0 & (n \bmod 2 = 0) \end{cases} n = 1, 2 \ldots, N. \tag{8}$$

By using the above pilot, on the one hand, we can reduce the interference experienced by the pilot as possible. In addition, for a practical FBMC system, one parameter called peak-to-average power ratio (PAPR) is a key factor for multicarrier systems. Generally speaking, a larger PAPR value leads to a larger input backoff value of high power amplifier (HPA), leading to lower power amplifier efficiency. Otherwise, multicarrier systems will suffer from nonlinear distortion by HPA. Fortunately, the training sequence generated by ICM is with low PAPR value.

In the receiver, suppose the signal on the pilot is $s[n]$. Let $\hat{H}[k]$ denotes the estimated channel gain at the kth subcarrier obtained by Least Square (LS) method:

$$H[k] = s[2k]/z[2k], \quad k = 1, 2, \ldots, 512. \tag{9}$$

Then, take the IDFT of $\{\hat{H}[k]\}_{k=1}^{N}$,

$$IDFT\{\hat{H}[k]\} = h[n] + \omega[n] = \hat{h}[n], \quad n = 1, 2, \ldots, N. \tag{10}$$

where $\omega[n]$ denotes the noise component in the time domain. Ignoring the coefficients $\{\hat{h}[n]\}$ that contain the noise only, define the coefficients for the maximum channel delay L as

$$\hat{h}_{DFT}[n] = \begin{cases} h[n] + \omega[n], & n = 1, 2, \ldots, L; \\ 0, & otherwise. \end{cases} \tag{11}$$

And transform the remaining L elements back to the frequency domain as follows

$$\hat{H}_{DFT}[k] = DFT\{\hat{h}_{DFT}[n]\}. \tag{12}$$

3.4   Equalization Technology

Although there are many FBMC equalization techniques, in order to better and easier reflect FBMC performance, Zero Forcing (ZF) equalization is used in this experiment. The demodulated data after ZF equalization as follows:

$$\tilde{x}_{ZF} = \left(H^H H\right)^{-1} H^H y, \tag{13}$$

where H is the channel response in frequency domain obtained by channel estimation, y represents the receiver data in frequency domain. $\tilde{x}_{ZF}$ represents the data after ZF equalization.

4   SDR Platform and Experiment

The testbench setup and the transmission chain can be separated into software and hardware parts. The hardware platform consists of the NI-PXIe and USRP RIO-2953R. The USRP product family is intended to be a comparatively inexpensive hardware platform for software radio, and is commonly used by research labs, universities, and hobbyists. USRPs are commonly used with the GNU Radio software suite to create complex software-defined radio systems. Because a USRP RIO include two transmitter and two receivers, a USRP N-2953 is able to meet our needs in the demonstration project. The experimental setup in the laboratory is shown as in Fig. 5. The software platform is LABVIEW 2014. LabVIEW (Laboratory Virtual Instrument Engineering Workbench) is a system-design platform and development environment for a visual programming language from National Instruments.

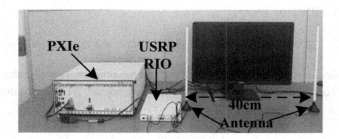

Fig. 5. Experimental setup in the laboratory

A. Experiment Parameter Settings

According to the frame structure designed in Sect. 3. A frame is constituted by two training sequences and five FBMC symbols. The length of FFT is 1024, and the frame length is 7168. The prototype filter we choose PHYDYAS filter, and the overlap factor $K = 4$ [12]. In total, the systematic parameters are shown in Table 1.

B. Experiment Result and Analysis

The experiment consists of a complete chain of FBMC radio transmission reception as it is depicted in Fig. 5. This is an indoor scenario where the environment is almost static. The RF parameters at transmitter and receivers are configured to the values shown in Table 1. The obtained results are shown by Figs. 6, 7, 8, 9 and 10, respectively.

Table 1. Experiment parameter settings

Parameters	Value
Number of symbols	7
FFT size	1024
Modulation	QPSK/OQAM
Prototype filter	PHYDYAS K = 4
Bandwidth	10M
Carrier frequency	2.4 GHz
Frame length	7168

Figure 6 shows the Power Spectrum Density of FBMC and OFDM with the length of cyclic prefix (CP) is 1/8 FFT length. One can see the spectrum level drops more rapidly compared to the OFDM one. This advantage provides to the FBMC a good opportunity to substitute the OFDM in next generation technologies [13].

Figure 7 represents synchronization correlation peak. In our experiments, we employ two the identical ZCZ sequence whose length is 512 in the transmitter. In the receiver, the local sequence is used to do sliding correlation with received signal. According to the autocorrelation of ZCZ sequences, it will produce three peaks, and the samples interval of each two peaks is 512. Therefore, the highest peak position denotes the starting point of one frame.

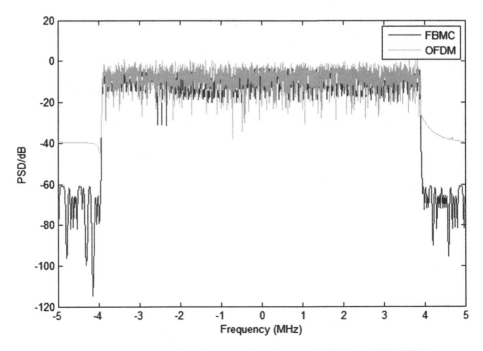

Fig. 6. Power spectrum density comparison between FBMC and CP-OFDM

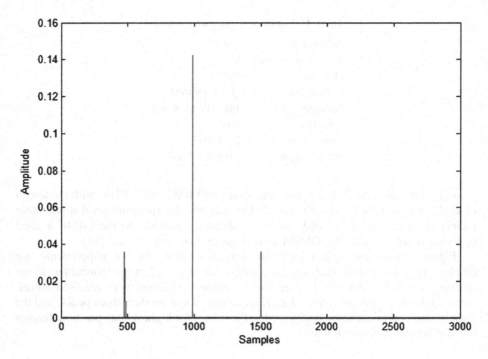

Fig. 7. Synchronization correlation peak

Figure 8 shows the estimated channel impulse response in frequency domain and time domain. In our laboratory environment, realistic channel model is usually less than three paths. And in this experiment result, the channel environment is two fading channel as shown from channel impulse response (CIR) in frequency domain. Judging from the CIR in time domain, there are two impulses on samples 0 and samples 1, represents $h[0]$ and $h[1]$ respectively. And there also exists some tiny value v_n in other samples, $h[n] = v_n, n = 3, 4, \ldots, 512$, in fact, these values can be regarded as noise coefficients.

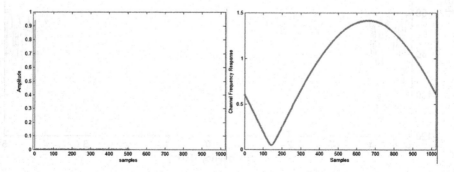

Fig. 8. Estimated channel impulse response in our scenario

Figure 9 represents the 4-QAM constellation after ZF equalization. As can be seen from the constellation, the data signal can be demodulated perfectly in the receiver, it indicates that the testbench can work effectively, meanwhile, it also demonstrates that

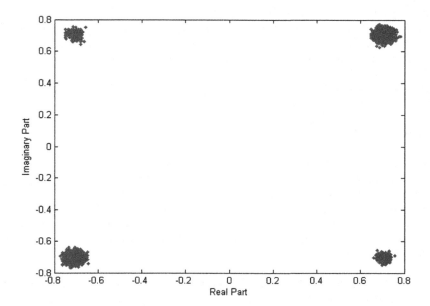

Fig. 9. 4-QAM constellation after equalization

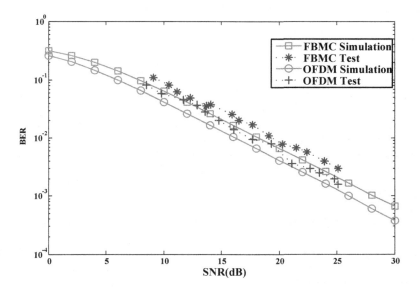

Fig. 10. Performance comparison between OFDM and FBMC

frame synchronization method and channel estimation technologies we employed are valid. Next, we are able to demodulate bit streams easily and apply them to calculate BER.

Figure 10 shows the BER performance comparison between OFDM and FBMC. When using MATLAB simulation, assuming that the channel is two-path Rayleigh fading channel. This is because our lab channel environment is usual two-path channel. And the length of CP in OFDM is 1/8 length of FFT. In this experiment, the Signal to Noise Ratio (SNR) is calculated reference to the method in [14]. One can see BER performance in actual environment is worse than simulation. Besides, if we don't consider spectral efficiency, the BER performance of CP-OFDM is better than the FBMC. In fact, if spectral efficiency is taken into account, BER performances of both systems are comparable.

5   Conclusion

In this paper, the hardware implementation of FBMC systems is presented. We have solved the problems of time-frequency synchronization, channel estimation and equalization techniques in FBMC prototyping. Finally, numerical analysis and simulation results show that FBMC is more spectrum-efficient than OFDM with CP. In the next work, we will transmit text, image and video by using FBMC technique. Furthermore, we will combine multiple input multiple output (MIMO) technology with FBMC systems and implement it.

Acknowledgement. The work is jointly supported by the MOST Program of International S&T Cooperation (Grant No. 2016YFE0123200), National Natural Science Foundation of China (Grant No. 61471100/61101090/61571082), Science and Technology on Electronic Information Control Laboratory (Grant No. 6142105040103) and Fundamental Research Funds for the Central Universities (Grant No. ZYGX2015J012/ZYGX2014Z005).

References

1. Gao, X., Wang, W., Xia, X., Au, E.K.S., You, X.: Cyclic prefixed OQAM-OFDM and its application to single-carrier FDMA. IEEE Trans. Commun. **59**(5), 1467–1480 (2011)
2. Andrews, J.G., Ghosh, A., Muhamed, R.: Fundamentals of WIMAX: Understanding Broadband Wireless Networking. Prentice-Hall, Upper Saddle River (2007)
3. Villemaud, G., Zhou, W., Risset, T.: Full duplex prototype of OFDM on GNU radio and USRPs. In: IEEE Radio Wireless Symposium, pp. 217–219 (2014)
4. 5G News and Article National Instruments. http://www.ni.com/tutorial/51986/en/. 2015.12.14
5. Bolcskei, H.: Orthogonal frequency division multiplexing based on offset QAM. In: Feichtinger, H.G., Strohmer, T. (eds.) Advances in Gabor Analysis, pp. 321–352. Birkhauser, Boston (2003). doi:10.1007/978-1-4612-0133-5_12
6. Du, J., Signell, S.: Time frequency localization of pulse shaping filters in OFDM/OQAM systems. In: 6th International Conference on Information, Communications and Signal Processing, pp. 1–5 (2007)

7. Massey, J.L.: Optimum frame synchronization. IEEE Trans. Commun. **20**(2), 115–119 (1972)
8. Xuefei, H., Jie, C.: Implementation frame synchronization for MIMO-OFDM system with ZCZ-codes. In: Proceedings of IEEE International Symposium MAPE, vol. 1, pp. 241–244 (2005)
9. van de Beek, J.-J., Sandell, M., Isaksson, M., Ola Borjesson, P.: Low-complex frame synchronization in OFDM systems. In: Proceedings of IEEE International Conference Universal Personal Communications, Tokyo, Japan, 6–10 November 1995, pp. 982–986 (1995)
10. Hu, J., Chen, Y., Huang, Q.: Synchronization of FBMC based on CAZAC sequence. In: 2011 IEEE 2nd International Conference on Software Engineering and Service Science, pp. 116–119 (2011)
11. Hu, S., Wu, G., Li, T., Xiao, Y., Li, S.: Preamble design with ICI cancellation for channel estimation in OFDM/OQAM systems. IEICE Trans. Commun. **93**(1), 211–214 (2010)
12. FP7-ICT PHYDYAS: Physical layer for dynamic spectrum access and cognitive radio. http://www.ict-phydyas.org
13. FBMC physical layer: a primer. Documents D2.1 and D3.1, July 2008. www.ict-phydyas.org
14. Serafimovski, N., Younis, A., Mesleh, R.: Practical implementation of spatial modulation. IEEE Trans. Veh. Technol. **62**, 4511–4523 (2013)
15. Kofidis, E.: Channel estimation in filter bank-based multicarrier systems: challenges and solutions. In: IEEE 6th International Symposium on Communications, Control and Signal Processing, pp. 453–456 (2014)
16. Savaux, V., Bader, F.: Mean square error analysis and linear minimum mean square error application for preamble-based channel estimation in orthogonal frequency division multiplexing/offset quadrature amplitude modulation systems. IET Commun. **9**(14), 1763–1773 (2015)

A Location Prediction-based Physical Layer Security Scheme for Suspicious Eavesdroppers

Yuqi Tian[1], Yan Huo[1(✉)], Chunqiang Hu[2,3], Qinghe Gao[1,3], and Tao Jing[1]

[1] School of Electronics and Information Engineering,
Beijing Jiaotong University, Beijing, China
yhuo@bjtu.edu.cn
[2] Key Laboratory of Dependable Service Computing in Cyber Physical Society,
Chongqing University, Chongqing, China
[3] Department of Computer Science, The George Washington University,
Washington, DC, USA

Abstract. This paper aims to help save energy when legitimate users exploit physical layer security techniques to guarantee security, which can suit resource limited systems more. It proposes a risk prediction scheme in a communication scene with a mobile eavesdropper, whose CSI (Channel State Information) is unknown to legitimate users. The scheme can predict where the eavesdropper will be later and decide whether security measures should be taken to against it. The security measures are only taken when the prediction result shows there will be risks in the communication process. Based on the proposed scheme, resources can be saved to a large degree as well as the security guaranteed.

Keywords: Physical layer security · Markov prediction · Outage

1 Introduction

Nowadays, wireless networks have become an important part of our lives. Due to the properties of broadcast communication and signal superposition in wireless scenarios [1,2], it is difficult to shield transmitted signals from unauthorized receivers and protect legitimate receivers from unintended overlapping of multiple signals [3]. These natures make security become a vital issue. So far, many works which mainly exploit cryptographic techniques at the upper layers of wireless networks have been done [4–6]. As a complement, physical layer security is proposed and has been widely discussed in recent years. In this field, strategies of anti-eavesdropping have been studied substantially [7–11], however, few of recent works consider a mobile eavesdropper, whose CSI is unknown to legitimate users.

We believe legitimate users do not have to act in a defensive way during the whole communication process when facing the mobile eavesdropper. Thus we propose a risk prediction scheme. We first derive the expression of the secrecy outage probability as the security metric, and set a performance target. Next, the Markov Chain is exploited to set up a Markov mobile model of the eavesdropper

© Springer International Publishing AG 2017
L. Ma et al. (Eds.): WASA 2017, LNCS 10251, pp. 854–859, 2017.
DOI: 10.1007/978-3-319-60033-8_72

to predict its mobile path. Then we perform the prediction by exploiting the history movement information of the eavesdropper. And we use the result to decide whether the eavesdropper will harm the communication later. If it will be, corresponding security measures will be taken. At last, we demonstrate the effectiveness and the performance of our scheme via a simulation study.

2   System Model

Considering a wireless network shown in Fig. 1, we assume there exist a transmitter (Alice), a receiver (Bob) and an eavesdropper (Eve). Alice is sending messages to Bob via the legitimate channel, while Eve is moving around Alice to achieve eavesdropping. We assume each node is equipped with a single omnidirection antenna, and the legitimate users' CSI is available for all nodes, while Eve's CSI is unknown to legitimate users because of its unexpected movement.

We define d_{ab} as the distance between Alice and Bob, and d_{ae} as the distance between Alice and Eve. The channel between Alice and Bob is denoted by h_{ab}, and the channel between Alice and Eve is denoted by h_{ae}. We assume both the channels are modeled as Rayleigh fading channels. They can be expressed as

$$h = \frac{c \cdot f(G)}{d^{\alpha}}, \tag{1}$$

where c is the path-loss constant, d represents the distance between the communicating nodes, α denotes the path-loss exponent, and $f(G)$ is the channel power fading coefficient that follows the exponential distribution. When Alice sends a message s to Bob, the SNRs (Signal to Noise Ratio) at Bob and at Eve can be written as follow respectively:

$$SNR_{ab} = \frac{P_s \|h_{ab}\|^2}{\sigma_n^2}, \quad SNR_{ae} = \frac{P_s \|h_{ae}\|^2}{\sigma_n^2},$$

where P_s is the available power, σ_n^2 is the variance of AWGN signals. According to [12], we can get the expression of secrecy outage probability, written as:

$$P_{out}(R_s) = 1 - \frac{SNR_{ab}}{SNR_{ab} + 2^{R_s} SNR_{ae}} exp(-\frac{2^{R_s} - 1}{SNR_{ab}}). \tag{2}$$

From former equations, we can see $P_{out}(R_s)$ is a function of d_{ab} and d_{ae}. Since Alice and Bob are settled, secrecy outage probabilities of other positions in the network can be calculated. If we can predict the position where Eve will be later, we can calculate the secrecy outage probability of the predicted position and decide whether it may steal the information. With the decision, we can take measures to guarantee security beforehand.

3   The Risk Prediction Scheme on Eve

In this section, we propose a scheme to predict where Eve will be in its later movement by exploiting the Markov Chain. We predict the position of Eve at

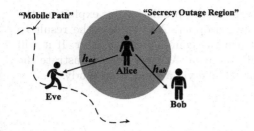
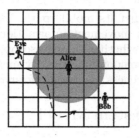

Fig. 1. Description of the network layout.   **Fig. 2.** The grid division of the network.

intervals of one moment, where one moment is set to be 1 length of time. When Eve moves from one position to another position from the current moment to the next moment, we call it as one step of movement. We define $t-1$ as the current moment; t as the next moment; and so on. We assume the history movement information of Eve is known. To operate the prediction more efficiently and lower the computation complexity, we divide the network into an $N \times N$ gridding, as shown in Fig. 2. We define each grid as a state. When Eve moves in the same grid, we consider it stays at the same state. The length of every grid is set to be 1. The distance between each pairs of adjacent grids is set to be 1. And we assume the grid is the minimum unit of the network space.

We use N_{total} to denote the number of grids, where $N_{total} = N \times N$. The state space is $SP = \{c_1, c_2, \cdots, c_{N_{total}}\}$. The transition matrix is a $N_{total} \times N_{total}$ matrix. We use p_{ij} $(1 \leq i, j \leq N_{total})$ to denote the transition probability in the ith row and the jth column of the transition matrix P. Every p_{ij} can be calculated based on the statistics of history movement information. We use N_{ij} $(1 \leq i, j \leq N_{total})$ to denote the total number of times that Eve moves from grid c_i to grid c_j in its movement history, thus p_{ij} can be expressed as

$$p_{ij} = \frac{N_{ij}}{\sum_{j=1}^{N_{total}} N_{ij}} \quad (1 \leq i, j \leq N_{total}). \tag{3}$$

After we get P, we can further derive the n-step transition matrix $P(n)$. By exploiting $C - K$ equation, we can see that

$$P(n) = P \cdot P(n-1) = P(n-1) \cdot P = P^n. \tag{4}$$

We believe the probabilities of positions at the next moment are related to P and Eve's k steps of states before the next moment. So we use a weighted way to do the calculation, that is

$$X(t) = a_1 S(t-1)P + a_2 S(t-2)P^2 + \cdots + a_k S(t-k)P^k, \tag{5}$$

where $X(t)$ is a $1 \times N_{total}$ matrix, containing the probabilities of all the states. And $S(m)$ $(t - k \leq m \leq t - 1)$ is a set containing the information of states. It represents the state Eve was at the former mth moment before the next moment. It is also a $1 \times N_{total}$ matrix, and the value at the first row, the mth column is 1, while other values are 0. $a_1, a_2, \cdots a_k$ are weighted coefficients, representing different influence degrees that movements at the former 1th, 2th, $\cdots$, kth moment before the next moment have on the next moment's movement, respectively. Noting that we consider that the influence degree is a relative value, thus the summation of $a_1, a_2, \cdots a_k$ is not 1.

After obtaining $X(t)$, we compare the probabilities. We assume Eve can only move form current grid to adjacent grids or stay still, thus probabilities of unreachable states can be set to 0, and we only have to compare the probabilities of potential states. The state with the maximum probability is where Eve will be at the next moment. And we use the result to decide whether we should take security measures. The whole decision process is summarized as Algorithm 1.

Algorithm 1. The Risk Prediction Rule

Initialization:
    $SP = \{c_1, c_2, \ldots, c_{N_{total}}\}$;
    $S = \{s_1, s_2, \ldots, s_t\}$;
    $N_{ij}\ (1 \le i \le N_{total}, 1 \le j \le N_{total})$.
  1: Calculate transition probabilities P_{ij} by N_{ij};
  2: Calculate n step transition matrix $(1 \le n \le k)$, $P, P^2, \ldots, P^k$;
  3: Calculate the predicted probabilities $X(t)$;
  4: Set $X_v \leftarrow 0$
     (v are sequence numbers of unreachable states);
  5: Find $(X_m ax = max(X(t)))$
  6: Calculate $P_{out}(R_s)$ with max;
  7: **if** $P_{out}(R_s) > \gamma_{th}$ **then**
  8:    Take secure measures against Eve;
  9: **else**
10:    Break;
11: **end if**
12: Modify N_{ij} for the next time prediction.

Here, we consider the miss probability P_m and the false alarm probability P_f to evaluate the performance. P_m means when the prediction says the communication is secure, but Eve is actually in the secrecy outage region. And P_f means the opposite. To present the performance simpler and clearer, we define an index P_e written as follow to represent the error level of our scheme.

$$P_e = P_m \cdot P_f. \tag{6}$$

4 Numerical Simulation

In this section, simulation results are shown to verify the effectiveness of our scheme. We observe the error probability P_e in scenarios with different parameter values. We respectively divide the network space into a 10×10, 20×20 and

30×30 gridding, which is denoted by N_{total}. And we set k to be $3, 5, 10$ and the number of history movements N_M to be $2000, 4000, 8000$. The target secrecy outage probability γ_{th} is set to be 0.8.

Figure 3 gives a description of P_e with different N_{total} and k. We can see P_e is monotonously decreasing with N_{total}. It is reasonable because dividing the network space with large grids can lead to a take-security-measure decision when Eve moves around the edge of the target secrecy outage region. And when grids goes smaller, the number of paths in the same grid goes smaller. Thus more history movement information can be get to perform a more accurate prediction. Besides, Fig. 3 also shows that as the value of k increases, the value of P_e goes down at first, and then goes up. The value of P_e is at the minimum when $k = 5$. It indicates considering more former steps may not achieve a better performance.

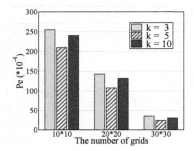
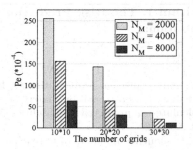

Fig. 3. P_e vs. N_{total} and k. Parameters setting: $N_M = 2000$, $N_{total} = 10 \times 10, 20 \times 20, 30 \times 30$, $k = 3, 5, 10$.

Fig. 4. P_e vs. N_{total} and N_M. Parameters setting: $k = 3$, $N_{total} = 10 \times 10, 20 \times 20, 30 \times 30$, $N_M = 2000, 4000, 8000$.

In Fig. 4, we present a description of P_e with different N_{total} and N_M. It shows P_e is monotonously decreasing with N_M. This is because history movements are crucial to the generation of the transition matrix. More history movements can provide more information about the mobile characteristics of Eve, thus the prediction result can be more accurate.

5   Conclusion

The paper proposes a risk prediction scheme in the communication scene with a mobile eavesdropper, whose CSI is unknown to legitimate users. We use the secrecy outage probability as the security metric, and perform the prediction by using the Markov Chain. Simulation results show the prediction scheme is with low error probability, which verifies its security performance. As for future work, we are going to re-investigate such issue in a MIMO network, and propose a specific physical layer security strategy.

Acknowledgments. We are very grateful to all reviewers who have helped improve the quality of this paper. This work was supported by the National Natural Science Foundation of China (Grant Nos. 61572070, 61471028, 61371069), the Specialized Research Fund for the Doctoral Program of Higher Education (Grant No. 20130009110015), and the Fundamental Research Funds for the Central Universities (Grant No. 2016JBZ003).

References

1. Zheng, X., Cai, Z., Gao, H.: Location-privacy-aware review publication mechanism for local business service systems. In: the 36th Annual IEEE International Conference on Computer Communications, pp. 1–9 (2017)
2. Cai, Z., He, Z., Guan, X., Li, Y.: Collective data-sanitization for preventing sensitive information inference attacks in social networks. IEEE Trans. Dependable Secure Comput. **PP**(99), 1 (2016)
3. Zheng, X., Cai, Z., Yu, J., Wang, C., Li, Y.: Follow but no track: privacy preserved profile publishing in cyber-physical social systems. IEEE Internet Things J. **PP**(99), 1 (2017)
4. Zhang, L., Cai, Z., Wang, X.: FakeMask: a novel privacy preserving approach for smartphones. IEEE Trans. Netw. Serv. Manage. **13**(2), 335–348 (2016)
5. Cai, J.Z., Ai, C., Yang, D., Gao, H., Cheng, X.: Differentially private k-anonymity: achieving query privacy in location-based services. In: The International Conference on Identification, Information and Knowledge in the Internet of Things (2016)
6. Li, J., Cai, Z., Yan, M., Li, Y.: Using crowdsourced data in location-based social networks to explore influence maximization. In: the 35th Annual IEEE International Conference on Computer Communications, pp. 1–9 (2016)
7. Li, Z., Jing, T., Cheng, X., Huo, Y., Zhou, W., Chen, D.: Cooperative jamming for secure communications in MIMO cooperative cognitive radio networks. In: 2015 IEEE International Conference on Communications, pp. 7609–7614 (2015)
8. Lin, P.-H., Lai, S.-H., Lin, S.-C., Su, H.-J.: On secrecy rate of the generalized artificial-noise assisted secure beamforming for wiretap channels. IEEE J. Sel. Areas Commun. **31**, 1728–1740 (2013)
9. Wang, J., Lee, J., Wang, F., Quek, T.Q.S.: Jamming-aided secure communication in massive mimo Rician channels. IEEE Trans. Wireless Commun. **14**, 6854–6868 (2015)
10. Li, Z., Jing, T., Ma, L., Huo, Y., Qian, J.: Worst-case cooperative jamming for secure communications in CIOT networks. Sensors **16**, 339 (2016)
11. Gao, Q., Huo, Y., Ma, L., Xing, X., Cheng, X., Jing, T., Liu, H.: Optimal stopping theory based jammer selection for securing cooperative cognitive radio networks. In: IEEE Global Communications Conference, pp. 1–6 (2016)
12. Li, H., Wang, X., Hou, W.: Security enhancement in cooperative jamming using compromised secrecy region minimization. In: 2013 13th Canadian Workshop on Information Theory, pp. 214–218 (2013)

Structural Holes Theory-Based Influence Maximization in Social Network

Jinghua Zhu[1], Xuming Yin[1], Yake Wang[1], Jinbao Li[1],
Yingli Zhong[1(⊠)], and Yingshu Li[2]

[1] School of Computer Science and Technology,
Heilongjiang University, Harbin 150008, China
zhongyingli@hlju.edu.cn
[2] Georgia State University, Atlanta, GA, USA

Abstract. Influence Maximization has been applied to marketing, advertising and public opinion monitoring. Most of the existed influence maximization algorithms are greedy or heuristic algorithms which are too time consuming. Based on the observation that the structural hole nodes are much more influential, we develop *structural holes theory*-based influence maximization algorithm SG with an emphasis on time efficiency. We conduct experiments to verify our algorithm's time efficiency and accuracy, the experimental results show that comparing with the existing algorithms, our algorithms are much faster and scalable.

Keywords: Social network · Influence maximization · Structural hole · Greedy

1 Introduction

Influence maximization is a fundamental research problem in social networks [1–3]. It selects a set of k nodes as seeds in order to maximize the propagation of ideas, opinions and products etc. al. The problem of Influence maximization is NP-hard, the widely used baseline methods for computing influence spread are based on Monte Carlo simulation or heuristic algorithms. Most of the existing methods only take consider of the influence on nodes and propagation probability on edges, while ignoring the structure feature of nodes in social networks. In fact, some structure positions act as bridge between individuals of different communities and have more control over information diffusion.

The absence of ties between two parts of social network is called *structural holes*. Two parts can only make connections indirectly by the connection to the third individual. In this case, there is a hole between these two parts in terms of structure, which is called **structural hole**. However, nodes might not be selected as seed node by the traditional influence maximization algorithms due to its low influence or propagation probability.

In this paper, we develop *Structural Holes* based *Influence Maximization* algorithm SG. The intuition behind SG is opinion leaders play a key role in spreading information within a community, while structure hole spanners are more important for spreading information between communities. We first identify structure holes whose structure

© Springer International Publishing AG 2017
L. Ma et al. (Eds.): WASA 2017, LNCS 10251, pp. 860–864, 2017.
DOI: 10.1007/978-3-319-60033-8_73

hole value above the given threshold. And then we compute the influence capability of each structure hole. At last, we select the top-k seeds by combining the structure hole value and influence value. By this way, a large amount of non-structure holes can be filtered out. Furthermore, the spread of information can be improved by combination of structure hole value and influence value.

The contributions of this paper are as follows:

- We propose structural hole theory-based algorithm SG to solve the problem of influence maximization.
- We propose SHF algorithm to compute the structural hole value of nodes based on Spectral graph theory.
- We conduct experiments to verify the time efficiency and influence spread of our algorithm.

2 Related Works

Leskovec [4] presented CELF algorithm, an improved greedy algorithm. Chen [5] proposed NewGreedy algorithm to filter those nodes that have little contributions for information propagation. Zhang [6] solved the structural hole finding problem by Fiedler vector in Laplacian matrix and designed DGSH algorithm to detect structural holes. Su [7] used domain structural holes to detect most influential nodes and proposed N-Burt algorithm to accurately evaluate importance of nodes. Lou and Tang [8] took advantage of information propagation probability to mine structural holes and designed HIS and MaxD model to find structural holes owners. Their methods relied on cluster-based network.

3 Structural Hole Theory Based Influence Maximization Problem

3.1 Propagation Model

Graph Model: :The social network can be treated as a directed graph G(V, E, W, S), here V stands for the set of vertices and E is the set of edges. W is weights on edges representing influential probabilities among users. S is set of structural hole values corresponding each node.

Propagation Model: We use Independent Cascading (IC) Model as our propagation model.

We use $\sigma(S)$ to represent the influential spread of seed set S. Given a social network graph $G(V, E, W, S)$, a positive integer k, a positive real number $\alpha(0 < \alpha < 1)$, α represents user's preference. The structural hole theory based Influence maximization problem is to find top-k influential nodes under the IC model.

3.2   Structural Hole Value

Structural Holes: Nodes which function as bridge in social networks.

Structural Holes Value: Areal number to evaluate the probability of node be structural hole.

Given a network graph, the adjacent matrix is a widely used data structure to represent the network. The element a_{ij} of the adjacent matrix A can be computed as the following:

$$A = \begin{cases} a_{ij} = 1 & if\ E(i,j) = 1 \\ 0 & otherwise \end{cases} \tag{1}$$

The degree matrix D is a diagonal matrix formed by the following way:

$$D = \begin{cases} d_i = p_i & if\quad i = j \\ 0 & otherwise \end{cases} \text{here } p_i = \sum_{j=1}^{n} a_{ij} \tag{2}$$

The Laplacian Matrix is

$$L = D - A \tag{3}$$

L has many properties, we can compute the Eigen value and eigenvector of matrix L. The node which corresponds to the second smallest value is the best structural hole node and we defined the value as structural hole value SH.

$$SH = \min_2\{|F|\} \tag{4}$$

3.3   Solution to Compute Structural Hole Value

We design SHF algorithm to calculate SH for each node as shown in Algorithm 1 and a greedy algorithm to get the most influential k seed nodes.

4   Experiments and Analysis

We select 10 thousands nodes and 342732 edges from Twitter. In all experiments, the total rounds of Monte Carlo simulation is set to be 20000.

Structural Hole Detection Algorithms: We compare the performance of SHF, DGSH, HIS and MaxD in terms of time cost. As shown in Fig. 1(a), our SHF is the fastest one.

Algorithm1: SHF	Algorithm2: SG
Input: G(V, E,W,S), θ	Input: G(V, E,S,W), k, α, θ
Output: G_1	Output: S (|S|=k)
1) u.SH=0, $\forall u \in V$;	1) S=$\varnothing$
2) Build the Laplacian Matrix LG;	2) SHVCalculate(G, θ);
3) Get the Federal vector F;	3) for $i = 1$ to k do
4) u←$\min_2${|F[i].value |} $1 \le i \le n$;	4) CI_v=0; (v∈V)
5) u.SH =$\min_2${|F[i].value|};	5) for $j = 1$ to R do
6) F[i].value=1;	6) for all v∈V do
7) V=V-{u};	7) σ_v(S)=σ_v(S) ∪ {v}-σ(S);
8) while(V≠$\varnothing$)	8) CI_v= CI_v+αSH_v+(1-α)σ_v(S);
9) GoTo Line 4	9) v_{max}=maxCI_v/R;
10) for $\forall u \in V$ do	10) S=S ∪ { v_{max} };
11) G_1←G\{u|u.inf< θ 且u.SH=0};	
12) return G_1.	11) return S.

Effect of Alpha: We evaluate influence range by varying the values of alpha. As shown in Fig. 1(b), when alpha is closed to 0.5, the influence range reached to the maximum. However, alpha has no effect on time costs when selecting seeds.

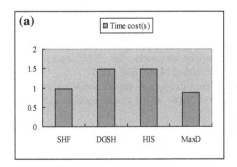
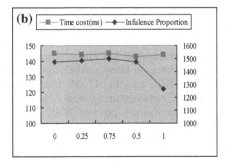

Fig. 1. (a) Time cost of detecting structure holes (b) Effect of α on performance

Influence Maximization Algorithm Comparison: We compare the influential range of different influence maximization algorithms. As shown in Fig. 2(a), our SG algorithm can influence more nodes because it considers nodes structure in network.

We compare time efficiency of various algorithms. We can see from Fig. 2(b) that SG is better than MG in terms of time efficiency and results quality. CELF has the perfect time efficiency while the seeds from CELF is not the best because it doesn't care about structural features.

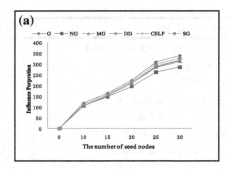 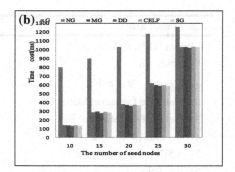

Fig. 2. (a) Influence spread of different algorithms (b) Time cost of different algorithms

5 Conclusion

In this paper, we propose a novel algorithm to solve the problem of influence maximization based on structure hole theory. we propose SHF to compute the structural hole values of nodes and propose SG algorithm to select the most influential k seed nodes. We conduct experiments to verify time efficiency and accuracy of our algorithm.

Acknowledgment. This work was supported in part by the National Science Foundation of China (61632010, 61100048, 61370222), the Natural Science Foundation of Heilongjiang Province (F2016034), the Education Department of Heilongjiang Province (12531498).

References

1. He, Z., Cai, Z., Wang, X.: Modeling propagation dynamics and developing optimized countermeasures for rumor spreading in online social networks. In: IEEE International Conference on Distributed Computing Systems, pp. 205–214. IEEE (2015)
2. Cai, J.L.Z., Yan, M., Li, Y.: Using crowdsourced data in location-based social networks to explore influence maximization. In: IEEE INFOCOM 2016 - IEEE Conference on Computer Communications, pp. 1–9. IEEE (2016)
3. Shi, T., Cheng, S., Cai, Z., et al.: Retrieving the maximal time-bounded positive influence set from social networks. Pers. Ubiquit. Comput. **20**(5), 717–730 (2016)
4. Leskovec, J., Krause, A., Guestrin, C., et al.: Cost-effective outbreak detection in networks. In: ACM SIGKDD International Conference on Knowledge Discovery and Data Mining, pp. 420–429. ACM (2007)
5. Chen, W., Wang, Y., Yang, S.: Efficient influence maximization in social networks. In: ACM SIGKDD International Conference on Knowledge Discovery and Data Mining KDD, Paris, France, 28 June–July, pp. 199–208 (2009)
6. Zhang, E., Wang, G., Gao, K., et al.: Generalized structural holes finding algorithm by bisection in social communities. In: Sixth International Conference on Genetic and Evolutionary Computing, pp. 276–279. IEEE (2012)
7. Xiao-Ping, S., Yu-Rong, S.: Leveraging neighborhood "structural holes" to identifying key spreaders in social networks. Acta Physica Sinica -Chinese Edition- **64**(2), 1–11 (2015)
8. Lou, T., Tang, J.: Mining structural hole spanners through information diffusion in social networks. In: The International Conference, pp. 825–836 (2013)

Layout Optimization for a Long Distance Wireless Mesh Network: An Industrial Case Study

Jintao Wang[1,2], Xi Jin[1], Peng Zeng[1,3](✉), Zhaowei Wang[1,2], and Changqing Xia[1]

[1] State Key Laboratory of Robotics, Shenyang Institute of Automation, Chinese Academy of Sciences, Shenyang 110016, China
zp@sia.cn
[2] University of Chinese Academy of Sciences, Beijing 100049, China
[3] Shenyang Institute of Automation, Guangzhou, Chinese Academy of Sciences, Guangzhou 511458, China

Abstract. In the deployment of industrial wireless network, nodes can only be deployed in some special regions due to the restriction of the environment in the factory, thus failing to effectively elude occlusions, and restricting the performance of the network. Therefore, optimization should be made for layout of the network. An optimization is made on nodes layout in this paper based on the architecture of IEEE 802.11 WIFI Long-Distance multi-hop mesh networks. The optimization objectives are the network throughput and the network construction cost with the delay of traffics as constraint. For the scene with small network size, a hierarchical traversal method is adopted to get the optimal solution; and for that with large one, a hierarchical heuristic method is proposed to get the approximate solution. Finally, we carried out experiments via simulation and the scene constructed in the actual environment of the factory. The results show that the algorithms proposed in this paper can obtain effective solutions, and the heuristic algorithm has shorter computing time.

Keywords: Mesh network · P-median model · Layout optimization

1 Introduction

In the practical deployment process of the network, nodes can only be deployed in some special regions due to the restriction of realistic environment in the factory. Meanwhile, high tower cannot be erected in some factories and antenna can only be erected at the top of some buildings or existing lamp pole. In this way, antenna of the network node fails to effectively elude some occlusions, thus restricting the transmission performance. Therefore, it is necessary to consider the proper location, number of nodes, angle of antenna and other factors, so as to optimize network bandwidth and guarantee the performance of network.

© Springer International Publishing AG 2017
L. Ma et al. (Eds.): WASA 2017, LNCS 10251, pp. 865–870, 2017.
DOI: 10.1007/978-3-319-60033-8_74

This problem can be included into the P-median facility location problem [1]. The problem in this paper is closest to the problem of P-median, and the difference lies in that: 1. The traditional P-median problem is to gain the minimum sum of the weight from demand points to facility location, while in the network model of this paper, consideration should be given not only on the weight from demand points (gateway node) to facilities (switch nodes), but also on the weight between facilities that the traffic flow passes through; 2. Only one single objective (weight) is considered in traditional P-median, while the model in this paper targets at optimizing the overall bandwidth and system cost to optimize the layout of network nodes.

This paper based on the heterogeneous industrial monitoring network. The wireless network (including WirelessHART [2], WIA-PA [3] and ZigBee [4]) applied in each factory is regarded as each subnet of the heterogeneous network. For IEEE 802.11 WIFI Long-Distance multi-hop mesh networks (WiLD networks) [5] can realize the long-distance transmission of traffics, each subnet is connected via the industrial backhaul network [6] based on WiLD nodes. The traffic is transmitted between the control center and subnet gateways through backhaul network.

2   System Model and Problem Formulation

WiLD network is expressed with $G = (V, E)$, where V and E refer to the set of node and edge in the network respectively. $e_{ij} \in E$ means the link between node $v_i \in V$ and $v_j \in V$. Suppose there are N locations can place node in the factory finitely, and the location capable of placing WiLD node is written as p_i $(i = 1, 2, \cdots, N)$, where $p_i = \begin{cases} 1, & place\ node \\ 0, & others \end{cases}$. M locations in N must be placed with nodes to execute the function of gateway node. We define variable $a_{ij} = \begin{cases} 1, & \exists e_{ij} \in E \\ 0, & others \end{cases}$, and the antenna number of each node v_i is $a_i = \sum\limits_{j \neq i \in [1,N]} a_{ij}$, where $0 \leq a_i \leq \frac{2\pi}{\theta + \frac{\pi}{6}}$. Suppose the basic construction cost of each node is α (the cost of each single node without antenna), and the cost added by each antenna is β, the construction cost of nodes can be expressed as $c_i = \alpha + \beta \cdot a_i$. The total cost of node construction in the network is $\sum\limits_{i=1}^{N} p_i c_i$.

Occlusion is measured by the bandwidth of received signal. The transmission bandwidth of traffic in link $e_{ij} \in E$ is B_{ij}. The end-to-end signal transmission bandwidth of the path that traffic f_k goes through from source node v_i $(i \in [1, M])$ to destination node σ is w^{f_k}, where $w^{f_k} = \min\limits_{\forall e_{ij}^{f_k}, i, j \in [1,N]} w_{ij}^{f_k} \cdot x_{ij}$ is the transmission rate of traffic f_k on link $e_{ij} \in E$, ϕ_k is the minimum transmission bandwidth demand of traffic f_k. $x_{ij} = 1$ refers to node v_i can be connected to v_j, otherwise, $x_{ij} = 0$.

Optimization Objectives

The optimization objective is to gain the maximum and minimum value respectively, namely $u_1 = \max\limits_{f_k \in F} \sum w^{f_k}$, $u_2 = \min \sum\limits_{i=1}^{N} p_i c_i$. So we suppose $u(p, a) = \dfrac{\sum\limits_{f_k \in F} w^{f_k}}{\sum\limits_{i=1}^{N} p_i c_i}$. Then, the optimization objective is $\max u(p, a)$.

Constraints:

Real-Time. According to the analysis of [7], The delay of each hop is fixed when using 2P MAC protocol and written as τ. Then, the end-to-end delay of the traffic f_k can be expressed as $\tau \cdot K_{f_k}$, where $K_{f_k} = \sum\limits_{i \neq j, i, j \in [1, N]} e_{ij}^{f_k}$ is the hop count that f_k passes through, and $e_{ij}^{f_k}$ is the link that traffic f_k passes through. Suppose the end-to-end delay demand of traffic f_k is μ_k, then $\tau \cdot K_{f_k} \leq \mu_k$.

Bandwidth Demand. Bandwidth provided by the transmission path for the traffic must meet the bandwidth demand of this traffic, namely $\min\limits_{\forall e_{ij}^{f_k}, i, j \in [1, N]} w_{ij}^{f_k} \cdot x_{ij} \geq d_i$.

Capacity Constraint of Each Link. $\forall i, j \in [1, N], j \neq i, \sum\limits_{\forall f_k \in F} w_{ij}^{f_k} \leq B_{ij}$.

Gateway Node Setting. $p_i = 1, i \in [1, M]$.

Node Setting. If node $v_j, j \in [1, N]$ can be connected with node $v_i, i \in [1, N]$, then node v_i must be the node that has been set. That is $x_{ij} \leq p_i$, $x_{ij}, p_{ij} \in \{0, 1\}$.

It has been proved that universal facility location problem is NP-hard problem [8], so the problem in this paper is also NP-hard problem. Thus, we use traversal and heuristic methods to solve it.

3   Solutions

3.1   Hierarchical Traversal Solving Method Based on P-Median Model (P-HTM)

The total number of nodes in need of location is $N - M - 1$ at most. We define a variable $P \in [1, N - M - 1]$, and establish the P-median model. Starting from $P = N - M - 1$, the hierarchical iteration based P-median solving method is used for solution. This algorithm is calculated by adding the restricted condition of uncertain node number set $p = \sum\limits_{i=1}^{N-M-1} p_i$ and adopting traversal method.

The basic idea of the algorithm mainly includes the following contents.

Initialization. The bandwidth w_{ij} occupied of each link e_{ij} that the traffic passing through is set as 0 at the beginning. Set a virtual node v_s in network, and add a link with bandwidth capacity $+\infty$ between v_s and each gateway node.

Construction of Augmenting Path. Starting from v_s, if there is an augmenting path between v_s and σ, find the path starting from v_s and with the least intermediate node number (the shortest augmenting path) from v_s to σ along the link with the most residual bandwidth.

Link Bandwidth Occupation Adjustment. Set δ as the minimum value of residual bandwidth of each link on the augmenting path selected, and add δ to the bandwidth occupation of all links in this augmenting path.

Starting from σ, we conduct reverse query for each node on path along the selected augmenting path in turn. For a certain node v_i on this augmenting path, if it is a surplus node [9]. Keep the path from v_s to v_i in the original augmenting path unchanged, select the shortest path from v_i to σ along v_i, then conduct link bandwidth occupation adjustment for path $v_s \rightarrow v_i \rightarrow \sigma$ again.

Calculation. Before each link bandwidth occupation adjustment, we calculate $\sum\limits_{f_k \in F} w^{f_k}$ and $\sum\limits_{i=1}^{N} p_i c_i$, and get $u(p, a)$. Then, we can get $maxu(p, a)$ according to each $u(p, a)$.

The overall complexity of the algorithm is $o\left(|E| \cdot N^2 \cdot (N - M - 1)\right)$.

3.2   P-Median Model Based Hierarchical Heuristic Solving Method (P-HHM)

For the P-HTM uses the traversing method, when the network size is relatively large, the computing complexity is very high. Therefore, we propose a P-median model based hierarchical heuristic solving method (P-HHM). The main idea of the P-HHM is:

Construction of Spinning Tree. Based on the traditional Kruskal's algorithm [10], and setting the bandwidth that the link can provided as its link weight, we get the maximum bandwidth spanning tree rooted at the data center node σ. Thus, we can get the available path $\Re_i$ from each gateway node $v_i, i \in [1, M]$ in G to the data center node σ. Then, we can calculate $u(p, a)$ at this point.

Deletion of Nodes. Set $P = P - 1$, and subtract a node from the spanning tree of the last step respectively. Then, connect the branch nodes that connected with this node initially to the adjacent node with largest bandwidth still in the spanning tree (N-1 times are required for this process). Find out $u(p, a)$ in these $N - 1$ conditions.

Bandwidth and Overhead Calculation. As P reduces, $\max\limits_{f_k \in F} \sum w^{f_k}$ and $\min \sum\limits_{i=1}^{N} p_i c_i$ will continue to reduce. When $\max\limits_{f_k \in F} \sum w^{f_k}$ reduces to the threshold value, the algorithm ends and then we get the max $u(p, a)$ from these $u(p, a)$.

The time complexity of algorithm P-HHM is $o\left((N - M - 1)^2\right)$.

4   Experiment and Analysis

In this section, the performance of algorithms proposed in this paper are verified via the simulation and real experiment. Network is randomly generated in the area of 2 km * 2 km. Set the maximum transmission bandwidth of the link between nodes is 30 M, the bandwidth of links linearly reduces with the increase of node distance. A comparison is made between P-HTM and P-HHM algorithm proposed in this paper with Genetic Algorithm (GA), and the results are shown in Fig. 1.

Figure 1(a) shows the computing time with each algorithm when solving based on different optional locations. It can prove that, P-HTM algorithm is more suitable for small size network. It can be seen from Fig. 1(b), (c) and (d) that the results from P-HTM, P-HHM and GA algorithm are basically identical. They show that we can get right solutions with shorter computing time via P-HTM and P-HHM.

To further verify the performance of algorithms, a real network is set in Fushun Olefin Factory, Sinopec Group, as shown in Fig. 2(a). Plants and equipment in the factory are distributed within the scope of 1.5 km * 1.5 km, and

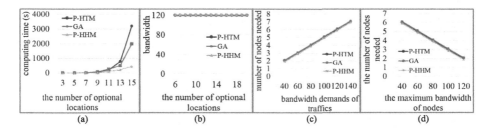

Fig. 1. Calculation results of P-HTM, GA and P-HHM algorithms ((a) computing time of each algorithm under different optional locations. (b) Maximum bandwidth provided under different optional locations. (c) Number of nodes required under different traffic bandwidth demands. (d) Number of nodes required under the different maximum bandwidth of nodes (traffic bandwidth demand is 120))

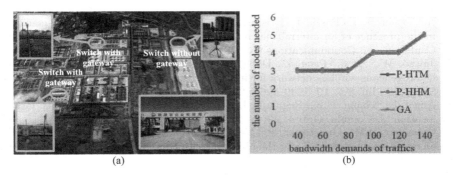

Fig. 2. (a) Actual node layout in the factory. (b) Nodes required under different traffic bandwidth demands in the factory (Unit: M)

occlusions include buildings, metal tanks and pipelines in the factory. There are 14 locations in the factory that can be selected to set nodes, of which 2 nodes should be connected with gateway nodes. A test is made under different bandwidth demands of two gateway nodes, and the node number required is get by applying different algorithms, as shown in Fig. 2(b). It can be seen from Fig. 2(b) that, the solution of network model can be get via both P-HTM and P-HHM algorithm.

5   Conclusions

To solve the node layout problem in industrial long distance wireless mesh network, we put forward a hierarchical P-median optimization method based on the traditional P-median model. For the scene with small network size, a hierarchical traversal method is adopted to get the optimal solution; for that with large one, a hierarchical heuristic method is proposed to get the approximate solution. Finally, we verified the performance of the algorithms proposed in this paper based on simulations and a real experiment.

References

1. Gendron, B., Khuong, P.V., Semet, F.: A Lagrangian-based branch-and-bound algorithm for the two-level uncapacitated facility location problem with single-assignment constraints. Transp. Sci. **50**(4), 1286–1299 (2016)
2. Li, Y.C., Hong, S.H., Huang, X., et al.: Implementation of a Powerlink-WirelessHART gateway for industrial automation. In: 2016 13th International Conference on Electrical Engineering/Electronics, Computer, Telecommunications and Information Technology (ECTI-CON), pp. 1–6. IEEE (2016)
3. Wang, P., Zhang, C., Wang, H., et al.: A TR069 WAN management protocol for WIA-PA wireless sensor Networks. In: 2016 25th Wireless and Optical Communication Conference (WOCC), pp. 1–4. IEEE (2016)
4. Yang, P., Yan, Y., Li, X.Y., et al.: Taming cross-technology interference for Wi-Fi and ZigBee coexistence networks. IEEE Trans. Mob. Comput. **15**(4), 1009–1021 (2016)
5. Hussain, M.I., Ahmed, Z.I., Sarma, N., et al.: An efficient TDMA MAC protocol for multi-hop WiFi-based long distance networks. Wirel. Pers. Commun. **86**(4), 1971–1994 (2016)
6. Achleitner, S., La Porta, T., Krishnamurthy, S.V., et al.: Network coding efficiency in the presence of an intermittent backhaul network. In: 2016 IEEE International Conference on Communications (ICC), pp. 1–6. IEEE (2016)
7. Jintao, W., Xi, J., Peng, Z., Dong, L.: End-to-end delay analysis in wide-area heterogeneous wireless network for industrial monitoring and control applications. Sci. Chin.: Inf. Sci. **10**, 1249–1262 (2015)
8. Angel, E., Thang, N.K., Regnault, D.: Improved local search for universal facility location. J. Combin. Optim. **29**(1), 237–246 (2015)
9. Colmenar, J.M., Greistorfer, P., Mart, R., et al.: Advanced greedy randomized adaptive search procedure for the obnoxious p-median problem. Eur. J. Oper. Res. **252**(2), 432–442 (2016)
10. Arroyo, J.E.C., Vieira, P.S., Vianna, D.S.: A GRASP algorithm for the multi-criteria minimum spanning tree problem. Ann. Oper. Res. **159**(1), 125–133 (2008)

Mobility Intention-Based Relationship Inference from Spatiotemporal Data

Feng Yi[1,2], Hong Li[1], Hongtao Wang[1,2], Hui Wen[1(✉)], and Limin Sun[1]

[1] Beijing Key Laboratory of IOT Information Security,
Institute of Information Engineering, CAS, Beijing 100093, China
wenhui@iie.ac.cn
[2] School of Cyber Security, University of Chinese Academy of Sciences,
19 A Yuquan Rd, Shijingshan District, Beijing 100049, People's Republic of China

Abstract. Inferring social relationship based on co-occurrence has become a focal point in the last decade. Many studies indicate that more frequently two users co-occur at non-public locations, the higher probability they are acquaintances. We find that in some spatiotemporal datasets collected by Internet of Things (IOT) devices in public locations, it's hard to distinguish co-occurrences between acquaintances and strangers. In this paper, we propose a mobility intention-based relationship inference model (MIRI) to address above challenge. We utilize mobility intention to characterize co-occurrences and propose a classification model for social relationship inference. The experimental results on real-world dataset demonstrate not only the superiority of our model, but also improve the effectiveness.

Keywords: Social relationship · Spatiotemporal data · Mobility intention

1 Introduction

Inferring social relationship is crucial to many applications, such as friends recommendation [1], target advertising [2], epidemiology spreading [3] and identifying members of a criminal gang. Along with the increasing amount of human spatiotemporal data, inferring social relationship based on ***co-occurrence*** has become a focal point in social relationship research. The co-occurrence refers to the phenomenon that two people have been to the same places at the same time [1].

In the past few years, many inference models based on co-occurrence are proposed. These models employed spatial features of co-occurrence like location entropy [1, 2, 4] to infer social relationship. The basic idea is that co-occurring at non-public places implies strong social strength. With the development of Internet of Things (IOT), a rich passively collected spatiotemporal data are being produced by IOT's devices, such as the *Smart Card Data* (SCD) of public transport, the traffic surveillance, bank notes. These devices are deployed in public places and all co-occurrences recorded by them happen in public locations.

© Springer International Publishing AG 2017
L. Ma et al. (Eds.): WASA 2017, LNCS 10251, pp. 871–876, 2017.
DOI: 10.1007/978-3-319-60033-8_75

Hence, existing models can not be applied to the passively collected spatiotemporal datasets.

In this paper, we propose a novel inference model called the Mobility Intention based Relationship Inference (MIRI) model. We adopt mobility intention to analyze co-occurrence behaviors and exploit their contributions to social relationship. In general, human mobility is fundamentally driven by diverse mobility intentions, such as family party, shopping and dining. If two people frequently co-occur for same mobility intentions, they are acquaintances with high probability. If the mobility intentions of each co-occurrence between tow users are different, they are likely to be strangers and the co-occurrences should be coincidences. Moreover, it is obvious that social relationship of two people who often co-occur for shopping or entertainment is much closer than two people who only co-occur for commuting.

The MIRI model consists of two stages: (1) extracting mobility intentions from a spatiotemporal dataset and mapping every co-occurrence to a mobility intention dyad; and (2) training an SVM classifier for social relationship inference. After SVM classifier is trained, given co-occurrences of two people, then we can infer whether they are acquaintances or strangers.

2   Related Work and Problem Definition

2.1   Related Work

There are many works aiming at inferring social relationship by co-occurrences during the past several years. The relation between social relationship and co-occurrence was first studied by Crandall et al. [5]. Nonetheless, different co-occurrences do not contribute equally to social relationship. Some spatial features of co-occurrence were adopted to decide the contribution to social relationship. Location entropy which measures the popularity of a location was a widely used spatial feature [1,2,4]. Some works consider other features of co-occurrences. The time interval between two continuous co-occurrence was considered in literature [6]. Zhou et al. [7] proposed a TAI model which used co-occurrence distribution on locations. Though existing inference models have shown how social relationship correlates to co-occurrence, they can not be applied to the situation which all co-occurrences of pair users happen in public locations. In contrast, our proposed MIRI model determines co-occurrence's contribution by corresponding mobility intentions and therefore overcomes the drawbacks in previous works.

2.2   Problem Definition

Given a spatiotemporal dataset of N users, a footprint of a user i is denoted by $o_k^i = (loc_k^i, t_k^i)$ which states user i visited loc_k^i at time t_k^i. The footprint history of user i is represented as a sequence of footprints: $O_i = (o_1^i, o_2^i, \ldots, o_n^i)$.

We consider two users have a *co-occurrence* if they both visited a location at almost the same time.

Definition 1: Co-occurrence. The footprint $(loc_r^i, t_r^i) \in O_i$ and $(loc_s^j, t_s^j) \in O_j$ of user i and j can form a co-occurrence $c = (o_r^i, o_s^j)$ if they satisfy both spatial condition $dist(loc_r^i, loc_s^j) < \delta$ and temporal condition $|t_r^i - t_s^j| < \tau$. δ and τ are distance and time thresholds respectively which are empirically decided by various application systems.

Let $C_{ij} = \{c_1, c_2, \cdots, c_w\}$ denote the set of w co-occurrences of user i and j. The problem of social inference is to infer whether they are acquaintances or strangers.

In this work, we use mobility intention to infer social relationship from spatiotemporal data. Formally, the mobility intention refers to a common cause which can explain why a user appeared in location loc at time t.

3   Social Relationship Inference

3.1   Characterized by Mobility Intention Extraction

In order to use mobility intention for social relationship inference, we need to know how many and what kinds of mobility intentions hide in a spatiotemporal dataset. The mobility patterns show a high degree of temporal and spatial regularity and can be considered as mobility intentions. For example, commuting which is a basic mobility pattern in many spatiotemporal datasets can be used to explain why a worker arrived at the work place around 9 a.m. on work days.

In this paper, we use `CANDECOMP/PARAFAC` (`CP`) decomposition algorithm to extract mobility patterns from a spatiotemporal dataset and consider them as mobility intentions. CP decomposition is an effective tool for analyzing the interrelationship between spatial and temporal attributes for spatiotemporal datasets [8]. In order to utilize CP algorithm, a three-dimensional tensor which is composed by `location-hour-day` is constructed. The element y_{r_i, t_j, d_k} of the three-way tensor $\mathcal{Y} \in \mathbb{R}^{M \times H \times D}$ can be computed as

$$y_{r_i, t_j, d_k} = \frac{Count(r_i, t_j, d_k)}{\sum\limits_{q=1}^{L} Count(r_q, t_j, d_k)} \tag{1}$$

where r_i, t_j, and d_k are the index of the location, the time bin and the day of month respectively; L is the total number of locations, and $Count(r_i, t_j, d_k)$ is the number of users who appeared at location r_i at time t_j on d_k-th days. In CP algorithm, the tensor $\mathcal{Y}$ is factorized into a sum of component rank-one tensors $\mathbf{Y}_r$. After decomposition, we manually label $\mathbf{Y}_r$ to summarize the mobility intention described by every rank 1 tensor and consider them as a mobility intension. We use m_i to denote the i-th mobility intention and $\mathcal{M} = \{m_i | 1 \leqslant i \leqslant q\}$ to represent the set of q mobility intentions.

We consider every mobility intention as one class. Each footprint $o_k^i = (loc_k^i, t_k^i)$ corresponds to one mobility intention m_k, in other words, belongs to a class. Then the mobility intention mapping can be considered as a multi-class classification problem.

In order to acquire good performance of multi-class classification, we perform a comprehensive feature engineering and model training. After analyzing vectors of rank one tensor and considering experiment results in feature engineering, we propose three kinds of exploited and distinguishable features: spatial features, hour features and day features, such as location entropy, time span and day type. Finally, with the three kinds of feature, we train an Adaboost model to map a footprint to a mobility intention. Then, we can characterize a co-occurrence $c = (o_r^i, o_s^j)$ with a mobility intention dyad (cm_r^i, cm_s^j).

3.2 Social Relationship Inference

So far, we can build the inference model which is based on the mobility dyads. The co-occurrence sequence C_{ij} of user i and user j can be characterized as the following sequence of mobility intention dyads:

$$\langle (cm_1^i, cm_1^j), \cdots, (cm_w^i, cm_w^j)\rangle, cm_k^i, cm_k^j \in \mathcal{M}, 1 \leqslant k \leqslant w.$$

where (cm_k^i, cm_k^j) are same or different mobility intentions. We construct a *mobility intention vector* **m** with following $q(q + 1)/2$ elements:

$$(Count(m_1, m_1), \cdots, Count(m_M, m_M), \cdots, Count(m_{M-1}, m_M))^{\mathrm{T}}$$

where $Count(m_r, m_s)$ is the number of mobility intention dyads (m_r, m_s).

Then, we can adopt virtually any existing binary classifier algorithm to distinguish acquaintances from strangers. In this paper, we use SVM as our binary classifier. After training is finished, given a pair of users and their co-occurrences, we first map them to mobility intentions dyads through the Adaboost model. Then we construct the mobility intention vector. Finally, we infer whether the two users are acquaintances or not through the trained classifier.

4   Experiment and Analysis

4.1 Settings

We use *Beijing Bus Smart Card* (BBSC) dataset in our experiment. The BBSC collects prepaid smart card records for public transportation in Beijing, China. We obtained a dataset with $275,951,094$ bus transaction records from October 1 2014 to October 31 2014. We identified 412 card users and 2,796 friend pairs among these card users. In our experiment, the two threshold parameters δ and τ are set to 20 (meters) and 10 (min) respectively.

The precision-recall curve is used to measure the accuracy of our model and make comparison with other baseline models. Let TR denote the set of ground truth friend pairs in the test set, and MR be the set of friend pairs reported by a social relationship inference model. The precision and recall are defined as:

$$\text{Precision} = \frac{|TR \cap MR|}{|MR|}, \quad \text{Recall} = \frac{|TR \cap MR|}{|TR|} \tag{2}$$

Three baseline models are chosen for performance comparison: EBM [1], PGT [2] and TAI [7].

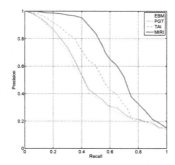

Fig. 1. Comparison with the state-of-the-art models

4.2 Results

In Fig. 1, the precision-recall curves of baseline models and MIRI illustrate that MIRI performs the best among all comparison models. The possible reason is that mobility intention is introduced and play a key role in differentiating co-occurrences between acquaintances and strangers. Our experiments demonstrates that the use of mobility intention improve the performance of social relationship inference.

After tensor decomposition, we extract 7 mobility intentions from BBSC dataset. They are shopping (Sh), dining (Dg), routing business (Rb), visiting (Vg), recreation (Rc), entertainment (En) and commuting (Cm). The top 5 positive and negative weights of mobility intention dyad are illustrated in Table 1. From the table, we can see that negative weights are generally more important than positive weights and they are not quite different. This provides evidence that two people are most likely strangers when they co-occurred for different mobility intentions. The positive weights are very different which mean different contribution to social relationship. There is only one negative weight in the same mobility intention dyads and it's "commuting-commuting". This probably due to the proportion of co-occurrences between acquaintances is much less than strangers in rush hours. In consequent two people are likely strangers if they co-occur only for commuting purpose.

Table 1. Top 5 most influential mobility intention pairs for social relationship inference

m_1	Sh	Dg	Sh	Rb	Dg	Vg	Dg	Rc	Sh	En
m_2	Vg	En	Rc	Vg	Rc	Vg	Dg	Rc	Sh	En
Weights	−0.0472	−0.0454	−0.0410	−0.0396	−0.0392	0.0323	0.0181	0.0125	0.0118	0.0112

5   Conclusions

In this paper, we have proposed a new social relationship inference model called MIRI, which considers the mobility intention dyads as features and adopts a classifier to infer whether two persons are acquaintances or not. The experiment results indicate that the proposed model significantly outperforms existing inference models. In our future work, we plan to exploit other mobility intention extraction methods and multi-classification methods to further improve the performance of mobility intention mapping.

Acknowledgments. This work was supported by the National Natural Science Foundation of China (Grant No. 61572231), the Major R&D Plan of Beijing Municipal Science & Technology Commission (Grant No. Z161100002616032), the Security Detection and Supervision for High Level Bio-Safety Laboratory Control System (Grant No. CXJJ-16Z234), the National Defense Basic Research Program of China (Grant No. JCKY2016602B001).

References

1. Pham, H., Shahabi, C., Liu, Y.: EBM: an entropy-based model to infer social strength from spatiotemporal data. In: Proceedings of the ACM SIGMOD International Conference on Management of Data, SIGMOD 2013, New York, NY, USA, 22–27 June 2013, pp. 265–276 (2013)
2. Wang, H., Li, Z., Lee, W.-C.: PGT: measuring mobility relationship using personal, global and temporal factors. In: 2014 IEEE International Conference on Data Mining, ICDM 2014, Shenzhen, China, 14–17 December 2014, pp. 570–579 (2014)
3. Liu, W., Li, H., Chen, Y., Zhu, H., Sun, L.: LARES: latency-reduced neighbour discovery for contagious diseases prevention. Int. J. Ad Hoc Ubiquit. Comput. **16**(1), 3–13 (2014)
4. Cranshaw, J., Toch, E., Hong, J.I., Kittur, A., Sadeh, N.M.: Bridging the gap between physical location and online social networks. In: Proceedings of the 12th International Conference Ubiquitous Computing, UbiComp 2010, Copenhagen, Denmark, 26–29 September 2010, pp. 119–128 (2010)
5. Crandall, D.J., Backstrom, L., Cosley, D., Suri, S., Huttenlocher, D., Kleinberg, J.: Inferring social ties from geographic coincidences. Proc. Nat. Acad. Sci. **107**(52), 22436–22441 (2010)
6. Cheng, R., Pang, J., Zhang, Y.: Inferring friendship from check-in data of location-based social networks. In: Proceedings of the 2015 IEEE/ACM International Conference on Advances in Social Networks Analysis and Mining, ASONAM 2015, Paris, France, 25–28 August 2015, pp. 1284–1291 (2015)
7. Zhou, N., Zhang, X., Wang, S.: Theme-aware social strength inference from spatiotemporal data. In: Li, F., Li, G., Hwang, S., Yao, B., Zhang, Z. (eds.) WAIM 2014. LNCS, vol. 8485, pp. 498–509. Springer, Cham (2014). doi:10.1007/978-3-319-08010-9_56
8. Fan, Z., Song, X., Shibasaki, R.: CitySpectrum: a non-negative tensor factorization approach. In: The 2014 ACM Conference on Ubiquitous Computing, UbiComp 2014, Seattle, WA, USA, 13–17 September 2014, pp. 213–223 (2014)

TACD: A Three-Stage Auction Scheme for Cloudlet Deployment in Wireless Access Network

Gangqiang Zhou, Jigang Wu$^{(\boxtimes)}$, and Long Chen

School of Computer Science and Technology, Guangdong University of Technology,
Guangzhou 510006, People's Republic of China
{gq_zhou,asjgwucn}@outlook.com, lonchen@mail.ustc.edu.cn

Abstract. Motivated by the group-buying behaviors in recent years, we suggest that Mobile Users (MUs) to gather in Access Point (AP) and bid for a cloudlet in a grouped way. In this paper, we proposed TACD, a three-stage auction to inspire cloudlets sharing their resources and manage the deal between MU, AP and cloudlet, which is efficient, flexible and truthful. This incentive mechanism aims at optimizing the social welfare, and ensures that all kinds of participants (MU, AP, cloudlet) can benefit from this auction. We also proposed TACDp, an improved algorithm base on TACD, which social welfare is markedly improved.

Keywords: Cloudlet · Mobile cloud computing · Auction · Resource allocation · Group-buying

1 Introduction

A cloudlet is constituted by a group of resource-rich and trusted computers which is well-connected with the Internet and is available by the nearby MUs [1]. Cloudlet can improve the performance of MUs' App by providing them with rich computing resources and low-latency access [2]. Meanwhile, many efficient algorithms have been proposed to place cloudlets in a given network [2,3], which can balance the workload between cloudlets and reduce MUs' delay significantly. But they ignore the cost of cloudlet and Access Point (AP) while performing offloading tasks to cloudlet through AP. Moreover, cloudlets and APs are usually selfish, they may not willing to share their resources to MUs. Therefore incentive mechanisms are introduced to inspire resource-holder to share their resources for MUs [4]. This work proposed flexible and stable model to manage deals between MU and resource holder. In this incentive mechanism, a MU always pays for a cloudlet independently. However, the ask price of cloudlet is usually too expensive for single MU, and the resource of a cloudlet often exceeds the

---

The corresponding author is Jigang Wu.

© Springer International Publishing AG 2017
L. Ma et al. (Eds.): WASA 2017, LNCS 10251, pp. 877–882, 2017.
DOI: 10.1007/978-3-319-60033-8_76

MU required which will waste lots of resources. Inspired by the group-buying in spectrum allocation [5], we introduce TACD, a three-stage auction model to place cloudlet in this paper. In TACD, several MUs connect with the Internet through one AP, and then we place cloudlets besides APs, a cloudlet can only be assign to one AP and can serve for all the MUs in this AP. And we also propose a higher performance algorithm named TACDp based on TACD.

2   System Model and Problem Formulation

2.1   Problem Formulation

There are K cloudlets in the given wireless access network, each of them have limited computation and storage resources to share with MUs. It will cost cloudlets much energy and resource when they share their resource to MUs, and the cost will increase with heavier workload. As similar as [6] we defined the cost of cloudlet C_k as

$$Cos(k) = c(k) \cdot w(k) \qquad (1)$$

$c(k)$ is the cost factor of C_k, and $w(k)$ is the workload brought by MUs. To inspire cloudlets sharing their computation and storage resources, we set that each cloudlet C_k have a reserve price r_k while sharing resource to MUs. If C_k is assigned to the i-th AP a_i in the auction, a_i must be charged with a clearing price $P_i \geq r_k$. Cap^k denotes C_k's resource capacity, it means C_k can only serve parts of MUs in AP a_i, and the sum workload which brought by those MUs is less than Cap^k. Cloudlets in this paper are heterogeneous, so we define that their capacity and cost factor are different with each other. We define cloudlet C_k's reserve price r_k as

$$r_k = c(k) \cdot Cap^k \qquad (2)$$

Cap_k, $c(k)$ and r_k are fixed number given in the beginning of auction, cloudlets can't change their value during the whole auction. By the way, cloudlet can change those values in the gap of the former auction and the later auction, cloudlets may improve their reserve price if the resource of cloudlet in the market in short supply, and they may reduce them while the resource is oversupply, but this studying rule is out of the scope of this paper, which will be left for future consideration.

There are n APs in the given network, each AP can be connected with at most n_i MUs. For each AP a_i, it's bandwidth is given, usually, it's bandwidth can meet MUs' networking requirements, to simplify the problem, we don't take APs' bandwidth into consideration during the three-stage auction. The number of MUs in each AP may be different at the same time, due to the moving MUs and the limited coverage area of AP. In the three-stage auction model, MUs can't connect with the cloudlet directly, they must connect with their local AP first, which means, MUs can't deal with cloudlets directly, they must access cloudlets through AP, and if cloudlet C_k is assigned to AP a_i, all the MUs which connected with a_i can only use C_k's resource. It is different from [3], where MU can request service from other cloudlets if it's local AP don't have cloudlet or the assigned cloudlet is out of service, which may cause significant delays. In this paper, if AP has assigned with cloudlet, the latency of cloudlet serving MUs will be very low, so we don't care about them in the auction.

In the auction, APs are agents and the deal is between cloudlets and MUs. Cloudlets are sellers and MUs are buyers. MUs' workload are different due to their various tasks. Intuitively, the workload is much less than cloudlet's capacity, which make MUs' group-buying significant. The MUs have different valuation on cloudlets depending on cloudlets' quality of service (QoS), they may set greater valuation on the cloudlet that has higher QoS. MU m_i^j is the j-th MU in AP a_i, m_i^j's valuation on cloudlet C_k is $v_i^j(k)$. The valuations are private information of MU, they will not commit collusion in the auction. On the other hand, they have various budget which is public information depending on their valuation.

2.2 System Model

APs are sellers to MUs and buyers to cloudlets. In the first stage, APs calculate the total budget of it's MUs to each cloudlet, we define the total budget as revenue for AP. The revenue AP a_i gets from it's MUs for cloudlet C_k is R_i^k, and MUs which contribute to the revenue will be regarded as potential winner set. In the second stage, APs will present a rational budget bid for each cloudlet depending on their revenues, and cloudlets will be assigned to APs at the clearing price after the deal between APs and cloudlets. The winner set of cloudlets is W', the winner set of APs is W, and the relationship between W' and W can be defined by the mapping function $\sigma()$, $\sigma(i) = k$ which means cloudlet C_k is assigned to AP a_i, their clearing price are P_i and P^k. After the deal between APs and cloudlets, winning APs will determine it's winner MUs and charge for them according to the potential winner set of the first stage. For AP a_i, it's winning MUs is w_i, and the winning MU m_i^j's clearing price is p_i^j.

We introduce utility to describe participants' QoS or profits they gained from the deal. The utility of MU m_i^j, Access Point a_i and cloudlet C_k are defined as follow:

$$u_i^j = \begin{cases} v_i^j(k) - p_i^j & if\ m_i^j \in w_i; \\ 0 & otherwise; \end{cases} \tag{3}$$

$$u_i = \begin{cases} R_i^k - P_i & if\ a_i \in W; \\ 0 & otherwise; \end{cases} \tag{4}$$

$$u^k = \begin{cases} P^k - Cos(k) & if\ C_k \in W'; \\ 0 & otherwise; \end{cases} \tag{5}$$

3 Auction Scheme

3.1 Stage I: APs Calculating Budget for Each Cloudlet

We call this stage ACBC, for each AP a_i, we calculate it's budget B_i^k for all cloudlets. The budget is collected from MUs which a_i connected with. We defined the mobile user m_i^j's performance price ratio on the k-th cloudlet c_k as

$$t_i^j(k) = \frac{b_i^j(k)}{l_i^j} \tag{6}$$

Which is to describe MU's unit budget on each cloudlet, l_i^j is m_i^j's workload which is a fixed number given in the beginning of auction, and $t_i^j(k)$ will be improved if m_i^j increasing the budget $b_i^j(k)$. The MU set A is a_i's mobile users sorted by their performance price ratio $t_i^j(k)$ in descending order. Such as, $m_i^a(k)$, $m_i^b(k)$, $m_i^c(k)$, ..., $m_i^{ni}(k)$, and it subjects to $t_i^a(k) \geq t_i^b(k) \geq t_i^c(k) \geq ... \geq t_i^{ni}(k)$. Let l_s to be the s-th MU's workload in A, and Sum to be the total workload of the first s MUs in A, i.e., $Sum = l_1 + l_2 + l_3 + ... + l_s$. To improve the utilization of cloudlet, we find a rational index s in A, to maximum Sum within Cap^k, subject to $Sum \leq Cap^k$ and $Sum + l_{s+1} > Cap^k$. If the sum of all MUs' workload in a_i is less than or equal to Cap^k, then $s = n_i$. In order to keep the auction truthfully, AP generates an independent integer m randomly, and $(s+1)/2 \leq m \leq s$. In our strategy, we will sacrifice the last m MUs in this stage, and send the first $n_i - m$ MUs to the next stage, their unit price p equals to the m-th MU's performance price ratio in A. Let $x = n_i - m$, then A_x is the first $n_i - m$ MUs in A, the sum workload of the first x MUs in A is L_x. Then AP a_i get the revenue $R_i^k = p \cdot L_x$, and it's budget in the next stage $B_i^k = R_i^k$ while a_i bid truthfully, A_x is the potential winner set for the k-th cloudlet A_i^k. By the way, the effect of independent integer m is to keep TACD truthful.

3.2   Stage II: APs' Auction to Select Rational Cloudlet

We call this stage ASC, in which APs deal with cloudlets depending on their budget B_i^k and cloudlets' fixed reserve price r_k. We assigned cloudlet to AP in a greedy manner, it's similar with *fixed price auction* in [7], which have been proved to be truthful, but ASC is more complex than it. At first, we sort APs randomly, let $C = C_k$ be the cloudlet set, for each AP in the random order, we try to map it with cloudlet C_k which is available to maximize the profit $B_i^k - r_k$, there is no doubt that this value must be a non-negative number, if ties, choose C_k with the smaller k. If there is another AP's bid B_j^k which $B_i^k \geq B_j^k \geq r_k$, or there are a few bids which $B_i^k \geq B_j^k \geq B_x^k \geq ... \geq r_k$, then the transaction between a_i and C_k is done and their clearing price is B_j^k, or a_i lost this auction.

3.3   Stage III: The Winning APs Ensure and Charge for Winning Mobile Users

In this stage, winning APs determine winning MUs base on it's potential winner set, and charge for them. For instance, if a_i wins C_k in ASC, then it's potential winner set for C_k will win the auction and they will be charged at their potential clearing price $p_i^j(k)$.

3.4   TACD Plus

In this subsection, we propose a more efficient algorithm to allocate cloudlets, which is named TACD plus (TACDp). TACDp is improved by changing the random integer m in ACBC base on TACD, the only difference between TACD and TACDp is the way we get number m. In TACD, m is randomly generated during $[(s + 1)/2, s]$, it will sacrifice many MUs to keep auction truthfulness, which may reduce the performance of TACD markedly. In TACDp, we get the random integer m by an algorithm named GTm, in the first stage of TACDp, as same as ACBC in TACD, we get the number s while a_i calculates the budget for C_k, then we generate the number m by GTm, and the rest steps are the same as ACBC in TACD. The number m generated by GTm can help TACDp get more budget for each AP, which can improve the social welfare significantly.

A is MUs in a_i which are sorted by their performance price ratio on C_k, the number of MUs which can benifit from C_k is no more than s for the resource in C_k is limited. In GTm, we can calculate a_i's budget for C_k if C_k only serve for the first x MUs in A, while the number x is from 1 to $s - 1$. Let array S to store the budget of all this $s - 1$ cases, then we sort S in descend order, and we save the first three cases as $tp1, tp2$ and $tp3$, their number of MUs are x_1, x_2 and x_3 respectively. Then we get a random number rnd from $\{tp1, tp2, tp3\}$, and $m = rnd + 1$.

3.5   Desired Properties

TACD and TACDp satisfied the desired properties: Truthfulness, Computational Efficiency, Budget Balance and Individual Rational. Due to limited space, verifications are omitted.

4   Numerical Results

4.1   Simulation Plan

We simulate our works on MATLAB R2014a, the number of APs and cloudlets is changing from 30 to 80. The capacity of cloudlet is subject to normal distribution N(25, 5) during [10, 30], i.e., $Cap^k \sim N(25,5)$ and $10 \leq Cap^k \leq 30$. Cloudlet C_k's cost factor $c(k)$ is subject to normal distribution N(0.75, 0.1) during [0.5, 1], i.e., $c(k) \sim N(0.75, 0.1)$ and $0.5 \leq c(k) \leq 1$. If $\sigma(i) = k$, we define C_k's utilization U^k as

$$U^k = \frac{\sum\limits_{j \in w_i} l_i^j}{Cap^k} \qquad (7)$$

The number of MUs in each AP subject to uniform distribution U(5, 30). For each MU, it's workload subject to normal distribution N(2, 1) during [1, 3], i.e., $l_i^j \sim N(2, 1)$ and $1 \leq l_i^j \leq 3$. MU's valuation for each cloudlet subject to uniform distribution U(1, 15), i.e., $b_i^j(k) \sim U(1, 15)$. We compare our works with the strategy Heaviest AP First (HAF) which mentioned in [3]. We sort APs by their MUs' total workload in descend order, and then sort cloudlets by their capacity in descend order, mapping cloudlets with APs in turn.

4.2   Simulation Results

The profits are shown in Fig. 1. We can find that TACD's social welfare is nearly equal to HAF, and TACDp is better than HAF, the distinction is more obviously while increasing the number of APs and cloudlets.

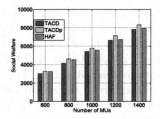

Fig. 1. Social welfare

Acknowledgement. This paper is supported by the National Natural Science Foundation of China (No. 61672171), R&D Major Project of Guangdong Province (No. 2015B010129014), Major Research Project of Educational Commission of Guangdong Province (No. 2016KZDXM052).

References

1. Satyanarayanan, M., Bahl, P., Cceres, R., Davies, N.: The case for VM-based cloudlets in mobile computing. IEEE Pervasive Comput. **8**(4), 14–23 (2009)
2. Jia, M., Liang, W., Xu, Z., Huang, M.: Cloudlet load balancing in wireless metropolitan area networks. In: IEEE INFOCOM 2016 - IEEE Conference on Computer Communications (2016)
3. Jia, M., Cao, J., Liang, W.: Optimal cloudlet placement and user to cloudlet allocation in wireless metropolitan area networks. IEEE Trans. Cloud Comput. **PP**(99), 1 (2015)
4. Jin, A.L., Song, W., Zhuang, W.: Auction-based resource allocation for sharing cloudlets in mobile cloud computing. IEEE Trans. Emerg. Topics Comput. **PP**(99), 1 (2015)
5. Lin, P., Feng, X., Zhang, Q., Hamdi, M.: Groupon in the air: a three-stage auction framework for spectrum group-buying. In: Proceedings - IEEE INFOCOM, vol. 12, no. 11, pp. 2013–2021 (2013)
6. Kang, X., Sun, S.: Incentive mechanism design for mobile data offloading in heterogeneous networks. In: IEEE International Conference on Communications (2015)
7. Goldberg, A.V., Hartline, J.D.: Competitive auctions for multiple digital goods. In: Heide, F.M. (ed.) ESA 2001. LNCS, vol. 2161, pp. 416–427. Springer, Heidelberg (2001). doi:10.1007/3-540-44676-1_35

Recognition of Electro-Magnetic Information Leakage of Computer Based on Multi-image Blind Deconvolution

Shanjing Yang[1,2(✉)], Jianlin Hu[1], and Weiqing Huang[1]

[1] Institute of Information Engineering,
Chinese Academy of Sciences, Beijing 100093, China
{yangshanjing,hujianlin,huangweiqing}@iie.ac.cn
[2] School of Cyber Security, University of Chinese Academy of Sciences,
Beijing 100049, China

Abstract. The security problem of screen image leakage from a display unit has become serious with the rapid speed of signal transmission technology. This paper presents a novel investigation on the characteristics of the power line compromising channel. Moreover, a measurement system has been actually developed for the leakage signal analyzing and image reconstruction. In order to overcome the degradation of reconstructed motion images and enhance the reconstructed image quality, a multi-image blind deconvolution method was proposed and test experiments were carried out to verify the effectiveness of the multi-image blind deconvolution algorithm based on the conducted signal from the power line.

Keywords: Recognition · Computer · Compromising emanations · Power line · Blind deconvolution

1 Introduction

All electronic equipments emit electromagnetic signals unintentionally and the electromagnetic radiations may contain information for Information Technology Equipments (ITEs). As an example of ITEs, computers have been widely used in our information society. For computers, one of the most important information sources is video display units. In the monitor, confidential information such as personal information may be often displayed. Thus, a target confidential information signal in the computer displays might be reproduced by receiving and analyzing this electromagnetic disturbance.

2 Related Work

The beginning of the studies about the eavesdropping risk of the displays was a research carried out by W. Van Eck in the Dr. Neher laboratories of Netherlands PTT [1]. He detected information that is displayed on a remote video screen placed in a building from a distance with a antenna, a receiver system and a television screen. In

© Springer International Publishing AG 2017
L. Ma et al. (Eds.): WASA 2017, LNCS 10251, pp. 883–889, 2017.
DOI: 10.1007/978-3-319-60033-8_77

[2, 3], standard PC plus flat panel are used as target information sources and display images reconstructed. In [4], with a near magnetic field probe and injection probe, laptop displays and LCDs are used as target and electromagnetic emanations are taken to reconstruct the images.

Recently, with the remarkable increase of information signal rates, the frequencies of such emissions tend to be higher and so are easier to radiate [5]. Besides the wireless channel, there can also be a potential information security threat for that the information can then be intercepted on the network cable [6] from a distance with no trace. Nevertheless, there are very little subject about research on information leakage of computer video based on power line cable that exists in every district or family use for which the security is often the most neglected.

In the following section, we will illustrate the EMC and compromising emanations of computer signals on the power line cable, and setup a system to analyze the conduct electromagnetic waves of computer display signals. Through a novel multi-channel blind image deblurring method, we have found that the detected signals show a serious eavesdropping risk of computer displays on the power line channel.

3 Multi-image Blind Deblurring Algorithm

In many practical scenarios we are presented with multiple pictures of the same scene under different imaging conditions. This is especially for receiving and reconstructing information leakage of computers via electromagnetic emanations. However, each reconstructed image may often contain blurring or motional noise. Thus, we proposed a Multi-image blind deconvolution algorithm to jointly utilize all available observations to produce a single sharp estimate of the underlying scene.

Considering L corrupted versions of a latent sharp image x, the uniform convolutional blur model assumes the observation process

$$y_\ell = k_\ell * x + n_\ell \quad \forall \ell \in \{1, \ldots, L\} \tag{1}$$

Given the case where we have a single image y. The observation model defines a Gaussian likelihood function $p(y/x, k)$ [7, 8]. Mathematically, this implies that $p(x) = \prod_{i=1}^m p(x_i)$, where m is the size of x (y is of size $n < m$)

$$p(x_i) = \max_{\gamma_i \geq 0} N(x_i; 0; \gamma_i) \exp[-\frac{1}{2} f(\gamma_i)] \tag{2}$$

The hyperparameter variances $\gamma = [\gamma_1 \ldots, \gamma_m]^T$ provide a convenient way of implementing several different estimation strategies. For instance, perhaps the most direct is a form of MAP estimation given by

$$\max_{x;\gamma;k \geq 0} p(y|x, k) \prod_i N(x_i; 0; \gamma_i) \exp[-\frac{1}{2} f(\gamma_i)] \tag{3}$$

The basic idea that extends to the blind deconvolution problem, is to first integrate out x, and then optimize over k, γ, as well as the noise level λ. And then the final latent sharp image can be recovered using the estimated kernel and noise level with standard non-blind deblurring algorithms. It can be shown that this alternative estimator is formally equivalent to solving

$$\min_{x,k,\lambda \geq 0} \frac{1}{\lambda_l} ||y - k * x||_2^2 + g(x, k, \lambda) \tag{4}$$

where

$$g(x, k, \lambda) = \min_{\gamma \geq 0} x^T \Gamma^{-1} x + \log |\lambda I + H\Gamma H^T| \tag{5}$$

To alleviate high-dimensional determinants involved with realistic sized images, a determinant identities and a diagonal approximation to $H\Gamma H$ was introduced, which leads to the simplified penalty function

$$g(x, k, \lambda) = \min_{\gamma \geq 0} \sum_i \left[\frac{x_i^2}{\gamma_i} + \log\left(\lambda + \gamma_i ||\mathbf{k}_l||_2^2\right) \right] \tag{6}$$

The cost function provides a transparent entry-point for multi-image deblurring. Assuming that all observations y_l are blurry or noisy measurements of the same underlying image x, and then γ may then justifiably be postulated shared across all l, which leads to the following revised multi-image optimization problem

$$\min_{x,\{k_l,\lambda_l \geq 0\}} \sum_{l=1}^{L} \frac{1}{\lambda_l} ||y_l - k_l * x||_2^2 + g(x, \{k_l, \lambda_l\}) \tag{7}$$

where the multi-image penalty function is now naturally defined as

$$g(x, \{k_l, \lambda_l\}) = \min_{\lambda \geq 0} \sum_{l=1}^{L} \sum_{i=1}^{m} \left[\frac{x_i^2}{\gamma_i} + \log\left(\lambda_l + \gamma_i ||k_l||_2^2\right) \right] \tag{8}$$

The resulting majorization-minimization approach is guaranteed to reduce or leave unchanged at each iteration. The multi-image blind deblurring algorithm, which is parameter-free and requires minimal user involvement are as follows.

Input : blurry images $\{y_l\}$, $l \in (1, L)$

Initialize : blur kenels $\{y_l\}$, noise levels $\{\lambda_l\}$

While stopping criteria is not satisfied, do

- **Update x** : $x \leftarrow \left[\sum_{l=1}^{L} \dfrac{H_l^T H_l}{L\lambda_l} + \Gamma^{-1}\right]^{-1} \sum_{l=1}^{L} \dfrac{H_l^T y_l}{L\lambda_l}$

where H_l is the convolution matrix of k_l

- **Update γ** : $\gamma_i \leftarrow x_i^2 + \dfrac{\sum_{l=1}^{L} z_{li}}{L}, \Gamma = diag(\gamma),$

$$z_{li} = \left(\left(\sum_j k_{lj}^2 \bar{I}_{ji}\right)\lambda_l^{-1} + \gamma_i^{-1}\right)^{-1}$$

- **Update** k_l :

$$k_l \leftarrow \arg\min k_l \geq 0 \; \frac{1}{\lambda_l} \parallel y_l - Wk_l \parallel_2^2 + \sum_j k_{lj}^2 \left(\sum_i z_{li} \bar{I}_{ji}\right)$$

with W the convolution matrix of x

- **Update noise levels** λ_l :

$$\lambda_l \leftarrow \frac{\parallel y_l - Wk_l \parallel_2^2 + \sum_i^m \sum_j k_{lj}^2 \sum_i z_{li} \bar{I}_{ji}}{n}$$

End

4 Experimental Results and Evaluation on Multi-image Blind Deconvolution Method for the Reconstruction Data

In order to analyze the leakage RGB signals of computer video in the power line and verify the transmission channel characteristic, test experiments were carried out to measure the conducted signal on the power line, which is shown in Fig. 1. The system is composed of a target PC Think Centre M8400t (1 GB separate display memory),

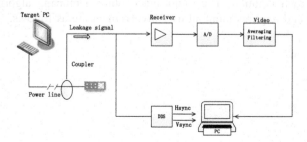

Fig. 1. Experiment and reconstruction system

a Think Vision LT2252wd LCD display, a coupler clamp, a spectrum receiver, a DDS sequence generator, and a reconstruct PC.

During the experiment setup, the display resolution and refresh rates of the PC were set to 1024×768 pixels at 60 Hz, with a video dot-frequency of 65.4 MHz. Table 1 shows the Horizontal and Vertical frequency of the DDS which were used to reconstruct the images on the power line.

Table 1. DDS signals for the information reconstruction

Signal type	Period	Frequency	Amplitude	Pulse-width
Vertical-sync	16.71 ms	59.822 Hz	4.96 V	16.58 ms
Horizontal -sync	20.74 µs	48.216 kHz	4.96 V	18.02 µs

In this experiment, we use a text image with resolution of 1024×768 pixels for image reconstruction and the test results are shown as Fig. 3. We construct a multi-observation test set with $l = 2$ blurry images by dividing the whole kernel set into two halves: $b_1 = \{1 \ldots 4\}$ and $b_2 = \{5 \ldots 8\}$. Estimated PSF pairs were shown in Fig. 2.

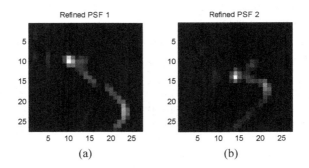

Fig. 2. The estimated PSFs: (a) image one, (b) image two

The images that reconstructed from conducted emission on the power line was evaluated by using a sample image text on the target PC. Figure 3(a) shows the original image of text displayed on the target PC. Figures 3(b), (c), show the reconstructed two image at receiving frequencies of 30 MHz without blind deconvolution processing. Figure 3(d) shows the final image with the multi-image blind deblurring algorithm of the two received images.

From the images reconstructed we can see that the target computer display can be successfully reconstructed by receiving the conducted emission on the power line. In addition, the multi-image blind deblurring algorithm can further enhanced the quality of reconstructed image. Thus the measurement system can be used in evaluating information leakage of a display image on a PC due to conducted emission on the power line cable.

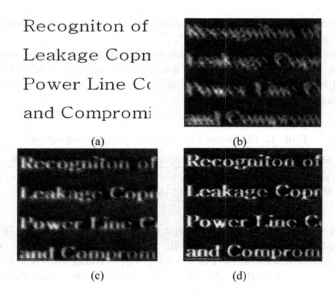

Fig. 3. The display image and reconstructed images before and after multi-image blind deblurring: (a) original image, (b) reconstructed image one, (c) reconstructed image two, (d) deconvolved image after processing.

5   Conclusions

In this paper, we have proposed a novel model for the eavesdropping attacks of computer displays on power line channel. In order to verify the characteristics of the power line channel, we also developed a system for the measurement of information leakage on the power line cable that was emitted by the switching RGB signals of display image. In addition, a multi-image blind deconvolution algorithm was proposed to reconstruct the display image from the conducted emission on the power line of a PC.

Acknowledgments. This work was supported by the National Natural Science Foundation of China (Y410041104) and Special Fund program for strategic technology, Chinese Academy of Sciences, China (No. XDA06010701).

References

1. Eck, W.V.: Electromagnetic radiation from video display units: an eavesdropping risk? Comput. Secur. 4(85), 269–286 (1985)
2. Kuhn, M.G.: Eavesdropping attacks on computer displays. Inf. Secur. Summit, 24–25 (2006). Prague

3. Kuhn, M.G.: Electromagnetic eavesdropping risks of flat-panel displays. In: Martin, D., Serjantov, A. (eds.) PET 2004. LNCS, vol. 3424, pp. 88–107. Springer, Heidelberg (2005). doi:10.1007/11423409_7
4. Tanaka, H., Takizawa, O., Yamamura, A.: A trial of the interception of display image using emanation of electromagnetic wave. J. Inst. Image Electron. Eng. Jpn **34**(1), 147–155 (2005)
5. Song, T.L., Jeong, Y.R., Yook, J.G.: Modeling of leaked digital video signal and information recovery rate as a function of SNR. IEEE Trans. Electromagn. Compat. **57**(2), 164–172 (2015)
6. Yu-Lei, D.U., Ying-Hua, L.U., Zhang, J.L.: Eavesdropping the display image from conducted emission on network cable of a PC. J. China Univ. Posts Telecommun. **20**, 78–84 (2013)
7. Miskin, J., Mackay, D.J.C.: Ensemble learning for blind image separation and deconvolution. In: Girolami, M. (ed.) Advances in Independent Component Analysis, pp. 123–141. Springer, London (2000)
8. Palmer, J.A., Wipf, D.P., Kreutz-Delgado, K., et al.: Variational EM algorithms for non-Gaussian latent variable models. In: International Conference on Neural Information Processing Systems, pp. 1059–1066. MIT Press (2005)

A Novel On-Line Association Algorithm in Multiple-AP Wireless LAN

Liang Sun, Lei Wang, Zhenquan Qin$^{(\boxtimes)}$, Zehao Ma, and Zhuxiu Yuan

School of Software, Dalian University of Technology, Dalian, China
{liang.sun,lei.wang,qzq}@dlut.edu.cn, johnmazehao@gmail.com,
zhuxiu.yuan@gmail.com

Abstract. Nowadays, wireless LAN has become the most widely deployed technology in mobile devices for providing Internet access. As a result, WLAN users usually find themselves covered by multiple access points and have to decide which one to associate with. In traditional implementations, most wireless stations would select the access point with the strongest signal, regardless of traffic load on that access point, which might result in heavy congestion and unfair load. In this paper, we propose a novel on-line association algorithm to deal with any sequence of STAs during a long-term time such as one day.

1 Introduction

Wireless local area networks (WLANs) have become a popular technology for access to the Internet and enterprise networks. In conventional implementations of WLANs, each station (STA) scans multiple wireless channels to detect the APs within the communication range, and chooses an AP that has the strongest received signal strength indicator (RSSI). The most apparent disadvantage of the RSSI-based STA association approach is that RSSI does not provide any information about the current traffic load of the AP [5]. Thus how to select an AP in a WLAN to guarantee high throughput and balance load for each STA is a challenging issue [6].

Obviously, the association algorithm can be used to achieve different objectives. For instance, it can be used to maximize the overall throughput of a system [9], achieve the network-wide bandwidth allocation fairness among STAs [4], and balance the load among APs. These plausible objectives can be obtained by one or two of the following parameters: the bit rate served by APs and the utilization of APs. Though these plausible objectives can be obtained by the two parameters by the periodical off-line optimal solutions, these are not desired feasible association algorithm which could be implemented in real-world situations. Consequently, more feasible association algorithms could deal with a sequence of STAs and maximize the overall traffic of a system.

The rest of the paper is organized as follows. In Sect. 2, we discuss the related work. In Sect. 3, we describe the system model considered in the paper. Section 4 gives the problem formulation of the AP association in WLANs and presents the

© Springer International Publishing AG 2017
L. Ma et al. (Eds.): WASA 2017, LNCS 10251, pp. 890–902, 2017.
DOI: 10.1007/978-3-319-60033-8_78

algorithm, followed by Sect. 5 which analyzes the proposed algorithm. We report the simulation and experimental results in Sect. 6. Finally, we conclude the paper in Sect. 7.

2   Related Work

Association algorithms for WLANs have been intensely studied by both the research community and the industry. Fairness and load balancing are two inter-related dimensions of the AP association problem.

None of the works mentioned above jointly considered the two interrelated dimensions in wireless LANs. Le *et al.* [7] proposed a distributed algorithm where each STA selected an appropriate contention window size to fairly share the channel occupancy time while maximizing the aggregated throughput of the network. Throughput based max-min fairness suffered from low network throughput in multi-rate wireless LANs [3].

Here we discuss a completely on-line algorithm with no need to run again when an STA is arriving or leaving. Actually, it is difficult to give consideration to the two interrelated dimensions at the same time. And there are many mechanisms to guarantee the quality of bandwidth allocated to the STAs [10]. Therefore, when we design an on-line association algorithm which could guarantee the quality of bandwidth of the associated STAs, we just consider the AP selection and the load balancing issues.

Mehta *et al.* [8] provided a simple framework to design a trade-off function between two factors in the on-line algorithm in. The paper proposed an on-line algorithm with competitive ratio $1 - 1/e$ to solve the AdWords problem among the Internet search engine companies. Based on the solution of the paper, we find that the capacity of each AP is limited, and the arrival and demand of the STAs are arbitrary. Therefore, we will apply this method to deal with the on-line case of our problem.

3   Network and System Description

3.1   Network Model

We consider an IEEE 802.11e based WLAN that comprises a large number of APs. Let A denote the set of APs and let N denote their quantity, i.e., $N = |A|$. All APs are attached to a controller, which makes the decision of which AP an STA should associate with. Each AP $a \in A$ has a theoretical traffic of C_a. Each AP has a limited transmission range and it can only serve STAs that reside in its service range.

We use S to denote the set of mobile STAs that have resided in the network range during a long-term time T. Our association algorithm is designed for the network in which STAs could arrive or depart freely. To the best of our knowledge, the network is regarded as stable when the time is measured in terms of tens of seconds. Therefore, we focus on a long-term time such as one day as the running time of the algorithm. Each STA is associated with a single AP to obtain service over a wireless channel. Because we don't take infrastructure into consideration, for STA $s \in S$ and AP $a \in A$, we use the maximal bit rate between STA and AP as the total bandwidth of the AP. In this paper, we first consider STAs with specified required bandwidth b_s and time t_s. APs will try to allocate the demanded bandwidth to its associated STAs, and STAs consume all bandwidth allocated to them and always have traffic to send or receive in their demanded time. Furthermore, we consider a general case where STAs can leave before their demanded time is used up.

3.2   System Description

We develop a centralized on-line association mechanism that determines the appropriate STA-AP associations to maximize the network traffic in a long-term time. We now discuss the main implementation aspects of an association control system. First, the system requires the relevant information of the session on each STA, such as the bandwidth and time demand of the session, the maximal bit rate that it experiences from each AP. Second, it needs an algorithm to determine the appropriate STA-AP association. Third, it needs a mechanism to enforce these decisions, including association, handover without user interference, and denial of service. We assume that such a mechanism is deployed at each AP, for instance, by using the emerging IEEE 802.11e extension [10] or any fair bandwidth allocation, and we build our association algorithm on top of it.

4   Algorithm Design

This section, we focus on the network scenario that each STA runs only one session which specifies a demanded bandwidth in its demanded time at one time.

4.1   Problem Definition

The AP association problem is the following: There are N APs, each with theoretical traffic C_a. S is a set of mobile STAs. Each AP a has the same total bandwidth b_a for STA $s \in S$ without concerning about the relative position between them and the interference. A sequence $s_1, s_2, \ldots, s_n$ of STAs $s_i \in S$ arrive on-line during T, and each STA s_i must specify required bandwidth b_{s_i} and time demand t_{s_i} according to its current session. The objective is to maximize the overall traffic of system at the end of T while respecting the quality of bandwidth of STAs. The notations and definitions to be used as summarized in Table 1. When a new STA s arrives at time t_s, we can divide the theoretical traffic into three parts in our association algorithm, the unused traffic before t_s, the allocated traffic and the remaining traffic after t_s as shown in Fig. 1. So the theoretical analysis based on the AdWords model will be incorrect. In our opinion, letting the unused part be small enough can be a reasonable solution to

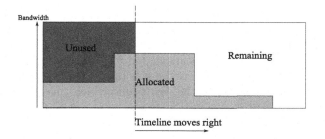

Fig. 1. The three parts of the theoretical traffic

Table 1. Notations

Symbol	Semantics
A	The set of all access points
S_a	The set of STAs which are associated with AP s
S	The set of all STAs
A_s	The set of candidate access points of STA s
C_a	The theoretical traffic of AP a
b_s	The demanded bandwidth of STA s
b'_s	The actual allocated bandwidth of STA s
t_s	The demanded time of STA s
b_a	The total bandwidth of AP a
$\psi(a)$	The tradeoff function on AP s
N	The number of APs in the network
n	The number of STAs which have associated with APs
t_s	The time a new STA s arrives
T	The running time of the association algorithm

adapt to the AdWords model. In order to achieve this, we define the "budget" for an AP as the theoretical traffic during a specified amount of time ("budget time"). We also suppose the amount of budget is the same for every AP, and call this a *budget window*. As our algorithm can only be valid during a short period of time at the beginning of budget window, we make the algorithm restart whenever the time-line reaches a specified short period (say, $1/k^2$ of "budget time") within budget window.

4.2   Algorithm

Now we will present our association algorithm when an STA s arrives in Algorithm 1. First, we define a trade-off function $\psi(x)$ of an AP as following:

$$\psi(x) = 1 - e^{-(1-x)}.$$

where x will be substituted with the ratio of allocated traffic within the total traffic of the AP's budget window. To make it clear, the allocated traffic is the traffic that this AP has used to communicate with its associated STAs, plus that which it has planned to use with its associated STAs in the future. And the total traffic of the AP's budget window is the size of the budget window. So on the other side, the ratio is related to the *free* traffic which this AP can allocate to upcoming STAs.

It's convenient to discretize the traffic into k equal parts, and we call each part a *slab*, so each slab contains $\frac{1}{k}$ of the total traffic in budget window. The AP allocates from lower slabs first, and when lower slabs are emptied, higher slabs will be used. The slab which the AP is currently allocating traffic from is called an *active* slab. We number each slab from 1 (lowest slab) to k (highest slab), and the active slab is $slab(i)$. Then we will get another form of the ψ function:

$$\psi_k(i) = 1 - e^{-(1-i/k)}.$$

When an STA s arrives, the STA s must notify the centralized AP controller its demanded bandwidth and time. Then each AP makes a bid to this STA. The bid is in the unit of traffic, that is, the bid equals the amount of traffic the AP can allocate. Of course, not all AP can satisfy the bandwidth demand of s, as the available bandwidth of an AP might be smaller than it (i.e., $b_a - \sum_{s \in S_a} b'_s < b_s$). In this case, the AP bid with traffic smaller than $b_s \times t_s$. If this AP gets associated, from the next moment until an STA leaves, its bandwidth will be fully utilized. Formally, this would be: (b'_s is the actual bandwidth allocated to the STA.)

$$b'_s = \begin{cases} b_s & b_a - \sum_{s \in S_a} b'_s \geq b_s; \\ b_a - \sum_{s \in S_a} b'_s & \text{otherwise.} \end{cases}$$

Algorithm 1. THE AP-ASSOCIATION ALGORITHM

Require: bandwidth and time demand of STA s, represented by b_s and t_s respectively.
Ensure: $max\_priority\_ap$ of STA s
1: $max\_priority \leftarrow -1$
2: **for** a in all APs **do**
3:     $bid \leftarrow b'_s \times t_s$
4:     **if** $max\_priority < bid \times \psi_k(slab(i))$ **then**
5:         $max\_priority \leftarrow bid \times \psi_k(slab(i))$
6:         $max\_priority\_ap \leftarrow a$
7:     **end if**
8: **end for**
9: $max\_priority\_ap$ is the chosen AP for STA s.

---

5   Theoretical Analysis

In this section we analyze the performance of our algorithm in the special case when all bids made by the candidate APs are equal. Then the association algorithm can be simplified to a new algorithm which is just based on the available traffic of the APs. For convenience, we call the new simplified algorithm as SIMPLIFIED-ASSOCIATION algorithm as shown in Algorithm 2.

Algorithm 2. THE SIMPLIFIED-ASSOCIATION ALGORITHM

Require: bandwidth and time demand of STA s, represented by b_s and t_s respectively.
Ensure: $max\_priority\_ap$ of STA s
1: $max\_priority \leftarrow -1$
2: **for** a in all APs **do**
3:    **if** $max\_priority < \psi_k(slab(i))$ **then**
4:       $max\_priority \leftarrow \psi_k(slab(i))$
5:       $max\_priority\_ap \leftarrow a$
6:    **end if**
7: **end for**
8: $max\_priority\_ap$ is the chosen AP for STA s.

We wish to give a lower bound of the total traffic achieved by SIMPLIFIED-ASSOCIATION ALGORITHM. Let us define the *type* of AP in a period according to the fraction of traffic served by that AP at the end of the algorithm SIMPLIFIED-ASSOCIATION ALGORITHM: say that the AP in some period is of type j if the fraction of its theoretical traffic spent at the end of the algorithm lies in the range $((j-1)/k, j/k)$, By convention an AP in some period who spends none of his budget is assigned type 1.

Lemma 1. *In some period, if OPT associates STA s with AP a of type $j \leq k-1$, then* SIMPLIFIED-ASSOCIATION ALGORITHM *lays all demanded traffic of s in some slab i such that $i \leq j$.*

The lemma follows immediately from the criterion used by SIMPLIFIED-ASSOCIATION ALGORITHM for associating STAs with APs: A has type $j \leq k-1$ and therefore transmits at most j/k fraction of his theoretical traffic at the end of SIMPLIFIED-ASSOCIATION ALGORITHM. It follows that when STA s arrives at the beginning of some period, A is available to SIMPLIFIED-ASSOCIATION ALGORITHM for associating with s, and therefore A must associate s with some AP who has transmitted at most j/k fraction of his total traffic in this period s.

For simplicity we will assume that the AP in each period of type i transmit exactly i/k fraction of their theoretical traffic, that the amount of traffic pieces of each STA do not straddle slabs. The second one is justified by fact the traffic piece is small compared to the traffic in each period (e.g. taking the piece to be smaller than $\frac{1}{k^2}$ of the traffic of each period). The total error resulting from this simplification is at most $\frac{(2n-1)N}{k}$ and is negligible, once we take k to be large enough. Now, for $i = 1, 2, \ldots, k-1$, let x_i be the number of periods for all APs of type(i). Let β_i denote the total traffic transmitted by the AP in each period from slab i in BALANCE. It is easy to see (Fig. 2) that $\beta_1 = (2n-1)N/k$, and for $2 \leq i \leq k$, $\beta_i = \frac{(2n-1)N}{k} - (x_1 + \ldots + x_{i_1})/k$.

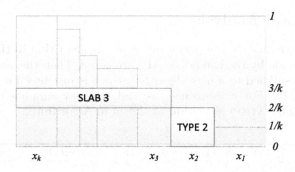

Fig. 2. The APs in each period are ordered from right to left in order of increasing type. We have labeled here the APs in each period of type 2 and the traffic in slab 3.

Lemma 2.

$$\forall\, i, 1 \le i \le k-1: \quad \sum_{j=1}^{i}(1 + \frac{i-j}{k})x_j \le \frac{i}{k}(2n-1)N.$$

From Lemma 1:

$$\sum_{j=1}^{i} x_j \le \sum_{j=1}^{i} \beta_j = \beta_1 + \sum_{j=2}^{i} \beta_j$$

$$= \frac{i}{k}(2n-1)N - \sum_{j=1}^{i} \frac{i-j}{k} x_j.$$

The traffic of Simplified-Association Algorithm is

$$\alpha - \text{AS} \ge \sum_{i=1}^{k-1} \frac{i}{k} x_i + [(2n-1)N - \sum_{i=1}^{k-1} x_i] - \frac{(2n-1)N}{k}$$

$$= (2n-1)N - \sum_{i=1}^{k-1} \frac{k-i}{k} x_i - \frac{(2n-1)N}{k}.$$

This gives the following LP, which we call L. In both the constraints below, i ranges from 1 to $k-1$.

$$\max \quad \Phi = \sum_{i=1}^{k-1} \frac{k-i}{k} x_i,$$

$$\text{subject to} \quad \forall i: \sum_{j=1}^{i}(1 + \frac{i-j}{k})x_j \le \frac{i}{k}(2n-1)N$$

$$\forall i: \ x_i \ge 0.$$

And the dual LP, D, will be used in the case of arbitrary demand bandwidth.

$$\min \quad \Phi = \sum_{i=1}^{k-1} \frac{i}{k}(2n-1)Ny_i,$$

$$\text{subject to} \quad \forall i: \sum_{j=i}^{k-1}(1 + \frac{j-i}{k})y_j \geq \frac{k-i}{k}$$

$$\forall i: \ y_i \geq 0.$$

According to the analysis in [8], the value of Φ of the programs L and D goes to $(2n-1)N/e$.

Lemma 3. *The competitive ratio of* SIMPLIFIED-ASSOCIATION ALGORITHM *is at least* $1 - \frac{1}{e}$.

Recall the traffic of SIMPLIFIED-ASSOCIATION ALGORITHM is at least $(2n-1)$ $N - \Phi - \frac{(2n-1)N}{k}$, hence it tends to $(2n-1)N(1 - \frac{1}{e})$. Since OPT is $(2n-1)N$, the competitive ratio is at least $1 - \frac{1}{e}$.

6   Evaluation

In this section, we test our association algorithm on Matlab [1] and a real TestBed respectively. We compare the performance of our algorithm with that of the following ones:

- Strongest Signal First (SSF): The default STA-AP association mechanism in the 802.11 standard.
- Largest Available Bandwidth (LAB): The STAs will associate with the APs which has the largest available bandwidth compared with the demanded bandwidth of the STAs based on 802.11e.

In order to compare our algorithm with other association algorithms in variety of settings, we select several different bandwidth allocation algorithms. The various cases of test algorithms are labeled in Table 2.

Table 2. Algorithm combinations

Label	Bandwidth allocation	Association algorithm
QoS_F/ALG	Fixed bandwidth	ALG
QoS_F/SSF	Fixed bandwidth	SSF
QoS_F/LAB	Fixed bandwidth	LAB

This set of algorithms are examined carefully according to the performance metrics listed in the following:

- Per-STA bandwidth in Mbps.
- The overall traffic of the network.
- The traffic on the APs in Mbps.
- The competitive ratio.

6.1 Simulations

We first consider a static network, which involves 2 fixed APs in the network, and each has a capacity of 4 Mbps. There are 4 STAs accessing the network successively. The parameters of the APs and the STAs are shown in Table 3. The algorithms, SSF and LAB, make greedy association decisions to satisfy the current STAs. The bandwidth allocated to the STAs is so unreasonable that the APs cannot provide the enough bandwidth for the coming STAs such as STA 4 as shown in Table 4. And ALG allows STA 4 associate with AP a to achieve more throughput in the system.

Table 3. Parameters of the APs and the STAs in scenario 2

STAs	Start(s)	End(s)	Demanded bandwidth (Mbps)	Max bit rate (Mbps)	
				AP a	AP b
1	0	200	1	4	2
2	50	200	1	2.7	2
3	100	200	2	2	4
4	150	200	2	3	4

Table 4. Scenario 1: dynamic STAs. The STA 4 could not associate with any AP in the network in the association algorithms, SSF and LAB

Metrics	Algorithms	APs							
		a (4 Mbps)				b (4 Mbps)			
		STAs				STAs			
		1	2	3	4	1	2	3	4
Association	QoS_F/ALG	√			√		√	√	
	QoS_F/SSF	√	√		⊗			√	⊗
	QoS_F/LAB	√	√		⊗			√	⊗
Traffic ($\times 10^3$ Mb)	QoS_F/ALG	0.2	0	0	0.1	0	0.15	0.2	0
	QoS_F/SSF	0.2	0.15	0	0	0	0	0.2	0
	QoS_F/LAB	0.2	0.15	0	0	0	0	0.2	0

Scenario 2 involves 9 APs and many mobile STAs in a $100 \times 100\,\mathrm{m}^2$ network. The locations of the APs are fixed as shown in Fig. 3. Each AP has a capacity of 54 Mbps. The arrival and departure of the STAs are subject to the normal distribution. There are two peak hours, 15 and 21, during a day (24 h) as shown in Fig. 4(a). The locations of the STAs are random in the network. We plot the network traffic under ALG and LAB as shown in Fig. 4(b). The network traffic in ALG improves about 37% compared with the LAB algorithm. And it is obvious that the traffic on each AP under ALG is more balancing compared with LAB as shown in Fig. 4(c) and (d).

Fig. 3. The topology of the static network

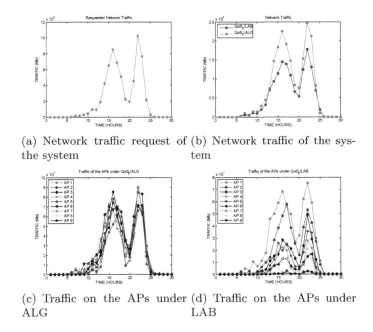

(a) Network traffic request of the system

(b) Network traffic of the system

(c) Traffic on the APs under ALG

(d) Traffic on the APs under LAB

Fig. 4. Scenario 3: dynamic network.

Scenario 3 involves 3 fixed APs in the network, each has a capacity of 4 Mbps as shown in Fig. 5. And the maximal bit rates between the APs and the STAs are the capacity of the APs. Then we can get the competitive ratio compared with SSF as shown in Fig. 6.

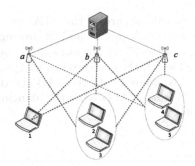

Fig. 5. The topology of the static network

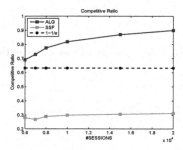

Fig. 6. Competitive ratio

6.2 Experiments

In this section, we will report our results of experiments which help us understand
the performance of our association algorithm. Experiments are conducted with
Thinkpad R61e laptops equipped with Atheros AR2425 802.11g wireless cards.
Each laptop is loaded with the modified Madwifi driver v0.9.4 [2] to collect
experimental data. The topology of the network is shown in Fig. 8.

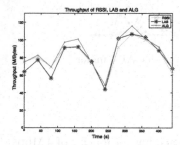

Fig. 7. Scenario 4: the network traffic
of the testbed.

Fig. 8. The topology of testbed

We compare the network traffic of our algorithm with that of LAB and SSF, and present that our algorithm has better performance than the other two as shown in Fig. 7. Actually, the network in the testbed is a worse case for our algorithm, because our association algorithm performs better in congested networks. Though this network is light-loaded because of the limited equipment, our algorithm still performs better than the other two.

7 Conclusions

In this paper, we propose a novel on-line association algorithm to deal with any sequence of STAs during a long-term period such as one day. One important advantage of our algorithm is that it does not need any periodical off-line optimal solutions. We give a strict proof that the competitive ratio of the algorithm is $1 - 1/e$ when APs allocate the demanded bandwidth of their associated STAs. Simulation results show that the proposed association algorithm can improve the network traffic by more than 37% when compared with conventional association algorithms. Our algorithm also performs better than SSF and LAB in the experiments even in a less congested network, which may improve more performance for other association algorithms than that of ours.

We plan to test and verify the performance of our association algorithm with more APs and more STAs in our testbed. In this condition, we try to find the difference between this experiment and the previous one to optimize our association algorithm. Meanwhile, interference which will influence the performance in a congested network will be taken into consideration in our model.

References

1. Matrix laboratory. http://www.mathworks.com
2. Multiband atheros driver for wifi. http://madwifi-project.org
3. Bejerano, Y., Han, S.J., Li, L.E.: Fairness and load balancing in wireless LANs using association control. In: Proceedings of the 10th Annual International Conference on Mobile Computing and Networking, MobiCom 2004, pp. 315–329. ACM, New York (2004). http://doi.acm.org/10.1145/1023720.1023751
4. Bredel, M., Fidler, M.: Understanding fairness and its impact on quality of service in IEEE 802.11. In: IEEE INFOCOM 2009, pp. 1098–1106. IEEE (2009)
5. He, Y., Perkins, D., Velaga, S.: Design and implementation of class: a cross-layer association scheme for wireless mesh networks. In: INFOCOM IEEE Conference on Computer Communications Workshops, pp. 1–6. IEEE (2010)
6. Kim, H., De Veciana, G., Yang, X., Venkatachalam, M.: Alpha-optimal user association and cell load balancing in wireless networks. In: 2010 Proceedings of IEEE INFOCOM, pp. 1–5. IEEE (2010)
7. Le, Y., Ma, L., Cheng, W., Cheng, X., Chen, B.: Maximizing throughput when achieving time fairness in multi-rate wireless LANs. In: 2012 Proceedings of IEEE INFOCOM, pp. 2911–2915. IEEE (2012)
8. Mehta, A., Saberi, A., Vazirani, U., Vazirani, V.: Adwords and generalized online matching. J. ACM **54**(5). http://doi.acm.org/10.1145/1284320.1284321

9. Nassiri, M., Heusse, M., Duda, A.: A novel access method for supporting absolute and proportional priorities in 802.11 WLANs. In: The 27th Conference on Computer Communications, INFOCOM 2008, pp. 709–717. IEEE (2008)
10. Ni, Q., Romdhani, L., Turletti, T.: A survey of QoS enhancements for IEEE 802.11 wireless LAN: research articles. Wirel. Commun. Mob. Comput. 4(5), 547–566 (2004). http://dx.doi.org/10.1002/wcm.v4:5

Near-Field Localization Algorithm Based on Sparse Reconstruction of the Fractional Lower Order Correlation Vector

Sen Li, Bin Lin$^{(\boxtimes)}$, Bing Li, and Rongxi He

Department of Information Science and Technology,
Dalian Maritime University, Dalian 116026, China
{listen, binlin, bingli, hrx}@dlmu.edu.cn

Abstract. This paper addresses the issue of joint direction-of-arrival (DOA) and range estimation of near-field signal under impulsive noise environments modeled by α-stable distribution. Since α-stable distribution does not have finite second-order statistics, the DOA and range estimation problem under impulsive noise environment can be decoupled in the fractional lower order correlation domain. Then, the two dimensional positioning problem is transformed into two one dimensional parameter estimation problems which can be solved by the sparse reconstruction of the fractional lower order correlation vector. The computer simulation results demonstrate that the proposed algorithm outperform the second order correlation-based methods.

Keywords: Near-filed · Direction of arrival · Range estimation · Impulsive noise · Sparse reconstruction · Fractional lower-order correlation

1 Introduction

Source localization is a hot research topic in array signal processing and has extensive applications in the microphone arrays, passive sonar, radar and wireless communications [1]. It has attracted many scholars' attention and a large amount of methods have been proposed to handle this issue. Most of these methods made the assumption that the sources are located in the far-filed region which is characterized by the direction of arrival (DOA). However, when the sources are located in the Fresnel region, the wavefront shape will not only be characterized by DOA but also by the range. Thus, existing methods based on the far-field assumption are not suitable to this situation. In view of the near-field source localization problem, researchers extended the conventional one-dimension MUSIC algorithm for DOA estimation to two-dimension MUSIC algorithm for joint range and DOA estimation [2]. Other methods, such as, higher-order statistics (HOS) based methods [3] and the weighted linear prediction method [4] had

This work was supported in part by the National Natural Science Foundation of China under Grants 61301228, 61371091 and the Fundamental Research Funds for the Central Universities under Grant 3132016331 and 3132016318.

© Springer International Publishing AG 2017
L. Ma et al. (Eds.): WASA 2017, LNCS 10251, pp. 903–908, 2017.
DOI: 10.1007/978-3-319-60033-8_79

also been proposed. Recently a very different framework, namely sparse signal recovery framework, is introduced in array signal processing. Method based on sparse signal recovery had been developed for near-field sources location [5].

One common assumption made by the above methods is that the ambient noise is assumed to be Gaussian distributed. However, in many real world applications the noise often exhibits non-Gaussian properties, sometimes accompanied by strong impulsiveness [6]. Under investigation, it is found that α-stable distribution is a suitable noise model to describe this type noise [7]. Since α-stable distribution has no finite second order statistics (SOS), the SOS-and HOS-based estimation methods are generally not applicable. Therefore, the fractional lower-order statistics (FLOS) was recently proposed such as the fractional lower order correlation (FLOC) and the phase fractional lower correlation (PFLOC) [8]. By using the PFLOC, [9] proposed a new search-free method for near-field source localization under impulsive noise.

So far as we know, there is no existing near-field parameter estimation methods based on sparse reconstruction in impulsive noise environments. Thus, in this paper, we propose a near-filed source location algorithm based on the sparse reconstruction of the FLOC vectors which are the output of the virtual far-field array. Computer simulation experiments are presented to illustrate the performance superiority of the proposed methods over the estimation method based on the sparse reconstruction of the correlation vectors under α-stable noise environments.

2   α-Stable Distribution

This section describes a noise model specified by α-stable distribution with its characteristic function specified by

$$\phi(t) = e^{\{jat - \gamma|t|^\alpha[1 + j\beta\mathrm{sgn}(t)\varpi(t,\alpha)]\}} \tag{1}$$

where γ and a are the dispersion and location parameters respectively and $\varpi(t,\alpha) = \tan\frac{\pi\alpha}{2}$ if $\alpha \neq 1$; $\varpi(t,\alpha) = \frac{2}{\pi}\log|t|$, if $\alpha = 1$, and $\mathrm{sgn}(t)$ is $|t|$ if $t \neq 0$ and 0 if $t = 0$. In particular, α ($0 < \alpha \leq 2$) is the characteristic exponent that measures the thickness of the tails of the distribution where the smaller α is, the thicker its tails. Also, β is the symmetry parameter, if $\beta = 0$, the distribution in which case the observation is referred to as the symmetry α-stable (SαS) distribution. When $\alpha = 2$ and $\beta = 0$, the α-stable distribution becomes a Gaussian distribution. An important difference between the Gaussian and the α-stable distribution is that only moments of order less than α exist for the α-stable distribution.

3   Problem Formulation

Consider the case of K independent narrowband sources are in the near-field of a symmetric uniform linear array (ULA) with $N = 2M + 1$ isotropic sensors. Set the array center being the phase reference point, the signal received by the mth sensor at time t can be expressed as

$$x_m(t) = \sum_{k=1}^{K} s_k(t)A_{mk} + n_m(t) = \sum_{k=1}^{K} s_k(t)e^{(j\tau_{mk})} + n_m(t), m = -M, \cdots, M \quad (2)$$

where, $s_k(t)$ and $n_m(t)$ is the source signal and additive noise, and τ_{mk} is phase shift of the kth source signal between phase reference point and sensor m. By Fresnel approximation, it can be given by

$$\tau_{mk} \approx w_k m + \phi_k m^2, \quad w_k = -\frac{2\pi d}{\lambda}\sin\theta_k, \quad \phi_k = \frac{\pi d\cos^2\theta_k}{\lambda r_k} \quad (3)$$

Herein, λ is the wavelength, d is the interspacing, (θ_k, r_k) represent the DOA and the range parameter of the kth source. Define the received data vector $X(t) = [x_{-M}(t), \cdots, x_0(t), \cdots, x_M(t)]^T$ which can be expressed as

$$X(t) = A(\theta, r)S(t) + N(t) \quad (4)$$

where $S(t) = [s_1(t), s_2(t), \cdots, s_K(t)]^T$, $N(t) = [n_{-M}(t), \cdots, n_0(t), \cdots, n_M(t)]^T$ and the manifold matrix $A(\theta, r) = [a(\theta_1, r_1), a(\theta_2, r_2), \cdots, a(\theta_K, r_K)]$ with $a(\theta_k, r_k) = [\exp(j((-M)w_k) + M^2\phi_k)), \cdots, 1, \cdots, \exp(j(Mw_k + M^2\phi_k))]^T$.

The FLOC between the mth and nth sensor output can be defined as:

$$c_x(m, n) = E\left\{x_m(t)|x_n(t)|^{p-2}x_n^*(t)\right\} = \sum_{k=1'}^{K} e^{j(w_k m + \phi_k m^2)}\Lambda_{kk}e^{-j(w_k n + \phi_k n^2)} + \xi\delta_{mn} \quad (5)$$

The definition of Λ_{kk} and ξ can be found in [8]. We can get it matrix form as $C = A(\theta, r)\Lambda A^H(\theta, r) + \xi I$ where $\Lambda = diag[\Lambda_{11}, \cdots, \Lambda_{KK}]$ and I is the identity matrix.

4 Proposed Two Step Estimation Method

Define $c_x = [c_x(-M, M), \ldots, c_x(-1, 1), c_x(1, -1) \ldots, c_x(M, -M)]^T \in C^{2M \times 1}$, a virtual far-field array model can be built as $c_x = A_w(\theta)\Lambda$ where c_x and Λ can be regarded as the received signal and source signals vector of the virtual far-field array, the manifold matrix can be expressed as $A_w(\theta) = [a_w(\theta_1), a_w(\theta_2), \cdots, a_w(\theta_K)] \in C^{2M \times K}$ with the virtual array steering vector $a_w(\theta_k) = [e^{-j2Mw_k}, \cdots, e^{-j2w_k}, e^{j2w_k}, \cdots, e^{j2Mw_k}]^T \in C^{2M \times 1}$.

4.1 Step-1: DOA Estimation

Define a potential DOAs set $\widehat{\theta} = \left[\widehat{\theta}_1, \widehat{\theta}_2 \cdots, \widehat{\theta}_{N_\theta}\right]$ and the number of the potential DOAs N_θ should be much greater than the number of sensors. Then, c_x can be rewritten as $c_x = A_w\left(\widehat{\theta}\right)v$ where $A_w\left(\widehat{\theta}\right) = \left[a_w\left(\widehat{\theta}_1\right), a_w\left(\widehat{\theta}_2\right), \cdots, a_w\left(\widehat{\theta}_{N_\theta}\right)\right]$ and the potential source signal vector $v = [v_1, v_2, \cdots, v_{N_\theta}]^T$ that have K nonzero elements, that is $v_k = $

Λ_{ii} if $\hat{\theta}_k = \theta_i, i = 1, \cdots, K$. Hence the DOA estimation can be reduced to finding the nonzero elements of vector v. Since v is sparse, so it can be obtained by solving the following sparse reconstruction problem:

$$\min\|v\|_1 \quad s.t. \quad \left\|c_x - A_w\left(\hat{\theta}\right)v\right\|_2 \leq \varepsilon \tag{6}$$

where ε is a parameter which means how much of the error we wish to allow.

4.2   Step-2: Range Estimation

Given a DOA $\bar{\theta}_k(k = 1, \cdots, K)$ which was estimated in Step-1, the FLOC matrix of the near-filed received signal can be written as

$$C_{\bar{\theta}_k} = A\left(\bar{\theta}_k, r\right)\Lambda A^H\left(\bar{\theta}_k, r\right) + \xi I \tag{7}$$

Applying the vectorization operator on Eq. (7), we have

$$y_{\bar{\theta}_k} = vect\left(C_{\bar{\theta}_k}\right) = B_{\bar{\theta}_k}(r)\Lambda + \xi vect(I) \in C^{N^2 \times 1} \tag{8}$$

$$B_{\bar{\theta}_k}(r) = \left[a^*\left(\bar{\theta}_k, r_1\right) \otimes a\left(\bar{\theta}_k, r_1\right), \cdots, a^*\left(\bar{\theta}_k, r_k\right) \otimes a\left(\bar{\theta}_k, r_k\right)\right] \in C^{N^2 \times k} \tag{9}$$

where $\otimes$ denotes Kronecker product. It is interesting to see that $y_{\bar{\theta}_k}$ in (8) can also be regarded as the virtual far-filed array output where $B_{\bar{\theta}_k}(r)$, Λ and $\xi vect(I)$ are the virtual manifold matrix, equivalent source signal vector and equivalent noise vector, respectively.

Using a similar approach as in Step-1, the virtual received signal vector $y_{\bar{\theta}_k}$ can be sparsely represented as the following form $y_{\bar{\theta}_k} = B_{\bar{\theta}_k}(\hat{r})p + \xi vect(I)$ where $B_{\bar{\theta}_k}(\hat{r}) \in C^{N^2 \times N_r}$ is the overcomplete basis on a set $\hat{r} = \left[\hat{r}_1, \hat{r}_2, \cdots, \hat{r}_{N_r}\right]$ with N_r is the number of the potential range parameters on the direction of $\bar{\theta}_k$, $p = [p_1, p_2, \cdots, p_{N_r}]^T$. is the potential source signal vector which is also sparse, so the range parameter can be estimated by solving the following optimization problem:

$$\min\|p\|_1 \quad s.t. \quad \left\|y_{\bar{\theta}_k} - B_{\bar{\theta}_k}(\hat{r})p - \xi vect(I)\right\|_2 \leq \varepsilon \tag{10}$$

where ξ can be estimated by the smallest eigenvalue of the eigenvalue decomposition of matrix $C_{\bar{\theta}_k}$.

5   Simulation Results

In this section, a series of numerical experiments under different conditions are conducted to compare the estimation performance of our proposed fraction lower order correlation-based sparse reconstruction method (FLOCSR) with that of the second order correlation-based sparse reconstruction method (SOCSR) [5]. Throughout this section, the convex optimization problem of (6) and (10) are resolved by using the software package CVX [10]. An $N = 15$ element ULA with an inter sensor spacing of a quarter wavelength is used. Two independent sources in the near-field region at locations $(\theta_1, r_1) = (20°, 1.5\lambda)$ and $(\theta_2, r_2) = (45°, 3.6\,\lambda)$ are considered. The direction grid is set to have $N_\theta = 181$ points sampled form $-90°$ to $90°$ with $1°$ intervals. The value scope of the range parameter is set to $[\lambda, 15\,\lambda]$ with the spacing is $0.1\,\lambda$, that is, $N_r = 141$.

The criterion used to assess the performance of the algorithms is the average root mean square error (RMSE) defined as $RMSE = \sqrt{\sum_{i=1}^{P} (\bar{x}(i) - x)^2 / P}$ where $\bar{x}(i)$ is the ith estimation of parameter and P is the number of Monte Carlo experiments. As the characteristic of the α-stable distribution makes the use of the standard SNR meaningless, a new SNR measure, generalized signal-to-noise ratio (GSNR) is defined as $GSNR = 10 \log_{10} (\sigma_s^2 / \gamma)$ [7], where σ_s is the variance of the signal, γ is the dispersion parameter of the α-stable noise.

Experiment 1: In this experiment, the characteristic exponent of noise was fixed at $\alpha = 1.5$ and the number of snapshots was $L = 1024$. Figure 1 shows the performance of the two methods for various GSNRs ranging from -5 to 20 dB. We see that the performance of two methods improved with the increase of GSNR, and the proposed FLOCSR method outperformed the SOCSR method when in low GSNR environments.

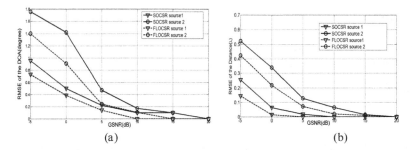

Fig. 1. Performance as a function of GSNR. (a) RMSE of DOA estimates, (b) RMSE of range estimates

Experiment 2: Figure 2 plots the performance of the two algorithms varying with different values of the characteristic exponent of the α- stable impulsive noise. The GSNR was kept at 10 dB, and the number of snapshots was 1024. As shown in Fig. 2 our proposed FLOCSR algorithm demonstrated its performance enhancement over SOCSR algorithm in the sense of RMSE of the DOA and range estimates under the highly impulsive noise environment.

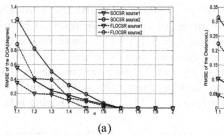 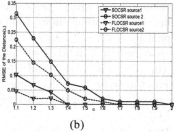

(a)   (b)

Fig. 2. Performance as a function of characteristic exponent α. (a) RMSE of DOA estimates, (b) RMSE of range estimates

6 Conclusion

In this paper, we have considered the problem of joint angle and range estimation for near-field sources in impulsive noise environments. By using the FLOC, we decomposed the joint two parameters estimation problem into two independent parameter estimation problems, and proposed a two-step near-filed source location algorithm based on the sparse reconstruction of the FLOC vector of the virtually far-filed array output. Simulation results are shown to demonstrate the effectiveness of the proposed method for a wide range of highly impulsive environments.

References

1. So, H.C.: Source localization: algorithms and analysis. In: Zekavat, R., Buehrer, R.M. (eds.) Handbook of Position Location: Theory Practice and Advances. Wiley-IEEE Press, New York (2011)
2. Zhi, W., Chia, M.Y.: Near-field source location via symmetric subarrays. IEEE Sig. Process. Lett. **14**(6), 409–412 (2007)
3. Xie, J., Tao, H., Rao, X., Su, J.: Passive localization of mixed far-field and near-field sources without estimating the number of sources. Sensors **15**, 3834–3853 (2015)
4. Grosicki, E., Meraim, A.K.: A weighted linear prediction method for near-field source localization. In: Proceedings of IEEE International Conference on Acoustics, Speech, Signal Processing, vol. 3, pp. 2957–2960 (2002)
5. Hu, K., Chepuri, S.P., Leus, G.: Near-field source localization: sparse recovery techniques and grid matching. In: Proceedings of the IEEE 8th Sensor Array and Multichannel Signal Processing Workshop (SAM), pp. 369–372, A Coruña, Spain, 22–25 June 2014
6. Button, M.D., Gardiner, J.G., Glover, I.A.: Measurement of the impulsive noise environment for satellite-mobile radio systems at 1.5 GHz. IEEE Trans. Veh. Technol. **51**(3), 551–560 (2002)
7. Nikias, C.L., Shao, M.: Signal processing with Alpha-stable distributions and applications. Wiely, New York (1995)
8. Li, S., He, R.X., Lin, B., Sun, F.: DOA Estimation based on sparse representation of the fractional lower order statistics in impulsive noise. IEEE/CAA J. Autom. Sin. (2016)
9. Qiu, T.S., Wang, P.: A novel method for near-field source localization in impulsive noise environments. Circuits Syst. Sig. Process. **35**, 4030–4059 (2016)
10. Grant, M., Boyd, S., Ye, Y.: CVX: matlab software for disciplined convex programming. CVX Research, Inc. (2008)

Author Index

Printed in the United States
By Bookmasters